T0190174

Lecture Notes in Computer Science   12657

More information about this subseries at http://www.springer.com/series/7409

Djoerd Hiemstra · Marie-Francine Moens ·
Josiane Mothe · Raffaele Perego ·
Martin Potthast · Fabrizio Sebastiani (Eds.)

Advances in Information Retrieval

43rd European Conference on IR Research, ECIR 2021
Virtual Event, March 28 – April 1, 2021
Proceedings, Part II

 Springer

Editors
Djoerd Hiemstra (iD)
Radboud University Nijmegen
Nijmegen, The Netherlands

Josiane Mothe (iD)
Toulouse Institute of Computer Science
Research
Toulouse, France

Martin Potthast (iD)
Leipzig University
Leipzig, Germany

Marie-Francine Moens (iD)
Department of Computer Science
Katholieke Universiteit Leuven
Heverlee, Belgium

Raffaele Perego (iD)
Istituto di Scienza e Tecnologie
dell'Informazione
Consiglio Nazionale delle Ricerche
Pisa, Italy

Fabrizio Sebastiani (iD)
Istituto di Scienza e Tecnologie
dell'Informazione
Consiglio Nazionale delle Ricerche
Pisa, Italy

ISSN 0302-9743   ISSN 1611-3349 (electronic)
Lecture Notes in Computer Science
ISBN 978-3-030-72239-5   ISBN 978-3-030-72240-1 (eBook)
https://doi.org/10.1007/978-3-030-72240-1

LNCS Sublibrary: SL3 – Information Systems and Applications, incl. Internet/Web, and HCI

This Springer imprint is published by the registered company Springer Nature Switzerland AG
The registered company address is: Gewerbestrasse 11, 6330 Cham, Switzerland

Preface

It is our great pleasure to welcome you to ECIR 2021, the 43rd edition of the annual BCS-IRSG European Conference on Information Retrieval.

ECIR 2021 was to be held in Lucca, Italy, but due to the COVID-19 pandemic emergence and the travel restrictions enforced worldwide, the conference was held entirely online. ECIR 2021 started on March 28 with a day of (full-day and half-day) tutorials, plus the Doctoral Consortium. The main conference took place in the three days that followed (March 28 – April 1). The technical program of the main conference included three exciting keynote talks, one per day: the first was presented by Francesca Rossi (IBM), the second by Ahmed Hassan Awadallah (Microsoft AI Research), as the winner of the BCS/Microsoft/BCS IRSG Karen Spärck Jones Award 2020, and the third by Ophir Frieder (Georgetown University). The technical program also consisted of research papers by contributors from Europe and the rest of the world. In total, 488 papers were submitted across all tracks, from 53 different countries. The program committees for the various tracks decided to accept 145 papers in total; the final scientific program thus included 50 full papers (a 24% acceptance rate), 39 short papers (25% acceptance rate), 15 demonstration papers (48% acceptance rate), and 11 reproducibility papers (52% acceptance rate). As in the previous edition, the technical program also included 12 "lab" (i.e., shared task) boosters from the CLEF 2021 conference, and the presentation of selected papers published in the 2020 issues of the Information Retrieval Journal. Symmetrically, the authors of a selection of ECIR 2021 papers will be invited to submit an extended version for publication in a special issue of the journal.

The last day of the conference (April 1) was devoted to 5 workshops and an exciting Industry Day. The workshops dealt with important topics such as algorithmic bias in search and recommendation (BIAS workshop), bibliometric-enhanced information retrieval (BIR workshop), conversational systems (MICROS workshop), online mis-information (ROMCIR workshop), and narrative extraction from texts (Text2Story workshop). This year the Industry Day was focused on the experience of Ph.D. interns in industrial contexts, and showcased success stories and positive experiences of former Ph.D. interns and former Ph.D. mentors. All submissions were peer reviewed by at least three international Program Committee members to ensure that only submissions of the highest quality were included in the final program. The acceptance decisions were further informed by discussions among the reviewers for each submitted paper, led by a senior Program Committee member or one of the track chairs. The accepted contributions covered the state of the art in IR: deep-learning–based information retrieval techniques, use of entities and knowledge graphs, recommender systems, retrieval methods, information extraction, question answering, topic and prediction models, multimedia retrieval, etc. In keeping with tradition, the ECIR 2021 program saw a high proportion of papers with students as first authors, and a balanced mix of papers from universities, public research institutes, and companies.

Putting everything together was hard teamwork. We want to thank everybody involved in making ECIR 2021 an exciting event. First and foremost, we want to thank our Program Chairs Djoerd Hiemstra and Marie-Francine (Sien) Moens for chairing the selection of the full papers. Many thanks also to the Short Papers Chairs Josiane Mothe and Martin Potthast, who managed not only the short paper submissions but also the CLEF papers submissions; to the Tutorials Chairs Richard McCreadie and Alejandro Moreo; to the Workshops Chairs Lorraine Goeuriot and Nicola Tonellotto; to the Reproducibility Track Chairs Maria Maistro and Gianmaria Silvello; to the Demo Chairs Nattiya Kanhabua and Franco Maria Nardini; to the Doctoral Consortium Chairs Claudio Lucchese and Guido Zuccon; to the Industry Day Chairs Roi Blanco and Fabrizio Silvestri; to the Sponsorship Chair Nicola Ferro; and to the Test-of-Time Award Chair Gabriella Pasi. Special thanks go also to our Publicity Chair Andrea Esuli and to our Proceedings Chair Ida Mele. All of them went to great lengths to ensure the high quality of this conference. Quite aside from the people who held chairing roles, lots of other people contributed to the scientific success of ECIR 2021: many thanks to the members of the Senior Program Committee, to the members of the Program Committees of the various tracks, to the mentors of the Doctoral Consortium Committee, and to all those who reviewed, in any capacity, full papers, short papers, reproducibility papers, tutorial and workshop proposals, and demo papers. Last but not least, we would like to thank all the members of the local organizing team at the National Research Council of Italy; in order to keep the registration fees as low as possible, no professional conference organization company was called in to help, which meant that this team took 100% of the organization upon them. We would thus like to thank our three Local Organization Chairs Cristina Muntean, Marinella Petrocchi and Beatrice Rapisarda. Thanks also to (in alphabetic order) Silvia Corbara, Andrea Esuli, Ida Mele, Alessio Molinari, Alejandro Moreo, Vinicius Monteiro de Lira, Franco Maria Nardini, Andrea Pedrotti, Nicola Tonellotto, Roberto Trani, and Salvatore Trani, for helping in various phases of the organization. They all invested tremendous efforts into making ECIR 2021 an exciting event by helping to create an enjoyable online and offline experience for authors and attendees. It is thanks to them that the organization of the conference was not just hard work, but also a pleasure. Finally, we would like to give heartfelt thanks to our sponsors and supporters: Bloomberg (platinum and best paper awards sponsor), Amazon, eBay, Google (gold sponsors), Textkernel (silver sponsor), Springer (test-of-time paper award sponsor), and Signal (industry impact award sponsor). We also gratefully acknowledge the generous support of the ACM Special Interest Group on Information Retrieval (ACM SIGIR) and of the ECIR 2020 organizers. We thank them all for their support and contributions to the conference, which allowed us to ask a low fee to paper authors only and to keep the registration free for all other attendees. Thanks also to the National Research Council of Italy, to the IMT School for Advanced Studies Lucca, to the British Computer Society's Information Retrieval Specialist Group (BCS-IRSG), and to the AI4Media project, for supporting our organizational work.

We hope you enjoy these proceedings of ECIR 2021!

March 28 to April 1, 2021   Raffaele Perego
                                                                  Fabrizio Sebastiani

Organization

General Chairs

Raffaele Perego   ISTI-CNR, Italy
Fabrizio Sebastiani   ISTI-CNR, Italy

Program Chairs

Djoerd Hiemstra   Radboud University, The Netherlands
Marie-Francine (Sien)   KU Leuven, Belgium
   Moens

Short Papers Chairs

Josiane Mothe   Université de Toulouse, France
Martin Potthast   Leipzig University, Germany

Tutorials Chairs

Richard McCreadie   University of Glasgow, UK
Alejandro Moreo   ISTI-CNR, Italy

Workshops Chairs

Lorraine Goeuriot   Université Grenoble Alpes, France
Nicola Tonellotto   Università di Pisa, Italy

Reproducibility Track Chairs

Maria Maistro   University of Copenhagen, Denmark
Gianmaria Silvello   Università di Padova, Italy

Demo Chairs

Nattiya Kanhabua   Upwork, Thailand
Franco Maria Nardini   ISTI-CNR, Italy

Industry Day Chairs

Roi Blanco   Amazon Research, Spain
Fabrizio Silvestri   Facebook, UK

Doctoral Consortium Chairs

Claudio Lucchese   Università di Venezia, Italy
Guido Zuccon   University of Queensland, Australia

Sponsorships Chair

Nicola Ferro   Università di Padova, Italy

Test-of-Time Award Chair

Gabriella Pasi   Università di Milano-Bicocca, Italy

Publicity Chair

Andrea Esuli   ISTI-CNR, Italy

Proceedings Chair

Ida Mele   IASI-CNR, Italy

Webmaster and Social Media Manager

Beatrice Rapisarda   IIT-CNR, Italy

Local Organization Chairs

Cristina Muntean   ISTI-CNR, Italy
Marinella Petrocchi   IIT-CNR, Italy
Beatrice Rapisarda   IIT-CNR, Italy

Local Organization Committee

Silvia Corbara   ISTI-CNR, Italy
Alessio Molinari   ISTI-CNR, Italy
Vinicius Monteiro de Lira   ISTI-CNR, Italy
Roberto Trani   ISTI-CNR, Italy
Salvatore Trani   ISTI-CNR, Italy
Andrea Pedrotti   ISTI-CNR, Italy

Organizing Institutions

Consiglio Nazionale delle Ricerche

ISTITUTO DI SCIENZA E TECNOLOGIE DELL'INFORMAZIONE "A. FAEDO"

Istituto di Informatica e Telematica

IMT SCHOOL FOR ADVANCED STUDIES LUCCA

Program Committee

Ahmed Abdelali	Hamid Bin Khalifa University
Karam Abdulahhad	GESIS - Leibniz Institute for the Social Sciences
Dirk Ahlers	Norwegian University of Science and Technology
Qingyao Ai	University of Utah
Ahmet Aker	University of Duisburg-Essen
Navot Akiva	Bar-Ilan University
Mehwish Alam	FIZ Karlsruhe - Leibniz Institute for Information Infrastructure, AIFB Institute, KIT
Dyaa Albakour	Signal AI
Mohammad Aliannejadi	University of Amsterdam
Pegah Alizadeh	École Supérieure d'Ingénieurs Léonard da Vinci
Satya Almasian	Heidelberg University
Omar Alonso	Instacart
İsmail Sengör Altıngövde	Bilkent University
Giambattista Amati	Fondazione Ugo Bordoni
Giuseppe Amato	ISTI-CNR
Linda Andersson	Artificial Researcher IT GmbH, TU Wien
Hassina Aouidad Aliane	CERIST
Ioannis Arapakis	Telefonica Research
Jaime Arguello	The University of North Carolina at Chapel Hill
Mozhdeh Ariannezhad	University of Amsterdam
Maurizio Atzori	University of Cagliari
Ebrahim Bagheri	Ryerson University
Seyed Ali Bahreinian	IDSIA
Krisztian Balog	University of Stavanger
Alexandros Bampoulidis	Research Studio Data Science - RSA FG
Mitra Baratchi	Leiden University
Alvaro Barreiro	University of A Coruña
Alberto Barrón-Cedeño	University of Bologna
Alejandro Bellogin	Universidad Autònoma de Madrid
Patrice Bellot	Aix-Marseille Université - CNRS (LSIS)
Alessandro Benedetti	Sease
Klaus Berberich	Saarbrücken University of Applied Sciences (htw saar)
Catherine Berrut	LIG, Université Joseph Fourier Grenoble I
Sumit Bhatia	IBM
Paheli Bhattacharya	Indian Institute of Technology Kharagpur
Roi Blanco	Amazon
Gloria Bordogna	National Research Council of Italy - CNR
Larbi Boubchir	University of Paris 8
Pavel Braslavski	Ural Federal University
David Brazier	Edinburgh Napier University
Timo Breuer	TH Köln (University of Applied Science)
Paul Buitelaar	Insight Centre for Data Analytics, National University of Ireland Galway

Fidel Cacheda	Universidade da Coruña
Sylvie Calabretto	LIRIS
Pável Calado	INESC-ID, University of Lisbon
Rodrigo Calumby	University of Feira de Santana
Ricardo Campos	Ci2 - Polytechnic Institute of Tomar; INESC TEC
Fazli Can	Bilkent University
Iván Cantador	Universidad Autónoma de Madrid
Annalina Caputo	Dublin City University
Zeljko Carevic	GESIS Leibniz Institute for the Social Sciences
Ben Carterette	Spotify
Pablo Castells	Universidad Autónoma de Madrid
Shubham Chatterjee	University of New Hampshire
Despoina Chatzakou	Information Technologies Institute, Centre for Research and Technology Hellas
Long Chen	University of Glasgow
Max Chevalier	IRIT
Adrian-Gabriel Chifu	Aix Marseille Univ, CNRS, LIS
Konstantina Christakopoulou	Google
Malcolm Clark	The University of the Highlands & Islands
Vincent Claveau	IRISA - CNRS
Jérémie Clos	University of Nottingham
Paul Clough	The University of Sheffield
Alessio Conte	University of Pisa
Fabio Crestani	University of Lugano (USI)
Bruce Croft	University of Massachusetts Amherst
Arthur Câmara	Delft University of Technology
Tirthankar Dasgupta	Tata Consultancy Services
Martine De Cock	University of Washington
Hélène De Ribaupierre	Cardiff University
Arjen de Vries	Radboud University
Yashar Deldjoo	Polytechnic University of Bari
Elena Demidova	Bonn University
José Devezas	University of Porto
Emanuele Di Buccio	University of Padua
Giorgio Maria Di Nunzio	University of Padua
Gaël Dias	University of Caen Normandie
Liviu Dinu	University of Bucharest
Vlastislav Dohnal	Masaryk University
Inês Domingues	IPO Porto + Universidade de Coimbra
Dennis Dosso	University of Padua
Pan Du	University of Montreal
Mehdi Elahi	University of Bergen
Tamer Elsayed	Qatar University
Ludwig Englbrecht	University of Regensburg
Liana Ermakova	HCTI EA-4249, Université de Bretagne Occidentale

José Alberto Esquivel	Primer.ai
Andrea Esuli	Istituto di Scienza e Tecnologie dell'Informazione
Ralph Ewerth	L3S Research Center, Leibniz Universität Hannover
Alessandro Fabris	University of Padova
Erik Faessler	University of Jena
Anjie Fang	Amazon.com
Hui Fang	University of Delaware
Hossein Fani	University of Windsor
Nicola Ferro	University of Padova
Sébastien Fournier	LSIS
Christoph M. Friedrich	University of Applied Sciences and Arts Dortmund
Ingo Frommholz	University of Wolverhampton
Norbert Fuhr	University of Duisburg-Essen
Michael Färber	Karlsruhe Institute of Technology
Luke Gallagher	RMIT University
Debasis Ganguly	IBM Ireland Research Lab
Darío Garigliotti	Aalborg University
Anastasia Giachanou	Utrecht University
Giorgos Giannopoulos	IMSI Institute, "Athena" Research Center
Alessandro Giuliani	University of Cagliari
Lorraine Goeuriot	Univ. Grenoble Alpes, CNRS, Grenoble INP, LIG
Marcos Gonçalves	Federal University of Minas Gerais
Julio Gonzalo	UNED
Kripabandhu Ghosh	IISER Kolkata
Michael Granitzer	University of Passau
Adrien Guille	Université de Lyon
Rajeev Gupta	Microsoft
Shashank Gupta	Flipkart
Cathal Gurrin	Dublin City University
Matthias Hagen	Martin-Luther-Universität Halle-Wittenberg
Lei Han	The University of Queensland
Allan Hanbury	Vienna University of Technology
Preben Hansen	Stockholm University
Donna Harman	NIST
Helia Hashemi	University of Massachusetts Amherst
Faegheh Hasibi	Radboud University
Claudia Hauff	Delft University of Technology
Jer Hayes	Accenture
Ben He	University of Chinese Academy of Sciences
Nathalie Hernandez	IRIT
Djoerd Hiemstra	Radboud University
Daniel Hienert	GESIS - Leibniz Institute for the Social Sciences
Gilles Hubert	IRIT
Ali Hürriyetoğlu	Koç University
Adrian Iftene	"Al.I.Cuza" University of Iasi

Dmitry Ignatov	National Research University Higher School of Economics
Bogdan Ionescu	University Politehnica of Bucharest
Radu Tudor Ionescu	University of Bucharest
Mihai Ivanovici	Transilvania University of Braşov
Adam Jatowt	University of Innsbruck
Jean-Michel Renders	Naver Labs Europe
Shiyu Ji	UCSB
Jiepu Jiang	University of Wisconsin-Madison
Gareth Jones	Dublin City University
Joemon Jose	University of Glasgow
Chris Kamphuis	Radboud University
Jaap Kamps	University of Amsterdam
Nattiya Kanhabua	Upwork
Jussi Karlgren	Spotify
Jaana Kekäläinen	Tampere University
Liadh Kelly	Maynooth University
Roman Kern	Graz University of Technology
Daniel Kershaw	Elsevier
Prasanna Lakshmi Kompalli	Gokaraju Rangaraju Institute of Engineering and Technology
Ralf Krestel	Hasso Plattner Institute, University of Potsdam
Kriste Krstovski	University of Massachusetts Amherst
Udo Kruschwitz	University of Regensburg
Vaibhav Kumar	Amazon Alexa AI, Carnegie Mellon University
Oren Kurland	Technion, Israel Institute of Technology
Saar Kuzi	University of Illinois at Urbana-Champaign
Léa Laporte	INSA Lyon - LIRIS
Teerapong Leelanupab	King Mongkut's Institute of Technology Ladkrabang
Jochen L. Leidner	University of Sheffield
Mark Levene	Birkbeck, University of London
Elisabeth Lex	Graz University of Technology
Jimmy Lin	University of Waterloo
Matteo Lissandrini	Aalborg University
Suzanne Little	Dublin City University
Haiming Liu	University of Bedfordshire
Fernando Loizides	Cardiff University
David Losada	University of Santiago de Compostela
Natalia Loukachevitch	Research Computing Center of Moscow State University
Claudio Lucchese	Ca' Foscari University of Venice
Bernd Ludwig	Universität Regensburg
Sean MacAvaney	University of Glasgow
Craig Macdonald	University of Glasgow
Andrew Macfarlane	City, University of London
Joel Mackenzie	The University of Melbourne

João Magalhães	Universidade NOVA de Lisboa
Walid Magdy	The University of Edinburgh
Marco Maggini	University of Siena
Shikha Maheshwari	Chitkara University
Maria Maistro	University of Copenhagen
Antonio Mallia	New York University
Thomas Mandl	University of Hildesheim
Behrooz Mansouri	University of Tehran
Jiaxin Mao	Renmin University of China
Stefano Marchesin	University of Padova
Rainer Martin	Institute of Communication Acoustics, Ruhr-Universität Bochum
Miguel Martinez	Signal AI
Bruno Martins	IST and INESC-ID - Instituto Superior Técnico, University of Lisbon
Fernando Martínez-Santiago	Universidad de Jaén
Yosi Mass	IBM Haifa Research Lab
Sérgio Matos	IEETA, Universidade de Aveiro
Philipp Mayr	GESIS
Richard McCreadie	University of Glasgow
Graham McDonald	University of Glasgow
Parth Mehta	IRSI
Edgar Meij	Bloomberg L.P.
Ida Mele	IASI-CNR
Massimo Melucci	University of Padova
Marcelo Mendoza	Universidad Técnica Federico Santa María
Zaiqiao Meng	University of Cambridge
Dmitrijs Milajevs	Queen Mary University of London
Malik Muhammad Saad Missen	The Islamia University of Bahawalpur
Bhaskar Mitra	Microsoft
Marie-Francine Sien Moens	Katholieke Universiteit Leuven
Mohand Boughanem	IRIT University Paul Sabatier Toulouse
Ludovic Moncla	LIRIS (UMR 5205 CNRS), INSA Lyon
Vinicius Monteiro de Lira	CNR - Pisa
Felipe Moraes	Delft University of Technology
José Moreno	IRIT/UPS
Alejandro Moreo	Istituto di Scienza e Tecnologie dell'Informazione "A. Faedo"
Yashar Moshfeghi	University of Strathclyde
Josiane Mothe	Université de Toulouse
Philippe Mulhem	LIG-CNRS
Cristina Ioana Muntean	ISTI CNR
Henning Müller	HES-SO
Preslav Nakov	Qatar Computing Research Institute, HBKU
Franco Maria Nardini	ISTI-CNR

Wolfgang Nejdl	L3S and University of Hannover
Jian-Yun Nie	University of Montreal
Andreas Nürnberger	Otto-von-Guericke University of Magdeburg
Kjetil Nørvåg	Norwegian University of Science and Technology
Neil O'Hare	Yahoo Research
Douglas Oard	University of Maryland
Michel Oleynik	Medical University of Graz
Anaïs Ollagnier	University of Exeter
Teresa Onorati	Universidad Carlos III de Madrid
Salvatore Orlando	Università Ca' Foscari Venezia
Iadh Ounis	University of Glasgow
Mourad Oussalah	University of Oulu
Deepak P.	Queen's University Belfast
Jiaul Paik	IIT Kharagpur
João Palotti	MIT
Girish Palshikar	Tata Consultancy Services
Polina Panicheva	National Research University Higher School of Economics, St Petersburg
Panagiotis Papadakos	Information Systems Laboratory - FORTH-ICS
Javier Parapar	University of A Coruña
Dae Hoon Park	Yahoo Research
Arian Pasquali	University of Porto
Bidyut Kr. Patra	NIT Rourkela
Pavel Pecina	Charles University in Prague
Filipa Peleja	Levi Strauss & Co.
Gustavo Penha	Delft University of Technology
Raffaele Perego	ISTI-CNR
Giulio Ermanno Pibiri	ISTI-CNR
Jeremy Pickens	OpenText
Karen Pinel-Sauvagnat	IRIT
Benjamin Piwowarski	CNRS/Sorbonne University Pierre and Marie Curie Campus
Martin Potthast	Leipzig University
Animesh Prasad	Amazon Alexa
Chen Qu	University of Massachusetts Amherst
Navid Rekab-Saz	Johannes Kepler University (JKU)
Kaspar Riesen	University of Applied Sciences and Arts Northwestern Switzerland
Kirk Roberts	The University of Texas Health Science Center at Houston
Paolo Rosso	Universitat Politècnica de València
Eric Sanjuan	Laboratoire Informatique d'Avignon- Université d'Avignon
Kamal Sarkar	Jadavpur University, Kolkata
Ramit Sawhney	Tower Research Capital
Philipp Schaer	TH Köln (University of Applied Sciences)

Ralf Schenkel	Trier University
Fabrizio Sebastiani	ISTI-CNR
Florence Sedes	I.R.I.T. Univ. P. Sabatier
Thomas Seidl	Ludwig-Maximilians-Universität München (LMU Munich)
Giovanni Semeraro	University of Bari
Procheta Sen	Dublin City University
Gautam Kishore Shahi	University of Duisburg-Essen, Germany
Mahsa S. Shahshahani	University of Amsterdam
Azadeh Shakery	University of Tehran
Eilon Sheetrit	Technion - Israel Institute of Technology
Jialie Shen	Queen's University Belfast
Kai Shu	Arizona State University
Mário J. Silva	Universidade de Lisboa
Gianmaria Silvello	University of Padua
Fabrizio Silvestri	Facebook
Laure Soulier	Sorbonne Université-LIP6
Marc Spaniol	Université de Caen Normandie
Günther Specht	University of Innsbruck
Damiano Spina	RMIT University
Andreas Spitz	Ecole Polytechnique Fédérale de Lausanne
Efstathios Stamatatos	University of the Aegean
Hanna Suominen	The ANU
Lynda Tamine	IRIT
Carla Teixeira Lopes	University of Porto
Gabriele Tolomei	Sapienza University of Rome
Antonela Tommasel	ISISTAN Research Institute, CONICET-UNCPBA
Nicola Tonellotto	University of Pisa
Salvatore Trani	ISTI-CNR
Alina Trifan	University of Aveiro
Manos Tsagkias	Apple
Theodora Tsikrika	Information Technologies Institute, CERTH
Ferhan Ture	Comcast Labs
Yannis Tzitzikas	University of Crete and FORTH-ICS
Md Zia Ullah	CNRS
Julián Urbano	Delft University of Technology
Daniel Valcarce	Google
Julien Velcin	ERIC Lyon 2, EA 3083, Université de Lyon
Suzan Verberne	Leiden University
Manisha Verma	VerizonMedia
Karin Verspoor	The University of Melbourne
Vishwa Vinay	Adobe Research
Marco Viviani	Università degli Studi di Milano-Bicocca
Duc Thuan Vo	Ryerson University
Stefanos Vrochidis	Information Technologies Institute
Shuohang Wang	Singapore Management University

Xi Wang	University of Glasgow
Christa Womser-Hacker	University of Hildesheim
Grace Hui Yang	Georgetown University
Min Yang	The Chinese Academy of Sciences
Andrew Yates	Max Planck Institute for Informatics
Emine Yilmaz	University College London
Hai-Tao Yu	University of Tsukuba
Ran Yu	GESIS - Leibniz Institute for the Social Sciences
Reza Zafarani	Syracuse University
Eva Zangerle	University of Innsbruck
Fattane Zarrinkalam	Ryerson University
Sergej Zerr	Leibniz Universität Hannover
Weinan Zhang	Shanghai Jiao Tong University
Xiangyu Zhao	Michigan State University
Xinyi Zhou	Syracuse University
Xiaofei Zhu	Chongqing University of Technology
Guido Zuccon	The University of Queensland

Additional Reviewers

Amigó, Enrique
Anand, Mayuresh
Apte, Manoj
Auersperger, Michal
Bakhshi, Sepehr
Bannihatti Kumar, Vinayshekhar
Bartscherer, Frederic
Basile, Pierpaolo
Bedathur, Srikanta
Bondarenko, Alexander
Boughanem, Mohand
Breuer, Timo
Busch, Julian
Christophe, Clément
Cresci, Stefano
Dadwal, Rajjat
Dalal, Dhairya
de Freitas, João
De Ribaupierre, Hélène
Dessì, Danilo
Dsouza, Alishiba
Efimov, Pavel
Essam, Marwa
Feng, Haoyun
Fournier, Sebastien

Fröbe, Maik
Gabler, Philipp
Gerritse, Emma
Ghahramanian, Pouya
Gourru, Antoine
Haak, Fabian
Hakimov, Sherzod
Haouari, Fatima
Hasanain, Maram
Hingmire, Swapnil
Hoppe, Anett
Iovine, Andrea
Jatowt, Adam
Julka, Sahib
Jullien, Sami
Kanungsukkasem, Nont
Kondapally, Ranganath
Kosmatopoulos, Andreas
Lal, Yash Kumar
Lee, Kai-Zhan
Loizides, Fernando
Lucchese, Claudio
Mavropoulos, Thanassis
Mayerl, Maximilian
Moumtzidou, Anastasia

Muntean, Cristina Ioana
Murauer, Benjamin
Mussard, Stéphane
Musto, Cataldo
Nardini, Franco Maria
Nikas, Christos
Noullet, Kristian
Nurbakova, Diana
Otto, Christian
Parveen, Daraksha
Pasricha, Nivranshu
Patil, Sangameshwar
Pawar, Sachin
Pegia, Maria Eirini
Perego, Raffaele
Pibiri, Giulio Ermanno
Polignano, Marco
Poux-Médard, Gaël
Pérez Vila, Miguel Anxo
Qiao, Yifan
Rahmani, Hossein A.
Repke, Tim
Roy, Nirmal
Saleh, Shadi
Santana, Brenda

Schaer, Philipp
Semedo, David
Sen, Bipasha
Shah, Shalin
Sharma, Himanshu
Skopek, Ondrej
Strauß, Niklas
Su, Ting
Suryawanshi, Shardul
Suwaileh, Reem
Syamala, Rama
Tavares, Diogo
Tempelmeier, Nicolas
Tonellotto, Nicola
Trani, Roberto
Truchan, Hubert
Venturini, Rossano
Vötter, Michael
Wang, Benyou
Witschel, Frieder
Yang, Min
Yang, Yingrui
Zerhoudi, Saber
Zhang, Zixun
Zühlke, Monty-Maximilian

Platinum and Best Paper Awards Sponsor

Bloomberg
`Engineering`

Bloomberg is building the world's most trusted information network for financial professionals. Our 6,000+ engineers, developers, and data scientists are dedicated to advancing and building new solutions and systems for the Bloomberg Terminal and other products in order to solve complex, real-world problems. Improving search and discovery of relevant content, functionality, and insights are critical focus areas for Bloomberg. To this end, we use Machine Learning, Deep Learning, Natural Language Processing, Information Retrieval, and Knowledge Graph technology across Bloomberg in several applications, including search, question answering, data integration, recommender systems, etc. to quickly understand and respond to major world events in order to predict when or how breaking business news will move markets – and why.

Gold Sponsors

Google   amazon | science   ebay

Silver Sponsor

textkernel

Test-of-Time Best Paper Award Sponsor

Springer

Test-of-Time Best Paper Award Sponsor

SIGNAL

With Generous Support from

SIGIR
Special Interest Group
on Information Retrieval

Contents – Part II

Short Papers

Demo Papers

CLEF 2021 Lab Descriptions

Doctoral Consortium Papers

Workshops

Contents – Part I

Reproducibility Track Papers

Cross-Domain Retrieval in the Legal and Patent Domains: A Reproducibility Study

Sophia Althammer[✉], Sebastian Hofstätter, and Allan Hanbury

TU Wien, Vienna, Austria
{sophia.althammer,sebastian.hofstatter,allan.hanbury}@tuwien.ac.at

Abstract. Domain specific search has always been a challenging information retrieval task due to several challenges such as the domain specific language, the unique task setting, as well as the lack of accessible queries and corresponding relevance judgements. In the last years, pretrained language models – such as BERT – revolutionized web and news search. Naturally, the community aims to adapt these advancements to cross-domain transfer of retrieval models for domain specific search. In the context of legal document retrieval, Shao et al. propose the BERT-PLI framework by modeling the **P**aragraph-**L**evel **I**nteractions with the language model BERT. In this paper we reproduce the original experiments, we clarify pre-processing steps and add missing scripts for framework steps, however we are not able to reproduce the evaluation results. Contrary to the original paper, we demonstrate that the domain specific paragraph-level modelling does not appear to help the performance of the BERT-PLI model compared to paragraph-level modelling with the original BERT. In addition to our legal search reproducibility study, we investigate BERT-PLI for document retrieval in the patent domain. We find that the BERT-PLI model does not yet achieve performance improvements for patent document retrieval compared to the BM25 baseline. Furthermore, we evaluate the BERT-PLI model for cross-domain retrieval between the legal and patent domain on individual components, both on a paragraph and document-level. We find that the transfer of the BERT-PLI model on the paragraph-level leads to comparable results between both domains as well as first promising results for the cross-domain transfer on the document-level. For reproducibility and transparency as well as to benefit the community we make our source code and the trained models publicly available.

Keywords: Information retrieval · Domain specific search · Reproducibility · Legal search · Patent search · Cross-domain retrieval

1 Introduction

Bringing the substantial effectiveness gains from contextualized language retrieval models from web and news search to other domains is paramount to the equitable use of machine learning models in Information Retrieval (IR).

© Springer Nature Switzerland AG 2021
D. Hiemstra et al. (Eds.): ECIR 2021, LNCS 12657, pp. 3–17, 2021.
https://doi.org/10.1007/978-3-030-72240-1_1

The promise of these pre-trained models is a cross-domain transfer with limited in-domain training data. Thus we investigate in this paper the document retrieval on two specific language domains, the legal and the patent domain, and study the transferability of the retrieval models between both domains.

In case law systems the precedent cases are a key source for lawyers, therefore it is essential for the lawyers' work to retrieve prior cases which support the query case. Similarly in the patent domain, patent examiners review patent applications and search for prior art, in order to determine what contribution the invention makes over the prior art. The recent advances in language modelling have shown that contextualized language models enhance the performance of information retrieval models in the web and news domain compared to traditional ad-hoc retrieval models [10,11]. However for legal and patent retrieval we have a different task setting as the documents contain longer text with a mean of 11,100 words per document. In document retrieval every passage may be relevant, therefore in a high-recall setting such as ours it is crucial for the retrieval model to take the whole document into account. This is a challenge for contextualized language retrieval models, which are only capable of computing short passages with a length up to 512 tokens [7,25,26].

Recently, Shao et al. [20] aimed to bring the gains of language modelling to legal document retrieval and tackle the challenge of long documents by proposing BERT-PLI, a multi-stage framework which models **P**aragraph-**L**evel **I**nteractions of queries and candidates with multiple paragraphs using BERT [6]. The document-level relevance of each query and candidate pair is predicted based on paragraph-level interaction of the query and candidate paragraphs which are aggregated with a recurrent neural network (LSTM or GRU). The BERT-PLI model is trained in two stages: first, BERT is trained on a paragraph entailment task, and second the recurrent aggregation component is trained on a binary classification task.

In this paper we reproduce the results for the legal retrieval task. We found shortcomings in the description of the data pre-processing and evaluation methods, after a discussion with the authors of the original paper we could clarify how the evaluation results are achieved. As the published code is missing crucial parts, we re-implement the pre-processing, the first stage BERT fine-tuning as well as the retrieval with BM25 in the second stage and the overall evaluation. Furthermore we analyze the ablation study of the original paper and answer the following research question:

RQ1 Does fine-tuning BERT on domain specific paragraphs improve the retrieval performance for document retrieval?

The original paper finds a 7–9% performance improvement of the BERT-PLI model for legal retrieval, when fine-tuning BERT on the legal paragraphs. Contrary to the original paper, we find that the paragraph-level modelling with BERT, fine-tuned on the domain specific paragraph-level modelling, does not appear to help the BERT-PLI model's performance on legal document retrieval. In line with that, we also demonstrate that the patent specific paragraph-level modelling harms the performance of the BERT-PLI model also for the patent retrieval task and remains a promising opportunity.

In order to analyze the proposed BERT-PLI model for another document retrieval task with long documents, we investigate following research question:

RQ2 To what extent is a BERT-PLI model, which is trained on patent retrieval, beneficial for document retrieval in the patent domain?

We find that the patent domain BERT-PLI model is outperformed by the BM25 baseline for the patent retrieval task. This shows that the document retrieval with BERT is not yet beneficial for the patent retrieval and stays a promising opportunity.

As the legal and patent documents come from similar language domains, it becomes an interesting question to what extent we can transfer the domain specific retrieval models from one to the other domain. Especially because of the restricted accessbility of domain specific, labelled retrieval data there is the need for studying cross-domain transfer of document retrieval models.

RQ3 To what extent is cross-domain transfer on paragraph- and document-level of the domain specific BERT-PLI model between legal and patent domain possible?

We show that the transfer of the domain specific paragraph-level interaction modelling is possible between the legal and patent domain with similar performance of the retrieval model. Furthermore we find on the document-level transfer that the zero-shot application of a patent domain specific BERT-PLI model for the legal retrieval task achieves a lower performance than the BM25 baseline. Showing first promising results, the cross-domain transfer of retrieval models stays an open and exciting research direction. Our main contributions are:

- We reproduce the experiments of Shao et al. [20] and investigate shortcomings in the data pre-processing and model methods. Contrary to the paper we find that domain specific paragraph-level modelling does not appear to help the performance of the BERT-PLI model for legal document retrieval
- We train a domain specific BERT-PLI model for the patent domain and demonstrate that it does not yet outperform the BM25 baseline
- We analyze the cross-domain transfer of the BERT-PLI model between the legal and patent domain with first promising results
- In order to make our results available for reproduction and to benefit the community, we publish the source code and trained models at: https://github.com/sophiaalthammer/bert-pli

2 Methods

2.1 Task Description

Document retrieval in the legal and patent domain are specialized IR tasks with the particularity that query and candidates are long documents which use domain specific language.

In legal document retrieval, the relevant documents are defined as the previous cases which should be noticed for solving the query case [17], in other words which support or contradict the query document [20]. The legal documents consist of long text containing the factual description of a case.

Relevance in the patent domain is defined for the prior art search task [15], i.e. it is the task to find documents in the corpus that are related to the new invention or describe the same invention. The patent documents consist of a title, an abstract, claims and a description as well as metadata like the authors or topical classifications. As we investigate retrieval and classification based on the textual information, we will only consider the textual data of the patent documents.

2.2   BERT-PLI Architecture Overview

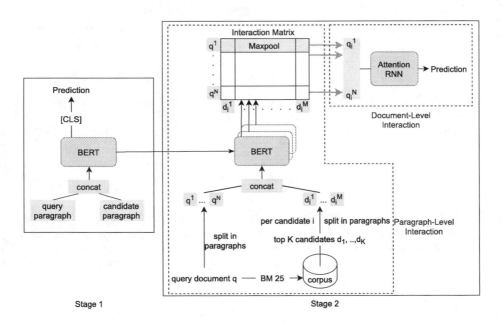

Fig. 1. BERT-PLI Multistage architecture

As the BERT model advanced the state-of-the-art in natural language processing and information retrieval, but has the restriction that it can only model the relation between short paragraphs, Shao et al. [20] propose a multi-stage framework model using BERT for the retrieval of long documents which is illustrated in Fig. 1. The training is separated into two stages. In stage 1, BERT is fine-tuned on a relevance prediction task on a paragraph-level. BERT takes the concatenated query and document paragraph as input and is then fine-tuned on predicting the relevance of the candidate paragraph to the query paragraph

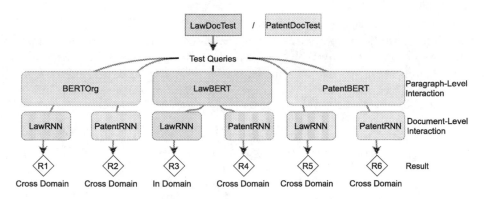

Fig. 2. Cross-domain evaluation approach

given the output vector of the special [CLS] token of BERT. Therefore this output vector is trained to be a relevance representation on a paragraph-level of the two concatenated input paragraphs.

This fine-tuned BERT model is used in stage 2, where the full document retrieval with paragraph-level interaction modelling takes place. For a query document q the top K candidates are retrieved from a corpus using BM25 [18], and the query document as well as the top K candidates are split into paragraphs. Then for each candidate $i \in 1, .., K$ the first N paragraphs of the query document and the first M paragraphs of the candidate are concatenated and their relevance representation is calculated with the BERT model from stage 1. This yields an interaction matrix between the query and candidate paragraphs. An additional Maxpooling layer captures the strongest matching signals per query paragraph and yields a document-level relevance representation of the query and the candidate. This document-level relevance representation is used to train an RNN model with a succeeding attention and fully-connected forward layer which we will refer to as Attention RNN. This Attention RNN yields the binary prediction of the relevance for the query and candidate document.

2.3 Cross-Domain Evaluation Approach

In the first stage of the BERT-PLI framework the BERT model learns to model the paragraph-level interaction. For the two different domains we fine-tune the BERT model on a paragraph-level relevance prediction task, which yields the paragraph-level interaction **LawBERT** model for the legal and the **Patent-BERT** model for the patent domain. In order to analyze the influence of the domain specific paragraph-level modelling, we compare the document retrieval models trained with the paragraph-level modelling of LawBERT or PatentBERT to document retrieval models trained on the paragraph-level modelling of the original BERT model. The paragraph-level modelling with the original BERT model is denoted with **BERT$_{\mathbf{ORG}}$** as in Fig. 2.

Based on these paragraph-level interaction representations we train an AttentionRNN on the legal as well as on the patent document-level retrieval task, which we denote with **LawRNN** or **PatentRNN** respectively. In order to isolate the impact of the different modelling of the paragraph-level interactions from LawBERT and PatentBERT, we additionally train an AttentionRNN on the patent document retrieval task given their LawBERT relevance representations and vice versa.

We evaluate the resulting models on the legal or the patent test document retrieval set, namely **LawDocTest** or **PatentDocTest**. This process is visualized in Fig. 2 and yields six evaluation results R1-6 for each test set. For example for LawDocTest, R3 is the in-domain evaluation result, whereas the other results denote cross domain evaluations. For LawDocTest the results R1, R3 and R5 are all from LawRNN document retrieval, but the LawRNNs differ in the paragraph-level relevance representation they are trained with. Therefore comparison of the results R1, R3 and R5 on LawDocTest shows the transferability of the paragraph-level modelling between the legal and patent domains and the difference of domain-specific paragraph-level modelling to the non-domain specific modelling. Furthermore to analyze the cross-domain transfer on the document-level, we compare the evaluation results of LawDocTest and PatentDocTest of R1 and R2, R3 and R4 as well as R5 and R6. This comparison shows the cross-domain transferability on the document-level as the LawRNN and PatentRNN share the same paragraph-level relevance representations, which they are trained on.

3   Experiments

3.1   Datasets

Legal Retrieval Dataset. Like Shao et al. [20], we use the legal retrieval collections from the COLIEE evaluation campaign 2019 [17], which consist of a paragraph-level and a document-level retrieval task. Both retrieval collections are based on cases from the Canadian case law system and are written in English. The paragraph-level task (COLIEE 2019 Task 2) involves the identification of a paragraph which entails the given query paragraph [17]. For this task the COLIEE evaluation campaign provides training and test queries with relevance judgements which we will refer to as **LawParaTrain** and **LawParaTest**. In the document-retrieval task (COLIEE 2019 Task 1) it is asked to find supporting cases from a provided set of candidate documents, which support the decision of the query document. As in the original paper we take 20% of the queries of the training set as validation set, denoted with **LawDocVal**. We will refer to the training and test datasets for the document retrieval as **LawDocTrain** and **LawDocTest**.

Patent Retrieval Dataset. For the patent retrieval queries and relevance judgments we use the datasets from the CLEF-IP evaluation campaign [14] as they provide a patent corpus and training and test collections for patent retrieval tasks on the paragraph- and document-level. The tasks contain English, French and German queries, we only consider the English queries and candidates. For the paragraph-level training and test collection we choose the provided queries and relevance judgements from the passage retrieval task starting from claims of the CLEF-IP 2013 [14] where the participants are asked to find passages from patent documents which are relevant to a given set of claims. We refer to these datasets as **PatentParaTrain** and **PatentParaTest**. As the document-level training and test collection we choose the queries and relevance judgements from the prior art candidate search from the CLEF-IP evaluation campaign 2011 [15] and refer to them as **PatentDocTrain** and **PatentDocTest**. As in the original paper, we take 20% of the training set as validation set, denoted with **PatentDocVal**. Both patent retrieval tasks retrieve paragraphs and documents from the patent corpus which consists of 3.5 million patent documents filed at the European Patent Office (EPO) or at the World Intellectual Property Office (WIPO).

The dataset statistics can be found in Table 1.

Table 1. Statistics of the training and test set for the paragraph the document-level retrieval task

	LawPara		LawDoc		PatentPara		PatentDoc	
	Train	Test	Train	Test	Train	Test	Train	Test
# of queries	181	41	285	61	44	42	351	100
avg # of candidates	32.12	32.19	200	200	3.5M	3.5M	3.5M	3.5M
avg # relevant candidates	1.12	1.02	5.21	5.41	43.52	76.3	3.27	2.85

3.2   Experiment Setting

Stage 1: BERT Fine-Tuning. In the first stage we fine-tune the BERT model[1] on the paragraph-level relevance classification for either the legal domain or the patent domain to attain LawBERT and PatentBERT. As there was no code open-sourced for fine-tuning BERT, we use the HuggingFace transformers library[2] and add the BERT fine-tuning script to the published code.

For LawBERT we use the LawParaTrain as training and LawParaTest as test queries and relevance judgements. In order to use the queries and relevance judgements for a binary classification task, we consider the paragraph pairs of the query and one relevant candidate as positive samples. It was not stated clearly in the original paper how the paragraph pairs of negative samples are constructed, therefore we investigate this data pre-processing decision. We find that taking all paragraph pairs constructed of the query and a non-relevant paragraph from the paragraph candidates as negatives, yields comparable results for fine-tuning the

---

[1] checkpoint from https://github.com/google-research/bert.
[2] https://github.com/huggingface/transformers.

BERT model on the legal domain as in the original paper. This negative sampling approach results in 3% positive and 97% negative samples in the training set. The queries and paragraph candidates have less than 100 words on average and are truncated symmetrically if they exceed the maximum input length of 512 tokens of BERT. For the training batch size we do a grid search and find that the F1-score of LawParaTest is the highest with a batch size of 2 (65.1% F1-Score) instead of 1 (63.4% F1-Score) after fine-tuning BERT for 3 epochs on LawParaTrain, contrary to the original paper: they report the highest F1-score of 65.2% without reporting the batch size. As stated in the original code, we assumed they used the batch size of 1, due to our comparison we use a batch size of 2 instead of 1. After a remark of the original authors it turns out the original implementation was done with a batch size of 16. For the learning rate we also do a grid search and find that the learning rate of $1e-5$ is optimal as in the original paper. As in the original paper, we fine-tune for 3 epochs and we do the final fine-tuning of the LawBERT model on the merged training and test set. This is permissible as we train and evaluate the BERT-PLI model on LawDocTrain and LawDocTest, the LawParaTrain and LawParaTest sets are only used for fine-tuning LawBERT.

For the PatentBERT fine-tuning we use the PatentParaTrain as training and PatentParaTest as test set. We construct the negative paragraph pairs by sampling randomly paragraphs (which are not the relevant paragraph) from the documents which contain a relevant paragraph to a query paragraph. Here we sample randomly 5 times the number of positive paragraphs as negatives, as otherwise the share of positive pairs is below 1% and in order to have a similar ratio as for the legal domain. We do a grid search for the training batch size and learning rate and find that a batch size of 2 with a learning rate of $2e-5$ yields the highest F1-score of 19.0%. We fine-tune PatentBERT solely on PatentParaTrain as it is common practice to hold out the test set.

Stage 2: Document Retrieval. In stage 2 the first step is to retrieve relevant documents from the given set of candidates (in the legal domain) or from the whole corpus (in the patent domain). As it was not clearly stated in the original paper nor was there code published, how to employ the BM25 algorithm [18] for this first step, we re-implement this step and use the BM25 algorithm [18] with $k_1 = 0.9$ and $b = 0.4$ implemented in the Pyserini toolkit[3]. Furthermore we do a grid search for the input length to the BM25 algorithm and find that the top $K = 50$ retrieval with input length of 250 leads to similar recall scores as the original paper for the LawDocTrain set (93.22%) and the LawDocTest (92.23%). Here we only consider recall scores as in the original paper, as the focus of the first step BM25 retrieval is to retrieve all relevant cases for re-ranking for the training and test set.

For patent document retrieval, the task is to retrieve relevant documents from the patent corpus with 3.5 million documents. As in the patent document

---

[3] https://github.com/castorini/pyserini.

retrieval task only 3.27 relevant patent documents per query document are contained and as the recall does not significantly increase when taking $K = 50$ candidates, we choose the top $K = 20$ from the BM25 retrieval, in order to have a similar ratio of positive and negative pairs as in the legal document retrieval for training the AttentionRNN. Here we find that the BM25 algorithm with the document input length of 250 reaches the highest recall score of 9.42% on Patent-DocTrain compared to other document input lengths. Due to the low recall score of the retrieved documents on PatentDocTrain we add the relevant documents from the relevance judgements to PatentDocTrain and sample randomly non-relevant documents from the BM25 candidates for the training dataset, so that we have in total 20 candidates. For PatentDocTest we retrieve the top 50 candidates as in the original implementation where we reach a recall of 10.66%, but we do not add the relevant candidates after the BM25 retrieval step. In order to reproduce the experiments for modelling the paragraph-level interaction and training the Attention RNN, we use the open-sourced repository[4] of the original paper. As in the original paper we set the number of paragraphs of the query $N = 54$ and the number of paragraphs of the candidate $M = 40$ for legal and patent retrieval. The query and candidate documents are split up in paragraphs of 256 tokens. We model the paragraph-level interactions of LawDocTrain, Law-DocTest, PatentDocTrain and PatentDocTest using LawBERT or PatentBERT or $BERT_{ORG}$. With these paragraph-level representations of each query and its candidate document we train an AttentionRNN network with either an LSTM [9] or a GRU network [3] as RNN on classifying the relevance between the query and candidate document. The AttentionRNN trained on the LawDocTrain is denoted with LawRNN, on PatentDocTrain it is denoted with PatentRNN. For training the AttentionRNN we use the same hyperparameter as in the original implementation, except for the PatentBERT LawRNN configuration, where we find that the learning rate of $1e-4$ is better suited, when evaluated on the LawDocVal set.

4   Evaluation and Analysis

4.1   In-Domain Evaluation for Legal Document Retrieval (RQ1)

Shao et al. [20] evaluate their models using the binary classification metrics precision, recall and F1-Score on the whole test set. Furthermore they compare their model performance to the two best runs from the COLIEE 2019 denoted by the team names JNLP [22] and ILPS [19]. As it was not clearly stated in the original paper, we assume that Shao et al. [20] evaluate the BERT-PLI models on the whole LawDocTest set with all 200 given candidates per query. With the first retrieval step, the top 50 query candidate pairs are retrieved for binary classification, therefore we assume the lower 150 candidates classified as irrelevant. As in [20], we use a cutoff value of 5 for the evaluation of ranking

---

[4] https://github.com/ThuYShao/BERT-PLI-IJCAI2020.

algorithms like BM25, this means the top 5 retrieved documents are classified as relevant, whereas the remaining 195 are considered irrelevant.

As Shao et al. [20] evaluate in their published code the top 50 candidates, we investigate the overall evaluation of our reproduced BERT-PLI models for all 200 candidates with the precision, recall and F1-score using the SciKitlearn classification report[5]. The results can be found in Table 2, we test the statistical significance compared to the BM25 baseline with the Student's paired, independent t-test [21,23]. Comparing the evaluation results stated in the original paper and our evaluation results, we find that our reproduced BERT-PLI Law-BERT LSTM and GRU model reach similar values. On the effect of domain specific paragraph-level modelling on the legal case retrieval task (RQ1), the original paper reports a 7–9% performance improvement for legal retrieval with the BERT-PLI model, when BERT is fine-tuned on the legal paragraph-level modelling compared to the original BERT. Contrary to that, we find that the domain specific paragraph-level modelling does not appear to help the performance of the legal case retrieval. Our reproduced $BERT_{ORG}$ LawRNN GRU model outperforms all other BERT-PLI models except on the recall, however this shows that contrary to the findings in the original paper, the domain specific paragraph-level modelling does not always improve the performance of the BERT-PLI model.

Table 2. Precision, Recall and F1-Score comparison of Shao et al. [20] and our reproduction, BM25 cutoff value of 5 as in [20], JNLP [22] and ILPS [19] denote the best two runs of the COLIEE 2019, [†] indicates statistically significant difference to BM25, $\alpha = 0.05$

Team/Model	Precision	Recall	F1-Score
JNLP [22]	0.6000	0.5545	0.5764
ILPS [19]	0.68	0.43	0.53
$BERT_{ORG}$ LawRNN LSTM [20]	0.5278	0.4606	0.4919
$BERT_{ORG}$ LawRNN GRU [20]	0.4958	0.5364	0.5153
LawBERT LawRNN LSTM [20]	0.5931	0.5697	0.5812
LawBERT LawRNN GRU [20]	**0.6026**	**0.5697**	**0.5857**
Reproduction			
BM25 (cutoff at 5)	0.5114	0.5360	0.5234
Repr $BERT_{ORG}$ LawRNN LSTM	$0.7053^{†}$	$0.5017^{†}$	$0.5863^{†}$
Repr $BERT_{ORG}$ LawRNN GRU	$\mathbf{0.8972^{†}}$	$0.4501^{†}$	$\mathbf{0.5995^{†}}$
Repr LawBERT LawRNN LSTM	$0.8620^{†}$	$0.4295^{†}$	$0.5733^{†}$
Repr LawBERT LawRNN GRU	$0.3826^{†}$	$\mathbf{0.6838^{†}}$	$0.4907^{†}$

---

[5] https://scikit-learn.org/stable/modules/generated/sklearn.metrics.classification_report.html.

4.2   In-domain Evaluation for Patent Document Retrieval (RQ2)

In order to investigate the applicability of the BERT-PLI model for information retrieval in the patent domain, we evaluate the PatentBERT PatentRNN
models trained on PatentDocTrain. The results can be found in Table 3, now
we analyze the in-domain evaluation for the PatentBERT PatentRNN models
on PatentDocTest. This shows that the in-domain, patent BERT-PLI model is
not beneficial for patent document retrieval, as it is outperformed by the BM25
baseline on all metrics. We reason this could be due to the number of considered
query and candidate paragraphs (N and M), which is fit to the legal retrieval
but not to the patent retrieval and could be unsuitable for patent retrieval as
PatentDocTrain and PatentDocTest contain on average more paragraphs than
LawDocTrain and LawDocTest. This demonstrates that the document retrieval
with contextualized language models for the patent domain is not yet beneficial and needs to be taken under further investigation. In line with the findings
regarding RQ1 for the legal document retrieval, we find that the paragraph-level
modelling with the PatentBERT model impairs the performance of the document retrieval compared to the paragraph-level modelling with $BERT_{ORG}$. This
shows that the domain specific paragraph-level modelling is not always beneficial
for BERT-PLI for the legal and patent document retrieval.

Table 3. In-domain and cross-domain evaluation on the legal and patent document
retrieval test set, in-domain evaluation for LawBERT LawRNN models on LawDocTest
and PatentBERT PatentRNN on PatentDocTest, R1-6 denote the result numbers from
Fig. 2, [†] indicates statistically significant difference to BM25, $\alpha = 0.05$

Model		LawDocTest			PatentDocTest		
		Prec	Rec	F1	Prec	Rec	F1
In-domain							
BM25 (cutoff at 5)		0.5114	0.5360	0.5234	**0.0500**	**0.3968**	**0.0888**
LawBERT LawRNN (R3)	**LSTM**	**0.8620**[†]	0.4295[†]	**0.5733**[†]	0.0207[†]	0.4761[†]	0.0398[†]
	GRU	0.3826[†]	**0.6838**[†]	0.4907[†]	0.0181[†]	0.4444[†]	0.0349[†]
PatentBERT PatentRNN (R6)	**LSTM**	0.7500[†]	0.2268[†]	0.3482[†]	0.0365[†]	0.1904[†]	0.0613[†]
	GRU	0.1153[†]	0.0412[†]	0.0607[†]	0.0416[†]	0.1904[†]	0.0683[†]
Cross-domain							
LawBERT PatentRNN (R4)	**LSTM**	0.1103[†]	0.5292[†]	0.1826[†]	0.0277[†]	0.1587[†]	0.0472[†]
	GRU	0.0961[†]	0.2749[†]	0.1424[†]	0.0246[†]	0.1904[†]	0.0436[†]
PatentBERT LawRNN (R5)	**LSTM**	0.8000[†]	0.4673[†]	0.5900[†]	0.0188[†]	0.3650[†]	0.0357[†]
	GRU	0.5460[†]	0.5704[†]	0.5579[†]	0.0233[†]	0.5555[†]	0.0448[†]
BERTOrg PatentRNN (R2)	**LSTM**	0.0000[†]	0.0000[†]	0.0000[†]	0.0602[†]	0.0793[†]	0.0684[†]
	GRU	0.0000[†]	0.0000[†]	0.0000[†]	**0.0769**[†]	0.0952[†]	0.0851[†]
BERTOrg LawRNN (R1)	**LSTM**	0.7053[†]	0.5017[†]	0.5863[†]	0.0160[†]	**0.8095**[†]	0.0314[†]
	GRU	**0.8972**[†]	0.4501[†]	**0.5995**[†]	0.0199[†]	0.4285[†]	0.0381[†]

4.3   Cross-Domain Evaluation (RQ3)

In order to analyze the cross-domain retrieval between the legal and patent domain, we evaluate each model on LawDocTest and PatentDocTest set as illustrated in Fig. 2 and compare for each test set the performance of the different models in order to gain insights about the transferability of the models between the legal and patent retrieval task and on the paragraph as well as on the document-level.

Analyzing the cross-domain transfer on the paragraph-level for LawDocTest, we see in Table 3 that the performance is similar for the LawRNNs when modelling the paragraph-level interaction with PatentBERT instead of LawBERT. An interesting result is the performance of the PatentBERT PatentRNN LSTM model, which was not trained on modelling legal paragraph-interactions nor legal document retrieval, but performs well on LawDocTest, however it does not outperform the domain independent BM25 baseline. On the document-level we see that the PatentRNN models have on average a 40% lower F1-Score than the LawRNN models with the same paragraph-level modelling, although we see a positive effect of modelling the paragraph-level interactions with $BERT_{ORG}$ instead of LawBERT or PatentBERT.

For the cross-domain evaluation on PatentDocTest, we find that each BERT-PLI model is outperformed by the BM25 baseline, except for the precision of the $BERT_{ORG}$ PatentRNN models and the recall of the $BERT_{ORG}$ LawRNN models. On the document-level transfer we see a consistent performance improvement of the PatentRNN models compared to the LawRNN models independent of the paragraph-level modelling, which leads to the conclusion that the domain specific training for patent document retrieval is beneficial here. On a paragraph-level transfer we can see a similar performance of the LawRNN models, independent of the paragraph-level modelling. For the PatentRNN models we find that the paragraph-level modelling with $BERT_{ORG}$ outperforms the modelling with PatentBERT and LawBERT.

5   Related Work

There are numerous evaluation campaigns for patent [15] and legal retrieval [2,8,17] with the goal to create and provide queries and relevance judgements for domain-specific retrieval and with this promote research in legal and patent IR. For legal retrieval, Cormack et al. [5] evaluate continuous, simple active and passive learning models in the TREC legal evaluation campaign [8] and propose an autonomous active learning framework [4]. In the COLIEE evaluation campaign, Rossi et al. [19] combine text summarization and a generalized language model to predict pairwise relevance for the legal case retrieval task, whereas Tran et al. [22] apply a summarization method and the extraction of lexical features. In the patent retrieval evaluation campaign CLEF-IP [14], Piroi et al. [16] report different approaches using the probabilistic BM25 model [18] as well as SVM-classifier trained on pretrained word-level representations.

As the language model BERT [6] advanced the state-of-the-art in language modeling, there are numerous approaches to apply BERT to IR tasks [12,25] and for cross-domain IR for web and news search [1] as well as for biomedical search [13,24].

6   Conclusion and Future Work

We reproduced the BERT-PLI model of Shao et al. [20] for the legal document retrieval task of the COLIEE evaluation campaign 2019 [17]. We have addressed shortcomings of the description of the data pre-processing and the second stage retrieval, which we investigated and for which we complemented the published code. Contrary to the original paper, we find that modelling the paragraph-level interactions with a BERT model fine-tuned on the domain does not appear to help the performance of the BERT-PLI model for document retrieval compared to modelling the paragraph-level interactions with the original BERT model. Furthermore we have analyzed the applicability of the BERT-PLI model for document retrieval in the patent domain, but we find that the BERT-PLI model does not yet improve the patent document retrieval compared to the BM25 baseline. We reason that the optimal number of query and candidate paragraphs to be considered for the interaction modelling could be a decisive hyperparameter to take into account. However bringing the gains from contextualized language model to patent document retrieval stays an open problem. We have investigated to what extend the BERT-PLI model is transferable between the legal and patent domain on the paragraph and document-level by evaluating the cross-domain retrieval of the BERT-PLI model. We show that the cross-domain transfer on the paragraph-level yields comparable performance between the legal and the patent domain. Furthermore the comparison on the document-level transfer shows first promising results when applying the BERT-PLI model trained on the patent domain to the legal domain. How to bring the benefits of contextualized language models to domain-specific search and how to transfer retrieval models across different domains remain open and exciting questions.

Acknowledgements. This work was supported by the EU Horizon 2020 ITN/ETN on Domain Specific Systems for Information Extraction and Retrieval (H2020-EU.1.3.1., ID: 860721).

References

1. Akkalyoncu Yilmaz, Z., Yang, W., Zhang, H., Lin, J.: Cross-domain modeling of sentence-level evidence for document retrieval. In: Proceedings of the 2019 Conference on Empirical Methods in Natural Language Processing and the 9th International Joint Conference on Natural Language Processing (EMNLP-IJCNLP), pp. 3490–3496. Association for Computational Linguistics, Hong Kong, China, November 2019. https://doi.org/10.18653/v1/D19-1352. https://www.aclweb.org/anthology/D19-1352

2. Bhattacharya, P., et al.: Fire 2019 AILA track: artificial intelligence for legal assistance. In: Proceedings of the 11th Forum for Information Retrieval Evaluation, FIRE 2019, pp. 4–6. Association for Computing Machinery, New York (2019). https://doi.org/10.1145/3368567.3368587
3. Cho, K., et al.: Learning phrase representations using RNN encoder-decoder for statistical machine translation. In: Proceedings of the 2014 Conference on Empirical Methods in Natural Language Processing (EMNLP), pp. 1724–1734. Association for Computational Linguistics, Doha, October 2014. https://doi.org/10.3115/v1/D14-1179. https://www.aclweb.org/anthology/D14-1179
4. Cormack, G., Grossman, M.: Autonomy and reliability of continuous active learning for technology-assisted review, April 2015
5. Cormack, G.V., Grossman, M.R.: Evaluation of machine-learning protocols for technology-assisted review in electronic discovery. In: Proceedings of the 37th International ACM SIGIR Conference on Research and Development in Information Retrieval, SIGIR 2014, pp. 153–162. Association for Computing Machinery, New York (2014). https://doi.org/10.1145/2600428.2609601
6. Devlin, J., Chang, M.W., Lee, K., Toutanova, K.: BERT: pre-training of deep bidirectional transformers for language understanding. In: Proceedings of the 2019 Conference of the North American Chapter of the Association for Computational Linguistics: Human Language Technologies, Volume 1 (Long and Short Papers), pp. 4171–4186. Association for Computational Linguistics, Minneapolis, June 2019. https://doi.org/10.18653/v1/N19-1423. https://www.aclweb.org/anthology/N19-1423
7. Gao, L., Dai, Z., Callan, J.: Modularized transfomer-based ranking framework. In: Proceedings of the 2020 Conference on Empirical Methods in Natural Language Processing (2020)
8. Hedin, B., Zaresefat, S., Baron, J., Oard, D.: Overview of the TREC 2009 legal track. In: The Eighteenth Text Retrieval Conference (TREC 2009) Proceedings, January 2009
9. Hochreiter, S., Schmidhuber, J.: Long short-term memory. Neural Comput. 9(8), 1735–1780 (1997). https://doi.org/10.1162/neco.1997.9.8.1735
10. Hofstätter, S., Hanbury, A.: Let's measure run time! Extending the IR replicability infrastructure to include performance aspects. In: Proceedings of OSIRRC (2019)
11. Hofstätter, S., Zlabinger, M., Hanbury, A.: Interpretable & time-budget-constrained contextualization for re-ranking. In: Proceedings of ECAI (2020)
12. Lee, K., Chang, M.W., Toutanova, K.: Latent retrieval for weakly supervised open domain question answering. In: Proceedings of the 57th Annual Meeting of the Association for Computational Linguistics, pp. 6086–6096. Association for Computational Linguistics, Florence, July 2019. https://doi.org/10.18653/v1/P19-1612. https://www.aclweb.org/anthology/P19-1612
13. MacAvaney, S., Cohan, A., Goharian, N.: SLEDGE-Z: a zero-shot baseline for COVID-19 literature search. In: Proceedings of the 2020 Conference on Empirical Methods in Natural Language Processing (EMNLP), pp. 4171–4179. Association for Computational Linguistics, November 2020. https://doi.org/10.18653/v1/2020.emnlp-main.341. https://www.aclweb.org/anthology/2020.emnlp-main.341
14. Piroi, F., Lupu, M., Hanbury, A.: Overview of CLEF-IP 2013 lab. In: Forner, P., Müller, H., Paredes, R., Rosso, P., Stein, B. (eds.) CLEF 2013. LNCS, vol. 8138, pp. 232–249. Springer, Heidelberg (2013). https://doi.org/10.1007/978-3-642-40802-1_25
15. Piroi, F., Lupu, M., Hanbury, A., Zenz, V.: CLEF-IP 2011: retrieval in the intellectual property domain, January 2011

16. Piroi, F., Tait, J.: CLEF-IP 2010: retrieval experiments in the intellectual property domain (2010)
17. Rabelo, J., Kim, M.-Y., Goebel, R., Yoshioka, M., Kano, Y., Satoh, K.: A summary of the COLIEE 2019 competition. In: Sakamoto, M., Okazaki, N., Mineshima, K., Satoh, K. (eds.) JSAI-isAI 2019. LNCS (LNAI), vol. 12331, pp. 34–49. Springer, Cham (2020). https://doi.org/10.1007/978-3-030-58790-1_3
18. Robertson, S., Zaragoza, H.: The probabilistic relevance framework: Bm25 and beyond. Found. Trends Inf. Retr. **3**(4), 333–389 (2009). https://doi.org/10.1561/1500000019
19. Rossi, J., Kanoulas, E.: Legal information retrieval with generalized language models (2019)
20. Shao, Y., et al.: BERT-PLI: modeling paragraph-level interactions for legal case retrieval. In: Bessiere, C. (ed.) Proceedings of the Twenty-Ninth International Joint Conference on Artificial Intelligence, IJCAI 2020, pp. 3501–3507. International Joint Conferences on Artificial Intelligence Organization, July 2020. Main track
21. Smucker, M.D., Allan, J., Carterette, B.: A comparison of statistical significance tests for information retrieval evaluation. In: Proceedings of the Sixteenth ACM Conference on Conference on Information and Knowledge Management, CIKM 2007, pp. 623–632. Association for Computing Machinery, New York (2007). https://doi.org/10.1145/1321440.1321528
22. Tran, V., Nguyen, M.L., Satoh, K.: Building legal case retrieval systems with lexical matching and summarization using a pre-trained phrase scoring model. In: Proceedings of the Seventeenth International Conference on Artificial Intelligence and Law, ICAIL 2019, pp. 275–282. Association for Computing Machinery, New York (2019). https://doi.org/10.1145/3322640.3326740
23. Urbano, J., Lima, H., Hanjalic, A.: Statistical significance testing in information retrieval: an empirical analysis of type i, type ii and type iii errors. In: Proceedings of the 42nd International ACM SIGIR Conference on Research and Development in Information Retrieval, SIGIR 2019, pp. 505–514. Association for Computing Machinery, New York (2019). https://doi.org/10.1145/3331184.3331259
24. Xiong, C., et al.: CMT in TREC-COVID round 2: mitigating the generalization gaps from web to special domain search. In: ArXiv preprint (2020)
25. Yang, W., et al.: End-to-end open-domain question answering with BERTserini. In: Proceedings of the 2019 Conference of the North American Chapter of the Association for Computational Linguistics (Demonstrations), pp. 72–77. Association for Computational Linguistics, Minneapolis, Minnesota, June 2019. https://doi.org/10.18653/v1/N19-4013
26. Zhang, Y., Nie, P., Geng, X., Ramamurthy, A., Song, L., Jiang, D.: DC-BERT: decoupling question and document for efficient contextual encoding (2020)

A Critical Assessment of State-of-the-Art in Entity Alignment

Max Berrendorf$^{(\boxtimes)}$ ⓘ, Ludwig Wacker, and Evgeniy Faerman

Ludwig-Maximilians-Universität München, Munich, Germany
{berrendorf,faerman}@dbs.ifi.lmu.de, l.wacker@campus.lmu.de

Abstract. In this work, we perform an extensive investigation of two state-of-the-art (SotA) methods for the task of Entity Alignment in Knowledge Graphs. Therefore, we first carefully examine the benchmarking process and identify several shortcomings, making the results reported in the original works not always comparable. Furthermore, we suspect that it is a common practice in the community to make the hyperparameter optimization directly on a test set, reducing the informative value of reported performance. Thus, we select a representative sample of benchmarking datasets and describe their properties. We also examine different initializations for entity representations since they are a decisive factor for model performance. Furthermore, we use a shared train/validation/test split for an appropriate evaluation setting to evaluate all methods on all datasets. In our evaluation, we make several interesting findings. While we observe that most of the time SotA approaches perform better than baselines, they have difficulties when the dataset contains noise, which is the case in most real-life applications. Moreover, in our ablation study, we find out that often different features of SotA method are crucial for good performance than previously assumed. The code is available at https://github.com/mberr/ea-sota-comparison.

Keywords: Knowledge Graph · Entity Alignment · Word embeddings

1 Introduction

The quality of information retrieval crucially depends on the accessible storage of information. Knowledge Graphs (KGs) often serve as such data structure [6]. Moreover, to satisfy diverse information needs, a combination of multiple data sources is often inevitable. Entity Alignment (EA) [2] is the discipline of aligning entities from different KGs. Once aligned, these entities facilitate information transfer between knowledge bases, or even fusing multiple KGs to a single knowledge base.

In this work, our goal is to analyze a SotA approach for the task of EA and identify which factors are essential for its performance. Although papers often use the same dataset in the evaluation and report the same evaluation metrics, the selection of SotA is not a trivial task: as we found out in our analysis, the usage

© Springer Nature Switzerland AG 2021
D. Hiemstra et al. (Eds.): ECIR 2021, LNCS 12657, pp. 18–32, 2021.
https://doi.org/10.1007/978-3-030-72240-1_2

of different types of external information for the initialization or train/test splits of different sizes[1] makes the results in different works incomparable. Therefore, while still guided by the reported evaluation metrics, we identified these common factors among strongly performing methods in multiple works:

- They are based on Graph Neural Networks (GNNs). GNNs build the basis of the most recent works [4,7,9,10,12,14,16–23,25].
- They utilize entity names in the model. Supported by recent advances in word embeddings, these attributes provide distinctive features.
- They consider different types of relations existing in KGs. Most GNNs ignore different relationship types and aggregate them in the preprocessing step.

Given these criteria, we selected Relation-aware Dual-Graph Convolutional Network (RDGCN) [17], as it also has demonstrated impressive performance in recent benchmarking studies [15,24]. Additionally, we include the recently published Deep Graph Matching Consensus (DGMC) [7] method in our analysis for two reasons: the studies mentioned above did not include it, and the authors reported surprisingly good performance, considering that this method does not make use of relation type information.

We start our study by reviewing the used datasets and discussing the initializations based on entity names. Although both methods utilize entity names, the actual usage differs. For comparison, we thus evaluate both methods on all datasets with all available initializations. We also report the zero-shot performance, i.e., when only using initial representations alone, as well as a simple GNN model baseline. Furthermore, we address the problem of hyperparameter optimization. Related works often do not discuss how they chose hyperparameters and, e.g., rarely report validation splits. So far, this problem was not addressed in the community. In the recent comprehensive survey [15], the authors use cross-validation for the estimation of the test performance. The models are either evaluated with hyperparameters recommended for other datasets or selected by not reported procedure. Also, in the published code of the investigated approaches, we could not find any trace of train-validation splits, raising questions about reproducibility and fairness of their comparisons. We thus create a shared split with a test, train, and validation part and extensively tune the model's hyperparameters for each of the dataset/initialization combinations to ensure that they are sufficiently optimized. Finally, we provide an ablation study for many of the parameters of a SotA approach (RDGCN), giving insight into the individual components' contributions to the final performance.

2   Datasets and Initialization

Table 1 provides a summary of a representative sample of datasets used for benchmarking of EA approaches. In the following, we first discuss each dataset's properties and, in the second part, the initialization of entity name attributes.

---

[1] Commonly used evaluation metrics in EA automatically become better with a smaller size of test set [3].

Table 1. Summary of the used EA datasets. We denote the entity set as $\mathcal{E}$, the relation set as $\mathcal{R}$, the triple set as $\mathcal{T}$, the aligned entities as $\mathcal{A}$ and the exclusive entities as $\mathcal{X}$.

Dataset	Subset	Graph	$|\mathcal{E}|$	$|\mathcal{R}|$	$|\mathcal{T}|$	$|\mathcal{A}|$	$|\mathcal{X}|$
DBP15k	zh-en	zh	19,388	1,701	70,414	15,000	4,388
		en	19,572	1,323	95,142	15,000	4,572
	ja-en	ja	19,814	1,299	77,214	15,000	4,814
		en	19,780	1,153	93,484	15,000	4,780
	fr-en	fr	19,661	903	105,998	15,000	4,661
		en	19,993	1,208	115,722	15,000	4,993
WK3l15k	en-de	en	15,126	1,841	209,041	9,783	5,343
		de	14,603	596	144,244	10,021	4,582
	en-fr	en	15,169	2,228	203,356	7,375	7,794
		fr	15,393	2,422	169,329	7,284	8,109
OpenEA	en-de	en	15,000	169	84,867	15,000	0
		de	15,000	96	92,632	15,000	0
	en-fr	en	15,000	193	96,318	15,000	0
		fr	15,000	166	80,112	15,000	0
	d-y	d	15,000	72	68,063	15,000	0
		y	15,000	21	60,970	15,000	0
	d-w	d	15,000	167	73,983	15,000	0
		w	15,000	121	83,365	15,000	0

2.1 Datasets

DBP15k. The DBP15k dataset is the most popular dataset for the evaluation of EA approaches. It has three subsets, all of which base upon DBpedia. Each subset comprises a pair of graphs from different languages. As noted by [2], there exist multiple variations of the dataset, sharing the same entity alignment but differing in the number of exclusive entities in each graph. The alignments in the datasets are always 1:1 alignments, and due to the construction method for the datasets, exclusive entities do not have relations between them, but only to shared entities. Exclusive entities complicate the matching process, and in real-life applications, they are not easy to identify. Therefore, we believe that this dataset describes a realistic use-case only to a certain extent. We found another different variant of DBP15k as part of the PyTorch Geometric repository[2], having a different set of aligned entities. This is likely due to extraction of alignments from data provided by [20] via Google Drive[3] as described in their

---

[2] https://github.com/rusty1s/pytorch_geometric/blob/d42a690fba68005f5738008a04f375ffd39bbb76/torch_geometric/datasets/dbp15k.py.

[3] https://drive.google.com/open?id=1dYJtj1_J4nYJdrDY95ucGLCuZXDXI7PL.

GitHub repository.[4] As a result, the evaluation results published in [7] are not directly comparable to other published results. In our experiments, we use the (smaller) JAPE variant with approximately 19–20k entities in each graph since it is the predominantly used variant.

OpenEA. The OpenEA datasets published by [15] comprise graph pairs from DBPedia, YAGO, and Wikidata obtained by iterative degree-based sampling to match the degree distribution between the source KG and the extracted subset. The alignments are exclusively 1:1 matchings, and there are no exclusive entities, i.e., every entity occurs in both graphs. We believe that this is a relatively unrealistic scenario. In our experiments, we use all graph pairs with 15k entities (`15K`) in the dense variant (`V2`), i.e., `en-de-15k-v2`, `en-fr-15k-v2`, `d-y-15k-v2`, `d-w-15k-v2`.

WK3l15k. The Wk3l datasets are multi-lingual KG pairs extracted from Wikipedia. As in [2], we extract additional entity alignments from the triple alignments. The graphs contain additional exclusive entities, and there are m:n matchings. We only use the 15k variants, where each graph has approximately 15k entities. There are two graph pairs, `en-de` and `en-fr`. Moreover, the alignments in the dataset are relatively noisy: for example, `en-de` contains besides valid alignments such as ("trieste", "triest"), or ("frederick i, holy roman emperor", "friedrich i. (hrr)"), also ambiguous ones such as ("1", "1. fc saarbrücken"), ("1", "1. fc schweinfurt 05"), and errors such as ("1", "157"), and ("101", "100"). While the noise aggravates alignment, it also reflects a realistic setting.

2.2 Label-Based Initializations

Prepared Translations (DBP15k). For DBP15k, we investigate label-based initializations based on prepared translations to English from [17] and [7] (which, in turn, originate from [20]). Afterwards, they use Glove [11] embeddings to obtain an entity representation. While [17] only provides the final entity representation vectors without further describing the aggregation, [7] splits the label into words (by white-space) and uses the sum over the words' embeddings as entity representation. [17] additionally normalizes the norm of the representations to unit length.

Prepared RDGCN Embeddings (OpenEA). OpenEA [15] benchmarks a large variety of contemporary entity alignment methods in a unified setting, also including RDGCN [17]. Since the graphs DBPedia and YAGO collect data from similar sources, the labels are usually equal. For those graph pairs, the authors propose to delete the labels. However, RDGCN requires a label based initialization. Thus, the authors obtain labels via attribute triples of a pre-defined set of

---

[4] https://github.com/syxu828/Crosslingula-KG-Matching/blob/56710f8131ae072f00 de97eb737315e4ac9510f2/README.md#how-to-run-the-codes.

Table 2. The statistics about label-based initialization in the OpenEA codebase: *attribute* denotes initialization via attribute values for a predefined set of "name attributes". *id* denotes initialization with the last part of the entity URI. For d-y this basically leaks ground truth, whereas, for Wikidata, the URI contains only a numeric identifier, thus rendering the initialization "label" useless.

Subset	Side	via attribute	via id	via id (%)
d-w	d	0	15,000	100.00%
	w	8,391	7,301	48.67%
d-y	d	2,883	12,122	80.81%
	y	15,000	0	0.00%

"name-attributes"[5]: skos:prefLabel, http://dbpedia.org/ontology/birthName for DBPedia-YAGO, and http://www.wikidata.org/entity/P373, http://www.wikidata.org/entity/P1476 for DBPedia-Wikidata.

However, when investigating the published code, we noticed that if the label is not found via attribute, the last part of the entity URI is used instead. For DBPedia/YAGO, this effectively leaks ground truth since they share the same label. For DBPedia/Wikidata, this results in useless labels for the Wikidata side since their labels are the Wikidata IDs, e.g., Q3391163. Table 2 summarizes the frequency of both cases. For d-w, DPBedia entities always use the ground truth label. For 49% of the Wikidata entities, useless labels are used for initialization. For d-y, YAGO entity representations are always initialized via an attribute triple. For DBPedia, in 81% of all cases, the ground truth label is used. We store these initial entity representations produced by the OpenEA codebase into a file and refer in the following to them as *Sun* initialization (since they are taken from the implementation of [15]).

Multi-lingual BERT (WK3l15k). Since we did not find related work with entity embedding initialization from labels on WK3l15k, we generated those using a pre-trained multi-lingual BERT model [5], BERT-Base, Multilingual Cased[6]. Following [5], we use the sum of the last four layers as token representation since it has comparable performance to the concatenation at a quarter of its size. To summarize the token representations of a single entity label, we explore sum, mean, and max aggregation as hyperparameters.

---

[5] https://github.com/nju-websoft/OpenEA/tree/2a6e0b03ec8cdcad4920704d1c38547a3ad72abe.

[6] https://github.com/google-research/bert/blob/cc7051dc592802f501e8a6f71f8fb3cf9de95dc9/multilingual.md.

3   Methods

We evaluate two SotA EA methods, RDGCN [17] which we reimplemented and DGMC [7] for which we used the original method implementation with adapted evaluation. In the following, we revisit their architectures and highlight differences between the architecture described in the paper and what we found in the published code.

Similarly to all GNN-based approaches, both models employ a Siamese architecture. Therefore, the same model with the same weights is applied to both graphs yielding representations of entities from both KGs. Given these entity representations, the EA approaches compute an affinity matrix that describes the similarity of entity representations from both graphs. Since the main difference between methods is the GNN model in the Siamese architecture, for brevity we only describe how it is applied on a single KG $\mathcal{G} = (\mathcal{E}, \mathcal{R}, \mathcal{T})$.

3.1   Relation-Aware Dual-Graph Convolutional Network (RDGCN)

Architecture. The RDGCN [17] model comprises two parts performing message-passing processes applied sequentially. The message passing process performed by the first part can be seen as *relation-aware*. The model tries to learn the importance of relations and weights the messages from the entities connected by these relations correspondingly. The message passing performed by the second component utilizes a simple adjacency matrix indicating the existence of any relations between entities, which we call *standard message passing*. Both components employ a form of skip connections: (weighted) residual connections [8] in the first part and highway layers [13] in the second part.

Relation-Aware Message Passing. The entity embeddings from the first component are computed by several *interaction rounds* comprising four steps

$$\mathbf{X_c} = RC(\mathbf{X_e}), \mathbf{X_c} \in \mathbb{R}^{|\mathcal{R}| \times 2d} \tag{1}$$

$$\mathbf{X_r} = DA(\mathbf{X_r}, \mathbf{X_c}), \mathbf{X_r} \in \mathbb{R}^{|\mathcal{R}| \times 2d} \tag{2}$$

$$\mathbf{X_e} = PA(\mathbf{X_e}, \mathbf{X_r}) \tag{3}$$

$$\mathbf{X_e} = \mathbf{X_e^0} + \beta_i \cdot \mathbf{X_e} \tag{4}$$

The first step, in (1), obtains a *relation context* (RC) $\mathbf{X_c}$ from the entity representations. For relation $r \in \mathcal{R}$, we extract its relation context as a concatenation of the mean entity representations for the head and the tail entities. By denoting the set of head and tail entities for relation r with H_r and T_r, we can thus express its computation as $(\mathbf{X_c})_i = \left[1/|H_i| \sum_{j \in H_i} (\mathbf{X_e})_j \| 1/|T_i| \sum_{j \in T_i} (\mathbf{X_e})_j \right]$ where $\|$ denotes the concatenation operation. An entity occurring multiple times as the head is weighted equally to an entity occurring only once.

The second step, in (2), is the *dual graph attention* (DA). The attention scores on the dual graph α_{ij}^D are computed by dot product attention with leaky ReLU activation: $\alpha_{ij}^D = J_{ij} \cdot LeakyReLU(\mathbf{W_L}(\mathbf{X_c})_i + \mathbf{W_R}(\mathbf{X_c})_j)$. Notice that

$\mathbf{W_L}(\mathbf{X_c})_i + \mathbf{W_R}(\mathbf{X_c})_j = (\mathbf{W_L}\|\mathbf{W_R})^T((\mathbf{X_c})_i\|(\mathbf{X_c})_j)$, where $\|$ denotes the concatenation operation. In the published code, we further found a weight sharing mechanism for $\mathbf{W_L}$ and $\mathbf{W_R}$ implemented, decomposing the projection weight matrices as $\mathbf{W_L} = \mathbf{W'_L}\mathbf{W_C}$ and $\mathbf{W_R} = \mathbf{W'_R}\mathbf{W_C}$ with $\mathbf{W'_L}, \mathbf{W'_R} \in \mathbb{R}^{1\times h}$, $\mathbf{W_C} \in \mathbb{R}^{h\times 2d}$ being trainable parameters, and $\mathbf{W_C}$ shared between both projections. J_{ij} denotes a fixed triple-based relation similarity score computed as the sum of the Jaccard similarities of the head and tail entity set for relation r_i and r_j: $J_{ij} := |H_i \cap H_j|/|H_i \cup H_j| + |T_i \cap T_j|/|T_i \cup T_j|$. The softmax is then computed only over those relations, where $J_{ij} > 0$, i.e., pairs sharing at least one head or tail entity. In the implementation, this is implemented as dense attention with masking, i.e. setting $\alpha_{ij}^D = -\infty$ (or a very small value) for $J_{ij} = 0$. While this increases the required memory consumption to $\mathcal{O}(|\mathcal{R}|^2)$, the number of relations is usually small compared to the number of entities, cf. Table 1, and thus this poses no serious computational problem. With $\tilde{\alpha}_{ij}^D$ denoting the softmax output, the new relation representation finally is $(\mathbf{X_r})_i = ReLU\left(\sum_j \tilde{\alpha}_{ij}^D(\mathbf{X_r})_j\right)$.

In the third step, in (3), the entity representations are updated. To this end, a relation-specific scalar score is computed as $\alpha_i^r = LeakyReLU(\mathbf{W}\mathbf{X_r} + b)$ with trainable parameters W and b. Based upon the relation-specific scores, an attention score between two entities e_i, e_j with at least one relation between them is given as $\alpha_{ij}^P = \sum_{r \in \mathcal{T}_{ij}} \alpha_i^r$. These scores are normalized with a sparse softmax over all $\{j \mid \exists r \in \mathcal{R} : (e_i, r, e_j) \in \mathcal{T}\}$: $\tilde{\alpha}_{ij}^P = \text{softmax}_{j'}(\alpha_{ij'}^P)_j$. The final output of the primal attention is $(\mathbf{X_e})_j = ReLU(\sum_i \tilde{\alpha}_{ij}(\mathbf{X_e})_j)$.

The fourth step, in (4), applies a skip connection from the initial representations to the current entity representation. The weight β_i is pre-defined ($\beta_1 = 0.1$, $\beta_2 = 0.3$) and not trained.

Standard Message Passing. The second part of the RDGCN consists of a sequence of GCN layers with highway layers. Each layer computes

$$\mathbf{X'_e} = ReLU(\mathbf{A}\mathbf{X_e}\mathbf{W}) \tag{5}$$

$$\beta = \sigma(\mathbf{W_g}\mathbf{X_e} + b_g) \tag{6}$$

$$\mathbf{X_e} = \beta \cdot \mathbf{X'_e} + (1 - \beta) \cdot \mathbf{X_e} \tag{7}$$

$\mathbf{A} \in \mathbb{R}^{|\mathcal{E}^L|\times|\mathcal{E}^L|}$ denotes the adjacency matrix of the primal graph. It is constructed by first creating an undirected, unweighted adjacency matrix where there is a connection between $e_i, e_j \in \mathcal{E}^L$ if there exists at least one triple $(e_i, r, e_j) \in \mathcal{T}^L$ for some relation $r \in \mathcal{R}^L$. Next, self-loops (e, e) are added for every entity $e \in \mathcal{E}^L$. Finally, the matrix is normalized by setting $\mathbf{A} = \mathbf{D}^{-1/2}\mathbf{A}\mathbf{D}^{-1/2}$ with $\mathbf{D}$ denoting the diagonal matrix of node degrees. When investigating the published code, we further found out that the weight matrix $\mathbf{W}$ is constrained to be a diagonal matrix and initialized as an identity matrix.

Training. Let $\mathbf{x}_i^L$ denote the final entity representation for $e_i^L \in \mathcal{E}^L$ and anologously $\mathbf{x}_j^R$ for $e_j^R \in \mathcal{E}^R$. RDGCN is trained with a margin-based loss formulation.

It adopts a hard negative mining strategy, i.e., the set of negative examples for one pair is the top k most similar entities of one of the entities according to the similarity measure used for scoring. The negative l_1 distance is used as similarity, the margin is 1, $k = 10$, and the negative examples are updated every 10 epochs.

3.2 Deep Graph Matching Consensus (DGMC).

DGMC [7] also comprises two parts, which we name *enrichment* and *correspondence refinement*. The enrichment part is a sequence of GNN layers enriching the entity representations with information from their neighborhood. Each layer computes $\phi(\mathbf{X}) = ReLU(norm(\mathbf{A})\mathbf{X}\mathbf{W_1} + norm(\mathbf{A}^T)\mathbf{X}\mathbf{W_2} + \mathbf{X}\mathbf{W_3})$, where $\mathbf{A} \in \mathbb{R}^{|\mathcal{E}^L| \times |\mathcal{E}^L|}$ denotes the symmetrically normalized adjacency matrix (as for second part of RDGCN), $norm$ the row-wise normalization operation, $\mathbf{X} \in \mathbb{R}^{\mathcal{E}^L \times d_{in}}$ the layer's input, and $\mathbf{W_1}, \mathbf{W_2}, \mathbf{W_3} \in \mathbb{R}^{d_{in} \times d_{out}}$ trainable parameters of the layer. An optional batch normalization and dropout follow this layer. For the enrichment phase's final output, all individual layers' outputs are concatenated before a learned final linear projection layer reduces the dimension to d_{out}.

The second phase, the *correspondence refinement*, first calculates the $k = 10$ most likely matches in the other graph for each entity as a sparse correspondence matrix $\mathbf{S} \in \mathbb{R}^{|\mathcal{E}^L| \times |\mathcal{E}^R|}$, normalized using softmax. Next, it generates random vectors for each entity $\mathbf{R} \in \mathbb{R}^{|\mathcal{E}^L| \times d_{rnd}}$ and sends these vectors to the probable matches via the softmax normalized sparse correspondence matrix, $\mathbf{S}^T\mathbf{R} \in \mathbb{R}^{|\mathcal{E}^R| \times d_{rnd}}$. A GNN layer ψ as in phase one distributes these vectors in the neighborhood of the nodes: $\mathbf{Y}^R = \psi(\mathbf{S}^T\mathbf{R})$. A two-layer MLP predicts an update for the correspondence matrix, given the difference between the representations $\mathbf{Y}^L$ and $\mathbf{Y}^R$. This procedure is repeated for a fixed number of refinement steps $L = 10$.

4 Experiments

Experimental Setup. For the general evaluation setting and description of metrics, we refer to [3]. Here, we primarily use Hits@1 (H@1), which measures the correct entity's relative frequency of being ranked in the first position. When investigating the published code of both, RDGCN [17][7] and DGMC [7][8], we did not find any code for tuning the parameters, nor a train-validation split. Also, the papers themselves do not mention a train-validation split. Thus, it is unclear how they choose the hyperparameters without a test-leakage by directly optimizing the test set's performance. We thus decided to create a shared test-train-validation split used by all our experiments to enable a fair comparison. Since DGMC already uses PyTorch, we could use their published code and extend it with HPO code. RDGCN was re-implemented in PyTorch in our codebase. We

---

[7] https://github.com/StephanieWyt/RDGCN.
[8] https://github.com/rusty1s/deep-graph-matching-consensus/.

Table 3. Investigated hyperparameters for all methods. * denotes that these parameters share the same value range but were tuned independently.

Common	
Parameter	Choices
Optimizer	Adam
Similarity	{cos, dot, l1 (bound inverse), l1 (negative), l2 (bound inverse), l2 (negative)}

RDGCN	
Parameter	Choices
(entity embedding) normalization	{always-l2, initial-l2, never}
(number of) GCN layers	{0, 1, 2, 3}
(number of) interaction layers	{0, 1, 2, 3}
Interaction weights	$\{0.1, 0.2, \ldots, 0.6\}$
Trainable embeddings	{False, True}
Hard negatives	{no, yes}
Learning rate	$[10^{-4}, 10^{-1}]$

DGMC	
Parameter	Choices
ψ_1 / ψ_2 dimension*	$[32, 64, \ldots, 1024]$
ψ_1 / ψ_2 (number of) GCN layers*	{1, 2, 3, 4, 5}
ψ_1 / ψ_2 batch normalization*	{False, True}
ψ_1 / ψ_2 layer concatenation*	{False, True}
ψ_1 dropout	$[0.00, 0.05, \ldots, 1.0]$
ψ_2 dropout	0.0
Trainable embeddings	False
(entity embedding) normalization	{never, always-l1, always-l2}
Learning rate	$[10^{-3}, 10^{-1}]$

GCN-Align*	
Parameter	Choices
Model output dimension	$[32, 64, \ldots, (embedding dimension)]$
(number of) GCN layers	{1, 2, 3}
Batch normalization	{False, True}
Layer concatenation	{False, True}
Final linear projection	{False, True}
Dropout	$\{0.0, 0.1, \ldots, 0.5\}$
Trainable embeddings	{False, True}
(entity embedding) normalization	{never, always-l1, always-l2}
(weight) sharing horizontal	{False, True}
Learning rate	$[10^{-3}, 10^{-1}]$

use the official train-test split for all datasets, which reserves 70% of the alignments for testing. We split the remaining part into 80% train alignments and 20% validation alignments.

We continued by tuning numerous model parameters (cf. Table 3) of all models on each of the datasets in Table 1 and each of the available initializations described in Sect. 2.2 to obtain sufficiently well-tuned configurations. We used random search due to its higher sample efficiency than grid search [1]. We additionally evaluate a baseline, which uses the GNN variant from DGMC without the neighborhood consensus refinement, coined *GCN-Align** due to its close correspondence to [16], and also evaluate the zero-shot performance of the initial node features.

For each tested configuration, we perform early stopping on validation H@1, i.e., select the epoch according to the best validation H@1. Across all tested configurations for a model-dataset-initialization combination, we then choose the best configuration according to validation H@1 and report the test performance in Table 4. We do not report performance for training on train+validation with the final configuration due to space restrictions. We decided to report performance when trained only on the train set to ensure that other works have performance numbers for comparison when tuning their own models.

4.1 Results

Table 4 presents the overall results. We can observe several points.

Table 4. Results in terms of H@1 for all investigated combinations of datasets, models, and initializations. Each cell represents the *test* performance of the best configuration of hyperparameters chosen according to *validation* performance.

		DBP15k (JAPE)				
init		Wu [18]			Xu [20]	
subset	fr-en	ja-en	zh-en	fr-en	ja-en	zh-en
Zero Shot	79.47	63.48	56.07	83.70	65.64	59.40
GCN-Align*	81.81	67.45	57.94	86.74	67.65	60.32
RDGCN	86.91	**72.90**	66.44	86.82	74.35	**69.54**
DGMC	**89.35**	72.17	69.98	**90.12**	**76.60**	68.76

		OpenEA		
init			Sun [15]	
subset	d-w	d-y	en-de	en-fr
Zero Shot	46.53	81.90	75.99	79.90
GCN-Align*	45.76	84.65	85.34	89.41
RDGCN	**64.28**	**98.41**	80.03	**91.52**
DGMC	51.29	88.60	**88.10**	89.40

	WK3l15k	
init	BERT	
subset	en-de	en-fr
Zero Shot	85.55	77.27
GCN-Align*	85.92	**78.22**
RDGCN	**86.76**	78.05
DGMC	84.08	73.92

Zero-Shot Performance. Generally, there is an impressive Zero-Shot performance, ranging from 39.15% for `OpenEA d-w` to 83.85% `WK3l15k en-de`. Thus, even in the weakest setting, approximately 40% of the entities can be aligned solely from their label, without any sophisticated method. Consequently, this highlights that comparison against methods not using this information is unfair. For `DBP15k`, we can compare the initialization from Wu et al. [17], used, e.g., by RDGCN to the performance of the initialization by Xu et al. [7], used, e.g., by DGMC. We observe that Wu's initialization is 7–9% points stronger than Xu's initialization. For `OpenEA d-w` we obtain 39.15% zero-shot performance, despite the original labels of the w side being meaningless identifiers. This is only due to using attribute triples with a pre-defined set of "name" attributes, cf. Table 2.

Model Performance. When comparing the performance of both analyzed models, we can observe that they have a clear advantage over both baselines in two of three datasets. However, we cannot identify a single winner among them. Although the performance of DGMC dropped compared to the results reported originally[9], it still leads by about 3–4 points on almost all DBP15k subsets. Therefore, it confirms our observation that a smaller test set automatically leads to better results. Furthermore, we can see that different initialization with entity name also affects model performance, which especially applies to the ja-en subset for DGMC or fr-en for GCN-Align*. RDGCN has a clear advantage on the OpenEA subsets extracted from DBPedia with a margin of between 10 and 13 points on both subsets. Note that we significantly improved results of RDGCN on the OpenEA dataset through our extensive hyperparameter search compared to the original evaluation [15]. Interestingly, as can be seen in the next section, the main reason is *not* the exploiting of information about different relations. The WK3L15k dataset constitutes an interesting exception. The performance of the DGMC method, which is supposed to be robust against noise due to its correspondence refinement, is not better than the zero-shot results. While DGMC and GCN-Align* can improve the results, the improvement by 1–2 points does not look very convincing. From these results, we conclude that there exists no silver bullet for the task of EA, and the method itself is still a hyperparameter. At the same time, we see that the most realistic dataset poses a real challenge for SotA methods.

4.2 Ablation: RDGCN

We additionally present the results of an ablation study for some model parameters of RDGCN on the OpenEA datasets in Table 5. For each presented parameter and each possible value, we fix this one parameter and select the best configuration among all configurations with the chosen parameter setting according to validation H@1. The cell then shows the validation and test performance of this configuration. We highlight the best setting on the respective graph pair in

---

[9] As a general rule, the results improve by 1–2 points when trained on train+ validation, and it is not going to change the picture.

Table 5. Ablation results for RDGCN on OpenEA datasets. The setting used by [17] is underlined. The first number is validation H@1, the second number test H@1. Bold highlights the best configuration. Please notice that due to the specialties of EA evaluation, the test and validation performance are *not* directly comparable [3].

Parameter	Value	Subset			
		d-w	d-y	en-de	en-fr
Normalization	Always	**84.06/64.28**	99.44/97.48	97.72/**93.56**	**96.89/91.52**
	Initial	82.67/62.58	**99.78**/98.41	97.67/93.02	95.56/89.50
	Never	78.39/61.77	99.72/**98.53**	**98.11**/80.03	95.44/90.14
GCN layers	0	57.33/50.79	92.33/83.83	**98.11**/80.03	92.22/86.94
	1	73.33/56.66	99.33/98.15	96.00/91.63	94.50/90.49
	2	78.39/61.77	99.56/98.16	97.72/**93.56**	**96.89/91.52**
	3	**84.06/64.28**	**99.78/98.41**	97.00/92.18	95.44/90.14
Interaction layers	0	78.11/60.53	99.72/**98.53**	97.72/**93.56**	95.33/89.08
	1	78.39/61.77	**99.78**/98.41	97.67/92.59	95.44/90.14
	2	82.67/62.58	99.56/98.16	**98.11**/80.03	**96.89/91.52**
	3	**84.06/64.28**	99.50/97.85	97.67/93.02	95.56/89.50
Trainable embeddings	No	**84.06/64.28**	99.72/**98.53**	97.72/**93.56**	**96.89/91.52**
	Yes	82.67/62.58	**99.78**/98.41	**98.11**/80.03	95.56/89.50
Similarity	Cos	82.67/62.58	99.56/98.16	**98.11**/80.03	95.56/89.50
	Dot	63.28/40.80	91.50/79.81	85.17/78.54	89.94/78.17
	l1 (inv.)	77.89/60.78	99.50/97.85	93.78/88.96	94.06/88.69
	l1 (neg.)	**84.06/64.28**	99.72/**98.53**	97.72/**93.56**	**96.89/91.52**
	l2 (inv.)	75.28/60.20	96.72/92.06	95.06/90.13	94.44/89.60
	l2 (neg.)	72.50/51.04	**99.78**/98.41	94.61/89.40	94.28/87.79
Hard negatives	No	82.67/62.58	**99.78/98.41**	**98.11**/80.03	**96.89/91.52**
	Yes	**84.06/64.28**	99.67/98.30	97.72/**93.56**	95.33/90.62

bold font. Note that the test performance numbers also coincide with the performance reported in Table 4 for OpenEA. We make the following interesting observations: for all but one graph pair, *always normalizing* the entity representations before passing them into the layers is beneficial. For d-y, where this is not the case, the difference in performance is small. For the *number of GCN layers*, we observe an increase in performance from 0 to 2 layers, and on some datasets (d-w, d-y) even beyond. Thus, aggregating the entities' neighborhood seems beneficial, highlighting the importance of the graph structure. For the *number of interaction layers*, which perform *relation-aware* message passing, we observe that for two of the four subsets (d-y, en-de) the best configuration does not use any interaction layer. However, the difference is small. None of the best configurations uses *trainable node embeddings*. The *negative l_1 similarity* is superior on all datasets, with most of the others being close to it. Using the dot product seems to be sub-optimal, maybe due to its unbound value range. Regarding *hard negative mining*, there is no clear tendency, but considering the hard negatives' expensive calculation (all-to-all kNN), its use might not be worthwhile.

Another observation is that sometimes there is a huge gap between the test performance for the best configuration according to validation performance and the best configuration according to test performance. For instance, if we had selected the hyperparameters according to test performance for `en-de`, we had obtained 93.53 H@1, while choosing them according to validation performance results in only 80.03 H@1 – a difference of 13.5% points. This difference emphasizes the need for a fair hyperparameter selection.

5   Conclusion

In this paper, we investigated state-of-the-art in Entity Alignment. Since we identified shortcomings in the commonly employed evaluation procedure, including the lack of validation sets for hyperparameter tuning and different initializations, we provided a fair and sound evaluation over a wide range of configurations. We additionally gave insight into the importance of individual components. Our results provide a strong, fair, and reproducible baseline for future works to compare against and offer deep insights into the inner workings of a GNN-based model.

We plan to investigate the identified weakness against noisy labelings in future work and increase the robustness. Moreover, we aim to improve the usage of relation type information in the message passing phase of models like RDGCN, which only use them in an initial entity representation refinement stage. For some datasets such as OpenEA d-y and en-de, optimal configurations did not consider the relational information. However, intuitively, this information should help to improve the structural description of entities. Potential improvements include establishing a relation matching between the two graphs or modifying the mechanism used to integrate relational information.

Acknowledgment. This work has been funded by the German Federal Ministry of Education and Research (BMBF) under Grant No. 01IS18036A. The authors of this work take full responsibilities for its content.

References

1. Bergstra, J., Bengio, Y.: Random search for hyper-parameter optimization. J. Mach. Learn. Res. **13**, 281–305 (2012)
2. Berrendorf, M., Faerman, E., Melnychuk, V., Tresp, V., Seidl, T.: Knowledge graph entity alignment with graph convolutional networks: lessons learned. In: Jose, J.M., et al. (eds.) ECIR 2020. LNCS, vol. 12036, pp. 3–11. Springer, Cham (2020). https://doi.org/10.1007/978-3-030-45442-5_1
3. Berrendorf, M., Faerman, E., Vermue, L., Tresp., V.: Interpretable and fair comparison of link prediction or entity alignment methods with adjusted mean rank. CoRR, abs/2002.06914 (2020)
4. Cao, Y., Liu, Z., Li, C., Liu, Z., Li, J., Chua, T.-S.: Multi-channel graph neural network for entity alignment. In: ACL (1), pp. 1452–1461. Association for Computational Linguistics (2019)

5. Devlin, J., Chang, M.-W., Lee, K., Toutanova, K.: BERT: pre-training of deep bidirectional transformers for language understanding. In: NAACL-HLT (1), pp. 4171–4186. Association for Computational Linguistics (2019)

6. Dietz, L., Xiong, C., Dalton, J., Meij, E.: Special issue on knowledge graphs and semantics in text analysis and retrieval. Inf. Retr. J. **22**(3–4), 229–231 (2019)

7. Fey, M., Lenssen, J.E., Morris, C., Masci, J., Kriege, N.M.: Deep graph matching consensus. In: 8th International Conference on Learning Representations, ICLR 2020, Addis Ababa, Ethiopia, 26–30 April 2020. OpenReview.net (2020)

8. He, K., Zhang, X., Ren, S., Sun, J.: Deep residual learning for image recognition. In: 2016 IEEE Conference on Computer Vision and Pattern Recognition, CVPR 2016, Las Vegas, NV, USA, 27–30 June 2016, pp. 770–778. IEEE Computer Society (2016)

9. Li, C., Cao, Y., Hou, L., Shi, J., Li, J., Chua, T.-S.: Semi-supervised entity alignment via joint knowledge embedding model and cross-graph model. In: EMNLP/IJCNLP (1), pp. 2723–2732. Association for Computational Linguistics (2019)

10. Mao, X., Wang, W., Xu, H., Lan, M., Wu, Y.: MRAEA: an efficient and robust entity alignment approach for cross-lingual knowledge graph. In: WSDM, pp. 420–428. ACM (2020)

11. Pennington, J., Socher, R., Manning, C.D.: Glove: global vectors for word representation. In: Moschitti, A., Pang, B., Daelemans, W. (eds.) Proceedings of the 2014 Conference on Empirical Methods in Natural Language Processing, EMNLP 2014, Doha, Qatar, 25–29 October 2014, A meeting of SIGDAT, a Special Interest Group of the ACL, pp. 1532–1543. ACL (2014)

12. Shi, X., Xiao, Y.: Modeling multi-mapping relations for precise cross-lingual entity alignment. In: EMNLP/IJCNLP (1), pp. 813–822. Association for Computational Linguistics (2019)

13. Srivastava, R.K., Greff, K., Schmidhuber, J.: Highway networks. CoRR, abs/1505.00387 (2015)

14. Sun, Z., et al.: Knowledge graph alignment network with gated multi-hop neighborhood aggregation. In: The Thirty-Fourth AAAI Conference on Artificial Intelligence, AAAI 2020, The Thirty-Second Innovative Applications of Artificial Intelligence Conference, IAAI 2020, The Tenth AAAI Symposium on Educational Advances in Artificial Intelligence, EAAI 2020, New York, NY, USA, 7–12 February 2020, pp. 222–229. AAAI Press (2020)

15. Sun, Z., et al.: A benchmarking study of embedding-based entity alignment for knowledge graphs. Proc. VLDB Endow. **13**(11), 2326–2340 (2020)

16. Wang, Z., Lv, Q., Lan, X., Zhang, Y.: Cross-lingual knowledge graph alignment via graph convolutional networks. In: EMNLP, pp. 349–357. Association for Computational Linguistics (2018)

17. Wu, Y., Liu, X., Feng, Y., Wang, Z., Yan, R., Zhao., D.: Relation-aware entity alignment for heterogeneous knowledge graphs. In: Kraus, S. (ed.) Proceedings of the Twenty-Eighth International Joint Conference on Artificial Intelligence, IJCAI 2019, Macao, China, 10–16 August 2019, pp. 5278–5284. ijcai.org (2019)

18. Wu, Y., Liu, X., Feng, Y., Wang, Z., Zhao., D.: Jointly learning entity and relation representations for entity alignment. In: EMNLP/IJCNLP (1), pp. 240–249. Association for Computational Linguistics (2019)

19. Xu, H., et al.: High-order relation construction and mining for graph matching. CoRR, abs/2010.04348 (2020)

20. Xu, K., et al.: Cross-lingual knowledge graph alignment via graph matching neural network. In: Korhonen, A., Traum, D.R., Màrquez, L. (eds.) Proceedings of the 57th Conference of the Association for Computational Linguistics, ACL 2019, Florence, Italy, July 28- August 2, 2019, Volume 1: Long Papers, pp. 3156–3161. Association for Computational Linguistics (2019)
21. Yang, H.-W., Zou, Y., Shi, P., Lu, W., Lin, J., Sun, X.: Aligning cross-lingual entities with multi-aspect information. In: EMNLP/IJCNLP (1), pp. 4430–4440. Association for Computational Linguistics (2019)
22. Ye, R., Li, X., Fang, Y., Zang, H., Wang, M.: A vectorized relational graph convolutional network for multi-relational network alignment. In: IJCAI, pp. 4135–4141. ijcai.org (2019)
23. Zhang, Q., Sun, Z., Hu, W., Chen, M., Guo, L., Qu, Y.: Multi-view knowledge graph embedding for entity alignment. In: IJCAI, pp. 5429–5435. ijcai.org (2019)
24. Zhao, X., Zeng, W., Tang, J., Wang, W., Suchanek, F.: An experimental study of state-of-the-art entity alignment approaches. IEEE Trans. Knowl. Data Eng. (01), 1 (2020)
25. Zhu, Q., Zhou, X., Wu, J., Tan, J., Guo, L.: Neighborhood-aware attentional representation for multilingual knowledge graphs. In: IJCAI, pp. 1943–1949. ijcai.org (2019)

System Effect Estimation by Sharding: A Comparison Between ANOVA Approaches to Detect Significant Differences

Guglielmo Faggioli[✉] and Nicola Ferro

Department of Information Engineering, University of Padua, Padua, Italy
guglielmo.faggioli@phd.unipd.it

Abstract. The ultimate goal of the evaluation is to understand when two IR systems are (significantly) different. To this end, many comparison procedures have been developed over time. However, to date, most reproducibility efforts focused just on reproducing systems and algorithms, almost fully neglecting to investigate the reproducibility of the methods we use to compare our systems. In this paper, we focus on methods based on ANalysis Of VAriance (ANOVA), which explicitly model the data in terms of different contributing effects, allowing us to obtain a more accurate estimate of significant differences. In this context, recent studies have shown how sharding the corpus can further improve the estimation of the system effect. We replicate and compare methods based on "traditional" ANOVA (tANOVA) to those based on a bootstrapped version of ANOVA (bANOVA) and those performing multiple comparisons relying on a more conservative Family-wise Error Rate (FWER) controlling approach to those relying on a more lenient False Discovery Rate (FDR) controlling approach. We found that bANOVA shows overall a good degree of reproducibility, with some limitations for what concerns the confidence intervals. Besides, compared to the tANOVA approaches, bANOVA presents greater statistical power, at the cost of lower stability. Overall, with this work, we aim at shifting the focus of reproducibility from systems alone to the methods we use to compare and analyze their performance.

1 Introduction

Comparing IR systems and identifying when they are significantly different is a critical task for both industry and academia [4,15,23]. In recent years, many fields have devoted a lot of effort to reproducing and generalizing their systems and algorithms [5,7,9,17]. Yet, the literature still lacks reproducibility studies on the statistical tools used to compare the performance of such systems and algorithms. Using reproducible – and thus trustworthy – statistical tools is crucial to drawing robust inferences and conclusions. In this respect, our work makes a first step toward the study of the reproducibility of evaluation methodologies themselves. In this context, ANalysis Of VAriance (ANOVA) [21] is a widely

© Springer Nature Switzerland AG 2021
D. Hiemstra et al. (Eds.): ECIR 2021, LNCS 12657, pp. 33–46, 2021.
https://doi.org/10.1007/978-3-030-72240-1_3

used technique, where we model performance as a linear combination of factors, such as topic and system effects, and, by developing more and more sophisticated models, we accrue higher sensitivity in determining significant differences among systems. We focus on two recently developed ANOVA models. Voorhees et al. [27] used sharding of the document corpus to obtain the replicates of the performance score for every (topic, system) pairs needed to develop a model accounting not only for the main effects, but also for the interaction between topics and systems; Voorhees et al. also used an ANOVA version based on residuals bootstrapping [6], which we call bANOVA. Given the absence, at the current time, of publicly available code, we are interested in replicating some of the results presented by Voorhees et al. Ferro and Sanderson [11] used document sharding as well but they developed a more comprehensive model, based on traditional ANOVA, which also accounts for the shard factor, the shard*system interaction, and the topic*shard interaction; we call this approach tANOVA. Another fundamental aspect to consider when comparing several IR systems is the need to adjust for *multiple comparisons* [12,22]. Indeed, when comparing just two systems, significance tests control the *Type-I error* at the significance level α. The Type-I error is the possibility to find a statistically significant difference between a pair of systems when they are not (also called *false positive*). However, when c simultaneous tests are carried out, the probability of committing at least one Type-I error increases up to $1 - (1 - \alpha)^c$. Several procedures have been developed for controlling Type-I errors when multiple comparisons are performed [14]. Voorhees et al. adopted a lenient False Discovery Rate (FDR) correction by Benjamini and Hochberg [2]; Ferro and Sanderson used a conservative Family-wise Error Rate (FWER) correction, using the Honestly Significant Difference (HSD) method by Tukey [25]. In conclusion, we identified three aspects that can impact the reproducibility of the above-mentioned ANOVA approaches: *i)* the strategy used to obtain replicates, *ii)* the kind of ANOVA used, and *iii)* the control procedure for the pairwise comparisons problem.

Our work is articulated in two research questions:

- **RQ1:** Given the absence of publicly available code, we are interested in determining the degree of replicability of the evaluation methodology proposed in Voorhees et al. [27][1];
- **RQ2:** We are interested in studying the behaviour of tANOVA and bANOVA under different experimental settings – with respect to the above-mentioned focal points – and the generalizability of their results.

The paper is organized as follows: Sect. 2 discusses the related works; Sect. 3 details on the replicated approach (i.e. Voorhees et al. [27]) and the experimental setup; Sects. 4 and 5 describe our efforts in generalizing the results by Voorhees et al. and Ferro and Sanderson; finally, Sect. 6 draws some conclusions and outlooks for future work.

---

[1] We already have access to the code and data used by Ferro and Sanderson, so we are not interested in their replicability.

2 Related Work

Tague-Sutcliffe and Blustein [24] used ANOVA to decompose performance into a topic and a system factor and adopted the Scheffe tests to compensate for multiple comparisons. Tague-Sutcliffe and Blustein were not able to model the topic*system interaction factor due to the lack of replicates for each (topic, system) pair but, later on, Banks et al. [1] suggested that the topic*system interaction should have been a large size effect. Bodoff and Li [3] used multiple relevance judgements to obtain replicates. Ferro et al. [8], Ferro and Sanderson [10,11], Voorhees et al. [27] investigated document shards as a mean to obtain replicates and develop more sophisticated ANOVA models. One problem when using document shards is that some topics may not have any relevant document in a shard and this prevents the computation of any performance measure on that shard. Voorhees et al. [27] solved this issue by resampling shards until all the topics have relevant documents on all the shards; they developed an ANOVA model consisting of a topic and system factors plus the topic*system interaction. Ferro et al. [8], Ferro and Sanderson [11] substituted missing values with an interpolated value. They developed models accounting for the topic, system, and shard factors as well as all their interactions. Ferro and Sanderson [11] (mathematically) proved that the system effect estimation is independent from the used interpolation value, when adopting the most accurate ANOVA model. Also Robertson and Kanoulas [20] explored the bootstrap usage to investigate the inter-topic variability and to obtain the replicates necessary to compute the interaction between topics and systems, while Robertson [19] investigated the usage of document sampling to estimate the stability of traditional IR evaluation. Multiple comparisons procedures aim at controlling either Family-wise Error Rate (FWER) [16] or False Discovery Rate (FDR) [2]. FWER is the probability of having at most one false positive among all rejected null hypoteses, and FWER-controlling procedures aim at keeping it equal to $1 - \alpha$. One of the most popular FWER correction approaches is the Honestly Significant Difference (HSD) by Tukey [25]. Given $\hat{\mu}_{.u.}$ and $\hat{\mu}_{.v.}$ the marginal means for two different systems, the test value for the HSD is computed as:

$$|tk| = \frac{|\hat{\mu}_{.u.} - \hat{\mu}_{.v.}|}{\sqrt{\frac{MS_{error}}{T \cdot S}}}$$

where: MS_{error} is the mean square error according to the ANOVA model and T and S are respectively the number of topics and shards. This test value is then compared against the critical value, obtained from $Q^{\alpha}_{R, df_{error}}$, the studentized range distribution , where R is the number of systems. Conversely, FDR-controlling procedures aim at keeping the false discovery rate (the number of false findings over all findings) at level α: this corresponds to allowing the number of false positives to increase, as long as the number of true discoveries increases. One of the most important FDR-controlling procedures is the Benjamini-Hochberg (BH) [2] procedure. It sorts in ascending order the p-values associated with N tested hypotheses. The greatest value of k for which

$p_{(k)} \leq \alpha \frac{k}{N}$ is then found: null hypotheses associated to p-values in ranks from 0 to k are rejected.

3   Approach

3.1   ANOVA Models

We consider the following ANOVA models:

$$y_{ijk} = \mu_{\ldots} + \tau_i + \alpha_j + \varepsilon_{ijk} \tag{MD1}$$

$$y_{ijk} = \mu_{\ldots} + \tau_i + \alpha_j + (\tau\alpha)_{ij} + \varepsilon_{ijk} \tag{MD2}$$

$$y_{ijk} = \mu_{\ldots} + \tau_i + \alpha_j + \beta_k + (\tau\alpha)_{ij} + (\tau\beta)_{ik} + (\alpha\beta)_{jk} + \varepsilon_{ijk} \tag{MD3}$$

where: $\mu_{\ldots}$ is the grand mean; τ_i is the effect of the i-th topic; α_j is the effect of the j-th system; β_k is the effect of the k-th shard; $(\tau\alpha)_{ij}$, $(\tau\beta)_{ik}$, and $(\alpha\beta)_{jk}$ are respectively interactions between topics and systems, topics and shards, and systems and shards; ε is the error committed by the model in predicting y. Our **(MD1)** is the model originally used by Tague-Sutcliffe and Blustein [24], it corresponds to the model in equation (2) of Voorhees et al. [27] and to (MD2) of Ferro and Sanderson [11]. Our **(MD2)** corresponds to the model in equation (3) of Voorhees et al. [27] and to (MD3) of Ferro and Sanderson [11]. Finally, our **(MD3)** corresponds to the model (MD6) of Ferro and Sanderson [11]. Voorhees et al. did not experimented with the latter model; so, its usage represents an aspect of generalizability.

3.2   Bootstrap ANOVA (bANOVA)

The bootstrap based version of ANOVA is the focus of our reproducibility study. It relies on bootstrap sampling of the residuals produced by a traditional ANOVA linear model. The use of bootstrap is motivated by the fact that, since it does not rely on the traditional F statistics, it allows for minimizing the assumptions imposed on the distribution of the data. To compute the bootstrap ANOVA, it is necessary to fit a traditional ANOVA linear model. Once the model is estimated, we can use it to compute the estimated performance $\hat{y}_{ijk}$, for the i-th topic, using the j-th system on the k-th shard. Note that estimated performance values can be organized in an estimated performance tensor $\hat{\mathbf{Y}}$, where $\hat{Y}_{ijk} = \hat{y}_{ijk}$. Afterwards, residuals are computed as $r_{ijk} = y_{ijk} - \hat{y}_{ijk}$, where y_{ijk} is the observed performance value. Called $\mathcal{R}$ the set of all residuals, B different perturbation tensors $\mathbf{R}^{(b)}$ are sampled, with $b \in \{0, ..., B-1\}$. In particular, $R_{ijk}^{(b)} = r_{ijk}^{(b)}$ where $r_{ijk}^{(b)}$ is sampled uniformly with replacement among all possible original ANOVA residuals $\mathcal{R}$. These perturbation tensors are then added to $\hat{\mathbf{Y}}$, producing B perturbed observation tensors $\tilde{\mathbf{Y}}^{(b)}$. Each perturbed observation tensor is then used to fit an ANOVA model, providing B new bootstrap sampled estimations for the effect of each system. Using these estimations, it is possible to fit a Probability Density Function (PDF) of the effect of the system. Note that, Voorhees et al. do not specify the approach to fit the PDF, and thus we used the Kernel Density Estimation (KDE) technique [28], using a Maximum Likelihood Estimation (MLE) approach. The average MLE bandwidth is 0.0016 and ranges between 0.0005 and 0.0033, according to the system, the number of shards, and model considered. Such distribution is used to compute the p-value associated with the null hypothesis that the system with greater effect is not statistically significantly better then the other (one-tail hypothesis). Once a p-value for each pairwise comparison is available, Voorhees et al. propose to apply Benjamini-Hochberg correction procedure to correct for multiple comparisons. Finally, using the information on the number of significant differences found, Voorhees et al. propose a strategy to compute an interval of confidence around the system effect, by trimming the vector of the bootstrap sampled estimations of the system effects. In particular, the proportion of samples removed from each side is $\alpha \frac{k}{2N}$, where N is the total number of pairwise comparisons between systems and k is the number of pairs of systems for which one of the two system has statistically larger effect size, according to the Benjamini-Hochberg procedure.

3.3   Experimental Setup

Akin Voorhees et al., we used two collections: the TREC-3 Adhoc track [13] and TREC-8 Adhoc track [26]. TREC-3 contains 50 topics and 40 runs for a total of 820 pairwise run comparisons. TREC-8 consists of 50 topics and 129 runs for a total of 8,256 pairwise run comparisons. We conducted all the experiments on both collections and we observed very similar behaviours. However, due to space constraints, the replicability results in Sect. 4 are reported on TREC-3, since Voorhees et al. provide more details on this collection; the generalizability results in Sect. 5 are reported on TREC-8, since it contains more runs. Note that the replicability experiments concern only bANOVA by Voorhees et al. and not also tANOVA by Ferro and Sanderson, since the latter is our own code. We use Average Precision (AP) and Precision (P) with the cutoff at 10 documents (P@10) as performance measure. The document corpus has been split in 2, 3, 5, 10 even-sized random shards and we repeated the sampling 5 times. For replicability in Sect. 4, we repeated the sampling until all the shards contain at least one relevant document for each topic; for generalizability in Sect. 5, if a shard does not contain any relevant document for a topic, we interpolate the missing value using 4 possible strategies: zero; lq, the value of the lower quartile of the measure scores; mean, the average value of the measure scores; and, one. Note that, for generalizability in Sect. 5, due to space constraints, we report only the case of 5-shards, being the others very similar. To ease the reproducibility of our experiments, the source code is publicly available at https://github.com/guglielmof/replicate_URIIRE.

4   Replicability of bANOVA

We tried to replicate the widths of the confidence intervals of the system effect and the number of s.s.d. pairs, i.e. systems for which one is significantly better than the other. Table 1 reports the results of our replicability analysis. Confidence intervals are much smaller, approximately halved, than those reported in the original paper. On the other hand, the number of s.s.d. pairs is slightly higher for both AP and P@10; however, this could be still considered within the bounds of the variability due to the random sharding, observed also by Voorhees et al.. To further investigate the interval size, we hypothesized that, even if the original paper describes a single-tailed test, its implementation might have used a more-strict two-tailed one, which is often the default in many statistical software libraries. Table 2 shows the results when using such a two-tailed test. We can note that the confidence intervals are still very similar to the case of Table 1 and, thus, the difference between one-tailed and two-tailed test is not the cause

Table 1. Confidence interval widths on systems effects and number of s.s.d. system pairs using one-tailed bANOVA on TREC-3. Between parentheses, values originally reported by Voorhees et al.; dashed values were not reported in the original paper.

Sample	Measure	No interactions (MD1)				Interactions (MD2)			
		Mean	Min	Max	s.s.d.	Mean	Min	Max	s.s.d.
2 shards	AP	0.045	0.044	0.045	683.80	0.016	0.016	0.017	749.00
		(0.075)	(0.071)	(0.082)	(—)	(0.029)	(0.026)	(0.031)	(743)
	P@10	0.078	0.076	0.080	666.00	0.038	0.037	0.039	728.00
		(0.130)	(0.122)	(0.140)	(—)	(0.065)	(0.061)	(0.069)	(712)
3 shards	AP	0.038	0.037	0.039	699.40	0.018	0.018	0.019	746.20
		(0.064)	(0.060)	(0.069)	(—)	(0.032)	(0.030)	(0.034)	(741)
	P@10	0.062	0.061	0.063	682.20	0.037	0.036	0.037	727.00
		(0.106)	(0.099)	(0.112)	(—)	(0.065)	(0.061)	(0.071)	(712)
5 shards	AP	0.033	0.032	0.033	714.40	0.020	0.020	0.021	742.20
		(0.055)	(0.052)	(0.058)	(—)	(0.033)	(0.031)	(0.034)	(—)
	P@10	0.046	0.045	0.047	697.00	0.031	0.030	0.032	723.00
		(0.081)	(0.076)	(0.086)	(—)	(0.055)	(0.052)	(0.060)	(—)

Table 2. Confidence intervals width on systems effects and number of s.s.d. system pairs using two-tailed bANOVA on TREC-3.

Sample	Measure	No interactions (MD1)				Interactions (MD2)			
		Mean	Min	Max	s.s.d.	Mean	Min	Max	s.s.d.
2 shards	AP	0.045	0.044	0.046	661.40	0.016	0.016	0.017	743.20
	P@10	0.078	0.076	0.080	639.60	0.038	0.037	0.039	717.40
3 shards	AP	0.038	0.038	0.039	678.80	0.019	0.018	0.019	739.60
	P@10	0.062	0.061	0.064	662.40	0.037	0.036	0.038	717.80
5 shards	AP	0.033	0.032	0.034	696.00	0.020	0.020	0.021	734.80
	P@10	0.047	0.046	0.048	677.60	0.031	0.030	0.032	712.00

of the observed discrepancy. On the other hand, the number of s.s.d. pairs is getting even closer to those of Voorhees et al.; a little bit less close in the case of P@10 but, as also observed by Voorhees et al., it is a less stable measure. To understand the issue with confidence interval sizes, we modified how they are computed. Instead of removing a percentage of the total number of samples, as described by Voorhees et al., we treated that number as an integer value, representing the actual number of samples to discard. Basically, this milder cut-off allows for removing just the most extreme values. Table 3 reports the result for such modification and we can now see that these modified confidence intervals are closer to those of Voorhees et al. To double-check the confidence intervals, we also tried the vice-versa, i.e. we used the intervals reported in Voorhees et al. to determine the number of s.s.d. pairs. Note that Voorhees et al. use the BH correction to determine the s.s.d. pairs and not the confidence intervals; in their case, they estimate confidence intervals in such a way that they should be consistent with the number of s.s.d. pairs obtained by the BH correction. Since we do not have the sizes of the original intervals, we use, for all the systems, in turn, the mean, minimum, and maximum interval widths reported by Voorhees et al. Table 4 reports the results of such analysis. The number of s.s.d. pairs is still lower compared to the expected one, in the range of 30 to 70 less, on average (cf. Table 2). This suggests that the original intervals are still a bit large to obtain the reported number of s.s.d. pairs; this might be due to the intrinsic

Table 3. Mean, Min and Max modified confidence intervals widths of systems effects on TREC-3, using 3 shards. Highlighted values are the closest to the original ones by Voorhees et al. (* for AP and ‡ for P@10).

Sample	Measure	No interactions (MD1)			Interactions(MD2)		
		Mean	Min	Max	Mean	Min	Max
Original	AP	0.064	0.060	0.069	0.032	0.030	0.034
	P@10	0.106	0.099	0.112	0.065	0.061	0.071
1	AP	0.065^*	0.061	0.071	0.033	0.030^*	0.035
	P@10	$0.106^\ddagger$	0.100	0.113	0.063	0.058	$0.069^\ddagger$
2	AP	0.065^*	0.061	0.072	0.032^*	0.030^*	0.034^*
	P@10	0.105	$0.099^\ddagger$	$0.112^\ddagger$	0.063	$0.060^\ddagger$	0.068
3	AP	0.068	0.065	0.073	0.037	0.034	0.041
	P@10	0.107	0.101	0.113	$0.066^\ddagger$	0.062	0.074
4	AP	0.065^*	0.060^*	0.070	0.030	0.028	0.033
	P@10	0.105	0.098	$0.112^\ddagger$	0.061	0.057	0.064
5	AP	0.065^*	0.059	0.069^*	0.030	0.026	0.032
	P@10	0.105	$0.099^\ddagger$	0.114	0.063	0.059	0.068
Avg	AP	0.066	0.061	0.071	0.032	0.030	0.035
	P@10	0.106	0.099	0.113	0.063	0.059	0.069

accuracy of the estimation procedure or to some differences in the implementation, as we hypothesized in Table 3. Overall, we can conclude that it is possible to fully replicate the bANOVA with BH correction and the resulting number of s.s.d. system pairs which, to us, is the core contribution of the paper and what is used in actual analyses. On the other hand, we were not able to replicate the derived estimation of the confidence intervals and remains an open issue.

5   Generalizability of tANOVA and bANOVA

5.1   Impact of the Multiple Comparison Strategies and Bootstrapping

To investigate the differences between ANOVA approaches, our first analysis compares the number of s.s.d. system pairs found by them. We consider the following multiple comparison procedures: HSD for tANOVA, as originally proposed by Ferro and Sanderson, indicated with tANOVA(HSD); BH for bANOVA, as originally proposed by Voorhees et al., indicated with bANOVA(BH); and, BH for tANOVA, indicated with tANOVA(BH). tANOVA with Benjamini-Hochberg correction is here employed and analyzed for the first time, representing a generalizability aspect. It takes the p-values on the difference between levels of the factors produced by the traditional ANOVA, but corrects them using the BH correction. The rationale behind it is that it enjoys the statistical properties provided by the ANOVA while granting a higher discriminative power f, due to the BH correction procedure. Finally, in this specific setting, such correction procedure allows us to investigate whether the differences between the bANOVA and tANOVA are due to the different ANOVA computation (bootstrap vs direct computation of F-statistics), or are due to the correction procedure applied (BH vs HSD) correction. `zero` has been used as interpolation strategy; in Sect. 5.3 we empirically show that the interpolation strategy has a negligible effect on the results. Finally, we experiment all the models from (MD1) to (MD3) with all the ANOVA approaches; note that (MD3) has not been studied before for bANOVA and this represents another generalizability aspect.

Table 4. s.s.d. system pairs as obtained by using the confidence intervals widths reported by Voorhees et al. Compare them with the ones reported in Table 1.

Sample	Measure	No interactions (MD1)			Interactions (MD2)		
		Mean	Min	Max	Mean	Min	Max
2 shards	AP	577.20	590.00	563.20	711.00	721.60	706.00
	P@10	544.60	558.20	528.80	670.40	678.80	661.40
3 shards	AP	608.80	622.80	592.00	702.80	708.60	695.00
	P@10	573.80	583.20	562.00	659.80	667.60	638.60
5 shards	AP	638.80	645.60	629.00	697.40	704.80	695.00
	P@10	597.00	608.20	586.40	656.80	663.60	644.00

Table 5. s.s.d. pairs of systems for different ANOVA approaches, using AP.

Model	Approach	bANOVA(BH)	tANOVA(BH)	tANOVA(HSD)
MD1	bANOVA(BH)	6866.60 ± 36.965	329.20 ± 22.027	2275.80 ± 39.844
	tANOVA(BH)	–	6537.40 ± 57.107	1946.60 ± 23.190
	tANOVA(HSD)	–	–	4590.80 ± 75.850
MD2	bANOVA(BH)	7231.80 ± 51.085	375.20 ± 17.436	2133.40 ± 70.456
	tANOVA(BH)	–	6856.60 ± 65.859	1758.20 ± 54.580
	tANOVA(HSD)	–	–	5098.40 ± 113.429
MD3	bANOVA(BH)	7563.40 ± 15.273	262.00 ± 11.681	1655.80 ± 25.377
	tANOVA(BH)	–	7301.40 ± 11.734	1393.80 ± 32.585
	tANOVA(HSD)	–	–	5907.60 ± 37.359

Table 5 reports the results averaged over the five samples of shards together with their confidence interval. Numbers on the diagonal of Table 5 describe how many pairs of systems are considered s.s.d. by a given approach; numbers above the diagonal are the additional s.s.d. pairs found by one method with respect to the other. Table 5 shows that, as the complexity of the model increases from (MD1) to (MD3), the pairs of systems deemed significantly different increase as well, confirming previous findings in the literature. tANOVA(HSD) controls tANOVA(BH) since all the s.s.d. pairs for tANOVA(HSD) are significant also for tANOVA(BH); this was expected since FWER controls FDR [14]. It is possible see this by considering the differences between approaches (above diagonal): by summing the difference between tANOVA(HSD) and tANOVA(BH) to the tANOVA(HSD) you obtain back the number of s.s.d. pairs identified by tANOVA(BH). However, this pattern holds also for bANOVA(BH) and tANOVA(BH), i.e. all the s.s.d. pairs of tANOVA(BH) are s.s.d. pairs for bANOVA(BH) too. While the relation between BH and HSD was expected, this finding sheds some light on the difference between using a traditional or a bootstrapped version of ANOVA. In summary, most of the increase in the s.s.d. pairs is due to the correction procedure rather than the use of bootstrap or not. Since bANOVA is more computationally demanding than tANOVA, due to its iterative nature, its use may be not worth if not when you really need to squeeze out all the possible s.s.d. pairs.

5.2   Effect of the Random Shards on the Stability of the Approaches

To assess the stability of different approaches against random resharding, we fix the number of shards (5 in the following analysis). We resampled the shards 5 times and we considered all the possible pairs of shard samples – i.e. 10 possible pairs of shards. To assess the stability with respect to random resharding, we consider the following counting measures proposed in [18]:

– Active Agreements (AA), i.e. the number of pairs of systems A and B for which an approach considers A to be significantly better than B on both samples of shards;

Table 6. Average PAA and PPA.

Model	Approach	Average PAA	Average PPA
MD1	bANOVA(BH)	0.979 ± 0.001	0.903 ± 0.005
	tANOVA(BH)	0.980 ± 0.001	0.924 ± 0.004
	tANOVA(HSD)	0.979 ± 0.002	0.973 ± 0.003
MD2	bANOVA(BH)	0.980 ± 0.001	0.866 ± 0.007
	tANOVA(BH)	0.979 ± 0.001	0.896 ± 0.006
	tANOVA(HSD)	0.977 ± 0.002	0.963 ± 0.004
MD3	bANOVA(BH)	0.982 ± 0.001	0.802 ± 0.012
	tANOVA(BH)	0.980 ± 0.001	0.850 ± 0.006
	tANOVA(HSD)	0.981 ± 0.001	0.953 ± 0.003

- Active Disagreements (AD), i.e. the number of pairs of systems A and B for which an approach considers A to be significantly better than B on a sample but B is significantly better than A on the other sample;
- Passive Agreements (PA), i.e. the number of pairs of systems A and B for which an approach considers A to not be significantly better than B on both samples of shards;
- Passive Disagreements (PD), i.e. the number of pairs of systems A and B for which an approach considers A to be significantly better than B on a sample but A is not significantly better than B on the other sample.

We did not find any occurrence of AD in any of our experiments, which would indicate a dependency of an approach on a specific random shard, raising some concerns about its stability. AA, PA, and PD are aggregated as follows:

- The Proportion of Active Agreements (PAA), given by $PAA = 2AA/(2AA + PD)$, represents how many times an approach agrees on two systems being s.s.d. concerning the total number of times two systems are claimed s.s.d.;
- The Proportion of Passive Agreements (PPA), given by $PPA = 2PA/(2PA + PD)$, shows how often an approach agrees on two systems not being s.s.d. compared to the total number of times two systems are not claimed s.s.d..

PAA and PPA indicate, respectively, the stability of the decisions about which systems are and are not s.s.d., independently from the shard samples. Overall, these two proportions indicate how much you would not change your mind when changing the random shard sample at hand.

Table 6 shows the PAA and PPA averaged over every possible pair of shards together with their confidence intervals. All the approaches have a very high PAA, suggesting that the conclusion about which systems are to be considered s.s.d. is quite stable. The PAA is also very close for all the approaches, slightly increasing as we adopt the more sophisticated (MD3) model but without notable differences between bootstrap and traditional ANOVA or between HSD and BH correction. On the other hand, tANOVA approaches lead to higher PPA than

Table 7. Average number of PD for ANOVA model MD2.

(MD2) approach	5 Shards				
	Interp.	zero	lq	mean	one
tANOVA(HSD)	zero	230.60 ± 21.55	23.00 ± 15.21	100.20 ± 74.45	89.80 ± 82.47
	lq	—	239.20 ± 22.56	77.20 ± 62.86	85.60 ± 96.98
	mean	—	—	253.20 ± 32.18	124.40 ± 92.81
	one	—	—	—	265.80± 53.21
bANOVA(BH)	zero	282.60 ± 13.70	5.80 ± 3.45	41.60 ± 24.44	33.20 ± 28.83
	lq	—	280.80 ± 12.99	35.80 ± 21.12	32.60 ± 30.75
	mean	—	—	285.00 ± 13.24	49.20 ± 40.73
	one	—	—	—	288.40 ± 18.59

bANOVA ones. The HSD correction produces notably higher PPA than the BH one. We hypothesize that the additional s.s.d. pairs brought in by bootstrap and BH are "corner cases" and the decision about them depends more on the actual shards at hand. We can also observe as the PPA tends to decrease as the models get more sophisticated from (MD1) to (MD3); also, in this case, a more complex model can identify more s.s.d. pairs, but some of them are "corner" cases subject to change from a random shard to another. Overall, the findings concerning PAA and PPA suggest that tANOVA with HSD correction is the most stable approach against different random shards. It should therefore be used when the goal is not the absolute number of s.s.d. pairs, but the accuracy of the decisions.

5.3 Stability of ANOVA Models with Respect to Different Interpolation Values

We study the impact of the interpolation strategy, i.e. how to substitute missing values for topics without any relevant document on a given shard, for the different approaches. Here, for space reasons, we report only the results for tANOVA(HSD) and bANOVA(BH), being the tANOVA(BH) midway between these two.

Ferro and Sanderson [11] mathematically proved that model (MD3) is independent of the adopted interpolation values while Voorhees et al. [27] did not experiment with interpolation values and did not consider this model at all. Tables 7 and 8 report the average PD counts together with their confidence interval (remember that AD turned out to be zero in our experiments), respectively for models MD2 and MD3. Values on the diagonal are the average PD observed using the same interpolation strategy, but over the pairs of shards samples. The upper triangle of the Table contains the average PD when using two different interpolation values. The PD counts on the diagonal are consistent with the findings of Table 6 in terms of PPA, confirming that bANOVA(BH) is more sensitive to the random sampling of shards than tANOVA(HSD). Table 7 shows what happens if, using model (MD2) by Voorhees et al., instead of re-sampling shards we use an interpolation value. We can note that the PD count on the diagonal, compared to the one of Table 8, slightly increases for both bANOVA(BH) and tANOVA(HSD). On the other hand, the values are in the same confidence interval,

Table 8. Average number of PD for ANOVA model MD3.

(MD3) approach	5 Shards				
	Interp.	zero	lq	mean	one
tANOVA(HSD)	zero	222.60 ± 15.392	0.00 ± 0.000	0.00 ± 0.000	0.00 ± 0.000
	lq	—	222.60 ± 15.392	0.00 ± 0.000	0.00 ± 0.000
	mean	—	—	222.60 ± 15.392	0.00 ± 0.000
	one	—	—	—	222.60± 15.392
bANOVA(BH)	zero	279.20 ± 16.60	0.00 ± 0.00	0.00 ± 0.00	0.00 ± 0.00
	lq	–	279.20 ± 16.60	0.00 ± 0.00	0.00 ± 0.00
	mean	–	–	279.20 ± 16.60	0.00 ± 0.00
	one	–	–	–	279.20 ± 16.60

and thus are not significantly different. We can also note that, as the interpolation value increases, the PD count on the diagonal tends to increase too. When it comes to the upper triangles, we interestingly find that bANOVA(BH) is much less sensitive to the interpolation values than tANOVA(HSD), being the PD counts substantially lower. Thus, Voorhees et al. could have used an interpolation value instead of re-sampling, without drastically changing the conclusions. The bootstrapped version of ANOVA (bANOVA) appears to be less stable with respect to the resharding. This phenomenon is likely due to its greater discriminative power: since a small evidence for bANOVA is enough to assess when two systems are different, the random resharding might produce spurious evidence and thus large variation among different samples. In Table 8, as expected from [11], the upper triangle for tANOVA(HSD) is zero, since tANOVA(HSD) with (MD3) is independent from the interpolation values. The most interesting finding is that also bANOVA(BH) with (MD3) is independent of the interpolation values. Indeed, the bANOVA approach samples the residuals and Ferro and Sanderson proved that they are independent of the interpolation value for (MD3). Therefore, using (MD3) also the bootstrap approach by Voorhees et al. does not need to re-sample shards.

6   Conclusions and Future Work

The aim of this paper is multi-folded: we wanted to replicate results by Voorhees et al., generalize the proposed method and compare it with other ANOVA approaches. We were able to replicate the number of s.s.d. found by bANOVA, i.e. the main contribution of the paper, but not the size of the confidence interval. Furthermore, we compared the tANOVA and bANOVA approaches under different conditions. We found out that tANOVA tends to be more robust than bANOVA with respect to the actual random shards used, suggesting more reliability in drawing the same conclusions. On the other hand, when using partial ANOVA models like (MD2) which are not able to deal with shards without relevant documents, bANOVA is more robust than tANOVA to the chosen interpolation value.

Regarding the multiple comparison strategy, we have found that tANOVA with HSD is more restrictive than bANOVA but tANOVA with BH correction behaves similarly to bANOVA. Overall, we can conclude that, the decision of the model and the correction technique depends on the final aim of the researcher. If you prioritize the stability of the results over the number of s.s.d. pairs found and you plan to use a full model like (MD3), it is preferable to use tANOVA(HSD), since it is more stable with respect to random shards and less computationally expensive. If instead, your focus is on the number of pairs, bANOVA(BH) gives you the maximum boost but at the price of less stability for random shards. If you plan to use a partial model, like (MD2), which is less expensive from the computational point of view, bANOVA(BH) frees you more from the dependency on topics without relevant documents on some shards. Future work will investigate the use of uneven-size random shards, instead of the even-size ones used in the literature so far.

Acknowledgments. We thank the reviewers for their comments.

The work is partially funded by the DAta BenchmarK for Keyword-based Access and Retrieval (DAKKAR) Starting Grants project sponsored by University of Padua and Fondazione Cassa di Risparmio di Padova e di Rovigo.

References

1. Banks, D., Over, P., Zhang, N.F.: Blind men and elephants: six approaches to TREC data. Inf. Retrieval **1**(1–2), 7–34 (1999)
2. Benjamini, Y., Hochberg, Y.: Controlling the false discovery rate: a practical and powerful approach to multiple testing. J. Royal Stat. Soc. **57**(1), 289–300 (1995)
3. Bodoff, D., Li, P.: Test theory for assessing IR test collections. In: Proceedings of SIGIR, pp. 367–374 (2007)
4. Carterette, B.A.: Multiple testing in statistical analysis of systems-based information retrieval experiments. ACM Trans. Inf. Syst. **30**(1), 4:1–4:34 (2012)
5. Clancy, R., Ferro, N., Hauff, C., Sakai, T., Wu, Z.Z.: The SIGIR 2019 open-source IR replicability challenge (OSIRRC 2019). In: Proceedings of SIGIR, pp. 1432–1434 (2019)
6. Efron, B., Tibshirani, R.J.: An Introduction to the Bootstrap. Chapman and Hall/CRC, Boca Raton (1994)
7. Ferrari Dacrema, M., Boglio, S., Cremonesi, P., Jannach, D.: A troubling analysis of reproducibility and progress in recommender systems research. User Modeling and User-Adapted Interaction (2019)
8. Ferro, N., Kim, Y., Sanderson, M.: Using collection shards to study retrieval performance effect sizes. ACM Trans. Inf. Syst. **37**(3), 30:1–30:40 (2019)
9. Ferro, N., Maistro, M., Sakai, T., Soboroff, I.: Overview of CENTRE@CLEF 2018: a first tale in the systematic reproducibility realm. In: Bellot, P., et al. (eds.) CLEF 2018. LNCS, vol. 11018, pp. 239–246. Springer, Cham (2018). https://doi.org/10.1007/978-3-319-98932-7_23
10. Ferro, N., Sanderson, M.: Sub-corpora impact on system effectiveness. In: Proceedings of SIGIR, pp. 901–904 (2017)
11. Ferro, N., Sanderson, M.: Improving the accuracy of system performance estimation by using shards. In: Proceedings of SIGIR, pp. 805–814 (2019)

12. Fuhr, N.: Some common mistakes in IR evaluation, and how they can be avoided. SIGIR Forum **51**(3), 32–41 (2017)
13. Harman, D.K.: Overview of the third text REtrieval conference (TREC-3). In: Proceedings of TREC, pp. 1–19 (1994)
14. Hsu, J.C.: Multiple Comparisons. Theory and Methods. Chapman and Hall/CRC, Boca Raton (1996)
15. Hull, D.A.: Using statistical testing in the evaluation of retrieval experiments. In: Proceedings of SIGIR, pp. 329–338 (1993)
16. Lehmann, E.L., Romano, J.P.: Generalizations of the Familywise Error Rate, pp. 719–735. Boston (2012)
17. Marchesin, S., Purpura, A., Silvello, G.: Focal elements of neural information retrieval models. An outlook through a reproducibility study. Inf. Process. Manage. **57**, 102–109 (2019)
18. Moffat, A., Scholer, F., Thomas, P.: Models and metrics: IR evaluation as a user process. In: Proceedings of ADCS, pp. 47–54 (2012)
19. Robertson, S.: On document populations and measures of IR effectiveness. In: Proceedings of the 1st International Conference on the Theory of Information Retrieval (ICTIR 2007), pp. 9–22. Foundation for Information Society (2007)
20. Robertson, S.E., Kanoulas, E.: On per-topic variance in IR evaluation. In: Proceedings of SIGIR, pp. 891–900 (2012)
21. Rutherford, A.: ANOVA and ANCOVA. A GLM Approach, 2nd edn. Wiley, New York (2011)
22. Sakai, T.: On Fuhr's guideline for IR evaluation. SIGIR Forum **54**(1), 14:1–14:8 (2020)
23. Savoy, J.: Statistical inference in retrieval effectiveness evaluation. Inf. Process. Manage. **33**(44), 495–512 (1997)
24. Tague-Sutcliffe, J.M., Blustein, J.: A statistical analysis of the TREC-3 data. In: Proceedings of TREC, pp. 385–398 (1994)
25. Tukey, J.W.: Comparing individual means in the analysis of variance. Biometrics **5**(2), 99–114 (1949)
26. Voorhees, E.M., Harman, D.K.: Overview of the Eigth Text REtrieval Conference (TREC-8). In: Proceedings of TREC, pp. 1–24 (1999)
27. Voorhees, E.M., Samarov, D., Soboroff, I.: Using replicates in information retrieval evaluation. ACM Trans. Inf. Syst. **36**(2), 12:1–12:21 (2017)
28. Wand, M.P., Jones, M.C.: Kernel Smoothing. Chapman and Hall/CRC, Boca Raton (1995)

Reliability Prediction for Health-Related Content: A Replicability Study

Marcos Fernández-Pichel[1]([⊠]) [iD], David E. Losada[1] [iD], Juan C. Pichel[1] [iD],
and David Elsweiler[2] [iD]

[1] Centro Singular de Investigación en Tecnoloxías Intelixentes (CiTIUS),
Universidade de Santiago de Compostela, 15782 Santiago de Compostela, Spain
{marcosfernandez.pichel,david.losada,juancarlos.pichel}@usc.es
[2] University of Regensburg, Regensburg, Germany
david@elsweiler.co.uk

Abstract. Determining reliability of online data is a challenge that has recently received increasing attention. In particular, unreliable health-related content has become pervasive during the COVID-19 pandemic. Previous research [37] has approached this problem with standard classification technology using a set of features that have included linguistic and external variables, among others. In this work, we aim to replicate parts of the study conducted by Sondhi and his colleagues using our own code, and make it available for the research community (https://github.com/MarcosFP97/Health-Rel). The performance obtained in this study is as strong as the one reported by the original authors. Moreover, their conclusions are also confirmed by our replicability study. We report on the challenges involved in replication, including that it was impossible to replicate the computation of some features (since some tools or services originally used are now outdated or unavailable). Finally, we also report on a generalisation effort made to evaluate our predictive technology over new datasets [20,35].

Keywords: Reliability · Language · Health-related content

1 Introduction

The emergence of digital media has brought a change in the way people inform themselves [33]. In many ways, this change has been positive, providing accessibility of information and speed of access, but we must also be aware of the dangers involved. The results offered can be unreliable [2], inaccurate [9], or of poor quality [34]. This can have a greater or lesser impact depending on the context [37], but is especially sensitive when it comes to **health-related content**, as Pogacar et al. [31] showed in a recent study.

Medical hoaxes, miracle diets, or advice given by unqualified people abound in this type of media [36] and can be highly dangerous if taken as true and

D. Hiemstra et al. (Eds.): ECIR 2021, LNCS 12657, pp. 47–61, 2021.
https://doi.org/10.1007/978-3-030-72240-1_4

applied without the supervision of a medical professional. This has become particularly evident in the context of the pandemic we are facing, with substantial information about **COVID-19** being either dubious or of poor quality [19,30].

Often, **language** is a powerful indicator of the veracity of the contents [24]. Hidden patterns can be discovered not only by analysing the latent topics discussed in a certain text but also by studying the use of certain words [28]. An example is the use of **technical terms** or formalisms, which is usually associated with documents of higher quality and, in many cases, of greater reliability.

In this work, we report on our endeavours to replicate the predictive technology developed in Sondhi et al. [37], based on Natural Language Processing (NLP) and Machine Learning techniques. We chose this study since, to our knowledge, it was the first one to address the issue of automatically assessing the reliability of webpages in the medical domain. They reduced this problem to a binary-classification task. Moreover, they also provided a test dataset and a set of features to be taken into account (see Sect. 3).

If the results could be recreated, the conclusions extracted in the original study would be verified and reinforced. This replication effort is worthwhile to establish the utility of current technology, and its potential to be applied in filtering non-reliable content.

To this end, we examined and, where possible, re-implemented the features proposed by the original authors. In order for the results to be comparable, we applied the same experimental methodology and performance metrics proposed in the original paper. A final section is also provided in which our experiments are extended and applied to two new datasets [20,35] for the sake of achieving generalisation.

2 Related Work

Several studies address the concept of the credibility of a webpage. Different teams have broadly analysed how online content credibility is assessed [10,26,40], and they have concluded that subjective ratings are very likely to rely on the user's background [26], e.g. their trust in technology, or on their reading skills [14].

Other researches focused on determining how the search engine result page (SERP) listings are used to determine credibility through user studies [22]. More specifically, several studies have been conducted related to assessing the credibility of health-related content on the web. For instance, Matthews et al. [25] analysed a corpus about alternative cancer treatments and found that almost 90% contained false claims. Liao and Fu [23] analysed age differences in credibility judgements and argued that older adults care less about the content of the site in comparison with younger ones.

Other teams focused on the association between different features and reliability. For example, Griffiths et al. [12] showed that algorithms like PageRank were unable to determine reliability on their own.

As can be seen, there are several concepts intimately related such as *reliabilty* [37], *trustworthiness* [20], *credibility* [35], or *veracity* [39]. Our reference study

Table 1. Class distribution in Sondhi's dataset.

	Sondhi et al.
# Reliable	180
% Reliable	50%
# Unreliable	180
% Unreliable	50%

will be Sondhi et al.'s [37] (which we will refer to from now on as the original paper), so we will use the same notion of reliability as them. For determining reliability, they defined their guidelines using the eight HONcode Principles[1]. For the generalisation experiments, we will consider the rest of the concepts (credibility, trustworthiness, etc.) as proxies of reliability (see Sect. 6).

3   Dataset

The original authors manually created a **fully balanced** dataset with reliable and unreliable webpages (see Table 1) that we directly used in our replicability task. This eases the classification task, but it is not very realistic since in real-world problems it is rare to find the same ratio among classes.

In the original paper, the authors randomly selected the positive pages from those websites accredited by HON[2] according to their principles. On the other hand, as HON does not report non-accredited sites, they searched the Web with a deliberate strategy to find poor quality pages. Using hand-crafted queries, such as *disease name + "miracle cure"*. To ensure that topical overlap between negative and positive instances (i.e. to avoid topic-bias classification), they conducted a topic analysis over the reliable corpus and extracted keywords related to diseases that occur in the set of reliable pages. For each keyword, they manually produced queries which involved terms like *treatment* or *miracle*. Finally, the authors checked and selected 180 unreliable pages from the search results. As the original download link for the dataset was no longer valid, the dataset was sourced via personal communication with the authors.

The main goal of the original paper was to build a **document-level classifier** using a standard supervised learning approach. We followed their experimental setup, in which the original authors argued that reliability can be represented as a binary value as the first approach to this problem.

3.1   Features

A variety of **features** were proposed based on style, content and external information such as links. As will be seen, we were not able to apply all of these in

---

[1] https://www.hon.ch/cgi-bin/HONcode/principles.pl?English.

[2] https://www.hon.ch/en/.

our experiments, since some tools or libraries were outdated, and other elements were not described in a sufficiently detailed way.

In the original paper, webpages were represented using several features, namely:

– **Link-based features:** the number and type of links are usually a good indicator of the type of website we are dealing with [4,5]. For example, as Sondhi and his colleagues exposed, a more reliable site tends to have more internal links, while a less reliable site tends to have more external links and advertisements [41]. On the other hand, the presence or absence of privacy policy information or contact links for the page author can be indicators of reliability. This is because the presence of these types of elements gives a sense of confidence to the user who consults the resource [11,21].
Based on these criteria five features were defined to be taken into account: normalised value of internal links, normalised value of external links, normalised value of total links, the presence or not of contact link (boolean), and the presence or not of privacy link (boolean). For the latter two, the original paper did not explain how they were computed. Therefore, we manually defined two lists of privacy[3] and contact[4] expressions, such as *Privacy Policy* or *Contact Us*, after performing a first exploratory analysis over the documents.
For normalisation, the original authors analysed a random sample of documents and they experimentally chose a large normalisation denominator (the link count was divided by Z_1, which was set to 200).
In our experiments, the links were extracted from the text using the Beautiful Soup[5] Python package.

– **Commercial features:** the presence of commercial interest and advertisings often indicates a low reputation [4,41]. Therefore, two characteristics were defined to be taken into account: the normalised value of commercial links and the normalised frequency of commercial words on the website.
For the latter, an initial list of indicative words of commercial interest was proposed in the article. We manually extend this list[6]. Since the original article was not explicit about word preprocessing, we followed a naive approach in which a word must match exactly with some of the words in the list to be taken into account in the final metric. This strategy can be improved in future versions by applying lemmatisation techniques, for example.
Regarding normalisation, the normalised value of commercial links was obtained dividing by the same Z_1 used above. The second feature consisted of dividing the number of commercial words found by the document length.

– **PageRank Features:** the authors of the original paper used this feature as an indicator of the relative importance of a website [3]. However, this service has been removed by Google, and all Python packages that used their

---

[3] https://github.com/MarcosFP97/Health-Rel/blob/master/lexicon/privacy.txt.
[4] https://github.com/MarcosFP97/Health-Rel/blob/master/lexicon/contact.txt.
[5] https://www.crummy.com/software/BeautifulSoup/bs4/doc/.
[6] https://github.com/MarcosFP97/Health-Rel/blob/master/lexicon/comm_list.txt.

endpoint cannot be applied. It would be still possible to manually compute PageRank based on the web graph. However, the current web graph does not reflect the situation of these pages when the collection was created (some pages are no longer accessible). Furthermore, previous work has shown that such features capture the popularity of a website, but fail to measure reliability [32].

- **Presentation features:** reliable content is usually presented carefully and clearly [11]. To evaluate this, the original paper employed *elinks*[7], a tool to extract the text of the webpage. Then, they defined two features based on the number of blank lines. However, in the final comparison, they did not include this feature set, so we did not take it into account in our replicability experiments.

- **Word-based features:** textual content and style are often good indicators of the reliability or reputation of a website [24,28]. Therefore, each word in a document was considered as a different dimension, taking its normalised frequency score. Since the original authors did not declare the use of any preprocessing stage, we applied no stemming or lemmatisation.

  We additionally considered two alternative pre-processing strategies, with and without *stopword* removal. To achieve this, the NLTK[8] English *stoplist* was manually extended[9] after a preliminary exploration of the documents.

  Finally, for each word we divided the number of occurrences of the word by the document length.

In addition to testing the feature sets in isolation, Sondhi and his colleagues also considered a final combination that merged **all features together**. In our case, we tested two variants of "all features" (one with word features extracted with stopword removal and another one with word features extracted with no stopword removal).

4 Experimental Setup

When carrying out the experimentation, a **vector support machine** was used as learning method. The original paper used a C++ implementation but, for compatibility reasons, we employed the SVMlight[10] Python wrapper. We are therefore facing a two-class classification problem.

To evaluate the results, we applied **5-fold cross validation**, as in the original study. When generating the predictions, there could be **two types of errors**: classifying a reliable page as non-reliable (FP) and classifying a non-reliable page as reliable (FN). The latter being the one we wish to avoid most. To make results comparable, the performance metric used is the same as in the original paper:

---

[7] http://elinks.or.cz.

[8] https://www.nltk.org/nltk_data.

[9] https://github.com/MarcosFP97/Health-Rel/blob/master/lexicon/stopwords.txt.

[10] https://bitbucket.org/wcauchois/pysvmlight.

$$Weighted\ Accuracy(\lambda) = \frac{(\lambda \times TP) + TN}{\lambda \times (TP + FN) + TN + FP} \tag{1}$$

Three variants were considered, corresponding to $\lambda \in \{1, 2, 3\}$. Moreover, following the original paper strategy, the SVM classifier was trained with a cost-factor set to the value of λ (the weighted accuracy $\lambda = 1$ was obtained with a SVM whose cost-factor was set to 1, the weighted accuracy $\lambda = 2$ was obtained with a SVM whose cost-factor was set to 2, and so forth). Such an approach tunes the classifier to the measure that would later evaluate its effectiveness.

We note that the experiments were performed on an Ubuntu 19.04 machine, with 32 GB of RAM, 240 GB of storage and an Intel(R) Core(TM) i7-9750H CPU @ 2.60 GHz. The Python version used was 3.7.3 in an Anaconda 4.8.0 environment. However, for the CLEF eHealth dataset experiments, detailed in Sect. 6.2.2, it was necessary to use a server due to the storage requirements. More specifically, we used a CentOS 7.6.1810 machine, with 377 GB of RAM, 15T of storage and Intel(R) Xeon(R) CPU E5-2630 v4 processor. The Python and Anaconda versions used were the same as in the local experiments.

5   Results

Sondhi et al.'s original results are shown in Table 2. In our experiments, we considered two variants for word-based representation: with and without *stopword* removal. Moreover, commercial features were not tested in isolation, but combined with link-based features. This is reasonable since they are intimately related to external and advertising links.

Our results (see Table 3) differ from the original ones, but the same conclusions can be drawn: word-based features and the merging all features achieve the best performance. Our comparison of the two word-based variants (with and without *stopwords*) suggests that keeping *stopwords* is the safest approach to estimate the reliability of a webpage.

We note that our best performance is higher than that obtained in the original work. More specifically, in our case, we observed a high increase in the performance obtained by merging all features together. This contrasts with the

Table 2. Sondhi et al. original paper results.

	Weighted accuracy (%)		
Features	$\lambda = 1$	$\lambda = 2$	$\lambda = 3$
Links	60.8	71.1	79.6
Links + Commercial	67.8	75.9	79.6
Words	**80.6**	**83.9**	85.0
All	80.0	83.2	**86.8**

Table 3. Our results for Sondhi et al. dataset.

	Weighted accuracy (%)		
Features	$\lambda = 1$	$\lambda = 2$	$\lambda = 3$
Links	70.5	80.0	73.5
Links + Commercial	69.7	79.4	74.3
Words (removing stopwords)	80.8	80.2	80.3
Words (keeping stopwords)	82.8	85.6	88.5
All (removing stopwords)	**97.5**	**98.3**	**98.6**
All (keeping stopwords)	96.1	96.3	96.5

original study, where the combination of features did not add value. This is perhaps the most surprising outcome of the replicability experiments, and the only plausible explanation we can derive is that this results from the setup differences between our experiments and the originals, as described in the previous sections.

6   Generalisation

To build on Sondhi et al.'s work and to determine the generalisability of their findings, we apply new **standardisation** techniques to the Sondhi et al. dataset and also test the methods with two **further datasets**.

6.1   Standardisation

The original paper authors did not report on how the **standardisation** of the features (to get 0 mean and 1 standard deviation) - commonly applied in machine learning [16] - could affect the algorithm performance. As such, we tested and report the results here (see Table 4).

As can be seen, the performance of all feature sets increases in comparison with results reported in Table 3. Of particular note, the models with word-based representation are most improved. By carrying out this procedure, in addition to the Z_1 normalisation per document previously described, we are favouring features or words that have a low average, that is, less-common or technical words (see Fig. 1). This evens out the differences between terms, and what really guides the classifier, is whether a feature of them deviates from its average in a particular document. For example, a word that is broadly used. This also explains why the best feature combination is word-based with *stopwords* being used.

6.2   New Test Datasets

The Web Search dataset by Schwarz et al. [35] and the CLEF eHealth consumer health search task 2018 [20] were used to further evaluate this classification technology. Both contain health-related content, but the first additionally addresses topics such as finance, politics, environment, and news about famous people.

Table 4. Our results for Sondhi et al. dataset (with standard scaler).

	Weighted accuracy (%)		
Features	$\lambda = 1$	$\lambda = 2$	$\lambda = 3$
Links	74.4	78.1	76.4
Links + Commercial	73.3	76.5	79.9
Words (removing stopwords)	97.2	**98.3**	98.5
Words (keeping stopwords)	**98.1**	**98.3**	**98.9**
All (removing stopwords)	97.2	**98.3**	98.5
All (keeping stopwords)	97.8	**98.3**	**98.9**

$$
\begin{array}{c}
\begin{array}{ccc} the & \cdots & hydroxychloroquine \end{array} \\
\begin{array}{c} D1 \\ D2 \\ \vdots \\ Dm \end{array}
\begin{pmatrix}
0,6 & \cdots & 0,1 \\
0,7 & \cdots & 0,2 \\
\vdots & \ddots & \vdots \\
0,8 & \cdots & 0,3
\end{pmatrix}
\end{array}
\xrightarrow{\frac{x-\mu}{\sigma}}
\begin{array}{c}
\begin{array}{ccc} the & \cdots & hydroxychloroquine \end{array} \\
\begin{array}{c} D1 \\ D2 \\ \vdots \\ Dm \end{array}
\begin{pmatrix}
0,07 & \cdots & 0,1 \\
0,07 & \cdots & 0 \\
\vdots & \ddots & \vdots \\
0,13 & \cdots & 0,1
\end{pmatrix}
\end{array}
$$

Fig. 1. Document-term matrix standardisation.

Schwarz et al. focused on credibility assessment to help people searching for information online. The CLEF eHealth task addresses a similar problem, but it is tighter to health-related online data. It must be noticed that these documents were not labelled in terms of reliability, but the notions of credibility and trustworthiness were used instead. However, we considered these concepts as proxies of reliability and attempted to see how generalisable the previous conclusions were against other datasets.

Schwarz et al. chose 1000 webpages related to multiple topics to be labelled in terms of credibility. They proposed a five-point Likert scale, from 1 to 5, to generate the ground-truth, and one of the authors of the paper rated the whole collection.

On the other hand, the CLEF eHealth consumer health search task dataset was created from webpages recovered from CommonCrawl[11]. The organisers of the task defined an initial list of potentially interesting sites and then, they submitted queries against a search engine to retrieve the final URLs. The initial list was extended by manually adding some reliable sites and other known to be unreliable. Finally, the corpus was divided into folders by domain.

In this CLEF task, it was decided to implement the RBP-based method proposed by Moffat et al. [27] to generate the assessment pool, instead of using a fixed-depth pooling strategy. After the pool was formed, human assessors from Amazon Mechanical Turk, with certain profiles, were selected. In the case of trustworthiness judgements, an eleven point scale, from 0 to 10, was used.

---

[11] http://commoncrawl.org.

It was necessary to relabel both datasets into a binary-class scale to fit with our 2-class technology. We removed the middle values (3 for Schwarz et al. and from 4 to 6 for CLEF) and mapped the extreme values to reliable and unreliable, respectively.

The main statistics of these datasets after performing this relabelling process are shown in Table 5. In both cases, we face an **imbalanced data** problem. This is particularly acute in the case of the Schwarz et al. data.

Table 5. Class distribution in the different datasets.

	Schwarz et al.	CLEF eHEALTH
# Reliable	75	9,879
% Reliable	93.75%	73.25%
# Unreliable	5	3,607
% Unreliable	6.25%	26.75%

Imbalanced learning is a common problem and there are multiple techniques to deal with the issue. In this case, we considered and compared two different approaches: introducing a **cost-factor** that applies a higher penalty to errors in the minority class and **resampling techniques** that try to balance the data by adding artificial instances or by removing some majority examples [6,15,17,18]. In this paper, only cost-factor techniques are reported since our preliminary experiments suggested that cost-factor methods outperform resampling methods in both datasets.

On the other hand, in imbalanced learning, it is common to use metrics, such as the **F1 measure**. Here, we report the micro-averaged F1, biased by the frequency of each class, and the value of F1 for each class. At the time of selecting the best feature combination for each collection, we gave priority to the minority class or unreliable F1.

Finally, it is worth noting that for both datasets the standardisation method described in Sect. 6.1 was applied.

6.2.1 Schwarz et al. Results

Due to the small dataset size, a stratified **2-fold cross validation** was used (instead of 5-folds). The obtained results are shown in Table 6. We note that in case of a tie, we always select the simplest feature set.

With **cost factor set to 1**, link-based features perform the best, but the classifier does not detect a single unreliable document. With this learning strategy, no combination is capable of correctly cataloguing examples from the minority class. This is not surprising given the low percentage of negative examples (6.25%).

Table 6. Our results for Schwarz et al. dataset.

Features	SVM cost factor	F1	F1 (reliable class)	F1 (non reliable class)	Weighted accuracy (%)		
					$\lambda = 1$	$\lambda = 2$	$\lambda = 3$
Links	1	**0.94**	**0.97**	0	**93.75**	–	–
	2	0.94	0.97	0	–	88.26	–
	3	0.94	0.97	0	–	–	83.4
Links + Commercial	1	**0.94**	**0.97**	0	**93.75**	–	–
	2	0.94	0.97	0	–	88.26	–
	3	0.94	0.97	0	–	–	83.4
Words (removing stopwords)	1	0.93	0.96	0	92.5	–	–
	2	0.91	0.95	0.25	–	87.01	–
	3	**0.91**	**0.95**	**0.33**	–	–	**85.42**
Words (keeping stopwords)	1	0.91	0.95	0	91.25	–	–
	2	0.91	0.95	0	–	85.88	–
	3	0.91	0.95	0.2	–	–	84.54
All (removing stopwords)	1	**0.94**	**0.97**	0	**93.75**	–	–
	2	0.91	0.95	0	–	85.88	–
	3	0.91	0.95	0	–	–	81.13
All (keeping stopwords)	1	0.93	0.96	0	92.5	–	–
	2	**0.91**	**0.95**	**0.25**	–	**87.02**	–
	3	**0.91**	**0.95**	**0.33**	–	–	**85.42**

With **cost factor 2**, the results were still even, but some feature combinations were able to detect the minority class. This was the case of the word-based model and for the model combining all features- keeping *stopwords*. The latter was selected as the best combination, due to a slight difference in the weighted accuracy performance.

With **cost factor 3**, the detection of the minority class is slightly improved. As for the combination of features, both the word-based and the combination of all features (maintaining the *stopwords*) offer the same performance, but the former was selected because it generates a simpler model.

6.2.2   CLEF eHealth Results

This was the largest dataset in our experiments, and it also presents an imbalance problem between classes. In contrast with Schwarz et al., a stratified **5-fold cross validation** could be applied given the larger number of data points. The obtained results are shown in Table 7.

For all cost factor values, the word-based model that maintains the *stopwords* was the one that offered the best results, with also reasonable minority or non-reliable class detection.

6.3 Generalisation Conclusions

Each of the studied datasets was different both in terms of content and task. Moreover, the original collection was fully balanced, while the others were clearly imbalanced. Nevertheless, some interesting conclusions can be drawn from the generalisation experiments.

Table 7. Our results for CLEF eHealth dataset.

Features	SVM cost factor	F1	F1 (reliable class)	F1 (non reliable class)	Weighted accuracy (%)		
					$\lambda = 1$	$\lambda = 2$	$\lambda = 3$
Links	1	0.73	0.85	0	73.15	–	–
	2	0.73	0.85	0	–	57.66	–
	3	0.46	0.39	0.28	–	–	50.39
Links + Commercial	1	0.73	0.85	0	73.15	–	–
	2	0.73	0.84	0	–	57.63	–
	3	0.3	0.12	0.41	–	–	51.74
Words (removing stopwords)	1	0.74	0.85	0.14	73.86	–	–
	2	0.68	0.79	0.38	–	61.57	–
	3	0.55	0.63	0.44	–	–	58.65
Words (keeping stopwords)	1	**0.75**	**0.85**	**0.24**	**74.63**	–	–
	2	**0.69**	**0.79**	**0.41**	–	**62.93**	–
	3	**0.59**	**0.68**	**0.45**	–	–	**59.81**
All (removing stopwords)	1	0.74	0.85	0.15	73.88	–	–
	2	0.68	0.79	0.38	–	61.58	–
	3	0.55	0.62	0.44	–	–	58.39
All (keeping stopwords)	1	0.75	0.85	0.24	74.53	–	–
	2	0.7	0.79	0.4	–	62.89	–
	3	0.59	0.67	0.45	–	–	59.72

The obtained results **reinforce** the main insights of the original study. In all of the experiments the best strategies are the bag-of-words approach or the one that merges all features set together. The evidence moreover suggests that keeping stopwords leads to enhanced performance.

7 Future Work

This work opens up a line of research that allows us to continue to study in-depth how unreliable information is transmitted in the Web and how it is perceived by users. A natural next step would be the application of our predictive technology to the case of **social media** [1,13,38], extracting known true and false claims from the labelled documents and seeing their impact on this media. This kind of news spreads very quickly in this media, which can help us to identify them or put them under suspicion.

We also intend to further analyse the effect of combining different features on performance and, additionally, plan to train new models using **BERT** [7]. This language modelling approach, which extracts a contextual representation of words, has been proven to be successful in the field of Natural Language Processing (NLP).

We will also perform transfer learning experiments among the different datasets available [8,29]. This can be helpful to understand whether or not training with one collection and testing with another reinforces the conclusions obtained.

8   Conclusions

In this work, a replicability study of reliability technology was presented. The main objective was to re-run the experiments and try to confirm the conclusions extracted from the original study. Our results reinforce the fact that word-based models or the ones that combine all available features are the most promising approaches to distinguish reliable from unreliable sites.

We have also tested this predictive technology against two further and highly different datasets and the conclusions remain the same. This gives us the confidence to state that the research presented in the original paper establishes a good reference for reliability detection in online data.

Finally, as a new test of its generalisation, this algorithm has been used by our team in the TREC 2020 Health Misinformation Track[12] to tackle misinformation about COVID-19 and its treatments. In order to replicate the experiments presented in this work, the code is available for the research community at Github[13].

Acknowledgements. This work was funded by FEDER/Ministerio de Ciencia, Innovación y Universidades – Agencia Estatal de Investigación/Project (RTI2018-093336-B-C21). This work has received financial support from the Consellería de Educación, Universidade e Formación Profesional (accreditation 2019–2022 ED431G-2019/04, ED431C 2018/29, ED431C 2018/19) and the European Regional Development Fund (ERDF), which acknowledges the CiTIUS-Research Center in Intelligent Technologies of the University of Santiago de Compostela as a Research Center of the Galician University System.

References

1. Abbasi, M.-A., Liu, H.: Measuring user credibility in social media. In: Greenberg, A.M., Kennedy, W.G., Bos, N.D. (eds.) SBP 2013. LNCS, vol. 7812, pp. 441–448. Springer, Heidelberg (2013). https://doi.org/10.1007/978-3-642-37210-0_48

---

[12] https://trec-health-misinfo.github.io.
[13] https://github.com/MarcosFP97/Health-Rel.

2. Abualsaud, M., Smucker, M.D.: Exposure and order effects of misinformation on health search decisions. In: Proceedings of the 42nd International ACM SIGIR Conference on Research and Development in Information Retrieval, Rome (2019)
3. Andersen, R., et al.: Robust pagerank and locally computable spam detection features. In: Proceedings of the 4th International Workshop on Adversarial Information Retrieval on the Web, pp. 69–76 (2008)
4. Becchetti, L., Castillo, C., Donato, D., Baeza-Yates, R., Leonardi, S.: Link analysis for web spam detection. ACM Trans. Web (TWEB) **2**(1), 1–42 (2008)
5. Borodin, A., Roberts, G.O., Rosenthal, J.S., Tsaparas, P.: Link analysis ranking: algorithms, theory, and experiments. ACM Trans. Internet Technol. (TOIT) **5**(1), 231–297 (2005)
6. Chawla, N.V., Bowyer, K.W., Hall, L.O., Kegelmeyer, W.P.: Smote: synthetic minority over-sampling technique. J. Artif. Intell. Res. **16**, 321–357 (2002)
7. Devlin, J., Chang, M.W., Lee, K., Toutanova, K.: Bert: pre-training of deep bidirectional transformers for language understanding. arXiv preprint arXiv:1810.04805 (2018)
8. Do, C.B., Ng, A.Y.: Transfer learning for text classification. Adv. Neural Inf. Process. Syst. **18**, 299–306 (2005)
9. Eysenbach, G.: Infodemiology: the epidemiology of (mis)information. Am. J. Med. **113**(9), 763–765 (2002)
10. Fogg, B.J.: Prominence-interpretation theory: explaining how people assess credibility online. In: CHI 2003 Extended Abstracts on Human Factors in Computing Systems, pp. 722–723 (2003)
11. Ginsca, A.L., Popescu, A., Lupu, M.: Credibility in information retrieval. Found. Trends Inf. Retr. **9**(5), 355–475 (2015). https://doi.org/10.1561/1500000046
12. Griffiths, K.M., Tang, T.T., Hawking, D., Christensen, H.: Automated assessment of the quality of depression websites. J. Med. Internet Res. **7**(5), e59 (2005)
13. Gupta, A., Kumaraguru, P., Castillo, C., Meier, P.: TweetCred: real-time credibility assessment of content on Twitter. In: Aiello, L.M., McFarland, D. (eds.) SocInfo 2014. LNCS, vol. 8851, pp. 228–243. Springer, Cham (2014). https://doi.org/10.1007/978-3-319-13734-6_16
14. Hahnel, C., Goldhammer, F., Kröhne, U., Naumann, J.: The role of reading skills in the evaluation of online information gathered from search engine environments. Comput. Hum. Behav. **78**, 223–234 (2018)
15. Haixiang, G., Yijing, L., Shang, J., Mingyun, G., Yuanyue, H., Bing, G.: Learning from class-imbalanced data: review of methods and applications. Expert Syst. Appl. **73**, 220–239 (2017)
16. Hastie, T., Tibshirani, R., Friedman, J.: The Elements of Statistical Learning. SSS. Springer, New York (2009). https://doi.org/10.1007/978-0-387-84858-7
17. He, H., Garcia, E.A.: Learning from imbalanced data. IEEE Trans. Knowl. Data Eng. **21**(9), 1263–1284 (2009)
18. Hoens, T.R., Chawla, N.V.: Imbalanced datasets: from sampling to classifiers. Imbalanced Learning: Foundations, Algorithms, and Applications, pp. 43–59 (2013)
19. Islam, M.S., et al.: Covid-19-related infodemic and its impact on public health: a global social media analysis. Am. J. Trop. Med. Hyg. **103**(4), 1621–1629 (2020)
20. Jimmy, J., Zuccon, G., Palotti, J., Goeuriot, L., Kelly, L.: Overview of the CLEF 2018 consumer health search task. In: International Conference of the Cross-Language Evaluation Forum for European Languages (2018)

21. Kakol, M., Nielek, R., Wierzbicki, A.: Understanding and predicting web content credibility using the content credibility corpus. Inf. Process. Manag. **53**(5), 1043–1061 (2017)
22. Kattenbeck, M., Elsweiler, D.: Understanding credibility judgements for web search snippets. Aslib J. Inf. Manag. **71**, 368–391 (2019)
23. Liao, Q.V., Fu, W.T.: Age differences in credibility judgments of online health information. ACM Trans. Comput.-Hum. Interact. (TOCHI) **21**(1), 1–23 (2014)
24. Matsumoto, D., Hwang, H.C., Sandoval, V.A.: Cross-language applicability of linguistic features associated with veracity and deception. J. Police Crim. Psychol. **30**(4), 229–241 (2015)
25. Matthews, S.C., Camacho, A., Mills, P.J., Dimsdale, J.E.: The Internet for medical information about cancer: help or hindrance? Psychosomatics **44**(2), 100–103 (2003)
26. McKnight, D.H., Kacmar, C.J.: Factors and effects of information credibility. In: Proceedings of the Ninth International Conference on Electronic Commerce, pp. 423–432 (2007)
27. Moffat, A., Zobel, J.: Rank-biased precision for measurement of retrieval effectiveness. ACM Trans. Inf. Syst. (TOIS) **27**(1), 1–27 (2008)
28. Mukherjee, S., Weikum, G.: Leveraging joint interactions for credibility analysis in news communities. In: Proceedings of the 24th ACM International on Conference on Information and Knowledge Management, pp. 353–362 (2015)
29. Pan, S.J., Yang, Q.: A survey on transfer learning. IEEE Trans. Knowl. Data Eng. **22**(10), 1345–1359 (2009)
30. Pennycook, G., McPhetres, J., Zhang, Y., Lu, J.G., Rand, D.G.: Fighting Covid-19 misinformation on social media: experimental evidence for a scalable accuracy-nudge intervention. Psychol. Sci. **31**(7), 770–780 (2020)
31. Pogacar, F.A., Ghenai, A., Smucker, M.D., Clarke, C.L.: The positive and negative influence of search results on people's decisions about the efficacy of medical treatments. In: Proceedings of the ACM SIGIR International Conference on Theory of Information Retrieval, pp. 209–216 (2017)
32. Popat, K., Mukherjee, S., Strötgen, J., Weikum, G.: Credibility assessment of textual claims on the web. In: Proceedings of the 25th ACM International on Conference on Information and Knowledge Management, pp. 2173–2178 (2016)
33. Reuters Institute, University of Oxford: Reuters Digital News Report 2020 (2020). https://www.digitalnewsreport.org/survey/2020. Accessed 16 Nov 2020
34. Rieh, S.Y.: Judgment of information quality and cognitive authority in the web. J. Am. Soc. Inf. Sci. Technol. **53**(2), 145–161 (2002)
35. Schwarz, J., Morris, M.: Augmenting web pages and search results to support credibility assessment. In: Proceedings of the SIGCHI Conference on Human Factors in Computing Systems, pp. 1245–1254 (2011)
36. Sharma, K., Qian, F., Jiang, H., Ruchansky, N., Zhang, M., Liu, Y.: Combating fake news: a survey on identification and mitigation techniques. ACM Trans. Intell. Syst. Technol. (TIST) **10**(3), 1–42 (2019)
37. Sondhi, P., Vydiswaran, V.G.V., Zhai, C.X.: Reliability prediction of webpages in the medical domain. In: Baeza-Yates, R., et al. (eds.) ECIR 2012. LNCS, vol. 7224, pp. 219–231. Springer, Heidelberg (2012). https://doi.org/10.1007/978-3-642-28997-2_19
38. Viviani, M., Pasi, G.: Credibility in social media: opinions, news, and health information-a survey. Wiley Interdiscip. Rev.: Data Min. Knowl. Discov. **7**(5), e1209 (2017)

39. Vydiswaran, V.V., Zhai, C., Roth, D.: Content-driven trust propagation framework. In: Proceedings of the 17th ACM SIGKDD International Conference on Knowledge Discovery and Data Mining, pp. 974–982 (2011)
40. Yamamoto, Y., Tanaka, K.: Enhancing credibility judgment of web search results. In: Proceedings of the SIGCHI Conference on Human Factors in Computing Systems, pp. 1235–1244 (2011)
41. Zha, W., Wu, H.D.: The impact of online disruptive ads on users' comprehension, evaluation of site credibility, and sentiment of intrusiveness. Am. Commun. J. **16**(2), 15–28 (2014)

An Empirical Comparison of Web Page Segmentation Algorithms

Johannes Kiesel[1]([✉])[iD], Lars Meyer[1][iD], Florian Kneist[1][iD], Benno Stein[1][iD], and Martin Potthast[2][iD]

[1] Bauhaus-Universität Weimar, Weimar, Germany
{johannes.kiesel,lars.meyer,florian.kneist,
benno.stein}@uni-weimar.de
[2] Leipzig University, Leipzig, Germany
martin.potthast@uni-leipzig.de

Abstract. Over the past two decades, several algorithms have been developed to segment a web page into semantically coherent units, a task with several applications in web content analysis. However, these algorithms have hardly been compared empirically and it thus remains unclear which of them—or rather, which of their underlying paradigms—performs best. To contribute to closing this gap, we report on the reproduction and comparative evaluation of five segmentation algorithms on a large, standardized benchmark dataset for web page segmentation: Three of the algorithms have been specifically developed for web pages and have been selected to represent paradigmatically different approaches to the task, whereas the other two approaches originate from the segmentation of photos and print documents, respectively. For a fair comparison, we tuned each algorithm's parameters, if applicable, to the dataset. Altogether, the classic rule-based VIPS algorithm achieved the highest performance, closely followed by the purely visual approach of Cormier et al. For reproducibility, we provide our reimplementations of the algorithms along with detailed instructions.

1 Introduction

When visiting a web page, a key step for human comprehension is to identify its semantic units. Eye-tracking studies show that participants identify such units immediately upon perceiving a web page, then inspect them one at a time, often starting with navigation elements [16]. To create a comprehensible web page, it is thus important for its author to group its content into such comprehensible semantic units that are easy to identify by its visitors. Though qualified web designers do so in a professional manner, every web page author possesses an intuitive understanding of the basic principles of Gestalt that apply here, as these principles form an integral part of human perception [8]. Naturally, these semantic units, then called web page segments, also form the basis for various web content analysis tasks, like content extraction [2], template detection [13], and design mining [11]. Consequently, several approaches for web page segmentation have been developed over the past two decades [10].

The ongoing and rapid development of web technologies like Cascading Style Sheets (CSS) and JavaScript (JS) has considerably increased the possibilities of web design over the past years. The elements of a web page encoded in its HTML source

© Springer Nature Switzerland AG 2021
D. Hiemstra et al. (Eds.): ECIR 2021, LNCS 12657, pp. 62–74, 2021.
https://doi.org/10.1007/978-3-030-72240-1_5

code can be more or less arbitrarily rearranged in its visual appearance in the browser, so that no correspondence between the linear order of elements in the source code and its visual ordering can be presumed. Since the focus of web page authors are mostly the human visitors and much less so web content analysis algorithms, there is hardly any incentive to emphasize the semantic units in the web page's HTML code. Web page segmentation algorithms thus increasingly focus on the visual rendition of a to-be-segmented web page; a recent algorithm completely disregards the HTML code [7]. But even the classic VIPS algorithm [3], which was introduced in 2003, uses the positions of elements in the rendered web page as features for its segmentation.

This reliance of algorithms on rendering the web page has limited the reproducibility of web page segmentation experiments, but the paper at hand demonstrates how to overcome this problem through the use of web archiving technology. In essence, several algorithms use JavaScript to segment the web page as it is rendered in a browser. However, to reproduce this situation properly, the following elements have to be kept constant: (1) the web page's complete source code (HTML, CSS, JS, images, etc.); (2) the browser, since different browsers and even different versions thereof render the same page differently; and (3) the browser's environment variables, like the date or random numbers, which the web page might request from the browser. These are not trivial requirements to meet, but modern web archiving technology can provide for a stable reproduction of web pages as they were rendered in the past [9].

We develop and present a reproducible empirical comparison of five segmentation algorithms, as well as an ensemble of them. The algorithms have been selected to represent and evaluate a variety of approaches and paradigms: two are rule-based, one is based entirely on visual edges, one has been originally developed for print documents, and one is a state-of-the-art approach in image segmentation of photos. For evaluation, we employ our Webis-WebSeg-20 dataset, which contains both a manually created segmentation ground-truth, and a web archive of 8490 web pages [10]. Moreover, we report on and show the importance of parameter tuning for the different algorithms. Documentation and provenance data of these experiments are available online.[1]

Among others, the results show that the classic VIPS algorithm still performs best when tuned to the dataset, but also that purely visual approaches can reach a competitive performance. Moreover, in adjusting the evaluation to the requirements of different downstream tasks of web page segmentation, we find that purely visual approaches are already the new state-of-the-art for downstream tasks that rely on pixel-based segments, like design mining. One of these purely visual approaches, the MMDetection algorithm, is able to reach this high performance despite being trained for a very different kind of input document than web pages: photos. The ensemble of four of the algorithms under consideration, however, does not outperform its base algorithms. Upon closer inspection, most of the ground-truth segments are identified by at least one of the algorithms.

After a brief literature review of web page segmentation experiments in Sect. 2, we detail our evaluation setup in Sect. 3 and the employed algorithms—including their parameter tuning—in Sect. 4. Section 5 discusses the empirical comparison of the algorithms.

---

[1] Code + documentation: https://github.com/webis-de/ecir21-an-empirical-comparison-of-web-page-segmentation-algorithms
Provenance data: https://doi.org/10.5281/zenodo.4146889.

2 Related Work

A number of publications that propose a new web page segmentation algorithm compare it with the classic VIPS algorithm [3] (e.g., [7, 14, 17]), which can thus be considered closest to a standard baseline. In the original publication, VIPS has been evaluated with a three-scale human assessment on only 140 web pages: According to the assessors, 61% of web pages were segmented "perfectly," whereas just 3% "failed." Such an assessment is unfortunately hardly reproducible. Zeleny et al. [17] perform an empirical comparison of their algorithms with VIPS on 800 semi-automatically annotated web pages. Their performance measure, F, is closely related to $F_{B^3}^*$ (nodes), employed in this paper (Sect. 5), and indeed, a similar performance is measured for VIPS: 0.71 by Zeleny et al., and 0.70 here. For their visual-edge-based algorithm, Cormier et al. [7] compare its segmentations with that of VIPS on 47 web pages using an adapted Earth Mover's Distance as performance measure. They find, that, though there is some agreement, their algorithm "tends to produce results significantly different from VIPS." Our evaluation in Sect. 5 also shows such a difference. Manabe and Tajima [14] compare the performance of their HEPS algorithm with that of VIPS for the task of identifying web page blocks—i.e., textual segments with headings. In their comparison on 1219 web pages, they find that HEPS clearly outperforms VIPS for exactly identifying such blocks: block precision is 0.59 (HEPS) vs. 0.22 (VIPS), and block recall is 0.56 vs. 0.07. This is in contrast to our results, which indicate a superior performance of VIPS over HEPS, not only for a text-based evaluation. A possible explanation lies in their different approach to ground-truth creation, which is tailored towards the mentioned header-based blocks.

However, no large-scale comparison of web page segmentation algorithms exists so far. Kiesel et al. [10] attribute this situation to a lack of generic, standardized datasets, a lack of a common view on how to measure algorithm performance, and a lack of reproducible evaluation procedures. Reviewing the related work beyond the aforementioned papers, evaluation datasets and performance measures have usually been created in an ad-hoc manner, and with respect to just one of the various downstream tasks of web page segmentation, which has led to several very focused datasets and many incompatible performance measures. The problem of reproducibility has, to the best of our knowledge, scarcely been tackled in the relevant literature so far: Only Zeleny et al. [17] attempt to reduce the influence of different browsers by using the same rendering engine for all algorithms. Recently, web archiving technology has been considered for web page segmentation, addressing its reproducibility problem for the first time [9]. This technology has been used to create the new Webis-WebSeg-20 dataset [10], which is nearly an order of magnitude larger than previous ones, and which has been annotated without specific downstream tasks involving web page segmentation in mind, based on human perception only. Moreover, the use of this dataset as a new evaluation framework is proposed, capturing the existing views on how to measure algorithm performance within a unified evaluation measure that can be adapted to various downstream tasks. This paper builds on this framework, and uses it for a first empirical comparison of segmentation algorithms.

3   Experiment Setup

For the empirical comparison of web page segmentation algorithms, this paper employs the 8490 web pages of the Webis-WebSeg-20 dataset [10]. The web pages have been sampled from a variety of sites, 4824 in total [9]. The dataset contains for each web page a ground-truth segmentation, which is fused from the segmentations of five human annotators. Furthermore, the dataset contains a web archive file for each web page, which allows to re-render the web page as if viewed at the time of the archiving. For algorithms that need no complete re-rendering, the dataset also provides for each page the DOM HTML, a screenshot, and the list of DOM nodes mapped to their coordinates on the screenshot. The latter allows to convert between segment descriptions as screenshot coordinates and as sets of DOM nodes. As the ground-truth uses a flat segmentation for all web pages but some algorithms produce hierarchical segmentations, we flatten such hierarchical segmentations for the evaluation.

Our evaluation discusses the achieved P_{B^3}, R_{B^3}, and $F_{B^3}^*$ for each algorithm. The have been introduced by Kiesel et al. [10]. They are straightforward adaptations of the respective extended BCubed measures from clustering theory [1]. In a nutshell, P_{B^3} is based on the elements that are segmented together in both the ground-truth and algorithmically created segmentations (the "true positives" in the usual definition of precision) divided by the number of all elements segmented together in the algorithmically created segmentations (the "positives"). R_{B^3} has the same numerator, but is divided by the number of all elements segmented together in the ground-truth segmentation. As usual, F_{B^3} is the harmonic mean of both for one web page. We here report the values averaged over all web pages, and $F_{B^3}^*$ is then the harmonic mean of the averaged P_{B^3} and R_{B^3}. As discussed by Kiesel et al., P_{B^3} decreases if algorithmically created segments extend beyond ground-truth segments, whereas R_{B^3} decreases in the inverse case. Put another way, P_{B^3} ignores cases of over-segmentation—where the algorithmically created segmentation is more fine-grained than the ground-truth segmentation—, whereas R_{B^3} ignores cases of under-segmentation. A segmentation of one segment that contains the entire page would thus achieve an R_{B^3} of the maximum value of 1, whereas a segmentation that puts every element into an own segment would achieve a P_{B^3} of 1.

In order to provide results that are applicable for various downstream tasks of web page segmentation, we execute all experiments for each of the five types of atomic elements defined by Kiesel et al. Different downstream tasks of web page segmentation weigh certain errors differently. For example, although for most downstream tasks it does not matter how background space is segmented, it is important for tasks that consider the spacing between segments, like design mining. P_{B^3} and R_{B^3} can be adapted to a downstream task by calculating them specifically for the type of elements of the web page that is relevant for that task. To cover a wide variety of tasks, this paper uses the five types suggested by Kiesel et al.: all pixels (*pixels*), all pixels at visual edges as per an edge detection algorithm in both a coarse (*edges$_C$*) and fine settings (*edges$_F$*), all visible DOM nodes (*nodes*), and all textual characters (*chars*).

We provide all code for the evaluation in the repository of this paper, and all generated segmentations as a new data resource (cf. Sect. 1). In very rare cases (at most 0.2% per algorithm), some algorithms failed (cf. Sect. 4): in these cases we used the baseline segmentation—a single segment that covers the entire page—as fallback.

4   Algorithms and Parameter Tuning

This section describes the segmentation algorithms that are compared in our experiments, and reports on the results of a corresponding parameter tuning for the algorithms. Table 1 gives an overview of the algorithms in the experiments, which are chosen as representatives for different segmentation paradigms and tasks. For web page segmentation, we evaluate the classic DOM-based VIPS (cf. Sect. 4.1), the specifically heading-based HEPS (cf. Sect. 4.2), and the purely visual algorithm of Cormier et al. (cf. Sect. 4.3). Inspired by the impressive recent advances in image understanding, we also evaluate the performance of one state-of-the-art algorithm of this field for the task of web page segmentation: MMDetection (cf. Sect. 4.4). Furthermore, as the tasks of web page segmentation is conceptually similar to the task of print document segmentation, we also evaluate the performance of a state-of-the-art approach for that task, the neural network of Meier et al. (cf. Sect. 4.5). Moreover, we report results for a voting-based ensemble of the algorithms (cf. Sect. 4.6). To contextualize the results, we include a naive baseline for comparison (cf. Sect. 4.7). We found that the algorithms do fail for a few web pages, for example, due to a web page's own JavaScript code interfering with the JavaScript code of the segmentation algorithm. As described in Sect. 3, we use the segmentation of the baseline in this case as a fallback.

Table 1. Overview of the five compared segmentation algorithms with respect to the kind of input documents they were created for, the features they use, and the format of the output segmentation.

Name	Ref.	Document	Features	Output
VIPS	[3]	Web page	Tree, style, location	Rectangle tree
HEPS	[14]	Web page	Tree, style	Node set
Cormier et al.	[6]	Web page	Screenshot	Rectangle tree
MMDetection	[4]	Photo	Screenshot	Pixel masks
Meier et al.	[15]	Article page	Screenshot, text-mask	Mask

4.1   VIPS

The "VIsion-based Page Segmentation algorithm" [3] is the de-facto standard for web page segmentation. Starting from one segment that covers the entire page, VIPS creates a hierarchical tree of segments based on the DOM tree of a web page. The rectangular segments are split based on their so-called degree of coherence, which is computed through heuristic rules based on the tag names, background colors, and sizes of DOM nodes, as well as visual separators: segments are split if their so-called degree of coherence is less than the permitted degree of coherence (PDoC), which is the single parameter of the algorithm. Previous implementations of VIPS rely on web rendering frameworks that are no longer maintained and render modern pages incorrectly. We thus ported one implementation[2] to JavaScript so that every modern browser can run it.

---

[2] Our port of https://github.com/tpopela/vips_java is available in the code repository of this paper.

For the experiments, we then used the reproduction mode of the Webis-Web-Archiver to have a Chrome browser run VIPS on the web pages as they are re-rendered from the web archives. Though Cai et al. [3] described the degree of coherence to range from 0 to 1, the implementation we ported and thus ours alike use an integer range from 1 to 11, since the heuristic rules suggest the corresponding 11 thresholds. The VIPS algorithm failed for 14 web pages (0.2%) due to rendering errors or due to interference of the web page's and VIPS' JavaScript code.

In a 10-fold cross-validation, the optimal value for PDoC was consistently 6. Figure 1 shows the average number of segments and performance for all values from 1 to 11 over all web pages. As the top graph shows, the number of segments stays almost the same for PDoC from 1 to 6, but increases considerably beyond that. The graphs are very similar for all types of atomic elements, with the notable exception of P_{B^3}—and thus also $F^*_{B^3}$—for *pixels*, which is considerable worse. We discuss this observation in Sect. 5. Compared to the default value for PDoC of 8 for the original implementation, $F^*_{B^3}$ increases by up to 0.20, which highlights the importance of parameter tuning.

4.2 HEPS

The "HEading-based Page Segmentation algorithm" [14] uses heading detection to identify segments. The authors define a heading as both visually prominent and describing the topic of a segment. HEPS does not solely rely on the HTML heading tags, as the authors found that headings are frequently defined by other means, and that heading tags are frequently used for other purposes. Instead, HEPS identifies headings and their corresponding segments through heuristic rules based on their position in the DOM tree, tag name, font size, and weight. The algorithm first identifies candidate headings using text nodes and images, and after that their corresponding blocks. It then creates a hierarchical segmentation based on the identified blocks. We use the original JavaScript implementation by the authors of the algorithm[3] in the same manner as our reimplementation of VIPS. For consistency with the other algorithms in this comparison, we merge the extracted headings with their associated segments. The HEPS algorithm originally failed for 211 web pages (2.5%) due to rendering errors or due to interference of the web page's and HEPS' JavaScript code, but we were able to reduce this amount to just 5 web pages (0.06%) through slight changes in handling of arrays in the code.

4.3 Cormier et al.

Cormier et al. implement a purely visual algorithm to web page segmentation that uses edge detection to find semantically significant edges, used to synthesize a coherent segmentation [6]. The algorithm takes a screenshot of the web page as input, and therefore does not require to re-render the page. It first calculates for each pixel the probability of a "locally significant edge," which is based on how different the horizontal or vertical image gradients at the pixel are from those of the surrounding pixels. After that, the algorithm composes horizontal and vertical line segments from these edge pixels, up to a maximum length of t_l. Note that the larger t_l, the larger the "gap" that visual

---

[3] https://github.com/tmanabe/HEPS.

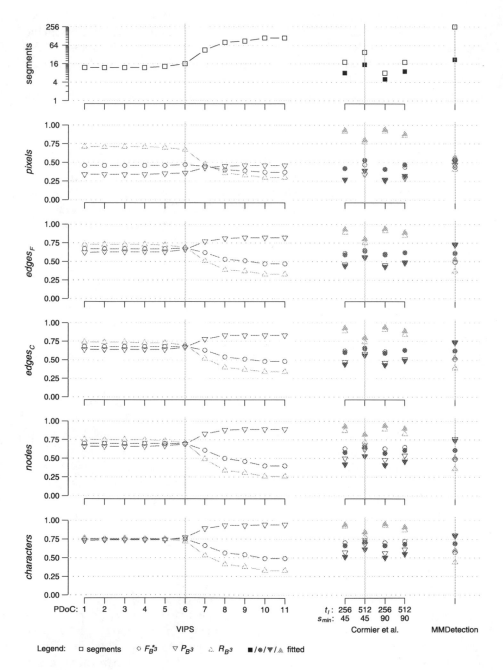

Fig. 1. Number of segments (top plot), $F_{B^3}^*$, P_{B^3}, and R_{B^3} for different parameters for the algorithms of VIPS, Cormier et al. and MMDetection. Filled symbols correspond to the values after fitting the segmentation to DOM nodes. The vertical lines show the overall best-performing parameter setting for each algorithm after fitting, as measured by $F_{B^3}^*$.

edges can have to still be considered one line segment. The algorithm then starts with the entire page as one segment, and recursively splits the segments into two by choosing the vertical or horizontal line that is the most "semantically significant," i.e., that has the most and clearest edge pixels. The algorithm stops if there are no semantically significant lines in a segment, or if a split would result in a segment with one side being less than s_{min} long. The authors thankfully provided us with their implementation for our experiments. The algorithm is computationally expensive, and requires up to 1 h for the larger web pages of the dataset on a modern CPU, but could likely be sped up considerably through the use of multi-threading and GPUs.

Due to the runtime requirements of the current implementation, we only tested four parameter settings that the original authors suggested to us: each combination of $t_l \in 256, 512$ and $s_{min} \in 45, 90$. The algorithm contains another parameter t_p that is used as a threshold for determining semantically significant line segments, but we always use $t_p = 0.5$ as suggested by the authors. Figure 1 shows the average number of segments and performance over all web pages. For a fair comparison, we follow Kiesel et al. and fit the visual segmentations to DOM nodes, which has for most cases just a minor effect on the performance, though it does increase $F_{B^3}^*$ for the best parameter setting $(t_l = 512, s_{min} = 45)$ for *pixels* by 0.06. This setting is used in our further experiments.

4.4   MMDetection

The Hybrid Task Cascade models [5] from the MMDetection toolbox [4] jointly segment real-world images (photos) and detect objects in them. At the time of our experiments, this algorithm led the MSCOCO [12] detection task leaderboard[4] and can thus be considered state-of-the-art for photo segmentation. The neural network model[5] features an intricate cascading structure. In spot checks, we found that the algorithm detected only segments within images that were included in the web pages. We found that this is due to a separate filtering step that classifies segments as containing real-world objects, so we disabled this step since its purpose does not exist in web page segmentation. Otherwise, the algorithm is the same as the original and no re-training is performed to investigate the similarities of photos and web pages. As segments can be arbitrarily formed in our evaluation setup, we use the corresponding instance segmentation output of the algorithm instead of the more coarse bounding boxes. Like for Cormier et al., we fit the resulting pixel mask segmentation to DOM nodes, which results in performance increases up to 0.12 in $F_{B^3}^*$. MMDetection found no segments for 103 web pages (1%), which we treated like segmentations of one segment that contains the entire page.

4.5   Meier et al.

The convolutional neural network by Meier et al. [15] is state-of-the-art in segmenting digitized newspaper pages. We reimplemented it in contact with the authors,[6] but

---

[4] https://cocodataset.org/#detection-leaderboard.

[5] We use the model with X-101-64x4d-FPN backbone and c3-c5 DCN as available and suggested at https://github.com/open-mmlab/mmdetection/blob/master/configs/htc.

[6] The authors reported an erratum in their publication to us, so we used the corrected kernel size of 3×3 instead of 5×5 for layers `conv6-1` and `conv7-1`.

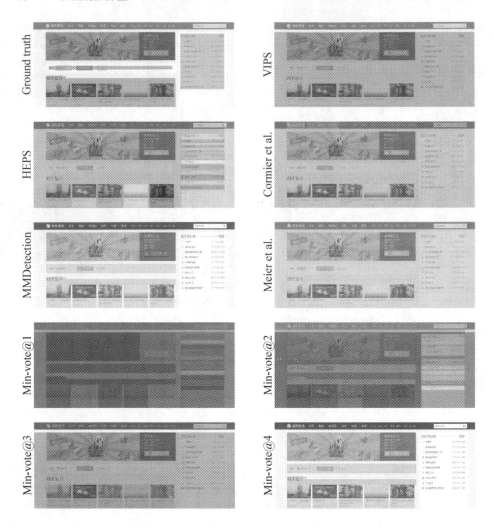

Fig. 2. Ground truth and algorithmic segmentations of the top of the same web page.

instead of determining the position of text through optical character recognition (OCR) we use the positions of text nodes from the corresponding list of nodes that accompanies the Webis-WebSeg-20. As the algorithm requires the input to be always of the same size, we had to crop or extend the web page screenshots to a uniform height. As a compromise between extremes, we selected a height that covers about 2/3 of pages, namely 4096 pixels. We then scaled the pages to 256x768 pixels to match the input width of the original approach. Since no pre-trained model is available, we use standard 10-fold cross-validation in the evaluation, and assure that all pages of a website are in the same fold. The training stopped when the loss did not improve for ten consecutive epochs, which led to a training of 20.8 epochs on average.

As the algorithm processes cropped web pages, its results are not fully comparable to those of the other algorithms. For this reason, we report the obtained measurements with some reservations and do not include the segmentations in the ensemble described below. The algorithm found no segments for 4 web pages (0.05%), which we treated like segmentations of one segment that contains the entire page.

4.6   Min-Vote@n

We also employ an ensemble of four of these algorithms, excluding the algorithm of Meier et al. as explained above. The ensemble algorithm is identical to the algorithm that was employed to fuse the human annotations to a single ground-truth for the Webis-WebSeg-20 [10]—just treating the algorithms as annotators. To filter out noise, the algorithm first removes all elements from consideration which less than n algorithms placed into segments. After that, the algorithm performs standard classic hierarchical agglomerative clustering, with the similarity of two elements being the ratio of algorithms that placed the elements in the same segment. In line with Kiesel et al., we use a similarity threshold of $\theta_a = \frac{n-0.5}{k}$, where $k = 4$ is the number of algorithms. The algorithm thus tends to put elements in one segment if at least n algorithms did so. We report results for all plausible values for n, namely 1 to 4.

4.7   Baseline

To put the performance of the algorithms into perspective, we report results for the naive approach of segmenting a web page into one single segment. This approach reaches always the maximum recall of 1 at the cost of the lowest possible precision. Both VIPS and the algorithm of Cormier et al. use this segmentation as their starting point.

5   Results of the Comparison

Table 2 shows the performance of each of the algorithms detailed in Sect. 4 on the Webis-WebSeg-20 dataset (cf. Sect. 3). The reported values all reflect the results after tuning the respective parameters of the algorithms.

The single algorithms, excluding baseline, Meier et al. and the ensemble, generate between 15.3 and 36.1 segments on average. This difference can be explained by the algorithms working at different levels of granularity. If successful, using more segments should increase the P_{B^3}. However, this is not necessarily the case: Though HEPS is clearly working at a finer level of granularity than VIPS (cf. Table 2 and Fig. 2), both algorithms perform similar in terms of P_{B^3}.

The highest $F_{B^3}^*$ scores are reached for *chars* and the smallest for *pixels*. This difference is likely due to web page segmentation algorithms being developed for information extraction purposes mainly, and thus mostly optimized for text. However, for applications like design mining, even the spacing between elements needs to be segmented correctly. New algorithms will be required for such and similar downstream tasks.

Conversely, the results differ only marginally between $edges_F$ and $edges_C$, despite the visually very different edge detection [10]. This result is very convenient for future

Table 2. Average number of segments per web page and evaluation results for each discussed algorithm on the Webis-WebSeg-20 dataset (Baseline, VIPS, HEPS, Cormier et al., MMDetection, Meier et al., and the Min-vote@n ensembles): average F_1-score (F_{B3}), precision (P_{B3}), recall (R_{B3}), as well as the harmonic mean of the averaged precision and recall (F_{B3}^*) for each type of atomic elements. The ground truth contains 9.1 segments on average. The highest score in each row (excluding the baseline) is highlighted in bold. The results of Meier et al. are shown in gray as its evaluation is not fully comparable.

Measure		Baseline	VIPS	HEPS	Corm.	MMD.	Meier	MV@1	MV@2	MV@3	MV@4
Segments		1.0	16.1	36.1	15.3	23.0	4.6	6.5	18.7	36.5	69.5
pixels	F_{B3}	0.24	0.38	0.33	0.36	**0.42**	0.32	0.30	0.39	0.30	0.28
	F_{B3}^*	0.28	0.47	0.44	0.53	**0.54**	0.50	0.35	0.50	0.45	0.42
	P_{B3}	0.16	0.36	0.36	0.39	0.51	0.48	0.22	0.38	0.60	**0.68**
	R_{B3}	1.00	0.67	0.56	0.80	0.57	0.52	**0.96**	0.72	0.36	0.30
$edges_F$	F_{B3}	0.44	**0.59**	0.48	0.51	0.53	0.41	0.50	0.56	0.39	0.34
	F_{B3}^*	0.49	**0.68**	0.58	0.65	0.61	0.55	0.56	0.66	0.49	0.45
	P_{B3}	0.32	0.66	0.61	0.55	0.73	0.55	0.40	0.61	0.81	**0.87**
	R_{B3}	1.00	0.69	0.55	0.80	0.53	0.55	**0.96**	0.71	0.36	0.30
$edges_C$	F_{B3}	0.45	**0.61**	0.49	0.53	0.54	0.42	0.51	0.57	0.39	0.35
	F_{B3}^*	0.49	**0.68**	0.59	0.66	0.62	0.56	0.56	0.67	0.50	0.46
	P_{B3}	0.32	0.67	0.62	0.56	0.74	0.55	0.40	0.63	0.82	**0.88**
	R_{B3}	1.00	0.70	0.56	0.80	0.53	0.57	**0.96**	0.72	0.36	0.31
nodes	F_{B3}	0.42	**0.63**	0.43	0.52	0.52	0.44	0.49	0.54	0.34	0.31
	F_{B3}^*	0.46	**0.70**	0.54	0.65	0.61	0.56	0.55	0.65	0.44	0.42
	P_{B3}	0.30	0.69	0.63	0.53	0.74	0.52	0.38	0.64	0.85	**0.88**
	R_{B3}	1.00	0.71	0.46	0.82	0.51	0.61	**0.96**	0.65	0.29	0.27
chars	F_{B3}	0.52	**0.67**	0.50	0.61	0.61	0.50	0.59	0.62	0.40	0.39
	F_{B3}^*	0.57	**0.75**	0.60	0.71	0.69	0.61	0.64	0.71	0.50	0.49
	P_{B3}	0.39	0.77	0.73	0.61	0.79	0.59	0.48	0.72	0.90	**0.92**
	R_{B3}	1.00	0.72	0.51	0.84	0.60	0.63	**0.96**	0.71	0.35	0.33

evaluations, as it indicates that (1) the parametrization of the edge detector does not play a major role, and (2) it is sufficient to evaluate for one parametrization of the edge detector. We recommend to employ $edges_F$ in the future, as it produces fewer segments that have no edges and which are thus not considered in the evaluation.

The best-performing algorithm from the literature for most types of atomic elements is the VIPS algorithm, reaching a F_{B3}^* of up to 0.75 and convincingly beating the baseline in all cases. It thus comes closest to human annotators—and also relatively close in terms of the average number of segments, which is 9.1 for the ground-truth. Moreover, for a higher value of PDoC it can reach a very high P_{B3} of up to 0.94 for *chars* (cf. Fig. 1), which is close to human agreement (cf. [10]). Therefore, PDoC can indeed be used to adjust the level of segmentation granularity. Nevertheless, P_{B3} is considerably lower at the optimal value for PDoC, which suggests that VIPS can benefit from an adaptation of PDoC to the (part of the) web page at hand. Though VIPS performs similarly well for most types of atomic elements, its precision is rather low for *pixels*. This difference is likely due to background pixels on the left and right of the actual content of the web pages: whereas VIPS includes such pixels in the segments, the human annotators did not (cf. Fig. 2 for one example).

However, both the algorithm by Cormier et al. and MMDetection reach a similar performance to VIPS in terms of $F_{B^3}^*$, which demonstrates the viability of purely visual approaches to web page segmentation. By comparison, the algorithm by Meier et al. fails to compete with the other algorithms, even though it had a clear advantage over the other algorithms by being trained on the data. Its poor performance might be due to the required adjustment of the input screenshots.

The results for the min-vote ensembles show that even a basic voting scheme can be employed to efficiently fuse the output of different algorithms. Remarkably, Min-vote@2 reaches a $F_{B^3}^*$ scores very similar to those of VIPS. Like PDoC for VIPS, the parameter n here fulfills the role of selecting the desired level of granularity. This is especially helpful as some algorithms, like HEPS, do not have such a parameter. The ensemble therefore allows to incorporate the HEPS heuristic (and others without such a parameter) and still to select a level of granularity.

A special ensemble is that of Min-vote@4, which puts elements in one segment if and only if all four single algorithms did so. We want to highlight that P_{B^3} is about 0.9 for all types of atomic elements except *pixels*, which indicates that most segments of these types of elements are indeed separated from others by at least one of the algorithms. However, *pixels* are an exception here, which shows a deficit that needs to be addressed by future algorithms.

6   Conclusion

As we contrast and discuss the results of our evaluation for each type of atomic page elements, it becomes clear that the classical VIPS algorithm is still the overall best option, unless the downstream task requires pixel-based segments. In that case, purely visual page segmentation performs better, whereas otherwise it is a close second to VIPS. MMDetection performed especially well for being designed and trained for photographic images. Interestingly, the state-of-the-art approaches for such images as well as for newspaper page segmentation both employ deep learning, while the approaches for web page segmentation rely mostly on hand-crafted heuristics and observations. We believe that this difference mainly stems from the fact that no large-scale datasets for web page segmentation have been available in the past. With this paper, we lay the foundation for the development of new approaches that may improve over the long-standing, yet heretofore unknown champion, VIPS.

Acknowledgements. We thank the anonymous reviewers for their helpful comments and the authors of the respective algorithms for providing us with either their code and/or their support for our re-implementations, as stated in the respective section.

References

1. Amigó, E., Gonzalo, J., Artiles, J., Verdejo, F.: A comparison of extrinsic clustering evaluation metrics based on formal constraints. Inf. Retr. **12**(4), 461–486 (2009). https://doi.org/10.1007/s10791-008-9066-8
2. Arias, J., Deschacht, K., Moens, M.F.: Language independent content extraction from web pages. In: Proceedings of the 9th Dutch-Belgian Information Retrieval Workshop, pp. 50–55. University of Twente, Enschede (2009)

3. Cai, D., Yu, S., Wen, J.-R., Ma, W.-Y.: Extracting content structure for web pages based on visual representation. In: Zhou, X., Orlowska, M.E., Zhang, Y. (eds.) APWeb 2003. LNCS, vol. 2642, pp. 406–417. Springer, Heidelberg (2003). https://doi.org/10.1007/3-540-36901-5_42

4. Chen, K., et al.: MMDetection: open MMLab detection toolbox and benchmark. CoRR abs/1906.07155 (2019). http://arxiv.org/abs/1906.07155

5. Chen, K., et al.: Hybrid task cascade for instance segmentation. CoRR abs/1901.07518 (2019). http://arxiv.org/abs/1901.07518

6. Cormier, M., Mann, R., Moffatt, K., Cohen, R.: Towards an improved vision-based web page segmentation algorithm. In: 14th Conference on Computer and Robot Vision, CRV 2017, pp. 345–352 (2017). https://doi.org/10.1109/CRV.2017.38

7. Cormier, M., Moffatt, K., Cohen, R., Mann, R.: Purely vision-based segmentation of web pages for assistive technology. Comput. Vis. Image Underst. 148, 46–66 (2016). https://doi.org/10.1016/j.cviu.2016.02.007

8. Goldstein, E.B.: Sensation and Perception. Cengage Learning, 8th edn. (2009). ISBN 9780495601494

9. Kiesel, J., Kneist, F., Alshomary, M., Stein, B., Hagen, M., Potthast, M.: Reproducible web corpora: interactive archiving with automatic quality assessment. J. Data Inf. Qual. (JDIQ) 10(4), 17:1–17:25 (2018). https://doi.org/10.1145/3239574. https://dl.acm.org/authorize?N676358

10. Kiesel, J., Kneist, F., Meyer, L., Komlossy, K., Stein, B., Potthast, M.: Web page segmentation revisited: evaluation framework and dataset. In: d'Aquin, M., Dietze, S., Hauff, C., Curry, E., Cudré-Mauroux, P. (eds.) 29th ACM International Conference on Information and Knowledge Management (CIKM 2020), pp. 3047–3054. ACM (October 2020). https://doi.org/10.1145/3340531.3412782

11. Kumar, R., et al.: Webzeitgeist: design mining the web. In: Mackay, W.E., Brewster, S.A., Bødker, S. (eds.) 2013 ACM SIGCHI Conference on Human Factors in Computing Systems, CHI 2013, pp. 3083–3092. ACM (2013). https://doi.org/10.1145/2470654.2466420

12. Lin, T.-Y., et al.: Microsoft COCO: common objects in context. In: Fleet, D., Pajdla, T., Schiele, B., Tuytelaars, T. (eds.) ECCV 2014. LNCS, vol. 8693, pp. 740–755. Springer, Cham (2014). https://doi.org/10.1007/978-3-319-10602-1_48

13. Ma, L., Goharian, N., Chowdhury, A.: Automatic data extraction from template generated web pages. In: Arabnia, H.R., Mun, Y. (eds.) Proceedings of the International Conference on Parallel and Distributed Processing Techniques and Applications, PDPTA 2003, pp. 642–648. CSREA Press (2003)

14. Manabe, T., Tajima, K.: Extracting logical hierarchical structure of HTML documents based on headings. PVLDB 8(12), 1606–1617 (2015)

15. Meier, B., Stadelmann, T., Stampfli, J., Arnold, M., Cieliebak, M.: Fully convolutional neural networks for newspaper article segmentation. In: 2017 14th IAPR International Conference on Document Analysis and Recognition (ICDAR), vol. 1, pp. 414–419. IEEE (2017)

16. Nielsen, J., Pernice, K.: Eyetracking Web Usability. Pearson Education, London (2010). ISBN 9780321714077

17. Zeleny, J., Burget, R., Zendulka, J.: Box clustering segmentation: a new method for vision-based web page preprocessing. Inf. Process. Manag. 53(3), 735–750 (2017). https://doi.org/10.1016/j.ipm.2017.02.002

Re-assessing the "Classify and Count" Quantification Method

Alejandro Moreo$^{(\boxtimes)}$ ⓘ and Fabrizio Sebastiani ⓘ

Istituto di Scienza e Tecnologie dell'Informazione,
Consiglio Nazionale delle Ricerche, 56124 Pisa, Italy
{alejandro.moreo,fabrizio.sebastiani}@isti.cnr.it

Abstract. *Learning to quantify* (a.k.a. *quantification*) is a task concerned with training unbiased estimators of class prevalence via supervised learning. This task originated with the observation that "Classify and Count" (CC), the trivial method of obtaining class prevalence estimates, is often a biased estimator, and thus delivers suboptimal quantification accuracy. Following this observation, several methods for learning to quantify have been proposed and have been shown to outperform CC. In this work we contend that previous works have failed to use properly optimised versions of CC. We thus reassess the real merits of CC and its variants, and argue that, while still inferior to some cutting-edge methods, they deliver near-state-of-the-art accuracy once (a) hyperparameter optimisation is performed, and (b) this optimisation is performed by using a truly quantification-oriented evaluation protocol. Experiments on three publicly available binary sentiment classification datasets support these conclusions.

Keywords: Learning to quantify · Quantification · Prevalence estimation · Classify and count

1 Introduction

Learning to quantify (a.k.a. *quantification*) consists of training a predictor that returns estimates of the relative frequency (a.k.a. *prevalence*, or *prior probability*) of the classes of interest in a set of unlabelled data items, where the predictor has been trained on a set of labelled data items [13]. When applied to text, quantification is important for several applications, e.g., gauging the collective satisfaction for a certain product from textual comments [8], establishing the popularity of a given political candidate from blog posts [17], predicting the amount of consensus for a given governmental policy from tweets [4], or predicting the amount of readers who will find a product review helpful [5].

The rationale of this task is that many real-life applications of classification suffer from *distribution shift* [22], the phenomenon according to which the distribution $p_y(U)$ of the labels in the set of unlabelled test documents U is different from the distribution $p_y(L)$ that the labels have in the set of labelled training documents L. It has been shown that, in the presence of distribution shift, the trivial strategy of using a standard classifier to classify all the unlabelled documents in U and counting the documents that have been assigned to each class

© Springer Nature Switzerland AG 2021
D. Hiemstra et al. (Eds.): ECIR 2021, LNCS 12657, pp. 75–91, 2021.
https://doi.org/10.1007/978-3-030-72240-1_6

(the "Classify and Count" (CC) method), delivers poor class prevalence estimates. The reason is that most supervised learning methods are based on the IID assumption, which implies that the distribution of the labels is the same in L and U. "Classify and Count" is considered a *biased estimator* of class prevalence, since the goal of standard classifiers is to minimise (assuming for simplicity a binary setting) *classification* error measures such as (FP + FN), while the goal of a quantifier is to minimise *quantification* error measures such as |FP − FN|. (In this paper we tackle binary quantification, so FP and FN denote the numbers of false positives and false negatives, resp., from a binary contingency table.) Following this observation, several quantification methods have been proposed, and have been experimentally shown to outperform CC.

In this paper we contend that previous works, when testing advanced quantification methods, have used as baselines versions of CC that had not been properly optimised. This means that published results on the relative merits of CC and other supposedly more advanced methods are still unreliable. We thus reassess the real merits of CC by running extensive experiments (on three publicly available sentiment classification datasets) in which we compare properly optimised versions of CC and its three main variants (PCC, ACC, PACC) with a number of more advanced quantification methods. In these experiments we properly optimise all quantification methods, i.e., (a) we optimise their hyperparameters, and (b) we conduct this optimisation via a truly quantification-oriented evaluation protocol, which also involves minimising a quantification loss rather than a classification loss. Our results indicate that, while still inferior to some cutting-edge quantification methods, CC and its variants deliver near-state-of-the-art quantification accuracy once hyperparameter optimisation is performed properly. We make available all the code and the datasets that we have used for our experiments.[1]

2 "Classify and Count" and Its Variants

In this paper we use the following notation. We assume a binary setting, with the two classes $\mathcal{Y} = \{\oplus, \ominus\}$ standing for Positive and Negative. By $\mathbf{x}$ we denote a document drawn from a domain $\mathcal{X}$ of documents; by $L \subset \mathcal{X}$ we denote a set of labelled documents, that we typically use as a training set, while by U we denote a sample of unlabelled documents, that we typically use as the sample to quantify on. By $p_y(\sigma)$ we indicate the true prevalence of class y in sample σ, by $\hat{p}_y(\sigma)$ we indicate an estimate of this prevalence[2], and by $\hat{p}_y^M(\sigma)$ we indicate the estimate of this prevalence as obtained via quantification method M. Of course, for any method M it holds that $\hat{p}_\ominus^M(U) = (1 - \hat{p}_\oplus^M(U))$.

An obvious way to solve quantification is by aggregating the scores assigned by a classifier to the unlabelled documents. We first define two different aggregation methods, one that uses a "hard" classifier (i.e., a classifier $h_\oplus : \mathcal{X} \to \{0, 1\}$

---

[1] https://github.com/AlexMoreo/CC.

[2] Consistently with most mathematical literature, we use the caret symbol (ˆ) to indicate estimation.

that returns binary decisions, 0 for $\ominus$ and 1 for $\oplus$) and one that uses a "soft" classifier (i.e., a classifier $s_\oplus : \mathcal{X} \rightarrow [0,1]$ that returns posterior probabilities $\Pr(\oplus|\mathbf{x})$, representing the probability that the classifier attributes to the fact that $\mathbf{x}$ belongs to the $\oplus$ class). Of course, $\Pr(\ominus|\mathbf{x}) = (1 - \Pr(\oplus|\mathbf{x}))$. The *classify and count* (CC) and the *probabilistic classify and count* (PCC) [3] methods then consist of computing

$$\hat{p}_\oplus^{\text{CC}}(U) = \frac{\sum_{\mathbf{x} \in U} h_\oplus(\mathbf{x})}{|U|} \qquad \hat{p}_\oplus^{\text{PCC}}(U) = \frac{\sum_{\mathbf{x} \in U} s_\oplus(\mathbf{x})}{|U|} \qquad (1)$$

Two popular, alternative quantification methods consist of applying an *adjustment* to the $\hat{p}_\oplus^{\text{CC}}(U)$ and $\hat{p}_\oplus^{\text{PCC}}(U)$ estimates. It is easy to show that, in the binary case, the true prevalence $p_\oplus(U)$ is such that

$$p_\oplus(U) = \frac{\hat{p}_\oplus^{\text{CC}}(U) - \text{FPR}_h}{\text{TPR}_h - \text{FPR}_h} \qquad p_\oplus(U) = \frac{\hat{p}_\oplus^{\text{PCC}}(U) - \text{FPR}_s}{\text{TPR}_s - \text{FPR}_s} \qquad (2)$$

where TPR_h and FPR_h (resp., TPR_s and FPR_s) here stand for the *true positive rate* and *false positive rate* that the classifier $h_\oplus$ (resp., $s_\oplus$) has on U. The values of TPR_h and FPR_h (resp., TPR_s and FPR_s) are unknown, but can be estimated via k-fold cross-validation on the training data. In the binary case this amounts to using the results that $h_\oplus(\mathbf{x})$ (resp., $s_\oplus(\mathbf{x})$) obtains in the k-fold cross-validation (i.e., when $\mathbf{x}$ ranges on the training documents) in equations

$$\hat{\text{TPR}}_h = \frac{\sum_{\mathbf{x} \in \oplus} h_\oplus(\mathbf{x})}{|\oplus|} \qquad \hat{\text{FPR}}_h = \frac{\sum_{\mathbf{x} \in \ominus} h_\oplus(\mathbf{x})}{|\ominus|}$$
$$\hat{\text{TPR}}_s = \frac{\sum_{\mathbf{x} \in \oplus} s_\oplus(\mathbf{x})}{|\oplus|} \qquad \hat{\text{FPR}}_s = \frac{\sum_{\mathbf{x} \in \ominus} s_\oplus(\mathbf{x})}{|\ominus|} \qquad (3)$$

We obtain $\hat{p}_\oplus^{\text{ACC}}(U)$ and $\hat{p}_\oplus^{\text{PACC}}(U)$ estimates, which define the *adjusted classify and count* (ACC) [11] and *probabilistic adjusted classify and count* (PACC) [3] quantification methods, resp., by replacing TPR_h and FPR_h (resp., TPR_s and FPR_s) in Eq. 2 with their estimates from Eq. 3.

3   Quantification and Parameter Optimisation

3.1   Unsuitable Parameter Optimisation and Weak Baselines

The reason why we here reassess CC and its variants we have described above, is that we believe that, in previous papers where these methods have been used as baselines, their full potential has not been realised because of *missing or unsuitable optimisation* of the hyperparameters of the classifier on which the method is based.

Specifically, both CC and its variants rely on the output of a previously trained classifier, and this output usually depends on some hyperparameters. Not only the quality of this output heavily depends on whether these hyperparameters have been optimised or not (on some held-out data or via k-fold cross-validation), but *it also depends on what evaluation measure this optimisation has used as a criterion for model selection.* In other words, given that hyperparameter optimisation chooses the value of the parameter that minimises error, it would make sense that, for a classifier to be used for quantification purposes, "error" is measured via a function that evaluates *quantification* error, and not classification error. Unfortunately, in most previous quantification papers, researchers either do not specify whether hyperparameter optimisation was performed at all [9,11,14,15,17,19,26,27], or leave the hyperparameters at their default values [1,3,10,16,21], or do not specify which evaluation measure they use in hyperparameter optimisation [8,12], or use, for this optimisation, a classification-based loss [2,25]. In retrospect, we too plead guilty, since some of the papers quoted here are our own.

All this means that CC and their variants, when used as baselines, have been turned into *weak* baselines, and this means that the merits of more modern methods relative to them have possibly been exaggerated, and are thus yet to be assessed reliably. In this paper we thus engage in a reproducibility study, and present results from text quantification experiments in which, contrary to the situations described in the paragraph above, we compare *carefully optimised* versions of CC and its variants with a number of (*carefully optimised* versions of) more modern quantification methods, in an attempt to assess the relative value of each in a robust way.

3.2   Quantification-Oriented Parameter Optimisation

In order to perform quantification-oriented parameter optimisation we need to be aware that there may exist two types of parameters that require estimation and/or optimisation, i.e., (a) the hyperparameters of the classifier on which the quantification method is based, and (b) the parameters of the quantification method itself.

The way we perform hyperparameter optimisation is the following. We assume that the dataset comes with a predefined split between a training set L and a test set U. (This assumption is indeed verified for the datasets we will use in Sect. 4.) We first partition L into a part L_{Tr} that will be used for training purposes and a part L_{Va} that will be used as a held-out validation set for optimising the hyperparameters of the quantifier. We then extract, from the validation set L_{Va}, several random validation samples, each characterised by a predefined prevalence of the $\oplus$ class; here, our goal is allowing the validation to be conducted on a variety of scenarios characterised by widely different values of class prevalence, and, as a consequence, by widely different amounts of distribution shift.[3] In order to do this, we extract each validation sample σ by randomly undersampling one or both classes in L_{Va}, in order to obtain a sample with

---

[3] Note that this is similar to what we do, say, in classification, where the different hyperparameter values are tested on many validation documents; here we test these hyperparameter values on many validation *samples*, since the objects of study of text quantification are document samples inasmuch as the objects of study of text classification are individual documents.

prespecified class prevalence values. We draw samples with a desired prevalence value and a fixed amount q of documents; in order to achieve this, in some cases only one class needs to be undersampled while in some other cases this needs to happen for both classes. We use random sampling without replacement if the number of available examples of $\oplus$ (resp. $\ominus$) is greater or equal to the number of required ones, and with replacement otherwise. We extract samples with a prevalence of the $\oplus$ class in the set $\{\pi_1, ..., \pi_n\}$; for each of these n values we generate m random samples consisting of q validation documents each. Let Θ be the set of hyperparameters that we are going to optimise. Given the established grid of value combinations $\theta_1, ..., \theta_n$ that we are going to test for Θ, for each θ_i we do the following, depending on whether the quantification method has its own parameters (Case 1 below) or not (Case 2 below):

1. If the quantification method M we are going to optimise requires some parameters λ_i to be estimated, we first split L_{Tr} into a part $L_{\text{Tr}}^{\text{Tr}}$ and a part $L_{\text{Tr}}^{\text{Va}}$, training the classifier on $L_{\text{Tr}}^{\text{Tr}}$ using the chosen learner parameterised with θ_i, and estimate parameters λ_i on $L_{\text{Tr}}^{\text{Va}}$.[4] Among the variants of CC, this applies to methods ACC and PACC, which require the estimation of (the hard or soft version of) TPR and FPR. Other methods used in the experiments of Sect. 4 and that also require some parameter to be estimated are HDy and QuaNet (see Sect. 4.3.2).
2. If the quantification method M we are going to optimise does not have any parameter that requires estimation, then we train our classifier on L_{Tr}, using the chosen learner parameterised with θ_i, and use quantification method M on all the samples extracted from L_{Va}.

In both cases, we measure the quantification error via an evaluation measure for quantification that combines (e.g., averages) the results across all the validation samples. As our final value combination for hyperparameter set Θ we choose the θ_i for which quantification error is minimum.

Note that, in the above discussion, each time we split a labelled set into a training set and a validation set for parameter estimation/optimisation purposes, we could instead perform a k-fold cross validation; the parameter estimation/optimisation would be more robust, but the computational cost of the entire process would be k times higher. While the latter method is also, from a methodological standpoint, an option, in this paper we stick to the former method, since the entire parameter optimisation process is, from a computational point of view, already very expensive.

---

[4] Note that we do *not* retrain the classifier on the entire L_{Tr}. While this might seem beneficial, since L_{Tr} contains more training data than $L_{\text{Tr}}^{\text{Tr}}$, we need to consider that the estimates $\hat{\text{TPR}}_h$ and $\hat{\text{FPR}}_h$ have been computed on L_{Tr} and not on $L_{\text{Tr}}^{\text{Tr}}$.

Table 1. The three datasets used in our experiments; the columns indicate the class prevalence values of the $\oplus$ and $\ominus$ classes, and the numbers of documents contained in the training set L and the test set U.

	$\oplus$	$\ominus$	L	L_{Tr}	L_{Va}	U
IMDB	0.500	0.500	25,000	15,000	10,000	25,000
KINDLE	0.917	0.083	3,821	2,292	1,529	21,592
HP	0.982	0.018	9,533	5,720	3,813	18,401

4   Experiments

In order to conduct our experiments we use the same datasets and experimental protocol as used in [7]. Specifically, we run our experiments on three sentiment classification datasets, i.e., (i) IMDB, the popular *Large Movie Review Dataset* [20]; (ii) KINDLE, a set of reviews of Kindle e-book readers [7], and (iii) HP, a set of reviews of the books from the Harry Potter series [7].[5] For all datasets we adopt the same split between training set L and test set U as in [7]. The IMDB, KINDLE, and HP datasets are examples of balanced, imbalanced, and severely imbalanced datasets, since the prevalence values of the $\oplus$ class in the training set L are 0.500, 0.917, 0.982, resp. Some basic statistics from these datasets are reported in Table 1. We refer the reader to [7] for more details on the genesis of these datasets.

In our experiments, from each set of training data we randomly select 60% of the documents for training purposes, leaving the remaining 40% for the hyperparameter optimisation phase; these random splits are stratified, meaning that the two resulting parts display the same prevalence values as the set that originated them. In this phase (see Sect. 3.2) we use $n = 21$, $m = 10$, and $q = 500$, i.e., we generate $m = 10$ random samples of $q = 500$ documents each, for each of the $n = 21$ prevalence values of the $\oplus$ class in $\{0.00, 0.05, ..., 0.95, 1.00\}$.

In order to evaluate a quantifier over a wide spectrum of test prevalence values, we use essentially the same process that we have discussed in Sect. 3.2 for hyperparameter optimisation; that is, along with [7,11], we repeatedly and randomly undersample one or both classes in the test set U in order to obtain testing samples with specified class prevalence values. Here we generate $m = 100$ random testing samples of $q = 500$ documents each, for each of the $n = 21$ prevalence values of the $\oplus$ class in $\{0.00, 0.05, ..., 0.95, 1.00\}$.

---

[5] The three datasets are available at https://doi.org/10.5281/zenodo.4117827 in preprocessed form. The raw versions of the HP and KINDLE datasets can be accessed from http://hlt.isti.cnr.it/quantification/, while the raw version of IMDB can be found at https://ai.stanford.edu/~amaas/data/sentiment/.

4.1   Evaluation Measures

As the measures of quantification error we use *Absolute Error* (AE) and *Relative Absolute Error* (RAE), defined as

$$\text{AE}(p,\hat{p}) = \frac{1}{|\mathcal{Y}|} \sum_{y \in \mathcal{Y}} |\hat{p}_y - p_y| \qquad\qquad \text{RAE}(p,\hat{p}) = \frac{1}{|\mathcal{Y}|} \sum_{y \in \mathcal{Y}} \frac{|\hat{p}_y - p_y|}{p_y} \qquad (4)$$

where $\mathcal{Y}$ is the set of classes of interest ($\mathcal{Y} = \{\oplus, \ominus\}$ in our case) and the sample σ is omitted for notational brevity. Note that RAE is undefined when at least one of the classes $y \in \mathcal{Y}$ is such that its prevalence in U is 0. To solve this problem, in computing RAE we smooth both all p_y's and $\hat{p}_y$'s via additive smoothing, i.e., we take $\underline{p}_y = \frac{\epsilon + p_y}{\sum_{y \in \mathcal{Y}}(\epsilon + p_y)}$, where $\underline{p}_y$ denotes the smoothed version of p_y and the denominator is just a normalising factor (same for the $\hat{p}(y)$'s); following [11], we use the quantity $\epsilon = \frac{1}{2|U|}$ as the smoothing factor. We then use the smoothed versions of p_y and $\hat{p}_y$ in place of their original non-smoothed versions in Eq. 4; as a result, RAE is always defined.

The reason why we use AE and RAE is that from a theoretical standpoint they are, as it has recently been argued [28], the most satisfactory evaluation measures for quantification.

4.2   Data Processing

We preprocess our documents by using the stop word remover and default tokeniser available within the `scikit-learn` framework[6]. In all three datasets we remove all terms occurring less than 5 times in the training set and all punctuation marks, and lowercase the text. As the weighting criterion we use a version of the well-known tfidf method, i.e.,

$$\text{tfidf}(f, \mathbf{x}) = \log(\#(f, \mathbf{x}) + 1) \times \log \frac{|L|}{|\mathbf{x}' \in L : \#(f, \mathbf{x}') > 0|} \qquad (5)$$

where $\#(f, \mathbf{x})$ is the raw number of occurrences of feature f in document $\mathbf{x}$; weights are then normalised via cosine normalisation.

Among the learners we use for classification (see below), the only one that does not rely on a tfidf-based representation is CNN. This learner simply converts all documents into lists of unique numeric IDs, indexing the terms in the vocabulary. We pad the documents to the first 300 words.

---

[6] http://scikit-learn.org/.

4.3   The Quantifiers

We here describe all the quantification systems we have used in this work.

4.3.1   CC and Its Variants

In our experiments we generate versions of CC, ACC, PCC, and PACC, using five different learners, i.e., support vector machines (SVM), logistic regression (LR), random forests (RF), multinomial naive Bayes (MNB), and convolutional neural networks (CNN). For the first four learners we rely on the implementations available from `scikit-learn`, while the CNN deep neural network is something we have implemented ourselves using the `pytorch` framework.[7] The setups that we use for these learners are the following:

– SVM: We use soft-margin SVMs with linear kernel and L2 regularisation, and we explicitly optimise the C parameter (in the range $C \in \{10^i\}$ with $i \in \{-4, -3, \ldots, 4, 5\}$) that determines the tradeoff between the margin and the training error (default: $C = 1$). We also optimise the $J_\oplus$ and $J_\ominus$ "rebalancing" parameters, which determine whether to impose that misclassifying a $\oplus$ document has a different cost than misclassifying a $\ominus$ document (in this case one sets $J_\oplus = \frac{p_\ominus(L)}{p_\oplus(L)}$ and $J_\ominus = 1$), or not (in this case one sets $J_\oplus = J_\ominus = 1$, which is the default configuration) [23].
– LR: As in SVM, we use L2 regularisation, and we explicitly optimise the rebalancing parameters and the regularisation coefficient C (default values are as in SVM).
– RF: we optimise the number of estimators in the range $\{10, 50, 100, 250, 500\}$, the max depth in $\{5, 15, 30, \max\}$,[8] and the splitting function in $\{\text{Gini}, \text{Entropy}\}$ (default: (100, max, Gini)).
– MNB: We use Laplace smoothing, and we optimise the additive factor α in the range $\{0.00, 0.05, \ldots, 0.95, 1.00\}$ (default: $\alpha = 1$).
– CNN: we use a single convolutional layer with γ output channels for three window lengths of 3, 5, and 7 words. Each convolution is followed by a ReLU activation function and a max-pooling operation. All convolved outputs are then concatenated and processed by an affine transformation and a sigmoid activation that converts the outputs into posterior probabilities. We use the Adam optimiser (with learning rate $1E^{-3}$ and all other parameters at their default values) to minimise the balanced binary cross-entropy loss, set the batch size to 100, and train the net for 500 epochs, but we apply an early stop after 20 consecutive training epochs showing no improvement in terms of F_1 for the minority class on the validation set. We explore the dimensionality of the embedding space in the range $\{100, 300\}$ (default: 100), the number of output channels γ in $\{256, 512\}$ (default: 512), whether to apply dropout to the last layer (with a drop probability of 0.5) or not (default: "yes"), and whether to apply weight decay (with a factor of $1E^{-4}$) or not (default: "no").

---

[7] https://pytorch.org/.
[8] When the depth is set to "max" then nodes are expanded until all leaves belong to the same class.

Since we perform hyperparameter optimisation via grid search, the number of validations (i.e., combinations of hyperparameters) that we perform amounts to 20 for SVMs, 20 for LR, 40 for RF, 21 for MNB, and 16 for CNN.

In the following, by the notation M_l^m we will indicate quantification method M using learner l whose parameters have been optimised using measure m (where $M_l^{\varnothing}$ indicates that no optimisation at all has been carried out). We will test, on all three datasets, all combinations in which M ranges on {CC, ACC, PCC, PACC}, l ranges on {SVM, LR, RF, MNB, CNN}, and m ranges on {A, F_1, AE}, where A denotes vanilla accuracy, F_1 is the well-known harmonic mean of precision and recall, and AE is absolute error. We stick to the tradition of computing F_1 with respect to the minority class, which always turns out to be $\ominus$ in all three datasets (this means that, e.g., the true positives of the contingency table are the documents that the classifier assigns to $\ominus$ and that indeed belong to $\ominus$).

Note that PCC requires the classifier to return posterior probabilities. Since SVMs does not produce posterior probabilities, for PCC_{SVM} and $PACC_{SVM}$ we calibrate the confidence scores that SVMs return by using Platt's method [24].

4.3.2   Advanced Quantification Methods

As the advanced methods that we test against CC and its variants, we use a number of more sophisticated systems that have been top-performers in the recent quantification literature.

- We use the Saerens-Latinne-Decaestecker method [6,27] (SLD), which consists of training a probabilistic classifier and then exploiting the EM algorithm to iteratively shift the estimation of $p_y(U)$ from the one that maximises the likelihood on the training set to the one that maximises it on the test data. As the underlying learner for SLD we use LR, since (as MNB) it returns posterior probabilities (which SLD needs), since these probabilities tend to be (differently from those returned by MNB) well-calibrated, and since LR is well-known to perform much better than MNB.
- We use methods SVM(KLD), SVM(NKLD), SVM(Q), SVM(AE), SVM(RAE), from the "structured output learning" camp. Each of them is the result of instantiating the SVM_{perf} structured output learner [18] to optimise a different loss function. SVM(KLD) [10] minimises the Kullback-Leibler Divergence (KLD); SVM(NKLD) [9] minimises a version of KLD normalised via the logistic function; SVM(Q) [1] minimises the harmonic mean of a classification-oriented loss (recall) and a quantification-oriented loss (RAE). We also add versions that minimise AE and RAE, since these latter are now, as indicated in Sect. 4.1, the evaluation measures for quantification considered most satisfactory, and the two used in this paper for evaluating the quantification accuracy of our systems. We optimise the C parameter of SVM_{perf} in the range $C \in \{10^i\}$, with $i \in \{-4, -3, \ldots 4, 5\}$. In this case we do not optimise the $J_{\oplus}$ and $J_{\ominus}$ "rebalancing" parameters since this option is not available in SVM_{perf}.
- We use the HDy method of [15]. The method searches for the prevalence values that minimise the divergence (as measured via the Hellinger Distance)

between two cumulative distributions of posterior probabilities returned by the classifier, one for the unlabelled examples and the other for a validation set. The latter is a mixture of the distributions of posterior probabilities returned for the $\oplus$ and $\ominus$ validation examples, respectively, where the parameters of the mixture are the sought class prevalence values. We use LR as the classifier for the same reasons as discussed for SLD.

– We use the QuaNet system, a "meta-"quantification method based on deep learning [7]. QuaNet takes as input a list of document embeddings, together with and sorted by the classification scores returned by a classifier. A bidirectional LSTM processes this list and produces a quantification embedding that is then concatenated with a vector of predictions produced by an ensemble of simpler quantification methods (we here employ CC, ACC, PCC, PACC, and SLD). The resulting vector passes through a set of fully connected layers (followed by ReLU activations and dropout) that return the estimated class prevalence values. We use CNN as the learner since, among the learners we use in this paper, it is the only one that returns both posterior probabilities and document embeddings (we use the last layer of the CNN as the document embedding). We set the hidden size of the bidirectional LSTM to $128 + 128 = 256$ and use two stacked layers. We also set the hidden sizes of the fully connected layers to 1024 and 512, and the dropout probability to 0.5. We train the network for 500 epochs, but we apply early stopping with a patience of 10 consecutive validations without improvements in terms of mean square error (MSE). Each training epoch consists of 200 quantification predictions, each of which for a batch of 500 randomly drawn documents at a prevalence sampled from the uniform distribution. In our case, validation epochs correspond to 21 quantification predictions for batches of 500 documents randomly sampled to have prevalence values $0.00, 0.05, \ldots, 0.95, 1.00$. We use Adam as the optimiser, with default parameters, to minimise MSE. In order to train QuaNet, we split (using a $40\%/40\%/20\%$ stratified split) the training set L_{Tr} in three sets $L_{\text{Tr}}^{\text{CTr}}$, for training the classifier; $L_{\text{Tr}}^{\text{QTr}}$, for training QuaNet; and $L_{\text{Tr}}^{\text{QVa}}$, for validating QuaNet. When optimising QuaNet we do not explore any additional hyperparameter apart from those for the CNN.

– We also report results for *Maximum Likelihood Probability Estimation* (MLPE), the trivial baseline for quantification which makes the IID assumption and thus simply assumes that $p_{\oplus}(U)$ is identical to the training prevalence $p_{\oplus}(L)$ irrespectively of the set U.

Note that ACC, PACC, HDy, and QuaNet need to estimate their own parameters on a validation set, which means that their performance depends on exactly which documents this set consists of. In order to mitigate the impact of this random choice, for these methods we run each experiment 10 times, each time with a different random choice. The results we report are the average scores across these 10 runs.

Table 2. Results showing how the quantification error of CC changes according to the measure used in hyperparameter optimization; a negative percentage indicates a reduction in error with respect to using the method with default parameters. The background cell color indicates improvement (green) or deterioration (red), while its tone intensity is proportional to the absolute magnitude.

	IMDB		KINDLE		HP	
	AE	RAE	AE	RAE	AE	RAE
$CC^{\varnothing}_{SVM}$	0.065	6.029	0.305	15.928	0.471	24.058
CC^{A}_{SVM}	0.059 (-9.6%)	5.408 (-10.3%)	0.245 (-19.8%)	13.220 (-17.0%)	0.401 (-14.9%)	20.645 (-14.2%)
$CC^{F_1}_{SVM}$	0.059 (-9.5%)	5.523 (-8.4%)	0.108 (-64.5%)	7.192 (-54.8%)	0.236 (-50.0%)	13.590 (-43.5%)
CC^{AE}_{SVM}	0.065 (+0.3%)	6.091 (+1.0%)	0.100 (-67.1%)	7.555 (-52.6%)	0.119 (-74.8%)	10.593 (-56.0%)
$CC^{\varnothing}_{LR}$	0.059	5.477	0.470	23.990	0.500	25.508
CC^{A}_{LR}	0.062 (+6.0%)	5.839 (+6.6%)	0.202 (-57.0%)	11.215 (-53.3%)	0.451 (-9.8%)	23.035 (-9.7%)
$CC^{F_1}_{LR}$	0.062 (+5.3%)	5.725 (+4.5%)	0.163 (-65.3%)	9.278 (-61.3%)	0.229 (-54.3%)	13.505 (-47.1%)
CC^{AE}_{LR}	0.062 (+6.1%)	5.745 (+4.9%)	0.094 (-80.0%)	7.087 (-70.5%)	0.110 (-78.0%)	10.304 (-59.6%)
$CC^{\varnothing}_{RF}$	0.155	13.388	0.448	22.988	0.493	25.196
CC^{A}_{RF}	0.080 (-48.1%)	7.446 (-44.4%)	0.463 (+3.5%)	23.744 (+3.3%)	0.500 (+1.3%)	25.482 (+1.1%)
$CC^{F_1}_{RF}$	0.079 (-49.1%)	7.396 (-44.8%)	0.451 (+0.7%)	23.142 (+0.7%)	0.499 (+1.2%)	25.469 (+1.1%)
CC^{AE}_{RF}	0.079 (-48.8%)	7.487 (-44.1%)	0.464 (+3.6%)	23.721 (+3.2%)	0.500 (+1.3%)	25.487 (+1.2%)
$CC^{\varnothing}_{MNB}$	0.096	8.147	0.500	25.513	0.500	25.510
CC^{A}_{MNB}	0.098 (+1.6%)	8.529 (+4.7%)	0.443 (-11.4%)	22.641 (-11.3%)	0.499 (-0.2%)	25.459 (-0.2%)
$CC^{F_1}_{MNB}$	0.097 (+0.8%)	8.311 (+2.0%)	0.444 (-11.3%)	22.731 (-10.9%)	0.499 (-0.2%)	25.470 (-0.2%)
CC^{AE}_{MNB}	0.097 (+0.9%)	8.431 (+3.5%)	0.443 (-11.4%)	22.701 (-11.0%)	0.499 (-0.2%)	25.464 (-0.2%)
$CC^{\varnothing}_{CNN}$	0.072	6.683	0.087	8.138	0.255	17.042
CC^{A}_{CNN}	0.073 (+2.0%)	6.620 (-1.0%)	0.107 (+23.8%)	8.680 (+6.7%)	0.159 (-37.5%)	14.255 (-16.4%)
$CC^{F_1}_{CNN}$	0.078 (+8.7%)	7.142 (+6.9%)	0.085 (-2.2%)	7.951 (-2.3%)	0.149 (-41.5%)	14.030 (-17.7%)
CC^{AE}_{CNN}	0.074 (+3.2%)	6.613 (-1.0%)	0.109 (+26.2%)	8.591 (+5.6%)	0.343 (+34.3%)	19.008 (+11.5%)

4.4 Results

Tables 2, 3, 4, and 5 report the results obtained for CC, ACC, PCC, and PACC. At a first glance, the results do not seem to give any clearcut indication on how the CC variants should be optimised. However, a closer look reveals a number of patterns. One of these is that SVM and LR (the two best-performing classifiers overall) tend to benefit from optimised hyperparameters, and tend to do so to a greater extent when the loss used in the optimisation is quantification-oriented. Somehow surprisingly, not all methods improve after model selection in every case. However, there tends to be such an improvement especially for ACC and PACC. A likely reason for this is the possible existence of a complex tradeoff between obtaining a more accurate classifier and obtaining more reliable estimates for the TPR and FPR quantities.

Regarding the different datasets, it seems that there is no clear improvement from performing model selection when the training set is balanced (see IMDB), neither by using a classification-oriented measure nor by using a quantification-oriented one. A possible reason is that any classifier (with or without hyperparameter optimisation) becomes a reasonable quantifier if it learns to pay equal importance to positive and negative examples, i.e., if the errors it produces are unbiased towards either $\oplus$ or $\ominus$. In this respect, RF and MNB prove strongly biased towards the majority class, and only when corrected via an adjustment (ACC or PACC) they deliver results comparable to those obtained for other learners.

Table 3. Same as Table 2, but with ACC instead of CC.

	IMDB		KINDLE		HP	
	AE	RAE	AE	RAE	AE	RAE
$ACC_{SVM}^{\varnothing}$	0.023	1.084	0.068	2.958	0.341	17.350
ACC_{SVM}^{A}	0.019 (-17.6%)	0.889 (-18.0%)	0.070 (+4.1%)	3.093 (+4.6%)	0.181 (-47.0%)	9.245 (-46.7%)
$ACC_{SVM}^{F_1}$	0.022 (-5.2%)	1.153 (+6.3%)	0.052 (-22.9%)	2.309 (-21.9%)	0.110 (-67.8%)	7.019 (-59.5%)
ACC_{SVM}^{AE}	0.020 (-11.4%)	0.933 (-13.9%)	0.069 (+1.6%)	3.193 (+7.9%)	0.108 (-68.4%)	7.225 (-58.4%)
$ACC_{LR}^{\varnothing}$	0.017	0.569	0.279	9.997	0.500	25.508
ACC_{LR}^{A}	0.020 (+21.2%)	0.933 (+63.9%)	0.060 (-78.6%)	2.628 (-73.7%)	0.185 (-62.9%)	9.629 (-62.3%)
$ACC_{LR}^{F_1}$	0.019 (+15.9%)	0.896 (+57.4%)	0.057 (-79.5%)	2.507 (-74.9%)	0.098 (-80.5%)	6.534 (-74.4%)
ACC_{LR}^{AE}	0.018 (+10.8%)	0.850 (+49.3%)	0.065 (-76.9%)	2.891 (-71.1%)	0.092 (-81.7%)	5.849 (-77.1%)
$ACC_{RF}^{\varnothing}$	0.034	1.254	0.136	4.199	0.439	23.528
ACC_{RF}^{A}	0.021 (-38.7%)	0.643 (-48.8%)	0.180 (+31.7%)	6.603 (+57.3%)	0.482 (+9.7%)	24.654 (+4.8%)
$ACC_{RF}^{F_1}$	0.019 (-42.7%)	0.526 (-58.1%)	0.155 (+13.4%)	4.282 (+2.0%)	0.460 (+4.7%)	24.205 (+2.9%)
ACC_{RF}^{AE}	0.019 (-43.0%)	0.554 (-55.8%)	0.197 (+44.2%)	6.057 (+44.3%)	0.499 (+13.5%)	25.436 (+8.1%)
$ACC_{MNB}^{\varnothing}$	0.049	2.316	0.473	23.280	0.500	25.508
ACC_{MNB}^{A}	0.051 (+4.4%)	2.479 (+7.0%)	0.189 (-59.9%)	9.065 (-61.1%)	0.435 (-13.1%)	22.170 (-13.1%)
$ACC_{MNB}^{F_1}$	0.049 (+0.5%)	2.404 (+3.8%)	0.197 (-58.3%)	9.285 (-60.1%)	0.428 (-14.5%)	22.025 (-13.7%)
ACC_{MNB}^{AE}	0.051 (+3.9%)	2.591 (+11.9%)	0.213 (-54.9%)	10.376 (-55.4%)	0.451 (-9.7%)	23.146 (-9.3%)
$ACC_{CNN}^{\varnothing}$	0.021	1.082	0.074	1.596	0.173	10.642
ACC_{CNN}^{A}	0.019 (-8.2%)	0.811 (-25.0%)	0.064 (-12.7%)	1.515 (-5.1%)	0.223 (+28.6%)	9.939 (-6.6%)
$ACC_{CNN}^{F_1}$	0.023 (+10.1%)	1.067 (-1.4%)	0.061 (-17.4%)	1.424 (-10.8%)	0.182 (+5.3%)	10.344 (-2.8%)
ACC_{CNN}^{AE}	0.023 (+9.1%)	1.072 (-0.9%)	0.068 (-7.8%)	1.399 (-12.4%)	0.174 (+0.7%)	10.810 (+1.6%)

Table 4. Same as Table 2, but with PCC instead of CC.

	IMDB		KINDLE		HP	
	AE	RAE	AE	RAE	AE	RAE
$PCC_{SVM}^{\varnothing}$	0.101	9.460	0.255	14.514	0.375	20.158
PCC_{SVM}^{A}	0.100 (-0.4%)	9.517 (+0.6%)	0.283 (+10.9%)	16.174 (+11.4%)	0.385 (+2.6%)	20.653 (+2.5%)
$PCC_{SVM}^{F_1}$	0.101 (+0.0%)	9.425 (-0.4%)	0.251 (-1.8%)	14.239 (-1.9%)	0.385 (+2.7%)	20.594 (+2.2%)
PCC_{SVM}^{AE}	0.100 (-0.4%)	9.484 (+0.2%)	0.254 (-0.6%)	14.461 (-0.4%)	0.386 (+2.8%)	20.607 (+2.2%)
$PCC_{LR}^{\varnothing}$	0.122	11.564	0.356	20.405	0.464	24.608
PCC_{LR}^{A}	0.091 (-25.5%)	8.563 (-26.0%)	0.279 (-21.5%)	15.031 (-26.3%)	0.352 (-24.2%)	18.605 (-24.4%)
$PCC_{LR}^{F_1}$	0.092 (-25.0%)	8.606 (-25.6%)	0.172 (-51.6%)	11.222 (-45.0%)	0.212 (-54.2%)	16.117 (-34.5%)
PCC_{LR}^{AE}	0.079 (-35.3%)	7.348 (-36.5%)	0.154 (-56.6%)	13.066 (-36.0%)	0.211 (-54.6%)	19.597 (-20.4%)
$PCC_{RF}^{\varnothing}$	0.199	18.865	0.376	21.592	0.461	24.267
PCC_{RF}^{A}	0.198 (-0.7%)	18.753 (-0.6%)	0.368 (-2.0%)	21.209 (-1.8%)	0.482 (+4.7%)	25.349 (+4.5%)
$PCC_{RF}^{F_1}$	0.195 (-2.1%)	18.459 (-2.2%)	0.372 (-0.9%)	21.319 (-1.3%)	0.466 (+1.1%)	24.563 (+1.2%)
PCC_{RF}^{AE}	0.196 (-1.4%)	18.565 (-1.6%)	0.366 (-2.5%)	21.088 (-2.3%)	0.462 (+0.3%)	24.379 (+0.5%)
$PCC_{MNB}^{\varnothing}$	0.171	15.928	0.478	24.702	0.498	25.453
PCC_{MNB}^{A}	0.168 (-1.7%)	15.663 (-1.7%)	0.381 (-20.3%)	20.396 (-17.4%)	0.497 (-0.2%)	25.397 (-0.2%)
$PCC_{MNB}^{F_1}$	0.167 (-2.2%)	15.617 (-2.0%)	0.380 (-20.4%)	20.369 (-17.5%)	0.473 (-5.0%)	24.487 (-3.8%)
PCC_{MNB}^{AE}	0.160 (-6.4%)	14.907 (-6.4%)	0.380 (-20.4%)	20.396 (-17.4%)	0.473 (-5.0%)	24.479 (-3.8%)
$PCC_{CNN}^{\varnothing}$	0.110	9.994	0.111	10.448	0.257	18.368
PCC_{CNN}^{A}	0.105 (-4.8%)	9.893 (-1.0%)	0.154 (+39.2%)	10.775 (+3.1%)	0.389 (+51.6%)	21.093 (+14.8%)
$PCC_{CNN}^{F_1}$	0.099 (-10.3%)	9.377 (-6.2%)	0.111 (+0.3%)	9.474 (-9.3%)	0.251 (-2.2%)	17.005 (-7.4%)
PCC_{CNN}^{AE}	0.145 (+31.3%)	11.146 (+11.5%)	0.148 (+33.8%)	14.017 (+34.2%)	0.156 (-39.3%)	14.644 (-20.3%)

CNN works well on average almost in all cases, and seems to be the least sensitive learner to model selection.

Table 5. Same as Table 2, but with PACC instead of CC.

	IMDB		KINDLE		HP	
	AE	RAE	AE	RAE	AE	RAE
$PACC^{\emptyset}_{SVM}$	0.021	1.166	0.059	2.464	0.137	8.368
$PACC^{A}_{SVM}$	0.021 (-3.2%)	1.215 (+4.3%)	0.065 (+10.0%)	2.893 (+17.4%)	0.106 (-22.8%)	6.425 (-23.2%)
$PACC^{F_1}_{SVM}$	0.021 (-3.4%)	1.202 (+3.1%)	0.066 (+11.4%)	2.979 (+20.9%)	0.148 (+8.2%)	8.723 (+4.2%)
$PACC^{AE}_{SVM}$	0.022 (+5.1%)	1.363 (+17.0%)	0.059 (-1.4%)	2.333 (-5.3%)	0.114 (-16.6%)	7.497 (-10.4%)
$PACC^{\emptyset}_{LR}$	0.017	0.846	0.064	2.456	0.119	9.639
$PACC^{A}_{LR}$	0.021 (+22.0%)	1.087 (+28.4%)	0.053 (-16.7%)	2.177 (-11.4%)	0.147 (+23.1%)	8.316 (-13.7%)
$PACC^{F_1}_{LR}$	0.021 (+24.5%)	1.176 (+39.0%)	0.065 (+2.2%)	2.060 (-16.1%)	0.091 (-23.2%)	7.748 (-19.6%)
$PACC^{AE}_{LR}$	0.021 (+26.5%)	1.237 (+46.3%)	0.068 (+5.5%)	2.253 (-8.3%)	0.104 (-12.3%)	8.812 (-8.6%)
$PACC^{\emptyset}_{RF}$	0.030	1.221	0.074	2.923	0.168	10.322
$PACC^{A}_{RF}$	0.022 (-28.4%)	0.877 (-28.2%)	0.082 (+10.4%)	3.367 (+15.2%)	0.180 (+7.1%)	11.095 (+7.5%)
$PACC^{F_1}_{RF}$	0.021 (-29.8%)	0.952 (-22.0%)	0.079 (+6.9%)	3.331 (+13.9%)	0.160 (-5.1%)	10.350 (+0.3%)
$PACC^{AE}_{RF}$	0.020 (-33.2%)	0.914 (-25.1%)	0.081 (+8.9%)	3.286 (+12.4%)	0.140 (-17.1%)	10.067 (-2.5%)
$PACC^{\emptyset}_{MNB}$	0.055	3.253	0.180	7.352	0.195	10.930
$PACC^{A}_{MND}$	0.058 (+4.8%)	3.412 (+4.9%)	0.130 (-27.7%)	6.058 (-17.6%)	0.335 (+71.6%)	17.883 (+63.6%)
$PACC^{F_1}_{MNB}$	0.060 (+8.1%)	3.487 (+7.2%)	0.122 (-32.2%)	5.570 (-24.2%)	0.363 (+86.0%)	18.138 (+65.9%)
$PACC^{AE}_{MNB}$	0.063 (+14.9%)	3.815 (+17.3%)	0.144 (-19.6%)	6.626 (-9.9%)	0.248 (+27.2%)	13.999 (+28.1%)
$PACC^{\emptyset}_{CNN}$	0.022	1.205	0.064	1.414	0.181	9.808
$PACC^{A}_{CNN}$	0.019 (-11.1%)	0.970 (-19.5%)	0.079 (+23.0%)	1.664 (+17.7%)	0.161 (-11.3%)	9.293 (-5.3%)
$PACC^{F_1}_{CNN}$	0.019 (-14.4%)	0.928 (-23.0%)	0.073 (+13.0%)	1.464 (+3.5%)	0.169 (-6.5%)	9.034 (-7.9%)
$PACC^{AE}_{CNN}$	0.018 (-17.3%)	0.830 (31.2%)	0.069 (+6.9%)	1.367 (-3.3%)	0.165 (-9.1%)	8.829 (-10.0%)

In order to better understand whether or not, on average and across different situations, CC and its variants benefit from performing model selection using a quantification-oriented loss, we have submitted our results to a statistical significance test. Table 6 shows the outcome of a two-sided t-test on *related* sets of scores, across datasets and learners, from which we can compare pairs of model selection methods. The test reveals that optimising AE works better than

Table 6. Two-sided t-test results on *related* samples of error scores across datasets and learners. For a pair of optimization measures X vs. Y, symbol ≫ (resp. >) indicates that method X performs better (i.e., yields lower error) than Y, and that the difference in performance, as averaged across pairs of experiments on all datasets and learners, is statistically significant at a confidence score of $\alpha = 0.001$ (resp. $\alpha = 0.05$). Symbols ≪ and < have a similar meaning but indicate that X performs worse (i.e., yields higher error) than Y. Symbol ~ instead indicates that the differences in performance between X and Y are not statistically significantly different, i.e., that p-value ≥ 0.05.

	CC		ACC		PCC		PACC	
	AE	RAE	AE	RAE	AE	RAE	AE	RAE
AE vs F_1	≫	~	≪	≪	≫	≪	≫	≫
AE vs A	≫	≫	≫	>	≫	≫	≫	≫
AE vs $\emptyset$	≫	≫	≫	≫	≫	≫	≫	~
F_1 vs A	≫	≫	≫	≫	≫	≫	~	~
F_1 vs $\emptyset$	≫	≫	≫	≫	≫	≫	≪	≪
A vs $\emptyset$	≫	≫	≫	≫	≫	≫	≪	≪

Table 7. Results showing how CC and its variants, once optimised using a quantification-oriented measure, compare with more modern quantification methods. **Boldface** indicates the best method. For columns AE and RAE, the best/worst results are highlighted in bright green/red; the colour for the other scores is a linearly interpolation between these two extremes. For columns r_{AE} and r_{RAE}, green/red is used to denote methods which have obtained higher/lower rank positions once the CC variants have been optimised for AE, with respect to the case in which they have not been optimised at all. All scores are different, in a statistically significant sense, from the best one according to a paired sample, two-tailed t-test at a confidence level of 0.001.

	IMDB		KINDLE		HP		IMDB		KINDLE		HP	
	AE	RAE	AE	RAE	AE	RAE	r_{AE}	r_{RAE}	r_{AE}	r_{RAE}	r_{AE}	r_{RAE}
CC_{SVM}^{AE}	0.065	6.091	0.100	7.555	0.119	10.593	20 (20)	20 (20)	13 (21)	15 (21)	8 (22)	11 (20)
ACC_{SVM}^{AE}	0.020	0.933	0.069	3.193	0.108	7.225	7 (8)	7 (6)	8 (6)	9 (9)	5 (16)	4 (15)
PCC_{SVM}^{AE}	0.100	9.484	0.254	14.461	0.386	20.607	25 (23)	25 (23)	24 (19)	24 (20)	21 (17)	22 (18)
$PACC_{SVM}^{AE}$	0.022	1.363	0.059	2.333	0.114	7.497	9 (6)	11 (7)	3 (3)	7 (7)	7 (5)	5 (3)
CC_{LR}^{AE}	0.062	5.745	0.094	7.087	0.110	10.304	14 (14)	15 (14)	12 (26)	14 (26)	6 (29)	10 (28)
ACC_{LR}^{AE}	0.018	0.850	0.065	2.891	0.092	5.849	4 (2)	5 (3)	4 (20)	8 (17)	3 (28)	3 (27)
PCC_{LR}^{AE}	0.079	7.348	0.154	13.066	0.211	19.597	22 (25)	22 (25)	19 (22)	22 (22)	16 (21)	20 (22)
$PACC_{LR}^{AE}$	0.021	1.237	0.068	2.253	0.104	8.812	8 (3)	10 (4)	5 (4)	6 (6)	4 (3)	6 (5)
CC_{RF}^{AE}	0.079	7.487	0.464	23.721	0.500	25.487	23 (26)	23 (26)	29 (25)	28 (24)	29 (24)	29 (23)
ACC_{RF}^{AE}	0.019	0.554	0.197	6.057	0.499	25.436	5 (11)	3 (11)	21 (14)	11 (10)	27 (19)	26 (19)
PCC_{RF}^{AE}	0.196	18.565	0.366	21.088	0.462	24.379	28 (28)	28 (28)	25 (23)	26 (23)	24 (20)	24 (21)
$PACC_{RF}^{AE}$	0.020	0.914	0.081	3.286	0.140	10.067	6 (10)	6 (10)	10 (9)	10 (8)	10 (6)	9 (7)
CC_{MNB}^{AE}	0.097	8.431	0.443	22.701	0.499	25.464	24 (22)	24 (22)	28 (29)	27 (29)	28 (26)	28 (29)
ACC_{MNB}^{AE}	0.051	2.591	0.213	10.376	0.451	23.146	12 (12)	12 (12)	23 (27)	20 (25)	23 (27)	23 (26)
PCC_{MNB}^{AE}	0.160	14.907	0.380	20.396	0.473	24.479	27 (27)	27 (27)	26 (28)	25 (27)	25 (25)	25 (25)
$PACC_{MNB}^{AE}$	0.063	3.815	0.144	6.626	0.248	13.999	16 (13)	13 (13)	16 (17)	12 (12)	19 (10)	17 (9)
CC_{CNN}^{AE}	0.074	6.613	0.109	8.591	0.343	19.008	21 (21)	21 (21)	14 (11)	17 (14)	20 (14)	19 (14)
ACC_{CNN}^{AE}	0.023	1.072	0.068	1.399	0.174	10.810	10 (5)	8 (5)	6 (8)	3 (3)	13 (7)	12 (8)
PCC_{CNN}^{AE}	0.145	11.146	0.148	14.017	0.156	14.644	26 (24)	26 (24)	17 (12)	23 (18)	11 (15)	18 (16)
$PACC_{CNN}^{AE}$	0.018	0.830	0.069	1.367	0.165	8.829	2 (7)	4 (9)	7 (5)	2 (2)	12 (8)	7 (6)
SLD_{LR}^{AE}	**0.014**	**0.216**	**0.048**	1.606	**0.042**	**0.195**	1 (1)	1 (1)	1 (1)	4 (4)	1 (1)	1 (1)
$SVM(KLD)^{AE}$	0.064	5.936	0.122	7.866	0.185	12.185	18 (18)	18 (18)	15 (13)	16 (13)	14 (9)	14 (11)
$SVM(NKLD)^{AE}$	0.065	5.927	0.085	6.693	0.121	9.566	19 (19)	16 (16)	11 (10)	13 (11)	9 (4)	8 (4)
$SVM(Q)^{AE}$	0.064	5.928	0.208	11.384	0.386	19.956	17 (17)	17 (17)	22 (18)	21 (19)	22 (18)	21 (17)
$SVM(AE)^{AE}$	0.060	5.572	0.159	9.705	0.219	13.090	13 (15)	14 (15)	20 (16)	19 (16)	17 (12)	15 (12)
$SVM(RAE)^{RAE}$	0.063	5.957	0.152	9.242	0.239	13.575	15 (16)	19 (19)	18 (15)	18 (15)	18 (13)	16 (13)
HDy_{LR}^{AE}	0.018	0.420	0.055	**1.027**	0.058	2.970	3 (4)	2 (2)	2 (2)	1 (1)	2 (2)	2 (2)
$QuaNet_{CNN}^{AE}$	0.027	1.175	0.070	2.119	0.210	11.433	11 (9)	9 (8)	9 (7)	5 (5)	15 (11)	13 (10)
$MLPE_{\emptyset}$	0.262	24.874	0.429	25.266	0.484	25.447	29 (29)	29 (29)	27 (24)	29 (28)	26 (23)	27 (24)

optimising A or than using default settings ($\emptyset$). The test does not clearly say whether optimising AE or F_1 is better, but it suggests that PACC (the strongest CC variant) works better when optimised for AE than when optimised for F_1.

Finally, Table 7 compares the CC variants against more recent state-of-the-art quantification systems. Columns AE and RAE indicate the error of each method for each dataset. Columns r_{AE} and r_{RAE} show the rank positions for each pair (dataset, error) and, in parentheses, the rank position each method would have obtained in case the CC variants had not been optimised.

Interestingly, although some advanced quantification methods (specifically: SLD and HDy) stand as the top performers, many among the (supposedly more sophisticated) quantification methods fail to improve over CC's performance. At a glance, most quantification methods tend to obtain lower ranks when compared with properly optimised CC variants. Remarkable examples of rank variation include CC and ACC with SVM and LR: when evaluated on KINDLE and HP, they climb several positions (up to 25), often entering the group of the 10 top-performing methods. In the most extreme case, ACC_{LR}^{AE} moves from position 28 (out of 29) to position 3 once properly optimised for quantification.

5   Conclusions

One of the takeaway messages from the present work is that, when using CC and/or its variants as baselines in their research on learning to quantify, researchers should properly optimise these baselines (i.e., use a truly quantification-oriented protocol, which includes the use of a quantification oriented loss, in hyperparameter optimisation), lest these baselines become strawmen. The extensive empirical evaluation we have carried out shows that, in general, the performance of CC and its variants improves when the underlying learner has been optimised with a quantification-oriented loss (AE). The results of our experiments are less clear about whether optimising AE or F_1 (which, despite being a *classification*-oriented loss, is one that rewards classifiers that balance FPs and FNs) is better, although they indicate that optimising AE is preferable for PACC, the strongest among the variants of CC.

Acknowledgments. The present work has been supported by the SoBigData++ project, funded by the European Commission (Grant 871042) under the H2020 Programme INFRAIA-2019-1, and by the AI4Media project, funded by the European Commission (Grant 951911) under the H2020 Programme ICT-48-2020. The authors' opinions do not necessarily reflect those of the European Commission.

References

1. Barranquero, J., Díez, J., del Coz, J.J.: Quantification-oriented learning based on reliable classifiers. Pattern Recognit. **48**(2), 591–604 (2015). https://doi.org/10.1016/j.patcog.2014.07.032
2. Barranquero, J., González, P., Díez, J., del Coz, J.J.: On the study of nearest neighbor algorithms for prevalence estimation in binary problems. Pattern Recognit. **46**(2), 472–482 (2013). https://doi.org/10.1016/j.patcog.2012.07.022
3. Bella, A., Ferri, C., Hernández-Orallo, J., Ramírez-Quintana, M.J.: Quantification via probability estimators. In: Proceedings of the 11th IEEE International Conference on Data Mining (ICDM 2010), Sydney, AU, pp. 737–742 (2010). https://doi.org/10.1109/icdm.2010.75
4. Borge-Holthoefer, J., Magdy, W., Darwish, K., Weber, I.: Content and network dynamics behind Egyptian political polarization on Twitter. In: Proceedings of the 18th ACM Conference on Computer Supported Cooperative Work and Social Computing (CSCW 2015), Vancouver, CA, pp. 700–711 (2015)
5. Card, D., Smith, N.A.: The importance of calibration for estimating proportions from annotations. In: Proceedings of the 2018 Conference of the North American Chapter of the Association for Computational Linguistics (HLT-NAACL 2018), New Orleans, US, pp. 1636–1646 (2018). https://doi.org/10.18653/v1/n18-1148

6. Esuli, A., Molinari, A., Sebastiani, F.: A critical reassessment of the Saerens-Latinne-Decaestecker algorithm for posterior probability adjustment. ACM Trans. Inf. Syst. **19**(2), 1–34 (2020). Article 19, https://doi.org/10.1145/3433164
7. Esuli, A., Moreo, A., Sebastiani, F.: A recurrent neural network for sentiment quantification. In: Proceedings of the 27th ACM International Conference on Information and Knowledge Management (CIKM 2018), Torino, IT, pp. 1775–1778 (2018). https://doi.org/10.1145/3269206.3269287
8. Esuli, A., Moreo, A., Sebastiani, F.: Cross-lingual sentiment quantification. IEEE Intell. Syst. **35**(3), 106–114 (2020). https://doi.org/10.1109/MIS.2020.2979203
9. Esuli, A., Sebastiani, F.: Explicit loss minimization in quantification applications (preliminary draft). In: Proceedings of the 8th International Workshop on Information Filtering and Retrieval (DART 2014), Pisa, IT, pp. 1–11 (2014)
10. Esuli, A., Sebastiani, F.: Optimizing text quantifiers for multivariate loss functions. ACM Trans. Knowl. Discov. Data **9**(4), 1–27 (2015). Article 27, https://doi.org/10.1145/2700406
11. Forman, G.: Quantifying counts and costs via classification. Data Min. Knowl. Discov. **17**(2), 164–206 (2008). https://doi.org/10.1007/s10618-008-0097-y
12. Gao, W., Sebastiani, F.: From classification to quantification in tweet sentiment analysis. Soc. Netw. Anal. Min. **6**(19), 1–22 (2016). https://doi.org/10.1007/s13278-016-0327-z
13. González, P., Castaño, A., Chawla, N.V., del Coz, J.J.: A review on quantification learning. ACM Comput. Surv. **50**(5), 74:1–74:40 (2017). https://doi.org/10.1145/3117807
14. González, P., Díez, J., Chawla, N., del Coz, J.J.: Why is quantification an interesting learning problem? Prog. Artif. Intell. **6**(1), 53–58 (2017). https://doi.org/10.1007/s13748-016-0103-3
15. González-Castro, V., Alaiz-RodríÂguez, R., Alegre, E.: Class distribution estimation based on the Hellinger distance. Inf. Sci. **218**, 146–164 (2013). https://doi.org/10.1016/j.ins.2012.05.028
16. Hassan, W., Maletzke, A., Batista, G.: Accurately quantifying a billion instances per second. In: Proceedings of the 7th IEEE International Conference on Data Science and Advanced Analytics (DSAA 2020), Sydney, AU (2020)
17. Hopkins, D.J., King, G.: A method of automated nonparametric content analysis for social science. Am. J. Polit. Sci. **54**(1), 229–247 (2010). https://doi.org/10.1111/j.1540-5907.2009.00428.x
18. Joachims, T.: A support vector method for multivariate performance measures. In: Proceedings of the 22nd International Conference on Machine Learning (ICML 2005), Bonn, DE, pp. 377–384 (2005)
19. Levin, R., Roitman, H.: Enhanced probabilistic classify and count methods for multi-label text quantification. In: Proceedings of the 7th ACM International Conference on the Theory of Information Retrieval (ICTIR 2017), Amsterdam, NL, pp. 229–232 (2017). https://doi.org/10.1145/3121050.3121083
20. Maas, A.L., Daly, R.E., Pham, P.T., Huang, D., Ng, A.Y., Potts, C.: Learning word vectors for sentiment analysis. In: Proceedings of the 49th Annual Meeting of the Association for Computational Linguistics (ACL 2011), Portland, US, pp. 142–150 (2011)
21. Milli, L., Monreale, A., Rossetti, G., Giannotti, F., Pedreschi, D., Sebastiani, F.: Quantification trees. In: Proceedings of the 13th IEEE International Conference on Data Mining (ICDM 2013), Dallas, US, pp. 528–536 (2013). https://doi.org/10.1109/icdm.2013.122

22. Moreno-Torres, J.G., Raeder, T., Alaíz-Rodríguez, R., Chawla, N.V., Herrera, F.: A unifying view on dataset shift in classification. Pattern Recognit. **45**(1), 521–530 (2012). https://doi.org/10.1016/j.patcog.2011.06.019
23. Morik, K., Brockhausen, P., Joachims, T.: Combining statistical learning with a knowledge-based approach. A case study in intensive care monitoring. In: Proceedings of the 16th International Conference on Machine Learning (ICML 1999), Bled, SL, pp. 268–277 (1999)
24. Platt, J.C.: Probabilistic outputs for support vector machines and comparison to regularized likelihood methods. In: Smola, A., Bartlett, P., Schölkopf, B., Schuurmans, D. (eds.) Advances in Large Margin Classifiers, pp. 61–74. The MIT Press, Cambridge (2000)
25. Pérez-Gállego, P., Castaño, A., Quevedo, J.R., del Coz, J.J.: Dynamic ensemble selection for quantification tasks. Inf. Fusion **45**, 1–15 (2019). https://doi.org/10.1016/j.inffus.2018.01.001
26. Pérez-Gállego, P., Quevedo, J.R., del Coz, J.J.: Using ensembles for problems with characterizable changes in data distribution: a case study on quantification. Inf. Fusion **34**, 87–100 (2017). https://doi.org/10.1016/j.inffus.2016.07.001
27. Saerens, M., Latinne, P., Decaestecker, C.: Adjusting the outputs of a classifier to new a priori probabilities: a simple procedure. Neural Comput. **14**(1), 21–41 (2002). https://doi.org/10.1162/089976602753284446
28. Sebastiani, F.: Evaluation measures for quantification: an axiomatic approach. Inf. Retr. J. **23**(3), 255–288 (2020). https://doi.org/10.1007/s10791-019-09363-y

Reproducibility, Replicability and Beyond: Assessing Production Readiness of Aspect Based Sentiment Analysis in the Wild

Rajdeep Mukherjee[1]([✉]), Shreyas Shetty[2], Subrata Chattopadhyay[1],
Subhadeep Maji[3], Samik Datta[3], and Pawan Goyal[1]

[1] Indian Institute of Technology Kharagpur, Kharagpur, India
rajdeep1989@iitkgp.ac.in, pawang@cse.iitkgp.ac.in
[2] Flipkart Internet Private Limited, Bengaluru, India
shreyas.shetty@flipkart.com
[3] Amazon India Private Limited, Bengaluru, India

Abstract. With the exponential growth of online marketplaces and user-generated content therein, aspect-based sentiment analysis has become more important than ever. In this work, we critically review a representative sample of the models published during the past six years through the lens of a practitioner, with an eye towards deployment in production. First, our rigorous empirical evaluation reveals poor reproducibility: an average 4–5% drop in test accuracy across the sample. Second, to further bolster our confidence in empirical evaluation, we report experiments on two challenging data slices, and observe a consistent 12–55% drop in accuracy. Third, we study the possibility of transfer across domains and observe that as little as 10–25% of the domain-specific training dataset, when used in conjunction with datasets from other domains within the same locale, largely closes the gap between complete cross-domain and complete in-domain predictive performance. Lastly, we open-source two large-scale annotated review corpora from a large e-commerce portal in India in order to aid the study of replicability and transfer, with the hope that it will fuel further growth of the field.

Keywords: Aspect based sentiment analysis · Aspect polarity detection · Reproducibility · Replicability · Transferability

1 Introduction

In recent times, online marketplaces of goods and services have witnessed an exponential growth in terms of consumers and producers, and have proliferated in a wide spectrum of market segments, such as e-commerce, food delivery,

R. Mukherjee and S. Shetty—Equal contribution.
S. Maji and S. Datta—Work done while at Flipkart.

D. Hiemstra et al. (Eds.): ECIR 2021, LNCS 12657, pp. 92–106, 2021.
https://doi.org/10.1007/978-3-030-72240-1_7

healthcare, ride sharing, travel and hospitality, to name a few. The Indian e-commerce market segment alone is projected to grow to 300–350M consumers and \$100–120B revenue by 2025[1]. In the face of ever-expanding choices, purchase decision-making is guided by the reviews and ratings: Watson et al. [29] estimates that the average product rating is the most important factor in making purchase decisions for 60% of consumers. Similarly, the academic research on Aspect Based Sentiment Analysis (ABSA) has come a long way since its humble beginning in the SemEval-2014[2]. Over the past 6 years, the accuracy on a benchmark dataset for *aspect term polarity* has grown by at least 11.4%. We ask, is this progress enough to support the burgeoning online marketplaces?

We argue on the contrary. On one hand, industrial-strength systems need to demonstrate several traits for smooth operation and delightful consumer experience. Breck et al. [1] articulates several essential traits and presents a rubric of evaluation. Notable traits include: (a) "All hyperparameters have been tuned"; (b) "A simpler model is not better"; (c) "Training is reproducible"; and (d) "Model quality is sufficient on important data slices". On the other hand, recent academic research in several fields has faced criticisms from within the community on similar grounds: Dhillon et al. [6] points out the inadequacy of benchmark dataset and protocol for few-shot image classification; Dacrema et al. [4] criticises the recent trend in recommendation systems research on the ground of lack of reproducibility and violations of (a)–(c) above; Li et al. [14] criticises the recent trend in information retrieval research on similar grounds. A careful examination of the recent research we conduct in this work reveals that the field of ABSA is not free from these follies.

To this end, it is instructive to turn our attention to classic software engineering with the hope of borrowing from its proven safe development practises. Notably, Kang et al. [10] advocates the use of *model assertions* – an abstraction to monitor and improve model performance during the development phase. Along similar lines, Ribeiro et al. [20] presents a methodology of large-scale comprehensive testing for NLP, and notes its effectiveness in identifying bugs in several (commercial) NLP libraries, that would not have been discovered had we been relying solely on test set accuracy. In this work, in addition to the current practice of reporting test set accuracies, we report performance on two challenging data slices – e.g., *hard set* [31], and, *contrast set* [7] – to further bolster the comprehensiveness of empirical evaluation.

For widespread adoption, data efficiency is an important consideration in real-world deployment scenarios. As an example, a large e-commerce marketplace in India operates in tens of thousands of categories, and a typical annotation cost is 3¢ per review. In this work, we introduce and open-source two additional large-scale datasets curated from product reviews in lifestyle and appliance categories to aid replicability of research and study of transfer across domains and locales (text with similar social/linguistic characteristics). In particular, we note that

---

[1] *How India Shops Online* – Flipkart and Bain & Company.
[2] SemEval-2014 Task 4.

just a small fraction of the in-domain training dataset, mixed with existing in-locale cross-domain training datasets, guarantees comparable test set accuracies.

In summary, we make the following notable contributions:

- Perform a thorough reproducibility study of models sampled from a public leaderboard[3] that reveals a consistent 4–5% drop in reported test set accuracies, which is often larger than the gap in performance between the winner and the runner-up.
- Consistent with the practices developed in software engineering, we bolster the empirical evaluation rigour by introducing two challenging data slices that demonstrates an average 12–55% drop in test set accuracies.
- We study the models from the perspective of data efficiency and note that as little as 10–25% of the domain-specific training dataset, when used in conjunction with existing cross-domain datasets from within the same locale, largely closes the gap in terms of test set accuracies between complete cross-domain training and using 100% of the domain-specific training instances. This observation has immense implications towards reduction of annotation cost and widespread adoption of models.
- We curate two additional datasets from product reviews in lifestyle and appliances categories sampled from a large e-commerce marketplace in India, and make them publicly accessible to enable the study of replicability.

2   Desiderata and Evaluation Rubric

Reproducibility and replicability have been considered the gold-standard in academic research and has witnessed a recent resurgence in emphasis across scientific disciplines: see for e.g., McArthur et al. [18] in the context of biological sciences and Stevens et al. [23] in the context of psychology. We follow the nomenclature established in [23] and define *reproducibility* as the ability to obtain same experimental results when a different analyst uses an identical experimental setup. On the other hand, *replicability*, is achieved when the same experimental setup is used on a different dataset to similar effect. While necessary, these two traits are far from sufficient for widespread deployment in production.

Breck et al. [1] lists a total of 28 traits spanning the entire development and deployment life cycle. Since our goal is only to assess the production readiness of a class of models. We decide to forego all 14 data-, feature- and monitoring-related traits. We borrow 1 ("Training is reproducible") and 2 ("All hyperparameters have been tuned" and "Model quality is sufficient on important data slices") traits from the infrastructure- and modeling-related rubrics, respectively.

Further, we note that the ability to transfer across domains/locales is a desirable trait, given the variety of market segments and the geographic span of online marketplaces. In other words, this expresses data efficiency and has implications towards lowering the annotation cost and associated deployment hurdles. Given the desiderata, we articulate our production readiness rubric as follows:

---

[3] *Papers With Code*: ABSA on SemEval 2014 Task 4 Sub Task 2.

- *Reproducibility.* A sound experimental protocol that minimises variability across runs and avoids common pitfalls (e.g., hyperparameter-tuning on the test dataset itself) should reproduce the reported test set accuracy within a reasonable tolerance, not exceeding the reported performance gap between the winner and the runner-up in a leaderboard. Section 6 articulates the proposed experimental protocol and Sect. 7 summarises the ensuing observations.
- *Replicability.* The aforementioned experimental protocol, when applied to a different dataset, should not dramatically alter the conclusions drawn from the original experiment; specifically, it should not alter the relative positions within the leaderboard. Section 4 details two new datasets we contribute in order to aid the study of replicability, whereas Sect. 7 contains the ensuing observations.
- *Performance.* Besides overall test-set accuracy, an algorithm should excel at challenging data slices such as hard- [31] and contrast sets [7]. Section 7 summarises our findings when this checklist is adopted as a standard reporting practice.
- *Transferability.* An algorithm must transfer gracefully across domains within the same locale, i.e. textual data with similar social/linguistic characteristics. We measure it by varying the percentage of in-domain training instances from 0% to 100% and locating the inflection point in test set accuracies. See Sect. 7 for additional details.

Note that apart from the "The model is debuggable" and "A simpler model is not better" traits, the remaining traits as defined by Breck et al. [1] are independent of the choice of the algorithm and is solely a property of the underlying system that embodies it, which is beyond the scope of the present study. Unlike [1], we refrain from developing a numerical scoring system.

3   Related Work

First popularised in the SemEval-2014 Task 4 [19], ABSA has enjoyed immense attention from both academic and industrial research communities. Over the past 6 years, according to the cited literature on a public leaderboard[4], the performance for the subtask of *Aspect Term Polarity* has increased from 70.48% in Pontiki et al. [19], corresponding to the winning entry, to 82.29% in Yang et al. [32] on the laptop review corpus. The restaurant review corpus has witnessed a similar boost in performance: from 80.95% in [19] to 90.18% in [32].

Not surprisingly, the field has witnessed a phase change in terms of the methodology: custom feature engineering and ensembles that frequented earlier [19] gave way to neural networks of ever-increasing complexity. Apart from this macro-trend, we notice several micro-trends in the literature: the year 2015 witnessed a proliferation of LSTM and its variants [24]; years 2016 and 2017 respectively witnessed the introduction [25] and proliferation [2,3,16,26] of memory networks and associated attention mechanisms; in 2018 research focused on

---

[4] *Papers With Code*: ABSA on SemEval 2014 Task 4 Sub Task 2.

CNN [31], transfer learning [13] and transformers [12], while memory networks and attention mechanisms remained in spotlight [9,11,15,27]; transformer and BERT-based models prevailed in 2019 [30,33], while attention mechanisms continued to remain mainstream [22].

While these developments appear to have pushed the envelope of performance, the field has been fraught with "winner's curse" [21]. In addition to the replicability and reproducibility crises [18,23], criticisms around inadequacy of baseline and unjustified complexity [4,6,14] applies to this field as well. The practice of reporting performance in challenging data slices [31] has not been adopted uniformly, despite its importance to production readiness assessment [1]. Similarly, the study of transferability and replicability has only been sporadically performed: e.g., Hu et al. [8] uses a dataset curated from Twitter along with the ones introduced in Pontiki et al. [19] for studying cross-domain transferability.

4   Dataset

For the *Reproducibility* rubric, we consider the datasets released as part of the SemEval 2014 Task 4 - Aspect Based Sentiment Analysis[5] for our experiments, specifically the Subtask 2 - Aspect term Polarity. The datasets come from two domains – Laptop and Restaurant. We use their versions made available in this Github[6] repository which forms the basis of our experimental setup.

The guidelines used for annotating the datasets were released as part of the challenge. For the *Replicability* rubric, we tagged two new datasets from the e-commerce domain viz., Men's T-shirt and Television, using similar guidelines.

The statistics for these four datasets are presented in Table 1. As we can observe, the sizes of the Men's T-shirt and Television datasets are comparable to the laptop and restaurant datasets, respectively.

Table 1. Statistics of the datasets showing the no. of sentences with corresponding sentiment polarities of constituent aspect terms.

Dataset	Train				Test			
	Positive	Negative	Neutral	Total	Positive	Negative	Neutral	Total
Laptop	994	870	464	2328	341	128	169	638
Restaurant	2164	807	637	3608	728	196	196	1120
Men's T-shirt	1122	699	50	1871	270	186	16	472
Television	2540	919	287	3746	618	257	67	942

For the *Performance* rubric, we evaluate and compare the models on two challenging subsets viz., *hard* as defined by Xue et al. [31] and *contrast* as defined by Gardner et al. [7]. We describe below the process to obtain these datasets:

---

[5] SemEval 2014: Task 4 http://alt.qcri.org/semeval2014/task4/.

[6] https://github.com/songyouwei/ABSA-PyTorch.

Table 2. Statistics of the Hard test sets

Dataset	Positive	Negative	Neutral	Total (% of Test Set)
Laptop	31	24	46	101 (15.8%)
Restaurants	81	60	83	224 (20.0%)
Men's T-shirt	23	24	1	48 (10.2%)
Television	43	40	19	102 (10.8%)

– **Hard data slice:** Hard examples have been defined in Xue et al. [31] as the subset of review sentences containing multiple aspects with different corresponding sentiment polarities. The number of such hard examples from each of the datasets are listed in Table 2.
– **Contrast data slice:** In order to create additional test examples, Gardner et al. [7] adds perturbations to the test set, by modifying only a couple of words to flip the sentiment corresponding to the aspect under consideration. For e.g., consider the review sentence: "I was happy with their service and food". If we change the word "happy" with "dissatisfied", the sentiment corresponding to the aspect "food" changes from positive to negative. We take a random sample of 30 examples from each of the datasets and add similar perturbations as above to create 30 additional examples. These 60 examples for each of the four datasets thus serve as our contrast test sets.

5   Models Compared

As part of our evaluation, we focus on two families of models which cover the major trends in the ABSA research community: (i) memory network based, and (ii) BERT based. Among the initial set of models for the SemEval 14 challenge, memory network based models had much fewer parameters compared to LSTM based approaches and performed comparatively better. With the introduction of BERT [5], work in NLP has focused on leveraging BERT based architectures for a wide spectrum of tasks. In the ABSA literature, the leaderboard[7] has been dominated by BERT based models, which have orders of magnitude more parameters than memory network based models. However, due to pre-training on large corpora, BERT models are still very data efficient in terms of number of labelled examples required. We chose three representative models from each family for our experiments and briefly describe them below:

– **ATAE-LSTM** [28] represents aspects using target embeddings and models the context words using an LSTM. The context word representations and target embeddings are concatenated and combined using an attention layer.

---

[7] https://paperswithcode.com/sota/aspect-based-sentiment-analysis-on-semeval.

- **Recurrent Attention on Memory (RAM)** [2] represents the input review sentence using a memory network, and the memory cells are weighted using the distance from the target word. The aspect representation is then used to compute attention scores on the input memory, and the attention weighted memory is refined iteratively using a GRU (recurrent) network.
- **Interactive Attention Networks (IAN)** [17] uses separate components for computing representations for both the target (aspect) and the context words. The representations are pooled and then used to compute an attention score on each other. Finally the individual attention weighted representations are concatenated to obtain the final representation for the 3-way classification task, with *positive*, *negative*, and *neutral* being the three classes.
- **BERT-SPC** [5] is a baseline BERT model that uses "[CLS] + context + [SEP] + target + [SEP]" as input for the sentence pair classification task, where '[CLS]' and '[SEP]' represent the tokens corresponding to *classification* and *separator* symbols respectively, as defined in Devlin et al. [5].
- **BERT-AEN** [22] uses an attentional encoder network to model the semantic interaction between the context and the target words. Its loss function uses a label smoothing regularization to avoid overfitting.
- **The Local Context Focus (LCF-BERT)** [33] is based on Multi-head Self-Attention (MHSA). It uses Context features Dynamic Mask (CDM) and Context features Dynamic Weighted (CDW) layers to focus more on the local context words. A BERT-shared layer is adopted to LCF design to capture internal long-term dependencies of local and global context.

6 Experimental Setup

We present an extensive evaluation of the aforementioned models across the four datasets: Laptops, Restaurants, Men's T-shirt and Television, as per the production readiness rubrics defined in Sect. 2. While trying to reproduce the reported results for the models, we faced two major issues; (i) the official implementations were not readily available, and (ii) the exact hyperparameter configurations were not always specified in the corresponding paper(s). In order to address the first, our experimental setup is based on a community designed implementation of recent papers available on GitHub[8]. Our choice for this public repository is guided by its thoroughness and ease of experimentation. As an additional social validation, the repository had 1.1k stars and 351 forks on GitHub at the time of writing. For addressing the second concern, we consider the following options; (a) use commonly accepted default parameters (for e.g., using a learning rate of $1e^{-4}$ for Adam optimizer). (b) use the public implementations to guide the choice of hyperparameters. The exact hyperparameter settings used in our experiments are documented and made available with our supporting code repository[9] for further reproducibility and replicability of results.

---

[8] https://github.com/songyouwei/ABSA-PyTorch.
[9] https://github.com/rajdeep345/ABSA-Reproducibility.

From the corresponding experimental protocols described in the original paper(s), we were not sure if the final numbers reported were based on the training epoch that gave the best performance on the test set, or whether the hyperparameters were tuned on a separate held-out set. Therefore, we use the following two configurations; (i) the test set is itself used as the held out set, and the model used for reporting the results is chosen corresponding to the training epoch with best performance on the test set; and (ii) 15% of the training data is set aside as a held out set for tuning the hyperparameters and the optimal training epoch is decided corresponding to the best performance on the held out set. Finally the model is re-trained, this time with all the training data (including 15% held out set), for the optimal no of epochs before evaluating the test set. For both the cases, we report mean scores over 5 runs of our experiments.

7   Results and Discussion: Production Readiness Rubrics

7.1   Reproducibility and Replicability

Tables 3(a) and 3(b) show our *reproducibility* study for the Laptop and Restaurant datasets, respectively. For both the datasets, we notice a consistent 1–2% drop in accuracy and macro-f1 scores when we try to reproduce the reported numbers in the corresponding papers. Only exceptions were LCF-BERT for Laptop and BERT-SPC for Restaurant dataset, where we got higher numbers than the reported ones. For ATAE-LSTM, the drop observed was much larger than other models. We notice an additional 1–2% drop in accuracy when we use 15% of the training set as a held-out set to pick the best model. These numbers indicate that the actual performance of the models is likely to be slightly worse than what is quoted in the papers, and the drop sometimes is larger than the difference between the performance of two consecutive methods on the leaderboard.

To study the *replicability*, Tables 3(c) and 3(d) summarise the performance of the individual models on the Men's T-shirt and Television datasets, respectively. We introduce these datasets for the first time and report the performance of all 6 models under the two defined configurations: test set as held out set, and 15% of train set used as held out set. We notice a similar drop in performance when we follow the correct experimental procedure (hyperparameter tuning on 15% train data as held-out set). Therefore, following a consistent and rigorous experimental protocol helps us to get a better sense of the true model performance.

7.2   Performance on the Hard and Contrast Data Slices

As per the *performance* rubric, we investigate the performance of all 6 models on both *hard* and *contrast* test sets, using the correct experimental setting (15% train data as held out set). The results are shown in brackets (in same order) in the last two columns of Tables 3(a), 3(b), 3(c), and 3(d) for the four datasets, respectively. We observe a large drop in performance on both these challenging data slices across models. LCF-BERT consistently performs very well on these test sets. Among memory network based models, RAM performs the best.

Table 3. Performance of the models on the four datasets. The first two dataset correspond to the reproducibility study, while the next two datasets correspond to the replicability study. Towards performance study, results on the hard and contrast data slices are respectively enclosed in brackets in the last two columns. All the reproduced and replicated results are averaged across 5 runs.

Model	Reported		Reproduced		Reproduced using 15% held out set	
	Accuracy	Macro-F1	Accuracy	Macro-F1	Accuracy	Macro-F1
ATAE-LSTM	68.70	-	60.28	44.33	58.62 (33.47, 26.00)	43.27 (29.01, 22.00)
RAM	74.49	71.35	72.82	68.34	70.97 (56.04, 46.00)	65.31 (55.81, 43.16)
IAN	72.10	-	69.94	62.84	69.40 (48.91, 34.67)	61.98 (48.75, 33.40)
BERT-SPC	78.99	75.03	78.72	74.52	77.24 (59.21, 52.00)	72.80 (59.44, 48.67)
BERT-AEN	79.93	76.31	78.65	74.26	75.71 (46.53, 37.33)	70.02 (45.22, 36.20)
LCF-BERT	77.31	75.58	79.75	76.10	77.27 (62.57, 54.67)	72.86 (62.71, 49.56)

(a) Laptop

Model	Reported		Reproduced		Reproduced using 15% held out set	
	Accuracy	Macro-F1	Accuracy	Macro-F1	Accuracy	Macro-F1
ATAE-LSTM	77.20	-	73.71	55.87	73.29 (52.41, 38.71)	54.59 (47.35, 33.13)
RAM	80.23	70.80	78.21	65.94	76.36 (59.29, 56.77)	63.15 (56.36, 56.12)
IAN	78.60	-	76.80	64.24	76.52 (57.05, 50.32)	63.84 (55.11, 48.19)
BERT-SPC	84.46	76.98	85.04	78.02	84.23 (68.84, 57.42)	76.28 (68.11, 57.23)
BERT-AEN	83.12	73.76	81.73	71.24	80.07 (51.70, 45.81)	69.80 (48.97, 46.88)
LCF-BERT	87.14	81.74	85.94	78.97	84.20 (69.38, 56.77)	76.28 (69.64, 57.81)

(b) Restaurant

Model	Replicated		Replicated using 15% held out set	
	Accuracy	Macro-F1	Accuracy	Macro-F1
ATAE-LSTM	83.13	55.98	81.65 (58.33, 40.67)	54.84 (39.25, 30.54)
RAM	90.51	61.93	88.26 (83.33, 46.00)	59.67 (56.01, 33.85)
IAN	87.58	59.16	87.41 (63.75, 42.67)	58.97 (42.85, 31.94)
BERT-SPC	93.13	73.86	92.42 (89.58, 66.00)	73.83 (60.62, 56.90)
BERT-AEN	88.69	72.25	87.54 (50.42, 58.67)	59.14 (32.96, 43.00)
LCF-BERT	93.35	72.19	91.99 (91.67, 71.33)	72.13 (62.30, 59.70)

(c) Men's T-shirt

Model	Replicated		Replicated using 15% held out set	
	Accuracy	Macro-F1	Accuracy	Macro-F1
ATAE-LSTM	81.10	53.71	79.68 (53.92, 25.33)	52.78 (39.13, 16.80)
RAM	84.29	58.68	83.02 (64.31, 53.33)	58.50 (50.07, 45.51)
IAN	82.42	57.15	80.49 (54.31, 32.00)	56.78 (41.67, 25.16)
BERT-SPC	89.96	74.68	88.56 (80.20, 62.67)	74.81 (74.32, 60.25)
BERT-AEN	87.09	67.92	85.94 (50.39, 50.66)	65.65 (38.08, 45.75)
LCF-BERT	90.36	76.01	90.00 (80.98, 66.67)	75.86 (73.72, 64.15)

(d) Television

7.3 Transferability Rubric: Cross Domain Experiments

In a production readiness setting, it is very likely that we will not have enough labelled data across individual categories and hence it is important to understand how well the models are able to transfer across domains. To understand the transferability of models across datasets, we first experiment with cross domain combinations. For each experiment, we fix the test set (for e.g., Laptop) and train three separate models, each with one of the other three datasets as training sets (Restaurant, Men's T-shirt, and Television in this case). Consistent with our experimental settings, for each such combination, we use 15% of the cross-domain data as held-out set for hyperparameter tuning, re-train the corresponding models with all the cross-domain data and obtain the scores for the in-domain set (here Laptop) averaged across 5 different runs of the experiment.

Table 4. Transferability: Average drop between in-domain and cross-domain accuracies for each dataset pair for (a) BERT based and (b) Memory network based models. Rows correspond to the train set. Columns correspond to the test set.

	Laptop	Restaurant	Men's T-shirt	Television
Laptop	0	4.50	3.84	3.53
Restaurant	2.17	0	3.49	3.68
Men's T-shirt	9.59	7.57	0	2.00
Television	3.85	5.65	2.08	0

(a) BERT based models

	Laptop	Restaurant	Men's T-shirt	Television
Laptop	0	7.18	15.75	9.89
Restaurant	5.29	0	10.7	10.3
Men's T-shirt	8.34	10.02	0	3.48
Television	4.5	7.5	6.77	0

(b) Memory network based models

Table 4 summarises the results averaged across the BERT-based models and Memory network based models, respectively on the four datasets. The rows and columns correspond to the train and test sets, respectively. The diagonals correspond to the in-domain experiments (denoted by 0) and each off-diagonal entry denotes the average drop in model performance for the cross-domain setting compared to the in-domain combination.

From Table 4 we observe that on an average the models are able to generalize well across the following combinations, which correspond to a lower drop in the cross domain experiments: (i) Laptops and Restaurants, and (ii) Men's T-shirt and Television. For instance, when testing on the Restaurant dataset, BERT based and memory network based models respectively show an average of ∼4 and ∼7 point absolute drops in % accuracies, when trained using the Laptop dataset. The drops are higher for the other two training sets. Interestingly, the generalization is more pronounced across locales rather than domains, contrary to what one would have expected. For e.g., we notice better transfer from Men's T-shirt → Television (similarity in locale) than in the expected Laptop → Television (similarity in domain). Given that our task is that of detecting sentiment polarities of aspect terms, this observation might be attributed to the similarity in social/linguistic characteristics of reviews from the same locale.

Further, in the spirit of *transferability*, we consider the closely related locales as identified above – {Laptop, Restaurant} and {Men's T-shirt, Television}, and conduct experiments to understand the incremental benefits of adding in-domain data on top of cross domain data, i.e., what fraction of the in-domain training instances can help to cover the gap between purely in-domain and purely

Table 5. Transferability: Results on including incremental in-domain training data. The rows correspond to cross-domain performance (0), adding 10%, 25% and 50% in-domain dataset to the cross-domain. To improve illustration, we repeat in-domain results. Inflection points for each dataset are boldfaced.

% in-domain	Laptop	Restaurant	Men's T-shirt	Television
0	74.6 (73.6, 74.6, 75.5)	78.3 (77.3, 77.8, 79.9)	88.6 (86.3, 89.6, 89.8)	86.1 (83.5, 87.5, 87.4)
10	**76.5** (73.9, 76.6, 78.9)	**81.6** (80.1, 81.5, 83.3)	88.9 (85.7, 90.6, 90.4)	83.8 (82.0, 86.1, 83.2)
25	76.3 (74.8, 77.0, 77.0)	82.1 (79.8, 82.8, 83.7)	**90.0** (87.2, 91.7, 91.0)	86.3 (83.8, 86.8, 88.2)
50	78.2 (76.4, 79.2, 78.9)	82.9 (80.8, 83.6, 84.4)	90.1 (86.8, 91.3, 92.3)	**87.2** (85.5, 88.2, 87.8)
In-domain	76.7 (75.7, 77.2, 77.3)	82.8 (80.1, 84.2, 84.2)	90.6 (87.5, 92.4, 92.0)	88.2 (85.9, 88.6, 90.0)

(a) Variance across BERT based models (BERT-AEN, BERT-SPC, LCF-BERT) is small.

% in-domain	Laptop	Restaurant	Men's T-shirt	Television
0	61.0 (58.6, 60.9, 63.6)	68.2 (68.3, 68.0, 68.3)	79.0 (76.6, 78.6, 81.9)	77.6 (75.4, 77.8, 79.6)
10	**65.1** (60.7, 65.6, 69.1)	**73.0** (70.1, 74.1, 74.9)	**83.8** (80.3, 84.1, 86.9)	**79.1** (77.1, 79.1, 81.2)
25	65.3 (59.9, 66.2, 69.8)	74.8 (72.2, 75.4, 76.6)	85.1 (82.9, 86.0, 86.4)	80.0 (78.7, 79.8, 81.5)
50	66.2 (60.5, 68.7, 69.5)	75.0 (72.9, 75.3, 76.8)	85.8 (82.7, 86.1, 88.4)	80.6 (78.8, 80.7, 82.4)
In-domain	66.3 (58.6, 69.4, 71.0)	75.4 (73.3, 76.5, 76.4)	85.8 (81.7, 87.4, 88.3)	81.1 (79.7, 80.5, 83.0)

(b) Variance across Memory network models (ATAE-LSTM, IAN, RAM) is significant.

cross-domain performance largely. For each test dataset, we take examples from the corresponding cross-domain dataset in the same locale as training set and incrementally add in-domain (10%, 25% and 50%) examples to evaluate the performance of the models. Table 5 summarises the results from these experiments for the BERT based models (a) and memory network based models (b). For instance, on the Restaurant dataset, the average cross-domain performance (i.e., trained on Laptop) across the three BERT-based models is 78.3 (first row), while the purely in-domain performance is 82.8 (last row). We observe that among all increments, adding 10% of the in-domain dataset (second row) gives the maximum improvement, and is accordingly defined as the inflection point, which is marked in bold. In Table 5(a), we report the accuracy scores (averaged over 5 runs) for the individual BERT based models (BERT-AEN, BERT-SPC, LCF-BERT) in brackets, in addition to the average numbers. As we can see, the variability in the numbers across models is low. For the memory network based models, on the other hand, the variability is not so low, and the corresponding scores have been shown in Table 5(b) in the order (ATAE-LSTM, IAN, RAM).

Interestingly, we notice that in most of the cases, the inflection point is obtained upon adding just 10% in-domain examples and the model performance reaches within 0.5–2% of purely in-domain performance, as shown in Table 6. While in a few cases, it happens by adding 25–50% in-domain samples. This is especially useful from the production readiness perspective since considerably good performance can be achieved by using limited in-domain labelled data on top of cross-domain annotated data from the same locale.

Table 6. Performance scorecard in accordance with the rubric: *reproducibility* – % drop in test set accuracy across Laptop and Restaurant, resp.; *replicability* – rank in leaderboard for Men's T-shirt and Television, resp. (rank obtained from avg. test set accuracy on Laptop and Restaurant); *performance* – % drop in test set accuracy (averaged across all four datasets) with hard and contrast-set data slices, resp.; *transferability* – % drop in test set accuracy in cross-domain setting, and upon adding in-domain training instances as per the inflection point, resp. (averaged over the four datasets)

Model	Reproducibility	Replicability	Performance	Transferability
ATAE-LSTM	(14.67, 5.06)	6, 6 (6)	(33.07, 55.31)	(4.60, 1.44)
RAM	(4.73, 4.82)	3, 4 (4)	(17.88, 36.12)	(8.06, 2.06)
IAN	(3.74, 2.64)	5, 5 (5)	(28.64, 48.93)	(9.22, 3.55)
BERT-SPC	(2.22, 0.27)	1, 2 (2)	(13.53, 30.58)	(3.83, 1.33)
BERT-AEN	(5.28, 3.67)	4, 3 (3)	(39.44, 41.88)	(2.61, 0.83)
LCF-BERT	(0.05, 3.37)	2, 1 (1)	(11.75, 27.55)	(3.14, 0.64)

7.4   Summary Comparison of the Different Models Under the Production Readiness Rubrics

We now make an overall comparison across different models considered in this study under our production readiness rubrics. Table 6 shows the various numbers across these rubrics. Under *reproducibility*, we observe a consistent drop in performance even for the BERT-based models, atleast for one of the two datasets, viz. Laptop and Restaurant. For Memory network based models, while there is a considerable drop across both the datasets, the drop for the Laptop dataset is quite noteworthy. Under *replicability*, we observe that the relative rankings of the considered models remain quite stable for the two new datasets, which is a good sign. Under *performance*, we note a large drop in test set accuracies for all the models across the two challenging data slices, with a minimum drop of 11–27% for LCF-BERT. Surprisingly, BERT-AEN suffered a huge drop in performance for both hard as well as contrast data slices. This is a serious concern and further investigation is needed to identify the issues responsible for this significant drop. Under *transferability*, while there is consistent drop in cross-domain scenario, the drop with the inflection point, corresponding to a meager addition of 10–25% of in-domain data samples, is much smaller.

7.5   Limitations of the Present Study

While representative of the modern trend in architecture research, memory network- and BERT-based models do not cover the entire spectrum of the ABSA literature. Important practical considerations, such as debuggability, simplicity and computational efficiency, have not been incorporated into the rubric. Lastly, a numeric scoring system based on the rubric would have made its interpretation objective. We leave them for a future work.

8   Conclusion

Despite the limitations, the present study takes an important stride towards closing the gap between empirical academic research and its widespread adoption and deployment in production. In addition to further strengthening the rubric and judging a broader cross-section of published ABSA models in its light, we envision to replicate such study in other important NLP tasks. We hope the two contributed datasets, along with the open-source evaluation framework, shall fuel further rigorous empirical research in ABSA. We make all the codes and datasets publicly available[10].

References

1. Breck, E., Cai, S., Nielsen, E., Salib, M., Sculley, D.: The ML test score: a rubric for ml production readiness and technical debt reduction. In: 2017 IEEE International Conference on Big Data (Big Data), pp. 1123–1132 (2017). https://doi.org/10.1109/BigData.2017.8258038
2. Chen, P., Sun, Z., Bing, L., Yang, W.: Recurrent attention network on memory for aspect sentiment analysis. In: Proceedings of the 2017 Conference on Empirical Methods in Natural Language Processing, Copenhagen, Denmark, pp. 452–461. Association for Computational Linguistics, September 2017. https://doi.org/10.18653/v1/D17-1047
3. Cheng, J., Zhao, S., Zhang, J., King, I., Zhang, X., Wang, H.: Aspect-level sentiment classification with heat (hierarchical attention) network. In: Proceedings of the 2017 ACM on Conference on Information and Knowledge Management, CIKM 2017, pp. 97–106. Association for Computing Machinery, New York (2017). https://doi.org/10.1145/3132847.3133037
4. Dacrema, M.F., Cremonesi, P., Jannach, D.: Are we really making much progress? A worrying analysis of recent neural recommendation approaches. In: Proceedings of the 13th ACM Conference on Recommender Systems, RecSys 2019, pp. 101–109. Association for Computing Machinery, New York (2019). https://doi.org/10.1145/3298689.3347058
5. Devlin, J., Chang, M.W., Lee, K., Toutanova, K.: BERT: pre-training of deep bidirectional transformers for language understanding. In: Proceedings of the 2019 Conference of the North American Chapter of the Association for Computational Linguistics: Human Language Technologies, Volume 1 (Long and Short Papers), Minneapolis, Minnesota, pp. 4171–4186. Association for Computational Linguistics, June 2019. https://doi.org/10.18653/v1/N19-1423
6. Dhillon, G.S., Chaudhari, P., Ravichandran, A., Soatto, S.: A baseline for few-shot image classification. In: International Conference on Learning Representations (2020)
7. Gardner, M., et al.: Evaluating models' local decision boundaries via contrast sets. In: Findings of the Association for Computational Linguistics: EMNLP 2020, pp. 1307–1323. Association for Computational Linguistics, November 2020. https://doi.org/10.18653/v1/2020.findings-emnlp.117

---

[10] https://github.com/rajdeep345/ABSA-Reproducibility.

8. Hu, M., Wu, Y., Zhao, S., Guo, H., Cheng, R., Su, Z.: Domain-invariant feature distillation for cross-domain sentiment classification. In: Proceedings of the 2019 Conference on Empirical Methods in Natural Language Processing and the 9th International Joint Conference on Natural Language Processing (EMNLP-IJCNLP), Hong Kong, China, pp. 5559–5568. Association for Computational Linguistics, November 2019. https://doi.org/10.18653/v1/D19-1558

9. Huang, B., Ou, Y., Carley, K.M.: Aspect level sentiment classification with attention-over-attention neural networks. In: Thomson, R., Dancy, C., Hyder, A., Bisgin, H. (eds.) SBP-BRiMS 2018. LNCS, vol. 10899, pp. 197–206. Springer, Cham (2018). https://doi.org/10.1007/978-3-319-93372-6_22

10. Kang, D., Raghavan, D., Bailis, P., Zaharia, M.: Model assertions for monitoring and improving ML models. In: Proceedings of the 3rd MLSys Conference, Austin, TX, USA (2020)

11. Li, L., Liu, Y., Zhou, A.: Hierarchical attention based position-aware network for aspect-level sentiment analysis. In: Proceedings of the 22nd Conference on Computational Natural Language Learning, Brussels, Belgium, pp. 181–189. Association for Computational Linguistics, October 2018

12. Li, X., Bing, L., Lam, W., Shi, B.: Transformation networks for target-oriented sentiment classification. In: Proceedings of the 56th Annual Meeting of the Association for Computational Linguistics (Volume 1: Long Papers), Melbourne, Australia, pp. 946–956. Association for Computational Linguistics, July 2018

13. Li, Z., Wei, Y., Zhang, Y., Zhang, X., Li, X., Yang, Q.: Exploiting coarse-to-fine task transfer for aspect-level sentiment classification. CoRR abs/1811.10999 (2018)

14. Lin, J.: The neural hype and comparisons against weak baselines. SIGIR Forum **52**(2), 40–51 (2019). https://doi.org/10.1145/3308774.3308781

15. Liu, Q., Zhang, H., Zeng, Y., Huang, Z., Wu, Z.: Content attention model for aspect based sentiment analysis. In: Proceedings of the 2018 World Wide Web Conference, WWW 2018. International World Wide Web Conferences Steering Committee, Republic and Canton of Geneva, Switzerland, pp. 1023–1032 (2018). https://doi.org/10.1145/3178876.3186001

16. Ma, D., Li, S., Zhang, X., Wang, H.: Interactive attention networks for aspect-level sentiment classification. In: Proceedings of the Twenty-Sixth International Joint Conference on Artificial Intelligence, IJCAI 2017, pp. 4068–4074 (2017). https://doi.org/10.24963/ijcai.2017/568

17. Ma, D., Li, S., Zhang, X., Wang, H.: Interactive attention networks for aspect-level sentiment classification. In: Proceedings of the 26th International Joint Conference on Artificial Intelligence, IJCAI 2017, pp. 4068–4074. AAAI Press (2017)

18. McArthur, S.L.: Repeatability, reproducibility, and replicability: tackling the 3R challenge in biointerface science and engineering. Biointerphases **14**(2), 020201 (2019). https://doi.org/10.1116/1.5093621

19. Pontiki, M., Galanis, D., Pavlopoulos, J., Papageorgiou, H., Androutsopoulos, I., Manandhar, S.: SemEval-2014 task 4: aspect based sentiment analysis. In: Proceedings of the 8th International Workshop on Semantic Evaluation (SemEval 2014), Dublin, Ireland, pp. 27–35. Association for Computational Linguistics, August 2014. https://doi.org/10.3115/v1/S14-2004

20. Ribeiro, M.T., Wu, T., Guestrin, C., Singh, S.: Beyond accuracy: behavioral testing of NLP models with CheckList. In: Proceedings of the 58th Annual Meeting of the Association for Computational Linguistics, pp. 4902–4912. Association for Computational Linguistics, July 2020. https://doi.org/10.18653/v1/2020.acl-main.442

21. Sculley, D., Snoek, J., Wiltschko, A.B., Rahimi, A.: Winner's curse? On pace, progress, and empirical rigor. In: ICLR (2018)

22. Song, Y., Wang, J., Jiang, T., Liu, Z., Rao, Y.: Targeted sentiment classification with attentional encoder network. In: Tetko, I.V., Kůrková, V., Karpov, P., Theis, F. (eds.) ICANN 2019. LNCS, vol. 11730, pp. 93–103. Springer, Cham (2019). https://doi.org/10.1007/978-3-030-30490-4_9

23. Stevens, J.R.: Replicability and reproducibility in comparative psychology. Front. Psychol. **8**, 862 (2017). https://doi.org/10.3389/fpsyg.2017.00862

24. Tang, D., Qin, B., Feng, X., Liu, T.: Effective LSTMs for target-dependent sentiment classification. In: Proceedings of COLING 2016, the 26th International Conference on Computational Linguistics: Technical Papers, Osaka, Japan, pp. 3298–3307. The COLING 2016 Organizing Committee, December 2016

25. Tang, D., Qin, B., Liu, T.: Aspect level sentiment classification with deep memory network. In: Proceedings of the 2016 Conference on Empirical Methods in Natural Language Processing, Austin, Texas, pp. 214–224. Association for Computational Linguistics, November 2016. https://doi.org/10.18653/v1/D16-1021

26. Tay, Y., Tuan, L.A., Hui, S.C.: Dyadic memory networks for aspect-based sentiment analysis. In: Proceedings of the 2017 ACM on Conference on Information and Knowledge Management, pp. 107–116. ACM (2017)

27. Wang, B., Lu, W.: Learning latent opinions for aspect-level sentiment classification. In: McIlraith, S.A., Weinberger, K.Q. (eds.) Proceedings of the Thirty-Second AAAI Conference on Artificial Intelligence (AAAI 2018), New Orleans, Louisiana, USA, 2–7 February 2018, pp. 5537–5544. AAAI Press (2018)

28. Wang, Y., Huang, M., Zhu, X., Zhao, L.: Attention-based LSTM for aspect-level sentiment classification. In: Proceedings of the 2016 Conference on Empirical Methods in Natural Language Processing, Austin, Texas, pp. 606–615. Association for Computational Linguistics, November 2016. https://doi.org/10.18653/v1/D16-1058

29. Watson, J., Ghosh, A.P., Trusov, M.: Swayed by the numbers: the consequences of displaying product review attributes. J. Mark. **82**(6), 109–131 (2018). https://doi.org/10.1177/0022242918805468

30. Xu, H., Liu, B., Shu, L., Yu, P.: BERT post-training for review reading comprehension and aspect-based sentiment analysis. In: Proceedings of the 2019 Conference of the North American Chapter of the Association for Computational Linguistics: Human Language Technologies, Volume 1 (Long and Short Papers), Minneapolis, Minnesota, pp. 2324–2335. Association for Computational Linguistics, June 2019. https://doi.org/10.18653/v1/N19-1242

31. Xue, W., Li, T.: Aspect based sentiment analysis with gated convolutional networks. In: Proceedings of the 56th Annual Meeting of the Association for Computational Linguistics (Volume 1: Long Papers), Melbourne, Australia, pp. 2514–2523. Association for Computational Linguistics, July 2018. https://doi.org/10.18653/v1/P18-1234

32. Yang, H., Zeng, B., Yang, J., Song, Y., Xu, R.: A multi-task learning model for Chinese-oriented aspect polarity classification and aspect term extraction. arXiv preprint arXiv:1912.07976 (2019)

33. Zeng, B., Yang, H., Xu, R., Zhou, W., Han, X.: LCF: a local context focus mechanism for aspect-based sentiment classification. Appl. Sci. **9**, 3389 (2019)

Robustness of Meta Matrix Factorization Against Strict Privacy Constraints

Peter Muellner[1(✉)], Dominik Kowald[1], and Elisabeth Lex[2]

[1] Know-Center GmbH, Graz, Austria
{pmuellner,dkowald}@know-center.at
[2] Graz University of Technology, Graz, Austria
elisabeth.lex@tugraz.at

Abstract. In this paper, we explore the reproducibility of MetaMF, a meta matrix factorization framework introduced by Lin et al. MetaMF employs meta learning for federated rating prediction to preserve users' privacy. We reproduce the experiments of Lin et al. on five datasets, i.e., Douban, Hetrec-MovieLens, MovieLens 1M, Ciao, and Jester. Also, we study the impact of meta learning on the accuracy of MetaMF's recommendations. Furthermore, in our work, we acknowledge that users may have different tolerances for revealing information about themselves. Hence, in a second strand of experiments, we investigate the robustness of MetaMF against strict privacy constraints. Our study illustrates that we can reproduce most of Lin et al.'s results. Plus, we provide strong evidence that meta learning is essential for MetaMF's robustness against strict privacy constraints.

Keywords: Recommender systems · Privacy · Meta learning · Federated learning · Reproducibility · Matrix factorization

1 Introduction

State-of-the-art recommender systems learn a user model from user and item data and the user's interactions with items to generate personalized recommendations. In that process, however, users' personal information may be exposed, resulting in severe privacy threats. As a remedy, recent research makes use of techniques like federated learning [2,4,6] or meta learning [7,20] to ensure privacy in recommender systems. In the federated learning paradigm, no data ever leaves a user's device, and as such, the leakage of their data by other parties is prohibited. With meta learning, a model gains the ability to form its hypothesis based on a minimal amount of data.

Similar to recent work [5,15], MetaMF by Lin et al. [16] combines federated learning with meta learning to provide personalization and privacy. Besides, MetaMF exploits collaborative information among users and distributes a private rating prediction model to each user. Due to MetaMF's recency and its clear focus on increasing privacy for users via a novel framework, we are interested

© Springer Nature Switzerland AG 2021
D. Hiemstra et al. (Eds.): ECIR 2021, LNCS 12657, pp. 107–119, 2021.
https://doi.org/10.1007/978-3-030-72240-1_8

in the reproducibility of Lin et al.'s research. Additionally, we aim to contribute our own branch of research regarding privacy, i.e., MetaMF's robustness against strict privacy constraints. This is motivated by a statement of Lin et al. about one critical limitation of MetaMF, i.e., its sensitivity to data scarcity that could arise when users employ strict privacy constraints by withholding a certain amount of their data. In this regard, every user has a certain privacy budget, i.e., a budget of private data she is willing to share. Thus, in our paper at hand, the privacy budget is considered a measure of how much data disclosure a user tolerates and is defined as the fraction of rating data she is willing to share with others. Thereby, employing small privacy budgets and thus, withholding data, serves as a realization of strict privacy constraints.

Our work addresses MetaMF's limitation against data scarcity and is structured in two parts. First, we conduct a study with the aim to reproduce the results given in the original work by Lin et al. Concretely, we investigate two leading research questions, i.e., *RQ1a: How does MetaMF perform on a broad body of datasets?* and *RQ1b: What evidence does MetaMF provide for personalization and collaboration?* Second, we present a privacy-focused study, in which we evaluate the impact of MetaMF's meta learning component and test MetaMF's performance on users with different amounts of rating data. Here, we investigate two more research questions, i.e., *RQ2a: What is the role of meta learning in the robustness of MetaMF against decreasing privacy budgets?* and *RQ2b: How do limited privacy budgets affect users with different amounts of rating data?* We address *RQ1a* and *RQ1b* in Sect. 3 by testing MetaMF's predictive capabilities on five different datasets, i.e., Douban, Hetrec-MovieLens, MovieLens 1M, Ciao, and Jester. Here, we find that most results provided by Lin et al. can be reproduced. In Sect. 4, we elaborate on *RQ2a* and *RQ2b* by examining MetaMF in the setting of decreasing privacy budgets. Here, we provide strong evidence of the important role of meta learning in MetaMF's robustness. Besides, we find that users with large amounts of rating data are substantially disadvantaged by decreasing privacy budgets compared to users with few rating data.

2   Methodology

In this section, we illustrate our methodology of addressing *RQ1a* and *RQ1b*, i.e., the reproducibility of Lin et al. [16], and *RQ2a* and *RQ2b*, i.e., MetaMF's robustness against decreasing privacy budgets.

2.1   Approach

MetaMF. Lin et al. recently introduced a novel matrix factorization framework in a federated environment leveraging meta learning. Their framework comprises three steps. First, collaborative information among users is collected and subsequently, utilized to construct a user's collaborative vector. This collaborative vector serves as basis of the second step. Here, in detail, the parameters of a private rating prediction model are learned via meta learning. Plus, in parallel, personalized item embeddings, representing a user's personal "opinion" about the items, are computed. Finally, in the third step, the rating of an item is predicted utilizing the previously learned rating prediction model and item embeddings. We resort to MetaMF to address *RQ1a*, *RQ1b*, and *RQ2b*, i.e., the reproducibility of results presented by Lin et al. and the influence of decreasing privacy budgets on users with different amounts of rating data.

NoMetaMF. In our privacy-focused study, *RQ2a* addresses the role of meta learning in MetaMF's robustness against decreasing privacy budgets. Thus, we conduct experiments with and without MetaMF's meta learning component. For the latter kind of experiments, we introduce NoMetaMF, a variant of MetaMF with no meta learning. In MetaMF, a private rating prediction model is generated for each user by leveraging meta learning. The authors utilize a hypernetwork [11], i.e., a neural network, coined meta network, that generates the parameters of another neural network. Based on the user's collaborative vector c_u, the meta network generates the parameters of the rating prediction model, i.e., weights $\mathbf{W}_l^u$ and biases $\mathbf{b}_l^u$ for layer l and user u. This is given by

$$\mathbf{h} = \mathrm{ReLU}(\mathbf{W}_h^* \mathbf{c}_u + \mathbf{b}_h^*) \tag{1}$$

$$\mathbf{W}_l^u = \mathbf{U}_{W_l^u}^* \mathbf{h} + \mathbf{b}_{W_l^u}^* \tag{2}$$

$$\mathbf{b}_l^u = \mathbf{U}_{b_l^u}^* \mathbf{h} + \mathbf{b}_{b_l^u}^* \tag{3}$$

where $\mathbf{h}$ is the hidden state with the widely-used $\mathrm{ReLU}(x) = \max(0, x)$ [8,12] activation function, $\mathbf{W}_h^*$, $\mathbf{U}_{W_l^u}^*$, $\mathbf{U}_{b_l^u}^*$ are the weights and $\mathbf{b}_h^*$, $\mathbf{b}_{W_l^u}^*$, $\mathbf{b}_{b_l^u}^*$ arc the biases of the meta network. NoMetaMF excludes meta learning by disabling backpropagation through the meta network in Eqs. 1–3. Thus, meta parameters $\mathbf{W}_h^*$, $\mathbf{U}_{W_l^u}^*$, $\mathbf{U}_{b_l^u}^*$, $\mathbf{b}_h^*$, $\mathbf{b}_{W_l^u}^*$, $\mathbf{b}_{b_l^u}^*$ will not be learned in NoMetaMF. While backpropagation is disabled in the meta network, parameters W_l^u and b_l^u are learned over those non-meta parameters in NoMetaMF to obtain the collaborative vector. Hence, the parameters of the rating prediction models are still learned for each user individually, but without meta learning.

Lin et al. also introduce a variant of MetaMF, called MetaMF-SM, which should not be confused with NoMetaMF. In contrast to MetaMF, MetaMF-SM does not generate a private rating prediction model for each user individually, but instead utilizes a shared rating prediction model for all users. Our NoMetaMF model generates an individual rating prediction model for each user but operates without meta learning. Furthermore, we note that in our implementation of NoMetaMF, the item embeddings are generated in the same way as in MetaMF. With NoMetaMF, we aim to investigate the impact of meta learning on the robustness of MetaMF against decreasing privacy budgets, i.e., *RQ2a*.

2.2 Datasets

In line with Lin et al., we conduct experiments on four datasets: Douban [14], Hetrec-MovieLens [3], MovieLens 1M [13], and Ciao [10]. We observe that none of these datasets comprises a high average number of ratings per item, i.e., 22.6 (Douban), 85.6 (Hetrec-MovieLens), 269.8 (MovieLens 1M), and 2.7 (Ciao). To increase the diversity of our datasets, we include a fifth dataset to our study, i.e., Jester [9] with an average number of ratings per item of 41,363.6. Furthermore, Lin et al. claimed that several observations about Ciao may be explained by its low average number of ratings per user, i.e., 38.3. Since Jester exhibits a similarly low average number of ratings per user, i.e., 56.3, we utilize Jester to verify Lin et al.'s claims. To fit the rating scale of the other datasets, we scale Jester's ratings to a range of [1, 5]. Descriptive statistics of our five datasets are outlined in detail in the following lines. *Douban* comprises 2,509 users with 893,575 ratings for 39,576 items. *Hetrec-MovieLens* includes 10,109 items and 855,598 ratings of 2,113 users. The popular *MovieLens 1M* dataset includes 6,040 users, 3,706 items and 1,000,209 ratings. *Ciao* represents 105,096 items, with 282,619 ratings from 7,373 users. Finally, our additional *Jester* dataset comprises 4,136,360 ratings for 100 items from 73,421 users.

We follow the evaluation protocol of Lin et al. and thus, perform no cross-validation. Therefore, each dataset is randomly separated into 80% training set R_{train}, 10% validation set R_{val} and 10% test set R_{test}. However, we highlight that in the case of Douban, Hetrec-MovieLens, MovieLens 1M, and Ciao, we utilize the training, validation and test set provided by Lin et al.

Identification of User Groups. In *RQ2b*, we study how decreasing privacy budgets influence the recommendation accuracy of user groups with different user behavior. That is motivated by recent research [1,19], which illustrates differences in recommendation quality for user groups with different characteristics. As an example, [19] measures a user group's mainstreaminess, i.e., how the user groups' most listened artists match the most listened artists of the entire population. The authors split the population into three groups of users with low, medium, and high mainstreaminess, respectively. Their results suggest that low mainstream users receive far worse recommendations than mainstream users.

In a similar vein, we also split users into three user groups: *Low*, *Med*, and *High*, referring to users with a low, medium, and a high number of ratings, respectively. To precisely study the effects of decreasing privacy budgets on each user group, we generate them such that the variance of the number of ratings is low, but yet, include a sufficiently large number of users. For this matter, each of our three user groups includes 5% of all users. In detail, we utilize the 5% of users with the least ratings (i.e., *Low*), the 5% of users with the most ratings (i.e., *High*) and the 5% of users, whose number of ratings are the closest to the median (i.e., *Med*). Thus, each user group consists of 125 (Douban), 106 (Hetrec-MovieLens), 302 (MovieLens 1M), 369 (Ciao), and 3,671 (Jester) users.

2.3   Recommendation Evaluation

In concordance to the methodology of Lin et al., we minimize the mean squared error (MSE) between the predicted $\hat{r} \in \hat{R}$ and the real ratings $r \in R$ as the objective function for training the model. Additionally, we report the MSE and the mean absolute error (MAE) on the test set R_{test} to estimate our models' predictive capabilities. Since we dedicate parts of this work to shed light on MetaMF's and NoMetaMF's performance in settings with different degrees of privacy, we illustrate how we simulate decreasing privacy budgets and how we evaluate a model's robustness against these privacy constraints.

Simulating Different Privacy Budgets. To simulate the reluctance of users to share their data, we propose a simple sampling procedure in Algorithm 1. Let β be the privacy budget, i.e., the fraction of data to be shared. First, a user u randomly selects a fraction of β of her ratings without replacement. Second, the random selection of ratings R_u^β is then shared by adding it to the set R^β. That ensures that (i) each user has the same privacy budget β and (ii) each user shares at least one rating to receive recommendations. The set of shared ratings R^β without held back ratings then serves as a training set for our models.

Algorithm 1: Sampling procedure for simulating privacy budget β.

Input: Ratings R, Users U and privacy budget β.
Result: Shared ratings R^β, with a fraction of β of each user's ratings.
$R^\beta = \{\}$
for $u \in U$ **do**
  $\quad R_u^\beta = \{R_u' \subseteq R_u : |R_u'|/|R_u| = \beta\}$
  $\quad R^\beta = R^\beta \cup R_u^\beta$
end

Measuring Robustness. Our privacy-focused study is concerned with discussing MetaMF's robustness against decreasing privacy budgets. We quantify a model's robustness by how the model's predictive capabilities change by decreasing privacy budgets. In detail, we introduce a novel accuracy measurement called ΔMAE@β, which is a simple variant of the mean absolute error.

Definition 1 (ΔMAE@β). *The relative mean absolute error ΔMAE@β measures the predictive capabilities of a model M under a privacy budget β relative to the predictive capabilities of M without any privacy constraints.*

$$\text{MAE@}\beta = \frac{1}{|R_{test}|} \sum_{r_{u,i} \in R_{test}} |(r_{u,i} - M(R_{train}^\beta, \theta)_{u,i})| \tag{4}$$

$$\Delta\text{MAE@}\beta = \frac{\text{MAE@}\beta}{\text{MAE@1.0}} \tag{5}$$

where $M(R_{train}^\beta, \theta)_{u,i}$ is the estimated rating for user u on item i for M with parameters θ being trained on the dataset R_{train}^β and $|\cdot|$ is the absolute function. Please note that the same R_{test} is utilized for different values of β.

Table 1. MetaMF's error measurements (reproduced/original) for our five datasets alongside the MAE (mean absolute error) and the MSE (mean squared error) reported in the original paper. The non-reproducibility of the MSE on the Ciao dataset can be explained by the particularities of the MSE and the Ciao dataset. All other measurements can be reproduced (*RQ1a*).

Dataset	MAE	MSE
Douban	0.588/0.584	0.554/0.549
Hetrec-MovieLens	0.577/0.571	0.587/0.578
MovieLens 1M	0.687/0.687	0.765/0.760
Ciao	0.774/0.774	1.125/1.043
Jester	0.856/-	1.105/-

Furthermore, it is noteworthy that the magnitude of $\Delta MAE@\beta$ measurements does not depend on the underlying dataset, as it is a relative measure. Thus, one can compare a model's $\Delta MAE@\beta$ measurements among different datasets.

2.4   Source Code and Materials

For the reproducibility study, we utilize and extend the original implementation of MetaMF, which is provided by the authors alongside the Douban, Hetrec-MovieLens, MovieLens 1M, and Ciao dataset samples via BitBucket[1]. Furthermore, we publish the entire Python-based implementation of our work on GitHub[2] and our three user groups for all five datasets on Zenodo[3] [18].

We want to highlight that we are not interested in outperforming any state-of-the-art approaches on our five datasets. Thus, we refrain from conducting any hyperparameter tuning or parameter search and utilize precisely the same parameters, hyperparameters, and optimization algorithms as Lin et al. [16].

3   Reproducibility Study

In this section, we address *RQ1a* and *RQ1b*. As such, we repeat experiments by Lin et al. [16] to verify the reproducibility of their results. Therefore, we evaluate MetaMF on the four datasets Douban, Hetrec-MovieLens, MovieLens 1M, and Ciao. Additionally, we measure its accuracy on the Jester dataset. Please note that we strictly follow the evaluation procedure as in the work to be reproduced.

We provide MAE (mean absolute error) and MSE (mean squared error) measurements on our five datasets in Table 1. It can be observed that we can reproduce the results by Lin et al. up to a margin of error smaller than 2%. Only in

---

[1] https://bitbucket.org/HeavenDog/metamf/src/master/, Last accessed Oct. 2020.

[2] https://github.com/pmuellner/RobustnessOfMetaMF.

[3] https://doi.org/10.5281/zenodo.4031011.

the case of the MSE on the Ciao dataset, we obtain different results. Due to the selection of random batches during training, our model slightly deviates from the one utilized by Lin et al. Thereby, also, the predictions are likely to differ marginally. As described in [21], the MSE is much more sensitive to the variance of the observations than the MAE. Thus, we argue that the non-reproducibility of the MSE on the Ciao dataset can be explained by the sensitivity of the MSE on the variance of the observations in each batch. In detail, we observed in Sect. 2.2 that Ciao comprises very few ratings but lots of items. Thus, the predicted ratings are sensitive to the random selection of training data within each batch. However, it is noteworthy that we can reproduce the more stable MAE on the Ciao dataset. Hence, we conclude that our results provide strong evidence of the originally reported measurements being reproducible, enabling us to answer *RQ1a* in the affirmative.

Next, we study the rating prediction models' weights and the learned item embeddings. Again, we follow the procedure of Lin et al. and utilize the popular t-SNE (t-distributed stochastic neighborhood embedding) [17] method to reduce the dimensionality of the weights and the item embeddings to two dimensions. Since Lin et al. did not report any parameter values for t-SNE, we rely on the default parameters, i.e., we set the perplexity to 30 [17]. After the dimensionality reduction, we standardize all observations $x \in X$ by $\frac{x-\mu}{\sigma}$, where μ is the mean and σ is the standard deviation of X. The rating prediction model of each user is defined as a two-layer neural network. However, we observe that Lin et al. did not describe what layer's weights they visualize. Correspondences with the leading author of Lin et al. clarified that in their work, they only describe the weights of the first layer of the rating prediction models. The visualizations of the first layer's weights of the rating prediction models on our five datasets are given in Fig. 1.

In line with Lin et al., we discuss the weights and the item embeddings with respect to personalization and collaboration. As the authors suggest, personalization leads to distinct weight embeddings and collaboration leads to clusters within the embedding space. First, we observe that MetaMF tends to generate different weight embeddings for each user. Second, the visualizations exhibits well-defined clusters, which indicates that MetaMF can exploit collaborative information among users. However, our visualizations of the weights deviate slightly from the ones reported by Lin et al. Similar to the reproduction of the accuracy measurements in Table 1, we attribute this to the inability to derive the exact same model as Lin et al. Besides, t-SNE comprises random components and thus, generates slightly varying visualizations. However, the weights for the Ciao dataset in Fig. 1d illustrate behavior that contradicts Lin et al.'s observations. In the case of the Ciao dataset, they did not observe any form of clustering and attributed this behavior to the small number of ratings per user in the Ciao dataset. To test their claim, we also illustrate the Jester dataset with a similarly low number of ratings per user. In contrast, our visualizations indeed show well-defined clusters and different embeddings. We note that Jester exhibits many more clusters than the other datasets due to the much larger

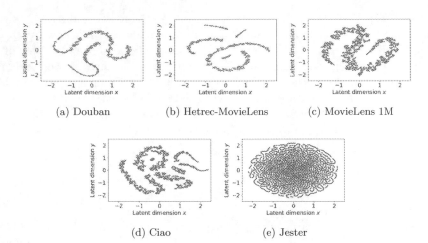

Fig. 1. MetaMF's weights embeddings of the first layer of the rating prediction models. One observation corresponds to an individual user ($RQ1b$).

number of users. Overall, we find that both, Ciao and Jester, do not support the claim made by Lin et al. However, we see the possibility that this observation may be caused by randomness during training.

Due to space limitations, we refrain from visualizing the item embeddings. It is worth noticing that our observations on the weights also hold for the item embeddings. In detail, our visualizations exhibit indications of collaboration and personalization for all datasets. Overall, we find the visualizations of the weights and the item embeddings presented by Lin et al. to be reproducible for the Douban, Hetrec-MovieLens, and MovieLens 1M datasets and thus, we can also positively answer $RQ1b$.

4   Privacy-Focused Study

In the following, we present experiments that go beyond reproducing Lin et al.'s work [16]. Concretely, we explore the robustness of MetaMF against decreasing privacy budgets and discuss $RQ2a$ and $RQ2b$. More detailed, we shed light on the effect of decreasing privacy budgets on MetaMF in two settings: (i) the role of MetaMF's meta learning component and (ii) MetaMF's ability to serve users with different amounts of rating data equally well.

First, we compare MetaMF to NoMetaMF in the setting of decreasing privacy budgets. Therefore, we utilize our sampling procedure in Algorithm 1 to generate datasets with different privacy budgets. In detail, we construct 10 training sets, i.e., $\{R_{train}^{\beta} : \beta \in \{1.0, 0.9, \ldots, 0.2, 0.1\}\}$, on which MetaMF and NoMetaMF are trained on. Then, we evaluate both models on the test set R_{test}. It is worth noticing that R_{test} is the same for all values of β to enable a valid comparison. Our results in Fig. 2a illustrate that for all datasets, MetaMF preserves its

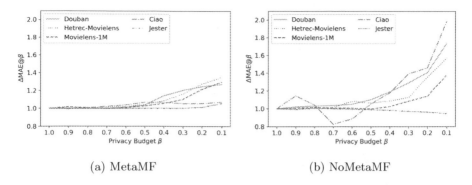

(a) MetaMF   (b) NoMetaMF

Fig. 2. ΔMAE@β measurements on (a) MetaMF and (b) NoMctaMF, in which meta learning is disabled. Especially for small privacy budgets, MetaMF yields a much more stable accuracy than NoMetaMF (*RQ2a*).

predictive capabilities well, even with decreasing privacy budgets. However, a privacy budget of $\approx 50\%$ sccms to be a critical threshold. The ΔMAE@β only marginally increases for $\beta > 0.5$, but rapidly grows for $\beta \leq 0.5$ in the case of the Douban, Hetrec-MovieLens, and MovieLens 1M dataset. In other words, a user could afford to withhold $\leq 50\%$ of her data and still get well-suited recommendations. Additionally, the ΔMAE@β remains stable for the Ciao and Jester dataset. Similar observations can be made about the results of NoMetaMF in Fig. 2b. Again, the predictive capabilities remain stable for $\beta > 0.5$ in the case of Douban, Hetrcc-MovieLens, and MovieLens 1M, but dccrcasc trcmcndously for higher levels of privacy. Our side-by-side comparison of MetaMF and NoMetaMF in Fig. 2 suggests that both methods exhibit robust behavior for large privacy budgets (i.e., $\beta > 0.5$), but exhibit an increasing MAE for less data available (i.e., $\beta \leq 0.5$). However, we would like to highlight that the increase of the MAE is much worse for NoMetaMF than for MetaMF. Here, the ΔMAE@β indicates that the MAE for NoMetaMF increases much faster than the MAE for MetaMF for decreasing privacy budgets. This observation pinpoints the importance of meta learning and personalization in settings with a limited amount of data per user, i.e., a high privacy level. Thus, concerning *RQ2a*, we conclude that MetaMF is indeed more robust against decreasing privacy budgets than NoMetaMF, but yet, requires a sufficient amount of data per user.

Next, we compare MetaMF to NoMetaMF with respect to their ability for personalization and collaboration in the setting of decreasing privacy budgets. As explained in Sect. 3, we refer to Lin et al., which suggest that personalization leads to distinct weight embeddings and collaboration leads to clusters within the embedding space. In Fig. 3, we illustrate the weights of the first layer of the rating prediction models of MetaMF and NoMetaMF for the MovieLens 1M dataset for different privacy budgets (i.e., $\beta \in \{1.0, 0.5, 0.1\}$). Again, we applied t-SNE to reduce the dimensionality to two dimensions, followed by standardization to ease the visualization. In the case of MetaMF, we observe that it preserves the

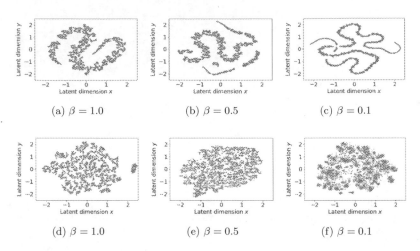

Fig. 3. Weights of the first layer of the rating prediction models for the MovieLens 1M dataset. (a), (b), (c) depict MetaMF, whereas (d), (e), (f) depict NoMetaMF, in which meta learning is disabled. No well-defined clusters are visible for NoMetaMF, which indicates the inability to exploit collaborative information among users (*RQ2a*).

ability to generate different weights for each user for decreasing privacy budgets. Similarly, well-defined clusters can be seen, which indicates that MetaMF also preserves the ability to capture collaborative information among users. In contrast, our visualizations for NoMetaMF do not show well-defined clusters. This indicates that NoMetaMF loses the ability to exploit collaborative information among users. Due to limited space, we refrain from presenting the weights of the first layer of the rating prediction models for the other datasets. However, we observe that MetaMF outperforms NoMetaMF in preserving the collaboration ability for decreasing privacy budgets on the remaining four datasets, which is also in line with our previous results regarding *RQ2a*.

In the following, we elaborate on how the high degree of personalization in MetaMF impacts the recommendations of groups of users with different amounts of rating data. In a preliminary experiment, we measure the MAE on our three user groups *Low*, *Med*, and *High* on our five datasets in Table 2. Except for the Ciao dataset, our results provide evidence that *Low* is served with significantly worse recommendations than *High*. In other words, users with lots of ratings are advantaged over users with only a few ratings.

To detail the impact of decreasing privacy budgets on these user groups, we monitor the ΔMAE@β on *Low*, *Med*, and *High*. The results for our five datasets are presented in Fig. 4. Surprisingly, *Low* seems to be much more robust against small privacy budgets than *High*. Here, we refer to our observations about MetaMF's performance on the Ciao and Jester dataset in Fig. 2a. In contrast to the other datasets, Ciao and Jester comprise only a small average number of ratings per user, i.e., 38 (Ciao) and 56 (Jester), which means that they share a common property with our *Low* user group. Thus, we suspect a relationship

Table 2. MetaMF's MAE (mean absolute error) measurements for our three user groups on the five datasets. Here, we simulated a privacy budget of $\beta = 1.0$. According to a one-tailed t-Test, *Low* is significantly disadvantaged over *High*, indicated by *, i.e., $\alpha = 0.05$ and ****, i.e., $\alpha = 0.0001$ (*RQ2b*).

Dataset	Low	Med	High
Douban*	0.638	0.582	0.571
Hetrec-MovieLens****	0.790	0.603	0.581
MovieLens 1M****	0.770	0.706	0.673
Ciao	0.773	0.771	0.766
Jester****	1.135	0.855	0.811

between the robustness against decreasing privacy budgets and the amount of rating data per user. The most prominent examples of *Low* being more robust than *High* can be found in Figs. 4a, 4b and 4c. Here, the accuracy of MetaMF on *High* substantially decreases for small privacy budgets. On the one hand, MetaMF provides strongly personalized recommendations for users with lots of ratings, which results in a high accuracy for these users (i.e., *High*). On the other hand, this personalization leads to a serious reliance on the data, which has a negative impact on the performance in settings with small privacy budgets. Thus, concerning *RQ2b*, we conclude that users with lots of ratings receive better recommendations than other users if they can take advantage of their abundance

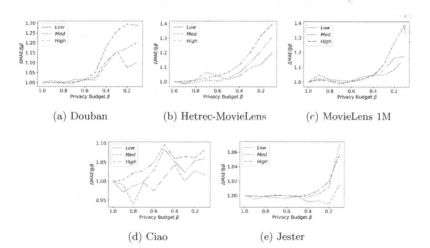

(a) Douban   (b) Hetrec-MovieLens   (c) MovieLens 1M

(d) Ciao   (e) Jester

Fig. 4. MetaMF's ΔMAE@β measurements for the (a) Douban, (b) Hetrec-MovieLens, (c) MovieLens 1M, (d) Ciao, and (e) Jester dataset for all three usergroups. Especially (a), (b), and (c) illustrate that *High* is sensitive to small privacy budgets. In contrast, *Low* can afford a high degree of privacy, since the accuracy of its recommendations only marginally decreases (*RQ2b*).

of data. In settings where a high level of privacy is required, i.e., a low privacy budget, and thus, users decide to hold back the majority of their data, users are advantaged who do not require as much personalization from the recommender system.

5   Conclusions and Future Work

In our study at hand, we conducted two lines of research. First, we reproduced results presented by Lin et al. in [16]. Besides, we introduced a fifth dataset, i.e., Jester, which, in contrast to the originally utilized datasets, has plenty of rating data per item. We found that all accuracy measurements are indeed reproducible (*RQ1a*). However, our reproduction of the t-SNE visualizations of the embeddings illustrated potential discrepancies between our and Lin et al.'s work (*RQ1b*). Second, we conducted privacy-focused studies. Here, we thoroughly investigated the meta learning component of MetaMF. We found that meta learning takes an important role in preserving the accuracy of the recommendations for decreasing privacy budgets (*RQ2a*). Furthermore, we evaluated MetaMF's performance with respect to decreasing privacy budgets on three user groups that differ in their amounts of rating data. Surprisingly, the accuracy of the recommendations for users with lots of ratings seems far more sensitive to small privacy budgets than for users with a limited amount of data (*RQ2b*).

Future Work. In our future work, we will research how to cope with incomplete user profiles in our datasets, as users may already have limited the amount of their rating data to satisfy their privacy constraints. Furthermore, we will develop methods that identify the ratings a user should share based on the characteristics of the data.

Acknowledgements. We thank the Social Computing team for their rich feedback on this work. This work is supported by the H2020 project TRUSTS (GA: 871481) and the "DDAI" COMET Module within the COMET – Competence Centers for Excellent Technologies Programme, funded by the Austrian Federal Ministry for Transport, Innovation and Technology (bmvit), the Austrian Federal Ministry for Digital and Economic Affairs (bmdw), the Austrian Research Promotion Agency (FFG), the province of Styria (SFG) and partners from industry and academia. The COMET Programme is managed by FFG.

References

1. Abdollahpouri, H., Mansoury, M., Burke, R., Mobasher, B.: The unfairness of popularity bias in recommendation. In: Workshop on Recommendation in Multistakeholder Environments in Conjunction with RecSys 2019 (2019)
2. Ammad-Ud-Din, M., et al.: Federated collaborative filtering for privacy-preserving personalized recommendation system. arXiv preprint arXiv:1901.09888 (2019)
3. Cantador, I., Brusilovsky, P., Kuflik, T.: Second international workshop on information heterogeneity and fusion in recommender systems. In: RecSys 2011 (2011)

4. Chen, C., Zhang, J., Tung, A.K., Kankanhalli, M., Chen, G.: Robust federated recommendation system. arXiv preprint arXiv:2006.08259 (2020)
5. Chen, F., Luo, M., Dong, Z., Li, Z., He, X.: Federated meta-learning with fast convergence and efficient communication. arXiv preprint arXiv:1802.07876 (2018)
6. Duriakova, E., et al.: PDMFRec: a decentralised matrix factorisation with tunable user-centric privacy. In: RecSys 2019 (2019)
7. Finn, C., Abbeel, P., Levine, S.: Model-agnostic meta-learning for fast adaptation of deep networks. In: ICML 2017 (2017)
8. Glorot, X., Bordes, A., Bengio, Y.: Deep sparse rectifier neural networks. In: AIS-TATS 2011 (2011)
9. Goldberg, K., Roeder, T., Gupta, D., Perkins, C.: Eigentaste: a constant time collaborative filtering algorithm. Inf. Retrieval 4(2), 133–151 (2001)
10. Guo, G., Zhang, J., Thalmann, D., Yorke-Smith, N.: ETAF: an extended trust antecedents framework for trust prediction. In: ASONAM 2014 (2014)
11. Ha, D., Dai, A., Le, Q.V.: Hypernetworks. In: ICLR 2016 (2016)
12. Hahnloser, R.H., Sarpeshkar, R., Mahowald, M.A., Douglas, R.J., Seung, H.S.: Digital selection and analogue amplification coexist in a cortex-inspired silicon circuit. Nature 405(6789), 947–951 (2000)
13. Harper, F.M., Konstan, J.A.: The movielens datasets: history and context. ACM Trans. Interact. Intell. Syst. (TIIS) 5(4), 1–19 (2015)
14. Hu, L., Sun, A., Liu, Y.: Your neighbors affect your ratings: on geographical neighborhood influence to rating prediction. In: SIGIR 2014 (2014)
15. Jiang, Y., Konečný, J., Rush, K., Kannan, S.: Improving federated learning personalization via model agnostic meta learning. In: International Workshop on Federated Learning for User Privacy and Data Confidentiality in conjunction with NeurIPS 2019 (2019)
16. Lin, Y., et al.: Meta matrix factorization for federated rating predictions. In: SIGIR 2020 (2020)
17. Maaten, L.V.D., Hinton, G.: Visualizing data using t-SNE. J. Mach. Learn. Res. 9(Nov), 2579–2605 (2008)
18. Müllner, P., Kowald, D., Lex, E.: User Groups for Robustness of Meta Matrix Factorization Against Decreasing Privacy Budgets (2020). https://doi.org/10.5281/zenodo.4031011
19. Schedl, M., Bauer, C.: Distance-and rank-based music mainstreaminess measurement. In: UMAP 2017 (2017)
20. Snell, J., Swersky, K., Zemel, R.: Prototypical networks for few-shot learning. In: NIPS 2017 (2017)
21. Willmott, C.J., Matsuura, K.: Advantages of the mean absolute error (MAE) over the root mean square error (RMSE) in assessing average model performance. Climate Res. 30(1), 79–82 (2005)

Textual Characteristics of News Title and Body to Detect Fake News: A Reproducibility Study

Anu Shrestha[✉] and Francesca Spezzano

Computer Science Department, Boise State University, Boise, ID, USA
anushrestha@u.boisestate.edu, francescaspezzano@boisestate.edu

Abstract. Fake news, a deliberately designed news to mislead others, is becoming a big societal threat with its fast dissemination over the Web and social media and its power to shape public opinion. Many researchers have been working to understand the underlying features that help identify these fake news on the Web. Recently, Horne and Adali found, on a small amount of data, that news title stylistic and linguistic features are better than the same type of features extracted from the news body in predicting fake news. In this paper, we present our attempt to reproduce the same results to validate their findings. We show which of their findings can be generalized to larger political and gossip news datasets.

Keywords: Misinformation detection on the web · Fake news · Linguistic analysis

1 Introduction

Social media and online news sources have become the major source of news diet for the increasingly large population instead of traditional media. In 2019, the Pew Research Center reported that more than half (55%) of American adults consume news from online platforms often or sometimes, which is 8% increase since 2018 [13]. With its increase in popularity, social media have also been proven to be an effective platform for fake news proliferation due to its lower cost and convenience of further sharing [16], which has attracted the attention of researchers, making it a global topic of interest. Several studies have been carried out to determine the validity of news relying on linguistic cues derived from the readability and lexical information of the news content [7,11,12].

Horne and Adali [7] conducted a study to understand and analyze the associated language patterns of the title and content of fake news. This paper has gained a lot of attention by the research community, with over 200 citations according to Google Scholar, and became the reference reading to understanding textual content differences between real and fake news. Horne and Adali witnessed that the general assumption about fake news that it is written to camouflage with real news and deceive the reader who does not care about the

D. Hiemstra et al. (Eds.): ECIR 2021, LNCS 12657, pp. 120–133, 2021.
https://doi.org/10.1007/978-3-030-72240-1_9

news sources' veracity is actually not true. In fact, they found the fake news is more similar to satire than to real news, and the focus of fake news is on users who are unlikely to read beyond the title. This sheds light on the necessity of research to understand the significant difference between the title of fake and real news separately from the news body content to mitigate the possible diffusion of the fake news. However, these claims were established based on a small data used in which labels were assigned according to the credibility of the news source, instead of fact-checking, which does not consider the fact that a news source can have mixed credibility and publish both real and fake information.

Thus, we decided to reproduce the paper by Horne and Adali [7] to validate their findings on larger state-of-the-art datasets with labels provided by professional journalists who have fact-checked the news, namely PolitiFact and GossipCop [15] and BuzzFeedNews [12]. Because the news trends continuously evolve, we analyze, similarly to Horne and Adali, news text (from body and title) by focusing on linguistic style, text complexity, and psychological aspects of the text, rather than topic-dependent representations of documents (e.g., [3]). In addition, we expanded the set of emotion features considered in the original paper to explore this aspect of the text further, given that Ghanem et al. [4] recently showed emotions play a key role in detecting false information. We also compare the classification performance of different classifiers beyond linear SVM (the only model used in [7]), and we discuss textual differences between two news domains, namely political and gossip news.

Our experiments confirm most of the original paper's findings regarding title and body feature differences between fake and real news, e.g., fake political news packs a lot in the title. However, differently from Horne and Adali, we found that fake titles contain more stop words than real titles. When using linear SVM to classify fake vs. real news, we confirm that title features outperform body features, but we observe the opposite results if we consider a non-linear and more expressive classifier such as Random Forest.

Furthermore, we show new patterns that were not present in the paper by Horne and Adali, namely fake news title and body express more negative emotions and sentiment than real news, and real news articles are more descriptive than fake news ones. Also, we highlight some differences between two different news domains: political and gossip. For instance, among stylistic, psychology, and complexity features in the news title, psychology features are the most important group of features for gossip news, while the most important group for political news is the one containing stylistic features. This shows how gossip news titles tend to be more persuasive than other news domains.

2   Overview of the Paper by Horne and Adali

In this section, we provide an overview of the approach, features, and findings by Horne and Adali [7].

2.1 Approach

Horne and Adali conducted a content analysis to study fake news by analyzing three small datasets: (i) a dataset (DS1) created by Buzzfeed leading to the 2016 U.S. elections which contains 36 real news stories and 35 fake news stories; (ii) a dataset (DS2) created by using Zimdars' list of fake and misleading news websites [18] and fact-checking website like snopes.com [7], containing 75 stories for each category: real, fake and satire sources; (iii) a dataset (DS3) containing 4000 real and 233 satire articles from a previous study [2]. During the experiments, they considered features from both news body and title for determining the veracity of news and comparing real news vs. fake news vs. satire.

2.2 Features

This research focused on three groups of features, including stylistic features (syntax, text style, and grammatical elements measured by 2015 Linguistic Inquiry and Word Count (LIWC) [10] and the Python Natural Language Toolkit Part of Speech tagger [1]), complexity features to capture details about how complex the article or title is (e.g., words per sentence, syntax tree depth determined by the Stanford Parser and readability level of text), and psychological features to capture emotional (positive/negative), social, and cognitive processes incorporated in news body or title computed by using the LIWC tool. Sentiment analysis was done through SentiStrength [17].

Feature Selection and Anaysis. The goal of feature selection is to avoid overfitting and increase generalizability. Because the datasets were small and the features generated were large, Horne and Adali performed feature selection by leveraging the one-way ANOVA test for those normally distributed features and the Wilcoxon rank-sum test for those that did not pass the normality test. This feature selection concluded with the selection of top 4 features for news body (number of nouns, lexical diversity (TTR), word count, and number of quotes) and news title (percentage of stop words, number of nouns, average word length, and Flesh-Kincaid Grade Readability Index).

Besides, they also used the above mentioned statistical tests to uncover statistically significant feature value differences among news with different labels (fake, satire, and real). If the value of a feature was higher (on average) for real news articles as compared to fake news articles, they denoted this by $R > F$ (and $F > R$ vice versa). We used the same notation while reproducing this experiments in Tables 2 and 3.

2.3 Observation and Evaluation

Horne and Adali's findings show how real news is different from fake and satire news and that fake news and satire have a lot in common across several dimensions. Regarding real vs. fake news (which is the scope of our reproducibility paper), they found that:

(f1) fake news articles tend to be shorter in terms of content, but use repetitive language,[1] smaller words, less punctuation, and fewer quotes (these results is consistent between datasets DS1 and DS2);

(f2) fake news articles require a lower educational level to read, use fewer analytic words, use more personal pronouns and adverbs, but fewer nouns (this result is not consistent between datasets DS1 and DS2 and it is less significative);

(f3) fake titles are longer, contain shorter words, use more all capitalized words, fewer stop words, and fewer nouns overall but more proper nouns (these results is consistent between datasets DS1 and DS2);

(f4) titles are a strong differentiating factor between fake and real news. They performed a binary classification of real vs. fake news separately on news body content and title on dataset DS2. They used the top 4 features from the feature selection process to run a linear SVM model with 5-fold cross-validation. The classification results show 71% accuracy for news body content and 78% accuracy for the title. Thus, they argued that the title is more important in predicting fake vs. real news, and the title and the body of the news should be analyzed separately.

3 Reproducibility

In this section, we describe in detail our attempt to reproduce and generalize findings (f1)–(f4) shown by Horne and Adali in their paper [7].

3.1 Datasets

There is generally limited availability of large scale benchmarks for fake news detection, especially where the ground truth labels are assigned via fact-checking, which is a time-consuming activity. FakeNewsNet [15] and BuzzFeedNews [12] are the only publicly available datasets having fact-checked labels. Thus, in this paper, we use these datasets to conduct our study (Table 1).

FakeNewsNet: PolitiFact and GossipCop. FakeNewsNet consists of two datasets, PolitiFact and GossipCop, from two different domains, i.e., politics and entertainment gossip, respectively. Thus, we used these two datasets separately in our study. Each of these datasets contains details about news content, publisher information, and social engagement information. We only used news content information in this paper.

---

[1] Repetitive language is measured by using the Type-Token Ratio (TTR) which is the number of unique words in the document by the total number of words in the document. A low TTR means more repetitive language, while a high TTR means more lexical diversity. Horne and Adali claim fake news has more repetitive language but show the opposite result in their paper, i.e., TTR is on average higher for fake than real news (cf. Table 4 in [7]), indicating more lexical diversity for fake than real news. Our results confirms more lexical diversity for fake news as shown in Table 2.

Table 1. Size of datasets used in our study.

Dataset	# Total News	# Fake News	# Real News
PolitiFact	838	378	460
BuzzFeedNews	1,561	299	1,262
GossipCop	19,759	4,734	15,025

PolitiFact contains news with known ground truth labels collected from the fact-checking website PolitiFact.[2] After cleaning the dataset from missing news bodies or titles, we obtained a total of 838 news articles, 378 fake and 460 real.

The GossipCop dataset contains fake news collected from GossipCop[3], which is a fact-checking website for entertainment stories and real news collected from E!Online,[4] a trusted media website for entertainment stories. After cleaning the dataset from missing news bodies or title, we obtained a total of 19,759 news articles, 4,734 fake and 15,025 real.

BuzzFeedNews Dataset. The BuzzFeedNews dataset contains news regarding the 2016 U.S. election published on Facebook by nine news agencies. This dataset[5] contains 1,262 articles that are mostly true, 212 that are a mixture of true and false, and 87 that are false, after cleaning the dataset from missing news bodies or titles. Ground truth is derived from professional journalists at BuzzFeed who have fact-checked the news in the dataset. As also done in the other datasets, we considered false news and news with a mixture of true and false as fake news and mostly true news as real news.

3.2   Features

This section describes the set of features we used in the paper to analyze real vs. fake news. In our implementation, we consider features similar to Horne and Adali [7], namely stylistic features, text complexity features, and psychology features. These features are computed for both the title and body text of the news.

Stylistic Features. We used the subset of LIWC features that represent the functionality of text, including word count (WC), words per sentence (WPS), time orientation (e.g., focus on past (focuspast) and focus on future (focusfuture)), number of personal (I, we, you, she/he – one feature each) and impersonal pronouns, number of quantifying words (quant), number of comparison words

---

[2] https://www.politifact.com/.

[3] https://www.gossipcop.com/.

[4] https://www.eonline.com/ap.

[5] The BuzzFeedNews dataset is available at https://zenodo.org/record/1239675#. X5riw0JKgXA.

(compare), number of exclamation marks (exlam), number of negations (negate), e.g., no, never, not, number of swear words (swear), number of online slang terms (netspeak), e.g., lol, brb, number of interrogatives, e.g., how, what, why (interrog), number of punctuation symbols (allPunc), number of quotes (quote).

Regarding the part of speech features, we used the Python Natural Language Toolkit part of speech (POS) tagger to compute the number of nouns (NN), proper nouns (NNP), personal pronouns (PRP), possessive pronouns (PRP$), Wh-pronoun (WP), determinants (DT), Wh-determinants (WDT), cardinal numbers (CD), adverbs (RB), interjections (UH), verbs (VB), Adjective (JJ), past tense verbs (VBD), gerund or present participle verbs (VBG), past participle verbs (VBN), non-3rd person singular present verbs (VBP), and third-person singular present verbs (VBZ).

This stylistic group of features also includes the upper case word count (all caps) and percent of stop words (per_stop).

Psychology Features. We computed these features by using the LIWC tool and include the number of analytic words (analytic), insightful words (insight), causal words (cause), discrepancy words (discrep), tentative words (tentat), certainty words (certain), differentiation words (differ), affiliation words (affil), power words, reward words, risk words, personal concern words (work, leisure, religion, money, home, death – one each), anxiety-related words (anx), emotional tone words (tone), and negative (negemo) and positive (posemo) emotional words. This group of features also includes positive (pos) and negative (neg) sentiment metrics as computed by the VADER sentiment analysis tool [5]. We also investigated the importance of features describing emotions expressed through the text, as Ghanem et al. [4] recently showed emotions play a key role in deceiving the reader and can successfully be used to detect false information. Thus, in addition to some emotion features provided by the LIWC tool (as described above), we computed additional emotion features such as anger, joy, sadness, fear, disgust, anticipation, surprise, and trust by using the Emotion Intensity Lexicon (NRC-EIL) [9] and the approach proposed in [8].

Complexity Features. The complexity of text in natural language processing depends on how easily the reader can read and understand a text. We used popular readability measures as complexity features in our analysis: Flesh Kincaid Grade Level (FK), Gunning Fog Index (GI), Simple Measure of Gobbledygook Index (SMOG). Higher scores of these readability measures indicate that the text is easier to read. This group of features also includes lexical diversity or Type-Token Ratio (TTR) and the average length of each word (avg wlen).

3.3 Analysis

Considering all the features from each group, we have a total of 68 features, which can still be too many for the size of the considered datasets (PolitiFact,

BuzzFeedNews, and GossipCop) to perform a real vs. fake news articles classification. Therefore, we used the same statistical tests (ANOVA and Wilcoxon
rank-sum) used by Horne and Adali to perform feature selection and analysis.
For each dataset, features are sorted by F-value in descending order to determine the importance, and only features where the two averages (real vs. fake)
were significantly different according to the statistical test (p-value < 0.05) were
considered. Among these features, we selected a number of features up to the
square root of the training set size (rule of thumb) for both news body and title
to feed the classification algorithm.

Instead of just using the linear SVM classifier as done by Horne and Adali, we
compared the performances of different classification algorithms, namely Logistic
Regression (LR) classifier with L2 regularization, linear Support Vector Machine
(SVM), and Random Forest (RF), with default parameters. As the datasets we
considered are not balanced, we used class weighting to deal with class imbalance,
stratified 5-fold cross-validation, and results are reported by using AUROC and
average precision (AvgP).

3.4 Results

Feature Statistical Analysis. We start our analysis by checking whether
Horne and Adali's findings (f1), (f2), and (f3) reported in Sect. 2.3 are confirmed in the three larger datasets we considered, namely PolitiFact and BuzzFeed (political news datasets), and GossipCop (gossip news dataset). To analyze
these findings we refer to the results reported in Table 2 for news body text and
Table 3 for news title.

Regarding finding (f1) (cf. Table 2), we confirm that fake news articles have a
shorter content (WC) and use less punctuation (allPunc) than real news articles
in all the three datasets we considered, and fake political articles have more
lexical diversity (TTR) than real political articles. Our analysis does not allow
us to generalize the finding that fake news articles use smaller words (avg wlen)
and fewer quotes (true in BuzzFeedNews, but not in Politifact and GossipCop).

Regarding finding (f2) (cf. Table 2), we can generalize the finding that fake
news articles use fewer analytic words (true in BuzzFeedNews and GossipCop).
We found that fake news articles require a lower educational level to read (as
measured by FK, GI, and SMOG readability indexes) only in one dataset (BuzzFeedNews) while the opposite trend holds for GossipCop dataset; the use of
more personal pronouns (PRP), adverbs (RB), and proper nouns (NNP) in fake
news articles is not confirmed in our analysis. We observe fake titles containing
more proper nouns (NNP) in all the three datasets considered.

Regarding finding (f3) (cf. Table 3), we confirm that fake titles have more
proper nouns (NNP) than real titles in all the three datasets we considered and
have fewer nouns (NN) in BuzzFeedNews and GossipCop. Also, we confirm that
fake political titles are longer (WC and WPS), use more capitalized words (all
caps) (they also use more possessive pronouns – PRP\$), and contain shorter
words (avg wlen). Our analysis does not confirm the fact that fake titles contain

Table 2. Features that differ in body of news content. All differences are statistically significant ($p < 0.05$).

Features	PolitiFact	BuzzFeed	GossipCop	Features	PolitiFact	BuzzFeed	GossipCop
allPunc	$R > F$	$R > F$	$R > F$	analytic	$F > R$	$R > F$	$R > F$
exclam	$F > R$	$F > R$	$F > R$	quote	$F > R$	$R > F$	$F > R$
tone	$R > F$	$R > F$	$R > F$	WC	$R > F$	$R > F$	$R > F$
WPS		$R > F$	$R > F$	affect		$F > R$	$R > F$
affil	$R > F$		$F > R$	cause		$F > R$	$F > R$
certain		$F > R$	$F > R$	all caps	$R > F$	$R > F$	$R > F$
differ	$R > F$	$F > R$	$F > R$	discrep	$R > F$	$F > R$	$F > R$
FK		$R > F$		focusfuture			$F > R$
GI		$R > F$	$F > R$	i			$R > F$
insight		$F > R$		interrog			$R > F$
leisure	$F > R$		$R > F$	TTR	$F > R$	$F > R$	
money	$R > F$			negate		$F > R$	$F > R$
netspeak			$R > F$	JJ	$R > F$	$R > F$	$R > F$
RB	$R > F$	$R > F$		CD	$R > F$	$R > F$	$R > F$
DT	$R > F$	$R > F$	$R > F$	UH	$R > F$		
NN	$R > F$	$R > F$	$R > F$	NNP	$R > F$	$R > F$	$R > F$
PRP	$R > F$	$R > F$	$R > F$	PRP$	$R > F$	$R > F$	
VBD	$R > F$	$R > F$	$R > F$	VBG	$R > F$	$R > F$	
VBN	$R > F$	$R > F$		VBP	$R > F$	$R > F$	$R > F$
VBZ	$R > F$	$R > F$		VB	$R > F$	$R > F$	$R > F$
WP	$R > F$	$R > F$	$R > F$	WDT	$R > F$	$R > F$	$R > F$
per_stop	$F > R$	$F > R$	$F > R$	power		$R > F$	$R > F$
quant	$R > F$			relig	$F > R$	$F > R$	$R > F$
reward			$R > F$	risk			$F > R$
sheshe	$F > R$		$F > R$	SMOG		$R > F$	$F > R$
swear	$F > R$	$F > R$		tentat		$F > R$	$F > R$
we	$R > F$		$R > F$	avg wlen		$R > F$	
work	$R > F$	$R > F$		you	$R > F$	$F > R$	$R > F$
compare		$R > F$		focuspast	$F > R$		$F > R$
neg	$F > R$	$F > R$	$F > R$	surprise	$F > R$		
disgust	$F > R$	$F > R$	$F > R$	negemo	$F > R$	$F > R$	$F > R$
pos	$R > F$		$R > F$	fear	$F > R$	$F > R$	
posemo	$R > F$		$R > F$	anx	$F > R$	$F > R$	$F > R$
sadness	$F > R$	$F > R$	$F > R$	anger		$F > R$	$F > R$
trust			$F > R$	joy			$F > R$

fewer stop words (per_stop). Similarly, we observe that fake news articles contain more stop words.

Furthermore, our results in Tables 2 and 3 highlight new patterns that were not present in the analysis performed by Horne and Adali. Specifically, we found that real news articles use a more positive tone and more nouns (NN), determinants (DT), wh-determinants (WDT), verbs (VB), past tense verbs (VBD), Wh-pronouns (WP), and adjectives (JJ) in all the three datasets considered.

Table 3. Features that differ in the title of news content. All differences are statistically significant ($p < 0.05$).

Features	PolitiFact	BuzzFeed	GossipCop	Features	PolitiFact	BuzzFeed	GossipCop
WC	F > R	F > R		avg wlen	R > F	R > F	F > R
quote	F > R	F > R	F > R	allPunc	R > F		F > R
exclam	F > R	F > R	F > R	tone	R > F	R > F	R > F
WPS	F > R	F > R	R > F	affect	F > R		R > F
affil			F > R	compare	F > R		R > F
differ			F > R	discrep	F > R		F > R
focusfuture	F > R		F > R	focuspast	F > R	F > R	
insight		F > R		interrog			R > F
leisure			R > F	TTR	F > R		F > R
money		R > F		negate			F > R
netspeak	R > F		R > F	JJ		R > F	R > F
UH			F > R	GI	F > R		F > R
FK	F > R		F > R	SMOG	F > R		F > R
analytic		R > F	R > F	all caps	F > R	F > R	
NN		R > F	R > F	NNP	F > R	F > R	F > R
PRP	F > R	F > R		PRP$	F > R	F > R	R > F
DT			R > F	RB	F > R		F > R
VBD	F > R			VBG	F > R		F > R
VBN	F > R			VBP	F > R	F > R	
VBZ	F > R	R > F		VB	F > R		F > R
WP		F > R		per_stop	F > R	F > R	
quant			R > F	relig	F > R	F > R	
reward			R > F	risk			F > R
work	R > F	R > F		i	F > R		R > F
you			R > F	shehe	F > R	F > R	
CD			R > F	fear	F > R	F > R	F > R
neg	F > R	F > R	F > R	sadness	F > R	F > R	F > R
surprise	F > R	R > F		anger	F > R	F > R	F > R
negemo	F > R		F > R	trust	R > F		R > F
disgust	F > R	F > R	F > R	pos			R > F
posemo			R > F	anx			F > R
joy			R > F				

This indicates that real news articles are more descriptive than fake news articles. Also, fake news titles and bodies use more exclamation marks (exclam) than real news titles (true in all the three datasets considered).

In addition, we observe that fake titles express more negative emotions (anger, sadness, fear, and disgust) and negative sentiment (neg) than real titles consistently across all the three considered datasets. This pattern is also true for fake news body. In contrast, real titles tend to express more positive emotions (trust, posemo, joy) and positive sentiment (pos), but this is less consistent across datasets. When selecting information, people have a sensitivity to negative information [6]. This negativity bias induces people to pay more attention

Table 4. News title vs. news body features for detecting fake news on the PolitiFact, BuzzFeedNews, and GossipCop datasets: stylistic, psychology, and complexity features. Best results for both news title and body are in bold. Best overall results between news title and body are shaded.

Features	PolitiFact		BuzzFeedNews		GossipCop	
	AUROC	AvgP	AUROC	AvgP	AUROC	AvgP
News body (SVM)	0.583	0.466	0.614	0.257	0.623	0.327
News body (LR)	0.855	0.809	0.728	0.351	0.703	0.437
News body (RF)	**0.911**	**0.878**	**0.785**	**0.417**	**0.782**	**0.630**
News Title (SVM)	0.833	0.804	0.669	0.317	0.588	0.309
News Title (LR)	0.849	0.813	0.787	0.423	0.663	0.380
News Title (RF)	**0.867**	**0.823**	**0.812**	**0.424**	**0.715**	**0.490**

Table 5. News title vs. news body features for detecting fake news on the PolitiFact, BuzzFeedNews, and GossipCop datasets: same four features as in Horne and Adali [7] NN, TTR, WC, and Quote for news body and FK, NN, per_stop, and avg wlen for title. Best results for both news title and body are in bold. Best overall results between news title and body are shaded.

Features	PolitiFact		BuzzFeedNews		GossipCop	
	AUROC	AvgP	AUROC	AvgP	AUROC	AvgP
News Body (SVM)	0.544	0.445	0.678	0.292	0.500	0.232
News Body (LR)	0.754	0.663	0.691	0.297	0.534	0.251
News Body (RF)	**0.861**	**0.803**	**0.708**	**0.342**	**0.631**	**0.42**
News Title (SVM)	0.649	0.531	0.713	**0.342**	0.528	0.250
News Title (LR)	0.643	0.530	**0.716**	**0.342**	0.530	0.251
News Title (RF)	**0.735**	**0.612**	0.706	0.330	**0.582**	**0.332**

to negative news, hence fake news tiles, bodies, and even associated images [14] express negative emotions to be catchier and circulate more among people.

Furthermore, there are some differences between political and gossip news. We found that fake political news articles have more religion-related words (relig) than real political news articles, while fake gossip news articles have fewer religion-related words; fake political news titles contain shorter words (avg wlen), and more words per sentence (WPS) and possessive pronouns (PRP$) than real political news titles, while this is the opposite for gossip news titles.

Real vs. Fake News Classification. Finding (f4) by Horne and Adali claims that title features are more informative (i.e., achieve higher accuracy) than news body features in classifying fake vs. real news with a linear SVM. Table 4 shows our classification results by comparing three classifiers, and when we used a number of features up to the square root of the training set size. We observe

Table 6. Feature group ablation for news title and body when the best classifier (Random Forest) is used on the PolitiFact, BuzzFeedNews, and GossipCop datasets. Best results for both news title and body are in bold.

Features	PolitiFact		BuzzFeedNews		GossipCop	
	AUROC	AvgP	AUROC	AvgP	AUROC	AvgP
News body						
Stylistic (RF)	**0.882**	**0.838**	**0.753**	**0.382**	**0.752**	**0.590**
Psychology (RF)	0.723	0.662	0.681	0.319	0.713	0.509
Complexity (RF)	0.804	0.708	0.630	0.285	0.000	0.000
News title						
Stylistic (RF)	**0.819**	**0.729**	**0.805**	**0.433**	0.634	0.365
Psychology (RF)	0.791	0.691	0.645	0.320	**0.651**	**0.407**
Complexity (RF)	0.583	0.486	0.555	0.257	0.553	0.287

that when we consider the linear SVM classifier, finding (f4) is confirmed, i.e., AUROC and average precision scores are higher for the title than the news body. However, Random Forest is the best classifier for both news body and title and outperforms linear SVM. When we consider Random Forest as the classifier, finding (f4) is reversed, i.e., AUROC and average precision scores are higher for news body than news title (this is true for two out of three of the datasets considered). We observe a similar trend also when we consider only the four features chosen by Horne and Adali to perform the classification (see results reported in Table 5). Of course, considering more than four features as we did in Table 4 results in better AUROC and average precision in all the three datasets.

Thus, our experiments reveal that whether or not the title is more informative than the news body depends on the chosen classifier. A non-linear classifier such as Random Forest has higher expressive power and outperforms linear SVM. Thus, if we choose the best classifier, namely Random Forest, finding (f4) does not hold in the larger datasets we considered. Having more information helps the Random Forest classifier to increase classification performances.

In addition, we performed feature ablation by feature group (style, psychology, and complexity) when the best classifier (Random Forest) is used. Results are reported in Table 6. We observe that stylistic features are the most important features in both title and news body for political news. For gossip news, stylistic features are the most important news body features, while psychology features are the most important features in title. Interestingly, this validates the definition of gossip as "small talk" that is originated from evolutionary psychology and has the basic intent to share information about third persons to indulge people in some discussion. Also, the reason people like gossip is because it is tempting and fun. Thus, the news title of gossip stories are written with more psychological words like tone and affect, e.g., "Angelina Jolie Can't Get Over

Heartbreak Of Losing Brad Pitt—Real Reason For Fury, Says Source" to catch readers attention even though the body text is not that engaging.

4 How to Reproduce Our Experiments

For reproducibility propose, we made our code available in a GitHub repository.[6] Because we did not directly collect the datasets, we are not uploading them in our repository, but we provide instructions on finding and downloading them. In our repository, we make our code available for extracting the features that are considered in this paper, including complexity, stylistic and psychology features extracted using NLTK part-of-speech, VADER Sentiment Analyser and the Emotion Intensity Lexicon (NRC-EIL),[7] except LIWC features as the LIWC tool has proprietary dictionaries whose licence should be purchased. LIWC features can be computed in two ways: (1) by using the software tool to compute the features, or (2) by downloading the dictionary provided by the tool for which we have provided code to extract features using the dictionary. In addition, we also provide code for the statistical test performed in this paper to reproduce Tables 2 and 3. Likewise we also provide code for the classification to reproduce Tables 4, 5 and 6.

5 Conclusions

In this paper, we reproduced the study by Horne and Adali [7] of the relative importance of news body and title in detecting fake news. We extended their experimental setting by using larger real and fake news datasets with ground truth at the news level, considering additional features describing emotions expressed through the text, comparing different classification algorithms, and highlighting differences between political and gossip news domains. Our experiments have shown that some of the original paper's observations are not the same as the trend of news writing is continuously evolving. For instance, the finding that the news title is more informative and plays an important role in discerning the news's veracity is confirmed if we use the same classifier, linear SVM, as in [7], but using a non-linear classifier such as Random Forest reverses the finding. Finally, we provide evidence that fake news title and body attract readers' attention with more negative emotions and sentiment, while real news articles are more descriptive.

Acknowledgements. This work has been supported by the National Science Foundation under Award no. 1943370. We thank Ashlee Milton and Maria Soledad Pera for providing us the code used in their paper [8] to compute emotional features.

---

[6] https://github.com/shresthaanu/ECIR21TextualCharacteristicsOfFakeNews.

[7] The NRC-EIL lexicon should be downloaded at https://www.saifmohammad.com/ WebPages/AffectIntensity.htm.

References

1. Bird, S.: NLTK: the natural language toolkit. In: Proceedings of the COLING/ACL on Interactive Presentation Sessions, pp. 69–72 (2006)
2. Burfoot, C., Baldwin, T.: Automatic satire detection: are you having a laugh? In: Proceedings of the ACL-IJCNLP 2009 Conference Short Papers, pp. 161–164 (2009)
3. Devlin, J., Chang, M.W., Lee, K., Toutanova, K.: Bert: pre-training of deep bidirectional transformers for language understanding. arXiv preprint arXiv:1810.04805 (2018)
4. Ghanem, B., Rosso, P., Rangel, F.: An emotional analysis of false information in social media and news articles. ACM Trans. Internet Technol. (TOIT) **20**(2), 1–18 (2020)
5. Gilbert, C., Hutto, E.: Vader: A parsimonious rule-based model for sentiment analysis of social media text. In: Eighth International Conference on Weblogs and Social Media (ICWSM 2014), vol. 81, p. 82 (2014)
6. Hills, T.T.: The dark side of information proliferation. Perspect. Psychol. Sci. **14**(3), 323–330 (2019)
7. Horne, B.D., Adali, S.: This just in: fake news packs a lot in title, uses simpler, repetitive content in text body, more similar to satire than real news. In: The 2nd International Workshop on News and Public Opinion at ICWSM (2017)
8. Milton, A., Batista, L., Allen, G., Gao, S., Ng, Y., Pera, M.S.: "Don't judge a book by its cover": exploring book traits children favor. In: RecSys 2020: Fourteenth ACM Conference on Recommender Systems, Virtual Event, Brazil, 22–26 September 2020, pp. 669–674. ACM (2020)
9. Mohammad, S.: Word affect intensities. In: Proceedings of the Eleventh International Conference on Language Resources and Evaluation (LREC 2018), Miyazaki, Japan, 7–12 May 2018 (2018)
10. Pennebaker, J.W., Boyd, R.L., Jordan, K., Blackburn, K.: The development and psychometric properties of LIWC2015. Technical report (2015)
11. Pérez-Rosas, V., Kleinberg, B., Lefevre, A., Mihalcea, R.: Automatic detection of fake news. In: Proceedings of the 27th International Conference on Computational Linguistics, pp. 3391–3401 (2018)
12. Potthast, M., Kiesel, J., Reinartz, K., Bevendorff, J., Stein, B.: A stylometric inquiry into hyperpartisan and fake news. In: Proceedings of the 56th Annual Meeting of the Association for Computational Linguistics, ACL 2018, Melbourne, Australia, 15–20 July 2018, Volume 1: Long Papers, pp. 231–240 (2018)
13. Shearer, E., Grieco, E.: Americans are wary of the role social media sites play in delivering the news (2019)
14. Shrestha, A., Spezzano, F., Gurunathan, I.: Multi-modal analysis of misleading political news. In: van Duijn, M., Preuss, M., Spaiser, V., Takes, F., Verberne, S. (eds.) MISDOOM 2020. LNCS, vol. 12259, pp. 261–276. Springer, Cham (2020). https://doi.org/10.1007/978-3-030-61841-4_18
15. Shu, K., Mahudeswaran, D., Wang, S., Lee, D., Liu, H.: Fakenewsnet: a data repository with news content, social context, and spatiotemporal information for studying fake news on social media. Big Data **8**(3), 171–188 (2020)
16. Shu, K., Sliva, A., Wang, S., Tang, J., Liu, H.: Fake news detection on social media: a data mining perspective. ACM SIGKDD Explor. Newsl. **19**(1), 22–36 (2017)

17. Thelwall, M., Buckley, K., Paltoglou, G., Cai, D., Kappas, A.: Sentiment strength detection in short informal text. J. Am. Soc. Inform. Sci. Technol. **61**(12), 2544–2558 (2010)
18. Zimdars: False, misleading, clickbait-y, and satirical news sources (2016). https://docs.google.com/document/d/10eA5-mCZLSS4MQY5QGb5ewC3VAL-6pLkT53V_81ZyitM/preview

Federated Online Learning to Rank with Evolution Strategies: A Reproducibility Study

Shuyi Wang$^{(\boxtimes)}$, Shengyao Zhuang , and Guido Zuccon

The University of Queensland, St Lucia, Australia
{shuyi.wang,s.zhuang,g.zuccon}@uq.edu.au

Abstract. Online Learning to Rank (OLTR) optimizes ranking models using implicit users' feedback, such as clicks, directly manipulating search engine results in production. This process requires OLTR methods to collect user queries and clicks; current methods are not suited to situations in which users want to maintain their privacy, i.e. not sharing data, queries and clicks.

Recently, the federated OLTR with evolution strategies (FOLtR-ES) method has been proposed to provide a solution that can meet a number of users' privacy requirements. Specifically, this method exploits the federated learning framework and ϵ-local differential privacy. However, the original research study that introduced this method only evaluated it on a small Learning to Rank (LTR) dataset and with no conformity with respect to current OLTR evaluation practice. It further did not explore specific parameters of the method, such as the number of clients involved in the federated learning process, and did not compare FOLtR-ES with the current state-of-the-art OLTR method. This paper aims to remedy to this gap.

Our findings question whether FOLtR-ES is a mature method that can be considered in practice: its effectiveness largely varies across datasets, click types, ranker types and settings. Its performance is also far from that of current state-of-the-art OLTR, questioning whether the maintained of privacy guaranteed by FOLtR-ES is not achieved by seriously undermining search effectiveness and user experience.

Keywords: Online learning to rank · Federated machine learning · Differential privacy

1 Introduction

Online learning to rank (OLTR) exploits users queries and interactions with search engine result pages (SERPs) to iteratively train and update a ranker in production [16]. In particular, OLTR relies on implicit user feedback from interactions on SERPs, e.g., clicks, rather than editorial relevance labels. Several methods for OLTR exist that attempt to address the specific challenges of online

© Springer Nature Switzerland AG 2021
D. Hiemstra et al. (Eds.): ECIR 2021, LNCS 12657, pp. 134–149, 2021.
https://doi.org/10.1007/978-3-030-72240-1_10

learning [7,9,16,30]: from making sense of the implicit feedback, to exploring the space of feature weights, accounting for biases in the click signal, reducing the impact of the online learning process on user experience, among others.

An aspect that has not been received wide attention in OLTR is how the privacy of users could be guaranteed. Current OLTR methods in fact assume that a central server collects all queries and interactions of all users of the search system, and it is this central server that is responsible for the indexing of the collection, the training of the ranker and the production of the SERPs. A recent work by Kharitonov, however, has attempted to provide a mechanism for OLTR that preserves the privacy of users [10]. The method, called FOLtR-ES, relies on the federated learning paradigm [27], in which data (collection, queries, interactions) is maintained at each client's side along with a copy of the ranker, and updates to the rankers that are learned from the interaction on the client side are shared to the central server, which is responsible for aggregating the update signal from clients and propagate the aggregated ranker update. In this specific case, all users observe and act on the same feature space; each user however retains control of their own data, which includes the collection, the queries and the interactions. FOLtR-ES uses evolutionary strategies akin to those in genetic algorithms to make client rankers explore the feature space, and a parametric privacy preserving mechanism to further anonymise the feedback signal that is shared by clients to the central server.

This paper aims to replicate and then reproduce the experiments from the original work of Kharitonov [10], investigating the effect different configurations of that federated OLTR method have on effectiveness and user experience, extending and generalising its evaluation to different settings commonly used in OLTR and to different collections. Specifically, we address the following research questions:

RQ1: *Does the performance of FOLftR-ES generalise beyond the MQ2007/2008 datasets?* The original method was only evaluated using MQ2007/2008 [18], while current OLTR practice is to use larger datasets that are feature richer and that contain typical web results.

RQ2: *How does the number of clients involved in FOLtR-ES affect its performance?* FOLtR-ES was previously evaluated using a set number of clients involved in the federated OLTR process ($n = 2,000$), and it was left unclear whether considering more or less client would impact performance.

RQ3: *How does FOLtR-ES compare with current state-of-the-art OLTR methods?* Compared to OLTR methods, FOLtR-ES preserves user privacy, but it is unclear to what expense in terms of search performance: the original work compared FOLtR-ES to rankers in non-federated settings, but the rankers used in there were not the current state-of-the-art in OLTR.

RQ4: *How does FOLtR-ES performance generalise to the evaluation settings commonly used for OLTR evaluation, i.e. measuring offline and online performance, with respect to nDCG and with relevance labels?* The original evaluation of FOLtR-ES considered an unusual setting for OLTR, consisting of using MaxRR [19] as evaluation measure in place of nDCG, computed on simulated clicks instead of on relevance labels.

The results of our empirical investigation of FOLtR-ES help understanding the specific settings in which this technique works, and the trade-offs between user privacy and search performance (in terms of effectiveness and user experience). They also unveil that more work is require to devise effective federated methods for OLTR that can guarantee some degree of user privacy without sensibly compromising search performance.

2   Federated OLTR with Evolution Strategies

We provide a brief overview of the FOLtR-ES method, which extends online LTR to federated learning; this is done by exploiting evolution strategies optimization, a widely used paradigm in Reinforcement Learning. The FOLtR-ES method consists of three parts. First, it casts the ranking problem into the federated learning optimization setting. Second, it uses evolution strategies to estimate gradients of the rankers. Finally, it introduces a privatization procedure to further protect users' privacy.

2.1   Federated Learning Optimization Setting

The federated learning optimization setting consists in turn of several steps, and assumes the presence of a central server and a number of distributed clients. First, a client downloads the most recently updated ranker from the server. Afterwards, the client observes B user interactions (search queries and examination of SERPs) which are served by the client's ranker. The performance metrics of these interactions are averaged by the client and a privatized message is sent to the centralized server. After receiving messages from N clients, the server combines them to estimate a single gradient g and performs an optimization step to update the current ranker. Finally, the clients download the newly updated ranker from the server.

2.2   Gradient Estimation

The method assumes that the ranker comes from a parametric family indexed by vector $\theta \in R^n$. Each time a user u has an interaction a, the ranking quality is measured; this is denoted as f. The goal of optimization is to find the vector θ^* that can maximize the mean of the metric f across all interactions a from all users u:

$$\theta^* = \arg\max_\theta F(\theta) = \arg\max_\theta \mathbb{E}_u \mathbb{E}_{a|u,\theta} f(a; \theta, u) \qquad (1)$$

Using Evolution Strategies (ES) [20], FOLtR-ES considers a population of parameter vectors which follow the distribution with a density function $p_\phi(\theta)$.

The objective aims to find the distribution parameter ϕ that can maximize the expectation of the metric across the population:

$$\mathbb{E}_{\theta \sim p_\phi(\theta)} [F(\theta)] \tag{2}$$

The gradient g of the expectation of the metric across the population (Eq. 2) is obtained in a manner similar to REINFORCE [24]:

$$g = \nabla_\phi \mathbb{E}_\theta[F(\theta)] = \nabla_\phi \int_\theta p_\phi(\theta)F(\theta)d\theta = \int_\theta F(\theta)\nabla_\phi p_\phi(\theta)d\theta$$

$$= \int_\theta F(\theta)p_\phi(\theta)\left(\nabla_\phi \log p_\phi(\theta)\right)d\theta = \mathbb{E}_\theta \left[F(\theta) \cdot \nabla_\phi \log p_\phi(\theta)\right] \tag{3}$$

Following the Evolution Strategies method, FOLtR-ES instantiates the population distribution $p_\phi(\theta)$ as an isotropic multivariate Gaussian distribution with mean ϕ and fixed diagonal covariance matrix $\sigma^2 I$. Thus a simple form of gradient estimation is denoted as:

$$g = \mathbb{E}_{\theta \sim p_\phi(\theta)} \left[F(\theta) \cdot \frac{1}{\sigma^2}(\theta - \phi)\right] \tag{4}$$

Based on the federated learning optimization setting, θ is sampled independently on the client side. Combined with the definition of $F(\theta)$ in Eq. 1, the gradient can be obtained as:

$$g = \mathbb{E}_u \mathbb{E}_{\theta \sim p_\phi(\theta)} \left[\left(\mathbb{E}_{a|u,\theta} f(a;\theta,u)\right) \cdot \frac{1}{\sigma^2}(\theta - \phi)\right] \tag{5}$$

To obtain the estimate $\hat{g}$ of g from Eq. 5, $\hat{g} \approx g$, the following steps are followed: (i) each client u randomly generates a pseudo-random seed s and uses the seed to sample a perturbed model $\theta_s \sim \mathbb{N}\left(\phi, \sigma^2 I\right)$, (ii) the average of metric f over B interactions is used to estimate the expected loss $\hat{f} \approx \mathbb{E}_{a|u,\theta_s} f(a;\theta_s,u)$ from Eq. 5, (iii) each client communicates the message tuple $(s, \hat{f})$ to the server, (iv) the centralized server computes the estimate $\hat{g}$ of Eq. 5 according to all message sent from the N clients.

To reduce the variance of the gradient estimates, means of antithetic variates are used in FOLtR-ES: this is a common ES trick [20]. The algorithm of the gradient estimation follows the standard ES practice, except that the random seeds are sampled at the client side.

2.3   Privatization Procedure

To ensure that the clients' privacy is fully protected, in addition to the federated learning setting, FOLtR-ES also proposes a privatization procedure that introduces privatization noise in the communication between the clients and the server.

Assume that the metric used on the client side is discrete or can be discretized if continuous. Then, the metric takes a finite number (n) of values, $f_0, f_1, ..., f_{n-1}$.

For each time the client experiences an interaction, the true value of the metric is denoted as f_0 and the remaining $n-1$ values are different from f_0. When the privatization procedure is used, the true metric value f_0 is sent with probability p. Otherwise, with probability $1-p$, a randomly selected value $\hat{f}$ out of the remaining $n-1$ values is sent. To ensure the same optimization goal described in Sect. 2.2, FOLtR-ES assumes that the probability $p > 1/n$.

Unlike other federated learning methods, FOLtR-ES adopts a strict notion of ϵ-local differential privacy [10], in which the privacy is considered at the level of the client, rather than of the server. Through the privatization procedure, ϵ-local differential privacy is achieved, and the upper bound of ϵ is:

$$\epsilon \leq log\frac{p(n-1)}{1-p} \tag{6}$$

This means that, thanks to the privatization scheme, at least $log[p(m-1)/(1-p)]$-local differential privacy can be guaranteed. At the same time, any ϵ-local differential private mechanism also can obtain ϵ-differential privacy [3].

3   Experimental Settings

3.1   Datasets

The original work of Kharitonov [10] conducted experiments on the MQ2007 and MQ2008 learning to rank datasets [18], which are arguably small and outdated. In our work, we instead consider more recent and lager datasets: MSLR-WEB10k [18] and Yahoo! Webscope [1], which are commonly-used in offline and online learning to rank [6,7,16,30]. Compared to MQ2007/2008, both MSLR-WEB10k and Yahoo! use 5-level graded relevance judgements, ranging from 0 (not relevant) to 4 (perfectly relevant). Each dataset contains many more queries and corresponding candidate documents than MQ2007/2008: MSLR-WEB10k has 10,000 queries, with each query having 125 assessed documents on average, while Yahoo! has 29,921 queries with 709,877 documents. In addition, both datasets have much richer and numerous features. MSLR-WEB10k has 136 features and Yahoo! 700. For direct comparison with the original FOLtR-ES work, we also use MQ2007/2008.

3.2   Simulation

It is common practice in OLTR to use LTR datasets and simulate user interactions [6,22]. This is because no public dataset with LTR features and clicks is available; in addition OLTR methods directly manipulate the rankings that have to be shown to users, so even if a public dataset with LTR features and clicks was to be available, this could not be used for OLTR. Thus, we simulate users and their reaction with the search results using labelled offline learning to rank datasets, akin to previous work [6,22].

For the experiment, we follow the same method used by the original FOLtR-ES work. We sample B queries for each client randomly and use the local perturbed model to rank documents. The length for each ranking list is limited to 10 documents. After simulating users clicks, we record the quality metric for each interaction and perform the privatization procedure with probability p. Next, we send the averaged metric and pseudo-random seed to optimize the centralized ranker. Finally, each client receives the updated ranker.

For simulating users' clicks, we use the Cascade Click Model (CCM) [5], as in the original FOLtR-ES work. We run instances of CCM using the same click probabilities and stop probabilities for MSLR-WEB10K and Yahoo!. Under CCM, the users are assumed to examine a SERP from top to bottom. Each document is examined and clicked with click probability $P(click = 1|r)$, conditioned on the relevance label r. After a click occurs, the user stops with stop probability $P(stop = 1|r)$, or continues otherwise. It is common practice in OLTR to consider three instantiations of the CCM: a *perfect* user with very reliable feedback, a *navigational* user searching for reasonably relevant documents, and an *informational* user with the noisiest feedback among three instantiations. Table 1 summarises the parameters of three click models. For simulating clicks for the MQ2007/2008, we use the same parameter settings from Table 1 in the original FOLtR-ES paper [10]: these are partially different from those used for MSLR-WEB10K and Yahoo! because relevance labels in these datasets are five-graded, while they are three-graded in MQ2007/2008.

Table 1. The three click model instantiations used for the MSLR-WEB10K and Yahoo! datasets.

R	$p(click = 1|R)$					$p(stop = 1|R)$				
	0	1	2	3	4	0	1	2	3	4
$perf$	0.0	0.2	0.4	0.8	1.0	0.0	0.0	0.0	0.0	0.0
nav	0.05	0.3	0.5	0.7	0.95	0.2	0.3	0.5	0.7	0.9
inf	0.4	0.6	0.7	0.8	0.9	0.1	0.2	0.3	0.4	0.5

3.3   Evaluation Metric

For direct comparison with the original FOLtR-ES work, we use the reciprocal rank of the highest clicked result in each interaction (MaxRR [19]). This metric is computed on the clicks produced by the simulated users on the SERPs.

The evaluation setting above is unusual for OLTR. In RQ4, we also consider the more commonly used normalised Discounted Cumulative Gain (nDCG), as FOLtR-ES is designed to allow optimization based on any absolute measures of ranking quality. We thus record the nDCG@10 values from the relevance labels of the SERP displayed to users during interactions. This is referred to as online nDCG and the scores represent users' satisfaction [6]. We also record the nDCG@10 of the final learned ranker measured a heldout test set: this is refer to as offline nDCG.

3.4 FOLtR-ES and Comparison OLTR Methods

In all experiments, we adopt the same models and optimization steps used by Kharitonov [10], and rely on the well document implementation made publicly available by the author. The two ranking models used by FOLtR-ES are a linear ranker and a neural ranker with a single hidden layer of size 10. For optimization, we use Adam [11] with default parameters.

To study how well FOLtR-ES compares with current state-of-the-art OLTR (RQ3), we implemented the Pairwise Differentiable Gradient Descent (PDGD) [16]. Unlike many previous OLTR methods that are designed for linear models, PDGD also provides effective optimization for non-linear models such as neural rankers. During each interaction, a weighted differentiable pairwise loss is constructed in PDGD and the gradient is directly estimated by document pairs preferences inferred from user clicks. PDGD has been empirically found to be significantly better than traditional OLTR methods in terms of final convergence, learning speed and user experience during optimization, making PDGD the current state-of-the-art method for OLTR [7,16,30].

4 Results and Analysis

4.1 RQ1: Generalisation of FOLtR-ES Performance Beyond MQ2007/2008

For answering RQ1 we replicate the results obtained by Kharitonov [10] on the MQ2007 and MQ2008 datasets; we then reproduce the experiment on MSLR-WEB10k and Yahoo datasets, on which FOLtR-ES has not been yet investigated, and we compare the findings across datasets. For these experiments we use antithetic variates, set the number of interactions $B = 4$ and simulate 2,000 clients, use MaxRR as reward signal and for evaluation on clicked items.

Figure 1a reports the results obtained by FOLtR-ES on the MQ2007 dataset[1] with respect to the three click models considered, various settings for the privatization parameter p, and the two FOLtR-ES methods (linear and neural). Our results fully replicate those of Kharitonov [10] and indicate the following findings: (1) FOLtR-ES allows for the iterative learning of effective rankers; (2) high values of p (lesser privacy) provide higher effectiveness; (3) the neural ranker is more effective than the linear ranker when $p \rightarrow 1$ (small to no privacy), while the linear model is equivalent, or better (for informational clicks) when $p = 0.5$.

However, not all these findings are applicable to the results obtained when considering MSLR-WEB10k and Yahoo!, which are displayed in Figs. 1b and 1c. In particular, we observe that (1) the results for MSLR-WEB10k (and to a lesser extent also for Yahoo!) obtained with the informational click model are very

---

[1] Similar results were obtained for MQ2008 and are omitted for space reasons.

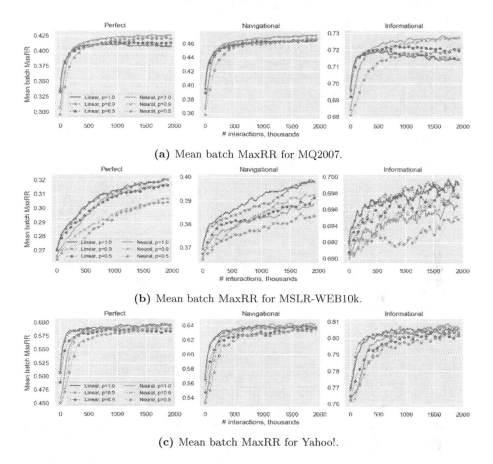

(a) Mean batch MaxRR for MQ2007.

(b) Mean batch MaxRR for MSLR-WEB10k.

(c) Mean batch MaxRR for Yahoo!.

Fig. 1. Results for RQ1: performance of FOLtR-ES across datasets under three different click models (averaged across all dataset splits).

unstable, and, regardless of the click model, FOLtR-ES requires more data than with MQ2007/2008 to arrive at a stable performance, when it does; (2) the neural ranker is less effective than the linear ranker, especially on MSLR-WEB10k. We believe these findings are due to the fact that query-document pairs in MSLR-WEB10k and Yahoo! are represented by a larger number of features than in MQ2007/2008. Thus, more data is required for effective training, especially for the neural model; we also note that FOLtR-ES is largely affected by noisy clicks in MSLR-WEB10k.

4.2   RQ2: Effect of Number of Clients on FOLtR-ES

To answer RQ2 we vary the number of clients involved in FOLtR-ES; we investigate the values {50, 1,000, 2,000}. Kharitonov [10] used 2,000 in the original experiments, and the impact of the number of clients has not been studied. To be able to fairly compare results across number of clients, we fixed the total number of ranker updates to 2,000,000; we also set $B = 4$ and $p = 0.9$. We perform these experiments on all three datasets considered in this paper, but we omit to report results for Yahoo! due to space limitations.

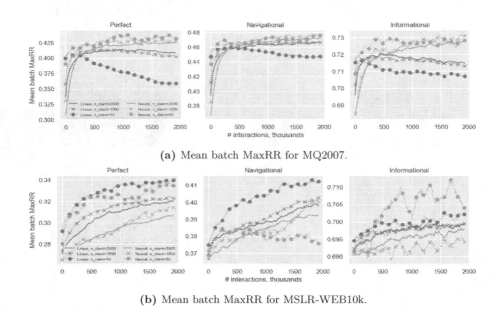

(a) Mean batch MaxRR for MQ2007.

(b) Mean batch MaxRR for MSLR-WEB10k.

Fig. 2. Results for RQ2: performance of FOLtR-ES with respect to number of clients (averaged across all dataset splits).

The results of these experiments are reported in Fig. 2, and they are mixed. For MQ2007, the number of clients have little effect on the neural ranker used in FOLtR-ES, although when informational clicks are provided this ranker is less stable, although often more effective, if very few clients (50) are used. Having just 50 clients, instead, severally hits the performance of the linear ranker, when compared with 1,000 or 2,000 clients. The findings on MSLR-WEB10k, however, are different. In this dataset, a smaller number of clients (50), is generally better than larger numbers, both for linear and neural ranker. An exception to this is when considering navigational clicks: in this case the linear ranker obtains by far the best performance with a small number of clients, but the neural ranker obtains the worst performance. This suggest that the number of clients greatly affects FOLtR-ES: but trends are not consistent across click types and datasets.

4.3   RQ3: Comparing FOLtR-ES to State-of-the-Art OLTR Methods

The original study of FOLtR-ES did not compared the method with non-federated OLTR approaches. To contextualise the performance of FOLtR-ES and to understand the trade-off between privacy and performance when designing FOLtR-ES, we compare this method with the current state-of-the-art OLTR method, the Pairwise Differentiable Gradient Descent (PDGD) [16]. For fair comparison, we set the privatization parameter $p = 1$ (lowest privacy) and the number of clients to 2,000. In addition note that in normal OLTR settings, rankers are updated after each user interaction: however in FOLtR-ES, rankers are updated in small batches. For fair comparison, we adapt PDGD to be updated in batch too. Instead of updating the ranker after each interaction (batch size 1), we accumulate gradients computed on the same batch size as for FOLtR-ES. Specifically, with 2000 clients for FOLtR-ES, the batch size of each update is 8,000 iterations ($4 \times 2,000$). We then compute the updated gradients for PDGD on 8,000 interactions too. We perform these experiments on all three datasets considered in this paper, but we omit to report results for Yahoo! due to space limitations.

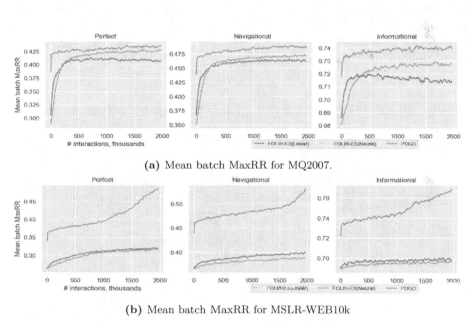

(a) Mean batch MaxRR for MQ2007.

(b) Mean batch MaxRR for MSLR-WEB10k

Fig. 3. Results for RQ3: performance of FOLtR-ES and PDGD across datasets with privatization parameter $p = 1$ and 2,000 clients (averaged across all dataset splits).

Results are shown in Fig. 3: regardless of linear or neural ranker, FOLtR-ES is less effective than PDGD. The gap in performance is greater in larger datasets like MSLR-WEB10k than in the smaller MQ2007/2008. This gap becomes even bigger, especially for the first iterations, if the PDGD ranker was updated after each iteration (not shown here), rather than after a batch has been completed. This highlights that FOLtR-ES has the merit of being the first privacy preserving federated OLTR approach available; however, more work is needed to improve the performance of FOLtR based methods so as to close the gap between privacy-oriented approaches and centralise approaches that do not consider user privacy.

4.4 RQ4: Extending FOLtR-ES Evaluation to Common OLTR Practice

In the original work and in the sections above, FOLtR-ES was evaluated using MaxRR computed with respect to the clicks performed by the simulated users (click models). This is an unusual evaluation for OLTR because: (1) usually nDCG@10 is used in place of MaxRR as metric, (2) nDCG is computed with respect to relevance labels, and not clicks, and on a withheld portion of the dataset, not on the interactions observed – this is used to produce learning curves and is referred to as offline nDCG, (3) in addition online nDCG is measured from the relevance labels in the SERPs from which clicks are obtained, and either displayed as learning curves or accumulated throughout the sessions – these values represent how OLTR has affected user experience. We then consider this more common evaluation of OLTR next, where we set the number of clients to 2,000 and experiment with $p = \{0.5, 0.9, 1.0\}$; we omit to report results for Yahoo! due to space limitations.

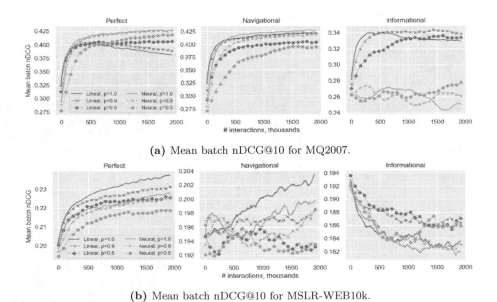

(a) Mean batch nDCG@10 for MQ2007.

(b) Mean batch nDCG@10 for MSLR-WEB10k.

Fig. 4. Results for RQ4: performance of FOLtR-ES in terms of online nDCG@10 computed using relevance labels and the SERPs used for obtaining user iterations (averaged across all dataset splits).

Results are reported in Fig. 4. It is interesting to compare these plots with those in Fig. 1, that relate to the unusual (for OLTR) evaluation setting used

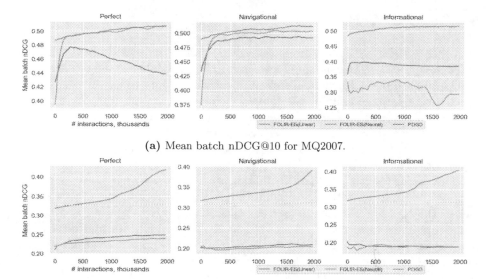

(a) Mean batch nDCG@10 for MQ2007.

(b) Mean batch nDCG@10 for MSLR-WEB10k.

Fig. 5. Results for RQ4: performance of FOLtR-ES and PDGD in terms of offline nDCG@10 with privatization parameter $p = 1$ and 2,000 clients (averaged across all dataset splits).

in the original FOLtR-ES work. By comparing the figures, we note that for MQ2007, FOLtR-ES can effectively learn rankers for perfect and navigational clicks. However, when the clicks become noisier (informational clicks), then FOLtR-ES learning is effective for the linear ranker but no learning occurs for the neural ranker: this is unlikely in the evaluation settings of the original work (Fig. 1). We note this finding repeating also for MSLR-WEB10k, but this time this affects both linear and neural rankers; we also note that the online performance in MSLR-WEB10k on navigational clicks is also quite unstable and exhibits little learning for specific values of p and ranker type. The online performance on MSLR10k for informational clicks (noisiest clicks) even exhibits a decreasing trend as iterations increase.

We further investigate the performance of FOLtR-ES with respect to offline nDCG@10. Results are shown in Fig. 5, and are plotted along with the offline nDCG@10 of PDGD for additional context. Also the offline performance confirm that FOLtR-ES does not provide stable learning across click settings, datasets and ranker types. We also note that the performance of PDGD are sensibly higher than that of FOLtR-ES, apart for the neural ranker on MQ2007 when perfect and navigational clicks are considered.

These findings suggest that FOLtR-ES is yet far from being a solution that can be considered for use in practice, and more research is required for devising effective federated, privacy-aware OLTR techniques.

5   Related Work

Learning to rank (LTR) consists of the application of supervised machine learning techniques to learn a ranking function from a set of labelled query-document pair examples, represented by features. A key limitation of LTR is the reliance on explicit relevance annotations (labels), which require substantial effort and cost to collect [1,18]. Editorial labelling also poses ethical issue when needing labels for private data [23], e.g., emails; in addition user preferences may not agree with that of annotators [21] and these labels cannot reflect evolving user preferences and search intents [15].

The use of implicit feedback in the form of, e.g., clicks has been suggested as a way to go beyond the above limitations [8]; this is the type of signal that the methods studied in this paper consider. This setting however presents a number of challenges: clicks are affected by a number of biases and noise, e.g., position bias and noisy clicks [4,9,17]. Approaches that exploit click feedback can be divided into counterfactual learning to rank (CLTR) [9] and online learning to rank (OLTR) [28]. CLTR relies on historical click through logs, treated as pure binary relevance labels, and commonly inverse propensity scoring (IPS) is used to re-weight clicks to minimise the impact of biases. Rankers are then trained in an offline manner and deployed online after training. OLTR instead, interactively updates rankers after each user interaction, in an online manner, and rankers explicitly manipulate SERPs to guide the learning process. This is the setup we consider in this paper, where rankers are iteratively updated in an online fashion following user interactions. A key aspect of OLTR is that the online interventions performed by rankers to guide the learning process carry the risk of displaying non optimal SERPs directly to the user, thus hurting user experience. It is important then for OLTR to rapidly learn a high quality ranker so as to not displaying low quality SERPs to a large number of users.

Little attention has been put on the fact that OLTR requires the search engine to monitor and collect user behaviour, thus not being appropriate when users want to preserve their privacy. In fact, current OLTR methods consider a central server that produces SERPs, collects queries and implicit user feedback, and updates a central ranker. An exception is the work of Kharitonov [10], considered in this paper, that instead exploits federate learning to de-centralise the collection of user data and computation of gradient updates to the ranker; a central server is still required, but this only observes the federated gradient updates, which are then applied to the central ranker which is then distributed to the clients at each update iteration (more details in Sect. 2). Federated (machine) learning was recently introduced by Konecny et al. [12,13]; in this framework models are learnt based on datasets distributed across different locations (clients) without the need to share the actual data, and with mechanisms to guarantee data leakage [27]. Privacy preservation is a topic of growing interest in information retrieval, with related workshops and tutorials being held in relevant venues [25,26], but its main focus so far has been on query log anonymisation and privacy-preservation when sharing logs [2,14,29], rather than on integrating privacy preservation mechanisms within the ranking algorithms, as the work of Kharitonov instead does [10].

6   Conclusions

In this paper we considered the federated online learning to rank with evolutionary strategies (FOLtR-ES) method recently proposed by Kharitonov [10]. This is an interesting method because privacy requirements have been so far ignored in OLTR, and FOLtR-ES represents the first method of its kind.

We set to explore four research questions related to FOLtR-ES. RQ1 aimed to investigate the generalisability of the original results obtained by FOLtR-ES on the MQ2007/2008 dataset to other datasets used in current OLTR practice. Our experiments on MQ2007/2008 show consistent findings with that of Kharitonov [10]. However, when larger LTR datasets are considered, results change. In particular, the neural ranker used in FOLtR-ES is less effective than the linear ranker, especially on MSLR-WEB10k.

RQ2 aimed to investigate the effect varying the number of clients involved in FOLtR-ES has on the effectiveness of the method. Our experiments show mixed results with respect to the number of clients: the effect largely varies depending on dataset, ranker type and click settings.

RQ3 aimed to compare FOLtR-ES with current OLTR state-of-the-art methods to understand the gap required to be paid for maintaining privacy. Our experiments show that FOLtR-ES lags behind the current OLTR state-of-the-art in terms of ranking performance: differences become more substantial when noisy clicks or larger datasets are considered.

RQ4 aimed to investigate the generalisability of the original results obtained for FOLtR-ES to common evaluation practice in OLTR. Our experiments show that if the common evaluation settings used in OLTR are used to evaluate FOLtR-ES, then thee method shows high variability in effectiveness across datasets, rankers and clicks types – and overall that FOLtR-ES is unreliable on large datasets and noisy clicks. This finding suggests that more research and improvements are needed before a federated OLTR method, and FOLtR-ES in particular, can be used in practice.

Code, experiment scripts and further results are provided at https://github.com/ielab/foltr.

Acknowledgements. Shuyi Wang is sponsored by a China Scholarship Council (CSC) scholarship. Associate Professor Guido Zuccon is the recipient of an Australian Research Council DECRA Research Fellowship (DE180101579) and a Google Faculty Award.

References

1. Chapelle, O., Chang, Y.: Yahoo! learning to rank challenge overview. In: Chapelle, O., Chang, Y., Liu, T. (eds.) Proceedings of the Yahoo! Learning to Rank Challenge, held at ICML 2010, Haifa, Israel, June 25, 2010. JMLR Proceedings, JMLR.org, vol. 14, pp. 1–24 (2011)
2. Cooper, A.: A survey of query log privacy-enhancing techniques from a policy perspective. ACM Trans. Web (TWEB) 2(4), 1–27 (2008)
3. Dwork, C., et al.: The algorithmic foundations of differential privacy. Found. Trend Theor. Comput. Sci. 9(3–4), 211–407 (2014)
4. Guan, Z., Cutrell, E.: An eye tracking study of the effect of target rank on web search. In: Proceedings of the SIGCHI Conference on Human Factors in Computing Systems, pp. 417–420 (2007)
5. Guo, F., Liu, C., Wang, Y.M.: Efficient multiple-click models in web search. In: Proceedings of the Second International Conference on Web Search and Web Data Mining, WSDM 2009, Barcelona, Spain, February 9–11, 2009, pp. 124–131. ACM (2009)
6. Hofmann, K., Schuth, A., Whiteson, S., De Rijke, M.: Reusing historical interaction data for faster online learning to rank for IR. In: Proceedings of the Sixth ACM International Conference on Web Search and Data Mining, pp. 183–192 (2013)
7. Jagerman, R., Oosterhuis, H., de Rijke, M.: To model or to intervene: a comparison of counterfactual and online learning to rank from user interactions. In: Proceedings of the 42nd International ACM SIGIR Conference on Research and Development in Information Retrieval, pp. 15–24 (2019)
8. Joachims, T.: Optimizing search engines using clickthrough data. In: Proceedings of the Eighth ACM SIGKDD International Conference on Knowledge Discovery and Data Mining, pp. 133–142 (2002)
9. Joachims, T., Swaminathan, A., Schnabel, T.: Unbiased learning-to-rank with biased feedback. In: Proceedings of the Tenth ACM International Conference on Web Search and Data Mining, pp. 781–789 (2017)
10. Kharitonov, E.: Federated online learning to rank with evolution strategies. In: Proceedings of the Twelfth ACM International Conference on Web Search and Data Mining, pp. 249–257 (2019)
11. Kingma, D.P., Ba, J.: Adam: a method for stochastic optimization. arXiv preprint arXiv:1412.6980 (2014)
12. Konecný, J., McMahan, H.B., Ramage, D., Richtárik, P.: Federated optimization: distributed machine learning for on-device intelligence. arXiv preprint arXiv:1610.02527 (2016)
13. Konecný, J., McMahan, H.B., Yu, F.X., Richtárik, P., Suresh, A.T., Bacon, D.: Federated learning: Strategies for improving communication efficiency. arXiv preprint arXiv:1610.05492 (2016)
14. Korolova, A., Kenthapadi, K., Mishra, N., Ntoulas, A.: Releasing search queries and clicks privately. In: Proceedings of the 18th International Conference on World Wide Web, pp. 171–180 (2009)
15. Lefortier, D., Serdyukov, P., De Rijke, M.: Online exploration for detecting shifts in fresh intent. In: Proceedings of the 23rd ACM International Conference on Conference on Information and Knowledge Management, pp. 589–598 (2014)
16. Oosterhuis, H., de Rijke, M.: Differentiable unbiased online learning to rank. In: Proceedings of the 27th ACM International Conference on Information and Knowledge Management, pp. 1293–1302 (2018)

17. Pan, B., Hembrooke, H., Joachims, T., Lorigo, L., Gay, G., Granka, L.: In google we trust: users' decisions on rank, position, and relevance. J. Comput. Mediated Commun. **12**(3), 801–823 (2007)
18. Qin, T., Liu, T.: Introducing LETOR 4.0 datasets. arXiv preprint arXiv:1306.2597 (2013)
19. Radlinski, F., Kleinberg, R., Joachims, T.: Learning diverse rankings with multi-armed bandits. In: Proceedings of the 25th International Conference on Machine Learning, pp. 784–791 (2008)
20. Salimans, T., Ho, J., Chen, X., Sidor, S., Sutskever, I.: Evolution strategies as a scalable alternative to reinforcement learning. arXiv preprint arXiv:1703.03864 (2017)
21. Sanderson, M.: Test collection based evaluation of information retrieval systems. Now Publishers Inc (2010)
22. Schuth, A., Oosterhuis, H., Whiteson, S., de Rijke, M.: Multileave gradient descent for fast online learning to rank. In: Proceedings of the Ninth ACM International Conference on Web Search and Data Mining, San Francisco, CA, USA, February 22–25, 2016, pp. 457–466. ACM (2016)
23. Wang, X., Bendersky, M., Metzler, D., Najork, M.: Learning to rank with selection bias in personal search. In: Proceedings of the 39th International ACM SIGIR Conference on Research and Development in Information Retrieval, pp. 115–124 (2016)
24. Williams, R.J.: Simple statistical gradient-following algorithms for connectionist reinforcement learning. Mach. Learn. **8**(3–4), 229–256 (1992)
25. Yang, G.H., Zhang, S.: Differential privacy for information retrieval. In: Proceedings of the ACM SIGIR International Conference on Theory of Information Retrieval, pp. 325–326 (2017)
26. Yang, H., Soboroff, I., Xiong, L., Clarke, C.L., Garfinkel, S.L.: Privacy-preserving IR 2016: differential privacy, search, and social media. In: Proceedings of the 39th International ACM SIGIR Conference on Research and Development in Information Retrieval, pp. 1247–1248 (2016)
27. Yang, Q., Liu, Y., Chen, T., Tong, Y.: Federated machine learning: concept and applications. ACM Trans. Intell. Syst. Technol. (TIST) **10**(2), 1–19 (2019)
28. Yue, Y., Joachims, T.: Interactively optimizing information retrieval systems as a dueling bandits problem. In: Proceedings of the 26th Annual International Conference on Machine Learning, pp. 1201–1208 (2009)
29. Zhang, S., Yang, H., Singh, L.: Anonymizing query logs by differential privacy. In: Proceedings of the 39th International ACM SIGIR conference on Research and Development in Information Retrieval, pp. 753–756 (2016)
30. Zhuang, S., Zuccon, G.: Counterfactual online learning to rank. In: Jose, J.M., et al. (eds.) ECIR 2020. LNCS, vol. 12035, pp. 415–430. Springer, Cham (2020). https://doi.org/10.1007/978-3-030-45439-5_28

Comparing Score Aggregation Approaches for Document Retrieval with Pretrained Transformers

Xinyu Zhang[1]([✉]) , Andrew Yates[2], and Jimmy Lin[1]

[1] David R. Cheriton School of Computer Science,
University of Waterloo, Waterloo, Canada
[2] Max Planck Institute for Informatics, Saarbrücken, Germany

Abstract. While BERT has been shown to be effective for passage retrieval, its maximum input length limitation poses a challenge when applying the model to document retrieval. In this work, we reproduce three passage score aggregation approaches proposed by Dai and Callan [5] for overcoming this limitation. After reproducing their results, we generalize their findings through experiments with a new dataset and experiment with other pretrained transformers that share similarities with BERT. We find that these BERT variants are not more effective for document retrieval in isolation, but can lead to increased effectiveness when combined with "pre–fine-tuning" on the MS MARCO passage dataset. Finally, we investigate whether there is a difference between fine-tuning models on "deep" judgments (i.e., fewer queries with many judgments each) vs. fine-tuning on "shallow" judgments (i.e., many queries with fewer judgments each). Based on available data from two different datasets, we find that the two approaches perform similarly.

1   Introduction

In the context of text retrieval, pretrained transformers such as BERT [6] have been shown to substantially improve ranking effectiveness across many domains, tasks, and settings [10]. Adapting BERT to passage retrieval is straightforward: it can be used as a classifier to predict the relevance of a passage with respect to a query, and such a relevance prediction model can be used to rerank candidate passages retrieved by an efficient first-stage keyword-based ranking method like BM25. However, BERT's maximum length limitation of 512 tokens prevents this approach from directly being applied to longer input texts like full-length documents. Several solutions have been proposed to address this issue by breaking a document into passages and then aggregating passage-level relevance to arrive at a document relevance score [1,5,9,12].

In this paper, we reproduce one such approach proposed by Dai and Callan [5]. Their approach segments documents into passages that can each be scored independently. At inference time, Dai and Callan [5] use one of three approaches to aggregate passage-level scores, called FirstP, MaxP, and SumP, which either

© Springer Nature Switzerland AG 2021
D. Hiemstra et al. (Eds.): ECIR 2021, LNCS 12657, pp. 150–163, 2021.
https://doi.org/10.1007/978-3-030-72240-1_11

takes the score of the first passage as the document score, the score of the maximum passage, or the sum of all passage scores, respectively. Dai and Callan [5] considered title and description queries on the Robust04 and ClueWeb09 test collections, finding that taking the maximum passage score as the document score (i.e., MaxP) was the most effective approach except when using description queries on ClueWeb09. However, the differences between MaxP and SumP were small in all settings.

Instead of replicating these results using the code[1] provided by Dai and Callan [5], we first independently reproduce their findings on Robust04 by implementing their approach with the Capreolus toolkit [18]. Note that our focus here is not to exactly obtain the same ranking metrics as their paper, but to attempt to reproduce their findings about the relative effectiveness of the various score aggregation approaches. Our Tensorflow v2 implementation is completely independent from the original code, which used Tensorflow v1 with an entirely different pipeline. In addition to the three approaches proposed in the paper, we introduce a new aggregation approach, AvgP, to compare with SumP and investigate the impact of document length. Our results show that the original findings are reproducible, though we observe much larger differences between MaxP and SumP than in the original work. In our results, MaxP consistently and significantly outperforms FirstP, SumP, and AvgP. As in the original work, we also find that BERT is more effective with description queries than with keyword queries.

Given that we are able to reproduce the results of Dai and Callan [5] on Robust04, we omit experiments on the ClueWeb09 collection. Instead, to further generalize the above findings and to provide a reference for the community, we apply the four aggregation approaches to the GOV2 test collection.[2] While we continue to observe a larger gap between MaxP and SumP than previously reported, our findings on GOV2 are consistent with those on Robust04: (1) MaxP is more effective than FirstP, SumP, and AvgP, and (2) description queries are more effective than keyword queries.

Since Dai and Callan [5] first demonstrated the effectiveness of MaxP for document retrieval, several BERT variants have been proposed that claim to improve BERT's effectiveness on NLP tasks by making architectural changes, e.g., sharing the same weights across all transformer layers [8] and changes to the pretraining setup such as removing the next sentence prediction task [11]. It is natural to ask whether retrieval can benefit from these model improvements and, if so, how much of an increase in effectiveness can be provided by using an improved variant. To answer this question, we repeated the above experiments with MaxP, the most effective aggregation approach, with different pretrained neural language models: RoBERTa [11], ALBERT [8], and ELECTRA [4].

In addition to the finding that pretrained language models improve effectiveness on ranking tasks, Dai and Callan [5] found that "pre–fine-tuning" BERT on Bing search log data further improves effectiveness (i.e., fine-tuning BERT on Bing data before further fine-tuning on the target dataset). Li et al. [9] pro-

---

[1] https://github.com/AdeDZY/SIGIR19-BERT-IR.
[2] http://ir.dcs.gla.ac.uk/test_collections/gov2-summary.htm.

vide further support for the benefit of pre–fine-tuning, and found that the MS MARCO passage dataset is more effective for this task than the Bing search logs. Furthermore, Zhang et al. [20] found that pre–fine-tuning BERT$_{Base}$ improves effectiveness regardless of the amount of data used to fine-tune for the downstream task. To validate these findings and to compare the impact of pretraining and pre–fine-tuning, we additionally consider whether the effectiveness of MaxP increases with pre–fine-tuning on MS MARCO.

Finally, we investigate the impact of different strategies for gathering relevance judgments on the effectiveness of MaxP. Traditionally, the Text REtrieval Conferences (TRECs) build test collections with "deep" judgments, in which a large number of judgments are obtained for a relatively small number of queries (typically, around 50). However, neural models are often trained on relevant query–document pairs or triples (queries with positive and negative instances), so it is unclear whether the "deep" approach of TREC is preferable to using many more queries but with fewer judgments per query (i.e., a "shallow" judgment approach). The recent MS MARCO dataset takes this shallow approach by providing a large number of queries that are associated with only one relevant document on average [3]. This dataset has become popular for training neural models. Similarly, the TREC 2007 Million Query dataset [2] provides shallow judgments and has also been used to train neural models for this reason [7,14]. To provide a more comprehensive view of how to best apply the BERT–MaxP model, we investigate the effectiveness of these two types of training data. Interestingly, based on available data from two different datasets, we find that the two approaches perform similarly (unlike Yilmaz and Robertson [19]).

In summary, the contributions of this work are:

1. We reproduce and confirm the findings of Dai and Callan [5] on Robust04 and further generalize the findings to the GOV2 test collection.
2. We investigate two approaches to obtaining "free" improvements in ranking effectiveness: using improved BERT variants or "pre–fine-tuning" on another retrieval dataset. The different BERT variants we examined bring no significant improvements, but pre–fine-tuning with MS MARCO data does improve effectiveness.
3. We investigate the impact of "deep" vs. "shallow" judgments on BERT–MaxP. At least for the datasets and sample sizes we explore, both approaches obtain similar levels of effectiveness.

2   Related Work

2.1   Passage Aggregation

Prior work has investigated several approaches for overcoming BERT's maximum length limitation by segmenting long documents into shorter passages. However, no consensus has been reached on how per-passage results should be aggregated. Dai and Callan [5] were the first to propose and evaluate different strategies for aggregating document scores. To do so, Dai and Callan [5] segment each document into N overlapping passages; each passage receives the relevance label of the document at training time. They compared three approaches to aggregate passage-level scores at inference time: FirstP, MaxP, and SumP. Given N passage scores from the same document, FirstP uses the score of the first passage as the document score, MaxP uses the highest passage score, and SumP uses the sum of all passage scores. Even though FirstP only uses the first passage from the document when computing document scores, it is not identical to truncating all documents in the corpus since the model is trained using all passages from the document. That is, although most passages do not directly contribute to the document score, they contribute to model fine-tuning.

Birch [1], another approach for aggregating passage scores, improves effectiveness by interpolating the top-k sentence-level scores, where $k \in 1, 2, 3$. To train the Birch model, datasets with passage-level judgments are used (e.g., MS MARCO and tweets). The model is then adapted for a target domain with longer documents by learning only the weights for the top-k scores as well as an interpolation weight for the first-stage ranker. Note that before these approaches, monoBERT [13] considered passage datasets where all "documents" were shorter than the model length limit, and thus the entire text can be fed into BERT at both training and inference time.

Rather than aggregating passage scores, MacAvaney et al. [12] concatenate the term representations BERT produces for each passage in order to form a document vector. This document vector is then used to construct a similarity matrix, which is used to compute a relevance score. Some variants of this approach additionally include the average of BERT's [CLS] representation of each passage. Li et al. [9] investigate additional approaches for aggregating passage representations instead of aggregating passage scores directly. They find that several strategies can improve over score aggregation.

In this work, we reproduce and extend the experiments in Dai and Callan [5] on different aggregation approaches. Note that since we apply other BERT variants to initialize this model (see Sect. 2.2), we use MaxP when referring to the general model architecture to avoid ambiguity and only use BERT–MaxP when the model is initialized with BERT$_{\text{Base}}$.

2.2   BERT Variants

While Devlin et al. [6] proposed several BERT variants with different model sizes (e.g., 110M weights with BERT$_{\text{Base}}$ and 330M weights with BERT$_{\text{Large}}$), additional variants have been proposed that purport to improve the model in different ways. RoBERTa [11] found that BERT's effectiveness on NLP tasks can be improved by modifying the training data and tuning pretraining hyperparameters. Additionally, RoBERTa eliminates the Next Sentence Prediction (NSP) objective as it was found to be ineffective for improving downstream tasks.

ALBERT [8] proposed to reduce BERT's parameters by factorizing word embedding into smaller matrices and sharing the parameters of each BERT layer. They found that, while these strategies compress the model size and accelerate pretraining given the same model configuration, the pretrained model still performs roughly on par with BERT$_{\text{Base}}$. This work additionally replaced the NSP task with Sentence Ordering Prediction (SOP), where the model is given two segments from the same document and learns to discriminate whether the two segments have been swapped. They found that the SOP task improves effectiveness on most of the downstream NLP tasks considered.

ELECTRA [4] improved representation learning efficiency by replacing the Masked Language Modeling (MLM) task with a new task called replaced token detection. In this task the model classifies whether *each* output token was generated by another small "generator" model or was the original token. The generator is a small two-layer BERT model that predicts masked tokens. While this approach requires training the generator model as well as the ELECTRA model, the new objective enables the model to learn from the output at all the positions, rather than just the 15% of the positions that are randomly masked in BERT's pretraining.

3   Experimental Setup

In this section, we describe in detail the BERT score aggregation approaches in our study, our approach for experimenting with other BERT variants, our methodology for generating deep and shallow judgments, and finally the experiment configurations.

3.1   BERT with MaxP, FirstP, SumP, and AvgP Aggregation

To apply BERT as a relevance classifier for text ranking, Nogueira and Cho [13] proposed feeding a query q and passage p to BERT to obtain a vector E$_{\text{CLS}}$ representing the interactions between them. To do so, a special [CLS] token is prepended to the input sequence, and a special [SEP] token is placed before and after the passage. This usage of the [CLS] vector follows the approach for applying a pretrained BERT model to classification tasks proposed by Devlin et al. [6]. This [CLS] vector is then fed to a fully-connected layer with two outputs followed by a softmax. The score of the positive class serves as the relevance score s used to rank the passages.

This approach is referred to as monoBERT. BERT's maximum input length limitation of 512 tokens[3] prevents this strategy from being directly applied to longer documents, however. In the work we are reproducing, Dai and Callan [5] proposed overcoming this limitation by converting a document d into a series of passages p_i, applying BERT as a relevance classifier to each passage p_i to obtain a series of relevance scores s_i, and then applying a score aggregation approach

---

[3] The length of BERT's inputs cannot exceed 512 tokens. This includes the query, the passage, and the three special tokens. This limitation comes from the fact that position embeddings are used to encode BERT's input; these position embeddings were only pretrained for sequences up to length 512.

to arrive at a final document relevance score s_d. To generate the passages, Dai and Callan [5] used a sliding window of 150 terms with a stride of 75.

Given this sequence of passages, one of three aggregation approaches was applied: taking the maximum passage score as the document score (MaxP), taking the first passage's score (FirstP), or taking the sum of all passage scores (SumP). We additionally consider an AvgP variant in which the sum of scores is divided by the number of passages in the document.

3.2   BERT Variants

In the original work, Dai and Callan [5] used BERT$_{Base}$ as a relevance classifier to obtain the scores s_i for aggregation. In addition to conducting experiments in this setting, we also experiment with using the larger BERT$_{Large}$ model provided by Devlin et al. [6], as well as the RoBERTa [11], ALBERT [8], and ELECTRA [4] models in their "base" sizes. Apart from the general-purpose pretrained models, we fine-tune BERT$_{Base}$ and ELECTRA$_{Base}$ using the MS MARCO passage dataset and add these pre–fine-tuned weights into our comparisons. These models can be viewed as drop-in replacements for BERT; to use them, we simply replace BERT$_{Base}$ with a different variant when computing E$_{CLS}$.

In the experiments investigating each pretrained model, we use the models available in the HuggingFace model hub [15], with names bert-base-uncased, bert-large-uncased, google/electra-base-discriminator, albert-base-v2 and roberta-base. For the experiment investigating the impact of MS MARCO pre–fine-tuning, we use the BERT$_{Base}$ weights provided by Nogueira and Cho [13] and the ELECTRA$_{Base}$ weights provided by Li et al. [9].

3.3   Deep and Shallow Sampling

In order to investigate whether it is preferable to use "deep and narrow" or "shallow and wide" judgments for training, we sample judgments from an existing test collection to simulate both cases. To accomplish this, we prepare ten smaller datasets from each of the Robust04[4] and GOV2[5] datasets by sampling the relevance judgments in a "shallow" or "deep" manner with a sampling rate r, described below.

Given the same number of judgments, the shallow setting contains more queries and fewer labeled documents per query, whereas the deep setting contains fewer queries with more labeled documents per query. The shallow setting is used in MS MARCO [3], whereas the deep setting is traditionally used in TREC evaluations. Shallow and deep sampling are two sampling schemes that we adopted to simulate these two labeling styles, respectively. The sampling approach we adopted in previous work [20] can be viewed as deep sampling, which provides a reference point for this paper.

---

[4] https://trec.nist.gov/data/robust/04.guidelines.html.
[5] http://ir.dcs.gla.ac.uk/test_collections/gov2-summary.htm.

Specifically, given a dataset with Q queries, D documents per query, and M judgments in total, where $M = Q \cdot D$, the r-sampled dataset always contains $r \cdot D$ judgments. Deep sampling accomplishes this by dropping queries with higher priority, while shallow sampling only drops the documents associated with each query and always preserves the original number of queries.

We achieve this with a two-step process. In the first step, deep sampling randomly preserves around $\lceil r \cdot Q \rceil$ queries, and shallow sampling randomly preserves $\lceil r \cdot D \rceil$ documents per query. At this point, both sampling mechanisms should produce slightly more than $r \cdot M$ judgments. In the second step, we eliminate the extra judgments by looping over the queries and randomly dropping one of its labeled documents until exactly $r \cdot D$ judgments are left.

Note that we use cross-validation in our experiments and the sampled datasets are only used in the training and validation folds. Test folds always contain the original judgments. That is, while the model is trained and validated on sampled data, it is evaluated with all available judgments to make fair comparisons.

3.4   Experimental Details

All the configurations are run on both the Robust04 and GOV2 datasets. Robust04 is a TREC collection with documents from the news domain that the original work [5] used in their evaluation. GOV2 contains documents crawled from .gov websites, which forms a different domain from Robust04. As in the original work, we use 5-fold cross-validation for Robust04 collection, with three folds for training, one fold for validation, and the other fold for evaluation. While Dai and Callan [5] did make their Robust04 folds available,[6] we opted to instead use the folds from Yang et al. [17] in order to ensure that the choice of folds does not affect the original findings. We randomly assign the queries in GOV2 into three groups and applied 3-fold cross-validation, with one fold for training, one fold for validation, and the other fold for evaluation.

We implement our experiments with the Capreolus toolkit [18]. To produce candidate documents for reranking, we use the Anserini BM25 implementation [16] with default parameters $k_1 = 0.9$ and $b = 0.4$ (i.e., the first-stage ranker). At training time we construct training instances from the top 1000 documents retrieved by BM25. We consider the top 100 documents at inference time since this setting is substantially more efficient (i.e., reranking 1000 documents takes ten times longer). This setting differs from the original work, which used a query-likelihood model as the first-stage ranker. As with the change in folds used, this allows us to provide evidence that the original work's findings are robust to minor changes in the experimental setup.

Following the original work, we generate passages from each document using a 150-term sliding window with a 75-term stride. The maximum number of passages per document is set to 30. During training, passages after the first

---

[6] http://boston.lti.cs.cmu.edu/appendices/SIGIR2019-Zhuyun-Dai/.

passage are randomly preserved with probability 0.1.[7] We use pairwise hinge loss and fine-tune the models over 36 epochs, with each epoch containing 256 batches of 16 training triples (i.e., a query, a positive document, and a negative document). We run validation every 4 epochs and preserve the best model in terms of nDCG@20 to mitigate overfitting. All experiments are fine-tuned using the Adam optimizer with $lr = 10^{-3}$ for non-BERT parameters and $lr = 10^{-5}$ for BERT parameters. The dropout rate for all fully-connected layers[8] is set to 0.1 except for ALBERT, where the dropout rate is set to 0.

For the reproduction and BERT variant experiments, we consider both keyword queries (title field) and description queries (desc field) on both datasets and report mAP, P@20, and nDCG@20, whereas for experiments comparing sampling mechanisms, we only report nDCG@20 on keyword queries. Our code and instructions are available on GitHub.[9]

4   Results and Discussion

4.1   Reproduction and Generalization of Aggregation Approaches

We report results from our attempts to reproduce Dai and Callan [5] in Table 1, which consist of the FirstP, MaxP, SumP, and AvgP score aggregation approaches with both keyword and description queries on the Robust04 and GOV2 datasets. All models are initialized from $BERT_{Base}$. Table 1a shows the Robust04 results copied from the original paper; Table 1b presents our results.

The nDCG@20 column under Robust04 in Table 1b shows that the original work's finding that MaxP outperforms FirstP on Robust04 is reproducible. In fact, we achieve slightly higher results for both methods, which confirms the correctness of our implementation. While MaxP continues to outperform SumP, the difference between these two methods is greater than in the original work. That is, Table 1a shows a tiny difference between the two with both approaches outperforming FirstP. However, in our results, SumP is not more effective than FirstP. Given that the implementation differences between these approaches are very small,[10] we attribute this finding to changes in our experimental setup (e.g., different folds and a different first-stage ranker). This suggests that MaxP is a more robust approach. In our results, MaxP almost always significantly outperforms the other approaches regardless of the query type or the dataset.

4.2   MaxP with BERT Variants

Results when initializing MaxP from different pretrained and pre–fine-tuned (denote "pFT") checkpoints are shown in Table 2. From the table, it can be

---

[7] https://github.com/AdeDZY/SIGIR19-BERT-IR/blob/master/run_qe_classifier.
py#L468-L471.

[8] The hidden_dropout_prob configuration in HuggingFace's library.

[9] https://github.com/crystina-z/MaxP-Reproduction.

[10] See line 58 of tools/bert_passage_result_to_trec.py in the original code.

Table 1. Results from the original work and our experiments for each passage score aggregation approach.

(a) The nDCG@20 metrics reported by Dai and Callan [5] on Robust04.

	Title			Desc		
	FirstP	MaxP	SumP	FirstP	MaxP	SumP
	0.444	0.469	0.467	0.491	0.529	0.524

(b) Our results with BERT–FirstP, BERT–MaxP, BERT–SumP, and BERT–AvgP. The underlined scores correspond to the values reported in Table 1a (i.e., nDCG@20 on Robust04). The best results are in **bold**. The † symbol indicates the score is significantly lower than the corresponding MaxP score according to a two-tailed t-test ($p < 0.01$) after Bonferroni correction.

		Robust04			GOV2		
		mAP@100	P@20	nDCG@20	mAP@100	P@20	nDCG@20
Title	FirstP	0.2163†	0.3821	0.4493	0.1730	0.5564	0.4911
	MaxP	**0.2384**	**0.4068**	**0.4767**	**0.1855**	**0.603**	**0.5175**
	SumP	0.2123†	0.3837	0.4476†	0.1679	0.5423	0.4679
	AvgP	0.2083†	0.3749	0.4383	0.1732	0.5594	0.4826
Desc	FirstP	0.2445†	0.4239†	0.5095	0.1811†	0.5803†	0.5213
	MaxP	**0.2646**	**0.4504**	**0.5303**	**0.1942**	**0.6292**	**0.5480**
	SumP	0.2113†	0.3821†	0.4436 †	0.1686†	0.5567†	0.4825†
	AvgP	0.2356†	0.4161†	0.4931†	0.1796†	0.5896	0.5099

Table 2. Results of MaxP models initialized with various pretrained or pre–fine-tuned weights. The † symbol indicates the score is significantly higher than the corresponding BERT$_{Base}$ score ($p < 0.01$) after Bonferroni correction. The best results among all pretrained models are underlined, and the best among all are in **bold**. Note that the $_{Base}$ subscript is omitted when there is no ambiguity.

		Robust04			GOV2		
		mAP@100	P@20	nDCG@20	mAP@100	P@20	nDCG@20
Title	BERT$_{Base}$	0.2384	0.4068	0.4767	0.1855	0.6030	0.5175
	BERT$_{Large}$	0.2424	0.4120	0.4875	0.1865	0.5990	0.5161
	ELECTRA	0.2437	0.4253	0.4959	0.1810	0.5718	0.4841
	RoBERTa	0.2425	0.4259	0.4938	0.1696	0.5591	0.4679
	ALBERT	0.2326	0.4006	0.4632	0.1925	0.6114	0.5354
	BERT$_{Base}$ (pFT)	0.2401	0.4207	0.4857	0.1958	0.6322	0.5473
	ELECTRA (pFT)	**0.2575**	**0.4482†**	**0.5225†**	**0.1998**	**0.6466**	**0.5624**
Desc	BERT$_{Base}$	0.2646	0.4504	0.5303	0.1942	0.6292	0.5480
	BERT$_{Large}$	0.2672	0.4655	0.5448	0.1968	0.6272	0.5420
	ELECTRA	0.2726	0.4584	0.5480	0.1895	0.6081	0.5152
	RoBERTa	0.2692	0.4671	0.5489	0.1928	0.6195	0.5370
	ALBERT	0.2637	0.4542	0.5400	0.1977	0.6309	0.5459
	BERT$_{Base}$ (pFT)	0.2719	0.4624	0.5476	0.2046†	0.6550	0.5788
	ELECTRA (pFT)	**0.2865†**	**0.4779†**	**0.5741†**	**0.2100†**	**0.6822†**	**0.6062†**

observed that although each BERT variant *can* achieve an improvement over BERT, such improvements are neither significant nor consistent across datasets or query types. On Robust04, BERT$_{Large}$, ELECTRA, and RoBERTa show some improvement over BERT$_{Base}$ for both query types, but their results on GOV2 are only on par with or even worse than BERT$_{Base}$. On the other hand, ALBERT is less effective than BERT on Robust04 with keyword queries and GOV2 with description queries, but improves over BERT$_{Base}$ in the other settings.

Compared with the inconsistent improvements brought by different BERT variants, the benefits of pre–fine-tuning on MS MARCO are much more stable. While the differences are significant only on GOV2, the pre–fine tuned BERT$_{Base}$ numerically outperforms the vanilla BERT$_{Base}$ across different query types and datasets. Moreover, the pre–fine-tuned ELECTRA yields an improvement with significant increases in a variety of settings.

4.3   Deep vs. Shallow Relevance Judgments

Table 3 shows the training effectiveness of MaxP across a spectrum of training and validation data sizes. Table 3a shows several baselines to put the results in context, including a BERT-MaxP model fine-tuned on only the MS MARCO collection (i.e., the pre–fine-tuned setting without further fine-tuning on the target domain) and the BERT-MaxP scores previously reported by Dai and Callan [5] and Li et al. [9]. Table 3b shows the BERT-MaxP metrics obtained by fine-tuning with each deep or shallow sampled dataset at different sampling

Table 3. Results of deep and shallow sampling experiments.

	Robust04	GOV2
BM25	0.4240	0.4740
BM25RM3	0.4310	0.4851
Zero-shot [20]	0.4751	0.5007
BERT$_{Base}$ [5]	0.4690	-
BERT$_{Base}$ (pFT) [9]	0.4931	0.5600

(a) nDCG@20 of baselines and prior work. The zero-shot setting uses the BERT$_{Base}$ checkpoint fine-tuned on the MS MARCO passage dataset.

	Robust04				GOV2			
	BERT$_{Base}$		BERT$_{Base}$ (pFT)		BERT$_{Base}$		BERT$_{Base}$ (pFT)	
	shallow	deep	shallow	deep	shallow	deep	shallow	deep
$r = 0.1$	0.4087	0.4111	0.4314	0.4427	0.4692	0.4538	0.5034	0.5197
$r = 0.3$	0.4592	0.4507	0.4658	0.4702	0.4861	0.4923	0.5290	0.5236
$r = 0.5$	0.4730	0.4593	0.4807	0.4725	0.5062	0.5039	0.5402	0.5384
$r = 0.7$	0.4779	0.4750	0.4821	0.4807	0.5106	0.5169	0.5358	0.5373
$r = 0.9$	0.4812	0.4711	0.4867	0.4787	0.5222	0.5202	0.5488	0.5429
$r = 1.0$	0.4767		0.4857		0.5175		0.5473	

(b) nDCG@20 on original and pre-fine-tuned (pFT) BERT$_{Base}$: results of fine-tuning BERT-MaxP using "deep" and "shallow" r-sampled judgments.

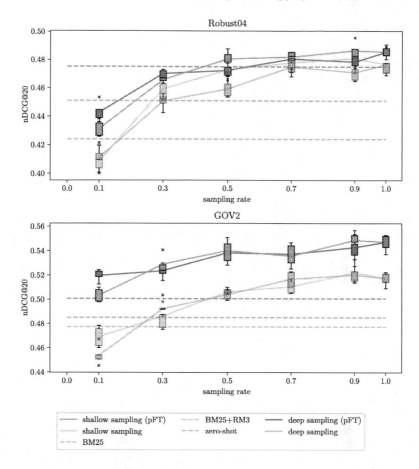

Fig. 1. Plots of baselines and our experiments with deep and shallow sampling.

rates r. As mentioned in Sect. 3.4, we report the median nDCG@20 of the five experiments under the same settings.

By plotting the scores in Fig. 1, it can be observed that while effectiveness benefits from more training and validation labels, there is no clear trend in terms of the superiority of the two schemes. It is not the case that one judgment scheme consistently yields better effectiveness than the other. This observation applies regardless of whether the model is pre–fine-tuned on MS MARCO. This is an interesting finding that differs from the results of Yilmaz and Robertson [19], who conducted similar experiments, but in a feature-based learning-to-rank context. Note that an important caveat here is that our sampling schemes apply only to sampling *training* data—in all cases, our test data are "complete". We have not explored the case where the test data are also sampled, in which case there may be differences between the two schemes for *evaluating* effectiveness.

5   Conclusion

In this work, we reproduced the three passage score aggregation approaches proposed in Dai and Callan [5]. We found that the MaxP aggregation approach is the most effective, and furthermore, the differences between MaxP and AvgP are larger than in the original work. We generalized this finding by conducting the same experiments on the GOV2 dataset and reaching the same conclusion. We found that MaxP can further benefit from pre–fine-tuning the model on the MS MARCO passage dataset, but does not necessarily benefit from replacing BERT with a newer variant. While none of the *general-purpose pretrained* models consistently improved over BERT, the pre–fine-tuned ELECTRA model achieved significant improvements under many settings. Finally, we explored the impact of fine-tuning BERT with shallow or deep judgments via sampling, finding that the model performed similarly regardless of which judgment scheme was used.

Acknowledgments. This research was supported in part by the Canada First Research Excellence Fund and the Natural Sciences and Engineering Research Council (NSERC) of Canada. In addition, we would like to thank Google Cloud and TensorFlow Research Cloud for credits to support this work.

References

1. Akkalyoncu Yilmaz, Z., Yang, W., Zhang, H., Lin, J.: Cross-domain modeling of sentence-level evidence for document retrieval. In: Proceedings of the 2019 Conference on Empirical Methods in Natural Language Processing and the 9th International Joint Conference on Natural Language Processing (EMNLP-IJCNLP), pp. 3481–3487 (2019)
2. Allan, J., Carterette, B., Aslam, J.A., Pavlu, V., Dachev, B., Kanoulas, E.: Million query track 2007 overview. In: Proceedings of TREC 2007 (2007)
3. Bajaj, P., et al.: MS MARCO: a human generated machine reading comprehension dataset. arXiv preprint arXiv:1611.09268v3 (2018)
4. Clark, K., Luong, M.T., Le, Q.V., Manning, C.D.: ELECTRA: pre-training text encoders as discriminators rather than generators. arXiv preprint arXiv:2003.10555 (2020)
5. Dai, Z., Callan, J.: Deeper text understanding for IR with contextual neural language modeling. In: Proceedings of the 42nd Annual International ACM SIGIR Conference on Research and Development in Information Retrieval (SIGIR 2019), pp. 985–988 (2019)
6. Devlin, J., Chang, M.W., Lee, K., Toutanova, K.: BERT: pre-training of deep bidirectional transformers for language understanding. In: Proceedings of the 2019 Conference of the North American Chapter of the Association for Computational Linguistics: Human Language Technologies, Volume 1 (Long and Short Papers), pp. 4171–4186 (2019)
7. Fan, Y., Guo, J., Lan, Y., Xu, J., Zhai, C., Cheng, X.: Modeling diverse relevance patterns in ad-hoc retrieval. In: Proceedings of the 41st International ACM SIGIR Conference on Research and Development in Information Retrieval, pp. 375–384 (2018)

8. Lan, Z., Chen, M., Goodman, S., Gimpel, K., Sharma, P., Soricut, R.: ALBERT: a lite BERT for self-supervised learning of language representations. arXiv preprint arXiv:1909.11942 (2019)

9. Li, C., Yates, A., MacAvaney, S., He, B., Sun, Y.: PARADE: passage representation aggregation for document reranking. arXiv preprint arXiv:2008.09093 (2020)

10. Lin, J., Nogueira, R., Yates, A.: Pretrained transformers for text ranking: BERT and beyond. arXiv preprint arXiv:2010.06467 (2020)

11. Liu, Y., et al.: RoBERTa: a robustly optimized BERT pretraining approach. arXiv preprint arXiv:1907.11692 (2019)

12. MacAvaney, S., Yates, A., Cohan, A., Goharian, N.: CEDR: contextualized embeddings for document ranking. In: Proceedings of the 42nd International ACM SIGIR Conference on Research and Development in Information Retrieval, pp. 1101–1104 (2019)

13. Nogueira, R., Cho, K.: Passage re-ranking with BERT. arXiv preprint arXiv:1901.04085 (2019)

14. Pang, L., Lan, Y., Guo, J., Xu, J., Xu, J., Cheng, X.: DeepRank: a new deep architecture for relevance ranking in information retrieval. In: Proceedings of the 2017 ACM on Conference on Information and Knowledge Management, pp. 257–266 (2017)

15. Wolf, T., et al.: HuggingFace's transformers: state-of-the-art natural language processing. arXiv preprint arXiv:1910.03771 (2019)

16. Yang, P., Fang, H., Lin, J.: Anserini: enabling the use of Lucene for information retrieval research. In: Proceedings of the 40th Annual International ACM SIGIR Conference on Research and Development in Information Retrieval (SIGIR 2017), pp. 1253–1256 (2017)

17. Yang, W., Lu, K., Yang, P., Lin, J.: Critically examining the "neural hype" weak baselines and the additivity of effectiveness gains from neural ranking models. In: Proceedings of the 42nd International ACM SIGIR Conference on Research and Development in Information Retrieval (SIGIR 2019), pp. 1129–1132 (2019)

18. Yates, A., Jose, K.M., Zhang, X., Lin, J.: Flexible IR pipelines with Capreolus. In: Proceedings of the 29th ACM International Conference on Information and Knowledge Management, pp. 3181–3188 (2020)

19. Yilmaz, E., Robertson, S.E.: Deep versus shallow judgments in learning to rank. In: Proceedings of the 32nd Annual International ACM SIGIR Conference on Research and Development in Information Retrieval (SIGIR 2009), pp. 662–663 (2009)

20. Zhang, X., Yates, A., Lin, J.: A little bit is worse than none: Ranking with limited training data. In: Proceedings of SustaiNLP: Workshop on Simple and Efficient Natural Language Processing, pp. 107–112 (2020)

Short Papers

Transformer-Based Approach Towards Music Emotion Recognition from Lyrics

Yudhik Agrawal[(✉)] [ID], Ramaguru Guru Ravi Shanker[ID], and Vinoo Alluri[ID]

International Institute of Information Technology, Hyderabad, Hyderabad, India
{yudhik.agrawal,ramaguru.guru}@research.iiit.ac.in,
vinoo.alluri@iiit.ac.in

Abstract. The task of identifying emotions from a given music track has been an active pursuit in the Music Information Retrieval (MIR) community for years. Music emotion recognition has typically relied on acoustic features, social tags, and other metadata to identify and classify music emotions. The role of lyrics in music emotion recognition remains under-appreciated in spite of several studies reporting superior performance of music emotion classifiers based on features extracted from lyrics. In this study, we use the transformer-based approach model using XLNet as the base architecture which, till date, has not been used to identify emotional connotations of music based on lyrics. Our proposed approach outperforms existing methods for multiple datasets. We used a robust methodology to enhance web-crawlers' accuracy for extracting lyrics. This study has important implications in improving applications involved in playlist generation of music based on emotions in addition to improving music recommendation systems.

Keywords: Music emotion recognition · Lyrics · Valence-arousal · Transformers

1 Introduction

Information retrieval and recommendation, be it related to news, music, products, images, amongst others, is crucial in e-commerce and on-demand content streaming applications. With the staggering increase in paid subscribers for music streaming platforms over the years, and especially in these Covid times [1], MIR systems have increased need and relevancy. Music Emotion Recognition has gained prominence over the recent years in the field of MIR, albeit relying on acoustic features [11,29] and social tags [6] to identify and classify music emotions. Lyrics have been largely neglected despite the crucial role they play in especially eliciting emotions [14], a vital factor contributing to musical reward [25], in addition to reflecting user traits and tendencies [34] which in turn are related to musical preferences [26]. Despite a handful of studies reporting the superior performance of music emotion classifiers based on features extracted from lyrics than audio [16,38], the role of lyrics in music emotion recognition remains under-appreciated.

© Springer Nature Switzerland AG 2021
D. Hiemstra et al. (Eds.): ECIR 2021, LNCS 12657, pp. 167–175, 2021.
https://doi.org/10.1007/978-3-030-72240-1_12

Analyzing lyrics and its emotional connotations using advanced Natural Language Processing (NLP) techniques would make for a natural choice. However, NLP in MIR has been used for topic modelling [20], identifying song structure via lyrics [13], and mood classification [16]. In the context of Music emotion recognition [23,38], typically traditional NLP approaches have been used, which are limited to word-level representations and embeddings, as opposed to more modern NLP techniques that are based on context and long-term dependencies such as transformers [10,40]. Lyrics can be treated as narratives rather than independent words or sentences, which therefore renders the use of transformers a natural choice in mining affective connotations. In this study, we use transformer model which, till date, has not been used for identifying emotional connotations of music based on lyrics.

2   Related Work

Analyzing affective connotations from text, that is, sentiment analysis, has been actively attempted in short contexts like reviews [4,30], tweets [3,7], news articles [35] amongst others with limited application to lyrics. Sentiment analysis has come a long way from its inception based on surveys and public opinions [21] to use of linguistic features like character n-grams [15], bag-of-words [4] and lexicons like SentiWordNet [27] to state-of-the-art that employ context-based approaches [10,33] for capturing the polarity of a text. The task of sentiment analysis has been approached using several deep learning techniques like RNN [7,31], CNN [7], and transformers [10,18] and have shown to perform remarkably better than traditional machine-learning methods [19].

Music emotion classification using lyrics has been performed based on traditional lexicons [16,17]. The lexicons not only have very limited vocabulary but also the values have to be aggregated without using any contextual information. In recent years the use of pre-trained models like GloVe [32], ELMO [33], transformers [10,37] are fast gaining importance for large text corpus has shown impressive results in downstream several NLP tasks. Authors in [2,9] perform emotion classification using lyrics by applying RNN model on top of word-level embedding. The MoodyLyrics dataset [5] was used by [2] who report an impressive F_1-score of 91.00%. Recurrent models like LSTMs work on Markov's principle, where information from past steps goes through a sequence of computations to predict a future state. Meanwhile, the transformer architecture eschews recurrence nature and introduces self-attention, which establishes longer dependency between each step with all other steps. Since we have direct access to all the other steps (self-attention) ensures negligible information loss. In this study, we employ Multi-task setup, using XLNet as the base architecture for classification of emotions and evaluate the performance of our model on several datasets that have been organized by emotional connotations solely based on lyrics. We demonstrate superior performance of our transformer-based approach compared to RNN-based approach [2,9]. In addition, we propose a robust methodology for extracting lyrics for a song.

3   Methodology

3.1   Datasets

MoodyLyrics [5]: This dataset comprises 2595 songs uniformly distributed across the 4 quadrants of the Russell's Valence-Arousal (V-A) circumplex model [36] of affect where emotion is a point in a two-dimensional continuous space which has been reported to sufficiently capture musical emotions [12]. Valence describes pleasantness and Arousal represents the energy content. The authors used a combination of existing lexicons such as ANEW, WordNet, and WordNet-Affect to assign the V-A values at a word-level followed by song-level averaging of these values. These were further validated by using subjective human judgment of the mood tags from AllMusic Dataset [24]. Finally, the authors had retained songs in each quadrant only if their Valence and Arousal values were above specific thresholds, thereby rendering them to be highly representative of those categories.

MER Dataset [24]: This dataset contains 180 songs distributed uniformly among the 4 emotion quadrants of the 2-D Russell's circumplex model. Several annotators assigned the V-A values for each song solely based on the lyrics displayed without the audio. The Valence and Arousal for each song were computed as the average of their subjective ratings. Also, this dataset was reported to demonstrate high internal consistency making it highly perceptually relevant.

3.2   Lyrics Extraction

Due to copyright issues, the datasets do not provide lyrics, however, the URLs from different lyric websites are provided in each of the datasets. In order to mine the lyrics, one approach is to write a crawler for each of the websites present in the datasets. However, some of those URLs were broken. Hence, in order to address this concern, we provide a robust approach for extracting lyrics using the Genius website. All the existing APIs, including Genius API require the correct artist and track name for extracting the lyrics. However, if the artist or track names are misspelled in the dataset, the API fails to extract the lyrics. We handled this issue by introducing a web crawler to obtain the Genius website URL for the lyrics of the song instead of hard-coding the artist and track name in Genius API. Using the web crawler, we were able to considerably improve the number of songs extracted from 60%–80% for the different datasets to ∼99% for each dataset.

3.3   Proposed Architecture

We describe a deep neural network architecture that, given the lyrics, outputs the classification of Emotion Quadrants, in addition to Valence and Arousal Hemispheres. The entire network is trained jointly on all these tasks using weight-sharing, an instance of multi-task learning. Multi-task learning acts as a regularizer by introducing inductive bias that prefers hypotheses explaining all the tasks. It overcomes the risk of overfitting and reduces the model's ability to accommodate random noise during training while achieving faster convergence [41]. Figure 1 displays the architecture of our proposed method.

We use XLNet [40] as the base network, which is a large bidirectional transformer that uses improved training methodology, larger data and more computational power. XLNet improves upon BERT [10] by using the Transformer XL [8] as its base architecture. The added recurrence to the transformer enables the network to have a deeper understanding of contextual information.

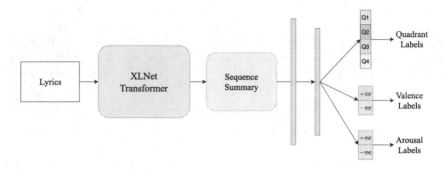

Fig. 1. Overview of our method

The XLNet transformer Model outputs raw hidden states, which are then passed on to *SequenceSummary* block, which computes a single vector summary of a sequence of hidden states, followed by one more hidden Fully-Connected (FC) layer which encodes the information into a vector of length 8. This layer finally branches out into three complementary tasks via a single FC layer on top for classification of Quadrant, Valence, and Arousal separately. As we feed input data, the entire pre-trained XLNet model and the additional untrained classification layers are trained for all three tasks. We use the following loss function to train our network.

$$L = (\lambda_1 * L_Q) + (\lambda_2 * L_V) + (\lambda_3 * L_A) \tag{1}$$

where L_Q, L_V, and L_A represents the classification loss on Quadrants, Valence, and Arousal, respectively.

Implementation Details. We use the AdamW optimizer [22] with an initial learning rate of $2e^{-5}$ and a dropout regularization with a 0.1 discard probability for the layers. We use Cross-Entropy Loss for calculating loss. A batch size of 8 was used. We also restrict the length of the lyrics to 1024 words. Lyrics of more than 99% of the songs had less than 1024 words. We leverage the rich information of pre-trained (XLNet-base-cased) model as they are trained on big corpora. As the pre-trained model layers already encode a rich amount of information about language, training the classifier is relatively inexpensive [37]. We also run our network on single-task classification and compare the results as part of our ablation study in a later section.

4   Experiment and Results

4.1   Evaluation Measures

For evaluating the effectiveness of our proposed model, we use the standard recall, precision, and F_1 measures. We provide results for both macro-averaged F_1 and micro-averaged F_1. The micro-average F_1 is also the classifier's overall accuracy. We use Macro-averaged F_1 ($\mathcal{F}_1$-score) [39] as given in Eq. 2. The scores are first computed for the binary decisions for each individual category and then are averaged over categories.

$$F1_x = 2\frac{P_x R_x}{P_x + R_x}; \qquad \mathcal{F}_1 = \frac{1}{n}\sum_x F1_x \qquad (2)$$

where $F1_x$, P_x, R_x denote F1-score, precision and recall with respect to class x. This metric is significantly more robust towards the error type distribution as compared to the other variants of the Macro-averaged F_1 [28].

4.2   Results

We use multi-task setup to compare our performance on various datasets. For a fair evaluation of our method, we use the data splits for respective datasets, as mentioned in respective studies. All the results reported hereon are the average of multiple data splits. Tables 1 and 2 compares the results of our approach on MoodyLyrics and MER dataset respectively. These results demonstrate the far superior performance of our method when compared to studies that have attempted the same task.

We also compare the performance of our approach by validating on an additional dataset, the AllMusic dataset comprising 771 songs provided by [24]. We follow the same procedure of training on the MER dataset and evaluating on the AllMusic dataset as mentioned by the authors. We get an improved $\mathcal{F}_1$-score of 75.40% compared to their reported 73.60% on single-task Quadrant classification in addition to improved Accuracy of 76.31% when compared to

Table 1. Results of classification by Quadrants on MoodyLyrics dataset.

Approach	Accuracy	Precision	Recall	$\mathcal{F}_1$-score
Naive Bayes [2]	83.00%	87.00%	81.00%	82.00%
BiLSTM + Glove [2]	91.00%	92.00%	90.00%	91.00%
Our method	94.78%	94.77%	94.75%	94.77%

Table 2. Results of classification on MER dataset.

Classification	Approach	Accuracy	Precision	Recall	$\mathcal{F}_1$-score
Quadrant	CBF + POS tags, Structural and Semantic features [24]	–	–	–	80.10%
Quadrant	Our method	88.89%	90.83%	88.75%	88.60%
Valence	CBF + POS tags, Structural and Semantic features [24]	–	–	–	90.00%
Valence	Our method	94.44%	92.86%	95.83%	93.98%
Arousal	CBF + POS tags, Structural and Semantic features [24]	–	–	–	88.30%
Arousal	Our method	88.89%	90.00%	90.00%	88.89%

Table 3. Ablation study on MoodyLyrics

Classification	Accuracy		$\mathcal{F}_1$-score	
	Multi-task	Single-task	Multi-task	Single-task
Quadrant	94.78%	95.68%	94.77%	95.60%
Valence	95.73%	96.51%	95.67%	96.46%
Arousal	94.38%	94.38%	94.23%	94.35%

the reported Accuracy of 74.25%, albeit on a subset of the AllMusic dataset, in [5]. Our Multi-task method demonstrated comparable $\mathcal{F}_1$-score and accuracy of 72.70% and 73.95% when compared to our single-task Quadrant classification.

Ablation Study: Owing to its large size and quadrant representativeness of the MoodyLyrics dataset, we perform extensive analysis with different architecture types and sequence lengths. In the initial set of experiments, we aimed to find the best model where we compared our baseline model with BERT transformer with same sequence length of 512, which resulted in inferior performance of an $\mathcal{F}_1$-score down by around 1.3%. We also compare the performance of our baseline model with our multi-task setup. Table 3 shows that we perform similar to our baseline method, but we saw a huge improvement in training speed as the latter converge faster. This also requires training different tasks from scratch every time, which makes it inefficient.

5   Conclusion

In this study, we have demonstrated the robustness of our novel transformer-based approach for music emotion recognition using lyrics on multiple datasets when compared to hitherto used approaches. Our multi-task setup helps in faster convergence and reduces model overfitting, however, the single-task setup performs marginally better albeit at the expense of computational resources. This study can help in improving applications like playlist generation of music with similar emotions. Also, hybrid music recommendation systems, which utilize predominantly acoustic content-based and collaborative filtering approaches can further benefit from incorporating emotional connotations of lyrics for retrieval. This approach can be extended in future to multilingual lyrics.

References

1. Spotify hits 130 million subscribers amid COVID-19. https://www.bbc.com/news/technology-52478708
2. Abdillah, J., Asror, I., Wibowo, Y.F.A., et al.: Emotion classification of song lyrics using bidirectional LSTM method with glove word representation weighting. Jurnal RESTI (Rekayasa Sistem Dan Teknologi Informasi) 4(4), 723–729 (2020)
3. Agarwal, A., Xie, B., Vovsha, I., Rambow, O., Passonneau, R.J.: Sentiment analysis of Twitter data. In: Proceedings of the Workshop on Language in Social Media (LSM 2011), pp. 30–38 (2011)
4. Barry, J.: Sentiment analysis of online reviews using bag-of-words and LSTM approaches. In: AICS, pp. 272–274 (2017)
5. Çano, E., Morisio, M.: Moodylyrics: a sentiment annotated lyrics dataset. In: Proceedings of the 2017 International Conference on Intelligent Systems, Metaheuristics & Swarm Intelligence, pp. 118–124 (2017)
6. Çano, E., Morisio, M., et al.: Music mood dataset creation based on Last.fm tags. In: 2017 International Conference on Artificial Intelligence and Applications, Vienna, Austria (2017)
7. Cliche, M.: BB_twtr at SemEval-2017 task 4: Twitter sentiment analysis with CNNs and LSTMs. arXiv preprint arXiv:1704.06125 (2017)
8. Dai, Z., Yang, Z., Yang, Y., Carbonell, J., Le, Q.V., Salakhutdinov, R.: Transformer-xl: attentive language models beyond a fixed-length context. arXiv preprint arXiv:1901.02860 (2019)
9. Delbouys, R., Hennequin, R., Piccoli, F., Royo-Letelier, J., Moussallam, M.: Music mood detection based on audio and lyrics with deep neural net. arXiv preprint arXiv:1809.07276 (2018)
10. Devlin, J., Chang, M.W., Lee, K., Toutanova, K.: Bert: pre-training of deep bidirectional transformers for language understanding. arXiv preprint arXiv:1810.04805 (2018)
11. Eerola, T., Lartillot, O., Toiviainen, P.: Prediction of multidimensional emotional ratings in music from audio using multivariate regression models. In: ISMIR, pp. 621–626 (2009)
12. Eerola, T., Vuoskoski, J.K.: A comparison of the discrete and dimensional models of emotion in music. Psychol. Music 39(1), 18–49 (2011)
13. Fell, M., Nechaev, Y., Cabrio, E., Gandon, F.: Lyrics segmentation: textual macrostructure detection using convolutions. In: Proceedings of the 27th International Conference on Computational Linguistics, pp. 2044–2054 (2018)
14. Greasley, A., Lamont, A.: Musical preferences. In: Oxford Handbook of Music Psychology, pp. 263–281 (2016)
15. Han, Q., Guo, J., Schuetze, H.: Codex: combining an SVM classifier and character n-gram language models for sentiment analysis on Twitter text. In: Second Joint Conference on Lexical and Computational Semantics (* SEM), Volume 2: Proceedings of the Seventh International Workshop on Semantic Evaluation (SemEval 2013), pp. 520–524 (2013)

16. Hu, X., Downie, J.S.: When lyrics outperform audio for music mood classification: a feature analysis. In: ISMIR, pp. 619–624 (2010)

17. Hu, Y., Chen, X., Yang, D.: Lyric-based song emotion detection with affective lexicon and fuzzy clustering method. In: ISMIR (2009)

18. Huang, Y.H., Lee, S.R., Ma, M.Y., Chen, Y.H., Yu, Y.W., Chen, Y.S.: EmotionX-IDEA: emotion BERT-an affectional model for conversation. arXiv preprint arXiv:1908.06264 (2019)

19. Kansara, D., Sawant, V.: Comparison of traditional machine learning and deep learning approaches for sentiment analysis. In: Vasudevan, H., Michalas, A., Shekokar, N., Narvekar, M. (eds.) Advanced Computing Technologies and Applications. AIS, pp. 365–377. Springer, Singapore (2020). https://doi.org/10.1007/978-981-15-3242-9_35

20. Kleedorfer, F., Knees, P., Pohle, T.: Oh oh oh whoah! towards automatic topic detection in song lyrics. In: ISMIR, pp. 287–292 (2008)

21. Knutson, A.L.: Japanese opinion surveys: the special need and the special difficulties. Public Opin. Q. **9**(3), 313–319 (1945)

22. Loshchilov, I., Hutter, F.: Decoupled weight decay regularization. arXiv preprint arXiv:1711.05101 (2017)

23. Malheiro, R., Panda, R., Gomes, P., Paiva, R.: Music emotion recognition from lyrics: a comparative study. In: 6th International Workshop on Machine Learning and Music (MML 2013). Held in . . . (2013)

24. Malheiro, R., Panda, R., Gomes, P., Paiva, R.P.: Emotionally-relevant features for classification and regression of music lyrics. IEEE Trans. Affect. Comput. **9**(2), 240–254 (2016)

25. Mas-Herrero, E., Marco-Pallares, J., Lorenzo-Seva, U., Zatorre, R.J., Rodriguez-Fornells, A.: Individual differences in music reward experiences. Music Percept.Interdisc. J. **31**(2), 118–138 (2012)

26. Melchiorre, A.B., Schedl, M.: Personality correlates of music audio preferences for modelling music listeners. In: Proceedings of the 28th ACM Conference on User Modeling, Adaptation and Personalization, pp. 313–317 (2020)

27. Ohana, B., Tierney, B.: Sentiment classification of reviews using SentiWordNet. In: 9th IT&T Conference, vol. 13, pp. 18–30 (2009)

28. Opitz, J., Burst, S.: Macro F1 and macro F1. arXiv preprint arXiv:1911.03347 (2019)

29. Panda, R., Malheiro, R., Rocha, B., Oliveira, A., Paiva, R.P.: Multi-modal music emotion recognition: a new dataset, methodology and comparative analysis. In: International Symposium on Computer Music Multidisciplinary Research (2013)

30. Pang, B., Lee, L.: A sentimental education: Sentiment analysis using subjectivity summarization based on minimum cuts. arXiv preprint cs/0409058 (2004)

31. Patel, A., Tiwari, A.K.: Sentiment analysis by using recurrent neural network. In: Proceedings of 2nd International Conference on Advanced Computing and Software Engineering (ICACSE) (2019)

32. Pennington, J., Socher, R., Manning, C.D.: Glove: global vectors for word representation. In: Proceedings of the 2014 Conference on Empirical Methods in Natural Language Processing (EMNLP), pp. 1532–1543 (2014)

33. Peters, M.E., et al.: Deep contextualized word representations. arXiv preprint arXiv:1802.05365 (2018)

34. Qiu, L., Chen, J., Ramsay, J., Lu, J.: Personality predicts words in favorite songs. J. Res. Pers. **78**, 25–35 (2019)

35. Raina, P.: Sentiment analysis in news articles using sentic computing. In: 2013 IEEE 13th International Conference on Data Mining Workshops, pp. 959–962. IEEE (2013)

36. Russell, J.A.: A circumplex model of affect. J. Pers. Soc. Psychol. **39**(6), 1161 (1980)

37. Sun, C., Qiu, X., Xu, Y., Huang, X.: How to fine-tune BERT for text classification? In: Sun, M., Huang, X., Ji, H., Liu, Z., Liu, Y. (eds.) CCL 2019. LNCS (LNAI), vol. 11856, pp. 194–206. Springer, Cham (2019). https://doi.org/10.1007/978-3-030-32381-3_16

38. Xia, Y., Wang, L., Wong, K.F.: Sentiment vector space model for lyric-based song sentiment classification. Int. J. Comput. Process. Lang. **21**(04), 309–330 (2008)

39. Yang, Y., Liu, X.: A re-examination of text categorization methods. In: Proceedings of the 22nd Annual International ACM SIGIR Conference on Research and Development in Information Retrieval, pp. 42–49 (1999)

40. Yang, Z., Dai, Z., Yang, Y., Carbonell, J., Salakhutdinov, R.R., Le, Q.V.: XLNet: generalized autoregressive pretraining for language understanding. In: Advances in Neural Information Processing Systems, pp. 5753–5763 (2019)

41. Zhang, Y., Yang, Q.: An overview of multi-task learning. Natl. Sci. Rev. **5**(1), 30–43 (2018)

BiGBERT: Classifying Educational Web Resources for Kindergarten-12th Grades

Garrett Allen[1]([⊠]), Brody Downs[1], Aprajita Shukla[1], Casey Kennington[1], Jerry Alan Fails[1], Katherine Landau Wright[2], and Maria Soledad Pera[1]

[1] Department of Computer Science, Boise State University, Boise, ID, USA
garrettallen@boisestate.edu
[2] Department of Literacy, Language and Culture, Boise State University, Boise, ID, USA

Abstract. In this paper, we present BiGBERT, a deep learning model that simultaneously examines URLs and snippets from web resources to determine their alignment with children's educational standards. Preliminary results inferred from ablation studies and comparison with baselines and state-of-the-art counterparts, reveal that leveraging domain knowledge to learn domain-aligned contextual nuances from limited input data leads to improved identification of educational web resources.

Keywords: Web classification · BERT · Educational standards

1 Introduction

Web resource classification is a well-explored area in Information Retrieval [15]. Recently, the field has seen an influx of research related to domain-specific classification, especially within the legal, financial and medical domains [11,18,36]. Classification in the domain of *education*, however, remains relatively unexplored. As a broad term, education applies to a variety of classification tasks. Prior work includes classifying educational resources based on "the strength of the educative resource [as] a property evaluated cumulatively by the target audience of the resource (e.g., students or educational experts)" using a Support Vector Machine (SVM) [16]. This model, however, relies heavily on manually-annotated data and is applicable only to computer science education. Xia [32] also uses an SVM to classify resources supporting instruction, whereas EduBERT [7] detects college-level forum posts written by struggling students. In general, efforts in this area classify resources for unspecified age groups, adult students, limited subject areas, instructors or institutional-level insights. There is a gap in the literature regarding recognizing educational web resources for children ages 6–18 in grades Kindergarten-12 (**K-12**). Educational standards, such as the United States' Common Core State Standards (CCSS) and the Next Generation Science Standards (NGCS), provide learning outcomes for K-12 students. For example, a grade 1 learning outcome from CCSS states "Identify the main topic and retell

D. Hiemstra et al. (Eds.): ECIR 2021, LNCS 12657, pp. 176–184, 2021.
https://doi.org/10.1007/978-3-030-72240-1_13

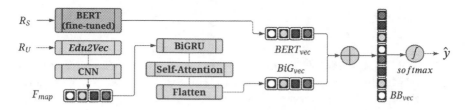

Fig. 1. BiGBERT architecture (R_U and R_S denote the URL and snippet, resp.).

key details of a text" [19]. We posit that domain knowledge obtained from these standards can inform the classification of children's educational web resources.

Regardless of the domain, classifiers tend to rely on features inferred from HTML page content [9,28]. Processing full web pages requires high computational power, large data storage, and time to retrieve [25] as web pages are often dynamic and contain pictures, videos, or scripts in addition to text [26]. To address some of these constraints, state-of-the-art approaches examine only URLs [14,26]. Unfortunately, URLs are not always comprised of meaningful tokens (i.e., valid terms), which may cause misclassifications. Consider the URL https://www.youtube.com/watch?v=pX3V9hoX1eM for a YouTube video by National Geographic For Kids related to animals. In this case, meaningful tokens include "youtube" and "watch," neither of which indicates the corresponding resource is child-friendly.

Mindful of the aforementioned limitations, in this paper, we introduce **BiG-BERT**, a **Bi**directional **G**ated Recurrent Unit (BiGRU) with BERT that recognizes educational web resources for children. In particular, we focus on educational resources that inform on subjects for grades K-12, such as language arts, science and social studies, described in CCSS, NGCS, and Idaho Content Standards (ICS). As illustrated in Fig. 1, BiGBERT has two main components: a URL and a snippet vectorizer. To vectorize URLs, we combine the domain-specific embeddings from *Edu2Vec* [3] with a BiGRU and a self attention layer. Shen et al. [27] show that using summaries instead of full page content results in comparable classification performance, thus we use snippets in place of full content. To vectorize snippets, we fine tune the transformer model BERT [8] using educational standards. Last, we concatenate the snippet and URL vectors and apply a softmax function to determine the class of a web resource.

With our work, we seek to answer these research questions: **RQ1**: Do URLs provide sufficient indication that resources are educational?; **RQ2**: Do snippets along with URLs help identify educational resources?; and **RQ3**: Does domain-specific knowledge affect identification of educational resources? Our main contribution is a hybrid strategy that simultaneously considers resource URL and snippet, while informing domain-dependent learning with minimal educational data for determining resource alignment to K-12 educational standards. We envision BiGBERT (https://github.com/BSU-CAST/BiGBERT) as groundwork to support other Information Retrieval tasks, e.g., easing access to online resources supporting K-12 curriculum-related information discovery tasks.

2   BiGBERT

In this section, we detail how BiGBERT simultaneously leverages features from the URL (R_U) and snippet (R_S) of a web resource R for classification purposes. BiGBERT is trained using a batch size of 128, binary cross-entropy loss function, and RMSProp optimizer [30] with momentum=0.2 and learning rate=0.001.

URL Vectorizer. BiGBERT tokenizes R_U into a sequence of terms T by splitting on non-alphanumeric symbols (e.g., periods, dashes and forward slashes) and using SymSpell [13] to perform word segmentation as URLs tend to compound words together (e.g., changing *stackoverflow* to *stack overflow*). Each token $t_i \in T$ is mapped to its corresponding word embedding. If t_i is not part of the embedding dictionary, we attribute this to a possible misspelling or spelling variation, and thus attempt a correction using a single edit distance operation (i.e., replacing, adding, or removing a character). If t_i is still not in the dictionary, we discard it to ensure only meaningful tokens remain.

To learn a representation of R_U, BiGBERT uses the *Edu2Vec* word embeddings dictionary [3] as it incorporates domain knowledge from NGCS, CCSS, and ICS. These standards serve as structured knowledge sources to identify terms, topics, and subjects for K-12 grades, enabling BiGBERT to emphasize K-12 curriculum concepts in R_U that may be overlooked by general-purpose pre-trained embeddings. Rather than analyzing independent embeddings, we design BiGBERT to scrutinize context-sensitive indications from T. Inspired by Rajalakshmi et al. [24] and in response to URLs not following traditional language syntax, we examine groups of embeddings (i.e., trigrams) using a Convolutional Neural Network (CNN)–a fast, effective, and compact method [20] to generate feature vectors from trigrams. The convolution results in a feature map $F_{map} = <F_1, F_2, ..., F_x>, \forall_{f=1..x} F_f = relu(w.x_{i:i+m-1} + b_u)$, where the rectified linear function $relu$ is applied to the dot product of a kernel w with a window of embeddings $x_{i:i+m-1}$ in T of size $m = 3$; b_u is a bias term. To explore long term dependencies of features that may appear far apart BiGBERT uses a BiGRU network, as it captures context information in a forwards and backwards direction. A self-attention layer then determines the importance of features identified by the CNN and BiGRU. This is followed by a flatten and dense layer that yields a single feature vector representation of R_U of size 128, denoted $\boldsymbol{BiG_{vec}}$.

Snippet Encoding. As snippets are a few sentences long, unlike URLs which are at most a few words, we require a model that can scrutinize each snippet as a whole. Hence, we incorporate the state-of-the-art transformer model BERT [8] into BiGBERT's design. BERT's ability to process sequences up to a maximum size of 512 tokens enables BiGBERT to exploit the sequential, contextual information within R_S in its entirety. Additionally, BERT's architecture consisting of 12 transformer blocks and self-attention heads ensures the learning of rich contextual information from each snippet. As such, we tokenize R_S into a sequence of sentences, encode it to BERT's specifications, and use BERT to attain an aggregate feature vector representation of size 768, denoted $\boldsymbol{BERT_{vec}}$.

On domain-dependent tasks like the one we address here, BERT benefits from fine-tuning [29]. Thus, we adjust traditional BERT to our definition of education by exploiting established educational standards. We perform fine-tuning as described in [29], training[1] BERT embeddings as an educational text classifier by adding a linear classification layer which uses binary cross entropy as loss and the Adam optimizer with learning rate $= 1e^{-5}$.

Classification. To leverage evidence of educational alignment inferred from R_U and R_S, we concatenate BiG_{vec} with $BERT_{vec}$ as BB_{vec}. BiGBERT then invokes a fully connected layer on BB_{vec} that uses a softmax activation function to produce a probability distribution $\hat{y}$ over each class, educational and not, such that $\hat{y} \in [0,1]$. This function ensures that the sum of the probabilities per class adds up to one. The class predicted for R is the one with the highest probability.

3   Experiments and Discussion

We conducted empirical explorations to answer the research questions that guided our work. Below we discuss our experimental set up and results.

Set-up. There is no **dataset**[2] we can use to assess the proposed task. Thus, we build one using URLs (with text in English) from *Alexa Top Sites* [2]–based on the well-known Open Directory Project (ODP) [6,22]. We treat as educational the 1,273 URLs in subcategories *Pre-School* and *School Time* from *Kids & Teens*. We also randomly select 3,998 non-educational URLs uniformly distributed among *Adult*, *Business*, *Recreation*, and *Games*. To validate that dataset labels align (or not) with our definition of educational, an education expert annotated a representative sample (n = 527). As in [23], we calculate the accuracy between the two annotations (Alexa vs. expert) per sample, obtaining an inter-annotator agreement of 94.7%. For performance assessment, we use **Accuracy**, a common classification metric, along with False Positive (**FPR**) and False Negative (**FNR**) ratios, to offer insights on the type of misclassified resources.

To the best of our knowledge, there are no domain-specific classifiers that we can use to contextualize BiGBERT's performance. Thus, we optimize and adapt several classifiers to detect K-12 web resources: (i) **BoW**[3] [14], a bag-of-words model that computes cosine similarity between a vectorized resource URL and ODP category descriptions to determine the resource's respective category (note that we use the text of learning outcomes from educational standards in lieu of category descriptions); (ii) **BGCNN** [26], a model based on a BiGRU with a CNN which identifies child-friendly URLs; (iii) **BERT4TC** [35], a text classifier that uses a BERT encoder to perform topic and sentiment classification, and (iv)

---

[1] For fine-tuning we use 2,655 text passages from NGCS, CCSS, and ICS along with 2,725 from the Brown corpus [5,12].

[2] Due to Terms of Use for Alexa Top Sites, we are unable to share this dataset.

[3] We explored SVM as an additional baseline, which performed similarly to BoW and is excluded for brevity.

Table 1. Experimental results. **U** and **S** applied to URL and snippet only; **E** augmented with educational data. * and † significant w.r.t. BiGBERT and non-educational counterpart, resp. Significance determined with McNemar's test, $p < 0.05$.

Row	Type	Models	Accuracy	FPR	FNR
1	Baseline	BoW	.7205 *	.115	.796
2	State-of the-art	BGCNN	.8399 *	.073	.432
3		BERT4TC	.9353 *	.041	.140
4		Hybrid-NB	.8600 *	.145	.123
5	Ablation study	BiGBERT-U	.8276 *	.073	.484
6		BiGBERT-U-E	.8287 * †	.072	.483
7		BiGBERT-S	.9374 *	.027	.175
8		BiGBERT-S-E	.9334 *	.038	.155
9		BiGBERT-U-S	.9381 *	.035	.146
10		**BiGBERT**	**.9533** †	**.027**	**.106**

Hybrid-NB [1], a hybrid model which examines both URL and content of websites to determine their target audience (i.e., Algerian users). Reported results for BGCNN and BERT4TC are the average of 5-fold cross validation. Additionally, we explore **variations** of BiGBERT where **U**, **S**, and **E** indicate when BiGBERT examines only URLs, snippets, and infuses educational information, respectively. Finally, through an ablation study, we showcase the contributions of the URL and snippet vectorizers towards the overall architecture of BiGBERT.

Results and Discussion. We summarize our results in Table 1.

Do URLs provide sufficient indication that resources are educational? Reports in [26] showcase the effectiveness of only examining URLs to identify sites as child-friendly. This motivates us to study the applicability of the approach for detecting educational web resources targeting K-12 populations. The accuracy of BoW does not surpass the 75% mark attained via a naive baseline (one always predicting non-educational due to the unbalanced nature of our dataset). BGCNN, BiGBERT-U, and BiGBERT-U-E outperform more traditional models with accuracies in the low 80 percentile. We attribute the increase in performance to the fact that state-of-the-art models do not assume URL token independence, unlike BoW. Results from our analysis indicate that when semantic and context-rich information is available, URLs are a valuable source to inform classification. The number of misclassified educational resources in this case, however, is high as nearly half of educational samples, which comprise 25% of our data, are being labelled non-educational (see respective FNR). This leads us to investigate additional information sources that can contribute to the classification process.

Do snippets along with URLs help identify educational resources? As content analysis is a staple of classification, it is logical to consider knowledge inferred from snippets to better support the classification of K-12 educational web resources. This is demonstrated by significant performance improvements of Hybrid-NB, BiGBERT-U-S, and BiGBERT over counterparts solely looking at URLs (BoW and BGCNN). In fact, BiGBERT significantly outperforms hybrid models in accuracy and FPR. Fewer false positives means lower likelihood for potentially inappropriate sites being labelled educational, which is of special importance given the domain and audience of our work. The results suggest that snippets, combined with URLs, do help identify educational resources. However, the higher FNR of BiGBERT-U-S compared to Hybrid-NB, again points to the misclassification of educational resources. This can be seen on samples like www.sesamestreet.org, recognized as educational by Hybrid-NB but overlooked by BiGBERT-U-S. This would suggest that the lack of explicit domain knowledge is a detriment to BiGBERT-U-S.

Does domain-specific knowledge affect identification of educational resources? BiGBERT's accuracy increases when using Edu2Vec and fine-tuned BERT embeddings (rows 9 vs 10 in Table 1). To determine whether the improvement is the result of explicitly infusing educational knowledge into the classification process, we compare BiGBERT-U and BiGBERT-S with educationally-augmented counterparts. Our experiments reveal a significant decrease in FPR and FNR between BiGBERT-U and BiGBERT-U-E; non significant between BiGBERT-S and BiGBERT-S-E. Unlike for URL variations, BiGBERT-S-E's performance improved only in FNR after augmentation. We attribute this to the relatively small training set used for fine-tuning in comparison to the initial pre-training set for BERT, leading to less new contextual information learned by the standard transformer model. Nonetheless, the significant increases in accuracy and decreases in FPR and FNR for BiGBERT when compared to BiGBERT-U-S suggest that domain-specific knowledge can have a positive effect on the classification of educational resources. This is illustrated by the URL www.xpmath.com, a site to support math education in grades 2–9, that is labelled non-educational by BiGBERT-U-S, yet it is correctly recognized as educational by BiGBERT.

4   Conclusion and Future Work

In this paper, we focused on a relatively unexplored area: identification of educational web resources for K-12 populations. We introduced BiGBERT based on a hybrid, deep learning architecture that relies on contextual analysis strategies alongside educational knowledge sources to capture features that best showcase resource alignment with K-12 subjects. Results from our experiments demonstrate that classifiers of educational K-12 web resources benefit from concurrently accounting for snippets and URLs. Further, via an ablation study we validate BiGBERT's design; specifically the need for the infusion of educational domain knowledge. Outcomes from our work align with [21], regarding leveraging scarce labelled data to better support classification.

Our findings can help improve how children can access educational content online. In particular, we will explore the effectiveness of BiGBERT when applied to re-ranking search results on educational alignment as a step toward supporting search as learning among K-12 students [17,31,33]. BiGBERT provides a foundation to support research in other Information Retrieval areas, e.g., identification of resources that teachers may use in the classroom [10], automatic curation of resources for educational search engines similar to Infotopia [4], and identification of educational questions on question answering sites [34].

Acknowledgments. Work funded by NSF Award # 1763649. The authors would like to thank Dr. Ion Madrazo Azpiazu for his valuable feedback.

References

1. Abdessamed, O., Zakaria, E.: Web site classification based on URL and content: algerian vs. non-algerian case. In: Proceedings of the 12th International Symposium on Programming and Systems (ISPS), pp. 1–8. IEEE (2015)
2. Amazon, I.: Alexa top sites (2020). https://www.alexa.com/topsites/category. Accessed 17 Sept 2020
3. Anuyah, O., Azpiazu, I.M., Pera, M.S.: Using structured knowledge and traditional word embeddings to generate concept representations in the educational domain. In: Companion Proceedings of the World Wide Web Conference, pp. 274–282 (2019)
4. Bell, C., Bell, M.: Infotopia (2020). https://wwww.infotopia.info. Accessed 17 Aug 2020
5. Bird, S., Klein, E., Loper, E.: Natural Language Processing with Python: Analyzing Text with the Natural Language Toolkit. O'Reilly Media Inc., Newton (2009)
6. Chen, W., Cai, F., Chen, H., De Rijke, M.: Personalized query suggestion diversification in information retrieval. Front. Comput. Sci. **14**(3), 1–14 (2019). https://doi.org/10.1007/s11704-018-7283-x
7. Clavié, B., Gal, K.: Edubert: pretrained deep language models for learning analytics. arXiv preprint arXiv:1912.00690 (2019)
8. Devlin, J., Chang, M.W., Lee, K., Toutanova, K.: Bert: Pre-training of deep bidirectional transformers for language understanding. arXiv preprint arXiv:1810.04805 (2018)
9. Eickhoff, C., Serdyukov, P., de Vries, A.P.: Web page classification on child suitability. In: Proceedings of the 19th ACM International Conference on Information and Knowledge Management, pp. 1425–1428 (2010)
10. Ekstrand, M.D., Wright, K.L., Pera, M.S.: Enhancing classroom instruction with online news. Aslib J. Inf. Manag. **72**(5), 725–744 (2020)
11. Elnaggar, A., Gebendorfer, C., Glaser, I., Matthes, F.: Multi-task deep learning for legal document translation, summarization and multi-label classification. In: Proceedings of the 2018 Artificial Intelligence and Cloud Computing Conference, pp. 9–15 (2018)
12. Francis, W.N., Kucera, H.: Brown corpus manual. Lett. Editor **5**(2), 7 (1979)
13. Garbe, W.: Symspell (2020). https://github.com/wolfgarbe/SymSpell
14. Geraci, F., Papini, T.: Approximating multi-class text classification via automatic generation of training examples. In: Gelbukh, A. (ed.) CICLing 2017. LNCS, vol. 10762, pp. 585–601. Springer, Cham (2018). https://doi.org/10.1007/978-3-319-77116-8_44

15. Hashemi, M.: Web page classification: a survey of perspectives, gaps, and future directions. Multimedia Tools Appl. 79, 11921–11945 (2020)

16. Hassan, S., Mihalcea, R.: Learning to identify educational materials. ACM Trans. Speech Lang. Process. (TSLP) **8**(2), 1–18 (2008)

17. Hoppe, A., Holtz, P., Kammerer, Y., Yu, R., Dietze, S., Ewerth, R.: Current challenges for studying search as learning processes. In: Proceedings of Learning and Education with Web Data (2018)

18. Hughes, M., Li, I., Kotoulas, S., Suzumura, T.: Medical text classification using convolutional neural networks. Stud. Health Technol. Inf. **235**, 246–50 (2017)

19. Initiative, CCSSO: Common core state standards for English language arts & literacy in history/social studies, science, and technical subjects (2020). http://www.corestandards.org/wp-content/uploads/ELA_Standards1.pdf

20. Kastrati, Z., Imran, A.S., Yayilgan, S.Y.: The impact of deep learning on document classification using semantically rich representations. Inf. Process. Manag. **56**(5), 1618–1632 (2019)

21. Liu, G., Guo, J.: Bidirectional LSTM with attention mechanism and convolutional layer for text classification. Neurocomputing **337**, 325–338 (2019)

22. Nimmagadda, S.L., Zhu, D., Rudra, A.: Knowledge base smarter articulations for the open directory project in a sustainable digital ecosystem. In: Companion Proceedings of the International Conference on World Wide Web, pp. 1537–1545 (2017)

23. Nowak, S., Rüger, S.: How reliable are annotations via crowdsourcing: a study about inter-annotator agreement for multi-label image annotation. In: Proceedings of the International Conference on Multimedia Information Retrieval, pp. 557–566 (2010)

24. Rajalakshmi, R., Aravindan, C.: A Naive Bayes approach for URL classification with supervised feature selection and rejection framework. Comput. Intell. **34**(1), 363–396 (2018)

25. Rajalakshmi, R., Tiwari, H., Patel, J., Kumar, A., Karthik, R.: Design of kids-specific URL classifier using recurrent convolutional neural network. Procedia Comput. Sci. **167**, 2124–2131 (2020)

26. Rajalakshmi, R., Tiwari, H., Patel, J., Rameshkannan, R., Karthik, R.: Bidirectional GRU-based attention model for kid-specific URL classification. In: Deep Learning Techniques and Optimization Strategies in Big Data Analytics, pp. 78–90. IGI Global (2020)

27. Shen, D., et al.: Web-page classification through summarization. In: Proceedings of the 27th International ACM SIGIR Conference on Research and Development in Information Retrieval, pp. 242–249 (2004)

28. Sreenivasulu, T., Jayakarthik, R., Shobarani, R.: Web content classification techniques based on fuzzy ontology. In: Peng, S.-L., Son, L.H., Suseendran, G., Balaganesh, D. (eds.) Intelligent Computing and Innovation on Data Science. LNNS, vol. 118, pp. 189–197. Springer, Singapore (2020). https://doi.org/10.1007/978-981-15-3284-9_22

29. Sun, C., Qiu, X., Xu, Y., Huang, X.: How to fine-tune BERT for text classification? In: Sun, M., Huang, X., Ji, H., Liu, Z., Liu, Y. (eds.) CCL 2019. LNCS (LNAI), vol. 11856, pp. 194–206. Springer, Cham (2019). https://doi.org/10.1007/978-3-030-32381-3_16

30. Tieleman, T., Hinton, G.: Lecture 6.5–RmsProp: divide the gradient by a running average of its recent magnitude. COURSERA: Neural Netw. Mach. Learn. **4**(2), 26–31 (2012)

31. Usta, A., Altingovde, I.S., Vidinli, I.B., Ozcan, R., Ulusoy, Ö.: How k-12 students search for learning? Analysis of an educational search engine log. In: Proceedings of the 37th International ACM SIGIR Conference on Research & Development in Information Retrieval, pp. 1151–1154 (2014)
32. Xia, T.: Support vector machine based educational resources classification. Int. J. Inf. Educ. Technol. **6**(11), 880 (2016)
33. Yigit-Sert, S., Altingovde, I.S., Macdonald, C., Ounis, I., Ulusoy, Ö.: Explicit diversification of search results across multiple dimensions for educational search. J. Assoc. Inf. Sci. Technol. (2020). https://doi.org/10.1002/asi.24403
34. Yilmaz, T., Ozcan, R., Altingovde, I.S., Ulusoy, Ö.: Improving educational web search for question-like queries through subject classification. Inf. Process. Manag. **56**(1), 228–246 (2019)
35. Yu, S., Su, J., Luo, D.: Improving BERT-based text classification with auxiliary sentence and domain knowledge. IEEE Access **7**, 176600–176612 (2019)
36. Zhao, W., Zhang, G., Yuan, G., Liu, J., Shan, H., Zhang, S.: The study on the text classification for financial news based on partial information. IEEE Access **8**, 100426–100437 (2020)

How Do Users Revise Zero-Hit Product Search Queries?

Yuki Amemiya[1]([✉]), Tomohiro Manabe[2], Sumio Fujita[2], and Tetsuya Sakai[1]

[1] Waseda University, Tokyo, Japan
yukiamemiya@fuji.waseda.jp, tetsuyasakai@acm.org
[2] Yahoo Japan Corporation, Tokyo, Japan
{tomanabe,sufujita}@yahoo-corp.jp

Abstract. A product search on an e-commerce site can return zero hits for several reasons. One major reason is that a user's query may not be appropriately expressed for locating existing products. To enable successful product purchase, an ideal e-commerce site should automatically revise the user query to avoid zero hits. We investigate what kinds of query revision strategies turn a zero-hit query into a successful query, by analyzing data from a major Japanese e-commerce site. Our analysis shows that about 99% of zero-hit queries can be turned into successful queries that lead to product purchase by *term dropping* (27%), *term replacement* (29%), *rephrasing* (17%), and *typo correction* (26%). The results suggest that an automatic rewriter for avoiding zero-hit product queries may be able to achieve satisfactory coverage and accuracy by focusing on the above four revision strategies.

Keywords: E-commerce search · Zero hits · Revision strategy

1 Introduction

According to a McKinsey report from July 2020, after the advent of COVID-19, more people are relying on online shopping, and plan to continue to do so[1]. However, while shopping sites provide product search capabilities for users, product searches often result in zero hits. There are several reasons behind this failure, such as the site not selling the product being sought or the product being out of stock. Among them, the most serious situation for the shopping sites is that the user's query may not be appropriately expressed for locating existing relevant products; this means that vendors lose customers' business even though they have the products to sell. Therefore, our final goal is to resolve this situation by automatically rewriting the user's query to avoid zero hits. To build an automatic query rewriter, the first and the most crucial step is to learn how users revise zero-hit queries to yield successful ones that lead to an actual

---

[1] https://www.mckinsey.com/business-functions/marketing-and-sales/our-insights/
a-global-view-of-how-consumer-behavior-is-changing-amid-covid-19.

D. Hiemstra et al. (Eds.): ECIR 2021, LNCS 12657, pp. 185–192, 2021.
https://doi.org/10.1007/978-3-030-72240-1_14

purchase. However, there is no comprehensive work that covers effective revision strategies and addresses zero-hit queries in the e-commerce search realm.

In light of this, we investigate what kinds of query revision strategies turn a zero-hit query into a successful query, by analyzing data from a major Japanese e-commerce site. Our analysis shows that about 99% of zero-hit product queries can be turned into successful queries that lead to product purchase by *term dropping* (27%), *term replacement* (29%), *rephrasing* (17%), and *typo correction* (26%). The results suggest that an automatic rewriter for zero-hit product queries may be able to achieve satisfactory coverage and accuracy by focusing on the above four revision strategies.

Section 2 discusses previous work related to the present study. Section 3 describes how we collected zero-hit queries and the corresponding successful queries with similar intents for our analysis. Section 4 describes the four major query revision strategies we have identified by analysing the pairs of zero-hit and successful queries. Section 5 analyzes the distribution of zero-hit queries over the four strategies. Finally, Sect. 6 concludes this paper.

2 Related Work

Understanding and rewriting zero-hit product queries is not a new problem. For example, Singh *et al.* [13] reported that zero-hit queries tend to be long, and one cause of zero hits is vocabulary mismatch between buyers and sellers. Parikh *et al.* [11] built a semantic query network to recover from zero-hit queries. Singh *et al.* [12] developed a system that drops some unimportant terms from the query and uses temporal feedback to rewrite zero-hit queries. Yang *et al.* [15] built a classifier to delete unimportant query terms, while Tan *et al.* [14] proposed term dropping and term replacement algorithms for query rewriting. Maji *et al.* [9] proposed a supervised classification method that rewrites queries into semantically similar ones with a high click-through rate. Manchanda *et al.* [10] proposed a query refinement approach that can suggest effective query terms that are not present in the original query. However, most of the above studies focus on a particular revision strategy or two for zero-hit queries.

Query refinement taxonomies help us understand queries and serve as the basis for automatic query reformulation. Huang *et al.* [3] developed a taxonomy for query refinement, which featured 13 reformulation types. Manchanda *et al.* [10] also divided e-commerce query transitions into five categories, including *transition from a general to a specific intent* and *transition from an incomplete to a complete query*. Hirsch *et al.* [2] analyzed the characteristics of the three reformulation types for e-commerce queries: *add*, *remove*, and *replace*. Unlike the above studies, we specifically focus on the problem of turning a zero-hit query into a successful one to enable product purchase.

Table 1 presents a comparison of our revision strategies for zero-hit product queries and query reformulation types in previous studies. Although we relied on Japanese queries to analyze revision strategies for zero-hit product queries, we believe that the strategies are language-independent, as they are a subset of existing generic query reformulation types (that are not specific to zero-hit product queries).

Table 1. A comparison of our revision strategies for zero-hit product queries and query reformulation types in previous studies

Present study	Hirsch et al. [2]	Yang et al. [15]	Tan et al. [14]	Jones et al. [5]	Hasan et al. [1] Zhou et al. [16]	Huang et al. [3]
Term dropping	Remove	Query term deletion	Query term dropping	–	–	Remove words
Term replacement	Replace	–	Query term replacement	Phrase substitution	–	Word substitution
Rephrasing	–	–	–			
Typo correction	–	–	–	–	Spelling correction	Spelling correction

3   Collecting Zero-Hit and Successful Queries with Similar Intents

For analyzing which revision strategies are effective for turning zero-hit queries into successful ones, we used a two-month search log of the Yahoo! JAPAN Shopping site. The queries used for the analysis include human-performed searches and exclude those from query suggestions or web crawlers.

We first extracted user sessions from the query logs. Following previous work [7,8], we limit the user session length to 30 min and break up sessions that are longer than this threshold because search intents may change within long sessions. From the user sessions, we extracted query pairs q and q', where q is a zero-hit query and q' is a *successful* query, which is defined as a query obtained by rewriting q in the same user session and resulting in an actual purchase. For privacy concerns, we ensured that both q and q' were observed in the data for at least two users, respectively. Henceforth, we denote a query transition from the zero-hit query q to the successful query q' as $q \mapsto q'$. We thus obtained 3,438 query pairs.

To identify effective revision strategies for zero-hit product queries, we first filtered the aforementioned 3,438 query pairs (q, q') to ensure that q (zero-hit query) and q' (successful query) have the same or similar intent. To this end, we hired crowd workers on the Yahoo! JAPAN Crowdsourcing site and let three assessors independently label query pairs as either "similar" or "not similar." We showed each query pair (q, q') to the assessors. We instructed the assessors to label it as "similar" if it is likely that q and q' will return at least one product in common, assuming that neither of them returns zero hits. The final label was obtained by majority voting. Consequently, we obtained 1,922 query pairs, where q and q' are considered to have similar intents.

It should be noted that our Japanese queries were processed by morphological analysis (MeCab[2]) before they were shown to the crowd workers in all of

---

[2] http://taku910.github.io/mecab/.

our experiments. This is because Japanese texts do not contain white spaces between words [4]: after morphological analysis, we can identify query terms and thereby consider existing query revision strategies such as *term dropping* and *term replacement*, as described below.

4   Four Revision Strategies for Zero-Hit Product Queries

By analyzing the above query pairs, we first observed that many users utilized the following two revision strategies for their zero-hit queries at the term level.

(1) *Term dropping*

In *term dropping*, a successful query q' is generated when any number of terms is removed from the zero-hit query q; that is, the terms included in the successful query q' are a subset of those included in the zero-hit query q.

Example (translated): *smartphone grip chick* $\mapsto$ *smartphone grip*

(2) *Term replacement*

In *term replacement*, a successful query q' is generated by replacing at least one term in the zero-hit query q with a new term.

Example (translated): *CASIO keyboard leg* $\mapsto$ *CASIO keyboard stand*

We conducted a preliminary analysis of how *term dropping* and *term replacement* actually occur as follows. First, from the 1,922 query pairs mentioned in Sect. 3, we automatically extracted pairs that are likely to have gone through *term dropping* and *term replacement* by comparing the set of query terms from the zero-hit query with that from the corresponding successful query for each pair. We thus obtained 364 and 787 query pairs that are likely to be *term dropping* and *term replacement* cases, respectively. We then examined the *positions* of query terms that were dropped or replaced; if multiple query terms within a zero-hit query were dropped or replaced, all of these were recorded. Figure 1

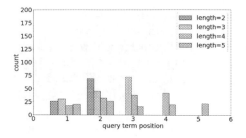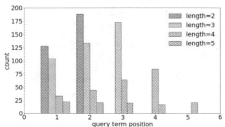

Fig. 1. Positions of query terms dropped (left) or replaced (right) from zero-hit queries.

visualizes the counts of query term positions summed across the aforementioned query pair sets where term dropping or replacement occurred, for original query lengths 2–5. It is clear that when the query length is between 2 and 4, term dropping and replacement tend to occur near the end of the original zero-hit query. Interestingly, this trend does not hold when the query length is 5.

Another query revision strategy we frequently observed in our query pairs is when the user modifies the entire query, as defined below.

(3) *Rephrasing*

In *rephrasing*, a successful query q' is generated by replacing all the terms in the zero-hit query q with other words. *Rephrasing* is similar to *term replacement*, but there is no term overlap between q and q'.

Example (translated): *enekeep* $\mapsto$ *dry cell type portable battery charger*

The fourth revision strategy we frequently observed in our query pairs was revision at the character level rather than term level. There are several reasons that this type of revision occurs, as discussed below.

(4) *Typo correction*

In *typo correction*, the user corrects a query that was not originally spelt correctly for some reason. The reasons include misspellings and typos, omitting white spaces between English terms, and inadvertently entering an incomplete query.

- Misspellings and typographical errors

  Example: *wearoot* $\mapsto$ *webroot*

- Omitting white spaces between English terms

  Example: *edfir* $\mapsto$ *edfir*

- Inadvertently entering an incomplete query

  Example: *cnstor* $\mapsto$ *cnstore*

Because the *typo correction* category occurs at the character level, automatically classifying zero-hit queries based on term-level comparisons as we have done for Fig. 1 is not sufficient if we want to classify our query pairs based on all four categories that we have mentioned. For example, given an instance *CASIO keyboard legg* $\mapsto$ *CASIO keyboard leg*, we would like to consider this as a *typo correction* rather than *term replacement*. Hence in Sect. 5, we manually classify our query pairs using the four revision strategies.

5   Coverage of the Four Revision Strategies

In this section, we analyze how many zero-hit queries can be remedied by the four revision strategies formulated in Sect. 4. To this end, we also used Yahoo! JAPAN Crowdsouring to label each of the 1,922 query pairs as one of *term dropping*, *term replacement*, *rephrasing*, *typo correction*, or *others*. The fifth category is to ensure that we capture all query revision phenomena. In this experiment, five workers independently classified each query pair into the five categories, and the final gold category was determined based on majority voting. The four categories are not strictly mutually exclusive: for example, there was an actual query pair *seven lens seed disposable* ↦ *7 lens* (translated), where two terms were dropped, while one term was replaced (from *seven* to *7*). However, we let assessors choose exactly one revision strategy for each query pair, as mutually exclusive categories are more convenient for analysing the distribution of queries over them. We ensured that at least three assessors agreed for each query pair; consequently, we were left with 1,530 pairs. The inter-assessor agreement in terms of Krippendorff's α [6] for nominal labels was 0.337, which we find satisfactory.

Table 2 shows the distribution of the 1,530 pairs over the five categories. It can be observed that the query pairs are reasonably evenly spread across *term dropping*, *term replacement*, *rephrasing*, and *typo correction*. To be more specific, *term dropping*, *term replacement*, and *typo correction* each cover about 26–29% of the zero-hit queries, while *rephrasing* covers about 17%. As *rephrasing* is substantially less frequently occurring than the other three revision strategies, we can say that users (who adhere to their original search intents) tend to reuse parts of their original queries rather than to completely rewrite them. Together, the four revision strategies cover 99% of our zero-hit queries and turn them into successful queries. As for the *others* category, we found that many of the instances are artifacts of morphological analysis applied to the Japanese queries. For example, we had a query pair *btsdvd* ↦ *bts dvd*. However, after morphological analysis, both the zero-hit and the successful queries became *bts dvd* and therefore the crowd workers were shown a pair of seemingly identical queries.

Table 2. The results of labeling each of the query pairs with the gold revision strategy

Strategy	# of zero-hit queries	Percentage
Term dropping	405	26.5%
Term replacement	438	28.6%
Rephrasing	261	17.1%
Typo correction	404	26.4%
Others	22	1.4%
Total	1,530	100%

6   Conclusions and Future Research

By analyzing query pairs consisting of zero-hit and successful queries based on a query log from the Yahoo! JAPAN Shopping site, we investigated what kinds of query revision strategies turn a zero-hit query into a successful query that lead to product purchase. Our analysis shows that about 99% of zero-hit product queries can be turned into successful queries by *term dropping* (27%), *term replacement* (29%), *rephrasing* (17%), and *typo correction* (26%). The results suggest that an automatic rewriter for zero-hit product queries may be able to achieve satisfactory coverage and accuracy by focusing on the above four strategies. We also found that *term dropping* and *term replacement* tend to occur near the end of the zero-hit query. For future research, we plan to construct an automatic zero-hit query rewriter that incorporates these four revision strategies.

References

1. Hasan, S., Heger, C., Mansour, S.: Spelling correction of user search queries through statistical machine translation. In: Proceedings of EMNLP 2015, pp. 451–460 (2015)
2. Hirsch, S., Guy, I., Nus, A., Dagan, A., Kurland, O.: Query reformulation in e-commerce search. In: Proceedings of ACM SIGIR 2020, pp. 1319–1328 (2020)
3. Huang, J., Efthimiadis, E.N.: Analyzing and evaluating query reformulation strategies in web search logs. In: Proceedings of ACM CIKM 2009, pp. 77–86 (2009)
4. Jones, G.J., Sakai, T., Kajiura, M., Sumita, K.: Experiments in Japanese text retrieval and routing using the NEAT system. In: Proceedings of ACM SIGIR 1998, pp. 197–205 (1998)
5. Jones, R., Rey, B., Madani, O., Greiner, W.: Generating query substitutions. In: Proceedings of WWW 2006, pp. 387–396 (2006)
6. Krippendorff, K.: Content Analysis: An Introduction to Its Methodology. Sage Publications, Thousand Oaks (2018)
7. Liu, Z., Singh, G., Parikh, N., Sundaresan, N.: A large scale query logs analysis for assessing personalization opportunities in e-commerce sites. In: WSCD Workshop at WSDM 2014 (2014)
8. Madvariya, A., Borar, S.: Discovering similar products in fashion e-commerce. In: Proceedings of ACM SIGIR 2017 Workshop on eCommerce (ECOM 2017) (2017)
9. Maji, S., Kumar, R., Bansal, M., Roy, K., Kumar, M., Goyal, P.: Addressing vocabulary gap in e-commerce search. In: Proceedings of ACM SIGIR 2019, pp. 1073–1076 (2019)
10. Manchanda, S., Sharma, M., Karypis, G.: Intent term selection and refinement in e-commerce queries. arXiv preprint arXiv:1908.08564 (2019)
11. Parikh, N., Sundaresan, N.: Inferring semantic query relations from collective user behavior. In: Proceedings of ACM CIKM 2008, pp. 349–358 (2008)
12. Singh, G., Parikh, N., Sundaresan, N.: Rewriting null e-commerce queries to recommend products. In: Proceedings of WWW 2012, pp. 73–82 (2012)
13. Singh, G., Parikh, N., Sundaresn, N.: User behavior in zero-recall ecommerce queries. In: Proceedings of ACM SIGIR 2011, pp. 75–84 (2011)
14. Tan, Z., Xu, C., Jiang, M., Yang, H., Wu, X.: Query rewrite for null and low search results in ecommerce. In: Proceedings of ACM SIGIR 2017 Workshop on eCommerce (ECOM 2017) (2017)

15. Yang, B., Parikh, N., Singh, G., Sundaresan, N.: A study of query term deletion using large-scale e-commerce search logs. In: de Rijke, M., et al. (eds.) ECIR 2014. LNCS, vol. 8416, pp. 235–246. Springer, Cham (2014). https://doi.org/10.1007/978-3-319-06028-6_20
16. Zhou, Y., Porwal, U., Konow, R.: Spelling correction as a foreign language. In: Proceedings of ACM SIGIR 2019 Workshop on eCommerce (ECOM 2019) (2019)

Query Performance Prediction Through Retrieval Coherency

Negar Arabzadeh[(⊠)], Amin Bigdeli, Morteza Zihayat, and Ebrahim Bagheri

Rryerson University, Toronto On, Canada
{narabzad,abigdeli,mzihayat,bagheri}@ryerson.ca

Abstract. Post-retrieval Query Performance Prediction (QPP) methods benefit from the characteristics of the retrieved set of documents to determine query difficulty. While existing works have investigated the relation between query and retrieved document spaces, as well as retrieved document scores, the association between the retrieved documents themselves, referred to as *coherency*, has not been extensively investigated for QPP. We propose that the coherence of the retrieved documents can be formalized as a function of the characteristics of a network that represents the associations between these documents. Based on experiments on three corpora, namely Robust04, Gov2 and ClueWeb09 and their TREC topics, we show that our coherence measures outperform existing metrics in the literature and are able to significantly improve the performance of state of the art QPP methods.

1 Introduction

The task of predicting the performance of a retrieval method is often known as Query Performance Prediction (QPP). A class of QPP methods, known as post-retrieval QPP, relies on the characteristics of the retrieved set of documents by the retrieval method to determine query performance. Existing post-retrieval QPP methods mainly rely on the relationship between the query and document spaces based on some measure of association such as the distribution of the document retrieval scores [1–6,14], or the degree of divergence between the characteristics of the retrieved documents and those of the entire corpus [7,8]. The intuition for such methods is that a higher association between query, retrieved document, and corpus spaces would be an indication of a query that is easier to satisfy. There are also QPP methods that capitalize on retrieval robustness [7]. These methods inject noise into the original query and measure retrieval robustness despite the noise. Furthermore, embeddings have also been used to incorporate semantics for estimating query performance [9–13].

We address QPP by considering the association between the retrieved set of documents. While the literature has extensively considered associations between the query and the retrieved documents [1–4], as well as the relation between the corpus and the retrieved documents [7,8], to the best of our knowledge, the association among the retrieved set of documents themselves has not been extensively explored. Motivated by the *Cluster hypothesis* [20], we put forth that

© Springer Nature Switzerland AG 2021
D. Hiemstra et al. (Eds.): ECIR 2021, LNCS 12657, pp. 193–200, 2021.
https://doi.org/10.1007/978-3-030-72240-1_15

the *coherency* of the retrieved set of documents can be an indication of query difficulty. In other words, a coherent set of retrieved documents shows that the retrieval method has been able to discriminate between relevant and non-relevant documents. [15] is among the only works that use coherence-based measures for QPP, by considering each query term as an aspect of the query. They find the coherence of the top-k documents retrieved for each query term by their three proposed coherence measures, namely QC1-3, separately, and count the number of the document pairs that have a similarity value above a threshold.

We propose a framework for defining a host of coherence measures based on the graphical modeling of the retrieved documents. We build a weighted undirected document association network that captures the retrieved documents and their similarities. We propose that query *coherence* can be measured as a function of the characteristics of the document association network. The **novelty of our work** is that it gives way to a host of coherence measures, among which the QC1-3 metrics [15] are special cases of the proposed coherence framework.

Our experiments are structured around four Research Questions (RQs): (**RQ1**) Would the consideration of network characteristics lead to the development of coherence measures with better performance compared to existing coherence measures; (**RQ2**) From existing QPP methods, which, if any, experience the most significant performance improvement as a result of incorporating the proposed coherence measures; (**RQ3**) Among the set of proposed coherence measures, which would lead to a significant and consistent improvement on QPP; (**RQ4**) Would the interpolation of coherence measures with base QPP methods lead to statically significant improvements over the state of the art QPP methods.

2   Proposed Approach

Our objective is to develop a predictor such as $\mu(q, D_q^k, C)$ that would predict the performance of query q against corpus C by considering the top-k documents retrieved denoted as D_q^k. we define a Document Association Network based on D_q^k as follows: For a given q, the Document Association Network G for a list of documents D_q^k is a weighted undirected

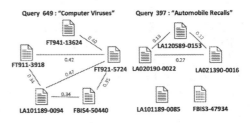

Fig. 1. Document association network for easy query (Left) vs hard query (Right).

graph $\mathbb{G}(q, D_q^k) = \{\mathbb{V}_G, \mathbb{E}_G, W\}$ where $\mathbb{V}_G = \{d \in D_q^k\}$ and $\mathbb{E}_G = \{e_{d_i d_j} : \forall d_i, d_j \in \mathbb{V}_G\}$. The function for edge weights is defined as $\mathbb{E}_G \rightarrow [0, 1]$ where the edge weight between two nodes d_i and d_j denotes similarity between documents d_i and d_j.

Document Association Network is a fully connected graph that finds all pairwise document similarities in D_q^k. We define our coherence measures over the document association network based on network measures. Given the fact that some

Table 1. Coherence based on document association network where node neighbourhood is defined as $\mathbb{N}_{d_i} = \{d_j | e_{d_i d_j} \in \mathbb{E}_G\}$ and k_i is the number of neighbours of d_i.

Method name	Description	Formula
Average Clustering Coefficient (ACC)	Average completeness of each node's neighborhood in the network	$\frac{1}{n} \sum\limits_{i=1}^{n} \frac{2|\{e_{d_j d_k} | d_j, d_k \in N_{d_i}; e_{d_j d_k} \in \mathbb{E}_G\}|}{k_i(k_i-1)}$
Average Degree Connectivity (ADC)	Average nearest neighbor degree of nodes with specific degree	$\frac{1}{n} \sum\limits_{i=1}^{n} (\frac{1}{degree(v_{d_i})} \sum\limits_{j \in N_{d_i}} w_{d_i d_j} k_j)$
Average Neighbour Degree (AND)	Average degree of the neighborhood of each node generalized over the whole network	$\frac{1}{n} \sum\limits_{i=1}^{n} (\frac{1}{k_i} \sum_{j \in N_{d_i}} k_j)$
Density (D)	The number of observed edges over the number of possible edges in a fully connected graph	$\frac{2|\mathbb{E}_G|}{|\mathbb{V}_G|(|\mathbb{V}_G|-1)}$

network measures are agnostic to edge weights and consider edges equally regardless of the edge weight, we prune the network through thresholding. As suggested in [16], adopting an adaptive thresholding strategy is quite useful where edges below the overall average edge weights in the graph are pruned. This produces a sparser network that does not consist of document associations with negligible similarities. We visualize the document association network of two queries from TREC topics in Fig. 1. Each network consists of the top-5 documents related to the query where edges are adaptively pruned as explained earlier. The network for the easier query has higher edge weights and enjoys a higher number of document associations. In contrast, the more difficult query is disconnected, has a sparse edge set and the edge weights are quite low. This example shows that network density metrics could be suitable coherence measures for QPP. Therefore, we focus on network density metrics introduced in Table 1 to define coherence measures [17]: (1) **Average Clustering Coefficient (ACC)** (2) **Average Degree Connectivity (ADC)** (3) **Average Neighbour Degree (AND)** and, (4) **Density (D)**. It is also possible to consider edge weights when computing ACC, ADC, AND and D and hence develop WACC, WADC, WAND, and WD measures. We further note that the QC metrics, QC1-3 [15] can be considered a special case of the D measure when applied over the document association network. However, He et al. assume that each multi-term query with n terms can be broken down into n separate terms for each of which top-k documents containing that term will be retrieved. The QC metrics are then defined as the count of number of edges weighted above a threshold averaged over n query terms. In contrast, we do not see each query as a decomposable unit and rather build the document association network over one set of top-k documents retrieved for the full query. The downside of QC1-3 is that they assume queries that are composed of hard query subsets will essentially translate into hard multi-term queries, which may not be the case in practice. For instance, consider the query 'apple corporation'. The query consists of two hard terms 'apple' and 'corporation'. The term 'apple' is a hard query as it is ambiguous with multiple senses and 'corporation' is also a hard query as it is non-specific

Table 2. Comparison of our coherence measures to the baselines based Pearson correlation. All results statistically significant at $\alpha = 0.05$ compared to actual AP values.

	Baseline coherence metrics			Unweighted				Weighted			
	QC-1	QC-2	QC-3	ACC	AND	ADC	D	WACC	WAND	WADC	WD
Robust04	0.205	0.188	0.181	0.253	0.286	0.326	0.233	0.149	0.300	0.284	0.221
ClueWeb09	0.222	0.194	0.269	0.184	0.183	0.215	0.239	0.236	0.290	0.163	0.296
GOV2	0.222	0.233	0.256	0.206	0.291	0.345	0.369	0.275	0.248	0.260	0.325

[13]. However, when used in conjunction, the multi-term query 'apple corporation' turns into an easy query since the two query terms qualify each other and become quite discriminative. Our approach is able to discern between the difficulty of the two individual terms and the multi-term query.

Furthermore, recent work suggest that the interpolation of measures that compute complementary aspects of a query can lead to improved QPP [13]. Hence, to investigate the complementarity of our proposed coherence measures to the baselines, we apply min-max normalization and then interpolate our coherence measures defined over G, denoted by $Coh(G)$, and existing QPP methods as follows where λ is an interpolation weight in $\{0, 0.1, ..., 1\}$:

$$\mu(q, D_q^k, C) = \lambda QPP(q, D_q^k, C) + (1 - \lambda)Coh(G) \qquad (1)$$

3   Experiments

Experimental Setup: We employed three corpora, namely, Robust04, Gov2, and ClueWeb09 and their TREC topics: 301–450 and 601–700 for Robust04, 1–200 for Clueweb09 and 701–850 for Gov2. We predict the Average Precision of each topic computed using Query Likelihood (QL) implemented in Anserini [19]. Edge weights are computed based on tf-idf similarities. For performance evaluation, we compute correlation coefficients between the list of queries (1) ordered by their difficulty for the retrieval method, and (2) ordered by the QPP metric. Hyper-parameters are set using 10-fold cross-validation optimized for Pearson ρ.

Baselines: For all the baselines as well as our proposed methods, we selected $k \in \{5, 10, 25, 50, 100, 250, 500, 750, 1000\}$ using 10-fold cross-validation. In terms of the selected baselines, some focus on the divergence between the top-K retrieved documents and the Corpus. Among which the **WIG** method [7] predicts query difficulty by measuring the *divergence* between the mean retrieval score of top-K documents and the corpus. The **Clarity** method [8] also measures the divergence between the language model of the retrieved documents and the corpus. The Query Feedback (**QF**) method [7] is proposed based on the *robustness* of the result list. QF measures the number of common documents between the top retrieved documents from the original query and a revised query, formed based on terms with the highest contribution to Clarity. We selected the cut-off parameter of QF from $n \in \{5, 10, 25, 50, 100\}$ through 10-fold cross-validation.

Another group of metrics targets the standard deviation between the retrieval score of top-K documents. **NQC** [2], σ_K [1], $n(\sigma_{X\%})$ [6], **SMV** [3] and **RSD** [4] belong to this group of metrics and each use an alternative form of the standard deviation of the retrieval scores of the top-K retrieved documents. Among these metrics, the bootstrapping-based approach RSD_{WIG} has a number of parameters to be tuned. We selected the sample size and the number of samples as suggested in [4], i.e., the number of bootstrap samples N = 100 and we select each document sample size $l \in \{30, 50, 100, 150, 200\}$ through 10-fold cross validation. We also consider the utility estimation framework (**UEF**) [21], which operates over baseline QPP methods for which we selected from WIG, Clarity, QF, and NQC. Finally, we include the work by Roy et al. who proposed $P_{clarity}$ based on the idea of clustering neural embeddings based on their vector similarity [13]. As suggested by the authors, we report $P_{clarity}$ after interpolation with NQC. We perform linear interpolation based on 10-fold cross-validation. Finally, we also compare against existing coherence-based QPP metrics by He et al. [15]. For its threshold, as suggested by the authors, we randomly sampled documents and calculated the average of the top 5% similarities as the cut-off point.

Findings:[1] In **RQ1**, we are interested in finding out whether the proposed coherence metrics are more effective than existing coherence metrics, i.e., QC1-3 by He et al. We make **two important observations** in Table 2: (1) Overall, the proposed host of coherence measures based on the document association network are more effective than the QC metrics regardless of the adopted network density metric, and (2) While the QC metrics are essentially similar to the Weighted Density (WD) metric, they do not show as strong a performance. As mentioned earlier, we find that this is due to the fact that QC metrics decompose the query into separate terms while in our work, we consider each query to be non-decomposable. Now, in **RQ2**, we are interested in determining the impact of our coherence metrics on the baseline QPP methods as a result of interpolation. The results of the interpolation per baseline QPP method is reported in Table 3 (left), which reports the best improvements observed for each baseline method. Our results report **two main findings**, namely (1) the interpolation of the coherence measures with baseline QPP methods will, in the majority of cases, lead to positive improvements; and, (2) most notably, baseline QPP methods that are based on the standard deviation of the retrieved document scores enjoy consistent improved performance when interpolated with our proposed coherence measure. Specifically, the SMV baseline reports the highest improvement percentage compared to all methods while $n(\sigma_{X\%})$ shows the best overall performance after being interpolated with our coherence measures.

Further, we study the performance of the different coherence measures when interpolated with the different QPP baselines in **RQ3**. Table 3 (right) reports the best performance observed by each coherence measure for the different corpora. While not all coherence measures can always show improved performance

---

[1] https://github.com/Narabzad/QPP-Retrieval-Coherency.

Table 3. The best Pearson correlation obtained after interpolation with coherence measures reported by (left) QPP method, (right) coherence measure. * indicates statistically significance at $\alpha = 0.05$.

	Robust04		ClueWeb09		Gov2	
	value	%Δ	value	%Δ	value	%Δ
WIG	0.57	13.6%*	0.41	26.5%*	0.55	1.6%
Clarity	0.51	−2.1%	0.35	10.9%*	0.49	8.7%
QF	0.41	−6.2%	0.28	47.6%*	0.55	23.9%*
NQC	0.55	20.3%*	0.36	68.7%*	0.46	−4.4%
σ_K	0.53	4.9%*	0.33	43.0%	0.50	8.9%*
$n(\sigma_{X\%})$	0.60	7.8%	0.32	18.5%*	0.62	8.6%*
SMV	0.54	22.8%*	0.33	15.4%*	0.55	45.6%*

		Robust04		ClueWeb09		Gov2	
		value	%Δ	value	%Δ	value	%Δ
UnWeighted	ACC	0.56	1.6%*	0.25	−7.0%	0.47	−17.0%
	ADC	0.56	0.7%*	0.35	29.5%*	0.57	−1.1%
	AND	0.57	3.6%*	0.26	−3.3%	0.54	−4.5%
	D	0.54	−2.0%	0.35	28.4%*	0.59	2.8%*
Weighted	WACC	0.55	−0.2%	0.40	48.7%*	0.43	−24.3%
	WADC	0.54	−2.0%	0.35	27.3%*	0.55	−3.3%
	WAND	0.60	7.8%*	0.32	18.4%*	0.62	8.6%*
	WD	0.57	3.3%	0.43	58.7%*	0.58	1.6%*

Table 4. Comparison between baselines and the interpolation of our coherence measures. Bold values are the best in each column. † is statistically significant improvement over the best baseline; * denotes statistically significant correlation with AP ($\alpha = 0.05$).

	Pearson Rho			Kendall Tau		
	RB04	CW09	GOV2	RB04	CW09	GOV2
WIG	0.500*	0.324*	0.545*	0.350*	0.257*	0.398*
Clarity	0.524*	0.312*	0.450*	0.371*	0.227*	0.285*
NQC	0.458*	0.214*	0.478*	0.364*	0.115*	0.343*
QF	0.435*	0.187*	0.443*	0.339*	0.120*	0.306*
UEF	0.528*	0.270*	0.500*	0.402*	0.187*	0.339*
SMV	0.439*	0.286*	0.377*	0.320*	0.221*	0.316*
σ_K	0.507*	0.230*	0.459*	0.327*	0.180*	0.347*
n(X%)	0.552*	0.271*	0.571*	0.373*	0.219*	0.393*
$P_{Clarity}$	0.541*	0.337*	0.547*	0.3937*	0.216*	0.364*
RSD_{WIG}	0.433*	0.211*	0.486*	0.356*	0.118*	0.356*
WAND[n(X%)]	**0.595*†**	0.321*	**0.620*†**	**0.408*†**	0.192*	**0.465*†**
WD[n(X%)]	0.570*	**0.430*†**	0.580*†	0.376*	0.270*†	0.451*†
WAND[SMV)]	0.495*†	0.218*	0.493*†	0.376*†	0.132*	0.391*†
WD[SMV)]	0.539*†	0.330*†	0.549*†	0.390*†	**0.288*†**	0.369*†

over the baseline methods, our **main observation** is that the weighted version of the AND (WAND) and Density (WD) measures are the ones that show consistent positive improvement over the baselines regardless of the dataset. In other words, these two proposed coherence measures will consistently improve their baseline QPP methods after interpolation. Finally, in **RQ4**, we are interested in the overall impact of our proposed coherence measures on post-retrieval QPP. We would like to investigate whether the consideration of coherence measures would significantly outperform existing QPP methods. For this purpose, we report the results of the interpolation of the best performing baseline QPP method identified in RQ2, i.e., $n(\sigma_{X\%})$, and the best proposed coherence measures in RQ3, i.e., WAND and WD, in Table 4. We find that both interpolations, lead to improved performance compared to the state of the art. More specifically, $WAND[n(\sigma_{X\%})]$ is statistically-speaking significantly better than the best baseline on both Pearson and Kendall correlations for Robust04 and Gov2. Furthermore, WD $[n(\sigma_{X\%})]$ is significantly better than the best baseline on both correlation measures on CW09. When not the best, both interpolations are competitive with the best baseline QPP method. Overall, our **main finding** from Table 4 is that our best performing coherence measures are able to improve the base QPP methods and lead to significantly better performing predictors. It should be noted that in our experiments λ was never determined to be at 1, i.e., no impact by the coherence measures (please see http://bit.ly/35zmTTr).

4   Concluding Remarks

We define coherence as a function of density metrics computed over a document association network. Our experiments performed on three TREC corpora identify **impactful findings**: **(1)** our proposed coherence measures show a consistently better performance compared to existing coherence measures in the literature; **(2)** standard deviation-based predictors experience a consistent positive impact when interpolated with our proposed coherence measures; **(3)** there are two of our coherence measures that consistently improve all baseline methods; **(4)** the interpolation of two of our coherence measures with standard deviation-based methods leads to significant improvement over the state of the art QPP methods.

References

1. Pérez-Iglesias, J., Araujo, L.: Standard deviation as a query hardness estimator. In: Chavez, E., Lonardi, S. (eds.) SPIRE 2010. LNCS, vol. 6393, pp. 207–212. Springer, Heidelberg (2010). https://doi.org/10.1007/978-3-642-16321-0_21
2. Shtok, A., Kurland, O., Carmel, D.: Predicting query performance by query-drift estimation. In: Azzopardi, L., et al. (eds.) ICTIR 2009. LNCS, vol. 5766, pp. 305–312. Springer, Heidelberg (2009). https://doi.org/10.1007/978-3-642-04417-5_30
3. Tao, Y., Wu, S.: Query performance prediction by considering score magnitude and variance together. In: Proceedings of the 23rd ACM International Conference on Conference on Information and Knowledge Management, pp. 1891–1894 (2014)
4. Roitman, H., Erera, S., Weiner, B.: Robust standard deviation estimation for query performance prediction. In: Proceedings of the ACM SIGIR International Conference on Theory of Information Retrieval, pp. 245–248 (2017)
5. Roitman, H.: ICTIR tutorial: modern query performance prediction: theory and practice. In: Proceedings of the 2020 ACM SIGIR on International Conference on Theory of Information Retrieval, pp. 195–196 (2020)
6. Cummins, R., Jose, J., O'Riordan, C.: Improved query performance prediction using standard deviation. In: Proceedings of the 34th International ACM SIGIR Conference on Research and Development in Information Retrieval, pp. 1089–1090 (2011)
7. Zhou, Y., Croft, W.B.: Query performance prediction in web search environments. In: Proceedings of the 30th Annual International ACM SIGIR Conference on Research and Development in Information Retrieval, pp. 543–550 (2007)

8. Cronen-Townsend, S., Zhou, Y., Croft, W.B.: Predicting query performance. In: Proceedings of the 25th Annual International ACM SIGIR Conference on Research and Development in Information Retrieval, pp. 299–306 (2002)
9. Arabzadeh, N., Zarrinkalam, F., Jovanovic, J., Bagheri, E.: Neural embedding-based metrics for pre-retrieval query performance prediction. In: Jose, J.M., et al. (eds.) ECIR 2020. LNCS, vol. 12036, pp. 78–85. Springer, Cham (2020). https://doi.org/10.1007/978-3-030-45442-5_10
10. Khodabakhsh, M., Bagheri, E.: Semantics-enabled query performance prediction for ad hoc table retrieval. Inf. Process. Manag. 58(1), 102399 (2021)
11. Bagheri, E., Arabzadeh, N., Zarrinkalam, F., Jovanovic, J., Al-Obeidat, F.: Neural embedding-based specificity metrics for pre-retrieval query performance prediction. Inf. Process. Manag. 57(4), 102248 (2020)
12. Zamani, H., Croft, W.B., Culpepper, J.S.: Neural query performance prediction using weak supervision from multiple signals. In: The 41st International ACM SIGIR Conference on Research and Development in Information Retrieval, pp. 105–114 (2018)
13. Roy, D., Ganguly, D., Mitra, M., Jones, G.J.: Estimating gaussian mixture models in the local neighbourhood of embedded word vectors for query performance prediction. Inf. Process. Manag. 56(3), 1026–1045 (2019)
14. Diaz, F.: Performance prediction using spatial autocorrelation. In: Proceedings of the 30th Annual International ACM SIGIR Conference on Research and Development in Information Retrieval, pp. 583–590 (2007)
15. He, J., Larson, M., de Rijke, M.: Using coherence-based measures to predict query difficulty. In: Macdonald, C., Ounis, I., Plachouras, V., Ruthven, I., White, R.W. (eds.) ECIR 2008. LNCS, vol. 4956, pp. 689–694. Springer, Heidelberg (2008). https://doi.org/10.1007/978-3-540-78646-7_80
16. Christophides, V., Efthymiou, V., Stefanidis, K.: Entity resolution in the web of data. Synth. Lect. Semant. Web 5(3), 1–122 (2015)
17. Marsden, P.V.: The reliability of network density and composition measures. Soc. Netw. 15(4), 399–421 (1993)
18. Song, F., Croft, W.B.: A general language model for information retrieval. In: Proceedings of the Eighth International Conference on Information and Knowledge Management, pp. 316–321 (1999)
19. Yang, P., Fang, H., Lin, J.: Anserini: enabling the use of lucene for information retrieval research. In: Proceedings of the 40th International ACM SIGIR Conference on Research and Development in Information Retrieval, pp. 1253–1256 (2017)
20. Kurland, O.: The cluster hypothesis in information retrieval. In: de Rijke, M., et al. (eds.) ECIR 2014. LNCS, vol. 8416, pp. 823–826. Springer, Cham (2014). https://doi.org/10.1007/978-3-319-06028-6_105
21. Shtok, A., Kurland, O., Carmel, D.: Using statistical decision theory and relevance models for query-performance prediction. In: Proceedings of the 33rd International ACM SIGIR Conference on Research and Development in Information Retrieval, pp. 259–266 (2010)

From the Beatles to Billie Eilish: Connecting Provider Representativeness and Exposure in Session-Based Recommender Systems

Alejandro Ariza[1]([⊠]) [iD], Francesco Fabbri[2,3] [iD], Ludovico Boratto[2] [iD], and Maria Salamó[1]

[1] Universitat de Barcelona, Barcelona, Spain
{alejandro.ariza14,maria.salamo}@ub.edu
[2] Eurecat - Centre Tecnológic de Catalunya, Barcelona, Spain
[3] Pompeu Fabra University, Barcelona, Spain
francesco.fabbri@eurecat.org, ludovico.boratto@acm.org

Abstract. Session-based recommender systems consider the evolution of user preferences in browsing sessions. Existing studies suggest as next item the one that keeps the user engaged as long as possible. This point of view does not account for the providers' perspective. In this paper, we highlight side effects over the providers caused by state-of-the-art models. We focus on the music domain and study how artists' exposure in the recommendation lists is affected by the input data structure, where different session lengths are explored. We consider four session-based systems on three types of datasets, with long, short, and mixed playlist length. We provide measures to characterize disparate treatment between the artists, through a systematic analysis by comparing (i) the exposure received by an artist in the recommendations and (ii) their input representation in the data. Results show that artists for which we can observe a lot of interactions, but offering less items, are mistreated in terms of exposure. Moreover, we show how input data structure may impact the algorithms' effectiveness, possibly due to preference-shift phenomena

Keywords: Session-based recommender systems · Provider exposure

1 Introduction

Recommender systems (RS) are key tools to support users in online platforms [16]. Recent literature has focused on monitoring the users in their browsing sessions, to generate adaptive recommendations in so called *session-based RS* [14]. Instead of considering only the historical interactions between users and items, session-based systems adapt in real time to user preferences.

The first two authors contributed equally to this work.

© Springer Nature Switzerland AG 2021
D. Hiemstra et al. (Eds.): ECIR 2021, LNCS 12657, pp. 201–208, 2021.
https://doi.org/10.1007/978-3-030-72240-1_16

While session-based systems focus on user effectiveness as their main goal, recently a multi-stakeholder perspective has become central, for both recommender and ranking systems [1,17]. RS can support this paradigm and consider providers' needs, by giving them a certain *exposure* when their items are recommended. However, recommendation technologies do not consider the provider perspective, thus overexposing popular providers [7,13], often leading to unfair outcomes [5,12]. In addition, the exposure in a ranking does not always match the expected one [4,15]. Despite the growing interest on fairness in recommendation, session-based RS received less attention [7] and no study tackled the exposure generated by a given data distribution.

Contribution. In this work, we analyze how the input data distribution impacts over RS quality, focusing also on the final exposure given to providers. As use-case, we consider the music streaming scenario, considering data coming from user-song interactions in Last-FM [18]. We sample three datasets, characterized by short, long, and mixed session lengths. Inspired by recent studies comparing the effectiveness of neural and non-neural approaches [11], we also focus on these two classes, considering four session-based systems, two for each class. In our study, we go beyond provider popularity, trying to understand if the *representation* of an artist (i.e., how many items they have in their catalog) affects the exposure they are given. Our results show that size of input representation plays an important role, with big providers in terms of representation (e.g., number of items in the catalog) being exposed not only more than unpopular ones, but also more than *popular-but-smaller* ones. We quantify this effect showing a systematic bias against providers having less items, which get lower chances of being recommended, despite being very popular. In other words, new but very popular artists like Billie Eilish, with billions of streams in music platforms, would be recommended less than very popular but bigger acts in terms of representation, such as The Beatles.

In a summary, (i) we characterize the effectiveness of session-based RS, comparing different algorithms and datasets, (ii) we provide a measure of *expected exposure* and characterize its connection with *provider representativeness* and *relevance*, (iii) we delve into the causes behind disparate exposure.

2   Metrics and Algorithms

Nowadays, streaming music services process user-item interactions as time-framed sequences, known as *sessions*. Considering a session s_n as an ordered list of user-item interactions of length n, a RS tries to predict the interaction i_{n+1} at time $n + 1$, suggesting a top-k list of most likely future interactions.

Performance assessment. In addition to traditional metrics, such as precision (P@K), recall (R@K), and mean average precision (MAP@K), metrics such as mean reciprocal rank (MRR@K) and hit rate (HR@K) have been introduced to focus only on the single highest-ranked relevant item [8,14]. These metrics optimize model performances in terms of user preferences, without accounting for the other stakeholders, such as the item providers. For this reason, we introduce a metric to quantify the goodness of the tested models w.r.t. the artist's utility.

Provider Exposure. Provider exposure assesses the quality of the models from the perspective of the searched/recommended individuals [19]. We consider each session s_n of length n as a query, $q(s_n)$, submitted to the RS; each query is processed by the recommendation algorithm that returns a top-k list of items L, ordered by interaction probability. Hence, we can define the probability distribution of interactions as $\sum_{i \in \mathcal{I}} p(i|q(s_n))$, with $\mathcal{I}$ as the set of items, and $p(i|q(s_n))$ as the probability that the user will interact with the item i, defined as:

$$p(i|q(s_n)) = \frac{1/\log_2(pos_i + 1)}{\sum_{j \in L} 1/\log_2(pos_j + 1)}$$

Where pos_j is the position of the item j in the list L. After processing a relevant number of queries $\mathcal{Q}$, it is possible to aggregate all the probabilities involving the item i, defining the related *expected exposure*:

$$e_i(\mathcal{Q}) = \sum_{q \in \mathcal{Q}} p(i|q(s_n))$$

This measure is inspired by the one by Diaz et al. [19]; in presence of a relevant number of queries, it expresses the expected amount of interactions for an item.

Assuming to group items by providers, where $\mathcal{I}_p \subseteq \mathcal{I}$ is the subset of items sold by the provider p, we can define the *expected provider exposure* as:

$$e_p(\mathcal{Q}) = \sum_{i \in \mathcal{I}_p} \sum_{q \in \mathcal{Q}} p(i|q(s_n))$$

For brevity, since we consider the same set of queries for each dataset, we use e_p. The expected provider exposure can be compared with the one in the input data, indicated as e_p^*, which is the number of times items from a provider p have been selected within the test-set. In the next section, we explore how these new exposure measures differ, depending on different input data and $|\mathcal{I}_p|$.

3 Experiments

3.1 Data and Algorithms

We analyze listening events of the *last.fm* platform. The dataset contains 1B listening events, 32M items, and 3M providers [18]. Since listenings come with a timestamp, we can aggregate them in sessions, fixing a threshold to split them in ordered lists. Initial tests led us to choose 15 min as cut-off. We extract three samples from the dataset. In each case, we randomly sample 200k sessions and keep those with at least 3 listenings. We obtain the following datasets (details in Table 1): (*i*) **LFM-S** is composed by short sessions, with length in the range

Table 1. Summary of sampled listenings data with dataset name, number of listenings, number of distinct items and number of providers

Name	Events	|S|	|I|	Providers
LFM-S	1,087,808	154,452	148,591	18,464
LFM-L	4,846,552	95,672	477,991	46,310
LFM-M	2,451,790	171,341	278,195	30,311

[5, 25]; (ii) **LFM-L** contains long sessions, with length in the range [40, 200]; (iii) **LFM-M** does not show differences in terms of session length.

As algorithms, we considered two neural and two non-neural approaches [11]. Association rules (**AR**), a non-neural one, considers co-occurrences at pairwise level. The second non-neural approach is a nearest-neighbour algorithm at session level (**S-KNN**). One of the neural approaches is based on recurrent neural networks (**GRU4REC**) [9]. The other, (**NARM**) (supposedly an improvement of GRU4REC), uses attention mechanisms [10]. The last 20% of the sessions of each dataset is used as test set and we generate top-20 lists. Hyperparameters are tuned as in the last benchmark paper [11].

3.2   Results

Algorithms' Evaluation. We look at both accuracy metrics and our new exposure metrics. The distribution of the expected exposure (e_p) generated by the recommendations, is normalized by the real one (e_p^*). This metric is assumed to be constant and close to 1 in the best scenario, where the recommender is able to predict in the long run the exposure of each artist. Table 2 summarizes our findings. For each dataset and column, we indicate in bold the best model. The last two columns show the average of e_p/e_p^* and the relative standard deviation.

As the first three columns show, S-KNN is the most effective approach in all datasets, minus the long-session one (LFM-L), which shows slightly better MAP and R values with the AR algorithm. Our results confirm recent findings, with the neural-based approaches outperformed by the memory-based ones. Indeed, neural approaches are optimized to predict the next item. Surprisingly, also considering the metrics coherent with their neural approaches' optimisation (HR@20 and MRR@20), the neural approaches do not always outperform the other methods. When comparing the datasets, the short-session one (LFM-S) produces the most effective predictions. Hence, when sessions get longer, algorithms cannot capture users' interests and understand what might be relevant for them. These results can be better understood by considering the metrics referred to the ratio between expected and real exposure, in the last two columns. Long sessions present the worst disparate exposure, confirming the algorithms are not able to catch drifts in user interests along the session. This leads to unstable exposure along the providers, leading to the highest values for $\mu(e_p/e_p^*)$ and $\sigma(e_p/e_p^*)$. Another interesting phenomenon in the last two columns is that NARM returns a distribution of providers exposure closest to the test, thus creating a trade-off between recommendation effectiveness and distribution of providers.

Table 2. Performance for four algorithms tested on three different datasets, in terms of accuracy and providers exposure.

Name	Algorithm	MAP@20	P@20	R@20	HR@20	MRR@20	$\mu(e_p/e_p^*)$	$\sigma(e_p/e_p^*)$
LFM-S	AR	0.0421	0.0848	0.3769	0.4630	0.1789	0.8907	0.6952
$|S| = 154{,}452$	S-KNN	**0.0446**	**0.0905**	**0.4110**	**0.5153**	0.1410	0.7679	**0.5787**
$\bar{s}_l = 7.04$	GRU4Rec	0.0254	0.0588	0.2882	0.4328	**0.3262**	1.1792	1.4163
	NARM	0.0301	0.0680	0.3234	0.4505	0.2641	**0.8909**	0.9757
LFM L	AR	**0.0243**	0.1418	**0.1332**	**0.3349**	0.0915	1.1913	2.4121
$|S| = 95{,}672$	S-KNN	0.0226	**0.1460**	0.1174	0.2747	0.0663	0.6277	**1.1023**
$\bar{s}_l = 50.66$	GRU4Rec	0.0084	0.0672	0.0665	0.3130	**0.2292**	1.7210	16.9100
	NARM	0.0129	0.0976	0.0789	0.1936	0.0537	**1.0195**	4.2379
LFM-M	AR	0.0302	0.1098	0.2258	0.3743	0.1219	1.0840	3.5950
$|S| = 171{,}341$	S-KNN	**0.0339**	**0.1295**	**0.2481**	0.3974	0.1019	0.5953	**0.6412**
$\bar{s}_l = 14.31$	GRU4Rec	0.0186	0.0796	0.1802	0.3770	**0.3262**	1.2481	1.8928
	NARM	0.0261	0.1064	0.2116	0.3740	0.1540	**0.9506**	4.6853

Impact of Provider Representativeness. Since the last two columns in Table 2 showed a clear instability of the algorithms to connect consistently expected artists' exposure with the ground truth, we investigate the possible sources of this effect. We look at the impact of the *provider representativeness* $\mathcal{I}_p$ and input relevance $rel_p = log_{10}(|\mathcal{E}_p|)$, where $\mathcal{E}_p$ is the number of events within the training data, which involve an item of a provider p. We generate, for each use-case, a scatter plot, where each point presents on the x-axis the logarithm of provider representativeness, $log_{10}(|\mathcal{I}_p|)$, and on the y-axis the ratio of expected and real exposure, $log_{10}(e_p/e_p^*)$. The dots are colored by the provider relevance rel_p and logarithmic scale is needed for the two axes, so that we can have an homogeneous representation, including also the possible outliers in the analysis. From Fig. 1, a common pattern emerges: artists with a higher value of $|\mathcal{I}_p|$, are also the most relevant. Interesting is also the fact that providers with bigger $|\mathcal{I}_p|$ (right side of the plots) present a fair value of e_p/e_p^* and are not overexposed. However, being a relevant provider, but not having many items in the market $|\mathcal{I}_p|$ (like emerging artists) may impact negatively on the e_p/e_p^* value. This means that a small *provider representativeness* affects the ability to return a fair value of e_p/e_p^* (i.e., in the plot, it is fair when close to 0). The left part of all the scatters shows how blurry are the sections of dots involving relevant and non-relevant artists, revealing how all the algorithms are unable to catch differences in relevance among artists having small $|\mathcal{I}_p|$. The neural approaches, which present higher $\sigma(e_p/e_p^*)$ in Table 2, confirm to be the most challenged. Among them, S-KNN is the most stable along the datasets and GRU4REC the worst.

Impact of Session Length. The three datasets, characterized by different ranges of session length, raise concerns on the limitations and common issues of state-of-the-art session-based algorithms. Longer-session data (LFM-L), reveals that longer sequences of interactions increase the unpredictability for the user, leading to a precarious artists representation. All the models present higher range of e_p/e_p^* if compared with the other two datasets. On the other hand, shorter-session data (LFM-S) helps the model to provide more stable recommendations, where representativeness is consistently decoupled from relevance in all the approaches.

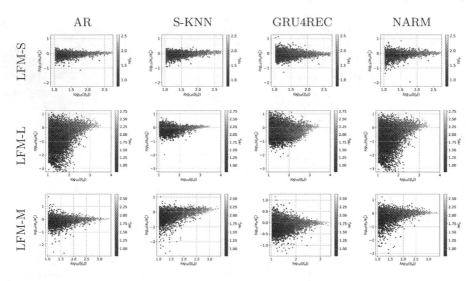

Fig. 1. Scatter plot, capturing the relationship between exposure, representativeness, and relevance of each provider. Over the x-axis the number of items produced by the provider p, over the y-axis the ratio between exposure by recommendations and one by test-set; each dot is colored with the relevance of the provider in the training set.

4   Conclusions

In this paper, we analyzed session-based RS, uncovering performance limitations due to different input data characteristics. Our findings align with recent work that sheds light on the limited progress of state-of-the-art models; in addition, we introduce the role of data distribution in this conversation. For the consumer-side, if we do not account for distribution of longer and shorter sessions, the effectiveness evaluation may be misleading. In addition, optimizing the accuracy leads to mistreatment and disparate exposure for providers. This finding connects our work to algorithmic fairness, by showing the incapability of models to calibrate the output, given the provider input relevance and representativeness. In the future, we will consider group-based scenarios, for both providers and consumers. We will also consider different datasets and session-based domains [2,3,6], with multiple definitions of exposure. From the algorithmic fairness perspective, we expect to design new session-based algorithms to meet exposure policies based on statistical parity or disparate treatment.

Acknowledgments. This research was partially funded by project 2017-SGR-341, MISMIS-LANGUAGE (grant No. PGC2018-096212-B-C33) from the Spanish Ministry of Science and Innovation, and NanoMoocs (grant No. COMRDI18-1-0010) from ACCI. L. Boratto and F. Fabbri acknowledge ACCI, for its support under project "Fair and Explainable Artificial Intelligence (FX-AI)".

References

1. Abdollahpouri, H., et al.: Beyond personalization: Research directions in multi-stakeholder recommendation. CoRR abs/1905.01986 (2019)
2. Barra, S., Marras, M., Fenu, G.: Continuous authentication on smartphone by means of periocular and virtual keystroke. In: Au, M.H., et al. (eds.) NSS 2018. LNCS, vol. 11058, pp. 212–220. Springer, Cham (2018). https://doi.org/10.1007/978-3-030-02744-5_16
3. Dessì, D., Fenu, G., Marras, M., Reforgiato Recupero, D.: COCO: semantic-enriched collection of online courses at scale with experimental use cases. In: Rocha, Á., Adeli, H., Reis, L.P., Costanzo, S. (eds.) WorldCIST'18 2018. AISC, vol. 746, pp. 1386–1396. Springer, Cham (2018). https://doi.org/10.1007/978-3-319-77712-2_133
4. Diaz, F., Mitra, B., Ekstrand, M.D., Biega, A.J., Carterette, B.: Evaluating stochastic rankings with expected exposure. CoRR abs/2004.13157 (2020)
5. Fenu, G., Lafhouli, H., Marras, M.: Exploring algorithmic fairness in deep speaker verification. In: Gervasi, O., et al. (eds.) ICCSA 2020. LNCS, vol. 12252, pp. 77–93. Springer, Cham (2020). https://doi.org/10.1007/978-3-030-58811-3_6
6. Fenu, G., Marras, M.: Leveraging Continuous Multi-modal Authentication for Access Control in Mobile Cloud Environments. In: Battiato, S., Farinella, G.M., Leo, M., Gallo, G. (eds.) ICIAP 2017. LNCS, vol. 10590, pp. 331–342. Springer, Cham (2017). https://doi.org/10.1007/978-3-319-70742-6_31
7. Ferraro, A., Jannach, D., Serra, X.: Exploring longitudinal effects of session-based recommendations. arXiv preprint arXiv:2008.07226 (2020)
8. Hidasi, B., Karatzoglou, A.: Recurrent neural networks with top-k gains for session-based recommendations. In: Proceedings of the 27th ACM International Conference on Information and Knowledge Management, pp. 843–852. ACM (2018)
9. Hidasi, B., Karatzoglou, A.: Recurrent neural networks with top-k gains for session-based recommendations. In: Cuzzocrea, A., et al. (eds.) Proceedings of the 27th ACM International Conference on Information and Knowledge Management, CIKM 2018, Torino, Italy, October 22–26, 2018, pp. 843–852. ACM (2018). https://doi.org/10.1145/3269206.3271761
10. Li, J., Ren, P., Chen, Z., Ren, Z., Lian, T., Ma, J.: Neural attentive session-based recommendation. In: Proceedings of the 2017 ACM on Conference on Information and Knowledge Management, pp. 1419–1428 (2017)
11. Ludewig, M., Mauro, N., Latifi, S., Jannach, D.: Performance comparison of neural and non-neural approaches to session-based recommendation. In: Proceedings of the 13th International ACM RecSys Conference on Recommender Systems (2019)

12. Marras, M., Korus, P., Memon, N.D., Fenu, G.: Adversarial optimization for dictionary attacks on speaker verification. In: Kubin, G., Kacic, Z. (eds.) Interspeech 2019, 20th Annual Conference of the International Speech Communication Association, Graz, Austria, 15–19 September 2019, pp. 2913–2917. ISCA (2019). https://doi.org/10.21437/Interspeech.2019-2430

13. Mehrotra, R., McInerney, J., Bouchard, H., Lalmas, M., Diaz, F.: Towards a fair marketplace: Counterfactual evaluation of the trade-off between relevance, fairness & satisfaction in recommendation systems. In: Proceedings of the 27th ACM International Conference on Information and Knowledge Management, pp. 2243–2251. ACM (2018)

14. Quadrana, M., Cremonesi, P., Jannach, D.: Sequence-aware recommender systems. ACM Comput. Surv. **51**(4), 66:1–66:36 (2018)

15. Ramos, G., Boratto, L., Caleiro, C.: On the negative impact of social influence in recommender systems: A study of bribery in collaborative hybrid algorithms. Inf. Process. Manag. **57**(2) (2020). https://doi.org/10.1016/j.ipm.2019.102058

16. Ricci, F., Rokach, L., Shapira, B., Kantor, P.B.: Recommender Systems Handbook, 1st edn. Springer, Heidelberg (2010). https://doi.org/10.1007/978-0-387-85820-3

17. Saúde, J., Ramos, G., Caleiro, C., Kar, S.: Reputation-based ranking systems and their resistance to bribery. In: Raghavan, V., Aluru, S., Karypis, G., Miele, L., Wu, X. (eds.) 2017 IEEE International Conference on Data Mining, ICDM 2017, New Orleans, LA, USA, 18–21 November 2017, pp. 1063–1068. IEEE Computer Society (2017). https://doi.org/10.1109/ICDM.2017.139

18. Schedl, M.: The LFM-1b dataset for music retrieval and recommendation. In: Proceedings of the 2016 ACM on International Conference on Multimedia Retrieval, pp. 103–110 (2016)

19. Singh, A., Joachims, T.: Fairness of exposure in rankings. In: Proceedings of the 24th ACM SIGKDD International Conference on Knowledge Discovery & Data Mining, pp. 2219–2228. ACM (2018)

Bayesian System Inference
on Shallow Pools

Rodger Benham[1]($\boxtimes$) (ID), Alistair Moffat[2](ID), and J. Shane Culpepper[1](ID)

[1] RMIT University, Melbourne, Australia
{rodger.benham,shane.culpepper}@rmit.edu.au
[2] The University of Melbourne, Melbourne, Australia

Abstract. IR test collections make use of human annotated judgments. However, new systems that surface unjudged documents high in their result lists might undermine the reliability of statistical comparisons of system effectiveness, eroding the collection's value. Here we explore a Bayesian inference-based analysis in a "high uncertainty" evaluation scenario, using data from the first round of the TREC COVID 2020 Track. Our approach constrains statistical modeling and generates credible replicates derived from the judged runs' scores, comparing the relative discriminatory capacity of RBP scores by their system parameters modeled hierarchically over different response distributions. The resultant models directly compute risk measures as a posterior predictive distribution summary statistic; and also offer enhanced sensitivity.

1 Introduction

TREC COVID [20] is the first IR evaluation track to use the *residual collection scoring* pooling methodology described by Salton and Buckley [17]. The track judged multiple rounds of runs, with shallow judgments made available after each round, to allow tuning of systems in subsequent rounds. Several participants raised concerns about the generalizability of the first round judgment set, after the RBP $\phi = 0.5$ [13] residuals were found to be unacceptably high for systems not included in the judgment pool. Voorhees [19] investigated the effect that further judgments had on the system orderings between the complete set and the first round set, finding that a small portion of systems had significant changes – the worst being RMITBFuseM2 which rose 33 ranks on P@5. Shallow judgments are also used for the MS MARCO [14] runs, a collection with so many topics that deep judgment coverage would be very costly. When system scores are uncertain, practitioners might decide to only evaluate pooled systems.

In general, when attempting to ascertain whether a ranker outperforms one or many others, a statistical test is employed to mitigate against sampling error. Sakai [15] notes that the most popular statistical test at present is the Student t-test. However, it (and all other frequentist tests) assumes that the sample of scores are one of many repeated samples from a population of score differences. Hence, using a t-test, even if the systems were both pooled, might produce

© Springer Nature Switzerland AG 2021
D. Hiemstra et al. (Eds.): ECIR 2021, LNCS 12657, pp. 209–215, 2021.
https://doi.org/10.1007/978-3-030-72240-1_17

overconfident confidence intervals, as an entire population of unseen topics are inferred against based on scores derived from low-fidelity judgments. Conversely, Bayesian inference allows the predicted score replicates to be conditioned on the measured pooled system-topic scores only.

In this paper, we adapt models initially described by Carterette [3] to infer graded RBP $\phi = 0.8$ scores over multiple systems hierarchically [1], and analyze the relative power of the resulting models using the pooled TREC COVID first round submissions and judgments, finding increased sensitivity. Other recent work [1] has also investigated Bayesian "risk" overlays which penalize systems for relative effectiveness loss against a baseline by a linear scalar r. We explore a similar summary statistic using the posterior predictive distribution (PPD).

2   Related Work

Carterette [2] was the first to use Bayesian inference as an alternative to frequentist statistical testing for IR effectiveness scores. Carterette [3] then empirically evaluated the outcomes of these models on the TREC-8, Robust04, and TREC Web 2012 track datasets. Sakai [16] shows that Bayesian Markov Chain Monte Carlo (MCMC) simulation can also be used to generate complementary information about the effect size of different systems, by calculating Glass' Δ and expected *a posteriori* (EAP) values for one-to-one system comparisons.

In early work on risk measures, Collins-Thompson [4] explored methods to measure the risk of query drift in query expansion. Similarly, Wang et al. [21] defined URisk as a learning-to-rank objective function. Dinçer et al. [6] then extended the URisk measure to be an inferential risk measure using the t-distribution, calling the result TRisk. Dinçer et al. [7] noted that in this one-to-one risk evaluation setting, experimental system comparisons will be biased to the baseline ranking; prompting the development of ZRisk and GeoRisk [5].

Benham et al. [1] recently combined Bayesian inference and risk-adjusted score overlays at the system-topic level on multiple systems. However, they did not compare the relative system effectiveness inferences over statistical models that consider system-topic-rank gain scores in the way that was proposed by Carterette [2]. That gap is targeted in this work.

3   Statistical Models

Our primary goal is to understand how increasingly sophisticated models affect assessment as to which ranker is the most effective. Bayesian inference techniques effectively reverse-engineer the parameters required to generate the underlying score observations in a parametric way, conditioned on a set of priors. Those parameters can be inferentially evaluated directly using a hierarchical model, such as a system effect parameter, to infer which system(s) are better [12]. We use the brms front-end to the Stan statistical programming language, in the R programming language to specify the models.[1] In our simulations, we use the

---

[1] Code to reproduce available at: https://github.com/rmit-ir/bayesian-shallow.

default weakly-informative priors in **brms**, which are auto-scaled with MCMC to be credible fits against the observed score values. Benham et al. [1] explain the process of generating Bayesian inferences in greater detail.

Using the pooled runs submitted to 2020 TREC COVID Track, we compare statistical outcomes when treating observed RBP score values, assuming either Gaussian or Zero-One Inflated Beta (ZOiB) distributions. Additionally, we model the RBP gain values directly on a per-document basis (cutting each system-topic ranking to the pooling depth of 7 documents), similar to Carterette [3], and compare against a Gaussian approach. The Gaussian method is a useful reference point, as it is similar in response distribution to t-distributed values [2]. Note that it is the differences in per-topic effectiveness scores between two systems that are studentized – beyond those score pairs for multiple system comparisons, many pairs of tests are run and corrected for. Therefore this exercise cannot guarantee that one approach gives inferences that are more "truthful" than others, as such a proof does not exist. The bottom 25% of pooled systems were discarded, to avoid comparisons being performed against erroneous runs.

Linear Model. The first model, Gaussian, simplistically assumes that the underlying distribution of RBP values is normally distributed, and is a function of a system and topic effect[2]:

$$y_{ij} \sim N(\hat{\alpha}_i + \hat{\beta}_j, \sigma_y^2) \qquad\qquad \sigma_{\{y,\alpha,\beta,\alpha_i,\beta_j\}} \sim t(3,0,2.5)$$
$$\hat{\alpha}_i = \omega_{\alpha,\alpha_i}\mu_\alpha + (1 - \omega_{\alpha,\alpha_i})\alpha_i \qquad\qquad \mu_\alpha \sim N(0,\sigma_\alpha^2);\ \alpha_i \sim N(0,\sigma_{\alpha_i}^2)$$
$$\hat{\beta}_j = \omega_{\beta,\beta_j}\mu_\beta + (1 - \omega_{\beta,\beta_j})\beta_j \qquad\qquad \mu_\beta \sim N(0,\sigma_\beta^2);\ \beta_j \sim N(0,\sigma_{\beta_j}^2),$$

where y_{ij} is an RBP effectiveness score parameterized by topic j and system i. The topic and system effects, β_j and α_i respectively, are moderated by *partial pooling* in the corresponding $\hat{\beta}_j$ and $\hat{\alpha}_i$ [11], where $\omega_{Y,y}$ is the pooling factor that measures the simulated strength of the population Y versus the observed group effect y (topics for example, β is the topic population parameter averaged from all other topics in the model, and β_j is the specific topic effect for the y_{ij} observation, for example, topic 3)

$$\omega_{Y,y} = 1 - \frac{\sigma_Y^2}{\sigma_Y^2 + \sigma_y^2}.$$

The parameters provided to the standard deviation three-parameter Student t-distribution prior and hyperpriors correspond to the non-informative defaults in **brms** for the Gaussian family. The above approach is related to the Model 2 specified by Carterette [3], with marginally more informative priors than the Jeffreys prior ($\sigma \sim \log(1/\sigma)$).

ZOiB Model. Inspection of the PPD of the Gaussian model (top of Fig. 1a) indicates that the MCMC simulation converges towards a distribution that describes some characteristics of the underlying effectiveness data. However, as Gaussian

---

[2] This amends Benham et al. [1, Eqn. 3], which omitted the partial pooling notation.

values are in the range $(-\infty, \infty)$, the replicate effectiveness scores are frequently invalid. A Beta distribution can be used to model a rate in the range $(0, 1)$, and a ZOiB distribution extends that range to $[0, 1]$.[3] We thus model RBP scores with the ZOiB parameters

$$
y_{ij} \sim \begin{cases} \pi_0 & \text{if } y_{ij} = 0 \\ (1 - \pi_0)(1 - \pi_1)\beta(\mu_{ij}\phi, (1 - \mu_{ij})\phi) & \text{if } 0 < y_{ij} < 1 \\ \pi_1 & \text{if } y_{ij} = 1 \end{cases}
$$

$$\text{logit } \mu_{ij} \sim N(\hat{\alpha}_i + \hat{\beta}_j, \sigma_y^2) \qquad \sigma_{\{y,\alpha,\beta,\alpha_i,\beta_j\}} \sim t(3, 0, 2.5)$$

$$\pi_0, \pi_1 \sim \beta(1, 1)$$

$$\phi \sim \gamma(0.01, 0.01)$$

$$\hat{\alpha}_i = \omega_{\alpha,\alpha_i}\mu_\alpha + (1 - \omega_{\alpha,\alpha_i})\alpha_i \qquad \mu_\alpha \sim N(0, \sigma_\alpha^2); \; \alpha_i \sim N(0, \sigma_{\alpha_i}^2)$$

$$\hat{\beta}_j = \omega_{\beta,\beta_j}\mu_\beta + (1 - \omega_{\beta,\beta_j})\beta_j \qquad \mu_\beta \sim N(0, \sigma_\beta^2); \; \beta_j \sim N(0, \sigma_{\beta_j}^2),$$

where ϕ is the precision parameter of the Beta distribution β to be modeled with a Gamma distribution (another brms default), π_0 and π_1 are the Bernoulli probabilities that a score will be zero or one, and μ_{ij} is logit transformed to link the linear parameterization (described in Gaussian) to the Beta distribution.

ZOiB-Rank. The ZOiB model can be extended to model y_{ijk} per-position RBP gain scores by including k as a rank parameter, modeled as a population effect. ZOiB-Rank is therefore a small modification: $\text{logit } \mu_{ijk} \sim N(\hat{\alpha}_i + \hat{\beta}_j + k, \sigma_y^2)$. (Carterette [3] used the very similar Quasi-Binomial distribution to model RBP gain scores, a response family that is not available in brms.) Of interest is comparing the properties of the system effect inferences of this gain-based approach against traditional RBP scores.

Posterior Predictive Risk. The URisk overlay with a challenger system against a champion computes the value:

$$URisk_r = -(1/n) \cdot \left[\sum Wins - r \cdot \sum Losses \right]. \tag{1}$$

Benham et al. [1] inferentially evaluate risk-adjusted scores using a Bayesian approach, with increasing r resulting in increased uncertainty according to their system effects. That uncertainty stems from attempting to predict instances where an experimental system would outperform the baseline (also known as the model selection problem). Here, we note that risk measures are essentially a summary statistic. As we can predict scores from experimental and baseline systems in a joint statistical model that has already been implicitly corrected for multiple comparisons in the Bayesian way (via hierarchical modeling [9], noting that the technique and any other correction approach is not flawless [10]), the PPD of what is judged to be the best fitting measure can be used to analyze the spread of the URisk values [8]. That is, for each draw from the posterior $\theta_i \sim p(\theta \mid data)$, the set of point parameter estimates from that draw θ_i is used to form *a posteriori* replicate scores supplied to URisk: $data_i' \sim p(data \mid \theta_i)$ [12].

---

[3] https://rdrr.io/cran/brms/man/brmsfamily.html, accessed October 29, 2020.

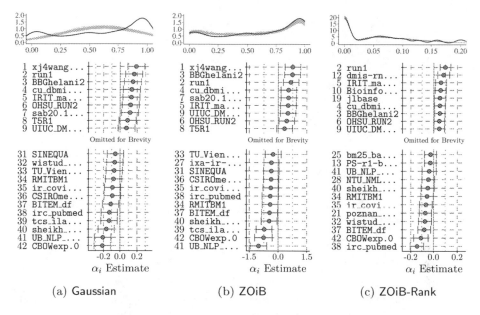

Fig. 1. RBP with $\phi = 0.8$: Bayesian analysis of system effects for three different models, with 95% credible intervals. The top graphs are described in the text. Numbers to the left of each system corresponds to the ordering the Gaussian model invoked as a reference. (Color figure online)

4   Analysis

Figure 1 plots the parametric inferences of the system effect for 95% credible intervals for the three models. The density plot above each column contains RBP topic scores amalgamated over all systems (blue solid line) or RBP gain scores combining all system-topic-rank scores (red solid line). Faint lines plotted behind these distributions are draws from the PPD which graphically indicates model fit – lines closer to the original distribution are preferable. As can be seen, the two ZOiB distributed models have a better fit than the Gaussian model. The best system can be distinguished from 17 other (poor) systems, and the worst system from 23 (good) systems with the Gaussian model; with the corresponding numbers being 17 and 29 for the ZOiB model, and 20 and 31 using the ZOiB-Rank model. For ZOiB-Rank, the 12th best system from the Gaussian model (dmis-rnd1-run3) moved up to 2nd place with ZOiB-Rank, and the run xj4wang_run1 moved from 1st to 10th. These shifts occur because ZOiB-Rank preferences systems more likely to report an RBP gain at any observed rank, rather than top-heavy systems that may return fewer relevant outcomes at the $\phi = 0.8$ expected viewing depth of 5 documents. Given that ZOiB visually fits the score distribution better than the Gaussian counterpart and does not draw unexpected predictions as in the ZOiB-Rank approach, the ZOiB model provides the most accurate description of system ranking dominance of the three tested, on the first round TREC COVID dataset.

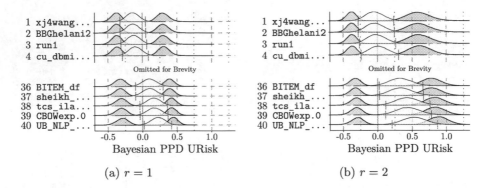

Fig. 2. RBP $\phi = 0.8$ EAP risk, URisk with two risk values r against the `bm25_baseline` run, 95% credible intervals, and with wins (blue), losses (orange), and run aggregates (yellow) plotted. (Color figure online)

Using the ZOiB model, Fig. 2 compares risk-free ($r = 1$) against risk-sensitive ($r = 2$) evaluation using EAP values. In Fig. 2a only `UB_NLP_RUN_1` (truncated) is able to be discriminated from the `bm25_baseline` run as the interval excludes zero, which is consistent with the extended parameter inference plot (without omitted systems) in Fig. 1b. In Fig. 2b, more challengers are statistically separable, while still being constrained to the observed outcomes in the pooled set. This EAP approach is therefore an improvement over the Benham et al. [1] approach, as it does not subsume the increased variance from the other challenger systems into the champion baseline system – providing more discriminative inferences in terms of the original URisk units.

5   Conclusion

Using the first round of the TREC COVID track, we modeled RBP scores via three separate distributions inspired by Carterette [3], and observed outcomes for many-to-many inferential system comparisons using a Bayesian hierarchical model. We found that the ZOiB method worked well for the corpus and smooth evaluation metrics considered, noting that further work is required to ascertain its applicability to other datasets (indeed, Urbano and Nagler [18] show that a one-size-fits-all model is rarely preferable). We also modeled risk inferentially using the PPD, which is more discriminative than modeling risk scores directly.

We posit that Bayesian hierarchical modeling may complement traditional IR statistical tests, and particularly recommend their use when there are fidelity concerns about the judgments used to form the evaluation scores. While these Bayesian methods are also amenable to more generalizing collection-based comparisons, they are not without limitations: they are orders of magnitude slower than traditional IR tests; and, in our observations to date, tend to require at least five systems to simulate the system parameters without divergent iterations.

Acknowledgments. This work was partially supported by Australian Research Council Grant DP190101113. The first author was supported by an RMIT VCPS.

References

1. Benham, R., Carterette, B., Culpepper, J.S., Moffat, A.: Bayesian inferential risk evaluation on multiple IR systems. In: Proceedings of the SIGIR, pp. 339–348 (2020)
2. Carterette, B.: Model-based inference about IR systems. In: Proceedings of the ICTIR, pp. 101–112 (2011)
3. Carterette, B.: Bayesian inference for information retrieval evaluation. In: Proceedings of the ICTIR, pp. 31–40 (2015)
4. Collins-Thompson, K.: Reducing the risk of query expansion via robust constrained optimization. In: Proceedings of the CIKM, pp. 837–846 (2009)
5. Dinçer, B.T., Macdonald, C., Ounis, I.: Risk-sensitive evaluation and learning to rank using multiple baselines. In: Proceedings of the SIGIR, pp. 483–492 (2016)
6. Dinçer, B.T., Macdonald, C., Ounis, I.: Hypothesis testing for the risk-sensitive evaluation of retrieval systems. In: Proceedings of the SIGIR, pp. 23–32 (2014)
7. Dinçer, B.T., Ounis, I., Macdonald, C.: Tackling biased baselines in the risk-sensitive evaluation of retrieval systems. In: Proceedings of the ECIR, pp. 26–38 (2014)
8. Gelman, A.: Two simple examples for understanding posterior p-values whose distributions are far from uniform. Electron. J. Statist. **7**, 2595–2602 (2013)
9. Gelman, A., Hill, J., Yajima, M.: Why we (usually) don't have to worry about multiple comparisons. J. Res. Int. Educ. **5**(2), 189–211 (2012)
10. Gelman, A., Loken, E.: The garden of forking paths: why multiple comparisons can be a problem, even when there is no "fishing expedition" or "p-hacking" and the research hypothesis was posited ahead of time. Department of Statistics, Columbia University (2013)
11. Gelman, A., Pardoe, I.: Bayesian measures of explained variance and pooling in multilevel (hierarchical) models. Technometrics **48**(2), 241–251 (2006)
12. Lambert, B.: A student's guide to Bayesian statistics. Sage (2018)
13. Moffat, A., Zobel, J.: Rank-biased precision for measurement of retrieval effectiveness. ACM Trans. Inf. Syst. **27**(1), 21–227 (2008)
14. Nguyen, T., et al.: MS MARCO: a human-generated machine reading comprehension dataset. In: Proceedings of the NIPS, pp. 96–105 (2016)
15. Sakai, T.: Statistical significance, power, and sample sizes: a systematic review of SIGIR and TOIS, 2006–2015. In: Proceedings of the SIGIR, pp. 5–14 (2016)
16. Sakai, T.: The probability that your hypothesis is correct, credible intervals, and effect sizes for IR evaluation. In: Proceedings of the SIGIR, pp. 25–34 (2017)
17. Salton, G., Buckley, C.: Improving retrieval performance by relevance feedback. J. Am. Soc. Inf. Sci. **41**(4), 288–297 (1990)
18. Urbano, J., Nagler, T.: Stochastic simulation of test collections: evaluation scores. In: Proceedings of the SIGIR, pp. 695–704 (2018)
19. Voorhees, E.: Effect on system rankings of further extending pools for TREC-COVID round 1 submissions (2020). https://ir.nist.gov/covidSubmit/papers/rnd1runs_j0.5-2.0.pdf
20. Voorhees, E., et al.: TREC-COVID: constructing a pandemic information retrieval test collection. SIGIR Forum **54**(1), 1–12 (2020)
21. Wang, L., Bennett, P.N., Collins-Thompson, K.: Robust ranking models via risk-sensitive optimization. In: Proceedings of the SIGIR, pp. 761–770 (2012)

Exploring Gender Biases in Information Retrieval Relevance Judgement Datasets

Amin Bigdeli[✉], Negar Arabzadeh, Morteza Zihayat, and Ebrahim Bagheri

Ryerson University, Toronto, Canada
{abigdeli,narabzad,mzihayat,bagheri}@ryerson.ca

Abstract. Recent studies in information retrieval have shown that gender biases have found their way into representational and algorithmic aspects of computational models. In this paper, we focus specifically on gender biases in information retrieval gold standard datasets, often referred to as relevance judgements. While not explored in the past, we submit that it is important to understand and measure the extent to which gender biases may be presented in information retrieval relevance judgements primarily because relevance judgements are not only the primary source for evaluating IR techniques but are also widely used for training end-to-end neural ranking methods. As such, the presence of bias in relevance judgements would immediately find its way into how retrieval methods operate in practice. Based on a fine-tuned **BERT** model, we show how queries can be labelled for gender at scale based on which we label MS MARCO queries. We then show how different psychological characteristics are exhibited within documents associated with gendered queries within the relevance judgement datasets. Our observations show that stereotypical biases are prevalent in relevance judgement documents.

1   Introduction

Extensive research in the psychology and sociology literature has shown that gender stereotypes can affect an individual's life descriptively and prescriptively [1,2]. These gender stereotypes not only affect the expectations of women and men about their behaviour, qualities, priorities, and personal needs implicitly, but can also influence the way they process information [3,4]. Besides, gender stereotypes can influence an individual's judgements, leading to unfair treatments and outcomes [5]. While individuals' perception of gender differences might be aligned with reality in certain cases, such perceptions often originate from gender stereotypes [6]. Recently, the impact of various biases has been a topic of interest among researchers in a variety of domains, including Information Retrieval (IR). [7–13]. For instance, given the wide adoption of neural embeddings in IR, various researchers have already begun investigating the impact of implicit biases that are embedded in neural embeddings. In [9], Bolukbasi et al. highlighted the fact that sexism implicit within pre-trained neural embeddings has the potential to pose the risk of introducing different types of biases in practically deployed applications; hence, reflecting gender stereotypes in real time.

© Springer Nature Switzerland AG 2021
D. Hiemstra et al. (Eds.): ECIR 2021, LNCS 12657, pp. 216–224, 2021.
https://doi.org/10.1007/978-3-030-72240-1_18

Given the impact of biases when seeking information, Rekabsaz et al. [7] have examined the degree of gender bias among several neural retrieval methods. They found that the utilization of already biased pre-trained embeddings considerably amplifies gender biases among the retrieved documents. In another important study [12], Fabris et al. proposed a word genderedness measure to detect and quantify how various types of information retrieval methods respond to gendered queries by retrieving documents that are inclined towards similar gender stereotypes. As a result of their experiments, the authors found that lexical, semantic, and neural models reinforce gender stereotypes in their results.

While biases among different retrieval methods and neural embeddings have been generally studied in IR, to the best of our knowledge, potential biases within gold standard benchmark datasets (often known as relevance judgements, aka *qrels*) have not yet been explored. We believe that it is important to study whether biases may have been introduced in gold standard datasets, which in essence govern how retrieval methods are trained and evaluated. An inclination towards a specific gender or the ascription of implicit biases towards them can result in a biased retrieval method. As such, the objective of this paper is to study potential stereotypical gender biases in information retrieval relevance judgements. The other distinguishing aspect of our work is that unlike earlier work [7,12], we do not propose a certain computational metric for measuring gender biases, but rather we measure various psychological characteristics of document content associated with gendered queries. This way, we quantify, if and when, systematic differences are exhibited between queries of different genders.

In summary, our work distinguishes itself from the literature by (1) offering an accurate and well-validated query gender classifier that can be used to label queries based on gender at scale; (2) studying potential biases at the level of gold standard relevance judgements through widely adopted psychological characteristics; and (3) revealing systematic biases aligned with perceptual stereotypes within query relevance judgements.

2   Methodology

We follow a three-staged methodological process in this paper: **(1)** In order to be able to determine query gender at scale, we benefit from the dataset of gendered queries provided by [7] to train a contextualized classifier to predict query gender. Subsequently, the trained model is used to label MS MARCO queries [14] (*c.f.* Sect. 2.2). **(2)** Based on these classified gendered queries from MS MARCO, we identify the associated relevant documents for each query and quantitatively measure various psychological characteristics of each such document using the well-established Linguistic Inquiry and Word Count (LIWC) toolkit (*c.f.* Sect. 2.3). **(3)** We report on gender stereotypical biases in information retrieval gold standards (query relevance judgements, i.e., qrels), which align with well-documented perceived biases in the psychological literature (*c.f.* Sect. 3). We note that all of our data, code, and results are made publicly accessible[1].

---

[1] https://github.com/aminbigdeli/gender-bias-in-relevance-judgements.

2.1   Datasets

Dataset for Query Gender Identification. We employed the publicly available gender-annotated dataset released by [7] that consists of queries labeled by one of the following classes: 1) non-gendered (neutral), 2) female, 3) male, and 4) other or multiple genders. The dataset consists of 742 female, 1,202 male and 1,765 neutral queries. We removed the 41 queries related to the 'Other or Multiple Genders' class as there were not sufficient instances to train a classifier. We also benefited from 32 pairs of gendered terms released by the same authors.

Dataset for Measuring Bias. For the purpose of measuring bias in relevance judgements, we adopted the queries in MS MARCO Dev set [14] that had at least one related human-judged relevance judgement document – equivalent to 51,827 queries. Note that, the queries from [7] were removed from this dataset to avoid unintended leakage.

Table 1. The accuracy and F1 score of each classifier by gender.

Category	Classifier	Accuracy	F1-Score		
			Female	Male	Neutral
Dynamic embeddings	BERT (base uncased)	**0.856**	**0.816**	**0.872**	**0.862**
	DistilBERT (base uncased)	0.847	0.815	0.861	0.853
	RoBERTa	0.810	0.733	0.820	0.836
	DistilBERT (base cased)	0.800	0.730	0.823	0.833
	BERT (base cased)	0.797	0.710	0.805	0.827
	XLNet (base cased)	0.795	0.710	0.805	0.826
Static embeddings	Word2Vec	0.757	0.626	0.756	0.809
	fastText	0.750	0.615	0.759	0.792

2.2   Query Gender Identification and Labeling

As the first step and in order to be able to label gendered queries at scale, we employ the dataset released by [7] to train relevant classifiers. We adopt two recent yet widely adopted techniques for this purpose, namely *dynamic embeddings* and *static embeddings*. More specifically, dynamic embeddings include models such as BERT [15], DistilBERT [16], RoBERTa [17], and XLNet [18], which are pre-trained models that have been trained on large corpora. For our work, we used the sequence classification class of BERT, DistilBERT, RoBERTa, and XLNet that have a linear layer over the pooled output, which is used to compute class likelihood scores. We used this fine tuning capability of these models with a batch size of 16 and the Adamw optimizer with learning rate $2e-5$. We set the number of epochs to 10 for BERT, DistilBERT, RoBERTa and 20 for XLNet.

Unlike dynamic embeddings, static embeddings such as `fastText` [19] and `Word2Vec` [20] create a single vector representation per token without regard for context. In order to train a `fastText` model, we used pre-trained vectors based on the Common Crawl dataset[2] and fine-tuned them based on the pair of gendered terms and the queries from [7]. As another model, we employed the pretrained Google News `Word2Vec` model and adopted the average of each query's term vectors to represent the query. Based on this, an `SVM` classifier with a polynomial kernel function was applied to classify the queries.

In order to evaluate the performance of the classifiers, we adopt a 5-fold cross-validation strategy. As shown in Table 1, the uncased fine-tuned `BERT` model shows the best performance for query gender identification. Now, using the uncased fine-tuned `BERT` model, we labeled all of the 51,827 queries in the MS MARCO query set. In total, we ended up with 48,200 neutral queries, 2,222 male queries, and 1,405 female queries. To have a balanced setup, we retained all 1,405 female queries and randomly selected 1,405 queries from each of the other two classes. We utilized 1,405 queries in each class and their associated relevance judgement documents to investigate the presence of stereotypical gender biases.

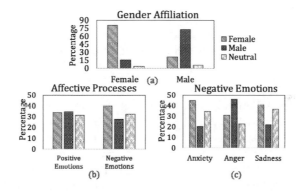

Fig. 1. (a) Percentage of female and male affiliations in relevant documents for each of the female, male and neutral query groups. (b) and (c) Differences between affective processes of relevance judgements for different gendered queries. The y-axis shows the percentage of each characteristic across female, male and neutral query sets.

2.3 Quantifying Psychological Characteristics

Our approach for quantifying bias is based on measuring different psychological characteristics of the relevance judgement documents associated with each query. We expect the measures of psychological characteristics across genders to align with findings from well-founded psychological experiments and not to exhibit behavior consistent with stereotypical biases associated with gender. To investigate this, we employ Linguistic Inquiry and Word Count (LIWC) [21] text

---

[2] https://bit.ly/3oBFTJ0.

analytics toolkit to compute the degree to which different psychological characteristics are observed in relevance judgement documents. We consider stereotypical biases relating to affective processes, cognitive processes, drive, and personal
concerns.

Before we present our findings, we benefit from LIWC to validate the performance of our BERT-based gender classifier. LIWC can be used to measure the
male or female affiliation of a document. We measure such gender affiliations
through LIWC for all relevance judgement documents and report the percentage
of gender affiliations related to each query gender type in Fig. 1(a). This figure
asserts the efficiency of the BERT-based gender classifier as it shows that female
queries are primarily associated with female affiliated documents, while male
queries are related to male affiliated documents. Furthermore, neutral queries
do not show affiliation with either gender. We consider the consistent behavior
between LIWC and the gender classifier as a sign of the utility of the gender
classifier as well as appropriateness of LIWC to be applied to such documents.

3   Findings

During information processing, individuals might make observations that are
compatible with their stereotypical mental presumptions [3]. We are interested
in exploring if such stereotypical biases are incorporated into gold standard relevance judgments, as they might pass biases onto retrieval methods.

Affective Processes are defined as the expression of positive and negative
emotions by an individual. We visualize the degree of positive and negative
emotions expressed in relevance judgement documents associated with gendered
queries in Fig. 1(b). As shown, the documents present a similar degree of positive
emotions regardless of the gender type of the query they are associated with.
However, when considering negative emotions, documents that are related to
female queries exhibit a higher degree of negativity compared to male and neutral

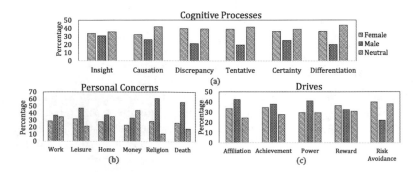

Fig. 2. Differences between the three psychological processes of relevance judgements
for different gendered queries. The y-axis is similar to Fig. 1.

queries. To further understand this, we explore the three sub-characteristics of negative emotions as described in [21], namely *anxiety, anger*, and *sadness*. We find that relevance documents associated with male queries exhibit higher rates of anger whereas higher degrees of anxiety and sadness are observed for documents associated with female queries. This implies that stereotypical biases can be observed in gold standard relevance judgements with regards to negative emotions of affective processes. Psychological studies [22, 23] have already shown that there are no systematic differences between males and females as it relates to affective processes such as the experience or expression of anger. Gao et al. [24] also reported that there were no significant gender differences in average depression and stress levels among female and male students. While the study did find significant gender differences in stress problems, it did report higher levels of anxiety for females consistent with the observations in Fig. 1(c).

Cognitive Processes are the higher-level functions of the brain and are represented through characteristics such as insight, causation, discrepancy, tentativeness, certainty, and differentiation within the LIWC toolkit. As shown in Fig. 2(a), documents associated with female queries show superior degrees of cognitive capacity compared to those related to male queries. However, based on psychological literature, males and females share similar cognitive abilities on most of cognitive functions [25]. Various researchers have argued that potentially observable differences between the sexes relating to intellectual and cognitive functions can be attributed to patterns of abilities as opposed to overall intellectual function of each gender [26–28]. Our observations show that there are implicit biases encoded within the relevance judgment documents associated with gendered queries in terms of psychological expression of cognitive processes.

Personal Concerns such as work, leisure, home, money, religion, and death are investigated and the findings presented in Fig. 2(b), reveal that relevance judgement documents associated with male queries have a higher degree of focus on personal concerns compared to female queries. This finding is aligned with the literature when it comes to personal concerns for leisure. The literature [29] reports that distribution of leisure time is significantly impacted by gender, especially for time allocated over the weekend. However, social psychology research has shown that such differences do not exist in other aspects of personal concern such as death, anxiety, and religiosity [30–33]. Furthermore, the literature reports that although the number of females has increased in the workplace and their presence in traditionally male-dominated professions has grown, there are still descriptive gender stereotypes in environments [34–38]. In another study [4], Heilam discussed that prescriptive and descriptive gender stereotypes result in gender bias in the workplace, which are unfounded. We find that such stereotypical biases do exist in relevance judgement documents and reflect biases that have been reported in the literature in the past.

Drives focus on characteristics of individuals that guide them towards achieving goals or accomplishing milestones. They can be defined with five key characteristics including affiliation, achievement, power, reward, and risk avoidance [21]. We find, as shown in Fig. 2(c), that relevance judgement documents associated with male queries express higher degrees of affiliation, achievement, and power compared to female queries, while the inverse is observed for reward and risk avoidance. These findings are supported by the literature that males seek for power and achievement more than females, but contradict studies that report higher degrees of affiliation for the female gender [39]. In addition, Byrens et al. have shown that males are more likely to take greater risks compared to females [40], which is compatible with our observations on degrees of risk avoidance.

Similar to other psychological characteristics, we find that differences can be observed regarding different personal drive characteristics between relevance documents associated with female and male queries. However, in this case, the differences are not due to stereotypical differences and have already been shown in the related literature that such personal drive characteristics are observed in practice for reasons such as physiological differences in gender.

4   Concluding Remarks

This paper investigated gender biases in gold standard IR relevance judgement datasets. We found that gender biases are prevalent in relevance judgements across a range of psychological processes. While some of the biases are expected as a result of physiological differences between genders, most gender biases are a result of the stereotypical perception of gender differences. We submit that regardless of the source of gender bias, be it stereotypical or physiological, IR relevance judgement documents should not show significant differences across various psychological processes based on the gender of the submitted query. Unbiased gold standards will ensure that gender biases do not get translated into representation and algorithmic aspects of retrieval methods.

References

1. Burgess, D., Borgida, E.: Who women are, who women should be: descriptive and prescriptive gender stereotyping in sex discrimination. Psychol. Public Policy Law **5**(3), 665 (1999)
2. Heilman, M.E.: Description and prescription: how gender stereotypes prevent women's ascent up the organizational ladder. J. Soc. Issues **57**(4), 657–674 (2001)
3. Ellemers, N.: Gender stereotypes. Annu. Rev. Psychol. **69**, 275–298 (2018)
4. Heilman, M.E.: Gender stereotypes and workplace bias. Res. Organ. Behav. **32**, 113–135 (2012)
5. Swim, J., Borgida, E., Maruyama, G., Myers, D.G.: Joan McKay versus John McKay: do gender stereotypes bias evaluations? Psychol. Bull. **105**(3), 409 (1989)
6. Huddy, L., Terkildsen, N.: Gender stereotypes and the perception of male and female candidates. Am. J. Polit. Sci. **37**, 119–147 (1993)

7. Rekabsaz, N., Schedl, M.: Do Neural Ranking Models Intensify Gender Bias? arXiv preprint arXiv:2005.00372 (2020)
8. Sun, T., et al.: Mitigating gender bias in natural language processing: literature review. arXiv preprint arXiv:1906.08976 (2019)
9. Bolukbasi, T., Chang, K.-W., Zou, J.Y., Saligrama, V., Kalai, A.T.: Man is to computer programmer as woman is to homemaker? Debiasing word embeddings. In: Advances in Neural Information Processing Systems, pp. 4349–4357 (2016))
10. Zhao, J., Zhou, Y., Li, Z., Wang, W., Chang, K.-W.: Learning gender-neutral word embeddings. arXiv preprint arXiv:1809.01496 (2018)
11. Rekabsaz, N., Henderson, J., West, R., Hanbury, A.: Measuring Societal Biases in Text Corpora via First-Order Co-occurrence. arXiv preprint arXiv:1812.10424 (2018)
12. Fabris, A., Purpura, A., Silvello, G., Susto, G.A.: Gender stereotype reinforcement: measuring the gender bias conveyed by ranking algorithms. Inf. Process. Manage. **57**, 102377 (2020)
13. Caliskan, A., Bryson, J.J., Narayanan, A.: Semantics derived automatically from language corpora contain human-like biases. Science **356**(6334), 183–186 (2017)
14. Nguyen, T., et al.: MS MARCO: a human-generated machine reading comprehension dataset (2016)
15. Devlin, J., Chang, M.-W., Lee, K., Toutanova K.: Bert: Pre-training of deep bidirectional transformers for language understanding. arXiv preprint arXiv:1810.04805 (2018)
16. Sanh, V., Debut, L., Chaumond, J., Wolf, T.: DistilBERT, a distilled version of BERT: smaller, faster, cheaper and lighter. arXiv preprint arXiv:1910.01108 (2019)
17. Liu, Y., et al.: Roberta: a robustly optimized Bert pretraining approach. arXiv preprint arXiv:1907.11692 (2019)
18. Yang, Z., Dai, Z., Yang, Y., Carbonell, J., Salakhutdinov, R.R., Le, Q.V.: XLNet: generalized autoregressive pretraining for language understanding. In: Advances in Neural Information Processing Systems, pp. 5753–5763 (2019)
19. Bojanowski, P., Grave, E., Joulin, A., Mikolov, T.: Enriching word vectors with subword information. Trans. Assoc. Comput. Ling. **5**, 135–146 (2017)
20. Mikolov, T., Sutskever, I., Chen, K., Corrado, G.S., Dean, J.: Distributed representations of words and phrases and their compositionality. In: Advances in Neural Information Processing Systems, pp. 3111–3119 (2013)
21. Pennebaker, J.W., Francis, M.E., Booth, R.J.: Linguistic inquiry and word count: LIWC 2001. Mahway Lawrence Erlbaum Associates **71**(2001), 2001 (2001)
22. Milovchevich, D., Howells, K., Drew, N., Day, A.: Sex and gender role differences in anger: an Australian community study. Personality Individ. Differ. **31**(2), 117–127 (2001)
23. Deffenbacher, J.L., et al.: State-trait anger theory and the utility of the trait anger scale. J. Couns. Psychol. **43**(2), 131 (1996)
24. Gao, W., Ping, S., Liu, X.: Gender differences in depression, anxiety, and stress among college students: a longitudinal study from China. J. Affect. Disord. **263**, 292–300 (2020)
25. Hyde, J.S.: Sex and cognition: gender and cognitive functions. Current Opinion Neurobiol. **38**, 53–56 (2016)
26. Halpern, D.F.: Sex Differences in Cognitive Abilities, 4th edn. Psychology Press, New York (2012)
27. Collins, D.W., Kimura, D.: A large sex difference on a two-dimensional mental rotation task. Behav. Neurosci. **111**(4), 845 (1997)

28. Mollet, G.A.: Fundamentals of human neuropsychology. J. Undergrad. Neurosci. Educ. **6**(2), R3 (2008)
29. Shaw, S.M.: Gender and leisure: inequality in the distribution of leisure time. J. Leisure Res. **17**(4), 266–282 (1985)
30. Dickstein, L.S.: Attitudes toward death, anxiety, and social desirability. OMEGA-J. Death Dying **8**(4), 369–378 (1978)
31. McDonald, R.T., Hilgendorf, W.A.: Death imagery and death anxiety. J. Clin. Psychol. **42**(1), 87–91 (1986)
32. Francis, L.J.: The personality characteristics of Anglican ordinands: feminine men and masculine women? Personality Individ. Differ. **12**(11), 1133–1140 (1991)
33. Deconchy, J.-P.: Boys and Girls Choices for A Religious Group. Psychology and Religion, pp. 284–300. Penguin, Harmondsworth (1973)
34. Schein, V.E.: A global look at psychological barriers to women's progress in management. J. Soc. Issues **57**(4), 675–688 (2001)
35. Heilman, M.E., Block, C.J., Martell, R.F.: Sex stereotypes: do they influence perceptions of managers? J. Soc. Behav. Pers. **10**(4), 237 (1995)
36. Heilman, M.E., Block, C.J., Martell, R.F., Simon, M.C.: Has anything changed? Current characterizations of men, women, and managers. J. Appl. Psychol. **74**(6), 935 (1989)
37. Brenner, O.C., Tomkiewicz, J., Schein., V.E.: The relationship between sex role stereotypes and requisite management characteristics revisited. Acad. Manage. J. **32**(3), 662–669 (1989)
38. Dodge, K.A., Gilroy, F.D., Mickey Fenzel, L.: Requisite management characteristics revisited: two decades later. J. Soc. Behav. Pers. **10**(4), 253 (1995)
39. Denzinger, F., Backes, S., Job, V., Brandstätter, V.: Age and gender differences in implicit motives. J. Res. Pers. **65**, 52–61 (2016)
40. Byrnes, J.P., Miller, D.C., Schafer, W.D.: Gender differences in risk taking: a meta-analysis. Psychol. Bull. **125**(3), 367 (1999)

Assessing the Benefits of Model Ensembles in Neural Re-ranking for Passage Retrieval

Luís Borges[1,2(✉)], Bruno Martins[1], and Jamie Callan[2]

[1] Instituto Superior Técnico and INESC-ID, University of Lisbon, Lisbon, Portugal
[2] Carnegie Mellon University, Pittsburgh, USA

Abstract. Our work aimed at experimentally assessing the benefits of model ensembling within the context of neural methods for passage re-ranking. Starting from relatively standard neural models, we use a previous technique named Fast Geometric Ensembling to generate multiple model instances from particular training schedules, then focusing or attention on different types of approaches for combining the results from the multiple model instances (e.g., averaging the ranking scores, using fusion methods from the IR literature, or using supervised learning-to-rank). Tests with the MS-MARCO dataset show that model ensembling can indeed benefit the ranking quality, particularly with supervised learning-to-rank although also with unsupervised rank aggregation.

Keywords: Model ensembling · Rank fusion · Passage re-ranking

1 Introduction

Ensemble methods are known to typically perform better than individual systems. In the field of information retrieval, several rank aggregation techniques have for instance been proposed to combine the results of different ranking methods [1,7,12,13], with previous studies showing that ensembles indeed lead to superior results. Ensemble methods are also common in the machine learning literature. Specifically within the context of learning with deep neural networks, ensembling algorithms such as Fast Geometric Ensembling (FGE) have recently been proposed and successfully applied to multiple tasks [11], using particular learning rate updating schedules to create multiple neural networks with no additional training cost, which can afterwards be combined (e.g., by averaging the scores from the resulting models) for improved performance.

In this paper, we assess the benefits of ensemble approaches within the context of neural models for passage re-ranking. We specifically leverage the

This research was supported by Fundação para a Ciência e Tecnologia (FCT), through the Ph.D. scholarship with reference SFRH/BD/150497/2019, and the INESC-ID multi-annual funding from the PIDDAC programme (UIDB/50021/2020).

D. Hiemstra et al. (Eds.): ECIR 2021, LNCS 12657, pp. 225–232, 2021.
https://doi.org/10.1007/978-3-030-72240-1_19

FGE approach together with relatively standard neural retrieval models [14], corresponding to re-ranking approaches based on recurrent neural networks, or instead based on Transformer-based models like RoBERTa [15]. With ensembles, we focused our attention on different approaches for combining the results, and we compared strategies based on (a) averaging the scores (i.e., the relevance estimates) produced by the multiple models, (b) combining the rankings from the multiple models with rank fusion approaches, or (c) using supervised learning-to-rank as a meta-learning strategy to combine the model scores.

We evaluated the different approaches on the well-known MS-MARCO passage re-ranking task [2]. The obtained results show that model ensembling indeed leads to improvements over individual neural ranking models, particularly with supervised learning-to-rank and/or in the case of RoBERTa models.

2   Passage Re-ranking with Neural Ensembles

Within our general approach, we first train a neural ranking model with the Fast Geometric Ensembling (FGE) technique, which outputs N different model checkpoints, saved at different phases of the training process. The different checkpoints are used to re-rank initial lists with the top 1000 passages for each test query, resulting in the generation of N ranked lists. For the initial rankings, we used the DeepCT first-stage retrieval algorithm, which extends BM25 with context-aware term weights derived from a BERT model [8]. Finally, the N different ranked lists are used as input to a fusion method, which combines the scores to produce a final re-ranked list. The following sub-sections describe the FGE technique and the different fusion methods that were considered.

2.1   Fast Geometric Model Ensembling

Fast Geometric Ensembling (FGE) consists of an ensembling technique for deep neural networks that generates multiple points in the weight space (i.e., multiple model instances, resulting from different checkpoints during training), that share a similar low test error [11]. The approach is inspired on the observation that the optima for the loss functions being optimized while training neural models are often connected by simple curves, over which the training/test accuracy are nearly constant. FGE uses a training procedure that leverages this geometric intuition, discovering points (i.e., model checkpoints) within the high-accuracy pathways through a particular learning rate update schedule.

The FGE algorithm starts with model weights corresponding to an initial training of the neural network, and resumes the training with a cyclical learning rate defined as follows, where α_1 and α_2 are the minimum and maximum values for the learning rate, while $\alpha(i)$ represents the learning rate at iteration i.

$$\alpha(i) = \begin{cases} (1 - 2 \times t(i)) \times \alpha_1 + 2 \times t(i) \times \alpha_2 & 0 < t(i) \leq 0.5 \\ (2 - 2 \times t(i)) \times \alpha_2 + (2 \times t(i) - 1) \times \alpha_1 & 0.5 < t(i) \leq 1 \end{cases} \quad (1)$$

Each iteration corresponds to processing one mini-batch. The parameter $t(i)$ can be defined with basis on the number of iterations c corresponding to a cycle.

$$t(i) = \frac{1}{c} \times (\mathrm{mod}(i-1, c) + 1) \tag{2}$$

In the middle of each cycle, when the learning rate reaches its minimum value α_2, the model weights are collected to form a checkpoint. After training, the checkpoints can be individually evaluated on a test set, and the corresponding results can afterwards by combined to form ensemble predictions.

2.2   Rank Fusion Methods

Multiple methods for fusing lists into a final consensus ranking have been proposed in the information retrieval literature [1]. As a simple approach, one can for instance rank instances according to the average of the scores associated to the different lists. Other approaches often leverage instead the ranking positions.

One example is Reciprocal Rank Fusion [7], which is based on summing the multiplicative inverse of the original rankings. Given a set of instances P (i.e., the passages to be retrieved) and multiple rankings R for a given query, the instances can be sorted according to the following score:

$$\mathrm{RRFscore}(p \in P) = \sum_{r \in R} \frac{1}{k + r(p)} \tag{3}$$

In Eq. 3, k is a smoothing constant often set to the constant value of 60 [7], and $r(p)$ is the rank of passage p in the ranked list $r()$. A simple variation, named MAP Fusion, was proposed by Lillis et al. [13] and involves weighting the contribution of each ranked list according its Mean Average Precision (MAP) score, as measured over a held-out set of queries:

$$\mathrm{MAPFscore}(p \in P) = \sum_{r \in R} \frac{1 \times \mathrm{MAP}_r}{k + r(p)} \tag{4}$$

Previous studies have also advanced probabilistic data fusion techniques, using training queries to estimate the probability that a resource is relevant to a given query, and leveraging those probabilities in order to create new ranking scores. One of those probabilistic techniques is SlideFuse [12], which first estimates the probability that a passage p, occurring in position i of a ranked list produced through a procedure r, is relevant. This can be computed according to the following equation, where Q_p is the set of training queries for which at least i instances were returned in lists produced through procedure r, and where $\mathrm{Rel}(p_i, q)$ is 1 if p_i is relevant to query q, and 0 otherwise.

$$P(p_i | r) = \frac{\sum_{q \in Q_i} \mathrm{Rel}(p_i, q)}{Q_i} \tag{5}$$

The final aggregated score for each document also considers a sliding window around each position of the rankings to be merged:

$$\text{SlideFscore}(p \in P) = \sum_{r \in R} \text{P}(p_{i,w}|r) \tag{6}$$

In the previous equation, $\text{P}(p_{i,w}|r)$ is the probability of relevance of passage p in position i, this time considering a window of w documents around each side of i. This can be estimated as follows, where the values a and b correspond to the window limits for every position i, considering N as the total number of documents for each query.

$$\text{P}(p_{i,w}|r) = \frac{\sum_{j=a}^{b} \text{P}(p_j|r)}{b-a+1}, \text{ with}$$

$$a = \begin{cases} i-w & i-w \geq 0 \\ 0 & i-w < 0 \end{cases} \text{ and } b = \begin{cases} i+w & i+w < N \\ N-1 & i+w \geq N \end{cases} \tag{7}$$

Variations on SlideFuse, weighting the contribution of individual ranked lists, are also possible. For instance Eq. 6 can be adapted in the same way as Eq. 4 extends from Eq. 3, weighting each system by the corresponding MAP score, and resulting in a MAP SlideFuse approach.

Besides rank aggregation methods we also experimented with a supervised learning-to-rank approach, specifically the LambdaRank [5] implementation from the XGBoost[1] package. In this case, for each training query, we collected the relevant passage and two other passages in the top 1000 list, ranked according to DeepCT. The LambdaRank model was trained on this data, using as features the DeepCT scores plus those from the FGE snapshots, together with the average and standard deviation, and attempting to optimize the MAP metric.

Still on what regards experimental settings, the SlideFuse method considered a window size of 6, and the LambdaRank algorithm used the default parameters from the XGBoost library, except in the choice of MAP as the optimized metric.

3   Neural Ranking Models

We experimented with two distinct types of neural ranking models, respectively leveraging recurrent neural networks, and Transformer-based language models.

The first model is inspired on a previous proposal for encoding and matching textual contents [4]. A sentence encoder is used to compute fixed-size vector representations for input sequences, leveraging pre-trained FastText [3] word embeddings together with two layers of bi-directional LSTM units with short-cut connections between them, and a max-pooling operation over the sequence produced by the second bi-LSTM. The query is processed through the aforementioned encoder, which outputs the corresponding representation. In turn, each sentence that composes the passage is also processed through the same encoder,

---

[1] https://github.com/dmlc/xgboost.

generating a sequence of representations. This sequence of sentence representations is then fed as input to a different encoder, using a similar structure (except for the initial FastText embedding layer) to produce a single fixed-size representation for the passage. The representations for the query and the passage are combined through different operations (i.e., vector concatenation, difference, and element-wise product), and the result is feed into a final feed-forward layer, which outputs the relevance score of the passage towards the query.

For the second neural ranking approach, we fine-tune RoBERTa-base [15] to our ranking problem, passing as input to the model the concatenation of the query and the passage text, separated by a special [SEP] token. We concatenate the vector representation of the special [CLS] token, together with the result of a max-pooling operation over the last sequence of hidden states output by RoBERTa-base, feeding the result to a final feed-forward layer which outputs the relevance score of the passage towards the query.

When training our models, we first use a fast approach (i.e., DeepCT [8]) to retrieve the top 1000 passages for the provided training queries. The loss function takes as input the scores between a query and a relevant passage, a non-relevant passage sampled from the top 25 passages retrieved for the query, and a negative passage sampled from the remaining 975 passages in the top 1000. The loss is formally defined as follows, where p is the score between the query and a positive passage, n_{25} is the score between the query and the passage sampled from the top 25, and n_{975} is the score between the query and the passage sampled from the remaining 975 passages.

$$\text{loss} = \text{hinge}(p, n_{25}) + \text{hinge}(p, n_{975}) + 0.25 \times \text{hinge}(n_{25}, n_{975}), \text{ with}$$
$$\text{hinge}(p, n) = \max(0, 1 - p + n) \tag{8}$$

For our RNN-based model, we used a dimensionality of 300 in the representations produced by the recurrent units. For RoBERTa-base, we used the default base parameters as defined in the Huggingface Transformers library[2]. We trained our models for a total of 15 epochs with the AdaMod [10] optimizer. The first five epochs produced the initial weights for the Fast Geometric Ensembling (FGE) technique. In the remaining ten epochs with FGE, we used cycles of $c = 4$ epochs, with a cyclic learning rate between $\alpha_1 = 2 \cdot 10^{-5}$ and $\alpha_2 = 2 \cdot 10^{-7}$, hence generating five different checkpoints.

4   Experimental Evaluation

Our experiments relied on the passage ranking data from MS-MARCO [2]. For each test query, a first-stage ranker (in our case, DeepCT [8]) retrieves a set of possibly relevant passages from the whole collection, and the top k results are then re-ranked through a second more expensive model.

Table 1 presents a comparison between the different alternatives described in Sects. 2 and 3, with results measured over the development portion of the MS-MARCO dataset. We specifically measured the Mean Average Precision (MAP),

---

[2] https://github.com/huggingface/transformers.

Table 1. Results over the MS-MARCO development dataset. Statistical significance tests were used to compare ensembles against individual models for re-ranking the DeepCT results, both for RNN (†) and RoBERTa-base (‡) models, as well as to compare the learning-to-rank ensembles against the second best ensemble (∗). The methods whose difference is statistically significant, for a p-value of 0.05, are marked on the table. Although this is not reported on the table, not including DeepCT scores in the FGE ensembles is consistently worse (i.e., approx. 0.01 points lower in terms of MRR@10 for RoBERTa-base ensembles, and up to 0.1 points lower for RNN ensembles).

Method	MAP	MRR	MRR@10
BM25	0.1835	0.1867	0.1758
DeepCT	0.2506	0.2546	0.2425
RNN	0.2127	0.2160	0.2010
RoBERTa-base	0.3356	0.3403	0.3311
RNN + DeepCT	0.2888	0.2936	0.2821
RoBERTa-base + DeepCT	0.3326	0.3378	0.3285
RNN FGE + DeepCT + Average[†]	0.3000	0.3056	0.2952
RNN FGE + DeepCT + RRFuse	0.2845	0.2891	0.2769
RNN FGE + DeepCT + MAPFuse	0.2847	0.2893	0.2771
RNN FGE + DeepCT + SlideFuse	0.2738	0.2781	0.2645
RNN FGE + DeepCT + MAPSlideFuse[†]	0.2741	0.2784	0.2649
RNN FGE + DeepCT + Learning-to-Rank[†∗]	0.3131	0.3181	0.3080
RoBERTa-base FGE + DeepCT + Average[‡]	0.3354	0.3411	0.3324
RoBERTa-base FGE + DeepCT + RRFuse[‡]	0.3819	0.3879	0.3813
RoBERTa-base FGE + DeepCT + MAPFuse[‡]	0.3818	0.3874	0.3806
RoBERTa-base FGE + DeepCT + SlideFuse[‡]	0.3787	0.3844	0.3774
RoBERTa-base FGE + DeepCT + MAPSlideFuse[‡]	0.3789	0.3844	0.3774
RoBERTa-base FGE + DeepCT + Learning-to-Rank[‡∗]	0.3856	0.3913	0.3846

Mean Reciprocal Rank (MRR), and MRR@10. The first two lines of Table 1 compare two first-stage retrieval approaches, returning 1000 possibly relevant passages for each development query. DeepCT outperformed BM25 in this initial task, and the remaining experiments focused on re-ranking the top 100 passages retrieved by DeepCT. A separate round of tests, not detailed in this paper, showed that re-ranking the top 100 passages lead to consistently better results than re-ranking the entire set of 1000 passages per query.

The second group of rows in Table 1 compares the results for both types of neural models, trained for a total of 15 epochs. The model based on RoBERTa-base clearly outperformed the RNN-based model, which even failed to outperform DeepCT. We also attempted to combine the rankings from each of these models and DeepCT, through the MAPFuse strategy. The results, given in the third group of rows, showed that the combination improved results for the RNN model, but not for the RoBERTa-base model.

The remaining rows from Table 1 show the results achieved with FGE ensembles, leveraging different types of techniques for combining the rankings. The results show that model ensembling has clear benefits for RoBERTa-base models, with mixed results for RNN models. Few differences were measured between the alternative rank aggregation approaches, and significantly better results were obtained with learning-to-rank. We expect that similar benefits from ensembling can be expected for larger models than RoBERTa-base.

5   Conclusions and Future Work

We tested the use of Fast Geometric Ensembling (FGE) with neural passage re-ranking models, comparing different fusion methods to combine the rankings from FGE checkpoints. Results over MS-MARCO show that model ensembling indeed leads to consistent improvements over individual models, thus constituting a viable approach to further improve state-of-the-art approaches.

For future work, we plan to conduct similar tests with other datasets, including TREC CAR [9] and WikiPassageQA [6], in addition to testing different ensembling methods, such as the Auto-Ensembling approach from Jun et al. [16].

References

1. Anava, Y., Shtok, A., Kurland, O., Rabinovich, E.: A probabilistic fusion framework. In: Proceedings of the ACM International on Conference on Information and Knowledge Management (2016)
2. Bajaj, P., et al.: MS-MARCO: A human generated machine reading comprehension dataset. arXiv preprint 1611.09268 (2016)
3. Bojanowski, P., Grave, E., Joulin, A., Mikolov, T.: Enriching word vectors with subword information. Trans. Assoc. Comput. Ling. 5, 135–146 (2017)
4. Borges, L., Martins, B., Calado, P.: Combining similarity features and deep representation learning for stance detection in the context of checking fake news. J. Data Inf. Qual. 11(3), 1–26 (2019)
5. Burges, C.J.: From RankNet to LambdaRank to LambdaMART: an overview. Learning 11(23–581), 81 (2010)
6. Cohen, D., Yang, L., Croft, W.B.: WikiPassageQA: a benchmark collection for research on non-factoid answer passage retrieval. In: Proceedings of the International ACM SIGIR Conference on Research and Development in Information Retrieval (2018)
7. Cormack, G.V., Clarke, C.L.A., Buettcher, S.: Reciprocal rank fusion outperforms Condorcet and individual rank learning methods. In: Proceedings of the International ACM SIGIR conference on Research and Development in Information Retrieval (2009)
8. Dai, Z., Callan, J.: Context-aware sentence/passage term importance estimation for first stage retrieval. arXiv preprint 1910.10687 (2019)
9. Dietz, L., Gamari, B., Dalton, J., Craswell, N.: TREC complex answer retrieval overview. In: Proceedings of the Text REtrieval Conference (2018)
10. Ding, J., Ren, X., Luo, R., Sun, X.: An adaptive and momental bound method for stochastic learning. arXiv preprint 1910.12249 (2019)
11. Garipov, T., Izmailov, P., Podoprikhin, D., Vetrov, D.P., Wilson, A.G.: Loss surfaces, mode connectivity, and fast ensembling of DNNs. In: Proceedings of the Annual Conference on Neural Information Processing Systems (2018)

12. Lillis, D., Toolan, F., Collier, R., Dunnion, J.: Extending probabilistic data fusion using sliding windows. In: Macdonald, C., Ounis, I., Plachouras, V., Ruthven, I., White, R.W. (eds.) ECIR 2008. LNCS, vol. 4956, pp. 358–369. Springer, Heidelberg (2008). https://doi.org/10.1007/978-3-540-78646-7_33

13. Lillis, D., Zhang, L., Toolan, F., Collier, R.W., Leonard, D., Dunnion, J.: Estimating probabilities for effective data fusion. In: Proceedings of the International ACM SIGIR conference on Research and Development in Information Retrieval (2010)

14. Lin, J., Nogueira, R., Yates, A.: Pretrained transformers for text ranking: BERT and beyond. arXiv preprint arXiv:2010.06467 (2020)

15. Liu, Y., et al.: RoBERTa: a robustly optimized BERT pretraining approach. arXiv preprint 1907.11692 (2019)

16. Yang, J., Wang, F.: Auto-ensemble: an adaptive learning rate scheduling based deep learning model ensembling. arXiv preprint 2003.11266 (2020)

Event Detection with Entity Markers

Emanuela Boros[1]($\boxtimes$)(iD), Jose G. Moreno[1,2](iD), and Antoine Doucet[1](iD)

[1] University of La Rochelle, L3i, 17000 La Rochelle, France
{emanuela.boros,antoine.doucet}@univ-lr.fr
[2] University of Toulouse, IRIT, UMR 5505 CNRS, 31000 Toulouse, France
jose.moreno@irit.fr

Abstract. Event detection involves the identification of instances of specified types of events in text and their classification into event types. In this paper, we approach the event detection task as a relation extraction task. In this context, we assume that the clues brought by the entities participating in an event are important and could improve the performance of event detection. Therefore, we propose to exploit entity information explicitly for detecting the event triggers by marking them at different levels while fine-tuning a pre-trained language model. The experimental results prove that our approach obtains state-of-the-art results on the ACE 2005 dataset.

Keywords: Information extraction · Event extraction · Event Detection

1 Introduction

Event detection (ED) aims to identify the instances of specified types of events in text. An event is represented by an *event mention* (a text that contains an event of a specific type and subtype), an *event trigger* (the word that expresses the event mention), an *event argument* (a participant in the event of a specific type), and an *argument role* (the role of the entity in the event). For instance, according to the ACE 2005 annotation guidelines[1], in the sentence "*She's been convicted of obstruction of justice*.", an event detection system should be able to recognize the word *convicted* as a trigger for the specific event type **Convict**.

A main challenge intervenes when the same event might appear in the form of various trigger expressions and an expression might represent different event types in different contexts. For example, *transfer* could refer to transferring ownership of an item, transferring money, or transferring personnel from one location to another. Each sense of the word is linked with an event type. In the same manner, *fired* can correspond to an **attack** type of event as in "*an American tank fired on the street*" or it can express the **dismissal** of an employee from a job as in "*Hillary Clinton was fired from the House Judiciary Committee's Watergate investigation*".

---

[1] https://www.ldc.upenn.edu/sites/www.ldc.upenn.edu/files/english-events-guidelines-v5.4.3.pdf.

© Springer Nature Switzerland AG 2021
D. Hiemstra et al. (Eds.): ECIR 2021, LNCS 12657, pp. 233–240, 2021.
https://doi.org/10.1007/978-3-030-72240-1_20

Therefore, we would assume that, in such cases, significant clues can be given by the context of a candidate trigger and by the presence of the participants at the event in this context, e.g. named entities. For analyzing the importance of these indicators of the existence of an event in a sentence, we adopt a relation extraction model to perform event detection by taking advantage of the participants in the event (event arguments).

2   Related Work

Most current state-of-the-art systems perform event detection individually [2,6,17], where the entities are either ignored or considered helpful in joint models.

Some works made use of gold-standard entities in different manners. Higher results can be obtained with gold-standard entity types [17], by concatenating randomly initialized embeddings for the entity types. A graph neural network (GNN) based on dependency trees [18] has also been proposed to perform event detection with a pooling method that relies on entity mentions aggregating the convolution vectors. Arguments provided significant clues to this task in the supervised attention mechanism proposed to exploit argument information explicitly for event detection [11], while also using events from FrameNet.

Although some joint learning-based methods have been proposed, which tackled event detection and argument extraction simultaneously, these approaches usually only make significant improvements on the argument extraction, but insignificant to event detection. These methods usually combine the loss functions of these two tasks and are jointly trained under the supervision of annotated triggers and arguments. Event triggers and their arguments are predicted at the same time in a joint framework [15] with bidirectional recurrent neural networks (Bi-RNNs) and a convolutional neural network (CNN) and systematically investigate the usage of memory vectors/matrices to store the prediction information during the course of labeling sentence features.

The architecture adopted in [12] was to jointly extract multiple event triggers and event arguments by introducing syntactic shortcut arcs derived from the dependency parsing trees to enhance the information flow in an attention-based graph convolution network (GCN) model. The gold-standard entity types are embedded as features for trigger and argument prediction. The argument information was also exploited in [11] explicitly for event detection by experimenting with different strategies for adding supervised attention mechanisms. The authors exploit the annotated entity information by concatenating the token embeddings with randomly initialized entity type embeddings.

Recently, different approaches that include external resources and features at a sub-word representation level have been proposed. Thus, generative adversarial networks (GANs) have been applied in event detection [8,24]. Besides, reinforcement learning (RL) is used in [24] for creating an end-to-end entity and event extraction framework. The approach attempted in [23] based on the BERT model with an automatic generation of labeled data by editing prototypes and filtering out the labeled samples through argument replacement by ranking their quality. A similar framework is proposed by [22] but information is encoded by BERT or a CNN suggesting a growing interest in adversarial models. Simultaneously, an integration of a distillation technique to enhance the adversarial prediction was explored in [13].

Although recent advances are focused on multiple techniques, several BERT-based architectures have been proposed [21–23]. In this work, we demonstrate that the advantages of BERT can be improved by adding extra information by explicitly marking the entities in the input text. We continue with the presentation of our proposed model in Sect. 3. The experimental setup and the results are detailed in Sect. 4 and we finalize with some conclusions and perspectives in Sect. 5.

3 Approach

We implemented the BERT-based model with *EntityMarkers*[2] We adapt the method presented in [19] applied for relation classification, to perform event detection. First, our model extends the BERT [3] model applied to sequential data. BERT itself is a stack of Transformer layers [20]. We refer the readers to the original paper for a more detailed description. We modify BERT by adding a conditional random fields (CRF) layer instead of the dense one, which is commonly used in other works on sequential labeling [9,14] to ensure output consistency. Next, the *EntityMarkers* model [19] consists in augmenting the input data with a series of special tokens. Thus, if we consider a sentence $x = [x_0, x_1, \ldots, x_n]$ with n tokens, we augment x with two reserved word pieces to mark the beginning and the end of each event argument mention in the sentence.

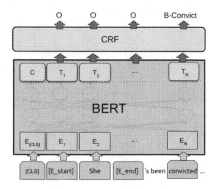

Fig. 1. The BERT-based model with *Entity Position Markers* and a CRF top layer.

In the ACE 2005 dataset, an event argument is defined as an entity mention, a temporal expression or a value (e.g. *Crime, Sentence, Job-Title*) that is

---

[2] We only used the input type representation and consider a complex output based on tokens which is not considered in [19].

involved in an event (as participants or attributes with a specific role in an event mention). An event argument has an entity type and a role. For example, in a *Conflict.Attack* event type, one event argument can be an *Attacker* with three possible types: PER, ORG, GPE (Person, Organization, Geo-political Entity). Thus, we introduce three types of markers: (1) *Entity Position Markers*, e.g. $[E_{start}]$ and $[E_{end}]$ where E represents an entity of any type, (2) *Entity Type Markers*, e.g. PER_{start} and PER_{end} where PER represents an entity of type Person, and (3) we also test that, in the case of the event argument roles are known beforehand, the *Argument Role Markers*, e.g. $[Defendant_{start}]$, $[Defendant_{end}]$ where Defendant is an event argument role. We modify x to give:

$$x = [x_0, x_1, \ldots, [MARKER_{start}] x_i \ldots x_{j-1} [MARKER_{end}], \ldots, x_n]$$ and we feed this token sequence into BERT instead of x. We also update the entity indices $E = (i + 1, j + 1)$ to account for the inserted tokens, as shown in Fig. 1 for the model with *Entity Position Markers*.

As an example, in the sentence *"**She**'s been convicted of **obstruction of justice**."*, where *She* has the argument role of a **Defendant** and *obstruction of justice* is an argument of type **Crime**, the sentence is augmented as follows:

(1) $[E_{start}]$ **She** $[E_{end}]$*'s been convicted of* $[E_{start}]$ **obstruction of justice** $[E_{end}]$.
(2) $[PER_{start}]$ **She** $[PER_{end}]$*'s been convicted of* $[Crime_{start}]$ **obstruction of justice** $[Crime_{end}]$.
(3) $[Defendant_{start}]$ **She** $[Defendant_{end}]$*'s been convicted of* $[Crime_{start}]$ **obstruction of justice** $[Crime_{end}]$.

For the *Argument Role Markers*, if an entity has different roles in different events that are present in the same sentence, we mark the entity with all the argument roles that it has.

4   Experiments and Results

The evaluation is conducted on the annotated data ACE 2005 corpus. For comparison purposes, we use the same test set with 40 news articles (672 sentences), the same development set with 30 other documents (863 sentences), and the same training set with the remaining 529 documents (14,849 sentences) as in previous studies of this dataset [15,17].

The ACE 2005 corpus has 8 types of events, with 33 subtypes (e.g. the event type *Conflict* has two subtypes *Attack, Demonstrate*) that, along with one

Table 1. Evaluation of the BERT-based models on the blind test data.

Models	Precision	Recall	**F1**
BERT-base-uncased	71.6	68.4	70.0
BERT-base-cased	71.3	72.0	71.6
BERT-large-uncased	72.0	72.9	72.5
BERT-large-cased	69.3	77.1	73.0

Table 2. Evaluation of our models and comparison with state-of-the-art systems for event detection on the blind test data. $^+$with gold-standard arguments. Change improvements w.r.t. our models are showed in columns "F1 Improvement (%)". Improvements greater than 10% are highlighted with background color. Statistical significance is measured with McNemar's test. * denotes a significant improvement at $p \leq 0.01$.

Models	Precision	Recall	F1	F1 Improvement (%)		
				(1)	(2)	(3)
CNN [17]	71.9	63.8	67.6	12.72%	16.12%	17.75%
CNN$^+$[17]	71.8	66.4	69.0	10.43%	13.77%	15.36%
Dynamic multi-pooling CNN [2]	75.6	63.6	69.1	10.27%	13.60%	15.20%
Joint RNN [15]	66.0	73.0	69.3	9.96%	13.28%	14.86%
CNN with document context [6]	77.2	64.9	70.5	8.09%	11.35%	12.91%
Non-Consecutive CNN [16]	N/A	N/A	71.3	6.87%	10.10%	11.64%
Attention-based$^+$ [11]	78.0	66.3	71.7	6.28%	9.48%	11.02%
GAIL [24]	74.8	69.4	72.0	5.83%	9.03%	10.56%
Gated Cross-Lingual Attention [10]	78.9	66.9	72.4	5.25%	8.43%	9.94%
Graph CNN [18]	77.9	68.8	73.1	4.24%	7.39%	8.89%
Seed-based [1]	80.6	67.1	73.2	4.10%	7.24%	8.74%
Hybrid NN [7]	**84.6**	64.9	73.4	3.81%	6.95%	8.45%
Attention-based GCN [12]	76.3	71.3	73.7	3.39%	6.51%	8.01%
Δ-learning [13]	76.3	71.9	74.0	2.97%	6.08%	7.57%
DEEB-RNN3y [25]	72.3	75.8	74.0	2.97%	6.08%	7.57%
BERT-base-uncased+LSTM [21]	N/A	N/A	68.9	10.60%	13.93%	15.53%
BERT-base-uncased [21]	N/A	N/A	69.7	9.33%	12.63%	14.20%
BERT-base-uncased [5]	67.1	73.2	70.0	8.86%	12.14%	13.71%
BERT-QA [5]	71.1	73.7	72.3	5.39%	8.58%	10.10%
DMBERT [22]	77.6	71.8	74.6	2.14%	5.23%	6.70%
DMBERT+Boot [22]	77.9	72.5	75.1	1.46%	4.53%	5.99%
BERT-large-cased	69.3	77.1	73.0	4.38%	7.53%	9.04%
BERT-large-cased+*Entity Position Markers*$^+$ (1)	75.9	76.6	76.2*	–	3.02%	4.46%
BERT-large-cased+*Entity Type Markers*$^+$ (2)	79.3	77.8	78.5*	–	–	1.40%
BERT-large-cased+*Argument Role Markers*$^+$ (3)	78.9	**80.4**	**79.6***	–	–	–

class "O" for the non-trigger tokens, constitutes a 34-class classification problem. Following the same line of works, we consider that a trigger is correct if its event type, subtype, and offsets match those of a reference trigger. We use precision (P), recall (R), and F-measure (F1) to evaluate the overall performance.

We first consider four baselines based on the BERT language model, applied in a similar way to [4] for the named entity recognition (NER) task, with the recommended hyperparameters. We test four widely used pre-trained English language models, two based on BERT-base and two based on BERT-large, *cased* (trained on the original words) and *uncased* (trained on lowercased words). tion is connected to the recognition of named entities, that are usually considered important to detect event mentions.

We compare our proposed models with markers with several state-of-the-art neural-based models proposed for event detection, that do not use external resources, more specifically with the following models based on CNNs and RNNs: the CNN-based model [17] with and without the addition of gold-standard entities, the dynamic multi-pooling CNN model [2], the bidirectional joint RNNs [15], the non-consecutive CNN in [16], the hybrid model [7], the GAIL model [24], the gated cross-lingual attention model [10], and the graph CNN [18]. We also compare our approach with recent proposed BERT-based models, the fine-tuned baseline BERT-base-uncased [5], the QA-BERT [5] where the task has been approached as a question answering task, the two models with adversarial training for weakly supervised event detection [22], and the BERT and LSTMs approaches [21] that models text spans and captures within-sentence and cross-sentence context.

Between the BERT-based baseline models presented in Table 1, it is worth noticing that the *cased* models perform better than the *uncased* ones, which could confirm that named entities that are usually capitalized are an important clue for the event detection task[3]. Moreover, the results are similar to the BERT-base-uncased in [5] (the same F1 value and similar precision and recall scores) and [21].

Full results of our model and its comparison against state of the art is presented in Table 2. There is a significant gain with the trigger classification of 9.04% higher over the stand-alone BERT-based model and 5.99% to the best reported previous models. These results demonstrate the effectiveness of our method to incorporate the argument information.

Moreover, the improvements are consistent regardless of the type of encoder (BERT or other) used to represent the inputs. For our first model (*Entity Position Markers*), where the entities are surrounded by a general marker that does not depend on the entity type, the results are improved with three percentage points revealing that the position of the entities is relevant for the trigger detection task. Furthermore, when we mark the entities with their argument roles (*Argument Role Markers*), the recall and F1 increase with around one absolute percentage point. However, this case is substantially optimistic as it assumes that argument roles were correctly identified and typed.

5   Conclusions and Perspectives

We presented an approach for integrating entity information for the event detection task by adding different levels of entity markers, their positions, their types, and finally, their argument roles. Considering the results, we can conclude that marking entities in a sentence can significantly improve the F1 scores and obtain state-of-the-art values. Further analysis remains to be done in order to understand in which cases the markers bring informative features. As future work, we propose to tackle the drawbacks of our current model by introducing the recognition and typing of the entities in our model.

---

[3] An amount of around 30% of the entities and 3% of the event triggers have the first token capitalized.

Acknowledgments. This work has been supported by the European Union's Horizon 2020 research and innovation program under grants 770299 (NewsEye) and 825153 (Embeddia).

References

1. Bronstein, O., Dagan, I., Li, Q., Ji, H., Frank, A.: Seed-based event trigger labeling: How far can event descriptions get us? In: ACL (2), pp. 372–376 (2015)
2. Chen, Y., Xu, L., Liu, K., Zeng, D., Zhao, J.: Event extraction via dynamic multi-pooling convolutional neural networks. In: Proceedings of the 53rd Annual Meeting of the Association for Computational Linguistics and the 7th International Joint Conference on Natural Language Processing, vol. 1, pp. 167–176 (2015)
3. Devlin, J., Chang, M.W., Lee, K., Toutanova, K.: BERT: pre-training of deep bidirectional transformers for language understanding. arXiv preprint arXiv:1810.04805 (2018)
4. Devlin, J., Chang, M.W., Lee, K., Toutanova, K.: BERT: pre-training of deep bidirectional transformers for language understanding. In: 2019 Conference of the North American Chapter of the Association for Computational Linguistics: Human Language Technologies (NAACL-HLT 2019), pp. 4171–4186. Association for Computational Linguistics, Minneapolis, June 2019
5. Du, X., Cardie, C.: Event extraction by answering (almost) natural questions. arXiv preprint arXiv:2004.13625 (2020)
6. Duan, S., He, R., Zhao, W.: Exploiting document level information to improve event detection via recurrent neural networks. In: Eighth International Joint Conference on Natural Language Processing (IJCNLP 2017), pp. 352–361. Asian Federation of Natural Language Processing (2017)
7. Feng, X., Huang, L., Tang, D., Ji, H., Qin, B., Liu, T.: A language-independent neural network for event detection. In: Proceedings of the 54th Annual Meeting of the Association for Computational Linguistics (Volume 2: Short Papers), vol. 2, pp. 66–71 (2016)
8. Hong, Y., Zhou, W., Zhang, J., Zhou, G., Zhu, Q.: Self-regulation: employing a generative adversarial network to improve event detection. In: Proceedings of the 56th Annual Meeting of the Association for Computational Linguistics (Volume 1: Long Papers), pp. 515–526 (2018)
9. Lample, G., Ballesteros, M., Subramanian, S., Kawakami, K., Dyer, C.: Neural architectures for named entity recognition. arXiv preprint arXiv:1603.01360 (2016)
10. Liu, J., Chen, Y., Liu, K., Zhao, J.: Event detection via gated multilingual attention mechanism. In: Thirty-second AAAI Conference on Artificial Intelligence (AAAI 2018) (2018)
11. Liu, S., Chen, Y., Liu, K., Zhao, J.: Exploiting argument information to improve event detection via supervised attention mechanisms. In: 55th Annual Meeting of the Association for Computational Linguistics (ACL 2017), pp. 1789–1798. Vancouver, Canada (2017)
12. Liu, X., Luo, Z., Huang, H.: Jointly multiple events extraction via attention-based graph information aggregation. arXiv preprint arXiv:1809.09078 (2018)
13. Lu, Y., Lin, H., Han, X., Sun, L.: Distilling discrimination and generalization knowledge for event detection via delta-representation learning. In: Proceedings of the 57th Annual Meeting of the Association for Computational Linguistics, pp. 4366–4376 (2019)

14. Ma, X., Hovy, E.: End-to-end sequence labeling via bi-directional LSTM-CNNS-CRF. arXiv preprint arXiv:1603.01354 (2016)
15. Nguyen, T.H., Cho, K., Grishman, R.: Joint event extraction via recurrent neural networks. In: Proceedings of NAACL-HLT, pp. 300–309 (2016)
16. Nguyen, T.H., Fu, L., Cho, K., Grishman, R.: A two-stage approach for extending event detection to new types via neural networks. ACL **2016**, 158 (2016)
17. Nguyen, T.H., Grishman, R.: Event detection and domain adaptation with convolutional neural networks. In: Proceedings of the 53rd Annual Meeting of the Association for Computational Linguistics and the 7th International Joint Conference on Natural Language Processing, pp. 365–371 (2015)
18. Nguyen, T.H., Grishman, R.: Graph convolutional networks with argument-aware pooling for event detection. In: Thirty-Second AAAI Conference on Artificial Intelligence (AAAI 2018) (2018)
19. Soares, L.B., FitzGerald, N., Ling, J., Kwiatkowski, T.: Matching the blanks: distributional similarity for relation learning. arXiv preprint arXiv:1906.03158 (2019)
20. Vaswani, A., et al.: Attention is all you need. In: Advances in Neural Information Processing Systems, pp. 5998–6008 (2017)
21. Wadden, D., Wennberg, U., Luan, Y., Hajishirzi, H.: Entity, relation, and event extraction with contextualized span representations. arXiv preprint arXiv:1909.03546 (2019)
22. Wang, X., Han, X., Liu, Z., Sun, M., Li, P.: Adversarial training for weakly supervised event detection. In: Proceedings of the 2019 Conference of the North American Chapter of the Association for Computational Linguistics: Human Language Technologies, Volume 1 (Long and Short Papers), pp. 998–1008 (2019)
23. Yang, S., Feng, D., Qiao, L., Kan, Z., Li, D.: Exploring pre-trained language models for event extraction and generation. In: Proceedings of the 57th Annual Meeting of the Association for Computational Linguistics, pp. 5284–5294 (2019)
24. Zhang, T., Ji, H., Sil, A.: Joint entity and event extraction with generative adversarial imitation learning. Data Intell. **1**(2), 99–120 (2019)
25. Zhao, Y., Jin, X., Wang, Y., Cheng, X.: Document embedding enhanced event detection with hierarchical and supervised attention. In: Proceedings of the 56th Annual Meeting of the Association for Computational Linguistics (Volume 2: Short Papers), pp. 414–419 (2018)

Simplified TinyBERT: Knowledge Distillation for Document Retrieval

Xuanang Chen[1,2(✉)], Ben He[1,2(✉)], Kai Hui[3], Le Sun[2], and Yingfei Sun[1(✉)]

[1] University of Chinese Academy of Sciences, Beijing, China
chenxuanang19@mails.ucas.ac.cn, {benhe,yfsun}@ucas.ac.cn
[2] Institute of Software, Chinese Academy of Sciences, Beijing, China
sunle@iscas.ac.cn
[3] Amazon Alexa, Berlin, Germany
kaihuibj@amazon.com

Abstract. Despite the effectiveness of utilizing the BERT model for document ranking, the high computational cost of such approaches limits their uses. To this end, this paper first empirically investigates the effectiveness of two knowledge distillation models on the document ranking task. In addition, on top of the recently proposed TinyBERT model, two simplifications are proposed. Evaluations on two different and widely-used benchmarks demonstrate that Simplified TinyBERT with the proposed simplifications not only boosts TinyBERT, but also significantly outperforms BERT-Base when providing 15× speedup.

Keywords: Document retrieval · BERT · Knowledge distillation

1 Introduction

Contextual pre-trained model, like BERT [3], demonstrates its effectiveness in ranking tasks [2,11,19]. However, the vast number of parameters in BERT make it expensive or even infeasible for serving [6,8], which is especially important when the model is used to re-rank thousands of search results. In the meantime, studies [7,13–18] have demonstrated that knowledge distillation (KD) can be used to learn smaller BERT models without compromising effectiveness too much, wherein a full-sized BERT model, like BERT-Base, is used as the teacher model and a small student model is trained to imitate it. More specifically, Tiny-BERT [7] is proposed to distill on both prediction layer and intermediate layers in a two-stage distillation method, and has achieved effectiveness that is close to the teacher model on multiple NLP tasks. However, it is unclear whether such distillation models are still effective on the document ranking task.

To bridge this gap, in this work, we first investigate the uses of the standard knowledge distillation model [5] and the more recent TinyBERT [7] on the document ranking task. In addition, we propose two simplifications for TinyBERT,

K. Hui—This work has been done before joining Amazon.

D. Hiemstra et al. (Eds.): ECIR 2021, LNCS 12657, pp. 241–248, 2021.
https://doi.org/10.1007/978-3-030-72240-1_21

hoping to further improve the effectiveness of the distilled ranking models. To this end, on the document ranking task in MS MARCO [10] and TREC 2019 DL Track [1], we demonstrate the potentials in employing knowledge distillation for document retrieval, and also confirm the superior effectiveness of the proposed Simplified TinyBERT which will be described in Sect. 3.

The contributions of this work are twofold. (1) To the best of our knowledge, this is the first effort to employ knowledge distillation for the document ranking task, by empirically investigating the effectiveness of standard knowledge distillation model [5] and TinyBERT [7] on two document ranking benchmarks; and, (2) Two simple but effective modifications have been proposed on top of TinyBERT. The student model distilled with the proposed Simplified TinyBERT not only can boost TinyBERT, but also significantly outperform BERT-Base when providing 15× speedup. The source code is available at https://github.com/cxa-unique/Simplified-TinyBERT.

2 Background

Passage-Level BERT-Based Document Re-ranking. Given a query and a document, the document is first split into overlapping passages, before a BERT model consumes the concatenation of query and passage through multiple transformer layers, and ultimately generates a score to indicate the relevance of the passage relative to the query. After that, the score of a document can be produced by its best passage (BERT-MaxP [2]), which is used to re-rank the documents.

Knowledge Distillation (KD). Due to the expensive computation cost of BERT during inference, some KD methods on BERT have been proposed, such as DistilBERT [13], BERT-PKD [14], TinyBERT [7], and MiniLM [18]. Early KD method [5] relies on the soft label from the teacher model, wherein a loss function is designed to make the student model directly simulate the output of the teacher model. In the meantime, the actual annotations are also considered in the loss function as in [5,14,16]. These two kinds of cross-entropy losses are coined as the soft loss, denoted as $\mathcal{L}_{soft}$, and the hard loss, denoted as $\mathcal{L}_{hard}$, respectively.

In **TinyBERT** [7], the pre-training and fine-tuning knowledge is distilled from a pre-trained BERT and the fine-tuned BERT on target tasks in the general stage and the task-specific stage, respectively. It employs three MSE losses to make the student model learn from three kinds of internal weights of the teacher model, namely, the attention weights, the hidden state weights, and the embedding weights in different layers, which are correspondingly denoted as $\mathcal{L}_{attn}$, $\mathcal{L}_{hidn}$ and $\mathcal{L}_{emb}$, in addition to $\mathcal{L}_{soft}$. The intermediate layers are distilled with $\mathcal{L}_{attn}$, $\mathcal{L}_{hidn}$ and $\mathcal{L}_{emb}$ in both stages, and the prediction layer is distilled with $\mathcal{L}_{soft}$ only in the task-specific stage.

3   Simplified TinyBERT for Ranking

In this Section, we propose two simplifications for the TinyBERT model, hoping to achieve better performance on the document ranking task.

3.1   Method

Merge Two Steps in the Task-Specific Stage into One Step. As described in Sect. 2, TinyBERT involves two stages, and there are two steps in the second stage, wherein the training process is time-consuming. Through our empirical investigations, however, we find that the two steps could be merged into one step by simply optimizing all losses at once as described in Eq. (1). This simplification not only brings down the training time, but also boosts the ranking performance as can be seen in Table 1. This implies that the student model could learn the prediction layer together with the intermediate layers more effectively. Actually, we also find that one could further simplify TinyBERT distillation process by merging two stages into one, namely, employing a pre-trained BERT model, if available, and using its first k layers to initialize the student model in place of the general distillation stage. For example, the student model coined as L6_H768 in Table 1 could also be distilled with only one stage by initializing the student model with the first six layers from BERT-Base, without compromising performance. We will leave further investigations on this part in future work.

$$\mathcal{L} = \mathcal{L}_{attn} + \mathcal{L}_{hidn} + \mathcal{L}_{emb} + \mathcal{L}_{soft} \tag{1}$$

Include Hard Label in the Loss Function. Inspired by existing models from [5,14,16], we conjecture that the hard labels could help to distinguish the relevant and non-relevant documents better. Therefore, we include the hard loss during distillation by adding it into Eq. (1), ending up with Eq. (2).

$$\mathcal{L}_h = \mathcal{L}_{attn} + \mathcal{L}_{hidn} + \mathcal{L}_{emb} + \mathcal{L}_{soft} + \mathcal{L}_{hard} \tag{2}$$

3.2   Implementation Details

Use BERT-Base as the Teacher Model. In BERT-PKD [14], it has been demonstrated that the uses of BERT-Base model are as effective as when using the three-times larger BERT-Large model. Thereby, we employ BERT-Base as the teacher model in this work, wherein the checkpoint which is trained on MS MARCO passage dataset from [11] is used to initialize the model as in [20]. The teacher model can be further fine-tuned on MS MARCO document dataset, but is omitted in our experiments, as both teacher models with or without the further fine-tuning step produce similar student models.

TinyBERT and Simplified TinyBERT. For the general distillation, we use 3.5G raw text from English Wikipedia, where the losses for distilling the intermediate layer, namely, $\mathcal{L}_{attn}$, $\mathcal{L}_{hidn}$, and $\mathcal{L}_{emb}$, are used. The hyper-parameter temperature T is fixed as 1 for both TinyBERT and the Simplified TinyBERT in the task-specific distillation stage, akin to the configuration in [7].

Table 1. The results for different distilled models. L and H refer to the number of layers and the dimension of hidden states, respectively. Statistical significance at p-value <0.01 (0.05) is marked with $T(t)$ and $B(b)$ for comparisons to TinyBERT and the teacher model BERT-Base (L12_H768), respectively. Note that MS MARCO Dev and TREC 2019 DL Test contain 4466 and 43 queries, respectively.

Model (Size)	MS MARCO Dev		TREC 2019 DL Test			FLOPs
	MRR	MRR@10	MRR	NDCG@10	MAP	(Speedup)
L12_H768 (109M)	0.3589	0.3523	0.9341	0.6644	0.2861	22.9G (1×)
L6_H768 (67M)						11.5G (2×)
Standard KD	0.3570^T	0.3498^T	0.9341	0.6408	0.2783	
TinyBERT	0.3711^B	0.3646^B	0.9380	0.6627	0.2821	
+ hard label	0.3767^{tB}	0.3701^{tB}	0.9380	0.6659	0.2777	
+ use one step	0.3701^B	0.3634^B	**0.9496**	0.6620	0.2843	
Simplified TinyBERT	$\mathbf{0.3908}^{TB}$	$\mathbf{0.3848}^{TB}$	**0.9496**	**0.6774**	**0.2847**	
L3_H384 (17M)						1.5G (15×)
Standard KD	0.3234^{TB}	0.3148^{TB}	0.9225	0.6042^B	0.2567^B	
TinyBERT	0.3527	0.3453	0.8973	0.6230^b	0.2755	
+ hard label	0.3544	0.3470	0.9263	0.6361^t	0.2721^B	
+ use one step	0.3630^T	0.3560^T	0.9263	0.6479^t	0.2776^b	
Simplified TinyBERT	$\mathbf{0.3683}^{Tb}$	$\mathbf{0.3614}^{Tb}$	**0.9554**	$\mathbf{0.6698}^T$	**0.2804**	

Training. The models are trained on up to four TITAN RTX 24G GPUs with Mixed Precision Training [9], using Adam optimizer with a weight decay of 0.01. In the general stage, we train for three epochs, setting learning rate 1e−6 and batch size 128. In the task-specific stage, we perform distillation up to two epochs. We train with batch size equaling to 128, and learning rate to 1e−6 for Standard KD and the second step of TinyBERT, meanwhile using 64 and 5e−5 for Simplified TinyBERT and the first step of TinyBERT. We do model selection according to MRR@10 on validation set, apart from the general stage and the first step in the task-specific stage of TinyBERT, for which the last model is chosen for further distillation.

4 Experiments

4.1 Experimental Setup

Dataset. According to our experiments, a relatively huge amount of training data is required to distill a small but effective BERT re-ranker. Meanwhile, recent work [4] also demonstrates that about 5-10M training examples are required to distill a model that is comparable to BERT-Base on the passage ranking task. Thus, we employ MS MARCO document ranking dataset due to its largest available number of training samples, which contains 367,013 training queries, 5,193 development (dev) queries and 5,793 test queries (for leaderboard). In addition, TREC 2019 DL Track [1] provides 43 test queries with more annotated relevant documents (compared with MS MARCO) based on the manual judgments from NIST assessors. We report our experiment results on the above two benchmarks.

Data Preprocessing. For training, after splitting the documents, we use the teacher model to filter passages from relevant documents, and reserve the five top-ranked passages as positive samples. Meanwhile, a negative passage is randomly sampled from irrelevant documents for every positive sample, to balance the positive and negative samples. Thereby, the actual training set includes about 3.3M query-passage pairs. For evaluation, due to the lack of annotations for test queries, we randomly reserve 727 dev queries for validation, and use the remaining 4,466 dev queries as our test set (but also denoted as MS MARCO Dev). The max length of the input tokens in BERT re-ranker is set as 256. Statistical significance in terms of paired two-tailed t-test is reported.

Models in Comparison. The distilled models are compared under two configurations, namely, distilling BERT-Base (L12_H768) into a medium-size model (L6_H768) which provides 2× speedup relative to BERT-Base; and into a even smaller model (L3_H384) with only three layers, which provides 15× speedup. Several distillation models are included in Table 1 for comparisons. **Standard KD** distills the teacher model only using the prediction layer, namely, training the student model with $\alpha \mathcal{L}_{soft} + (1 - \alpha)\mathcal{L}_{hard}$. We perform grid search on validation set over temperature $T = \{1, 5, 10\}$ and $\alpha = \{0.2, 0.5, 0.7\}$ on a parameters-fixed student model as in [14]; **TinyBERT** distills the teacher model following a two-stage method as in [7], **Simplified TinyBERT** is the modified TinyBERT as described in Sect. 3. In addition, + **hard label** and + **use one step** in Table 1 indicate the results when applying one simplification on top of TinyBERT.

4.2   Results

In this section, we discuss the re-ranking performance of Standard KD, Tiny-BERT, and our Simplified TinyBERT.

Distilled Models Perform Well on Document Ranking Task. We first examine the performance of Standard KD and TinyBERT. For L6_H768, from Table 1, it can be seen that TinyBERT outperforms BERT-Base (L12_H768) significantly on our MS MARCO Dev set, and behaves on par with BERT-Base on TREC 2019 DL Test set, when providing 2× speedup. For L3_H384, with 15× speedup, TinyBERT performs significantly worse than BERT-Base on shallow pool, and is comparable with BERT-Base on deep pool. Compared with Standard KD, TinyBERT improves almost all metrics consistently, highlighting the strength of the distillation framework in TinyBERT. Overall, according to our experiments, we confirm that both TinyBERT and Standard KD could dramatically reduce the model size meanwhile preserving most of the effectiveness.

Simplified TinyBERT Provides Better Re-ranking Effectiveness and 15× Speedup at the Same Time. We further examine the performance of the proposed Simplified TinyBERT, by comparing it with BERT-Base and Tiny-BERT. From Table 1, on our MS MARCO Dev set, our Simplified TinyBERT could consistently outperform both BERT-Base and TinyBERT significantly under both model configurations. On TREC 2019 DL Test set, when distilling a medium-size student model (L6_H768), Simplified TinyBERT performs on par with BERT-Base and TinyBERT; meanwhile, it outperforms TinyBERT on shallow pool in terms of NDCG@10, whereas TinyBERT performs significantly worse than BERT-Base, when the student model is very small (L3_H384).

Table 2. Re-ranking the documents at different depth using distilled L3_H384 models. The MRR@10 on our MS MARCO Dev set (4466 queries) is reported. The superscripts for statistical significance test are the same as in Table 1.

Depth	L12_H768	TinyBERT	Simplified TinyBERT
10	0.2896	0.2892	0.2970^{Tb}
20	0.3195	0.3188	0.3288^{TB}
50	0.3395	0.3359	0.3509^{TB}
100	0.3523	0.3453	0.3614^{Tb}

Table 3. Training time of the second stage in TinyBERT and Simplified TinyBERT.

Model	TinyBERT (two steps)	Simplified TinyBERT (one step)
L6_H768	29.95 h (2.08×)	14.37 h (1×)
L6_H384	20.45 h (1.81×)	11.30 h (1×)
L3_H768	18.93 h (1.88×)	10.05 h (1×)
L3_H384	15.87 h (1.72×)	9.22 h (1×)

Robustness at Different Re-ranking Depth. We also examine the effectiveness of the 3-layer student model (L3_H384) at different re-ranking depth, namely, top-10, 20, 50, and 100 documents. As shown in Table 2, the original TinyBERT behaves on par with BERT-Base, whereas our Simplified TinyBERT can outperform BERT-Base significantly at all re-ranking depth. This further confirms the superior effectiveness of the proposed simplifications.

Ablation Study on Two Simplifications. As shown in Table 1, both the simplifications could boost the metric scores, meanwhile two simplifications together gain even higher ranking performance. Thus, training using Eq. (2) could bring significant boost, wherein both simplifications contribute.

Simplified TinyBERT can be Trained Faster. As described in Sect. 2, the training of TinyBERT is decomposed into two stages, and the second stage further includes two steps. In our Simplified TinyBERT, as described in Sect. 3, we merge the two steps in the second stage. The training time of the second stage in the original TinyBERT and our Simplified TinyBERT is summarized in Table 3, where the proposed one-step simplification could save around 42–52% training time. This is important when training on large datasets, like MS MARCO dataset used in this work.

5 Conclusion

In this paper, we demonstrated that the BERT-Base re-ranker model can be compressed using knowledge distillation technique, without compromising too much ranking effectiveness. Furthermore, a simplified TinyBERT is proposed, the student model from whom could outperform the more expensive teacher model significantly. For the future work, we would like to study the distillation of more advanced ranking models like T5 [12] using the proposed knowledge distillation method.

References

1. Craswell, N., Mitra, B., Yilmaz, E., Campos, D., Voorhees, E.M.: Overview of the TREC 2019 deep learning track. CoRR abs/2003.07820 (2020)
2. Dai, Z., Callan, J.: Deeper text understanding for IR with contextual neural language modeling. In: SIGIR, pp. 985–988. ACM (2019). https://doi.org/10.1145/3331184.3331303
3. Devlin, J., Chang, M., Lee, K., Toutanova, K.: BERT: pre-training of deep bidirectional transformers for language understanding. In: NAACL-HLT (1), pp. 4171–4186. Association for Computational Linguistics (2019). https://doi.org/10.18653/v1/n19-1423
4. Gao, L., Dai, Z., Callan, J.: Understanding BERT rankers under distillation. In: ICTIR, pp. 149–152. ACM (2020)
5. Hinton, G.E., Vinyals, O., Dean, J.: Distilling the knowledge in a neural network. CoRR abs/1503.02531 (2015)
6. Hofstätter, S., Hanbury, A.: Let's measure run time! extending the IR replicability infrastructure to include performance aspects. In: OSIRRC@SIGIR. CEUR Workshop Proceedings, vol. 2409, pp. 12–16. CEUR-WS.org (2019)
7. Jiao, X., et al.: TinyBERT: distilling BERT for natural language understanding. In: EMNLP (Findings), pp. 4163–4174. Association for Computational Linguistics (2020). https://doi.org/10.18653/v1/2020.findings-emnlp.372
8. MacAvaney, S., Yates, A., Cohan, A., Goharian, N.: CEDR: contextualized embeddings for document ranking. In: SIGIR, pp. 1101–1104. ACM (2019). https://doi.org/10.1145/3331184.3331317
9. Micikevicius, P., et al.: Mixed precision training. In: ICLR (Poster). OpenReview.net (2018)
10. Nguyen, T., Rosenberg, M., Song, X., Gao, J., Tiwary, S., Majumder, R., Deng, L.: MS MARCO: a human generated machine reading comprehension dataset. In: CoCo@NIPS. CEUR Workshop Proceedings, vol. 1773. CEUR-WS.org (2016)

11. Nogueira, R., Cho, K.: Passage re-ranking with BERT. CoRR abs/1901.04085 (2019)
12. Nogueira, R., Jiang, Z., Pradeep, R., Lin, J.: Document ranking with a pretrained sequence-to-sequence model. In: EMNLP (Findings), pp. 708–718. Association for Computational Linguistics (2020). https://doi.org/10.18653/v1/2020.findings-emnlp.63
13. Sanh, V., Debut, L., Chaumond, J., Wolf, T.: Distilbert, a distilled version of BERT: smaller, faster, cheaper and lighter. CoRR abs/1910.01108 (2019)
14. Sun, S., Cheng, Y., Gan, Z., Liu, J.: Patient knowledge distillation for BERT model compression. In: EMNLP/IJCNLP (1), pp. 4322–4331. Association for Computational Linguistics (2019). https://doi.org/10.18653/v1/D19-1441
15. Sun, Z., Yu, H., Song, X., Liu, R., Yang, Y., Zhou, D.: MobileBERT: a compact task-agnostic BERT for resource-limited devices. In: ACL, pp. 2158–2170. Association for Computational Linguistics (2020). https://doi.org/10.18653/v1/2020.acl-main.195
16. Tang, R., Lu, Y., Liu, L., Mou, L., Vechtomova, O., Lin, J.: Distilling task-specific knowledge from BERT into simple neural networks. CoRR abs/1903.12136 (2019)
17. Turc, I., Chang, M., Lee, K., Toutanova, K.: Well-read students learn better: the impact of student initialization on knowledge distillation. CoRR abs/1908.08962 (2019)
18. Wang, W., Wei, F., Dong, L., Bao, H., Yang, N., Zhou, M.: MiniLM: deep self-attention distillation for task-agnostic compression of pre-trained transformers. In: NeurIPS (2020)
19. Yang, W., Zhang, H., Lin, J.: Simple applications of BERT for ad hoc document retrieval. CoRR abs/1903.10972 (2019)
20. Yilmaz, Z.A., Wang, S., Yang, W., Zhang, H., Lin, J.: Applying BERT to document retrieval with birch. In: EMNLP/IJCNLP (3), pp. 19–24. Association for Computational Linguistics (2019). https://doi.org/10.18653/v1/D19-3004

Improving Cold-Start Recommendation via Multi-prior Meta-learning

Zhengyu Chen[1,2(✉)], Donglin Wang[2], and Shiqian Yin[3]

[1] Zhejiang University, Hangzhou, China
[2] School of Engineering, Westlake University, Hangzhou, China
{chenzhengyu,wangdonglin}@westlake.edu.cn
[3] Cornell University, Ithaca, USA

Abstract. Optimization-based meta-learning has been applied in cold-start recommendations, where a good initialization of meta learner is obtained from past experiences and then reused for fast adaptation to new tasks. However, when dealing with various users with diverse preferences, meta-learning with a single prior might fail in cold-start recommendations due to its insufficient capability for adaptation. To address this problem, a multi-prior meta-learning (MPML) approach is proposed in this paper and applied in cold-start recommendations. More concretely, we integrate a novel accuracy-based task clustering scheme with double gradient to learn multiple priors. Experiments demonstrate the effectiveness of MPML.

1 Introduction

Recommender systems commonly deal with a variety of distinct datasets that contain highly personalized historical data of users. Collaborative filtering based systems estimate user response by collecting the preference information of numerous users [1,16,17]. This kind of prediction for a target user is built upon the existing rating of other users. However, such recommendation is incapable of dealing with cold-start scenarios where the information of user-item interaction is lacking.

Content-based systems are introduced [10] to solve the cold-start problem. These systems utilize user profile information (e.g. gender, nationality and religion) and the contents of items to make recommendations. Each item is recommended to new users who own similar profile information [2,8]. Nevertheless, collecting personal profile information is difficult due to privacy issues [18]. To alleviate this cold-start problem, many systems take advantage of evidence candidates for recommendations [12], where only a few items and corresponding ratings are required to achieve fast adaptation of the recommendation model. Recently, deep learning methods are also applied to make recommendations in this scenario to improve performance [3,8]. However, the cold-start problem still remains unsolved for new users who have rated on only a few items.

Optimization-based meta-learning algorithms learn to efficiently solve new tasks by exploiting prior experiences [7], which have been recently considered

© Springer Nature Switzerland AG 2021
D. Hiemstra et al. (Eds.): ECIR 2021, LNCS 12657, pp. 249–256, 2021.
https://doi.org/10.1007/978-3-030-72240-1_22

in recommendations to overcome cold-start problem [5,12,14]. As the first try, Vartak et al. [14] propose a model-agnostic meta-learning (MAML) based recommendation for binary-item cases, which results in comparatively large limitations in real applications. Du et al. [5] combine scenario-specific learning with MAML to mitigate the cold-start problem in online recommendations. Once more, by utilizing MAML as a meta learner to estimate the preference of cold-start users, Lee et al. [12] propose the MeLU method, which can rapidly predict a new user's preference with a few consumed items. All these works above provide a single prior of meta learner for cold-start recommendations.

Although a single common prior of meta learner is good for tasks that are drawn from a fixed distribution, it is not sufficient to attain fast learning for a wide range of potential tasks that require multi-modality [15]. Specifically, in recommender systems, owing to the difference of users' nationality, religion, education, past experience, location and so on, a single model might not be sufficient to characterize diverse preferences of different users [4,11,13]. Koren [11] proposes a combined model, which estimates ratings based on the combination of both global and local models. Lee et al. [13] propose a method that calculates the rating by a weighted combination of multiple estimated local models. Christakopoulou et al. [4] propose to assign the users into different subsets based on their rating patterns and then estimate specific local models using the subset of users. Inspired by these works above, *we aim to learn multiple priors in meta learner to support multi-modality recommendation tasks*, where each prior corresponds to a single but different recommendation model for each subset of users.

Only one existing work [15] considers multi-modality meta learning but never deals with the recommendation problem. Differently, we propose a multi-prior meta-learning (MPML) approach for cold-start recommendations by integrating a novel task-clustering scheme with MAML. Without task-identity information, the challenge is how to identify a category of tasks and how to associate it with a specific prior. To address this, we propose an accuracy-based task clustering scheme that estimates the accuracy of a task using each prior. The category to which a task belongs is labelled by the prior with the highest accuracy. After task clustering, meta update using double-gradient descent [7], is applied to learn multiple priors. The MPML *alternately* clusters tasks and updates each prior in the meta-learner.

Contribution: Our primary contribution is a novel MPML approach with multiple priors for cold-start recommendations, where we propose an effective task clustering scheme by measuring the accuracy. Experiments demonstrate the effectiveness of MPML for fast adaptation to new tasks in wide-range domains.

2 Methodology

2.1 Framework of MPML

In meta-learning based recommendations, the model takes user content and item content as input, and generates the preference of users for items as output [12]. In this paper, MPML can *generate multiple priors in a single meta-learner*. Meta-learner M trains recommendation models so that each model can adapt quickly to new users in a single domain using only small amounts of data. Denote by $M(\theta)$ meta-learner with an prior parameters θ. Suppose that meta-learner learns K priors θ_k, $k = 1, 2, \cdots, K$, the recommendation model associated with $M(\theta_k)$ is denoted by f_{θ_k}.

Figure 1 shows MPML framework providing a general meta-learning solution for cold-start recommendations, independent of specific model and data format. As seen, MPML consists of two modules: task clustering and meta update. In *task clustering*, a task consists of data from a user, which is models' input. The resulting accuracy is taken as a measure for whether the task should be assigned to a category represented by a prior. Finally, each task is labelled by the prior with the highest accuracy. In *meta update*, a double-gradient descent method, as in MAML [7], is considered for the update of each prior by sampling the corresponding category of tasks.

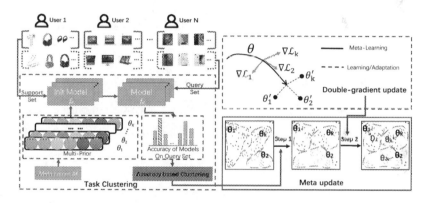

Fig. 1. Framework of MPML.

2.2 Accuracy-Based Task Clustering

The optimization-based meta-learner is usually trained by sampling tasks from the whole dataset to learn a common prior [7]. However, considering tasks mixed from multiple different domains, sampling the whole dataset cannot generate a good prior. It can only realize fast adaptation for close tasks rather than all tasks.

Accuracy-based task clustering is essentially a direct and but effective scheme to identify tasks in each of different domains. MPML attempts to learn multiple priors by sampling tasks in diverse distributions. Specifically, the task clustering module takes each task T_i as input to learn the most suitable prior θ^*. Denote by $T_{sup}^{(i)}$ the support set and $T_{que}^{(i)}$ the query set in T_i.

First, the support set $T_{sup}^{(i)}$ of task T_i is input into every recommendation model f_{θ_k}, $k = 1, 2, \cdots, K$, which is optimized by minimizing the loss of

$f_{\theta_k}\left(T_{sup}^{(i)}\right)$. Secondly, after fast adaptation using one or a few gradient updates, the model f_{θ_k} becomes $f_{\theta'_k}$ to fit query set $T_{que}^{(i)}$. Thirdly, the query set $T_{que}^{(i)}$ of task T_i is input into every recommendation model $f_{\theta'_k}$ for evaluation. We calculate the accuracy of every recommendation model $f_{\theta'_k}\left(T_{que}^{(i)}\right)$, where the accuracy is measured by the following MSE loss: $\mathcal{L}_{T_{que}^{(i)}}\left(f_{\theta'_k}\left(T_{que}^{(i)}\right)\right) = \sum (y_{i,j} - \hat{y}_{i,j})^2$, where $y_{i,j}$ is the preference of user i for item j, and $\hat{y}_{ij}$ is the preference predicted by recommendation model $f_{\theta'_k}\left(T_{que}^{(i)}\right)$. Finally, the task T_i is assigned to the cluster represented by prior θ^* that generates the highest accuracy :
$\theta^* = \arg\min_{\theta_k} \mathcal{L}_{T_{que}^{(i)}}\left(f_{\theta'_k}\left(T_{que}^{(i)}\right)\right).$

In summary, the procedure is represented as $\theta^* = Cluster\,(T_i, f_{\theta_k})$.

2.3   Meta Update

In training phase, MPML is optimized by a double-gradient descent method [7]. In test phase, or cold-start recommendation phase, MPML selects the learned prior to quickly adapt to individual users. The MPML is summarized in **Algorithm 1**.

Training Phase. The meta-training process proceeds in an episodic manner. In each episode, a batch of users are sampled from a large training population (line 5 in **Algorithm 1**). After performing task clustering (line 7), the prior θ^* is updated by minimizing the loss $\mathcal{L}(\cdot)$ using the support set $T_{sup}^{(i)}$. So we have

$$\arg\min_{\theta^*} \sum_{i=1}^{S} \mathcal{L}_{T_{sup}^{(i)}}\left(f_{(\theta^*)'}\right) = \sum_{i=1}^{S} \mathcal{L}_{T_{sup}^{(i)}}\left(f_{\theta^* - \alpha\nabla_{\theta^*}\mathcal{L}_{T_{sup}^{(i)}}(f_{\theta^*})}\right), \quad (1)$$

where, α is a step size, S is the number of sampled tasks labelled by θ^*, $(\theta^*)' \triangleq \theta^* - \alpha\nabla_{\theta^*}\mathcal{L}_{T_{sup}^{(i)}}(f_{\theta^*})$ and the inner gradient $\nabla_{\theta^*}\mathcal{L}(\cdot)$ is calculated based on a small mini-batch of data from $T_{sup}^{(i)}$.

Then, stochastic gradient descent is used to solve the across-task optimization [7]. To update each meta parameter θ_k, $k = 1, 2, \cdots, K$, we firstly find all tasks labelled by θ_k and then aggregate their query sets as $T_{que,k}$. The prior θ_k is updated using the aggregated query set $T_{que,k}$ as follows

$$\theta_k \leftarrow \theta_k - \beta \sum \nabla_{\theta_k}\mathcal{L}_{T_{que,k}}\left(f_{\theta'_k}\right), \quad (2)$$

where β is the meta step size.

Test Phase. Identical task clustering procedure is used for both meta-training and meta-test. The only difference is that in test phase task clustering C takes as input Sup_s and Sup_q, where Sup_s and Sup_q are splits from the support test set because the query test set remains unknown for evaluation.

In test phase, firstly, tasks are clustered using Sup_s and Sup_q, and a good prior θ_m is selected for the test task. Then, for test task $\mathcal{T}_t$, the model f_{θ_m} quickly adapts to the objective of support set $\mathcal{T}_{sup,t}$ using Eq. (1). Finally, using the query set $\mathcal{T}_{que,t}$, the preference of users for items are calculated by the model $f_{\theta'_m}$.

2.4   Complexity Analysis

The computational complexity of MAML is known as $O(H * N)$ [6], where H is the number of iterations and N is the number of tasks. On this basis, the complexity of our MPML is obtained as $O(I * H * N)$, where I is the number of clusters after accuracy-based task clustering. Fortunately, the number of clusters I is usually comparatively small so MPML approximately lies in the same level as MAML in terms of complexity.

3   Experiment

3.1   Experimental Setup

Datasets. We evaluate our method on two benchmark datasets: **MovieLens** [9] and **Bookcrossing** [19] that are frequently used for recommendations. Both datasets provide basic side information, such as user's age and item's publication year. Similar to [12], we divide users into two groups (existing/new) to evaluate the performance under user-cold-start condition. The same grouping is used for items.

Baselines. In order to evaluate the performance, we consider the following baselines in our experiments: **Wide & Deep (WD)** [3]: predicts whether a user likes an item. We use it as a regression model to estimate preferences; **DeepFM** [8]: combines deep learning and factorization machines to learn features in a new network architecture; **MeLU** [12]: applies MAML in the user preference estimator to predict cold-start user preference. Please be noted that we do not consider collaborative-filtering based approaches as baselines because they fail to estimate preferences for new users or new items.

3.2   Experimental Results

Performance Comparison: We conducted experiments on three scenarios: **regular recommendation** with existing items and users, **new-user recommendation** with existing items, and **new-item recommendation** with existing users, and compare our MPML with baselines. Table 1 shows RMSE, MAE and NDCG@10, which demonstrates that MPML achieves the best performance for all cases.

Visualization of Task Clustering: We use MovieLens to show the effect of task clustering in MPML. As observed, four categories of tasks can be learned

Table 1. Recommendation results.

Type	Method	MovieLens			Bookcrossing		
		MAE	RMSE	NDCG	MAE	RMSE	NDCG
Recommendation of existing items for existing users	WD	0.7206	0.9107	0.4577	0.9976	1.3904	0.4195
	DeepFM	0.7244	0.9152	0.4592	0.9894	1.3824	0.4177
	MeLU	0.7137	0.9082	0.4654	0.9807	1.3624	0.4288
	MPML	**0.7068**	**0.8953**	**0.4759**	**0.9752**	**1.2997**	**0.4357**
Recommendation of existing items for new users	WD	0.9385	1.1520	0.4252	1.3863	1.7623	0.3996
	DeepFM	0.9530	1.1666	0.4217	1.3824	1.7673	0.3916
	MeLU	0.9080	1.0767	0.4357	1.4663	1.6352	0.4011
	MPML	**0.8643**	**1.0654**	**0.4476**	**1.3727**	**1.5872**	**0.4168**
Recommendation of new items for existing users	WD	0.9515	1.1720	0.3796	1.5440	1.9438	0.3878
	DeepFM	0.9497	1.1723	0.3726	1.5464	1.9438	0.3807
	MeLU	0.9275	1.1006	0.3878	1.5303	1.7273	0.3923
	MPML	**0.8758**	**1.0307**	**0.3988**	**1.4538**	**1.6645**	**0.4017**

in MPML, denoted as *cluster k*, $k = 1, 2, 3, 4$. For fair comparison, we consider the same categories of tasks for MeLU. MeLU generates a single prior for four categories of tasks while MPML learns four different priors for each of them. Figure 2 show the t-SNE visualization of the $(\theta^*)'$ in Eq. (1). Compared with MeLU, the results indicate that our task clustering module are able to effectively identify the tasks in different clusters.

Ablation Study: In order to further study how MPML improves performance for cold-start recommendations, MPML without task clustering (MPML_w/o_TC) is evaluated in terms of MAE. Its performance is shown in Fig. 3 and compared to MPML.

Similar to *Visualization of Task Clustering*, four categories of tasks can be learned in MPML. For fair comparison, we consider four identical categories for MPML_w/o_TC. MPML_w/o_TC generates a single prior for all four categories while MPML learns four different priors for each of them. It is observed from Fig. 3 that MPML outperforms MPML_w/o_TC for all clusters, where we achieve the most substantial improvement on *cluster* 2. The reason might be that tasks in *cluster* 2 are not close to the common prior in MPML_w/o_TC while MPML can provide a customized prior for *cluster* 2 so that fast adaptation is achieved.

Sensitivity on Number of priors k: Figure 4 shows how the number of priors affects the performance on two datasets. It is observed that the best performance on MovieLens is achieved at $k = 4$, indicating that MovieLens can be thought of as a dataset containing 4 different domains. Similarly, Bookcrossing dataset can be thought of as a dataset containing 2 different domains so the best performance is achieved at $k = 2$. With k deviating from the best value above, the performance drops increasingly on both datasets.

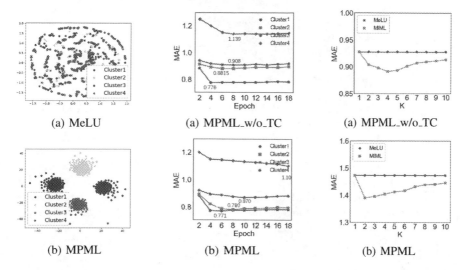

(a) MeLU

(a) MPML_w/o_TC

(a) MPML_w/o_TC

(b) MPML

(b) MPML

(b) MPML

Fig. 2. t-SNE of clustering

Fig. 3. Ablation study

Fig. 4. Number of priors

4 Conclusion

MPML is proposed to learn multiple priors and applied in cold-start recommendations. Experiments show that our proposed MPML and task clustering scheme do improve the performance of recommendations, in comparison to state-of-the-art baselines.

References

1. Chen, Z., Gai, S., Wang, D.: Deep tensor factorization for multi-criteria recommender systems. In: 2019 IEEE International Conference on Big Data (Big Data), Los Angeles, CA, USA, December 9–12, 2019, pp. 1046–1051 (2019)
2. Chen, Z., Xu, Z., Wang, D.: Deep transfer tensor decomposition with orthogonal constraint for recommender systems. In: The Thirty-Fifth AAAI Conference on Artificial Intelligence, AAAI 2021 (2021)
3. Cheng, H.T., et al.: Wide & deep learning for recommender systems. In: Proceedings of the 1st Workshop on Deep Learning for Recommender Systems, pp. 7–10. ACM (2016)
4. Christakopoulou, E., Karypis, G.: Local latent space models for top-n recommendation. In: 24th ACM SIGKDD, pp. 1235–1243 (2018)
5. Du, Z., Wang, X., Yang, H., Zhou, J., Tang, J.: Sequential scenario-specific meta learner for online recommendation. In: Proceedings of the 25th ACM SIGKDD, pp. 2895–2904 (2019)
6. Fallah, A., Mokhtari, A., Ozdaglar, A.: On the convergence theory of gradient-based model-agnostic meta-learning algorithms. arXiv preprint arXiv:1908.10400 (2019)

7. Finn, C., Abbeel, P., Levine, S.: Model-agnostic meta-learning for fast adaptation of deep networks. In: 34th ICML (2017)

8. Guo, H., Tang, R., Ye, Y., Li, Z., He, X.: DeepFM: a factorization-machine based neural network for CTR prediction. In: 26th IJCAI, pp. 1725–1731 (2017)

9. Harper, F.M., Konstan, J.A.: The MovieLens datasets: history and context. ACM TIIS **5**(4), 1–19 (2015)

10. Hu, L., Jian, S., Cao, L., Gu, Z., Chen, Q., Amirbekyan, A.: Hers: modeling influential contexts with heterogeneous relations for sparse and cold-start recommendation. In: Proceedings of the AAAI Conference on Artificial Intelligence, vol. 33, pp. 3830–3837 (2019)

11. Koren, Y.: Factorization meets the neighborhood: a multifaceted collaborative filtering model. In: Proceedings of the 14th ACM SIGKDD, pp. 426–434 (2008)

12. Lee, H., Im, J., Jang, S., Cho, H., Chung, S.: MeLU: meta-learned user preference estimator for cold-start recommendation. In: 25th ACM SIGKDD 2019, Anchorage, AK, USA, August 4–8, 2019, pp. 1073–1082 (2019)

13. Lee, J., Bengio, S., Kim, S., Lebanon, G., Singer, Y.: Local collaborative ranking. In: Proceedings of the 23rd WWW, pp. 85–96 (2014)

14. Vartak, M., Thiagarajan, A., Miranda, C., Bratman, J., Larochelle, H.: A meta-learning perspective on cold-start recommendations for items. In: NeurIPS, 4–9 December 2017, Long Beach, CA, USA, pp. 6904–6914 (2017)

15. Vuorio, R., Sun, S.H., Hu, H., Lim, J.J.: Multimodal model-agnostic meta-learning via task-aware modulation. In: NeurIPS, pp. 1–12 (2019)

16. Xiao, T., Liang, S., Meng, Z.: Hierarchical neural variational model for personalized sequential recommendation. In: The World Wide Web Conference, WWW 2019, San Francisco, CA, USA, May 13–17, 2019, pp. 3377–3383 (2019)

17. Xiao, T., Liang, S., Shen, W., Meng, Z.: Bayesian deep collaborative matrix factorization. In: The Thirty-Third AAAI Conference on Artificial Intelligence, AAAI 2019, The Thirty-First Innovative Applications of Artificial Intelligence Conference, IAAI 2019, The Ninth AAAI Symposium on Educational Advances in Artificial Intelligence, EAAI 2019, Honolulu, Hawaii, USA, January 27–February 1, 2019, pp. 5474–5481 (2019)

18. Yargic, A., Bilge, A.: Privacy risks for multi-criteria collaborative filtering systems. In: 2017 26th ICCCN, pp. 1–6. IEEE (2017)

19. Ziegler, C.N., McNee, S.M., Konstan, J.A., Lausen, G.: Improving recommendation lists through topic diversification. In: Proceedings of the 14th WWW, pp. 22–32. ACM (2005)

A White Box Analysis of ColBERT

Thibault Formal[1,2(✉)], Benjamin Piwowarski[1], and Stéphane Clinchant[2]

[1] LIP6, Sorbonne Université, 75005 Paris, France
benjamin.piwowarski@lip6.fr
[2] Naver Labs Europe, Meylan, France
{thibault.formal,stephane.clinchant}@naverlabs.com

Abstract. Transformer-based models are nowadays state-of-the-art in adhoc Information Retrieval, but their behavior are far from being understood. Recent work has claimed that BERT does not satisfy the classical IR axioms. However, we propose to dissect the matching process of ColBERT, through the analysis of term importance and exact/soft matching patterns. Even if the traditional axioms are not formally verified, our analysis reveals that ColBERT (i) is able to capture a notion of term importance; (ii) relies on exact matches for important terms.

Keywords: Information retrieval · Term matching · Transformer · BERT

1 Introduction

Over the last two years, Natural Language Processing has been shaken by the release of large pre-trained language models based on self-attention, like BERT [4]. Ranking models based on BERT are currently state-of-the-art in adhoc IR, ranking first on leaderboards[1] of the MSMARCO passage and document (re-)ranking tasks by a large margin [11], as well as on more standard IR datasets such as Robust04 [3,10,12]. It is thus interesting to understand better what is happening inside those models, and what phenomena are captured. Some works have been conducted in this direction [2,13], but focused on whether IR axioms are respected – or not – by neural and transformer-based models. In [2], BERT has been shown to not fully respect axioms that have proved to be important for standard IR models, such as the axiom stating that words occurring in more documents are less important (IDF effect). [9] extended the diagnosis to properties like word order or fluency. Instead of investigating whether these models behave like standard ones, we make a step towards understanding *how* they manage to improve over traditional models through their specific matching process.

There exists a wide variety of BERT-based ranking models, as summarized in the recent overview [8]. Canonical BERT models are difficult to analyse because they require a thorough analysis of attention mechanisms, which is a complex

---

[1] https://microsoft.github.io/msmarco/.

© Springer Nature Switzerland AG 2021
D. Hiemstra et al. (Eds.): ECIR 2021, LNCS 12657, pp. 257–263, 2021.
https://doi.org/10.1007/978-3-030-72240-1_23

task [1]. We rather choose to focus on contextual interaction models [6,7,10], where query and document are encoded *independently*. Among such models, ColBERT [7] exhibits the best trade-off between effectiveness and efficiency, with performance on par with standard BERT, suggesting that the power of these models comes from learning rich contextual representations, rather than modeling complex matching patterns. Moreover, the structure of ColBERT (sum over query terms of some similarity scores) is similar to standard IR models like BM25, and makes the analysis easier, as the contribution for each term is explicit.

In this paper, we hence focus on ColBERT, and look at two research questions. In Sect. 3, we investigate the link between term importance as computed by standard IR models, and the one computed by (Col)BERT. In Sect. 4, we look at how (Col)BERT is dealing with exact and soft matches as this is known to be critical for IR systems.

2   Experimental Setting

Dataset. For our analysis, we use the passage retrieval tasks from TREC-DL 2019 and 2020 [15] (400 queries in total). We consider a re-ranking setting, where for a given query q, the model needs to re-rank a set of documents S_q selected by a first stage ranker. Following the MSMARCO setting, we consider candidates from BM25, and $|S_q| \leq 1000$. In order to study the model properties, we are interested in *how it attributes scores to each query token, for documents in S_q*.

ColBERT. We now introduce the variant of ColBERT [7] we used to simplify the analysis – we checked each time that the drop in performance was minor. In particular, we did not include query/document specific tokens, since they could bias the term representations. Second, while query augmentation has been shown to be beneficial in [5,7], we omit this component to avoid the analysis of the induced implicit query expansion mechanism. We however keep the compression layer, that projects token representations from the BERT space ($d = 768$) to the ColBERT space ($d = 128$). By fine-tuning our model in a similar fashion to [7], we obtain a MRR@10 of 0.343 on MSMARCO dev set (versus 0.349). This shows that the above simplifications are negligible performance-wise, and would not invalidate our analysis. In order to understand what is learned during training, we also consider a non fine-tuned version of the model (without compression layer), that relies on the output of a pre-trained BERT model.

The formal definition of ColBERT, given the BERT embeddings $E_q = (E_{q_i})_i$ for the query q (after WordPiece tokenization) and $E_d = (E_{d_j})_j$ for the document d, is given by the following relevance score:

$$s(q,d) = \sum_{i \in q} \max_{j \in d} \cos(E_{q_i}, E_{d_j}) = \sum_{i \in q} \max_{j \in d} C_{ij} = \sum_{i \in q} C_{id}^{\star} \tag{1}$$

In the following, we say that *a query token i matches the document token j^** if $C_{ij^*} = C_{id}^{\star}$. We denote this token j^* by $d_i^{\star}$.

3   ColBERT Term Importance

Our first research question focuses on comparing term importance in standard IR models (e.g. BM25) with term importance as determined by ColBERT. With respect to the former, given that documents are small passages, term frequency is close to 1 for most terms ($\mathrm{avg}(tf) \approx 1.1$). Moreover, passage length does not vary much, and is caped at 512 tokens. Hence, we can reasonably assume that a term BM25 score roughly corresponds to its IDF – this might not be true for terms with low IDF, but it is a good enough approximation for other terms.

For ColBERT, it is difficult to measure the importance of a term, as it depends on both document and query contexts. We hence resort to an indirect mean, by measuring the correlation between the original ColBERT ranking and the ranking obtained when we remove from the sum in Eq. (1) all the *contributions* of subwords that compose the corresponding term. Another option would be to directly mask the input term, but we would loose the query structure. Finally, to compare rankings, we use AP-correlation[2] τ_{AP} [16], which is akin to Kendall rank correlation, but gives more importance to the top of the ranking. Values close to 1 indicate a strong correlation, meaning that the two rankings are similar, implying a low contribution of the term in the ranking process. Note that such measure of importance is query dependent: when the term appears in several queries, we consider the average as a final measure of importance.

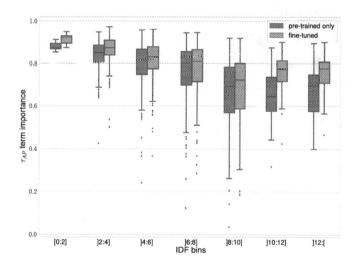

Fig. 1. ColBERT term importance (as computed using τ_{AP}) with respect to IDF.

In Fig. 1, we show how IDF and τ_{AP} are connected. There is a linear negative correlation between both metrics (Pearson correlation coefficient $r = -0.4$), showing that (Col)BERT implicitly captures IDF. Note that words with higher

---

[2] using the Python implementation provided by [14].

IDF tend to be longer, and hence to be split into multiple subwords more often – increasing the importance of such terms.

We also observe that the link between IDF and term importance is not so direct for high IDF values (>8). We believe that there are three reasons explaining this behavior: (i) ColBERT has correctly learned that this term was not *so* important; (ii) as most of the documents contain the term, the effect on τ_{AP} might not be high; (iii) another query term (with no semantics) is bearing the same semantics as the target one. The first hypothesis is probably true since ColBERT improves over BM25. As for the second one, this is a more general observation regarding the re-ranking setting, where IR axioms might not fully apply. Finally, to investigate (iii), we looked, for each query token, at the frequency of exact matching (i.e. the max similarity is obtained with the same token in a document) and at the frequency with which it matches in documents *other* query terms. We observed that stopwords (*the*, *of*, etc.) did indeed match terms in the documents that were other query terms. For instance, in the query (and associated τ_{AP}) "*the (0.94) symptoms (0.87) of (0.93) shingles (0.88)*", the word "of" actually mostly matches with "shingles" in documents from $\mathcal{S}_q$.

4   Analysis of Exact and Soft Matches

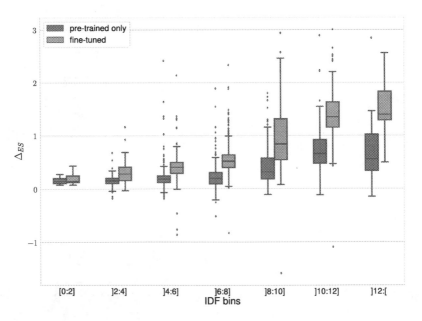

Fig. 2. Δ_{ES} with respect to IDF: we observe a moderate correlation (0.667), showing that the less frequent a term is, the more it is likely to be matched exactly.

After having looked at term importance, we now turn our attention into the issue of exact matches, i.e. how exact string matching is processed by ColBERT.

We need to define a measure indicating when ColBERT asserts whether a term should favor an exact match or not (i.e., soft match). To do so, we compute, for each query term i, the difference between the average ColBERT scores when i matches the same term within a document (i.e., when $d_i^\star \to t$) or not (i.e., when $d_i^\star \not\to t$). We then average at the query level, to obtain one measure per term (for terms appearing in several queries). This measure is formally defined as:

$$\Delta_{ES}(t) = \operatorname*{mean}_{i,q/i \to t} \left(\operatorname*{mean}_{d \in \mathcal{S}_q/d_i^\star \to t} \{C_{id}^\star\} - \operatorname*{mean}_{d \in \mathcal{S}_q/d_i^\star \not\to t} \{C_{id}^\star\} \right) \tag{2}$$

where $j \to t$ means that the jth token corresponds to token t.

For a term w composed of several WordPiece components $t_1, \ldots, t_n$, we use $\sum_{t \in w} \Delta_{ES}(t)$, which corresponds to the way ColBERT operates (summing over subwords). Then, for each query term w, we plot $\Delta_{ES}(w)$ with respect to $IDF(w)$ (Fig. 2). Higher Δ tends to indicate that a match value is higher if the terms appears in the document (exact match), as the model learns to widen the gap (in average) between exact and soft scores. We can observe a moderate positive correlation between terms focusing more on exact matching –larger Δ_{ES}– and IDF ($r = 0.667$). Interestingly, this effect is already observable for BERT, but fine-tuning has an important impact for words with an IDF above 8: ColBERT thus learns to emphasize on exact matches for such words. For instance, in the query (and associated Δ_{ES}) *"causes (0.35) of (0.11) left (0.64) ventricular (1.14) hypertrophy (1.62)"*, the model mostly relies on exact match for the last two terms.

To explain this behavior, our hypothesis is that exact matches correspond to contextual embeddings that do not vary much: hence, the cosine similarity between the query term and the document term would be closer to 1, and ColBERT will tend to select this term. On the contrary, terms that carry less "information" are more heavily influenced by their context (they act as some sort of reservoirs to encode concepts of the sequence), and thus their embeddings vary a lot. To check this hypothesis, we conducted a spectral analysis of contextual term embeddings. More specifically, we use an SVD decomposition of the matrix composed of all the contextual representations for a given term t, on the test documents, and look at the relative magnitude of the singular values $\lambda_1 \geq \ldots \geq \lambda_d$ where d is the dimension of the embedding space. If the magnitude of λ_1 is much larger than the others, it means that all the contextual representations point to the same direction in the embedding space. In Fig. 3, we report the ratio of the first eigenvalue λ_1 with respect to $\sum_k \lambda_k$ for terms that appear in the test queries. It confirms the above hypothesis, as the ratio increases with the subword IDF (correlation $r = 0.77$). Moreover, this effect is much stronger when fine-tuning, indicating that training on relevance indeed promotes exact matches in ColBERT. By looking at the distribution of singular values (not shown here), we can confirm this trend. In particular, words with a low IDF tend to point in different directions, showing that what they capture is more about their context. For instance, in the query *"when did family feud come out ?"* (a TV show), the term "come", for all the documents in $\mathcal{S}_q$, matches 97%

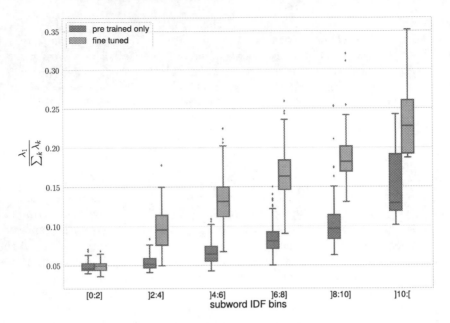

Fig. 3. Ratio of the first eigenvalue to the sum of the eigenvalues with respect to IDF (subword level). The less frequent the term is, the higher the ratio is, *showing that the contextualized embeddings for a rare term are concentrated in the same direction.*

of the time to terms that are not in the query, but are synonyms (in a broad sense) e.g. {*july, happen, item, landing, released, name, en, going, it, rodgers*}.

5   Conclusion

While the axiomatic approach is appropriate to analyze traditional IR models, its application to BERT-based models remains limited and somehow inadequate. To the best of our knowledge, our study is one of the first to shed light on matching behavior of BERT, through the analysis of a simpler counterpart, ColBERT. We showed that (i) even if the IDF effect from the axiomatic theory is not enforced, (Col)BERT does have a notion of term importance; (ii) exact matching remains an important component of the model, especially for important terms; (iii) our analysis gave some hints on the properties of frequent words which tend to capture the contexts in which they appear.

Although this work is a first step towards understanding matching properties of BERT in IR, we believe there is much more to uncover by either analyzing a wider range of models, or by extending our analysis of ColBERT to first stage ranking, where retrieval axioms might be more critical.

References

1. Brunner, G., Liu, Y., Pascual, D., Richter, O., Ciaramita, M., Wattenhofer, R.: On identifiability in transformers (2020)
2. Câmara, A., Hauff, C.: Diagnosing BERT with retrieval heuristics. In: Jose, J.M., et al. (eds.) ECIR 2020. LNCS, vol. 12035, pp. 605–618. Springer, Cham (2020). https://doi.org/10.1007/978-3-030-45439-5_40
3. Dai, Z., Callan, J.: Deeper text understanding for IR with contextual neural language modeling. CoRR abs/1905.09217 (2019). http://arxiv.org/abs/1905.09217
4. Devlin, J., Chang, M., Lee, K., Toutanova, K.: BERT: pre-training of deep bidirectional transformers for language understanding. CoRR abs/1810.04805 (2018). http://arxiv.org/abs/1810.04805
5. Hofstätter, S., Althammer, S., Schröder, M., Sertkan, M., Hanbury, A.: Improving efficient neural ranking models with cross-architecture knowledge distillation (2020)
6. Hofstätter, S., Zlabinger, M., Hanbury, A.: Interpretable & time-budget-constrained contextualization for re-ranking (2020)
7. Khattab, O., Zaharia, M.: Colbert: efficient and effective passage search via contextualized late interaction over BERT. In: Proceedings of the 43rd International ACM SIGIR Conference on Research and Development in Information Retrieval, SIGIR 2020, pp. 39–48. Association for Computing Machinery, New York (2020). https://doi.org/10.1145/3397271.3401075
8. Lin, J., Nogueira, R., Yates, A.: Pretrained transformers for text ranking: BERT and beyond. arXiv:2010.06467 (October 2020)
9. MacAvaney, S., Feldman, S., Goharian, N., Downey, D., Cohan, A.: ABNIRML: analyzing the behavior of neural IR models (2020)
10. MacAvaney, S., Yates, A., Cohan, A., Goharian, N.: CEDR: contextualized embeddings for document ranking. In: SIGIR (2019)
11. Nogueira, R., Cho, K.: Passage re-ranking with BERT (2019)
12. Nogueira, R., Jiang, Z., Lin, J.: Document ranking with a pretrained sequence-to-sequence model (2020)
13. Rennings, D., Moraes, F., Hauff, C.: An axiomatic approach to diagnosing neural IR models. In: Azzopardi, L., Stein, B., Fuhr, N., Mayr, P., Hauff, C., Hiemstra, D. (eds.) ECIR 2019. LNCS, vol. 11437, pp. 489–503. Springer, Cham (2019). https://doi.org/10.1007/978-3-030-15712-8_32
14. Urbano, J., Marrero, M.: The treatment of ties in AP correlation. In: Proceedings of the ACM SIGIR International Conference on Theory of Information Retrieval, ICTIR 2017, pp. 321–324. Association for Computing Machinery, New York (2017). https://doi.org/10.1145/3121050.3121106
15. Voorhees, E.M., Ellis, A. (eds.): Proceedings of the Twenty-Eighth Text REtrieval Conference, TREC 2019, Gaithersburg, Maryland, USA, November 13–15, 2019, vol. 1250. NIST Special Publication, National Institute of Standards and Technology (NIST) (2019). https://trec.nist.gov/pubs/trec28/trec2019.html
16. Yilmaz, E., Aslam, J.A., Robertson, S.: A new rank correlation coefficient for information retrieval. In: Proceedings of the 31st Annual International ACM SIGIR Conference on Research and Development in Information Retrieval, SIGIR 2008, pp. 587–594. Association for Computing Machinery, New York (2008). https://doi.org/10.1145/1390334.1390435

Diversity Aware Relevance Learning
for Argument Search

Michael Fromm[✉], Max Berrendorf, Sandra Obermeier, Thomas Seidl,
and Evgeniy Faerman

Database Systems and Data Mining, LMU Munich, Munich, Germany
fromm@dbs.ifi.lmu.de

Abstract. In this work, we focus on retrieving relevant arguments for
a query claim covering diverse aspects. State-of-the-art methods rely on
explicit mappings between claims and premises and thus cannot utilize
extensive available collections of premises without laborious and costly
manual annotation. Their diversity approach relies on removing duplicates via clustering, which does not directly ensure that the selected
premises cover all aspects. This work introduces a new multi-step approach for the argument retrieval problem. Rather than relying on ground-
truth assignments, our approach employs a machine learning model to
capture semantic relationships between arguments. Beyond that, it aims
to cover diverse facets of the query instead of explicitly identifying duplicates. Our empirical evaluation demonstrates that our approach leads to
a significant improvement in the argument retrieval task, even though it
requires fewer data than prior methods. Our code is available at https://
github.com/fromm-m/ecir2021-am-search.

Keywords: Argument similarity · Argument clustering · Argument
retrieval

1 Introduction

Argumentation is a paramount process in society, and debating on socially relevant topics requires high-quality and relevant arguments. In this work, we deal
with the problem of *argument search*, which is also known as *argument retrieval*.
The goal is to develop an Argument Retrieval System (ARS) which organizes
arguments, previously extracted from various sources [4,8,15,17], in an accessible form. Users then formulate a query to access relevant arguments retrieved
by the ARS. The query can be defined as a *topic*, e.g. *Energy* in which case the
ARS retrieves all possible arguments without further specification [10,15,17].
Our work deals with a more advanced case, where a query is formulated in the
form of a *claim*, and the user expects *premises* attacking or supporting this query

---

M. Fromm and M. Berrendorf—Equal contribution.

© Springer Nature Switzerland AG 2021
D. Hiemstra et al. (Eds.): ECIR 2021, LNCS 12657, pp. 264–271, 2021.
https://doi.org/10.1007/978-3-030-72240-1_24

claim. An example of a claim related to the topic *Energy* could be *"We should abandon Nuclear Energy"* and a supporting premise, e.g., *"Accidents caused by Nuclear Energy have longstanding negative impacts"*. A popular search methodology to find relevant premises is a similarity search, where the representations of the retrieved premises are similar to the representation of the (augmented) query claim [1,3,9,16]. However, as noted by [6,7], the relevance of a premise does not necessarily coincide with pure text similarity. Therefore, the authors of [6] advocate to utilize the similarity between the query claim and other claims in an ARS database and retrieve the premises assigned to the most similar claims. However, such ARS requires ground truth information about the premise to claim assignments and therefore has limited applicability: Either the information sources are restricted to those sources where such information is already available or can automatically be inferred, or expensive human annotations are required. To mitigate this problem and keep the original system's advantages, we propose to use a machine learning model *to learn* the relevance between premises and claims. Using this model, we can omit the (noisy) claim-claim matching step and evaluate the importance of (preselected) candidate premises directly for the query claim. Since the relevance is defined on the semantic level, we have to design an appropriate training task to enable the model to learn semantic differences between relevant and non-relevant premises. Furthermore, an essential subtask for an ARS is to ensure that the retrieved premises do not repeat the same ideas. Previous approaches [6] employ clustering to eliminate duplicates. However, clustering approaches often group data instances by other criteria than expected by the users [12], as also observed in Argument Mining (AM) applications [13]. For our method, we propose an alternative to clustering based on the idea of *core-sets* [14], where the goal is to cover the space of relevant premises as well as possible.

2   Preliminaries

In our setting, the query comes in the form of a claim, and an answer is a sorted list of *relevant* premises from the ARS database. A premise is considered relevant if it attacks or supports the idea expressed in the claim [11,19]. We denote the query claim by c_{query} and the list of premises retrieved by ARS by A, with the length being fixed to $|A| = k$. Besides relevance, another vital requirement for the ARS is that premises in A should have diverse semantic meaning. We consider a two-step retrieval process. First, in the *pre-filtering*, the system selects a set of candidate premises $\mathcal{T}$ with $|\mathcal{T}| > k$. This step should have a relatively high recall, i.e., find most of the relevant premises. For a fair comparison to previous approaches, we leave the pre-filtering step from [6] unchanged. We note that the current version of pre-filtering requires ground-truth matchings of premises to claims restricting its applicability and improving it in future work. The pre-filtering process described in [6] has several steps. When a query claim arrives, the system first determines *claims* from the database which have the highest Divergence from Randomness [2] similarity to the query claim. Next, the system receives the corresponding claim clusters of the claims found in the previous step, and all premises assigned to all claims from these clusters are collected in a candidate seed set $\mathcal{T}_{seed}$. Each premise $p \in \mathcal{T}_{seed}$ is then used as a query to obtain the most similar premises using the BM25 score, which are accumulated in a set $\mathcal{T}_{sim}$. The complete candidate set is then given as the union $\mathcal{T} = \mathcal{T}_{seed} \cup \mathcal{T}_{sim}$.

3 Our Approach for Candidate Refinement

Our work's primary focus is the second step in the retrieval process or the candidate refinement/ranking procedure. The candidates are analyzed more thoroughly in the refinement step, and non-relevant or redundant premises are discarded. Our refinement process comprises two components. The *relevance filter* component determines each premise's relevance from the candidate set $\mathcal{T}$ using an advanced machine learning model that keeps only the most relevant ones. The relevance filter thus maps the candidate set $\mathcal{T}$ to a subset thereof, denoted by $\mathcal{T}_{filtered} \subseteq \mathcal{T}$. The subsequent *premise ranker* selects and orders k premises from $\mathcal{T}_{filtered}$ to the result list A. An essential requirement for the premise ranker is that A does not contain semantically redundant premises. In the following, we describe both components in more detail.

3.1 Relevance Filter

Inference Given a set of candidate premises $\mathcal{T}$ and the query claim c_{query}, the *relevance filter* determines the relevance score of each candidate $p \in \mathcal{T}$ denoted as $r(p \mid c_{query})$. We keep only the most relevant candidates in the filtered candidate set $\mathcal{T}_{filtered} = \{p \in \mathcal{T} \mid r(p \mid c_{query}) > \tau\}$ with a relevance threshold τ. We interpret the relevance prediction as a binary classification problem and train a Transformer [18] model to solve this classification task given the concatenation of the candidate premise and the query claim. At inference time, we use the predicted likelihood as the relevance score and evaluate the model on the concatenation of each candidate premise with the query claim.

Training Task. For the training part, we assume that we have access to a (separate) dataset $D = (\mathcal{P}', \mathcal{C}', \mathcal{R}^+)$ containing a set of premises $\mathcal{P}'$, a set of claims $\mathcal{C}'$ and a set of relevant premise-claim pairs $\mathcal{R}^+ \subseteq \mathcal{P}' \times \mathcal{C}'$. In fact, several datasets fulfill this requirement, e.g., [7,20]. Since the relevance filter receives as input the remaining candidate premises after the pre-filtering, we assume that the non-relevant premises appear similar to the relevant ones. Therefore, the training task must be designed very carefully to enable the model to learn semantic differences between relevant and non-relevant premises. We use the ground truth premise-claim pairs $\mathcal{R}^+$ as instances of the positive class (i.e., an instance of matching pairs). For each positive instance $(p^+, c) \in \mathcal{R}^+$, we generate L instances of the negative class $(p_i^-, c) \in \mathcal{R}^-$. For p_i^-, we choose the L most similar premises according to a premise similarity *psim*, which do not co-occur with c in the database. We use the cosine similarity $psim(p, p') = \cos(\phi(p), \phi(p'))$

Algorithm 1: Biased Coreset

Data: candidates $\mathcal{T}$, relevances R, similarity $psim$, $k \in \mathbb{N}$, $\alpha \in [0,1]$
Result: premise list A
for $i = 1$ **to** k **do**
    if $|A| = 0$ **then** $a = \underset{p \in \mathcal{T}}{\operatorname{argmax}}\, \alpha \cdot R[p]$;
    else $a = \underset{p \in \mathcal{T}}{\operatorname{argmax}}\, \alpha \cdot R[p] - (1 - \alpha) \cdot \underset{a \in A}{\max}\, psim(a, p)$;
    $A.append(a)$; $\mathcal{T} = \mathcal{T} \setminus \{a\}$
end

---

between the premise representations $\phi(p)$ obtained from a pre-trained BERT model without any fine-tuning as premise similarity.[1] The transformer model, which predicts the premise-claim relevance, is initialized with weights from a pre-trained BERT model [5].

3.2 Premise Ranker

The *premise ranker* receives a set of relevant premises with the corresponding relevance scores and makes the final decision about the premises and the order they are returned to the user. Since the two relevance filtering steps have been applied, we assume that most remaining candidates are relevant. Thus, the main task of this component is to avoid semantic duplicates. While related approaches [6] advocate for the utilization of clustering for the detection of duplicates and expect that premises with the same meaning end up in the same clusters, we pursue a different idea. Instead of explicitly detecting the duplicates, we aim to identify k premises that adequately represent all premises in $\mathcal{T}_{filtered}$. Therefore, we borrow the idea of core-sets from [14] and aim to select k premises from the final candidate set $\mathcal{T}_{filtered}$ such that for each candidate premise $p \in \mathcal{T}_{filtered}$ there is a similar premise in the result A. More formally, we denote $Q(p, A) = \max_{a \in A} psim(p, a)$ as a measure of how well p is represented by A, using the premise similarity $psim$. Thus, $\bar{Q}(A) = \min_{p \in \mathcal{T}_{filtered}} Q(p, A)$ denotes the worst representation of any premise $p \in \mathcal{T}_{filtered}$ by A. Hence, we aim to maximize $\bar{Q}$ such that every premise p is well represented. This min-max objective ensures that every premise is well-represented at not only the majority of premises. To solve the selection problem, we adopt the greedy approach from [14]. Since our goal is not only that the selected premises represent the remaining candidates well, but also that the selected premises have high relevance, we start with the most relevant premise and also consider the relevance score r for the next assignments, with a weighting parameter $\alpha \in [0,1]$. $\alpha = 0$ scores only according to the coreset criterion, while $\alpha = 1$ uses only the relevance. The full algorithm is presented in Algorithm 1.

---

[1] Using average pooling of the second-to-last hidden layer over all tokens.

Premise Representation. The premise ranker requires a meaningful similarity measure to compare premises with each other. As also noted in [6], semantically similar premises might often be expressed differently. Therefore, an essential requirement for the similarity function is that it captures semantic similarities. We investigate two approaches to obtain vector representations on which we compute similarities using $l1$, $l2$, or cos similarity. Previous works demonstrated that BERT models pre-trained on language modeling can capture argumentative context [10]. Thus, our first *BERT* similarity function employs a BERT model without fine-tuning to encode the premises. We abbreviate these representations with *BERT*. As an alternative, we propose representing each premise by a vector of relevance scores to selected claims in the database. While we can use randomly selected claims or cluster all claims in the database, many databases already contain topic information about the claims, such as e.g., "Energy." Thus, we restrict the selection of claims for each premise to the same high-level topic of interest. In this case, all premises retrieved for a single query belong to the same topic. We do not consider it a substantial restriction since arguments always exist in some context, and it rarely makes sense to retrieve premises from different topics for the same query. We utilize our relevance filter model to compute relevance scores for the premise and each of the selected claims. We call the resulting vector of stacked similarities *CLAIM-SIM* representation. We hypothesize that a similar relationship to the selected claims is a good indicator of semantically similar premises.

4 Evaluation

Experimental Setting. The training dataset of the relevance filter is a subset of 160,000 positive (relevant) claim-premise sentence pairs of the dataset described in [7]. Additionally, we generated 320,000 negatives (not-relevant) claim-premise pairs as described in Sect. 3.1. For the evaluation of our approach and comparison with the baselines, we utilize the dataset from [6]. The evaluation set consists of 1,195 triples $(c_{query}, c_{result}, p_{result})$ each labeled as "very relevant" (389), "relevant" (139) or "not relevant" (667). The 528 "very relevant" and "relevant" premises were assigned to groups with the same meaning by human annotators. In contrast to [6] we do *not* utilize the ground truth assignments of $c_{result} \leftrightarrow p_{result}$ in our approach. Therefore our method can utilize newly arriving premises without an assignment to c_{result}. To select the optimal hyperparameters for our approach and avoid test leakage, we use leave-one-out cross-validation: For each query claim with corresponding premises, we use the rest

Table 1. Modified NDCG score for $k = 5$ and $k = 10$.

k	[6]			top-k			k-means		Biased coreset	
	First	Sent	Sliding	Zero-shot	Same topic	Ours	BERT	CLAIM-SIM	BERT	CLAIM-SIM
5	.399	.378	.455	.437	.373	.447	.428	.465	.437	**.475**
10	.455	.429	.487	.476	.448	.502	.515	.513	.520	**.526**

of the evaluation dataset to select the hyperparameters and then evaluate this hold-out query. To obtain a final score, we average over all splits. As an evaluation metric, we use the modified nDCG from [6]: Only the first occurrence from a premise ground truth cluster yields positive gain; duplicates do not give any gain. In Table 1, we summarize the results of the argument retrieval task. The numbers represent the modified NDCG scores for $k = 5$ and $k = 10$. The first three columns show the evaluation results for the methods from [6].[2] In the next three columns denoted as *top-k*, we present the results when premises with the highest score are returned directly, without de-duplication. With the *zero-shot* approach, we investigate the assumption that similarity between query and claim is not a sufficient indicator for relevance. Thus, we use the similarity between representations obtained from a pre-trained BERT model without training on claim-premise relevance. The second column, *same topic*, denotes the performance of the relevance model trained in the same setting as our approach with the only difference that negative instances for the training are selected from the same topic. Finally, *ours* denotes the setting, where k instances have the highest probability to be relevant estimated by our model (more precisely, the *relevance filter*). Given these results, we observe a strong performance of the *zero-shot* approach, which comes close to the approaches by [6]. We emphasize that this is even though this baseline approach neither uses ground truth premise-claim relevance data as [6], nor any other external premise-claim relevance data. Moreover, we observe that we can achieve good performance in terms of the *modified* NDCG despite not filtering duplicates. At the same time, we observe that our model can still improve the similarity-based approach by several points. In contrast, the model learned with negatives instances from the same topic performs much worse than *zero-shot*, which underlines the correct task's importance. Finally, the columns denoted as *Biased Coreset* present our final results. The results are from the *premise ranker* applied to the different premise representations of the most relevant premises selected by *relevance filter*. For comparison, we also report the results, where k-means is used as *premise ranker* on the same representations, where we select at most one premise per cluster according to the similarity. The *claim-sim* premise representation always outperforms *bert* and our *biased-coreset* premise ranker is better than the k-means clustering.

5   Conclusion

In this work, we have presented a novel approach for the retrieval of *relevant* and *original* premises for the query claims. Our new approach can be applied more flexibly than previous methods since it does not require mappings between premises and claims in the database. Thus, it can also be applied in an inductive

---

[2] For the evaluation, we have used interim results provided by the authors of the original publication. Since we had obtained deviations from the originally reported results, we have contacted the authors and came together to the conclusion that our numbers are correct. We thank the authors for their help.

setting, where new premises can be used without the need first to associate them with relevant claims manually. At the same time, it achieves better results than approaches that make use of this information.

Acknowledgment. This work has been funded by the German Federal Ministry of Education and Research (BMBF) under Grant No. 01IS18036A and by the Deutsche Forschungsgemeinschaft (DFG) within the project Relational Machine Learning for Argument Validation (ReMLAV), Grant NumberSE 1039/10-1, as part of the Priority Program "Robust Argumentation Machines (RATIO)" (SPP-1999). The authors of this work take full responsibility for its content.

References

1. Akiki, C., Potthast, M.: Exploring argument retrieval with transformers. In: Working Notes Papers of the CLEF 2020 Evaluation Labs (September 2020)
2. Amati, G., Van Rijsbergen, C.J.: Probabilistic models of information retrieval based on measuring the divergence from randomness. ACM Trans. Inf. Syst. (TOIS) **20**(4), 357–389 (2002)
3. Bondarenko, A., et al.: Overview of Touché 2020: argument retrieval. In: Arampatzis, A., et al. (eds.) CLEF 2020. LNCS, vol. 12260, pp. 384–395. Springer, Cham (2020). https://doi.org/10.1007/978-3-030-58219-7_26
4. Chernodub, A., et al.: Targer: neural argument mining at your fingertips. In: Proceedings of the 57th Annual Meeting of the Association for Computational Linguistics: System Demonstrations, pp. 195–200 (2019)
5. Devlin, J., Chang, M.W., Lee, K., Toutanova, K.: BERT: pre-training of deep bidirectional transformers for language understanding. In: Proceedings of the 2019 Conference of the North American Chapter of the Association for Computational Linguistics: Human Language Technologies, Volume 1 (Long and Short Papers), pp. 4171–4186. Association for Computational Linguistics, Minneapolis (June 2019). https://doi.org/10.18653/v1/N19-1423, https://www.aclweb.org/anthology/N19-1423
6. Dumani, L., Neumann, P.J., Schenkel, R.: A framework for argument retrieval. In: Jose, J.M., et al. (eds.) ECIR 2020. LNCS, vol. 12035, pp. 431–445. Springer, Cham (2020). https://doi.org/10.1007/978-3-030-45439-5_29
7. Dumani, L., Schenkel, R.: A systematic comparison of methods for finding good premises for claims (2019)
8. Ein-Dor, L., et al.: Corpus wide argument mining-a working solution. In: AAAI, pp. 7683–7691 (2020)
9. Feger, M., Steimann, J., Meter, C.: Structure or content? Towards assessing argument relevance. In: Proceedings of the 8th International Conference on Computational Models of Argument (COMMA 2020), p. 135 (2020)
10. Fromm, M., Faerman, E., Seidl, T.: TACAM: topic and context aware argument mining. In: Barnaghi, P.M., Gottlob, G., Manolopoulos, Y., Tzouramanis, T., Vakali, A. (eds.) 2019 IEEE/WIC/ACM International Conference on Web Intelligence, WI 2019, Thessaloniki, Greece, October 14–17, 2019, pp. 99–106. ACM (2019). https://doi.org/10.1145/3350546.3352506

11. Habernal, I., Gurevych, I.: Which argument is more convincing? Analyzing and predicting convincingness of web arguments using bidirectional LSTM. In: Proceedings of the 54th Annual Meeting of the Association for Computational Linguistics (Volume 1: Long Papers), pp. 1589–1599. Association for Computational Linguistics, Berlin (August 2016). https://doi.org/10.18653/v1/P16-1150, https://www.aclweb.org/anthology/P16-1150

12. Kriegel, H.P., Kröger, P., Zimek, A.: Clustering high-dimensional data: a survey on subspace clustering, pattern-based clustering, and correlation clustering. ACM Trans. Knowl. Discov. Data (TKDD) **3**(1), 1–58 (2009)

13. Reimers, N., Schiller, B., Beck, T., Daxenberger, J., Stab, C., Gurevych, I.: Classification and clustering of arguments with contextualized word embeddings. In: Proceedings of the 57th Annual Meeting of the Association for Computational Linguistics, pp. 567–578. Association for Computational Linguistics, Florence (July 2019). https://doi.org/10.18653/v1/P19-1054, https://www.aclweb.org/anthology/P19-1054

14. Sener, O., Savarese, S.: Active learning for convolutional neural networks: a core-set approach. arXiv preprint arXiv:1708.00489 (2017)

15. Stab, C., Miller, T., Schiller, B., Rai, P., Gurevych, I.: Cross-topic argument mining from heterogeneous sources. In: Proceedings of the 2018 Conference on Empirical Methods in Natural Language Processing, pp. 3664–3674. Association for Computational Linguistics, Brussels (October–November 2018). https://doi.org/10.18653/v1/D18-1402, https://www.aclweb.org/anthology/D18-1402

16. Staudte, C., Lange, L.: SentArg: a hybrid Doc2Vec/DPH model with sentiment analysis refinement. In: CLEF (2020)

17. Trautmann, D., Fromm, M., Tresp, V., Seidl, T., Schütze, H.: Relational and fine-grained argument mining. Datenbank-Spektrum **20**, 1–7 (2020)

18. Vaswani, A., et al.: Attention is all you need. In: Advances in Neural Information Processing Systems, pp. 5998–6008 (2017)

19. Wachsmuth, H., et al.: Computational argumentation quality assessment in natural language. In: Proceedings of the 15th Conference of the European Chapter of the Association for Computational Linguistics: Volume 1, Long Papers, pp. 176–187 (2017)

20. Wachsmuth, H., et al.: Building an argument search engine for the web. In: Proceedings of the 4th Workshop on Argument Mining, pp. 49–59 (2017)

SQE-GAN: A Supervised Query Expansion Scheme via GAN

Tianle Fu, Qi Tian, and Hui Li[✉] [iD]

School of Cyber Engineering, Xidian University, Xi'an, China
{futianle,qitian}@stu.xidian.edu.cn, hli@xidian.edu.cn

Abstract. Existing Supervised Query Expansion (SQE) spends much time in term feature extraction but generates sub-optimal expanded terms. In this paper, we introduce Generative Adversarial Nets (GANs) and propose a GAN-based SQE method (SQE-GAN) to get helpful query expansion terms. We unify two types of models in query expansion: the generative model and the discriminative one. The generative (resp., discriminative) model focuses on predicting relevant terms (resp., relevancy) given a query (resp., a query-term pair). We iteratively optimize both models with a game between them. Besides, a BiLSTM layer is adopted to encode the utility of a term with respect to the query. As a result, the costly feature calculation in SQE schemes is avoided, such that the efficiency can be significantly improved. Moreover, by introducing GAN into expansion, the expanded terms are possible to be more effective with respect to the eventual needs of the user. Our experimental results demonstrate that SQE-GAN can be 37.3% faster than state-of-the-art SQE solutions while outperforming some recently proposed neural models in the retrieval quality.

Keywords: Supervised Query Expansion · GAN · Word embedding

1 Introduction

The query words entered by the user are often short, unclear or even ambiguous and cannot fully express his needs, resulting in the fact that the retrieved documents can't be sorted according to his true intent. Query Expansion (QE) is designed to solve this problem, which expands or reconstructs original queries with extra terms to be more in line with the user's actual query needs [15].

Existing work in QE can be categorized into two groups, Unsupervised Query Expansion (UQE) and Supervised Query Expansion (SQE). Many classical algorithms [1,18] belong to the first group. However, recent studies [3,11] show that a large portion of expansion terms selected by UQE algorithms are proved

This work is supported by National Natural Science Foundation of China (No. 61972309), CCF-Huawei Database System Innovation Research Plan (No. 2020010B), Key Scientific Research Program of Shaanxi Provincial Department of Education (No. 20JY014), and Natural Science Basic Research Program of Shaanxi (No. 2020JM-575).

© Springer Nature Switzerland AG 2021
D. Hiemstra et al. (Eds.): ECIR 2021, LNCS 12657, pp. 272–279, 2021.
https://doi.org/10.1007/978-3-030-72240-1_25

as noisy or even harmful. SQE is proposed to solve the problem with the power of supervised learning, which has recently become the state-of-the-art in the QE literature. Most SQE solutions [3,6,11,14] utilize the classical machine learning algorithms and conduct carefully designed term feature engineering to improve the effectiveness. Although SQE can provide more effective expanded terms, they have to sacrifice much response time comparing to UQE. Recently, due to recent research achievements in word embedding [16] and deep neural networks, there are new opportunities for many information retrieval tasks, including QE. In particular, word embedding may help us avoid the time-consuming feature extraction phase in SQE. Besides, recent progress in deep learning may help us encode the correlation between an arbitrary pair of query and expanded term. [7] proposed a neural network architecture for classifying terms based on their effectiveness in query expansion. [21] applied seq2seq [13] model in query expansion for the first time, showing the feasibility, flexibility and scalability of the generative model in QE tasks. Moreover, it is possible for us to learn the underlying true relevance distribution of terms with respect to a query.

Learning the underlying distribution of some variables is a general task in traditional machine learning. There are plenty of solutions in this field, among which GAN (Generative Adversarial Nets) shows the most promising performance in many areas (*e.g.,* computer vision [10]) by modeling the learning task as a game between a pair of discriminator and generator. Inspired by GAN, we found that QE task can also be decomposed into a pair of discriminative model and generative model. The former one can be described as $f_\phi(query, term)$, and learns a expansion term ranking function implicitly from labeled data. The latter one can be described as $p(term|query)$, and is in charge of obtaining useful features from the massive unlabeled data. Based on that, we present a novel SQE framework, SQE-GAN. The experimental results show that for the same dataset, our framework outperforms the latest neural SQE solutions in retrieval quality and response time in the benchmarking dataset.

2   Framework

In traditional pseudo relevance feedback (PRF) scenario [4], let C denote the target corpus upon which retrieval is performed. Assuming a retrieval algorithm (e.g. TFIDF) is utilized, then the typical procedure of QE in retrieval is summarized into three steps: (1) retrieve original query q on corpus C; (2) select expanded terms $\{t^e\}$ from the top k documents returned; (3) obtain the final results by performing an expanded query q^e over corpus C. Depending on whether the model to select expanded terms $\{t^e\}$ (in Step **(2)**) is supervised or not, QE can be classified as SQE and UQE. Generally, Algorithm 1 shows a common pipeline of SQE that have been followed by a series of works [3,6,11,22].

According to the general procedure of SQE, we have a set of original queries $\{q_1, ..., q_n\}$, and a set of terms $\{t_1, ..., t_M\}$, which are generated by UQE (*e.g.,* KL [1]). For an arbitrary query q_i, the expanded terms may be classified as positive and negative. The underlying true relevance distribution can be expressed as the conditional probability $p_{true}(t|q,r)$, which describes the query preference term distribution. In this work, we follow Pointwise-based Learning to rank (LTR) framework [2,8], which contains a pair of models as follows.

Generative Model. $p_\theta(t|q,r)$ tries to select top k relevant terms from the candidate ones given a query q. We denote the task of generative model as $q \rightarrow t$, where q,t refer to the original query and the relevant term, respectively.

Algorithm 1: General SQE Procedure	**Algorithm 2:** SQE-GAN Algorithm

▷ Training SQE model $\hbar$
 1: For training query q, record its retrieval accuracy r_q.
    Select M candidate terms $\{t_c^i | i = 1 : M\}$ via UQE.
 2: Each time, a single candidate term t_c is appended to q,
    i.e., $q^c = q \cup t^c$; record its retrieval accuracy r_c^q ; then
    $\triangle r_c^q = r_c^q - r^q$ is the label for t^c .
 3: Process data and train a specific model using the labels
 ▷ Testing
 1: For testing query q, use UQE to select M candidate terms
 2: Use $\hbar$ (the trained model) to get top m terms
	Require: generator $p_\theta(t|q,r)$; discriminator $f_\phi(t,q_n)$; training dataset S;
	 1: Initialize $p_\theta(t|q,r)$,$f_\phi(t,q_n)$ with random weights.
	 2: Pre-train $p_\theta(t|q,r)$,$f_\phi(t,q_n)$ using S.
	 3: **repeat**
	 4: **for** g-steps **do**
	 5: $p_\theta(t|q,r)$ generates K term pairs for each query
	 6: Update generator parameters via policy gradient.
	 7: **end for**
	 8: **for** d-steps **do**
	 9: Use the current $p_\theta(t|q,r)$ to generates negative term pairs and combine with the positive term pairs
	 10: Train discriminator $f_\phi(t,q_n)$
	 11: **end for**
	 12: **until** the two models converge

Discriminative Model. $f_\phi(q,t)$, in contrary, tries to discriminate well-matched query-term tuples (q,t) from ill-matched ones, where the goodness of matching given by $f_\phi(q,t)$ depends on the relevance of t with respect to q. We denote the task of discriminative model as $q \oplus t \rightarrow r$, where r and $\oplus$ refers to the relevancy and combination of features, respectively. It's obvious that terms and queries are jointly fed into the model as features, then the discriminative model is inferred and their relevancy prediction is produced.

Model Definition. We then construct a game between them: the generative model would try to generate relevant expanded terms that look like the ground-truth ones in order to fool the discriminative model. In the contrary, the discriminative model would try to draw a clear distinction between the ground-truth relevant terms and the generated ones. The score given by the discriminator will be used as a criterion to judge generator's current performance, providing necessary information to train the generator. It is proportional to the similarity between the generated terms and the ground-truth ones. The overall loss function of SQE-GAN is defined as follows:

$$J^{G^*,D^*} = \min_\theta \max_\phi \sum_{n=1}^N (\mathbb{E}_{t \sim p_{true}(t|q_n,r)}[log D(t|q_n)] + \mathbb{E}_{t' \sim p_\theta(t'|q_n,r)}[log(1 - D(t'|q_n))])$$

(1)

where the generative model G is denoted as $p_\theta(t|q_n,r)$, and the discriminative model $D(t|q_n)$ estimates the probability of t being relevant to query q_n, which is given by the sigmoid function of the discriminator score. t and t' refer to the true and the generated term with respect to query q_n, respectively.

The probability that a term t being correctly ranked (*i.e.*, $D(t|q_n)$) can be estimated by the discriminative model through a sigmoid function of $f_\phi(t, q)$. Besides, the generative model $p_\theta(t|q, r)$ is defined as a softmax function of $g_\theta(q, t)$, which reflects the chance of the term t being generated from q.

Training the Discriminator. With the observed relevant terms, and the ones sampled from $p_\theta(t|q, r)$, one can then obtain the optimal parameters for the discriminator $D(t|q)$ by maximizing the following objective:

$$\phi^* = arg\max_\phi \sum\nolimits_{n=1}^N (\mathbb{E}_{t\sim p_{true}(t|q_n,r)}[log\sigma(f_\phi(t, q_n))] + \mathbb{E}_{t'\sim p_\theta(t'|q_n,r)}[log(1 - \sigma(f_\phi(t', q_n)))]) \tag{2}$$

We can use stochastic gradient descent (SGD) to train the discriminative model if the function f_ϕ is differentiable with respect to ϕ.

Training the Generator. On the other hand, $p_\theta(t|q, r)$ intends to minimize the objective. Specifically, while keeping the discriminator $f_\phi(q, t)$ fixed after its minimization in Eq. 1, we learn the generative model via minimizing:

$$\theta^* = arg\min_\theta \sum\nolimits_{n=1}^N (\mathbb{E}_{t\sim p_{true}(t|q_n,r)}[log\sigma(f_\phi(t, q_n))] + \mathbb{E}_{t'\sim p_\theta(t'|q_n,r)}[log(1 - \sigma(f_\phi(t', q_n)))])$$
$$= arg\max_\theta \sum\nolimits_{n=1}^N \underbrace{\mathbb{E}_{t'\sim p_\theta(t'|q_n,r)}[log(1 + exp(f_\phi(t', q_n)))]}_{J^G(q_n)} \tag{3}$$

As the sampling of t is discrete, it cannot be directly learned by SGD. We propose to use policy gradient based reinforcement learning [19,20] as follows.

$$\nabla_\theta J^G(q_n) = \nabla_\theta \mathbb{E}_{t\sim p_\theta(t'|q,r)}[log(1 + exp(f_\phi(t', q_n)))]$$
$$= \sum\nolimits_{i-1}^M \nabla_\theta p_\theta(t_i'|q_n, r)log(1 + exp(f_\phi(t_i', q_n)))$$
$$= \sum\nolimits_{i=1}^M p_\theta(t_i'|q_n, r)\nabla_\theta log p_\theta(t_i'|q_n, r)log(1 + exp(f_\phi(t_i', q_n))) \tag{4}$$
$$= \mathbb{E}_{t\sim p_\theta(t'|q_n,r)}[\nabla_\theta log p_\theta(t'|q_n, r)log(1 + exp(f_\phi(t', q_n)))]$$
$$\simeq \sum\nolimits_{i=1}^K \nabla_\theta log p_\theta(t_k'|q_n, r)log(1 + exp(f_\phi(t_k', q_n)))$$

Lastly, we sample the top k terms from the generator $p_\theta(t'|q_n, r)$. It's obvious that the parameter update of G is not from the data sample itself (*i.e.*, not to infer the likelihood of data), but from a back propagation gradient of discriminant model D. With reinforcement learning, the term $log(1 + exp(f_\phi(t'|q_n)))$ acts as the reward for the policy taking an action d in the environment q_n. The overall logic of our proposed SQE-GAN model is summarized in Algorithm 2.

3 Applying SQE-GAN in the Query

In this section, we will illustrate the process of applying SQE-GAN in retrieval task. As formulated in Eq. 3, the generator G's conditional distribution $p_\theta(t|q, r)$

fully depends on the scoring function $g_\theta(q,t)$. In the sampling stage, the parameter τ is incorporated in Eq. 3 as: $p_\theta(t|q,r) = \frac{exp(g_\theta(q,t)/\tau)}{\sum_t exp(g_\theta(q,t)/\tau)}$.

The discriminator's ranking of terms, *i.e.*, Eq. 2, is fully determined by the scoring function $f_\phi(t,q_n)$. The implementation of these two scoring functions, *i.e.*, $g_\theta(q,t)$ and $f_\phi(t,q_n)$, can be different. In spite of that, in order to focus more on adversarial training, we choose the same scoring function (with different sets of parameters) in SQE-GAN: $g_\theta(q,t) = s_\theta(q,t), f_\phi(q,t) = s_\phi(q,t)$.

We employ a BiLSTM encoder [12] to compute the score between a query and an expanded term. Herein, the word embedding[1] of t (L2-normalized) and q_i are fed into the encoder, which can be then denoted as $U_a = [\vec{u_a}; \overleftarrow{u_a}]$, where $\vec{u_a} = \overrightarrow{LSTM}(u_{a-1}, [q_a; q_a * t_a; |q_a - t_a|])$ and $\overleftarrow{u_a} = \overleftarrow{LSTM}(u_{a+1}, [q_a; q_a * t_a; |q_a - t_a|])$. Herein, u_{a-1} denotes the LSTM hidden state, the size of which is set to 50, at time step $a - 1$. U_a is the concatenated representation of the forward and backward process. An affine layer projects U_a to a space with fixed length (*e.g.*, 20). After that, the output of BiLSTM is then fed into a fully connected layer. Depending on whether it is the generator or discriminator, a softmax layer or a sigmoid layer is employed then. The output of the softmax layer refers to the probability distribution about the chance of term t being generated from q, while that of the sigmoid reflects the probability of t being relevant to query q.

4   Experiments

Datasets and Settings. We use *TREC Robust 2004* for evaluating our model, which contains approximately 528,000 high-quality documents and provides 250 queries (301–450 and 601–700) for experiments. We use *Terrier V4.2*, one of the academic search systems, to index all corpora in the form of inverted index. Porter stemmer is applied for stemming, and standard InQuery stopwords are removed. We use Word2Vec's Continuous Bag-of-Words (CBOW) approach [16] that represents terms in a vector space based on their co-occurrence in windows of text. The dimension of query and expansion term are both set to 100. Learning rate is set to 0.001. For all the approaches, the number of candidate terms generated by UQE are set as $M = 100$, from which 20 terms are finally selected as expansion ones. For all the query sets, we randomly select 40% queries to train the models, 10% to validate, while the remaining 50% are used for testing.

We use TFIDF as the basic retrieval model for all the experiments below. For response time, state-of-the-art SQE schemes, namely SQE-TFS [22] and traditional UQE method (*i.e.*, KL divergence) are used as baselines. For the retrieval effect, we compare SQE-GAN with UQE [1], RankSVM [9] and some recently proposed competitive neural networks [7,21]. In addition, we have also designed a neural-network-based discriminative model using different score functions as the baselines (*i.e.*, LSTM(DIS): BiLSTM is used in the discriminative model. ATTEN(DIS): "Query-to-Term Attention", aiming at calculating which term are most relevant to each query word.). We evaluate the

---

[1] Any embedding technique can be adopted, *e.g.*, BERT [5], ELMo [17], Word2Vec [16].

query performance in terms of MAP (Mean Average Precision), Precision@k, NDCG and time cost (in seconds). In experimental comparison, for all the baselines, we adopt their best performance in terms of query efficacy and efficiency.

Table 1. Retrieval performance on TREC dataset

	MAP	%	Prec@5	%	Prec@10	%	NDCG	%
UQE (KL divergence)	0.2544	0	0.4458	0	0.3992	0	0.5284	0
SQE-RankSVM	0.2595	+2.00%	0.4613	+3.48%	0.4016	+0.60%	0.5334	+0.95%
LSTM (DIS)	0.2540	−0.16%	0.4919	+10.34%	0.4194	+5.06%	0.5257	−0.51%
ATTEN (DIS)	0.2563	+0.75%	0.4903	+9.98%	0.4250	+6.46%	0.5354	+1.32%
DEC [7]	0.2358	−7.31%	–	–	0.4057	+1.63%	–	–
AAAI2019 [21]	0.2581	+1.45%	–	–	–	–	–	–
SQE-GAN	**0.2618**	+2.91%	**0.4919**	+10.34%	**0.4274**	+7.06%	**0.5410**	+2.38%

Effectiveness and Efficiency. Table 1 shows the query performance over all approaches. SQE-GAN with BiLSTM as the score model in both discriminator and generator achieves the best performance across all metrics. For the variants of the score model of SQE-GAN, they also perform better than UQE method and SQE-RankSVM in both Precision@5 and NDCG. The phenomenon also indicates that simply adding attention mechanism into SQE-GAN may not necessarily improve the query performance, which has also been justified in [21].

[22] reported that the main time cost of applying SQE algorithms comes from term feature extraction and SQE-TFS can significantly reduce the time cost for SQE-RankSVM, while maintaining its good effectiveness. We evaluate the major inefficient part (*i.e.*, term feature extraction for SQE-RankSVM, Word embedding for SQE-GAN, [7] and [21]) for different SQE models. Through the test, UQE, SQE-TFS and SQE-GAN spends 0.302, 1.76 and 1.104 s in average, respectively. Comparing with SQE-TFS, SQE-GAN has a 37.3% improvement in major time cost. The reason is easy to interpret, we do not need to perform feature calculation but word embedding, which is much more efficient. Taking into account that the BiLSTM setting exhibits the best query performance, we are happy to find that SQE-GAN with BiLSTM for both discriminator and generator is superior to the state-of-the-art SQE models. Moreover, given a corpus, we can pre-compute and index word embeddings for all terms that may be generated from UQE as candidates. In that case, the efficiency can be further significantly improved for SQE-GAN.

5   Conclusions

In this paper, we propose a novel SQE scheme, namely SQE-GAN, based on word embedding and GAN such that the costly feature calculation can be avoided. It firstly employs UQE to get expanded terms. After that, word embedding technique is used to fill the score of GAN, where we propose a generative model and a discriminative model. Both models iteratively optimize each other as a game. Empirical studies show that the proposed framework can significantly improve the efficiency of SQE solutions. In addition, SQL-GAN also improves the result quality compared with the latest deep learning-based QE solutions.

References

1. Amati, G.: Probability models for information retrieval based on divergence from randomness. Univ. Glasgow **20**(4), 357–389 (2003)
2. Burges, C.J.C., et al.: Learning to rank using gradient descent. In: ICML, pp. 89–96 (2005)
3. Cao, G., Nie, J.Y., Gao, J., Robertson, S.: Selecting good expansion terms for pseudo-relevance feedback. In: SIGIR, pp. 243–250 (2008)
4. Carpineto, C., Romano, G.: A survey of automatic query expansion in information retrieval. ACM Comput. Surv. **44**(1), 1–50 (2013)
5. Devlin, J., Chang, M., Lee, K., Toutanova, K.: BERT: pre-training of deep bidirectional transformers for language understanding. In: NAACL, pp. 4171–4186 (2019)
6. Gao, J., Xu, G., Xu, J.: Query expansion using path-constrained random walks. In: SIGIR, pp. 563–572 (2013)
7. Imani, A., Vakili, A., Montazer, A., Shakery, A.: Deep neural networks for query expansion using word embeddings. In: ECIR, pp. 203–210 (2019)
8. Joachims, T.: Optimizing search engines using clickthrough data. In: KDD, pp. 133–142 (2002)
9. Joachims, T.: Training linear SVMs in linear time. In: KDD, pp. 217–226 (2006)
10. Karras, T., Laine, S., Aila, T.: A style-based generator architecture for generative adversarial networks. In: CVPR, pp. 4401–4410 (2019)
11. Lee, C.J., Chen, R.C., Kao, S.H., Cheng, P.J.: A term dependency-based approach for query terms ranking. In: CIKM, pp. 1267–1276 (2009)
12. Li, J., Luong, M., Jurafsky, D.: A hierarchical neural autoencoder for paragraphs and documents. In: ACL, pp. 1106–1115 (2015)
13. Luong, T., Pham, H., Manning, C.D.: Effective approaches to attention-based neural machine translation. In: EMNLP, pp. 1412–1421 (2015)
14. Lv, Y., Zhai, C.X., Chen, W.: A boosting approach to improving pseudo-relevance feedback. In: SIGIR, pp. 165–174 (2011)
15. Manning, C.D.: Introduction to information retrieval. J. Am. Soc. Inf. Sci. Technol. **61**, 852–853 (2009)
16. Mikolov, T., Chen, K., Corrado, G., Dean, J.: Efficient estimation of word representations in vector space. In: ICLR (2013)
17. Peters, M.E., et al.: Deep contextualized word representations. In: NAACL, pp. 2227–2237 (2018)
18. Victor Lavrenko, W.B.C.: Relevance-based language models. In: SIGIR, pp. 120–127 (2001)
19. Wang, J., et al.: IRGAN: a minimax game for unifying generative and discriminative information retrieval models. In: SIGIR, pp. 515–524 (2017)
20. Williams, R.J.: Simple statistical gradient-following algorithms for connectionist reinforcement learning. Mach. Learn. **8**, 229–256 (1992)

21. Zaiem, S., Sadat, F.: Sequence to sequence learning for query expansion. In: AAAI, pp. 10075–10076 (2019)
22. Zhang, Z., Wang, Q., Si, L., Gao, J.: Learning for efficient supervised query expansion via two-stage feature selection. In: SIGIR, pp. 265–274 (2016)

Rethink Training of BERT Rerankers in Multi-stage Retrieval Pipeline

Luyu Gao[✉], Zhuyun Dai, and Jamie Callan

Language Technologies Institute, Carnegie Mellon University, Pittsburgh, USA
{luyug,zhuyund,callan}@cs.cmu.edu

Abstract. Pre-trained deep language models (LM) have advanced the state-of-the-art of text retrieval. Rerankers fine-tuned from deep LM estimates candidate relevance based on rich contextualized matching signals. Meanwhile, deep LMs can also be leveraged to improve search index, building retrievers with better recall. One would expect a straightforward combination of both in a pipeline to have additive performance gain. In this paper, we discover otherwise and that popular reranker cannot fully exploit the improved retrieval result. We, therefore, propose a Localized Contrastive Estimation (LCE) for training rerankers and demonstrate it significantly improves deep two-stage models (Our codes are open sourced at https://github.com/luyug/Reranker.).

1 Introduction

Recent state-of-the-art retrieval systems are pipelined, consisting of a first-stage heuristic retriever such as BM25 that efficiently produces an initial set of candidate results followed by one or more heavy rerankers that rerank the most promising candidates [11]. Neural language models (LM) such as BERT [7] have had a major impact on this architecture by providing more effective index terms [12] and term weights [5] for heuristic retriever and providing rich contextualized matching signals between query and document for rerankers [4,10].

Intuitively, a better initial ranking provides later stage neural rerankers with more relevant documents to pull up to the top of the final ranking. In a perfect world, a neural reranker recognizes the relevant documents in its candidate pool, inheriting all of the successes of previous retriever. However, simply forming the pipeline by appending a BERT reranker to an effective first-stage retriever does not guarantee an effective final ranking. An improved candidate list sometimes causes inferior reranking. When the candidate list improves, false positives can become harder to recognize as they tend to share confounding characteristics with the true positives. A discriminative reranker should be able to handle the top portion of retriever results and avoid relying on those confounding features.

In this paper, we introduce Localized Contrastive Estimation (LCE) learning. We *localize* negative sample distribution by sampling from the target retriever top results. Meanwhile, we use a *contrastive* form loss which penalizes signals

D. Hiemstra et al. (Eds.): ECIR 2021, LNCS 12657, pp. 280–286, 2021.
https://doi.org/10.1007/978-3-030-72240-1_26

generated from confounding characteristics, preventing the reranker from collapsing.

Experiments on the MSMARCO document ranking dataset show that LCE can better exploit the LMs capability. With the same BERT model, LCE achieves significantly higher accuracy without incurring training or inference overhead.

2 Background

Separation of retrieval into stages was introduced naturally due to efficiency-effectiveness trade-off among different ranking models: fast but less accurate model (e.g. BM25) retrieves from the entire corpus while slower but more accurate ones (e.g. BERT) refines ranking in the top candidate list.

Heuristic retrievers like BM25 use matching signals exclusively from exact match and therefore can use inverted list data structure for low latency full corpus retrieval. They are limited by document statistics for scoring. As a fix, deep language models can be leveraged to re-estimate term weights in search index [5,6]. An alternative is adding probable query terms to document [12].

Pre-trained deep LMs [7,14] have demonstrated strong supervised transfer performance on reranking tasks. Popular recent works [4,10] fine-tune BERT [7] with binary classification objective and show it significantly outperforms earlier models. In this paper, we however question if this simple paradigm is sufficient to realize BERT's full potential, especially for high performance deep retrievers that generate candidates consisting of harder negatives.

Alternatives to binary classification objective are the contrastive learning objectives that directly take negatives into account [8]. The popular NCE loss computes scores of a positive instance and several negatives instances, normalize them into probabilities and train the model to give higher probability to the positive instance [16]. The incorporation of negatives in loss prevents the model from collapsing. While contrastive loss has been widely studied in representation learning [2,16], there are few prior works adopting it to train deep LM rerankers.

3 Methodologies

Preliminaries. We aim to train a BERT reranker to score a query document pair,

$$s = \text{score}(q, d) = \mathbf{v}_p^\intercal \, cls(\text{BERT}(\mathbf{concat}(q, d))) \tag{1}$$

where cls extracts BERT's [CLS] vector and $\mathbf{v}_p$ is a projection vector. We refer to the training technique popularly adopted [4,10] as the *Vanilla method*. It samples query document pairs independently and compute on each individual query-document pair using binary cross entropy (BCE) based on query q document d and corresponding label $(+/-)$,

$$\mathcal{L}_v := \begin{cases} \text{BCE}(\text{score}(q, d), +) & \text{d is positive} \\ \text{BCE}(\text{score}(q, d), -) & \text{d is negative} \end{cases} \tag{2}$$

Vanilla method treats reranker training as a general binary classification problem. However, reranker is unique in nature; it deals with the very top portion of retriever results, each of which may contain many confounding signatures. The reranker is expected to,

– Exile at handling top portion of retriever results.
– Avoid collapsing onto matching with confounding features.

To this end, in this section, we introduce Localized Contrastive Estimation (LCE) loss. The contrastive loss prevents collapsing and localized negative samples focus the reranker on top retriever results.

Localized Negatives from Target Retriever. Given a target initial stage retriever and a set of training queries, we use the retriever to retrieve from the entire corpus, generating a set of document rankings for the queries. For each query q then sample from the set R_q^m of top ranked m documents, n non-relevant documents as negatives examples. All sampled documents together form the negative training set. As will be shown in Sect. 6, re-building training set based on the specific target retriever is critical to ensure robust training.

Contrastive Loss. After aggregating all negatives sampled from target retriever, we form for each query q a group G_q with a single relevant positive d_q^+ and sampled non-relevant negative documents from R_q^m. We treat the BERT scoring function as a deep distance function,

$$dist(q, d) = \text{score}(q, d) = \mathbf{v}_\text{p}^\mathsf{T} \, cls(\text{BERT}(\mathbf{concat}(q, d))) \tag{3}$$

with which we define the contrastive loss for one query q as,

$$\mathcal{L}_q := -log \frac{exp(dist(q, d_q^+))}{\sum_{d \in G_q} exp(dist(q, d))} \tag{4}$$

Importantly, here loss and gradient condition not only on the relevant pair but also the retrieved negatives. This effectively helps prevent collapsing onto simple confounding matchings.

LCE Batch Update. Putting it all together, we can define the Localized Contrastive Estimation (LCE) loss on a training batch of a set of query Q as,

$$\mathcal{L}_{\text{LCE}} := \frac{1}{|Q|} \sum_{q \in Q, G_q \sim R_q^m} -log \frac{exp(dist(q, d_q^+))}{\sum_{d \in G_q} exp(dist(q, d))} \tag{5}$$

Compared to a standard noise contrastive estimation (NCE) loss, LCE uses the target retriever to localize negative samples and focus learning on top portion instead of randomly sampled noisy negatives.

Table 1. Document ranking performance measured on MSMARCO dev (left table) and eval set (right table). † indicates statistical significance over Vanilla using a t-test with $p < 0.05$. As the leaderboard eval set only reports aggregated metrics, we cannot report statistical significance.

Method	MSMARCO Dev			
	MRR@100			
	Indri	BM25	BM25*	HDCT
Vanilla	38.34	36.97	39.28	40.84
LCE	39.55†	39.66†	42.23†	43.38†

Method	MSMARCO Eval
	MRR@100
PROP (ensemble)[a]	40.1
BERT-m1 (ensemble)[b]	39.8
Indri + Vanilla	33.8
HDCT + LCE (single)	38.2
HDCT + LCE (ensemble)	**40.5** (1st place)

[a] PROP_step400K base (ensemble v0.1)
[b] BERT-m1 base + classic IR + doc2query (ensemble)

4   Experiment Methodologies

Dataset and Tasks. We use the MSMARCO [1] *document* ranking dataset. The dataset contains 3 million documents. A document consists of 3 fields (title, URL, and body) with around 900 words. Models are trained on the train set of 0.37M training pairs. As recommended by MSMARCO organizers, we use the dev set for analysis.

Initial Stage Retriever. We experimented with four initial retrievers: Indri, un-tuned BM25, tuned BM25 (denoted as BM25*), and HDCT [5]. The Indri search results come from MSMARCO organizers[1]. We build BM25 indices with the Anserini toolkit [17], from which we produce two sets of search results with the toolkit's default BM25 parameters and a set of tuned parameters suggested by the toolkit authors[2]. HDCT is the SOTA method for augmenting document search indices with term weights re-estimated with BERT; we use the rankings provided by the authors [3]. We input top 100 candidate lists to rerankers.

Implementation. Following [4]'s BERT-FirstP setup, we input the concatenated document title, url and body's first 512 queries to the rerankers. Our rerankers are built and trained in mixed precision with PyTorch [13] and based on Huggingface's BERT implementation [15]. We sample negatives from the target retriever's top ranked $m = 100$ documents similar to reranking depth. We train on 4 RTX 2080 ti GPUs, each with a batch of 8 documents. We train for 2 epochs, with a 1e−5 learning rate and a warmup portion 0.1.

5   Document Ranking Performance

In Table 1, we summarize ranking performance on MSMARCO document ranking Dev and Eval (leaderboard) queries. Here, both vanilla and LCE use negatives from target retriever. On the dev set, we test rerankers trained with vanilla

---

[1] https://microsoft.github.io/msmarco/.
[2] https://github.com/castorini/anserini.
[3] http://boston.lti.cs.cmu.edu/appendices/TheWebConf2020-Zhuyun-Dai/.

and LCE loss on each type of the first-stage retriever. We see LCE significantly improves performance with all retrievers. Meanwhile, we see that gain using LCE enlarges as the retriever grows stronger, suggesting it can capture more complicated matching in the improved candidate list, while not being confused by the harder negatives.

The leader board results confirmed the effectiveness of LCE. HDCT+LCE pipeline outperformed the vanilla basline by a large margin. Following other recent leaderboard submissions, we further incorporate model ensemble. Our ensemble entry uses an LCE trained ensemble of BERT, RoBERTa [9] and ELECTRA [3] to rerank HDCT top 100. This submission got first place, achieving the state-of-the-art performance[4].

6   Analysis

In this section, we first analyze the effect of number of sampled documents per query in LCE, then the influence of the negative sample localization.

Fig. 1. Effect of LCE sample size We plot MRR@100 against sizes.

Effect of LCE Sample Size. In Fig. 1, we study the effect of varying the number of sampled documents per query in the LCE loss. We observe a big improvement from size 2 (1 positive, 1 negative) that compute loss scale with a single negative, to size 4 where loss weights are computed with 3 negatives. Further increase in sample size can generate some additional improvements.

Influence of Negative Localization. LCE samples negatives from top ranked documents retrieved by target retriever. Here we quantitatively evaluate its importance. Denote retriever used in training for negative sampling *train retriever* and in testing for candidate generation *test retriever*. We use all rerankers from Sect. 5 to rank candidate lists generated by all retrievers and plot results in a heat map Fig. 2. We plot rerankers using different train retrievers on the **horizontal** axis and test retrievers on the **vertical** axis. Each 4 × 4 sub-grid corresponds to a training strategy, and sub-grid diagonals correspond to Sect. 5 results. We observe localization benefits both LCE and vanilla methods. The performance of the Vanilla trained reranker *drops* severely when negatives are not localized by test retriever but from a weaker train retriever. Similarly,

---

[4] On the camera ready date (January 20th, 2021).

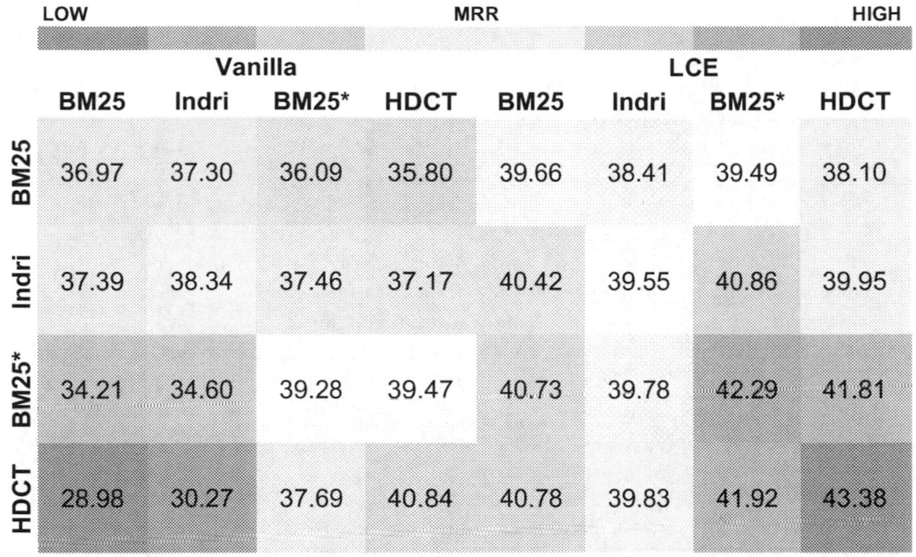

LOW   MRR   HIGH

| | Vanilla | | | | LCE | | | |
	BM25	Indri	BM25*	HDCT	BM25	Indri	BM25*	HDCT
BM25	36.97	37.30	36.09	35.80	39.66	38.41	39.49	38.10
Indri	37.39	38.34	37.46	37.17	40.42	39.55	40.86	39.95
BM25*	34.21	34.60	39.28	39.47	40.73	39.78	42.29	41.81
HDCT	28.98	30.27	37.69	40.84	40.78	39.83	41.92	43.38

Fig. 2. Effects of Train Retriever. The **horizontal** axis is the retriever that generates negatives for training (train retriever); the **vertical** axis is the retriever that generates candidates for testing (test retriever).

rerankers trained with LCE loss also perform better with localization. Interestingly, we do find that the LCE loss can bring some degrees of adaptability to the reranker, making it robust when the test retriever is different from the train retriever.

7 Conclusion

Recent research shows promising results on using deep LMs to improve initial retrievers. However, we discovered that previous BERT rerankers could not fully exploit the improved initial rankings. We propose Localized Contrastive Estimation (LCE) learning, to localize training negatives with target retriever, and to use a contrastive loss to penalize matching with confounding characteristics.

Experimental results demonstrate that reranker trained with LCE significantly outperforms its vanilla method trained counterpart using the same LM. Our analysis shows that localizing negatives and having an expressive loss with multiple contrastive negatives are both critical for the success of LCE.

The positive results show that, instead of adopting more advanced LM, it is also possible to improve the performance of existing deep LMs with better learning methods. Meanwhile, before this work, there are few existing work studying the interaction between different deep retrievers and reranker in pipelined retrieval systems. We believe this paper will encourage the community to conduct more systematic research on pipelined IR systems.

References

1. Campos, D.F., et al.: Ms marco: A human generated machine reading comprehension dataset. arXiv:abs/1611.09268 (2016)
2. Chen, T., Kornblith, S., Norouzi, M., Hinton, G.E.: A simple framework for contrastive learning of visual representations. arXiv:abs/2002.05709 (2020)
3. Clark, K., Luong, M.T., Le, Q.V., Manning, C.D.: Electra: pre-training text encoders as discriminators rather than generators. arXiv:abs/2003.10555 (2020)
4. Dai, Z., Callan, J.: Deeper text understanding for ir with contextual neural language modeling. In: Proceedings of the 42nd International ACM SIGIR Conference on Research and Development in Information Retrieval (2019)
5. Dai, Z., Callan, J.P.: Context-aware document term weighting for ad-hoc search. In: Proceedings of The Web Conference 2020 (2020)
6. Dai, Z., Callan, J.: Context-aware term weighting for first stage passage retrieval. In: Proceedings of the 43rd International ACM SIGIR Conference on Research and Development in Information Retrieval (2020)
7. Devlin, J., Chang, M.W., Lee, K., Toutanova, K.: Bert: pre-training of deep bidirectional transformers for language understanding. In: NAACL-HLT (2019)
8. Hadsell, R., Chopra, S., LeCun, Y.: Dimensionality reduction by learning an invariant mapping. In: 2006 IEEE Computer Society Conference on Computer Vision and Pattern Recognition (CVPR 2006), vol. 2, pp. 1735–1742 (2006)
9. Liu, Y., et al.: Roberta: a robustly optimized Bert pretraining approach. arXiv:abs/1907.11692 (2019)
10. Nogueira, R., Cho, K.: Passage re-ranking with Bert. arXiv:abs/1901.04085 (2019)
11. Nogueira, R., Yang, W., Cho, K., Lin, J.: Multi-stage document ranking with bert. ArXiv abs/1910.14424 (2019)
12. Nogueira, R., Yang, W., Lin, J., Cho, K.: Document expansion by query prediction. arXiv:abs/1904.08375 (2019)
13. Paszke, A., et al.: Pytorch: An imperative style, high-performance deep learning library. In: Advances in Neural Information Processing Systems, vol. 32, pp. 8024–8035. Curran Associates, Inc. (2019). http://papers.neurips.cc/paper/9015-pytorch-an-imperative-style-high-performance-deep-learning-library.pdf
14. Peters, M.E., et al.: Deep contextualized word representations. arXiv:abs/1802.05365 (2018)
15. Wolf, T., et al.: Huggingface's transformers: state-of-the-art natural language processing. arXiv:abs/1910.03771 (2019)
16. Wu, Z., Xiong, Y., Yu, S., Lin, D.: Unsupervised feature learning via nonparametric instance discrimination. In: 2018 IEEE/CVF Conference on Computer Vision and Pattern Recognition, pp. 3733–3742 (2018)
17. Yang, P., Fang, H., Lin, J.: Anserini: enabling the use of Lucene for information retrieval research. In: Proceedings of the 40th International ACM SIGIR Conference on Research and Development in Information Retrieval (2017)

Should I Visit This Place? Inclusion and Exclusion Phrase Mining from Reviews

Omkar Gurjar[1(✉)] and Manish Gupta[1,2]

[1] IIIT-Hyderabad, Hyderabad, India
omkar.gurjar@students.iiit.ac.in, manish.gupta@iiit.ac.in
[2] Microsoft, Hyderabad, India
gmanish@microsoft.com

Abstract. Although several automatic itinerary generation services have made travel planning easy, often times travellers find themselves in unique situations where they cannot make the best out of their trip. Visitors differ in terms of many factors such as suffering from a disability, being of a particular dictary preference, travelling with a toddler, etc. While most tourist spots are universal, others may not be inclusive for all. In this paper, we focus on the problem of mining inclusion and exclusion phrases associated with 11 such factors, from reviews related to a tourist spot. While existing work on tourism data mining mainly focuses on structured extraction of trip related information, personalized sentiment analysis, and automatic itinerary generation, to the best of our knowledge this is the first work on inclusion/exclusion phrase mining from tourism reviews. Using a dataset of 2000 reviews related to 1000 tourist spots, our broad level classifier provides a binary overlap F1 of ~80 and ~82 to classify a phrase as inclusion or exclusion respectively. Further, our inclusion/exclusion classifier provides an F1 of ~98 and ~97 for 11-class inclusion and exclusion classification respectively. We believe that our work can significantly improve the quality of an automatic itinerary generation service.

1 Introduction

Hundreds of millions of visitors travel across the globe every year resulting into trillions of dollars of spending. Number of international tourist arrivals has seen a steady increase over the past few decades[1]. Thanks to the availability of multiple online services like web maps, travel and stay booking, and automatic planning, tourism has become a lot comfortable in recent years.

Automated itinerary planning systems[2] provide a holistic solution enabling transportation, lodging, sights, and food recommendations. However such recommendation systems cannot incorporate subtle user constraints like a claustrophobic user, visitors travelling with a toddler, visitors of a particular ethnicity

---

[1] https://data.worldbank.org/indicator/ST.INT.ARVL.
[2] http://itineree.com/top-online-travel-planners/.

© Springer Nature Switzerland AG 2021
D. Hiemstra et al. (Eds.): ECIR 2021, LNCS 12657, pp. 287–294, 2021.
https://doi.org/10.1007/978-3-030-72240-1_27

with visa restrictions, etc. Indeed, many of them, do not even incorporate tourist spot specific properties like what time of day is best to visit, temporary ad hoc closures due to local vacations or maintenance work, visitor height/gender restrictions, vegetarian friendly or not, etc.

Tourist review websites are a gold mine of data related to very subtle restrictions (or exclusions) associated with a tourist spot. In this work, we focus on the following 11 different factors regarding inclusion or exclusion nature of tourist spots. (1) Age/Height: Disallow visitors of a particular age/height group: too old, or too young, too short. (2) Claustrophobia: Some spots consist of a lot of confined spaces and hence unsuitable for claustrophobic visitors. (3) Couples/Family: Some spots are family/kids friendly versus not. (4) Crowd: Some spots are often heavily crowded, which may be repulsive to some visitors. (5) Food: Some spots may serve low quality food, non-vegetarian food only, may not serve any food, may not allow any external food, may not allow alcoholic drinks, etc. (6) Handicap: Some spots may not allow facilities for disabled folks like lifts, ramps, etc. The terrain may not be wheel-chair or stroller friendly. (7) Hygiene: Some spots may be filthy, e.g., unclean toilets, littered beaches, etc. (8) Parking: Unavailability and ease of parking. (9) Price: Some spots may be very expensive for tourists. (10) Queues: Some spots may exhibit large queues leading to long wait times. Visitors on a tight schedule may want to avoid such places, or visit them in low wait time durations. (11) Time: Various spots have a preferred visit timings, such as early morning, late evening, on Wednesdays, from Sep-Dec, etc. This category also includes ad hoc closures due to maintenance or other reasons.

In this paper, we focus on two related tasks: (1) Task 1 pertains to mining inclusion/exclusion phrases from tourism reviews. A phrase which pertains to any of the exclusions as mentioned above is labeled as an exclusion phrase, while a phrase related to inclusion of the above factors is labeled as an inclusion phrase. (2) Task 2 is about fine-grained classification of inclusion/exclusion phrases into one of the above 11 categories. "I had my kids who loved this museum" and "elevators for those whom stairs are problematic" are examples of age and handicap inclusion phrases. "place was very crowded", "would not recommend the area for young children" are examples of crowd and age exclusion phrases.

We are the first to propose the problem of extracting inclusion/exclusion phrases from tourism review data. The problem is challenging: (1) There can be many types of exclusions as discussed above. (2) These factors can be expressed in lots of different ways. (3) There could be multiple indirect references (e.g. if the place allows gambling, likely kids are not allowed) or unrelated references (e.g., a review talking about a tour guide's "family" rather than if "families" are allowed at the spot).

Overall, we make the following contributions in this paper: (1) We propose a novel task of mining inclusion/exclusion phrases from online tourist reviews, and their fine-grained classification. (2) We model the first task as a sequence labeling problem, and the second one as a multi-class classification. We investigate the effectiveness of CRFs (Conditional Random Fields), BiLSTMs (Bidirectional

Long Short-Term Memory networks), and Transformer models like BERT (Bidirectional Encoder Representations from Transformers). (3) We make the code and the manually labeled dataset (2303 phrases mined from ~2000 reviews) publicly available[3]. Our experiments show that the proposed models lead to practically usable classifiers.

2   Related Work

Tourism Data Mining: Work on tourism data mining has mostly focused on structured extraction of trip related information [18], mining reviews (personalized sentiment analysis of tourist reviews [15], establishing review credibility [1,7]), and automatic itinerary generation [2,3,5,8]. Popescu et al. [18] extract visit durations or information like "what can I visit in one day in this city?" from Flickr data. Pantano et al. [15] predict tourists' future preferences from reviews. Ayeh et al. [1] examine the credibility perceptions and online travelers' attitude towards using user-generated content (UGC). Filieri et al. [7] study the impact of source credibility, information quality, website quality, customer satisfaction, user experience on users' trust towards UGC. The automatic itinerary generation problem has been studied extensively from multiple perspectives. Friggstad et al. [8] model the problem as an orienteering problem on a graph of tourist spots. Chang et al. [2] weigh different factors like spot name, popularity, isRestaurant, isAccomodation, etc. based on user interactions to optimize the process of trip planning. De et al. [5] aggregate across geo-temporal breadcrumbs data for multiple users to construct itineraries. Clearly, our system can be an important sub-module to generate automated itineraries which are exclusion-sensitive.

Sequence Labeling: Sequence labeling involves predicting an output label sequence given an input text sequence. A label is generated per input token. Popular sequence labeling models include CRFs [13], LSTMs [9], LSTM-CRFs [11], and Transformer models like BERT [6]. Many NLP tasks can be modeled as sequence labeling tasks including opinion mining [12], part-of-speech tagging, etc. The labels for such tasks are typically encoded using BIO (begin, inside, outside) labeling. In this paper, we investigate the effectiveness of such sequence labeling approaches for the inclusion/exclusion phrase mining task.

Aspect Extraction: Aspect extraction has been studied widely in the past decade, mainly for product reviews, using supervised [19], semi-supervised [14] as well as unsupervised [10] methods. In this work, we study aspect extraction for reviews in the tourism domain.

3   Proposed Approach

3.1   Dataset

We first obtained a list of top 1000 tourist spots from lonelyplanet.com (a popular tourist website). Next, we obtained a maximum of 2000 reviews corresponding to

---

[3] https://github.com/omkar2810/Inclusion_Exclusion_Phrase_Mining.

each of these spots from tripadvisor.com. Further, we broadly filtered out reviews (and then sentences) that could be potentially related to the eleven factors mentioned in Sect. 1 using a manually produced keyword list for each category. We provide the full keyword list per category as part of the dataset. These ~2000 reviews were then manually labeled for inclusion/exclusion phrases using the BIO tagging, as well as their fine categorization into one of the 11 categories. A total of 2303 phrases were labeled with one of the 11 categories. The distribution across the categories is as follows: Age/Height: 324, Claustrophobia: 217, Couples/Family: 151, Crowd: 307, Food: 313, Handicap: 204, Hygiene: 95, Parking: 65, Price: 351, Queues: 185, and Time: 91. For the inclusion/exclusion phrase mining task, a total of 2303 phrases from 2154 sentences were labeled. Phrases in these sentences which are not inclusion/exclusion are marked as others. Across these phrases, the word label distribution is as follows: B_EXC: 1176, B_INC: 1223, EXC: 5713, INC: 5455, O: 29976, where INC and EXC denote inclusion and exclusion respectively. We make the code and the manually labeled dataset publicly available[3]. On a small set of 115 instances, we measured the inter-annotator agreement and found the Cohen's Kappa to be 0.804 and 0.931 for the first and the second tasks respectively, which is considered as very good.

3.2 Methods

We experiment with two different word embedding methods: GloVe (Global Vectors for Word Representation) [16] and ELMo (Embeddings from Language Models) [17]. We use CRFs, BiLSTMs, BiLSTM-CRFs and BERT for the first sequence labeling task. We use traditional machine learning (ML) classifiers like XGBoost and Support Vector Machines (SVMs) and deep learning (DL) models like BiLSTMs, LSTM-CNN and BERT for the multi-class classification task.

CRFs [13]: Conditional Random Fields (CRFs) are prediction models for tasks where contextual information or state of the neighbors affect the current prediction. They are a type of discriminative undirected probabilistic graphical model.

BiLSTMs [9]: Bidirectional LSTMs are the most popular traditional deep learning models for sequence modeling. They model text sequences using recurrence and gate-controlled explicit memory logic. Bidirectionality helps propagate information across both directions leading to improved accuracies compared to unidirectional LSTMs.

BiLSTM-CNNs [4]: BiLSTM-CNNs use character-based CNNs to first generate the word embeddings. These word embeddings are further used by the LSTM to generate the embedding for the text sequence. This is then connected to a dense layer and then finally to the output softmax layer.

BiLSTM-CRFs [11]: We combine a BiLSTM network and a CRF network to form a BiLSTM-CRF model. This network can efficiently use past input features via a LSTM layer and sentence level tag information via a CRF layer.

BERT [6]: BERT is a Transformer-encoder model trained in a bidirectional way. BERT has been shown to provide very high accuracies across a large number of NLP tasks. For the sequence labeling task, we connect the semantic output for each position to an output softmax layer. For multi-class classification, we connect semantic representation of CLS token to the output softmax layer.

4 Experiments

For BiLSTM experiments, we used three layers, ReLU activation for hidden layers and softmax for output, SGD optimizer (with momentum $= 0.7$, learning rate $= 1e-5$, batch size $= 8$), and cross-entropy loss. We trained for 50 epochs. We used GloVe 200D word vectors. For BERT, we used the pretrained BERT BASE model with 12 Transformer layers, Adam optimizer with learning rate $= 3e-5$, max sequence length $= 128$, batch size $= 8$, and categorical cross entropy loss.

4.1 Results

Table 1 shows results for the inclusion/exclusion phrase mining task. As discussed in [12], we use two metrics: (1) Binary Overlap which counts every overlapping match between a predicted and true expression as correct, and (2) Proportional Overlap which imparts a partial correctness, proportional to the overlapping amount, to each match. BERT based method outperforms all other methods. This is because the 12 layers of self-attention help significantly in discovering the right inclusion/exclusion label for each word. Also, precision values are typically lower than recall, which means that our models can detect that the text implies some inclusion or exclusion but find it difficult to differentiate between the two.

Table 1. Inclusion/exclusion phrase mining accuracy results

Model	Inclusion						Exclusion					
	Precision		Recall		F1		Precision		Recall		F1	
	Prop	Bin	Prop	Bin	Prop	Bin	Prop	Bin	Prop	Bin	Prop	Bin
CRF + GloVe	0.354	0.417	0.531	0.758	0.425	0.538	0.372	0.392	0.524	0.728	0.435	0.512
BiLSTM + GloVe	0.456	0.590	0.573	0.643	0.508	0.615	0.506	0.638	0.570	0.668	0.536	0.650
BiLSTM CRF + GloVe	0.490	0.625	0.613	0.714	0.545	0.666	0.516	0.649	0.654	0.788	0.577	0.712
BiLSTM + ELMo	0.580	0.645	0.604	0.770	0.590	0.701	0.602	0.678	0.566	0.738	0.579	0.703
BERT	**0.677**	**0.748**	**0.765**	**0.869**	**0.718**	**0.804**	**0.664**	**0.756**	**0.801**	**0.908**	**0.726**	**0.825**

We present the results of our 11-class phrase classification in Table 2. We observe that typically the accuracy is better for inclusion phrases rather than exclusion phrases. Deep learning based methods like LSTMs and BERT are better than traditional ML classifiers. BERT outperforms all other methods by a large margin for both the inclusion and exclusion phrases.

Further, we performed an end-to-end evaluation of our system. For each sentence in the test set, we first obtained BIO predictions using our phrase mining system. Then, we perform 11-class classification on these mined phrases. Golden label for our predicted inclusion/exclusion phrase is set to the ground truth label for the phrase with maximum intersection. For predicted phrases which have no intersection with any golden phrase, we assume them to belong to a special "sink" class, and they count towards loss in precision. Golden phrases not detected by our system count towards loss in recall. Such an evaluation leads to an overall F1 of 0.748 (P = 0.695, R = 0.812), inclusion F1 of 0.739 (P = 0.691, R = 0.795) and an exclusion F1 of 0.759 (P = 0.700, R = 0.830).

Table 2. 11-class categorization accuracy results

Model	Total			Inclusion			Exclusion		
	Precision	Recall	F1	Precision	Recall	F1	Precision	Recall	F1
SVM	0.725	0.631	0.626	0.759	0.635	0.649	0.665	0.626	0.604
XGBoost	0.802	0.796	0.797	0.802	0.785	0.786	0.817	0.806	0.806
BiLSTM + GloVe	0.890	0.885	0.884	0.921	0.917	0.916	0.862	0.852	0.853
BiLSTM-CNN + GloVe	0.895	0.892	0.891	0.903	0.900	0.900	0.889	0.883	0.883
BiLSTM Attn + GloVe	0.914	0.911	0.911	0.938	0.934	0.934	0.894	0.887	0.889
BERT	**0.978**	**0.978**	**0.978**	**0.983**	**0.982**	**0.982**	**0.975**	**0.973**	**0.973**

Next, we present two examples of the output from our system. Consider the sentence: "The wheelchair wouldn't go through the turnstile which was disappointing". Our inclusion/exclusion phrase mining BERT classifier outputs "B_EXC EXC EXC EXC EXC EXC EXC O O O" while our 11-class classifier labels this as "Handicap". Our system was able to smartly associate "wheelchair wouldn't go through" with "handicap" category. Consider another example, "We came to Eiffel Tower to celebrate twenty five years of togetherness". Our two classifiers predict "O O O O O O O INC INC INC INC INC" and "Couples/Family". Interestingly, it can relate "togetherness" with "Couples/Family".

4.2   Error Analysis

We performed a manual analysis of some of the errors made by our best model. We found the following interesting patterns. (1) It is difficult to predict the right label when the phrase can be provided multiple labels. E.g. "If you don't like crowds or feel claustrophobic being on narrow walkways full of groups of people ..." can be labeled into either of the Crowd or Claustrophobia categories. (2) Conflicting opinions mentioned in same review. "... Well worth the $25 ... The cost of the day was very expensive compared to Australian water parks." In this review, from a price perspective, it is difficult to figure out whether the spot is cheap or expensive. Similarly, consider another review: "Wednesday night is bike night in Beale Street so a lot of noise from at least 1000 bikes many highly decorated. It was fun and the usual bar street of many cities." Can't really make out whether one should visit during the night or not. (3) References to other unrelated things: Consider this review: "... I was lucky enough to have a descendant who gave the garden tour and tell about the family (more than you might usually get) ..." The word "family" here does not indicate anything about inclusion/exclusion wrt families for the spot.

5   Conclusion

In this paper, we proposed a novel task for mining of inclusion/exclusion phrases and their detailed categorization. We investigated the effectiveness of various deep learning methods for the task. We found that BERT based methods lead to a binary overlap F1 of ~80 and ~82 for the sequence labeling task, and an F1 of ~98 and ~97 for 11-class inclusion and exclusion classification respectively. In the future, we plan to integrate this module as a part of a personalized automated itinerary recommendation system.

References

1. Ayeh, J.K., Au, N., Law, R.: "Do we believe in TripAdvisor?" Examining credibility perceptions and online travelers' attitude toward using user-generated content. J. Travel Res. **52**(4), 437–452 (2013)
2. Chang, H.T., Chang, Y.M., Tsai, M.T.: ATIPS: automatic travel itinerary planning system for domestic areas. Comput. Intell. Neurosci. (2016)
3. Chen, G., Wu, S., Zhou, J., Tung, A.K.: Automatic itinerary planning for traveling services. IEEE Trans. Knowl. Data Eng. **26**(3), 514–527 (2013)
4. Chiu, J.P., Nichols, E.: Named entity recognition with bidirectional LSTM-CNNS. Trans. Assoc. Comput. Linguist. **4**, 357–370 (2016)
5. De Choudhury, M., Feldman, M., Amer-Yahia, S., Golbandi, N., Lempel, R., Yu, C.: Automatic construction of travel itineraries using social breadcrumbs. In: Proceedings of the 21st ACM conference on Hypertext and hypermedia, pp. 35–44 (2010)
6. Devlin, J., Chang, M.W., Lee, K., Toutanova, K.: Bert: Pre-training of deep bidirectional transformers for language understanding. arXiv preprint arXiv:1810.04805 (2018)
7. Filieri, R., Alguezaui, S., McLeay, F.: Why do travelers trust tripadvisor? antecedents of trust towards consumer-generated media and its influence on recommendation adoption and word of mouth. Tourism Manage. **51**, 174–185 (2015)
8. Friggstad, Z., Gollapudi, S., Kollias, K., Sarlos, T., Swamy, C., Tomkins, A.: Orienteering algorithms for generating travel itineraries. In: Proceedings of the Eleventh ACM International Conference on Web Search and Data Mining, pp. 180–188 (2018)
9. Graves, A., Jaitly, N., Mohamed, A.R.: Hybrid speech recognition with deep bidirectional LSTM. In: 2013 IEEE Workshop on Automatic Speech Recognition and Understanding, pp. 273–278. IEEE (2013)
10. He, R., Lee, W.S., Ng, H.T., Dahlmeier, D.: An unsupervised neural attention model for aspect extraction. In: Proceedings of the 55th Annual Meeting of the Association for Computational Linguistics (Volume 1: Long Papers), pp. 388–397 (2017)
11. Huang, Z., Xu, W., Yu, K.: Bidirectional LSTM-CRF models for sequence tagging. arXiv preprint arXiv:1508.01991 (2015)
12. Irsoy, O., Cardie, C.: Opinion mining with deep recurrent neural networks. In: Proceedings of the 2014 Conference on Empirical Methods in Natural Language Processing (EMNLP), pp. 720–728 (2014)

13. Lafferty, J.D., McCallum, A., Pereira, F.C.: Conditional random fields: probabilistic models for segmenting and labeling sequence data. In: Proceedings of the Eighteenth International Conference on Machine Learning, pp. 282–289 (2001)
14. Mukherjee, A., Liu, B.: Aspect extraction through semi-supervised modeling. In: Proceedings of the 50th Annual Meeting of the Association for Computational Linguistics (Volume 1: Long Papers). p,. 339–348 (2012)
15. Pantano, E., Priporas, C.V., Stylos, N.: 'you will like it!' using open data to predict tourists' response to a tourist attraction. Tourism Manage. **60**, 430–438 (2017)
16. Pennington, J., Socher, R., Manning, C.D.: Glove: global vectors for word representation. In: Proceedings of the 2014 Conference on Empirical Methods in Natural Language Processing (EMNLP), pp. 1532–1543 (2014)
17. Peters, M.E., et al.: Deep contextualized word representations. arXiv preprint arXiv:1802.05365 (2018)
18. Popescu, A., Grefenstette, G.: Deducing trip related information from Flickr. In: Proceedings of the 18th International Conference on World wide Web, pp. 1183–1184 (2009)
19. Wang, W., Pan, S.J., Dahlmeier, D., Xiao, X.: Recursive neural conditional random fields for aspect-based sentiment analysis. arXiv preprint arXiv:1603.06679 (2016)

Dynamic Cross-Sentential Context Representation for Event Detection

Dorian Kodelja⬛, Romaric Besançon⬛, and Olivier Ferret(✉)⬛

Université Paris-Saclay, CEA, List, 91120 Palaiseau, France
{dorian.kodelja,romaric.besancon,olivier.ferret}@cea.fr

Abstract. In this paper, which focuses on the supervised detection of event mentions in texts, we propose a method to exploit a large context through the representation of distant sentences selected based on coreference relations between entities. We show the benefits of extending a neural sentence-level model with this representation through evaluation carried out on the TAC Event 2015 reference corpus.

Keywords: Information extraction · Event detection · Global context

1 Introduction

This study focuses on the supervised event extraction from text, which consists in identifying in texts the words or the sequences of words, called event mentions, that mark the presence of a predefined type of events. For instance, the word *pow-wow* for an event of type MEET in:

> Putin had invited Tony Blair to the **pow-wow** in Saint Petersburg's Grand Hotel Europe.

The best methods for achieving this task are generally based on neural models and operate at the sentence level, similarly to [13]. However, the sentence level is not always sufficient to get all the elements for detecting an event mention. Two main types of studies already explored the possibility to exploit information at a larger scale: on the one hand, methods that use document level information to perform event extraction at a local scale; on the other hand, methods that achieve event extraction globally at the document level through joint approaches [3,10,15,18]. Our work takes place among the first type of methods, which can be broken down into methods using specific information at the document scale between events [8,9] or event and entities [6] and methods exploiting a more global representation of documents, either through generic models such as *Doc2Vec* [4] or models specifically trained for the target task as in [19].

In this article, our contribution is a new method for taking into account the document context for event extraction. More precisely, we exploit the coreference

Work partly supported by ANR under project ASRAEL (ANR-15-CE23-0018) with the FactoryIA supercomputer supported by the Ile-de-France Regional Council.

D. Hiemstra et al. (Eds.): ECIR 2021, LNCS 12657, pp. 295–302, 2021.
https://doi.org/10.1007/978-3-030-72240-1_28

links from the entities surrounding a candidate mention to dynamically build its context from selected event-related distant sentences. The representations of those sentences are then integrated into a sentence-level model that, similarly to recent studies [1,11,13,17], is based on Graph Convolution Networks (GCN) [7].

2   Model

Classically, we frame event detection as a multi-class classification task for each word in a document. The label is either one of the 38 event types of the DEFT Rich ERE taxonomy [2] or the *NONE* label for the absence of event mention.

2.1   Intra-sentential GCN

Our intra-sentential model is a GCN relying on syntactic dependencies, similarly to [13]. In this model, we consider as candidate each word w_t in a sentence $S = (w_1, w_2, \ldots, w_n)$, where w_i is the i-th word in the sentence, associated with an entity type e_i (with $e_i = O$ if w_i is not an entity head). Each of these words is represented as a real-valued vector $X = x_1, x_2, \ldots, x_n$ built by concatenating three kinds of embeddings: a word embedding for representing the word itself, a position embedding for its relative distance to the candidate, and an entity embedding for its entity type e_i. A BiLSTM is applied to the target sentence S (focused on w_t through the position embedding) for producing a first contextual representation of each word. A GCN made of K convolution layers is then used for producing a contextual representation of each word taking into account the influence of distant words of S through up to K syntactic dependencies. It relies on a directed graph G where the nodes are the words of S and each edge (w_i, w_j) is associated with a label $L(w_i, w_j)$ corresponding to a syntactic dependency between w_i and w_j. The last step consists in aggregating the sequence $h_{w_1}^K, h_{w_2}^K, \ldots h_{w_n}^K$ at the last convolution layer into a final representation p_t of the target word w_t that can be fed to a dense layer with a softmax for the classification. [13] introduces a new pooling strategy that focuses on entities, with the assumption that entities carry a special interest for the task.

With a similar goal, we propose *syntactic pooling*, which also considers multiple specific words in the sentence while not requiring a prior annotation of named entities. In this case, the pooling is focused on the target word and all nouns (n), verbs (v), and adjectives (a) in the sentence:

$$p_t = maxpool(\{h_{w_t}^K\} \cup \{h_{w_i,1 \leqslant i \leqslant n}^K : pos(w_i) \in \{n, v, a\}\}) \qquad (1)$$

2.2   Cross-Sentential Context Representation

Contrary to work integrating a global representation of the document [4,19], we chose to take into account the context of a target sentence in a more selective way, both for improving the disambiguation of candidate event mentions and limiting the parameters of the model. For the task of event extraction, the presence of common named entities is a good indicator of the contextual association of the sentences since they are typically possible arguments of similar events (for instance, different legal events concerning the same person), related events in a chronological succession (an injure event followed by a die event) or even two mentions of the same event. In the example given in the introduction, *pow-wow* is not a frequent word for a MEET event but the event is also mentioned with less ambiguous occurrences in the same document, in sentences sharing common entities, such as *Saint Petersburg*:

> But the *Saint Petersburg* **summit** ended without any formal declaration on Iraq.

Context Representation. Our context representation relies on the integration of a contextual representation of each entity mention e_i^j of the target sentence S^j. For selecting the context linked to e_i^j, we define the function $links(S^j, S^k, i)$, that gives the set of positions l in a context sentence S^k of its entity mentions that are in a coreference relation with the considered entity mention e_i^j:

$$links(S^j, S^k, i) = \{l \colon E(e_i^j) = E(e_l^k)\} \quad {\scriptstyle 1 \leqslant l \leqslant n} \qquad (2)$$

where $E(e)$ denotes the entity referred by the mention e. The context of e_i^j is then built from the set of pairs (context sentence, mention of $E(e_i^j)$) defined as:

$$Links(S^j, i) = \{(S^k, l) \colon l \in links(S^j, S^k, i)\} \quad {\scriptstyle 1 \leqslant l \leqslant n,\ k \neq j} \qquad (3)$$

For each pair (S^k, l) of this context, we produce an input representation, noted $X^{k,l} = x_1^{k,l}, x_2^{k,l}, \ldots, x_n^{k,l}$, similar to the one in Sect. 2.1, except for the position embeddings: in this case, the position vector of each word of S^k represents the distance to the position l of the entity mention e_l^k. A BiLSTM is then applied to this input representation. Two extraction methods for the representation of each pair (S^k, l) are considered: the *Final* mode (Eq. 4), which concatenates the final representations of the two LSTMs, and the *Mention* mode (Eq. 5), which extracts the representations at the position of the entity mention e_l^k.

$$\textbf{Final: } h_{\textbf{context}}(S^k, l) = [h_{\text{forward}}(x_n^{k,l}); h_{\text{backward}}(x_1^{k,l})] \qquad (4)$$

$$\textbf{Mention: } h_{\textbf{context}}(S^k, l) = [h_{\text{forward}}(x_l^{k,l}); h_{\text{backward}}(x_l^{k,l})] \qquad (5)$$

Context Integration. The context representation of the entity mention e_i^j is then integrated into the local context at two possible levels, as illustrated by Fig. 1: either as an additional embedding in the local input representation of the entity mention, or as an additional node in the graph, associated with the node of the entity mention by a specific relation. For both integration modes, the expected representation is a vector that we obtain by aggregating the vectors of all contextual entity mentions through max-pooling:

$$context(e_i^j) = maxpool(\{h_{\textbf{context}}(S^k, l) \colon (S^k, l) \in Links(S^j, i)\}) \qquad (6)$$

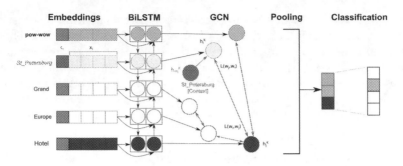

Fig. 1. Two solutions for integrating the context representation (in red) of an entity mention into the GCN model: at the input level or by adding a node to the graph. (Color figure online)

For the integration as a node, we modify the dependency graph G by adding a node cn_i^j merging all the context representations of e_i^j and having $h_{cn_i^j}^0 = context(e_i^j)$ as initial representation. We then define a new *Context* edge type between the local entity mentions and their context representation and add the corresponding edge (w_i^j, cn_i^j) in G. For the integration at the embedding level, the context representation is concatenated to the other embeddings. For the words having no context representation, a default representation $c_{default}$ is used, initialized randomly, and modified during training. The context vector defined in (6) is then generalized to all the words of the sentence with:

$$c_i^j = \begin{cases} context(e_i^j) & \text{if } |Links(S^j, i)| > 0 \\ c_{default} & \text{otherwise} \end{cases} \tag{7}$$

and the input sequence is redefined as $X^j = ([x_0^j, c_0^j], [x_1^j, c_1^j], \dots, [x_n^j, c_n^j])$.

3 Experiments

3.1 Data and Preprocessing

Our training dataset is composed of 58 documents from the TAC 2015 training dataset and 288 documents from the DEFT Rich ERE (R2 V2 and V2) dataset. The validation set is composed of the remaining 100 documents from the TAC 2015 training dataset. We evaluate our proposed model on the test set of TAC 2015 to compare it with the graph model of [13].

We use the Stanford CoreNLP tool [12] for named entity recognition (NER), coreference resolution, and syntactic analysis to produce dependency graphs from its *Basic dependencies*. At the document level, an entity is defined as a group of mentions in coreference. For increasing the coverage of the automatic coreference system, we merge entities mentions of which are identical.

Example Generation. To facilitate access to content-bearing words in the graph convolution, we filter some categories of words: punctuations, symbols, numbers, determiners, prepositions, conjunctions, or interjections. We also use a prediction mask: only nouns, verbs, and adjectives are associated with a predicted category; the other words are associated with the NONE class.

Hyperparameters. The word embeddings are initialized with pretrained GloVe embeddings [14]. The position and the entity type embeddings are of size 50 while the dimensions of the local BiLSTM layer and the two graph convolution layers are 400 and 300 respectively. The embeddings for the words, entities, and distances are the same for the target sentences and the context sentences. The model is trained using SGD with momentum and batches of 10 examples. All average performances are computed on 10 runs with the same parameters.

3.2   Study of Model's Parameters

We first evaluate the influence of the different choices for the model's parameters:

- **Intra-sentential pooling**: *Syntactic/Entity*
- **Context representation extraction**: *Final/Mention*
- **Context representation integration**: *Embedding/Node*

We searched for the best values of these parameters on the validation set together with the values of less specific optimization parameters (learning rate, l2 regularization, dropout, momentum). Concerning the model's parameters, the best result is obtained using *Syntactic* pooling, *Final* extraction, and *Embedding* integration. These parameters are also the best, in general, in each tested configuration, but since we cannot show all results, we present in Table 1 the results for this best model, noted C-GCN, and the variations of this model when changing each of the other parameters.

Table 1. Performances on the validation set for the main model's parameters ($P_{avg.}$, $R_{avg.}$, $F_{avg.}$: average values from 10 runs of precision, recall, and F-score; F_σ: F-score standard deviation; $F_{max.}$: F-score maximal value).

	$P_{avg.}$	$R_{avg.}$	$F_{avg.}$	F_σ	$F_{max.}$
C-GCN	75.6	**50.4**	**60.5**	0.6	**60.4**
Pooling - *Entity*	74.8	49.2	59.3	0.9	60.2
Extraction - *Mention*	75.0	48.8	59.1	1.2	58.1
Integration - *Node*	**76.9**	48.1	59.1	1.2	59.3

We observe, with a weakly significant difference ($p = 0.058$), that the *entity* pooling is slightly worse than the *Syntactic* pooling, which indicates that the use of a larger set of context words benefits to an enriched representation of the target word. On the contrary, the *overall* pooling in [13] performs worse than the *entity* pooling while it also considers more words than that pooling. However, this difference may come from the use of different NER tools.

Concerning the context extraction, the poor results obtained with the *Mention* mode could also be related to the quality of the entities or to the fact that the final representations of the context sentences are more informative than the specific representations of the entity mentions. Finally, the integration of the context representation as a node does not degrade the results in a significant way but produces a less balanced performance between precision and recall.

3.3 Comparison with State-of-the-Art

We compare in this section our proposed model to the original model from [13], noted GCN_{nguyen}, and to the best model of the TAC evaluation campaign, RPI_BLENDER, proposed by [5], based on a MaxEnt classifier using a large set of lexical, syntactic and entity features. To further prove the interest of having a specific context for each example, we train a model $C\text{-}GCN_{generic}$ that uses all the sentences of the document as context. In this case, there is no position embedding for the context sentences, and the same representation is used as an embedding for all the words in the considered sentence.

Table 2. Results on TAC 2015 test set ($F_{max./dev}$: F-score for the best parameters on the dev. set; for the two reference systems, P and R are *max./dev* values; average values for the others).

	P	R	$F_{avg.}$	F_σ	$F_{max./dev}$
RPI_BLENDER	75.2	47.7	–	–	58.4
GCN_{nguyen}	70.3	**50.6**	–	–	58.8
GCN_{repro}	**78.5**	47.0	58.7	0.8	59.1
$C\text{-}GCN_{generic}$	74.5	48.4	58.6	0.6	59.0
C-GCN	75.6	50.4	**60.5**	0.6	**60.4**

The results presented in Table 2 prove the interest of our proposition: our implementation of the GCN model, noted GCN_{repro}, achieve results similar to the ones reported by [13][1] and we obtain a gain of 1.8 F-score on this baseline when using the context representation ($p < 0.0001$). We also see that the integration of the context in $C\text{-}GCN_{generic}$ does not yield better results, which confirms our intuition on the interest of defining a context specific to each example.

4 Conclusion and Perspectives

We propose in this article a method allowing a neural model for event extraction to take into account a cross-sentential context. The approach consists in enriching

---

[1] We note that we do not have exactly the same train/dev datasets because we also used the DEFT dataset as training, which can explain the slight gain in F-score.

the representation of entity mentions in a target sentence with a contextual embedding built using information from distant sentences where these entities also occur. The evaluation of the approach on the dataset TAC 2015 proves the interest of the method, with a significant gain over the initial model. One perspective would be to use an attention mechanism as an alternative to the max-pooling to aggregate the representations of all the mentions of an entity, which could lead to better discriminate and filter context sentences. Another one could be the use of a more elaborated GCN model able to take into account the type of the relations in the graph, such as Relational GCN [16].

References

1. Balali, A., Asadpour, M., Campos, R., Jatowt, A.: Joint event extraction along shortest dependency paths using graph convolutional networks. Knowl.-Based Syst. **210**, (2020). https://doi.org/10.1016/j.knosys.2020.106492

2. Bies, A., et al.: A comparison of event representations in DEFT. In: Fourth Workshop on Events, pp. 27–36 (2016)

3. Chen, Y., Yang, H., Liu, K., Zhao, J., Jia, Y.: Collective event detection via a hierarchical and bias tagging networks with gated multi-level attention mechanisms. In: 2018 Conference on Empirical Methods in Natural Language Processing (EMNLP 2018), Brussels, Belgium, pp. 1267–1276. ACL (2018). https://doi.org/10.18653/v1/D18-1158

4. Duan, S., He, R., Zhao, W.: Exploiting document level information to improve event detection via recurrent neural networks. In: Eighth International Joint Conference on Natural Language Processing (IJCNLP 2017), pp. 352–361 (2017)

5. Hong, Y., et al.: RPI_BLENDER TAC-KBP2015 system description. In: Proceedings of the 2015 Text Analysis Conference (2015)

6. Hong, Y., Zhang, J., Ma, B., Yao, J., Zhou, G., Zhu, Q.: Using cross-entity inference to improve event extraction. In: 49th Annual Meeting of the Association for Computational Linguistics: Human Language Technologies (ACL 2011), pp. 1127–1136. ACL (2011)

7. Kipf, T.N., Welling, M.: Semi-supervised classification with graph convolutional networks. In: 5th International Conference on Learning Representations (ICLR 2017), Toulon, France (2017)

8. Kodelja, D., Besançon, R., Ferret, O.: Exploiting a more global context for event detection through bootstrapping. In: 41st European Conference on Information Retrieval (ECIR 2019), pp. 763–770 (2019)

9. Liao, S., Grishman, R.: Using document level cross-event inference to improve event extraction. In: 48th Annual Meeting of the Association for Computational Linguistics (ACL 2010), pp. 789–797. ACL, Uppsala, Sweden (2010)

10. Liu, S., Liu, K., He, S., Zhao, J.: A probabilistic soft logic based approach to exploiting latent and global information in event classification. In: Thirtieth AAAI Conference on Artificial Intelligence (AAAI 2016), Phoenix, AZ, USA. AAAI Press (2016)

11. Liu, X., Luo, Z., Huang, H.: Jointly multiple events extraction via attention-based graph information aggregation. In: 2018 Conference on Empirical Methods in Natural Language Processing (EMNLP 2018), Brussels, Belgium, pp. 1247–1256 (2018)

12. Manning, C.D., Surdeanu, M., Bauer, J., Finkel, J., Bethard, S.J., McClosky, D.: The Stanford CoreNLP natural language processing toolkit. In: 52nd Annual Meeting of the Association for Computational Linguistics (ACL 2014), System Demonstrations, pp. 55–60 (2014)

13. Nguyen, T.H., Grishman, R.: Graph convolutional networks with argument-aware pooling for event detection. In: Thirty-Second AAAI Conference on Artificial Intelligence (AAAI 2018), New Orleans, LA, USA. AAAI Press (2018)

14. Pennington, J., Socher, R., Manning, C.: Glove: Global Vectors for Word Representation. In: 2014 Conference on Empirical Methods in Natural Language Processing (EMNLP 2014), Doha, Qatar, pp. 1532–1543. ACL (2014)

15. Reichart, R., Barzilay, R.: Multi-event extraction guided by global constraints. In: 2012 Conference of the North American Chapter of the Association for Computational Linguistics: Human Language Technologies (NAACL HLT 2012), Montréal, Canada, pp. 70–79 (2012)

16. Schlichtkrull, M., Kipf, T.N., Bloem, P., van den Berg, R., Titov, I., Welling, M.: Modeling relational data with graph convolutional networks. In: Gangemi, A., et al. (eds.) ESWC 2018. LNCS, vol. 10843, pp. 593–607. Springer, Cham (2018). https://doi.org/10.1007/978-3-319-93417-4_38

17. Yan, H., Jin, X., Meng, X., Guo, J., Cheng, X.: Event detection with multi-order graph convolution and aggregated attention. In: 2019 Conference on Empirical Methods in Natural Language Processing and the 9th International Joint Conference on Natural Language Processing (EMNLP-IJCNLP 2019), Hong Kong, China, pp. 5766–5770 (2019)

18. Yang, B., Mitchell, T.M.: Joint extraction of events and entities within a document context. In: 2016 Conference of the North American Chapter of the Association for Computational Linguistics: Human Language Technologies (NAACL HLT 2016), San Diego, California, pp. 289–299. ACL (2016)

19. Zhao, Y., Jin, X., Wang, Y., Cheng, X.: Document embedding enhanced event detection with hierarchical and supervised attention. In: 56th Annual Meeting of the Association for Computational Linguistics (Short Papers) (ACL 2018), Melbourne, Australia, pp. 414–419. ACL (2018)

Transfer Learning and Augmentation
for Word Sense Disambiguation

Harsh Kohli[(✉)] [iD]

SalesKen, Bengaluru, India
harshkohli@salesken.ai

Abstract. Many downstream NLP tasks have shown significant improvement through continual pre-training, transfer learning and multi-task learning. State-of-the-art approaches in Word Sense Disambiguation today benefit from some of these approaches in conjunction with information sources such as semantic relationships and gloss definitions contained within WordNet. Our work builds upon these systems and uses data augmentation along with extensive pre-training on various different NLP tasks and datasets. Our transfer learning and augmentation pipeline achieves state-of-the-art single model performance in WSD and is at par with the best ensemble results.

Keywords: Word Sense Disambiguation · Multi-task training · Transfer learning

1 Introduction

Word Sense Disambiguation or WSD is the task of gleaning the correct sense of an ambiguous word given the context in which it was used. It is a well-studied problem in NLP and has seen several diversified approaches over the years including techniques leveraging Knowledge-Based Systems, Supervised learning approaches and, more recently, end-to-end deep learnt models. WSD has found application in various kinds of NLP systems such as Question Answering, IR, and Machine Translation.

WordNet 3.0 is the most popular and widely used sense inventory that consists of over 109k synonym sets or synsets and relationships between them such as hypernym, anotnym, hyponym, entailment etc. Most training and evaluation corpora used in supervised systems today consist of sentences where words are manually annotated and mapped to a particular synset in WordNet. We use these sources in addition to other publicly available datasets to tune our model for this task. Through transfer learning from these datasets and other augmentation and pre-processing techniques we achieve state-of-the-art results on standard benchmarks.

© Springer Nature Switzerland AG 2021
D. Hiemstra et al. (Eds.): ECIR 2021, LNCS 12657, pp. 303–311, 2021.
https://doi.org/10.1007/978-3-030-72240-1_29

2   Related Work

Traditional approaches to WSD relied primarily on Knowledge-Based Systems. Lexical similarity over dictionary definitions or Gloss for each synset was first used in [10] to estimate the correct sense. Graph based approaches such as [18] were also proposed which leverage structural properties of lexico-semantic sources treating the knowledge graph as a semantic network. One major advantage of using such unsupervised techniques was that they eliminated the need of having large annotated training corpora. Since annotation is expensive given the large number of fine-grained word senses, such methods were the de facto choice for WSD systems. Recently, however, approaches for semi-automatic [27] and automatic [21] sense annotation have been proposed to partially circumvent the problem of manually annotating a sizeable training set.

Supervised methods, on the other hand, relied on a variety of hand-crafted features such as a neighbouring window of words and their corresponding part of speech (POS) tags etc. Commonly referred to as word expert systems, they involved training a dedicated classifier for each individual lemma [34]. The default or first sense was usually returned when the target lemma was not seen during training. While these were less practical in real application, they often yielded better results on common evaluation sets.

[8] and [24] were the first neural architectures for WSD which consisted of Bidirectional LSTM models and Seq2Seq Encoder-Decoder architectures with attention. These architectures optionally included lexical and POS features which yielded better results. Due to strong performance of contextual embeddings such as BERT [3] on various NLP tasks, recent approaches such as [30] and [5] have used these to achieve significant gains in WSD benchmarks. We leverage the ideas presented in GlossBERT [5] and improve upon the results with a multi-task pre-training procedure and greater semantic variations in the train dataset through augmentation techniques.

3   Data Preparation Pipeline

3.1   Source Datasets

We use the largest manually annotated WSD corpus SemCor 3.0 [17] consisting of over 226k sense tags for training our models. In keeping with most neural architectures today such as [14], we use the SemEval-2007 corpus [22] as our dev set and SemEval-2013 [20], SemEval-2015 [19], Senseval-2 [4], and Senseval-3 [26] as our test sets.

3.2   Data Preprocessing

GlossBERT [5] utilizes context gloss pairs with weak supervision to achieve state-of-the-art single model performance on the evaluation sets. We follow the same pre-processing procedure as GlossBERT. The context sentence along with each of the gloss definitions of senses of the target word are considered as a pair. Thus, for a sentence containing an ambiguous word with N senses, we consider all N senses with as many sentence pairs. Only the correct sense is marked as a positive sample while all others are considered negative inputs to our pairwise sentence classifier. As this formulation relies on the gloss definition of a synset and not just the synset tag or key, it is more robust to keys that do not occur or are under-represented in training.

Context Sentence	Gloss Definition	Label
How long has it been since you reviewed the " objectives " of your benefit and service program ?	objectives : the lens or system of lenses in a telescope or microscope that is nearest the object being viewed	0
How long has it been since you reviewed the " objectives " of your benefit and service program ?	objectives : the goal intended to be attained (and which is believed to be attainable)	1
How long has it been since you reviewed the " objectives " of your benefit and service program ?	objectives : undistorted by emotion or personal bias; based on observable phenomena	0
How long has it been since you reviewed the " objectives " of your benefit and service program ?	objectives : serving as or indicating the object of a verb or of certain prepositions and used for certain other purposes	0
How long has it been since you reviewed the " objectives " of your benefit and service program ?	objectives : belonging to immediate experience of actual things or events	0
How long has it been since you reviewed the " objectives " of your benefit and service program ?	objectives : emphasizing or expressing things as perceived without distortion of personal feelings, insertion of fictional matter, or interpretation	0

Fig. 1. Context-Gloss Pairs with Weak Supervision

Figure 1 above shows an example of context-gloss pairs for a single context sentence with the target word - objectives. The highlighted text represent the weak supervised signals which help identify the target word both in the gloss definition, as well as in the context sentence. In the context sentence, the target word may appear more than once, and the signal helps associate each occurrence with the definition independently.

3.3 Data Augmentation

Given the large number of candidate synsets for each target lemma, the train dataset has a large class imbalance. The ratio of negative samples to positives is nearly 8:1. Rather than adopting a simple oversampling strategy, we use data augmentation through back translation. Back translation is a popular method for generating paraphrases involving translating a source sentence to one of several target languages and then translating the sentence back into the source language. Approaches described in [16,23,32] have successfully leveraged modern Neural Machine Translation systems to generate paraphrases for a variety of tasks. We use this technique to introduce greater diversity and semantic variation in our training set and augment examples in our minority class.

The Transformers library [33] provides MarianMT models [7] for translation to and from several different languages. Each model is a 6-layer transformer [29] encoder-decoder architecture. For best results, we select from a number of high-resource languages such as French, German etc. and apply simple as well as chained back-translation (e.g. English - Spanish - English - French - English). From our pool of back-translated sentences, we retain sentences where the target word occurs exactly once in the original as well as back-translated sentence. This way, we generate several paraphrased examples for each positive example in our train set. We randomly select n augmented samples for each original sample at train time, where n was treated as a hyper-parameter during our training experiments. We achieve best results when $n = 3$.

4   Model

We use the MT-DNN [12] architecture for training our model. The network consists of shared layers and task-specific layers. Through cross-task training, the authors demonstrate how the shared layers of the network learn more generalized representations and are better suited to adapt to new tasks and domains. Multi-task learning using large amount of labelled data across tasks has a regularization effect on the network and the model is able to better generalize to new domains with relatively fewer labelled training examples than simple pre-trained BERT. It is this property of MT-DNN that we leverage to improve performance on WSD.

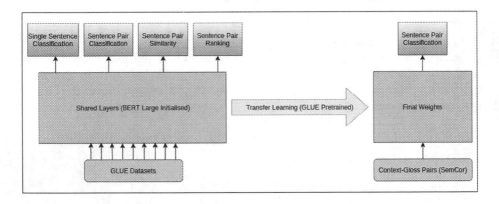

Fig. 2. Pre-training and Tuning methodology

The pre-training procedure for MT-DNN is similar to that of BERT which used two supervised tasks - masked LM and next sentence prediction. Using BERT Large model (24 layers, 1024 dim, 335 m trainable parameters) as our base model, we then tune on all tasks in the GLUE benchmark [31]. While [5] reported better performance using BERT base (12 layers, 768 dim, 110 m trainable parameters), we found that the larger BERT model performed significantly better in our experiments. We attribute this behaviour to our pre-training procedure which learns better, more generalized representations thus preventing a larger, more expressive model from overfitting on the train dataset.

Four different task-specific output layers are constructed corresponding to single sentence classification, pairwise text similarity, pairwise text classification, and pairwise text ranking. These are illustrated in Fig. 2. Learning objectives differ for each task - single-sentence and pairwise classification tasks are optimized using cross-entropy loss, pairwise text similarity is optimized on the mean squared error between the target similarity value and semantic representations of each of the sentences in the input pair, and pairwise text ranking follows the pairwise learning-to-rank paradigm in minimizing the negative log likelihood of a positive example given a list of candidates [2]. The pairwise text classification output layer uses a stochastic answer network (SAN) [11] which maintains a memory state and employs K-step reasoning to iteratively improve upon predictions. We use the same pairwise classification head when tuning the network for our WSD task. At inference time, we run context-gloss pairs for each sense of the target lemma and the candidate synset with the highest score is considered the predicted sense.

5   Implementation Details

Examples from each of the 9 datasets in GLUE are input to the network and passed to the correct output layer given the task-type. 5 epochs of pre-training are thus carried out using GLUE data. The best saved checkpoint is then selected and, thereafter, context-gloss pairs as described above are input to the model for tuning on WSD. Model weights of shared layers are carried over from multi-task training on GLUE. Adamax [9] optimizer is used to tune the weights and a low learning rate of $2e-5$ is used to facilitate a slower, but smoother convergence. A batch size of 256 is maintained and the architecture is tuned on 8x Tesla V100 GPU's with 16 GB of VRAM each for a total of 128 GB GPU memory.

6   Results

We summarize the results of our experiments in Table 1. We compare our results against the Most Frequent Sense Baseline as well as different approaches, Knowledge Based - Lesk (ext+emb) [1] and Babelfly [18], Word-Expert Supervised Systems - IMS [34] and IMS+emb[6], Neural Models - Bi-LSTM [8], Bi-LSTM + att + lex +pos [24], CAN/HCAN [14], GAS [15], SemCar/SemCor+WNGC, hypernyms [30] and GlossBERT [5]. We exclude results from ensemble systems marked in Table 1 as these results were obtained using a geometric mean of predictions across 8 independent models. We achieve the best results for any single model across all evaluation sets and POS types.

While [30] supplement their train corpus with the Wordnet Gloss Corpus (WNGC) and also use 8 different models for their ensemble, our overall results are at par with theirs on test datasets and slightly better on the dev set. The fact that such results were achieved with fewer training examples (without the use of WNGC) further enforces the generalization and domain adaptation capabilities of our pre-training methodology.

Table 1. Final Results. * Result excluded from consideration as it uses an ensemble

System	SE07	SE2	SE3	SE13	SE15	Noun	Verb	Adj	Adv	All
MFS Baseline	54.5	65.6	66.0	63.8	67.1	67.7	49.8	73.1	80.5	65.5
Lesk$_{ext+emb}$	56.7	63.0	63.7	66.2	64.6	70.0	51.1	51.7	80.6	64.2
Babelfly	51.6	67.0	63.5	66.4	70.3	68.9	50.7	73.2	79.8	66.4
IMS	61.3	70.9	69.3	65.3	69.5	70.5	55.8	75.6	82.9	68.9
IMS$_{+emb}$	62.6	72.2	70.4	65.9	71.5	71.9	56.6	75.9	84.7	70.1
Bi-LSTM	–	71.1	68.4	64.8	68.3	69.5	55.9	76.2	82.4	68.4
Bi-LSTM$_{+att.+LEX+POS}$	64.8	72.0	69.1	66.9	71.5	71.5	57.5	75.0	83.8	69.9
GAS$_{ext}$(Linear)	–	72.4	70.1	67.1	72.1	71.9	58.1	76.4	84.7	70.4
GAS$_{ext}$(Concatenation)	–	72.2	70.5	67.2	72.6	72.2	57.7	76.6	85.0	70.6
CAN	–	72.2	70.2	69.1	72.2	73.5	56.5	76.6	80.3	70.9
HCAN	–	72.8	70.3	68.5	72.8	72.7	58.2	77.4	84.1	71.1
SemCor,hyp	–	–	–	–	–	-	–	–	–	75.6
SemCor,hyp(ens)*	69.5	77.5	77.4	76.0	78.3	79.6	65.9	79.5	85.5	76.7
SemCor+WNGC,hyp	–	–	–	–	–	–	–	–	–	77.1
SemCor+WNGC,hyp(ens)*	73.4	79.7	77.8	78.7	82.6	81.4	68.7	83.7	85.5	79.0
BERT(Token-CLS)	61.1	69.7	69.4	65.8	69.5	70.5	57.1	71.6	83.5	68.6
GlossBERT(Sent-CLS)	69.2	76.5	73.4	75.1	79.5	78.3	64.8	77.6	83.8	75.8
GlossBERT(Token-CLS)	71.9	77.0	75.4	74.6	79.3	78.3	66.5	78.6	84.4	76.3
GlossBERT(Sent-CLS-WS)	72.5	77.7	75.2	76.1	80.4	79.3	66.9	78.2	86.4	77.0
MTDNN+Gloss	**73.9**	**79.5**	**76.6**	**79.7**	**80.9**	**81.8**	**67.7**	**79.8**	**86.5**	**79.0**

7   Conclusion and Future Work

We use the pre-processing steps and weak-supervision over context-gloss pairs as described in [5] and improve upon the results through simple and chained back-translation as a means of data augmentation and multi-task training and transfer learning from different data sources. Better and more generalized representations achieved by leveraging the GLUE datasets allows us to train a larger model with nearly thrice as many trainable parameters. Through these techniques we are able improve upon existing SOTA on standard benchmark.

Additional data from WNGC or OMSTI [27] has shown to aid model performance in various systems and could be incorporated in training. Recent work such as [28] indicates that cost-sensitive training is often effective when training BERT when there is a class imbalance. Given the nature of the problem, a triplet loss function similar to [25] could be used to further improve performance. Online hard or semi-hard sampling strategies could be experimented with to sample the negative sysnets. Finally, RoBERTa [13] has shown improved performance on many NLP tasks and could be used as a base model that is input to our multi-task pre-training pipeline. All of these techniques could be used in conjunction with our context-gloss pairwise formulation to improve performance further.

References

1. Basile, P., Caputo, A., Semeraro, G.: An enhanced Lesk word sense disambiguation algorithm through a distributional semantic model. In: Proceedings of COLING 2014, the 25th International Conference on Computational Linguistics: Technical Papers, Dublin, Ireland, pp. 1591–1600. Dublin City University and Association for Computational Linguistics, August 2014. https://www.aclweb.org/anthology/C14-1151

2. Burges, C., et al.: Learning to rank using gradient descent. In: Proceedings of the 22nd International Conference on Machine Learning, ICML 2005, pp. 89–96, New York, NY, USA. Association for Computing Machinery (2005). https://doi.org/10.1145/1102351.1102363, https://doi.org/10.1145/1102351.1102363

3. Devlin, J., Chang, M.W., Lee, K., Toutanova, K.: Bert: pre-training of deep bidirectional transformers for language understanding. arXiv:abs/1810.04805 (2019)

4. Edmonds, P., Cotton, S.: SENSEVAL-2: overview. In: Proceedings of SENSEVAL-2 Second International Workshop on Evaluating Word Sense Disambiguation Systems, Toulouse, France, pp. 1–5. Association for Computational Linguistics, July 2001. https://www.aclweb.org/anthology/S01-1001

5. Huang, L., Sun, C., Qiu, X., Huang, X.: Glossbert: Bert for word sense disambiguation with gloss knowledge. arXiv:abs/1908.07245 (2019)

6. Iacobacci, I., Pilehvar, M.T., Navigli, R.: Embeddings for word sense disambiguation: an evaluation study. In: Proceedings of the 54th Annual Meeting of the Association for Computational Linguistics (Volume 1: Long Papers), Berlin, Germany, pp. 897–907. Association for Computational Linguistics, August 2016. https://doi.org/10.18653/v1/P16-1085, https://www.aclweb.org/anthology/P16-1085

7. Junczys-Dowmunt, M., et al.: Marian: Fast neural machine translation in C++. In: Proceedings of ACL 2018, System Demonstrations, Melbourne, Australia, pp. 116–121. Association for Computational Linguistics, July 2018. http://www.aclweb.org/anthology/P18-4020

8. Kågebäck, M., Salomonsson, H.: Word sense disambiguation using a bidirectional LSTM. In: Proceedings of the 5th Workshop on Cognitive Aspects of the Lexicon (CogALex - V), Osaka, Japan, pp. 51–56. The COLING 2016 Organizing Committee, December 2016. https://www.aclweb.org/anthology/W16-5307

9. Kingma, D., Ba, J.: Adam: a method for stochastic optimization. In: International Conference on Learning Representations, December 2014

10. Lesk, M.E.: Automatic sense disambiguation using machine readable dictionaries: how to tell a pine cone from an ice cream cone. In: SIGDOC 1986 (1986)

11. Liu, X., Duh, K., Gao, J.: Stochastic answer networks for natural language inference, April 2018

12. Liu, X., He, P., Chen, W., Gao, J.: Multi-task deep neural networks for natural language understanding. In: Proceedings of the 57th Annual Meeting of the Association for Computational Linguistics, Florence, Italy, pp. 4487–4496. Association for Computational Linguistics, July 2019. https://www.aclweb.org/anthology/P19-1441

13. Liu, Y., et al.: Roberta: a robustly optimized BERT pretraining approach. CoRR abs/1907.11692 (2019). http://arxiv.org/abs/1907.11692

14. Luo, F., Liu, T., He, Z., Xia, Q., Sui, Z., Chang, B.: Leveraging gloss knowledge in neural word sense disambiguation by hierarchical co-attention. In: Proceedings of the 2018 Conference on Empirical Methods in Natural Language Processing, Brussels, Belgium, pp. 1402–1411. Association for Computational Linguistics, October–November 2018. https://doi.org/10.18653/v1/D18-1170, https://www.aclweb.org/anthology/D18-1170

15. Luo, F., Liu, T., Xia, Q., Chang, B., Sui, Z.: Incorporating glosses into neural word sense disambiguation. In: Proceedings of the 56th Annual Meeting of the Association for Computational Linguistics (Volume 1: Long Papers), Melbourne, Australia , pp. 2473–2482. Association for Computational Linguistics, July 2018. https://doi.org/10.18653/v1/P18-1230, https://www.aclweb.org/anthology/P18-1230

16. Mallinson, J., Sennrich, R., Lapata, M.: Paraphrasing revisited with neural machine translation. In: Proceedings of the 15th Conference of the European Chapter of the Association for Computational Linguistics: Volume 1, Long Papers, Valencia, Spain, pp. 881–893. Association for Computational Linguistics, April 2017. https://www.aclweb.org/anthology/E17-1083

17. Miller, G.A., Leacock, C., Tengi, R., Bunker, R.T.: A semantic concordance. In: Human Language Technology: Proceedings of a Workshop Held at Plainsboro, New Jersey, March 21–24, 1993 (1993). https://www.aclweb.org/anthology/H93-1061

18. Moro, A., Raganato, A., Navigli, R.: Entity linking meets word sense disambiguation: a unified approach. Trans. Assoc. Comput. Linguist. **2**, 231–244 (2014)

19. Moro, A., Navigli, R.: SemEval-2015 task 13: multilingual all-words sense disambiguation and entity linking. In: Proceedings of the 9th International Workshop on Semantic Evaluation (SemEval 2015), Denver, Colorado, pp. 288–297. Association for Computational Linguistics, June 2015. https://doi.org/10.18653/v1/S15-2049, https://www.aclweb.org/anthology/S15-2049

20. Navigli, R., Jurgens, D., Vannella, D.: SemEval-2013 task 12: multilingual word sense disambiguation. In: Second Joint Conference on Lexical and Computational Semantics (*SEM), Volume 2: Proceedings of the Seventh International Workshop on Semantic Evaluation (SemEval 2013), Atlanta, Georgia, USA, pp. 222–231. Association for Computational Linguistics, June 2013. https://www.aclweb.org/anthology/S13-2040

21. Pasini, T., Navigli, R.: Train-o-matic: Large-scale supervised word sense disambiguation in multiple languages without manual training data, pp. 78–88, January 2017. https://doi.org/10.18653/v1/D17-1008

22. Pradhan, S., Loper, E., Dligach, D., Palmer, M.: SemEval-2007 task-17: English lexical sample, SRL and all words. In: Proceedings of the Fourth International Workshop on Semantic Evaluations (SemEval-2007), Prague, Czech Republic, pp. 87–92. Association for Computational Linguistics, June 2007. https://www.aclweb.org/anthology/S07-1016

23. Prakash, A., Hasan, S.A., Lee, K., Datla, V., Qadir, A., Liu, J., Farri, O.: Neural paraphrase generation with stacked residual LSTM networks. In: Proceedings of COLING 2016, the 26th International Conference on Computational Linguistics: Technical Papers, Osaka, Japan, pp. 2923–2934. The COLING 2016 Organizing Committee, December 2016. https://www.aclweb.org/anthology/C16-1275

24. Raganato, A., Delli Bovi, C., Navigli, R.: Neural sequence learning models for word sense disambiguation. In: Proceedings of the 2017 Conference on Empirical Methods in Natural Language Processing, pp. 1156–1167, Copenhagen, Denmark. Association for Computational Linguistics, September 2017. https://doi.org/10.18653/v1/D17-1120, https://www.aclweb.org/anthology/D17-1120

25. Schroff, F., Kalenichenko, D., Philbin, J.: Facenet: a unified embedding for face recognition and clustering. In: 2015 IEEE Conference on Computer Vision and Pattern Recognition (CVPR), pp. 815–823 (2015)
26. Snyder, B., Palmer, M.: The English all-words task. In: Proceedings of SENSEVAL-3, the Third International Workshop on the Evaluation of Systems for the Semantic Analysis of Text, Barcelona, Spain, pp. 41–43. Association for Computational Linguistics, July 2004. https://www.aclweb.org/anthology/W04-0811
27. Taghipour, K., Ng, H.T.: One million sense-tagged instances for word sense disambiguation and induction. In: Proceedings of the Nineteenth Conference on Computational Natural Language Learning, Beijing, China, pp. 338–344. Association for Computational Linguistics, July 2015. https://doi.org/10.18653/v1/K15-1037, https://www.aclweb.org/anthology/K15-1037
28. Tayyar Madabushi, H., Kochkina, E., Castelle, M.: Cost-sensitive BERT for generalisable sentence classification on imbalanced data. In: Proceedings of the Second Workshop on Natural Language Processing for Internet Freedom: Censorship, Disinformation, and Propaganda, Hong Kong, China, pp. 125–134. Association for Computational Linguistics, November 2019. https://doi.org/10.18653/v1/D19-5018, https://www.aclweb.org/anthology/D19-5018
29. Vaswani, A., et al.: Attention is all you need. In: Guyon, I., et al. (eds.) Advances in Neural Information Processing Systems, vol. 30, pp. 5998–6008. Curran Associates, Inc. (2017). http://papers.nips.cc/paper/7181-attention-is-all-you-need.pdf
30. Vial, L., Lecouteux, B., Schwab, D.: Sense vocabulary compression through the semantic knowledge of wordnet for neural word sense disambiguation. CoRR abs/1905.05677 (2019). http://arxiv.org/abs/1905.05677
31. Wang, A., Singh, A., Michael, J., Hill, F., Levy, O., Bowman, S.: GLUE: a multi-task benchmark and analysis platform for natural language understanding. In: Proceedings of the 2018 EMNLP Workshop BlackboxNLP: Analyzing and Interpreting Neural Networks for NLP, Brussels, Belgium, pp. 353–355. Association for Computational Linguistics, November 2018. https://doi.org/10.18653/v1/W18-5446, https://www.aclweb.org/anthology/W18-5446
32. Wieting, J., Gimpel, K.: ParaNMT-50M: pushing the limits of paraphrastic sentence embeddings with millions of machine translations. In: Proceedings of the 56th Annual Meeting of the Association for Computational Linguistics (Volume 1: Long Papers), Melbourne, Australia, pp. 451–462. Association for Computational Linguistics, July 2018. https://doi.org/10.18653/v1/P18-1042, https://www.aclweb.org/anthology/P18-1042
33. Wolf, T., et al.: Huggingface's transformers: state-of-the-art natural language processing, arXiv:abs/1910.03771 (2019)
34. Zhong, Z., Ng, H.T.: It makes sense: a wide-coverage word sense disambiguation system for free text. In: Proceedings of the ACL 2010 System Demonstrations, Uppsala, Sweden, pp. 78–83. Association for Computational Linguistics, July 2010. https://www.aclweb.org/anthology/P10-4014

Cross-modal Memory Fusion Network for Multimodal Sequential Learning with Missing Values

Chen Lin[(✉)], Joyce C. Ho, and Eugene Agichtein

Emory University, Atlanta, GA 30322, USA
{chen.lin,joyce.c.ho,eugene.agichtein}@emory.edu

Abstract. Information in many real-world applications is inherently multi-modal, sequential and characterized by a variety of missing values. Existing imputation methods mainly focus on the recurrent dynamics in one modality while ignoring the complementary property from other modalities. In this paper, we propose a novel method called cross-modal memory fusion network (CMFN) that explicitly learns both modal-specific and cross-modal dynamics for imputing the missing values in multi-modal sequential learning tasks. Experiments on two datasets demonstrate that our method outperforms state-of-the-art methods and show its potential to better impute missing values in complex multi-modal datasets.

Keywords: Multi-modal information · Sequential learning · Missing value imputation · Recurrent neural networks

1 Introduction and Related Work

1.1 Introduction

In many real-world scenarios, information and data are multi-modal (e.g. heterogeneous features collected from multi-typed sensors for air quality surveillance [1,8,20]; and multi-modal perception for face-to-face communication [16,19]). In these scenarios, features from different modalities are seamlessly used together for classification/regression purposes. However, multi-modal sequential data is often incomplete due to various reasons, such as broken sensors, failed data transmission or low sampling rate. For example, Fig. 1a shows two time series of air quality data at Atlanta Fire Station #8, where two-thirds of fine particulate matter ($PM_{2.5}$) data is missing while relative humidity data is complete. Relative humidity data, as shown in Fig. 1a, is promising for improving daily $PM_{2.5}$ surveillance because of its high correlation and low missing rate. Many previous studies [2,3,13,15] have been developing models that could impute missing values in multivariate sequential data by either constructing local statistics or utilizing local and global recurrent dynamics. Although these methods have achieved remarkable success in multivariate sequential data of one modality, they can not

© Springer Nature Switzerland AG 2021
D. Hiemstra et al. (Eds.): ECIR 2021, LNCS 12657, pp. 312–319, 2021.
https://doi.org/10.1007/978-3-030-72240-1_30

be naturally adapted to multi-modal sequential data. Specifically, they are not designed to incorporate the information from modalities with lower missing rates for imputing the missing values of modalities with higher missing rates.

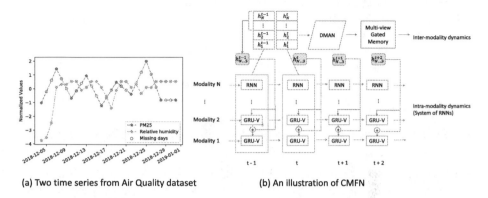

(a) Two time series from Air Quality dataset   (b) An illustration of CMFN

Fig. 1. Two time series from $PM_{2.5}$ monitoring station at Atlanta Fire Station #8 (left) and an illustraion of CMFN (right).

Previous studies [9,16,17] in multi-modal sequential learning have been proved successful in exploring intra-modality and inter-modality dynamics for more robust and accurate prediction. The strategies for multi-modal sequential learning can be classified into three categories. The first strategy is early fusion, which simply concatenates multi-modal features at the input level [10,12]. This fusion strategy could not efficiently model the intra-modality dynamics because the complex inter-modality dynamics can dominate the learning process or result in overfitting. The second strategy is late fusion, which trains unimodal classifiers independently and performs decision voting [14,19]. This strategy could lead to inefficient exploration of inter-modality dynamics by relying on the simple weighted averaging of multiple classifiers. The last strategy is to design models that could learn both the intra-modality and inter-modality end-to-end [9,16,17]. It has been shown that by exploring the consistency and complementary properties of different modalities, the third strategy is a more effective and promising way of multi-modal sequential learning. However, there is few studies examining the condition when there are missing values in one or more modalities and how to leverage the intra-modality and inter-modality dynamics for missing value imputation remains an under-explored problem.

To address the aforementioned problems, we propose a novel cross-modal memory fusion network (CMFN) for multi-modal sequential learning with missing values. CMFN extends the memory fusion network [17], where recurrent neural networks (RNNs) are leveraged for learning intra-modality dynamics and attention-based modules are leveraged for learning inter-modality dynamics. Since the original RNN is unable to handle incomplete input, we introduced a novel variant of gated recurrent units (GRU) [5] called GRU-V to impute the missing values by leveraging modal-specific and cross-modal dynamics. The main contributions of the paper are:

- We study a new problem of multi-modal sequential learning with missing values by leveraging intra-modality and inter-modality dynamics.
- We propose a novel framework CMFN, with a GRU-V module to impute missing values in multi-modal sequential learning.
- We conduct experiments on both real-world datasets and synthetic datasets to validate the proposed approach.

1.2 Related Work

We now briefly review related work to place our contribution in context.

Multivariate Sequential Learning with Missing Values. A variety of imputation methods such as statistical imputation (e.g., mean, median), EM-based imputation [11], K-nearest neighborhood [6] and tensor factorization [4] have been applied to estimate missing values. However, these approaches fail to model the sequential pattern of data and are independent of the training process, which often leads to sub-optimal results. To tackle this issue, recent studies [2,3,13] propose end-to-end frameworks that jointly estimate missing values and make the prediction. For example, Che *et al.* [3] introduced the GRU-D model to impute missing values in a single modality using the linear combination of statistical features, which is under strong assumptions that missing values could be learned by assigning weights between the last observed value and statistical mean value.

Multi-modal Sequential Learning. Previous studies dealing with multi-modal sequential data have largely focused on three major types of models as mentioned in Sect. 1.1. The third category of models [9,17,18] relies on collapsing the time dimension from sequences by learning a temporal representation for each of the different modalities. Memory fusion network (MFN) [17] is one of these models, which uses a special attention mechanism called the Delta-memory Attention Network (DMAN) and a Multi-view Gated Memory to identify the cross-modal interactions. Experiments show that these models [16–18] achieve remarkable success on a variety of tasks, including multi-modal sentiment analysis and emotion recognition; however, none of them can handle input with missing values in one or more modalities.

2   Methodology

In this section, we first define the problem setting, and then we present the model architecture in detail.

2.1   Problem Formulation

The input is multi-modal sequential data with $N \geq 2$ modalities. For those N modalities, we order them from high missing rate to low missing rate as modality 1, modality 2, ..., modality N. For each modality k, the input data is denoted as $X_k = \left[x_k^t : t \leq T, x_k^t \in R^{d_{x_k}} \right]$, where d_{x_k} is the input dimensionality of modality k. We also input the masking matrix $M_k = \{ m_1, m_2, \ldots, m_t \}, m_i \in \{0, 1\}^{d_{x_k}}$ to denote missing status ($m = 0$ means missing) and the time interval matrix $D_k = \{ \delta_1, \delta_2, \ldots, \delta_t \}, \delta_i \in R^{d_{x_k}}$ to denote the number of time steps since last observation.

2.2   Model Architecture

The Cross-modal Memory Fusion Network (CMFN) is a recurrent model for multi-modal sequential learning with missing values, which consists of two main components: 1) A system of RNNs consisting of multiple RNNs for learning intra-modality dynamics. 2) DMAN and Multi-view Gated Memory [17] for learning inter-modality dynamics. As shown in Fig. 1b, RNNs such as GRU and long short-term memory (LSTM) [7] are applied for modalities without missing values, GRU-V is applied for imputing the missing values with intra-modality and inter-modality dynamics for modalities with missing values.

GRU-V is inspired by the structure of GRU-D proposed by Che *et al.* [3]. To explain the procedure of missing value imputation, we assume that the input for modality 1 is feature matrix X_1, masking matrix M_1 and time interval matrix D_1. As shown in Fig. 1b, at time step t, for the $N - 1$ modalities with lower missing values, we concatenate their hidden outputs $\{ h_2^t, h_3^t, \ldots, h_{N-1}^t \}$ as $h_{N \ldots 2}^t$ to represent cross-modal dynamics. For modality 1, we have the hidden output h_1^{t-1} at last time step to represent modal-specific dynamics. We then concatenate the cross-modal and modal-specific dynamics, denoted as $c^{[h_1^{t-1}, h_{N \ldots 2}^t]}$, and pass the concatenated tensor to a neural network $\mathcal{D}_v : R^{d_c} \mapsto R^{d_{x_1}}$ to infer the variance of the missing values from its empirical mean $\tilde{X}_1$ in modality 1 as:

$$V_{X_1}^t = \mathcal{D}_v \left(c^{[h_1^{t-1}, h_{N \ldots 2}^t]]} \right) \tag{1}$$

$V_{X_1}^t$ are softmax activated scores, which is then used to infer the missing values as:

$$\mathcal{X}_1^t = \tilde{X}_1 + 2K \cdot (V_{X_1}^t - 0.5) \tag{2}$$

$\mathcal{X}_1^t$ are the inferred values, and we rescale $V_{X_1}^t$ from $[0, 1]$ to $[-K, K]$ using rescale parameter K. Because all the input values are normalized, we set $K = 3$ to represent the variance of input values. Following GRU-D, we then use a weight decay function $\Gamma_{D_1^t}$ to assign weights between the last observed value $X_1^{t'}$ and the inferred value $\mathcal{X}_1^t$ and get final imputed value $\hat{X}_1^t$ as:

$$\Gamma_{D_1^t} = \exp \left\{ -\max \left(\tilde{\Gamma}, W_\Gamma D_1^t + b_\Gamma \right) \right\} \tag{3}$$

$$\hat{X}_1^t = \Gamma_{D_1^t} X_1^{t'} + (1 - \Gamma_{D_1^t}) \cdot \mathcal{X}_1^t \tag{4}$$

where W_Γ and b_Γ are model parameters that we train jointly with other parameters of the GRU. $\tilde{\Gamma}$ is the default weight decay, which is set as a hyper-parameter in range $[0, 1]$.

3   Experiments

In this section, we describe experiments in four parts. First, we describe the datasets. Second, we present the baseline models. Then we describe the experimental setup. Last, we summarize experimental results comparing with state-of-the-art baselines.

3.1   Datasets

Air Quality Dataset. Air Quality dataset is time series of daily measurement of $PM_{2.5}$ and meteorological data (i.e. relative humidity and temperature) in Atlanta Fire Station #8 monitoring site from Jan 1, 2011 to Dec 31, 2018. This dataset consists of two modalities and it facilitates a regression task of predicting $PM_{2.5}$ concentration based on data of the past 7 days.

CMU-MOSI Dataset. Multimodal Opinion Sentiment Intensity (CMU-MOSI) dataset [19] is a collection of 93 opinion videos from online sharing websites with three modalities: language, vision, and acoustic. Each video consists of multiple opinion segments and each segment is annotated with sentiment in the range $[-3, 3]$. This benchmark dataset facilitates three prediction tasks: 1) Binary Sentiment classification 2) Seven-Class sentiment classification 3) Sentiment regression in range $[-3, 3]$. This dataset contains no missing values, so we synthetically introduce missing values by randomly masking 50% percent of the values in acoustic modality. We construct the synthetic datasets in two ways to test our model under different conditions. Synthetic Dataset #1: For 5 features in acoustic modality, We randomly mask values separately, which means this modality is partly masked when selected. Synthetic Dataset #2: We mask values for all 5 features randomly, which means this modality is masked totally when selected.

3.2   Baseline Models

Here, we use the following models for baselines and ablation studies.

- EFLSTM: LSTM model using early fusion strategy. The missing values are simply imputed by the last observed values and all modalities are concatenated into a single modality at the input level.
- MFN: State-of-the-art multi-modal learning model that learns the temporal representation for each modality using an RNN. The missing values are simply imputed by the last observed values.

- GRU-D: Baseline for multivariate sequential learning with missing values. All modalities are concatenated into a single modality using early fusion method at the input level.
- MFN-GRUD: This model is proposed for the ablation study and the RNNs in MFN are replaced with the GRU-D. Thus, it is a multi-modal learning architecture that imputes the missing values based only on intra-modality dynamics.

3.3   Experimental Setup

For the Air Quality dataset, we split the training (2011–2016), validation (2017) and testing (2018) sets chronologically. For the CMU-MOSI dataset, there are 1284, 229, and 686 samples in the training, validation, and testing sets respectively. We implement our models using Pytorch[1]. For all the experiments, the batch size is set to be 32 and all the parameters are tuned by the validation dataset.

3.4   Performance Comparison

Table 1. Comparison with state-of-the-art approaches for multi-modal sequential learning with missing values.

Task	Air Quality		CMU-MOSI Dataset #1					CMU-MOSI Dataset #2				
Metric	MAE	MSE	BA	F1	MA(7)	MAE	r	BA	F1	MA(7)	MAE	r
ELLSTM	3.19	15.5	0.726	0.725	0.325	1.051	0.584	0.739	0.735	0.343	1.021	0.623
MFN	3.17	15.35	0.739	0.735	0.322	1.012	0.618	0.749	0.745	0.327	1.008	0.616
GRUD	3.13	15.22	0.739	0.738	0.294	1.037	0.620	0.755	0.750	0.331	**0.957**	0.652
MFN-GRUD	3.07	14.8	0.736	0.729	0.321	**0.996**	**0.621**	0.755	0.753	**0.354**	0.987	0.626
CMFN	**3.04**	**14.21**	**0.755**	**0.751**	**0.354**	1.007	0.615	**0.767**	**0.759**	0.353	0.958	**0.660**

Table 1 summarizes the comparison between CMFN and proposed baselines for all the multi-modal sequential learning tasks. For the regression tasks, we report mean absolute error (MAE), mean squared error (MSE) and Pearson's correlation r. For binary classification, we report binary accuracy (BA) and binary F1 score. For multiclass classification, we report multiclass accuracy MA(k) where k denotes the number of classes. The results show that CMFN outperforms all the baseline methods in 8/12 tasks. For the CMU-MOSI dataset, when the features in acoustic modality are either partly missing (Dataset #1) or completely missing (Dataset #2), CMFN can robustly impute the missing values and outperform the compared methods. For the ablation study, the difference between CMFN and MFN-GRUD is that the latter only uses intra-modality dynamics for missing value imputation. The results show that CMFN outperforms MFN-GRUD in 9/12 tasks, which suggests that cross-modal dynamics can improve the missing value imputation performance.

---

[1] https://pytorch.org.

4   Conclusion

In this paper, we investigate a novel problem of exploring intra-modality and inter-modality dynamics for multi-modal sequential learning with missing values. We propose a new framework CMFN, which adopts modality-specific and cross-modal information for imputing missing values. To validate the framework, we instantiated a setup incorporating real-world data and synthetic data on benchmark multi-modal learning data. Our result outperforms existing state-of-the-arts models, with ablation studies to show architectural advantages.

References

1. Cabaneros, S.M.S., Calautit, J.K., Hughes, B.R.: A review of artificial neural network models for ambient air pollution prediction. Environ. Modell. Software **119**, 285–304 (2019). https://doi.org/10.1016/j.envsoft.2019.06.014
2. Cao, W., Wang, D., Li, J., Zhou, H., Li, L., Li, Y.: BRITS: Bidirectional Recurrent Imputation for Time Series. arXiv (2018)
3. Che, Z., Purushotham, S., Cho, K., Sontag, D., Liu, Y.: Recurrent neural networks for multivariate time series with missing values. Sci. Rep. **8**(1), 6085 (2018). https://doi.org/10.1038/s41598-018-24271-9
4. Chen, X., He, Z., Chen, Y., Lu, Y., Wang, J.: Missing traffic data imputation and pattern discovery with a Bayesian augmented tensor factorization model. Transp. Res. Part C: Emerging Technol. **104**, 66–77 (2019). https://doi.org/10.1016/j.trc. 2019.03.003
5. Cho, K., Merrienboer, B.v., Bahdanau, D., Bengio, Y.: On the properties of neural machine translation: encoder-decoder approaches. arXiv (2014)
6. Friedman, J., Hastie, T., Tibshirani, R.: The elements of statistical learning, vol. 1. Springer, New York (2001). https://doi.org/10.1007/978-0-387-21606-5
7. Hochreiter, S., Schmidhuber, J.: Long short-term memory. Neural Comput. **9**(8), 1735–1780 (1997)
8. Li, V.O.K., Lam, J.C.K., Chen, Y., Gu, J.: deep learning model to estimate air pollution using M-BP to fill in missing proxy urban data. In: GLOBECOM 2017– 2017 IEEE Global Communications Conference, pp. 1–6 (2017). https://doi.org/ 10.1109/glocom.2017.8255004
9. Liang, P.P., Liu, Z., Tsai, Y.H.H., Zhao, Q., Salakhutdinov, R., Morency, L.P.: Learning representations from imperfect time series data via tensor rank regularization. arXiv (2019)
10. Morency, L.P., Mihalcea, R., Doshi, P.: Towards multimodal sentiment analysis: harvesting opinions from the web, pp. 169–176 (2011). https://doi.org/10.1145/ 2070481.2070509
11. Nelwamondo, F.V., Mohamed, S., Marwala, T.: Missing data: a comparison of neural network and expectation maximization techniques. Current Sci. 1514–1521 (2007)
12. Poria, S., Chaturvedi, I., Cambria, E., Hussain, A.: Convolutional MKL based multimodal emotion recognition and sentiment analysis. In: 2016 IEEE 16th International Conference on Data Mining (ICDM), pp. 439–448 (2016). https://doi.org/ 10.1109/icdm.2016.0055

13. Tang, X., Yao, H., Sun, Y., Aggarwal, C., Mitra, P., Wang, S.: Joint modeling of local and global temporal dynamics for multivariate time series forecasting with missing values (2019)
14. Wang, H., Meghawat, A., Morency, L.P., Xing, E.P.: Select-additive learning: improving generalization in multimodal sentiment analysis. arXiv (2016)
15. Yi, X., Zheng, Y., Zhang, J., Li, T.: St-mvl: filling missing values in geo-sensory time series data (2016)
16. Zadeh, A., Chen, M., Poria, S., Cambria, E., Morency, L.P.: Tensor fusion network for multimodal sentiment analysis. arXiv (2017)
17. Zadeh, A., Liang, P.P., Mazumder, N., Poria, S., Cambria, E., Morency, L.P.: Memory fusion network for multi-view sequential learning. arXiv (2018)
18. Zadeh, A., Mao, C., Shi, K., Zhang, Y., Liang, P.P., Poria, S., Morency, L.P.: Factorized multimodal transformer for multimodal sequential learning. arXiv (2019)
19. Zadeh, A., Zellers, R., Pincus, E., Morency, L.P.: MOSI: multimodal corpus of sentiment intensity and subjectivity analysis in online opinion videos. arXiv (2016)
20. Zhao, X., Zhang, R., Wu, J.L., Chang, P.C.: A deep recurrent neural network for air quality classification. J. Inf. Hiding Multimed. Sig. Proc. **9**, 346–354 (2018)

Social Media Popularity Prediction of Planned Events Using Deep Learning

Sreekanth Madisetty[✉] and Maunendra Sankar Desarkar

Department of Computer Science and Engineering, Indian Institute of Technology Hyderabad, Hyderabad, Telangana, India
{cs15resch11006,maunendra}@iith.ac.in

Abstract. Early prediction of popularity is crucial for recommendation of planned events such as concerts, conferences, sports events, performing arts, etc. Estimation of the *volume of* social media discussions related to the event can be useful for this purpose. Most of the existing methods for social media popularity prediction focus on estimating tweet popularity i.e. predicting the number of retweets for a given tweet. There is less focus on predicting event popularity using social media. We focus on predicting the popularity of an event much before its start date. This type of early prediction can be helpful in event recommendation systems, assisting event organizers for better planning, dynamic ticket pricing, etc. We propose a deep learning based model to predict the social media popularity of an event. We also incorporate an extra feature indicating how many days left to the event start date to improve the performance. Experimental results show that our proposed deep learning based approach outperforms the baseline methods.

Keywords: Popularity prediction · Event popularity · Twitter

1 Introduction

Identifying which information goes viral or popular in social media is an important and challenging task. This information may be tweets, Facebook posts, images, videos, news articles, etc. Identifying this type of information helps in many applications (tweet outbreak prediction [9], news popularity [1], viral videos [11], viral images [8], online petitions [10], advertising, marketing, etc.). Most of the existing works in this line focus on the popularity of individual posts or tweets. This may not be sufficient for estimating the popularity of events. By the word event, we refer to planned events, which are real-world incidents that happen at a particular place, time, and is of interest to several people. Examples of planned events are music concerts, conferences, movie launches, product launches, etc.

In the context of predicting the popularity of planned events, it is useful to predict the volume of the discussions centered around the event. Such discussions would include new tweets generated as well as the retweets or sharing of

© Springer Nature Switzerland AG 2021
D. Hiemstra et al. (Eds.): ECIR 2021, LNCS 12657, pp. 320–326, 2021.
https://doi.org/10.1007/978-3-030-72240-1_31

the posts. The sizes of such discussion cascades can be used as a proxy to the popularity of the event. In this paper, we focus on predicting the number of posts or tweets for a given planned event. As planned events are time bound, it is important to predict this well before the occurrence of the event. Estimating this popularity very close to the event date or after the event is over will not be helpful for recommendation purposes. To the best of our knowledge, this is the first published work towards the formulation and development of methods towards *early prediction of future popularity* of planned events. Predicting the popularity of an event helps in many ways. It plays important role in event recommendation, assisting event organizers for better planning of the event, taking traffic management decisions, setting dynamic ticket pricing, arrangement of additional services, etc.

2   Related Work

In this section, we describe the literature work related to popularity prediction. A comparison of methods for viral information cascade prediction is described in [6]. The authors compared the methods based on three categories: point process based, feature based, and centrality based methods. They showed that feature based methods outperform centrality and point process based methods. A neural network approach to predict the popularity of social media content is proposed in [3]. It makes use of tweet text, users, and time series information for prediction.

A feature based method for tweet cascade growth prediction is designed in [4]. The authors have used content features, author features, retweeters features, structural properties, and temporal features. A method to predict retweet cascade and citation cascade is proposed in [2]. The authors make use of Hawkes process and deep learning models for this problem. A deep stacking model for predicting the image popularity in social media is proposed in [8]. This layer-wise deep stack model stacks multiple regression models. A CNN based model for predicting the popularity of online petitions is described in [10]. The UK and US governments online petition datasets are used in their work.

A method to find cross-platform event popularity is proposed in [7]. The authors proposed the model to predict the popularity of an event based on the information of the event in another platform. An RNN based approach for tweet outbreak prediction is proposed in [9]. The authors have used handcrafted features like tweet information, user information are combined with deep learning models LSTM and GRU for tweet outbreak prediction.

3   Problem Definition and Methodology

In this section, we provide the mathematical definition of our proposed formulations and describe the proposed methodology. Let T be the start date of the event. Also, let S_t denote the number of tweets relevant to the event generated on day t. $t = 0$ can be set by the recommendation system. It can refer to the day on which the relevant tweets for the event were collected for the first time, or

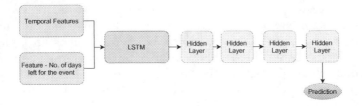

Fig. 1. Block diagram of the proposed architecture for popularity prediction

the date on which a reasonable number of relevant tweets were gathered in/by the system.

$C_{m:n}$ denotes the total number of tweets related to the event generated between day m and n (both inclusive) with $m < n$. In other words, $C_{m:n} = \sum_{i=m}^{n} S_i$. Since we are concerned with *early prediction of future popularity*, we assume each of m, n and t to be $\leq T$. We now provide our proposed formulations for the event popularity estimation problem.

Problem 1 (Running count prediction problem): *Let T be the start date of an event. Given the counts till S_{t-k}, predict the value of $C_{0:t}$, where $t \leq T$.*

Problem 2 (Total count prediction problem): *Given the tweet counts up to S_{t-k} predict the value of $C_{0:T}$.*

For both the problems, we consider an additional setting in which cumulative tweet counts ($C_{0:t-k}$) are passed as the inputs. The value of k can be set to any value depending on the exact domain, task and availability of data. In our work, we consider the value of k to be 10. The *Running count prediction* can be useful for setting dynamic ticket pricing, making advertisements or outreach related activities, etc. *Total count prediction* can be used for recommendation, traffic planning, decisions regarding additional services, etc.

In this paper, we propose an LSTM-based approach for predicting the event popularity. Our proposed architecture consists of one LSTM layer, four hidden dense layers, one dropout layer, and a final dense layer. We use temporal features in LSTM to predict the popularity of an event. To improve the performance of the system, we also use one extra feature i.e. number of days left to the event start date. Let this feature be f_{dl}. As we explain later in the evaluation section, this extra feature improves the performance of the proposed method. The block diagram of the proposed approach is shown in Fig. 1.

4   Experiments

There are not many datasets that can be used for the particular task considered in this work. The only dataset which can be directly used for this task is the CLEF dataset [5], and we have used it for our experiments. This dataset contains 70 million tweets which are collected over a 18 months long period. These tweets are in different languages. This dataset is related to festivals. We have used 25 events which have good number of relevance labels around the event time.

Table 1. k-days ahead Running count prediction, based on *tweet counts* only.

(a) With only temporal features

Method	MAE	RMSE	MAPE
LR	223.046	291.562	43.916
RNN	216.831	286.958	44.882
LSTM	**148.293**	**197.292**	**30.510**

(b) With temporal features + extra feature f_{dl}

Method	MAE	RMSE	MAPE
LR-F	150.948	197.315	69.966
RNN-F	141.985	182.669	62.97
LSTM-F	**93.228**	**135.919**	**18.336**

Table 2. k-days ahead Running count prediction, based on *cumulative tweet count*.

(a) With only temporal features

Method	MAE	RMSE	MAPE
LR	223.046	291.562	43.916
RNN	240.492	327.761	40.836
LSTM	**181.812**	**242.879**	**37.560**

(b) With temporal features + extra feature f_{dl}

Method	MAE	RMSE	MAPE
LR-F	150.948	197.315	69.966
RNN-F	120.027	158.001	35.770
LSTM-F	**98.467**	**143.982**	**20.365**

4.1   Results and Analysis

We have experimented on the following two input types: (a) *Prediction based on tweet count*: In this input type, for an event the absolute tweet count for each day is given as input to the model, and (b) *Prediction based on tweet cumulative count*: In this input type, for an event the cumulative tweet count on each day is given as input to the model. All reported results are based on 5-fold cross validation. We use *Linear Regression (LR)* and *Recurrent Neural Networks (RNN)* as the baseline methods. We refer to the proposed methods as *LSTM* and *LSTM-F*. *LSTM* refers to the method with our proposed architecture in Sect. 3. *LSTM F* refers to the method that uses the same *LSTM* architecture but uses an additional feature (number of days left to the event) as input.

Results for *Running Count Prediction* with input based on absolute tweet counts and only temporal features are shown in Table 1a. The RNNs perform better for MAE and RMSE evaluation metrics compared to linear regression method. Our proposed LSTM based method outperforms both the LR and RNNs for all the evaluation metrics. The results with temporal features and extra feature f_{dl} are shown in Table 1b. After adding the extra feature all the three methods improve the performance in MAE and RMSE. Both the baseline methods MAPE value is increased after adding the extra feature f_{dl} i.e. performance decreased. However our proposed method LSTM-F performance is improved for MAPE metric also. The extra feature f_{dl} and our proposed architecture plays an important role for better performance in our proposed method LSTM-F.

The results of *Running Count Prediction* based on tweet cumulative counts with only temporal features and with temporal features and extra feature f_{dl} are shown in Tables 2a and 2b respectively. The results of tweet absolute counts are better than tweet cumulative counts for most of the methods. However for *Running Count Prediction* RNN results with temporalfeatures and feature f_{dl} for tweet cumulative counts are better than results of tweet absolute count. For tweet cumulative count also our proposed methods LSTM and LSTM-F performance is better than both the baseline methods.

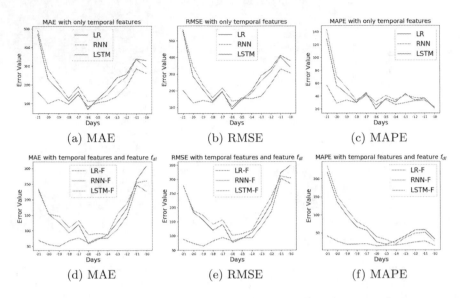

Fig. 2. Day-wise error plots for k-days-ahead Running Count Prediction. Figures (a), to (c) correspond to models with temporal features only. Figures (c), to (e) correspond to models with the extra feature f_{dl}. Tweet absolute counts were considered in input.

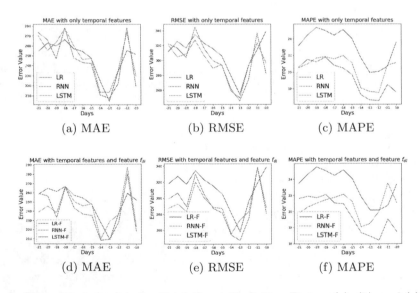

Fig. 3. Day-wise error plots for *Total Count Prediction*. Figures (a), (b), and (c) correspond to models with temporal features only. Figures (c), (d), and (e) correspond to models with the extra feature f_{dl}. Tweet absolute counts were considered in input.

Day-wise error analysis plots for *Running Count Prediction* with only temporal features and with temporal features and feature f_{dl} are shown in Fig. 2. The plot for *Running Count Prediction* MAE with only temporal features is shown in Fig. 2a. Several observations can be made from the plots. It can be seen from the plots that, barring very few cases, the curve for LSTM always lies below the curves for other methods. It indicates that LSTM (and LSTM-F) are better candidates for the prediction tasks than the competitor methods.

We also see sudden jumps in the MAE and RMSE values towards the later parts of the curves. However, the MAPE values continue to come down. This indicates that the number of posts related to the events increase as we approach closer to the event date. Hence, even though the errors in terms of count increases, the percentage error comes down. This is a typical scenario expected for discussions related to planned events. The discussions pick up as the event date approaches, as more and more people start talking about their anticipation and expectations about the event. Additionally, the organizers also spend extra effort in releasing teasers or promotions around this time. This trend is very specific to planned events and makes it characteristically different from other temporal sequence data. This is one reason why adding the number of days left to the event as a model parameter helps in achieving better performances.

Day-wise error analysis plots for *Total Count Prediction* is shown in Fig. 3. From the Figs. 3a, 3b, and 3c we can observe that day-wise errors are almost similar or the proposed method performs better for MAE and RMSE evaluation metrics. For MAPE evaluation metric LSTM performs better than LR and RNN. The error plots for *Total Count Prediction* with temporal features and extra feature f_{dl} are shown in Fig. 3d, 3e, and 3f respectively. We notice that the magnitudes of MAE and RMSE values are higher for total count prediction as compared to the running count prediction problem. This is because the cumulative counts have higher values than the individual day-wise counts. However, MAPE is in similar range for both the problems, which is expected.

As mentioned earlier, to the best of our knowledge, this is the first work on early prediction of future popularity of planned events using social media data. There are multiple scopes for improvement in the proposed models and architectures. We observe from the dataset that all the events are of similar types, or they are homogeneous in nature. In reality, when we have heterogeneous type of events (mix of concerts, performing arts, academic conferences, sports events etc.), the nature of the event, the organizers, the performers or players etc. have significant influence on the amount of discussion about the event. If these additional signals can be incorporated in the model, then we expect the predictions to be even better. Since the events in the considered dataset were homogeneous, we did not include these factors in the model.

5   Conclusion

In this paper, we proposed an LSTM based approach to predict the popularity of an event much before its start date. We showed that adding extra feature f_{dl}

improves the performance of the model. We experimented on the CLEF dataset. Our proposed methods outperformed the baseline methods in terms of both aggregate measures and day-wise performance analysis. In future, we plan to use additional signals related to event metadata in the modeling exercise, and also to explore other deep learning algorithms to further improve the predictions.

References

1. Bandari, R., Asur, S., Huberman, B.A.: The pulse of news in social media: forecasting popularity. In: Sixth International AAAI Conference on Weblogs and Social Media (2012)
2. Cao, Q., Shen, H., Cen, K., Ouyang, W., Cheng, X.: Deephawkes: bridging the gap between prediction and understanding of information cascades. In: Proceedings of the 2017 ACM on Conference on Information and Knowledge Management, pp. 1149–1158 (2017)
3. Chen, G., Kong, Q., Xu, N., Mao, W.: NPP: a neural popularity prediction model for social media content. Neurocomputing **333**, 221–230 (2019)
4. Elsharkawy, S., Hassan, G., Nabhan, T., Roushdy, M.: Towards feature selection for cascade growth prediction on twitter. In: Proceedings of the 10th International Conference on Informatics and Systems, pp. 166–172 (2016)
5. Goeuriot, L., Mothe, J., Mulhem, P., Murtagh, F., SanJuan, E.: Overview of the CLEF 2016 cultural micro-blog contextualization workshop. In: Fuhr, N., Quaresma, P., Gonçalves, T., Larsen, B., Balog, K., Macdonald, C., Cappellato, L., Ferro, N. (eds.) CLEF 2016. LNCS, vol. 9822, pp. 371–378. Springer, Cham (2016). https://doi.org/10.1007/978-3-319-44564-9_30
6. Guo, R., Shakarian, P.: A comparison of methods for cascade prediction. In: 2016 IEEE/ACM International Conference on Advances in Social Networks Analysis and Mining (ASONAM), pp. 591–598. IEEE (2016)
7. Liao, M., Gao, X., Peng, X., Chen, G.: CROP: an efficient cross-platform event popularity prediction model for online media. In: Hartmann, S., Ma, H., Hameurlain, A., Pernul, G., Wagner, R.R. (eds.) DEXA 2018. LNCS, vol. 11030, pp. 35–49. Springer, Cham (2018). https://doi.org/10.1007/978-3-319-98812-2_3
8. Lin, Z., Huang, F., Li, Y., Yang, Z., Liu, W.: A layer-wise deep stacking model for social image popularity prediction. World Wide Web **22**(4), 1639–1655 (2018). https://doi.org/10.1007/s11280-018-0590-1
9. Roy, S., Suman, B.K., Chandra, J., Dandapat, S.K.: Forecasting the future: leveraging rnn based feature concatenation for tweet outbreak prediction. In: Proceedings of the 7th ACM IKDD CoDS and 25th COMAD, pp. 219–223 (2020)
10. Subramanian, S., Baldwin, T., Cohn, T.: Content-based popularity prediction of online petitions using a deep regression model. arXiv preprint arXiv:1805.06566 (2018)
11. Xu, J., Van Der Schaar, M., Liu, J., Li, H.: Forecasting popularity of videos using social media. IEEE J. Selected Top. Signal Process. **9**(2), 330–343 (2014)

Right for the Right Reasons: Making Image Classification Intuitively Explainable

Anna Nguyen$^{(\boxtimes)}$, Adrian Oberföll, and Michael Färber

Karlsruhe Institute of Technology (KIT), Karlsruhe, Germany
{anna.nguyen,michael.faerber}@kit.edu, adrian.oberfoell@student.kit.edu

Abstract. The effectiveness of Convolutional Neural Networks (CNNs) in classifying image data has been thoroughly demonstrated. In order to explain the classification to humans, methods for visualizing classification evidence have been developed in recent years. These explanations reveal that sometimes images are classified correctly, but for the wrong reasons, i.e., based on incidental evidence. Of course, it is desirable that images are classified correctly for the right reasons, i.e., based on the actual evidence. To this end, we propose a new *explanation quality metric* to measure *ob*ject *al*igned *ex*planation in image classification which we refer to as the *ObAlEx* metric. Using object detection approaches, explanation approaches, and ObAlEx, we quantify the focus of CNNs on the actual evidence. Moreover, we show that additional training of the CNNs can improve the focus of CNNs without decreasing their accuracy.

1 Introduction

Convolutional Neural Networks (CNNs) have been demonstrated to be very effective in image classification tasks, achieving high accuracy. However, methods to explain classifications performed by CNNs have shown that sometimes image data has been classified for incidental evidences, undermining the trust between humans and machines [7]. Previous attempts to fix this problem have included a human-in-the-loop approach [10], a pre-processing step for removing features of the input that are deemed irrelevant for the classification task at hand (such as images' backgrounds) [5], or the introduction of a new loss function that incorporates an explanation approach during training [8]. Although the latter work constrains the explanation of the model in the loss function penalizing the input gradients, it uses explanations only based on input gradients which is not ideal for all use cases, especially in image classification, where individual pixels are difficult to interpret. Overall, we believe that there is a lack of a metric which quantifies if an intuitive explanation can be gained.

In this paper, we propose an *ob*ject *al*igned *ex*planation quality metric, called *ObAlEx*. ObAlEx quantifies to which degree the object mask of an image is consistent with the obtained evidence of explanation methods and thus, imitates

© Springer Nature Switzerland AG 2021
D. Hiemstra et al. (Eds.): ECIR 2021, LNCS 12657, pp. 327–333, 2021.
https://doi.org/10.1007/978-3-030-72240-1_32

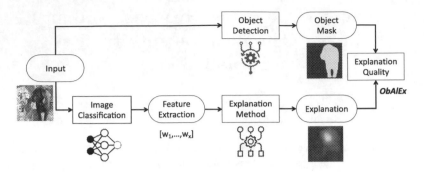

Fig. 1. The pipeline of our metric.

human behavior to classify images according to the objects contained. The proposed metric is independent of the used explanation method (e.g., occlusion [13], LIME [7], or Grad-cam [11]) and object detection method and can therefore be applied together with arbitrary explanation methods and object detection methods. Our approach to identify the focus on the relevant input regions requires neither human interaction nor pre-processing. Based on extensive experiments, we demonstrate the effectiveness of the proposed metric while training CNNs, ensuring both high accuracy and a focus on the relevant input regions.

Our main contributions are as follows:

1. We propose an object aligned explanation metric, ObAlEx, to quantify explanations of image classification models intuitively. Our metric is applicable to different explanation methods and neither requires human interaction nor interference in the model's architecture.
2. In extensive experiments,[1] we show that our metric can be used for making CNN models for image classification more intuitive while keeping the accuracy.

In the following section, we outline our metric. We then present our extensive experiments. Finally, we close with some concluding remarks.

2　ObAlEx Metric

The metric ObAlEx is designed as a relative metric which depends on the explanation method and the classifier used. Based on the change of the explanation quality during training, it can be evaluated if a certain training strategy leads to an improvement or deterioration of the model's intuitive explanation. By explanation quality, we define the degree of alignment between object to be classified and explanation of the classification model.

The pipeline to calculate ObAlEx is outlined in Fig. 1. Given an input image on which an object should be detected, we first apply an object detection method

---

[1] We provide the source code online at https://github.com/annugyen/ObAlEx.

(e.g., Mask R-CNN) to obtain the image regions of the object itself (i.e., object mask). We define regions of the explanation that lie outside of the object mask as indicative of a classification for the wrong reasons, and conversely, that regions of the explanation that lie inside of the object mask as indicative of a classification for the right reasons. The mask of objects on images can be obtained with a high accuracy nowadays (see Sect. 3).

Simultaneously, an image classifier (e.g., pretrained VGG16) is applied to obtain labels of recognized objects (e.g., "dog"). An explanation method (e.g., Grad-Cam) then outputs the image regions which are most influential given the extracted features from the CNN and the input image.

Both the object mask and the explanation output is then used to compute the metric ObAlEx and thus, to improve the explanation quality. Since existing explanation methods support different highlighting levels, our score is constructed in such a way that the score is the higher the more of the highlighted explanation aligns with the object mask. In the following, we describe the computation of the explanation quality formally.

Given a data set D with correctly classified images and an image $d \in D$ with pixels p_{ij}^d, width w^d, and height h^d, let A^d denote the matrix whose values a_{ij}^d equals the activation of the pixels of the object mask, where $i \in \{1, \ldots, h^d\}$, $j \in \{1, \ldots, w^d\}$, $h^d, w^d \in \mathbb{N}$. We regard A^d as a fuzzy set, i.e. whose values have degrees of membership depicted as a_{ij}^d. We define $a_{ij}^d \in \mathbb{R}$ with $0 \leq a_{ij}^d \leq 1$. In our experiments, we set $a_{ij}^d = 1$ if the pixel p_{ij}^d of the input image belongs to the object mask and $a_{ij}^d = 0$, otherwise. Similarly, let B^d be the matrix whose values b_{ij}^d equals the activation of the pixels of the explanation. We additionally normalize the values b_{ij}^d between zero and one, i.e. $0 \leq b_{ij}^d \leq 1$ where $b_{ij}^d = 1$ if the pixel p_{ij}^d of the input image belongs to the highest activation and $b_{ij}^d = 0$ otherwise. Our metric ObAlEx is, then, defined as follows:

$$\text{ObAlEx}(A^d, B^d) = \frac{\sum_{i,j} a_{ij}^d b_{ij}^d}{\sum_{i,j} b_{ij}^d} \in [0, 1] \tag{1}$$

To get the explanation quality of an image classifier, ObAlEx can be applied on all images in a data set D. We then calculate the average of all values of the explanation quality of each picture for an image collection. In doing so, we weight all images equally. The explanation quality of the classifier is defined as

$$\text{AvgObAlEx}(D) = \frac{1}{n} \sum_{d=1}^{n} \text{ObAlEx}(A^d, B^d) \in [0, 1], \tag{2}$$

where $n \in \mathbb{N}$ is the number of images in data set D. AvgObAlEx only considers the scores of images classified correctly by the model, otherwise the metric would get skewed. Therefore, images which are classified wrong are excluded.

3   Evaluation

3.1   Evaluation Setting

To evaluate ObAlEx, we apply pre-trained CNN models. We focus on three state-of-the-art image classification models: *VGG16* [12], *ResNet50* [3], and *MobileNet* [4]. The models are pre-trained on the ILSVRC2012 data set [9] which is also known as ImageNet. We adapt each model's upper output dense layers to the specific data set (i.e., number of categories in the used image classification data sets *Dogs vs. Cats* and *Caltech 101*, respectively). To show the universal applicability of ObAlEx, we use different well-known explanation methods such as occlusion [13], LIME [7], Grad-Cam [11], and Grad-Cam++ [1]. In our experiments, the AvgObAlEx settled around a fixed value after 50 images. For that reason and due to high computing power costs in case of LIME, we calculate the AvgObAlEx for 50 images per epoch in the following experiments. Our experiments are executed on a server with 12 GB of GPU RAM. We use TensorFlow and the Keras deep learning library for implementation. We use the following data sets in our evaluation:

Dogs vs. Cats data set[2] contains 3,000 dog and cat images, 1,500 per class. We use Mask R-CNN [2] to create the object masks. The quality of the object masks is important for the validity of the proposed metric ObAlEx. Therefore, we manually evaluated the computed object masks for 200 randomly chosen images regarding the overlap of the whole object. The accuracy was 91%. Thus, we argue that the pre-trained Mask R-CNN performs well for our purpose.

Given the data set size, we used 70% of the images for training and 30% for testing. We first adjust the output layer of all CNN models to the two categories (dog and cat) and train them for 10 epochs on the Dogs vs. Cats data set (where all layers except output layer are frozen). After that, we freeze different combinations of layers for further training. In the original papers of the above mentioned models, the convolutional layers are divided into five blocks. For simplification and comparability, we use this convention for our strategies. We also summarize the last dense layers to one block. Thus, we always set whole blocks of layers to either be trainable or non-trainable. We train every strategy for another 10 epochs. We investigate the following strategies: (a) train the last dense layers which we denote as dense block, (b) train the last two convolutional blocks (i.e. the fourth and fifth), (c) train the first three convolutional blocks, and (d) train all layers, i.e. all convolutional and dense blocks.

Caltech 101 data set [6] has 101 object categories. We create a uniform distributed data set by drawing random sampling from the categories resulting in a total of 6,060 images with 60 images per class. We use a test split of 0.25. This data set is provided with hand-labeled object masks for all images. Thus, we use those labeled object masks. We perform another experiment inspired by [8,10]. To actively force the model to be more intuitive and thus, to provide a

---

[2] https://www.kaggle.com/c/dogs-vs-cats, last accessed: 2020-10-28.

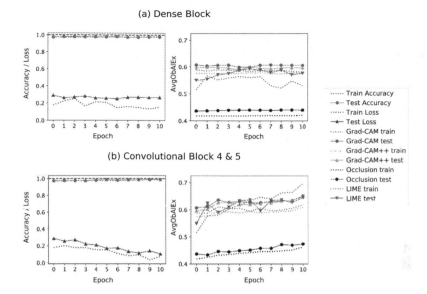

Fig. 2. VGG16 Results. Transfer learning strategies with VGG16 with explanation methods Occlusion, LIME and Grad-Cam/Grad-Cam++.

more interpretable explanation, we followed a naïve approach by using artificial images. We edit the images in a way that they contain the object to classify and masked out the background with random pixels. This should force the model to focus more on the object and increase the explanation quality.

3.2   Evaluation Results

Dogs vs. Cats. Figure 2 shows the results for VGG16 with training strategies (a) and (b). We can see that the performance of the model measured with accuracy did not change within 10 epochs (see Fig. 2 (a)/(b) left graph). However, we observed a change in AvgObAlEx (see Fig. 2 (a)/(b) right graph). The explanation quality after 10 epochs computed with any explanation method for strategy (b) is significantly higher than the explanation quality for strategy (a). This fits to the common knowledge that complex structures in the input images are learned in the later convolutional blocks and are, therefore, more decisive for the classification. Moreover, Fig. 2 (b) shows with increasing number of epochs a decrease in the loss, while the AvgObAlEx increases simultaneously. This indicates the effectiveness of the model for right predictions based on the right reasons. The results of strategy (d) and (b) and the results of strategy (c) and (a) are similar to each other respectively, which emphasizes the common knowledge. Without using the proposed metric ObAlEx this improvement would not be evident since the accuracy of all models stays the same during training.

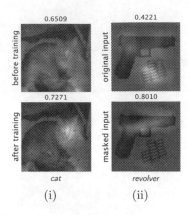

(i)   (ii)

Fig. 3. Examples from (i) Dogs vs. Cats and (ii) Caltech 101 with quality scores shown above.

In Fig. 3(i), we provide an example of the explanation visualized with Grad-Cam with strategy (b) on VGG16. We can see that the explanation quality increases after training and that the visualized explanation has a stronger focus on the object. With only 10 epochs of additional training, we were able to improve the model in a way that it utilizes more important features such as the face of the animal. Without ObAlEx, it would be obvious to not train the model any further due to the non-changing accuracy. We observed similar results on the experiments with ResNet50 and MobileNet, and also on the Caltech 101 data set but omit them due to page limitations (See footnote 1).

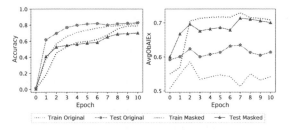

Fig. 4. Training on Caltech 101.

Caltech 101. Figure 4 shows the results for 10 epochs of training VGG16 on Caltech 101 with the original and masked images as input. As we can observe in the left graph, training with the original images results in a higher accuracy than training with the masked images. However, the AvgObAlEx (computed with Grad-Cam as explainer, see graph on the right) of the model trained with masked input images is significantly higher than the AvgObAlEx of the model trained with the original input images. This indicates that more background information was used in the classification. Thus, evaluating image classifiers beyond accuracy can be valuable to real-world cases where specific background information is unavailable.

Figure 3 (ii) shows an example image with Grad-Cam on VGG16. Despite high accuracy, we can see that the explanation for the image with masked out background (image at the bottom) is more intuitive and more focused on the actual object than the original input image.

4   Conclusion

In this paper, we focused on evaluating CNN image classifiers with different explanation approaches. We introduced a novel explanation quality score metric to support the training process besides accuracy and loss function. We have shown in our experiments that our metric ObAlEx can be used to indicate cases where a model makes its predictions based on wrong reasons. Overall, ObAlEx facilitates more generalized models which can increase the user's trust in the model by object aligned explanations.

References

1. Chattopadhyay, A., Sarkar, A., Howlader, P., Balasubramanian, V.N.: Grad-cam++: generalized gradient-based visual explanations for deep convolutional networks. In: 2018 IEEE Winter Conference on Applications of Computer Vision, WACV 2018, pp. 839–847. IEEE Computer Society (2018)
2. He, K., Gkioxari, G., Dollár, P., Girshick, R.B.: Mask R-CNN. IEEE Trans. Pattern Anal. Mach. Intell. **42**(2), 386–397 (2020)
3. He, K., Zhang, X., Ren, S., Sun, J.: Deep residual learning for image recognition. In: 2016 IEEE Conference on Computer Vision and Pattern Recognition, CVPR 2016, pp. 770–778. IEEE Computer Society (2016)
4. Howard, A.G., et al.: Mobilenets: efficient convolutional neural networks for mobile vision applications. CoRR abs/1704.04861 (2017)
5. Jia, S., Lansdall-Welfare, T., Cristianini, N.: Right for the right reason: training agnostic networks. In: Duivesteijn, W., Siebes, A., Ukkonen, A. (eds.) IDA 2018. LNCS, vol. 11191, pp. 164–174. Springer, Cham (2018). https://doi.org/10.1007/978-3-030-01768-2_14
6. Li, F., Fergus, R., Perona, P.: Learning generative visual models from few training examples: an incremental bayesian approach tested on 101 object categories. Comput. Vis. Image Understand. **106**(1), 59–70 (2007)
7. Ribeiro, M.T., Singh, S., Guestrin, C.: "why should I trust you?": explaining the predictions of any classifier. In: Proceedings of the 22nd ACM SIGKDD International Conference on Knowledge Discovery and Data Mining, 2016, pp. 1135–1144. ACM (2016)
8. Ross, A.S., Hughes, M.C., Doshi-Velez, F.: Right for the right reasons: training differentiable models by constraining their explanations. In: Proceedings of the Twenty-Sixth International Joint Conference on Artificial Intelligence, IJCAI 2017, pp. 2662–2670. ijcai.org (2017)
9. Russakovsky, O., et al.: Imagenet large scale visual recognition challenge. Int. J. Comput. Vis. **115**(3), 211–252 (2015)
10. Schramowski, P., et al.: Right for the wrong scientific reasons: revising deep networks by interacting with their explanations. CoRR abs/2001.05371 (2020)
11. Selvaraju, R.R., Das, A., Vedantam, R., Cogswell, M., Parikh, D., Batra, D.: Grad-cam: why did you say that? visual explanations from deep networks via gradient-based localization. CoRR abs/1610.02391 (2016)
12. Simonyan, K., Zisserman, A.: Very deep convolutional networks for large-scale image recognition. In: 3rd International Conference on Learning Representations, ICLR 2015, Conference Track Proceedings (2015)
13. Zeiler, M.D., Fergus, R.: Visualizing and understanding convolutional networks. In: Fleet, D., Pajdla, T., Schiele, B., Tuytelaars, T. (eds.) ECCV 2014. LNCS, vol. 8689, pp. 818–833. Springer, Cham (2014). https://doi.org/10.1007/978-3-319-10590-1_53

Weakly Supervised Label Smoothing

Gustavo Penha$^{(\boxtimes)}$ and Claudia Hauff

TU Delft, Delft, The Netherlands
{g.penha-1,c.hauff}@tudelft.nl

Abstract. We study Label Smoothing (LS), a widely used regularization technique, in the context of neural learning to rank (L2R) models. LS combines the ground-truth labels with a uniform distribution, encouraging the model to be less confident in its predictions. We analyze the relationship between the non-relevant documents—specifically how they are sampled—and the effectiveness of LS, discussing how LS can be capturing *"hidden similarity knowledge"* between the relevant and non-relevant document classes. We further analyze LS by testing if a curriculum-learning approach, i.e., starting with LS and after a number of iterations using only ground-truth labels, is beneficial. Inspired by our investigation of LS in the context of neural L2R models, we propose a novel technique called *Weakly Supervised Label Smoothing* (WSLS) that takes advantage of the retrieval scores of the negative sampled documents as a weak supervision signal in the process of modifying the ground-truth labels. WSLS is simple to implement, requiring no modification to the neural ranker architecture. Our experiments across three retrieval tasks—passage retrieval, similar question retrieval and conversation response ranking—show that WSLS for pointwise BERT-based rankers leads to consistent effectiveness gains. The source code is available at https://github.com/Guzpenha/transformer_rankers/tree/wsls.

1 Introduction

Neural Learning to Rank (L2R) models are traditionally trained using large amounts of strongly labeled data, i.e., human generated relevance judgements. For example, in ad hoc retrieval each instance is comprised of a query, a document and a relevance judgment. All the other documents in the collection that were not labeled as (non-)relevant for the query, while not specified explicitly, can be viewed as non-relevant for the query. Since utilizing an entire corpus for training a L2R model is practically infeasible, the typical procedure is to rely on the top-k ranked documents for a query obtained from an efficient (but less effective) retrieval model such as BM25. While research has shown that the negative sampler (NS), i.e. the technique to select documents to use as negative samples for a query, matters a great deal in the effectiveness of the learned ranker [1,2,10,14,22] there has been no work on how to make use of the *scores* of the NS, which are currently ignored in the training of L2R models—only the content of the documents are employed.

© Springer Nature Switzerland AG 2021
D. Hiemstra et al. (Eds.): ECIR 2021, LNCS 12657, pp. 334–341, 2021.
https://doi.org/10.1007/978-3-030-72240-1_33

In this work we first aim to understand, in the realm of neural L2R[1], a widely used and successful [21, 26, 27] regularization technique called Label Smoothing [20] (LS), that penalizes the divergence between the predictions and a uniform distribution. We begin by looking into how the choice of NS impacts LS, since in the binary relevance prediction problem LS penalizes the model less than normal training when predicting a negative document as relevant and vice versa. We also analyze whether it is beneficial to use a curriculum-learning inspired procedure for the hyper-parameter that controls the LS strength as shown by recent work on understanding LS in other domains [4, 23]. This initial exploration to understand LS leads to the following research question: *RQ1 Is label smoothing an effective regularizer for neural L2R (and if so, under what conditions)?* Our experimental results on three different retrieval tasks reveal that LS is indeed an effective regularization technique for neural L2R, specifically when **(a)** there is similarity between the relevant and the non-relevant sampled documents, i.e. when we use BM25 as the NS technique, and **(b)** a curriculum-like approach is used to control the strength of the smoothing.

Inspired by our findings, we propose the Weakly Supervised Label Smoothing (WSLS) technique which exploits the NS retrieval scores, as opposed to LS where all labels are smoothed equally, for training neural L2R models. Instead of interpolating the ground-truth label distribution with a uniform distribution (as done in LS), we interpolate it with the NS score distribution. WSLS has two benefits compared to using the ground-truth labels: (a) it regularizes the neural ranker by penalizing overconfident predictions and (b) it provides additional supervision signal through weak supervision [3] for the negative sampled documents. WSLS is simple to implement, and requires no modification to the neural ranker architecture, but only to the labels using weak supervision scores that are readily available. Our experiments to answer our second research question (*RQ2 Is WSLS more effective than LS for training neural L2R models?*) reveal that WSLS is a better way of smoothing the labels by providing additional weak supervision obtained from the negative sampling procedure. We reach relative gains of 0.5% in effectiveness across tasks.

2   Background: Label Smoothing (LS)

Given an input instance x (a query and document combination), two classes ($k = 0$ means not relevant and $k = 1$ relevant, and thus here $K = 2$), a ground truth distribution $q(k \mid x)$ and predictions from the neural L2R model $p(k \mid x) = \frac{\exp(z_k)}{\sum_{i=1}^{K} \exp(z_i)}$, where z_i are the logits, we can use the cross entropy loss for training: $\ell = -\sum_{k}^{K} \log(p(k))q(k)$, where $q(k) = \delta_{k,y}$, and $\delta_{k,y}$ is Dirac delta (equals 1 for $z = y$ and 0 otherwise). Maximizing the log-likelihood of the correct label is approached if the logit corresponding to the ground-truth label is much greater than all other logits: $z_y \gg z_k$ for all $k \neq y$. This encourages the model

---

[1] Binary relevance prediction is quite different from other domains such as image classification and language modelling which employ up to thousands of distinct classes.

to be overconfident in its predictions, which might not generalize well. Label smoothing [20] is a regularization mechanism to encourage the model to be less confident. Given a distribution $u(k)$, *independent* of the training example x, and a smoothing parameter ϵ, for a training example with ground-truth label y, we replace the label distribution $q(k \mid x) = \delta_{k,y}$ with $q'(k \mid x) = (1 - \epsilon)\delta_{k,y} + \epsilon u(k)$. In LS the uniform distribution is employed, i.e. $u(k) = 1/K$.

While LS is a widely used technique to regularize models, the reasons underlying its successes [21,26,27] and failures [12,19] remain unclear. Müller et al. [17] showed that while LS impairs teacher models to do knowledge distillation [8] it improves the models' calibration, i.e. how representative the predictions are with respect to the true likelihood of correctness [7].

Curriculum Learning for Label Smoothing (T-LS). Xu et al. [23] argued that given the empirical evidence of LS ineffectiveness in certain cases, it is natural to combine LS with the ground-truth labels during training in a two-stage training procedure and thus proposed T-LS: start training with LS, i.e. $\epsilon > 0$, and after X training instances use normal training, i.e. $\epsilon = 0$ (the unmodified ground-truth labels are used). Similarly, Dogan et al. [4] proposed to move from a distribution of labels smoothed by the similarity between label classes towards the ground-truth labels with a curriculum leaning procedure. In this paper we resort to T-LS[2] [23] to test whether a curriculum learning inspired approach for ϵ is required or not in the training of neural L2R models.

3   Weakly Supervised Label Smoothing (WSLS)

We propose to replace the uniform distribution $u(k)$ that is independent of the example x, with a weakly supervised function $w(k \mid x)$, which is readily available for documents with label 0 as part of the negative sampling procedure of L2R, at no additional cost: the negative sampler (NS) score. Specifically, $q'(k \mid x) = (1-\epsilon)\delta_{k,y} + \epsilon NS(k \mid x)$, where $NS(k \mid x)$ is the negative sampling procedure score for instance x and label class k. If we use $BM25$ to retrieve negative samples[3], then for $k = 0$ we have $q'(k \mid x) = (1 - \epsilon)\delta_{k,y} + \epsilon BM25(x)$ and when $k = 1$ we fall back to LS since we have strong labeled data: $q'(k \mid x) = (1 - \epsilon)\delta_{k,y} + \epsilon\frac{1}{K}$. In the same way we can induce a curriculum learning procedure for LS resulting in T-LS (see Sect. 2), we can do it for WSLS, for which we refer to as T-WSLS.

4   Experimental Setup

Tasks and Datasets: In order to evaluate our research questions, we resort to the three following retrieval tasks: passage retrieval using the 2020 Deep Learning track of TREC (TREC-DL) dataset (we split the dev set into dev and test), similar question retrieval with the Quora Question Pairs [9] (QQP) dataset and conversation response ranking with the MANtIS [18] dataset. We use them

---

[2] Initial experiments where we decreased ϵ linearly [4] were as effective as T-LS [23].

[3] Since the BM25 scores are not between 0 and 1 we apply min-max scaling.

due to the large amount of labeled examples (required for training neural ranking models) and diversity of tasks.

Implementation Details and Evaluation: We use BERT-based ranking as a strong neural L2R baseline. We follow previous research [15] and fine-tune BERT using the [CLS] token to predict binary relevance—the query and the document are concatenated using the [SEP] token and used as input—using the cross-entropy loss and Adam optimizer [11] with $lr = 5^{-6}$ and $\epsilon = 1^{-8}$. We train with a batch size of 32 and fine-tune the models for 50000 training instances. We train and test each model 5 times using different random seeds with 10 total candidate documents by query. We resort to a standard evaluation metric in conversation response ranking [6,24]: recall at position K with n candidates: $R_n@K$. Since all tasks here are concerned with re-ranking $R_n@K$ is a sampled metric [13] suitable to compare models on how high the relevant documents are ranked when having only n candidates. We resort to a robust and widely used NS to obtain such candidates: BM25. We refer to using the query as input to BM25 and select the top $n - 1$ ranked documents as NS^{BM25}. We also use random sampling (NS^{random})—which samples candidate documents from the whole collection with the same probability and thus returns documents that are quite different from the relevant one—to better understand LS.

Table 1. Average $R_{10}@1$ and the standard deviation results of 5 runs with different random seeds for BERT with label smoothing (w. LS) and BERT with two-stage label smoothing (w. T-LS) for different negative samplers during training (NS^{BM25} and NS^{random}) and $\epsilon = 0.2$ for the development set. Bold indicate the highest values for each dataset and ▲/▾ superscripts indicate significant gains and losses respectively over the baseline (BERT) using paired Student's t-test with confidence level of 0.95.

	NS^{BM25}			NS^{random}		
	TREC-DL	QQP	MANtIS	TREC-DL	QQP	MANtIS
BERT	0.568±.00	0.581±.03	0.612±.01	**0.385±.01**	0.444±.01	**0.350±.01**
w. LS	0.564±.01▾	0.593±.01▲	0.612±.01	0.304±.05▾	0.440±.03▾	0.348±.01▾
w. T-LS	**0.570±.01▲**	**0.598±.01▲**	0.612±.01	0.382±.02▾	0.444±.01	0.345±.01▾

5 Results

Effectiveness of Label Smoothing for Neural Ranking (RQ1). Table 1 displays the dev. set results[4] for the LS and T-LS techniques when changing the NS. The results reveal that when training BERT with NS^{random} to sample negative documents, it is not effective to use any type of label smoothing. In fact there is a consistent and statistically significant decrease in the effectiveness compared to BERT. In contrast, when we sample documents to train with

---

[4] Since we do not do any hyper-parameter tuning for RQ1, we resort to the dev. set to avoid overusing the test set.

NS^{BM25} we observe that there are significant gains to train BERT with T-LS, with the exception of MANtIS where there is no statistical difference. When we compare LS with T-LS, we see that it is indeed beneficial to use a curriculum-learning approach for label smoothing (T-LS), which indicates that being more permissive of the mistakes in the first half of training is effective—this is in line with results obtained in other domains [4,23]. **This answers our first RQ positively: label smoothing is an effective regularization technique to train neural L2R models, with gains of 1% of R_{10}@1 compared to standard training (BERT) on average across three different retrieval tasks when (a) using NS^{BM25} and (b) a curriculum learning approach for LS**.

We hypothesize that label smoothing is effective for training neural L2R models if the negative documents are similar to the relevant documents for the query. Our results when changing from NS^{BM25} to NS^{random} support this hypothesis. Intuitively, if the negative document is random and thus very dissimilar to the query, using a label smoothing regularizer will penalize the model less for this mistake, which might hinder learning. When using label smoothing with a negative document that was sampled using BM25, we are penalizing the model less for choosing a document that is similar to the query in terms of exact matching words. In this way we are teaching the model the similarity between the classes relevant and non-relevant by means of documents that are closer to the classification frontier. A similar reasoning can be found in recent work which discusses that the similarity between classes on the wrong responses, i.e. *"hidden similarity knowledge"* [8], is helpful for learning better neural networks [4,5,25]. Our findings also align with [16]: training with topically similar (but non-relevant) documents—as opposed to random documents—allows the model to better discriminate between documents provided by an earlier retrieval stage.

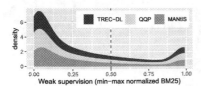

Fig. 1. Stacked and smoothed weak supervision distributions used for WSLS from the min-max normalized scores of NS^{BM25}. The dashed vertical line indicates the distribution used by LS (uniform with $K = 2$).

Table 2. Average R_{10}@1 and the standard deviation results of 5 runs with different random seeds for the test set. ▲/▼ and △/▽ superscripts indicate significant gains and losses over the baselines (BERT) and (BERT w. T-LS) respectively using paired Student's t-test with confidence level of 0.95 and Bonferroni correction.

	TREC-DL	QQP	MANtIS
BERT	0.599±.00	0.595±.01	0.609±.01
w. T-LS	0.601±.00▲	0.596±.01	0.607±.01
w. T-WSLS	**0.604±.00▲△**	**0.598±.01▲△**	0.609±.01△

Effectiveness of Weakly Supervised Label Smoothing (RQ2). Before we dive into the effectiveness of T-WSLS[5], we investigate the distribution of the normalized weak supervision scores from NS^{BM25} in Fig. 1. There is a high density for low scores indicating that only a few of the sampled documents receive scores close to the maximum of the list (0.99 score after min-max scaling) and most of them are closer to the minimum (0.00). This is very different from the uniform distribution used by T-LS (dashed vertical line), which does not change according to the sample, and with two classes ($K = 2$) is equal to 0.5, whereas the mean of the weak supervision distribution is 0.33. This suggests that the optimal ϵ for T-WSLS is different from T-LS.

Based on this observation, we test different values of ϵ on the dev. set in order to tune this hyper-parameter and use it on the test set. Figure 2 displays the effect of ϵ on the effectiveness of the proposed approach. The highest $R_{10}@1$ values are observed for T-WSLS: 0.574 (+1% over the baseline w/o T-WSLS) for TREC-DL when $\epsilon = 0.4$, 0.600 (+3.2%) for QQP when $\epsilon = 0.2$ and 0.6151 (+0.5%) for MANtIS when $\epsilon = 0.4$. When we apply the best models (for both T-LS and T-WSLS) found using the dev. set on the test set, we see in Table 2 that BERT w. T-WSLS outperforms both BERT and BERT w. LS with statistical significance (with the exception of MANtIS where there is no difference). **This answers RQ2 indicating that WSLS is indeed more effective than LS with statistically significant gains on all tasks against T-LS and with an average of 0.5% improvement over BERT.**

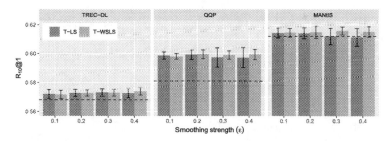

Fig. 2. T-LS and T-WSLS sensitivity to the hyperparameter ϵ for the dev. set. Error bars indicate the 95% confidence intervals for $R_{10}@1$ over 5 runs with different random seeds. Dashed horizontal lines indicate the baseline w/o label smoothing ($\epsilon = 0$).

6   Conclusion

We studied LS in the context of neural L2R models. Our findings indicate that LS is effective when there is similarity between relevant and non-relevant documents and that using curriculum learning for the strength of the regularization is effective. We proposed a technique that combines the weak supervision scores of negative sampled documents with label smoothing (WSLS) which outperforms

---

[5] Based on RQ1 results we use the two-stage approaches here (T-LS and T-WSLS).

LS on different retrieval tasks. In future work we will explore WSLS in a wider range of retrieval models and tasks.

Acknowledgements. This research has been supported by NWO projects SearchX (639.022.722) and NWO Aspasia (015.013.027).

References

1. Aslam, J.A., Kanoulas, E., Pavlu, V., Savev, S., Yilmaz, E.: Document selection methodologies for efficient and effective learning-to-rank. In: Proceedings of the 32nd International ACM SIGIR Conference on Research and Development in Information Retrieval, pp. 468–475 (2009)
2. Cohen, D., Jordan, S.M., Croft, W.B.: Learning a better negative sampling policy with deep neural networks for search. In: Proceedings of the 2019 ACM SIGIR International Conference on Theory of Information Retrieval, pp. 19–26 (2019)
3. Dehghani, M., Zamani, H., Severyn, A., Kamps, J., Croft, W.B.: Neural ranking models with weak supervision. In: Proceedings of the 40th International ACM SIGIR Conference on Research and Development in Information Retrieval, pp. 65–74 (2017)
4. Dogan, U., Deshmukh, A.A., Machura, M., Igel, C.: Label-similarity curriculum learning. arXiv preprint arXiv:1911.06902 (2019)
5. Furlanello, T., Lipton, Z.C., Tschannen, M., Itti, L., Anandkumar, A.: Born again neural networks. arXiv preprint arXiv:1805.04770 (2018)
6. Gu, J.C., et al.: Speaker-aware Bert for multi-turn response selection in retrieval-based chatbots. arXiv preprint arXiv:2004.03588 (2020)
7. Guo, C., Pleiss, G., Sun, Y., Weinberger, K.Q.: On calibration of modern neural networks. arXiv preprint arXiv:1706.04599 (2017)
8. Hinton, G., Vinyals, O., Dean, J.: Distilling the knowledge in a neural network. arXiv preprint arXiv:1503.02531 (2015)
9. Iyer, S., Dandekar, N., Csernai, K.: First quora dataset release: question pairs (2017)
10. Karpukhin, V., et al.: Dense passage retrieval for open-domain question answering. arXiv preprint arXiv:2004.04906 (2020)
11. Kingma, D.P., Ba, J.: Adam: a method for stochastic optimization. arXiv preprint arXiv:1412.6980 (2014)
12. Kornblith, S., Shlens, J., Le, Q.V.: Do better imagenet models transfer better? In: Proceedings of the IEEE Conference on Computer Vision and Pattern Recognition, pp. 2661–2671 (2019)
13. Krichene, W., Rendle, S.: On sampled metrics for item recommendation. In: Proceedings of the 26th ACM SIGKDD International Conference on Knowledge Discovery & Data Mining, pp. 1748–1757 (2020)
14. Li, J., Tao, C., Feng, Y., Zhao, D., Yan, R., et al.: Sampling matters! an empirical study of negative sampling strategies for learning of matching models in retrieval-based dialogue systems. In: Proceedings of the 2019 Conference on Empirical Methods in Natural Language Processing and the 9th International Joint Conference on Natural Language Processing (EMNLP-IJCNLP), pp. 1291–1296 (2019)
15. Lin, J., Nogueira, R., Yates, A.: Pretrained transformers for text ranking: Bert and beyond. arXiv preprint arXiv:2010.06467 (2020)

16. Mitra, B., Diaz, F., Craswell, N.: Learning to match using local and distributed representations of text for web search. In: Proceedings of the 26th International Conference on World Wide Web, pp. 1291–1299 (2017)
17. Müller, R., Kornblith, S., Hinton, G.E.: When does label smoothing help? In: Advances in Neural Information Processing Systems, pp. 4694–4703 (2019)
18. Penha, G., Balan, A., Hauff, C.: Introducing mantis: a novel multi-domain information seeking dialogues dataset. arXiv preprint arXiv:1912.04639 (2019)
19. Seo, J.W., Jung, H.G., Lee, S.W.: Self-augmentation: generalizing deep networks to unseen classes for few-shot learning. arXiv preprint arXiv:2004.00251 (2020)
20. Szegedy, C., Vanhoucke, V., Ioffe, S., Shlens, J., Wojna, Z.: Rethinking the inception architecture for computer vision. In: Proceedings of the IEEE Conference on Computer Vision and Pattern Recognition, pp. 2818–2826 (2016)
21. Vaswani, A., et al.: Attention is all you need. In: Advances in Neural Information Processing Systems, pp. 5998–6008 (2017)
22. Xiong, L., et al.: Approximate nearest neighbor negative contrastive learning for dense text retrieval. arXiv preprint arXiv:2007.00808 (2020)
23. Xu, Y., Xu, Y., Qian, Q., Li, H., Jin, R.: Towards understanding label smoothing. arXiv preprint arXiv:2006.11653 (2020)
24. Yuan, C., et al.: Multi-hop selector network for multi-turn response selection in retrieval-based chatbots. In: EMNLP, pp. 111–120 (2019)
25. Yuan, L., Tay, F.E., Li, G., Wang, T., Feng, J.: Revisiting knowledge distillation via label smoothing regularization. In: Proceedings of the IEEE/CVF Conference on Computer Vision and Pattern Recognition, pp. 3903–3911 (2020)
26. Zeyer, A., Irie, K., Schlüter, R., Ney, H.: Improved training of end-to-end attention models for speech recognition. arXiv preprint arXiv:1805.03294 (2018)
27. Zoph, B., Vasudevan, V., Shlens, J., Le, Q.V.: Learning transferable architectures for scalable image recognition. In: Proceedings of the IEEE Conference on Computer Vision and Pattern Recognition, pp. 8697–8710 (2018)

Neural Feature Selection
for Learning to Rank

Alberto Purpura[1](✉), Karolina Buchner[2], Gianmaria Silvello[1],
and Gian Antonio Susto[1]

[1] University of Padua, Padua, Italy
{purpuraa,silvello,sustogia}@dei.unipd.it
[2] Apple, Cupertino, USA
kbuchner@apple.com

Abstract. LEarning TO Rank (LETOR) is a research area in the field of
Information Retrieval (IR) where machine learning models are employed
to rank a set of items. In the past few years, neural LETOR approaches
have become a competitive alternative to traditional ones like LambdaMART. However, neural architectures performance grew proportionally to their complexity and size. This can be an obstacle for their adoption in large-scale search systems where a model size impacts latency and
update time. For this reason, we propose an architecture-agnostic approach based on a neural LETOR model to reduce the size of its input by
up to 60% without affecting the system performance. This approach also
allows to reduce a LETOR model complexity and, therefore, its training
and inference time up to 50%.

Keywords: Learning to rank · Feature selection · Deep learning

1 Introduction

LEarning TO Rank (LETOR) is a research area in the field of Information
Retrieval (IR) where machine learning techniques are applied to the task of
ranking a set of items [10]. The input to a LETOR system is a set of real-valued
vectors representing the items to be ranked – in decreasing order of relevance –
in return to a certain user query. The output of such systems is usually a set of
relevance scores – one for each item in input – which estimate the relevance of
each item and are used to rank them. In the recent years, the attention on neural
approaches for this task has grown proportionally to their performance. Starting
from [2], where the authors propose to employ a recurrent neural layer to model
documents list-wise interactions, to [12], where the now popular self-attention
transformer architecture is used. Also, the performance of neural models [12,

A. Purpura—Work done as part of Apple internship.
G. Silvello—Work supported by the ExaMode project, as part of the European Union
Horizon 2020 program under Grant Agreement no. 825292.

D. Hiemstra et al. (Eds.): ECIR 2021, LNCS 12657, pp. 342–349, 2021.
https://doi.org/10.1007/978-3-030-72240-1_34

20] recently became competitive with approaches such as LambdaMART [4] which is often one of the first choices for LETOR tasks. However, neural models performance grew at the expense of their complexity and this hampers their application in large-scale search systems. Indeed, in such context, model latency and update time are as important as model performance. Reducing the input size can help decreasing model architectural complexity, number of parameters, and consequently training and inference time. Also, previous works [5,6,8] showed that the document representations used for LETOR can sometimes be redundant and often reduced [6] without impacting the ranking performance.

Existing feature selection approaches can be organized into three main groups: *filter*, *embedded*, and *wrapper* methods [6][1]. Filter methods, such as the Greedy Search Algorithm (GAS) [5], compute one score for each feature – independently from the LETOR model that is going to be used afterwards – and select the top ones according to it. In GAS the authors minimize feature similarity (Kendall Tau) and maximize feature importance. They rank the input items using only one of the features at a time and consider as importance score the MAP or nDCG@k value. Embedded approaches, such as the one presented in [15], incorporate the feature selection process in the model. In [15], the authors propose to apply different types of regularizations – such as L1 norm regularization – on the weights of a neural LETOR model to reduce redundancy in the hidden representations of the model and improve its performance. Finally, wrapper methods such as the ones presented in [6] and the proposed approach, rely on a LETOR model to estimate feature importance and then perform a selection.

We reimplemented the two best-performing approaches proposed in [6] and consider them as our baselines: eXtended naive Greedy search Algorithm for feature Selection (XGAS) – which relies on LambdaMART to estimate feature relevance – and Hierarchical agglomerative Clustering Algorithm for feature Selection (HCAS) employing single likage [7] – which relies on Spearman's correlation coefficient between feature pairs as a proxy for feature importance. To the best of our knowledge, our approach is the first feature selection technique for LETOR specifically targeted to neural models. The main contributions of this paper are the following:

- we propose an architecture-agnostic Neural Feature Selection (NFS) approach which uses a neural LETOR model to estimate feature importance;
- we evaluate the quality of our approach on two public LETOR collections;
- we confirm the robustness of the extracted feature set evaluating the performance of the proposed neural reranker and of a LambdaMART model using subsets of features of different sizes computed with the proposed approach.

Our experimental results show that the document representations used for LETOR can sometimes be redundant and reduced to up to 40% [6] of the total without impacting the ranking performance.

---

[1] We purposely omit a comparison with other dimensionality reduction approaches such as PCA since these methods often compute a *combination* of the features to reduce the representation size which is beyond the scope of this paper.

2   Proposed Approach

The proposed Neural Feature Selection (NFS) approach is organized in the following three steps. We first train a neural model for the LETOR task, i.e. to compute a relevance score for each item in the input set to be used to rank it. Second, we use the trained model to extract the most significant features groups considered by the model to rank each item. Finally, we perform feature selection using the previously computed feature information.

Neural Model Training. The NFS model architecture is composed of n self-attention layers [19], followed by two fully-connected layers. We train this model using the ApproxNDCG loss [3]. Before feeding the document vectors to the self-attention layer we apply the same feature transformation strategy described in [20]. In [20], the authors apply three different feature transformations to each feature in the input data and then combine them through a weighted sum. The weights for each transformation are learned by the model so that the best feature transformation strategy for each feature could be used each time. The model architecture is depicted in Fig. 1. Also, we apply batch normalization to the input of each feed-forward layer and dropout on the output of each hidden layer. Note that, since our approach for feature selection is *architecture-agnostic*, we can easily make changes to this neural architecture without impacting the following steps for feature selection.

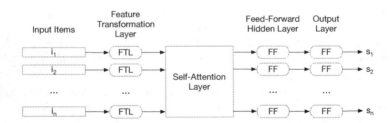

Fig. 1. Architecture of the neural architecture employed in our evaluation.

Feature Groups Mining. At this step, we use the model trained in the previous step to select the most important features used to rank each item in our training data. To do so, we compute the saliency map – a popular approach in the computer vision field to understand model predictions [1,16,17] – i.e. the gradient w.r.t. the each input item feature, corresponding to each item in the training dataset. We then apply min-max normalization on each saliency map M_i to map the values in each vector to the same range $[0,1]$. Afterwards, we select from each saliency map the groups of features g which have a *saliency* score higher than a threshold t. The set of feature groups G extracted at this step are the most significant features sets that our neural model learned to rely on to compute the relevance score of each item. These features however might not be the same for any possible input instance and – as also pointed out in [1]

– saliency maps can often be noisy and not always represent the behavior of a neural model. For this reason, we propose to apply a further selection step to prune less reliable feature groups similarly to what proposed in [18] where the authors compute the statistical significance of groups of items by comparing their frequency of occurrence in real data to the one in randomly generated datasets. We compute K random sets of saliency maps, each of the same cardinality of the experimental dataset employed. For example, if a dataset contains N queries, each with R documents to be ranked, then we will generate K random datasets, each containing $N \times R$ saliency maps. Then, we apply the same feature groups extraction process on the random saliency maps and compute K different sets of feature groups. The saliency maps are computed sampling values from a uniform distribution with support $[0, 1]$. According to this modeling strategy, each feature can be considered as salient in the current random saliency map with probability $1 - t$; where t is the threshold we used in the previous step to select salient features. Once we computed these K sets of random feature groups $\hat{G}_k$ we use their frequency to prune the original ones. In particular, we consider the frequency f_{g_i} of group $g_i \in G$ and compare it to its frequency in each of the K random datasets $f_{g_{i,k}}$ – the frequency $f_{g_{i,k}}$ might also be 0 if the feature group g_i does not appear in the random dataset k. If $f_{g_i} \leq f_{g_{i,k}}$ in more than $2\%^2$ of the randomly generated feature groups $\hat{G}_k$, we discard feature group g_i, considering it as noise.

Feature Selection. In this final step, we rely on the feature groups extracted in the previous step and their frequency in the saliency maps to compute a feature similarity matrix. We then use this similarity matrix to perform feature selection. Each feature pair similarity value is computed counting the times the two features appear in the same feature group and normalizing that score by the total number of groups where that feature appears. Finally, we rely on this similarity matrix to perform hierarchical clustering as done in [6]. We consider the number of clusters as the stopping criterion for the single linkage hierarchical clustering algorithm. The final set of features to keep is computed selecting the most frequently occurring feature in the previously computed feature groups, from each feature cluster.

3   Experimental Setup

We evaluate our approach on the first fold of the MSLR-WEB30K [13] and on the whole OHSUMED [14] dataset where the items to rank are represented by 136 and 45 features, respectively[3]. We use the LambdaMART implementation available in the LightGBM[4] library [9] and train and test the proposed neural

---

[2] This value was set empirically to yield a reasonable number of feature groups for the following feature extraction step.

[3] https://www.microsoft.com/en-us/research/project/letor-learning-rank-information-retrieval.

[4] https://github.com/microsoft/LightGBM.

model considering only the top 128 results returned by LambdaMART. We tuned the LightGBM model parameters on the validation sets of both datasets, optimizing the ndcg@3 metric[5]. The proposed neural reranking model is trained for 500 epochs – 100 epochs on the OHSUMED dataset – with batch size 128, using Adam optimizer and a learning rate 0.0005. We consider a feature embedding size of 128 in the feature transformation layer on the MSLR-WEB30K dataset – while we removed it for the experiments on the OHSUMED collection due to its much smaller size and number of features which limited the benefits of it – 4 self-attention heads on the MSLR-WEB30K and 1 on the OHSUMED dataset and a hidden size of 128 for the hidden feed-forward layer. Since each attention head has an output size equal to the total number of features divided by the number of attention heads, to compute the results reported in Table 1, we reduce the number of attention heads to 1 when using 5% and 10% of all the available features (6 and 13 features respectively), we use 4 attention heads when considering 30% (27 features), and 3 when using 40% (54 features). The batch normalization momentum we use is 0.4 and the dropout probability is $p = 0.5$. In the feature groups mining step, we generate 5000 random datasets and the threshold t to extract the feature groups is empirically set to 0.95. For the evaluation of the approach we consider the nDCG@3 measure, similar results are obtained with nDCG at different cutoffs.

4   Experimental Results

In Table 1, we report the results of our experiments on the MSLR-WEB30K dataset. We trained both a LambdaMART model and the proposed neural reranking one on different subsets of features of increasing size. From these experiments, we observe that the proposed Neural Feature Selection (NFS) approach always outperforms all the other baselines when the selected features are used to train a LambdaMART model, and in most of the cases when used with the proposed neural model. The evaluation results on the OHSUMED dataset reported in Table 2 are computed as the previous case. Here, we consider 60%, 70%, 80%, and 90% of the total features in the collection since the total number of feature is much smaller than in the previous dataset. In our evaluation, NFS outperforms HCAS in the majority of the cases, even though the latter approach is slightly more competitive than before.

The main advantage of using a subset of features to represent the inputs to a neural model is that we can reduce the model complexity. We observe this effect mainly when our data is represented by a large number of features as in the MSLR-WEB30K collection. For example, when using 40% of the features of the dataset, the number of attention heads in our model was reduced from 4 to 3 and, since we were considering only 54 out of 136 features, the number of parameters of the self-attention heads – the first layer of our model – was also

---

[5] We set the learning rate to 0.05, the number of leaves to 200 and the number of trees to 1000 (500) on the MSLR-WEB30K (OHSUMED) collection.

Table 1. Evaluation of the proposed Neural Feature Selection (NFS) approach on the MSLR-WEB30K dataset. We report the ndcg@3 values obtained by LambdaMART and the proposed Neural Reranking model employing different subsets of features.

LambdaMART				Neural reranker		
Features Perc.	XGAS	HCAS (single)	NFS	XGAS	HCAS (single)	NFS
5%	0.3580	0.3589	**0.3753**	**0.3768**	0.3595	0.3749
10%	0.3701	0.4044	**0.4195**	0.3826	0.3923	**0.4117**
20%	0.3781	**0.4672**	**0.4672**	0.3831	**0.4444**	0.4434
30%	0.4169	0.4655	**0.4713**	0.4085	**0.4478**	0.4236
40%	0.4387	0.4709	**0.4730**	0.3943	0.4516	**0.4559**
100%	0.4731	0.4731	0.4731	0.4526	0.4526	0.4526

reduced. As a consequence, training time was halved and inference time also decreased.

Table 2. Evaluation of the proposed Neural Feature Selection (NFS) approach on the OHSUMED dataset. We report the ndcg@3 values obtained by LambdaMART and the proposed Neural Reranking model employing different subsets of features.

LambdaMART				Neural reranker		
Features Perc.	XGAS	HCAS (single)	NFS	XGAS	HCAS (single)	NFS
60%	0.3669	0.3781	**0.3950**	0.4210	**0.4275**	0.4242
70%	0.3669	0.3781	**0.3860**	0.4243	0.4431	**0.4437**
80%	0.3669	0.3993	**0.4007**	0.4374	**0.4369**	0.4205
90%	0.3669	**0.4050**	0.3959	0.3669	0.4050	**0.4221**
100%	0.3968	0.3968	0.3968	0.4973	0.4973	0.4973

It is also interesting to observe the differences between the features selected by the proposed NFS approach and other baselines. We focus on the top 3 features selected from the OHSUMED collection by each of the considered feature selection algorithms over the 5 different dataset folds and refer the reader to [14] for a more detailed description of each feature. NFS most frequently selected features computed with popular retrieval models such as BM25 or QLM [11] (features 4, 12 and 28) based on the document abstract or title. On the other hand, HCAS selected simpler features derived from raw frequency counts of the query terms in each document's title and abstract (features 23, 40 and 36). Finally, XGAS selected a mix of features computed with traditional retrieval approaches such as QL, and simpler frequency counts (features 2, 44 and 13). We conclude that the advantage of NFS is likely due to its ability to recognize and select the most sophisticated and useful matching scores thanks to the information learned during training.

5 Conclusions

In the recent years, neural models became a competitive alternative to traditional Learning TO Rank (LETOR) approaches. Their performance however, grew at the expense of their efficiency and complexity. In this paper, we propose an approach for feature selection for Learning TO Rank (LETOR) based on a neural ranker. Our approach is specifically designed to optimize the performance of neural LETOR models without the need to change their architecture. In our experiments, the proposed approach improved the efficiency of a sample neural LETOR model and decreased its training time without impacting its performance. We also validated the robustness of the selected features testing them using a different – non neural – model such as LambdaMART. We performed our evaluation on two popular LETOR datasets – i.e. MSLR-WEB30K and OHSUMED – comparing our approach to three state-of-the-art techniques from [6]. The proposed approach outperformed the selected baselines in the majority of the experiments on both datasets.

References

1. Adebayo, J., Gilmer, J., Muelly, M., Goodfellow, I., Hardt, M., Kim, B.: Sanity checks for saliency maps. In: Advances in Neural Information Processing Systems, pp. 9505–9515 (2018)
2. Ai, Q., Bi, K., Guo, J., Croft, W.: Learning a deep listwise context model for ranking refinement. Proc. SIGIR **2018**, 135–144 (2018)
3. Bruch, S., Zoghi, M., Bendersky, M., Najork, M.: Revisiting approximate metric optimization in the age of deep neural networks. Proc. SIGIR **2019**, 1241–1244 (2019)
4. Burges, C.J.: From ranknet to lambdarank to lambdamart: an overview. Learning **11**(23–581), 81 (2010)
5. Geng, X., Liu, T., Qin, T., Li, H.: Feature selection for ranking. Proc. SIGIR **2007**, 407–414 (2007)
6. Gigli, A., Lucchese, C., Nardini, F., Perego, R.: Fast feature selection for learning to rank. Proc. ICTIR **2016**, 167–170 (2016)
7. Gower, J.C., Ross, G.: Minimum spanning trees and single linkage cluster analysis. J. Royal Stat. Soc. Ser. C (Appl. Stat.) **18**(1), 54–64 (1969)
8. Han, X., Lei, S.: Feature selection and model comparison on microsoft learning-to-rank data sets. arXiv preprint arXiv:1803.05127 (2018)
9. Ke, G., et al.: Lightgbm: a highly efficient gradient boosting decision tree. In: Advances in Neural Information Processing Systems, pp. 3146–3154 (2017)
10. Liu, T.: Learning to rank for information retrieval. Springer Science & Business Media (2011)
11. Manning, C., Schütze, H., Raghavan, P.: Introduction to Information Retrieval. Cambridge University Press, Cambridge (2008)
12. Pobrotyn, P., Bartczak, T., Synowiec, M., Białobrzeski, R., Bojar, J.: Context-aware learning to rank with self-attention. arXiv preprint arXiv:2005.10084 (2020)
13. Qin, T., Liu, T.: Introducing letor 4.0 datasets. arXiv preprint arXiv:1306.2597 (2013)

14. Qin, T., Liu, T.Y., Xu, J., Li, H.: Letor: a benchmark collection for research on learning to rank for information retrieval. Inf. Retrieval **13**(4), 346–374 (2010)
15. Rahangdale, A., Raut, S.: Deep neural network regularization for feature selection in learning-to-rank. IEEE Access **7**, 53988–54006 (2019)
16. Shrikumar, A., Greenside, P., Shcherbina, A., Kundaje, A.: Not just a black box: learning important features through propagating activation differences. arXiv preprint arXiv:1605.01713 (2016)
17. Simonyan, K., Vedaldi, A., Zisserman, A.: Deep inside convolutional networks: visualising image classification models and saliency maps. arXiv preprint arXiv:1312.6034 (2013)
18. Tonon, A., Vandin, F.: Permutation strategies for mining significant sequential patterns. In: Proceedings of ICDM 2019, pp. 1330–1335. IEEE (2019)
19. Vaswani, A., et al.: Attention is all you need. In: Advances in Neural Information Processing Systems, pp. 5998–6008 (2017)
20. Zhuang, H., Wang, X., Bendersky, M., Najork, M.: Feature transformation for neural ranking models. In: Proceedings of SIGIR 2020 (2020)

Exploring the Incorporation of Opinion Polarity for Abstractive Multi-document Summarisation

Dominik Ramsauer$^{(\boxtimes)}$ and Udo Kruschwitz

University of Regensburg, Regensburg, Germany
{dominik.ramsauer,udo.kruschwitz}@ur.de

Abstract. Abstractive multi-document summarisation (MDS) remains a challenging task. Part of the problem is the question as to how to preserve a document's polarity in the summary. We propose an opinion polarity attention model for MDS, which incorporates a polarity estimator based on a BERT-GRU sentiment analysis network. It captures the impact of opinions expressed in the source documents and integrates it in the attention mechanism. Experimental results using a state-of-the-art MDS approach and a common benchmark test collection demonstrate that this model has a measurable positive effect using a range of metrics.

Keywords: Multi-document summarisation · Neural abstractive summarisation · Opinion polarity · Sentiment analysis

1 Introduction

Text summarisation is a core problem of natural language processing which also plays a central role in modern information retrieval systems. The focus has shifted from extractive to abstractive approaches. In this context, encoder-decoder architectures have been shown to work well for single document summarisation (SDS) [13,22]. Recent studies have started to explore extractive summarisation applied in a MDS setting. Moving from one to several documents raises new challenges, the most common one being (de)duplication. But documents are also written in different styles, have different lengths, and they vary in many other ways. One such aspect is the opinion expressed by the author of an article. Take the examples in Table 1, which both report on the same story, but one with a degree of judgement and the other fairly neutral. This opinion could potentially be relevant for the reader which suggests that we might want to preserve it in a summary. It has in fact been shown that opinion diversity and controversiality can play a critical role for abstractive MDS [5].

We want to explore the contribution opinionated contents in documents might offer for abstractive MDS. To do so we present an end-to-end neural abstractive approach to perform MDS based on a pointer-generator network

© Springer Nature Switzerland AG 2021
D. Hiemstra et al. (Eds.): ECIR 2021, LNCS 12657, pp. 350–358, 2021.
https://doi.org/10.1007/978-3-030-72240-1_35

which incorporates an opinion polarity classifier for adjusting attention weights of the source texts. In order to benchmark the model it is compared to several baselines, giving improvements to a state-of-the-art MDS approach on a common benchmark dataset.

Table 1. Examples from the Multi-News summarisation dataset.

Source 1
President Donald Trump quietly signed a bill into law Tuesday rolling back an Obama-era regulation that made it harder for people with mental illnesses to purchase a gun.
The rule, which was...

Source 2
President Donald Trump signed a measure nixing a regulation aimed at keeping guns out of the hands of some severely mentally ill people.
The original rule was...

2 Related Work

State-of-the-art abstractive multi-document summarisation tends to be based on neural models that harness the graph structure of cross-document relationships, such as semantic units that fit together or discourse relations [14,15,17,20,27]. For scoring of sentences a common theme is to combine extractive and abstractive methods by incorporating extractive scoring within abstractive approaches [12,15]. Interestingly, opinion mining has so far not been the centre of attention when it comes to summarisation. The field has been around for quite some time now [19] but still faces major challenges, e.g. [3,25]. Opinion does however play a major role in news articles. Historical backgrounds, anecdotal facts, future forecasts, evaluations and expectations are often core part of such articles [7] and opinion summarisation has also been investigated, though with a different focus, namely on opinion summarisation in customer reviews [1,24].

Given that most recent approaches to abstractive MDS are attention-based models that concentrate on exploiting the graph structure of relationships between discourse elements but disregard the possible contribution of opinionated statements, we propose to adopt a state-of-the-art neural abstractive MDS architecture which is expanded by incorporating an opinion polarity module.

3 Proposed Model

In this section details of the proposed opinion polarity attention Pointer-generator (OP-AP) model for neural abstractive MDS are provided[1]. The model

---

[1] All code, model files and outputs are available at https://github.com/dramsauer/Summarizing-Opinions.

consists of a pointer-generator network and an opinion polarity module, as shown in Fig. 1.

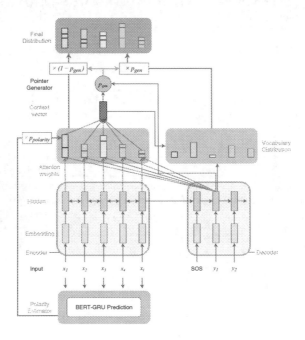

Fig. 1. The overview of the proposed model. The approach incorporates a BERT-GRU model, which scores the input by opinion polarity. These scores are taken into account in the attention mechanism of a pointer-generator model.

Pointer-Generator Network: The pointer-generator network [22] is a well-established sequence-to-sequence summarisation model which relies on the encoder-decoder concept and uses attention [2]. It is a hybrid model that can copy words from the input text *(pointing)* and can output novel words from a vocabulary *(generator)*. The pointing mechanism helps to preserve the exact wording and information of the input text while the generator ensures to produce new phrases. All input tokens w_i of a source article are given to the encoder creating a sequence of *hidden encoder states* h_i. For each step t, the decoder obtains an embedding of the previous word and a *decoder state* d_t. Analogous to [2], an *attention distribution* a^t is calculated in order to get a *context vector* h_t^* as follows:

$$e_i^t = v^T tanh(W_h h_i + W_d d_t + b_{attn})$$
$$a^t = softmax(e^t)$$
$$h_t^* = \sum_i a_i^t h_i^t$$

(1)

HiMAP: As an extension to the pointer-generator network (PGN), the hierarchical MMR-attention PGN network (HiMAP) [12] aims to integrate the maximal marginal relevance (MMR) [4] into the pointer-generator network. MMR is an extractive summarisation approach that combines query-relevance with information-novelty. In order to adapt MMR for PGN, a sentence-level representation is introduced additionally via LSTM cells. The idea behind MMR is to rank sentences by trading off their relevance to redundancy to the query.

Opinion Polarity Estimator: To expand the original pointer generator model [22] with an opinion-sensitive mechanism, a sentiment analysis model is trained initially. As training corpus, the MPQA Opinion Corpus dataset [8] was used. As a subtask, they detected opinion polarity within the data. The dataset consists of 10,606 sentences, that have been extracted from news articles on a broad range of news sources. The sentences are labelled with respect to their overall sentiment polarities with two class labels. With 3,311 positive documents and 7,293 negative documents, this is an imbalanced dataset.

For setting up a sentiment analysis model, we deploy BERT [9], a pre-trained contextual language model based on transformers [26] which has been shown to push the state of the art in a variety of NLP tasks. Due to training complexity we use the BERT-Base model. In order to use BERT as a sentiment classifier, a multi-layer bi-directional Gated recurrent unit (GRU) is used. GRUs [6] are a gating mechanism in recurrent neural networks with fewer parameters to train than LSTMs but with similar results on certain NLP tasks [23]. Since the idea is to capture the overall polarity within the source, the focus is not on differentiating between positive and negative sentiment but on how distinct it is. Therefore, the network output is chosen to scale in a range of $\phi(v_i) \in [0;1]$, with 0 corresponding to low polarity and 1 to high polarity. To achieve this, the absolute value of the hyperbolic tangent is used as activation function:

$$\phi(v_i) = |tanh(v_i)| \tag{2}$$

The choice fell on the hyperbolic tangent since it has low gradients at its extrema. The network output will therefore not be overly sensitive to polarity[2]. This polarity score is intended to adjust the attention weights at summarisation:

$$a^t = a^t \phi(v_i) \tag{3}$$

4   Experiment

Dataset: For the experiment the Multi-News dataset [12] was chosen – a recently published large-scale multi-document news summarisation dataset that includes abstractive gold-standard summaries. The summaries have been collected from newser.com[3], a human-powered American news aggregation website. Since the summaries are human-written the dataset is appropriate here and has already been used for abstractive MDS [15,17].

---

[2] A conceivable way to penalise opinionated content might be to choose $1 - |tanh(v_i)|$.
[3] https://www.newser.com/.

Metrics and Baselines: ROUGE scores [18] are used as metrics for evaluation of the experiment. Since the focus of the project lies on news articles, ROUGE F1 is reported on the Multi-News [12] dataset, which is also used in most recent related work. To assess the proposed model, it gets compared to several common baselines and recently published approaches. Baselines are the first sentences of the source articles as extractive summary: Lead-1 (only first sentence) and Lead-3 (first three sentences), LexRank [11], TextRank [21], MMR [4].

Following [12], the scores of PG-BRNN and CopyTransformer are reported as reference. The PG-BRNN model is a pointer-generator implementation from OpenNMT[4], an open source framework for neural machine translation. It follows the approach of [13] and uses a 1-layer bi-LSTM both for encoder and decoder. The dimensions of the LSTMs are 128 for the encoder and 512 for the decoder. The HiMAP model [12] is based on this approach, which is reported with scores of their results and our re-implementation for comparison. CopyTransformer, also published in [13], is a model which replaces the LSTM which a 4-layer transformer with dimensions of 512 both for encoder and decoder. GraphSum [17] is a recently published graph-based model, which uses graph encoding and decoding layers together with transformer stacks for encoding and decoding. It also splits large documents in multiple paragraphs, as suggested in [20]. MGSum [15], also recently published, treats documents, sentences and words as semantic units of different granularities and depict them within a three-staged hierarchical relation graph. This enables an architecture which can combine extractive and abstractive summarisation techniques. For interaction between these hierarchical levels they employ attention mechanisms.

Experimental Setting and Implementation Details: In order to test the proposed approach several model combinations were trained. Firstly, the attempt was to reproduce the results of [12] of their HiMAP model and the underlying PG-BRNN model as suggested in [13]. Since the approach in this work is based on these models, this was done in order to get comparable baselines. The results of these two models are depicted as the first two rows in the bottom section in Table 2. Both of these models were then combined with the opinion polarity model that had been trained in advance. For training the opinion polarity model, standard parameters have been chosen. The hidden dimension size was set to 256 with two bidirectional layers, a dropout rate of 0.25 and a batch size of 128. As optimiser Adam [16] was chosen with learning rate 0.001, $\beta_1 = 0.9$, $\beta_2 = 0.999$.

For all of the four trained MDS models, the same parameter set was chosen. As basis for the parameters (both for pre-processing and training) the same ones were chosen as in [12] to ensure comparability: For pre-processing, the input articles are truncated to 500 tokens as suggested by [12]. As training parameters, learning rate was set to 0.15 with a batch size of 2. The chosen optimiser was in these cases Adagrad [10] with an accumulator value of 0.1.

---

[4] https://github.com/OpenNMT/OpenNMT-py/blob/master/docs/source/
examples/Summarization.md.

Automatic Evaluation: For evaluation, ROUGE scores [18] are reported, that measure the overlap of unigrams (ROUGE-1), overlap of bigrams (ROUGE-2) and the longest common subsequence (ROUGE-L) at sentence-level (Table 2). The first block of the table shows common extractive baseline models, the second block includes pointer-generator networks and recently published hierarchical and graph-based models. The last block shows the results of the conducted experiments. The initial experiment was to reproduce the results of the HiMAP approach. As can be seen, despite following the exact same settings and training regime we do not achieve the results reported in [12].[5] Nevertheless, both trained models with integrated polarity estimation managed to improve our HiMAP scores. The model with disabled MMR even scored slightly better than the one with both MMR- and polarity-weighted attention enabled. Our conclusion is that incorporating polarity does improve the overall summary quality obtained by a state-of-the-art MDS approach and we hypothesise that this will also hold for an improved benchmark performance (i.e., HiMAP) – to be investigated further. It can be assumed that very recently published models such as MGSum and GraphSum might also benefit from embedding polarity, but we also leave this for future work. Obviously, we only use ROUGE scores to draw our conclusions, and a human evaluation of the summaries should also be conducted to confirm the results. Finer integration of the opinion polarity estimation, starting at the phrase- or sentence-level are also worthwhile future directions.

Table 2. ROUGE F1 scores for models trained and tested on the Multi-News dataset. Bottom section includes experiment results. We report the sentence-level ROUGE-L value. Results with * mark are replicated from the corresponding papers.

Model	R-1	R-2	R-L
Lead-1	27.50	7.80	20.18
Lead-3	36.49	22.54	32.09
LexRank [11]	41.34	13.71	37.21
TextRank [21]	41.51	13.75	37.46
MMR [4]	44.25	14.81	39.84
HiMAP [12]	43.47*	14.89*	40.40
PG-BRNN [13]	44.10	15.45	39.80
CopyTransformer [13]	44.79	15.23	40.45
GraphSum [17]	45.02*	16.69*	——
MGSum [15]	**46.00***	**16.81***	——
HiMAP (ours)	42.68	14.76	38.31
Opinion Pol. + HiMAP (OP-HiMAP)	43.68	15.06	39.29
Opinion Pol. Attention PG-BRNN (OP-AP)	**43.84**	**15.07**	**39.48**

---

[5] The basic PG-BRRN approach was also reproduced with similarly lower results, which raises the question of reproducibility in general. There have also been attempts to reproduce MGSum and GraphSum, but without success.

5   Conclusion

We propose an opinion polarity attention pointer-generator model for neural abstractive MDS. Fine-tuned on an opinion-annotated corpus, a BERT-GRU network is used therein as a polarity estimator. This allows the model to incorporate both objective and the author's (subjective) contents. Incorporating opinion polarity has shown to give improvements to a state-of-the-art MDS approach (with the caveat that we could not exactly reproduce the originally reported results). Results suggest that recently proposed state-of-the-art methods can benefit from an integration of polarity estimation leaving scope for plenty of future work.

References

1. Amplayo, R.K., Lapata, M.: Unsupervised opinion summarization with noising and denoising. In: Proceedings of the 58th Annual Meeting of the Association for Computational Linguistics, pp. 1934–1945. Association for Computational Linguistics, Online, July 2020 (2020). https://doi.org/10.18653/v1/2020.acl-main.175
2. Bahdanau, D., Cho, K.H., Bengio, Y.: Neural machine translation by jointly learning to align and translate. In: 3rd International Conference on Learning Representations, ICLR 2015 - Conference Track Proceedings, pp. 1–15. International Conference on Learning Representations, ICLR, San Diego, CA, USA (2015). https://arxiv.org/abs/1409.0473v7
3. Barnes, J., Øvrelid, L., Velldal, E.: Sentiment analysis is not solved! Assessing and probing sentiment classification. In: Proceedings of the Second BlackboxNLP Workshop on Analyzing and Interpreting Neural Networks for NLP, pp. 12–23. Association for Computational Linguistics, Florence, Italy (2019). https://doi.org/10.18653/v1/W19-4802
4. Carbonell, J., Goldstein, J.: Use of MMR, diversity-based reranking for reordering documents and producing summaries. In: Proceedings of the 21st Annual International ACM SIGIR Conference on Research and Development in Information Retrieval (SIGIR 1998), pp. 335–336. Association for Computing Machinery, Melbourne, Australia (1998). https://doi.org/10.1145/290941.291025
5. Carenini, G., Cheung, J.C.K., Pauls, A.: Multi-document summarization of evaluative text. Comput. Intell. **29**(4), 545–576 (2013). https://doi.org/10.1111/j.1467-8640.2012.00417.x
6. Cho, K., et al.: Learning phrase representations using RNN encoder-decoder for statistical machine translation. In: EMNLP 2014–2014 Conference on Empirical Methods in Natural Language Processing, Proceedings of the Conference, pp. 1724–1734. Association for Computational Linguistics (ACL), Doha, Qatar (2014). https://doi.org/10.3115/v1/d14-1179
7. Choubey, P.K., Lee, A., Huang, R., Wang, L.: Discourse as a function of event: profiling discourse structure in news articles around the main event. In: Proceedings of the 58th Annual Meeting of the Association for Computational Linguistics, pp. 5374–5386. Association for Computational Linguistics, Online (2020). https://doi.org/10.18653/v1/2020.acl-main.478

8. Deng, L., Wiebe, J.: MPQA 3.0: an entity/event-level sentiment corpus. In: Proceedings of the 2015 Conference of the North American Chapter of the Association for Computational Linguistics: Human Language Technologies, pp. 1323–1328. Association for Computational Linguistics, Denver, Colorado (2015). https://doi.org/10.3115/v1/N15-1146

9. Devlin, J., Chang, M.W., Lee, K., Google, K.T., Language, A.I.: BERT: pre-training of deep bidirectional transformers for language understanding. In: Proceedings of NAACL-HLT, pp. 4171–4186. Association for Computational Linguistics, Minneapolis, Minnesota (2019). https://doi.org/10.18653/v1/N19-1423, https://github.com/google-research/bertwww.aclweb.org/anthology/N19-1423

10. Duchi, J., Hazan, E., Singer, Y.: Adaptive subgradient methods for online learning and stochastic optimization * Elad Hazan. J. Mach. Learn. Res. **12**(61), 2121–2159 (2011). www.jmlr.org/papers/volume12/duchi11a/duchi11a.pdf?source=post_page

11. Erkan, G., Radev, D.R.: LexRank: graph-based lexical centrality as salience in text summarization. J. Artif. Intell. Res. **22**, 457–479 (2011). https://doi.org/10.1613/jair.1523, http://arxiv.org/abs/1109.2128

12. Fabbri, A.R., Li, I., She, T., Li, S., Radev, D.R.: Multi-News: a large-scale multi-document summarization dataset and abstractive hierarchical model. In: Proceedings of the 57th Annual Meeting of the Association for Computational Linguistics, pp. 1074–1084. Association for Computational Linguistics, Florence, Italy (2019). https://doi.org/10.18653/v1/P19-1102, https://www.aclweb.org/anthology/P19-1102.pdf

13. Gehrmann, S., Deng, Y., Rush, A.M.: Bottom-up abstractive summarization. In: Proceedings of the 2018 Conference on Empirical Methods in Natural Language Processing, EMNLP 2018, pp. 4098–4109. Association for Computational Linguistics, Brussels, Belgium (2018). http://arxiv.org/abs/1808.10792

14. Huang, L., Wu, L., Wang, L.: Knowledge graph-augmented abstractive summarization with semantic-driven cloze reward. In: Proceedings of the 58th Annual Meeting of the Association for Computational Linguistics, pp. 5094–5107. Association for Computational Linguistics, Online (2020). https://doi.org/10.18653/v1/2020.acl-main.457

15. Jin, H., Wang, T., Wan, X.: Multi-granularity interaction network for extractive and abstractive multi-document summarization. In: Proceedings of the 58th Annual Meeting of the Association for Computational Linguistics, pp. 6244–6254. Association for Computational Linguistics, Online (2020). https://doi.org/10.18653/v1/2020.acl-main.556

16. Kingma, D.P., Ba, J.L.: Adam: a method for stochastic optimization. In: 3rd International Conference on Learning Representations, ICLR 2015 - Conference Track Proceedings, pp. 1–15. International Conference on Learning Representations, ICLR, San Diego, CA, USA (2015). https://arxiv.org/abs/1412.6980v9

17. Li, W., Xiao, X., Liu, J., Wu, H., Wang, H., Du, J.: Leveraging graph to improve abstractive multi-document summarization. In: Proceedings of the 58th Annual Meeting of the Association for Computational Linguistics, pp. 6232–6243. Association for Computational Linguistics, Online (2020). https://doi.org/10.18653/v1/2020.acl-main.555

18. Lin, C.Y.: ROUGE: a package for automatic evaluation of summaries. In: Text Summarization Branches Out, pp. 74–81. Association for Computational Linguistics, Barcelona, Spain (2004). https://www.aclweb.org/anthology/W04-1013

19. Liu, B.: Sentiment Analysis and Opinion Mining. Synthesis Lectures Hum. Lang. Technol. **5**(1), 1–167 (2012). http://citeseerx.ist.psu.edu/viewdoc/download? doi=10.1.1.244.9480&rep=rep1&type=pdf

20. Liu, Y., Lapata, M.: Hierarchical transformers for multi-document summarization. In: Proceedings of the 57th Annual Meeting of the Association for Computational Linguistics, vol. 5070, pp. 5070–5081. Association for Computational Linguistics (ACL), Florence, Italy (2019). https://doi.org/10.18653/v1/p19-1500, https://github.com/nlpyang/hiersumm

21. Mihalcea, R., Tarau, P.: TextRank: bringing order into texts. In: Proceedings of the 2004 Conference on Empirical Methods in Natural Language Processing, pp. 404–411. Association for Computational Linguistics, Barcelona, Spain (2004). https://www.aclweb.org/anthology/W04-3252

22. See, A., Liu Google Brain, P.J., Manning, C.D.: Get to the point: summarization with pointer-generator networks. In: Proceedings of the 55th Annual Meeting of the Association for Computational Linguistic, pp. 1073–1083. Association for Computational Linguistics, Vancouver, Canada (2017). https://doi.org/10.18653/v1/P17-1099

23. Su, Y., Kuo, C.C.J.: On extended long short-term memory and dependent bidirectional recurrent neural network. Neurocomputing **356**, 151–161 (2018). https://doi.org/10.1016/j.neucom.2019.04.044, http://arxiv.org/abs/1803.01686dx.doi.org/10.1016/j.neucom.2019.04.044

24. Suhara, Y., Wang, X., Angelidis, S., Tan, W.C.: OpinionDigest: a simple framework for opinion summarization. In: Proceedings of the 58th Annual Meeting of the Association for Computational Linguistics, pp. 5789–5798. Association for Computational Linguistics, Online (2020). https://doi.org/10.18653/v1/2020.acl-main.513, https://www.aclweb.org/anthology/2020.acl-main.513

25. Tan, X., Cai, Y., Zhu, C.: Recognizing conflict opinions in aspect-level sentiment classification with dual attention networks. In: Proceedings of the 2019 Conference on Empirical Methods in Natural Language Processing and the 9th International Joint Conference on Natural Language Processing, pp. 3426–3431. Association for Computational Linguistics, Hong Kong, China (2019). https://doi.org/10.18653/v1/D19-1342

26. Vaswani, A., et al.: Attention is all you need. In: Advances in Neural Information Processing Systems, pp. 5998–6008. Curran Associates Inc, Long Beach, California (2017). http://papers.nips.cc/paper/7181-attention-is-all-you-need.pdf

27. Xu, S., Li, H., Yuan, P., Wu, Y., He, X., Zhou, B.: Self-attention guided copy mechanism for abstractive summarization. In: Proceedings of the 58th Annual Meeting of the Association for Computational Linguistics, pp. 1355–1362. Association for Computational Linguistics, Online (2020). https://doi.org/10.18653/v1/2020.acl-main.125

Multilingual Evidence Retrieval and Fact Verification to Combat Global Disinformation: The Power of Polyglotism

Denisa A. Olteanu Roberts[(✉)] [iD]

AI SpaceTime, New York, NY, USA
d.roberts@aispacetime.org

Abstract. This article investigates multilingual evidence retrieval and fact verification as a step to combat global disinformation, a first effort of this kind, to the best of our knowledge. The goal is building multilingual systems that retrieve in evidence - rich languages to verify claims in evidence - poor languages that are more commonly targeted by disinformation. To this end, our EnmBERT fact verification system shows evidence of transfer learning ability and a 400 example mixed English - Romanian dataset is made available for cross - lingual transfer learning evaluation.

Keywords: Multilingual evidence retrieval · Disinformation · Natural language inference · Transfer learning · mBERT

1 Introduction

The recent COVID−19 pandemic broke down geographical boundaries and led to an *infodemic* of fake news and conspiracy theories [43]. Evidence based fact verification (English only) has been studied as a weapon against fake news and disinformation [36]. Conspiracy theories and disinformation can propagate from one language to another and some languages are more evidence rich (English). During the US 2020 elections, evidence of online Spanish language disinformation aimed at Latino-American voters was reported [27]. Polyglotism is not uncommon. According to a 2017 Pew Research study, 91% of European students learn English in school[1]. Furthermore, recent machine translation advances are increasingly bringing down language barriers [17,22]. Disinformation can be defined as intentionally misleading information [12,13]. The "good cop" of the Internet [8], Wikipedia has become a source of ground truth as seen in the recent literature on evidence-based fact verification. There are more than 6mln English Wikipedia articles[2] but resources are lower in other language editions, such as Romanian (400K). As a case study we evaluate a claim about Ion Mihai Pacepa,

---

[1] https://www.pewresearch.org/fact-tank/2020/04/09/most-european-students-learn-english-in-school/.

[2] https://meta.wikimedia.org/wiki/List_of_Wikipedias.

© Springer Nature Switzerland AG 2021
D. Hiemstra et al. (Eds.): ECIR 2021, LNCS 12657, pp. 359–367, 2021.
https://doi.org/10.1007/978-3-030-72240-1_36

former agent of the Romanian secret police during communism, author of books on disinformation [25,26]. Related conspiracy theories can be found on internet platforms, such as rumors about his death [1], or Twitter posts in multiple languages, with strong for or against language, such as (English and Portuguese)[3] or (English and Polish)[4]. Strong language has been associated with propaganda and fake news [44]. In the following sections we review the relevant literature, present our methodology, experimental results and the case study resolution, and conclude with final notes. We make code, datasets, API, and trained models available[5].

2   Related Work

The literature review touches on three topics: online disinformation, multilingual NLP and evidence based fact verification. **Online Disinformation.** Previous disinformation studies focused on election related activity on social media platforms like Twitter, botnet generated hyperpartisan news, 2016 US presidential election [3–5,15]. To combat online disinformation one must retrieve reliable evidence at scale since fake news tend to be more viral and spread faster [29,32,37,44]. **Multilingual NLP Advances.** Recent multilingual applications leverage pre-training of massive language models that can be fine-tuned for multiple tasks. For example, the cased multilingual BERT (mBERT) [11],[6] is pretrained on a corpus of the top 104 Wikipedia languages, with 12 layers, 768 hidden units, 12 heads and 110M parameters. Cross-lingual transfer learning has been evaluated for tasks such as: natural language inference [2,9], document classification [30], question answering [7], fake Indic language tweet detection [18]. **English-Only Evidence Retrieval and Fact Verification.** Fact based claim verification is framed as a natural language inference (NLI) task that retrieves its evidence. An annotated dataset was shared [35] and a task [36] was set up to retrieve evidence from Wikipedia documents and predict claim verification status. Recently published SotA results rely on pre-trained BERT flavors or XLNet [39]. DREAM [41], GEAR [42] and KGAT [23] achieved SotA with graphs. Dense Passage Retrieval [19] is used in RAG [21] in an end-to-end approach for fact verification.

3   Methodology

The system depicted in Fig. 1 is a pipeline with a multilingual evidence retrieval component and a multilingual fact verification component. Based on input claim c_{l_i} in language l_i the system retrieves evidence E_{l_j} from Wikipedia edition in language l_j and supports, refutes or abstains (not enough info). We employ English

---

[3] https://twitter.com/MsAmericanPie_/status/1287969874036379649.

[4] https://twitter.com/hashtag/Pacepa.

[5] https://github.com/D-Roberts/multilingual_nli_ECIR2021.

[6] https://github.com/google-research/bert/blob/master/multilingual.md.

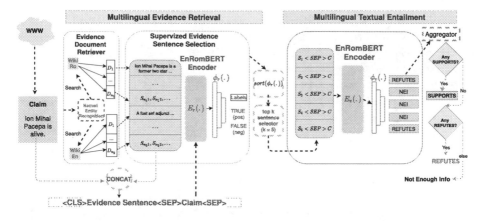

Fig. 1. Overview of the multilingual evidence retrieval and fact verification system.

and Romanian as sample languages. We use all the annotated $110K$ verifiable claims provided in the initial FEVER task [35] for training the end to end system in Fig. 1. **Multilingual Document Retrieval.** To retrieve top Wikipedia n_l documents D_{c,n_l} per claim for each evidence language l, we employ an ad-hoc entity linking system [16] based on named entity recognition in [10]. Entities are parsed from the (English) claim c using the AllenNLP [14] constituency parser. We search for the entities and retrieve 7 English [16] and 1 Romanian Wikipedia pages (higher number of Romanian documents did not improve performance) using MediaWiki API[7] each. Due to the internationally recognized nature of the claim entities, 144.9K out of 145.5K training claims have Romanian Wikipedia search results. **Multilingual Sentence Selection.** All sentences $\cup_{n_l}\{S_{D_{c,n_l}}\}$ from each retrieved document are supplied as input to the sentence selection model. We removed diacritics in Romanian sentences [31] and prepended evidence sentences with the page title to compensate for the missed co-reference pronouns [33,40]. We frame the multilingual sentence selection as a two-way classification task [16,28]. One training example is a pair of an evidence sentence and the claim [40,42]. The annotated evidence sentence-claim pairs from FEVER are given the True label. We randomly sample 32 sentences per claim from the retrieved documents as negative sentence-claim pairs (False label). We have 2 flavors of the fine-tuned models: EnmBERT only includes English negative sentences and EnRomBERT includes 5 English and 27 Romanian negative evidence sentences. The architecture includes an mBERT encoder $E_r(\cdot)$ [38][8] and an MLP classification layer $\phi(\cdot)$. During training, all the parameters are fine-tuned and the MLP weights are trained from scratch. The encoded first $<CLS>$ token, is supplied to the MLP classification layer. For each claim, the system outputs all the evidence sentence-claim pairs ranked in the order of the predicted probability of success $P(\mathbf{y}=1|\mathbf{x}) = \phi(E_r(\mathbf{x}))$ (pointwise ranking [6]).

---

[7] https://www.mediawiki.org/wiki/API:Main_page.
[8] https://github.com/huggingface/transformers.

Multilingual Fact Verification. The fact verification step (NLI) training takes as input the 110K training claims paired with each of the 5 selected evidence sentences (English only for EnmBERT or En and Ro for EnRomBERT), and fine-tunes the three-way classification of pairs using the architecture in Fig. 1). We aggregate the predictions made for each of the 5 evidence sentence-claim pairs based on logic rules [24] (see Fig. 1) to get one prediction per claim. Training of both sentence selection and fact verification models employed the Adam optimizer [20], batch size of 32, learning rate of $2e-5$, cross-entropy loss, and 1 and 2 epochs of training, respectively. **Alternative Conceptual End-to-End Multilingual Retrieve-Verify System.** The entity linking approach to document retrieval makes strong assumptions about the presence of named entities in the claim. Furthermore, the employed constituency parser [14] assumes that claims are in English. To tackle these limitations, we propose a conceptual end-to-end multilingual evidence retrieval and fact verification approach inspired by the English-only RAG [21]. The system automatically retrieves relevant evidence passages in language l_j from a multilingual corpus corresponding to a claim in language l_i. In Fig. 1, the 2-step multilingual evidence retrieval is replaced with a multilingual version of dense passage retrieval (DPR) [19] with mBERT backbone. The retrieved documents form a latent probability distribution. The fact verification step conditions on the claim x_{l_i} and the latent retrieved documents z to generate the label y, $P(y|x_{l_i}) = \sum_{z \in D_{top-k,l_j}} p(z|x_{l_i})p(y|x_{l_i},z)$. The multilingual retrieve-verify system is jointly trained and the only supervision is at the fact verification level. We leave this promising avenue for future experimental evaluation.

4   Experimental Results

In the absence of equivalent end-to-end multilingual fact verification baselines, we compare performance to English-only systems using the official FEVER scores[9] on the original FEVER datasets [35]. Furthermore, the goal of this work is to use multilingual systems trained in evidence rich languages to combat disinformation in evidence poor languages. To this end we evaluate the transfer learning ability of the trained verification models on an English-Romanian translated dataset. We translated 10 supported and 10 refuted claims (from the FEVER developmental set) together with 5 evidence sentences each (retrieved by the EnmBERT system) and combined in a mix and match development set of 400 examples. **Calibration results on FEVER development and test sets.** In Table 1 and Fig. 2 we compare EnmBERT and EnRomBERT verification accuracy (LA-3) and evidence recall on the fair FEVER development (dev) set, the test set and on a golden-forcing dev set. The fair dev set includes all the claims in the original FEVER dev set and all the sentences from the retrieved documents (English and/or Romanian). The golden forcing dev set forces all ground truth evidence into the sentence selection step input, effectively giving perfect

---

[9] https://github.com/sheffieldnlp/fever-scorer.

document retrieval recall [23]. On the fair dev set, the EnmBERT system reaches within 5% accuracy of English-only BERT-based systems such as [33] (LA-3 of 67.63%). We also reach within 5% evidence recall (Table 1 88.60%) as compared to English-only KGAT [23] and better than [33]. Note that any of the available English-only systems with BERT backbone such as KGAT [23] and GEAR [42] can be employed with an mBERT (or another multilingual pre-trained) backbone to lift the multilingual system performance.

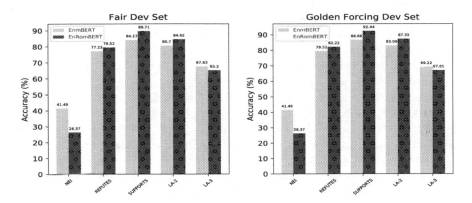

Fig. 2. Error analysis per class. 'LA-2' is Accuracy for 'Supports' & 'Refutes' Claims

Table 1. Calibration of models evaluation using the official FEVER scores % in [35].

Dataset	Model	Prec@5	Rec@5	FEVER	LA-3 Acc
Fair-Dev	EnmBERT-EnmBERT	25.54	**88.60**	64.62	**67.63**
Fair-Dev	EnRomBERT-EnRomBERT	25.20	88.03	61.16	65.20
Test	EnmBERT-EnmBERT	25.27	87.38	62.30	65.26
Test	EnRomBERT-EnRomBERT	24.91	86.80	58.78	63.18

To better understand strengths and weaknesses of the system performance and the impact of including Romanian evidence in training EnRomBERT, we present a per class analysis in Fig. 2. We also calculate accuracy scores for only 'SUPPORTS' and 'REFUTES' claims (FEVER-2). The English-only SotA label accuracy (LA-2) on FEVER-2 is currently given in RAG [21] at 89.5% on the fair dev set and our EnRomBERT system reaches within 5%. We postulate that the noise from including Romanian sentences in training improves the FEVER-2 score (see Fig. 2), EnRomBERT coming within 5% of [34] English-only FEVER-2 SotA of 92.2% on the golden-forcing dev set. In the per-class analysis, on 'SUP-PORTS' and 'REFUTES' classes in Fig. 2, EnRomBERT outperforms Enm-BERT on both fair and golden-forcing dev sets. To boost the NEI class per-formance, future research may evaluate the inclusion of all claims, including

NEI, in training. Furthermore, retrieval in multiple languages may alleviate the absence of relevant evidence for NEI claims.**Transfer Learning Performance** Table 2 shows EnmBERT and EnRomBERT transfer learning ability evaluated directly in the fact verification step using the previously retrieved and manually translated 400 mixed claim-evidence pairs. We report the classification accuracy on all 400 mixed examples, and separately for En-En (English evidence and English claims), En-Ro, Ro-En and Ro-Ro pairs. EnmBERT's zero-shot accuracy on Ro-Ro is 85% as compared to 95% for En-En, better than EnRomBERT's. EnmBERT outperforms EnRomBERT as well for Ro-En and En-Ro pairs. We recall that Romanian evidence sentences were only included in EnRomBERT training as negative evidence in the sentence retrieval step. If selected in the top 5 evidence sentences, Romanian sentences were given the NEI label in the fact verification step. Hence, EnRomBERT likely learned that Romanian evidence sentences are NEI, which led to a model bias against Romanian evidence. **Disinformation Case Study** We employ EnmBERT to evaluate the claim "Ion Mihai Pacepa, the former Securitate general, is alive". The document retriever retrieves Wikipedia documents in English, Romanian and Portuguese. Page summaries are supplied to the EnmBERT sentence selector, which selects top 5 evidence sentences (1XEn, 2XRo, 2XPt). Based on the retrieved evidence, the EnmBERT fact verification module predicts 'SUPPORTS' status for the claim. For illustration purposes, the system is exposed as an API[10].

Table 2. Fact verification accuracy (%) for translated parallel claim - evidence sentences.

Model	Mixed	En-En	En-Ro	Ro-En	Ro-Ro
EnmBERT	95.00	95.00	50.00	65.00	85.00
EnRomBERT	95.00	95.00	25.00	0.00	50.00

5   Final Notes

In this article we present a first approach to building multilingual evidence retrieval and fact verification systems to combat global disinformation. Evidence poor languages may be at increased risk of online disinformation and multilingual systems built upon evidence rich languages in the context of polyglotism can be an effective weapon. To this end, our trained EnmBERT system shows cross-lingual transfer learning ability for the fact verification step on the original FEVER-related claims. This work opens future lines of research into end-to-end multilingual retrieve-verify systems for disinformation suspect claims, in multiple languages, with multiple reliable evidence retrieval sources available in addition to Wikipedia.

---

[10] https://github.com/D-Roberts/multilingual_nli_ECIR2021.

References

1. Andrei, A.: impact.ro (2020). https://www.impact.ro/exclusiv-ce-se-intampla-acum-cu-ion-mihai-pacepa. Accessed 28 Oct 2020
2. Artetxe, M., Schwenk, H.: Massively multilingual sentence embeddings for zero-shot cross-lingual transfer and beyond. Trans. Assoc. Comput. Linguist. **7**, 597–610 (2019)
3. Bastos, M.T., Mercea, D.: The Brexit botnet and user-generated hyperpartisan news. Soc. Sci. Comput. Rev. **37**(1), 38–54 (2019)
4. Bessi, A., Ferrara, E.: Social bots distort the 2016 US Presidential election online discussion. First Monday **21**(11–7), 56 (2016)
5. Brachten, F., Stieglitz, S., Hofeditz, L., Kloppenborg, K., Reimann, A.: Strategies and influence of social bots in a 2017 German state election-a case study on Twitter. arXiv preprint arXiv:1710.07562 (2017)
6. Cao, Z., Qin, T., Liu, T.Y., Tsai, M.F., Li, H.: Learning to rank: from pairwise approach to listwise approach. In: Proceedings of the 24th International Conference on Machine Learning, pp. 129–136 (2007)
7. Clark, J.H., et al.: TyDi QA: a benchmark for information-seeking question answering in typologically diverse languages. arXiv preprint arXiv:2003.05002 (2020)
8. Cohen, N.: Conspiracy videos? Fake news? Enter Wikipedia, the 'good cop' of the Internet. The Washington Post (2018)
9. Conneau, A., et al.: XNLI: evaluating cross-lingual sentence representations. arXiv preprint arXiv:1809.05053 (2018)
10. Cucerzan, S.: Large-scale named entity disambiguation based on Wikipedia data. In: Proceedings of the 2007 Joint Conference on Empirical Methods in Natural Language Processing and Computational Natural Language Learning (EMNLP-CoNLL), pp. 708–716 (2007)
11. Devlin, J., Chang, M., Lee, K., Toutanova, K.: BERT: pre-training of deep bidirectional transformers for language understanding. CoRR abs/1810.04805 (2018). http://arxiv.org/abs/1810.04805
12. Fallis, D.: What is disinformation? Library Trends **63**(3), 401–426 (2015)
13. Fetzer, J.H.: Disinformation: the use of false information. Mind. Mach. **14**(2), 231–240 (2004)
14. Gardner, M., et al.: AllenNLP: a deep semantic natural language processing platform. arXiv preprint arXiv:1803.07640 (2018)
15. Grinberg, N., Joseph, K., Friedland, L., Swire-Thompson, B., Lazer, D.: Fake news on Twitter during the 2016 US presidential election. Science **363**(6425), 374–378 (2019)
16. Hanselowski, A., et al.: UKP-Athene: multi-sentence textual entailment for claim verification. In: Proceedings of the First Workshop on Fact Extraction and VERification (FEVER), pp. 103–108 (2018)
17. Johnson, M., et al.: Google's multilingual neural machine translation system: enabling zero-shot translation. Trans. Assoc. Comput. Linguist. **5**, 339–351 (2017)
18. Kar, D., Bhardwaj, M., Samanta, S., Azad, A.P.: No rumours please! A multi-Indic-lingual approach for COVID fake-tweet detection. arXiv preprint arXiv:2010.06906 (2020)
19. Karpukhin, V., et al.: Dense passage retrieval for open-domain question answering. arXiv preprint arXiv:2004.04906 (2020)
20. Kingma, D.P., Ba, J.: Adam: a method for stochastic optimization. arXiv preprint arXiv:1412.6980 (2014)

21. Lewis, P., et al.: Retrieval-augmented generation for knowledge-intensive NLP tasks. arXiv preprint arXiv:2005.11401 (2020)
22. Liu, Y., et al.: Multilingual denoising pre-training for neural machine translation. arXiv preprint arXiv:2001.08210 (2020)
23. Liu, Z., Xiong, C., Sun, M., Liu, Z.: Fine-grained fact verification with kernel graph attention network. In: Proceedings of the 58th Annual Meeting of the Association for Computational Linguistics, pp. 7342–7351 (2020)
24. Malon, C.: Team Papelo: transformer networks at FEVER. In: Proceedings of the First Workshop on Fact Extraction and VERification (FEVER), pp. 109–113 (2018)
25. Pacepa, I.M.: Red Horizons: Chronicles of a Communist Spy Chief. Gateway Books (1987)
26. Pacepa, I.M., Rychlak, R.J.: Disinformation: Former Spy Chief Reveals Secret Strategy for Undermining Freedom, Attacking Religion, and Promoting Terrorism. Wnd Books (2013)
27. Rogers, K., Longoria, J.: Why a Gamer Started a Web of Disinformation Sites Aimed at Latino Americans (2020). https://fivethirtyeight.com/features/why-a-gamer-started-a-web-of-disinformation-sites-aimed-at-latino-americans. Accessed 18 Jan 2021
28. Sakata, W., Shibata, T., Tanaka, R., Kurohashi, S.: FAQ retrieval using query-question similarity and BERT-based query-answer relevance. In: Proceedings of the 42nd International ACM SIGIR Conference on Research and Development in Information Retrieval, pp. 1113–1116 (2019)
29. Schroepfer, M.: Creating a data set and a challenge for deepfakes. Facebook Artificial Intelligence (2019)
30. Schwenk, H., Li, X.: A corpus for multilingual document classification in eight languages. arXiv preprint arXiv:1805.09821 (2018)
31. Sennrich, R., Haddow, B., Birch, A.: Edinburgh neural machine translation systems for WMT 16. arXiv preprint arXiv:1606.02891 (2016)
32. Silverman, C.: This Analysis Shows How Viral Fake Election News Stories Outperformed Real News on Facebook (2016). https://www.buzzfeednews.com/article/craigsilverman/viral-fake-election-news-outperformed-real-news-on-facebook. Accessed 28 Oct 2020
33. Soleimani, A., Monz, C., Worring, M.: BERT for evidence retrieval and claim verification. In: Jose, J.M., et al. (eds.) ECIR 2020. LNCS, vol. 12036, pp. 359–366. Springer, Cham (2020). https://doi.org/10.1007/978-3-030-45442-5_45
34. Thorne, J., Vlachos, A.: Avoiding catastrophic forgetting in mitigating model biases in sentence-pair classification with elastic weight consolidation. arXiv preprint arXiv:2004.14366 (2020)
35. Thorne, J., Vlachos, A., Christodoulopoulos, C., Mittal, A.: FEVER: a large-scale dataset for fact extraction and verification. arXiv preprint arXiv:1803.05355 (2018)
36. Thorne, J., Vlachos, A., Cocarascu, O., Christodoulopoulos, C., Mittal, A.: The fact extraction and verification (FEVER) shared task. arXiv preprint arXiv:1811.10971 (2018)
37. Vosoughi, S., Roy, D., Aral, S.: The spread of true and false news online. Science 359(6380), 1146–1151 (2018)
38. Wolf, T., et al.: HuggingFace's transformers: state-of-the-art natural language processing. arXiv arXiv:1910 (2019)
39. Yang, Z., Dai, Z., Yang, Y., Carbonell, J., Salakhutdinov, R.R., Le, Q.V.: XLNet: generalized autoregressive pretraining for language understanding. In: Advances in Neural Information Processing Systems, pp. 5753–5763 (2019)

40. Yoneda, T., Mitchell, J., Welbl, J., Stenetorp, P., Riedel, S.: UCL machine reading group: four factor framework for fact finding (HexaF). In: Proceedings of the First Workshop on Fact Extraction and VERification (FEVER), pp. 97–102 (2018)
41. Zhong, W., et al.: Reasoning over semantic-level graph for fact checking. arXiv preprint arXiv:1909.03745 (2019)
42. Zhou, J., et al.: GEAR: graph-based evidence aggregating and reasoning for fact verification. arXiv preprint arXiv:1908.01843 (2019)
43. Zhou, X., Mulay, A., Ferrara, E., Zafarani, R.: ReCOVery: a multimodal repository for COVID-19 news credibility research. arXiv preprint arXiv:2006.05557 (2020)
44. Zhou, X., Zafarani, R.: A survey of fake news: fundamental theories, detection methods, and opportunities. ACM Comput. Surv. (CSUR) 53(5), 1–40 (2020)

How Do Active Reading Strategies Affect Learning Outcomes in Web Search?

Nirmal Roy[(⊠)], Manuel Valle Torre, Ujwal Gadiraju, David Maxwell,
and Claudia Hauff

Delft University of Technology, Delft, The Netherlands
{n.roy,m.valletorre,u.k.gadiraju,d.m.maxwell,c.hauff}@tudelft.nl

Abstract. Prior work in education research has shown that various active reading strategies, notably highlighting and note-taking, benefit learning outcomes. Most of these findings are based on observational studies where learners learn from a *single* document. In a *Search as Learning (SAL)* context where learners have to iteratively scan and explore a large number of documents to address their learning objective, the effect of these active reading strategies is largely unexplored. To address this research gap, we carried out a crowd-sourced user study, and explored the effects of different highlighting and note-taking strategies on learning during a complex, learning-oriented search task. Out of five hypotheses derived from the education literature we could confirm three in the SAL context. Our findings have important design implications on aiding learning through search. Learners can benefit from search interfaces equipped with active reading tools—but some learning strategies employing these tools are more effective than others. (This research has been supported by *DDS (Delft Data Science)* and *NWO* projects *SearchX* (639.022.722) and *Aspasia* (015.013.027).)

1 Introduction and Prior Work

In the education literature, *active reading tools* such as highlighting and note-taking have been shown to improve learning outcomes in both low-level recall-oriented tasks [2,24,26], and high-level critical tasks [10]. These works also explore different strategies by which learners *use* these tools and their effects on learning outcomes [1,11,14,26]. However, in most of these works, learners are tasked to learn from a single document—often on paper. The effects of these strategies are unexplored in a *Search as Learning (SAL)* [5] context, where learners engage in an iterative exploration of the web, scanning and processing a number of documents with the goal of gaining knowledge pertaining to their learning objectives.

Previously, several *information organisational tools* have been developed for web search engines [3,8]. However, the effect that these tools have on learning has not been explicitly measured, nor do they study if participants employed different strategies while using these tools. Moreover, contemporary web search engines do not employ highlighting or note-taking tools—despite their benefits in learning [10,26]. In order to address these shortcomings, we utilise data obtained

© Springer Nature Switzerland AG 2021
D. Hiemstra et al. (Eds.): ECIR 2021, LNCS 12657, pp. 368–375, 2021.
https://doi.org/10.1007/978-3-030-72240-1_37

from a crowd-sourced user study [21] to investigate how different highlighting and note-taking strategies (shown to be beneficial in learning outside of a SAL setup) affect learning outcomes during a complex, learning-oriented search task.

In this work we investigate whether five hypotheses (summarised in Table 1), inspired from the education literature, hold up in our SAL setup too.

Table 1. The five hypotheses and rationalisations used for this exploratory study.

Hypothesis		Rationale
H1	Learners who consider highlighting to be an important active reading strategy benefit less from it than learners who do not	According to [26], learners who are *less* accustomed to highlighting put more effort into the act of highlighting and ultimately a better learning outcome is recorded for them
H2	Learners directly copying considerable portions of their notes from documents they have viewed benefit less than participants who rephrase content in their own way	Copying large portions of text reduces the attention of learners to critical details [1]. Rephrasing text while note-taking leads to a deeper processing and understanding of the said text while writing summaries [10]
H3	The number or amount of highlights by learners is *not* an indicator of learning outcomes	Prior studies [12,17,26] have shown that the amount of highlights is not an indicator of learning outcomes
H4	Learners who take wordier notes cover more facts in their essays	Prior works [11,18] depict conflicting observations regarding wordy notes. For this study, we assume that wordier notes contain more facts [18]
H5	Trained highlighters and note-takers learn significantly more than their untrained counterparts	[14] and [4] trained learners on effective highlighting and note-taking strategies respectively. They observed that the trained group of learners had significantly greater learning outcomes compared to control groups

2   Study Design

User Data, Topics and System. In this work we make use of data collected during a user study conducted by Roy et al. [21]. The user study follows the setup by Moraes et al. [16], making use of the open source retrieval system, SearchX [20]. The standard interface, facilitated by the *Bing Search API*, provides a series of widgets, quality control features and generates fine-grained search logs, allowing us to capture a number of key behavioural measures. On top of the standard widgets of SearchX, we incorporate *highlighting* and *note-taking* tools, with a screenshot of the tools available in Fig. 1 of Roy et al. [21]. In order to systematically evaluate the effect of active reading strategies (from our hypotheses) on learning, we consider four experimental conditions, namely:

- CONTROL: The standard SearchX search interface is provided *without* highlighting or note-taking tools.
- NOTE: In this condition, only the note-taking tool is enabled.

- HIGH: In this condition, only the highlighting tool is enabled.
- HIGH+NOTE: Both the highlighting and note-taking tools are enabled.

In line with prior works [15,22], learners are assessed based on a learning-oriented *critical task*. Two topics—*Genetically Modified Organisms* (**GMO**) and *Urban Water Cycle* (**UWC**) inspired from Câmara et al. [7]—are used, and we ask learners to write a summary criticising and evaluating ideas from multiple perspectives [13]. In the data collected from the user study [21] (where highlighting and note-taking tools (*not* strategies) were examined over learning and search behaviour), we used: the text learners highlighted; the notes they have taken; the total time spent in taking notes; and their written essays. Depending on the experimental condition, learners had access to their saved documents (CONTROL and NOTE), their highlights together with the documents (HIGH and HIGH+NOTE) or their notes (NOTE and HIGH+NOTE) while writing the essays.

We collected data from $N = 115$ participants (referred to as *learners*) [21]; 71 of whom were assigned to the **GMO** topic, with the remaining 44 assigned to the **UWC** topic. In order to evaluate the learning outcomes from the essays, we employ two metrics inspired from Wilson and Wilson [25]. Specifically, we use **F-Fact**, which counts the number of individual facts present in the essays, and **T-Depth**, which rates the extent to which certain subtopics of the topics is covered in a summary essay, on a scale of 0–3 (from not covered at all, to covered with great focus). Both these measures were shown to be good indicators of learning. Three annotators (this paper's authors) split the 115 essays for manual annotation; 18 essays were analysed by all. They obtained a Pearson correlation of 0.78 ($p = 0.002$) for **T-Depth** scores and a correlation of 0.76 ($p = 0.002$) for **F-Fact** scores. We also calculated the Flesch-Kincaid[1] scores of the essays in order to assess their readability. A high score indicates that the essay is simple to read; a low score indicates a complicated text, best read by a graduate. After obtaining the essay scores, we operationalised our five hypotheses based on our collected data as follows:

H1: Learners were asked *Do you think highlighting is useful?* during the pre-questionnaire. This was an open question; we manually analysed their answers and divide them into *pro, unsure* and *anti* highlighters[2].

H2: We calculated how many terms from the learners' notes are taken verbatim from the documents they read. The more terms that overlapped, the more we assumed text was directly taken from the examined documents.

H3: We divided (median-split) learners into *heavy* and *light* highlighters based on two separate conditions: *(i)* the total number of highlighting actions; and *(ii)* the total number of words highlighted.

H4: We divided (median-split) learners into *heavy* and *light* note-takers based on the total number of words written in their note-taking tool.

---

[1] We use textstat for computing the Flesch readability score.
[2] Pro - *A great extent*; Unsure -*It's a mild benefit to me*; Anti - *I don't think highlighting itself helps me all that much.*

Table 2. Mean (standard error) of learning metrics and metrics pertaining to active reading strategies across all participants in each condition. [†] Indicates two-way ANOVA significance, while ^{C},^{H},^{N},^{B} indicate post-hoc significance (TukeyHSD pairwise test, $p < 0.05$) increases vs. CONTROL, HIGH, NOTE and HIGH+NOTE respectively.

Measure		CONTROL	HIGH	NOTE	HIGH+NOTE
I	#users	32	29	29	25
II	Session duration (min)	23 m 40 s (1 m 51 s)	28 m 19 s (1 m 48 s)	20 m 3 s (1 m 15 s)	29 m 17 s (3 m 3 s)
III	T-Depth scores of essays[†]	1.2 (0.1)^{H}	1.6 (0.1)^{C}	1.4 (0.1)	1.5 (0.1)
IV	F-Fact scores of essays[†]	14.6 (1.8)^{N}	16.6 (1.0)	19.6 (1.6)^{C}	15.9 (1.6)
V	Flesch scores of essays[†]	32.2 (7.0)	21.4 (11.6)	15.9 (11.4)^{B}	46.4 (3.3)^{N}
VI	#essay terms	181.6 (13.5)	200.8 (15.9)	225.9 (20.9)	193.0 (17.6)
VII	#highlight actions	—	56.8 (45.0)	—	54.9 (48.4)
VIII	#words highlighted	—	1625.8 (406.1)	—	1533.6 (290.5)
IX	Frac. essay terms in highlights	—	0.4 (0.0)	—	0.5 (0.0)
X	Overlap notes w/ documents	—	—	10% (0.0)	10% (0.0)
XI	#words in note-pad	—	—	1000.1 (460.0)	372.3 (181.0)
XII	Frac. essay terms in notes[†]	—	—	0.4 (0.0)^{B}	0.2 (0.1)^{N}

H5: We make two assumptions to distinguish between trained and untrained highlighters and note-takers: *(i)* learners who frequently engaged in highlighting and note-taking prior to the study are considered to be trained (learners were asked the open question: *How often do you highlight and take notes while learning?* during the pre-questionnaire)[3]; and *(ii)* based on their education level—learners having a bachelor's, master's or a doctorate degree are considered to be trained.

3   Results and Discussion

The basic learner statistics for each condition are shown in Table 2. We observe that HIGH learners cover significantly more subtopics in their essays (**T-Depth, III**), whereas NOTE learners write significantly more facts than their CONTROL counterparts (**F-Fact, IV**). Essays written by NOTE learners were also significantly more complex to read compared to HIGH+NOTE learners (**Flesch, V**). Incorporating both highlighting and note-taking tools does not lead to a significant improvement in learning outcomes.

---

[3] Trained - *Almost always if I see something very new to me*; Untrained - *Rarely*.

Table 3. H1: Learners are divided into *pro-highlighters*, *unsure* or *anti-highlighters*. † Indicates two-way ANOVA significance, while ^{C}, ^{H}, ^{B} indicate post-hoc significance (TukeyHSD pairwise test, **p < 0.05**) with Holm-Bonferroni correction.

		CONTROL			HIGH			HIGH+NOTE		
		Pro	Unsure	Anti	Pro	Unsure	Anti	Pro	Unsure	Anti
I	#users	9	13	10	13	11	5	11	7	7
II	#words highli.	—	—	—	1529.8 (333.1)	1944.6 (1018.2)	1174.2 (126.6)	1703.0 (319.0)	1826.7 (790.1)	974.1 (490.3)
III	F-Fact	13.1 (1.9)	16.3 (3.9)	13.6 (3)	17.1 (1.3)	14.6 (1.5)	19.6 (3.6)	16.2 (2.4)	17.9 (3.7)	13.6 (2.5)
IV	T-Depth†	1.2 (0.2)	1.2 (0.1)^{H,B}	1.2 (0.1)^{H}	1.4 (0.1)	1.6 (0.1)^{C}	2.3 (0.2)^{C}	1.2 (0.2)	1.7 (0.1)^{C}	1.8 (0.3)
V	Flesch	35.7 (7.7)	25.9 (12.1)	37.3 (15.4)	8.0 (18.4)	27.3 (21.7)	43.3 (3.1)	48.9 (5.2)	41.7 (2.9)	47.2 (8.7)

H1: We did not observe a significant difference (Table 3) for Flesch scores (**V**) and F-Fact (**III**) between the three groups of highlighters belonging to HIGH and HIGH+NOTE when compared to the three groups of CONTROL. However, we observed significant differences for T-Depth ($F(2,77) = 6.44, p = 0.002$). Post-hoc tests revealed that unsure highlighters belonging to both HIGH and HIGH+NOTE cover significantly more subtopics in their essays than their CONTROL counterparts. Anti-highlighters belonging to HIGH show better learning outcomes compared to anti-highlighters belonging to CONTROL, whereas pro-highlighters belonging to HIGH and HIGH+NOTE gain no benefits. This is in line with the findings of [26] and shows evidence *for* our hypothesis. This might be attributed to the fact that learners who are not sure about the benefits of highlighting put more effort in the act of highlighting itself. This also indicates that highlighting makes some learners process text in a way different from how they normally would, which eventually leads to a better understanding of the text.

H2: From Table 2, we find that notes of learners from both NOTE and HIGH+NOTE on average have 10% overlap with the documents they read (row **X**). Hence, when we combine all note-takers, we see that those who have more than 10% of their notes overlapped with the viewed documents, covered significantly more facts (F-Facts) than whose notes overlapped less than 10% ($t(38) = 2.04, p = 0.04$), which shows evidence *against* our hypothesis. However, the former explored less subtopics and wrote more complex essays (although not significantly) than the latter. This shows that although copying considerable portions of text into notes might not be beneficial for certain aspects of essay writing like topical coverage, they can be useful when the essays require more factual information.

H3: Again from Table 2, we observe no significant difference between learners of HIGH and HIGH+NOTE when comparing learning metrics, the number of highlight actions (**VII**) and words highlighted (**VIII**). Following this, dividing learners into *heavy* and *light* highlighters, we see from Table 4 the amount of highlighting is not an indicator of learning since there is no significant difference between *heavy* and *light* highlighters (**I, II**), thereby providing evidence *for* our hypothesis. This indicates that the act of highlighting alone does not benefit learning—it has to be coupled with a deeper cognitive processing of the text.

Table 4. H3, H4: Learners are divided into two groups (*heavy* and *light*) based on the median values for each active reading strategy. The learning metrics are computed separately for each group. The significant differences obtained from TukeyHSD pairwise test are highlighted in **bold**.

		F-Fact		T-Depth		Flesch Scores	
		Heavy	Light	Heavy	Light	Heavy	Light
I.	#Highlight Actions	15.9 (1.2)	16.6 (1.4)	1.5 (0.1)	1.6 (0.1)	32.4 (7.1)	33.5 (11.3)
II.	#Highlighted Words	17.0 (1.3)	15.5 (1.3)	1.4 (0.1)	1.7 (0.1)	26.4 (9.5)	39.5 (9.2)
III.	#Words in Note-pad	**20.0 (1.8)**	**15.7 (1.4)**	1.4 (0.1)	1.5 (0.1)	**11.6 (12.0)**	**48.4 (2.8)**

Table 5. H5: Participants are divided into two groups (*trained* and *non-trained*) based on their self reported highlighting and note-taking frequency and also based on their education level. The learning metrics are computed separately for each group. The significant differences obtained from TukeyHSD pairwise tests are highlighted in **bold**.

		F-Fact		T-Depth		Flesch scores	
		Trained	Non-trained	Trained	Non-trained	Trained	Non-trained
I.	Prior highlighting frequency	16.8 (1.3)	15.8 (1.3)	**1.4 (0.1)**	**1.7 (0.1)**	28.8 (12.2)	36.6 (6.5)
II.	Highlighter education level	16.4 (1.2)	15.7 (1.5)	1.7 (0.1)	1.5 (0.1)	36.6 (8.8)	27.4 (10.8)
III.	Prior note-taking frequency	18.9 (1.5)	16.6 (1.8)	1.6 (0.1)	1.3 (0.1)	28.7 (8.8)	31.8 (10.3)
IV.	Note-taker education level	19.5 (1.6)	15.7 (1.7)	1.5 (0.1)	1.4 (0.1)	23.8 (10.8)	36.9 (6.4)

H4: NOTE learners cover significantly more facts in their essays compared to their CONTROL counterparts (**IV**), cover significantly more essay terms in their notes (**XI**), and write more complex essays (**V**) than their HIGH+NOTE counterparts (Table 2). Furthermore, albeit not significantly, NOTE learners write wordier notes (**XI**) compared to HIGH+NOTE learners (Table 2). This shows evidence *for* our hypothesis that wordy notes benefit learners in our given task. Table 4 further corroborates our hypothesis where we see that learners who take wordier notes (*heavy* note-takers) cover significantly more facts in their essays, and write significantly more complex essays (**III**). This indicates that taking wordy notes and having access to them while writing their essays help learners to cover more factual information.

H5: When we divide learners based on their prior highlighting experience, we observe a significant difference for T-Depth (Table 5)—untrained highlighters cover more subtopics in their essays (**I**). Prior note-taking experience does not benefit learners. We also do not see any significant learning difference between trained and untrained highlighters/note-takers when we divide them based on their education level. These results show evidence *against* our hypothesis that being trained in highlighting and note-taking benefits learners. This indicates that if learners are prevented from learning using strategies they employ, the cost of prevention does not outweigh the benefits of using a highlighting or a note-taking tool. Although these results do not follow the observations from [4,14], it needs to be considered that in those studies, the experimental groups of learners were trained specifically about efficient highlighting and note-taking strategies.

Contributions and Conclusions. In our work we investigated the extent to which five findings (i.e. our hypotheses) from the education literature [2,4,14,26] hold up in a SAL context. We confirmed three of those hypotheses, and showed that while engaging in complex learning-oriented search tasks on the web, the acts of highlighting and note-taking themselves may not benefit learners. Rather, it is *how* these tools change the way the learners scan and processes text that is more important for learning while searching. The observations from this work has design implications for search interfaces, where we must consider incorporating active reading tools within web search engines. For future work, we will build on existing literature that looks into search behaviours as proxies for learning [6,9, 16,19,23]. This can be done by analysing if active reading strategies can also be used to predict learning outcomes.

References

1. Bauer, A., Koedinger, K.: Pasting and encoding: note-taking in online courses. In: Sixth IEEE International Conference on Advanced Learning Technologies (ICALT 2006), pp. 789–793. IEEE (2006)
2. Ben-Yehudah, G., Eshet-Alkalai, Y.: The contribution of text-highlighting to comprehension: a comparison of print and digital reading. J. Educ. Multimedia Hypermedia **27**(2), 153–178 (2018)
3. Bharat, K.: Searchpad: explicit capture of search context to support web search. Comput. Netw. **33**(1–6), 493–501 (2000)
4. Boyle, J.R.: Thinking strategically to record notes in content classes. Am. Second. Educ. **40**, 51–66 (2011)
5. Collins-Thompson, K., Hansen, P., Hauff, C.: Search as learning (dagstuhl seminar 17092). Dagstuhl Rep. **7**, 135–162 (2017)
6. Collins-Thompson, K., Rieh, S.Y., Haynes, C.C., Syed, R.: Assessing learning outcomes in web search: a comparison of tasks and query strategies. In: Proceedings of the 2016 ACM on Conference on Human Information Interaction and Retrieval, pp. 163–172. ACM (2016)
7. Câmara, A., Roy, N., Maxwell, D., Hauff, C.: Searching to learn with instructional scaffolding. In: Proceedings of the 6th ACM CHIIR (2021)
8. Donato, D., Bonchi, F., Chi, T., Maarek, Y.: Do you want to take notes? identifying research missions in yahoo! search pad. In: Proceedings of the 19th WWW, pp. 321–330 (2010)
9. Eickhoff, C., Teevan, J., White, R., Dumais, S.: Lessons from the journey: a query log analysis of within-session learning. In: Proceedings of the 7th ACM WSDM, pp. 223–232 (2014)
10. Hagen, Å.M., Braasch, J.L., Bråten, I.: Relationships between spontaneous note-taking, self-reported strategies and comprehension when reading multiple texts in different task conditions. J. Res. Reading **37**(S1), S141–S157 (2014)
11. Howe, M.J.: Using students' notes to examine the role of the individual learner in acquiring meaningful subject matter. J. Educ. Res. **64**(2), 61–63 (1970)
12. Lauterman, T., Ackerman, R.: Overcoming screen inferiority in learning and calibration. Comput. Hum. Behav. **35**, 455–463 (2014)
13. Lee, H., Lee, J., Makara, K., Fishman, B.J., Hong, Y.: Does higher education foster critical and creative learners? An exploration of two universities in South Korea and the USA. High. Educ. Res. Dev. **34**(1), 131–146 (2015)

14. Leutner, D., Leopold, C., den Elzen-Rump, V.: Self-regulated learning with a text-highlighting strategy. Zeitschrift für Psychologie/J. Psychol. **215**(3), 174–182 (2007)
15. Liu, H., Liu, C., Belkin, N.: Investigation of users' knowledge change process in learning-related search tasks. Proc. ASIS&T **56**(1), 166–175 (2019)
16. Moraes, F., Putra, S.R., Hauff, C.: Contrasting search as a learning activity with instructor-designed learning. In: CIKM 2018, pp. 167–176. ACM (2018)
17. Norman, E., Furnes, B.: The relationship between metacognitive experiences and learning: is there a difference between digital and non-digital study media? Comput. Hum. Behav. **54**, 301–309 (2016)
18. Nye, P.A., Crooks, T.J., Powley, M., Tripp, G.: Student note-taking related to university examination performance. High. Educ. **13**(1), 85–97 (1984)
19. Pardi, G., von Hoyer, J., Holtz, P., Kammerer, Y.: The role of cognitive abilities and time spent on texts and videos in a multimodal searching as learning task. In: Proceedings of the 5th ACM CHIIR, pp. 378–382 (2020)
20. Putra, S.R., Grashoff, K., Moraes, F., Hauff, C.: On the development of a collaborative search system. In: DESIRES, pp. 76–82 (2018)
21. Roy, N., Valle, M., Gadiraju, U., Maxwell, D., Hauff, C.: Searching to learn with instructional scaffolding. In: Proceedings of the 6th ACM CHIIR (2021)
22. Song, X., Liu, C., Liu, H.: Characterizing and exploring users' task completion process at different stages in learning related tasks. Proc. Assoc. Inf. Sci. Technol. **55**(1), 460–469 (2018)
23. Syed, R., Collins-Thompson, K.: Exploring document retrieval features associated with improved short-and long-term vocabulary learning outcomes. In: Proceedings of the 3rd ACM CHIIR, pp. 191–200 (2018)
24. Wang, S., Unal, D., Walker, E.: MindDot: Supporting effective cognitive behaviors in concept map-based learning environments. In: Proceedings of the 38th ACM CHI, pp. 1–14 (2019)
25. Wilson, M., Wilson, M.: A comparison of techniques for measuring sensemaking and learning within participant-generated summaries. JASIST **64**(2), 291–306 (2013)
26. Yue, C.L., Storm, B.C., Kornell, N., Bjork, E.L.: Highlighting and its relation to distributed study and students' metacognitive beliefs. Educ. Psychol. Rev. **27**(1), 69–78 (2015)

Fine-Tuning BERT for COVID-19 Domain Ad-Hoc IR by Using Pseudo-qrels

Xabier Saralegi[✉] and Iñaki San Vicente[ID]

Elhuyar fundazioa, Zelai Haundi 3, 20170 Usurbil, Spain
{x.saralegi,i.sanvicente}@elhuyar.eus
http://hizkuntzateknologiak.elhuyar.eus

Abstract. This work analyzes the feasibility of training a neural retrieval system for a collection of scientific papers about COVID-19 using pseudo-qrels extracted from the collection. We propose a method for generating pseudo-qrels that exploits two characteristics present in scientific articles: a) the relationship between title and abstract, and b) the relationship between articles through sentences containing citations. Through these signals we generate pseudo-queries and their respective pseudo-positive (relevant documents) and pseudo-negative (non-relevant documents) examples. The article retrieval process combines a ranking model based on term-maching techniques and a neural one based on pre-trained BERT models. BERT models are fine-tuned to the task using the pseudo-qrels generated. We compare different BERT models, both open domain and biomedical domain, and also the generated pseudo-qrels with the open domain MS-Marco dataset for fine-tuning the models. The results obtained on the TREC-COVID collection show that pseudo-qrels provide a significant improvement to neural models, both against classic IR baselines based on term-matching and neural systems trained on MS-Marco.

Keywords: Ad-hoc IR · Ranking neural models · Weak supervised learning · COVID-19

1 Introduction

During the last few years, different neural architectures have been proposed to address the task of ad-hoc Information Retrieval (IR), to retrieve both documents [17] and passages [11]. However, those architectures require large amounts of qrels training data composed of queries and their corresponding judgments of relevance on a collection.

Datasets including qrels such as MS-Marco [10] and CAR [5] have been successfully used for training neural systems based on BERT. This work addresses to what extent these datasets are sufficient for training an ad-hoc IR system of a very specific domain collection including scientific papers on COVID-19, i.e.

© Springer Nature Switzerland AG 2021
D. Hiemstra et al. (Eds.): ECIR 2021, LNCS 12657, pp. 376–383, 2021.
https://doi.org/10.1007/978-3-030-72240-1_38

CORD19 [15], and whether it is possible to generate synthetic domain training data from signals coming from the target collection. Specifically, we will study two signals to generate pairs of queries and relevant judgements: a) Title-abstract pairs; and b) Pairs composed of a citation and the abstract of the cited article.

Similar to other authors in the literature [11,17], we deal with the task of ad-hoc information retrieval using a two step approach. First, we obtain a preliminary ranking of relevant documents using a term-matching based approach [12]. Second, the candidates in the ranking are re-ranked by means of a neural model with a pointwise learning objective applied to the query and the abstracts. We have fine-tuned existing pre-trained BERT models for the task of ranking pairs of queries and relevant texts through cross-entropy loss. For the purpose of fine-tuning, we have compared the use of general domain training data (MS-Marco) versus using domain specific synthetic training data generated by the above-mentioned methods from the target collection (CORD19). We also compare the use as basis of general pretrained models (BERT Base and BERT Large) versus a clinical domain pretrained model (CBERT [1]).

The contribution of this paper is twofold: i) we show that it is possible to generate competitive training qrel data in a synthetic way from the target collection; and ii) we test to what extent is the use of a in-domain pre-trained model like CBERT decisive.

The article is structured as follows. Section 2 reviews related works. Next, we present the methods implemented for the generation of synthetic qrel data from the target collection. The adopted IR strategy is explained in Sect. 3. The experiments carried out and the results obtained are discussed next. Finally, we draw the main conclusions extracted from this work.

2   Related Works

Over the past four years, different neural architectures have been proposed to address the task of ad-hoc IR [6,7,9,11,16,17]. Among the proposed approaches stand out those based on pre-trained language models such as [11] and [17], as they offer a significant improvement over classic IR systems. In those approaches the neural model is used to rerank an initial ranking generated by a classical information retrieval model based on term-matching techniques.

[11] propose a neural reranker based on BERT Large to address the task of passage retrieval. Specifically, they use the BERT Large model as a binary classification model, adding a single layer neural network fed by the [CLS] vector in order to obtain a relevance probability. The pretrained BERT model is fine-tuned for the classification task using the cross-entropy loss. [17] adopt a similar strategy to address the ad-hoc document retrieval task, dividing the documents into sentences, and adding their scores, since the length of the documents exceeds the maximum length of BERT's input.

Neural architectures require a large number of query relevances (qrels) for training, but their manual generation is very expensive. Some authors [11,17] use qrel data oriented to passage retrieval such as MS-Marco [10] and TREC-CAR [5]. Another alternative is to generate pseudo-qrels automatically. [3], for example, propose to train neural models for ranking using pseudo-qrels generated by unsupervised models like BM25. The TREC-CAR dataset [5] itself is automatically generated from the structure (article, section and paragraph) of the Wikipedia articles. [8] generate pseudo-qrels from a news collection, using the titles as pseudo-queries and their content as relevant text. Other authors [2,18] use the signal produced by anchor-document relationships to simulate qrels.

This work analyzes the feasibility of implementing a neural information retrieval system for a collection of scientific papers of restricted domain (CORD-19), by fine-tuning BERT models (both general and domain adapted) to the task by means of pseudo-qrels extracted from the collection. For the generation of pseudo-qrels we have analyzed two specific signals from collections of scientific papers: a) the relationship between a title and its abstract, and b) the relationship between articles through sentences containing citations. The task of document retrieval has been implemented following a similar strategy to the one proposed by [11], but using an approach based on language models [12], and applied to the whole document, for the elaboration of the preliminary ranking.

3   Approach

3.1   Pseudo-qrels from TREC-COVID Collection

To train the neural rerank a set of queries and their respective relevant and non-relevant documents are needed. The objective is to learn the classification -the relevance of the second text respect to the first- of a pair of texts.

The method for generating pseudo-qrels that we present aims to generate pairs including queries and corresponding pseudo-positive (relevant) and pseudo-negative (not relevant) documents. The method is fully automatic and does not require any set of previously generated queries, since pseudo-queries are extracted from the target collection. Relevant and non-relevant documents are also extracted from the target collection. In this work we have used as target collection the CORD-19 version used in the final round of the TREC-COVID shared task[1]. The dataset contains 192K scientific articles.

To generate the pseudo-queries and their respective pseudo-relevances we use two signals present in collection of scientific papers: a) the relationship between a title and its abstract, and b) the relationship between a sentence that including a citation and the abstract of the paper referenced in the citation.

Relationship Between Title and Abstract (Title): The title of the scientific articles is usually brief and at the same time descriptive of the content. Therefore, it is very similar to the queries used in search systems, and can be used as a pseudo-query. Its corresponding abstract constitutes a good candidate to be a relevant text (pseudo-positive) to that pseudo-query. We take (title, abstract) pairs to generate (pseudo-query,pseudo-positive) pairs.

Relationships Based on Citations (cites): Other papers are often cited in the content of scientific papers, and the sentences including citations are usually

---

[1] Release of July 16th, 2020.

descriptive of the content -in whole or in part- of the article they cite. These sentences and the abstracts of the cited articles are suitable material for the generation of pairs of pseudo-query and relevant texts (pseudo-positives). In order to keep "query like" sentences we select those whose length is between 50 and 250 characters, after removing authors and year from the reference. In addition, those sentences that cite works not included in the same collection are removed to ensure their linkage to the domain.

Non-relevant (pseudo-negative) texts are generated by randomly selecting abstracts from the collection. The optimal number of negatives n has been established $n = 2$ from experiments conducted on the development set (see Sect. 4). In this way we generate one pseudo-positive and two pseudo-negatives for each pseudo-query. As an alternative to randomly selecting negatives in order to include hard negatives, we also implemented the method proposed by [3] which consists on obtaining BM25 rankings for the queries, and using the documents on the lower ranks as negatives. Several variants of this method were tested over the development set selecting different lower rank ranges, but the neural rerankers trained on this data do not provide good results.

3.2   IR Approach

The task of recovery is approached in two steps. First, from the collection of full texts of the scientific articles, we obtain a preliminary ranking for the query with an approach based on language models [12], specifically, the Indri search engine [14]. Second, for each candidate document in the ranking a pair formed by the query[2] and the candidate's abstract are processed with a BERT-based relevance classifier. Using the abstract, and not the whole document, allows us to feed the BERT classifier without exceeding the 512 token limitation.

The relevance classifier is a pretrained BERT model that has been fine-tuned (using the vector [CSL] as an input to a single-layer neural network) for the binary task (pointwise learning objective) of classifying the relevance corresponding to a pair of short texts (relevance of the second text with respect to the first). The classifier returns a relevance probability that is linearly combined with the score of the first ranking according to a coefficient k, and the ranking is rearranged based on that new value.

The fine-tuning of the pretrained BERT model is done by the cross-entropy loss on the pseudo-qrels presented in the previous section. All fine-tunings were performed using original BERT Tensorflow implementation on Google cloud V3-8 TPUs. Training was done for 4 epochs with a learning rate of 2e-5 and a batch size of 32. Code, fine-tuned models and datasets are available at https://github.com/Elhuyar/covid19-ir-pseudoqrels.

4   Experiments

All the experiments are carried out over the CORD-19 dataset used in the final round of TREC-COVID, using the final set of topics and relevance judgements

---

[2] Query and question fields in TREC-COVID topics are joined as query sentence.

for development and testing. We divide the set of 50 topics in two random splits: 10 topics are used as dev set and the other 40 are reserved as test set.

Six sets of pseudo-qrels were generated: using both methods *title* and *cite* (see Sect. 3), and pseudo-negatives per query in the range $n = [1, 2, 5]$. Development set was used to optimize both the number of negatives and the coefficient k used for the linear combination of the reranker output with the initial Indri ranking. Optimal negative number value is $n = 2$ based on dev results, and thus results over test set are computed with retrieval systems trained on 1:2 negative ratio qrels. k is optimized for each system on the dev set, taking *ndcg* measure as reference. Optimum values of k are stable across metrics[3].

We implemented several systems in order to evaluate the following aspects:

i. The quality of the reranker. For that aim we implemented two baselines without any reranker. One using Indri with default parameters over the full collection of documents and the second one adding pseudo-relevance feedback (PRF)[4]. The Baseline using PRF is used for producing the candidates for the neural rerankers, and computing the linear combinations.

ii. Compare open domain BERT models vs. Domain specific models. Original BERT (base and large) [4] and Clinical BERT (CBERT) [1] models were used as the basis for our fine-tunings.

iii. Evaluate the methods to generate pseudo-qrels: *titles* and *cites*. For comparison with the state of the art of neural rerankers we also include BERT fine-tuned on Ms-Marco [11].

With respect to the metrics used for evaluation, we selected map, ndcg and ndcg@20. The first two take into account the first 1000 candidates of the ranking, while ndcg@20 focuses on the top positions.

Table 1 shows the results obtained for the different BERT pretained models on the development and test sets[5]. First, all neural systems clearly outperform both Indri baselines (statistically significant -$p < 0.01$-). The second results that stands out is the fact that the generated pseudo-qrels indeed are suitable to adapt pretrained neural models to the COVID-19 domain. All neural models trained on pseudo-qrels outperform the two models trained solely on MS-Marco (statistically significant -$p < 0.05$- for ndcg and map metrics).

With respect to pretrained BERT models used as the basis for neural rerankers, if we look at the results on the development set (columns 3–5 in Table 1) using *titles* pseudo-qrels, CBERT obtains the best result for all three metrics, excluding the combination. However, that superiority is not repeated on the test set, where CBERT *titles* is only best in terms of ndcg@20.

With the results obtained on the development set in hand, we limited the fine-tuning with *cites* pseudo-qrels to CBERT. CBERT *cites* performs poorly on the dev set, compared to CBERT *title*, but surpasses it on the test in terms of ndcg. Finally, combining both pseudo signals further improves (statistically

---

[3] MAP, BPREF, P@[5, 10, 20], ndcg and ndcg@[10, 20] were considered.

[4] Parameters tuned on dev: $weight = 0.5$, $fbterms = 25$, $fbdocs = 45$.

[5] Significance tests are done using Paired Randomization Test [13].

Table 1. Results on the test-set of topic.

	k	Dev			Test		
		ndcg	ndcg@20	Map	ndcg	ndcg@20	Map
Baselines							
Indri	–	45.96	48.98	20.33	47.15	63.86	23.54
Indri+PRF	–	48.15	58.97	22.87	49.75	68.73	25.84
General domain models							
BERT-base *title*	0.9	55.46	66.00	30.56	55.92	74.38	33.15
BERT-large *title*	0.3	54.84	69.62	29.20	55.20	74.49	32.35
BERT-base-msmarco	0.2	51.05	61.76	25.52	53.29	70.52	29.46
BERT-large-msmarco	0.9	51.47	64.16	27.10	54.05	73.28	30.41
BERT-base-msmarco-*title*	0.9	54.64	67.84	30.17	56.15	74.16	33.60
BERT-large-msmarco-*title*	0.9	54.52	65.76	30.29	56.07	73.47	33.65
Domain specific models							
CBERT *title*	0.9	55.97	70.51	31.00	55.83	**75.00**	32.81
CBERT *cites*	0.2	54.01	60.74	27.85	56.85	71.06	32.83
Combination							
CBERT *title+cites*	1.0	**56.33**	**71.9**	**32.85**	**57.5**	68.65	**34.41**

significant at $p < 0.05$ with respect to CBERT *title*) the performance of the reranker, as the last row on Table 1 shows. These results suggest that both strategies for generating pseudo-qrels provide complementary knowledge.

As a final notice, "large" models do not provide any clear gain over their "base" counterparts.

5   Conclusions

This work shows that it is feasible to train a neural retrieval system based on BERT pretrained models for COVID-19 domain using pseudo-qrels extracted from the target collection.

We have presented two alternatives to generate pseudo qrel data from the target collection, exploiting title-abstract relation and cites to other papers. These pseudo-qrels are used to train neural classifiers which are part of an ad-hoc IR system. Experiments on TREC-COVID shared task data show that the training data generated in this manner provides significant improvement over robust baselines. There are no significant differences between using general pretrained models such as BERT and domain specific models such as CBERT.

Acknowledgement. This work has been partially funded by the Basque Government (DeepText, (Elkartek grant no. KK-2020/00088) and by VIGICOVID project FSuperaCovid-5 (Fondo Supera COVID-19/CRUE-CSIC-Santander). We also acknowledge the support of Googles's TFRC program.

References

1. Alsentzer, E., Murphy, J., Boag, W., Weng, W.H., Jin, D., Naumann, T., McDermott, M.: Publicly available clinical BERT embeddings. In: Proceedings of the 2nd Clinical Natural Language Processing Workshop, Minneapolis, Minnesota, USA, pp. 72–78. Association for Computational Linguistics, June 2019. https://doi.org/10.18653/v1/W19-1909. https://www.aclweb.org/anthology/W19-1909
2. Asadi, N., Metzler, D., Elsayed, T., Lin, J.: Pseudo test collections for learning web search ranking functions. In: Proceedings of the 34th International ACM SIGIR Conference on Research and Development in Information Retrieval, pp. 1073–1082 (2011)
3. Dehghani, M., Zamani, H., Severyn, A., Kamps, J., Croft, W.B.: Neural ranking models with weak supervision. In: Proceedings of the 40th International ACM SIGIR Conference on Research and Development in Information Retrieval, pp. 65–74 (2017)
4. Devlin, J., Chang, M.W., Lee, K., Toutanova, K.: Bert: pre-training of deep bidirectional transformers for language understanding. arXiv preprint arXiv:1810.04805 (2018)
5. Dietz, L., Verma, M., Radlinski, F., Craswell, N.: TREC complex answer retrieval overview. In: TREC (2017)
6. Guo, J., Fan, Y., Ai, Q., Croft, W.B.: A deep relevance matching model for ad-hoc retrieval. In: Proceedings of the 25th ACM International on Conference on Information and Knowledge Management, pp. 55–64 (2016)
7. Hui, K., Yates, A., Berberich, K., De Melo, G.: CO-PACRR: a context-aware neural IR model for ad-hoc retrieval. In: Proceedings of the Eleventh ACM International Conference on Web Search and Data Mining, pp. 279–287 (2018)
8. MacAvaney, S., Hui, K., Yates, A.: An approach for weakly-supervised deep information retrieval. arXiv preprint arXiv:1707.00189 (2017)
9. Mitra, B., Diaz, F., Craswell, N.: Learning to match using local and distributed representations of text for web search. In: Proceedings of the 26th International Conference on World Wide Web, pp. 1291–1299 (2017)
10. Nguyen, T., Rosenberg, M., Song, X., Gao, J., Tiwary, S., Majumder, R., Deng, L.: Ms marco: a human-generated machine reading comprehension dataset. arXiv preprint arXiv:1611.09268 (2016)
11. Nogueira, R., Cho, K.: Passage re-ranking with BERT. arXiv preprint arXiv:1901.04085 (2019)
12. Ponte, J.M., Croft, W.B.: A language modeling approach to information retrieval. In: Proceedings of the 21st annual international ACM SIGIR Conference on Research and Development in Information Retrieval, pp. 275–281 (1998)
13. Smucker, M.D., Allan, J., Carterette, B.: A comparison of statistical significance tests for information retrieval evaluation. In: CIKM 2007: Proceedings of the Sixteenth ACM Conference on Conference on Information and Knowledge Management, New York, NY, USA, pp. 623–632. ACM (2007). http://doi.acm.org/10.1145/1321440.1321528
14. Strohman, T., Metzler, D., Turtle, H., Croft, W.B.: Indri: a language model-based search engine for complex queries. In: Proceedings of the International Conference on Intelligent Analysis, vol. 2, pp. 2–6. Citeseer (2005)
15. Wang, L.L., et al.: Cord-19: the covid-19 open research dataset. ArXiv (2020)
16. Xiong, C., Dai, Z., Callan, J., Liu, Z., Power, R.: End-to-end neural ad-hoc ranking with kernel pooling. In: Proceedings of the 40th International ACM SIGIR Conference on Research and Development in Information Retrieval, pp. 55–64 (2017)

17. Yang, W., Zhang, H., Lin, J.: Simple applications of BERT for ad hoc document retrieval. arXiv preprint arXiv:1903.10972 (2019)
18. Zhang, K., Xiong, C., Liu, Z., Liu, Z.: Selective weak supervision for neural information retrieval. In: Proceedings of The Web Conference 2020, pp. 474–485 (2020)

Windowing Models for Abstractive Summarization of Long Texts

Leon Schüller[1], Florian Wilhelm[2], Nico Kreiling[2], and Goran Glavaš[1(✉)]

[1] Data and Web Science Group, University of Mannheim, Mannheim, Germany
goran@informatik.uni-mannheim.de
[2] inovex GmbH, Pforzheim, Germany
{fwilhelm,nkreiling}@inovex.de

Abstract. Neural summarization models have a fixed-size input limitation: if text length surpasses the model's maximal input length, some document content (possibly summary-relevant) gets truncated. Independently summarizing windows of maximal input size disallows for information flow between windows and leads to incoherent summaries. We propose windowing models for neural abstractive summarization of (arbitrarily) long texts. We extend the sequence-to-sequence model augmented with pointer generator network by (1) allowing the encoder to slide over different windows of the input document and (2) sharing the decoder and retaining its state across different input windows. We explore two windowing variants: Static Windowing precomputes the number of tokens for the decoder to generate from each window (based on training corpus statistics); in Dynamic Windowing the decoder learns to emit a token signaling the shift to the next input window. Empirical results render our models effective in intended use-case: summarizing long texts with relevant content not bound to document beginning.

Keywords: Abstractive summarization · Dynamic long text summarization

1 Background and Motivation

While extractive summarization selects and copies the most relevant source phrases and sentences to the summary, abstractive summarization (AS) aims to capture the source meaning and generate summaries not necessarily containing portions of the source texts [13], holding promise of producing summaries more like human created ones. State-of-the-art neural AS models [11,12,14–16,18] extend a standard sequence-to-sequence (Seq2Seq) architecture, using either recurrent (RNN) [1] or Transformer-based [17] encoder and decoder components. See et al. [15] extend the standard Seq2Seq model with a pointer-generator network (PG-Net), providing the model with extractive capabilities, i.e., allowing it to choose between generating a token and copying source text tokens. Tan et al. [16] propose a hierarchical model that introduces an additional graph-based attention mechanism which serves to model interactions between encoded

© Springer Nature Switzerland AG 2021
D. Hiemstra et al. (Eds.): ECIR 2021, LNCS 12657, pp. 384–392, 2021.
https://doi.org/10.1007/978-3-030-72240-1_39

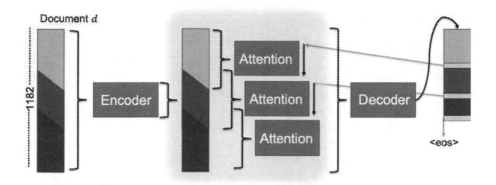

Fig. 1. High-level illustration of the windowing model for long document summarization.

sentence representations. Paulus et al. [14] incorporate a reward expectation based on reinforcement learning into a mixed training objective to steer the model towards predicting globally meaningful sequences.

With respect to long-document summarization, Celikyilmaz et al. [2] distribute the encoding task to multiple collaborating encoder agents, whereas Cohan et al. [3] propose a hierarchical encoder that captures the document's discourse structure, and an attentive discourse-aware decoder that generates the summary. The latter requires a predefined discourse structure and is designed for domain-specific texts (e.g., scientific publications). Despite multiple encoders operating on different document segments, these models still limit the maximal document length at inference.

In this work, we address a prominent limitation of neural AS models: they cannot summarize texts longer than the maximal input length T_x set during model training. At inference, documents longer than T_x tokens are truncated, which renders the (potentially summary-relevant) truncated content inaccessible to the model. We propose novel AS models based on windowing of source text: we sequentially shift encoder's attention over different windows of source text. The decoder is shared across windows, thereby preserving semantic information from a previous window when decoding the next. We investigate two windowing strategies: (1) Static Windowing Model (SWM) precomputes, based on the training corpus statistics, the number of tokens the decoder is to generate from each source window; (2) for the Dynamic Windowing Model (DWM), we first heuristically, based on semantic similarity between source text and summary sentences, inject special *window-shift* tokens into the training reference summaries and then let the decoder learn to emit window-shift tokens during generation. Signaling the window shift by generating a special token, allows DWM to summarize arbitrarily long texts during inference. Evaluation on the WikiHow corpus [8] of long texts with more balanced distribution of summary-relevant content renders our windowing models effective.

2   Windowing as Models

Figure 1 contains the high-level depiction of the windowing AS model. We start from the attention-based Seq2Seq model with recurrent components [1],[1] which maps the input sequence $x_1, ..., x_{T_x}$ into an output sequence $y_1, ..., y_{T_y}$. A bidirectional LSTM (Bi-LSTM) encoder produces contextualized representations $h_j = [\overrightarrow{h}_j; \overleftarrow{h}_j]$ for each input token. Decoder's state is initialized with the concatenation of the end states of encoder's LSTMs ($s_0 = [\overrightarrow{h}_{T_x}; \overleftarrow{h}_1]$). We apply an attention mechanism similar to Luong et al. [10]. However, instead of learning a local attention span around each source text position – which would limit the model to a fixed-size input during training – we attend over a window of T_w tokens and sequentially slide the window over the long text. This way the decoder learns to model transitions between content windows, allowing to summarize arbitrarily long documents at inference.

Window size T_w and a stride step ss, divide the source text (T_x tokens) into overlapping windows.[2] We use the same decoder, retaining its state, across all input windows. Sharing a decoder across input windows allows the flow of semantic information between adjacent windows and holds promise of retaining summary coherence. At each decoding step t, we attend over the window representations, using the decoder's hidden state s_t as the attention query, and obtain the conditioned window encoding c_t (for the decoding step t): $c_t = \sum_{j \in T_w} \alpha_{t,j} h_j$, with attention weight $\alpha_{t,j}$ computed as the softmax-normalized value of the dot-product $s_t^\top h_j$ between the encoded token h_j and the decoder's state s_t. Decoder outputs the embedding l_t via feed-forward projection of the concatenation of the attended input representation c_t and its own hidden state s_t: $l_t = W_l \tanh([c_t; s_t]) + b_l$, with $W_l \in \mathbb{R}^{d \times 2d}, b_l \in \mathbb{R}^d$ as parameters. The output probability distribution P_V (over training vocabulary V) is then simply computed by applying the softmax function on the vector of dot-product values computed between l_t and each of the (pretrained) word embeddings.

We augment the Seq2Seq model with the pointer-generator network (PG-Net), as in [15], allowing decoder to choose in each step between generating a token from the training vocabulary and copying a token from the source document, with the generation probability computed from context vector c_t, decoder's state s_t, and decoder's input x_t:

$$p_{gen} = \sigma(w_c^\top c_t + w_s^\top s_t + w_x^\top x_t + b_{ptr}) \qquad (1)$$

with $w_c, w_s \in \mathbb{R}^d, w_x \in \mathbb{R}^{d_{emb}}, b_{ptr} \in \mathbb{R}$ as parameters. The output probability for a word x from the extended vocabulary $\hat{V}$ (union of V and source text words) interpolates between generation and copying distributions:

$$P_{\hat{V}}(x) = p_{gen} \cdot P_V(x) + (1 - p_{gen}) \sum_{j:x_j=x} \alpha_{t,j} \qquad (2)$$

---

[1] We experimented also with Transformer [17] encoder/decoder, but obtained worse results.
[2] We pad the last window(s), if shorter than T_w tokens.

This specifies the PG-Net-augmented Seq2Seq AS model that operates on a window (T_w tokens). We next specify when to transition from one window of source text to another.

2.1 Static Windowing

The Static Windowing Model precomputes the number of tokens the decoder needs to generate for each input window. Let $\{w_1, w_2, \ldots, w_N\}$ be the equally-sized source windows (determined with T_w and ss). We use the following function to determine the importance (weight) for each window: $e_s(w_i) = \exp(-k(1 + i \cdot d^i))$, with k and d as parameters defining the shape of the summary distribution over windows.[3] The unnormalized weights $e_s(w_i)$ are converted into probabilities using the softmax function. We next compute the expected summary length for a given document, based on the document length and training corpus statistics. Let D be the set of documents and S the set of their respective reference summaries in the training corpus. We compute the expected summary length for a new document d as:

$$\mathbb{E}(|s|)_d = majority(|S|) \cdot \frac{|d|}{majority(|D|)} \tag{3}$$

where $majority(|D|)$ is the length that covers 90% of training documents (i.e., 90% of $d \in D$ are at most $majority(|D|)$) and $Majority(|S|)$ is the length that covers 90% of reference summaries from S. The number of tokens the decoder is to generate for a window w_i is now simply a product of $\mathbb{E}(|s|)_d$ and the normalized weight $c_s(w_i)$.

2.2 Dynamic Windowing

SWM still relies on the document (and summary) lengths of the training corpus, and the number of summary tokens decoded for a window does not depend it's content. Dynamic Windowing Model (DWM) aims to be more flexible, by allowing the decoder to dynamically signal, via a special token, the saturation of the current window and shift to the next. Because (1) the decoder needs to learn to emit this window-shift token ($\rightarrow$), and (2) we still want an end-to-end trainable AS model, we need to somehow inject window-shift tokens ($\rightarrow$) into reference summaries of the training corpus. We achieve this heuristically, by computing semantic similarity scores between source text sentences and reference summary sentences. We simply obtain the sentence embedding as a sum of word embeddings and compute the cosine similarity between sentence embeddings.[4]

---

[3] For example, with $d = 1.2$ and $k = 0.8$, the early windows will receive larger weights than the later windows.

[4] This is a rudimentary method for computing semantic sentence similarity. We will experiment with cutting-edge sentence embedding models [4,5,9,19, *inter alia*] in subsequent work.

For every reference summary sentence, we identify the most similar source document sentence and determine its respective window.[5] This way we map each reference summary sentence to one source window. The order of windows assigned to summary sentences is, however, not necessarily sequential (e.g., $[1, 3, 2, 4, 3]$ for some reference summary with five sentences). Since our model allows only sequential window shifts, we first make the window order sequential by replacing sequence-breaking windows with accumulated maximums (e.g., $[1, 3, 2, 4, 3]$ becomes $[1, 3, 3, 4, 4]$). We then inject window-shift tokens ($\rightarrow$) between summary sentences with different assigned source windows (e.g., for the window assignment $[1, 3, 3, 4, 4]$ we inject $\rightarrow \rightarrow$ between the first and second summary sentence and $\rightarrow$ between the third and fourth sentence). During inference, the input window is shifted whenever the decoder outputs the $\rightarrow$ token.

3   Evaluation

Data. We evaluate our windowing models on two benchmark datasets: (1) CNN/Dailymail news corpus, created by [12] from the question answering dataset of Hermann et al. [6] and (2) WikiHow corpus [8]. News place the most relevant information at the beginning (the so-called lead-and-body principle): the standard models that truncate long documents are thus likely to perform well in the CNN/Dailymail evaluation. The WikiHow dataset does not have such a construction bias – summary-relevant information is more evenly distributed across the texts.

Experimental Setup. We use the negative log likelihood objective and optimize the models by maximizing the ROUGE-L performance on development sets. We use a batch-level beam search decoder with beam size $B = 3$. Unlike standard beam search, B does not decrease when the end-of-summary token (<eos>) is predicted. Longer yet incomplete partial hypotheses can thus take over completed beams whenever they prevail in terms of length-normalized log probability. We set the hidden state sizes for both encoder's LSTMs and decoder's LSTM to 256. We employ the Adam optimizer [7] ($\beta_1 = 0.9$, $\beta_2 = 0.999$, and $\epsilon = 1e-8$). For word representations, we use pretrained 300-dim. fastText embeddings (50,000 most frequent words)[6]

Baselines. We compare different variants of SWM and DWM against the standard PG-Net Seq2Seq model (STAN) with the fixed-size input [15], as well as against the commonly employed LEAD-3 baseline, which simply copies the first three document sentences to the summary.

Results and Discussion. Table 1 contains the results on the CNN/Dailymail dataset. Unsurprisingly, the simple LEAD-3 baseline outperforms *Stan* and both our static and dynamic windowing models. This is because in CNN/Dailymail

---

[5] Depending on T_w and ss, a sentence can appear in more than one window. In such cases, we map the sentence to its last containing window.

[6] https://tinyurl.com/y3y69h3z.

Table 1. Results on the CNN/Dailymail test set: summaries of $T_y = 125$ tokens; STAN trained with fixed-size input of $T_x = 400$ tokens; SWM ($d = 1.2$, $k = 0.8$) & DWM trained on $T_x = 1160$ tokens, with windows of $T_w = 400$ tokens (stride $ss = 380$).

Model	R-1	R-2	R-L
LEAD-3	39.89	17.22	36.08
STAN	37.85	16.48	34.95
Static Windowing (SWM)	37.11	16.01	34.37
Dynamic Windowing (DWM)	36.02	15.67	33.28

documents almost all of the summary-relevant content is found at the very beginning of the document. The ability to process all windows does not benefit to SWM and DWM in this setting as there is virtually no summary-relevant content in later windows.

In Table 2 we display the results on the WikiHow dataset, which is bound to be more appropriate for the windowing models, because of the more even distribution of the summary-relevant content across the source documents. On the WikiHow dataset, the windowing models – SWM and DWM – generally have an edge over the standard PG-Net Seq2Seq model (STAN) when the fixed-size input for STAN matches the windows size of the windowing models. For a larger input size $T_x = 400$, STAN performs comparably to DWM with the same window size $T_w = 400$. Notably, the DWM has the advantage of being able to process longer overall input. Lowering T_x for STAN to 200 and comparing it against SWM/DWM with windows of the same size $T_w = 200$, we see that the windowing models clearly prevail. This renders our windowing models as a more appropriate solution for summarization of documents for which the following two properties hold: (1) the document length massively surpasses the maximal number of tokens we can feed to the fixed-input-size model and (2) summary-relevant information is present all across the document, and not just at its beginning. SWM seems to outperform DWM, but in practice it cannot really summarize arbitrarily long texts. Despite transitioning across windows, SWM adapts to summary lengths seen in training corpus and generates the <eos> token too early during inference

Table 2. Results on the WikiHow dataset ($T_y = 125$, $d = 0$ for SWM).

Model	T_x	T_w/ss	R-1	R-2	R-L
LEAD-3	–	–	24.24	5.31	21.86
STAN	200	–	22.84	7.89	22.38
Dynamic Windowing (DWM)	740	200/180	26.15	8.63	25.48
STAN	400	–	27.54	9.59	26.85
Static Windowing (SWM)	780	400/380	28.25	9.71	27.55
Dynamic Windowing (DWM)	780	400/380	27.23	9.51	26.49

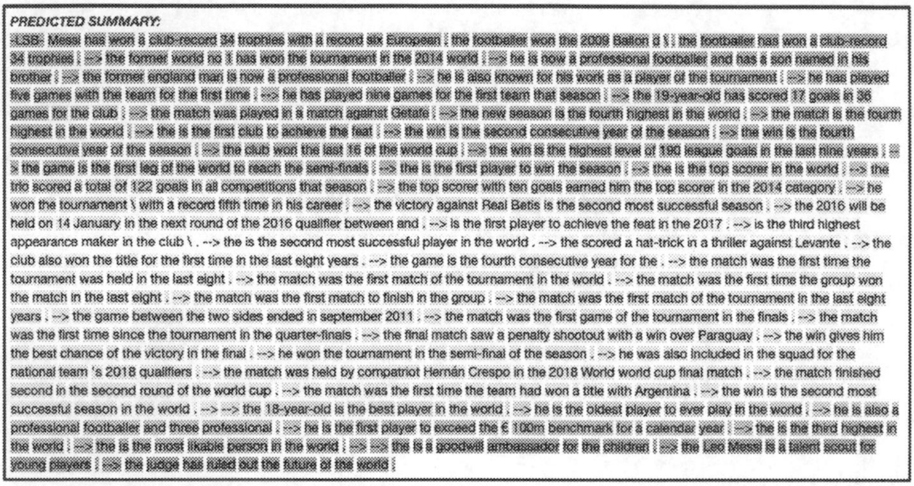

PREDICTED SUMMARY:
-LSB- Messi has won a club-record 34 trophies with a record six European : the footballer won the 2009 Ballon d'\ : the footballer has won a club-record 34 trophies : --> the former world no 1 has won the tournament in the 2014 world : --> he is now a professional footballer and has a son named in his brother : --> the former england man is now a professional footballer : --> he is also known for his work as a player of the tournament : --> he has played five games with the team for the first time : --> he has played nine games for the first team that season : --> the 19-year-old has scored 17 goals in 36 games for the club : --> the match was played in a match against Getafe : --> the new season is the fourth highest in the world : --> the match is the fourth highest in the world : --> the is the first club to achieve the feat : --> the win is the second consecutive year of the season : --> the win is the fourth consecutive year of the season : --> the club won the last 16 of the world cup : --> the win is the highest level of 190 league goals in the last nine years : --> the game is the first leg of the world to reach the semi-finals : --> the is the first player to win the season : --> the is the top scorer in the world : --> the trio scored a total of 122 goals in all competitions that season : --> the top scorer with ten goals earned him the top scorer in the 2014 category : --> he won the tournament \ with a record fifth time in his career : --> the victory against Real Betis is the second most successful season : --> the 2016 will be held on 14 January in the next round of the 2016 qualifier between and . --> is the first player to achieve the feat in the 2017 : --> is the third highest appearance maker in the club \ . --> the is the second most successful player in the world . --> the scored a hat-trick in a thriller against Levante . --> the club also won the title for the first time in the last eight years . --> the game is the fourth consecutive year for the . --> the match was the first time the tournament was held in the last eight . --> the match was the first match of the tournament in the last eight . --> the match was the first time the group won the match in the last eight . --> the match was the first match to finish in the group . --> the match was the first match of the tournament in the last eight years . --> the game between the two sides ended in september 2011 . --> the match was the first game of the tournament in the finals . --> the match was the first time since the tournament in the quarter-finals . --> the final match saw a penalty shootout with a win over Paraguay . --> the win gives him the best chance of the victory in the final . --> he won the tournament in the semi-final of the season . --> he was also included in the squad for the national team 's 2018 qualifiers . --> the match was held by compatriot Hernán Crespo in the 2018 World world cup final match . --> the match finished second in the second round of the world cup . --> the match was the first time the team had won a title with Argentina . --> the win is the second most successful season in the world . --> --> the 18-year-old is the best player in the world . --> he is the oldest player to ever play in the world . --> he is also a professional footballer and three professional : --> he is the first player to exceed the € 100m benchmark for a calendar year : --> the is the third highest in the world : --> the is the most likable person in the world : --> the is a goodwill ambassador for the children : --> the Leo Messi is a talent scout for young players : --> the judge has ruled but the future of the world :

Fig. 2. Summary for the Wikipedia page "Lionel Messi" (13.607 tokens) produced by DWM trained on CNN/Dailymail ($T_x = 1.160$ tokens). Colors correspond to different source text windows over which the decoder attended during generation.

on the long texts. In contrast, the Dynamic Windowing Model can truly generate summaries for arbitrarily long texts at inference time, regardless of the observed lengths of training document. Figure 2 depicts the summary of a very long document (13.607 tokens), produced by a DWS model trained on an order of magnitude shorter documents ($T_x = 1.160$ tokens).

4   Conclusion

Neural summarization models fix the length of the source texts in training (e.g., based on the average source document length in the training set), forcing documents longer than this threshold to be truncated at inference. In this work, we proposed windowing summarization models, which allow to process arbitrarily long documents at inference, taking into account full source text. Our models are effective in summarizing long texts with evenly distributed summary-relevant content.

Acknowledgment. The work of Goran Glavaš is supported by the Baden Württemberg Stiftung (Eliteprogramm, AGREE grant).

References

1. Bahdanau, D., Cho, K., Bengio, Y.: Neural machine translation by jointly learning to align and translate. In: Proceedings of ICLR (2015). http://arxiv.org/abs/1409. 0473
2. Celikyilmaz, A., Bosselut, A., He, X., Choi, Y.: Deep communicating agents for abstractive summarization. In: Proceedings of the 2018 Conference of the North American Chapter of the Association for Computational Linguistics: Human Language Technologies, volume 1 (Long Papers), pp. 1662–1675 (2018)
3. Cohan, A., Dernoncourt, F., Kim, D.S., Bui, T., Kim, S., Chang, W., Goharian, N.: A discourse-aware attention model for abstractive summarization of long documents. In: Proceedings of the 2018 Conference of the North American Chapter of the Association for Computational Linguistics: Human Language Technologies, vol. 2 (Short Papers), pp. 615–621 (2018)
4. Conneau, A., Kiela, D., Schwenk, H., Barrault, L., Bordes, A.: Supervised learning of universal sentence representations from natural language inference data. In: Proceedings of the 2017 Conference on Empirical Methods in Natural Language Processing, pp. 670–680 (2017)
5. Devlin, J., Chang, M.W., Lee, K., Toutanova, K.: Bert: pre-training of deep bidirectional transformers for language understanding. In: Proceedings of the 2019 Conference of the North American Chapter of the Association for Computational Linguistics: Human Language Technologies, Volume 1 (Long and Short Papers), pp. 4171–4186 (2019)
6. Hermann, K.M., et al.: Teaching machines to read and comprehend. In: Advances in Neural Information Processing Systems, pp. 1693–1701 (2015)
7. Kingma, D.P., Ba, J.: Adam: a method for stochastic optimization. In: ICLR (2015)
8. Koupaee, M., Wang, W.Y.: Wikihow: a large scale text summarization dataset. CoRR abs/1810.09305 (2018). http://arxiv.org/abs/1810.09305
9. Kusner, M., Sun, Y., Kolkin, N., Weinberger, K.: From word embeddings to document distances. In: International Conference on Machine Learning, pp. 957–966 (2015)
10. Luong, M., Pham, H., Manning, C.D.: Effective approaches to attention-based neural machine translation. In: Proceedings of EMNLP, pp. 1412–1421 (2015). http://arxiv.org/abs/1508.04025
11. Makino, T., Iwakura, T., Takamura, H., Okumura, M.: Global optimization under length constraint for neural text summarization. In: Proceedings of the 57th Annual Meeting of the Association for Computational Linguistics, pp. 1039–1048 (2019). https://www.aclweb.org/anthology/P19-1099
12. Nallapati, R., Xiang, B., Zhou, B.: Sequence-to-sequence RNNs for text summarization. In: Proceedings of ICLR: Workshop Track (2016). http://arxiv.org/abs/1602.06023
13. Nenkova, A., McKeown, K.R.: Automatic summarization. Found. Trends Inf. Retr. 5(2–3), 103–233 (2011)
14. Paulus, R., Xiong, C., Socher, R.: A deep reinforced model for abstractive summarization. In: Proceedings of ICLR (2018). http://arxiv.org/abs/1705.04304
15. See, A., Liu, P.J., Manning, C.D.: Get to the point: summarization with pointer-generator networks. In: Proceedings of the 55th Annual Meeting of the Association for Computational Linguistics (Volume 1: Long Papers), pp. 1073–1083 (2017)

16. Tan, J., Wan, X., Xiao, J.: Abstractive document summarization with a graph-based attentional neural model. In: Proceedings of the 55th Annual Meeting of the Association for Computational Linguistics (Volume 1: Long Papers), pp. 1171–1181. Association for Computational Linguistics (2017). https://doi.org/10.18653/v1/P17-1108. http://aclweb.org/anthology/P17-1108
17. Vaswani, A., et al.: Attention is all you need. In: Proceedings of NeurIPS (2017)
18. You, Y., Jia, W., Liu, T., Yang, W.: Improving abstractive document summarization with salient information modeling. In: Proceedings of the 57th Annual Meeting of the Association for Computational Linguistics, pp. 2132–2141 (2019). https://www.aclweb.org/anthology/P19-1205
19. Zhelezniak, V., Savkov, A., Shen, A., Moramarco, F., Flann, J., Hammerla, N.Y.: Don't settle for average, go for the max: fuzzy sets and max-pooled word vectors. In: Proceedings of ICLR (2019)

Towards Dark Jargon Interpretation in Underground Forums

Dominic Seyler[1]([✉]), Wei Liu[1], XiaoFeng Wang[2], and ChengXiang Zhai[1]

[1] University of Illinois at Urbana-Champaign, Champaign, IL, USA
{dseyler2,weil8,czhai}@illinois.edu
[2] Indiana University Bloomington, Bloomington, USA
xw7@indiana.edu

Abstract. Dark jargons are benign-looking words that have hidden, sinister meanings and are used by participants of underground forums for illicit behavior. For example, the dark term "rat" is often used in lieu of "Remote Access Trojan". In this work we present a novel method towards automatically identifying and interpreting dark jargons. We formalize the problem as a mapping from dark words to "clean" words with no hidden meaning. Our method makes use of interpretable representations of dark and clean words in the form of probability distributions over a shared vocabulary. In our experiments we show our method to be effective in terms of dark jargon identification, as it outperforms another baseline on simulated data. Using manual evaluation, we show that our method is able to detect dark jargons in a real-world underground forum dataset.

Keywords: Dark jargon · Hidden meaning interpretation · NLP

1 Introduction

When bad actors communicate in underground forums (e.g., Silk Road [5]), they often use jargons to obfuscate their true intentions. They make use of dark jargons, which are benign-looking words that have hidden, sinister meanings, especially among communities in underground forums. For example, when a user posts a thread wanting a "rat", what he/she might really want is malware, i.e., "Remote Access Trojan". As those jargons facilitate an enormous underground economy [18], identifying the real meaning of dark words is essential for understanding cybercrime activities and is an important step in order to measure, monitor and mitigate illicit activity.

Recently, there has been substantial research interest in the intersection of Cybersecurity, Information Retrieval [7–9,11,12,15,16,19], and Natural Language Processing [13,17,22–24]. However, dark jargon detection and interpretation has not been well studied since only two works are directly related: Yang et al. [20] proposes to detect dark jargon by utilizing a search engine. The authors scrape data from pages that tend to contain dark terms, filter out key words and use the search engine's similar search function to discover new dark words. Yuan

© Springer Nature Switzerland AG 2021
D. Hiemstra et al. (Eds.): ECIR 2021, LNCS 12657, pp. 393–400, 2021.
https://doi.org/10.1007/978-3-030-72240-1_40

et al. [21] leverages the context of a word as a representation for the word's meaning. The intuition is that dark words in dark forums appear in drastically different contexts compared to reputable online corpora (e.g., Wikipedia). Dark words are categorized into five general classes. For example, "blueberry" is categorized as "drug" and not as "marijuana", which would be more beneficial for interpretation. We address this limitation as our method provides more interpretable meaning representations by utilizing probability distributions over context words. Another shortcoming of previous approaches is that the actual meaning of the identified dark jargon is mostly unknown. We alleviate this problem by making our framework more expressive and allow dark terms to be mapped to any word/category where the meaning is known. Furthermore, our framework is completely general as it does not require external resources, such as Wikipedia or a search engine.

We formalize the problem of finding underground jargon into a general framework of finding a probabilistic mapping function of dark words to word meanings. We investigate a specific case of this general framework where we find binary mappings of dark words to "clean" words, which are words that have no hidden meaning. Further, we develop novel methodology to find dark jargon words in underground forums automatically using the difference in word distributions. This methodology enables us to create interpretable representations of jargon words that can be used to further explain their hidden meanings. In our experiments we make use of a dark corpus of underground forums and evaluate our methodology. We find that our method successfully identifies dark words in a simulated and a real-world setting.

2   Approach

2.1   General Framework

In our general framework we use words with no hidden meanings as an direct explanation for the hidden meaning of dark jargon words. Thus, in the most general sense we are interested in a mapping function $hidden\_meaning(V_{dark})$ that takes as input a vocabulary of dark words V_{dark} and outputs a mapping to a vocabulary of "clean" words V_{clean}, with no hidden meaning. This mapping can be a probability distribution, which expresses the probability of relatedness of a dark word in V_{dark} to all clean words in V_{clean}.

In this work, we investigate the specific case where the probability distribution is forced to have only a single element with probability 1.0. Thus, we are interested in a binary mapping from V_{dark} to V_{clean}. However, it is possible to retrieve a more fine-grained distribution, which we leave for future work.

2.2   Problem Setup

Our problem setup is as follows: given two text corpora, a dark corpus C_{dark} and a clean corpus C_{clean}, the goal is to find the words that are likely to have hidden meanings in the dark corpus and identify their true meaning. We further build a joint vocabulary V, which is the most frequent N words from the union of C_{dark} and C_{clean}. Then, for each word $w_d \in C_{dark}$ we want to find a word $w_c \in C_{clean}$, such that w_c expresses the hidden meaning of w_d.

We first get a word vector for each word in both corpora, such that every word $w \in V$ has two word vectors w_d and w_c. Second, for each w_d, we rank all clean word vectors, such that we find the words in C_{clean} that are most similar to w_d, thereby assuming that the meaning of w_d is related to closeness of words in C_{clean} according to some similarity measure.

We propose to use two methodologies for achieving this mapping. We first introduce a novel method based on word distributions and Kullback-Leibler-divergence [10]. We then find another suitable method in cross-context lexical analysis [14]. In our experiments we compare both methods to understand which one is more performance for our task.

2.3   Word Distribution Modeling and KL-Divergence

We start by introducing the word distribution and KL-divergence method. The intuition is that a dark word, e.g., "rat", will appear in different contexts than the clean word "rat". It will therefore have a context more similar to a clean word like "malware", as it would have to "mouse". When we represent word contexts as probability distributions over words, we find that "rat" in the dark corpus and "malware" in the clean corpus have the most similar distributions.

For each word in our vocabulary V, we build a unigram probability distribution of all other words in V. In order to build this probability distribution we make use of a sliding window technique, where we look at k words before and after the occurrence of the word under consideration. We choose to employ this technique, since we are interested in a word's immediate context, as compared to the entire document, which is often used in unigram language modes.

More specifically, to build a word distribution for a word $w \in V$, we first get a length $|V|$ all zero word count vector, with each entry mapped to a word in V. We then go through the whole corpus C, and for each occurrence of w, we look at k words before and after it, increase the value of the counter vector at corresponding indices. To get a probability distribution over context words, we perform maximum-likelihood estimation and divide each element in the vector by the sum of all vector elements. We further employ smoothing to handle the zero-value probability problem, where we smooth the word distribution of w. We get two word distributions for each word $w \in V$: One distribution estimated from the dark text $P(w_d|C_{dark})$ and one from the clean text $P(w_c|C_{clean})$. To get two words' dissimilarity $dissim(w_d, w_c)$, we calculate the KL-Divergence between the two probability distributions as in Eq. 1. Finally, for each dark jargon we define it's hidden meaning as the clean word with the lowest dissimilarity to our target dark word w_d (Eq. 2).

$$dissim(w_d, w_c) = KL(P(w_d|C_{dark})||P(w_c|C_{clean})) \tag{1}$$

$$hidden\_meaning_{KL}(w_d) = \underset{w_c \in C_{clean}}{\arg\min} \; dissim(w_d, w_c) \tag{2}$$

2.4   Cross-context Lexical Analysis

Another suitable method for our problem setup is cross-context lexical analysis (CCLA) [14]. Here, the goal is to analyze differences and similarities of words across different contexts. Contexts are usually defined over document collections, which is very akin to our problem setting. Therefore, we can directly apply this methodology to our problem, where the two corpora under consideration are our dark and clean corpora C_{dark} and C_{clean}, respectively. Using CCLA as a framework, we can leverage it as yet another method to measure the difference of words in a clean and dark context.

Following Massung [14], we define a scoring function as in Eq. 3, where $cos(w_1, w_2, C)$ is the cosine similarity of the word vector of w_1 and w_2 computed over corpus C. $NN(w, C, k)$ is the corresponding length-k vector, where each entry has the value of the cosine similarity of w's word vector and the k closest word vectors. W_{common} is the intersection of the set of k words in corpus C with highest similarity to the word vectors w_d and w_c (Eq. 4). Note that our function is a slight variation of Massung [14], as we modify it to be suitable for two input words (w_d, w_c), rather than just a single input word. Essentially, ϕ measures the similarity of the usage of w_d and w_c across C_{dark} and C_{clean}. To generalize, for each word in $w_d \in C_{dark}$, we find a $w_c \in C_{clean}$ that maximizes ϕ, which is then used as the mapping for w_d (Eq. 5).

$$\phi(w_d, w_c, C_{dark}, C_{clean}, k) = \frac{\Sigma_{w \in W_{common}} cos(w, w_d, C_{dark}) * cos(w, w_c, C_{clean})}{||NN(w_d, C_{dark}, k)|| * ||NN(w_c, C_{clean}, k)||} \tag{3}$$

$$W_{common}(w_d, w_c, C_{dark}, C_{clean}, k) = W(w_d, C_{dark}, k) \bigcap W(w_c, C_{clean}, k) \tag{4}$$

$$hidden\_meaning_{CCLA}(w_d) = \underset{w_c \in C_{clean}}{\arg\max} \; \phi(w_d, w_c, C_{dark}, C_{clean}, k) \tag{5}$$

3   Experiments

3.1   Experimental Setup

We aim to answer three research questions: (1) What is the performance of the word distribution method? (2) What is the performance of CCLA compared to the word distribution method? (3) What are the qualitative results in terms of dark jargons identified?

Table 1. Clean-clean Evaluation of the Word Distribution (KL) and Cross-context Lexical Analysis (CCLA) Methods using the Mean Reciprocal Rank (MRR) metric.

Method	MRR all words	MRR dark words
KL	0.909	**0.892**
CCLA	**0.974**	0.479

Datasets. We make use of two datasets in our experiments, where each dataset has stowords and punctuation removed, words are lower-cased and stemmed: (1) *Dark Corpus.* Taken from Yuan et al. [21], our dark corpus contains user posts scraped from four major underground forums: Silk Road [5], Nulled [3], Hackforums [2] and Dark0de [1]. The combined corpus contains 376,989 posts. (2) *Clean Corpus.* The clean corpus contains a web scrape of 1.2 million reddit [4] threads from 1,697 top subreddits in terms the number of subscribers.

Evaluation Environments. In order to answer our research questions, we build two evaluation environments: The first environment aims to evaluate the quantitative performance of our method. Since no gold standard data is available for this task, we decided to simulate the dark jargons in the dataset. The second environment aims to measure the quality of the dark jargons identified on real data. Here, we manually check if the model can find real meanings of dark words on non-simulated data. The two environments are created as follows:

(1) *Clean-Clean*: We randomly split the documents in the clean corpus into two splits. In the first split, namely $clean_1$, we randomly select 500 words and prefix them with a dash ("_"). For example, if the word "strawberry" was selected, a sentence like "John loves **strawberry** milkshakes" would be turned into "John loves **_strawberry** milkshakes". The second split, namely $clean_2$, remains unmodified. Once we run the models on this corpus, for each word in the vocabulary in $clean_1$, we get its corresponding ranking list of nearest words in $clean_2$. We separately investigate the dashed words (words with "_"). For those words, the top-ranked word should be the word itself, i.e., the original word without the dash ("_"). We calculate the mean reciprocal rank (MRR) as a performance evaluation metric for the clean-clean dataset. We separately measure MRR for all words in the vocabulary and for our simulated dark words.

(2) *Dark-Clean*: For the real world dataset, we run our word distribution method and get a ranked list of nearest words in *clean* for each word in *dark*. We then do a manual evaluation of random dark words our method retrieves to find out their hidden meanings.

Hyperparameters. We use the following parameters for our methods, which we empirically found to perform best: We use a vocabulary size of 10,000. For the word distribution method, we use a sliding window size k of 10 and *Laplace*[1]

---

[1] We found that Dirichlet smoothing was less effective.

Table 2. Dark-clean Manual Evaluation based on our Word Distribution Method.

Dark Word	Clean word	Meaning
gdp	kush	Grand Daddy Purps (type of marijuana)
blueberry	kush	Type of marijuana
coke	cocaine	Nickname for cocaine
klonopin	xanax	Sedative medication
shrooms	lsd	Hallucinogenic drug similar to LSD
bubba	kush	Type of marijuana
ecstasy	mdma	Nickname for mdma
dilaudid	oxy, morphine	Strong painkiller (aka: hospital heroin)
pineapple	kush	Type of marijuana
zeus	botnet	Botnet malware
rat	malware	Remote Access Trojan (malware)

smoothing with $\alpha = 1$. For CCLA, we use an embedding size of 300 and a neighborhood size k of 100.

3.2   Experimental Results

We now move on to our experimental results and answer our three research questions. Table 1 shows the results of our proposed word distribution method (KL) and CCLA for all words in the vocabulary and our simulated dark words. To answer our first research question, we see that the KL method performs well, with an MRR around 0.9 for all words in the vocabulary and the simulated dark words. To answer research question two, we find that the CCLA method performs better for all words, however, it is performing much worse for the simulated dark words. Since finding dark words is the goal of our research, we can conclude that KL outperforms CCLA for our task.

To answer research question three, we perform a manual evaluation into the dark words that were identified by our method on a real-world corpus. In Table 2, we present a list of dark words identified by our word distribution method and the clean word that was mapped to the corresponding dark word. We also show the meaning that we manually identified using a slang dictionary or by searching for the highest ranked clean words online. As can be seen from the table, our method retrieves meaningful results since our analysis finds many drug-related and malware-related terms. We take these results as evidence for the potential of our method for finding dark term meanings in a real-world setting.

4   Conclusion and Future Work

We have shown that our approach based on word distributions derived from a word's context is effective for jargon detection and it outperformed a related method based on cross-context lexical analysis. Furthermore, our method leverages word distributions and is therefore inherently interpretable, as individual word probabilities can be thought of as importance weights of a word's context. In the future, we plan to further improve interpretability of dark terms by leveraging external large-scale knowledge resources that define the meaning of slang words, such as Urban Dictionary [6].

Acknowledgment. This material is based upon work supported by the National Science Foundation under Grant No. 1801652.

References

1. Dark0de (forum). https://en.wikipedia.org/wiki/Dark0de
2. Hackforums.https://hackforums.net
3. Nulled (forum). https://www.nulled.to
4. reddit (forum). https://www.reddit.com
5. Silk Road (marketplace). https://en.wikipedia.org/wiki/Silk_Road_(marketplace)
6. Urban dictionary. https://urbandictionary.com
7. Husari, G., Al-Shaer, E., Ahmed, M., Chu, B., Niu, X.: TTPDrill: automatic and accurate extraction of threat actions from unstructured text of CTI sources. In: Proceedings of the 33rd Annual Computer Security Applications Conference, pp. 103–115 (2017)
8. Husari, G., Niu, X., Chu, B., Al-Shaer, E.: Using entropy and mutual information to extract threat actions from cyber threat intelligence. In: International Conference on Intelligence and Security Informatics (ISI), pp. 1–6 (2018)
9. Khandpur, R.P., Ji, T., Jan, S., Wang, G., Lu, C.T., Ramakrishnan, N.: Crowdsourcing cybersecurity: cyber attack detection using social media. In: Proceedings of the Conference on Information and Knowledge Management, pp. 1049–1057 (2017)
10. Kullback, S., Leibler, R.A.: On information and sufficiency. Ann. Math. Stat. **22**(1), 79–86 (1951)
11. Liao, X., Yuan, K., Wang, X., Li, Z., Xing, L., Beyah, R.: Acing the IOC game: toward automatic discovery and analysis of open-source cyber threat intelligence. In: Proceedings of the Conference on Computer and Communications Security, pp. 755–766 (2016)
12. Liao, X., et al.: Seeking nonsense, looking for trouble: efficient promotional-infection detection through semantic inconsistency search. In: Symposium on Security and Privacy (SP) (2016)
13. Lim, S.K., Muis, A.O., Lu, W., Ong, C.H.: MalwaretextDB: a database for annotated malware articles. In: Proceedings of the 55th Annual Meeting of the Association for Computational Linguistics, pp. 1557–1567 (2017)
14. Massung, S.A.: Beyond topic-based representations for text mining. Ph.D. thesis, University of Illinois at Urbana-Champaign (2017)
15. Mittal, S., Das, P.K., Mulwad, V., Joshi, A., Finin, T.: Cybertwitter: using twitter to generate alerts for cybersecurity threats and vulnerabilities. In: Proceedings of the International Conference on Advances in Social Networks Analysis and Mining, pp. 860–867 (2016)

16. Mulwad, V., Li, W., Joshi, A., Finin, T., Viswanathan, K.: Extracting information about security vulnerabilities from web text. In: Proceedings of the International Conferences on Web Intelligence and Intelligent Agent Technology, pp. 257–260 (2011)
17. Seyler, D., Li, L., Zhai, C.: Semantic text analysis for detection of compromised accounts on social networks. In: Proceedings of the International Conference on Advances in Social Network Analysis and Mining (2020)
18. Thomas, K., et al.: Framing dependencies introduced by underground commoditization. In: Workshop on the Economics of Information Security (2015)
19. Tsai, F.S., Chan, K.L.: Detecting cyber security threats in weblogs using probabilistic models. In: Pacific-Asia Workshop on Intelligence and Security Informatics, pp. 46–57 (2007)
20. Yang, H., et al.: How to learn klingon without a dictionary: Detection and measurement of black keywords used by the underground economy. In: Symposium on Security and Privacy (SP), pp. 751–769 (2017)
21. Yuan, K., Lu, H., Liao, X., Wang, X.: Reading thieves' cant: automatically identifying and understanding dark jargons from cybercrime marketplaces. In: USENIX Security Symposium (2018)
22. Zhou, S., Long, Z., Tan, L., Guo, H.: Automatic identification of indicators of compromise using neural-based sequence labelling. In: 32nd Pacific Asia Conference on Language, Information and Computation (2018)
23. Zhu, Z., Dumitras, T.: Featuresmith: automatically engineering features for malware detection by mining the security literature. In: Proceedings of the Conference on Computer and Communications Security, pp. 767–778 (2016)
24. Zhu, Z., Dumitras, T.: Chainsmith: Automatically learning the semantics of malicious campaigns by mining threat intelligence reports. In: European Symposium on Security and Privacy (EuroS&P), pp. 458–472 (2018)

Multi-span Extractive Reading Comprehension Without Multi-span Supervision

Takumi Takahashi[✉], Motoki Taniguchi, Tomoki Taniguchi,
and Tomoko Ohkuma

Fuji Xerox Co., Ltd., Tokyo, Japan
{takahashi.takumi,motoki.taniguchi,
taniguchi.tomoki,ohkuma.tomoko}@fujixerox.co.jp

Abstract. This study focuses on multi-span reading comprehension (RC), which requires answering questions with multiple text spans. Existing approaches for extracting multiple answers require an elaborate dataset that contains questions requiring multiple answers. We propose a method for rewriting single-span answers extracted using several different models to detect single/multiple answer(s). With this approach, only a simple dataset and models for single-span RC are required. We consider multi-span RC with zero-shot learning. Experimental results using the DROP and QUOREF datasets demonstrate that the proposed method improves the exact match (EM) and F1 scores by a large margin on multi-span RC, compared to the baseline models. We further analyzed the effectiveness of combining different models and a strategy for such combinations when applied to multi-span RC.

Keywords: Reading comprehension · Multi-span extraction · Zero-shot learning

1 Introduction

Reading comprehension (RC) is an automatic answering task based on questions from a given context. In extractive RC tasks such as SQuAD [9,10], several models have shown superior performance over humans [4,8,14]. However, such tasks are restricted to answering questions with a single text span (i.e., single-span RC), and questions requiring multiple answers (i.e., multi-span RC) remain unsolved. Multi-span RC increases the difficulty in addressing questions owing to the number of expected answers [5]. Studies on multi-span RC [1,6,11] have required an elaborate dataset that contains questions requiring multiple answers. Although preparing such datasets is demanding, numerous single-span RC datasets [7,9,10,13,15] exist. Therefore, models that can extract multiple answers from a context without multi-span supervision (i.e., zero-shot learning) are worth exploring. This is the first attempt to tackle multi-span RC only with single-span supervision.

© Springer Nature Switzerland AG 2021
D. Hiemstra et al. (Eds.): ECIR 2021, LNCS 12657, pp. 401–409, 2021.
https://doi.org/10.1007/978-3-030-72240-1_41

We hypothesize that simple models for single-span RC can extract fragments of multiple answers from a context individually. To examine the assumption, we performed a preliminary experiment to show the behavior of several RC models. In Fig. 1 (left) we observed that several answers extracted by single-span RC models, including correct and incorrect spans, were scattered within the context. Similarly, unique predictions extracted by several RC models on multi-span RC were more divergent than those on single-span RC, as shown in the right panel of Fig. 1. Therefore, we assume that multiple answers in a specific context can be found through the following operations: *extracting* and *rewriting*.

In this study, we leverage a behavior in which answers extracted by several models are often different on multi-span RC. Specifically, we use single-span RC models to find fragments of multiple answers (*extracting*). Then, our method rewrites the fragments to obtain well-formed answers (*rewriting*). To implement this idea, only a simple dataset and models for single-span RC are required. Our main contributions are as follows:

1. We propose a method for rewriting single-span answers extracted by several single-span RC models to detect single/multiple answer(s) *without* multi-span supervision.
2. We show that the proposed method improves the performance of multi-span RC compared to the baseline models, beyond the limitations of single-span RC models.
3. We analyze a combination of different structural models on multi-span RC including the effectiveness of such models and methods to efficiently combine them.

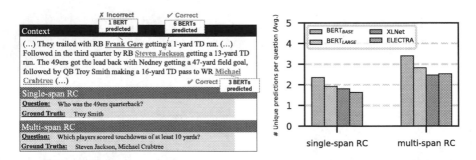

Fig. 1. Left: Example of single/multi-span RC. Underlined text strings in the context are predictions of multi-span RC using ten fine-tuned BERT$_{BASE}$ models. **Right:** Average number of unique predicted answers that were extracted by ten fine-tuned models. The number of unique predictions in a question is equal to 1 if all predictions are completely matched. In both cases, we used DROP (**Dev.**) described in Sect. 3.1.

2   Methodology

We leverage a behavior in which answers extracted by several models are frequently different on multi-span RC. The proposed method is composed of two components: Extractive QA and RC-rewriter. Extractive QA, a set of simple models for single-span RC, is trained *only* on a single-span RC dataset (i.e., zero-shot setting for multi-span RC). To detect answers to a question, RC-rewriter integrates several text spans extracted by Extractive QA into single/multiple answer(s).

Extractive QA

This component extracts fragments of single/multiple answer(s) to a question from a context. Extractive QA is composed of a set of N different extractive RC models, $M = \{m_1, ..., m_N\}$, where each model is trained *only* on a single-span RC dataset in advance. Because Extractive QA admits arbitrary models, m_* is trained using its training procedure, as described in the RC models [4,12,16].

For prediction, the i-th model m_i extracts an answer a_i with a single text span from a given context c as $a_i = m_i(q, c)$, where q is a given question. Finally, a set of detected answers $A^* = \{a_1, ..., a_N\}$ is fed into the RC-rewriter to integrate individually detected answers into well-formed single/multiple answer(s).

RC-Rewriter

This component rewrites a set of extracted answers A^* to obtain single/multiple answer(s). As the key idea of this component, the actual answer A will be a **single answer** if a set of extracted answers A^* is converged in a specific span, and A will be **multiple answers** if A^* is diverged into separated spans.

First, we compute the convergence rate $F = \{f_1, ..., f_{|c|}\}$ of A^* over tokens $T = \{t_1, ..., t_{|c|}\}$ in the context c. Specifically, the convergence rate f_j between the j-th token t_j and A^* is computed as follows:

$$f_j = \frac{1}{|A^*|} \sum_{a \in A^*} \mathbb{1}_{[g_b(a) \leq j \leq g_e(a)]},$$

where $\mathbb{1}_{[\cdot]}$ is an indicator function that returns a value of 1 if the input condition is true, and 0 otherwise. In addition, $g_b(\cdot)$ and $g_e(\cdot)$ are functions that return the start and end positions of its input.

Second, RC-rewriter classifies the j-th token t_j into **single-span**, **multi-span**, or **no-span** as an intermediate label, which is a clue for detecting the final answers. Specifically, the intermediate label s_j of the j-th token t_j is computed as follows: (1) s_j is **single-span** if $f_j \geq u$, (2) s_j is **multi-span** if $u > f_j \geq l$, or (3) s_j is **no-span** if $l > f_j$, where u and l are the thresholds categorizing t_j into three classes. In the first and second steps, these operations are performed on all tokens of T to obtain $S = \{s_1, ..., s_{|c|}\}$.

Finally, the answer A is detected based on intermediate labels S. For multiple spans, A is composed of a set of sequentially continuous tokens classified as **multi-span** if there is no token classified as **single-span**. Otherwise, we obtain sequentially continuous tokens classified as **single-span**.

3   Experiment

3.1   Dataset and Evaluation Metrics

We used the DROP [5] and QUOREF [3] datasets to evaluate our models and compare them to competing approaches. We sampled extractive RC examples from the official dataset and split them into multi-span RC and single-span RC. Because no test split was applied to the official dataset, we used random sampling to divide the official training split into **Train** and **Dev.** at a ratio of 9:1. In the experiment, the official development split was used as **Test**. Because multi-span RC (**train**) was used to train only the fully supervised model described in Sect. 3.2, multi-span RC (**train**) was not used for training other models. The preprocessing was applied to the DROP and QUOREF datasets. The statistics of the datasets are listed in Table 1. To compare our models to competing models, we used the exact match (EM) and F1 scores following the original DROP evaluation metrics [5].

Table 1. Number of triplets of a question, context, and their answers used in the experiment. The training split of multi-span RC (†) is used to train only the fully supervised models.

Dataset	Single-span RC			Multi-span RC		
	Train	Dev.	Test	Train	Dev.	Test
DROP	20,620	2,448	2,749	$4,141^{\dagger}$	477	553
QUOREF	15,758	1,654	2,197	$1,777^{\dagger}$	210	221

3.2   Compared Models

Single-Span Baseline. We used BERT [4], XLNet [14], and ELECTRA [2] as single-span baselines that extract an answer with a single text span. These models predict start and end positions of an answer via two fully connected layers. All models were trained and validated only on single-span RC. Henceforth, ♣, ♢, ♡, and ♠ refer to $BERT_{BASE}$, $BERT_{LARGE}$, XLNet, and ELECTRA, respectively.

Fully Supervised Model. We implemented Multi-span Extractor based on MTMSN [6], which can extract answers with multiple text spans. This model repeatedly extracted multiple answers until the number of extracted spans was the same as the predicted number of spans. Several models, ♣, ♢, ♡, and ♠, were employed as an encoder and span extractor. In addition, a span number predictor was implemented on top of the encoder. This model differs from MTMSN in terms of not containing arithmetic headers because its focus is mainly on span extraction. Note that both single- and multi-span RC were used to train and validate the model.

Oracle$_{single}$**.** We prepared an oracle to evaluate the limitations of single-span RC models. The oracle extracts a correct answer from a list of gold answers where the extracted answer has the highest F1 score.

3.3 Model Configurations

For the Extractive QA, we trained 20 single-span RC models with different random seeds. We used the optimal model validated on single-span RC (**Dev.**) as a single-span baseline. We used Adam with a learning rate of 3e-5 to train all models. For the RC-rewriter, the thresholds u and l were set to 1.0 and 0.2, respectively, by validating with few examples.[1] For other hyperparameters, we used 12, 24, and 32 as the batch sizes of ♣, ◇/♡, and ♠, respectively. The numbers of epochs were set to 20, 10, and 5 for ♣, ◇, and ♡/♠, respectively. The maximum sequence length was limited to 512 tokens. For the fully supervised models, the maximum number of spans was set to 8. Other hyperparameters of the model correspond to each single-span baseline.

Table 2. Performance of our models and the competing models on **Test**.

Model	DROP				QUOREF			
	Multi-span RC		Single-span RC		Multi-span RC		Single-span RC	
Single-span Baseline	EM	F1	EM	F1	EM	F1	EM	F1
BERT$_{BASE}$ (♣)	0	22.0	58.0	64.3	0	27.7	62.8	65.6
BERT$_{LARGE}$ (◇)	0	28.2	70.6	77.2	0	31.2	78.7	82.3
XLNet (♡)	0	**28.8**	73.1	79.5	0	30.9	79.5	83.2
ELECTRA (♠)	0	28.7	**75.6**	**81.9**	0	34.1	**83.2**	**86.2**
Fully Supervised Model	EM	F1	EM	F1	EM	F1	EM	F1
Multi-span Extractor ♣	8.3	38.5	56.5	63.2	21.7	49.7	60.3	63.5
Multi-span Extractor ◇	13.0	48.4	69.0	76.0	30.8	60.9	77.8	81.5
Multi-span Extractor ♡	**14.1**	**51.0**	71.9	77.9	34.8	63.6	79.5	82.7
Multi-span Extractor ♠	11.2	50.9	**75.7**	**82.2**	**39.8**	**67.9**	**82.2**	**85.1**
Zero-shot Multi-span Model	EM	F1	EM	F1	EM	F1	EM	F1
Proposed (♣ × 20 + RC-rewriter)	3.8	31.5	46.4	62.0	8.1	39.8	48.5	61.0
Proposed (◇ × 20 + RC-rewriter)	8.9	41.2	61.2	75.5	15.4	45.3	69.6	79.5
Proposed (♡ × 20 + RC-rewriter)	10.7	42.6	64.1	77.5	**22.2**	49.0	72.2	80.7
Proposed (♠ × 20 + RC-rewriter)	**13.7**	**45.1**	**68.0**	**80.4**	19.5	48.4	**76.0**	**83.7**
Single-span Oracle	EM	F1	EM	F1	EM	F1	EM	F1
Oracle$_{single}$	0	42.0	100	100	0	42.8	100	100

---

[1] 30 examples were randomly sampled from each single- and multi-span RC (**Dev.**). The best u and l were selected from $[0.5, 0.6, 0.7, 0.8, 0.9, 1.0]$ and $[0.1, 0.2, 0.3, 0.4, 0.5]$, respectively.

3.4   Experimental Results

Table 2 presents a summary of the performances of our models and those of the competing models for multi- and single-span RC on **Test**.

Multi-span RC. The proposed method drastically improved the performance of the single-span baselines on both datasets, whereas the single-span baselines indicated the 0% EM scores. In particular, the performance of ♠ × 20 + RC-rewriter on the DROP dataset reached values close to those of the fully supervised models, Multi-span Extractor, trained on both single- and multi-span RC. Furthermore, the proposed method based on ◇, ♡, and ♠ also outperformed Oracle$_{single}$. This indicates that the proposed method can achieve significant success beyond the capabilities of a single-span RC model, even *without* multi-span supervision.

Single-span RC. Compared to the single-span baselines, although the performances of the proposed method were maintained in terms of the F1 score, they decreased in terms of the EM. This is because the proposed method not only extracts the correct answer to a question but also extracts incorrect answers occasionally.[2] In contrast, suppose a naive top-k extractor[3] is applied to single-span RC, the EM of single-span RC is 0%. This suggests that to obtain significant results on both single- and multi-span RC, extracting several answers using different models and rewriting the answers are important in the zero-shot setting.

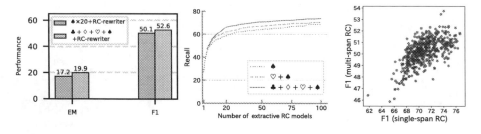

Fig. 2. Left: Effectiveness of combining models with different structures for multi-span RC in the DROP dataset. For a fair comparison, we used five models with different seeds per model. **Middle**: Relationship between recall and number of predictions using single-span RC models for multi-span RC in the DROP dataset. **Right**: Pearson correlation between F1 scores for single/multi-span RC in DROP ($r = 0.627$). Each plot corresponds to a combined model. The number of plots was 500. In all figures, we used the **Dev.** split.

---

[2] We found the error pattern of 36.0% from randomly sampled 100 error examples.

[3] A naive top-k extractor implemented on a single-span baseline repeatedly extracts top-k spans ($k \geq 2$) until the number of extracted spans is reached at the *fixed* number of spans.

3.5 Effectiveness of Combining Models with Different Structures

We analyzed the combination of different structural models to show its effectiveness.

First, we show the effectiveness of combining the different structural models. In Fig. 2 (left) we demonstrate that the combined model with different structures improved the performance of the best combined model with the same structure.

Second, its effectiveness was indicated by the recall curves, as illustrated in the middle panel of Fig. 2. We analyzed the recall curves of several single-span RC models without *rewriting*. The recall curves present the efficiency of extracting fragments of multiple answers, which suggests that combining different structural models enhances the performance of the Extractive QA.

Finally, we analyzed the Pearson correlation between F1 scores on single- and multi-span RC to identify the optimal combinations for multi-span RC. We randomly sampled 20 RC models from ♣, ◇, ♡, and ♠ with different seeds to generate several models and then evaluated the combined models. As shown in the right panel of Fig. 2, there is a moderate correlation between F1 scores. Therefore, we can identify the optimal combined model for multi-span RC only with the development split of single-span RC. Furthermore, we found that the high-performing models tend to employ a strong model (♠) while combining different structural models.

4 Conclusion

This study proposed a method for rewriting single-span answers extracted using simple models, to detect single/multiple answer(s) *without* multi-span supervision. The experimental results demonstrate that the proposed method outperforms the baseline models on multi-span RC and that combining different structural models improves the performance. As future work of this study, we will analyze the gap between beneficial and unbeneficial combinations to improve their performances.

References

1. Andor, D., He, L., Lee, K., Pitler, E.: Giving BERT a calculator: finding operations and arguments with reading comprehension. In: Proceedings of the 2019 Conference on Empirical Methods in Natural Language Processing and the 9th International Joint Conference on Natural Language Processing (EMNLP-IJCNLP), Hong Kong, China, pp. 5947–5952. Association for Computational Linguistics, November 2019. https://doi.org/10.18653/v1/D19-1609. https://www.aclweb.org/anthology/D19-1609
2. Clark, K., Luong, M.T., Le, Q.V., Manning, C.D.: Electra: Pre-training text encoders as discriminators rather than generators. In: International Conference on Learning Representations (2020). https://openreview.net/forum?id=r1xMH1BtvB

3. Dasigi, P., Liu, N.F., Marasović, A., Smith, N.A., Gardner, M.: Quoref: A reading comprehension dataset with questions requiring coreferential reasoning. In: Proceedings of the 2019 Conference on Empirical Methods in Natural Language Processing and the 9th International Joint Conference on Natural Language Processing (EMNLP-IJCNLP), Hong Kong, China, pp. 5925–5932. Association for Computational Linguistics, November 2019. https://doi.org/10.18653/v1/D19-1606. https://www.aclweb.org/anthology/D19-1606

4. Devlin, J., Chang, M.W., Lee, K., Toutanova, K.: BERT: Pre-training of deep bidirectional transformers for language understanding. In: Proceedings of the 2019 Conference of the North American Chapter of the Association for Computational Linguistics: Human Language Technologies, Volume 1 (Long and Short Papers), Minneapolis, Minnesota, pp. 4171–4186. Association for Computational Linguistics, June 2019. https://doi.org/10.18653/v1/N19-1423. https://www.aclweb.org/anthology/N19-1423

5. Dua, D., Wang, Y., Dasigi, P., Stanovsky, G., Singh, S., Gardner, M.: DROP: A reading comprehension benchmark requiring discrete reasoning over paragraphs. In: Proceedings of the 2019 Conference of the North American Chapter of the Association for Computational Linguistics: Human Language Technologies, Volume 1 (Long and Short Papers), Minneapolis, Minnesota, pp. 2368–2378. Association for Computational Linguistics, June 2019. https://doi.org/10.18653/v1/N19-1246. https://www.aclweb.org/anthology/N19-1246

6. Hu, M., Peng, Y., Huang, Z., Li, D.: A multi-type multi-span network for reading comprehension that requires discrete reasoning. In: Proceedings of the 2019 Conference on Empirical Methods in Natural Language Processing and the 9th International Joint Conference on Natural Language Processing (EMNLP-IJCNLP), Hong Kong, China, pp. 1596–1606. Association for Computational Linguistics, November 2019. https://doi.org/10.18653/v1/D19-1170.https://www.aclweb.org/anthology/D19-1170

7. Joshi, M., Choi, E., Weld, D., Zettlemoyer, L.: TriviaQA: A large scale distantly supervised challenge dataset for reading comprehension. In: Proceedings of the 55th Annual Meeting of the Association for Computational Linguistics (Volume 1: Long Papers), Vancouver, Canada, pp. 1601–1611. Association for Computational Linguistics, July 2017. https://doi.org/10.18653/v1/P17-1147. https://www.aclweb.org/anthology/P17-1147

8. Lan, Z., Chen, M., Goodman, S., Gimpel, K., Sharma, P., Soricut, R.: Albert: a lite BERT for self-supervised learning of language representations. arXiv preprint arXiv:1909.11942 (2019)

9. Rajpurkar, P., Jia, R., Liang, P.: Know what you don't know: unanswerable questions for SQuAD. In: Proceedings of the 56th Annual Meeting of the Association for Computational Linguistics (Volume 2: Short Papers), Melbourne, Australia, pp. 784–789. Association for Computational Linguistics, July 2018. https://doi.org/10.18653/v1/P18-2124. https://www.aclweb.org/anthology/P18-2124

10. Rajpurkar, P., Zhang, J., Lopyrev, K., Liang, P.: SQuAD: 100,000+ questions for machine comprehension of text. In: Proceedings of the 2016 Conference on Empirical Methods in Natural Language Processing, Austin, Texas, pp. 2383–2392. Association for Computational Linguistics, November 2016. https://doi.org/10.18653/v1/D16-1264. https://www.aclweb.org/anthology/D16-1264

11. Segal, E., Efrat, A., Shoham, M., Globerson, A., Berant, J.: A simple and effective model for answering multi-span questions. arXiv preprint arXiv:1909.13375v3 (2019)

12. Seo, M., Kembhavi, A., Farhadi, A., Hajishirzi, H.: Bidirectional attention flow for machine comprehension. arXiv preprint arXiv:1611.01603 (2016)
13. Trischler, A., Wang, T., Yuan, X., Harris, J., Sordoni, A., Bachman, P., Suleman, K.: NewsQA: A machine comprehension dataset. In: Proceedings of the 2nd Workshop on Representation Learning for NLP, Vancouver, Canada, pp. 191–200. Association for Computational Linguistics, August 2017. https://doi.org/10.18653/v1/W17-2623. https://www.aclweb.org/anthology/W17-2623
14. Yang, Z., Dai, Z., Yang, Y., Carbonell, J., Salakhutdinov, R., Le, Q.V.: XLNET: generalized autoregressive pretraining for language understanding. arXiv preprint arXiv:1906.08237 (2019)
15. Yang, Z., Qi, P., Zhang, S., Bengio, Y., Cohen, W., Salakhutdinov, R., Manning, C.D.: HotpotQA: a dataset for diverse, explainable multi-hop question answering. In: Proceedings of the 2018 Conference on Empirical Methods in Natural Language Processing, Brussels, Belgium, pp. 2369–2380. Association for Computational Linguistics, Oct-Nov 2018. https://doi.org/10.18653/v1/D18-1259, https://www.aclweb.org/anthology/D18-1259
16. Yu, A.W., Dohan, D., Luong, M.T., Zhao, R., Chen, K., Norouzi, M., Le, Q.V.: QANET: combining local convolution with global self-attention for reading comprehension. arXiv preprint arXiv:1804.09541 (2018)

Textual Complexity as an Indicator of Document Relevance

Anastasia Taranova and Martin Braschler[✉]

Zurich University of Applied Sciences, 8401 Winterthur, Switzerland
taranana@students.zhaw.ch, bram@zhaw.ch

Abstract. We study the textual complexity of documents as an aspect of the Information Retrieval process that influences retrieval effectiveness. Our experiments show that in many cases user queries allow determining which linguistic competency level best suits an underlying information need. The paper investigates promising first approaches on how to do so automatically and compares them to an idealistic baseline. By filtering out documents of unexpected textual complexity, we find improved search results mainly when using precision-oriented effectiveness measures.

Keywords: Information retrieval · Textual complexity · Document relevance

1 Introduction

Nowadays, information about every conceivable topic can be found digitally. Information Retrieval (IR) systems assist users in retrieving documents from large collections such as for example the World Wide Web. An IR system estimates a retrieval score for each document in a collection using a ranking function in accordance with a query criterion and returns the documents in decreasing order of estimated probability of relevance starting with the best ranked document [18].

To solve an IR problem or satisfy an information need, a user first verbalizes the information need based on their understanding of the problem. Initially, it would in most scenarios be paradoxical to assume that the user is aware of the "solution" [17]. This initial formulation rarely encapsulates all aspects that relevant documents may discuss. Next, the user initiates an interaction with an IR system by entering a query which is a coded form of that verbalization. As a consequence, the query is twice removed from the original information need of the user but forms the basis for the query/document matching. On the other end of this matching process, we observe that not every retrieved document that contains matching words with the query is relevant. Conversely, not every relevant document contains any of the query terms chosen by the user. These considerations explain why it is in practice unavoidable that the result list will contain irrelevant items. The user will, after consulting the result list,

© Springer Nature Switzerland AG 2021
D. Hiemstra et al. (Eds.): ECIR 2021, LNCS 12657, pp. 410–417, 2021.
https://doi.org/10.1007/978-3-030-72240-1_42

decide whether to reformulate the query and initiate a new retrieval cycle. In the following, we are concerned with document collections where the documents are mostly presented as natural language and, therefore, can be of different textual complexity depending on the content, used words, and sentence structures.

Research Question: *We explore whether there is a relation still present in the coded query between the information need and the textual complexity of relevant documents. In other words, we verify whether documents that solve the same problem or are relevant to the same information need share content and terminology to such an extent that they have similar textual complexity.*

We propose to estimate the complexity of retrieved documents by means of machine learning algorithms and use this information to improve the quality of the result lists. If a query attracts simple (or complex) documents in the top k retrieved documents, we believe it would be beneficial to eliminate complex (or simple) documents from the result list thereby making the list more homogeneous. In other words, we explore whether there are information needs that are best answered by sources that tend to have complex or simple language, respectively. To this end, we build a model for document complexity estimation and use complexity filters for choosing documents from a ranked list. We then verify that it is indeed in some cases possible to guess what complexity level the truly relevant documents are supposed to have according to a user's preferences by looking at top k retrieved documents, thus improving retrieval effectiveness.

2   Related Work

Most widely-known IR research related to textual complexity is centered around readability [11,14,15,22]. Readability is the sum total of all elements in a text that affect a reader's understanding, speed of reading, and interest in the text [8]. In IR, the readability measure is used to match a particular user to the retrieved documents that better suit the user's comprehension abilities. In this case, the relevance of a retrieved document is not the primary characteristic: even if the document turned out to be highly relevant, the user may not understand it.

The readability of medical information has been thoroughly studied [10,21]. In particular, CLEF eHealth organized labs [10] to support the development of techniques to aid people with different backgrounds and levels of education in grasping medical information and make health-centered decisions.

We, however, distinguish textual complexity from readability. Our complexity model does not take into account the user's level of knowledge and ability to comprehend. The goal is exclusively to leverage this "complexity" to help us improve the relevance of the ranked list assuming that documents from the list, which answer to the user's information need, share context and terminology.

Early works on the estimation of textual complexity employed heuristic measures [7,9] that are calculated as a weighted sum of simple textual features. Later the same features have been adopted by machine learning algorithms [14–16,23], where the complexity estimation is viewed as a classification problem. The previous work explored various combinations of features and classification algorithms such as k-NN, SVM, MLP. In this work, we use an MLP for classification.

3   Our Approach

The main idea of our approach is to estimate the textual complexity of retrieved documents (see Sect. 3.1) and use this information to improve retrieval effectiveness. We further build algorithms that selectively eliminate documents with "unexpected" complexity that are more likely to be irrelevant (see Sect. 3.2).

3.1   Complexity Estimation

We formulate the complexity estimation task as a probabilistic binary classification problem where each document belongs to a class of either simple or complex documents. The classification involves two steps (see Fig. 1): feature extraction, and utilization of extracted features as an input for a classification algorithm that outputs the probabilities of being in each of two classes. In this paper, we use a multi-layer neural network as a classifier: two hidden layers of 200 and 40 nodes, respectively, with the ReLU as the activation functions and the sigmoid at the output layer. Other classification algorithms can also be used.

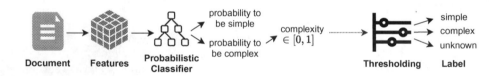

Fig. 1. Document complexity estimation pipeline.

Dataset for Classification. The Wikipedia dumps [1], which are available for both English and Simple English articles, are used for training and testing the binary classifier. The Simple English version is explicitly targeted to represent easily readable and understandable texts intended to reach a broad audience. However, we have observed that some pages from Simple English Wikipedia are more complex than the corresponding pages from the main English Wikipedia. Nonetheless, we assume the articles from Simple Wikipedia to be simple (low complexity) and the articles from English Wikipedia to be complex (high complexity). We train the classifier on 106744 pairs of articles using 5-fold cross-validation to predict what Wikipedia version each document belongs to.

Features Extraction. Features are characteristics possessed by a document and represented as numerical vectors. Extracting informative features greatly enhances the performance of a machine learning classification algorithm. We leverage document embeddings, which represent context information of a text as a fixed-length numerical vector. We use the doc2vec algorithm [12], which uses a neural network to learn semantic vector representations of a text. To our knowledge, the doc2vec algorithm has not been used to capture the complexity characteristics of texts before. The trained classifier achieves accuracy of 0.8907. We have also experimented with standard features that cover word-level, sentence-level, and discourse-level effects [19], and achieved similar performance. We report the findings on complexity estimation using doc2vec features, only.

In the binary classification, the decision for converting a predicted probability into a class label is governed by a decision threshold, which is 0.5 by default; a document with score less than 0.5 is categorized as simple, otherwise, it is complex. In this work, we use two thresholds and categorize documents into three groups: *simple, complex, and unknown (i.e., average)*. We label documents as complex only if the classifier assigns high probability to be complex for a document, and as simple only if the classifier assigns low probability to be complex for a document. If the predicted probability for a document is between two thresholds, we consider the document neither complex nor simple. The two thresholds are found using F1 thresholding [13] that determines thresholds given a required F1-score per class. We use F1 of 0.95, which resulted in 37.2% of documents to be of simple complexity, 38% - complex, 24.8% - unknown/average.

3.2   Complexity in IR: Analysis and Experiments

In this section, we study how textual complexity estimators can be utilized to improve quality of search result lists. First, we verify that complexity filters can be exploited to improve the relevance of such lists. Next, we examine queries on the complexity levels of retrieved documents. Finally, we build algorithms that apply the complexity filters automatically and show that they can be used to improve retrieval scores of the Indri search engine for a TREC dataset.

To show the potential of using documents' complexity, we establish five filters:

- *keep all* that keeps all documents;
- *keep complex* that eliminates all simple and unknown documents;
- *remove simple* that eliminates all simple documents;
- *remove complex* that eliminates all complex documents;
- *keep simple* that eliminates all complex and unknown documents.

Dataset. For the experiments we use the ClueWeb09 [2] dataset and TREC queries [3–6]. We work with the "Category A" part of the dataset, which is roughly 500 million English pages, and 200 queries provided by TREC. As a baseline, we use the Indri retrieval framework [20]. Overall, 30% of all analyzed pages from Indri baseline were simple, 28.5% - complex, and 41.5% - unknown.

Oracle-Based Complexity Filtering. To verify that the complexity filters can *in principle* improve retrieval effectiveness, we build an "all-knowing oracle". First, we apply the filters to a ranked list for each of 200 queries and

Table 1. Performance of the Oracle over the Indri baseline.

Metric	Indri	Filtering with the Oracle
P@20	0.2443	0.3134*
nDCG@20	0.1775	0.2364*
Bpref	0.1393	0.1521*

* indicates statistically significant difference; 2-tailed t-test, 0.025 level of significance.

compare several relevance scores for the lists before and after filtering. Next, we retrospectively choose the filter that maximizes the score for each list. Table 1 shows the result of applying the best-performed filters to the Indri baseline for various evaluation metrics. The result demonstrates that the filters produce substantial, statistically significant improvement of the evaluation scores over the baseline.

Table 2 provides specific queries and filters that have managed to increase the relevance of the result lists. For example, the query about PlayStation 2 games with the "keep simple" filter doubled the nDCG score. This confirms that the information need that was formulated as "ps2 game" is best fulfilled by sources that tend to have simple language. Similarly, the relevance of the ranked list for the Mitchell college query is improved using the "keep complex" filter.

Table 2. Queries that were improved with the filters.

Query	Best filter	nDCG before filtering	nDCG after filtering
ps 2 game	Keep simple	0.1191	0.2447
Mitchell college	Keep complex	0.1544	0.2098
Obama family tree	Remove simple	0.6088	0.6330

Complexity as an Aspect of an Information Need. To understand the information need implied in the queries, we analyze a perfect baseline that contains only relevant documents to each query. The perfect baseline is constructed from the query relevance files that are made by human assessors from TREC.

Table 3 shows queries that have high and low average complexity scores over the top 10 documents in the perfect baseline. For example, the "ps 2 games" query has a very low average complexity; it supports our hypothesis that the retrieved documents for some queries are supposed to be of specified complexity.

Automatic Application of Complexity Filters. *Consequently, we assume that the average complexity of the top documents in a ranked list provides a hint about the complexity of the sources that fulfill the underlying information need.* We build two approaches that choose a filter in consideration of the average complexity of the list. The first model (*Oracle Rule-based*) uses the average

Table 3. Example of queries with high and low mean (top 10) complexity scores.

QID	Complexity	Query	QID	Complexity	Query
Complex queries			Simple queries		
1	0.972	Obama family tree	9	0.150	Used car parts
24	0.953	Diversity	29	0.075	ps 2 games
60	0.927	Bellevue	49	0.053	Flame designs
157	0.995	The beatles rock band	182	0.141	Quit smoking

Algorithm 1. Rule-based filtering strategy

Input: Average complexity of the top k documents

1: **if** mean_complexity > threshold1 **then** *apply_keep_complex_filter*
2: **else if** mean_complexity > threshold2 **then** *apply_remove_simple_filter*
3: **else if** mean_complexity > threshold3 **then** *apply_keep_all_filter*
4: **else if** mean_complexity > threshold4 **then** *apply_remove_complex_filter*
5: **else** *apply_keep_simple_filter*

---

complexity estimation of the top 10 documents from the perfect list to choose a filter using four complexity thresholds (see Algorithm 1). The main idea of the algorithm is to select a filter to match the average complexity level of the perfect list. This is, however, an unrealistic setup since users do not have the perfect lists for their queries. The second model (*Rule-based*) fully relies on the average complexity of the *retrieved* documents. This approach does not take into account the complexity estimation of the perfect list and, therefore, represents the desired real-world setting.

We use the Algorithm 1 to distinguish five different scenarios. We found threshold values for both approaches using 5-fold cross-validation over queries for the Indri baseline. The found values for the *Oracle Rule-based* model are [0.8, 0.45, 0.24, 0.08], for the real-world *Rule-based* model are [0.59, 0.42, 0.07, 0.05].

Table 4 shows the evaluation scores after the application of the filtering strategies. For comparison, we use the "vanilla" Indri baseline and our oracle. Please note that any filtering will not be beneficial with respect to overall recall, so, by design, we expect to see most of the benefits for precision-oriented measures. The table indicates improvements when using the *Rule-based* strategy with no oracle for the P@20 and nDCG@20 measures, however, they are statistically insignificant. The *Oracle Rule-based* strategy, on the other hand, significantly increases the scores for the P@20 and nDCG@20 metrics. Nonetheless, Bpref scores have been reduced for all strategies but the *Oracle*, since the elimination of documents decreases the recall, as expected. Thus, we believe that the elimination of documents from the ranked list is a good strategy unless the problem is in a high recall situation.

Table 4. Improvements over Indri baseline using three strategies.

Metric	Indri	Oracle	Oracle Rule-based	Rule-based
P@20	0.2443	0.3134*	0.2631*	0.2541
nDCG@20	0.1775	0.2364*	0.1947*	0.1822
Bpref	0.1393	0.1521*	0.1296*	0.1240*

*statistically significant difference; 2-tailed t-test, 0.025 level of significance.

4 Conclusion

In this paper, we focused on the concept of textual complexity being a valuable indicator to determine document relevance. We leveraged complexity estimates of retrieved documents to infer the complexity level of a topic implied by an initial information need. The experiments showed that the elimination of documents based on their complexity from a search result can increase substantially the retrieval effectiveness in theory, and that there is also indication that we can leverage these improvements in practice. We hope that the paper will stimulate discussion and research on using complexity filters to improve document retrieval. For future work, we plan to build more sophisticated filtering strategies to improve the relevance of the search results.

References

1. Wikimedia downloads (2020). https://dumps.wikimedia.org/
2. Callan, J., Hoy, M., Yoo, C., Zhao, L.: The ClueWeb09 dataset (2009). http://www.lemurproject.org/clueweb09/clueweb09info.php
3. Clarke, C.L., Craswell, N., Soboroff, I.: Overview of the TREC 2009 Web track. Tech. rep, National Institute of Standards and Technology (2009)
4. Clarke, C.L., Craswell, N., Soboroff, I., Cormack, G.L.: Overview of the TREC 2010 Web track. Tech. rep, National Institute of Standards and Technology (2010)
5. Clarke, C.L., Craswell, N., Soboroff, I., Voorhees, E.M.: Overview of the TREC 2011 Web track. Tech. rep, National Institute of Standards and Technology (2011)
6. Clarke, C.L., Craswell, N., Voorhees, E.M.: Overview of the TREC 2012 Web track. Tech. rep, National Institute of Standards and Technology (2012)
7. Dale, E., Chall, J.S.: A formula for predicting readability: instructions. Educ. Res. Bull. 37–54 (1948)
8. Dale, E., Chall, J.S.: The concept of readability. Elemen. English **26**(1), 19–26 (1949)
9. Flesch, R.: A new readability yardstick. J. Appl. Psychol. **32**(3), 221 (1948)
10. Goeuriot, L., et al.: ShARe/CLEF eHealth Evaluation Lab 2013, task 3: Information retrieval to address patients' questions when reading clinical reports. CLEF 2013 Online Working Notes 8138 (2013)
11. Kane, L., Carthy, J., Dunnion, J.: Readability applied to information retrieval. In: Lalmas, M., MacFarlane, A., Rüger, S., Tombros, A., Tsikrika, T., Yavlinsky, A. (eds.) ECIR 2006. LNCS, vol. 3936, pp. 523–526. Springer, Heidelberg (2006). https://doi.org/10.1007/11735106_56

12. Le, Q., Mikolov, T.: Distributed representations of sentences and documents. In: International Conference on Machine Learning, pp. 1188–1196 (2014)
13. Lipton, Z.C., Elkan, C., Narayanaswamy, B.: Thresholding classifiers to maximize F1 score. arXiv preprint ArXiv:1402.1892 14 (2014)
14. Nakatani, M., Jatowt, A., Tanaka, K.: Adaptive ranking of search results by considering user's comprehension. In: Proceedings of the 4th International Conference on Uniquitous Information Management and Communication, pp. 1–10 (2010)
15. Newbold, N., McLaughlin, H., Gillam, L.: Rank by readability: document weighting for information retrieval. In: Cunningham, H., Hanbury, A., Rüger, S. (eds.) IRFC 2010. LNCS, vol. 6107, pp. 20–30. Springer, Heidelberg (2010). https://doi.org/10.1007/978-3-642-13084-7_3
16. Pantula, M., Kuppusamy, K.: A machine learning-based model to evaluate readability and assess grade level for the web pages. Comput. J. (2020)
17. Peters, C., Braschler, M., Clough, P.: Multilingual Information Retrieval: From Research to Practice. Springer, Heidelberg (2012). https://doi.org/10.1007/978-3-642-23008-0
18. Robertson, S.E.: Theories and models in information retrieval. J. Document. **33**(2), 126–148 (1977)
19. Van der Sluis, F., Van den Broek, E.L., Glassey, R.J., van Dijk, E.M., de Jong, F.M.: When complexity becomes interesting. J. Am. Soc. Inf. Sci. **65**(7), 1478–1500 (2014)
20. Strohman, T., Metzler, D., Turtle, H., Croft, W.B.: Indri: a language model-based search engine for complex queries. In: Proceedings of the International Conference on Intelligent Analysis, vol. 2, pp. 2–6 (2005)
21. Teixeira Lopes, C., Ribeiro, C.: Interplay of documents' readability, comprehension and consumer health search performance across query terminology. In: Proceedings of the 2019 Conference on Human Information Interaction and Retrieval, pp. 193–201 (2019)
22. Yan, X., Song, D., Li, X.: Concept-based document readability in domain specific information retrieval. In: Proceedings of the 15th ACM International Conference on Information and Knowledge Management, pp. 540–549 (2006)
23. Zhao, J., Kan, M.Y.: Domain-specific iterative readability computation. In: Proceedings of the 10th Annual Joint Conference on Digital Libraries, pp. 205–214 (2010)

A Comparison of Question Rewriting Methods for Conversational Passage Retrieval

Svitlana Vakulenko[1]([✉]), Nikos Voskarides[1], Zhucheng Tu[2], and Shayne Longpre[2]

[1] University of Amsterdam, Amsterdam, The Netherlands
{s.vakulenko,n.voskarides}@uva.nl
[2] Apple Inc., Cupertino, USA

Abstract. Conversational passage retrieval relies on question rewriting to modify the original question so that it no longer depends on the conversation history. Several methods for question rewriting have recently been proposed, but they were compared under different retrieval pipelines. We bridge this gap by thoroughly evaluating those question rewriting methods on the TREC CAsT 2019 and 2020 datasets under the same retrieval pipeline. We analyze the effect of different types of question rewriting methods on retrieval performance and show that by combining question rewriting methods of different types we can achieve state-of-the-art performance on both datasets (Resources can be found at https://github.com/svakulenk0/cast_evaluation.)

1 Introduction

Conversational search aims to provide automated support for natural and effective human–information interaction [1]. The TREC Conversational Assistance Track (CAsT) introduced the task of conversational (multi-turn) passage retrieval (PR) [3], where the goal is to retrieve short passages of text from a large passage collection that answer the information need at the current turn.

One prominent challenge in conversational PR is that the question at the current turn often requires information from the conversation history (questions and passages retrieved in previous turns) to be interpreted correctly. A proposed solution to this challenge is question rewriting (or resolution, QR), i.e., modifying the question such that it no longer depends on the conversation history. For instance, the question "What did he work on?" can be rewritten into "What did Bruce Croft work on?" based on the conversation history (see Table 4 for the complete example).

Recently proposed methods for QR in conversational PR can be categorized into two types, namely sequence generation and term classification. Sequence generation QR methods generate natural language sequences using the conversation history [7,9], while term classification QR methods add terms from the conversation history to the current turn question [5,8]. The former can be trained

© Springer Nature Switzerland AG 2021
D. Hiemstra et al. (Eds.): ECIR 2021, LNCS 12657, pp. 418–424, 2021.
https://doi.org/10.1007/978-3-030-72240-1_43

using human generated rewrites or data obtained from search sessions and heuristics [7,9], while the latter are either heuristic-based [5], or trained using human generated rewrites or distant supervision [8].

In this paper, we conduct a systematic evaluation of the state-of-the-art QR methods under the same retrieval pipeline on the CAsT 2019 and 2020 datasets. While CAsT 2019 only depends on the previous questions in the conversation, CAsT 2020 also includes questions that depend on the previously retrieved passages. Our results provide insights on the ability of the QR methods to account for the conversation history, as well as on the potential of combining QR methods of different types for improving retrieval effectiveness.

2   Task Definition

We model the conversational PR task as a sequence of two subtasks: (1) question rewriting (QR) and (2) passage retrieval (PR) [7–9]. In this paper, we focus on the QR subtask and investigate the impact of QR on PR performance.

In the QR subtask, we are given the current turn question Q_i and a sequence of question-answer pairs $H := [Q_1, A_1, \ldots, Q_{i-1}, A_{i-1}]$ (the conversation history). The current turn question Q_i may depend on the conversation history H and thus some information in H is required to correctly interpret Q_i. The goal of QR is to generate a question rewrite Q_i' that no longer depends on H.

In the PR subtask, we are given the question rewrite Q_i' and a passage collection C, and the goal is to retrieve a list of passages R sorted by their relevance to Q_i' from C. If Q_i' is semantically equivalent to $\langle Q_i, H \rangle$, we expect R to constitute relevant passages for $\langle Q_i, H \rangle$.

3   Experimental Setup

We aim to answer the following research questions:

RQ1. How do different QR methods perform on the two datasets we consider (CAsT 2019 and CAsT 2020)?

RQ2. Can we combine different QR models to improve retrieval performance?

Following previous work, we perform both intrinsic and extrinsic evaluation [2,8]. In intrinsic evaluation, we compare rewrites produced by QR methods with manual rewrites produced by human annotators using ROUGE-1 Precision (P), Recall (R) and F-measure (F) [2].[1] In extrinsic evaluation, we measure PR performance when using different QR methods using standard ranking metrics: NDCG@3, MRR and Recall@1000.

---

[1] We use ROUGE-1 to measure unigram overlap after punctuation removal, lower casing and Porter stemming. We use the following ROUGE implementation: https://github.com/google-research/google-research/tree/master/rouge.

3.1   Question Rewriting Methods

We compare the following question rewriting methods:

- **Original** The original current turn question without any modification.
- **Human** The gold standard rewrite of the current turn question produced by a human annotator.
- **Rule-Based** and **Self-Learn** model question rewriting as a sequence generation task and use GPT-2 to perform generation [9]. In order to gather training data, these methods convert ad-hoc search sessions to conversational search sessions either by using heuristic rules (**Rule-Based**) or by using self-supervised learning (**Self-Learn**).
- **Transformer++** [7] is a GPT-2 sequence generation model. It was trained on CANARD, a conversational question rewriting dataset [4].
- **QuReTeC** [8] models question rewriting as term classification, i.e., predicting which terms from the conversation history to add to the current turn question. It uses BERT to perform term classification and can be trained using human rewrites or distant supervision obtained from query-passage relevance labels. In this paper, we use the model trained on CANARD [4] to be comparable with **Transformer++**. Since **QuReTeC** does not generate natural language text but rather appends a bag-of-words (BoW) to the original question, we also introduce an oracle **Human-BoW** as an upper-bound for **QuReTeC** performance.

Table 1. Datasets statistics.

Dataset	#Topics	#Questions	#Copy	(%)
CAsT 2019	50	479	88	(21)
CAsT 2020	25	216	5	(3)

3.2   Datasets

We use the recently constructed TREC CAsT 2019 and CAsT 2020 datasets [3]. Table 1 shows basic statistics of the datasets. **Copy** indicates the number of questions for which the human rewrite is exactly the same as their corresponding original question. This statistic shows that in contrast to CAsT 2019, in CAsT 2020, only a very few questions can be copied verbatim and the majority of questions require extra terms.

Another major difference between the two datasets is that the current turn question in CAsT 2020 may also depend on the answer passage to the previous turn question (A_{i-1}), while in CAsT 2019 the current turn question depends only on the questions of the previous turns in the conversation history ($Q_1, Q_2, \ldots, Q_{i-1}$). Therefore, we experiment with two variations of input to the QR models: (1) all previous questions (indicated as **Q**) and (2) all previous questions and the answer passage to the previous turn question (indicated as **Q&A**).[2]

Table 2. Evaluation of question rewriting methods on CAsT 2019.

QR Method	Recall@1000	NDCG@3		ROUGE-1		
	Initial	Initial	Reranked	P	R	F
Original	0.417	0.131	0.266	0.92	0.76	0.82
Transformer++ Q	0.743	0.265	**0.525**	**0.96**	0.88	**0.91**
Self-Learn Q	0.725	0.261	0.513	0.93	0.89	0.90
Rule-Based Q	0.717	0.248	0.487	0.94	0.89	0.91
QuReTeC Q	**0.768**	**0.296**	0.500	0.89	**0.90**	0.89
Transformer++ Q + QuReTeC Q	**0.791**	0.300	**0.546**	**0.93**	0.91	**0.91**
Self-Learn Q + QuReTeC Q	0.785	0.293	0.519	0.90	**0.93**	**0.91**
Rule-Based Q + QuReTeC Q	0.783	**0.301**	0.534	0.91	**0.93**	**0.91**
Human-BoW Q	0.769	0.297	0.524	0.91	0.90	0.90
Human	0.803	0.309	0.577	1.00	1.00	1.00

3.3   Passage Retrieval Pipeline

All QR methods described in Sect. 3.1 were previously evaluated on CAsT 2019 using different retrieval pipelines. For a fair comparison, we evaluate the QR methods on both CAsT 2019 and CAsT 2020 using the same passage retrieval pipeline.

We use a standard two-stage pipeline for passage retrieval, consisting of an unsupervised ranker for initial retrieval performing efficient lexical match (BM25) and a supervised reranker (BERT) over the top-1000 passages returned by initial retrieval [6].[3] Both components were fine-tuned on a subset of the MS MARCO dataset ($k_1 = 0.82, b = 0.68$).[4]

4   Results

4.1   QR Methods Comparison

Here we answer **RQ1**: How do different QR methods perform on the two datasets we consider?

---

[2] We use the answer passage to the previous turn question retrieved by the *automatic* rewriting system provided by the TREC CAsT 2020 organizers.

[3] Note that our pipeline outperforms the official baseline provided by the TREC CAsT organizers for both 2019 and 2020 datasets for all query rewriting methods they considered. Since our focus is on comparing different query rewriting methods, we do not report those results for brevity.

[4] https://github.com/nyu-dl/dl4marco-bert.

CAsT 2019. In Table 2, we observe that QuReTeC outperforms all other methods in initial retrieval (Recall@1000 and NDCG@3). However, we see that Transformer++ Q outperforms QuReTeC in reranking (NDCG@3). This may indicate that the reranking component (BERT) is more sensitive to rewritten questions that do not resemble natural language text (produced by QuReTeC) than the initial retrieval component (BM25). This is also reflected in the ROUGE-1 metric variations: ROUGE-1 R is generally in agreement with initial retrieval performance. This is expected since our initial retrieval component is BoW and does not get substantially affected by missing or incorrect terms such as pronouns and stopwords, which are usually insignificant for lexical matching (see Human-BoW in Table 2). ROUGE-1 P, however, favours the sequence generation methods, and penalizes QuReTeC, since QuReTeC does not have a mechanism to delete or replace such terms from the original question.

Table 3. Evaluation of question rewriting methods on CAsT 2020.

QR Method	Recall@1000	NDCG@3		ROUGE-1		
	Initial	Initial	Reranked	P	R	F
Original	0.251	0.068	0.193	**0.87**	0.66	0.74
Transformer++ Q& A	0.351	0.098	0.252	0.75	0.69	0.70
Self-Learn Q& A	0.462	0.156	0.342	0.84	0.73	0.76
Rule-Based Q& A	0.455	0.137	0.339	0.84	0.75	**0.78**
QuReTeC Q& A	**0.531**	**0.171**	**0.370**	0.82	**0.77**	**0.78**
Transformer++ Q + QuReTeC Q& A	0.525	0.160	0.351	**0.83**	0.77	0.78
Self-Learn Q + QuReTeC Q& A	**0.567**	0.168	**0.375**	0.82	**0.79**	**0.79**
Rule-Based Q& A + QuReTeC Q& A	0.519	**0.173**	0.362	0.80	**0.79**	0.78
Human-BoW Q	0.579	0.189	0.465	0.89	0.81	0.84
Human-BoW Q& A	0.649	0.226	0.465	0.88	0.85	0.86
Human	0.707	0.240	0.531	1.00	1.00	1.00

CAsT 2020. In Table 3, we observe that the retrieval performance of Original and Human is much lower than in Table 2, which indicates that CAsT 2020 is more challenging than CAsT 2019.[5] We observe that QuReTeC outperforms all other methods in all ranking metrics. This indicates that QuReTeC better captures relevant terms both from the previous turn questions and the answer passage to the previous turn question than the other QR methods. Similarly to Table 2, ROUGE-1 R is in agreement with initial retrieval performance. As for ROUGE-1 P, we observe that it is not as important for retrieval as in Table 2. Next, we assess the contribution of the answer passage to the previous turn question on QR performance. In Fig. 1, we observe that most QR methods (except Transformer++) do benefit from using the answer passage, with QuReTeC having the biggest gain in initial retrieval. Table 4 shows examples of question rewrites produced by Rule-Based and QuReTeC.

---

[5] Recall that questions in CAsT 2020 may depend on the answer of the previous turn question, but this is not the case in CAsT 2019.

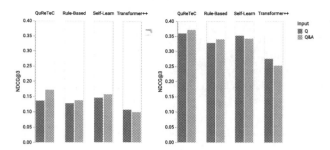

Fig. 1. Initial retrieval (left) and reranking (right) performance on CAsT 2020 when the answer passage to the previous turn question is used (Q&A) or not used (Q) as input to the QR methods.

Table 4. Example question rewrites for the topic in CAsT 2020 starting with "Who are some of the well-known Information Retrieval researchers?".

Answer passage	Original	Rule-Based Q& A	QuReTeC Q& A
Bruce Croft formed the Center	What did he work on?	What did Bruce Croft work on?	What did he work on? croft bruce
Karpicke and Janell R. Blunt (2011) followed up	Who are some important British ones?	Who are some important British ones?	Who are some important British ones? information retrieval

4.2   Combining QR Methods

Next we answer **RQ2**: Can we combine different QR models to improve performance? In order to explore whether combining QR methods of different types (sequence generation or term classification) can be beneficial, we simply append terms from the conversation history predicted as relevant by QuReTeC to the rewrite produced by one of the sequence generation methods. We found that by doing this we can improve upon individual QR methods and achieve state-of-the-art retrieval performance on CAsT 2019 by combining Transformer++ Q with QuReTeC Q (see Table 2), and on CAsT 2020 by combining Self-Learn Q and QuReTeC Q&A (see Table 3); however the gains on CAsT 2020 are smaller.

5   Conclusion

We evaluated alternative question rewriting methods for conversational passage retrieval on the CAsT 2019 and CAsT 2020 datasets. On CAsT 2019, we found that QuReTeC performs best in terms of initial retrieval, while Transformer++ performs best in terms of reranking. On CAsT 2020, we found that QuReTeC performs best both in terms of initial retrieval and reranking. Moreover, we achieved state-of-the-art ranking performance on both datasets using a simple method that combines the output of QuReTeC (a term classification method) with the output of a sequence generation method. Future work should focus on developing more advanced methods for combining term classification and sequence generation question rewriting methods.

Acknowledgements. We thank Raviteja Anantha for providing the rewrites of the Transformer++ model.

References

1. Anand, A., Cavedon, L., Joho, H., Sanderson, M., Stein, B.: Conversational search (dagstuhl seminar 19461). Dagstuhl Reports (2019)
2. Anantha, R., Vakulenko, S., Tu, Z., Longpre, S., Pulman, S., Chappidi, S.: Open-domain question answering goes conversational via question rewriting. arXiv preprint arXiv:2010.04898 (2020)
3. Dalton, J., Xiong, C., Callan, J.: Cast 2019: The conversational assistance track overview. In: TREC (2019)
4. Elgohary, A., Peskov, D., Boyd-Graber, J.: Can you unpack that? Learning to rewrite questions-in-context. In: EMNLP-IJCNLP (2019)
5. Mele, I., Muntean, C.I., Nardini, F.M., Perego, R., Tonellotto, N., Frieder, O.: Topic propagation in conversational search. In: SIGIR (2020)
6. Nogueira, R., Cho, K.: Passage re-ranking with BERT. arXiv preprint arXiv:1901.04085 (2019)
7. Vakulenko, S., Longpre, S., Tu, Z., Anantha, R.: Question rewriting for conversational question answering. In: WSDM (2021)
8. Voskarides, N., Li, D., Ren, P., Kanoulas, E., de Rijke, M.: Query resolution for conversational search with limited supervision. In: SIGIR (2020)
9. Yu, S., et al.: Few-shot generative conversational query rewriting. In: SIGIR (2020)

Predicting Question Responses to Improve the Performance of Retrieval-Based Chatbot

Disen Wang[1(✉)] and Hui Fang[1,2]

[1] Institute for Financial Services Analytics, University of Delaware, Newark, USA
{disen,hfang}@udel.edu
[2] Department of Electrical and Computer Engineering, University of Delaware,
Newark, USA

Abstract. Chatbot models are built to mimic a conversation between humans and fulfill different tasks. Retrieval-based chatbot models are designed to select the most appropriate response from a pool of candidates given a past conversation and current input. During the conversation, chatbots are expected to (1) provide direct assistant when the user request is clear or (2) ask clarification questions to gather more information to better understand the user's need. Despite its importance, few studies have looked at when to ask questions and how to retrieve relevant questions accordingly. As a result, existing retrieval-based chatbot models perform poorly when the correct response is a question. To overcome this limitation, we propose an adaptive response retrieval model. Specifically, we first predict whether the best response should be a question, and then apply different models to retrieve the responses accordingly. A novel question response retrieval model is proposed to better capture the matching patterns between question responses with the conversations. Experiments on two public data sets show the proposed adaptive model can significantly and consistently improve the retrieval performance in particular for the question responses.

1 Introduction

Chatbots have been playing an important role in many applications such as customer support and tutoring systems [3,8,10]. Retrieval-based chatbot models aim to select the most appropriate response from a pool of candidates. Given past conversations, a retrieval-based chatbot model computes the matching score for each candidate response in the candidate pool and returns the one with the highest matching score as the chosen response [6,14–17]. The goal of chatbot models is to fulfill the user's information needs. However, users often fail to formulate their complex needs in a single input. To better understanding the user's need, the chatbot models should be able to proactively asking questions under these situations. Figure 1 shows a pair of example conversations. Based on different user input, the chatbot should be able to choose either provide an answer or ask a question to better understanding the user's information need.

© Springer Nature Switzerland AG 2021
D. Hiemstra et al. (Eds.): ECIR 2021, LNCS 12657, pp. 425–431, 2021.
https://doi.org/10.1007/978-3-030-72240-1_44

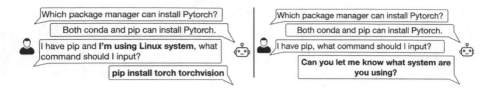

Fig. 1. Conversation examples

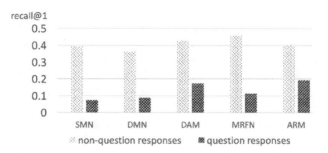

Fig. 2. Performance Comparison of State of the Art Models (SMN [15], DMN [16], DAM [17], MRFN [12], and ARM [14])

Unfortunately, none of the existing models [6,14–17] have considered the effect of question responses. In fact, they all assume the correct responses should be providing answers. To test the influence of ignoring question responses, we compared the retrieval performance of different correct response groups. As can be seen in Fig. 2, where the y-axis represents the retrieval performance, all existing models perform worse on question group than answer group. It is clear that the lack of considering question responses has limited the performance of existing models.

To overcome this limitation, we proposed an adaptive response retrieval model. Specifically, we first predict whether the best response should be asking a question for a given conversation. Based on the prediction, different retrieval models are used to retrieve the response. For the question responses, we propose a novel question response retrieval models to better capture the matching patterns between the question responses with respect to the input conversations. Experiment results demonstrate the effectiveness of both question response prediction and question response retrieval components in the proposed model.

2   Related Work

Many retrieval-based chatbot models have been proposed [12,14–17], but none of them has considered the scenario of question responses. A few related papers studied whether the current user input is answerable in the context of reading comprehension problems [4,5,9,11]. And Aliannejadi et al. [2] proposed a system to ask clarify questions in open-domain conversations and provided a dataset to

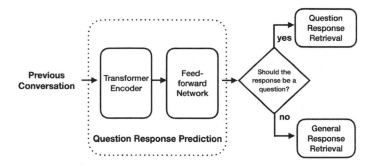

Fig. 3. Overview of the adaptive response retrieval model

evaluate the clarify questions prediction performance [1]. All these previous studies require a paragraph to generate the potential answer, which is inapplicable in our problem setup.

3   Adaptive Response Retrieval Models

Figure 3 shows an overview of our proposed adaptive response retrieval model. We first apply a prediction module to predict whether the correct response type should be a question or an answer. Based on the prediction, we will then feed candidate responses into different modules to retrieve the best response: a novel question response retrieval model is used for question responses, and the existing models are used for other response types.

3.1   Question Response Prediction

To improve the performance of response retrieval, it is crucial to understand the users' information needs. If a chatbot does not have enough information to identify relevant information, it needs to ask users questions to gather more information. The question response prediction aims to predict, given the current conversations, whether the desirable response should be a question or not.

We propose to use neural models to tackle this challenge. In particular, we first apply the Transformer model [13] to encode the previous conversation into low-dimensional dense vectors. The Transformer encoder is composed of a stack of multiple identical layers. Each layer has a multi-headed attention layer and a feed-forward layer. The attention mechanism provides a flexible way to learn the content that the model uses. After that, the encoded textual representation is fed to 3 layer feed-forward network using sigmoid activations with the final layer computing binary probability of the expected response type. The learned probability of a response being a question is denoted as p_q.

Given a response, if the probability output by the question prediction module is high enough (i.e., higher than a threshold), the chatbot system should retrieve relevant questions using our proposed question response models as described in Sect. 3.2. Otherwise, any existing retrieval models such as those mentioned in Sect. 2 can be leveraged to handle the general response retrieval.

3.2   Question Response Retrieval Module

As suggested in Fig. 2, existing models can not capture well the semantic relations between the question responses and the previous conversations. Thus, we propose a new way to capture the matching pattern between previous conversations and question response via a matching matrix.

We first apply Word2Vec algorithm [7] to generate the word embedding $e \in \mathbb{R}^d$ for each word, where d is the number of dimensions in the word embedding. The model looks up a pre-trained word embedding table to convert previous conversation $g = [w_{g,1}, w_{g,2}, ..., w_{g,n_g}]$ into $G = [e_{g,1}, e_{g,2}, ..., e_{g,n_g}]$, where $w_{g,i}$ is the i-th word and $e_{g,i}$ is the corresponding word embedding vector, and n_g is the length of g. The candidate response $r = [w_{r,1}, w_{r,2}, ..., w_{r,n_r}]$ is converted into $R = [e_{r,1}, e_{r,2}, ..., e_{r,n_r}]$ using identical method. Then we feed the word embedding vectors into the GRU network, where the hidden state is updates at each step. The final hidden state represents a summary of the input utterance, therefore we take the final hidden state h_{g,n_g} as a summary of the previous conversation, and take the final hidden state h_{r,n_r} as a summary of the candidate response using the identical method. We then calculate the matching score of the candidate response by using a matrix M:

$$s = \sigma(h_{g,n_g} M h_{r,n_r} + b),$$

where bias b and the matrix M are learned model parameters. We will train the question retrieval model using only part of the data where the correct responses are questions, therefore the matching matrix is able to capture the pattern between previous conversation and question responses. We will rank all candidate responses according to their matching scores s.

4   Experiments

4.1   Experiment Setup

We evaluate the performance of the proposed question response model on two publicly available data sets from the DSTC7 Response Selection Challenge[1]. (1) The first data set is the *Ubuntu dialogue corpus*, which contains conversations about solving an Ubuntu user's posted problem. (2) The second one is the *student-advisor data set*. In each conversation, the advisor will guide the student to pick courses. We assume a candidate response is a question if it includes a question mark. Following the previous studies [6,15], the primary evaluation measures are $R_{100}@k$, which means the probability of correct response being ranked in top k for given 100 candidate responses. k is set to 1 and 10.

The confidence scores of the question response prediction is computed as $c = p_q - p_a$. A response is considered to be a question response only when c is higher than a manually set threshold. We will discuss the impact of threshold on the performance in the later part of this section. For the question response

---

[1] https://github.com/IBM/dstc7-noesis.

Table 1. Performance on question-only datasets with confidence threshold $c = 0.85$. * means statistically significant difference over the original model with $p < 0.05$.

Model	Ubuntu dataset				Student-advisor dataset			
	Original model		Original model+QR		Original model		Original model+QR	
	$R_{100}@1$	$R_{100}@10$	$R_{100}@1$	$R_{100}@10$	$R_{100}@1$	$R_{100}@10$	$R_{100}@1$	$R_{100}@10$
SMN [15]	7.45%	31.52%	21.43%*	55.21%*	5.57%	22.39%	15.33%*	36.5%*
DMN [16]	8.75%	40.86%	23.86%*	54.6%*	4.6%	21.64%	16.25%*	35.31%*
DAM [17]	17.32%	42.29%	31.82%*	59.14%*	4.13%	26.32%	17.95%*	37.6%*
MRFN [12]	11.32%	43.85%	23.8%*	58.28%*	6.35%	22.28%	18.42%*	36.38%*
ARM [14]	19.4%	48.95%	31.15%*	61.36%*	5.74%	26.5 %	18.65%*	39.53%*
$ARM_B ERT$ [14]	23.28%	52.44%	34.21%*	63.35%*	8.32%	29.55 %	21.52%*	42.2%*

Table 2. Performance on full datasets with confidence $c = 0.85$. * means statistically significant difference over the original model with $p < 0.05$.

Model	Ubuntu dataset				Student-advisor dataset			
	Original model		Original model+QR		Original model		Original model+QR	
	$R_{100}@1$	$R_{100}@10$	$R_{100}@1$	$R_{100}@10$	$R_{100}@1$	$R_{100}@10$	$R_{100}@1$	$R_{100}@10$
SMN [15]	34.14%	71.52%	38.26%*	75.45%*	19.57%	52.39%	21.43%*	56.5%*
DMN [16]	33.91%	70.86%	39.64%*	74.46%*	19.6%	51.64%	20.35%*	55.13%*
DAM [17]	35.37%	72.29%	42.41%*	79.5%*	21.13%	53.32%	24.21%*	57.06%*
MRFN [12]	36.13%	73.85%	41.28%*	78.38%*	20.35%	52.28%	23.42%*	56.81%*
ARM [14]	38.53%	74.45%	43.14%*	78.36%*	22.74%	54.5 %	26.7%*	58.03%*
$ARM_B ERT$ [14]	44.81%	81.44%	45.24%*	82.35%*	26.42%	64.43 %	28.13%*	65.1%*

prediction, we set the dimension of position-wise feed-forward networks inner layer as 2048, the number of heads as 8 and the number of stacked layer as 6. For question response retrieval, we set the dimension of hidden states as 50. The hyper-parameters for the general response retrieval are set based on the previous work [12, 15–17].

4.2 Results and Analysis

Effectiveness of the Adaptive Response Retrieval Models: We evaluate the performance of the proposed adaptive response retrieval model. Given a conversation, the model first predicts whether the response needs to be a question, and then select different retrieval models based on the prediction results: (1) use the proposed question response (QR) retrieval model if the response is predicted to be a question; (2) use the state of the art models (i.e., SMN [15], DMN [16], DAM [17], MRFN [12], and ARM[14]) otherwise. Experiments are conducted over two versions of the original data sets: (1) question only version, which includes only conversations whose responses are a question; (2) full version, which includes all the conversations no matter their response types. Table 1 shows the performance comparison on the question-only versions with confidence threshold set to 0.85. These results demonstrate the effectiveness of the question

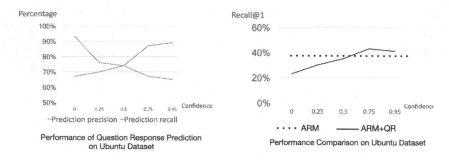

Fig. 4. Impact of the confidence threshold (Left: prediction; Right: retrieval)

response retrieval model as it can consistently and significantly outperform the state of the art models for question response retrieval. Furthermore, we conduct similar experiments but on the full versions of the data sets, and the results are shown in Table 2. Again, we can see the performance of the proposed model outperforms the performance of the state of the art models, which demonstrates the effectiveness of both question response prediction module as well as the question response retrieval module.

Impact of the Confidence Threshold: The confidence threshold in the proposed model affects the prediction accuracy as well as the retrieval performance. Figure 4 shows the parameter sensitivity with respect to the both tasks: QR prediction and QR retrieval. Similar patterns can be observed on other data sets. In the left plot, the red line corresponds to the prediction recall while the blue line corresponds to the prediction precision With the confidence threshold set to 0.85, the prediction module achieves 88% accuracy and can identify 65% question responses on the ubuntu data set. The right plot shows the retrieval performance with respect to different values of the confidence threshold. It is clear that the threshold needs to be set to a larger value (i.e., larger than 0.7) to ensure the effectiveness of the model.

5   Conclusion and Future Work

An intelligent chatbot system is expected to know when to ask questions to gather more information and when to deliver relevant information. This paper proposes an adaptive response model that first predicts the response type and then applies different retrieval models accordingly. Experiment results demonstrate the effectiveness of both the QR prediction and QR retrieval modules. For the future work, we plan to study more response type and extend the adaptive retrieval model accordingly.

Acknowledgement. The first author is grateful to the JP Morgan Chase scholarship he received from the Ph.D. Program in Financial Services Analytics to support this research.

References

1. Aliannejadi, M., Kiseleva, J., Chuklin, A., Dalton, J., Burtsev, M.: Convai3: generating clarifying questions for open-domain dialogue systems (clariq). arXiv (2020)
2. Aliannejadi, M., Zamani, H., Crestani, F., Croft, W.: Asking clarifying questions in open-domain information-seeking conversations. In: SIGIR, pp. 52–59 (2019)
3. Assefi, M., Liu, G., Wittie, M.P., Izurieta, C.: An experimental evaluation of apple siri and google speech recognition. In: ISCA SEDE, pp. 1–6 (2015)
4. Aubet, F.X., Danks, D., Zhu, Y.: Equant (enhanced question answer network). arXiv e-prints arXiv:1907.00708 (2019)
5. Hu, M., Wei, F., Peng, Y., Huang, Z., Yang, N., Zhou, M.: Read + verify: machine reading comprehension with unanswerable questions. In: AAAI, pp. 267–275 (2019)
6. Lowe, R., Pow, N., Vlad, I., Charlin, L., Liu, C.W., Pineau, J.: Training end-to-end dialogue systems with the ubuntu dialogue corpus. Dialog. Discourse **8**(1), 31–65 (2017)
7. Mikolov, T., Chen, K., Corrado, G., Dean, J.: Efficient estimation of word representations in vector space. In: ICLR, pp. 1–12 (2013)
8. Qiu, M., et al.: AliMe chat: a sequence to sequence and rerank based chatbot engine. In: ACL pp. 498–503 (2017)
9. Rajpurkar, P., Jia, R., Liang, P.: Know what you don't know: unanswerable questions for SQuAD. In: ACL, pp. 784–789 (2018)
10. Shum, H.Y., He, X., Li, D.: From eliza to xiaoice: challenges and opportunities with social chatbots. Front. Inf. Technol. Electron. Eng. **19**, 10–26 (2018). https://doi.org/10.1631/FITEE.1700826
11. Tan, C., Wei, F., Zhou, Q., Yang, N., Lv, W., Zhou, M.: I know there is no answer: Modeling answer validation for machine reading comprehension. In: NLPCC, pp. 21–29 (2018)
12. Tao, C., Wu, W., Xu, C., Hu, W., Zhao, D., Yan, R.: Multi-reprentation fusion network for multi-turn response selection in retrieval-based chatbots. In: WSDM, pp. 267–275 (2019)
13. Vaswani, A., et al.: Attention is all you need. CoRR, pp. 5998–6008 (2017)
14. Wang, D., Fang, H.: An adaptive response matching network for ranking multi-turn chatbot responses. In: NLDB, pp. 239–251 (2020)
15. Wu, Y., Wu, W., Xing, C., Xu, C., Li, Z., Zhou, M.: A sequential matching framework for multi-turn response selection in retrieval-based chatbots. In: ACL, pp. 496–505 (2017)
16. Yang, L., Huang, J., Chen, H., Croft, W.B.: response ranking with deep matching networks and external knowledge in information-seeking conversation systems. In: SIGIR, pp. 245–254 (2018)
17. Zhou, X., Li, L., Dong, D., Liu, Y., Chen, Y., Zhao, W.X., Yu, D., Wu, H.: Multi-Turn Response selection for chatbots with deep attention matching network. In: ACL, pp. 1118–1127 (2018)

Multi-head Self-attention with Role-Guided Masks

Dongsheng Wang$^{(\boxtimes)}$, Casper Hansen, Lucas Chaves Lima, Christian Hansen, Maria Maistro, Jakob Grue Simonsen, and Christina Lioma

Department of Computer Science, University of Copenhagen, Copenhagen, Denmark
{wang,c.hansen,lcl,chrh,mm,simonsen,c.lioma}@di.ku.dk

Abstract. The state of the art in learning meaningful semantic representations of words is the Transformer model and its attention mechanisms. Simply put, the attention mechanisms learn to attend to specific parts of the input dispensing recurrence and convolutions. While some of the learned attention heads have been found to play linguistically interpretable roles, they can be redundant or prone to errors. We propose a method to guide the attention heads towards roles identified in prior work as important. We do this by defining role-specific masks to constrain the heads to attend to specific parts of the input, such that different heads are designed to play different roles. Experiments on text classification and machine translation using 7 different datasets show that our method outperforms competitive attention-based, CNN, and RNN baselines.

Keywords: Self-attention · Transformer · Text classification

1 Introduction

The Transformer model has had great success in various tasks in Natural Language Processing (NLP). For instance, the state of the art is dominated by models such as BERT [5] and its extensions: RoBERTa [12], ALBERT [9], SpanBERT [8], SemBERT [24], and SciBERT [2], all of which are Transformer-based architectures. Due to this, recent studies have focused on developing approaches to understand how attention heads digest input texts, aiming to increase the interpretability of the model [4,14,20]. The findings of those analyses are aligned: while some attention heads of the Transformer often play linguistically interpretable roles [4,20], others are found to be less important and can be pruned without significantly impacting (indicating redundancy), or even improving (indicating potential errors contained in pruned heads), effectiveness [14,20].

While the above studies show that the effectiveness of the attention heads is, in part, derived from different head roles, only scant prior work analyze the impact of *explicitly* adopting roles for the multiple heads. Such an explicit guidance would force the heads to spread the attention on different parts of the input with the aim of reducing redundancy. This motivates the following research question: *What is the impact of explicitly guiding attention heads?*

D. Wang and C. Hansen—Equal contribution.

© Springer Nature Switzerland AG 2021
D. Hiemstra et al. (Eds.): ECIR 2021, LNCS 12657, pp. 432–439, 2021.
https://doi.org/10.1007/978-3-030-72240-1_45

To answer this question, we define role-specific masks to guide the attention heads to attend to different parts of the input, such that different heads are designed to play different roles. We first choose important roles based on findings from recent studies on interpretable Transformers roles; then we produce masks with respect to those roles; and finally the masks are incorporated into self-attention heads to guide the attention computation. Experimental results on both text classification and machine translation on 7 different datasets show that our approach outperforms competitive attention-based, CNN, and RNN baselines.

2   Related Work

The Transformer [19] was originally proposed as an encoder-decoder model, but has also been used successfully for transfer learning tasks, especially after being pre-trained on massive amounts of unlabeled texts. At the heart of the transformer lies the notion of multi-head self-attention, where the attention of each head is computed as:

$$\text{Attention}(Q, K, V) = \text{softmax}\left(\frac{QK^T}{\sqrt{d_k}}\right) V \tag{1}$$

where Q, is the query, K is the key, V is the value, and d_k is the key dimension. The input to each head is a head-specific linear projection, and the Transformer uses multi-heads such that the attention for each head is concatenated for a single output.

Recently, efforts have been made to explore how the Transformer attends over different parts of the input texts [4,7,20]. Clark et al. [4] investigate each attention head's linguistic roles, and find that particular heads refer to specific aspects of syntax. Voita et al. [20] study the importance of the different heads using layer-wise relevance propagation (LRP) [6], and characterize them based on the role they perform. Furthermore, Voita et al. [20] find that not all heads are equally important and choose to prune the heads using a L_0 regularizer, finding that most of the non-pruned heads have specialized roles.

Scant prior work exists on guiding the attention heads to have a specific purpose. Strubell et al. [18] train the multi-head model with the first head attending to a single syntactic parent token, while the rest being regular attention heads. In contrast, we explore multiple more complex predefined roles grounded in head roles discovered in recent work. Sennrich and Haddow [15] incorporate linguistic features (e.g. sub-word tags, POS tags, etc.) as additional features into an attention encoder and decoder model for the task of machine translation, in order to enrich the model. In contrast, our method also makes use of linguistic features, but instead of enriching the input, we use these linguistic features to define the role-specific masks for guiding the attention heads.

3   Multi-head Attention with Guided Masks

We incorporate role-specific masks for self-attention heads, constraining them to attend to specific parts of the input. By doing this, we aim to reduce the redundancy between the heads, and force the heads to have roles identified in previous work as important. Then, we adopt a weighted gate layer to aggregate the heads.

We first define the multi-head self-attention with role-specific masks in Sect. 3.1 followed by a description of each role in Sect. 3.2. We denote our final attention guided Transformer model as Transformer-Guided-Attn.

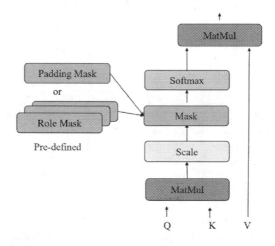

Fig. 1. Scaled-dot product with role mask or padding mask.

3.1 Multi-head Attention

We incorporate a role-specific mask into a masked attention head (mh) as:

$$mh(Q, K, V, M_r) = softmax\left(\frac{QK^T + M_r}{\sqrt{d_k}}\right) V \qquad (2)$$

where M_r is a role-specific mask used to constrain the attention head. For an input of length n, M_r is an n-by-n matrix where each element is either $-\infty$ (ignore) or 0 (include). For multi-head self-attention, we introduce N role-specific masks for the first N heads out of a total of H heads ($N \leq H$). If N is strictly less than H, then the remaining heads are regular attention heads. Based on this, the multi-head attention can be expressed as:

$$MultiHead(Q, K, V) = Concat(mh_1, mh_2, ..., mh_N, h_{N+1}, h_{N+2}, ..., h_H)W^O \qquad (3)$$

where mh_i is the head with a role mask, and h_i is a regular head computed using Eq. (1).

A visualization of using the masks is shown in Fig. 1, where we associate the standard padding mask to regular attention heads. The padding masks ensure that inputs shorter than the model allowed length are padded to fit the model.

3.2 Mask Roles

We adopt the roles detected as important by Voita et al. [20] and Clark et al. [4]. We categorize them as 1) specialized (rare words and separators), 2) syntactic (dependency syntax and major relations), and 3) window (relative position) roles (see [10,11] for a linguistic basis of this categorisation). We include the separator role as Clark et al. [4] found that over half of BERT's attention, in layer 6–10, focus on separators. We describe these 5 specific roles below, which are used for creating role-specific masks.

Rare words (RareW). The rare words role refers to the least frequent tokens in a text. As defined by Voita et al. [20], we compute IDF (inversed document frequency) scores for all tokens and use the 10% least frequent tokens (highest 10% values according to IDF) in the sentence as the target attentions.

Separator (Seprat). The separator role guides the head to point to only separators. We extend the separator from $\{[SEP], [START], [END]\}$ to common punctuation of {comma, semicolon, dot, question mark, exclamation point}.

Dependency syntax (DepSyn). Dependency syntax role guides the head to attend to tokens with syntactic dependency relations. We assume this role can guide the head to attend to those–not adjacent–but still relevant tokens, complementary to the Rel-Pos role (see below).

Major syntactic relations (MajRel). The major syntactic relations role guides the head to attend to the tokens involved with major syntactic relations. The four major relations defined by Voita et al. [20] are NSUBJ, DOBJ, AMOD, and ADVMOD.

Relative Position (RelPos). The relative position role guides the head to look at adjacent tokens, corresponding to scanning the text with a centered window of size 3.

For each role, we generate the guided mask for each input sentence by first producing an n-by-n matrix with all values as $-\infty$ (corresponding to ignoring all tokens initially). Then, we change the value of position (i, j) into 0.0, referring to the query token i with respect to the guided key token j, depending on the mask role.

4 Experiment

We experimentally compare our Transformer-Guided-Attn model to competitive baselines across 7 datasets in the tasks of text classification and machine translation. We make the source code publicly available on GitHub[1].

4.1 Classification Tasks

We consider two different classification tasks: sentiment analysis and topic classification. We compare our methods against six competitive baselines: the original Transformer [19]; multi-scale CNNs [22]; RNNs (BiLSTM) [3]; directional Self-attention (DiSAN) [17] that incorporates temporal order and multi-dimensional attention into the Transformer; phrase-level self-attention (PSAN) [23] which performs self-attention

---

[1] https://github.com/dswang2011/guided-attention-transformer.

across words inside a phrase; and Transformer-Complex-Order [21] that incorporates sequential order into the Transformer to capture ordered relationships between token positions. For the baselines implemented by us (marked in the Tables), we tune them as described in the original papers. For our Transformer-Guided-Attn, we consider a simple, but effective, way of selecting the combination of role-specific masks: For each layer, we fix 5 attention heads to be guided by the specific roles specified in Sect. 3.2, and let the remaining be regular heads. We tune the number of layers from $\{2, 4, 6, 8\}$ and number of additional regular heads from $\{1, 3\}$.

Dataset. The statistics of the datasets are shown in Table 1. We use the same splits as done by Wang et al. [21].

Results. As shown in Table 3, we observe consistent improvements compared to the best baseline for each dataset, except on MR where we perform as well as PSAN. Compared to the original Transformer model, we obtain accuracy gains of up to 2.96%, depending on the dataset, thus showing a notable performance impact from guiding the attention heads. Compared to DiSAN and PSAN, our proposed Transformer-Guided-Attn obtains consistent improvements over the original Transformer across all datasets, while DiSAN and PSAN both have lower performance for TREC and SUBJ (Table 2).

Table 1. Classification dataset statistics. CV means 10-fold cross validation.

Dataset	Train	Test	Task	Vocab.	Class
CR	4k	CV	Product review	6k	2
TREC	5.4k	0.5k	Question	10k	6
SUBJ	10k	CV	Subjectivity	21k	2
MPQA	11k	CV	Opinion polarity	6k	2
MR	11.9k	CV	Movie review	20k	2
SST	67k	2.2k	Movie review	18k	2

Table 2. Machine translation results. ⋆ marks scores reported from other papers.

Method	BLEU
Transformer [19]	34.3
AED + Linguistic [15] ⋆	28.4
AED + BPE [16] ⋆	34.2
Tensorized Transformer [13] ⋆	34.9
Transformer-Complex-Order [21] ⋆	35.8
Transformer-Guided-Attn (ours)	**38.8**

Table 3. Classification results (accuracy %). ⋆ marks scores reported from other papers.

Method	CR	TREC	SUBJ	MPAQ	MR	SST
Transformer [19]	82.0	91.8	93.2	88.6	77.7	81.8
Multi-scale CNNs [22]	81.2	93.1	93.3	89.1	77.8	80.9
BiLSTM [3]	82.6	92.4	93.6	88.9	78.4	81.1
DiSAN (Directional Self-Attention) [17]⋆	84.1	88.3	92.2	89.5	79.7	82.9
PSAN (phrase-level Self-Attention) [23]⋆	84.2	89.1	91.9	89.9	**80.0**	83.8
Transformer-Complex-Order [21]⋆	80.6	89.6	89.5	86.3	74.6	81.3
Transformer-Guided-Attn (ours)	**84.4**	**93.6**	**93.8**	**90.7**	**80.0**	**84.2**

4.2   Translation Task

We use the standard WMT 2016 English-German dataset [16] and use four baselines: Attentional encoder-decoder (AED) [15] with linguistic features including morphological, part-of-speech, and syntactic dependency labels as additional embedding space; AED with Byte-pair encoding (BPE) [16] subword segmentation for open-vocabulary translation; the tensorized Transformer [13]; and the Transformer-Complex-order [21]. The first two models are extensions on top of the basic AED [1]. For the models we implement, we follow the same tuning as in the classification experiments. We evaluate the machine translation performance using the Bilingual Evaluation Understudy (BLEU) measure.

Results. Our Transformer-Guided-Attn consistently outperforms the competitive baselines. Specifically, we observe gains of 8.2% compared to the best baseline, Transformer-Complex-Order, and close to 13% compared to the original Transformer. These gains are even larger than the results for the classification experiments, thus highlighting a significant performance impact from guiding the attention heads for the task of machine translation.

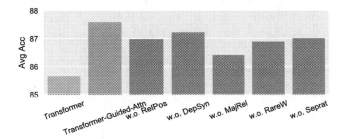

Fig. 2. Ablation study of Transformer-Guided-Attn when dropping each role individually.

4.3   Ablation Study

We now consider the performance impact associated with each role-specific mask. For each classification dataset, we run configurations of our Transformer-Guided-Attn with each role-specific mask excluded once and replaced with a default padding mask used in the Transformer. The average accuracy drop associated with excluding each role-specific mask is shown in Fig. 2, which also includes the average accuracy of the Transformer and our Transformer-Guided-Attn using all role-specific masks. We observe that the removal of each role has a negative impact on performance, where the major syntactic relations role (MajRel) has the largest impact. Thus, collectively all roles contribute to the performance of the full Transformer-Guided-Attn model.

5   Conclusion

We presented Transformer-Guided-Attn, a method to explicitly guide the attention heads of the Transformer using role-specific masks. The motivation of this explicit guidance is to force the heads to spread their attention on different parts of the input with the aim of reducing redundancy among the heads. Our experiments demonstrated that incorporating multiple role masks into multi-head attention can consistently improve performance on both classification and machine translation tasks.

As future work, we plan to explore additional roles for masking, as well as evaluating the impact of including it for pre-training language representation models such as BERT [5].

Acknowledgments. This work is supported by the European Union's Horizon 2020 research and innovation programme under the Marie Skłodowska-Curie grant agreement No. 721321 (QUARTZ project) and No. 893667 (METER project).

References

1. Bahdanau, D., Cho, K., Bengio, Y.: Neural machine translation by jointly learning to align and translate. In: Bengio, Y., LeCun, Y. (eds.) 3rd International Conference on Learning Representations, ICLR 2015, San Diego, CA, USA, May 7–9, 2015, Conference Track Proceedings (2015). http://arxiv.org/abs/1409.0473
2. Beltagy, I., Cohan, A., Lo, K.: Scibert: pretrained contextualized embeddings for scientific text. CoRR abs/1903.10676 (2019). http://arxiv.org/abs/1903.10676
3. Bin, Y., Yang, Y., Shen, F., Xu, X., Shen, H.T.: Bidirectional long-short term memory for video description. In: Proceedings of the 24th ACM international conference on Multimedia, pp. 436–440 (2016)
4. Clark, K., Khandelwal, U., Levy, O., Manning, C.D.: What does BERT look at? an analysis of BERT's attention. arXiv preprint arXiv:1906.04341 (2019)
5. Devlin, J., Chang, M., Lee, K., Toutanova, K.: BERT: pre-training of deep bidirectional transformers for language understanding. In: Burstein, J., Doran, C., Solorio, T. (eds.) Proceedings of the 2019 Conference of the North American Chapter of the Association for Computational Linguistics: Human Language Technologies, NAACL-HLT 2019, Minneapolis, MN, USA, 2–7 June 2019, Volume 1, pp. 4171–4186. Association for Computational Linguistics (2019). https://doi.org/10.18653/v1/n19-1423
6. Ding, Y., Liu, Y., Luan, H., Sun, M.: Visualizing and understanding neural machine translation. In: Proceedings of the 55th Annual Meeting of the Association for Computational Linguistics (Volume 1: Long Papers), pp. 1150–1159 (2017)
7. Hoover, B., Strobelt, H., Gehrmann, S.: exbert: a visual analysis tool to explore learned representations in transformers models. arXiv preprint arXiv:1910.05276 (2019)
8. Joshi, M., Chen, D., Liu, Y., Weld, D.S., Zettlemoyer, L., Levy, O.: Spanbert: improving pre-training by representing and predicting spans. Trans. Assoc. Comput. Linguist. **8**, 64–77 (2020)
9. Lan, Z., Chen, M., Goodman, S., Gimpel, K., Sharma, P., Soricut, R.: Albert: a lite BERT for self-supervised learning of language representations. In: International Conference on Learning Representations (2020)
10. Lioma, C., Blanco, R.: Part of speech based term weighting for information retrieval. In: Boughanem, M., Berrut, C., Mothe, J., Soule-Dupuy, C. (eds.) ECIR 2009. LNCS, vol. 5478, pp. 412–423. Springer, Heidelberg (2009). https://doi.org/10.1007/978-3-642-00958-7_37

11. Lioma, C., van Rijsbergen, C.J.K.: Part of speech n-grams and information retrieval. French Review of Applied Linguistics, Special issue on Information Extraction and Linguistics XII I(2008/1), 9–22 (2008). https://www.cairn-int.info/article-E_RFLA_131_0009-part-of-speech-n-grams-and-information.htm

12. Liu, Y., et al.: Roberta: a robustly optimized Bert pretraining approach. arXiv preprint arXiv:1907.11692 (2019)

13. Ma, X., et al.: A tensorized transformer for language modeling. In: Advances in Neural Information Processing Systems, pp. 2229–2239 (2019)

14. Michel, P., Levy, O., Neubig, G.: Are sixteen heads really better than one? In: Advances in Neural Information Processing Systems, pp. 14014–14024 (2019)

15. Sennrich, R., Haddow, B.: Linguistic input features improve neural machine translation. In: Proceedings of the First Conference on Machine Translation, WMT 2016, colocated with ACL 2016, August 11–12, Berlin, Germany, pp. 83–91. The Association for Computer Linguistics (2016). https://doi.org/10.18653/v1/w16-2209

16. Sennrich, R., Haddow, B., Birch, A.: Edinburgh neural machine translation systems for WMT 16. In: Proceedings of the First Conference on Machine Translation: Volume 2, Shared Task Papers, pp. 371–376. Association for Computational Linguistics, Berlin, Germany, August 2016. https://www.aclweb.org/anthology/W16-2323

17. Shen, T., Zhou, T., Long, G., Jiang, J., Pan, S., Zhang, C.: DISAN: directional self-attention network for RNN/CNN-free language understanding. In: Thirty-Second AAAI Conference on Artificial Intelligence (2018)

18. Strubell, E., Verga, P., Andor, D., Weiss, D., McCallum, A.: Linguistically-informed self-attention for semantic role labeling. In: Proceedings of the 2018 Conference on Empirical Methods in Natural Language Processing, pp. 5027–5038. Association for Computational Linguistics, Brussels, Belgium, October–November 2018. https://doi.org/10.18653/v1/D18-1548, https://www.aclweb.org/anthology/D18-1548

19. Vaswani, A., et al.: Attention is all you need. In: Advances in Neural Information Processing Systems, pp. 5998–6008 (2017)

20. Voita, E., Talbot, D., Moiseev, F., Sennrich, R., Titov, I.: Analyzing multi-head self-attention: Specialized heads do the heavy lifting, the rest can be pruned. In: Korhonen, A., Traum, D.R., Màrquez, L. (eds.) Proceedings of the 57th Conference of the Association for Computational Linguistics, ACL 2019, Florence, Italy, July 28- August 2, 2019, Volume 1: Long Papers. pp. 5797–5808. Association for Computational Linguistics (2019). https://doi.org/10.18653/v1/p19-1580

21. Wang, B., Zhao, D., Lioma, C., Li, Q., Zhang, P., Simonsen, J.G.: Encoding word order in complex embeddings. In: 8th International Conference on Learning Representations, ICLR 2020, Addis Ababa, Ethiopia, April 26–30, 2020. OpenReview.net (2020). https://openreview.net/forum?id=Hke-WTVtwr

22. Wang, D., Simonsen, J.G., Larsen, B., Lioma, C.: The Copenhagen team participation in the factuality task of the competition of automatic identification and verification of claims in political debates of the clef-2018 fact checking lab. CLEF (Working Notes) **2125** (2018)

23. Wu, W., Wang, H., Liu, T., Ma, S.: Phrase-level self-attention networks for universal sentence encoding. In: Proceedings of the 2018 Conference on Empirical Methods in Natural Language Processing. pp. 3729–3738 (2018)

24. Zhang, Z., et al.: Semantics-aware BERT for language understanding. CoRR abs/1909.02209 (2019). http://arxiv.org/abs/1909.02209

PGT: Pseudo Relevance Feedback Using a Graph-Based Transformer

HongChien Yu$^{(\boxtimes)}$, Zhuyun Dai, and Jamie Callan

Carnegie Mellon University, Pittsburgh, USA
{hongqiay,zhuyund,callan}@cs.cmu.edu

Abstract. Most research on pseudo relevance feedback (PRF) has been done in vector space and probabilistic retrieval models. This paper shows that Transformer-based rerankers can also benefit from the extra context that PRF provides. It presents PGT, a graph-based Transformer that sparsifies attention between graph nodes to enable PRF while avoiding the high computational complexity of most Transformer architectures. Experiments show that PGT improves upon non-PRF Transformer reranker, and it is at least as accurate as Transformer PRF models that use full attention, but with lower computational costs.

1 Introduction

Pseudo relevance feedback (PRF) uses context defined by the top-ranked documents of an initial retrieval to improve a subsequent retrieval. Most prior research has been done in vector space [20], probabilistic [19], and language modeling [13,16,23] retrieval models.

Recently the field has moved to Transformer-based rerankers [18] that are more accurate and computationally complex. Most Transformer-based rerankers learn contextualized representations from query-document pairs, but they have two limitations. First, the query-document pair provides limited context for query understanding. Second, most Transformers have computational complexity quadratic to the input sequence length, rendering longer context infeasible.

To overcome these limitations, we propose a PRF method using a graph-based Transformer (PGT). PGT constructs a graph of the query, the candidate document, and the feedback documents. It uses intra-node attention to contextualize the query according to each individual document, and it uses inter-node attention to aggregate information. With the graph approach, PGT can utilize richer relevance context using a configurable number of feedback documents. Its inter-node attention is sparsified, so it also saves computation.

This paper makes two contributions to the study of pseudo relevance feedback in Transformer architectures. First, it investigates several ways of using PRF documents as context for Transformer rerankers. It shows that PGT improves upon non-PRF Transformer rerankers, and that PGT is at least as accurate as Transformer PRF models that use full attention, while reducing computation.

D. Hiemstra et al. (Eds.): ECIR 2021, LNCS 12657, pp. 440–447, 2021.
https://doi.org/10.1007/978-3-030-72240-1_46

Second, it studies the impact of contextual interactions by adjusting the configuration of the graph. It shows that token-level interaction between the query and feedback documents is critical, while document-level interaction is sufficient to aggregate information from multiple documents.

2 Related Work

Pseudo-relevance feedback is a well-studied method of generating more effective queries. Typically pseudo-relevance feedback uses the top-ranked documents to add query terms and set query term weights. Well-known methods include Rocchio [20], BM25 expansion [19], relevance models [13], and KL expansion models [16,23]. A large body of work studies which documents to use for expansion (e.g., [3]). Most methods were designed for discrete bag-of-words representations.

Recent research also studies PRF in neural networks. Li et al. [15] present a neural PRF framework that uses a feed forward network to combine the relevance scores of feedback documents. Only marginal improvement was observed over simple score summation, indicating that the framework does not make the best use of the feedback documents' information.

Recently, pre-trained Transformer [21] language models, such as BERT [6], have improved the state-of-the-art for ad hoc retrieval. Most Transformer-based rerankers are applied to individual query-document pairs. Some research explores jointly modeling multiple top retrieved documents in a Transformer architecture for question clarification [11], question answering [10,14] or code generation [8]. The effectiveness of using top retrieved documents in Transformer rerankers remains to be studied.

While the Transformer-based architectures have achieved state-of-the-art results in multiple natural language tasks [6], the original self-attention mechanism incurs computational complexity quadratic to the length of the input sequence. Therefore, much recent work studies sparsifying Transformer attention [1,2,24]. Among these models, Transformer-XH [24] features an underlying graph structure, where each node represents a text sequence, which makes it a good candidate for multi-sequence tasks such as PRF.

Transformer-XH employs full-attention within each sequence, but it sparsifies inter-sequence attention. Specifically, for each document sequence s, the lth layer encoder calculates the intra-sequence, token-level attention by the standard self-attention. Inter-sequence, document-level attentions are calculated using the hidden representations of each sequence's first token [CLS]:

$$\hat{h}^l_{s,0} = \sum_{s' \in \mathcal{N}(s)} softmax_{s'}(\frac{\hat{q}^T_{s,0} \cdot \hat{k}_{s',0}}{\sqrt{d_k}}) \cdot \hat{v}_{s',0}, \tag{1}$$

where $\mathcal{N}(s)$ are the neighboring document sequences of s in the graph. This allows the [CLS] token to carry context from other neighboring sequences. Such information is propagated to other tokens in the sequence through the intra-sequence attention in the next layer. Hence Transformer-XH outputs a condensed representation that contains both the global graph-level information and the local sequence-level information.

Fig. 1. Right: Nodes in PGT contextualize the query using the candidate document d_c and the feedback documents d_i with intra-sequence, token-level attention. Left: The input graph is fully connected with inter-sequence attention among [CLS] tokens.

3   Proposed Method

We propose PGT, a PRF reranker with a graph-based Transformer. Given a query q, a candidate document d_c, and feedback documents d_1, ..., d_k retrieved by a first-stage retrieval algorithm, the goal is to predict the score of d_c by aggregating information from feedback documents. To achieve this goal, PGT adopts the Transformer-XH [24] architecture, and builds a graph of q, d_c and d_1, ..., d_k. Figure 1 illustrates the graph.

PGT has two types of nodes. The d_i nodes contextualize the query using feedback documents. As shown in Fig. 1 (right), the input to a d_i node is the text of d_i, with q and d_c prepended in order to extract information specific for predicting the relevance between q and d_c. The input text sequence is fed into a Transformer module with standard token-level self-attention. To distinguish different parts of the input, we associate segment id 0 with q and d_c, and 1 with d_i. In addition to the feedback document nodes, PGT also adopts a special node for the query-candidate pair (q, d_c). The input of the (q, d_c) node is the concatenation of the query and candidate document, which constitutes a typical input sequence to existing Transformer-based rerankers. We hypothesize that the (q, d_c) node will help the model focus more on the query-candidate pair.

PGT aggregates sequence-level information through inter-sequence attention. Within the sequence, the Transformer encodes the [CLS] token to represent the whole sequence (Fig. 1 right). Between the sequences, all [CLS] tokens attend to each other to gather information from other sequences (Fig. 1 left). We follow Zhao et al. [24] and incorporate inter-sequence attention in the last three Transformer encoder layers. The model is trained on a binary relevance classification task using cross-entropy loss, and it predicts the final relevance score using a weighted sum of all the [CLS] representations [24].

4   Experimental Setup

This section describes our datasets, baselines and other experimental settings.

4.1   Datasets

Experiments were done with the MS MARCO Passage Ranking task dataset [17]. It contains about 8.8 million passages and about 0.5 million queries with relevance judgments as training data. Each query has an equal number of relevant and non-relevant passages. We used the official evaluation query set from the TREC 2019 Deep Learning Track [4]. It contains 43 test queries manually annotated by NIST on a four-point scale. On average, a query has 95 relevant documents. We report NDCG@10, MAP@10, and MAP@100.

4.2   Baselines

We compare PGT to initial rankers, a non-PRF reranker, and PRF models.

- **BM25 (initial ranker):** We used Anserini's implementation [22]. k_1 and b were tuned using a parameter sweep on 500 training queries, following [5].
- **CLEAR (initial ranker):** This model combines BM25's lexical retrieval and BERT's dense embedding retrieval. It performs significantly better than BM25 on our dataset. We used the rankings provided by Gao, et al. [7].
- **BERT reranker (non-PRF reranker):** This is a standard BERT reranker, whose input is the concatenated sequence of the query q and the candidate document d_c. We trained the model following Nogueira and Cho [18].
- **RM3 (PRF):** This is a traditional language modeling PRF method [12,13].
- **BERT PRF (PRF):** This is the same as BERT reranker except that we concatenate $(q, d_c, d_1, d_2, ..., d_k)$ to form a PRF input sequence, with documents separated by [SEP]. Limited by the input length constraint of BERT [6], we used 5 feedback documents. Same as for PGT, we used segment id 0 for q and d_c, and 1 for d_i.

4.3   PGT Graph Variants

Modeling queries and documents in a graph gives control over how representations are contextualized. We examined 5 graph variants to study this effect.

- **PGT base** is the graph described in Sect. 3. The query is first contextualized by the candidate and feedback document at the token-level. Feedback information is then aggregated following the graph structure. The (q, d_c) node emphasizes q and d_c at the graph-level. This variant has the richest context.
- **PGT w/o pre d_c** removes prepended candidate from the d_i nodes, so each query is only contextualized by the feedback document at sequence-level.
- **PGT w/o pre q, d_c** removes both the prepended query and the prepended candidate from the feedback nodes. Each feedback document hence only contextualizes the query at the graph-level.

- **PGT w/o node d_c** removes candidate from the (q, d_c) node, so only q is emphasized again at the graph-level.
- **PGT w/o node q, d_c** removes the (q, d_c) node from the graph, so q and d_c are not emphasized again at the graph-level.

4.4   Training and Evaluation

We implement PGT based on the Transformer-XH [24] PyTorch implementation. The parameters for the intra-sequence attention are initialized from a pre-trained BERT base model [6], and those for the inter-sequence attention are initialized according to Xavier et al. [9]. We train the model for 2 epochs, with per-GPU batch size = 4 on 2 GPUs. The maximum node sequence length is 128, and the learning rate is 5e-6 with linear decay.

We train both BERT PRF and PGT using feedback documents from BM25. In order to test how Transformer-based PRF models generalize when different initial rankers are used, we evaluate them using both BM25 and CLEAR. We follow prior research [7, 18] and report the results at each model's best reranking depth r (Table 1).

5   Experimental Results

PRF vs. non-PRF Transformers. We study the effectiveness of PRF in Transformer-based models by comparing PGT and BERT PRF with BERT reranker. Table 1 shows that all PRF Transformers outperform BERT reranker on MAP@10 using either initial ranker. In particular, PGT achieves MAP@10 13.0% and 7.4% better than BERT reranker on BM25 and CLEAR respectively, with comparable NDCG@10. The results suggest that the richer context provided by PRF helps Transformers rank relevant documents to the very top.

PRF enables Transformers to exploit high-quality initial rankings better. Comparing BM25 and CLEAR results in Table 1, we found that when the initial ranker is stronger, PGT achieves the best performance across all metrics, closely followed by BERT PRF. In comparison, BERT reranker cannot make the best of the initial retrieval of CLEAR, as reported by prior research [7].

PGT vs. BERT PRF. While PGT rankings are at least as good as BERT PRF, it is more computationally efficient. Using $k = 5$ for a fair comparison, we calculated the number of multiplication and addition operations. PGT consumes 88% as many operations on each input example compared with BERT PRF. In addition, PGT requires smaller reranking depth (Table 1). Using BM25 as the initial ranker, the computational cost is hence only 44% of BERT PRF's.

Compared with BERT PRF, PGT allows flexible configurations on the graph structure (Table 1). As discussed in Sect. 4.3, the graph structure controls how relevance context flows across the graph. Contrary to our initial intuition, removing the (q, d_c) node partially or entirely (PGT w/o node d_c and PGT w/o node q, d_c) achieves the best results among all graph variants. q is an impoverished description of the information need compared to feedback documents $d_1 \ldots d_k$, which may explain why the comparison of q to d_c is less useful than comparisons between d_c and high-quality documents.

The number of feedback documents k is a parameter that is usually tuned. BERT's self-attention mechanism restricts the input sequence length, limiting BERT to 5 feedback documents on our dataset. PGT has no such restriction. Our experiments use $k = 7$ for PGT because it is more effective (Table 2).

Table 1. The evaluation results with BM25 and CLEAR as initial rankers. RM3 is shown for completeness, but it is not competitive, so it is not discussed. We report the results at each models' best reranking depth (r) according to prior research [7,18]. We use $k = 7$ feedback documents for PGT. $*$ and $\dagger$ indicate statistical significance over the initial ranker and BERT reranker using t-test with $p \leq 0.05$.

	BM25				CLEAR			
	NDCG	MAP	MAP		NDCG	MAP	MAP	
	@10	@10	@100	r	@10	@10	@100	r
Initial ranker	0.5058	0.1126	0.2993	–	0.6990	0.1598	0.4181	–
RM3	0.5180	0.1192	0.3370*	1K	$-^a$	–	–	–
BERT Reranker	0.6988*	0.1457*	0.3905*	1K	0.7127	0.1572	0.4134	20
BERT PRF	0.6862*	0.1495*	**0.4075***	1K	0.7188	0.1646	0.4203	20
PGT base	0.6712*	0.1542*	0.3927*	500	0.7238*	0.1660	0.4205	20
PGT w/o pre d_c	0.6693*	0.1523*	0.3563*	500	0.7146	0.1658	0.4194	20
PGT w/o pre q, d_c	0.6676*	0.1468*	0.3450*	500	0.7005	0.1572	0.4145	20
PGT w/o node d_c	0.6840*	0.1586*	0.3868*	500	0.7139	**0.1689***	0.4192	20
PGT w/o node q, d_c	**0.7078***	**0.1646*†**	0.3819*	500	**0.7326***	0.1654	**0.4220**	20

^{a} CLEAR jointly trains a hybrid of sparse and dense retrieval models. Running RM3 on CLEAR is an open question that is beyond the scope of this work.

Table 2. PGT base using different numbers of feedback documents (k)

	BM25			CLEAR		
	NDCG	MAP	MAP	NDCG	MAP	MAP
k	@10	@10	@100	@10	@10	@100
5	0.6344	0.1497	0.3536	0.6923	0.1653	0.4177
7	**0.6712**	**0.1542**	0.3927	**0.7238**	**0.1660**	**0.4205**
9	0.6538	0.1476	**0.3931**	0.6940	0.1636	0.4180

6   Conclusion

Most Transformer-based rerankers learn contextualized representations for query-document pairs, however queries are impoverished descriptions of information needs. This paper presents PGT, a pseudo relevance feedback method that uses a graph-based Transformer. PGT graphs treat feedback documents as additional context and leverage sparse attention to reduce computation, enabling them to use more feedback documents than is practical with BERT-based rerankers.

Experiments show that PGT improves upon non-PRF BERT rerankers. Experiments also show that PGT rankings are at least as good as BERT PRF rerankings, however they are produced more efficiently due to fewer computations per document and fewer documents reranked per query. PGT is robust, delivering effective rankings under varied graph structures and with two rather different initial rankers.

References

1. Beltagy, I., Peters, M.E., Cohan, A.: Longformer: the long-document transformer. arXiv preprint arXiv:2004.05150 (2020)
2. Child, R., Gray, S., Radford, A., Sutskever, I.: Generating long sequences with sparse transformers. arXiv preprint arXiv:1904.10509 (2019)
3. Collins-Thompson, K., Callan, J.: Estimation and use of uncertainty in pseudo-relevance feedback. In: Proceedings of the Thirtieth Annual International ACM SIGIR Conference on Research and Development in Information Retrieval (2007)
4. Craswell, N., Mitra, B., Yilmaz, E., Campos, D., Voorhees, E.M.: Overview of the TREC 2019 deep learning track. arXiv preprint arXiv:2003.07820 (2020)
5. Dai, Z., Callan, J.: Context-aware term weighting for first stage passage retrieval. In: Proceedings of the 43rd International ACM SIGIR conference on research and development in Information Retrieval, pp. 1533–1536. ACM (2020)
6. Devlin, J., Chang, M., Lee, K., Toutanova, K.: BERT: pre-training of deep bidirectional transformers for language understanding. In: Proceedings of the 2019 Conference of the North American Chapter of the Association for Computational Linguistics: Human Language Technologies, vol. 1, pp. 4171–4186. ACL (2019)
7. Gao, L., Dai, Z., Chen, T., Fan, Z., Durme, B.V., Callan, J.: Complement lexical retrieval model with semantic residual embeddings. arXiv preprint arXiv:2004.13969 (2020)
8. Gemmell, C., Rossetto, F., Dalton, J.: Relevance transformer: generating concise code snippets with relevance feedback. In: Proceedings of the 43rd International ACM SIGIR Conference on Research and Development in Information Retrieval, pp. 2005–2008. ACM (2020)
9. Glorot, X., Bengio, Y.: Understanding the difficulty of training deep feedforward neural networks. In: Proceedings of the Thirteenth International Conference on Artificial Intelligence and Statistics, AISTATS 2010. JMLR Proceedings, vol. 9, pp. 249–256. JMLR.org (2010)
10. Guu, K., Lee, K., Tung, Z., Pasupat, P., Chang, M.: REALM: retrieval-augmented language model pre-training. arXiv preprint arXiv:2002.08909 (2020)
11. Hashemi, H., Zamani, H., Croft, W.B.: Guided transformer: leveraging multiple external sources for representation learning in conversational search. In: Proceedings of the 43rd International ACM SIGIR Conference on Research and Development in Information Retrieval, pp. 1131–1140 (2020)
12. Jaleel, N.A., et al.: Umass at TREC 2004: novelty and HARD. In: Proceedings of the Thirteenth Text REtrieval Conference, TREC 2004. NIST Special Publication, vol. 500–261. NIST (2004)

13. Lavrenko, V., Croft, W.B.: Relevance-based language models. In: Proceedings of the 24th Annual International ACM SIGIR Conference on Research and Development in Information Retrieval, pp. 120–127. ACM (2001)
14. Lee, K., Chang, M., Toutanova, K.: Latent retrieval for weakly supervised open domain question answering. In: Proceedings of the 57th Conference of the Association for Computational Linguistics, vol. 1, pp. 6086–6096. ACL (2019)
15. Li, C., et al.: NPRF: a neural pseudo relevance feedback framework for ad-hoc information retrieval. In: Proceedings of the 2018 Conference on Empirical Methods in Natural Language Processing, pp. 4482–4491. ACL (2018)
16. Lv, Y., Zhai, C.: Revisiting the divergence minimization feedback model. In: Proceedings of the 23rd ACM International Conference on Conference on Information and Knowledge Management, CIKM 2014, pp. 1863–1866. ACM (2014)
17. Nguyen, T., et al.: MS MARCO: a human generated machine reading comprehension dataset. In: Proceedings of the Workshop on Cognitive Computation: Integrating neural and symbolic approaches 2016 co-located with the 30th Annual Conference on Neural Information Processing Systems (NIPS 2016). CEUR Workshop Proceedings, vol. 1773. CEUR-WS.org (2016)
18. Nogueira, R., Cho, K.: Passage re-ranking with BERT. arXiv preprint arXiv:1901.04085 (2019)
19. Robertson, S.E., Zaragoza, H.: The probabilistic relevance framework: BM25 and beyond. Found. Trends Inf. Retr. 3(4), 333–389 (2009)
20. Rocchio, J.J.: Relevance feedback in information retrieval. In: The SMART Retrieval System - Experiments in Automatic Document Processing, pp. 313–323. Prentice-Hall, Englewood Cliffs (1971)
21. Vaswani, A., et al.: Attention is all you need. In: Advances in Neural Information Processing Systems 30: Annual Conference on Neural Information Processing Systems, vol. 2017, pp. 5998–6008 (2017)
22. Yang, P., Fang, H., Lin, J.: Anserini: enabling the use of lucene for information retrieval research. In: Proceedings of the 40th International ACM SIGIR Conference on Research and Development in Information Retrieval, pp. 1253–1256. ACM (2017)
23. Zhai, C., Lafferty, J.D.: Model-based feedback in the language modeling approach to information retrieval. In: Proceedings of the 2001 ACM CIKM International Conference on Information and Knowledge Management, pp. 403–410. ACM (2001)
24. Zhao, C., Xiong, C., Rosset, C., Song, X., Bennett, P.N., Tiwary, S.: Transformer-XH: multi-evidence reasoning with extra hop attention. In: 8th International Conference on Learning Representations, ICLR 2020. OpenReview.net (2020)

Clustering-Augmented Multi-instance Learning for Neural Relation Extraction

Qi Zhang[1(✉)], Siliang Tang[2], Jinquan Sun[1], Yu Wang[1], and Lei Zhang[1]

[1] Alibaba Group Inc., Hangzhou, China
{mickey.zq,jinquan.sjq,tonggou.wangyu,lei.zhang.lz}@alibaba-inc.com
[2] Zhejiang University, Hangzhou, China
siliang@zju.edu.cn

Abstract. Despite its efficiency in generating training data, distant supervision for sentential relation extraction assigns labels to instances in a context-agnostic manner—a process that may introduce false labels and confuse sentential model learning. In this paper, we propose to integrate instance clustering with distant training, and develop a novel clustering-augmented multi-instance training framework. Specifically, for sentences labeled with the same relation type, we jointly perform clustering based on their semantic representations, and treat each cluster as a training unit for multi-instance training. Comparing to existing bag-level attention models, our proposed method does not restrict the training unit to be sentences with the same entity pair, as it may cause the selective attention to focus on instances with simple sentence context, and thus fail to provide informative supervision. Experiments on two popular datasets demonstrate the effectiveness of augmenting multi-instance learning with clustering.

Keywords: Relation extraction · Distant supervision · Clustering

1 Introduction

Relation Extraction (RE) aims to detect and classify the relations between entities in the given sentences, and provides the cornerstone for many downstream applications such as information extraction, knowledge base population, and question-answering. It is a challenging task partly because it requires elaborative human annotations [9], which could be slow or expensive to get.

To reduce such reliance, knowledge bases like Freebase have been leveraged to provide Distant Supervision (DS) automatically [8]. Although such supervision is efficient w.r.t. time and cost, it is generated in a context-agnostic manner, thus could contain massive noise for sentential RE and lead to a poor performance. Many attempts have been made to leverage multi-instance learning (MIL) [1] to protect the model from such noise. Specifically, they treat sentence bags as the training unit – each sentence bag is composed of an ordered entity pair with a relation type and all sentences containing that entity pair [5,9,10]. Specifically,

© Springer Nature Switzerland AG 2021
D. Hiemstra et al. (Eds.): ECIR 2021, LNCS 12657, pp. 448–454, 2021.
https://doi.org/10.1007/978-3-030-72240-1_47

by selecting instances from such bags, existing work can conduct training with sentences of a higher quality, reduce the effect of noisy labels and obtain obvious improvements [6].

At the same time, most existing methods use a static multi-instance structure, i.e., sentences containing the same entity pair are treated as the training unit. Due to the lack of flexibility, it could be relatively easy for neural models to "overfit", e.g., the model could treat some correct but relative complicated sentences as label noise and mainly fit to relative simple sentences. As Table 1 shows, the instance in the bottom line is a positive instance for relation type */location/location/contains*, but is ignored due to the low attention score caused by relatively complicated semantic expression.

In this paper, we go beyond those existing learning paradigms and propose a novel framework, Clustering-augmented Multi-Instance Learning (CAMIL). It leverages clustering to construct sentence bags and jointly trains the relation extractor. The integrated clustering module allows us to conduct multi-instance training in a dynamic manner and thus can leverage training data more effectively.

Table 1. Some examples of selective attention in NYT corpus

Attention	Instance For */location/location/contains*
0.91	Catering to craniacs is relatively new for **port_aransas** and rockport, the small **texas** towns near the aransas national wildlife refuge not far from corpus christi
0.09	Anywhere from four to six nights a week, the mckay brothers -lrb- hollin, 31, and noel, 36 -rrb- lead-foot it across **texas** in their chevy pickup, playing honky-tonks, dive bars and coffee shops from **port_aransas** to luckenbach to alpine, always returning home to hill country to sleep in their own beds

Specifically, we assume that the more instances a cluster has, the more reliable it is. Since a clustering bag contains instances with similar semantic, our assumption could be viewed as that the more instances are in a particular way of expression, the more likely this expression is a truthful expression of the relation. We create a nonlinear mapping between the clustering bag size and the reliability score. We use the reliability score as the prior to regularize the model's posterior distribution and form a unified Bayesian expected loss (Regularized Bag Loss, RBL).

We further conduct experiments on human annotated datasets. Our proposed method beats state-of-art neural relation extraction (NRE) model in sentential RE.

2   Methodology

Here, we introduce the Clustering-augmented Multi-Instance Learning framework. It has been developed upon the previous state-of-the art method, Selective

Attention Neural Relation Extraction (SA-NRE) [13]. Similar to SA-NRE, we leverage multi-instance learning to handle the label noise. Besides, we further integrate a clustering component to construct the basic bag dynamically. We will first introduce the SA-NRE model, then proceed to present the framework of CAMIL.

2.1 Selective Attention Neural Relation Extraction

SA-NRE first constructs word representations, then uses neural networks (e.g., CNN, PCNN, BiGRU, BiLSTM) to encode each sentence into a vector. Based on these vectors and a relation type assigned by distant supervision, selective attention determines the quality of each sentence and train the extractor with sentences of a relative high quality.

In particular, we construct sentence representations for SA-NRE as follows. We set the maximum length of a sentence to m, and pad all sentences to the same length. For a sentence $S = \{v_1, \cdots, v_m\}$, we refer to the pre-trained word embedding [7] for i_{th} word (v_i) as $\mathbf{v}_i$. Marking the two entity mentions in S as d_1 and d_2, we calculate the relative distance from each word to these two entities, construct their position embedding vectors and refer to the two vectors for v_i as $\mathbf{p}_{i,1}$ and $\mathbf{p}_{i,2}$ [12]. These position embedding vectors are randomly initialized and can be learned during the model training. Concatenating $\mathbf{v}_i$ together with $\mathbf{p}_{i,1}$ and $\mathbf{p}_{i,2}$, we can get our word representation $\mathbf{w}_i$. In this way, we can transform each sentence into a fix-sized matrix $S = \{\mathbf{w}_1, \mathbf{w}_2, ..., \mathbf{w}_m\}$, where $S \in R^{m \times |\mathbf{w}|}$. Taking this sentence as the input, the sentence-level encoder (e.g., PCNN and BiGRU) further constructs the sentence vector $\mathbf{x}$.

For a sentence bag with a relation type r, $B_i = \{\mathbf{x}_1, \cdots, \mathbf{x}_{n_i}\}$, selective attention is used to determine the quality of each sentence $\mathbf{x}_j$ by calculates an attention weight w.r.t. a relation type representation $\mathbf{r}$:

$$e_j = \mathbf{x}_j A \mathbf{r} \tag{1}$$

where A is the attention parameter and e_j is the weight for $\mathbf{x}_j$. Selective attention value could be further calculated as:

$$\alpha_j = \frac{e^{e_j}}{\sum_{k=1}^{n_i} e^{e_k}} \tag{2}$$

Finally, we can calculate the weighted sentence bag representation for B_i as follows:

$$\mathbf{b}_i = \sum_{j=1}^{n_i} \alpha_j \mathbf{x}_j \tag{3}$$

2.2 CAMIL

We now first introduce the overall framework of CAMIL and then discuss the training objective.

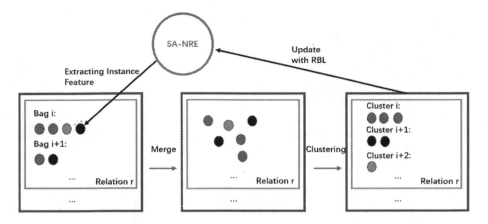

Fig. 1. Diagram of CAMIL

Overall Framework. As visualized in Fig. 1, during each iteration, we will first construct the representation for each instance with the encoder of SA-NRE. These representations are fed into the clustering module (e.g., DBSCAN [3]) to construct instance clusters. These clusters are further treated as the bag for multi-instance learning, and pass to SA-NRE to calculate loss and update parameters. Since the clustering module relies on the representation constructed by the neural encoder, and the neural encoder is trained based on the clustering results, these two modules could mutually enhance each other. Accordingly, as in Algorithm 1, we propose a unified framework and conduct training iteratively.

Regularized Bag Loss. Conducting training with sentence bag could also suffer from label noise, as in some cases, it's possible the clustered sentence bag is composed of unrelated sentences. To solve this problem, we proposed a regularization that based on the following hypothesis: the probability of a clustering bag that contains true positive instance will increase as the clustering bag size grows. The idea of this hypothesis is from the Bernoulli's Law of Large Numbers, which indicates that the empirical probability of success in a series of Bernoulli trials will converge to the theoretical probability. Finding a true positive instance in the data corpus is like a Bernoulli trial, the probability of success should have a certain relation with the number of trials. Therefore, we define a Clustering Bag Size Impact Factor (CBSIF) u to quantify the impact of clustering bag size as follows:

$$u_i = \tanh(\log(1 + \text{size}(i))) \tag{4}$$

where $\text{size}(i)$ represents the number of instances within the bag B_i. Equation (4) could ensure that a clustering bag with more instances will have a higher CBSIF within a certain range (i.e., $u_i \in [0, 1)$).

Based on this CBSIF factor, we can define a reliability score R_i as follows:

$$R_i = \lambda + (1 - \lambda)u_i \tag{5}$$

Data: Total Number of Relations: R;
Original DS Dataset: $\mathbf{B} = \{B^1, B^2, ..., B^R\}$;
For Relation r: $B^r = \{B_1^r, B_2^r, ..., B_{|B^r|}^r\}$;
For Bag i: $B_i^r = \{S_{i,1}^r, \cdots, S_{i,n_i}^r\}$;
Result: An CAMIL model
initialization SA-NRE model parameter θ_π;
Pre-train SA-NRE with Original Dataset $\mathbf{B}$;
for *Iteration m=1 to M* **do**
    Using encoder part of SA-NRE to encode all original instances $S_{i,j}^r$ to sentence representation $\mathbf{x}_{i,j}^r$;
    for *Relation r=1 to R* **do**
        Merge all bags in this relation $\overline{B^r} = B_1^r \cup \cdots \cup B_{|B^r|}^r$;
        Perform clustering on $\overline{B^r}$ using DBSCAN and get C_r cluster ;
    end
    Total number of clusters: $C = \sum_{r=1}^{R} C_r$;
    for *Batch batch_number=1 to C/n_{batch}* **do**
        Randomly choose a mini-batch of clusters and feed the clusters into the SA-NRE;
        Back-propagate RBL and update the parameter θ_π of SA-NRE via Adadelta;
    end
end

Algorithm 1: CAMIL

where λ is a hyperparameter representing the bound of the influence from u_i.

Finally, the Regularized Bag Loss stochastic with gradient descent over shuffled mini-batches can be calculated by:

$$RBL = -\frac{1}{n_{batch}} \sum_{i=1}^{n_{batch}} R_i log p(r_i|B_i) \tag{6}$$

where B_i means the i_{th} clustering bag in the mini-batch, and n_{batch} is the batch size. In the implementation, we employ dropout [4] on the output layer to prevent overfitting, and use Adadelta [11] to train our model.

3   Experiment

3.1   Dataset

In this work, we are primarily interested in sentential relation extraction. Following previous work focusing on sentential relation extraction [2,5], we use the manually annotated NYT dataset introduced by [5]. For a more meaningful comparison, we experiment with two versions of the dataset including NYTFB-68K [9] and NYTFB-280K [6].

3.2   Result

Our experiments are intended to provide evidence that supports the following hypotheses: the proposed CAMIL framework can improve the performance of the multi-instance learning and better handle the label noise in sentential NRE.

We treat the vanilla SA-NRE as our major baseline and compare our method with a structured method NMAR [2] which can be also jointly trained with SA-NRE. Following the previous work, we apply CAMIL to three typical SA-NRE models (i.e., PCNN, BiGRU and BiLSTM). Similar to previous NRE studies, we evaluate the model performance with F1-Measure.

In all of our experiments, we use a pre-trained 50-dimensional word vectors that are pre-trained by the Skip-gram [7] model[1] on the NYT data corpus. Our models are tuned by the three-fold cross-validation on the training set. With a grid search, we determine the optimal model parameters as follows: word vector size $d_v = 50$, position embedding size $d_p = 5$, batch size $n_{batch} = 200$, dropout probability $p = 0.5$, Adadelta parameter ρ, $\varepsilon = 0.95$, $1e^{-6}$, max iterations of CAMIL $M = 10$.

We report the F1-Measure in Table 2. We can observe that: SA-NRE with CAMIL brings significant performance improvements over the vanilla SA-NRE. This phenomenon verifies that CAMIL framework can help to handle the label noise and improve the performance of SA-NRE.

Table 2. Different performance comparison by F1-Measure on two datasets

Model	SA-NRE type	NYTFB-68K	NYTFB-280K
CAMIL	PCNN	0.889	0.856
	BiGRU	0.867	0.845
	BiLSTM	0.870	0.851
NMAR	PCNN	0.860	0.831
	BiGRU	0.851	0.829
	BiLSTM	0.839	0.817
Baselines	PCNN	0.764	0.721
	BiGRU	0.781	0.743
	BiLSTM	0.786	0.750

4   Conclusion

In this paper, we reveal a new potential problem in distant supervision and propose a novel framework to solve the problem in the sentential relation extraction. We believe CAMIL can be applied to any multi-instance learning method for relation extraction. The experimental results prove the efficiency of CAMIL, which significantly improves the performance of the state-of-the-art SA-NRE model.

---

[1] https://code.google.com/p/word2vec/.

References

1. Babenko, B.: Multiple instance learning: algorithms and applications. View Article PubMed/NCBI Google Scholar, pp. 1–19 (2008)
2. Bai, F., Ritter, A.: Structured minimally supervised learning for neural relation extraction (2019)
3. Ester, M., et al.: Density-based spatial clustering of applications with noise. In: International Conference on Knowledge Discovery and Data Mining, vol. 240 (1996)
4. Hinton, G.E., et al.: Improving neural networks by preventing co-adaptation of feature detectors. arXiv preprint arXiv:1207.0580 (2012)
5. Hoffmann, R., et al.: Knowledge-based weak supervision for information extraction of overlapping relations. In: Proceedings of the 49th Annual Meeting of the Association for Computational Linguistics: Human Language Technologies, vol. 1, pp. 541–550. Association for Computational Linguistics (2011)
6. Lin, Y., et al.: Neural relation extraction with selective attention over instances. In: Proceedings of the 54th Annual Meeting of the Association for Computational Linguistics (Volume 1: Long Papers), vol. 1, pp. 2124–2133 (2016)
7. Mikolov, T., et al.: Efficient estimation of word representations in vector space. arXiv preprint arXiv:1301.3781 (2013)
8. Mintz, M., et al.: Distant supervision for relation extraction without labeled data. In: Proceedings of the Joint Conference of the 47th Annual Meeting of the ACL and the 4th International Joint Conference on Natural Language Processing of the AFNLP: Volume 2, vol. 2, pp. 1003–1011. Association for Computational Linguistics (2009)
9. Riedel, S., Yao, L., McCallum, A.: Modeling relations and their mentions without labeled text. In: Balcázar, J.L., Bonchi, F., Gionis, A., Sebag, M. (eds.) ECML PKDD 2010. LNCS (LNAI), vol. 6323, pp. 148–163. Springer, Heidelberg (2010). https://doi.org/10.1007/978-3-642-15939-8_10
10. Surdeanu, M., et al.: Multi-instance multi-label learning for relation extraction. In: Proceedings of the 2012 Joint Conference on Empirical Methods in Natural Language Processing and Computational Natural Language Learning, pp. 455–465. Association for Computational Linguistics (2012)
11. Zeiler, M.D.: Adadelta: an adaptive learning rate method. arXiv preprint arXiv:1212.5701 (2012)
12. Zeng, D., et al.: Relation classification via convolutional deep neural network. In: Proceedings of COLING 2014, the 25th International Conference on Computational Linguistics: Technical Papers, pp. 2335–2344 (2014)
13. Zhou, P., et al.: Attention-based bidirectional long short-term memory networks for relation classification. In: Proceedings of the 54th Annual Meeting of the Association for Computational Linguistics (Volume 2: Short Papers), vol. 2, pp. 207–212 (2016)

Detecting and Forecasting Misinformation via Temporal and Geometric Propagation Patterns

Qiang Zhang[1(✉)], Jonathan Cook[1], and Emine Yilmaz[1,2]

[1] University College London, London, UK
qiang.zhang.16@ucl.ac.uk
[2] Alan Turing Institute, London, UK

Abstract. Misinformation takes the form of a false claim under the guise of fact. It is necessary to protect social media against misinformation by means of effective misinformation detection and analysis. To this end, we formulate misinformation propagation as a dynamic graph, then extract the temporal evolution patterns and geometric features of the propagation graph based on Temporal Point Processes (TPPs). TPPs provide the appropriate modelling framework for a list of stochastic, discrete events. In this context, that is a sequence of social user engagements. Furthermore, we forecast the cumulative number of engaged users based on a power law. Such forecasting capabilities can be useful in assessing the threat level of misinformation pieces. By jointly considering the geometric and temporal propagation patterns, our model has achieved comparable performance with state-of-the-art baselines on two well known datasets.

Keywords: Misinformation · Propagation graph · Point processes

1 Introduction

Social media has empowered human society in many ways. It is easier than ever to keep in touch with those we wish to, allowing an enormous variety of relationships to transcend physical isolation [19]. More so than ever before, social media has a responsibility for our mental wellbeing, as the arbiter of interactions between colleagues, friends and loved ones [13, 24]. It is therefore a matter of the utmost importance that we make this platform a safe environment, protected against those wishing to corrupt the service with *fake news* [20].

Various methods have been used to tackle the misinformation problem. Content-based misinformation analysis models apply natural language processing tools to the text content of claims [23]. Alone, content-based models fail to trace the dynamics of spread for tasks such as early detection or spread forecasting. Recent misinformation analysis models use static graph neural networks to extract geometric propagation patterns; others leverage time-series analysis by treating misinformation spread as a temporal event sequence [4, 15]. These

© Springer Nature Switzerland AG 2021
D. Hiemstra et al. (Eds.): ECIR 2021, LNCS 12657, pp. 455–462, 2021.
https://doi.org/10.1007/978-3-030-72240-1_48

two approaches each neglect the alternative propagation structure with neither leveraging both geometric and temporal dissemination features.

Propagation-based misinformation analysis makes use of patterns that can be attributed to the dynamics of spread. Our principal goal is to utilise the maximum space of these spreading features, so as to make the most effective use of the available data. Specifically, we first formulate misinformation propagation as a dynamic graph, then we employ a continuous-time temporal point process to extract the temporal evolution patterns and geometric features. Furthermore, we use a power law to model the growth in the temporal network scale, so as to forecast the future rate of spread for a claim identified as misinformation. The contributions of this study can thus be summarised as follows. (i) We formulate misinformation propagation as a dynamic graph. (ii) We then design temporal point processes (TPPs) to utilize both temporal and geometric features of the dynamic graph for misinformation detection. (iii) This study is the first to introduce forecasting of user engagements to misinformation analysis.

2   Related Work

To figure out the differences between true and false statements, most researchers conduct studies from three approaches: textual content, multimedia features and social context. Misinformation often contains opinionated language [2], which motivates textual content-based detection [1]. Sentiment features like positive words (e.g., love, sweet) and negating words (e.g., not, never) are reported to help detect rumours [6]. Misinformation also relies on sensational images to provoke an emotional response in consumers. As an example, Deepfakes [3] employed deep learning to generate fake images and videos to convey misleading information.

In social media, every piece of news is correlated to other posts and users. User engagements (e.g., commenting) provide rich reference evidence in two ways: by aggregation with relevant posts for a specific affair, and by temporal evolution. The first way relies on the "wisdom of crowds" to locate potential misinformation [1], while the second way captures temporal propagation patterns. For example, Hawkes processes are used to analyze how user stance changes temporally in [11]. However, these methods neglect geometric propagation features.

Graph neural networks can extract geometric propagation patterns. Graph Convolutional Networks (GCN) are used in [14] to encapsulate the propagation structure of heterogeneous data. Graph-Aware Co-Attention Network (GCAN) is proposed in [4,8] to utilise the co-attention mechanism in graph modeling. Each of these works use static graphs and researchers neglect temporal information.

3   Problem Formulation

This section gives definitions and describes notation. A source claim takes the form of $c = (x, t)$, where x is a concatenation of the posting user account features and the claim's text features, i.e. $x = [u \parallel M]$. Here, u is the user account representation and M is the text message representation. t is initially zero, as ensuing dissemination events are timestamped with respect to the source claim.

Suppose the claim c is accompanied by a sequence of social engagements $S = \{v_1, v_2, \ldots, v_j, \ldots, v_N\}$, where $v_j = (x_j, t_j)$. Similarly, x_j is the feature of an engaging node and t_j is the engagement time with respect to claim post time. Social engagements include all forms of interactions that users conduct with claims on social media platforms, such as reposting, commenting and tagging.

Our temporal, dynamic graph is represented as a sequence of time-stamped snapshots $\mathcal{G} = \{\mathcal{G}(t_0), \mathcal{G}(t_1), \cdots, \mathcal{G}(t_j), \cdots, \mathcal{G}(t_N)\}$, where the first snapshot simply represents the source claim node and further snapshots are added with each representing the state of the dissemination network when a new node is connected. Let $\mathcal{G}(t) = < \mathcal{V}(t), \mathcal{E}(t) >$ denote the state of the temporal graph $\mathcal{G}$ at time t, where $\mathcal{V}(t) = \{c, v_1, v_2, \ldots, v_j, \ldots, v_{N(t)}\}$, with $N(t)$ being the number of nodes to have directly or indirectly interacted with the claim c as of time t. A new graph snapshot $\mathcal{G}(t_{j+1})$ is generated when a node v_{j+1} is added to the sequence of social engagements. The graph structure of an exemplary false claim's dissemination tree is demonstrated in Fig. 1.

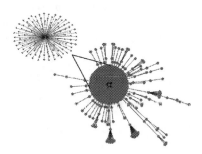

Fig. 1. Graph representation of source claim dissemination tree, where nodes represent interaction events such as comments and retweets.

4 Model Description

With the temporal evolution of the propagation graph $\mathcal{G}(t)$, new engagement nodes will establish edges with existing nodes and thus update the graph. To capture both geometric and temporal propagation features, we view the addition of new engagement nodes as the chronological events and develop a temporal point process that generates node embeddings of the dynamic graph $\mathcal{G}(t)$.

4.1 Propagation by Temporal Point Processes

A temporal point process (TPP) is a stochastic process that is realised as a list of discrete events in the continuous time domain $t \in \mathbb{R}^+$. TPPs usually rely on an intensity function, which is defined as the probability of the occurrence of an event in an infinitesimal time interval [22], to describe the temporal dynamics. They have been used to model dynamic graphs in [10,17,25].

In our propagation graph use-case, the timestamped event sequence comprises static graph snapshots. This static propagation graph represents the final state of the misinformation dissemination tree. Symbolically, $\mathcal{S} = \{(\boldsymbol{x}_j, t_j)\}_{j=1}^N$, where $\boldsymbol{x}_j$ are the event features (previously node features) and t_j is the timestamp of the jth event in the sequence $\mathcal{S}$. Intuitively, the added edge $\boldsymbol{e}_{i,j}$ between the source node $\boldsymbol{v}_i$ and the new node $\boldsymbol{v}_j$ are influenced by not only $\boldsymbol{v}_i$ and $\boldsymbol{v}_j$, but also the history nodes of $\boldsymbol{v}_i$. With this assumption, we define the intensity function associated with adding the new edge $\boldsymbol{e}_{i,j}$ as,

$$\lambda_{i,j}(t) = g(\boldsymbol{x}_i, \boldsymbol{x}_j) + \sum_{i' \in \mathcal{H}^i} \alpha_{i'j}(t) f(\boldsymbol{x}_{i'}, \boldsymbol{x}_j) \kappa(t - t_{i'}). \tag{1}$$

where $\mathcal{H}^i$ contains history events of the node i. The function $g(\cdot)$ calculates the affinity between two nodes, which is implemented as a bilinear interaction with the trainable parameter $\mathbf{W}_1$, i.e., $f(\boldsymbol{x}_i, \boldsymbol{x}_j) = \boldsymbol{x}_i * \mathbf{W}_1 * \boldsymbol{x}_j$. A non-linear activation ReLU is used to define the base intensity $g(\cdot) = ReLU(f(\cdot))$.

The influence from history nodes are measured via the self-attention mechanism as proposed in [21,22]. For history nodes before time t, we calculate attention weight for each node,

$$\alpha_{i'j} = \frac{\exp(f(\boldsymbol{x}_{i'}, \boldsymbol{x}_j))}{\sum_{k \in \mathcal{H}^i} \exp(f(\boldsymbol{x}_k, \boldsymbol{x}_j))}. \tag{2}$$

With the intensity function, we derive the probability of having a new node $\boldsymbol{v}_j$ following an existing node $\boldsymbol{v}_i$ at the timestamp t,

$$p\left(\boldsymbol{v}_i, \boldsymbol{v}_j \mid \mathcal{H}^i(t)\right) = \frac{\lambda_{i,j}(t)}{\sum_{i' \in \mathcal{H}^i(t)} \lambda_{i',j}(t)}. \tag{3}$$

The objective function to minimize is the negative log-likelihood of all the events in the sequence, $\mathcal{L}_{TPP} = -\sum_{t \in \mathcal{T}} \sum_{(v_i, v_j, t) \in \mathcal{E}} \log p\left(\boldsymbol{v}_i, \boldsymbol{v}_j \mid \mathcal{H}^i(t)\right)$. Negative sampling is used to generate non-existing edges in the objective function as done in [9], so that the learnt node embeddings are able to distinguish which two nodes are connected and which two are not, i.e., the geometric structure. Maximizing the intensity at occurrence timestamps while minimizing the intensity otherwise will enforce the node embeddings to capture temporal dynamics.

4.2   Predictive Task

Macro-dynamics describe the evolution pattern of the network scale. We assume the network scale can be described with a certain dynamics equation. Given a dynamic graph $\mathcal{G}$, we have the cumulative number of nodes $N(t)$ by timestamp t. We empirically find that $N(t)$ increases in a power law, which is presented in Sect. 5. To approximate the power law, we define the following predictive equation

$$\hat{N}(t) = N_{max} * (1 - \alpha * \exp(-\beta * t)), \qquad (4)$$

where N_{max}, α and β are learnable parameters. N_{max} is the maximum number of nodes that this graph will contain while α and β control how fast the graph scale will increase. Predictive loss is measured by $\mathcal{L}_{Pred} = (N(t) - \hat{N}(t))^2$.

4.3   Veracity Classification

We have designed a temporal point process to capture the geometric structure and temporal evolution of the propagation graph. With node embeddings, we obtain the graph embedding by concatenating the mean pooling and the maximum pooling of all nodes as well as the source claim being verified, $\boldsymbol{x}_G = [MeanPool(\mathcal{S})||MaxPool(\mathcal{S})||\boldsymbol{c}]$. The graph embedding is then concatenated by parameters in predictive tasks, i.e., $\boldsymbol{x} = [\boldsymbol{x}_G||N_{max}||\alpha||\beta]$. The veracity prediction is conducted by a Multi-Layer Perceptron (MLP) $\hat{\boldsymbol{y}} = \text{softmax}(\text{ReLU}(\mathbf{W}_2\boldsymbol{x} + \mathbf{b}))$, where $\mathbf{W}_2$ and $\mathbf{b}$ are trainable parameters. And the classification loss is calculated by cross-entropy: $\mathcal{L}_{MLP} = -y\log(\hat{y}_1) - (1-y)\log(1-\hat{y}_0)$. We take the weighted sum of the TPP loss, predictive loss and the MLP loss as the final loss function $\mathcal{L} = \mathcal{L}_{TPP} + \omega_1 * \mathcal{L}_{Pred} + \omega_2 * \mathcal{L}_{MLP}$.

5   Experiments

We use two Twitter datasets [12], i.e., Twitter15 and Twitter16, in the experiments. Each dataset has a collection of stories with a source tweet being verified and a sequence of its retweets. We pick "True" and "False" source tweets to make the experimental datasets, and split the dataset into training, validation and test sets with 70%, 10% and 20% respectively. We train the model with the training set, tune hyperparameters with the validation set and report performance on the test set. We crawl user information according to their user IDs via Twitter API (Table 1).

Table 1. Statistics of the used datasets.

	Twitter 15	Twitter 16
# Source Tweets	742	412
# True	372	205
# False	370	207
# Users	190,868	115,036
Avg retweet per story	202.19	208.70

As we set out to tackle the misinformation detection task, we compare our model with state-of-the-art baselines. RFC [5] is a random forest model with features from the source tweets and engaged user profiles. CRNN [7] combines convolutional neural networks and recurrent neural networks to extract features from engaged users and retweet texts. CSI [15] incorporates relevant articles and analyses the group behaviour of engaged users. dEFEND [16] uses a co-attention mechanism to study the source claims and user features. The graph-based baseline GCAN has been explained in Related Works.

6   Results and Analysis

To demonstrate the dissemination trends of true and false claims, we plotted the mean number of nodes within temporal graphs associated with each veracity classification at 5 min time intervals for the first 200 min following a source Tweet's posting time. In Fig. 2, we make three interesting observations. (1) Both claim veracity types exhibit a similar power-law trend of plateauing gradient. (2) Contrary to much of the misinformation literature, which suggests that fake news spreads faster than true news [18], within our datasets, true news stories spread faster and reach more users on average. (3) There is a far greater disparity between the mean spreading plots in the Twitter16 dataset than there is in the Twitter15 dataset. This would indicate that it is easier to extract temporal features that are consistent within a given veracity classification in Twitter16.

We show the misinformation detection performance of our model against state-of-the-art baselines on test subsets. From Table 2, we can tell that we are able to achieve comparable performance with GCAN. Specifically, we beat GCAN on the Twitter16 dataset. This can be explained by the fact that Twitter16 displays greater disparity between the mean spreading of true and false claims, and our model captures such patterns to reach higher performance.

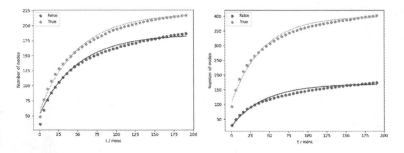

Fig. 2. Plots of average number of nodes comprising a dissemination tree with respect to time from the moment of source claim publication. The left is Twitter15 while the right is Twitter16. The solid curves follow the power law approximation.

Table 2. Test results on the two experimental datasets.

Model	Twitter15				Twitter16			
	F1	Recall	Precision	Accuracy	F1	Recall	Precision	Accuracy
RFC	0.4642	0.5302	0.5718	0.5385	0.6275	0.6587	0.7315	0.6620
CRNN	0.5249	0.5305	0.5296	0.5919	0.6367	0.6433	0.6419	0.7576
CSI	0.7174	0.6867	0.6991	0.6987	0.6304	0.6309	0.6321	0.6612
dFEND	0.6541	0.6611	0.6584	0.7383	0.6311	0.6384	0.6365	0.7016
GCAN	**0.8250**	**0.8295**	**0.8257**	**0.8767**	0.7593	0.7632	0.7594	0.8084
Ours	0.7698	0.7643	0.7754	0.7988	**0.7774**	**0.7741**	**0.808**	**0.8453**

7   Conclusion

This study sets out to detect and forecast misinformation. We model the misinformation propagation as a continuous-time dynamic graph, and employ Temporal Point Processes to capture geometric and temporal patterns of the graph. We also develop a power law equation to forecast the growth of the graph scale. Experiments show the effectiveness of our model to achieve state-of-the-art performance in misinformation detection tasks. Future works will investigate more comprehensive methods to combine temporal and geometric features for propagation-based misinformation detection.

Acknowledgments. This project was funded by the EPSRC Fellowship titled "Task Based Information Retrieval", grant reference number EP/P024289/1. We acknowledge the support of NVIDIA Corporation with the donation of the Titan Xp GPU.

References

1. Castillo, C., Mendoza, M., Poblete, B.: Information credibility on Twitter. In: Proceedings of the 20th International Conference on World Wide Web, pp. 675–684. ACM (2011)
2. Chen, Y., Conroy, N.J., Rubin, V.L.: Misleading online content: recognizing clickbait as false news. In: Proceedings of the 2015 ACM on Workshop on Multimodal Deception Detection, pp. 15–19. ACM (2015)
3. Floridi, L.: Artificial intelligence, deepfakes and a future of ectypes. Philos. Technol. **31**(3), 317–321 (2018)
4. Huang, Q., Yu, J., Wu, J., Wang, B.: Heterogeneous graph attention networks for early detection of rumors on twitter. arXiv preprint arXiv:2006.05866 (2020)
5. Kwon, S., Cha, M., Jung, K.: Rumor detection over varying time windows. PLoS ONE **12**(1), e0168344 (2017)
6. Kwon, S., Cha, M., Jung, K., Chen, W., et al.: Prominent features of rumor propagation in online social media. In: International Conference on Data Mining. IEEE (2013)
7. Liu, Y., Wu, Y.F.B.: Early detection of fake news on social media through propagation path classification with recurrent and convolutional networks. In: Thirty-Second AAAI Conference on Artificial Intelligence (2018)
8. Lu, Y.J., Li, C.T.: GCAN: graph-aware co-attention networks for explainable fake news detection on social media. arXiv preprint arXiv:2004.11648 (2020)
9. Lu, Y., Wang, X., Shi, C., Yu, P.S., Ye, Y.: Temporal network embedding with micro- and macro-dynamics. arXiv preprint arXiv:1909.04246 (2019)
10. Lu, Y., Wang, X., Shi, C., Yu, P.S., Ye, Y.: Temporal network embedding with micro-and macro-dynamics. In: Proceedings of the 28th ACM International Conference on Information and Knowledge Management, pp. 469–478 (2019)
11. Lukasik, M., Srijith, P., Vu, D., Bontcheva, K., Zubiaga, A., Cohn, T.: Hawkes processes for continuous time sequence classification: an application to rumour stance classification in Twitter. In: Proceedings of the 54th Annual Meeting of the Association for Computational Linguistics (Volume 2: Short Papers), pp. 393–398 (2016)

12. Ma, J., Gao, W., Wei, Z., Lu, Y., Wong, K.F.: Detect rumors using time series of social context information on microblogging websites. In: Proceedings of the 24th ACM International on Conference on Information and Knowledge Management, pp. 1751–1754. ACM (2015)
13. Ma, J., Gao, W., Wong, K.F.: Rumor detection on twitter with tree-structured recursive neural networks. In: Proceedings of the 56th Annual Meeting of the Association for Computational Linguistics (Volume 1: Long Papers), pp. 1980–1989. Association for Computational Linguistics (2018)
14. Monti, F., Frasca, F., Eynard, D., Mannion, D., Bronstein, M.M.: Fake news detection on social media using geometric deep learning. arXiv preprint arXiv:1902.06673 (2019)
15. Ruchansky, N., Seo, S., Liu, Y.: CSI: a hybrid deep model for fake news detection. In: Proceedings of the 2017 ACM on Conference on Information and Knowledge Management, pp. 797–806. ACM (2017)
16. Shu, K., Cui, L., Wang, S., Lee, D., Liu, H.: Defend: explainable fake news detection. In: Proceedings of the 25th ACM SIGKDD International Conference on Knowledge Discovery & Data Mining, pp. 395–405 (2019)
17. Trivedi, R., Farajtabar, M., Biswal, P., Zha, H.: Dyrep: learning representations over dynamic graphs. In: International Conference on Learning Representations (2019)
18. Vosoughi, S., Roy, D., Aral, S.: The spread of true and false news online. Science **359**, 1146–1151 (2018). https://doi.org/10.1126/science.aap9559
19. Weiss, K., Khoshgoftaar, T.M., Wang, D.D.: A survey of transfer learning. J. Big Data **3**(1), 1–40 (2016). https://doi.org/10.1186/s40537-016-0043-6
20. Zhang, Q., Liang, S., Lipani, A., Ren, Z., Yilmaz, E.: From stances' imbalance to their hierarchical representation and detection. In: The World Wide Web Conference, pp. 2323–2332 (2019)
21. Zhang, Q., Liang, S., Yilmaz, E.: Variational self-attention model for sentence representation. arXiv preprint arXiv:1812.11559 (2018)
22. Zhang, Q., Lipani, A., Kirnap, O., Yilmaz, E.: Self-attentive hawkes processes. arXiv preprint arXiv:1907.07561 (2019)
23. Zhang, Q., Lipani, A., Liang, S., Yilmaz, E.: Reply-aided detection of misinformation via Bayesian deep learning. In: The World Wide Web Conference, pp. 2333–2343. ACM (2019)
24. Zhang, Q., Yilmaz, E., Liang, S.: Ranking-based method for news stance detection. In: Companion Proceedings of the The Web Conference 2018. ACM Press (2018)
25. Zuo, Y., Liu, G., Lin, H., Guo, J., Hu, X., Wu, J.: Embedding temporal network via neighborhood formation. In: Proceedings of the 24th ACM SIGKDD International Conference on Knowledge Discovery & Data Mining, pp. 2857–2866 (2018)

Deep Query Likelihood Model
for Information Retrieval

Shengyao Zhuang$^{(\boxtimes)}$ (D), Hang Li (D), and Guido Zuccon (D)

The University of Queensland, St. Lucia, Brisbane, Australia
{shengyao.zhuang,hang.li,g.zuccon}@uq.edu.au

Abstract. The query likelihood model (QLM) for information retrieval has been thoroughly investigated and utilised. At the basis of this method is the representation of queries and documents as language models; then retrieval corresponds to evaluate the likelihood that the query could be generated by the document. Several approaches have arisen to compute such probability, including by maximum likelihood, smoothing and considering translation probabilities from related terms.

In this paper, we consider estimating this likelihood using modern pretrained deep language models, and in particular the text-to-text transfer transformer (T5) – giving rise to the QLM-T5. This approach is evaluated on the passage ranking task of the MS MARCO dataset; empirical results show that QLM-T5 significantly outperforms traditional QLM methods, as well as a recent ad-hoc methods that exploits T5 for this task.

1 Introduction

Language modelling has been introduced in Information Retrieval (IR) in the late '90s to score documents for a query [5,18] and as alternative to other popular methods such as TF-IDF and BM25. The most basic and popular form of language model used in IR is unigram language model, which defines a probability distribution over the words in the collection. A common way to exploit language models in IR is within the query likelihood model (QLM) [18], on which we base the method in this paper; alternative approaches include the relevance model of Lavrenko and Croft [9] and the risk minimization framework of Zhai and Lafferty [8].

QLM scores a document for retrieval by considering the likelihood that the query could be generated by the document. The basic form of QLM uses the maximum likelihood estimator (MLE) to compute the query likelihood; this however exposes the method to issues due to data sparseness [24], e.g., the estimated probability of a query term that does not appear in the document will be zero, rendering the overall score of the document to be zero. To overcome this issue, smoothing has been commonly used. Smoothing transfers probability mass from the probability associated with a query term appearing in the document to the

S. Zhuang and H. Li—Contributed equally to this work.

probability associated with that query term appearing in the collection. Extensively used smoothing methods include Jelinek–Mercer and Dirichlet smoothing [24], which interpolate, in a parametric manner, the likelihood of the term in the document with that associated with the term appearing in the collection. The optimal parameter values for these smoothing techniques are collection and application dependent [24]. Alternatives to these form of smoothing are methods that transfer probabilities across related terms (translation language models [1]) and others that use clusters and nearest neighbours [7,11].

Recent advances in natural language processing have seen the introduction of deep language models [2,12,19,20]; pre-trained versions of these models have been applied to search tasks demonstrating promising results [10]. Specifically, the common trend in IR is to obtain deep language models that have been pre-trained on a large text corpus and convert them to ranking models via fine-tuning on ranking tasks. An example is the work from Nogueira and Cho [16], where the raw text from a query-document pair is provided as input to the pre-trained deep language model BERT, which in turn outputs a relevance score. A notable benefit of using such deep language models is that no language preprocessing pipeline such as stemmers and stoppers is required. For example, different morphological variations are automatically handled by these deep language models by exploiting the knowledge gained from the pre-train and fine-tune steps.

In this paper we build upon the QLM tradition in IR, and create a novel QLM ranking method based on a specific deep language model. Our method, called QLM-T5, uses the text-to-text transfer transformer language model (T5) deep language model [20] in place of the MLE estimation in QLM; and, unlike in traditional QLM, it does so effectively without the need for further smoothing. T5 is an encoder-decoder model that has been shown effective for an array of natural language processing tasks. Our experimental results on the MS MARCO passage ranking task [15] show that QLM-T5 significantly outperforms traditional QLM methods, demonstrating the benefit of deep language models used within a QLM approach to IR.

2   T5 Query Language Model

The query likelihood model calculates the probability $P(Q|D)$ of generating the query Q from a given document D. Traditional approaches in IR use the maximum likelihood estimation (MLE) and smoothing methods to compute this probability [24]. Recent autoregressive deep language models such as generative pre-trained (GPT) [19] and text-to-text transfer transformer (T5) [20] can alternatively be used to calculate the likelihood of generating a target text given an input text using the teacher forcing inference mechanism: instead of taking the generated token as the input to the next time step, the target token is passed as the next input. The likelihood of generating an entire sequence of target tokens is then computed by the product of the sampling probabilities of the next target tokens from the output probability distributions of each time step.

In this work we focus on using the T5 deep language model, which has been already exploited in previous work in IR, but in an alternative form, i.e., to generate possible query variations to append to the document representation, which is then used for retrieval (doc2query-T5 method) [17].

The T5 model is an encoder-decoder architecture. When using the teacher forcing mechanism, the document text tokens $d_0, d_1...d_n \in D$ are provided as input to the encoder, while the target query text tokens $q_0, q_1...q_{|Q|} \in Q$ plus a decoder start of sentence token $<bos>$ at the beginning of the sequence are provided as input to the decoder. At each time step t, the decoder outputs the probability $P_{T5}(q_{t+1})$ of sampling the next target query token:

$$T5_t(Encoder(d_0, d_1...d_n), Decoder(<bos>, q_0, q_1...q_t)) = P_{T5}(q_{t+1}) \quad (1)$$

It is important to note that the probability of sampling the next query token is conditioned to the document text and all previous query tokens[1]:

$$P_{T5}(q_{t+1}) = P_{T5}(q_{t+1}|D, <bos>, q_0, q_1...q_t) \quad (2)$$

This is differ from the traditional unigram QLM, where the sampling probabilities of each token only depend on the document text, but somewhat resemble dependence language models [4,13] that provide a similar mechanism.

We take a similar approach to the traditional QLM to exploit T5 for retrieval. Specifically, we compute the query (log) likelihood for Q given the document D as

$$log(P_{QLM-T5}(Q, D)) = log(P_{T5}(<bos>)) + \sum_{i=0}^{|Q|-1} log(P_{T5}(q_i)) \quad (3)$$

3   Empirical Evaluation

We are interested to empirically verify the effectiveness of QLM-T5, compared to traditional forms of QLM; we further compare QLM-T5 to a recent method that also exploits T5 for ranking (doc2query-T5 [17]), but without casting T5 in the QLM framework. For this, we use the development portion of the MS MARCO Passage Ranking Dataset [15]. This portion consists of ≈8.8 million passages and 6980 unique queries; on average, each query has one relevant passage only.

Passages were indexed with Anserini [23] using the default parameters. Anserini was also used to produce runs for BM25 ($k1 = 0.82$ and $b = 0.68$), Query Language Models with Dirichlet (QLM-D, $\mu = 1,000$) and Jelinek Mercer (QLM-JM, $\lambda = 0.1$) smoothing, and Sequential Dependence Model using QLM-JM [13] (QLM-JM-SDM), retrieving the top 1,000 passages for each query. These form our first-stage retrieval baselines. We used QLM-JM-SDM to inform us regarding whether it may have been the inclusion of query term dependencies, rather than the actual deep language model, that produced gains over QLM-D/JM.

---

[1] The first query token q_0 only depends on the document text D plus the $<bos>$ token.

Because the inference stage of T5 is computationally expensive, in our experiments we used QLM-T5 as a second-stage re-ranker, with BM25 used as the first-stage ranker. We then also created runs where QLM-D and QLM-JM were used as second-stage re-ranker on top of BM25. For completeness, we also ran our QLM-T5 using QLM-D and QLM-JM as first-stage rankers. Although the aim of our experiments is to study the effectiveness of QLM-T5 with respect to other methods in the QLM framework, we also reproduced the doc2query-T5 model [17] to provide further context for the interpretation of our results. The doc2query-T5 model also relies on T5; furthermore, the same fine-tuned model was used[2]. However it does so by leveraging T5 to source possible query candidates that may be asked regarding a target document (passage in the case of these experiments). These query candidates are appended to the document to enhance its representation – retrieval is then performed with BM25 operated on the new representation of the documents.

As evaluation metrics, we use MRR@10, nDCG and INST. MRR@10[3] was used despite remarks that this is an unstable metric (Fuhr's argument [3], but perhaps more importantly Zobel&Rashidi's findings [25]) because this is the only metric used in the MS MARCO leaderboard, to which we want to allow comparison for further contextualisation of the results reported here. The use of nDCG for this task is less controversial (though note only binary relevance and mostly single-relevant documents for each query). The cut-offs considered were at 1 to model the use of the method for selecting an answer in context of e.g., a conversational search agent; at 3 and 10 to model a typical web search scenario; and at 1,000 to provide an evaluation of the complete ranking. We also computed INST [14] using the publicly available implementation from Koopman&Zuccon [6]. INST is a weighted precision metric where the probability of a user assessing a result at a specific rank depends on the rank position, the expected number of relevant documents T, and the actual number of relevant documents encountered up to that rank. This metric suits well the MS MARCO task, which is a question-answer based task with $T = 1$ (we use this value). Statistical analysis of results is performed using two-tailed paired t-test.

4   Results

Empirical results are reported in Table 1. The first four rows in the table show BM25 is superior to QLM-D, QLM-JM and QLM-JM-SDM on MS MARCO (differences statistical significant, $p < 0.01$); the superiority of BM25 with regards to QLM-D and QLM-JM is consistent with previous findings on other collections [21,22]. The next pair of rows shows that the traditional QLM methods are not effective second-stage rankers either.

---

[2] T5 model for MS MARCO from Nogueira et al. [17], fine-tuned to maximize query likelihood.

[3] I.e. the reciprocal rank value (averaged across all queries) up to rank 10 if a relevant document has been retrieved by then, otherwise zero.

Table 1. Effectiveness of first-stage and rerank methods. BM25+QLM-T5 is statistically significant better ($p < 0.01$) than all first-stage rankers, including doc2query-T5+BM25. BM25+QLM-T5 is statistically significant better ($p < 0.01$) than QLM-JM+QLM-T5 on metrics indicated by $\Diamond$, and BM25+QLM-T5 is statistically significant better ($p < 0.01$) than QLM-D+QLM-T5 on metrics indicated by §.

Method	ndcg@1	ndcg@3	ndcg@10	ndcg@1000	INST	MRR@10
BM25	0.1042	0.1736	0.2340	0.3161	0.0916	0.1874
QLM-JM	0.0960	0.1586	0.2181	0.2955	0.0849	0.1740
QLM-D	0.0831	0.1371	0.1874	0.2752	0.0730	0.1491
QLM-JM-SDM	0.1044	0.1674	0.2271	0.3032	0.0900	0.1825
BM25+QLM-JM	0.0960	0.1586	0.2181	0.3006	0.0849	0.1741
BM25+QLM-D	0.0831	0.1371	0.1875	0.2795	0.0730	0.1492
QLM-JM+QLM-T5	0.1765	0.2786	0.3577	0.4086	0.1485	0.2948
QLM-D+QLM-T5	0.1769	0.2790	0.3595	0.4123	0.1489	0.2960
BM25+QLM-T5	**0.1784**	**0.2823**$^\Diamond$	**0.3647**$^{\Diamond\,§}$	**0.4215**$^{\Diamond\,§}$	**0.1506**$^\Diamond$	**0.2997**$^{\Diamond\,§}$
doc2query-T5+BM25	0.1653	0.2600	0.3377	0.4139	0.1389	0.2768

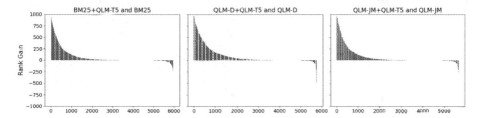

Fig. 1. Rank position gains/losses per query for QLM-T5 re-ranker compared to the respective first-stage retrieval method.

We now focus on the effectiveness of the proposed QLM-T5, which is used to re-rank results from a first-stage ranker (all results up to rank 1,000). We find that the use of QLM-T5 (irrespective of the first-stage method QLM-T5 uses) significantly outperforms first-stage retrieval runs, other re-rankers, and the doc2query-T5 model, which also relies on the T5 language model, on several evaluation metrics. Among all QLM-T5 runs, we find that the one that uses BM25 as first-stage ranker outperforms the others, and differences are statistically significant ($p < 0.01$) on several evaluation metrics.

Furthermore, in Fig. 1 we present the ranks gained (or lost) by QLM-T5 with respect to BM25, QLM-D and QLM-JM. Specifically, we measure how many rank positions the relevant passages have gained (lost) compared to the corresponding first-stage ranker method. Figure 1 indicates that QLM-T5 reranker sensibly improves rankings (movements of up to 991 ranks) for more than 50% of the queries for BM25, QLM-JM, and QLM-D, with more than $\approx 1,500$ queries exhibiting gains of over 100 rank positions. The method does however produce some losses: a small amount of queries appear to have rank losses for QLM-T5. Similar findings are obtained when nDCG was used in place of rank position.

To better understand when QLM-T5 worked and when it failed, we further analyzed the queries with the maximum (991) and minimum (−495) rank gains/losses between BM25+QLM-T5 and BM25. For query *"what does it mean when you dream about babies"*, QLM-T5 achieved the maximum rank gain of 991: the relevant passage is pushed from BM25's rank position 993 up to rank 2. We note that the passage placed by BM25+QLM-T5 at rank 1 also appears relevant to us: *"... Dreams that include babies are positive signs. Dreaming about interacting with a baby or simply seeing a baby in a dream can mean that pleasant surprises and fortuitous occurrences are about to occur in your life..."*,

For query *"how many tables can sql server join"*, QLM-T5 had the largest rank loss (−495): BM25 placed the relevant passage at rank 255 while BM25+QLM-T5 at rank 750. We further note, however, that the top passage by BM25+QLM-T5 is *"... A SQL Server JOIN is performed whenever two or more tables are joined in a SQL statement."*, which appears to us to be relevant to the query[4].

These examples suggest that (1) QLM-T5 can successfully capture the semantic meaning of queries and passages, and produce a good match; (2) losses observed for QLM-T5 might be because of unjudged passages in MS MARCO, (3) results on MS MARCO should be considered very carefully as the dataset does not contain information about unjudged documents (thus rendering impossible the computation of residuals, e.g., for INST) and assessments appear to be very shallow and primarily based on BM25.

5   Conclusion and Future Work

In this paper, we have adapted the T5 deep language model within the query likelihood model to rank passages. Results on the MS MARCO benchmark dataset show that QLM-T5 significantly outperforms traditional QLM methods, quantifying the benefits of using deep language models within QLM in place of MLE and smoothed estimators. We also show that QLM-T5 more effectively models query dependencies than sequential dependence models.

A drawback of QLM-T5 is its computational efficiency. The method, being based on a transformer based neural network, requires considerable running time at inference. In addition, unlike traditional QLM methods (but akin to sequential dependence models), the calculation of the likelihood of each query term is conditioned on all previous query terms: pre-computing and storing query term likelihoods independently of the query is then not possible. This makes it reasonable to execute the QLM-T5 as a second-stage reranker, but it is infeasible to use it as a first-stage ranker instead. However, we believe that this issue could be partially alleviated by storing outputs of the encoder layer of T5 in the index so

---

[4] The passage marked relevant in MS MARCO for this query is *"... A JOIN clause is used to combine rows from two or more tables, based on a related column between them..."*.

that at runtime the only inference needed is at the decoder level. Compared to other strong neural re-ranker baselines, such as BERT-based re-ranker [16], our model is outperformed in terms of MRR@10 (BERT-Large: 0.365 vs. QLM-T5: 0.300). Future work will explore this direction along with alternative avenues to improve the efficiency of QLM-T5, e.g., so that it becomes reasonable to apply it to document ranking tasks, besides the considered passage ranking.

Acknowledgements. Hang Li is funded by the Grain Research and Development Corporation (GRDC), project AgAsk (UOQ2003-009RTX). Associate Professor Guido Zuccon is the recipient of an Australian Research Council DECRA Research Fellowship (DE180101579) and a Google Faculty Award.

References

1. Berger, A., Lafferty, J.: Information retrieval as statistical translation. In: Proceedings of the 22nd Annual International ACM SIGIR Conference on Research and Development in Information Retrieval, pp. 222–229 (1999)
2. Devlin, J., Chang, M.W., Lee, K., Toutanova, K.: Bert: pre-training of deep bidirectional transformers for language understanding. In: Proceedings of the 2019 Conference of the North American Chapter of the Association for Computational Linguistics: Human Language Technologies, pp. 4171–4186 (2019)
3. Fuhr, N.: Some common mistakes in IR evaluation, and how they can be avoided. In: ACM SIGIR Forum, vol. 51, pp. 32–41. ACM, New York (2018)
4. Gao, J., Nie, J.Y., Wu, G., Cao, G.: Dependence language model for information retrieval. In: Proceedings of the 27th Annual International ACM SIGIR Conference on Research and Development in Information Retrieval, pp. 170–177 (2004)
5. Hiemstra, D.: A linguistically motivated probabilistic model of information retrieval. In: Nikolaou, C., Stephanidis, C. (eds.) ECDL 1998. LNCS, vol. 1513, pp. 569–584. Springer, Heidelberg (1998). https://doi.org/10.1007/3-540-49653-X_34
6. Koopman, B., Zuccon, G.: A test collection for matching patients to clinical trials. In: Proceedings of the 39th International ACM SIGIR Conference on Research and Development in Information Retrieval, SIGIR 2016, pp. 669–672. Association for Computing Machinery, New York (2016). https://doi.org/10.1145/2911451.2914672
7. Kurland, O., Lee, L.: Corpus structure, language models, and ad hoc information retrieval. In: Proceedings of the 27th Annual International ACM SIGIR Conference on Research and Development in Information Retrieval, pp. 194–201 (2004)
8. Lafferty, J., Zhai, C.: Document language models, query models, and risk minimization for information retrieval. In: Proceedings of the 24th Annual International ACM SIGIR Conference on Research and Development in Information Retrieval, SIGIR 2001, pp. 111–119. Association for Computing Machinery, New York (2001). https://doi.org/10.1145/383952.383970
9. Lavrenko, V., Croft, W.B.: Relevance based language models. In: Proceedings of the 24th Annual International ACM SIGIR Conference on Research and Development in Information Retrieval, SIGIR 2001, pp. 120–127. Association for Computing Machinery, New York (2001). https://doi.org/10.1145/383952.383972
10. Lin, J., Nogueira, R., Yates, A.: Pretrained transformers for text ranking: Bert and beyond. arXiv preprint arXiv:2010.06467 (2020)

11. Liu, X., Croft, W.B.: Cluster-based retrieval using language models. In: Proceedings of the 27th Annual International ACM SIGIR Conference on Research and Development in Information Retrieval, pp. 186–193 (2004)
12. Liu, Y., et al.: Roberta: a robustly optimized Bert pretraining approach. arXiv preprint arXiv:1907.11692 (2019)
13. Metzler, D., Croft, W.B.: A Markov random field model for term dependencies. In: Proceedings of the 28th Annual International ACM SIGIR Conference on Research and Development in Information Retrieval, pp. 472–479 (2005)
14. Moffat, A., Bailey, P., Scholer, F., Thomas, P.: Inst: an adaptive metric for information retrieval evaluation. In: Proceedings of the 20th Australasian Document Computing Symposium. ADCS 2015. Association for Computing Machinery, New York (2015). https://doi.org/10.1145/2838931.2838938
15. Nguyen, T., et al.: MS MARCO: a human-generated machine reading comprehension dataset (2016)
16. Nogueira, R., Cho, K.: Passage re-ranking with Bert. arXiv preprint arXiv:1901.04085 (2019)
17. Nogueira, R., Lin, J., Epistemic, A.: From doc2query to docTTTTTquery. Online preprint (2019)
18. Ponte, J.M., Croft, W.B.: A language modeling approach to information retrieval. In: Proceedings of the 21st Annual International ACM SIGIR Conference on Research and Development in Information Retrieval, pp. 275–281 (1998)
19. Radford, A., Wu, J., Child, R., Luan, D., Amodei, D., Sutskever, I.: Language models are unsupervised multitask learners. OpenAI blog 1(8), 9 (2019)
20. Raffel, C., et al.: Exploring the limits of transfer learning with a unified text-to-text transformer. arXiv preprint arXiv:1910.10683 (2019)
21. Robertson, S., Zaragoza, H.: The Probabilistic Relevance Framework: BM25 and Beyond. Now Publishers Inc (2009)
22. Speriosu, M., Tashiro, T.: Comparison of Okapi BM25 and language modeling algorithms for NTCIR-6. Justsystems Corporation 14 (2006)
23. Yang, P., Fang, H., Lin, J.: Anserini: enabling the use of lucene for information retrieval research. In: Proceedings of the 40th International ACM SIGIR Conference on Research and Development in Information Retrieval, pp. 1253–1256 (2017)
24. Zhai, C., Lafferty, J.: A study of smoothing methods for language models applied to information retrieval. ACM Trans. Inf. Syst. (TOIS) 22(2), 179–214 (2004)
25. Zobel, J., Rashidi, L.: Corpus bootstrapping for assessment of the properties of effectiveness measures. In: Proceedings of the 29th ACM International Conference on Information & Knowledge Management, CIKM 2020, pp. 1933–1952. Association for Computing Machinery, New York (2020). https://doi.org/10.1145/3340531.3411998

Tweet Length Matters: A Comparative Analysis on Topic Detection in Microblogs

Furkan Şahinuç and Cagri Toraman$^{(\boxtimes)}$ ⓘ

Aselsan Research Center, Ankara, Turkey
{fsahinuc,ctoraman}@aselsan.com.tr

Abstract. Microblogs are characterized as short and informal text; and therefore sparse and noisy. To understand topic semantics of short text, supervised and unsupervised methods are investigated, including traditional bag-of-words and deep learning-based models. However, the effectiveness of such methods are not together investigated in short-text topic detection. In this study, we provide a comparative analysis on topic detection in microblogs. We construct a tweet dataset based on the recent and important events worldwide, including the COVID-19 pandemic and BlackLivesMatter movement. We also analyze the effect of varying tweet length in both evaluation and training. Our results show that tweet length matters in terms of the effectiveness of a topic-detection method.

Keywords: Microblog · Short text · Topic detection · Tweet

1 Introduction

Online social networks, such as microblogs, are rich sources to share opinion and information, as well as collaborate with other users. Public discussion can be about various topics. Finding their topic labels can provide semantic basement and understanding for many applications; such as information filtering [2], new event detection and tracking [1], sentiment analysis [6], and opinion mining [10].

Microblogs are generally characterized as having short, informal, and noisy text. Tweets are one of the most popular example of microblogs. Finding their topics can be challenging due to the aforementioned characteristics. Given a set of microblogs, or tweets in this study, the task is to detect a single coarse-grained topic label for each one. We refer to this task as *tweet topic detection*.

Several methods are proposed for topic detection. Topic Detection and Tracking aims to monitor news stories not seen before, and group individual topics [1]. Topic modeling methods, such as LDA [4], discover thematic clusters of documents as mixture of probability distributions. Rather than finding topic groups in an unsupervised way, our task is a supervised classification. Traditional methods encode documents in the bag-of-words model, and employ state-of-the-art

© Springer Nature Switzerland AG 2021
D. Hiemstra et al. (Eds.): ECIR 2021, LNCS 12657, pp. 471–478, 2021.
https://doi.org/10.1007/978-3-030-72240-1_50

classifiers, such as SVM. However, such methods mostly rely on word occurrence, and thereby suffer from sparsity and vocabulary mismatch, which are likely to be observed in short text. With the recent developments in deep learning, documents can be encoded to capture advanced semantics with neural networks and word embeddings [17]. Words are not assumed to be independent as in bag-of-words. Text semantics are captured sequentially using word order and positions to get bidirectional contextual representations, as in the Transformer model [22].

There are many efforts to overcome sparsity and vocabulary mismatch in tweet classification. Tweet-specific features are extracted for classification [14]. Topic memory networks are employed for short text classification [25]. Topically enriched word embeddings are used for topic detection [14]. Neural models, such as RNN and LSTM, are employed to detect discrimination-related tweets [24], and CNN for Twitter sentiment analysis [12]. Transformer-based language models, such as BERT [9], are employed in disaster-related tweet detection [20].

Our contributions are the followings. (i) Although the existing studies cover various methods for tweet classification on different domains, there is still a lack of comparative analysis for tweet topic detection. We provide a comparative analysis of both traditional and recent methods for topic detection of short text, particularly tweets. (ii) Short text is mostly studied in terms of average length (number of words). We provide a detailed analysis for the effect of the length of short text in both evaluation and training. (iii) We construct a tweet dataset with topic labels related to recent and important events, including the COVID-19 pandemic and the BlackLivesMatter movement.

2   Topic Detection in Microblogs

In this section, we select and explain six methods related to tweet topic detection; namely, Boolean search [15], topic modeling [4], bag-of-words [15], word embeddings [5], neural network [13], and Transformer-based language model [9].

Boolean Search. Inverted index keeps a dictionary of words, and for each word, a list that holds the documents that words occur in [15]. Query keywords are searched efficiently on an inverted index by Boolean search operations. We assign topics to tweets based on any keyword match by the Boolean OR operator. We pre-determine five query keywords for each topic based on the most frequent hashtags. In case of matching more than one topic, we assign off-topic. To find more matches, words are stemmed with the Snowball stemmer for indexing.

Topic Modeling. Topic modeling is a probabilistic method that finds coherent topic distributions in the given documents in an unsupervised way. We use Latent Dirichlet Allocation (LDA) [4] for topic modeling. To utilize topic distributions for supervised topic detection, we use the topic distribution of a document as its feature vector. We then employ Support Vector Machines (SVM) for training.

Bag-of-Words. Bag-of-words is a document encoding method based on vector space model, where each document is represented in a fixed length of vectors [15]. Each vector consists of identifiers for terms in documents. We use TF-IDF

(Term Frequency-Inverse Document Frequency) term weighting [15]. We employ SVM for training. In this method, words are assumed to be independent, and grammar structure is not preserved.

Word Embeddings. Word embeddings are the encoded vector representations for words in an embedding space that projects semantical similarities [16]. Word embeddings are divided into contextual and non-contextual ones. Contextual embeddings have different vectors according to the text that they occur in, while non-contextual embeddings have static vectors regardless of context. This method considers non-contextual embeddings, while contextual ones are examined in Transformer-based language models. We use FastText [5], which is the successor of Word2Vec [16] and GloVe [19], but considers sub-word embeddings by n-grams. To obtain sentence embeddings for tweets, we get the average of word embeddings with L2 normalization, which divides the sum of embeddings by the length of a vector in the Euclidean space. We use a softmax layer to compute the probabilities for topic labels.

Neural Networks. Artificial neural networks have significant interest in the last decade, such as Recurrent Neural Network (RNN) and Convolutional Neural Networks (CNN), to process text sequentially and get neural embeddings. We select CNN that leverages local features in hidden layers of networks with convolving filters. CNN achieves remarkable results in natural language processing tasks [12,13]. Based on [13], we train CNN for sentence classification with one layer of convolution on randomly initialized word embeddings.

Transformer-Based Language Models. Transformer is a deep learning-based architecture that uses self-attention for each token over all tokens [22]. Similar to RNN and CNN, text order is preserved; but Transformer processes text sequence without recurrent neural structures, instead with self-attention that keeps positional embeddings. We select BERT [9], which is a deep learning-based language model built on bidirectional contextual representations of words by considering word positions and context with Transformer. To fine-tune BERT, we add a softmax layer with the cross-entropy loss function. The CLS sentence embeddings provided by the last layer of BERT are given as input to this additional layer.

3   Experiments

3.1   Experimental Setup

Dataset Construction. We collect around 100 million tweets in English, 21% of which have at least one hashtag, from Twitter API between April 07, 2020 and June 15, 2020. We select six important topics that occur in the top-100 most frequently used hashtags. The topics are the COVID-19 pandemic, "Black Lives Matter" (BLM) movement, Korean popular music (K-Pop), Bollywood movies and series, gaming consoles, and U.S. politics. We notice that many hashtags belong to the same topic. We assign topics to tweets according to the

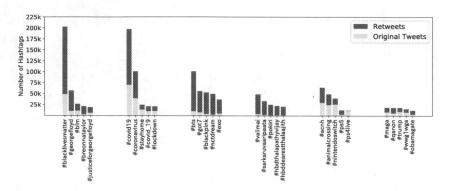

Fig. 1. The most frequently used five hashtags for each topic (BLM, COVID-19, K-pop, Bollywood movies, gaming, and U.S. politics, respectively).

predetermined set of hashtags for each topic. Figure 1 displays the top-5 most frequently used hashtags for each topic. A significant part of the hashtags are observed in retweets for K-Pop and Bollywood.

We apply the following cleaning steps to construct our dataset. (i) We exclude retweets, since duplicate contents would cause bias in results. (ii) We ignore the tweets with multiple hashtags from different topics, and the tweets with less than three words. (iii) We remove the words with less than three and more than 15 characters; as well as hashtags, mentions, and URLs. We keep words with only alpha-numeric characters. Words are lowercased. The NLTK lemmatization [3] is applied. (iv) We randomly select out-of-topic tweets that contain no related hashtag to our topics, which makes seven classes. The size of out-of-topic is chosen to be approximately 10% of the size of whole dataset. The final version of our dataset has 354,310 tweets[1]. The average length (number of words) is 13.4. The total numbers of tweets by topics are given in Table 1.

Table 1. The total number of tweets in our topic-detection dataset.

BLM	COVID-19	K-Pop	Bollywood	Gaming	U.S. Politics	Out-of-Topic	**Total**
61,672	139,036	45,817	9,661	36,613	26,373	35,138	**354,310**

Methodology. We use scikit-learn [18] for bag-of-words and topic modeling. We limit the vector size to 10,000 features, and remove the English stop words provided by scikit-learn. For LDA, we choose the number of topics as 50, based on the preliminary experiments. We use Linear SVC with one-vs-rest multi-classification for both models. For word embeddings, we use FastText's classification module [11] by choosing the vector dimension as 100. For neural networks, we follow CNN-based sentence classification [13], and use TensorFlow[2] with default parameters.

---

[1] The dataset can be accessed in https://github.com/avaapm/ECIR2021.
[2] https://github.com/dennybritz/cnn-text-classification-tf.

For Transformer-based models, we use DistilBERT [21] uncased model by Hug-gingFace [23] for the sake of efficiency.

We design two experiments: (i) We compare six important topic-detection methods, by applying 10-fold cross validation and reporting the weighted F1 score to evaluate effectiveness. The pairwise differences between the methods are statistically validated by using the two-tailed paired t-test at a 95% interval with Bonferroni correction. (ii) We analyze effectiveness for varying tweet lengths from 4 to 40 words to understand the behavior of the topic-detection methods.

3.2   Experimental Results

Comparison of Topic-Detection Methods. The comparison results are given in Table 2. We observe that (i) Boolean search has a poor performance, possibly due to dynamic dictionary in tweets. (ii) CNN-based topic detection statistically significantly outperforms other methods in short text, except BERT-based topic detection (we also validate that BERT statistically significantly outperforms others too, except CNN). We fine-tune BERT to provide a classification layer, but one can pre-train BERT for short and informal text to improve its effectiveness. (iii) Bag-of-words and topic modeling have lower scores, compared to CNN and BERT, possibly due to the sparsity of short text. (iv) FastText performs poor, possibly due to the fact that we employ pre-trained non-contextual word embeddings, not fine-tuned on the changing context of microblogs.

Table 2. The effectiveness results for topic detection in short text. The means of 10-fold cross-validation are reported. • indicates statistical significant difference at a 95% interval (with Bonferroni correction $p < 0.01$) in pairwise comparisons between the highest performing method and others (except the one with ○).

Method	Weighted F1 Score
Boolean search on inverted index	0.202 ± 0.0002
Topic modeling (LDA) with SVM	0.456 ± 0.0001
Bag-of-words (TF-IDF) with SVM	0.672 ± 0.0003
Word embeddings (FastText)	0.649 ± 0.0002
Neural networks (CNN)	$0.754• \pm 0.0019$
Transformer-based language models (BERT)	$0.739○ \pm 0.0002$

Effect of Tweet Length. In this experiment, we employ the highest performing four models. Figure 2 shows the effectiveness of each model for varying tweet length (number of words). In Fig. 2a, we keep all train instances regardless of their length to show the effect of tweet length in evaluation. In Fig. 2b, we use the distinct subsets of training data to show the effect of tweet length in training. Each subset contains tweets with the same length.

In Fig. 2a, we observe that (i) the effectiveness of all methods decreases as tweet length in evaluation gets shorter. We thereby state that tweet length matters in evaluation. BERT and CNN have better performance in shorter tweets, compared to the others. (ii) The highest results for all methods are seen when tweet length is between 20 and 30 words. (iii) The highest performing method is CNN, while BERT challenges especially in extremely short and long tweets.

In Fig. 2b, we observe that (i) unlike the previous results, CNN performs poor when training data is limited to the same length. We thereby state that tweet length matters in training. CNN applies padding to input embedding matrix according to the longest tweet length [13]. Since this setup focuses on a specific length in training, CNN does not apply padding and model size gets smaller, which could be the reason of its poor performance. (ii) BERT outperforms the others in this setup, i.e. BERT is more robust to text length in training. (iii) Since the number of train instances gets too small as text length increases, effectiveness gets deteriorated after 30 words. However, BERT is more robust to train size, compared to other methods. Bag-of-words has also good performance in longer text, as expected due to the lower degree of sparsity.

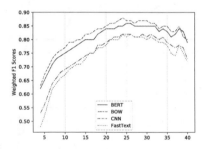 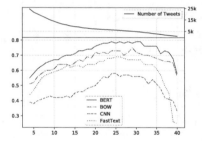

(a) Training set includes tweets with all lengths. X-axis represents tweet length in test set. Number of tweets for each length is the same for training.

(b) Training set includes tweets with the same length. X-axis represents tweet length in both training and test sets. Number of tweets for each length is given at the top.

Fig. 2. The effect of tweet length (number of words) on topic-detection methods.

4   Conclusion and Future Work

We provide a comparative analysis of traditional and recent methods for topic detection in short text. We construct a tweet dataset with the recent events, including the COVID-19 pandemic and BlackLivesMatter movement. Our experimental results show that the sentence embeddings based on a neural model (CNN) and a Transformer-based language model (BERT) obtain the highest effectiveness scores. We also show that tweet length matters in both evaluation and training for the effectiveness of a topic-detection method. In future work, we plan to investigate other sentence embeddings, such as InferSent [8] or Universal Sentence Encoder [7]. The effect of tweet length can be further analyzed in different short-text datasets, such as news snippets.

References

1. Allan, J., Papka, R., Lavrenko, V.: On-line new event detection and tracking. In: Proceedings of SIGIR, pp. 37–45 (1998). https://doi.org/10.1145/290941.290954
2. Belkin, N.J., Croft, W.B.: Information filtering and information retrieval: two sides of the same coin? Commun. ACM **35**(12), 29–38 (1992). https://doi.org/10.1145/138859.138861
3. Bird, S., Klein, E., Loper, E.: Natural Language Processing with Python: Analyzing Text with the Natural Language Toolkit. O'Reilly Media, Inc., Newton (2009)
4. Blei, D.M., Ng, A.Y., Jordan, M.I.: Latent Dirichlet allocation. J. Mach. Learn. Res. **3**(1), 993–1022 (2003). https://doi.org/10.5555/944919.944937
5. Bojanowski, P., Grave, E., Joulin, A., Mikolov, T.: Enriching word vectors with subword information. Trans. Assoc. Comput. Linguist. **5**, 135–146 (2017). https://doi.org/10.1162/tacl_a_00051
6. Van Canneyt, S., Claeys, N., Dhoedt, B.: Topic-dependent sentiment classification on Twitter. In: Hanbury, A., Kazai, G., Rauber, A., Fuhr, N. (eds.) ECIR 2015. LNCS, vol. 9022, pp. 441–446. Springer, Cham (2015). https://doi.org/10.1007/978-3-319-16354-3_48
7. Cer, D., et al.: Universal sentence encoder for English. In: Proceedings of EMNLP: System Demonstrations, pp. 169–174 (2018). https://doi.org/10.18653/v1/D18-2029
8. Conneau, A., Kiela, D., Schwenk, H., Barrault, L., Bordes, A.: Supervised learning of universal sentence representations from natural language inference data. In: Proceedings of EMNLP, pp. 670–680 (2017). https://doi.org/10.18653/v1/D17-1070
9. Devlin, J., Chang, M.W., Lee, K., Toutanova, K.: BERT: pre-training of deep bidirectional transformers for language understanding. In: Proceedings of NAACL-HLT, pp. 4171–4186 (2019). https://doi.org/10.18653/v1/N19-1423
10. Fang, A., Ounis, I., Habel, P., Macdonald, C., Limsopatham, N.: Topic-centric classification of Twitter user's political orientation. In: Proceedings of SIGIR, pp. 791–794 (2015). https://doi.org/10.1145/2766462.2767833
11. Joulin, A., Grave, E., Bojanowski, P., Douze, M., Jégou, H., Mikolov, T.: Fasttext.zip: compressing text classification models. arXiv preprint arXiv:1612.03651 (2016)
12. Kalchbrenner, N., Grefenstette, E., Blunsom, P.: A convolutional neural network for modelling sentences. In: Proceedings of ACL, pp. 655–665 (2014). https://doi.org/10.3115/v1/P14-1062
13. Kim, Y.: Convolutional neural networks for sentence classification. In: Proceedings of EMNLP, pp. 1746–1751 (2014). https://doi.org/10.3115/v1/D14-1181
14. Li, Q., Shah, S., Liu, X., Nourbakhsh, A., Fang, R.: Tweetsift: tweet topic classification based on entity knowledge base and topic enhanced word embedding. In: Proceedings of CIKM, pp. 2429–2432 (2016). https://doi.org/10.1145/2983323.2983325

15. Manning, C.D., Schütze, H., Raghavan, P.: Introduction to Information Retrieval. Cambridge University Press, Cambridge (2008). https://doi.org/10.1017/CBO9780511809071

16. Mikolov, T., Sutskever, I., Chen, K., Corrado, G.S., Dean, J.: Distributed representations of words and phrases and their compositionality. In: Proceedings of NIPS, pp. 3111–3119 (2013)

17. Onal, K.D., et al.: Neural information retrieval: at the end of the early years. Inf. Retrieval **21**(2–3), 111–182 (2018). https://doi.org/10.1007/s10791-017-9321-y

18. Pedregosa, F., et al.: Scikit-learn: machine learning in python. J. Mach. Learn. Res. **12**, 2825–2830 (2011)

19. Pennington, J., Socher, R., Manning, C.: GloVe: global vectors for word representation. In: Proceedings of EMNLP, pp. 1532–1543 (2014). https://doi.org/10.3115/v1/D14-1162

20. Ray Chowdhury, J., Caragea, C., Caragea, D.: Cross-lingual disaster-related multilabel tweet classification with manifold mixup. In: Proceedings of ACL: Student Research Workshop, pp. 292–298 (2020). https://doi.org/10.18653/v1/2020.acl-srw.39

21. Sanh, V., Debut, L., Chaumond, J., Wolf, T.: DistilBERT, a distilled version of BERT: smaller, faster, cheaper and lighter. In: NeurIPS EMC^2 Workshop (2019)

22. Vaswani, A., et al.: Attention is all you need. In: Proceedings of NIPS, pp. 5998–6008 (2017)

23. Wolf, T., et al.: Huggingface's transformers: state-of-the-art natural language processing. arXiv preprint arXiv:1910.03771 (2019)

24. Yuan, S., Wu, X., Xiang, Y.: Incorporating pre-training in long short-term memory networks for tweets classification. In: Proceedings of IEEE ICDM, pp. 1329–1334 (2016). https://doi.org/10.1109/ICDM.2016.0181

25. Zeng, J., Li, J., Song, Y., Gao, C., Lyu, M.R., King, I.: Topic memory networks for short text classification. In: Proceedings of EMNLP, pp. 3120–3131 (2018). https://doi.org/10.18653/v1/D18-1351

Demo Papers

repro_eval: A Python Interface to Reproducibility Measures of System-Oriented IR Experiments

Timo Breuer[1](✉), Nicola Ferro[2], Maria Maistro[3], and Philipp Schaer[1]

[1] TH Köln - University of Applied Sciences, Cologne, Germany
{timo.breuer,philipp.schaer}@th-koeln.de
[2] University of Padua, Padua, Italy
ferro@dei.unipd.it
[3] University of Copenhagen, Copenhagen, Denmark
mm@di.ku.dk

Abstract. In this work we introduce repro_eval - a tool for reactive reproducibility studies of system-oriented Information Retrieval (IR) experiments. The corresponding Python package provides IR researchers with measures for different levels of reproduction when evaluating their systems' outputs. By offering an easily extensible interface, we hope to stimulate common practices when conducting a reproducibility study of system-oriented IR experiments.

Keywords: Replicability · Reproducibility · Evaluation

1 Introduction

Reproduciblity is a cornerstone of scientific findings. However, many scientific fields are affected by reproducibility issues [2] and IR is not an exception [6]. In the previous decade, different communities from the computational sciences developed a range of tools supporting researchers in their attempts to make studies reproducible.

According to Potthast et al. [12] reproducibility efforts can be subdivided into either *proactive*, *reactive* or *supportive* actions. Many existing tools for reproducibility support *proactive* actions. More general examples include RoHub [11], CodaLab[1] (executable papers), ReproZip [4] (workflow tracking, data provenance), Process Migration Framework (system resource logging) [13], ReproMatch[2] (search engine for reproducibility tools), noWorkflow [10] (monitoring data provenance), yesWorkflow [9] and others. With special regards to system-oriented IR experiments, the implementations and requirements can be *proactively* packaged with virtual machines or as shown more recently with Docker

---

[1] https://codalab.org/.
[2] http://repromatch.poly.edu/tools/search/.

© Springer Nature Switzerland AG 2021
D. Hiemstra et al. (Eds.): ECIR 2021, LNCS 12657, pp. 481–486, 2021.
https://doi.org/10.1007/978-3-030-72240-1_51

containers as exemplified by TIRA [12] and the OSIRRC platform [5], respectively. On the other hand, the IR community promotes *reactive* reproducibility studies by archiving experimental data from evaluation campaigns at TREC [15] or CLEF [1]. Here, we can use the artifacts - or more specifically system runs - of previous experiments as points of reference to which we compare the results of our reimplementations. Tools of *supportive* actions have been realized as *Evaluation-as-a-Service* infrastructures and shared task platforms [8].

The presented software complements existing reproducibility tools by measuring the exactness of reproduced system runs in relation to their original counterparts. It is often not sufficient to compare system results based on their average retrieval performance (ARP), as the averaged scores may hide differences between the distributions of topic scores or the order of documents. In this sense, `repro_eval` supports researchers as part of their *reactive* approach when reimplementing another researcher's retrieval system. The implemented measures of `repro_eval` provide the reproducer with insights at different levels of reproduction. Under consideration of these insights, `repro_eval` contributes to the adequate use of reimplemented systems, for instance when they are used as baseline systems in experimental evaluations.

2   Evaluating Reimplementations with `repro_eval`

The presented Python package compiles system-oriented reproducibility measures we introduced in previous studies [3]. According to the ACM policy of *Artifact Review and Badging*[3], we align the system-oriented IR experiment to the terminology it introduces. More specifically, `repro_eval` can be used to evaluate the *reproducibility* with a reimplemented IR system in combination with the *same test collection* of the original experiments, whereas *replicability* considers the reimplementation in combination with a *different test collection*.

In this sense, `repro_eval` supports IR researchers who want to compare their systems to a reference or state-of-the-art system for which no source code or public artifact is available. Especially, when reference systems need to be evaluated in a different context (with a possibly different test collection), IR researchers cannot rely on the results reported in the original publication. With `repro_eval` they can evaluate their reimplemented reference system and gain insight into how similar the two systems are. With an increasing level of specificity, the Python package provides different measures that provide a more nuanced perspective on the degree of reproduction and replication. Figure 1 provides a hierarchical illustration of the different levels and corresponding measures.

Proceeding from the bottom to the top of this hierarchy, the specificity of reproduction (and replication) increases from the most general to the most specific. Note that some evaluations are limited to reproduced experiments only.

---

[3] https://www.acm.org/publications/policies/artifact-review-badging Previous versions of the policy basically swapped the meaning of the two terms *reproducibility* and *replicability*, which is why we used the terms vice versa in earlier studies.

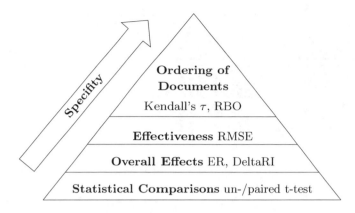

Fig. 1. Measures of `repro_eval` arranged with regard to their level of specificity

The ordering of documents can only be compared if all systems runs (possibly) contain the same documents or were derived from the same test collection. Likewise, the level of effectiveness can only be determined if reproduced runs are derived for the same topics as in the original experiment. Here, the Root Mean Square Error (RMSE) evaluates the closeness of the topic scores distributions between the reproduced and original results. In order to evaluate replicated runs, reimplementations need to be compared on more general levels. The overall effects are determined with the help of the Effect Ratio (ER) and the Delta Relative Improvement (DeltaRI). To do so, a replicated baseline run and an improved version of it (which we refer to as the advanced run) are required. The ER and DeltaRI measure how accurately the effects between the baseline and the advanced run can be replicated. At the most general level, it is possible to compare the topic score distributions of the reproduced and replicated runs with paired and unpaired t-tests, respectively. The p-values deliver information about the success of reproduction and replication. In case of a low p-value, there is a strong evidence that the repeated experiment has failed.

3   Case Study on the Evaluation of Reproducibility

Let us consider IR researchers reimplementing a retrieval system of another research group that provides no other artifacts except for the description in the publication and the original run files. Having reimplemented the system, the researchers want to know about the quality of their reproductions/replications. Since the publication lacks some details about optional processing steps or parameterizations, the researchers try different variations and end up having many runs. How do they know which one is the most exactly reproduced/replicated run? Intuitively, they can compare the runs by the ARP. However, equal (averaged) scores might hide differences between the topic score distributions or document orderings. Furthermore, replicated runs (derived from another test collection) cannot be compared at these two levels.

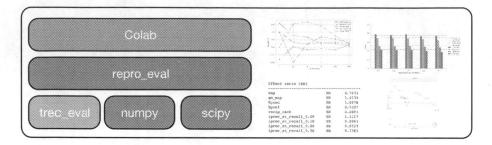

Fig. 2. repro_eval as a cornerstone for statistical and visual analytics of reproducibility studies with the help of Colab.

In this case, repro_eval provides a toolbox of different measures for reproducibility and replicability. It is a Python package which uses the Pytrec_eval [7] interface to trec_eval[4], as well as numpy [16] and scipy [14]. Once installed, repro_eval can be used either by a conventional command line call (similar to trec_eval) or by importing it into programs as exemplified by the Colab-based tool for visually analysing the reproducibility and replicability (see Fig. 2).

We provide an interactive demonstration in a Colab-based environment featuring example data that complies with the previously outlined use case[5]. Besides numerical outputs comparable to those of trec_eval, our demonstration showcases some plots that help researchers to gain a better understanding of the reproductions. Bar plots visualize conventional comparisons at the level of ARP, whereas the included plots of Kendall's τ Union and the RMSE illustrate the reproduction quality across the cut-off ranks. At the level of overall effects, the ER/DeltaRI plots are a valuable tool helping to explore the space of reproduction/replication. In theory, the best reproduction/replication yields (ER 1/DeltaRI 0). The included scatter plots visualize which runs resemble the originals in terms of P@10, AP, and nDCG the most.

4   Contributions and Conclusions

We introduce repro_eval, a tool for reproducibility studies of system-oriented IR experiments. This tool provides a Python package that can be used by researchers in their reactive approach to reimplement another researchers' experiments. The included reproducibility and replicability measures offer assistance when measuring the closeness of reimplemented systems' outputs compared to the original results. More technical details, installation instructions and a demonstration video of repro_eval can be found in our public GitHub repository[6].

---

[4] https://github.com/usnistgov/trec_eval.

[5] https://colab.research.google.com/github/irgroup/repro_eval/blob/master/example/demo.ipynb.

[6] https://github.com/irgroup/repro_eval.

Acknowledgements. This paper was partially supported by the EU Horizon 2020 research and innovation programme under the Marie Skłodowska-Curie grant agreement No. 893667, and by the German Research Foundation (No. 407518790).

References

1. Agosti, Maristella, Di Nunzio, Giorgio Maria, Ferro, Nicola, Silvello, Gianmaria: An innovative approach to data management and curation of experimental data generated through IR test collections. In: Ferro, N., Peters, C. (eds.) Information Retrieval Evaluation in a Changing World. TIRS, vol. 41, pp. 105–122. Springer, Cham (2019). https://doi.org/10.1007/978-3-030-22948-1_4
2. Baker, M.: 1,500 scientists lift the lid on reproducibility. Nature **533**, 452–454 (2016)
3. Breuer, T., et al.: How to measure the reproducibility of system-oriented IR experiments. In: Huang, J., et al. (eds.) Proceedings of the 43rd International ACM SIGIR Conference on Research and Development in Information Retrieval, SIGIR 2020, Virtual Event, China, 25–30 July 2020, pp. 349–358. ACM (2020). https://doi.org/10.1145/3397271.3401036
4. Chirigati, F., Rampin, R., Shasha, D.F., Freire, J.: Reprozip: computational reproducibility with ease. In: Özcan, F., Koutrika, G., Madden, S. (eds.) Proceedings of the 2016 International Conference on Management of Data, SIGMOD Conference 2016, San Francisco, CA, USA, 26 June–01 July 2016, pp. 2085–2088. ACM (2016). https://doi.org/10.1145/2882903.2899401
5. Clancy, R., Ferro, N., Hauff, C., Lin, J., Sakai, T., Wu, Z.Z.: The SIGIR 2019 open-source IR replicability challenge (OSIRRC 2019). In: Piwowarski, B., Chevalier, M., Gaussier, É., Maarek, Y., Nie, J., Scholer, F. (eds.) Proceedings of the 42nd International ACM SIGIR Conference on Research and Development in Information Retrieval, SIGIR 2019, Paris, France, 21–25 July 2019, pp. 1432–1434. ACM (2019). https://doi.org/10.1145/3331184.3331647
6. Ferro, N.: Reproducibility challenges in information retrieval evaluation. J. Data Inf. Qual. **8**(2), 8:1–8:4 (2017). https://doi.org/10.1145/3020206
7. Gysel, C.V., de Rijke, M.: Pytrec_eval: an extremely fast python interface to trec_eval. In: Collins-Thompson, K., Mei, Q., Davison, B.D., Liu, Y., Yilmaz, E. (eds.) The 41st International ACM SIGIR Conference on Research & Development in Information Retrieval, SIGIR 2018, Ann Arbor, MI, USA, 08–12 July 2018, pp. 873–876. ACM (2018). https://doi.org/10.1145/3209978.3210065
8. Hopfgartner, F., et al.: Evaluation-as-a-service for the computational sciences: overview and outlook. ACM J. Data Inf. Qual. **10**(4), 15:1–15:32 (2018). https://doi.org/10.1145/3239570
9. McPhillips, T.M., et al.: Yesworkflow: a user-oriented, language-independent tool for recovering workflow information from scripts. CoRR abs/1502.02403 (2015). http://arxiv.org/abs/1502.02403
10. Murta, L., Braganholo, V., Chirigati, F., Koop, D., Freire, J.: noWorkflow: capturing and analyzing provenance of scripts. In: Ludäscher, B., Plale, B. (eds.) IPAW 2014. LNCS, vol. 8628, pp. 71–83. Springer, Cham (2015). https://doi.org/10.1007/978-3-319-16462-5_6
11. Palma, R., Hołubowicz, P., Corcho, O., Gómez-Pérez, J.M., Mazurek, C.: ROHub — a digital library of research objects supporting scientists towards reproducible science. In: Presutti, V., et al. (eds.) SemWebEval 2014. CCIS, vol. 475, pp. 77–82. Springer, Cham (2014). https://doi.org/10.1007/978-3-319-12024-9_9

12. Potthast, M., Gollub, T., Wiegmann, M., Stein, B.: TIRA integrated research architecture. In: Ferro, N., Peters, C. (eds.) Information Retrieval Evaluation in a Changing World. TIRS, vol. 41, pp. 123–160. Springer, Cham (2019). https://doi.org/10.1007/978-3-030-22948-1_5

13. Rauber, A., Miksa, T., Mayer, R., Pröll, S.: Repeatability and re-usability in scientific processes: process context, data identification and verification. In: Kalinichenko, L.A., Starkov, S. (eds.) Selected Papers of the XVII International Conference on Data Analytics and Management in Data Intensive Domains (DAMDID/RCDL 2015), Obninsk, Russia, 13–16 October 2015. CEUR Workshop Proceedings, vol. 1536, pp. 246–256. CEUR-WS.org (2015). http://ceur-ws.org/Vol-1536/paper33.pdf

14. Virtanen, P., et al.: SciPy: Scipy 1.0-fundamental algorithms for scientific computing in python. CoRR abs/1907.10121 (2019). http://arxiv.org/abs/1907.10121

15. Voorhees, E.M., Rajput, S., Soboroff, I.: Promoting repeatability through open runs. In: Yilmaz, E., Clarke, C.L.A. (eds.) Proceedings of the Seventh International Workshop on Evaluating Information Access, EVIA 2016, a Satellite Workshop of the NTCIR-12 Conference, National Center of Sciences, Tokyo, Japan, 7 June 2016. National Institute of Informatics (NII) (2016). http://research.nii.ac.jp/ntcir/workshop/OnlineProceedings12/pdf/evia/04-EVIA2016-VoorheesE.pdf

16. van der Walt, S., Colbert, S.C., Varoquaux, G.: The numpy array: a structure for efficient numerical computation. Comput. Sci. Eng. 13(2), 22–30 (2011). https://doi.org/10.1109/MCSE.2011.37

Signal Briefings: Monitoring News Beyond the Brand

James Brill[1]([⊠]), Dyaa Albakour[1], José Esquivel[1], Udo Kruschwitz[2],
Miguel Martinez[1], and Jon Chamberlain[3]

[1] Signal AI, London, UK
james.brill@signal-ai.com
[2] University of Regensburg, Bavaria, Germany
[3] University of Essex, Colchester, UK

Abstract. Public relations (PR) professionals are responsible for managing an organisation's reputation through monitoring entities of interest and wider industry news. Monitoring and tracking wide news spaces such as industry news can cause a significant work load on PR professionals. We present Signal Briefings, a system which uses a combination of clustering and ranking to produce a small set of impactful articles distributed as a periodic email in a scalable and efficient manner.

1 Introduction

A public relations (PR) team, whether internal to a company or an external agency, is responsible for monitoring news articles that mention entities of interest. Typically this information is summarised in a curated digest of the latest articles identified as having relevance and potential impact on the decision making of the organisation. The PR team routinely monitors news about entities of interest such as their organisation and its competitors; however, short-term monitoring is also used for product releases, promotional campaigns, reputation management, and assessing the impact of disruptive events such as Brexit and Covid-19. Historically, media monitoring tools have used Boolean search [3] as the underpinning search technology. Moving away from Boolean search and to facilitate more accurate information retrieval, companies are using Natural Language Processing (NLP), for example, to identify entities and topics, e.g. *Signal AI news monitoring*[1] which analyses up to 3M news articles a day [6], or to automatically generate query suggestions [9].

Media monitoring products are designed to provide focused search results of the most relevance to the user; however, some articles may be excluded that contain important information due to the high volume of news content being released every day (other articles such as summary articles should in fact be excluded [2]). By increasing the search scope, the task of the PR team becomes exponentially harder and less-efficient. The focus on narrow searches hinders

---

[1] https://www.signal-ai.com/.

© Springer Nature Switzerland AG 2021
D. Hiemstra et al. (Eds.): ECIR 2021, LNCS 12657, pp. 487–491, 2021.
https://doi.org/10.1007/978-3-030-72240-1_52

PR teams who try to monitor news more widely (in what we describe as a *broad news space*) to anticipate policy amendments, industrial ecosystem change, and evolving customer habits. This must be achieved whilst only reading a small number of articles that are unique in content and up to date. Additionally, this information needs to be delivered inline with organisational procedure, typically being processed by the PR team first thing on a week-day morning and made available the same day within the organisation. In this paper, we describe *Signal Briefings* - a system for monitoring broad news spaces by PR professionals.

2   Architecture and Deployment

System Requirements: In order to identify key requirements for the system, 5 PR professionals were interviewed during a 3-week period in June 2019 in 30-minute informal interviews identifying four key aspects: (a) *Minimal noise*: show no duplicate information; (b) *Novel information*: provide information that would not otherwise be found; (c) *Important information*: identify the most important (*"impactful"*) articles within a broad news space; (d) *Authority of article*: report source reputation to reduce the need to check for misinformation.

Architecture: *Signal Briefings* identifies up to ten news articles from a set to represent the most impactful stories in the broad news space.[2] These are sent via email to users at a configured time. *Signal Briefings* was integrated into the news monitoring product of Signal, adding a layer on top of the existing concept-based search by grouping and filtering the search results to provide a more diverse representation of the news being monitored by users. The underlying model for this filtering layer consists of three stages: (1) clustering; (2) ranking the clusters; (3) selecting the best article from each cluster.

We use single-pass clustering [7] with nearest-neighbour classification [1] to assign each new document to the closest cluster or instantiate a new cluster if no clusters exist within a maximum distance. A key element of this stage is that documents are processed in chronological order and represented as a sparse TF-IDF vector (to keep computational costs low) with IDF derived from 3 months of data. Our representation of the cluster is the document that instantiates the cluster, allowing us to use cosine similarity as the distance metric to identify nearest neighbours. By clustering similar documents together and reducing duplication, we address user requirement (1): minimal noise. We define a custom ranking function (based on the user requirements) that outperforms typical baseline ranking – chronological ranking and BM25 [8]:

$$f(C) = |C| \cdot \sum_{a \in C} reach(a) + source\_ranking(a) \tag{1}$$

where $C = \{a_1, a_2, ..., a_n\}$ represents a cluster. At an article level, there are two main components *reach* and *source_ranking*. The *reach* function returns

---

[2] A demonstration video is available on https://tinyurl.com/y5txp6ap showing examples of Signal Briefings.

normalised readership figures for an article of a certain news type (print, online) obtained through third-party providers such as SimilarWeb[3]. The *reach* function seeks to model the 'size' of the story. The *source_ranking* is a manual proprietary reputation score of sources (ranging between 0–1) based on Signal's expertise of the PR domain, and reflects the value of a source to a PR professional. The ranking function is designed to address user requirements (2) and (3) (novel and important information) by prioritising *impactful* stories. It makes the assumption that stories will be reported on by reputable news sources and will have high readership figures.

The final stage is to select a single article to represent each cluster thereby increasing the number of news stories that can be covered in a single email (of up to ten stories). The article with the highest *source_ranking* is selected to represent each cluster with second preference being chronological order. This stage addresses user requirement (4): article provenance and source authority. *Reach* is excluded from selection as it does not model article provenance well; for example, a state-owned news company might have a weak reputation for journalistic quality but still maintain very high readership.

Scalable Deployment: The user requirement interviews indicated that organisations need this information first thing in the morning. An assessment of Signal's *Bulletins* product (a more traditional search alert system) showed that 87% of emails were sent out between 6am and 9am. The requirement for user retrieval requests to be completed at the same time places a very high demand on server processing and is not scalable without some form of parallelisation. To solve this problem, we ensure a light processing overhead at serve time. This was achieved by using a streaming approach where, instead of searching the index of the collection of documents for each request, each search request processes a constant stream of documents in small batches. For each new document added to the collection, we find the closest cluster it belongs to, update the cluster score, and store the document with the highest source ranking. By using a streaming approach, the majority of the processing work is not a function of the number of search requests, but the total number of documents flowing through the system.

3   Evaluation

The prototype system was integrated into Signal's email services within the live product in February 2020. The prototype could then be evaluated in a restricted but realistic setting with selected clients briefed on its function. The system was evaluated for user value and technical performance.

User Engagement and Value: The output emails were initially validated with five PR professionals (different from the user requirements interviewees). Subsequently, several restricted tests of the prototype on the live product were performed: (1) All Signal's user base were offered the chance to receive an email on up to 3 predefined search queries via an in-app poll; (2) The evaluation was

---
[3] https://www.similarweb.com/.

expanded to let the 44 users who volunteered from the previous stage use the unconstrained system for a limited time. This allowed us to better understand the value of the feature by empowering users to use it on their own searches; (3) The beta system was made available to all clients before being released as an additional premium feature.

The operational metrics [5] we used to monitor user engagement were *open rate* (whether the user opened the email that was sent) and *click rate* (whether the user clicked on an article within the email to read it). Over a 6-month period we assessed the relative differences between *Bulletins* and *Signal Briefings* and found an increase in the open rate of 41.4% and an increased click rate of 115.7% [4], i.e. a substantial boost in terms of both metrics (statistically significant in both cases using Mann-Whitney test at $p < 0.01$) Comparing the daily average number of *Signal Briefings* sent in terms of the first two weeks and the last two weeks showed there was an increase of 950%.

A sample of 4,384 *Signal Briefings* from one month were analysed to determine the number of duplicated articles in each one, and the proportion of unknown words in documents that pass through the pipeline. Identifying duplicate articles is vital to ensure novelty of information and the reduction of noise as identified in the four key requirements. Signal's existing de-duplication service, which uses locality sensitive hashing [4], was used to automatically detect duplicates. 94% of briefs contain no duplicates, and 6% contain 1 duplicate. Quantifying the proportion of unique unknown tokens demonstrates how well our vocabulary for vectorisation understands the documents that users search. A high proportion of unique unknown tokens would impact the performance of the clustering quality. Less than 10% of unique tokens were unknown in 99% of the 22,089,510 documents processed in a month period. The client user base contains PR professionals from every industry, hence the proportion of missing tokens are within acceptable limits and were not expected to impact clustering performance.

Technical Performance: The system uses a streaming approach for processing the document collection to collapse broad news spaces. The technical performance of the system was measured as the time taken to perform the retrieval task to produce each email containing the ten most impactful articles. Analysis during the 2-month test period with more than 10K requests shows that the median average time taken remains reasonably consistent at 0.25 s. On further inspection of our system, we find this is mostly due to the amount of data transfer needed at the time of serving a request. At serve time, the *Signal Briefings* database stores 6,333,526 articles in 1,084,580 clusters (for all the alerts setup at the time of writing). This is a compression of 83% in the amount of data transfer out of our systems to cluster, rank, and serve the articles in a briefing.

---

[4] Exact numbers are redacted due to company confidentiality.

4   Discussion and Conclusion

We have presented Signal's approach to solving an everyday challenge for PR professionals, *monitoring large news spaces with limited resources*. We found that this new feature has significantly more engagement than Signal AI's existing email alerting product. Additionally, the feature has proven to be valuable to Signal AI who created free *Signal Briefings* on COVID-19 based around different industry verticals. The feature was built around the user needs of Signal AI's clients who did not identify potential bias as a concern, thus addressing bias in news spaces was not a high priority in this context but it may be a concern in other systems. Validating the findings of the evaluation in a business-to-business environment with long sales cycles is difficult due to the many other factors involved and as a result, user satisfaction had to be estimated by measuring feature engagement, and other indicators of quality such as duplicate articles.

References

1. Cover, T., Hart, P.: Nearest neighbor pattern classification. IEEE Trans. Inf. Theory **13**(1), 21–27 (1967)
2. Fisher, M., Albakour, D., Kruschwitz, U., Martinez, M.: Recognising summary articles. In: Azzopardi, L., Stein, B., Fuhr, N., Mayr, P., Hauff, C., Hiemstra, D. (eds.) ECIR 2019. LNCS, vol. 11437, pp. 69–85. Springer, Cham (2019). https://doi.org/10.1007/978-3-030-15712-8_5
3. Frants, V.I., Shapiro, J., Taksa, I., Voiskunskii, V.G.: Boolean search: current state and perspectives. J. Am. Soc. Inf. Sci. **50**(1), 86–95 (1999)
4. Indyk, P., Motwani, R.: Approximate nearest neighbors: towards removing the curse of dimensionality. In: Proceedings of the Thirtieth Annual ACM Symposium on Theory of Computing, pp. 604–613 (1998)
5. Karlgren, J.: Adopting systematic evaluation benchmarks in operational settings. In: Ferro, N., Peters, C. (eds.) Information Retrieval Evaluation in a Changing World. TIRS, vol. 41, pp. 583–590. Springer, Cham (2019). https://doi.org/10.1007/978-3-030-22948-1_25
6. Martinez-Alvarez, M., Kruschwitz, U., Hall, W., Poesio, M.: Signal: advanced real-time information filtering. In: Hanbury, A., Kazai, G., Rauber, A., Fuhr, N. (eds.) ECIR 2015. LNCS, vol. 9022, pp. 793–796. Springer, Cham (2015). https://doi.org/10.1007/978-3-319-16354-3_87
7. van Rijsbergen, C.J.: Information retrieval. Butterworth (1979)
8. Robertson, S., Zaragoza, H.: The Probabilistic Relevance Framework: BM25 and Beyond. Now Publishers Inc (2009)
9. Verberne, S., Wabeke, T., Kaptein, R.: Boolean queries for news monitoring: suggesting new query terms to expert users. In: Martinez-Alvarez, M., et al. (eds.) Proceedings of the First International Workshop on Recent Trends in News Information Retrieval co-located with 38th European Conference on Information Retrieval (ECIR 2016), Padua, Italy, 20 March 2016. CEUR Workshop Proceedings, vol. 1568, pp. 3–8. CEUR-WS.org (2016). http://ceur-ws.org/Vol-1568/paper1.pdf

Time-Matters: Temporal Unfolding of Texts

Ricardo Campos[1,2(✉)] ⓘ, Jorge Duque[2], Tiago Cândido[2], Jorge Mendes[2],
Gaël Dias[3] ⓘ, Alípio Jorge[1,4] ⓘ, and Célia Nunes[5] ⓘ

[1] LIAAD – INESCTEC, Porto, Portugal
ricardo.campos@ipt.pt, amjorge@fc.up.pt
[2] Polytechnic Institute of Tomar, Ci2 - Smart Cities Research Center, Tomar, Portugal
{aluno19893,aluno20185,aluno19263}@ipt.pt
[3] Normandie Univ, UNICAEN, ENSICAEN, CNRS, GREYC, Caen, France
gael.dias@unicaen.fr
[4] FCUP, University of Porto, Porto, Portugal
[5] Center of Mathematics and Applications, University of Beira Interior, Covilhã, Portugal
celian@ubi.pt

Abstract. Over the past few years, the amount of information generated, consumed and stored on the Web has grown exponentially, making it impossible for
users to keep up to date. Temporal data representation can help in this process by
giving documents a sense of organization. Timelines are a natural way to showcase
this data, giving users the chance to get familiar with a topic in a shorter amount
of time. Despite their importance, little is known about their use in the context
of single documents. In this paper, we present Time-Matters, a novel system to
automatically explore arbitrary texts through temporal narratives in an interactive
fashion that allows users to get insights into the relevant temporal happenings of
a story through multiple components, including temporal annotation, storylines
or temporal clustering. In contrast to classical timeline multi-document summarization tasks, we focus on performing text summaries of single documents with
a temporal lens. This approach may be of interest to a number of providers such
as media outlets, for which automatically building a condensed overview of a text
is an important issue.

Keywords: Timeline generation · Temporal narratives · Temporal information

1 Introduction

Recent times have shown an abundance of textual content creating new challenges for
those who want to quickly get insights, without having to read entire documents. Much
of this text is in free form. Extracting information from it requires the use of computer
resources capable of understanding natural language. Presenting text using temporal
structures can help reduce the effort of the reader [4, 15]. For example, they can define the
time period of events in news articles [18, 21], play an important role in communication
platforms, such as Twitter [1–3] or Wikipedia [13], and help contextualize historical
texts [14] or legal documents [12]. Advances on these domains are partially due to the

© Springer Nature Switzerland AG 2021
D. Hiemstra et al. (Eds.): ECIR 2021, LNCS 12657, pp. 492–497, 2021.
https://doi.org/10.1007/978-3-030-72240-1_53

existence of temporal taggers, such as Heideltime [19] or SUTime [9]. Timelines appear in this context as a common approach that leverages the detected temporal signals to summarize the information spread over multiple documents in a temporal order fashion. However, little is known about their use in the scope of single documents [16, 20]. An optimal summary should cover all the important temporal aspects of a text while disregarding unimportant or irrelevant dates. However, manually building these timelines may be a laborious and time-consuming task, and an impossible effort for average users or professionals interested in making sense of an increasing volume of textual data. This slows down the process of text analytics and data understanding. In this paper, we present Time-Matters, a novel system that can give users an automatic overview of the most important time-periods and associated text stories in a short amount of time without having to read text-heavy documents. This can be very useful in several scenarios and domains and fits within the recent trend of automatically generating narratives from texts [8]. For instance, it may be of importance for media outlets [17], interested in telling stories and in reaching new audiences with alternative and appealing forms, but also for those interested in quickly extracting temporal information from long documents such as Wikipedia documents.

To accomplish this objective, we adapted a previously introduced version of Time-Matters [5] which worked over queries and multiple documents, to single texts. In particular, we aim to estimate the importance of the temporal expressions detected in a text and hence disregard the non-relevant ones. The goal is to not only provide a temporal annotation of the text with the corresponding scores given by the Time-Matters algorithm, but also to offer users the chance to interact with the system with a temporal storyline component that shows the most important stories of a text. We do this in an interactive fashion that includes a timeline and graphical elements likely related to parts of the story. Further possibilities include exploring the most relevant stories of the text through temporal clustering. Another important key aspect of our approach is that it is **unsupervised**, **domain** and **corpus-independent** as it does not require any training stage and builds upon local text statistical features extracted from single documents. Hence, it can readily be applied to any text. The core of Time-Matters is also **mostly language-independent**. While it anchors on Heideltime [19] to detect temporal expressions it can also use a simple rule-based approach (focused on years detection), which, while not as effective as Heideltime, may be a good solution when performance and language is an issue. As a contribution to the research community, we make available an **online demo** [http://time-matters.inesctec.pt], an **API** [http://time-matters.inesctec.pt/api], a **python package** [https://github.com/LIAAD/Time-Matters] and a **docker image** [https://hub.docker.com/r/liaad/time-matters] of Time-Matters. On the sidelines, we also make public a python package wrapper for **Heideltime** [https://github.com/JMendes1995/py_heideltime] which aims to facilitate the use of this well-known temporal tagger.

2   Time-Matters Algorithm

Our assumption is that the relevance of a candidate date d_j may be determined with regards to the relevant terms W_j^* that it co-occurs with in a given context (defined as a window of n terms in a sentence or the sentence itself). That is, the more a given candidate date is correlated with the most relevant keywords of a text t_i, the more relevant the candidate date is for the text at hand. To model this temporal relevance, we rely on the Generic Temporal Similarity measure (GTE) [5], which makes use of co-occurrences of keywords and temporal expressions as a means to identify relevant dates within a text. In this work, relevant keyphrases and temporal expressions are respectively detected by YAKE! keyword extractor [6, 7], and Heideltime temporal tagger [9]. GTE is formalized in Eq. 1 and ranges between 0 (irrelevant) and 1 (relevant), where IS is the InfoSimba similarity measure [10].

$$\text{GTE}(t_i, d_j) = \text{median}\big(\text{IS}(w_{\ell,j}, d_j)\big), w_{\ell,j} \in W_j^* \tag{1}$$

A fully detailed description of the underlying scientific approach and the evaluation methodology for the study of queries and multiple documents can be found in Campos et al. [5]. Readers are also recommended to refer to our wiki documentation [https://github.com/LIAAD/Time-Matters/wiki] for an in-depth understanding of the single document version explored in this demo.

3   Time-Matters Demonstration

We demonstrate our approach using an arbitrary text related to the 1st anniversary of the Haiti earthquake held on January 12, 2011. Texts can be given as input in the homepage or as an URL, in which case, we make use of the well-known Newspaper 3k library [https://newspaper.readthedocs.io] to extract contents. The resulting interface is divided into five major components: "Annotated Text"; "Storyline", "Temporal Clustering"; "Timeline"; and "Scores". In this paper, we put an emphasis on the first two, "Annotated Text" and "Storyline", due to space reasons.

Annotated Text. Figure 1 shows the "Annotated Text" component. At the top, we can observe the time spent to obtain the results, the number of relevant annotated temporal expressions instances and the text language. Time performance is highly dependent on the Heideltime component as computing GTE scores is a quick process. Each date is tagged with a 5-color Likert relevance scale, from least relevant dates (bold red) to most relevant ones (bold green). To get a sense of the relevance of the dates, users can also mouse over a given temporal expression. By default, only relevant temporal expressions, those with GTE scores equal or above 0.35 (according to the experiments conducted in [5]) are shown to the user. Scores close to 1 are considered highly relevant in the particular part of the text being analyzed. Equal date instances in different sentences can also result in different scores (one such approach can be explored in the advanced options section in the homepage). In addition to relevant dates, users can also ask for least relevant ones (scores < 0.35) as exemplified in Fig. 1 for the temporal expression "the afternoon of February 11, 1975" (marked in bold red), which is shown a score of 0. By doing this, we give users the opportunity to understand the effectiveness of the Time-Matters algorithm in filtering out non relevant dates initially marked by the temporal tagger. One can also observe, marked as bold, the relevant keyphrases co-occurring next to the date and that most contribute to the results of Time-Matters. By default, n-grams are set to 1, meaning that keywords will be formed by 1 single token only, though other options can be defined in the advanced options setting.

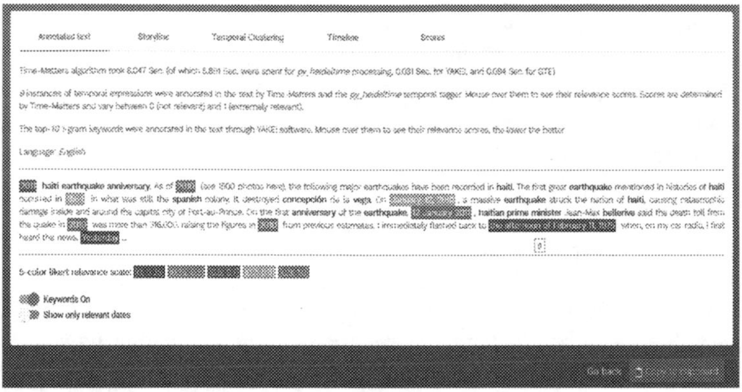

Fig. 1. "Annotated Text" interface. (Color figure online)

Storyline Visualization. The storyline interface (see Fig. 2) explores the different stories of a text through a temporal lens. The component at the top, highlights the relevant dates ("1564"), its score ("0.799"), the sentence where the date occurs and a summary of that particular part of the story ("great earthquake mentioned") given by YAKE! [6]. The story is also illustrated automatically with images. We leverage on the Portuguese web archive Arquivo.pt [11] images search API v1 [https://github.com/arquivo/pwa-tec hnologies/wiki]. While this API can obtain results for any language it naturally works better for its native language, Portuguese. Users can then navigate between the different time-periods by either clicking at the right row (labelled in this figure example as "Recorded in Haiti, 2010") or at the bottom timeline component which gives, per se, a temporal overview of the story.

Fig. 2. "Storyline" interface.

In this paper, we suggest a simple yet effective approach for summarizing a text through a temporal perspective, highlighting the most important temporal aspects of the text. As future research, we plan to investigate further elaborated solutions that study the correlation between the detected relevant dates and the relevant events found in the surroundings of the date. This can be used to improve not only the story description but also the retrieval of images.

Acknowledgements. Ricardo Campos and Alípio Jorge were financed by the ERDF – European Regional Development Fund through the North Portugal Regional Operational Programme (NORTE 2020), under the PORTUGAL 2020 and by National Funds through the Portuguese funding agency, FCT - Fundação para a Ciência e a Tecnologia within project PTDC/CCI-COM/31857/2017 (NORTE-01-0145-FEDER-03185). This funding fits under the research line of the Text2Story project. Célia Nunes was financed by the Fundação para a Ciência e a Tecnologia (Portuguese Foundation for Science and Technology) through projects UIDB/00212/2020.

References

1. Alonso, O., Shiells, K.: Timelines as summaries of popular scheduled events. In: Proceedings of the 22nd International Conference on World Wide Web (WWW 2013), Rio de Janeiro, Brazil, 13–17 May 2013, pp. 1037–1044 (2013)
2. Alonso, O., Tremblay, S.-E., Diaz, F.: Automatic generation of event timelines from social data. In: Proceedings of the 2017 ACM on Web Science Conference (WebSci 2017), New York, USA, 25–28 June 2017, pp. 207–211 (2017)
3. Alonso, O., Kandylas, V., Tremblay, S.-E.: How it happened: discovering and archiving the evolution of a story using social signals. In: Proceedings of the ACM/IESS Joint Conference on Digital Libraries (JCDL 2018), Texas, USA, 3–7 June 2018, pp. 193–202 (2018)
4. Campos, R., Dias, G., Jorge, A., Jatowt, A.: Survey of temporal information retrieval and related applications. ACM Comput. Surv. **47**(2), Article 15 (2014)
5. Campos, R., Dias, G., Jorge, A.M., Nunes, C.: Identifying top relevant dates for implicit time sensitive queries. Inf. Retrieval J. **20**(4), 363–398 (2017). https://doi.org/10.1007/s10791-017-9302-1
6. Campos, R., Mangaravite, V., Pasquali, A., Jorge, A.M., Nunes, C., Jatowt, A.: A text feature based automatic keyword extraction method for single documents. In: Pasi, G., Piwowarski, B., Azzopardi, L., Hanbury, A. (eds.) ECIR 2018. LNCS, vol. 10772, pp. 684–691. Springer, Cham (2018). https://doi.org/10.1007/978-3-319-76941-7_63
7. Campos, R., Mangaravite, V., Pasquali, A., Jorge, A., Nunes, C., Jatowt, A.: YAKE! keyword extraction from single documents using multiple local features. Inf. Sci. J. **509**, 257–289 (2020)
8. Campos, R., Jorge, A., Jatowt, A., Sumit, B.: Third International workshop on narrative extraction from texts (Text2Story'20). In: Jose, J., et al. (eds.) Proceedings of the 42nd European Conference on Information Retrieval (ECIR'20), pp. 648–653. Springer, Cham (2020). https://doi.org/10.1007/978-3-030-45442-5_86
9. Chang, A.X., Manning, C.D.: SUTIME: a library for recognizing and normalizing time expressions. In: Proceedings of the 8th International Conference on Language Resources and Evaluation (LREC 2012), Istambul, Turkey, 23–25 May 2012, pp. 3735–3740 (2012)
10. Dias, G., Alves, E., Lopes, J.: Topic segmentation algorithms for text summarization and passage retrieval: an exhaustive evaluation. In: Proceedings of the 22nd Conference on Artificial Intelligence (AAAI 2007), Vancouver, Canada, 22–26 July 2007, pp. 1334–1340. AAAI Press (2007)

11. Gomes, D., Cruz, D., Miranda, J., Costa, M., Fontes, S.: Search the past with the portuguese web archive. In: Proceedings of the 22nd International Conference on World Wide Web (WWW 2013), Rio de Janeiro, Brazil, 13–17 May 2013, pp. 321–324 (2013)

12. Hausner, P., Aumiller, D., Gertz, M.: Time-centric exploration of court documents. In: Proceedings of the 3rd International Workshop on Narrative Extraction from Texts (Text2Story20@ECIR 2020), Lisbon, Portugal, 14 April 2020, pp. 31–37 (2020)

13. Hausner, P., Aumiller, D., Gertz, M.: TiCCo: time-centric content exploration. In: Proceedings of the 29th ACM International Conference on Information & Knowledge Management (CIKM 2020), Virtual Event, Ireland, 19–23 October 2020, pp. 3413–3416. ACM Press (2020)

14. Jatowt, A., Campos, R., Bhowmick, S., Doucet, A.: Document in context of time (DICT): system that provides temporal context for analyzing old documents. In: Proceedings of the 28th ACM International Conference on Knowledge Management (CIKM 2019), Beijing, China, 03–07 November 2019, pp. 2869–2872. ACM Press (2019)

15. Kanhabua, N., Blanco, R., Nørvåg, K.: Temporal information retrieval. Found. Trends Inf. Retrieval **9**(2), 91–208 (2015)

16. Kanhabua, N., Romano, S., Stewart, A.: Identifying relevant temporal expressions for real-world events. In: Proceedings of the Workshop on Time-aware Information Access (TAIA'12@SIGIR'12), Portland, USA, 12–16 August 2012 (2012)

17. Martinez-Alvarez, M., et al.: First international workshop on recent trends in news information retrieval (NewsIR'16). In: Ferro, N., et al. (eds.) ECIR 2016. LNCS, vol. 9626, pp. 878–882. Springer, Cham (2016). https://doi.org/10.1007/978-3-319-30671-1_85

18. Pasquali, A., Mangaravite, V., Campos, R., Jorge, A.M., Jatowt, A.: Interactive system for automatically generating temporal narratives. In: Azzopardi, L., Stein, B., Fuhr, N., Mayr, P., Hauff, C., Hiemstra, D. (eds.) ECIR 2019. LNCS, vol. 11438, pp. 251–255. Springer, Cham (2019). https://doi.org/10.1007/978-3-030-15719-7_34

19. Strötgen, J., Gertz, M.: Multilingual and cross-domain temporal tagging. Lang. Resour. Eval. **47**(2), 269–298 (2013)

20. Strötgen, J., Alonso, O., Gertz, M.: Identification of top relevant temporal expressions in documents. In: Proceedings of the 2nd Temporal Web Analytics Workshop (Temp-Web12@WWW'12), Lyon, France, 17 April 2012, pp. 33–40 (2012)

21. Tran, G., Alrifai, M., Herder, E.: Timeline summarization from relevant headlines. In: Hanbury, A., Kazai, G., Rauber, A., Fuhr, N. (eds.) ECIR 2015. LNCS, vol. 9022, pp. 245–256. Springer, Cham (2015). https://doi.org/10.1007/978-3-319-16354-3_26

An Extensible Toolkit of Query Refinement Methods and Gold Standard Dataset Generation

Hossein Fani[1]([⊠])(iD), Mahtab Tamannaee[2], Fattane Zarrinkalam[2],
Jamil Samouh[2], Samad Paydar[2], and Ebrahim Bagheri[2]

[1] School of Computer Science, University of Windsor, Windsor, Canada
hfani@uwindsor.ca
[2] Laboratory for Systems, Software and Semantics (LS3), Ryerson University,
Toronto, Canada
{mtamannaee,fzarrinkalam,jsamouh,paydar,bagheri}@ryerson.ca

Abstract. We present an open-source extensible python-based toolkit that provides access to a (1) range of built-in unsupervised query expansion methods, and (2) pipeline for generating gold standard datasets for building and evaluating supervised query refinement methods. While the information literature offers abundant work on query expansion techniques, there is yet to be a tool that provides unified access to a comprehensive set of query expansion techniques. The advantage of our proposed toolkit, known as ReQue (refining queries), is that it offers one-stop shop access to query expansion techniques to be used in external information retrieval applications. More importantly, we show how ReQue can be used for building gold standards datasets that can be used for training supervised deep learning-based query refinement techniques. These techniques require sizeable gold query refinement datasets, which are not available in the literature. ReQue provides the means to systematically build such datasets.

1 Introduction

To improve retrieval performance, query refinement methods fill the gap between the language of the user's query and that of the relevant information by formulating an alternative set of terms for the original query either through an unsupervised approach, e.g., adding more synonyms with similar significance (see [2] for a comprehensive study), or via a supervised learning approach that learns how to reformulate the original query q to a refined version q' from a set of labeled training samples $(q \rightarrow q')$, e.g., neural-based models that have recently received more attention [6,11,19].

While the literature has extensively explored methods of supervised and unsupervised query expansion, there are two major limitations in this area: (1) while the implementation of some supervised query expansion methods are sporadically available by the authors, the implementation of many others are not

D. Hiemstra et al. (Eds.): ECIR 2021, LNCS 12657, pp. 498–503, 2021.
https://doi.org/10.1007/978-3-030-72240-1_54

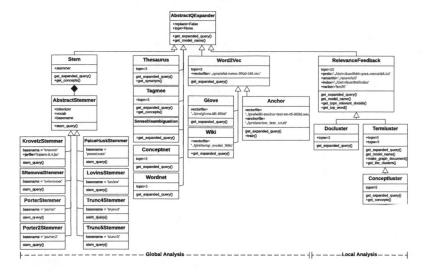

Fig. 1. Inheritance hierarchy for expanders available in ReQue.

available. The implementation of those available are also not compatible with each other and require substantial revision to be deployable; and (2) even though supervised query refinement methods require gold standard dataset for training, there is no known *truly* gold standard dataset for this purpose. Such methods are often benchmarked on session-based search history of the users such as aol [17] and msmarco [15] where the main underlying assumption is that the last query in the users' search session is a better reformulation of the original query and can be considered to be an acceptable *refined query*. The expectation is that the user has gradually revised her query over successive attempts to find relevant information within the same session. This assumption however has not been confirmed neither empirically nor theoretically in the literature. Indeed, intuitive counterexamples can be easily provided from real-world user search sessions as extracted from the msmarco dataset in [20]. In order to address these two major limitations, we make a python-based extensible toolkit, called ReQue, publicly available that offers the following capabilities:

1. Like similar efforts in the community such as MatchZoo [5], which offer an extensible platform of the design, comparison and sharing of deep text matching models, ReQue offers a platform to publicly share query expansion techniques. It comes with a host of implemented query expansion methods and offers an object-oriented structure that can easily facilitate and accommodate the addition of new query expansion methods;
2. Based on its set of built-in unsupervised query expansion methods, ReQue offers a pipeline to automatically generate gold standard datasets to be used for training supervised query refinement methods. This is a major advantage as most state of the art neural query refinement methods are now developed

```
# ./qe/expanders/abstractqexpander.py
class AbstractQExpander:
    def __init__(self,replace=False,topn=None):
        self.replace = replace
        self.topn = topn
    def get_expanded_query(self,q,args=None):
        return q

# ./qe/stemmers/abstractstemmer.py
class AbstractStemmer():
    def __init__(self): ...
    def stem_query(self,q): ...
```

```
# ./qe/expanders/relevancefeedback.py
class RelevanceFeedback(AbstractQExpander):
    def __init__(self, ranker, ..., topn=10):...
    def get_expanded_query(self, q, args): ...
    def get_topn_relevant_docids(self, qid): ...
    def get_top_word(self, tfidf): ...

# ./qe/expanders/stem.py
from stemmers.abstractstemmer import AbstractStemmer
class Stem(AbstractQExpander):
    def __init__(self, stemmer:AbstractStemmer):
        AbstractQExpander.__init__(self)
        self.stemmer = stemmer
    def get_expanded_query(self,q,args=None):
        return self.stemmer.stem_query(q)
```

(a)   (b)

Fig. 2. ReQue's code snippets for implementing expanders.

based on *silver* standard query datasets, which we have already shown to include considerable limitations [20].

ReQue has currently integrated a host of 21 state-of-the-art unsupervised query expansion methods including, but not limited to, lexical [18], semantic [7,16,21], embedding [9], corpus-based clustering [3,14], web-based [1,8,12], and pseudo-relevance feedback [10] methods. The methods are shown in the inheritance hierarchy of classes in Fig. 1 and can be classified into *global* and *local* analysis methods. The codebase along with the installation instructions and video tutorials as well as case studies on trec topics can be obtained at https://github.com/hosseinfani/ReQue/tree/ecir2021demo.

Demonstration. During the presentation of this work, we will (1) introduce the built-in query expansion methods that are offered by ReQue and how they can be used in other applications, (2) show how new query expansion methods can be easily integrated into ReQue, (3) demonstrate the workflow provided by ReQue for generating gold standard datasets to train and evaluate supervised query refinement methods [4,13,19], and (4) review the statistical characteristics of the gold standard datasets that are generated by ReQue.

2   Toolkit Overview

2.1   Query Expansion in ReQue

ReQue offers a set of query expansion methods, called *expanders*, to generate expanded queries for any input query. At its core, and as shown in Fig. 2a, ReQue includes the *identity* expander, called `AbstractQExpander`, as the abstract root of the class hierarchy whose main method `get_expanded_query()` is to be overridden by expanders. Adding a new expander to ReQue is as easy as extending an existing expander, and modifying `get_expanded_query()`, as shown in Fig. 2b for `RelevanceFeedback` and `Stem` expanders. The expanders are also able to revise the original query by either adding (`replace=False`) or replacing (`replace=True`) its terms with `topn` new related terms. ReQue currently

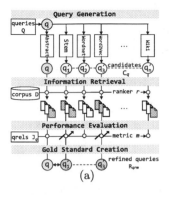

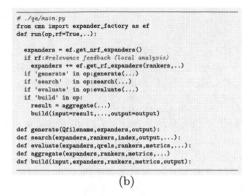

Fig. 3. ReQue's gold standard generation (a) workflow and (b) core engine.

has integrated a host of 21 state-of-the-art unsupervised query expansion methods (*c.f.* Fig. 1). Due to a modular design, the expanders can be easily combined/mixed into new expander mashups.

2.2   Gold Standard Generation in ReQue

ReQue adopts a simple yet effective approach to generate gold standard query refinement datasets on existing query sets such as those offered by trec competitions or msmarco [15]. Reque takes three inputs: 1) a set of queries $Q = \{q\}$ along with their associated relevance judgements (`qrels`) J_q in a corpus D, e.g., `robust04`, 2) an information retrieval method (ranker) r, e.g., `bm25`, and 3) an evaluation metric m, e.g., mean average precision (`map`). As shown in Fig. 3, a host of state-of-the-art expanders are used foremost to systematically generate a large number of revised candidate queries C_q for each original query q. Next, the revised candidate queries C_q are evaluated based on how they improve the performance of the given ranker r in terms of the evaluation metric m given the relevance judgments J_q for corpus D. Finally, given the performances of the revised candidate queries, those that provide better improvement compared to the original query q are selected as the refined queries $R_{qrm} \subseteq C_q$.

Out of the box, ReQue includes gold standard datasets for `robust04`, `gov2`, `clueweb09b` and `clueweb12b13` based on `bm25` and `qld` as the rankers and `map` as the evaluation metric along with benchmark results of 3 supervised query refinement methods [4,13,19]. Statistics including the average number of refined queries and the average `map` improvement rate for each of these gold standard datasets has been reported in [20] and show that for all the rankers, at least 1.44 refined queries exists on average for an original query while the best performance is for `robust04` over `bm25` with 4.24. Given the best refined query for each original query, the average `map` improvement rate is greater than 100% for all the gold standard datasets which means the best refined query for an original query almost *doubled* the performance of the ranker in terms of `map`.

3   Concluding Remarks

This paper introduces ReQue that benefits the IR community by the seamless access to query expansion methods as well as to the development of gold standard datasets for the task of supervised query refinement. Key contributions include:

1. ReQue is designed with extensibility in mind. While it already hosts a wide variety of unsupervised query expansion methods, it is quite easy to add new unsupervised query expansion methods, supervised query refinement models, or user-defined query refinement methods to it;
2. ReQue automatically generates gold standard datasets for training and evaluating supervised query refinement methods. It can be easily configured based on an original query set, its associated relevance judgements, a ranker of choice and an evaluation metric. It ensures refined queries improve the performance of the ranker in terms of the evaluation metric;
3. ReQue aids reproducibility and repeatability of the research work on shared gold standard datasets. As a part of its release, it includes gold standard datasets for each of the `robust04`, `gov2`, `clueweb09b` and `clueweb12b13` document collections and their associated trec topics based on `bm25` and `qld` as the rankers and `map` as the evaluation metric.

References

1. Al-Shboul, B., Myaeng, S.-H.: Wikipedia-based query phrase expansion in patent class search. Inf. Retrieval **17**(5–6), 430–451 (2013). https://doi.org/10.1007/s10791-013-9233-4
2. Azad, H.K., Deepak, A.: Query expansion techniques for information retrieval: a survey. Inf. Process. Manag. **56**(5), 1698–1735 (2019)
3. Carpineto, C., de Mori, R., Romano, G., Bigi, B.: An information-theoretic approach to automatic query expansion. ACM Trans. Inf. Syst. **19**(1), 1–27 (2001)
4. Dehghani, M., Rothe, S., Alfonseca, E., Fleury, P.: Learning to attend, copy, and generate for session-based query suggestion. In: 2017 ACM on Conference on Information and Knowledge Management, pp. 1747–1756 (2017)
5. Guo, J., Fan, Y., Ji, X., Cheng, X.: Matchzoo: a learning, practicing, and developing system for neural text matching. In: SIGIR 2019, pp. 1297–1300. ACM, New York (2019)
6. Han, F.X., Niu, D., Chen, H., Lai, K., He, Y., Xu, Y.: A deep generative approach to search extrapolation and recommendation. In: KDD 2019, pp. 1771–1779. ACM (2019)
7. Hsu, M.-H., Tsai, M.-F., Chen, H.-H.: Query expansion with ConceptNet and WordNet: an intrinsic comparison. In: Ng, H.T., Leong, M.-K., Kan, M.-Y., Ji, D. (eds.) AIRS 2006. LNCS, vol. 4182, pp. 1–13. Springer, Heidelberg (2006). https://doi.org/10.1007/11880592_1
8. Kraft, R., Zien, J.Y.: Mining anchor text for query refinement. In: WWW 2004, pp. 666–674. ACM (2004)
9. Kuzi, S., Shtok, A., Kurland, O.: Query expansion using word embeddings. In: CIKM 2016, pp. 1929–1932. ACM (2016)

10. Lee, K., Croft, W.B., Allan, J.: A cluster-based resampling method for pseudo-relevance feedback. In: Proceedings of the 31st Annual International ACM SIGIR Conference on Research and Development in Information Retrieval, SIGIR 2008, pp. 235–242. ACM (2008)
11. Li, R., Li, L., Wu, X., Zhou, Y., Wang, W.: Click feedback-aware query recommendation using adversarial examples. In: WWW 2019, pp. 2978–2984. ACM (2019)
12. Li, Y., Zheng, R., Tian, T., Hu, Z., Iyer, R., Sycara, K.P.: Joint embedding of hierarchical categories and entities for concept categorization and dataless classification. In: COLING 2016, pp. 2678–2688. ACL (2016)
13. Luong, T., Pham, H., Manning, C.D.: Effective approaches to attention-based neural machine translation. In: 2015 Conference on Empirical Methods in Natural Language Processing, EMNLP, pp. 1412–1421. The Association for Computational Linguistics (2015)
14. Natsev, A., Haubold, A., Tesic, J., Xie, L., Yan, R.: Semantic concept-based query expansion and re-ranking for multimedia retrieval. In: Proceedings of the 15th International Conference on Multimedia, pp. 991–1000. ACM (2007)
15. Nguyen, T., et al.: MS MARCO: a human generated machine reading comprehension dataset. In: NIPS 2016 (2016)
16. Pal, D., Mitra, M., Datta, K.: Improving query expansion using wordnet. J. Assoc. Inf. Sci. Technol. 65(12), 2469–2478 (2014)
17. Pass, G., Chowdhury, A., Torgeson, C.: A picture of search. In: Infoscale 2006, p. 1 (2006)
18. Schofield, A., Mimno, D.M.: Comparing apples to apple: the effects of stemmers on topic models. Trans. Assoc. Comput. Linguistics 4, 287–300 (2016)
19. Sordoni, A., Bengio, Y., Vahabi, H., Lioma, C., Simonsen, J.G., Nie, J.: A hierarchical recurrent encoder-decoder for generative context-aware query suggestion. In: CIKM 2015, pp. 553–562. ACM (2015)
20. Tamannaee, M., Fani, H., Zarrinkalam, F., Samouh, J., Paydar, S., Bagheri, E.: Reque: a configurable workflow and dataset collection for query refinement. In: CIKM2020, pp. 3165–3172. ACM (2020)
21. Tan, L.: Pywsd: python implementations of word sense disambiguation (WSD) technologies [software]. https://github.com/alvations/pywsd

CoralExp: An Explainable System to Support Coral Taxonomy Research

Jaiden Harding[1]([✉]), Tom Bridge[2,3], and Gianluca Demartini[1]

[1] University of Queensland, Brisbane, Australia
jaiden.harding@uq.net.au
[2] ARC Centre of Excellence for Coral Reef Studies, Douglas, Australia
[3] Queensland Museum Network, South Brisbane, Australia

Abstract. Thanks to the availability of large digital collections of coral images and because of the difficulty for experts to manually process all of them, it is possible and valuable to apply automatic methods to identify similar and relevant coral specimens in a coral specimen collection. Given the digital nature of these collections, it makes sense to leverage computer vision and information retrieval methods to support marine biology experts with their research.

In this paper we introduce CoralExp: a data exploration system aimed at supporting domain experts in marine biology by means of explainable computer vision and machine learning techniques in better understanding the reasoning behind automated classification decisions and thus providing insights on which coral properties should to be considered when designing future coral taxonomies.

1 Coral Taxonomies

Molecular studies of coral began to take place within the 1980s. This provided a new perspective on the relationship between species of coral. It was found that although some coral may be morphologically similar, on a molecular scale they are fundamentally different species. There are several morphological features that can be used to identify different species of coral. Computer vision algorithms could potentially extract these features from images of the coral, and subsequently use them to further identify other related species. From the common growth types, some of these key features include branches (splitting and non-splitting), plates of varying size and thickness, surface texture, and shapes.

In order to aid coral taxonomy researchers, in this paper we present an interactive system that can be used to explore a digital coral collection and to identify coral specimens with common morphological features. Also thanks to the use of explainable models, users can not only identify similar specimens, but also understand why the system considers them related by being presented with elements of the coral image that has lead to a certain classification decision.

© Springer Nature Switzerland AG 2021
D. Hiemstra et al. (Eds.): ECIR 2021, LNCS 12657, pp. 504–508, 2021.
https://doi.org/10.1007/978-3-030-72240-1_55

2   Processing Coral Images

Of the four main classes of image processing techniques (i.e., image enhancement, restoration, analysis, and compression), the system we present in this paper relies mainly on image enhancement and analysis. Given the need to determine underlying relationships and to cluster coral specimens purely based on common morphological features, the proposed system first leverages unsupervised learning to generate groups of similar specimens. Given the availability of a fully labelled digital collection, it is possible to train supervised models to classify new coral specimens into known classes. However, the aim of the presented human-in-the-loop system is to support domain expert exploration of the dataset and to discover coral attributes that may be indicative of belonging to certain coral families rather than providing a fully automated coral classification system.

Related Work. Recent work has explored the feasibility of using neural network architectures to extract important features of coral from specimen images [3]. The used dataset was obtained from various images of coral reefs throughout the world. The image dataset was manually labelled by experts prior to training. The learning architecture uses a cascade of layers to extract and transform image features and, at the lowest layer, the image is processed to find key features, such as circles, squares and edges [3]. The output is then passed onto the next layer, which searches for more complex features. Such a supervised approach is able to identify the key features that lead to a classification decision, but may lack in transparency and not enable the domain expert understanding of how decisions have been made thus not necessarily helping to progress coral taxonomy research. In contract, the system we introduce in this paper is designed to support marine biologists and their research by enabling the identification of important morphological features of coral. Other popular coral image datasets include CoralNet[1] which has been an enabler of computer vision research in this domain by serving as a hub to collect and share coral specimen images and annotations. CLEF has also recently run evaluation initiatives and created collections making use of coral image datasets. In 2019 [1] and 2020 [2] the available training sets contain 240 images (with 6670 different annotations) and the test sets contain 200 images. While the CLEF tasks make use of benthic substrate bounding box annotations, the system we propose aims at supporting experts in taxonomic coral classification.

Such a human-in-the-loop classification system is key for follow-up Information Retrieval tasks aiming, for example, to retrieve images for a specific family of corals and to map corals in the wild.

3   CoralExp System Design

Implementation. CoralExp has been developed using Python, utilising the scikit-learn libraries for clustering, dimensionality reduction, and t-sne projections.

---

[1] https://coralnet.ucsd.edu/.

Dash has been used as the application framework, allowing for full development of a prototype application, focused on usability and visualisation of results.

Dataset. The system is demonstrated by means of a digital coral collection provided by Queensland Museum containing 998 different coral specimens collected from reefs throughout the world for a total of 8'259 images. Each specimen is represented by images taken on the field (i.e., underwater) as well as in the lab once the specimen has been collected and catalogued.

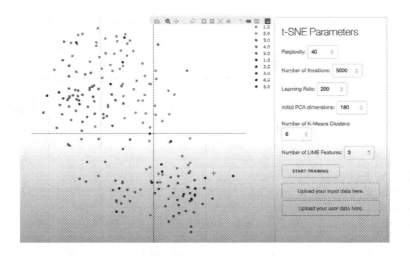

Fig. 1. Bi-dimensional t-sne projection of the digital coral collection.

Demo and User Interaction. The system allows to load a collection of coral images and it first performs a clustering of the available corals to generate groups based on extracted visual features. It then allows to visualise the multi-dimensional feature space by means of t-sne projections [4]. The user can interact with the projected collection which displays coral specimens as items on a two-dimensional space where proximity in the space indicates similarity (see Fig. 1). By clicking on a data item, the user is able to see an image of the selected coral specimen (see Fig. 2). The user is also able to ask for an explanation of the classification decision by asking the system to visualise which parts of the coral specimen are the most indicative for the decision the model has taken (see Fig. 3). Explanations are generated by means of LIME [5].

A video demonstration of the user interaction is available here: https://www.youtube.com/watch?v=4N4YC6LBA3g

4   Conclusions

We have introduced CoralExp: a new system to support experts in marine biology in exploring large collections of coral images with the purpose of conducting

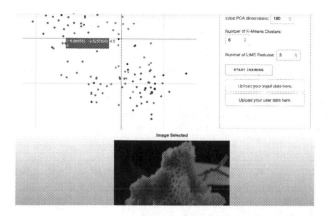

Fig. 2. One selected specimen from the digital coral collection.

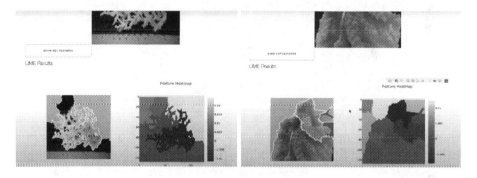

Fig. 3. Explanations of which features are considered most important by the automatic classification model for two example coral specimens.

research on which morphological features may be indicative of differentiating different coral species. Our system makes use of computer vision techniques as well as representational methods to present users with a summary overview of the digital collection enabling them to explore and drill down into similar specimens with common attributes.

Given the availability of labelled data, future extensions of the presented system may include the application of supervised classification models to unlabeled images. Using model classification confidence scores, coral specimen with high confidence may be automatically classified into a predetermined category structure. However, if the model was not confident, it could use detected features to cluster similar specimens and present them to a group of experts for a final classification decision.

Acknowledgements. This work is partially supported by the ARC Discovery Project (Grant No. DP190102141).

References

1. Chamberlain, J., Campello, A., Wright, J.P., Clift, L.G., Clark, A., García Seco de Herrera, A.: Overview of ImageCLEFcoral 2019 task. In: CLEF2019 Working Notes. CEUR Workshop Proceedings, vol. 2380. CEUR-WS.org (2019)
2. Chamberlain, J., Campello, A., Wright, J.P., Clift, L.G., Clark, A., García Seco de Herrera, A.: Overview of the ImageCLEFcoral 2020 task: automated coral reef image annotation. In: CLEF2020 Working Notes. CEUR Workshop Proceedings, Thessaloniki, Greece, 22–25 September 2020, vol. 1166. CEUR-WS.org
3. González-Rivero, M., et al.: Monitoring of coral reefs using artificial intelligence: a feasible and cost-effective approach. Remote Sens. **12**(3), 489 (2020)
4. Maaten, L.V.D., Hinton, G.: Visualizing data using t-SNE. J. Mach. Learn. Res. **9**(Nov), 2579–2605 (2008)
5. Ribeiro, M.T., Singh, S., Guestrin, C.: "Why should I trust you?" Explaining the predictions of any classifier. In: Proceedings of the 22nd ACM SIGKDD International Conference on Knowledge Discovery and Data Mining, pp. 1135–1144 (2016)

AWESSOME: An Unsupervised Sentiment Intensity Scoring Framework Using Neural Word Embeddings

Amal Htait$^{(\boxtimes)}$ and Leif Azzopardi

University of Strathclyde, Glasgow, UK
{amal.htait,leif.azzopardi}@strath.ac.uk

Abstract. Sentiment analysis (SA) is the key element for a variety of opinion and attitude mining tasks. While various unsupervised SA tools already exist, a central problem is that they are lexicon-based where the lexicons used are limited, leading to a vocabulary mismatch. In this paper, we present an unsupervised word embedding-based sentiment scoring framework for sentiment intensity scoring (SIS). The framework generalizes and combines past works so that pre-existing lexicons (e.g. VADER, LabMT) and word embeddings (e.g. BERT, RoBERTa) can be used to address this problem, with no require training, and while providing fine grained SIS of words and phrases. The framework is scalable and extensible, so that custom lexicons or word embeddings can be used to core methods, and to even create new corpus specific lexicons without the need for extensive supervised learning and retraining. The Python 3 toolkit is open source, freely available from GitHub (https://github.com/cumulative-revelations/awessome) and can be directly installed via *pip install awessome*.

Keywords: Sentiment intensity · Pre-trained language model · Lexicon · BERT · VADER

1 Introduction

With the increasing usage of social media platforms, there has been great interest from various sectors, such as sociology, psychology, and marketing, to analyse and monitor such streams in order to extract people's opinions, attitudes and emotions [2,6]. Consequently, numerous sentiment analysis (SA) techniques and methods have been proposed and developed over the years [3,6,11]. Given the daily streams of posts, tweets, blogs and reviews, where people talk about products, places, people, etc., the aim of SA techniques has been to either classify the content as positive, neutral or negative (Sentiment Classification), or to rate the intensity of the sentiment on a scale from strongly positive to strongly negative (Sentiment Intensity Scoring (SIS)). The later being the harder task, which can then be used for classification purposes. The extremely informal nature of online texts varies significantly from formal texts, creating challenges for traditional

© Springer Nature Switzerland AG 2021
D. Hiemstra et al. (Eds.): ECIR 2021, LNCS 12657, pp. 509–513, 2021.
https://doi.org/10.1007/978-3-030-72240-1_56

unsupervised SA techniques, which rely mainly on direct keyword matching and scoring using a highly curated sentiment lexicon (e.g. VADER [2], LabMT [1], LIWC [9]) combined with a series of crafted rules. While, these dictionary based approaches required no training and play an essential role in the fast and scalable analysis of large volumes of online posts, they are fundamentally limited. This is due to the vocabulary mismatch problem, as the vocabulary of the target text is different from the sentiment lexicons, reducing the effectiveness of methods trying to score the sentiment intensity of the phrase or sentence. This work aims to develop a framework for building SIS methods that: (1) addresses the vocabulary mismatch problem by using neural word embeddings, (2) capitalises on pre-existing lexicons for validated sentiment scores, (3) runs out of the box, without requiring any supervised training, and (4) is configurable, customisable and scalable.

1.1 Related Tools and Lexicons

While there are many approaches that have been proposed which are based on supervised machine learning, our focus is on unsupervised approaches. Largely unsupervised approaches are dictionary based - that is they draw upon a curated lexicon of {word, sentiment score} pairs - which are used in conjunction with hand-crafted rules: **SentiStrength**[1] [10] is a sentiment strength extraction tool, it classifies text based on a dual 5-point system for positive and negative sentiment. For that purpose, SentiStrength uses a sentiment dictionary and employs a range of well known non-standard spellings in addition to other common textual methods of expressing sentiment. **VADER** [2] is a widely used simple rule-based model for SA. It relies on a sentiment dictionary (7500 records) of gold-standard quality with human-validated valence scores that indicated both the sentiment polarity (positive/negative), and the sentiment intensity on a scale from -4 to $+4$ (e.g. *good* has a positive valence of 1.9, *great* is 3.1). VADER's sentiment lexicon was compared to seven well-known SA lexicons and it proved its well performance, particularly in the social media domain [2]. Another well known sentiment lexicon, **LabMT** [1] of 10,222 words with their average happiness (or positivity) calculated by combining word frequency distributions and an independently assessed numerical estimates of the *happiness* of over 10,000 words obtained using Amazon's Mechanical Turk[2]. An embeddings based approach, **ASID**[3] [4], was more recently proposed to score SIS. In their approach the sentence words were matched against positive and negative seed lists' terms via corpus based word embeddings, and then the average difference between the positive and negative lists were used to produce the final sentiment intensity score. In this work, we extend this approach to draw upon the lexicons previously developed and validated and to combine them with pre-existing neural word embeddings to create a generalized framework for SIS.

---

[1] http://sentistrength.wlv.ac.uk/.
[2] https://www.mturk.com/.
[3] https://github.com/amalhtait/ASID.

2   The AWESSOME Framework

The presented framework, *A Word Embedding Sentiment Scorer Of Many Emotions* (AWESSOME), has the purpose of predicting the sentiment intensity of words and sentences. The generalised framework is inspired by our previous work [4], which relies on using sentiment seed terms and word embeddings, where the similarity between the vector representation of two sentences is considered as a reflection of their sentiment similarity. For example, if we take the sentence (or word) X and we calculate its similarity with the word (1)*"happy"*, and then with the word (2) *"miserable"*. If X is more similar to (1) than to (2), that would suggest that X has a higher positive sentiment than negative. To apply the method, we need lists of seed terms with strong semantic orientation (i.e. positive and negative seed lists) but lack sensitivity to context [7] (e.g. good, bad), to use as a reference of sentiment polarity and compare the sentences to them. Pre-existing sentiment lexicons (e.g. VADER, LabMT, etc.) make a great choice to use as seed terms, and can be used whole or partially. For the similarity calculation, Htait et al. [4] used a Word2Vec word embedding model. However, Word2Vec lacks the ability to distinguish between the use of a same word in different contexts (e.g. *"bank"* is a riverside or a financial institution) or to understand negations or irony (e.g. *"not happy"*, or *"it was really good, NOT!"*). To solve these problems, we employ neural word embeddings through pre-trained language models (e.g. BERT, etc.) as they can capture the semantics of the entire sentence – which can then be compared to the embeddings of the seed terms. Our SIS method consists of the following components (see Fig. 1):

- **Lexicon for the positive and negative seed word lists**: Existing validated lexicons from VADER and LabMT can be used, or a custom specific lexicon can be imported.
- **Neural Transformer for Word Embeddings for the lower dimensional representation of words and sentences**: Using HuggingFace's Transformer library, different language model can be used directly (e.g. *bert-base-nli-mean-tokens*). Alternatively, such models can be fine tuned specifically to the corpus at hand.
- **Similarity Metric to compute the distance between seed words and target sentences**: So far two similarity metrics have been included: cosine and euclidean distance.
- **Weighting Seed Terms**: To amplify (or not) positive and negative terms, the intensity score of seed terms can be used in conjunction with the similarity score to boost/reduce their impact on the final score.
- **Aggregating function to combine the similarity scores**: To combine the scores of similarity with the terms of the seed lists, an aggregating function is employed: maximum, sum or average. The addition of other similarity metrics or aggregation functions can be easily added in through sub-classes.

Since large seed lists can be computationally expensive, the number of most positive and most negative seed terms from the lexicon can be set.

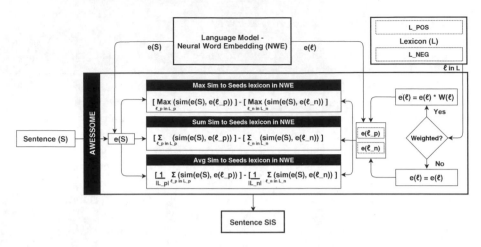

Fig. 1. The AWESSOME framework for SIS consists of three components: a kernel function (e.g. Max, Avg), a neural word embedding and a seed lexicon.

From experiments on three of SemEval's test collections: SemEval-2016 General English (SE16-GE: 2,999 phrases), SemEval-2016 Mixed Polarity (SE16-MP: 1,269 phrases) [5], and SemEval-2018 Task1 (SE18-Vreg: 937 tweets) [8], we found that approximately 500–1000 terms were needed in order to obtain the highest correlations with human annotated intensity scores. While we do not have space to report the details here, we found that the best configurations were by using **600** seed terms from **VADER**'s lexicon, with **BERT** pre-trained language model, while combining the **cosine** similarity scores using the **average** function. Table 1 presents a sample of our experiments results, with the following evaluation measures for correlation coefficient: Kendall's rank (SemEval-2016), and Pearson (SemEval-2018). AWESSOME is open source, freely available from GitHub[4] and can be directly installed via *pip install awessome*.

Table 1. Sample results: Correlation between human-annotations and predicted SIS.

Method	SE16-GE	SE16-MP	SE18-Vreg
Supervised -BERT+Linear Classifier	0.502	0.475	0.645
Unsupervised -VADER Module	0.586	0.365	0.517
AWESSOME (AVG, BERT, VADER-600)	**0.631**	**0.563**	**0.718**
AWESSOME (AVG, BERT, LabMT-600)	0.587	0.479	0.642

---

[4] https://github.com/cumulative-revelations/awessome.

3   Summary

In this paper, we presented a word embedding-based sentiment scoring framework. The framework combined past works so that pre-existing lexicons and word embeddings can be used to predict sentiment intensity, with no required training, and while providing SIS for words, phrases, and sentences. In another work, we have shown that the performance of the presented SIS methods is comparable or better than existing methods. Our Python 3 toolkit is open source and freely available from GitHub (see footnote 4).

Acknowledgement. *Cumulative Revelations of Personal Data.* This project is supported by the UKRI's EPSRC under Grant Numbers: EP/R033854/1.

References

1. Dodds, P.S., Harris, K.D., Kloumann, I.M., Bliss, C.A., Danforth, C.M.: Temporal patterns of happiness and information in a global social network: hedonometrics and Twitter. PLoS ONE **6**(12), e26752 (2011)
2. Gilbert, C., Hutto, E.: Vader: a parsimonious rule-based model for sentiment analysis of social media text. In: ICWSM 2014, vol. 81, p. 82 (2014)
3. Go, A., Bhayani, R., Huang, L.: Twitter sentiment classification using distant supervision. CS224N project report, Stanford **1**(12), 2009 (2009)
4. Htait, A., Fournier, S., Bellot, P., Azzopardi, L., Pasi, G.: Using sentiment analysis for pseudo-relevance feedback in social book search. In: Proceedings of the 2020 ACM SIGIR on International Conference on Theory of Information Retrieval, pp. 29–32 (2020)
5. Kiritchenko, S., Mohammad, S., Salameh, M.: SemEval-2016 task 7: determining sentiment intensity of English and Arabic phrases. In: Proceedings of the 10th International Workshop on Semantic Evaluation (SEMEVAL-2016), pp. 42–51 (2016)
6. Liu, B.: Sentiment analysis and opinion mining. Synth. Lect. Hum. Lang. Technol. **5**(1), 1–167 (2012)
7. Mikolov, T., Chen, K., Corrado, G., Dean, J.: Efficient estimation of word representations in vector space. In: ICLR Workshop (2013)
8. Mohammad, S.M., Bravo-Marquez, F., Salameh, M., Kiritchenko, S.: SemEval-2018 task 1: affect in tweets. In: Proceedings of International Workshop on Semantic Evaluation (SemEval-2018), New Orleans, LA, USA (2018)
9. Pennebaker, J.W., Francis, M.E., Booth, R.J.: Linguistic inquiry and word count: LIWC 2001. Mahway: Lawrence Erlbaum Assoc. **71**(2001), 2001 (2001)
10. Thelwall, M., Buckley, K., Paltoglou, G., Cai, D., Kappas, A.: Sentiment strength detection in short informal text. J. Am. Soc. Inform. Sci. Technol. **61**(12), 2544–2558 (2010)
11. Wang, Y., Huang, M., Zhu, X., Zhao, L.: Attention-based LSTM for aspect-level sentiment classification. In: Proceedings of the 2016 Conference on Empirical Methods in Natural Language Processing, pp. 606–615 (2016)

HSEarch: Semantic Search System for Workplace Accident Reports

Emrah Inan[1], Paul Thompson[1], Tim Yates[2], and Sophia Ananiadou[1(✉)]

[1] National Centre for Text Mining, University of Manchester, Manchester, UK
{emrah.inan,paul.thompson,sophia.ananiadou}@manchester.ac.uk
[2] Health and Safety Executive, HSE Science and Research Centre, Buxton, UK
tim.yates@hse.gov.uk

Abstract. Semantic search engines, which integrate the output of text mining (TM) methods, can significantly increase the ease and efficiency of finding relevant documents and locating important information within them. We present a novel search engine for the construction industry, HSEarch (http://www.nactem.ac.uk/hse/), which uses TM methods to provide semantically-enhanced, faceted search over a repository of workplace accident reports. Compared to previous TM-driven search engines for the construction industry, HSEarch provides a more interactive means for users to explore the contents of the repository, to review documents more systematically and to locate relevant knowledge within them.

Keywords: Construction industry · Hazard identification · Semantic search

1 Introduction

Ensuring safety in new construction projects requires an exploration of documents describing potential hazards and mitigations from previous projects that share similar sets of attributes. Text mining (TM) methods have been used in construction document retrieval systems to expand queries with additional semantically-related terms (e.g. [12]), to retrieve semantically similar documents (e.g., [20]) and to recognise concepts automatically (e.g., [7]). In other domains, semantic search systems allowing filtering of results based on various *facets* of semantic content have been effective (e.g., [17]).

In this paper, we present a novel search system for construction-related documents, HSEarch, which facilitates search over 3000 Reporting of Injuries, Diseases and Dangerous Occurrences Regulations (RIDDOR) workplace accident reports from the archive of the Health and Safety Executive (HSE). The system integrates standard keyword-based search with state-of-the-art TM methods to provide faceted search refinement at different levels of granularity, while automatic summarisation increases the efficiency of scanning longer documents for potential relevancy. Compared to other construction industry search systems, HSEearch provides a more interactive and flexible environment for efficient exploration and filtering of workplace accident reports from multiple perspectives.

D. Hiemstra et al. (Eds.): ECIR 2021, LNCS 12657, pp. 514–519, 2021.
https://doi.org/10.1007/978-3-030-72240-1_57

2   Related Work

Previous TM-based studies have aimed to ease the burden of retrieving and exploring construction documents, e.g., a search system over computer-aided design (CAD) documents uses similarity between text extracted from the documents and the input query as the basis for retrieval [10]. Automatic document classification approaches have used pre-defined topics from a construction information classification system [4] or different categorisations of injuries, incidents or hazards [1,8,16]. In [19], dictionaries and rules are used to recognise pre-defined injury-related concepts in texts. However, supervised Named Entity Recognition (NER) methods are more flexible, since they learn how to recognise mentions of concepts that never occur in the training data. A corpus of RIDDOR reports [18], manually annotated with 6 concept categories (e.g., hazards, consequences, and project attributes) facilitates supervised NER for the construction domain.

3   HSEarch

HSEarch was implemented using Elasticsearch[1]. It can be accessed from a web-based interface written in Flask[2], a microframework for web development.

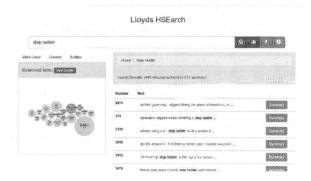

Fig. 1. HSEarch user interface

Figure 1 illustrates the three main components of the user interface, i.e., a search area (top); main search results pane (right); and content exploration pane (left), consisting of three different tabs (*word cloud*, *clusters* and *entities*), allowing the semantic content of the retrieved documents to be explored/filtered.

The left of Fig. 1 illustrates the word cloud resulting from a search for *slipped*. The cloud provides a dynamically-generated overview of the content of the

---

[1] https://www.elastic.co/products/elasticsearch.
[2] https://flask.palletsprojects.com/en/1.1.x/.

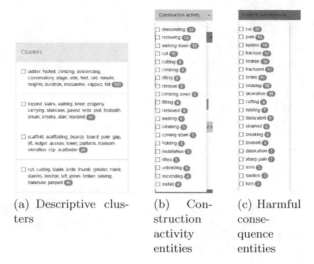

(a) Descriptive clusters

(b) Construction activity entities

(c) Harmful consequence entities

Fig. 2. Clusters and entity categories

retrieved documents, obtained using the widely-used TerMine tool [6], which automatically identifies the most important terms mentioned within a collection of documents. The *Summary* button displays a short summary of longer documents, produced using an entity enriched graph-based method [13] whose nodes including NEs and TerMine-identified terms. We compute similarity between the nodes, leveraging the Word2vec model [14] trained using the RIDDOR reports. After obtaining a weighted graph, we employ the PageRank [2] algorithm to rank the most representative sentences. We then apply Maximum Marginal Relevance (MMR) [5] to the ranked list to ensure that only sentences providing new information are added to the summary.

Figure 2(a) displays some clusters for the search term *slipped*, which provide a high-level overview of the most pertinent topics covered in the retrieved documents. Clicking a check box next to a cluster will filter the search results to retain only the documents in the selected cluster. We use a recently developed, self-tuned *descriptive clustering* approach [3], in which the set of topics is dynamically determined for each new search, and documents are automatically clustered according to these search-specific topics. While the first three clusters clearly correspond to slipping incidents where a fall took place, the documents in fourth cluster concern equipment slipping from a worker's grasp.

We apply a layered neural model [11] to the construction safety corpus [18][3] to recognise domain-relevant NEs. Figure 2(b) shows common NEs mentioned in documents containing the search term *slipped*. While most activities are concerned with ascending or descending, others, like lifting or unloading items, also carry a risk of slipping. Figure 2(c) shows the most frequent *Harmful consequence* NEs in documents containing the word *slipped*, which vary in severity

---

[3] Consult cited paper for details of documents and categories annotated.

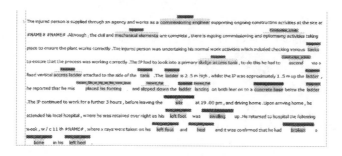

Fig. 3. Semantically-enhanced full text document view

from bruisings to breaks. This list could be used to prioritise exploration of the most severe consequences. Highlighting and colour-coding of NEs in documents (Fig. 3) makes it easy to focus on parts of the text containing different types of important information.

4   Evaluation

The relevance of retrieval results for 20 queries based on various aspects of accidents (e.g., risks, causes and equipment) were evaluated on a scale of 0–2 by 4 domain experts, following the TREC evaluation paradigm [9].

Table 1. Experimental retrieval results using the system.

Enquires	Expert 1		Expert 2		Expert 3		Expert 4		AVG	
Category	nDCG	P@5	nDCG	P@5	nDCG	P@5	nDCG	P@5	nDCG	P@5
Word-Based	0.674	0.77	0.608	0.67	0.578	0.54	0.619	0.66	0.619	0.66
Entity-Based	0.966	0.75	0.945	0.65	0.920	0.45	0.915	0.55	0.937	0.6

Table 1 compares experimental results for entity-indexed texts with traditional word-based indexing in Elasticsearch, using Trectools [15]. We used Fleiss' kappa (overall score 0.99) to verify the correlation between pairs of relevance assessments, and Kendall's tau (0.768) to verify system correlation between word and entity-based indexing. Although P@5 (precision for the first 5 results) is generally similar for both word and entity-based indexing, nDCG (normalised discounted cumulative gain) is significantly higher for entity-based indexing, showing that this method results in better ranked results. Furthermore, we carried out an initial usability study of the HSEarch system, in which we evaluated whether the semantically enhanced document view can be useful within a given user scenario, in terms of being able to capture the prevalence of a risk category. If a domain expert wants to find an answer to the query "How many cuts are caused by a Stanley knife blade?", then the fact that the search system identifies

"Stanley knife blade" as an NE of type "Equipment" allows the user to easily filter documents that mention this NE and explore what is being said about it.

References

1. Bertke, S., Meyers, A., Wurzelbacher, S., Bell, J., Lampl, M., Robins, D.: Development and evaluation of a naïve bayesian model for coding causation of workers' compensation claims. J. Safety Res. **43**(5–6), 327–332 (2012)
2. Brin, S., Page, L.: The anatomy of a large-scale hypertextual web search engine. In: WWW7: Proceedings of the Seventh International Conference on World Wide Web 7 (Amsterdam, The Netherlands, The Netherlands) (1998)
3. Brockmeier, A.J., Mu, T., Ananiadou, S., Goulermas, J.Y.: Self-tuned descriptive document clustering using a predictive network. IEEE Trans. Knowl. Data Eng. **30**(10), 1929–1942 (2018)
4. Caldas, C.H., Soibelman, L.: Automating hierarchical document classification for construction management information systems. Autom. Constr. **12**(4), 395–406 (2003)
5. Carbonell, J., Goldstein, J.: The use of MMR, diversity-based reranking for reordering documents and producing summaries. In: Proceedings of the 21st Annual International ACM SIGIR Conference on Research and Development in Information Retrieval, pp. 335–336 (1998)
6. Frantzi, K., Ananiadou, S., Mima, H.: Automatic recognition of multi-word terms: the C-value/NC-value method. Int. J. Digit. Libr. **3**(2), 115–130 (2000)
7. Gao, G., Liu, Y.S., Lin, P., Wang, M., Gu, M., Yong, J.H.: BIMTag: concept-based automatic semantic annotation of online BIM product resources. Adv. Eng. Inform. **31**, 48–61 (2017)
8. Goh, Y.M., Ubeynarayana, C.: Construction accident narrative classification: an evaluation of text mining techniques. Accid. Anal. Prev. **108**, 122–130 (2017)
9. Harman, D.: TREC-style evaluations. In: Agosti, M., Ferro, N., Forner, P., Müller, H., Santucci, G. (eds.) PROMISE 2012. LNCS, vol. 7757, pp. 97–115. Springer, Heidelberg (2013). https://doi.org/10.1007/978-3-642-36415-0_7
10. Hsu, J.Y., Yu, W.D.: Content-based text mining technique for retrieval of cad documents. Autom. Constr. **31**, 65–74 (2013)
11. Ju, M., Miwa, M., Ananiadou, S.: A neural layered model for nested named entity recognition. In: Proceedings of the 2018 Conference of the North American Chapter of the Association for Computational Linguistics: Human Language Technologies, vol. 1 (Long Papers), pp. 1446–1459 (2018)
12. Kim, T., Chi, S.: Accident case retrieval and analyses: using natural language processing in the construction industry. J. Constr. Eng. Manag. **145**(3), 04019004 (2019)
13. Mihalcea, R., Tarau, P.: Textrank: bringing order into text. In: Proceedings of the 2004 Conference on Empirical Methods in Natural Language Processing, pp. 404–411 (2004)
14. Mikolov, T., Sutskever, I., Chen, K., Corrado, G.S., Dean, J.: Distributed representations of words and phrases and their compositionality. Adv. Neural. Inf. Process. Syst. **26**, 3111–3119 (2013)
15. Palotti, J., Scells, H., Zuccon, G.: TrecTools: an open-source python library for information retrieval practitioners involved in TREC-like campaigns. In: SIGIR 2019. ACM (2019)

16. Taylor, J.A., Lacovara, A.V., Smith, G.S., Pandian, R., Lehto, M.: Near-miss narratives from the fire service: a Bayesian analysis. Accid. Anal. Prev. **62**, 119–129 (2014)
17. Thompson, P., et al.: Text mining the history of medicine. PLoS ONE **11**(1) (2016). https://doi.org/10.1371/journal.pone.0144717
18. Thompson, P., Yates, T., Inan, E., Ananiadou, S.: Semantic annotation for improved safety in construction work. In: Proceedings of the 12th Language Resources and Evaluation Conference, pp. 1990–1999 (2020)
19. Tixier, A.J.P., Hallowell, M.R., Rajagopalan, B., Bowman, D.: Automated content analysis for construction safety: a natural language processing system to extract precursors and outcomes from unstructured injury reports. Autom. Constr. **62**, 45–56 (2016)
20. Zou, Y., Kiviniemi, A., Jones, S.W.: Retrieving similar cases for construction project risk management using natural language processing techniques. Autom. Constr. **80**, 66–76 (2017)

Multi-view Conversational Search Interface Using a Dialogue-Based Agent

Abhishek Kaushik[1]([⊠]), Nicolas Loir[2], and Gareth J. F. Jones[1]

[1] ADAPT Centre, School of Computing, Dublin City University, Dublin, Ireland
abhishek.kaushik2@mail.dcu.ie, Gareth.Jones@dcu.ie
[2] IUT d'Orsay, Orsay, France

Abstract. We present a demonstration application for dialogue-based search. In this system, a conversational agent engages with the user of an online search tool to support their search activities. Agent-supported conversational search of this type represents a fundamental advance beyond current standard search engines, such as web search tools. Analogous to the role of a human librarian, the agent can direct the user to potentially interesting retrieved information and provide suggestions to help progress the searcher's activities.

Keywords: Conversational search · Multiview interface · Human Computer Interaction

1 Introduction

The concept of conversational search has received considerable attention in recent years within the information retrieval (IR) research community [6]. However, little attention has been given to the realization of demonstrations of conversational engagement in real search applications. We present an interactive demonstration of conversational search where the user's search activities are supported by a dialogue-based agent.

Our application combines a conversational search agent with an extended standard graphical search interface as shown in the link[1]. The agent takes the form of a *personal assistant* which works beside the user, rather than sitting between the user and the search engine [5]. The user is able to engage directly with the search engine, while receiving support from the assistant both to help them to form their query and to guide their interaction with retrieved content.

2 Conversational Search Prototype System

The interface for our prototype conversational search system is shown in Fig. 1. This interface includes the following components:

This work was supported by Science Foundation Ireland as part of the ADAPT Centre (Grant 13/RC/2106) at Dublin City University.
[1] https://tinyurl.com/y5phk9f9.

D. Hiemstra et al. (Eds.): ECIR 2021, LNCS 12657, pp. 520–524, 2021.
https://doi.org/10.1007/978-3-030-72240-1_58

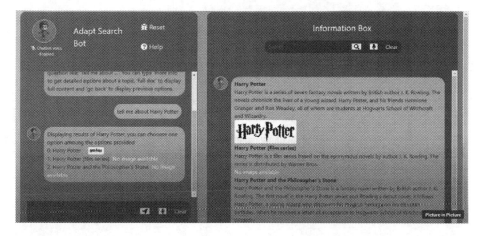

Fig. 1. Conversational search interface incorporates: chat display, chat box, information box, query box, Help-button and retrieved snippets and documents.

1. Help Button: Displays information of interface commands and functionality.
2. Chat Display: Shows dialogue between the agent and the user.
3. Chat Box: Enables the user to insert chat.
4. Information Box: Displays significant features of retrieved items.
5. Query Box: Enables use of standard search interaction by entering a query.
6. Action Button: Enables the following operations:
   (a) Enter: Enter text or query in Chat Box or Search Box.
   (b) Clear: Clear the text from the Chat Box.
   (c) Audio input: Allow the user to enter audio input (represented by the dark colour microphone sign)
   (d) Reset: Clear chat history from the chat box.
   (e) Chatbot voice enabled/disabled: Enable/disable audio response from the search agent.
   (f) Disable discussion: Disable the search agent, information panel then functions like a convectional search system.

The search agent communicates with the user via the Chat Box. Input and output interaction with the Chat Box can either be typed or spoken. The agent performs various actions, including seeking clarification of ambiguous queries, suggesting words for use in revised queries, or showing key details from retrieved items. The Information Box shows key information from retrieved items. Using this, the user's attention can be directed to key details in retrieved content.

2.1 System Implementation

The system is divided into two sections: a Web Interface and a Logical System.

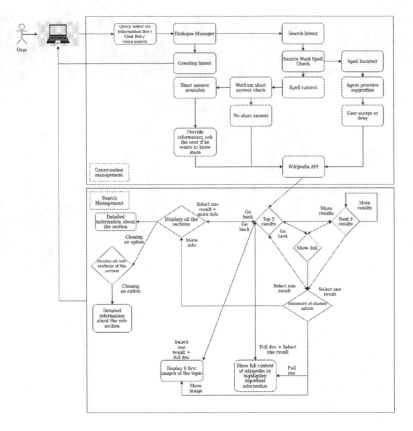

Fig. 2. Workflow of the conversational model

Web Interface. This is constructed using the lightweight WSGI web application python framework[2], with HTML, CSS, and JS toolkit known as bootstrap[3].

Logical System. This is responsible for conversation and search management. The RASA toolkit[4] powered by a fined tuned bert model and spacy is used to identify intent and entities to understand the user need, and to access the spell checking API[5]. The Wikipedia API is used to support the search process. The Wikipedia API[6] (long document) and wolfram alpha (fact based answers) is used to support the search process.

Operations. The search assistant can accept the following user commands:

---

[2] https://palletsprojects.com/p/flask/.
[3] https://getbootstrap.com/.
[4] https://rasa.com/.
[5] https://pypi.org/project/pyspellchecker/.
[6] https://pypi.org/project/wikipedia/.

1. Open {*Document or topic number or title*}: Show the snippet of selected document or topic.
2. More Info {*Document number or title*}: Displays all available metadata from the document, this allows users to explore a topic in depth.
3. Show Image {*Document or option number or title*}: Shows the images from the current document.
4. Go Back: Displays the previous results.
5. More Results: Displays more search results.
6. Search {*Query keyword*}: Starts search for new query, displays highest scoring results for the query.
7. Search Image {*Query keyword*}: Shows top scoring images from documents for the query using image captions.
8. Full Doc {*Document number or title*}: Shows full document with summary of highlighted top scoring sentences at top of document. Clicking on highlighted sentence navigates to corresponding paragraph.
9. Show Links: Display the links to complete documents

2.2 Dialogue Strategy and Taxonomy

After investigating user search behaviour [2] and dialogue systems [3,4,7,8], we developed a dialogue strategy and taxonomy to support conversational search. The dialogue process is divided into three phases with multiple states as discussed in our previous work [1]. The three phases are: identification of user information need, presentation of results in the chat system, and continuation of the dialogue until the user is satisfied or aborts the search. The agent can seek clarification from the user if they believe that the query may contain a typo. The user always has the option to end the current search dialogue by entering a new query. The communication finishes when the user ends the search with success (information need) or abandons with search failure.

The system workflow is divided into two sections: Conversation Management and Search Management, as shown in Fig. 2. Conversation management includes: a Dialogue Manager, a Spell Checker and an image search API. The Dialogue Manager validates the user input and decides to either send it to the RASA or self handle it. Search Management is responsible for search and displaying the top ranking search results to the user in the Information Box. It can give detailed information about a selected item or display more results. There is also an option to look at all available information about an item. In user engagement, the user commences a search from the Information Box, the assistant initiates a dialogue to assist them in the search process. The system also provides support to a user who wants to examine a specific retrieved item.

3 Concluding Remarks

We have introduced a prototype conversational search system. In comparison to the current state of the art in conversational information access tools. e.g.

Amazon Echo Show using Alexa, our prototype can be completely customized and moves beyond the question answering focus of existing conversational tools, to enable the use of conversational mechanisms in broad exploratory search.

References

1. Kaushik, A., Bhat Ramachandra, V., Jones, G.J.F.: An interface for agent supported conversational search. In: Proceedings of the 2020 Conference on Human Information Interaction and Retrieval, CHIIR 2020, pp. 452–456. Association for Computing Machinery, New York (2020)
2. Kaushik, A., Jones, G.J.F.: Exploring current user web search behaviours in analysis tasks to be supported in conversational search. In: Second International Workshop on Conversational Approaches to Information Retrieval (CAIR 2018), Ann Arbor Michigan, USA (2018)
3. Leech, G., Weisser, M.: Generic speech act annotation for task-oriented dialogues. In: Proceedings of the Corpus Linguistics 2003 Conference, vol. 16, pp. 441–446. Lancaster University, Lancaster (2003)
4. Loisel, A., Chaignaud, N., Kotowicz, J.P.: Modeling human interaction to design a human-computer dialog system. arXiv preprint arXiv:0911.5652 (2009)
5. Maes, P.: Agents that reduce work and information overload. Commun. ACM **37**(7), 30–40 (1994)
6. Radlinski, F., Craswell, N.: A theoretical framework for conversational search. In: Proceedings of the 2017 Conference on Conference Human Information Interaction and Retrieval, pp. 117–126. ACM (2017)
7. Sitter, S., Stein, A.: Modeling the illocutionary aspects of information-seeking dialogues. Inf. Process. Manag. **28**(2), 165–180 (1992)
8. Stein, A., Thiel, U.: A conversational model of multimodal interaction in information systems. In: Proceedings of the Eleventh National Conference on Artificial Intelligence, pp. 283–288. AAAI Press (1993)

LogUI: Contemporary Logging Infrastructure for Web-Based Experiments

David Maxwell$^{(\boxtimes)}$ and Claudia Hauff

Delft University of Technology, Delft, The Netherlands
{d.m.maxwell,c.hauff}@tudelft.nl

Abstract. Logging user interactions is fundamental to capturing and subsequently analysing user behaviours in the context of web-based *Interactive Information Retrieval (IIR)*. However, logging is often implemented within experimental apparatus in a piecemeal fashion, leading to incomplete or noisy data. To address these issues, we present the **LogUI** logging framework. We use (now ubiquitous) contemporary web technologies to provide an easy-to-use yet powerful framework that can capture virtually any user interaction on a webpage. **LogUI** removes many of the complexities that must be considered for effective interaction logging.

Keywords: Logging · Framework · Experimental infrastructure

1 Introduction

Contemporary *web applications* are complex and ubiquitous [17]. At their heart, a series of manipulations are undertaken on the *Document Object Model (DOM)*[1], where *HTML elements* are created and modified during the lifespan of a webpage. *Web-based* experimental apparatus is commonplace within the IIR community to examine an interface's usability and the behaviours exhibited by those who use it. Vital to these studies is the concept of *logging user interactions*. Interaction logs are generated by capturing and recording a user's interactions (or *events*) with webpage(s) during a search and/or browsing session.

Researchers often work on their own web-based apparatus, including their own logging infrastructure. Anecdotal observations highlight that logging is often achieved in a piecemeal fashion, often considered to be an afterthought leading on from the implementation of the main system. However, this is undesirable. Infrastructure can be complex to implement [1], with researchers forgetting to log key events, or misunderstanding implementation nuances. This can lead to low quality logs, with missing and/or noisy data—with the potential for *post-hoc* frustrations when interpreting the data. While attempts have been made to develop logging infrastructure over the years (refer to Sect. 2), we have failed

---

[1] The *DOM* is the tree-like structure of *HTML elements* that constitute a webpage.

© Springer Nature Switzerland AG 2021
D. Hiemstra et al. (Eds.): ECIR 2021, LNCS 12657, pp. 525–530, 2021.
https://doi.org/10.1007/978-3-030-72240-1_59

to find an easy-to-use (and affordable) solution that considers the necessary complexities to generate clean logs—and is able to exploit contemporary web technologies.

As such, we present in this paper the **LogUI** framework. The framework can capture and record high-quality, fine-grained user interaction data over the course of a search and/or browsing session. It can be easily integrated within any existing web application that is run on a contemporary web browser/framework, meaning support on both desktop and mobile platforms is possible.

2 Existing Approaches

While a large number of IIR studies report measures such as click depths (on *Search Engine Result Pages (SERPs)*), mouse trails and movements, dwell times, keypresses, and so forth, descriptions about how the underlying data are captured are seldom provided. Indeed, logging apparatus is often implemented *in situ* within the wider experimental system. A number of logging tools (and associated literature) exist. Phillips and Dumas [16] presented a number of criteria that effective logging infrastructure must comply with.

The mid-2000s to the mid-2010s saw a shift in focus from *platform-specific* [14,16,21] to *web-based* experimental apparatus, including interaction logging infrastructure that focused on examining the DOM. Examples of solutions from this period included *MLogger* [10], *PooDLE* [5], *Search-Logger* [18], *Wrapper* [13], *UsaProxy* [3,4], the framework by Hall and Toms [11], *WHOSE* [12], and *YASFIIRE* [20]. Some of these solutions required additional software to be installed (such as browser toolbars), while others made use of an intermediary *proxy server* to inject logging code, as used in subsequent studies [2,6,7,15].

Despite advancements, these approaches were less than ideal [8]. A second *browser war* led to a rise in prominence for client-side scripting (i.e., *ECMAScript*, or *JavaScript*), and in turn increased the capabilities of browsers. Existing solutions became redundant, with new, *JavaScript-only* solutions such as *ALF* [9]. In the commercial space, tools such as *Google Analytics*, *Hotjar*, *Matomo*, and *eTracker Analytics* are available. While useful, these tools offer either coarse-grained logging (for *SEO*); are prohibitively expensive; are not designed to be loosely coupled (leading to integration difficulties); or use outdated technologies. A more recent solution is *UXJs* [19], but it may still have issues when integrating with modern web applications using frameworks such as *React*. These modern frameworks use JavaScript to *'draw'* elements on a webpage; the fine-grained logging solutions mentioned above do not cater for elements drawn *after* the page initially loads. We believe that there is therefore a pertinent need for logging apparatus supported by researchers within the IIR community.

3   The LogUI Framework

With a high-level overview of **LogUI** shown in Fig. 1, we now present a brief discussion of the framework's architecture, highlighting the main components. This includes: the **client**; what can be logged; the **server**; and ease of integration. Note that all circled numbers (e.g., ❶) pertain to the component highlighted with the same number as in Fig. 1.

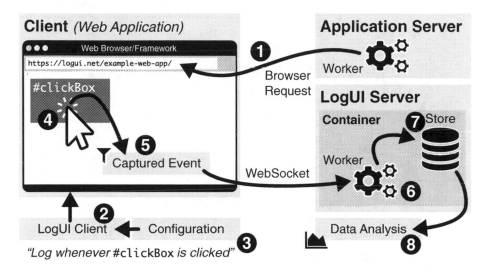

Fig. 1. Architecture diagram of the **LogUI** framework. Refer to Sect. 3 for a detailed explanation, along with descriptions of the eight highlighted components.

LogUI Client Library: The **LogUI** client is a JavaScript library that provides advanced functionality for the tracking of events associated with a specific element on a webpage, or associated with the webpage as a whole. To clarify, an *event* pertains to a specific action—such as the click of a user's mouse—on a specific *element*—such as a snippet as presented on a SERP. Events pertaining to the page as a whole could be, for example, the resizing of the web browser's viewport, tracking mouse movements, the scrolling of the page, or the web browser no longer being the user's active window *(losing focus)*. As previously mentioned, **LogUI** can be used in a contemporary web browser[2]; web-based application frameworks such as *Electron* are also supported if required.

Given an existing web application (such as experimental apparatus) where fine-grained event logging is required ❶, one can integrate **LogUI** by including the compiled **LogUI** client library ❷. A configuration object must be supplied to **LogUI** ❸. This tells the client library what elements on the page should be logged—and for what events (see below). When an event occurs ❹, the

---

[2] **LogUI** has been tested with *Chrome, Edge, Firefox, Opera,* and *Safari.*

LogUI client then packages up the data for the event (along with any specified *metadata*, see below) ❺, and sends the packaged data down the established *Websocket* connection to the listening **LogUI** server worker process ❻.[3]

Loggable Elements and Events: Standardised *CSS Selectors* are used in the configuration object ❸ to allow for the selection of *any* element within the DOM. Any standardised DOM events can also be used (such as `mouseover` or `keyup`). As mentioned, page-wide events can also be logged. Changes to the DOM are also incorporated, with **LogUI** watching for new elements matching a given CSS selector, and applying the necessary events.[4] We also include so-called *grouping*, where one or more events can be chained together to act as a single, managable event (e.g., `mouseover` and `mouseout` events would constitute a grouped `hover` event). This means that additional logic can be added to avoid logging *noisy* events, such as when scrolling. This is a novel and non-trivial feature, and while it affords additional complexity, it results in cleaner logs.

Metadata: One or more pieces of *metadata* may be required to be packaged with a logged event.[5] **LogUI** provides numerous *metadata sourcers*, allowing for the extraction of data from different locations (e.g., the attribute of the element, or localstorage). We also include sourcers for frameworks like React, allowing one to extract a `prop` or `state` value from the associated *component*.

LogUI Server: The server authenticates a **LogUI** client, and receives the packaged event data ❻. It is then placed in backing storage ❼ (with session IDs, allowing for filtering/merging). Captured data for search/browsing sessions can be then downloaded and used for data analysis ❽. The server is implemented within a containerised environment to aid portability.

Integration with Web Applications: **LogUI** can be seamlessly integrated within existing web applications. As it examines the DOM only, it is *framework agnostic*. The client is self-contained, meaning it does not interfere with other libraries. Logging is as easy as *1-2-3*: *(1)* include the client library within the web application; *(2)* specify what elements and events to log; and *(3)* start a server instance to receive the logged events. The framework provides support for web applications on a single webpage, or over multiple webpages. Interactions over multiple pages can therefore be counted as a single session. A simple API is also provided to start and stop the library, or reset the session as required.

---

[3] Note that the *Application Server* and *LogUI Server* are two entirely different processes, and can be run on separate computers (with *CORS* support enabled).

[4] **LogUI** therefore supports contemporary client-side web application frameworks.

[5] Metadata examples could include the `docid` for a document presented on a SERP, or, more generally, the condition a participant is assigned to in an *A/B test*.

Availability: Code is open source and available from GitHub. The client is accessible at https://github.com/logui-framework/client/, with server code at https://github.com/logui-framework/server/. Documentation for both components are also available in the respective repository.

4   Summary

We have described our new logging framework, **LogUI**. The complexity that the framework handles (along with the relative simplicity of using it) will provide a powerful new tool for researchers to deploy when logging user interactions as part of IIR experiments. We aim to continue developing the framework to support more advanced features[6], and will promote its use in a wide variety of experimental apparatus, leading to increased productivity for researchers.

Acknowledgements. This research has been supported by *NWO* projects *SearchX* (639.022.722) and *Aspasia* (015.013.027).

References

1. Alexander, J., Cockburn, A., Lobb, R.: AppMonitor: a tool for recording user actions in unmodified windows applications. Behav. Res. Methods **40**(2), 413–421 (2008)
2. Apaolaza, A., Harper, S., Jay, C.: Longitudinal analysis of low-level web interaction through micro behaviours. In: Proceedings of 26th ACM HT, pp. 337–340 (2015)
3. Atterer, R., Wnuk, M., Schmidt, A.: Knowing the user's every move: user activity tracking for website usability evaluation and implicit interaction. In: Proceedings of 15th WWW, pp. 203–212 (2006)
4. Atterer, R.: Logging usage of AJAX applications with the "UsaProxy" HTTP proxy. In: Workshop on Logging Traces of Web Activity, Proceedings of 15th WWW (2006)
5. Bierig, R., Gwizdka, J., Cole, M.J.: A user-centered experiment and logging framework for interactive information retrieval. In: Workshop on Understanding the User, Proceedings of 32nd ACM SIGIR, pp. 8–11 (2009)
6. Bigham, J., Cavender, A.: Evaluating existing audio captchas and an interface optimized for non-visual use. In: Proceedings of 27th ACM CHI, pp. 1829–1838 (2009)
7. Bilal, D., Gwizdka, J.: Children's eye-fixations on google search results. Proc. ASIS&T **53**(1), 1–6 (2016)
8. Dekel, U.: A framework for studying the use of wikis in knowledge work using client-side access data. In: Proceedings of 3rd WikiSym, pp. 25–30 (2007)
9. Doolan, M., Azzopardi, L., Glassey, R.: ALF: a client side logger and server for capturing user interactions in web applications. In: Proceedings of 35th ACM SIGIR, p. 1003 (2012)
10. Edmonds, A., White, R.W., Morris, D., Drucker, S.M.: Instrumenting the dynamic web. J. Web Eng. **6**(3), 244–260 (2007)

---

[6] Features could include a *UXJs*-style [19] analysis interface, or screen capturing.

11. Hall, M., Toms, E.: Building a common framework for IIR evaluation. In: Proceedings of 4th CLEF, pp. 17–28 (2013)
12. Hienert, D., van Hoek, W., Weber, A., Kern, D.: Whose - a tool for whole-session analysis in IIR. In: Proceedings of 37th ECIR, pp. 172–183 (2015)
13. Jansen, B.J., Ramadoss, R., Zhang, M., Zang, N.: Wrapper: an application for evaluating exploratory searching outside of the lab. In: Workshop on Evaluating Exploratory Search Systems, in Proceedings of 29th ACM SIGIR (2006)
14. Kukreja, U., Stevenson, W.E., Ritter, F.E.: RUI: recording user input from interfaces under Windows and Mac OS X. Behav. Res. Methods 38(4), 656–659 (2006)
15. Lassila, M., Pääkkönen, T., Arvola, P., Kekäläinen, J., Junkkari, M.: Unobtrusive mobile browsing behaviour tracking tool. In: Proceedings of 4th IIiX, pp. 278–281 (2012)
16. Philips, B.H., Dumas, D.J.S.: Usability testing: identifying functional requirements for data logging software. In: Proceedings of Human Factors Society Annual Meeting, vol. 34, no. 4, pp. 295–299 (1990)
17. Rossi, G., Urbieta, M., Distante, D., Rivero, J.M., Firmenich, S.: 25 years of model-driven web engineering. What we achieved, what is missing. CLEI Elec. J. 19(3), 5–57 (2016)
18. Singer, G., Norbisrath, U., Vainikko, E., Kikkas, H., Lewandowski, D.: Searchlogger: analyzing exploratory search tasks. In: Proceedings of 26th ACM SAC, pp. 751–756 (2011)
19. Solís-Martínez, J., Espada, J.P., González Crespo, R., Pelayo G-Bustelo, B.C., Cueva Lovelle, J.M.: UXJs: tracking and analyzing web usage information with a Javascript oriented approach. IEEE Access 8, 43725–43735 (2020)
20. Wei, X., Zhang, Y., Gwizdka, J.: Yasfiire: yet another system for IIR evaluation. In: Proceedings of 5th IIiX, pp. 316–319 (2014)
21. Westerman, S.J., et al.: Investigating the human-computer interface using the Datalogger. Behav. Res. Methods Instrum. Comput. 28(4), 603–606 (1996)

LEMONS: Listenable Explanations
for Music recOmmeNder Systems

Alessandro B. Melchiorre[1,2]([✉]) [iD], Verena Haunschmid[1] [iD], Markus Schedl[1,2] [iD],
and Gerhard Widmer[1,2] [iD]

[1] Johannes Kepler University (JKU), Linz, Austria
{alessandro.melchiorre,verena.haunschmid,
markus.schedl,gerhard.widmer}@jku.at
[2] Linz Institute of Technology (LIT), Linz, Austria

Abstract. Although current music recommender systems suggest new tracks to their users, they do not provide listenable explanations of why a user should listen to them. LEMONS (Demonstration video: https://youtu.be/giSPrPnZ7mc) is a new system that addresses this gap by (1) adopting a deep learning approach to generate audio content-based recommendations from the audio tracks and (2) providing listenable explanations based on the time-source segmentation of the recommended tracks using the recently proposed audioLIME.

Keywords: Music recommendation · Explainability · audioLIME · Content-based recommendation

1 Introduction

Motivated by the impact of explainability on transparency, user satisfaction, and scrutability [1,2], different types of explanations in recommender system (RS) research have been proposed [3,4]. The adopted explanation method depends on the type of model input (e.g., user-item interaction data, content features, or contextual information), the RS algorithm (e.g., CF or CBF), and the modality used to give explanations (e.g., textually [5–8], visually [9], or graph-based user preferences [4,10,11]), cf. [4]. In music RS, research on explaining recommendations has considered music data [12–14], user data [14,15], context information [16], or a combination of the above [6,14,17], which are predominantly used to create textual explanations (such as "because you like jazz", "because users with similar taste listen to it", or "because it's Monday morning", respectively). To the best of our knowledge, none of the existing approaches provides explanations in the same modality of music itself, i.e. listenable. We address this shortcoming in the LEMONS demo[1] at hand by (1) adopting an audio-based music recommender system and (2) providing listenable explanations of the recommended tracks. LEMONS is based on the recently proposed audioLIME method [18].

A. B. Melchiorre and V. Haunschmid—These authors contributed equally.
[1] https://github.com/cpjku/lemons.

© Springer Nature Switzerland AG 2021
D. Hiemstra et al. (Eds.): ECIR 2021, LNCS 12657, pp. 531–536, 2021.
https://doi.org/10.1007/978-3-030-72240-1_60

2   System Overview

Music Recommender System. Existing approaches in content-based music RS usually employ metadata or acoustic features extracted from the audio track to make recommendations, which, in turn, can be used to create explanations [13, 14]. However, these approaches lead to non-listenable explanations as the audio information is either lost or compressed. In contrast, we provide explanations a user can listen to with an audio-based recommendation model inspired by state-of-the-art approaches for music tagging [19,20]. Focusing on one user at a time, we train a fully convolutional neural network[2] to predict the relevance of a specific track for the user by using its audio as input. More precisely, we consider the tracks listened to by the user as relevant while randomly selected tracks never interacted with as non-relevant [21]. We split the tracks into train, validation, and test set in an 80-10-10 fashion and select the model that achieves the best results in terms of AUC and MAP on the validation set. The results on the test set averaged across the users are 0.734 ± 0.130 MAP and 0.758 ± 0.113 AUC.

Generating Listenable Explanations. Explanations are computed post-hoc using audioLIME [18], an extension of LIME [22] for audio data. audioLIME extracts interpretable components from audios by using source separation estimates and temporal segmentation [18,23]. These interpretable components are then used as input features to fit a simple linear model that mimics the underlying RS model. The components with a positive weight are interpreted as having a positive contribution to the recommended track relevance, while the opposite is true for negative weights. When computing explanations using audioLIME, we also care how well the linear model approximates the RS model, which is reported by the fidelity score, the coefficient of determination R^2 between the linear explanation model and the RS model.

Data. We use the Million Song Dataset (MSD) and the Taste Profile Dataset [24] for training the recommender systems, as they provide listening data for about 1 million users and 300,000 songs. For this demo, we carefully select 7 users who listened to more than 900 tracks and who differ by their music preferences. The music audio data was originally obtained from 7digital[3] and the snippets' durations range from 30s to 60s. We also include and test our system on the musdb18 dataset [25], which comprises 150 songs ($\sim$10 h) belonging to 9 different genres.

3   Demonstration Overview

The landing page of our demo is shown in Fig. 1. It first introduces the 7 users from the MSD that serve as different personas (e.g., a listener with very specific

---

[2] Details about training and architecture can be found in our GitHub repository.
[3] https://www.7digital.com/.

LEMONS: Listenable Explanations for Music recOmmeNder Systems

User/Persona Selection

Below you can explore the 7 users/personas of our demo. Each user is characterized by a distinctive music preference.

Which user?

| Elizabeth - (rock, alternative metal, heavy metal) | ▼ |

Selected user profile

Elizabeth
Her top 3 genres she likes are rock, alternative metal, and heavy metal.
She listened to 826 tracks (shown below sorted by playcount) for a total of 1918 listening events.

	title	artist	album	playcount	track
679	You Often Forget (malignant)...	Revolting Cocks	Big Sexy Land	37	TRWSVAT128F147B64
536	Never Enough	Five Finger Death Punch	The Way Of The Fist	23	TROFJAC128F932086
299	5.45	Gang Of Four	Entertainment	17	TROTJAW128F1466DC
1553	Crossing Over	Five Finger Death Punch	War Is The Answer	14	TRPOCPP129B3CAE12
655	Dresses In Decay	OXY	An Answer Can Be Found	14	TRVINSF128B07BE1C
238	Skin Ticket (Album Version)	Slipknot	Iowa	13	TRSGVCM128F4238A6
403	Return of the Tres	Delinquent Habits	Excess Alterlatina	13	TRWYUZT128F93118?
505	Salvation	Five Finger Death Punch	The Way Of The Fist	13	TRPQNVO128F9338B6
1585	Bodies	Drowning Pool	Sinner	12	TRILVCI129B3CCC98
681	Sermon	Drowning Pool	Sinner	12	TRLNLRD129B3CCC98
448					

Fig. 1. Introduction of personas' music taste, listening statistics, and listened to tracks.

genre taste, very diverse taste, or a chart music follower), from which one can be selected. The selected user's profile is then shown below along with a short description of their music preferences, some music listening statistics, and the tracks they listened to. On the left (not shown in the figure), a sidebar provides clarification on how the RS and the listenable explanations work. Thereafter, the music dataset from which recommendations are computed (either MSD or musdb18) can be selected. The recommended tracks are presented to the user as a ranked list, in decreasing order of relevance. The demo user can select a song, play it, and seek within a visualization of its waveform.

As shown in Fig. 2, we offer three types of listenable explanations for the selected song depending on the interpretable components used: (1) *time-based* explanations use time segmentation to split the audio into five equally long segments, (2) *source-based* explanations use Spleeter [26] to separate the audio into 5 sources (vocals, drums, bass, piano, and other), (3) *time-and-source-based* explanations combine both, resulting in 25 interpretable components. We also describe the selected type of explanation accompanied by an illustrating image.

When the *Compute Explanation* button is pressed, the system generates the explanation and provides the fidelity score. We present two interfaces for the listenable explanations: "Top Highlight" and "Top-3". Top Highlight allows listening to the single interpretable component that influences the recommendation the most. Top-3, instead, selects the 3 most influential components. A *time-and-source-based* explanation for a track could sound like drums and bass playing in the first segment and drums playing in the third segment.

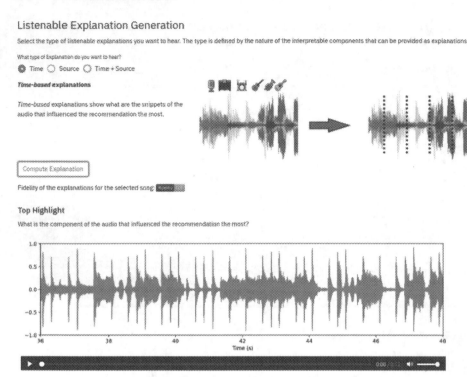

Fig. 2. Listenable Explanations: After having selected the explanation type (e.g. *time-based*), the demo shows the fidelity score and the listenable explanation interfaces. In this example, "Top Highlight" shows that the most influential component is the snippet from seconds 36 to 48.

4   Conclusion and Future Work

We presented a novel approach to generate listenable explanations for music recommender systems (LEMONS). For this purpose, we integrated audioLIME into a content-based recommender system, to uncover the pivotal components in the music audio signal which serve as explanations of why a track has been recommended to the user. As a next step, we plan to conduct a user study to investigate the quality and usefulness of the offered explanations from an end user's perspective. In addition, future work includes integrating a music segmentation technique to provide more meaningful segments for the time-based explanations (e.g., verse, chorus, or motif), and extending the purely content-based approach to a hybrid one by integrating collaborative listening data.

References

1. Tintarev, N., Masthoff, J.: Explaining recommendations: design and evaluation. In: Ricci, F., Rokach, L., Shapira, B. (eds.) Recommender Systems Handbook, pp. 353–382. Springer, Boston (2015). https://doi.org/10.1007/978-1-4899-7637-6_10

2. Balog, K., Radlinski, F.: Measuring recommendation explanation quality: the conflicting goals of explanations. In: Proceedings of the 43rd International ACM SIGIR Conference on Research and Development in Information Retrieval, pp. 329–338. Association for Computing Machinery (2020)

3. Arrieta, A.B., et al.: Explainable artificial intelligence (XAI): concepts, taxonomies, opportunities and challenges toward responsible AI. Inf. Fusion **58**, 82–115 (2020)

4. Zhang, Y., Chen, X.: Explainable recommendation: a survey and new perspectives. Found. Trends Inf. Retrieval **14**(1), 1–101 (2020)

5. Zhang, Y., Lai, G., Zhang, M., Zhang, Y., Liu, Y., Ma, S.: Explicit factor models for explainable recommendation based on phrase-level sentiment analysis. In: Proceedings of the 37th International ACM SIGIR Conference on Research & Development in Information Retrieval, pp. 83–92. Association for Computing Machinery (2014)

6. Tsukuda, K., Goto, M.: Explainable recommendation for repeat consumption. In: 14th ACM Conference on Recommender Systems, pp. 462–467. Association for Computing Machinery (2020)

7. Li, P., Wang, Z., Ren, Z., Bing, L., Lam, W.: Neural rating regression with abstractive tips generation for recommendation share on. In: Proceedings of the 40th International ACM SIGIR Conference on Research and Development in Information Retrieval, pp. 345–354. Association for Computing Machinery (2017)

8. Chang, S., Harper, F.M., Terveen, L.G.: Crowd-based personalized natural language explanations for recommendations. In: Proceedings of the 10th ACM Conference on Recommender Systems, pp. 175–182. Association for Computing Machinery (2016)

9. Chen, X., et al.: Personalized fashion recommendation with visual explanations based on multimodal attention network: towards visually explainable recommendation. In: Proceedings of the 42nd International ACM SIGIR Conference on Research and Development in Information Retrieval, pp. 765–774. Association for Computing Machinery (2019)

10. Kouki, P., Schaffer, J., Pujara, J., O'Donovan, J., Getoor, L.: User preferences for hybrid explanations. In: Proceedings of the 11th ACM Conference on Recommender Systems, pp. 84–88. Association for Computing Machinery (2017)

11. Herlocker, J.L., Konstan, J.A., Riedl, J.: Explaining collaborative filtering recommendations. In: Proceedings of the 2000 ACM Conference on Computer Supported Cooperative Work, pp. 241–250. Association for Computing Machinery (2000)

12. Vig, J., Sen, S., Riedl, J.: Tagsplanations: explaining recommendations using tags. In: Proceedings of the 14th International Conference on Intelligent User Interfaces, pp. 47–56. Association for Computing Machinery (2009)

13. Green, S.J., et al.: Generating transparent, steerable recommendations from textual descriptions of items. In: Proceedings of the 3rd ACM Conference on Recommender Systems, pp. 329–338. Association for Computing Machinery (2009)

14. Millecamp, M., Htun, N.N., Conati, C., Verbert, K.: To explain or not to explain: the effects of personal characteristics when explaining music recommendations. In: Proceedings of the 24th International Conference on Intelligent User Interfaces, pp. 397–407. Association for Computing Machinery (2019)

15. Sharma, A., Cosley, D.: Do social explanations work? Studying and modeling the effects of social explanations in recommender systems. In: Proceedings of the 22nd International Conference on World Wide Web, pp. 1133–1144. Association for Computing Machinery (2013)

16. Zhao, G., et al.: Personalized reason generation for explainable song recommendation. ACM Trans. Intell. Syst. Technol. **10**(4), 1–21 (2019)

17. Wang, X., Wang, D., Xu, C., He, X., Cao, Y., Chua, T.S.: Explainable reasoning over knowledge graphs for recommendation. In: Proceedings of the 33rd AAAI Conference on Artificial Intelligence, vol. 33, pp. 5329–5336. Association for the Advancement of Artificial Intelligence Press (2019)
18. Haunschmid, V., Manilow, E., Widmer, G.: audioLIME: listenable explanations using source separation. In: 13th International Workshop on Machine Learning and Music, pp. 20–24 (2020)
19. Won, M., Ferraro, A., Bogdanov, D., Serra, X.: Evaluation of CNN-based automatic music tagging models. In: Proceedings of 17th Sound and Music Computing (2020)
20. Choi, K., Fazekas, G., Sandler, M.: Automatic tagging using deep convolutional neural networks. In: Proceedings of the 17th International Conference on Music Information Retrieval (ISMIR 2016), pp. 805–811 (2016)
21. Pan, R., et al.: One-class collaborative filtering. In: 2008 Eighth IEEE International Conference on Data Mining, pp. 502–511. Institute of Electrical and Electronics Engineers (2008)
22. Ribeiro, M.T., Singh, S., Guestrin, C.: "Why should i trust you?": explaining the predictions of any classifier. In: Proceedings of the 22nd ACM SIGKDD International Conference on Knowledge Discovery and Data Mining, pp. 1135–1144. Association for Computing Machinery (2016)
23. Haunschmid, V., Manilow, E., Widmer, G.: Towards Musically Meaningful Explanations Using Source Separation. CoRR abs/2009.02051 (2020). https://arxiv.org/abs/2009.02051
24. Bertin-Mahieux, T., Ellis, D.P., Whitman, B., Lamere, P.: The million song dataset. In: Proceedings of the 12th International Conference on Music Information Retrieval (ISMIR 2011), pp. 591–596. University of Miami (2011)
25. Rafii, Z., Liutkus, A., Stöter, F.R., Mimilakis, S.I., Bittner, R.: MUSDB18 - A Corpus for Music Separation (2017)
26. Hennequin, R., Khlif, A., Voituret, F., Moussallam, M.: Spleeter: a fast and efficient music source separation tool with pre-trained models. J. Open Source Softw. 5(50), 2154 (2020)

Aspect-Based Passage Retrieval
with Contextualized Discourse Vectors

Jens-Michalis Papaioannou[1(✉)], Manuel Mayrdorfer[2], Sebastian Arnold[1],
Felix A. Gers[1], Klemens Budde[2], and Alexander Löser[1]

[1] Beuth University of Applied Sciences, Luxemburger Str. 10, 13353 Berlin, Germany
{michalis.papaioannou,sarnold,gers,aloeser}@beuth-hochschule.de
[2] Charité – Universitätsmedizin Berlin, Charitéplatz 1, 10117 Berlin, Germany
{manuel.mayrdorfer,klemens.budde}@charite.de

Abstract. Passage retrieval is the task of retrieving only the portions
of a document that are relevant to a particular information need. One
application medical doctors and researchers face is the challenge of reading a large amount of novel literature. For example, since the outbreak
of Coronavirus disease 2019 (COVID-19), tens of thousands of papers
have been published each month about the disease. We demonstrate
how we can support healthcare professionals in this exploratory research
task with our neural passage retrieval system based on Contextualized
Discourse Vectors (CDV). CDV captures the discourse of long documents on sentence level and allows to query a large corpus with medical
entities and aspects. Our demonstration covers over 27,000 diseases and
14,000 clinical aspects including symptoms, diagnostics, treatments and
medications. It returns passages and highlights sentences to effectively
answer clinical queries with up to 65% Recall@1. We showcase our system on the COVID-19 Open Research Dataset (CORD-19), Orphanet
and Wikipedia diseases corpora.

1 Introduction

In December 2019, starting in Wuhan, Hubei Province, China, an unprecedented
outbreak of pneumonia of unknown etiology emerged, resulting in an ongoing
pandemic [12]. Research groups all over the world contributed to thousands
of publications within mere weeks, making it demanding for scientists to keep
pace with the rapidly growing number of papers about the novel disease. In
this context, the Allen Institute for AI[1] with other partners created CORD-19
[18], a growing resource of scientific papers on COVID-19. Many search systems
were built over this resource. Two prominent examples are Google Research
Explorer[2], which gives short factual answers to questions posed by researchers
and Spike-CORD[3], which uses a sentence-level, context-aware extractive search.

---

[1] https://allenai.org/.

[2] https://covid19-research-explorer.appspot.com/.

[3] https://spike.covid-19.apps.allenai.org/search/covid19.

© Springer Nature Switzerland AG 2021
D. Hiemstra et al. (Eds.): ECIR 2021, LNCS 12657, pp. 537–542, 2021.
https://doi.org/10.1007/978-3-030-72240-1_61

In this paper we demonstrate a system that complements existing general-purpose search and question-answering solutions, which primarily focus on the document or paragraph level. Our system allows effective and efficient exploration of scientific publications and retrieves information on sentence level by decoding contextualized information about medical entities and their aspects, such as symptoms, medication or treatment options. It is based on our prior work on Contextualized Document Vectors (CDV) [2], a neural model that encodes discourse of long documents with sentence granularity[4]. Our approach is especially helpful for skimming long and complex documents like those in the medical domain and supports a structured query following the PICO principle [14] used in evidence based medicine [5]. To complement the experimental evaluation in the original paper, we showcase three demonstrators to prove the usefulness of our approach in a real world scenario. The demos are available online using CORD-19[5] [18], WikiSection[6] [3], and Orphanet[7] [9] as their resource accordingly. Due to space constraints, we focus on the first system here.

2   Demonstrating CORD-19 Literature Search

Prior to starting a new study, medical doctors should be aware of other scientific groups having studied the same or similar aspects of a disease, in order to be able to compare the results to others and to avoid looking for answers where well-assessed evidence already exists. Let's consider a researcher posing the query whether *coronaviruses* exist in *other species* that are in regular contact with humans. The goal of this query is to retrieve statements contained in publications about different animals as hosts for coronaviruses. This could be used as a starting point for a literature analysis addressing the needs mentioned above. The demonstration interface for this use case is shown in Fig. 1. It has two fields, one for a medical entity e.g. "SARS-CoV-2", and another for the aspect of interest e.g. "Other species" (1). The auto-complete supports the medical doctor to resolve known entities and aspects, but also allows free text. The system returns a list of similar entities, e.g. "Canine influenza" and "Bovine coronavirus infection", which can be clicked to refine the query (2). The search result contains up to 30 passages from different articles that match the query, shown with its semantic discourse similarity matching score in percent (3). By hovering over a sentence, its individual score is shown. For each article, the best matching sentence is highlighted in bold, e.g."During the SARS outbreak, masked palm civet cats (Paguma larvata) and raccoon dogs (Nyctereutes procyonoides) were found to carry SARSlike viruses, even before the virus was discovered in lesser bamboo bats (Tylonycteris pachypusa and Pipistrellus)" [6] (4). The medical doctor can open the original source article or read a larger part of the passage by clicking

---

[4] Code available at https://github.com/sebastianarnold/CDV.

[5] https://cord19.cdv.demo.datexis.com (We use all 11k documents from the PMC Commercial Use subset).

[6] https://wiki.cdv.demo.datexis.com.

[7] This resource is not publicly available due to licensing reasons.

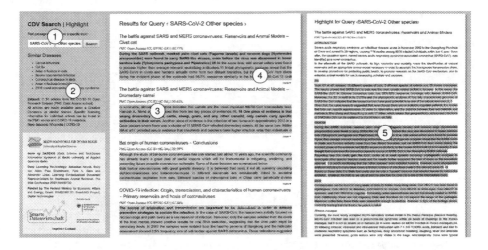

Fig. 1. Screenshot of the CDV search interface (left), result passages (center) and one document in highlight view (right).

"more" (5). Here, the entire article is shown, and the similarity score of each sentence with the query is indicated by a shade of blue. The more saturated the shade is, the more relevant the text excerpt is. While the first view highlights interesting passages for a query, the second view provides a medical doctor with the context of the entire research article.

3 CDV Passage Retrieval Process

The problem of passage retrieval has been extensively studied for decades [16]. In particular for long documents, passage retrieval needs to focus on retrieving small excerpts in response to the query statement of a user [1]. We have previously shown that CDV outperforms popular search methods, such as TF-IDF [10] and BM25 [15], but also recent neural approaches such as DSSM [8] and HAR [19] on this task in a zero-shot scenario [13] on nine English healthcare resources with up to 65.21% Recall@1 [2]. We use the CDV model as shown in Fig. 2 to deliver the requested information to a medical doctor or researcher following our prior work on Smart-MD [17]. The retrieval process is divided into three steps:

1. Discourse vector encoding. We apply a pre-trained CDV model to all documents in the data set following [2]: First, the text of each document is encoded into a sequence of sentence embeddings using BioBERT [11]. Next, we transform the word input space of T sentences per document into a contextualized discourse vector space using a bidirectional LSTM over the sentence embeddings [7]. Finally, all discourse vectors $\delta_t, t \in \{1, \ldots, T\}$ are indexed in an in-memory index. This step forms the discourse-aware document representation and embeds all necessary information to decode contextualized entity and aspect information for a document.

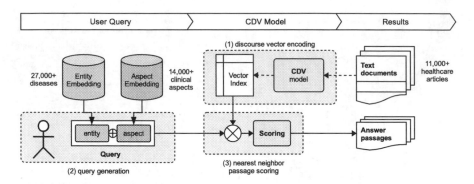

Fig. 2. CDV retrieval process: At load time, research articles are mapped to the same space as entities and aspects by the model and stored in a vector index (1). During retrieval, the medical doctor's query is matched with an embedding from the knowledge base or calculated on-the-fly (2). Next, we calculate semantic similarity for every sentence and the query (3). Finally, the scores are ranked and presented to the user.

2. Query generation. We encode entity and aspect of the query using pre-trained entity and aspect embeddings and represent the query Q as vector concatenation of the two embeddings. The models are trained with a Fasttext+BLSTM [4] architecture using descriptions from Wikipedia and other medical resources [2].

3. Nearest-neighbor passage scoring. Finally, to score every passage, we compute the cosine similarity between the query Q and every sentence δ_t of the documents in the index. The system averages the sentence score over passages and ranks the resulting passages according to the similarity score. Because the encoding of discourse-aware representations requires only a single pass through all documents at index time, the scoring step only takes a few hundred milliseconds [2].

4   Discussion

In [2], we have shown the effectiveness of our passage retrieval system. With this demonstration, we amplify this result by showing how CDV can support medical doctors in skimming long and complex documents in medical literature analysis tasks. The results delivered in this task were encouraging and pave the way for further investigation about the usefulness of our system in a clinical scenario. Future work includes the extension of the CDV model in order to enable more complex query compositions like a conjunction query, e.g. ⟨"COVID-19" AND "Kawasaki syndrome", "children"⟩ or another query paradigm like query-by-document or query-by-case.

Acknowledgements. Our work is funded by the German Federal Ministry for Economic Affairs and Energy (BMWi) under grant agreement 01MD19003B (PLASS) and 01MK2008D (Servicemeister).

References

1. Allan, J., Wade, C., Bolivar, A.: Retrieval and novelty detection at the sentence level. In: SIGIR 2003: Proceedings of the 26th Annual International ACM SIGIR Conference on Research and Development in Information Retrieval, pp. 314–321. ACM (2003). https://doi.org/10.1145/860435.860493
2. Arnold, S., van Aken, B., Grundmann, P., Gers, F.A., Löser, A.: Learning contextualized document representations for healthcare answer retrieval. In: WWW 2020: The Web Conference 2020, pp. 1332–1343. ACM/IW3C2 (2020). https://doi.org/10.1145/3366423.3380208
3. Arnold, S., Schneider, R., Cudré-Mauroux, P., Gers, F.A., Löser, A.: SECTOR: a neural model for coherent topic segmentation and classification. Trans. Assoc. Comput. Linguist. **7**, 169–184 (2019). https://doi.org/10.1162/tacl_a_00261
4. Bojanowski, P., Grave, E., Joulin, A., Mikolov, T.: Enriching word vectors with subword information. Trans. Assoc. Comput. Linguist. **5**, 135–146 (2017). https://transacl.org/ojs/index.php/tacl/article/view/999
5. Cheng, G.Y.: A study of clinical questions posed by hospital clinicians. J. Med. Libr. Assoc. **64**, 445–58 (2004)
6. Gong, S., Bao, L.: The battle against SARS and MERS coronaviruses: reservoirs and animal models. Anim. Models Exp. Med. **1**, 125–133 (2018)
7. Hochreiter, S., Schmidhuber, J.: Long short-term memory. Neural Comput. **9**(8), 1735–1780 (1997). https://doi.org/10.1162/neco.1997.9.8.1735
8. Huang, P., He, X., Gao, J., Deng, L., Acero, A., Heck, L.P.: Learning deep structured semantic models for web search using clickthrough data. In: 22nd ACM International Conference on Information and Knowledge Management, CIKM 2013, pp. 2333–2338. ACM (2013). https://doi.org/10.1145/2505515.2505665
9. INSERM: Orphanet: an online database of rare diseases and orphan drugs. Tech. rep., Copyright, INSERM (1997)
10. Jones, K.S.: A statistical interpretation of term specificity and its application in retrieval. J. Doc. **60**(5), 493–502 (2004). https://doi.org/10.1108/00220410410560573
11. Lee, J., Yoon, W., Kim, S., Kim, D., Kim, S., So, C.H., Kang, J.: BioBERT: a pre-trained biomedical language representation model for biomedical text mining. Bioinformatics **36**, 1234–1240 (2019)
12. Lu, H., Stratton, C.W., Tang, Y.W.: Outbreak of pneumonia of unknown etiology in Wuhan, China: the mystery and the miracle. J. Med. Virol. **92**, 401–402 (2020)
13. Palatucci, M., Pomerleau, D., Hinton, G.E., Mitchell, T.M.: Zero-shot learning with semantic output codes. In: Advances in Neural Information Processing Systems 22: 23rd Annual Conference on Neural Information Processing Systems 2009, pp. 1410–1418. Curran Associates, Inc. (2009). http://papers.nips.cc/paper/3650-zero-shot-learning-with-semantic-output-codes
14. Richardson, W.S., Wilson, M.C., Nishikawa, J.A., Hayward, R.S.A.: The well-built clinical question: a key to evidence-based decisions. ACP J. Club **123**(3), A12–A13 (1995)
15. Robertson, S.E., Walker, S., Hancock-Beaulieu, M.: Large test collection experiments on an operational, interactive system: okapi at TREC. Inf. Process. Manag. **31**(3), 345–360 (1995). https://doi.org/10.1016/0306-4573(94)00051-4
16. Salton, G., Allan, J., Buckley, C.: Approaches to passage retrieval in full text information systems. In: Proceedings of the 16th Annual International ACM-SIGIR Conference on Research and Development in Information Retrieval, pp. 49–58. ACM (1993). https://doi.org/10.1145/160688.160693

17. Schneider, R., Arnold, S., Oberhauser, T., Klatt, T., Steffek, T., Löser, A.: Smart-MD: neural paragraph retrieval of medical topics. In: Companion of the The Web Conference 2018 on The Web Conference 2018, WWW 2018, pp. 203–206. ACM (2018). https://doi.org/10.1145/3184558.3186979
18. Zhang, E., Gupta, N., Nogueira, R., Cho, K., Lin, J.: Rapidly deploying a neural search engine for the COVID-19 open research dataset: preliminary thoughts and lessons learned. CoRR abs/2004.05125 (2020). https://arxiv.org/abs/2004.05125
19. Zhu, M., Ahuja, A., Wei, W., Reddy, C.K.: A hierarchical attention retrieval model for healthcare question answering. In: The World Wide Web Conference, WWW 2019, pp. 2472–2482. ACM (2019). https://doi.org/10.1145/3308558.3313699

News Monitor: A Framework
for Querying News in Real Time

Antonia Saravanou[✉], Nikolaos Panagiotou, and Dimitrios Gunopulos

Department of Informatics and Telecommunications, National and Kapodistrian
University of Athens, Athens, Greece
{antoniasar,npanagio,dg}@di.uoa.gr

Abstract. News articles generated by online media are a major source
of information. In this work, we present News Monitor, a framework that
automatically collects news articles from a variety of web pages and performs various analysis tasks. The framework initially identifies fresh news
and clusters articles about the same incidents. For every story, it extracts
a Knowledge Base (KB) using open information extraction techniques
and utilizes this KB in order to build a summary for the user. News
Monitor allows the users to query the article in natural language using
the state-of-the-art framework BERT. Nevertheless, it allows the user
to perform queries also in the KB in order to identify relevant articles.
Finally, News Monitor crawls Twitter using a dynamic set of keywords in
order to retrieve relevant messages. The framework is distributed, online
and performs analysis in real-time.

Keywords: News monitoring · Event detection · Question answering

1 Introduction

News agencies such as CNN provide on daily basis a large amount of news articles
that cover the events happening in the whole world. Some events are localized
while other may have a global impact such as the recent COVID-19 pandemic.
For the readers, it is challenging to identify which news are fresh and in many
cases the readers are interested only for the summary of an article since their
time is limited. At the same time, other users on social media, such as Twitter,
actively discuss the various stories and provide further details or criticism about
the events. Thus, a news portal should provide two orthogonal functionalities:
(i) summarization of the articles, and (ii) exploration of social media feeds.

In this work we demonstrate our distributed framework News Monitor[1] with
the following advantages:

– Scalability: We analyse in real-time over 500 RSS streams under limited hard-
  ware exploiting randomized data structures ensuring constant complexity.
  Furthermore, we propose an elastic and distributed architecture.

---

[1] System demonstration available in: http://195.134.67.89/news_monitor/.

© Springer Nature Switzerland AG 2021
D. Hiemstra et al. (Eds.): ECIR 2021, LNCS 12657, pp. 543–548, 2021.
https://doi.org/10.1007/978-3-030-72240-1_62

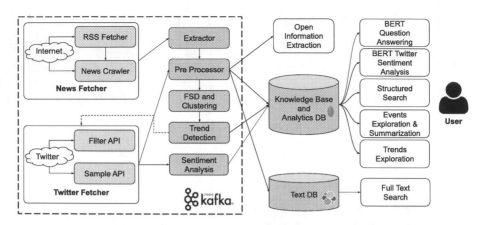

Fig. 1. The architecture of News Monitor.

- Usability: The framework provides to the users an interface that provides them with the tools in order to quickly explore an article. It addition, it allows them to directly search a Knowledge Base constructed from the news.
- Novelty: We integrate under a unified solution a variety of state-of-the-art techniques and provide a simple yet effective framework for exploring news.
- Comparison to state-of-the-art: News Monitor has further analytical features, including online question answering, graph summarization and sentiment analysis, in comparison to commercial systems such as Yahoo News.

2   Advancing the State of the Art

The first functionality of News monitor is first story detection (FSD). A variety of techniques [9,11–13,19] have been proposed in the recent literature that exploit nearest neighbor methods. News monitor uses the FSD framework proposed in our previous work [11] under real-time realistic settings. In terms of clustering documents for event detection online clustering techniques have been proposed, unsupervised [2,17] and supervised [20] methods, as well as ranking techniques [18]. More recent works focus on sub-event detection [8,16] in order to provide a timeline of the highlights of the detected events. One major component of News Monitor is the knowledge base construction exploiting open information extraction methods. For open information extraction a variety of techniques is proposed in the literature such as ReVerb [5], RelNoun [10] and SRLIE [3]. News Monitor uses ReVerb due to its simplicity and efficiency. Relevant applications to News Monitor but focused on event detection include Twitter Monitor [7], Twitter Stand [15], EveSense [14] and Jasmine [20]. The most relevant commercial application is the system Event Registry [6]. However, News Monitor provides online question answering and sentiment analysis using the framework BERT [4].

3   Architecture

The system architecture follows a distributed microservices perspective. That is, every analysis module is an independent component that runs on its own machine. The various components are integrated using the Apache Kafka message queue. Apache Kafka provides the mechanism for the components to communicate with each other in an efficient and fault tolerant way. Each component can subscribe to one or more topics and publish to one topic. The knowledge base as well as the analysis is stored in MongoDB instance. The architecture of News Monitor is illustrated in Fig. 1. The demonstration runs on two servers with 16 threads, and 32 GB of RAM. In addition, the deep learning algorithms use a NVIDIA 2070 GPU.

4   Features of the News Monitor

The News Monitor framework currently supports a variety of features that allow the registered users to explore news stories.

News and Twitter Fetcher: The most important components of the News Monitor system are the News and Twitter fetcher. These two components are responsible to provide the input data to the system. The News Fetcher, is periodically monitoring a list of RSS feeds. The Twitter Fetcher uses the streaming Twitter API in order to receive messages and tracks a list of keywords according to the output of the trend detection.

Preprocessing and Knowledge Base Construction: Each document provided by the Extractor module has an extracted content. This content is used by the Preprocessor module that performs various NLP tasks. The open information extraction output is a list of triplets of the form (argument1, relation ,argument 2). The tuples are stored to the MongoDB knowledge base. These tuples are used in order to create a summary of each article as a graph as shown in Fig. 2(b). The pre-processed tweets and the articles are stored in an ElasticSearch database.

First Story Detection: The stream that is provided by the News Crawler is provided to the First Story Detection component. This component uses the framework provided by the work [11] in order to examine if a document is a new story. In order to ensure scalability, the module uses multiple LSH indexes that have a capacity of 2000 documents in order to ensure constant processing time.

Trends Detection: The trends detection module examines all the prepossessed news articles in order to examine trending named entities. That is, for every window the references of named entities are stored. Then these counts are used in order to calculate the z-scores for every entity.

Question Answering: The question answering module allows the user to query in natural language. In the case the user is interested in performing queries in natural language, we use the BERT pretrained model [1] in the SQuAD dataset.

Fig. 2. (a) News monitor interface. (b) A graph summary provided by News Monitor.

5 Demonstration

A view of the interface is shown in Fig. 2(a). The framework fetches and analyzes news articles from over 500 RSS sources and Twitter messages relevant to these articles. The user can read the first stories that the system has identified. These stories describe the latest events reported by news and in addition, for each story the users will be able to view other articles about the same event. Thus, a curious reader could read multiple views about the same event.

For each of the news articles the system creates a summary in the form of a graph (as shown in Fig. 2(b)). This summary originates from the Knowledge Base that was constructed by the article. In addition, News Monitor allows users to define queries of interest, relevant to the article, in natural language. Then, News Monitor computes the answer in the form of a text chunk by using the state-of-the-art BERT [4] model. This is a novel feature that is not provided by existing systems such as Yahoo News or Event Registry.

As already mentioned, the News Monitor extracts for each article a Knowledge Graph in order to create a Knowledge Base. The users can search this Knowledge Base by using the structured search option that is searching in the extracted tuples. When a user finds a tuple interesting, she is able to further explore the document where the tuple exists. In addition the users could use the advanced search option to refine their queries. The ability to search directly the sub-events of an article is a novel feature of News Monitor.

Finally, during the users can explore Twitter messages analyzed by News Monitor. They are able to define a query and the framework will provide a collection of tweets that are relevant. For each tweet, the News Monitor provides the sentiment as calculated by the BERT framework. This is another novel aspect of News Monitor in comparison to Event Registry and Yahoo News.

Acknowledgments. The present work was co-funded by the European Union and Greek national funds through the Operational Program "Human Resources Development, Education and Lifelong Learning" (NSRF 2014-2020), under the call "Supporting Researchers with an Emphasis on Young Researchers - Cycle B" (MIS:5048149).

References

1. Pre-trained BERT model. https://huggingface.co/bert-large-uncased-whole-word-masking-finetuned-squad (2018). Accessed 20 Jan 2021
2. Abdelhaq, H., Sengstock, C., Gertz, M.: Eventweet: online localized event detection from twitter. Proc. VLDB Endow. **6**(12), 1326–1329 (2013)
3. Christensen, J., Soderland, S., Etzioni, O.: An analysis of open information extraction based on semantic role labeling. In: Proceedings of the Sixth International Conference on Knowledge Capture, pp. 113–120 (2011)
4. Devlin, J., Chang, M.W., Lee, K., Toutanova, K.: BERT: pre-training of deep bidirectional transformers for language understanding. In: Proceedings of the 2019 Conference of the North American Chapter of the Association for Computational Linguistics: Human Language Technologies, vol. 1 (Long and Short Papers), pp. 4171–4186. Association for Computational Linguistics, Minneapolis, Minnesota (2019). https://www.aclweb.org/anthology/N19-1423
5. Etzioni, O., Fader, A., Christensen, J., Soderland, S., Mausam, M.: Open information extraction: the second generation. IJCAI **11**, 3–10 (2011)
6. Leban, G., Fortuna, B., Brank, J., Grobelnik, M.: Event registry: learning about world events from news. In: Proceedings of the 23rd International Conference on World Wide Web, pp. 107–110 (2014)
7. Mathioudakis, M., Koudas, N.: Twittermonitor: trend detection over the twitter stream. In: Proceedings of the 2010 ACM SIGMOD International Conference on Management of data, pp. 1155–1158 (2010)
8. Meladianos, P., Nikolentzos, G., Rousseau, F., Stavrakas, Y., Vazirgiannis, M.: Degeneracy-based real-time sub-event detection in twitter stream. ICWSM **15**, 248–257 (2015)
9. Moran, S., McCreadie, R., Macdonald, C., Ounis, I.: Enhancing first story detection using word embeddings. In: Proceedings of the 39th International ACM SIGIR Conference on Research and Development in Information Retrieval, pp. 821–824 (2016)
10. Pal, H.: Demonyms and compound relational nouns in nominal open IE. In: Proceedings of the 5th Workshop on Automated Knowledge Base Construction, pp. 35–39 (2016)
11. Panagiotou, N.E., Akkaya, C., Tsioutsiouliklis, K., Kalogeraki, V., Gunopulos, D.: A general framework for first story detection utilizing entities and their relations. IEEE Trans. Knowl. Data Eng. **1**, 1 (2020)
12. Petrović, S., Osborne, M., Lavrenko, V.: Streaming first story detection with application to twitter. In: Human Language Technologies: The 2010 Annual Conference of the North American Chapter of the Association for Computational Linguistics, pp. 181–189 (2010)
13. Petrović, S., Osborne, M., Lavrenko, V.: Using paraphrases for improving first story detection in news and twitter. In: Proceedings of the 2012 Conference of the North American Chapter of the Association for Computational Linguistics: Human Language Technologies, pp. 338–346 (2012)
14. Saeed, Z., Ayaz Abbasi, R., Razzak, I.: EveSense: what can you sense from twitter? In: Jose, J.M., et al. (eds.) Advances in Information Retrieval, pp. 491–495. Springer, Cham (2020)
15. Sankaranarayanan, J., Samet, H., Teitler, B.E., Lieberman, M.D., Sperling, J.: Twitterstand: news in tweets. In: Proceedings of the 17th ACM SIGSPATIAL International Conference on Advances in Geographic Information Systems, pp. 42–51 (2009)

16. Saravanou, A., Katakis, I., Valkanas, G., Gunopulos, D.: Detection and delineation of events and sub-events in social networks. In: ICDE, pp. 1348–1351 (2018)
17. Saravanou, A., Katakis, I., Valkanas, G., Kalogeraki, V., Gunopulos, D.: Revealing the hidden links in content networks: an application to event discovery. In: Proceedings of the 2017 ACM on Conference on Information and Knowledge Management, pp. 2283–2286 (2017)
18. Saravanou, A., Stefanoni, G., Meij, E.: Identifying notable news stories. In: Jose, J.M., et al. (eds.) ECIR 2020. LNCS, vol. 12036, pp. 352–358. Springer, Cham (2020). https://doi.org/10.1007/978-3-030-45442-5_44
19. Saravanou, A., Valkanas, G., Gunopulos, D., Andrienko, G.: Twitter floods when it rains: a case study of the UK floods in early 2014. In: Proceedings of the 24th International Conference on World Wide Web, pp. 1233–1238 (2015)
20. Watanabe, K., Ochi, M., Okabe, M., Onai, R.: Jasmine: a real-time local-event detection system based on geolocation information propagated to microblogs. In: Proceedings of the 20th ACM International Conference on Information and Knowledge Management, pp. 2541–2544 (2011)

Chattack: A Gamified Crowd-Sourcing Platform for Tagging Deceptive & Abusive Behaviour

Emmanouil Smyrnakis[1(✉)], Katerina Papantoniou[1,2],
Panagiotis Papadakos[1,2] ⓘ, and Yannis Tzitzikas[1,2] ⓘ

[1] University of Crete, Heraklion, Greece
{csd3504,tzitzik}@csd.uoc.gr
[2] Information Systems Laboratory, FORTH-ICS, Heraklion, Greece
{papanton,papadako}@ics.forth.gr

Abstract. With the explosion of social networks, the web has been transformed into an arena of inappropriate interactions and content, such as fake news and misinformation, deception, hate speech, inauthentic online behaviour, proselytism, slander, and mobbing. In this demo we present `Chattack`, a first step towards our aim of providing publicly available datasets for accelerating research in the area of safer online conversations. `Chattack` is a crowd-sourcing web platform that allows the creation of textual dialogues containing inappropriate interactions or language. To make the platform sustainable and collect as many qualitative dialogues as possible, we build upon a gamified approach that can engage users and provide incentives for the completion of various tasks. We provide the details of our approach, present the functionality of the platform, stress its novel features, and discuss some preliminary results and the lessons learned. The platform is publicly available and we invite the participation of the community for its growth.

1   Introduction

The use of Facebook, Instagram, Twitter and many other social networking platforms is constantly increasing in today's society. These platforms offer the illusion of anonymity, more casual ways of communication, and an enormous load of information. However, despite the trust that users have to these platforms, they might witness deceptive and offensive behaviours ranging from immoral to outlaw actions [2,4]. Nowadays, such behaviours are becoming common and can have ruinous consequences for the victims. Numerous studies [5,6,8] show that apart from the financial ramifications, such incidents can result in mental disorders like depression, anxiety, self-harm, eating disorders and even suicidal thoughts. As a result, it is of utmost importance such incidents to be detected in real time. The current state-of-the-art approaches are based on machine and deep learning methods, requiring a large volume of training data which is currently lacking.

In this demo we present `Chattack`, a crowd-sourcing platform that allows the creation of textual dialogues containing inappropriate interactions or language, through a functionality that resembles popular platforms for online games (e.g.,

D. Hiemstra et al. (Eds.): ECIR 2021, LNCS 12657, pp. 549–553, 2021.
https://doi.org/10.1007/978-3-030-72240-1_63

lichess, chess.com and others). Such platforms let the users find opponents for online games, monitor played games, and engage them through various kinds of incentives like credits, to keep them playing. In the same manner, `Chattack` through its gamified approach tries to engage users to raise social awareness for the dark side of online communications. It enables users to participate and monitor games of two players, where the aim of one of the players, the attacker, is to lead a dialogue with abusive, offensive and/or deceptive characteristics in disguise; characteristics that should not be recognized by the other player, the defender. The platform let the players annotate at real time any offensive behaviour with tags from an ontology of related tags, while the rest of the community can rate their annotations, game performance and task completion. The engagement of users is done through points and badges, which they can earn by playing games, rating tags and games, or by completing various challenges. This gamified approach can help the sustainability of the platform, and in collecting as many qualitative dialogues as possible. `Chattack` stores all related data and metadata regarding every game, regarding the dialogue and its utterances, including their assigned tags and rates.

Although similar crowd-sourcing approaches have been made for recording and detecting abusive and deceptive behaviours in social networks [1,3,7], none of them is available online and supports the challenging task of collecting dialogues in a gamified manner. `Chattack` is publicly available with the objective to collect and provide crowd-sourced datasets of high quality 'inappropriate' dialogues of various troubling behaviour categories. By engaging the community, `Chattack` can potentially become a reference for the collection of datasets of such dialogues.

In a nutshell, the contributions of this paper are: (a) we introduce a crowd-sourcing approach that is based on gamification, adapted to the needs of creating tagged collections of abusive and deceptive dialogues, and (b) we present the design and implementation of a system that realizes this approach.

2   Description of the System `Chattack`

`Chattack` is a web application[1] in which users interact in pairs through matches, where the purpose of each match is to complete a specific task related to abusive, offensive and/or deceptive characteristics that might appear in online dialogues. Below we describe the main resources of the platform, which are tasks, users, matches, messages, tags, challenges, annotations and ratings Some screenshots of the platform are provided in Fig. 1.

Users. Users are the mainspring of our platform as our metadata depend on their actions. To gain access, users have to create a user account with which they can participate to the platform under three different roles: a) as workers that can play matches, b) as creators of new tasks for matches, and c) as annotators of

---

[1] The frontend was developed using React while the backend uses the javalin framework for micro-services.

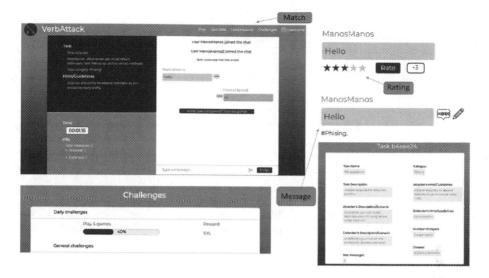

Fig. 1. Overview of the graphical user interface of Chattack

completed matches. Furthermore, a user can earn points and badges, according to its activity to the platform, and their goal is to earn as many points as possible in order to climb the leader board. Depending on their current active role (i.e., player, task administrator, or annotator), their profile page displays some statistics like the number of played games, created tasks, completed annotations, as well as their points and badges.

Tasks. Tasks embody the basis of each match that takes place in the platform. In more details, each task has an offense category and a description of its purpose, while the objectives of both attacker and defender are described. Hints and suggestions for the task are also provided for both attackers and defenders, while an optional maximum size of exchanged messages can be used for terminating and unsuccessful game.

Matches. A match is a live synchronous chat created for a specific task, where two users exchange messages and can report offenses. In this head-to-head conversation, each user has a role which can be either an Attacker or a Defender. Specifically, the attacker is assigned to harm, cheat, offend or fool the opposite user, while the defender needs to recognize and him/herself against any kinds of assaults. The purpose of a single match is the completion of either user's objective while there is always the "forfeit" option. If both of the opponents agree to terminate the game as the task is completed, they earn both 10 points and the game is tied. On the other hand, if one of them forfeits only the other one earns the 10 points of the game.

Messages. Messages are a significant part of a match between two users. There is a maximum number of messages that can be sent in a match and depends on the task used for the creation of the game. A message displays the sender name on top, the content of the message in the box and the report an offense tag option on the right side. Each message can be annotated by a set of tags which are shown below it.

Tags. Each user can also report any of the messages of the dialogue with an offense through the tags. Each tag has an offense category. The tag categories vary from racism, sexism to phishing and cheating. All tags are stored in a database where we can specify which messages where offensive and which was the offense. Currently, for every tag a user earns 2 points while every matching tag between the two opponents gives them 3 extra points.

Challenges. Each user can participate in various predefined challenges. Each challenge offers a reward, a progress and a description which indicates what the user has to achieve to earn the reward. The completion of such challenges let the users gain more points or even earn some badges that are shown in their avatar.

Annotations/Ratings. Users can also perform an annotation of a match in our platform, an action that can provide them and other users more points. Annotators can rate the messages of a match with ratings from 1–5 stars. Each star given to a message, earns a point for the sender of the message. Furthermore, an annotator can rate the attacker's and defender's playing style and rate the whole game. The annotator earns for every rating 2 points and 10 extra for every game annotation.

3   Concluding Remarks

In brief, the platform supports tasks in the form of an online chat (with attackers and offenders), various user roles (player, admin, annotator) and user statistics. The platform provides challenges as incentives, it supports a tag mechanism with offence categories, and a rewarding scheme. Moreover an annotation mechanism is provided and the users can rate individual messages as well as whole games. The platform is currently available at http://demos.isl.ics.forth.gr/chattack, and it is under continuous improvement. We plan to release it publicly, and to invite the community to participate, by December 2020. The annotated dataset is available at http://islcatalog.ics.forth.gr/dataset/deceptive-and-abusive-online-dialogs.

References

1. Antonios, A., Ioannis, M., Grigorios, T.: Hatebusters: a web application for actively reporting YouTube hate speech. In: Proceedings of the Twenty-Seventh International Joint Conference on Artificial Intelligence, IJCAI-18, pp. 5796–5798. International Joint Conferences on Artificial Intelligence Organization (2018)
2. Vidgen, A.H.B., Margetts, H.: How much online abuse is there?. Technical report, The Alan Turing Institute (2019)
3. Federico, B., Sara, T.: A 3D role-playing game for abusive language annotation. In Workshop on Games and Natural Language Processing, pp. 39–43, Marseille, France, May 2020. European Language Resources Association (2020)

4. The European Commission (Eurobarometer). Fake news and disinformation online. Technical report, European Union (2018)
5. Amnesty International. Amnesty reveals alarming impact of online abuse against women (2017). https://www.amnesty.org/en/latest/news/2017/11/amnesty-reveals-alarming-impact-of-online-abuse-against-women. Accessed 6 Oct 2020
6. Kelly, Y., Zilanawala, A., Booker, C., Sacker, A.: Social media use and adolescent mental health: findings from the UK millennium cohort study. EClinical Med. **6**, 59–68 (2018)
7. Haruna, O., Hitoshi, N., Takenobu, T., Hikaru, Y.: Gamification platform for collecting task-oriented dialogue data. In: LREC (2020)
8. Samantha, B.S., Maria, R., David, L.P., Philip, D.H.: Cyberbullying and its relationship to current symptoms and history of early life trauma: a study of adolescents in an acute inpatient psychiatric unit. J. Clinical Psychiatry **81**(1) (2020)

PreFace++: Faceted Retrieval of Prerequisites and Technical Data

Prajna Upadhyay$^{(\boxtimes)}$ and Maya Ramanath

Indian Institute of Technology, Delhi, India
{prajna.upadhyay,ramanath}@cse.iitd.ac.in

Abstract. While learning new technical material, a user faces difficulty encountering new concepts for which she does not have the necessary prerequisite knowledge. Determining the right set of prerequisites is challenging because it involves multiple searches on the web. Although a number of techniques have been proposed to retrieve prerequisites, none of them consider grouping prerequisites into interesting facets. To address this issue, we have developed a system called **PreFace++** (http://eval_teknowbase_for_ir.apps.iitd.ac.in/prerequisites/) which assists a user in learning new topics. PreFace++ is an extension of our previous system PreFace. It takes a query as input and returns (i) a prerequisite graph, where the nodes represent prerequisites for the query and edges indicate prerequisite relationship, ii) a set of interesting facets towards understanding the query (iii) prerequisites for the query and the facet and iv) a set of research papers and posts relevant for the query and the facet to explore relationship between the query and the facet. The backbone of PreFace++ is TeKnowbase, which is a knowledge base in Computer Science.

Keywords: Prerequisites · Facets · Knowledge base · Academic search

1 Introduction

When reading new technical material, a common problem faced by readers is encountering new and unknown concepts, to understand which the reader does not have the required prerequisite knowledge. A prerequisite for a concept a is another concept b that can be suggested for study before a for better understanding of a. For example, to understand artificial_neural_network, one needs to have a prerequisite knowledge of neuron. Also, a knowledge of software such as matlab is required to implement the query and improve her overall understanding. Identifying the right set of prerequisite concepts is challenging because retrieval systems only return relevant documents that may or may not contain prerequisites in them. Even if they do, the user may need to further refer to the prerequisite's prerequisite. This results in more queries, and essentially "knocking around" [10] trying to find appropriate reading material to understand the new concept. It would be helpful to have a retrieval system that, given an input concept, returns

© Springer Nature Switzerland AG 2021
D. Hiemstra et al. (Eds.): ECIR 2021, LNCS 12657, pp. 554–558, 2021.
https://doi.org/10.1007/978-3-030-72240-1_64

exactly the prerequisite concepts required to understand it. A number of techniques to determine prerequisites for a concept have been proposed over the years [2–6,8,9,14,15]. The main issue with these techniques is that they ignore the multiple facets of understanding of a query. For example, for artificial_neural_network, along with concepts such as neuron, exisiting techniques return concepts such as matlab or image_classification together. Instead, neuron should be recommended to be studied *before* artificial_neural_network, while matlab should be suggested if the user is interested in implementing artificial_neural_network, which need not necessarily be studied before artificial_neural_network. So, it is more desirable if concepts such as neuron, which *have to* studied before artificial_neural_network, are recommended in the form of a prerequisite graph. After that, the prerequisites relevant for multiple facets should be recommended in groups.

To address these issues, we have developed a system called PreFace++, which is an extension of our earlier system PreFace [13]. PreFace++ generates a prerequisite graph, where the nodes are *necessary prerequisites* – prerequisites which *have to* be studied before the concept. After that, it automatically identifies facets and prerequisites for the query using TeKnowbase, the Open Research Corpus[1] and the StackOverflow dataset[2].

2   System Architecture

Our system consists of 4 main parts.

TeKnowbase. TeKnowbase [11] is a knowledge base in the domain of Computer Science, consisting of entities which are concepts in Computer Science, such as genetic_algorithm. The relationships between the entities are domain-independent, such as typeof or domain-specific, such as application. It is used by the other two components of our system to generate the results.

Prerequisite Graph Generation. PreFace++ takes a query, which can be any technical entity in Computer Science, as input, and returns a prerequisite graph. The nodes in the graph are necessary prerequisites and the edges indicate a prerequisite relationship. To construct this graph, we constructed a tree by traversing the concepts mentioned in the first paragraph of the Wikipedia page of the query for two hops. However, not all the concepts mentioned in the first paragraphs qualify to be prerequisites. So, we first used *RefD* [3], an existing technique that identifies prerequisite relationship between a pair of concepts. A drawback of only using *RefD* is that it returns prerequisites for different facets together along with the necessary prerequisites. To remove such concepts, we used the idea of similar neighborhoods. We have observed that prerequisites relevant for different facets of the query share different neighborhoods in TeKnowbase. We captured the idea of neighborhoods using knowledge graph embeddings generated using Node2Vec [1] on TeKnowbase. Node2Vec assigns

---

[1] https://allenai.org/data/s2orc.
[2] https://archive.org/download/stackexchange.

vector representations closer to each other to concepts that share similar neighborhoods. So, concepts that are prerequisites for different facets get vector representations farther away from the query's. So, we retained only those concepts in the prerequisite graph whose similarity exceeds a given threshold from the queried concept. The cosine similarity between the vector representations of the concepts was used as a measure of the similarity between the concepts.

Facet Generation and Ranking. This component determines interesting facets and prerequisites for the query. We first generate the candidate facets by clustering the keyphrases relevant for the query. These keyphrases were extracted from the top-k relevant documents for the query retrieved using query likelihood model from the Open Research Corpus dataset. Additionally, we extracted more keyphrases from posts where the query has been tagged in 14 topics from the StackOverflow dataset. The procedure to generate candidate facets in [13] uses hierarchical clustering with complete linkage, which is a time consuming operation. So, we used a faster approach for generating candidate facets from the phrases. First, we tagged entities from TeKnowbase in keyphrases relevant for the query. Then, we represented the keyphrases using bag of words and entities, and expanded this set by adding entities situated at a 1-hop distance from already tagged entities in TeKnowbase to capture better context. Then, for each entity that was tagged, we chose a set of similar phrases based on the Jaccard similarity of the entity with the phrase until a given similarity threshold was crossed. So, we were finally left with a set of clusters of phrases which were returned as candidate facets. These facets and the query were then represented as language models (LM) [7] and ranked in increasing order of KL divergence between their LMs. The details about this procedure is given in [13].

Retrieval of Research Papers and Technical Posts. This component returns:
1) Sentences containing the query and the facet terms. To better understand the relationship between the query and the facet terms, PreFace++ returns sentences from the corpus where they occur together in a sentence.
2) Relevant research papers and technical posts. Not all the prerequisites identified for the facets co-occur with the query in a sentence. So, PreFace++ allows the user to explore research papers from Open Resesrch Corpus and technical posts from StackOverflow relevant for the query and the facet.

3   System Implementation

Front End. We used PHP and Javascript to develop the front end and the D3 library to render the prerequisite graph. The user interface provides autocompletion for the query as the user enters the terms in the search box. These are generated by querying for the entered string in the back-end database (MySQL) of entities using AJAX. Figure 1 shows the autocompletion options obtained for the string artificial_neur, the prerequisite graph, and 4 facets retrieved for artificial_neural_network.

Fig. 1. (a) Auto-completion options for the partially completed string artificial_neur, (b) Prerequisite graph returned for artificial_neural_network. The nodes in this graph are the necessary prerequisites. An edge from node a to b indicates that b is a prerequisite of a, (c) Four facets (software, cancer, function, and algorithm) with their prerequisites extracted for artificial_neural_network. The sentences where the facet terms and the query co-occur are also shown.

Back End. We used Apache Tomcat and Java Servelets to set up our server. The top-1000 documents relevant for the query were retrieved from Open Research Corpus indexed on Galago. We created indexes on StackOverflow data to retrieve posts relevant for the query. Next, we extracted keyphrases from these posts and documents using a Java implementation of RAKE[3]. We stored pre-extracted keyphrases and LMs for a set of around 8000 entities. The keyphrases and the LMs for the remaining entities were extracted on the fly and results stored to be reused later. Then, the facets were generated using the technique described in Sect. 2.3, represented as language models, and smoothed using additive smoothing techniques. We parallelized the computation of KL divergence of the candidate set of facets to obtain faster results.

4   Conclusion

In this demo paper, we described the construction of PreFace++, which assists a user in learning a new topic in the domain of Computer Science. PreFace++ takes a concept as input and returns a prerequisite graph for the concept along with interesting facets towards its understanding. It also allows the user to explore research papers and technical posts related to the query and the identified facets. In the future, we would like to extend this system to automatically generate personalized lecture notes for a query of interest. These will be generated by summarizing the prerequisite graph as well as the facets for the query.

References

1. Grover, A., Leskovec, J.: Node2Vec: scalable feature learning for networks. In: KDD (2016)

---

[3] https://github.com/Linguistic/rake.

2. Li, I., et al.: What should i learn first: introducing lecturebank for NLP education and prerequisite chain learning. In: AAAI (2019)
3. Chen, L., et al.: Measuring prerequisite relations among concepts. In: EMNLP (2015)
4. Chen, L., et al.: Recovering concept prerequisite relations from university course dependencies. In: AAAI (2017)
5. Chen, L., et al. Investigating active learning for concept prerequisite learning. In: EAAI (2018)
6. Pan, L., Li, C., Li, J., Tang, J.: Prerequisite relation learning for concepts in MOOCs. In: ACL (2017)
7. Jay, M.: Ponte and W. Bruce Croft. a language modeling approach to information retrieval. In: SIGIR (1998)
8. Roy, S., et al.: Inferring concept prerequisite relations from online educational resources. In: AAAI (2019)
9. Mohsen, S., et al.: Finding prerequisite relations using the wikipedia clickstream. WWW Companion (2019)
10. Tyson-Bernstein, H.: A conspiracy of good intentions: America's textbook fiasco. Council for Basic Education (1988)
11. Upadhyay, P., et al.: Construction and applications of teknowbase: a knowledge base of computer science concepts. In: WWW Companion (2018)
12. Prajna, U., et al.: Aspect-based academic search using domain-specific kb. In: ECIR (2020)
13. Prajna, U., Maya, R.: Preface: faceted retrieval of pre-requisites using domain-specific knowledge bases. In: ISWC (To appear) (2020)
14. Wang, S., Liu, L.: Prerequisite Concept Maps Extraction for Automatic Assessment. WWW Companion (2016)
15. Yang, Y., et al.: Concept graph learning from educational data. In: WSDM (2015)

Brief Description of COVID-SEE: The Scientific Evidence Explorer for COVID-19 Related Research

Karin Verspoor[1,2(✉)] ⓘ, Simon Šuster[2] ⓘ, Yulia Otmakhova[2,3], Shevon Mendis[2], Zenan Zhai[2], Biaoyan Fang[2], Jey Han Lau[2], Timothy Baldwin[2], Antonio Jimeno Yepes[2,3], and David Martinez[2,3]

[1] RMIT University, Melbourne, Australia
karin.verspoor@rmit.edu.au
[2] The University of Melbourne, Melbourne, Australia
[3] IBM Research Australia, Carlton, Australia

Abstract. We present COVID-SEE, a system for medical literature discovery based on the concept of information exploration, which builds on several distinct text analysis and natural language processing methods to structure and organise information in publications, and augments search through a visual overview of a collection enabling exploration to identify key articles of interest. We developed this system over COVID-19 literature to help medical professionals and researchers explore the literature evidence, and improve findability of relevant information. COVID-SEE is available at http://covid-see.com.

1 Introduction

The outbreak of COVID-19 led to a rapid and proactive response from research communities worldwide. In information retrieval and natural language processing, efforts have concentrated on building tools for efficiently managing the growing literature on COVID-19 [21]. While many tools emerged for article retrieval and question answering, relatively few systems go beyond returning a list of (relevant) documents, or leverage domain knowledge to organise and present information found within the literature [35]. Building on observations about the importance of *exploratory search* [25], with **COVID-SEE** (Scientific Evidence Explorer), we aim to fill this gap. We developed a web application that combines a search engine for COVID-19 medical literature with summary visualisations of document content. Our work is the first comprehensive system incorporating semantic search with visualisation of concepts, relations, and topics [34], extending the capabilities of systems such as SciSight [12,20] and SemViz [13,33] which provide more narrowly-scoped views of the literature (see summary in Table 2).

A typical usage scenario in COVID-SEE begins with a textual query over the COVID-19 literature, providing: (i) a list of *retrieved documents*, and (ii) a *visualisation dashboard*. As a user reviews and interacts with the information in these views, documents of interest can be selected and saved into a *collection* for later export or targeted visualisation. Our objective is to combine learning and investigation with direct

© Springer Nature Switzerland AG 2021
D. Hiemstra et al. (Eds.): ECIR 2021, LNCS 12657, pp. 559–564, 2021.
https://doi.org/10.1007/978-3-030-72240-1_65

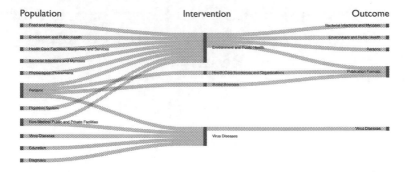

Fig. 1. Visualisation of PICO concepts and relations in articles retrieved for query *incubation period of COVID-19*. Links between concepts can be selected to reveal papers with those relations.

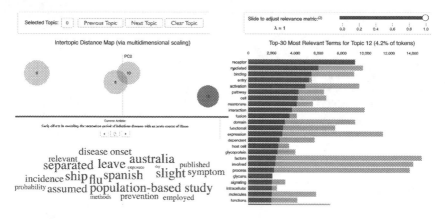

Fig. 2. Topic visualisation for articles retrieved for query *incubation period of COVID-19*. *Inset:* Word cloud view of an individual document showing 20 key concepts, including multi-word terms.

retrieval to support the known health information seeking behaviour of alternating between focused and exploratory search [28]. We facilitate exploration by providing views of document content – in terms of key concepts, relevant themes, and relations of medical interest observed in the articles – that provide a user with deeper insight into retrieved articles.

2   System Overview

The system adopts several well-established techniques, integrating them in a novel manner. After standard information retrieval based on query analysis, the dashboard represents the current active collection with three distinct *interactive views*. This draws on insights from research in information visualisation that demonstrate the value of multiple coordinated views of documents, with a specific emphasis on visually illustrating connections between entities [18, 32].

Table 1. Examples of extracted PICO textual spans and MeSH terms found in them. The PICO concepts we use are the PICO-typed MeSH terms (e.g. Vaccines+Intervention).

PICO snippet	PICO cat.	MeSH terms
Patients presenting with RTI	Population	Patients; Respiratory Tract Infections
Mass vaccination campaigns with parenteral vaccines	Intervention	Immunization Programs; Vaccines; Parenteral Nutrition
Cumulative COVID-19-related hospitalization and death rates	Outcome	Hospitalization; Mortality

Data: CORD-19 is currently the most extensive coronavirus literature corpus publicly available [36]. The dataset contains all COVID-19 and coronavirus-related research (e.g. SARS, MERS, etc.) from sources including PubMed Central full text articles, and bioRxiv and medRxiv pre-prints. As of 6 June it consisted of more than 130k documents.

Information Retrieval: Article retrieval is powered by an existing search engine developed for the CORD-19 dataset, COVIDEX [37]. After submitting a query, a list of retrieved documents is shown. Each document entry can be expanded to display its abstract as well as metadata (authors, journal, source, year, license). The user can also filter by criteria such as year and source. Articles can be selected and added to a collection, the set of documents a user wishes to keep track of, which can be visualised, versioned, and exported.

We also support *semantic search*, where search criteria can be defined in terms of the typed medical concepts we also use for our relational concept view (see below); boolean matching is used in this retrieval approach.

2.1 Visual Overviews

The first view is a **relational concept view** in which we organise the medical concepts found in the articles according to key categories of evidence-based medicine, known as PICO [30] (Population, Intervention, Comparator, Outcome). In this view, more salient relations – based on the number of supporting abstracts – carry more weight, and once a relation is clicked, the corresponding articles are revealed. We use an example based on the query *incubation period of COVID-19* to illustrate this functionality (Fig. 1). This view is a Sankey diagram frame, which shows which medical concepts are identified within PICO statements in the articles and illustrates how they co-occur in specific documents in the retrieved results.

To detect PICO statements, we train a BiLSTM-CRF model [22] on the EBM-NLP dataset [26] containing reports of randomised clinical trials annotated with textual spans that describe the PICO elements. As pretrained word representations for the model, we use 200-dimensional word2vec embeddings induced on PubMed abstracts and MEDLINE articles [19], obtaining comparable results to published figures. We then recognise medical terms from Medical Subject Headings (MeSH), a structured vocabulary maintained by the US National Library of Medicine, using the MetaMap tool [6,15]. Examples of extracted PICO concepts are shown in Table 1. In the Sankey diagram, we display pairwise relations based on article co-occurrence of Population–Intervention and Intervention–Outcome concepts.

Table 2. Comparison of COVID-SEE (1*) with related systems. (2) SciSight [20], (3) DOC Search [4], (4) COVID-19 Navigator [2], (5) LitCOVID [17], (6) SemViz [33], (7) WellAI [14], (8) COVID Intelligent Search [3], (9) Le Bras et al. [23], (10) COVID-19 LOVE [1], (11) Trial-streamer [27].

		(1*)	(2)	(3)	(4)	(5)	(6)	(7)	(8)	(9)	(10)	(11)
Search	NL/IR	✓	✗	✓	✗	✓	✗	✗	✓	✗	✗	✓
	Concepts	✓	✓	✓	✓	✓	✓	✓	✓	✓	✓	✓
	PICO	✓	✓	✓	✗	✗	✗	✗	✗	✗	✓	✓
Visualisation	Concepts	✓	?	?	✗	✗	✓	✗	✗	✗	✗	?
	Relations	✓	✓	✗	✗	✗	✓	✗	✗	✗	✗	✗
	Topics	✓	✗	✗	✗	✗	✗	✗	✗	?	✗	✗

The second, **topic view** (Fig. 2), is thematic and shows representative topics for the current collection. We trained a global topic model on medical concepts extracted from CORD-19. using Latent Dirichlet allocation (LDA) [16] to learn topics over the whole dataset, and display the topics in the retrieved subset of articles visually [9]. LDA represents each document as a mixture of topics, and each topic as a mixture of words. We chose 20 topics as optimal based on the C_v topic coherence measure [31].

Our third component is a **concept cloud view** (Fig. 2, Inset), showing the 20 most representative concepts for each active document in a wordcloud [11]. Concepts here correspond to pre-identified medical terms from the Unified Medical Language System (UMLS [24]), extracted using MetaMap [6]. To select discriminative concepts, concept distributions of articles in the collection are compared to those in the data set as a whole using the log-likelihood test [29]. Analysis is done over concepts rather than words, thereby capturing multi-word terms such as *intensive care unit*.

2.2 Technical Details

All data is stored in the graph database neo4j [7]. The front-end of our web application accesses it via the Cypher language and the py2neo library [8]. The website was built with React [10] and Flask [5], and topic visualisations are supported by pyLDAVis [9].

A screencast of the system can be viewed at https://youtu.be/vL_tXuTz-LU.

3   Conclusions and Future Work

COVID-SEE is designed to facilitate more interactive exploration of the COVID-19 literature, through integration of sub-collection thematic analysis, document-level visual concept summaries, and PICO-structured concept relations. Documents retrieved for a query are visually summarised through the relational and topic views, and the salient concepts in individual documents are highlighted through the word cloud views. Our system goes beyond other systems by coupling the relational structure of medical literature with collection-level visual summaries.

In future work, a recommendation system for articles which have similar topic distributions could be added. For visual representations, we will experiment with expanding beyond the MeSH term vocabulary to include more specific terminology, and more effective use of the hierarchical relationships that exist between terms. Finally, we are planning a user study with medical professionals to evaluate the potential of COVID-SEE as a knowledge discovery tool.

Acknowledgements. This research was conducted by the Australian Research Council Training Centre in Cognitive Computing for Medical Technologies (project number ICI70200030) and funded by the Australian Government.

References

1. COVID-19 Living OVerview of Evidence. https://app.iloveevidence.com/loves/5e6fdb9669c00e4ac072701d?utm=aile. Accessed 30 Oct 2020
2. COVID-19 Navigator. https://covid-19-navigator.mybluemix.net/. Accessed 30 Oct 2020
3. COVID Intelligent Search. https://covidsearch.sinequa.com. Accessed 30 Oct 2020
4. DOC Search. https://covid-search.doctorevidence.com. Accessed 30 Oct 2020
5. Flask application development framework. https://flask.palletsprojects.com/. Accessed 30 Oct 2020
6. MetaMap. http://metamap.nlm.nih.gov. Accessed 30 Oct 2020
7. neo4j graph database. http://neo4j.com. Accessed 30 Oct 2020
8. py2neo Python library. http://py2neo.org. Accessed 30 Oct 2020
9. pyLDAvis package. https://github.com/bmabey/pyLDAvis. Accessed 30 Oct 2020
10. React Javascript framework. https://reactjs.org/. Accessed 30 Oct 2020
11. React wordcloud package. https://github.com/chrisrzhou/react-wordcloud. Accessed 30 Oct 2020
12. SciSight. https://scisight.apps.allenai.org. Accessed 30 Oct 2020
13. SemViz. https://www.semviz.org/. Accessed 30 Oct 2020
14. WellAI. https://wellai.health/covid/. Accessed 30 Oct 2020
15. Aronson, A.R., Lang, F.M.: An overview of metamap: historical perspective and recent advances. J. Am. Med. Inform. Assoc. **17**(3), 229–236 (2010)
16. Blei, D.M., Ng, A.Y., Jordan, M.I.: Latent Dirichlet allocation. J. Machine Learn. Res. **3**, 993–1022 (2003)
17. Chen, Q., Allot, A., Lu, Z.: Keep up with the latest coronavirus research. Nature **579**(7798), 193 (2020). https://doi.org/10.1038/d41586-020-00694-1, https://www.ncbi.nlm.nih.gov/pubmed/32157233
18. Görg, C., et al.: Visualization and language processing for supporting analysis across the biomedical literature. In: International Conference on Knowledge-Based and Intelligent Information and Engineering Systems, pp. 420–429 (2010)
19. Hakala, K., Kaewphan, S., Salakoski, T., Ginter, F.: Syntactic analyses and named entity recognition for PubMed and PubMed central – up-to-the-minute. In: Proceedings of the 15th Workshop on Biomedical Natural Language Processing, pp. 102–107. Association for Computational Linguistics, Berlin, Germany (2016). https://doi.org/10.18653/v1/W16-2913, https://www.aclweb.org/anthology/W16-2913
20. Hope, T., et al.: SciSight: combining faceted navigation and research group detection for COVID-19 exploratory scientific search. bioRxiv (2020)
21. Hutson, M.: Artificial-intelligence tools aim to tame the coronavirus literature. Nature (2020). https://doi.org/10.1038/d41586-020-01733-7

22. Lample, G., Ballesteros, M., Subramanian, S., Kawakami, K., Dyer, C.: Neural architectures for named entity recognition. In: Proceedings of the 2016 Conference of the North American Chapter of the Association for Computational Linguistics: Human Language Technologies, pp. 260–270. Association for Computational Linguistics, San Diego, California (2016). https://doi.org/10.18653/v1/N16-1030, https://www.aclweb.org/anthology/N16-1030

23. Le Bras, P., Gharavi, A., Robb, D.A., Vidal, A.F., Padilla, S., Chantler, M.J.: Visualising COVID-19 Research. arXiv:2005.06380 (2020)

24. Lindberg, D.A., Humphreys, B.L., McCray, A.T.: The unified medical language system. Yearbook Med. Inform. **2**(01), 41–51 (1993)

25. Marchionini, G.: Exploratory search: From finding to understanding. Commun. ACM **49**(4), 41–46 (2006). https://doi.org/10.1145/1121949.1121979

26. Nye, B., et al.: A corpus with multi-level annotations of patients, interventions and outcomes to support language processing for medical literature. In: Proceedings of the 56th Annual Meeting of the Association for Computational Linguistics (volume 1: Long Papers), pp. 197–207. Association for Computational Linguistics, Melbourne, Australia (2018). https://doi.org/10.18653/v1/P18-1019, https://www.aclweb.org/anthology/P18-1019

27. Nye, B., Nenkova, A., Marshall, I., Wallace, B.C.: Trialstreamer: mapping and browsing medical evidence in real-time. In: Proceedings of the 58th Annual Meeting of the Association for Computational Linguistics: System Demonstrations, pp. 63–69. Association for Computational Linguistics, Online (2020). https://www.aclweb.org/anthology/2020.acl-demos.9

28. Pang, P.C.I., Verspoor, K., Chang, S., Pearce, J.: Conceptualising healthinformation seeking behaviours and exploratory search: result of aqualitative study. Health Technol. **5**(1), 45–55 (2015).https://doi.org/10.1007/s12553-015-0096-0, https://doi.org/10.1007/s12553-015-0096-0

29. Rayson, P., Garside, R.: Comparing corpora using frequency profiling. The Workshop on Comparing Corpora, pp. 1–6 (2000)

30. Richardson, W.S., Wilson, M.C., Nishikawa, J., Hayward, R.S., et al.: The well-built clinical question: a key to evidence-based decisions. Acp J Club **123**(3), A12–3 (1995)

31. Röder, M., Both, A., Hinneburg, A.: Exploring the space of topic coherence measures. In: Proceedings of the Eighth ACM International Conference on Web Search and Data Mining, pp. 399–408 (2015)

32. Stasko, J., Görg, C., Liu, Z.: Jigsaw: supporting investigative analysis through interactive visualization. Inf. Visual. **7**(2), 118–132 (2008). https://doi.org/10.1057/palgrave.ivs.9500180

33. Tu, J., Verhagen, M., Cochran, B., Pustejovsky, J.: Exploration and Discovery of the COVID-19 Literature through Semantic Visualization. arXiv:2007.01800 (2020)

34. Verspoor, K., et al.: Covid-see: Scientific evidence explorer for covid-19 related research (2020)

35. Wang, L.L., Lo, K.: Text mining approaches for dealing with the rapidly expanding literature on COVID-19. Brief. Bioinform. (2020). https://doi.org/10.1093/bib/bbaa296, https://doi.org/10.1093/bib/bbaa296

36. Wang, L.L., et al.: CORD-19: the COVID-19 open research dataset. In: Proceedings of the 1st Workshop on NLP for COVID-19 at ACL 2020. Association for Computational Linguistics, Online (2020). https://www.aclweb.org/anthology/2020.nlpcovid19-acl.1

37. Zhang, E., Gupta, N., Nogueira, R., Cho, K., Lin, J.: Rapidly Deploying a Neural Search Engine for the COVID-19 Open Research Dataset: Preliminary Thoughts and Lessons Learned. arXiv:2004.05125 (2020)

CLEF 2021 Lab Descriptions

Overview of PAN 2021: Authorship Verification, Profiling Hate Speech Spreaders on Twitter, and Style Change Detection
Extended Abstract

Janek Bevendorff[1(✉)], BERTa Chulvi[2], Gretel Liz De La Peña Sarracén[2],
Mike Kestemont[3], Enrique Manjavacas[3], Ilia Markov[3], Maximilian Mayerl[4],
Martin Potthast[5], Francisco Rangel[6], Paolo Rosso[2], Efstathios Stamatatos[7],
Benno Stein[1], Matti Wiegmann[1], Magdalena Wolska[1], and Eva Zangerle[4]

[1] Bauhaus-Universität Weimar, Weimar, Germany
pan@webis.de
[2] Universitat Politècnica de València, Valencia, Spain
[3] University of Antwerp, Antwerp, Belgium
[4] University of Innsbruck, Innsbruck, Austria
[5] Leipzig University, Leipzig, Germany
[6] Symanto Research, Nuremberg, Germany
[7] University of the Aegean, Samos, Greece
http://pan.webis.de

Abstract. The paper gives a brief overview of the three shared tasks to be organized at the PAN 2021 lab on digital text forensics and stylometry hosted at the CLEF conference. The tasks include authorship verification across domains, author profiling for hate speech spreaders, and style change detection for multi-author documents. In part the tasks are new and in part they continue and advance past shared tasks, with the overall goal of advancing the state of the art, providing for an objective evaluation on newly developed benchmark datasets.

1 Introduction

The PAN workshop series has been organized since 2007 and included shared tasks on specific computational challenges related to authorship analysis, computational ethics, and determining the originality of a piece of writing. Over the years, the respective organizing committees of the 51 shared tasks have assembled evaluation resources for the aforementioned research disciplines that amount to 48 datasets plus nine datasets contributed by the community.[1] Each new dataset introduced new variants of author identification, profiling, and author obfuscation tasks as well as multi-author analysis and determining the morality, quality, or originality of a text. The 2021 edition of PAN continues in the same vein, introducing new resources and previously unconsidered problems to the community.

---

[1] https://pan.webis.de/data.html.

ⓒ Springer Nature Switzerland AG 2021
D. Hiemstra et al. (Eds.): ECIR 2021, LNCS 12657, pp. 567–573, 2021.
https://doi.org/10.1007/978-3-030-72240-1_66

As in earlier editions, PAN is committed to reproducible research in IR and NLP and all shared tasks will ask for software submissions on our TIRA platform [10].

2   Author Profiling

Author profiling is the problem of distinguishing between classes of authors by studying how language is shared by people. This helps in identifying authors' individual characteristics, such as age, gender, and language variety, among others. During the years 2013–2020 we addressed several of these aspects in the shared tasks organised at PAN.[2] In 2013 the aim was to identify gender and age in social media texts for English and Spanish [16]. In 2014 we addressed age identification from a continuous perspective (without gaps between age classes) in the context of several genres, such as blogs, Twitter, and reviews (in Trip Advisor), both in English and Spanish [14]. In 2015, apart from age and gender identification, we addressed also personality recognition on Twitter in English, Spanish, Dutch and Italian [18]. In 2016, we addressed the problem of cross-genre gender and age identification (training on Twitter data and testing on blogs and social media data) in English, Spanish, and Dutch [19]. In 2017, we addressed gender and language variety identification in Twitter in English, Spanish, Portuguese, and Arabic [17]. In 2018, we investigated gender identification in Twitter from a multimodal perspective, considering also the images linked within tweets; the dataset was composed of English, Spanish, and Arabic tweets [15].

In 2019 the focus was on profiling bots and discriminating bots from humans on the basis of textual data only [13]. We used Twitter data both in English and Spanish. Bots play a key role in spreading inflammatory content and also fake news. Advanced bots that generated human-like language, also with metaphors, were the most difficult to profile. It is interesting to note that when bots were profiled as humans, they were mostly confused with males. In 2020 we focused on profiling fake news spreaders [11]. The ease of publishing content in social media has led to an increase in the amount of disinformation that is published and shared. The goal was to profile those authors who have shared some fake news in the past. Early identification of possible fake news spreaders on Twitter should be the first step towards preventing fake news from further dissemination.

Haters: Profiling Hate Speech Spreaders on Twitter at PAN'21

Hate speech (HS) is commonly defined as any communication that disparages a person or a group on the basis of some characteristic, such as race, colour, ethnicity, gender, sexual orientation, nationality, religion, or others [8]. Given the huge amount of user-generated content on the Web and, in particular, on social media, the problem of detecting and, if possible, contrasting the HS diffusion, is becoming fundamental, for instance, for fighting against misogyny and xenophobia [1]. Having previously profiled bots and fake news spreaders, at PAN'21 we

---

[2] To generate the datasets, we have followed a methodology that complies with the EU General Data Protection Regulation [12].

will focus on PROFILING HATE SPEECH SPREADERS in social media, more specifically on Twitter. We will address the problem both in English and Spanish, as we did in the previous author profiling tasks. The goal will be to identify those Twitter users that can be considered haters, depending on the number of tweets with hateful content that they had spread (tweets will be manually annotated). As an evaluation setup, we will create a collection that contains Spanish and English tweets posted by users on Twitter. One document will consist of a feed of tweets written by the same user. The goal will then be to classify the user as hater or not hater (binary classification). Given that we plan to create a balanced dataset (although this is not a realistic scenario,[3] we balance the dataset to reinforce the haters' view and to prevent machine/deep learning models from being skewed towards tweets), we will use accuracy as the evaluation metric for the binary classification.

3   Author Identification

Authentication is a major safety issue in today's digital world and in this sense it is unsurprising that (computational) author identification has been a longstanding task at PAN. Author identification still poses a challenging empirical problem in fields related to Information and Computer Science, but the underlying techniques are nowadays also frequently adopted as an auxiliary component in other application domains, such as literary studies or forensic linguistics. These scholarly communities are strongly dependent on reliable and transparent benchmark initiatives that closely monitor the state of the art in the field and enable progress [9]. Author identification is concerned with the automated identification of the individual(s) who authored an anonymous document on the basis of text-internal properties related to language and writing style [4,7,21]. At different editions of PAN since 2007, author identification has been studied in multiple incarnations: as authorship attribution (given a document and a set of candidate authors, determine which of them wrote the document; 2011–2012 and 2016–2020), authorship verification (given a pair of documents, determine whether they are written by the same author; 2013–2015), authorship obfuscation (given a document and a set of documents from the same author, paraphrase the former so that its author cannot be identified anymore; 2016–2018), and obfuscation evaluation (devise and implement performance measures that quantify the safeness, soundness, and/or sensibleness of obfuscation software; 2016–2018).

For the next edition, we will continue to capitalize on so-called fanfiction, as we did in previous years [5,6]. 'Fanfiction' or 'transformative literature' refers to the world-wide cultural phenomenon of (non-professional) writers producing (largely unauthorized) literary fiction in the tradition of well-known, influential

---

[3] In a realistic scenario, we would need to know a priori the distribution of haters vs non-haters: this information is unknown and impossible to calculate manually; one of the aims of this shared task is to foster research on profiling haters in order to address this problem automatically.

domains in culture, called 'fandoms', such as J.K. Rowling's Harry Potter or Sherlock Holmes [3]. Fanfiction is nowadays estimated to be the fastest growing form of online writing [2] and the abundance of data in this area is a major asset. Typically, fan writers actively aim to attract more readers and on most platforms (e.g. archiveofourown.org or fanfiction.net) the bulk of their writings can be openly accessed although the intellectual rights relating to these texts are convoluted [23]. Multilinguality of the phenomenon is another asset since fanfiction extends far beyond the Indo-European language area that is the traditional focus of shared tasks. Finally, fanfiction is characterized by a remarkable wealth of author-provided metadata related to the textual domain (the fandom), popularity (e.g. number of 'kudos'), time of publication, and even intended audience (e.g. maturity ratings).

Cross-domain Authorship Verification at PAN'21

Fanfiction provides an excellent source of material to study cross-domain attribution scenarios since users usually publish narratives that range over multiple domains, the previously-mentioned 'fandoms': Harry Potter, Twilight, Marvel comics, for instance. Previous editions of PAN, in particular the last one, have already included a cross-domain authorship attribution task set in the context of fanfiction. Two basic cross-domain setups specific to fanfiction (training and test documents from disjoint fandoms) were examined: closed-set attribution (the true author of a test document belongs to the set of candidates) and open-set attribution (the true author of a test document could not be one of the candidates). For the 2021 edition, we will focus on the (OPEN) AUTHORSHIP VERIFICATION scenario: given two documents belonging to different fandoms, determine whether they are written by the same, previously unseen author. This is a fundamental task in author identification and all cases, be it closed-set or open-set ones, and can be decomposed into a series of verification instances. Again exploiting fanfiction – where the topic is easily controlled and a larger volume (on the order of thousands) of verification instances can be produced covering multiple languages – we will also attempt to mitigate the effect of certain weaknesses identified in the evaluation framework of previous authorship verification evaluations (e.g., ensuring that each verification instance is handled separately).

4   Multi-Author Writing Style Analysis

The goal of the style change detection task is to identify – based on an intrinsic style analysis – the text positions within a given multi-author document at which the author switches. Detecting these positions is a crucial part of the authorship identification process and multi-author document analysis; multi-author documents have been largely understudied in general.

This task has been part of PAN since 2016, with varying task definitions, data sets, and evaluation procedures. In 2016, participants were asked to identify and group fragments of a given document that correspond to individual authors [20]. In 2017, we asked participants to detect whether a given document is multi-authored and, if this is indeed the case, to determine the positions at which authorship changes [22]. However, since this task was deemed as highly complex, in 2018 its complexity was reduced to asking participants to predict whether a given document is single- or multi-authored [6]. Following the promising results achieved, in 2019 participants were asked first to detect whether a document was single- or multi-authored and, if it was indeed written by multiple authors, to then predict the number of authors [25]. Based on the advances made over the previous years, in 2020 we decided to go back towards the original definition of the task, i.e., finding the positions in a text where authorship changes. Participants first had to determine whether a document was written by one or by multiple authors and, if it was written by multiple authors, they had to detect between which paragraphs the authors change [24].

Style Change Detection at PAN'21

In today's scientific practice, usually a team of researchers is involved in writing a paper and conducting the underlying research—research work is teamwork. Hence, a fundamental question is the following: If multiple authors together have written a text, can we find evidence for this fact, e.g., do we have a means to detect variations in the writing style? Answering this question belongs to the most difficult and most interesting challenges in author identification and is the only means to detect plagiarism in a document if no comparison texts are given; likewise, it can help to uncover gift authorships, to verify a claimed authorship, and to develop new technology for writing support. We tackle this challenge by providing STYLE CHANGE DETECTION tasks of increasing difficulty which will attract both novices and experts in the field of authorship analytics: (1) Single vs. Multiple authors: given a text, find out whether the text is written by a single author or by multiple authors, (2) Style Change Basic: given a text written by two authors that contains a single style change only, find the position of this change, i.e., cut the text into the two authors' texts; note that this task corresponds to authorship verification where the two authors are responsible for the beginning and the end of the text respectively, (3) Style Change Real-World: given a text written by two or more authors, find all positions of writing style change, i.e., assign all paragraphs of the text uniquely to some author out of the number of authors you assume for the multi-author document. For this year's edition, we will introduce a new type of corpus which is based on a publicly available dump of a Q&A platform and which is particularly suited for these tasks because of its topic homogeneity. For all three task variants, we will guarantee that each paragraph in a text is authored by a single author, in other words, a style change may be observed only at the beginning of a paragraph.

Acknowledgments. The work of the researchers from Universitat Politècnica de València was partially funded by the Spanish MICINN under the project MISMIS-FAKEnHATE on MISinformation and MIScommunication in social media: FAKE news and HATE speech (PGC2018-096212-B-C31), and by the Generalitat Valenciana under the project DeepPattern (PROMETEO/2019/121).

References

1. Basile, V., et al.: SemEval-2019 Task 5: multilingual detection of hate speech against immigrants and women in Twitter. In: Proceedings of the 13th International Workshop on Semantic Evaluation (SemEval-2019), co-located with the Annual Conference of the North American Chapter of the Association for Computational Linguistics: Human Language Technologies (NAACL-HLT 2019) (2019)
2. Fathallah, J.: Fanfiction and the Author. How FanFic Changes Popular Cultural Texts, Amsterdam University Press (2017)
3. Hellekson, K., Busse, K. (eds.): The Fan Fiction Studies Reader. University of Iowa Press (2014)
4. Juola, P.: Authorship attribution. Found. Trends Inf. Retr. **1**(3), 233–334 (2006)
5. Kestemont, M., Stamatatos, E., Manjavacas, E., Daelemans, W., Potthast, M., Stein, B.: Overview of the cross-domain authorship attribution task at PAN 2019. In: CLEF 2019 Labs and Workshops, Notebook Papers (2019)
6. Kestemont, M., et al.: Overview of the author identification task at PAN 2018: cross-domain authorship attribution and style change detection. In: CLEF 2018 Labs and Workshops, Notebook Papers (2018)
7. Koppel, M., Schler, J., Argamon, S.: Computational methods in authorship attribution. J. Am. Soc. Inform. Sci. Technol. **60**(1), 9–26 (2009)
8. Nockleby, J.T.: Hate speech. In: Levy, L.W., Karst, K.L., et al. (eds.) Encyclopedia of the American Constitution, 2nd edn., pp. 1277–1279. Macmillan, New York (2000)
9. Potthast, M., et al.: Who wrote the web? Revisiting influential author identification research applicable to information retrieval. In: Ferro, N., et al. (eds.) ECIR 2016. LNCS, vol. 9626, pp. 393–407. Springer, Cham (2016). https://doi.org/10.1007/978-3-319-30671-1_29
10. Potthast, M., Gollub, T., Wiegmann, M., Stein, B.: TIRA integrated research architecture. Information Retrieval Evaluation in a Changing World. TIRS, vol. 41, pp. 123–160. Springer, Cham (2019). https://doi.org/10.1007/978-3-030-22948-1_5
11. Rangel, F., Giachanou, A., Ghanem, B., Rosso, P.: Overview of the 8th author profiling task at PAN 2019: profiling fake news spreaders on twitter. In: CLEF 2020 Labs and Workshops, Notebook Papers. CEUR Workshop Proceedings (2020)
12. Rangel, F., Rosso, P.: On the implications of the general data protection regulation on the organisation of evaluation tasks. Language and Law / Linguagem e Direito **5**(2), 95–117 (2019)
13. Rangel, F., Rosso, P.: Overview of the 7th author profiling task at pan 2019: Bots and gender profiling. In: CLEF 2019 Labs and Workshops, Notebook Papers (2019)
14. Rangel, F., et al.: Overview of the 2nd author profiling task at PAN 2014. In: CLEF 2014 Labs and Workshops, Notebook Papers (2014)
15. Rangel, F., Rosso, P., Montes-y-Gómez, M., Potthast, M., Stein, B.: Overview of the 6th author profiling task at PAN 2018: multimodal gender identification in Twitter. In: CLEF 2019 Labs and Workshops, Notebook Papers (2018)
16. Rangel, F., Rosso, P., Moshe Koppel, M., Stamatatos, E., Inches, G.: Overview of the author profiling task at PAN 2013. In: CLEF 2013 Labs and Workshops, Notebook Papers (2013)

17. Rangel, F., Rosso, P., Potthast, M., Stein, B.: Overview of the 5th author profiling task at PAN 2017: Gender and language variety identification in Twitter. Working Notes Papers of the CLEF (2017)

18. Rangel, F., Rosso, P., Potthast, M., Stein, B., Daelemans, W.: Overview of the 3rd author profiling task at PAN 2015. In: CLEF 2015 Labs and Workshops, Notebook Papers (2015)

19. Rangel, F., Rosso, P., Verhoeven, B., Daelemans, W., Potthast, M., Stein, B.: Overview of the 4th author profiling task at PAN 2016: Cross-genre evaluations. In: CLEF 2016 Labs and Workshops, Notebook Papers (Sep 2016), ISSN 1613–0073

20. Rosso, P., Rangel, F., Potthast, M., Stamatatos, E., Tschuggnall, M., Stein, B.: Overview of PAN 2016–new challenges for authorship analysis: cross-genre profiling, clustering, diarization, and obfuscation. In: Experimental IR Meets Multilinguality, Multimodality, and Interaction. 7th International Conference of the CLEF Initiative (CLEF 2016) (2016)

21. Stamatatos, E.: A survey of modern authorship attribution methods. JASIST **60**(3), 538–556 (2009). https://doi.org/10.1002/asi.21001

22. Tschuggnall, M., et al.: Overview of the author identification task at PAN 2017: style breach detection and author clustering. In: CLEF 2017 Labs and Workshops, Notebook Papers (2017)

23. Tushnet, R.: Legal fictions: Copyright, fan fiction, and a new common law. Loyola Los Angel. Entertain. Law Rev. **17**(3) (1997)

24. Zangerle, E., Mayerl, M., Specht, G., Potthast, M., Stein, B.: Overview of the style change detection task at PAN 2020. In: CLEF 2020 Labs and Workshops, Notebook Papers (2020)

25. Zangerle, E., Tschuggnall, M., Specht, G., Stein, B., Potthast, M.: Overview of the style change detection task at PAN 2019. In: CLEF 2019 Labs and Workshops, Notebook Papers (2019)

Overview of Touché 2021:
Argument Retrieval
Extended Abstract

Alexander Bondarenko[1]([⊠]), Lukas Gienapp[2], Maik Fröbe[1], Meriem Beloucif[3],
Yamen Ajjour[1], Alexander Panchenko[4], Chris Biemann[3], Benno Stein[5],
Henning Wachsmuth[6], Martin Potthast[2], and Matthias Hagen[1]

[1] Martin-Luther-Universität Halle-Wittenberg, Halle, Germany
`touche@webis.de`
[2] Leipzig University, Leipzig, Germany
[3] Universität Hamburg, Hamburg, Germany
[4] Skolkovo Institute of Science and Technology, Moscow, Russia
[5] Bauhaus-Universität Weimar, Weimar, Germany
[6] Paderborn University, Paderborn, Germany
`https://touche.webis.de`

Abstract. Technologies for argument mining and argumentation analysis are maturing rapidly, so that, as a result, the retrieval of arguments in search scenarios becomes a feasible objective. For the second time, we organize the Touché lab on argument retrieval with two shared tasks: (1) argument retrieval for controversial questions, where arguments are to be retrieved from a focused debate portal-based collection and, (2) argument retrieval for comparative questions, where argumentative documents are to be retrieved from a generic web crawl. In this paper, we briefly summarize the results of Touché 2020, the first edition of the lab, and describe the planned setup for the second edition at CLEF 2021.

1 Introduction

Making informed decisions and forming personal opinions are everyday tasks, requiring one to choose between two or more options, or sides. This may be based on prior knowledge and experience, but more often requires the collection of new information first. The web is rife with documents comprising arguments and opinions on many controversial topics, as well as on products, services, etc. However, hardly any support is provided for individuals who specifically search for argumentative texts in order to support their decision making or opinion formation. Especially for controversial topics, search results are often riddled with populism, conspiracy theories, and one-sidedness, all of which arguably do not lead to the kind of insights that help individuals form well-justified informed opinions. But even straightforward tasks, such as comparing among two specific options for a product, are sometimes challenging to be solved with a web search

© Springer Nature Switzerland AG 2021
D. Hiemstra et al. (Eds.): ECIR 2021, LNCS 12657, pp. 574–582, 2021.
https://doi.org/10.1007/978-3-030-72240-1_67

engine, given that advertisers optimize their sales pages and compete with others for the top-most search result slots, displacing reasoned comparisons.

To foster research on argument retrieval in the scenarios of (1) opinion formation on controversial topics, and (2) personal "everyday" decision making, we organize the second edition of the Touché lab on Argument Retrieval at CLEF 2021.[1] Participants of the lab are asked to develop a technology that helps to retrieve "strong" arguments for decisions at the societal level (e.g., "Is climate change real and what to do?") and at the personal level (e.g., "Should I buy real estate or rent, and why?"). The corresponding two shared tasks are:

1. *Argument Retrieval for Controversial Questions.* Argument retrieval from a focused document collection (crawled from debate portals) to support opinion formation on controversial topics.
2. *Argument Retrieval for Comparative Questions.* Argument retrieval from a generic web crawl to support decision making in "everyday" choice situations.

Our goal is to establish an understanding of how to evaluate argument retrieval and what retrieval models or processing methods are effective. For instance, an important component of argument retrieval probably is the assessment of argument quality (i.e., whether a given argument is a "strong" one). Good argument retrieval approaches will not only allow for a better handling of argumentative information needs in search engines, but they may also become, in the long run, an enabling technology for automatic open-domain agents that convincingly discuss and interact with human users.

2   Task Definition

The Touché lab adopts the standard TREC-style setup and evaluation methodology, where document collections and a set of search topics are provided to the participants. Every topic is comprised of a search query, a detailed description of the search scenario, and hints on document relevance for assessors.

The second edition of the lab repeats the two shared tasks from the first edition with specific twists: (1) Topics and judgments from the first year are made available to the participants for training their models,[2] (2) new topics are composed and used for the evaluation of the submitted approaches, and (3) in addition to relevance, several argument quality dimensions are evaluated (cf. Sect. 2.4).

To allow for a high diversity of approaches, participating teams are allowed to submit up to five runs (differently ranked result lists) that then form part of the judgment pool passed to expert assessors. We encourage the participating teams to submit the software implementing their approaches within the evaluation platform TIRA [10] in order to maximize the reproducibility.

---

[1] 'Touché' is commonly "used to acknowledge a hit in fencing or the success or appropriateness of an argument, an accusation, or a witty point." [https://merriam-webster.com/dictionary/touche].

[2] Available for download on the lab website: https://touche.webis.de.

2.1   Task 1: Argument Retrieval for Controversial Questions

The first shared task focuses on the scenario of supporting individuals who search directly for arguments on controversial topics of general societal interest (e.g., immigration, climate change, or the use of plastic bottles). The retrieved arguments relevant to such topics should be useful in debating conversations, or be helpful in forming an opinion on the topic. Multiple online portals are centered around argumentative topics (e.g., debate portals), yet general web search engines do not offer an effective way to retrieve "strong" arguments from these platforms (cf. Sect. 2.4 for a more detailed description of argument strength). However, there are some prototypes of argument search engines, such as args.me [17], ArgumenText [14], and TARGER [5], that implement different paradigms to solve the task of argument retrieval. While the args.me approach first identifies a focused collection of arguments crawled from online debate portals and then indexes only these arguments, ArgumenText and TARGER follow a more "traditional" web-based retrieval approach and mine arguments from a query's result documents in a post-processing step.

In Task 1, to ensure a low entry barrier for participants, we use the existing args.me argument corpus [1]. This corpus is a focused crawl obtained from four online debate portals (idebate.org, debatepedia.org, debatewise.org, and debate.org) and thus mostly contains short and to-the-point arguments exchanged during an online debate. This way, participants of Task 1 do not necessarily need to manage a fully-fledged argument mining pipeline for participation. The corpus is available for download and can also be queried directly using the API of args.me [17].[3]

2.2   Task 2: Argument Retrieval for Comparative Questions

The second shared task aims to support users in personal decisions when choosing between different options. In particular, the task is to find relevant documents containing "strong" arguments for questions like "Is X better than Y for Z?". In their current form, web search engines do not provide much support for such comparative questions; they even sometimes retrieve one-sided answers from community question answering platforms. A state-of-the-art system to deal with comparative information needs is the comparative argumentation machine CAM [13], which takes two objects to be compared as well as a set of aspects of comparison as input, retrieves comparative sentences in favor of one or the other option from a 2016 Common Crawl version using BM25 as the retrieval model, and clusters the sentences to present a summary table. However, CAM cannot process queries represented as questions, it processes relevant information only on sentence level, and it does not account for argumentative aspects of answers. Improving retrieval models for systems like CAM is the objective of Task 2.

---

[3] https://www.args.me/api-en.html.

The participants of Task 2 are asked to retrieve documents from the general-purpose web crawl ClueWeb12[4] to help individuals come to an answer for some comparative question. Ideally, relevant documents should comprise "strong" arguments for or against one or the other option underlying the comparative question. For participants who do not want to index the ClueWeb12 at their site, a retrieval functionality is made accessible via the API of the (argumentation-agnostic) reference search engine ChatNoir [2].[5] Furthermore, the APIs of argument tagging tools like TARGER [5][6] may be used to identify argumentative units (i.e., claims and premises) in free text input.

2.3 Search Topics and Training Data

For each shared task, we provide 100 search topics (50 from the first lab edition for training and 50 new topics for evaluation), ensuring that respective information can be found in the focused crawl of debate portals and in the ClueWeb12, respectively. Every topic consists of (1) a *title* representing a question on some controversial topic or some choice problem, (2) a *description* providing a detailed definition of the respective scenario, and (3) a *narrative* that is part of the "guideline" used for relevance and argument quality labeling by expert assessors. The topics (previous and new) and the relevance judgments from the first lab edition (for 5,262 unique arguments in Task 1 and for 1,783 unique documents in Task 2) are available to the participants—to, for instance, allow training or fine-tuning of (neural) retrieval models. The participants' submitted ranked document lists (runs) are also available to analyze the submitted rankings. Given the relatively small training data, the participants may of course also exploit document relevance judgments collected at other shared tasks (e.g., various TREC tracks[7]) that, for instance, can be found in the Anserini GitHub repository [18].[8] Additionally, for argument quality assessment, corpora such as the ones published by Gienapp et al. [6], Gretz et al. [7], Toledo et al. [15], or Wachsmuth et al. [16] may be used.

2.4 Evaluation

The evaluation is based on the pooled top results of the participants' submitted runs. For these, human assessors label argumentative text passages or documents manually, both for their general topical relevance, and for argument quality dimensions found to be important for the evaluation of arguments [16].

For Task 1, we assess three such quality dimensions: whether an argumentative text is logically cogent, whether it is rhetorically well-written, and whether it contributes to the users' stance-building process (i.e., "dialectical quality",

---

[4] https://lemurproject.org/clueweb12/.
[5] https://www.chatnoir.eu/doc/api/.
[6] https://demo.webis.de/targer-api/apidocs/.
[7] https://trec.nist.gov/tracks.html.
[8] https://github.com/castorini/anserini/.

similar to the concept of "utility") [16]. For Task 2, in addition to a document's relevance, human assessors judge whether sufficient argumentative support is provided as defined by Braunstain et al. [4], and they evaluate the credibility of web documents as defined by Rafalak et al. [11]. Thus, a "strong" argument is defined as one that fulfills certain criteria of argument quality such as logical cogency, rhetorical quality, contribution to stance-building, level of support, and credibility. The studies carried out by Potthast et al. [9] and Gienapp et al. [6] suggest that argument quality assessment is feasible also via crowdsourcing, yet, challenging for untrained annotators. For this reason, we specifically pay attention to developing annotation instructions and quality control instruments (pilot judgments, assessing inter-annotator agreement, and recruiting assessors externally and internally).

The effectiveness of the participants' submitted approaches is measured in traditional ranking-based ways with respect to relevance and the qualitative aspects of arguments (e.g., nDCG [8] using the graded relevance or quality judgments).

3   Touché at CLEF 2020: Results and Findings

In the first edition of the Touché lab, 28 teams registered, from which 17 actively participated in the shared tasks by submitting approaches/results [3]. The majority of the participating teams used the TIRA platform [10] to submit software that then produced runs after being invoked at our site. The run output files follow the standard TREC-style format. The teams were allowed to submit several runs, but asked to give evaluation priorities in case more than one run was submitted. This resulted in 41 valid submitted runs from the 17 teams. From every team, at least the top five runs of highest priority were pooled for further evaluation. Additionally, we included rankings produced by two baseline systems in the evaluation: the Lucene implementation of query likelihood with Dirichlet-smoothed language models (DirichletLM [19]) for Task 1, and the BM25F-based [12] search engine ChatNoir [2] for Task 2. We briefly summarize the main results and findings here; the lab overview contains more specific information [3].

Task 1: Argument Retrieval for Controversial Questions. The submissions to Task 1 (13 teams submitted 31 runs, one additional baseline) mainly followed a general strategy consisting of three components: (1) a retrieval model, (2) an augmentation (either query expansion or an extension of an initially retrieved result set), and (3) a (re-)ranking approach based on some document features that boosted or modified the initial retrieval scores, or that were used directly to rank the initial results.

Most of the participating teams chose one of four retrieval models. In the evaluation, DirichletLM and DPH were much more effective than BM25 and TF-IDF. Half of the submitted approaches opted to integrate query or result augmentation by applying various strategies. Queries were expanded by synonyms or they were augmented with newly generated queries using large pre-trained language models. The retrieval results were sometimes post-processed using argument clustering (e.g., topic models or semantic clustering) and in a final re-ranking step, the majority of the approaches either exploited some notion of argument quality or utilized sentiment analysis. Other re-ranking features include premise prediction scores, text readability, presence of named entities, and credibility scores of argument authors in the corpus.

In the first lab edition, we evaluated only the relevance of the retrieved arguments (not their quality) using the nDCG [8] implementation provided by the *trec_eval* library[9] with an evaluation depth of five. Following annotation guidelines designed previously [6,9], we collected relevance judgments on Amazon Mechanical Turk for the 5,262 unique arguments in the top-5 pooling of the participants' runs. The most effective approach achieved an nDCG@5 of 0.81, the least effective 0.27, while the (argumentation-agnostic) baseline achieved an nDCG@5 of 0.77.

Task 2: Argument Retrieval for Comparative Questions. Five teams submitted eleven approaches to this task—all used the BM25F-based search engine ChatNoir [2] to access the ClueWeb12 and to retrieve an initial candidate ranking. For further re-ranking, models of different complexity were employed, basically in three steps: (1) represent documents and queries using language models, (2) identify arguments and comparative structures in documents, and (3) assess argument quality. Interestingly, only two approaches used query expansion techniques for retrieving the initial candidates.

Similar to the first task, we evaluated only the relevance of the retrieved documents. Using a top-5 pooling (10 submitted runs plus the additional ChatNoir baseline), a total of 1,783 unique results were judged by volunteers recruited internally. According to the evaluation, only one approach achieved a slightly better average nDCG@5 score than the ChatNoir baseline by using query expansion and taking credibility and argumentativeness into account in the re-ranking. The top-5 approaches (including the baseline) all had average nDCG@5 scores in the range of 0.55–0.58. Interestingly, the top-4 approaches relied on traditional feature engineering, while four out of the six lower-ranked approaches used deep learning-based language models. This difference in effectiveness could be caused by the absence of task-specific training data in the first lab edition. Using the relevance judgments created in the first lab may enable participants of the second lab edition to better train and fine-tune their (neural) re-ranking methods.

4 Conclusion

The main goal of Touché and its two shared tasks on argument retrieval for controversial and comparative questions is to establish a collaborative platform for researchers in the area of argument retrieval. By providing submission and evaluation tools as well as by organizing collaborative events such as workshops,

---

[9] https://trec.nist.gov/trec_eval/.

Touché aims to foster accumulating knowledge and developing new approaches in the field. All evaluation resources developed at Touché are shared freely, including search queries (topics), the assembled relevance judgments (qrels), and the participants' submitted ranked result lists (runs).

The evaluation of the approaches from 17 participating teams in the first Touché lab indicates that relatively basic, argumentation-agnostic baselines such as DirichletLM and BM25F-based retrieval are still almost as effective as the best approaches. Even though query expansion, argument quality assessment, or comparison features helped to (somewhat slightly) increase the overall retrieval effectiveness in the respective tasks' scenarios, there appears to be ample room for further improvement. More research on argument retrieval is thus well-justified.

In the second year of Touché, the participants are able to use the previously collected relevance judgments to develop and fine-tune new argument retrieval approaches, which may also allow for deploying state-of-the-art neural retrieval models. Moreover, we plan to have deeper judgment pools and to additionally evaluate argument quality dimensions, such as logical cogency and strength of support.

Acknowledgments. This work was partially supported by the DFG through the project "ACQuA: Answering Comparative Questions with Arguments" (grants BI 1544/7-1 and HA 5851/2-1) as part of the priority program "RATIO: Robust Argumentation Machines" (SPP 1999).

References

1. Ajjour, Y., Wachsmuth, H., Kiesel, J., Potthast, M., Hagen, M., Stein, B.: Data acquisition for argument search: the args.me corpus. In: Benzmüller, C., Stuckenschmidt, H. (eds.) KI 2019. LNCS (LNAI), vol. 11793, pp. 48–59. Springer, Cham (2019). https://doi.org/10.1007/978-3-030-30179-8_4

2. Bevendorff, J., Stein, B., Hagen, M., Potthast, M.: Elastic ChatNoir: search engine for the ClueWeb and the common crawl. In: Pasi, G., Piwowarski, B., Azzopardi, L., Hanbury, A. (eds.) ECIR 2018. LNCS, vol. 10772, pp. 820–824. Springer, Cham (2018). https://doi.org/10.1007/978-3-319-76941-7_83

3. Bondarenko, A., et al.: Overview of Touché 2020: argument retrieval. In: Arampatzis, A., et al. (eds.) CLEF 2020. LNCS, vol. 12260, pp. 384–395. Springer, Cham (2020). https://doi.org/10.1007/978-3-030-58219-7_26

4. Braunstain, L., Kurland, O., Carmel, D., Szpektor, I., Shtok, A.: Supporting human answers for advice-seeking questions in CQA sites. In: Ferro, N., et al. (eds.) ECIR 2016. LNCS, vol. 9626, pp. 129–141. Springer, Cham (2016). https://doi.org/10.1007/978-3-319-30671-1_10

5. Chernodub, A., et al.: TARGER: neural argument mining at your fingertips. In: Proceedings of the 57th Annual Meeting of the Association for Computational Linguistics, ACL 2019 (demos), pp. 195–200, Association for Computational Linguistics (2019). URL https://doi.org/10.18653/v1/p19-3031

6. Gienapp, L., Stein, B., Hagen, M., Potthast, M.: Efficient pairwise annotation of argument quality. In: Proceedings of the 58th Annual Meeting of the Association for Computational Linguistics, ACL 2020, pp. 5772–5781. Association for Computational Linguistics (2020). https://www.aclweb.org/anthology/2020.acl-main.511/

7. Gretz, S., et al.: A large-scale dataset for argument quality ranking: construction and analysis. In: Proceedings of The Thirty-Fourth Conference on Artificial Intelligence, AAAI 2020, The Thirty-Second Innovative Applications of Artificial Intelligence Conference, IAAI 2020, The Tenth Symposium on Educational Advances in Artificial Intelligence, EAAI 2020, pp. 7805–7813. AAAI Press (2020). https://aaai.org/ojs/index.php/AAAI/article/view/6285

8. Järvelin, K., Kekäläinen, J.: Cumulated gain-based evaluation of IR techniques. ACM Trans. Inf. Syst. **20**(4), 422–446 (2002). http://doi.acm.org/10.1145/582415.582418

9. Potthast, M., et al.: Argument search: assessing argument relevance. In: Proceedings of the 42nd International Conference on Research and Development in Information Retrieval, SIGIR 2019, pp. 1117–1120. ACM (2019). https://doi.org/10.1145/3331184.3331327

10. Potthast, M., Gollub, T., Wiegmann, M., Stein, B.: TIRA integrated research architecture. Information Retrieval Evaluation in a Changing World. TIRS, vol. 41, pp. 123–160. Springer, Cham (2019). https://doi.org/10.1007/978-3-030-22948-1_5

11. Rafalak, M., Abramczuk, K., Wierzbicki, A.: Incredible: is (almost) all web content trustworthy? Analysis of psychological factors related to website credibility evaluation. In: Proceedings of the 23rd International World Wide Web Conference, WWW 2014, Companion Volume, pp. 1117–1122. ACM (2014). https://doi.org/10.1145/2567948.2578997

12. Robertson, S.E., Zaragoza, H., Taylor, M.J.: Simple BM25 extension to multiple weighted fields. In: Proceedings of the 13th International Conference on Information and Knowledge Management, CIKM 2004, pp. 42–49. ACM (2004). https://doi.org/10.1145/1031171.1031181

13. Schildwächter, M., Bondarenko, A., Zenker, J., Hagen, M., Biemann, C., Panchenko, A.: Answering comparative questions: better than ten-blue-links? In: Proceedings of the Conference on Human Information Interaction and Retrieval, CHIIR 2019, pp. 361–365. ACM (2019). https://doi.org/10.1145/3295750.3298916

14. Stab, C., et al.: ArgumenText: searching for arguments in heterogeneous sources. In: Proceedings of the Conference of the North American Chapter of the Association for Computational Linguistics, NAACL 2018, pp. 21–25. Association for Computational Linguistics (2018). https://www.aclweb.org/anthology/N18-5005

15. Toledo, A., et al.: Automatic argument quality assessment - new datasets and methods. In: Proceedings of the Conference on Empirical Methods in Natural Language Processing and the 9th International Joint Conference on Natural Language Processing, EMNLP-IJCNLP 2019, pp. 5624–5634. Association for Computational Linguistics (2019). https://doi.org/10.18653/v1/D19-1564

16. Wachsmuth, H., et al.: Computational argumentation quality assessment in natural language. In: Proceedings of the 15th Conference of the European Chapter of the Association for Computational Linguistics (EACL), pp. 176–187. Association for Computational Linguistics (2017). https://doi.org/10.18653/v1/e17-1017

17. Wachsmuth, H., et al.: Building an argument search engine for the web. In: Proceedings of the Fourth Workshop on Argument Mining, ArgMining 2017, pp. 49–59. Association for Computational Linguistics (2017). https://doi.org/10.18653/v1/w17-5106

18. Yang, P., Fang, H., Lin, J.: Anserini: enabling the use of lucene for information retrieval research. In: Proceedings of the 40th International Conference on Research and Development in Information Retrieval, SIGIR 2017, pp. 1253–1256. ACM (2017). https://doi.org/10.1145/3077136.3080721
19. Zhai, C., Lafferty, J.D.: A study of smoothing methods for language models applied to ad hoc information retrieval. In: Proceedings of the 24th International Conference on Research and Development in Information Retrieval, SIGIR 2001, pp. 334–342. ACM (2001). https://doi.org/10.1145/383952.384019

Text Simplification for Scientific Information Access
CLEF 2021 SimpleText Workshop

Liana Ermakova[1]([✉]), Patrice Bellot[2], Pavel Braslavski[3], Jaap Kamps[4],
Josiane Mothe[5], Diana Nurbakova[6], Irina Ovchinnikova[7], and Eric San-Juan[8]

[1] Université de Bretagne Occidentale, HCTI - EA 4249, Brest, France
`liana.ermakova@univ-brest.fr`
[2] Aix Marseille Univ, Universite de Toulon, CNRS, LIS, Marseille, France
[3] Ural Federal University, Yekaterinburg, Russia
[4] University of Amsterdam, Amsterdam, The Netherlands
[5] Université de Toulouse, IRIT, Toulouse, France
[6] Institut National des Sciences Appliquées de Lyon, Lyon, France
[7] Sechenov University, Moscow, Russia
[8] Avignon Université, LIA, Avignon, France

Abstract. Modern information access systems hold the promise to give
users direct access to key information from authoritative primary sources
such as scientific literature, but non-experts tend to avoid these sources
due to their complex language, internal vernacular, or lacking prior background knowledge. Text simplification approaches can remove some of
these barriers, thereby avoiding that users rely on shallow information
in sources prioritizing commercial or political incentives rather than
the correctness and informational value. The CLEF 2021 SimpleText
track will address the opportunities and challenges of text simplification approaches to improve scientific information access head-on. We aim
to provide appropriate data and benchmarks, starting with pilot tasks
in 2021, and create a community of NLP and IR researchers working
together to resolve one of the greatest challenges of today.

Keywords: Scientific text simplification · (Multi-document)
summarization · Contextualization · Background knowledge

> Everything should be made as simple as
> possible, but no simpler
>
> *Albert Einstein*

1 Introduction

Scientific literacy, including health related questions, is important for people to
make right decisions, evaluate the information quality, maintain physiological
and mental health, avoid spending money on useless items. For example, the

D. Hiemstra et al. (Eds.): ECIR 2021, LNCS 12657, pp. 583–592, 2021.
https://doi.org/10.1007/978-3-030-72240-1_68

stories the individuals find credible can determine their response to the COVID-19 pandemic, including the application of social distancing, using dangerous fake medical treatments, or hoarding. Unfortunately, stories in social media are easier for lay people to understand than the research papers. Scientific texts such as scientific publications can also be difficult to understand for non domain-experts or scientists outside the publication domain. Improving text comprehensibility and its adaptation to different audience remains an unresolved problem. Although there are some attempts to tackle the issue of text comprehensibility, they are mainly based on readability formulas, which are not convincingly demonstrated the ability to reduce the difficulty of text [26].

To put a step forward to automatically reduce difficulty of text understanding, we propose a new workshop called SimpleText which aims to create a community interested in generating simplified summaries of scientific documents. Thus, the goal of this workshop is to connect researchers from different domains, such as Natural Language Processing, Information Retrieval, Linguistics, Scientific Journalism etc. in order to work together on automatic popularisation of science.

Improving text comprehensibility and its adaptation to different audience bring societal, technical, and evaluation challenges. There is a large range of important *societal challenges* SimpleText is linked to. Open science is one of them. Making the research really open and accessible for everyone implies providing it in a form that can be readable and understandable; referring to the "comprehensibility" of the research results, making science understandable [16]. Another example of those societal challenges is offering means to develop counter-speech to fake news based on scientific results. SimpleText also tackles *technical challenges* related to data (passage) selection and summarisation, comprehensibility and readability of texts.

To face these challenges, SimpleText provides an open forum aiming at answering questions like:

- **Information selection:** Which information should be simplified (e.g., in terms document and passage selection and summarisation)?
- **Comprehensibility:** What kind of background information should be provided (e.g., which terms should be contextualized by giving a definition and/or application)? What information is the most relevant or helpful?
- **Readability:** How to improve the readability of a given short text (e.g., by reducing vocabulary and syntactic complexity) without information distortion?

We will provide data and benchmarks, and address evaluation challenges underlying the technical challenges, including:

- How to evaluate information selection?
- How to evaluate background information?
- How to measure text simplification?

2   Information Selection, Comprehensibility, Readability

In order to simplify scientific texts, one have to (1) *select the information* to be included in a simplified summary, (2) decide whether the selected information is sufficient and *comprehensible* or he/she should provide some background knowledge, (3) improve the *readability* of the text. Our tasks are based on this pipeline.

2.1   Selecting the Information to Be Included in a Simplified Summary

People have to manage the constantly growing amount of information. According to several estimates the number of scientific journals is around 30,000, with about two million articles published per year [3]. About 180,000 articles on Covid-19 were published from January 2020 to October 2020 [1]. To deal with this data volume, one should have a concise overview, i.e. a summary. People prefer to read a short document instead of a long one. Thus, even single-document summarization is already a step of text simplification. Notice, that the information in a summary designed for a scientist from a specific field should be different from that adapted for general public.

Automatic summarization can simplify access to primary scientific documents – the resulting concise text is expected to highlight the most important parts of the document and thus reduces the reader's efforts. Evaluation initiatives in the 2000s such as Document Understanding Conference (DUC) and the Summarization track at the Text Analysis Conference (TAC) have focused primarily on the automatic summarization of news in various contexts and scenarios. Scientific articles are typically provided with a short abstract written by the authors. Thus, automatic generation of an abstract for a stand-alone article does not seem to be a practical task. However, if we consider a large collection of scientific articles and citations between them, we can come to a task of producing an abstract that would contain important aspects of a paper from the perspective of the community. Such a task has been offered to the participants of the TAC 2014 Biomedical Summarization Track[1], as well as of the CL-SciSumm shared task series. In particular, the 2020 edition of CL-SciSumm features LaySummary subtask, where a participating system must produce a text summary of a scientific paper intended for non-technical audience[2] without using technical jargon. However, in most cases, the names of the objects are not replaceable in the process of text transformation or simplification due to the risk of information distortion. In this case it is important to explain these complex concepts to a reader (see Sect. 2.2 Comprehensibility). Another close work is CLEF-IP 2012-2013: Retrieval in the Intellectual Property Domain[3] (novelty

---

[1] https://tac.nist.gov/2014/BiomedSumm/.

[2] https://ornlcda.github.io/SDProc/sharedtasks.html#laysumm.

[3] http://www.ifs.tuwien.ac.at/~clef-ip/tasks.shtml.

search). Given a claim, the task was to retrieve relevant passages from a document collection. However, CLEF-IP focused on extractive summarization only and did not consider text simplification.

Sentence compression can be seen as a middle ground between text simplification and summarization. The task is to remove redundant or less important parts of an input sentence, preserving its grammaticality and original meaning [18]. Thus, the main challenge is to *choose which information* should be included in a simplified text.

2.2   Comprehensibility

Comprehensibility of a simple text varies for different readership. Readers of popular science texts have a basic background, are able to process logical connections and recognize novelty [24]. In the popular science text, a reader looks for rationalization and clear links between well known and new [28]. To adopt the novelty, readers need to include new concepts into their mental representation of the scientific domain.

According to The Free Dictionary, *background knowledge* is "information that is essential to understanding a situation or problem" [2]. Lack of basic knowledge can become a barrier to reading comprehension [30]. In [30], the authors suggested that there is a knowledge threshold allowing reading comprehension. Background knowledge, along with content, style, location, and some other dimension, are useful for personalised learning [35]. In contrast to newspapers limited by the size of the page, digital technologies provide essentially unbounded capabilities for hosting primary-source documents and background information. However, in many cases users do not read these additional texts. It is also important to remember, that the goal is to keep the text simple and short, not to make it indefinitely long to discourage potential readers.

Entity linking (also known as Wikification) is the task of tying named entities from the text to the corresponding knowledge base items. A scientific text enriched with links to Wikipedia or Wikidata can potentially help mitigate the background knowledge problem, as these knowledge bases provide definitions, illustrations, examples, and related entities. However, the existing standard datasets for entity linking such as [23] are focused primarily on such entities as people, places, and organizations, while a lay reader of a scientific article needs rather assistance with new concepts, methods, etc. Wikification is close to the task of terminology and keyphrase extraction from scientific texts [4]. Searching for background knowledge is close to INEX/CLEF Tweet Contextualization track 2011–2014 [7] and CLEF Cultural micro-blog Contextualization 2016, 2017 Workshop [14], but SimpleText differs from them by making a focus on selection of notions to be explained and the helpfulness of the information provided rather than its relevance. The idea to contextualize news was further developed in Background Linking task at TREC 2020 News Track aiming at a list of links to the articles that a person should read next[4]. In contrast to that, SimpleText

---

[4] http://trec-news.org/guidelines-2020.pdf.

try to determine terms to be contextualized. SimpleText is similar to the Wikification task at TREC 2020 News Track since it also aims to evaluate whether the critical context for understanding is missing but the types of background knowledge are different since our target is a scientific text. Besides, we will rank terms to be contextualized rather than passages.

Thus, the main challenge of the comprehensibility is to *provide relevant background knowledge* to help a reader to understand a complex scientific text.

2.3 Readability

Readability is the ease with which a reader can understand a written text. Readability is different from legibility, which measures how easily a reader can distinguish characters from each other. Readability indices have been widely used to evaluate teaching materials, news, and technical documents for about a century [21, 45]. For example, Gunning fog index, introduced in 1944, estimates the number of years in a scholar system required to understand a given text on the first reading. Similarly, the Flesch–Kincaid readability test shows the difficulty of a text in English based on word length and sentence length [19]. Although these two metrics are easy to compute, they are criticized for the lack of reliability [36]. The very structure of the readability indices suggested to authors or editors how to simplify a text: organize shorter and more frequent words into short sentences. Later studies incorporate lexical, syntactic, and discourse-level features to predict text readability [33]. In NLP tasks, readability, coherence, conciseness, and grammar are usually assessed manually since it is difficult to express these parameters numerically [13]. However, several studies were carried out in the domain of automatic readability evaluation, including the application of language models [10,17,22,36] and machine learning techniques [17,32]. Traditional methods of readability evaluation are based on familiarity of terms [9,20,37] or their length [41] and syntax complexity (e.g. sentence length, the depth of a parse tree, omission of personal verb, rate of prepositional phrases, noun and verb groups etc.) [8,10,29,42,46]. Word complexity is usually evaluated by experts [9,20,38]. [6] computed average normalized number of words in valid coherent passages without syntactical errors, unresolved anaphora, and redundant information. Several researches argue also the importance of sentence ordering for text understanding [5,15].

Automatic text simplification might be the next step after estimation of text complexity. Usually, text simplification task is performed and assessed on the level of individual sentences. To reduce the reading complexity, in [11], the authors introduced a task of sentence simplification through the use of more accessible vocabulary and sentence structure. They provided a new corpus that aligns English Wikipedia with Simple English Wikipedia and contains simplification operations such as rewording, reordering, insertion and deletion. Accurate lexical choice presupposes unambiguous reference to the particular object leading to actualization of its connections with other objects in the domain. Domain complexity concerns the number of objects and concepts in the domain, and connections among them described by the terminology system (see a survey:

[25]). Names of the objects are not replaceable in the process of text transformation or simplification due to risk of information distortion [12,27]. For example, 'hydroxychloroquine' represents a derivative of 'chloroquine', so the substances are connected thanks to belonging to a set 'chloroquine derivatives'. However, it is impossible to substitute 'hydroxychloroquine' by 'chloroquine' while simplifying a medical text about a Covid-19 treatment because of the difference in their chemical composition. A hypernym 'drugs' can refer to the substances. The hypernym generalizes the information while omitting essential difference between the drugs; however, the generalization allows to avoid misinformation [40]. Science text simplification presupposes facilitation of readers' understanding of complex content by establishing links to basic lexicon, avoiding distortion connections among objects within the domain.

Ideally, the results undergo a human evaluation, since traditional readability indices can be misleading [43]. Automatic evaluation metrics have been proposed for the task: SARI [44] targets lexical complexity, while SAMSA estimates structural complexity of a sentence [39]. Formality style transfer is a cognate task, where a system rewrites a text in a different style preserving its meaning [34]. These tasks are frequently evaluated with BLEU metrics [31] to compare system's output against gold standard.

Thus, the main challenge of the readability improvement is to *reduce vocabulary and syntactic complexity* without information distortion while keeping the target genre.

3   Pilot Tasks

To start with, we will develop three pilot tasks that will help to better understand the challenges as well to discuss these challenges and the way to evaluate solutions. Details on the tasks, guideline and call for contributions can be found at www.irit.fr/simpleText, in this paper we just briefly introduce the planed pilot tasks. Note that the pilot tasks are means to help the discussions and to develop a research community around text simplification. Contributions will not exclusively rely on the pilot tasks.

3.1   Task 1: Ranking the Words/Sentences to Be Included in a Simplified Summary

Participants will be provided with scientific articles. This pilot task aims at automatically deciding which passages of these scientific articles should be included in extractive summaries in order to get a simplified summary of the initial texts. Note, that the information in a summary designed for an expert should be different from those for the general audience. To evaluate these results, we will rely on manual annotation and automatic metrics.

3.2   Task 2: Searching for Background Knowledge

The goal of this pilot task is to provide relevant background knowledge to help a reader to understand a complex scientific text. Participants should keep the text simple and short, not to make it indefinitely long to discourage potential readers. The participants have to answer two questions: (1) What kind of background information should be provided (e.g. which terms should be contextualized by giving a definition and/or application)? (2) What information is the most relevant (passage retrieval from an external source, e.g. Wikipedia)? The evaluation will be a combination of manual assessment and automatic metrics.

3.3   Task 3: Scientific Text Simplification

In this pilot task, the participants will be provided with the abstract of scientific papers. The goal will be to provide a simplified version of these abstracts. In this pilot task, we thus consider that the summarization part is already solved and that the main science nuggets are in the provided summaries. We will thus use scientific paper summaries which consist on context, aims, methodology, findings and discussion. Some medical papers will be used in this task. The guideline will detail the targeted simplification. Evaluation will be a combination of manual and automatic evaluation, the results of which will also be discussed during the workshop.

4   Conclusion

The paper introduced the CLEF 2021 SimpleText track, consisting of a workshop and pilot tasks on text simplification for scientific information access. Full details about the tasks and how to participate in the track can be found in the detailed call for papers and guidelines at the SimpleText website: https://www.irit.fr/simpleText/. Please join this effort and contribute by working on one of the greatest challenges of today!

References

1. "2019-nCoV" OR ... Publication Year: 2020 in Publications - Dimensions. https://covid-19.dimensions.ai/
2. Background knowledge. https://www.thefreedictionary.com/background+knowledge
3. Altbach, P.G., Wit, H.D.: Too much academic research is being published, July 2018. https://www.universityworldnews.com/post.php?story=20180905095203579
4. Augenstein, I., Das, M., Riedel, S., Vikraman, L., McCallum, A.: Semeval 2017 task 10: scienceie-extracting keyphrases and relations from scientific publications. arXiv preprint arXiv:1704.02853 (2017)
5. Barzilay, R., Elhadad, N., McKeown, K.R.: Inferring strategies for sentence ordering in multidocument news summarization. J. Artif. Intell. Res. **17**, 35–55 (2002)

6. Bellot, P., et al.: Overview of INEX. In: Information Access Evaluation. Multilinguality, Multimodality, and Visualization - 4th International Conference of the CLEF Initiative, CLEF 2013, Valencia, Spain, 23–26 September 2013. Proceedings, pp. 269–281 (2013)

7. Bellot, P., Moriceau, V., Mothe, J., SanJuan, E., Tannier, X.: INEX tweet contextualization task: evaluation, results and lesson learned. Inf. Process. Manage. **52**(5), 801–819 (2016). https://doi.org/10.1016/j.ipm.2016.03.002

8. Chae, J., Nenkova, A.: Predicting the fluency of text with shallow structural features: case studies of machine translation and human-written text. In: Proceedings of the 12th Conference of the European Chapter of the ACL, pp. 139–147 (2009)

9. Chall, J.S., Dale, E.: Readability revisited: The new Dale-Chall readability. Brookline Books, Cambridge (1995)

10. Collins-Thompson, K., Callan, J.: A language modeling approach to predicting reading difficulty. In: Proceedings of HLT/NAACL, vol. 4 (2004)

11. Coster, W., Kauchak, D.: Simple English Wikipedia: a new text simplification task. In: Proceedings of the 49th Annual Meeting of the Association for Computational Linguistics: Human Language Technologies, pp. 665–669 (2011)

12. Cram, D., Daille, B.: Terminology extraction with term variant detection. In: Proceedings of ACL-2016 System Demonstrations, Berlin, Germany, pp. 13–18. Association for Computational Linguistics, August 2016. https://doi.org/10.18653/v1/P16-4003, https://www.aclweb.org/anthology/P16-4003

13. Ermakova, L., Cossu, J.V., Mothe, J.: A survey on evaluation of summarization methods. Inf. Process. Manage. **56**(5), 1794–1814 (2019). https://doi.org/10.1016/j.ipm.2019.04.001, http://www.sciencedirect.com/science/article/pii/S0306457318306241

14. Ermakova, L., Goeuriot, L., Mothe, J., Mulhem, P., Nie, J.-Y., SanJuan, E.: CLEF 2017 microblog cultural contextualization lab overview. In: Jones, G.J.F., et al. (eds.) CLEF 2017. LNCS, vol. 10456, pp. 304–314. Springer, Cham (2017). https://doi.org/10.1007/978-3-319-65813-1_27

15. Ermakova, L., Mothe, J., Firsov, A.: A metric for sentence ordering assessment based on topic-comment structure (short paper). In: ACM SIGIR Special Interest Group on Information Retrieval (SIGIR), Tokyo, Japan, 07/08/2017-11/08/2017 (2017). selection rate 30

16. Fecher, B., Friesike, S.: Open science: one term, five schools of thought. In: Bartling, S., Friesike, S. (eds.) Opening Science, pp. 17–47. Springer, Cham (2014). https://doi.org/10.1007/978-3-319-00026-8_2

17. Feng, L., Jansche, M., Huenerfauth, M., Elhadad, N.: A comparison of features for automatic readability assessment. In: Proceedings of the 23rd International Conference on Computational Linguistics: Posters. COLING 2010, Stroudsburg, PA, USA, pp. 276–284, Association for Computational Linguistics (2010). http://dl.acm.org/citation.cfm?id=1944566.1944598

18. Filippova, K., Altun, Y.: Overcoming the lack of parallel data in sentence compression. In: Proceedings of the 2013 Conference on Empirical Methods in Natural Language Processing, pp. 1481–1491 (2013)

19. Flesch, R.: A new readability yardstick. J. Appl. Psychol. **32**(3), p221–233 (1948)

20. Fry, E.: A readability formula for short passages. J. Read. **8**(594–597), 33 (1990)

21. Fry, E.: The Varied Uses of Readability Measurement, April 1986

22. Heilman, M., Collins-Thompson, K., Eskenazi, M.: An analysis of statistical models and features for reading difficulty prediction. In: Proceedings of the Third Workshop on Innovative Use of NLP for Building Educational Applications. EANL 2008, Stroudsburg, PA, USA, pp. 71–79. Association for Computational Linguistics (2008). http://dl.acm.org/citation.cfm?id=1631836.1631845

23. Hoffart, J., et al.: Robust disambiguation of named entities in text. In: Proceedings of the 2011 Conference on Empirical Methods in Natural Language Processing, pp. 782–792 (2011)

24. Jarreau, P.B., Porter, L.: Science in the social media age: profiles of science blog readers. J. Mass Commun. Quart. **95**(1), 142–168 (2018). https://doi.org/10.1177/1077699016685558, publisher: SAGE Publications Inc

25. Ladyman, J., Lambert, J., Wiesner, K.: What is a complex system? European J. Philos. Sci. **3**(1), 33–67 (2013). https://doi.org/10.1007/s13194-012-0056-8

26. Leroy, G., Endicott, J.E., Kauchak, D., Mouradi, O., Just, M.: User evaluation of the effects of a text simplification algorithm using term familiarity on perception, understanding, learning, and information retention. J. Medical Internet Res. **15**(7), e144 (2013)

27. McCarthy, P.M., Guess, R.H., McNamara, D.S.: The components of paraphrase evaluations. Behav. Res. Methods **41**(3), 682–690 (2009). https://doi.org/10.3758/BRM.41.3.682

28. Molek-Kozakowska, K.: Communicating environmental science beyond academia: Stylistic patterns of newsworthiness in popular science journalism. Disc. Commun. **11**(1), 69–88 (2017). https://doi.org/10.1177/1750481316683294

29. Mutton, A., Dras, M., Wan, S., Dale, R.: Gleu: automatic evaluation of sentence-level fluency. In: ACL 2007, pp. 344–351 (2007)

30. O'Reilly, T., Wang, Z., Sabatini, J.: How much knowledge is too little? When a lack of knowledge becomes a barrier to comprehension. Psychol. Sci. (2019). https://doi.org/10.1177/0956797619862276, https://journals.sagepub.com/doi/10.1177/0956797619862276, publisher: SAGE PublicationsSage CA: Los Angeles, CA

31. Papineni, K., Roukos, S., Ward, T., Zhu, W.J.: Bleu: a method for automatic evaluation of machine translation. In: Proceedings of the 40th Annual Meeting of the Association for Computational Linguistics, pp. 311–318 (2002)

32. Petersen, S.E., Ostendorf, M.: A machine learning approach to reading level assessment. Comput. Speech Lang. **23**(1), 89–106 (2009). https://doi.org/10.1016/j.csl.2008.04.003, http://dx.doi.org/10.1016/j.csl.2008.04.003

33. Pitler, E., Nenkova, A.: Revisiting readability: A unified framework for predicting text quality (2008)

34. Rao, S., Tetreault, J.: Dear sir or madam, may i introduce the GYAFC dataset: Corpus, benchmarks and metrics for formality style transfer. In: Proceedings of the 2018 Conference of the North American Chapter of the Association for Computational Linguistics: Human Language Technologies, Volume 1 (Long Papers), pp. 129–140 (2018)

35. Shi, H., Revithis, S., Chen, S.S.: An agent enabling personalized learning in e-learning environments. In: Proceedings of the First International Joint Conference on Autonomous Agents and Multiagent Systems: Part 2. AAMAS 2002, New York, NY, USA, pp. 847–848. Association for Computing Machinery, July 2002. https://doi.org/10.1145/544862.544941

36. Si, L., Callan, J.: A statistical model for scientific readability. In: Proceedings of the Tenth International Conference on Information and Knowledge Management, CIKM 2001, pp. 574–576, New York, NY, USA. ACM (2001). https://doi.org/10.1145/502585.502695, http://doi.acm.org/10.1145/502585.502695

37. Stenner, A.J., Horablin, I., Smith, D.R., Smith, M.: The Lexile Framework. Metametrics, Durham, NC (1988)

38. Stenner, A., Horabin, I., Smith, D.R., Smith, M.: The Lexile Framework. Meta-Metrics, Durham, NC (1988)

39. Sulem, E., Abend, O., Rappoport, A.: Semantic structural evaluation for text simplification. In: Proceedings of the 2018 Conference of the North American Chapter of the Association for Computational Linguistics: Human Language Technologies, Volume 1 (Long Papers), pp. 685–696 (2018)

40. Søe, S.O.: Algorithmic detection of misinformation and disinformation: Gricean perspectives. J. Doc. **74**(2), 309–332 (2018). https://doi.org/10.1108/JD-05-2017-0075, publisher: Emerald Publishing Limited

41. Tavernier, J., Bellot, P.: Combining relevance and readability for INEX 2011 question-answering track, pp. 185–195 (2011)

42. Wan, S., Dale, R., Dras, M.: Searching for grammaticality: propagating dependencies in the Viterbi algorithm. In: Proceedings of the Tenth European Workshop on Natural Language Generation (2005)

43. Wubben, S., van den Bosch, A., Krahmer, E.: Sentence simplification by monolingual machine translation. In: Proceedings of the 50th Annual Meeting of the Association for Computational Linguistics (Volume 1: Long Papers), pp. 1015–1024 (2012)

44. Xu, W., Napoles, C., Pavlick, E., Chen, Q., Callison-Burch, C.: Optimizing statistical machine translation for text simplification. Trans. Assoc. Comput. Linguist. **4**, 401–415 (2016)

45. Zakaluk, B.L., Samuels, S.J.: Readability: its past, present, and future. International Reading Association, 800 Barksdale Rd (1988). https://eric.ed.gov/?id=ED292058

46. Zwarts, S., Dras, M.: Choosing the right translation: a syntactically informed classification approach. In: Proceedings of the 22nd International Conference on Computational Linguistics, pp. 1153–1160 (2008)

CLEF eHealth Evaluation Lab 2021

Lorraine Goeuriot[1]([✉])[iD], Hanna Suominen[2][iD], Liadh Kelly[3][iD],
Laura Alonso Alemany[4], Nicola Brew-Sam[5][iD], Viviana Cotik[6], Darío Filippo[7],
Gabriela Gonzalez Saez[1], Franco Luque[12], Philippe Mulhem[1][iD],
Gabriella Pasi[8][iD], Roland Roller[9][iD], Sandaru Seneviratne[5], Jorge Vivaldi[10],
Marco Viviani[8][iD], and Chenchen Xu[11]

[1] Univ. Grenoble Alpes, CNRS, Grenoble INP, LIG, 38000 Grenoble, France
{lorraine.goeuriot,gabriela.saez,philippe.mulhem}@univ-grenoble-alpes.fr
[2] The Australian National University (ANU), Data61/Commonwealth Scientific and
Industrial Research Organisation (CSIRO), and University of Turku,
Canberra, ACT, Australia
hanna.suominen@anu.edu.au
[3] Maynooth University, Co., Kildare, Ireland
liadh.kelly@mu.ie
[4] Universidad Nacional de Córdoba, Córdoba, Argentina
lauraalonsoalemany@unc.edu.ar
[5] The ANU, Canberra ACT, Australia
{nicola.brew-sam,sandaru.seneviratne}@anu.edu.au
[6] Universidad de Buenos Aires, CONICET, Buenos Aires, Argentina
vcotik@dc.uba.ar
[7] Hospital de Pediatría 'Prof. Dr. Juan P. Garrahan', Buenos Aires, Argentina
[8] University of Milano-Bicocca, Milan, Italy
{gabriella.pasi,marco.viviani}@unimib.it
[9] German Research Center for Artificial Intelligence (DFKI),
Kaiserslautern, Germany
roland.roller@dfki.de
[10] Institut de Lingüística Aplicada, Universitat Pompeu Fabra, Barcelona, Spain
jorge.vivaldi@upf.edu
[11] The ANU and Data61/CSIRO, Canberra, ACT, Australia
chenchen.xu@anu.edu.au
[12] Universidad Nacional de Córdoba, CONICET, Córdoba, Argentina
francolq@unc.edu.ar

Abstract. Motivated by the ever increasing difficulties faced by laypeople in retrieving and digesting valid and relevant information to make health-centred decisions, the CLEF eHealth lab series has offered shared tasks to the community in the fields of *Information Extraction* (IE), management, and *Information Retrieval* (IR) since 2013. These tasks have attracted large participation and led to statistically significant improvements in processing quality. In 2021, CLEF eHealth is calling for participants to contribute to the following two tasks: Task 1 on IE focuses on

LG, HS, & LK co-chair the CLEF eHealth lab and contributed equally to this paper.
Task 1 is led by LAA and VC, and organized by DF, FL, RR, and JV; Task 2 is led
by LG, GP, and HS, and organized by NB-S, GGS, LK, PM, SS, MV, and CX.

IE from noisy text. Participants will identify and classify Named Entities
in written ultrasonography reports, containing misspellings and inconsistencies, from a major public hospital in Argentina. Identified entities will
then have to be classified, which can be very challenging as it requires to
handle lexical variations. Task 2 is a novel extension of the most popular
and established task on consumer health search (CHS), aiming at retrieving relevant, understandable, and credible information for patients and
their next-of-kins. In this paper we describe recent advances in the fields
of IE and IR, and the subsequent offerings of this years CLEF eHealth
lab challenges.

Keywords: eHealth · Medical informatics · Information extraction ·
Information storage and retrieval

1   Introduction

The requirement to ensure that patients[1] can understand their official, privacy-
sensitive health information in their own *Electronic Health Records* (EHRs) is
stipulated by policies and laws [16]. Patients' better abilities to understand their
own EHR empowers them to take part in the related healthcare judgment, leading to their increased independence from healthcare providers, better healthcare
decisions, and decreased healthcare costs [16]. Improving patients' ability to
access and digest this content could mean paraphrasing the EHR-text, enriching
it with hyperlinks to term definitions, care guidelines, and further supportive
information on patient-friendly and reliable websites, helping them to discover
good search queries to retrieve more contents, and allowing not only text but
also speech as a query modality for example.

Information access conferences have organized evaluation labs on related
Electronic Health (eHealth) *Information Extraction* (IE), *Information Management* (IM), and *Information Retrieval* (IR) tasks for almost 20 years. Yet, with
rare exception, they have targeted the healthcare experts' information needs
only [4,5,11]. The *CLEF eHealth Evaluation-lab and Lab-workshop Series*[2] has
been organized every year since 2012 as part of the *Conference and Labs of
the Evaluation Forum* (CLEF) [7,8,10,12–14,19,22,23] with the primary goal
of supporting laypersons, and their next-of-kin, access to medical information.
This year, the lab proposes two tasks: one centered on Information Extraction
(identify and classify Named Entities in written ultrasonography reports); one
centered on Information Retrieval (*Consumer Health Search* (CHS)).

In this paper we overview the interest in the CLEF eHealth evaluation lab
series to-date. We then consider recent advances in IE and IR which inform the
offered CLEF eHealth 2021 IE and IR tasks. These IE and IR evaluation lab
challenge tasks are also described. The paper concludes with a vision for CLEF
eHealth beyond 2021.

---

[1] In the paper, we consider *patients*, *layperson* or *consumer*, to be system users with
no or little medical background.

[2] http://clefehealth.imag.fr.

2   CLEF eHealth in 2012–2020

The CLEF and other information access conferences have organized evaluation labs and shared tasks on eHealth IE, IR, and Information Management
for approximately two decades. Yet, their primary focus has been on healthcare
experts' information needs, with limited consideration of laypersons' difficulties
to retrieve and digest credible, topical, and easy-to-understand contents in their
preferred language to make health-centred decisions [4,5,11].

This niche of addressing patients, their families, health scientists, healthcare policy makers, and other laypersons' health information needs in a range
of languages in order to make health-centered decisions began stimulating the
annual CLEF eHealth Evaluation-lab and Lab-workshop Series in 2012. Its first
workshop took place in 2012 with an aim to organize an evaluation lab, and in
2013–2021, this lab with up to three shared tasks annually has preceded each
campaign-concluding CLEF eHealth workshop [7,8,10,12–14,19,22,23].

3   CLEF eHealth 2021 Information Extraction Task

3.1   Preceding Efforts

In 2020, the CodiEsp task of the CLEF eHealth evaluation lab mastered the
challenge of building a publicly available automatic clinical coding system for
Spanish documents, which is a step towards the final application of *natural language processing* (NLP) technologies in non-English speaking countries [10].
In contrast to previous clinical coding tasks using death certificates and non-
technical summaries of animal experimentations [14,20,21], the 2020 task was
able to use a collection of clinical case reports from a variety of medical disciplines chosen to constitute a corpus of *electronic health records* (EHRs; 1,000
documents from the *Spanish clinical case reports* (SPACCC) corpus). CodiEsp
shared tasks attracted participants from both Spanish and non-Spanish speaking
countries, with different backgrounds in the 51 teams registered for the tasks.
Thus, CodiEsp was able to prove that the language barrier (languages other
than English) does not necessarily make the tasks more restrictive, but presents
an opportunity to adapt well-known techniques to language-specific features.
The diversity in profiles led to the development of heterogeneous resources, with
a development of 167 novel clinical coding systems achieved. Finally, the 2020
task organizers' showed that individual task results could be combined, leading
to further performance gains.

The 2020 task on Spanish resources was popular to the extent that it set the
ground for the 2021 SpRadIE (Spanish Radiology Information Extraction) task
focusing on further sub-aspects of the Spanish language: text in the radiology
domain, image reports written under time constraints, resulting in misspellings
and inconsistencies, coming from a public hospital in South America, as elaborated in the next subsection. These particularities pose an interesting challenge of
domain and register adaptation for systems trained for general Spanish eHealth, in
their application to a specific setting. With this objective, we are calling for submissions from hospitals and private companies to supplement academic participants.

3.2   The Task in 2021: Multilingual Information Extraction

In 2021, the SpRadIE task will target Named Entity Recognition and Classification in the domain of radiological image reports, more concretely, pediatric ultrasonographies. These reports are written in haste, under time pressure in a public Argentinean hospital. They tend to be repetitive, probably due to an extensive use of copy and paste. Nevertheless, these are actual free text reports with no pre-determined structure, which results in great variations in size and content. No element is mandatory in the report except the age of the patient. Also, there are misspellings and inconsistencies in the usage of abbreviations, punctuation and line breaks.

The corpus consists of a total of 513 sonography reports, with over 17,000 annotated named entities with some class imbalance (the smallest class is a sixth of the majority class). Reports were manually annotated by clinical experts and then revised by linguists. Annotation guidelines and training were provided for both rounds of annotation. Interannotator (dis)agreement, detailed for each type of entity, will be used to better assess the performance of automatic annotators. Automatic annotators will be expected to perform well in those cases where human annotators have strong agreement, and worse in cases that are difficult for human annotators to identify consistently.

Five different classes of entities are distinguished: *Finding, Anatomical Entity, Location, Measure, Degree, Type of Measure* and *Abbreviation.* Hedges are also identified, distinguishing *Negation, Uncertainty, Condition and Conditional Temporal.* Entities can be embedded within other entities of different types. Moreover, entities can be discontinuous, and can span over sentence boundaries. The entity type *Finding* is particularly challenging, as it presents great variability in its textual forms. It ranges from a single word to more than ten words in some cases, and comprising all kinds of phrases. However, this is also the most informative type of entity for the potential users of these annotations. Other challenging phenomena are the regular polysemy observed between *Anatomical entities* and *Locations,* and the irregular uses of *Abbreviations.* In the manual annotation process, we have found that human annotators differ more on those categories than on the others, thus we expect automatic annotators will also have difficulties to consistently classify those as well.

For the SpRadIE 2021 task, submissions will be evaluated with different metrics, including exact and lenient match. The lenient evaluation will be carried out using a Jaccard Index, similarly as used in the 2013 BioNLP shared task [1]:

$$J_{(ref,pred)} = \frac{overlap_{(ref,pred)}}{length_{ref} + length_{pred} - overlap_{(ref,pred)}}$$

It takes the length (offsets) of the annotated reference concept, the predicted concept, as well as the overlap between them. This index amounts to 1 in the case of perfect match and 0 if there is no overlap between reference and prediction.

The official evaluation measures for the task are Slot Error Rate (SER) [15] with the Jaccard index as primary metric for entity match, and F1 for classification of matching entities within each type of entity.

4   CLEF eHealth 2021 Information Retrieval Task

4.1   Preceding Efforts

In 2020, the CHS task of CLEF eHealth consisted of an extension of the 2018 task. The use case was similar to previous years: helping patients and their next-of-kins find relevant health information online. The topics were extracted from query logs from the Health on the Net website and were representative of real information needs. The organizers oversaw the generation of spoken queries for these topics, and transcription of these spoken queries. Participants could submit their runs to two subtasks: one adhoc IR subtask using the textual queries; one spoken IR subtask using the spoken queries or their transcriptions. In each subtask, the effectiveness of the participants systems were evaluated considering three dimensions of relevance: topical relevance, understandability, and credibility. Three teams took part in the challenge, and all of them submitted runs to the 2 subtasks. However, none of them adapted the IR models used for each subtask – only the input query changed (textual query or transcription). This tendency was also observed in the previous multilingual tasks (running from 2014 until 2018), where only a few teams went further than adding a translation layer before the IR pipeline. Given the workload necessary to record and transcribe the topics the organizers have decided not to carry on this task that failed to bring together several communities, and in the end did not really address the challenge of varying input type for IR models.

A constant effort has been made in the task since 2014 to integrate relevance dimensions. This has led to many interesting publications in order to adapt IR models to these dimensions, as well as the evaluation framework itself. Since 2020, the credibility dimension has been considered too. Integrating a dimension that, in itself, is already challenging to define, assess, and measure, led to a variety of interesting and exciting research questions. The 2021 CHS tasks reflect these new challenges.

4.2   The Task in 2021: Consumer Health Search

The 2018 CLEF eHealth CHS document collection will be used in the 2021 IR task. This collection consists of Web pages acquired from Common Crawl,[3] which is augmented with additional pages collected from a number of known reliable health Websites and other known unreliable health Websites [9]. The topics for 2021 are manually created by medical professionals from realistic scenarios. Participants are challenged in the 2021 Task with retrieving the relevant documents from the provided document collection. A number of distinct subtasks can be completed using the considered queries and the provided labeled dataset: *ad-hoc search*, *credibility assessment*, and *personalized search based on multi-dimensional relevance assessment*.

---

[3] https://commoncrawl.org/.

Like in the 2020 IR task, the pool of documents to be assessed will be labelled with respect to three relevance dimensions: *topicality*, *understandability*, and *credibility*. The assessment guidelines will follow up on 2020 guidelines: assessors will be asked to assess if the documents are on the same topic as the query, how readable/understandable the document is to a layperson, and how credible it is. Credibility has been introduced in the 2020 IR task. When assessing the credibility of online information, we consider credibility as an objective characteristic of an information item (either it is true, false, or partially true/false) [25], which is subjectively perceived by individuals [18]. Hence, the assessors are required to consider distinct aspects related to [24]: the *source* that disseminates information (e.g., its *trustworthiness* [3]), some characteristics associated with the *message* diffused (e.g., syntactic, semantic, and stylistic aspects [17]), and some *social aspects* if the information is disseminated through a virtual community (e.g., to be part of an *echo chamber* [2]).

The official evaluation measures include classic IR measures such as Binary Preference, Mean Reciprocal Rank, or Normalized Discounted Cumulative Gain @ 1–10, measuring how well systems retrieve relevant documents at low ranks (which is in line with the CHS use case). In order to measure how well systems can adapt the retrieved content to the consumers knowledge, understandability and credibility Rank-biased Precision will also be considered as official metrics. For the credibility assessment subtask, reference will made to measures such as Accuracy and F-measure to establish the goodness of the classification between credible information or not.

5   A Vision for CLEF eHealth Beyond 2021

The general purpose of our lab throughout the years, as its 2021 IE and IR tasks demonstrate, has been to assist laypeople in finding and understanding health information in order to make enlightened decisions. Breaking language barriers has been our priority over the years, and this will continue in our multilingual tasks. Each year of the labs has enabled the identification of difficulties and challenges in IE, IM, and IR which have shaped our tasks. For example, our IR tasks have considered multilingual, contextualized, spoken queries, and query variants. However, further exploration of query construction, search scenario definition, aiming at a better understanding and management of CHS are still needed. The task will also further explore relevance dimensions, and work toward a better assessment of understandability and credibility, as well as methods to take these dimensions into consideration. Moreover, by better defining the search scenarios, the topics, and considering a document relevance in all its various aspects, the task will progress towards personalized and effective health search engines. As lab organizers, our purpose is to increase the impact and the value of the resources, methods and the community built by CLEF eHealth. Examining the quality and stability of the lab contributions will help the CLEF eHealth series to better understand where it should be improved and how. As future work, we intend continuing our analysis of the influence of the CLEF eHealth evaluation series from the perspectives of publications and data/software releases [6,20,21].

Acknowledgements. The lab has been supported in part by the CLEF Initiative and the Our Health in Our Hands (OHIOH) initiative of The Australian National University (ANU). OHIOH is a strategic initiative of The ANU which aims to transform healthcare by developing new personalised health technologies and solutions in collaboration with patients, clinicians, and healthcare providers. The lab has been supported in part by the bi-lateral Kodicare (Knowledge Delta based improvement and continuous evaluation of retrieval engines) project funded by the french ANR (ANR-19-CE23-0029) and Austrian FWF.

References

1. Bossy, R., Golik, W., Ratkovic, Z., Bessières, P., Nédellec, C.: BioNLP shared task 2013 - an overview of the bacteria biotope task. In: Proceedings of the BioNLP Shared Task 2013 Workshop. pp. 161–169. Association for Computational Linguistics, Sofia, Bulgaria, August 2013. https://www.aclweb.org/anthology/W13-2024
2. Bruns, A.: Echo chamber? What echo chamber? Reviewing the evidence (2017)
3. Ceravolo, P., Damiani, E., Viviani, M.: Adding a trust layer to semantic web metadata. In: Herrera-Viedma, E., Pasi, G., Crestani, F. (eds.) Soft Computing in Web Information Retrieval. Studies in Fuzziness and Soft Computing, vol. 197, pp. 87–104. Springer, Heidelberg (2006). https://doi.org/10.1007/3-540-31590-X_5
4. Demner-Fushman, D., Elhadad, N.: Aspiring to unintended consequences of natural language processing: a review of recent developments in clinical and consumer-generated text processing. Yearb. Med. Inform. **1**, 224–233 (2016)
5. Filannino, M., Uzuner, Ö.: Advancing the state of the art in clinical natural language processing through shared tasks. Yearb. Med. Inform. **27**(01), 184–192 (2018)
6. Goeuriot, L., et al.: An analysis of evaluation campaigns in ad-hoc medical information retrieval: CLEF eHealth 2013 and 2014. Inf. Retr. J. **21**, 507–540 (2018). https://doi.org/10.1007/s10791-018-9331-4
7. Goeuriot, L., et al.: Overview of the CLEF eHealth evaluation lab 2015. In: Mothe, J., et al. (eds.) CLEF 2015. LNCS, vol. 9283, pp. 429–443. Springer, Cham (2015). https://doi.org/10.1007/978-3-319-24027-5_44
8. Goeuriot, L., et al.: CLEF 2017 eHealth evaluation lab overview. In: Jones, G.J.F., et al. (eds.) CLEF 2017. LNCS, vol. 10456, pp. 291–303. Springer, Cham (2017). https://doi.org/10.1007/978-3-319-65813-1_26
9. Goeuriot, L., Liu, Z., Pasi, G., Saez, G.G., Viviani, M., Xu, C.: Overview of the CLEF eHealth 2020 task 2: consumer health search with ad hoc and spoken queries. In: Working Notes of Conference and Labs of the Evaluation (CLEF) Forum. CEUR Workshop Proceedings (2020)
10. Goeuriot, L., et al.: Overview of the CLEF eHealth evaluation lab 2020. In: Arampatzis, A., et al. (eds.) CLEF 2020. LNCS, vol. 12260, pp. 255–271. Springer, Cham (2020). https://doi.org/10.1007/978-3-030-58219-7_19
11. Huang, C.C., Lu, Z.: Community challenges in biomedical text mining over 10 years: success, failure and the future. Brief. Bioinform. **17**(1), 132–144 (2016)
12. Kelly, L., et al.: Overview of the CLEF eHealth evaluation lab 2016. In: Fuhr, N., et al. (eds.) CLEF 2016. LNCS, vol. 9822, pp. 255–266. Springer, Cham (2016). https://doi.org/10.1007/978-3-319-44564-9_24

13. Kelly, L., et al.: Overview of the ShARe/CLEF eHealth evaluation lab 2014. In: Kanoulas, E., et al. (eds.) CLEF 2014. LNCS, vol. 8685, pp. 172–191. Springer, Cham (2014). https://doi.org/10.1007/978-3-319-11382-1_17

14. Kelly, L., et al.: Overview of the CLEF eHealth evaluation lab 2019. In: Crestani, F., et al. (eds.) CLEF 2019. LNCS, vol. 11696, pp. 322–339. Springer, Cham (2019). https://doi.org/10.1007/978-3-030-28577-7_26

15. Makhoul, J., Kubala, F., Schwartz, R., Weischedel, R.: Performance measures for information extraction. In: Proceedings of DARPA Broadcast News Workshop, pp. 249–252 (1999)

16. McAllister, M., Dunn, G., Payne, K., Davies, L., Todd, C.: Patient empowerment: the need to consider it as a measurable patient-reported outcome for chronic conditions. BMC Health Serv. Res. **12**, 157 (2012)

17. Mukherjee, S., Weikum, G., Danescu-Niculescu-Mizil, C.: People on drugs: credibility of user statements in health communities. In: Proceedings of the 20th ACM SIGKDD International Conference on Knowledge Discovery and Data Mining, pp. 65–74 (2014)

18. Self, C.C.: Credibility. In: An Integrated Approach to Communication Theory and Research, pp. 449–470. Routledge (2014)

19. Suominen, H.: CLEFeHealth2012 – the CLEF 2012 workshop on cross-language evaluation of methods, applications, and resources for eHealth document analysis. In: Forner, P., Karlgren, J., Womser-Hacker, C., Ferro, N. (eds.) CLEF 2012 Working Notes. vol. 1178. CEUR Workshop Proceedings (CEUR-WS.org) (2012)

20. Suominen, H., Kelly, L., Goeuriot, L.: Scholarly influence of the conference and labs of the evaluation forum eHealth initiative: review and bibliometric study of the 2012 to 2017 outcomes. JMIR Res. Prot. **7**(7), e10961 (2018)

21. Suominen, H., Kelly, L., Goeuriot, L.: The scholarly impact and strategic intent of CLEF eHealth labs from 2012 to 2017. Information Retrieval Evaluation in a Changing World. TIRS, vol. 41, pp. 333–363. Springer, Cham (2019). https://doi.org/10.1007/978-3-030-22948-1_14

22. Suominen, H., et al.: Overview of the CLEF eHealth evaluation lab 2018. In: Bellot, P., et al. (eds.) Experimental IR Meets Multilinguality, Multimodality, and Interaction. LNCS, vol. 11018, pp. 286–301. Springer, Cham (2018). https://doi.org/10.1007/978-3-319-98932-7_26

23. Suominen, H., et al.: Overview of the ShARe/CLEF eHealth evaluation lab 2013. In: Forner, P., Müller, H., Paredes, R., Rosso, P., Stein, B. (eds.) CLEF 2013. LNCS, vol. 8138, pp. 212–231. Springer, Heidelberg (2013). https://doi.org/10.1007/978-3-642-40802-1_24

24. Viviani, M., Pasi, G.: A multi-criteria decision making approach for the assessment of information credibility in social media. In: Petrosino, A., Loia, V., Pedrycz, W. (eds.) WILF 2016. LNCS (LNAI), vol. 10147, pp. 197–207. Springer, Cham (2017). https://doi.org/10.1007/978-3-319-52962-2_17

25. Viviani, M., Pasi, G.: Credibility in social media: opinions, news, and health information–a survey. Wiley Interdisc. Rev. Data Min. Knowl. Discov. **7**(5), e1209 (2017)

LifeCLEF 2021 Teaser: Biodiversity Identification and Prediction Challenges

Alexis Joly[1](✉) , Hervé Goëau[2] , Elijah Cole[3] , Stefan Kahl[4],
Lukáš Picek[5] , Hervé Glotin[6] , Benjamin Deneu[1] ,
Maximilien Servajean[7] , Titouan Lorieul[8] , Willem-Pier Vellinga[9],
Pierre Bonnet[2] , Andrew M. Durso[10] , Rafael Ruiz de Castañeda[11] ,
Ivan Eggel[12], and Henning Müller[12]

[1] Inria, LIRMM, University of Montpellier, Montpellier, France
alexis.joly@inria.fr
[2] CIRAD, UMR AMAP, Montpellier, France
[3] Caltech, Pasadena, USA
[4] Center for Conservation Bioacoustics, Cornell Lab of Ornithology, Cornell
University, Ithaca, USA
[5] Dept. of Cybernetics, FAV, University of West Bohemia, Pilsen, Czechia
[6] Aix Marseille Univ, Université de Toulon, CNRS, LIS, DYNI, Marseille, France
herve.glotin@univ-tln.fr
[7] LIRMM, Université Paul Valéry, University of Montpellier, CNRS,
Montpellier, France
[8] INRA, UMR AMAP, Montpellier, France
[9] Xeno-canto Foundation, The Hague, The Netherlands
[10] Department of Biological Sciences,
Florida Gulf Coast University, Fort Myers, USA
[11] Institute of Global Health, Faculty of Medicine, University of Geneva,
Geneva, Switzerland
[12] HES-SO, Sierre, Switzerland

Abstract. Building accurate knowledge of the identity, the geographic distribution and the evolution of species is essential for the sustainable development of humanity, as well as for biodiversity conservation. However, the difficulty of identifying plants and animals in the field is hindering the aggregation of new data and knowledge. Identifying and naming living plants or animals is almost impossible for the general public and is often difficult even for professionals and naturalists. Bridging this gap is a key step towards enabling effective biodiversity monitoring systems. The LifeCLEF campaign, presented in this paper, has been promoting and evaluating advances in this domain since 2011. The 2021 edition proposes four data-oriented challenges related to the identification and prediction of biodiversity: (i) PlantCLEF: cross-domain plant identification based on herbarium sheets, (ii) BirdCLEF: bird species recognition in audio soundscapes, (iii) GeoLifeCLEF: location-based prediction of species based on environmental and occurrence data and (iv) Snake-CLEF: image-based snake identification.

Keywords: Biodiversity · Machine learning · AI · Species identification · Species prediction · Plant identification · Bird identification · Species distribution model · Snake identification

D. Hiemstra et al. (Eds.): ECIR 2021, LNCS 12657, pp. 601–607, 2021.
https://doi.org/10.1007/978-3-030-72240-1_70

1   Introduction

Accurately identifying organisms observed in the wild is an essential step in ecological studies. Unfortunately, observing and identifying living organisms requires high levels of expertise. For instance, plants alone account for more than 400,000 different species and the distinctions between them can be quite subtle. Since the Rio Conference of 1992, this *taxonomic gap* has been recognized as one of the major obstacles to the global implementation of the Convention on Biological Diversity [4]. In 2004, Gaston and O'Neill [12] discussed the potential of automated approaches for species identification. They suggested that, if the scientific community were able to (i) produce large training datasets, (ii) precisely evaluate error rates, (iii) scale up automated approaches, and (iv) detect novel species, then it would be possible to develop a generic automated species identification system that would open up new vistas for research in biology and related fields.

Since the publication of [12], automated species identification has been studied in many contexts [10,14,20–22,25,26,30]. This area continues to expand rapidly, particularly due to recent advances in deep learning [9,13,15,23,27–29]. In order to measure progress in a sustainable and repeatable way, the LifeCLEF [6] research platform was created in 2014 as a continuation and extension of the plant identification task [19] that had been run within the ImageCLEF lab [5] since 2011 [16–18]. LifeCLEF expanded the challenge by considering animals in addition to plants, and including audio and video content in addition to images. LifeCLEF 2021 consists of four challenges (PlantCLEF, BirdCLEF, GeoLifeCLEF, and SnakeCLEF), which we will now describe in turn.

2   PlantCLEF 2021 Challenge: Identifying Plant Pictures from Herbarium Sheets

Motivation: For several centuries, botanists have collected, catalogued and systematically stored plant specimens in herbaria. These physical specimens are used to study the variability of species, their phylogenetic relationship, their evolution, or phenological trends. One of the key step in the workflow of botanists and taxonomists is to find the herbarium sheets that correspond to a new specimen observed in the field. This task requires a high level of expertise and can be very tedious. Developing automated tools to facilitate this work is thus of crucial importance. More generally, this will help to convert these invaluable centuries-old materials into FAIR [8] data.

Data Collection: The task will rely on a large collection of more than 320,000 herbarium sheets used during the last PlantCLEF edition. The specimens were mostly collected in the Guiana shield and the Northern Amazon rainforest, focusing on about 1,000 plant species of the French Guiana flora. A valuable asset of this collection is that several herbarium sheets are accompanied by a few pictures of the same specimen in the field. New information such as morphological, ecological, phenological traits at the species level will be aggregated from various sources (EOL TraitBank, TRY Plant Trait Database, specimen annotations from "Herbier de Cayenne"), and will enrich the data collection this year.

Task Description: The challenge will be evaluated as a cross-domain classification task. The training set will consist of herbarium sheets whereas the test set will be composed of field pictures. To enable learning a mapping between the herbarium sheets domain and the field pictures domain, we will provide both herbarium sheets and field pictures for a subset of species. As was already anticipated in some promising methods evaluated in the last edition, morphological, ecological and phenological traits could potentially be directly integrated into the models and significantly improve the performances on this difficult task.

3   BirdCLEF 2021 Challenge: Bird Species Recognition in Audio Soundscapes

Motivation: Recognizing bird sounds in complex soundscapes is an important sampling tool that often helps to reduce the limitations of point counts. In the future, archives of recorded soundscapes will become increasingly valuable as the habitats in which they were recorded will be lost in the near future. This is already the case for soundscapes used for this competition and point counts to assess biodiversity from this particular location in South America will only be possible through soundscape analysis. It is imperative to develop new technologies that can cope with the increasing amount of audio data and that can help to accelerate the process of species diversity assessments. In the past few years, deep learning approaches have transformed the field of automated soundscape analysis. Yet, the results still lack reliability and submitted systems often yield very low scores particularly when the vocal density of species is high. The goal of this competition is to establish training and test datasets that can serve as real-world applicable evaluation scenarios and help the scientific community to advance their conservation efforts through automated bird sound recognition.

Data Collection: The 2021 dataset will closely resemble the previously used training and test data. However, we will establish a new subset of data to allow participants that are new to the evaluation campaign to quickly train and test their systems on an entry-level dataset. Training data will again be provided by the Xeno-canto community and will feature almost 1,000 bird species from three continents. The test data will contain expert annotated soundscapes with tens of thousands of labels and high overlap of bird vocalizations. The entry-level portion of the data will contain 20–50 species for training and soundscapes from a selected location in Germany with a runtime of only one hour. This approach reflects the feedback that we received from participants of the 2020 edition and we hope to attract more participating groups and a better turnout in terms of submitted runs and scores.

Task Description: The evaluation mode will closely resemble the 2020 test mode and we will use the same established metrics of class-wise and sample-wise mean average precision. However, we will alter the assessment of submitted results to better reflect false positives. The test data annotations have a coverage of 100% of all audio files and we will switch the evaluation mode to not only test for segments that have a label but also for segments that do not contain an annotation (e.g., nighttime recordings). Doing so will allow us to keep our current (well established) evaluation system in place while better reflecting real-world use cases.

4   GeoLifeCLEF 2021 Challenge: Location-Based Prediction of Species Based on Environmental and Occurrence Data

Motivation: Automatically predicting the list of species that are the most likely to be observed at a given location is useful for many scenarios in biodiversity informatics. First of all, it could improve species identification tools by reducing the list of candidate species that are observable at a given location (be they automated, semi-automated or based on classical field guides or flora). More generally, it could facilitate biodiversity inventories through the development of location-based recommendation services (typically on mobile phones), favor the involvement of non-expert nature observers, as well as accelerate the annotation or validation of species observed by non-experts to produce high quality datasets. Last but not least, it might serve educational purposes thanks to biodiversity discovery applications providing functionalities such as contextualized educational pathways.

Data Collection: The dataset used in 2020 [11] contained about 2 million plant and animal occurrences, each paired with high-resolution covariates (satellite, land cover, altitude) and environmental rasters (bioclimatic variables, soil type, etc.). This dataset of about 840GB took months to build and was delivered quite late to the participants. Training a model on it takes almost two weeks on a machine equipped with several modern GPUs. Last year, only two participants out of the 40 registered managed to submit runs. Therefore, we think it is necessary to keep the same dataset in 2021. However, to facilitate participation and foster consistent progress over last year, we will provide (i) new python tools and intermediate data formats facilitating the training of models, (ii) a validation set allowing participants to compare the performance they obtain with the one of the best method of last year, (iii) an entry-level subset of the whole dataset facilitating debugging before training large-scale models.

Task Description: Given the test set of locations (i.e. geo-coordinates) and corresponding high-resolution and environmental covariates, the goal of the task will be to return for each location a ranked list of species sorted according to the likelihood that they might have been observed at that location. The metric used will be the Average-30 accuracy [11].

5   SnakeCLEF 2021 Challenge: Image-Based Snake Identification

Motivation: Existence of a robust system for automatic snake species identification from photographs is essential for biodiversity conservation and global health. With over half a million victims of death and disability from venomous snakebite annually, understanding the global distribution of the more than 3800 snake species and differentiating species from images taken in developing countries could significantly improve epidemiology data and treatment outcomes. As the current snake image data is highly biased towards developed countries, the machine learning models trained with such data will most likely perform poorly on species with few or no images, many of which come from developing countries. To address this problem, we would like to improve the poor regularization for countries (or continents) with limited image data—mostly developing countries in Africa and Asia.

Data Collection: For this year's challenge, the same training dataset as the previous year will be used [24]. The most significant difference is related to the validation and test set. Both sets will be aligned with this competition's goal, following the uneven species distributions across all the countries included in the data. Additionally, the undisclosed test set will be extended with new data from 2020.

Task Description: given the set of images and corresponding two-level geographic locality information (country and continent), the task's goal will be to return for each image a ranked list of species sorted according to the likelihood that they are in the image and should have been observed at that location.

6   Timeline and Registration Instructions

All information about the timeline and participation in the challenges is provided on the LifeCLEF 2021 web pages [7]. The system used to run the challenges (registration, submission, leaderboard, etc.) is the AIcrowd platform [1].

7   Discussion and Conclusion

The long-term societal impact of boosting research on biodiversity informatics is difficult to overstate. To fully reach its objective, an evaluation campaign such as LifeCLEF requires a long-term research effort so as to (i) encourage non-incremental contributions, (ii) measure consistent performance gaps, (iii) progressively scale-up the problem and (iv), enable the emergence of a strong community. The 2021 edition of the lab will support this vision and will include the following innovations:

- The PlantCLEF task will be extended with traits information, i.e. structured tags or numerical values related to the morphological, ecological or phenological attributes of species.

– An entry-level dataset (in addition to the official data) will be delivered for
  the BirdCLEF task in order to allow new participants to quickly get results
  and progress more iteratively.
– New helper tools and more pre-formatted data will be provided for the Geo-
  LifeCLEF task in order to facilitate participation and build upon the best
  methods of previous year.
– New validation metric related to the country and continent level performance
  will be used to align with the SnakeCLEF goal - reliable performance in
  developing countries.

The results of this challenge will be published in the proceedings of the CLEF
2021 conference [3] and in the CEUR-WS workshop proceedings [2].

Acknowledgements. This work is supported in part by the SEAMED PACA project,
the SMILES project (ANR-18-CE40-0014), and an NSF Graduate Research Fellowship
(DGE-1745301). This work has received funding from the European Union's Horizon
2020 research and innovation program under grant agreement No 863463 (Cos4Cloud
project).

References

1. AICrowd. https://www.aicrowd.com/
2. CEUR-WS. http://ceur-ws.org/
3. CLEF 2021. https://clef2021.clef-initiative.eu/
4. Convention on Biodiversity. https://www.cbd.int/
5. ImageCLEF. http://www.imageclef.org/
6. LifeCLEF. http://www.lifeclef.org/
7. LifeCLEF 2021. https://www.imageclef.org/LifeCLEF2021
8. The FAIR Data Principles. https://www.force11.org/group/fairgroup/
   fairprinciples
9. Bonnet, P., et al.: Plant identification: experts vs. machines in the era of deep
   learning. In: Joly, A., Vrochidis, S., Karatzas, K., Karppinen, A., Bonnet, P. (eds.)
   Multimedia Tools and Applications for Environmental & Biodiversity Informatics.
   MSA, pp. 131–149. Springer, Cham (2018). https://doi.org/10.1007/978-3-319-
   76445-0_8
10. Cai, J., Ee, D., Pham, B., Roe, P., Zhang, J.: Sensor network for the monitoring of
    ecosystem: Bird species recognition. In: 3rd International Conference on Intelligent
    Sensors, Sensor Networks and Information, 2007. ISSNIP 2007 (2007). https://doi.
    org/10.1109/ISSNIP.2007.4496859
11. Cole, E., et al.: The geolifeclef 2020 dataset. arXiv preprint arXiv:2004.04192
    (2020)
12. Gaston, K.J., O'Neill, M.A.: Automated species identification: why not? Philosoph-
    ical Transactions of the Royal Society of London B: Biological Sciences **359**(1444),
    655–667 (2004)
13. Ghazi, M.M., Yanikoglu, B., Aptoula, E.: Plant identification using deep neural
    networks via optimization of transfer learning parameters. Neurocomputing **235**,
    228–235 (2017)

14. Glotin, H., LeCun, Y., Artiéres, T., Mallat, S., Tchernichovski, O., Halkias, X.: Proceedings of the Neural Information Processing Scaled for Bioacoustics, from Neurons to Big Data. NIPS International Conference on Tahoe USA (2013). http://sabiod.org/nips4b

15. Goeau, H., Bonnet, P., Joly, A.: Plant identification based on noisy web data: the amazing performance of deep learning (LifeCLEF 2017). In: CLEF 2017-Conference and Labs of the Evaluation Forum, pp. 1–13 (2017)

16. Goëau, H., et al.: The ImageCLEF 2013 plant identification task. In: CLEF. Valencia, Spain (2013)

17. Goëau, H., et al.: The ImageCLEF 2011 plant images classification task. In: CLEF 2011 (2011)

18. Goëau, H., et al.: ImageCLEF2012 plant images identification task. In: CLEF 2012, Rome (2012)

19. Goëau, H., et al.: The imageclef plant identification task 2013. In: Proceedings of the 2nd ACM International Workshop on Multimedia analysis for Ecological Data, pp. 23–28. ACM (2013)

20. ICML International Conference: Proceedings of the 1st workshop on Machine Learning for Bioacoustics - ICML4B (2013). http://sabiod.univ-tln.fr

21. Joly, A., et al.: Interactive plant identification based on social image data. Ecol. Inform. **23**, 22–34 (2014)

22. Lee, D.J., Schoenberger, R.B., Shiozawa, D., Xu, X., Zhan, P.: Contour matching for a fish recognition and migration-monitoring system. In: Optics East, pp. 37–48. International Society for Optics and Photonics (2004)

23. Lee, S.H., Chan, C.S., Remagnino, P.: Multi-organ plant classification based on convolutional and recurrent neural networks. IEEE Trans. Image Process. **27**(9), 4287–4301 (2018)

24. Picek, L., Ruiz De Castaneda, R., Durso, A.M., Sharada, P.: Overview of the snakeclef 2020: automatic snake species identification challenge. In: CLEF (Working Notes) (2020)

25. Towsey, M., Planitz, B., Nantes, A., Wimmer, J., Roe, P.: A toolbox for animal call recognition. Bioacoustics **21**(2), 107–125 (2012)

26. Trifa, V.M., Kirschel, A.N., Taylor, C.E., Vallejo, E.E.: Automated species recognition of antbirds in a Mexican rainforest using hidden Markov models. J. Acoust. Soc. Am. **123**, 2424 (2008)

27. Van Horn, G., et al.: The inaturalist species classification and detection dataset. In: CVPR (2018)

28. Wäldchen, J., Mäder, P.: Machine learning for image based species identification. Methods Ecol. Evol. **9**(11), 2216–2225 (2018)

29. Wäldchen, J., Rzanny, M., Seeland, M., Mäder, P.: Automated plant species identification–trends and future directions. PLoS Comput. Biol. **14**(4) (2018)

30. Yu, X., Wang, J., Kays, R., Jansen, P.A., Wang, T., Huang, T.: Automated identification of animal species in camera trap images. In: EURASIP Journal on Image and Video Processing (2013)

ChEMU 2021: Reaction Reference Resolution and Anaphora Resolution in Chemical Patents

Jiayuan He[1,3], Biaoyan Fang[1], Hiyori Yoshikawa[1,4], Yuan Li[1],
Saber A. Akhondi[2], Christian Druckenbrodt[5], Camilo Thorne[5], Zubair Afzal[2],
Zenan Zhai[1], Lawrence Cavedon[3], Trevor Cohn[1], Timothy Baldwin[1],
and Karin Verspoor[1,3(✉)]

[1] The University of Melbourne, Melbourne, Australia
[2] Elsevier B.V., Amsterdam, The Netherlands
[3] RMIT University, Melbourne, Australia
`karin.verspoor@rmit.edu.au`
[4] Fujitsu Laboratories Ltd., Kawasaki, Japan
[5] Elsevier Information Systems GmbH, Frankfurt am Main, Germany

Abstract. Chemical patents serve as an indispensable source of information about new discoveries of chemical compounds. The ChEMU (Cheminformatics Elsevier Melbourne University) lab addresses information extraction over chemical patents, and aims to advance the state of the art on this topic. ChEMU lab 2021, as part of the 12th Conference and Labs of the Evaluation Forum (CLEF-2021), will be the second ChEMU lab. ChEMU 2021 will provide two distinct tasks related to reference resolution in chemical patents. Task 1—Chemical Reaction Reference Resolution—focuses on paragraph-level references and aims to identify the chemical reactions or general conditions specified in one reaction description referred to by another. Task 2—Anaphora Resolution—focuses on expression-level references and aims to identify the reference relationships between expressions in chemical reaction descriptions. In this paper, we introduce ChEMU 2021, including its motivation, goals, tasks, resources, and evaluation framework.

Keywords: Reaction reference resolution · Anaphora resolution · Chemical patents · Text mining

1 Introduction

The discovery of new chemical compounds is perceived as a key driver of the chemical industry and many other industrial sectors, and information relevant for this discovery is found in chemical synthesis descriptions in natural language texts. In particular, patents serve as a critical source of information about new chemical compounds. Compared with journal publications, patents provide more timely and comprehensive information about new chemical compounds [1,4,18], since they are usually the first venues where new chemical compounds are disclosed. Despite the significant commercial and research value of the information

© Springer Nature Switzerland AG 2021
D. Hiemstra et al. (Eds.): ECIR 2021, LNCS 12657, pp. 608–615, 2021.
https://doi.org/10.1007/978-3-030-72240-1_71

in patents, manual extraction of such information is costly, considering the large volume of patents available [10,13]. Thus, developing automatic natural language processing (NLP) systems for chemical patents, which convert text corpora into structured knowledge about chemical compounds, has become a focus of recent research [11,14].

The ChEMU campaign focuses on information extraction tasks over chemical reactions in patents[1]. ChEMU 2020 [9,14] provided two information extraction tasks, named entity recognition (NER) and event extraction, and attracted 37 teams around the world to participate. In the ChEMU 2021 lab, we will provide two new information extraction tasks: chemical reaction reference resolution and anaphora resolution, focusing on reference resolution in chemical patents. Compared with previous shared tasks dealing with anaphora resolution, e.g., the CRAFT co-reference task [3], our proposed tasks extend the scope of reference resolution by considering reference relationships on both paragraph-level and expression-level (see Fig. 1). Specifically, our first task aims at the identification of reference relationships between reaction descriptions. Our second task aims at the identification of reference relationships between chemical expressions, including both co-reference and bridging. Moreover, we focus on chemical patents while the CRAFT co-reference task focused on journal articles.

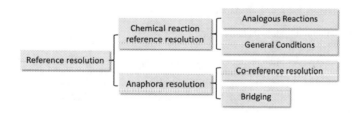

Fig. 1. Illustration of the task hierarchy.

The ChEMU lab 2021 will be a challenging opportunity for researchers to further improve the sophistication of information extraction systems for chemical patents. In this paper, we introduce our motivation and goals, a detailed description of the tasks, and our evaluation framework.

2   Related Shared Tasks

Several shared tasks have addressed reference resolution in scientific literature. BioNLP2011 hosted a subtask on protein co-reference [15]. CRAFT-CR 2019 hosted a subtask on co-reference resolution in biomedical articles [3]. However, these shared tasks differ from ours in several respects.

First, previous shared tasks considered different domains of scientific literature. For example, the dataset used in BioNLP2011 is derived from the GENIA

---

[1] Our main website is http://chemu.eng.unimelb.edu.au.

corpus [16], which primarily focuses on the biological domain, viz. gene/proteins and their regulations. The dataset used in CRAFT-CR co-reference shared task is based on biomedical journal articles in PubMed [2,5]. Our ChEMU shared task focuses by contrast on the domain of chemical patents. This difference entails the critical importance for this shared task: information extraction methodologies for general scientific literature or the biomedical domain will not be effective for chemical patents [12]. It is widely acknowledged that patents are written quite differently as compared with general scientific literature, resulting in substantially different linguistic properties. For example, patent authors may trade some clarity in wording for more protection of their intellectual property.

Secondly, our reference resolution tasks include both paragraph-level and entity-level reference phenomena. Our first task aims at identification of reference relationships between reaction descriptions, i.e., paragraph-level. This task is challenging because a reaction description may refer to an extremely remote reaction and thus requires processing of very long documents. Our second task aims at anaphora resolution, similarly to previous entity-level co-reference tasks. However, a key difference is that we extend the scope of this task by including both co-reference and bridging phenomena. That is, we not only aim at finding expressions referring to the same entity, but also expressions that are semantically related or associated.

3   Goals and Importance

The goals of ChEMU2021 are three-fold: We aim to (1) develop tasks that address fundamental challenges in automatic information extraction over chemical patents; (2) provide the community with a new dataset that can serve as benchmark datasets for future method development; and (3) advance the state-of-the-art technologies in information extraction over chemical patents together with worldwide NLP experts.

Our tasks provide an important opportunity for NLP experts to develop information extraction models for chemical patents and gain experience in analysing the linguistic properties of patent documents. The campaign will provide strong baselines as well as useful resources for future research in this area.

4   Tasks

Task 1: Chemical Reaction Reference Resolution. Given a reaction description, this task requires identifying references to other reactions that the reaction relates to, and to the general conditions that it depends on. Assume a set of reaction statements (RSs), each of which corresponds to a description of an individual chemical reaction or a general condition for the reaction. By identifying all the reference relationships amongst these reaction statements, the details of reactions can be fully specified by connecting related reaction statements. Two types of reference relationships are defined in this task, namely *Analogous Reactions* and *General Conditions*.

(a) Analogous reactions

ID	Text
RS1	**Prep. 2** 1(R)-Benzyl-6-methoxy-1(S)-(3-oxo-butyl)-3,4-dihydro-1H-naphthelen-2-one A solution of 62 g (0.23 mol) of the title product of Preparation 1 and 28 mL, ...
RS2	**Prep. 3** 1(S)-Benzyl-6-methoxy-1(R)-(3-oxo-butyl)-3,4-dihydro-1H-naphthelen-2-one **The title product of this preparation was prepared using a method analogous to Prep. 2**, using (R)-(+)-alphamethyl benzylamine in the initial imine formation ...

(b) General conditions

ID	Text
RS3	Preparation Examples (1) Step (A) 4-Bromobenzaldehyde and boronic acid were subjected to Suzuki cross coupling reaction using a palladium catalyst as shown in [Scheme 1a]... (2) Steps (B) and (C) ... (3) Preparation of salt ... 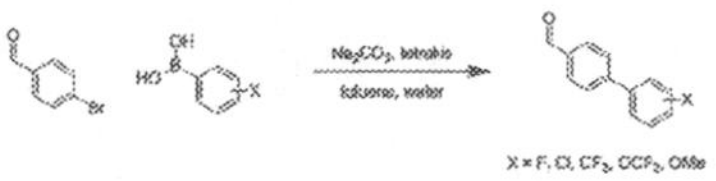
RS4	Example 1: Synthesis of (S)-2-(((2'-fluorobiphenyl-4-yl)methyl)amino) propanamide methanesulfonate White solid; yield: 90%; 1H NMR ...
RS5	Example 2: Synthesis of (S)-2-(((3'-fluorobiphenyl-4-yl)methyl)amino) propanamide methanesulfonate White solid; yield: 97%; 1H NMR ...

Fig. 2. Abbreviated examples of reaction references: (a) analogous reactions [6] and (b) general conditions [17].

Examples of the two types of reaction reference relationships are given in Fig. 2. In Fig. 2(a), the description of RS2 contains a statement "using a method analogous to Prep. 2" which is highlighted in bold. This indicates a reference relationship from RS2 to RS1. In Fig. 2(b), a standard procedure RS3 is first given. Unlike RS1 and RS2 in analogous reactions, RS3 is not associated with any specific reaction. In addition, Scheme 1a in the figure illustrates RS3 via Markush structures, with a variable X that can be replaced with several substructures. These indicate that the following chemical reactions RS4 and RS5 refer to this procedure. These two reactions should each be linked with their common procedure RS3.

Task 2: Anaphora Resolution. This task requires the resolution of general anaphoric dependencies between expressions in chemical patents. In this task, we define five types of anaphoric relationships, common in chemical patents:

1. *Co-reference*: two expressions/mentions that refer to the same entity.
2. *Transformed*: two chemical compound entities that are initially based on the same chemical components and have undergone possible changes through various conditions (e.g., pH and temperature).
3. *Reaction-associated*: the relationship between a chemical compound and its immediate sources via a mixing process. The immediate sources do need to be reagents, but they need to end up in the corresponding product. The source compounds retain their original chemical structure.

4. *Work-up*: the relationship between chemical compounds that were used for isolation or purification purposes, and their corresponding output products.
5. *Contained*: the association holding between chemical compounds and the related equipment in which they are placed. The direction of the relation is from the related equipment to the previous chemical compound.

[**Acetic acid (9.8 ml)**] and [**water (4.9 ml)**] were added to [**the solution**] in [**a flask**]. [**The mixture**]$_1$ was stirred for 3 hrs at 50°C and then cooled to 0°C . 2N-sodium hydroxide aqueous solution was added to [**the mixture**]$_2$ until the pH of [**the mixture**]$_3$ became 9. [**The mixture**]$_4$ was extracted with [**ethyl acetate**] for 3 times. [**The combined organic layer**] was washed with water and saturated aqueous sodium chloride.

ID	Relation type	Anaphor	Antecedent
AR1	Co-reference	[**The mixture**]$_4$	[**the mixture**]$_3$
AR2	Transformed	[**the mixture**]$_2$	[**The mixture**]$_1$
AR3	Reaction_associated	[**The mixture**]$_1$	[**water (4.9 ml)**]
AR4	Work-up	[**The combined organic layer**]	[**ethyl acetate**]
AR5	Contained	[**a flask**]	[**the solution**]

Fig. 3. Text snippet containing a chemical reaction, with its anaphoric relationships. The expressions that are involved are highlighted in **bold**. In the cases where several expressions have identical text form, subscripts are added according to their order of appearance.

Several anaphoric relationships can be extracted from the text snippet in Fig. 3. [**The mixture**]$_4$ and [**the mixture**]$_3$ refer to the same "mixture" and thus, form a co-reference relationship. The two expressions [**The mixture**]$_1$ and [**the mixture**]$_2$ are initially based on the same chemical components but the property of [**the mixture**]$_2$ changes after the "stir" and "cool" action. Thus, the two expressions should be linked as "Transformed". The expression [**The mixture**]$_1$ comes from mixing the chemical compounds prior to it, e.g., [**water (4.9 ml)**]. Thus, the two expressions are linked as "Reaction-associated". The expression [**The combined organic layer**] comes from the extraction of [**ethyl acetate**]. Thus, they are linked as "Work-up". Finally, the expression [**the solution**] is contained by the entity [**a flask**], and the two are linked as "Contained".

5   Data, Resources, and Evaluation

Dataset. A corpus extending the ChEMU 2020 dataset [19] is in development. The corpus contains patents from the European Patent Office and the United States Patent and Trademark Office, available in English in a digital format. The corpus is based on the Reaxys® database,[2] containing reaction entries for patent documents manually created by experts in chemistry.

---

[2] Reaxys® Copyright ©2020 Elsevier Limited except certain content provided by third parties. Reaxys is a trademark of Elsevier Limited. https://www.reaxys.com.

For Task 1, a collection of reaction descriptions will be provided with annotated reference relationships. A reaction entry in Reaxys has "locations" of the reaction in the corresponding patent document, mostly in terms of paragraph IDs. To date, a silver-standard dataset has been constructed using these locations and will be the foundation of a higher-quality gold-standard set. Existing work has established several baselines for this data [20].

For Task 2, the ChEMU-Ref corpus is in development [7,8]. This a collection of reaction snippets with the expression-level reference relationships annotated. A detailed annotation guideline has been developed; two chemical experts have been trained for the annotation task and annotation is in progress. Several baselines will also be made available, following [7].

Resources. A number of existing resources can be utilized by participants to develop their approaches to these tasks. These include the ChELMo pre-trained ELMo embeddings for chemical patents [21] and datasets for the ChEMU 2020 Named Entity Recognition and Event Extraction tasks [9,19].

Evaluation. For Task 1, we will use standard precision, recall, and F-score as our primary evaluation metrics. In addition, scores will be calculated for their *referrer detection* performance as well. This measure should reflect how well the model detects reactions that refer to at least one reaction description or a general condition.

In Task 2, we consider two types of co-reference linking, i.e., (1) surface co-reference linking and (2) atomic co-reference linking, due to the existence of *transitive co-reference relationships*. By transitive co-reference relationships we mean multi-hop co-reference such as a link from an expression T1 to T3 via an intermediate expression T2, viz., "T1→T2→T3". Surface co-reference linking will restrict attention to one-hop relationships, viz., to: "T1 ›T2" and "T2→T3". Whereas atomic co-reference linking will tackle co-reference between an anaphoric expression and its first antecedent, i.e., intermediate antecedents will be collapsed. Thus, these two links will be used for the above example, "T1→T3" and "T2→T3". Note that we only consider transitive linking in co-reference relationships. In addition, the criteria of both exact and relaxed text-span matching will be used. We will use F-score in terms of exact text-span matching and surface linking as the primary system ranking metric for Task 2.

6 Conclusions

In this paper, we introduced our upcoming lab ChEMU 2021. As the second instance of our ChEMU lab series, ChEMU 2021 will provide two new tasks focusing on reference resolution in chemical patents. Our first task aims at identification of reference relationships between chemical reaction descriptions, and our second task aims at identification of reference relationships between expressions in chemical reactions. We look forward to seeing innovative approaches to these complex tasks.

Acknowledgements. Funding for the ChEMU project is provided by an Australian Research Council Linkage Project, project number LP160101469, and Elsevier.

References

1. Akhondi, S.A., et al.: Automatic identification of relevant chemical compounds from patents. In: Database (2019)
2. Bada, M., et al.: Concept annotation in the CRAFT corpus. BMC Bioinform. **13**, 161 (2012). https://doi.org/10.1186/1471-2105-13-161. https://www.ncbi.nlm.nih.gov/pubmed/22776079
3. Baumgartner Jr, W.A., et al.: CRAFT shared tasks 2019 overview–integrated structure, semantics, and coreference. In: Proceedings of The 5th Workshop on BioNLP Open Shared Tasks, pp. 174–184 (2019)
4. Bregonje, M.: Patents: a unique source for scientific technical information in chemistry related industry? World Patent Inf. **27**(4), 309–315 (2005)
5. Cohen, K.B., et al.: Coreference annotation and resolution in the Colorado Richly Annotated Full Text (CRAFT) corpus of biomedical journal articles. BMC Bioinform. **18**(1), 1–14 (2017)
6. Dow, R.L., Liu, K.K.C., Morgan, B.P., Swick, A.G.: Glucocorticoid receptor modulators. European patent no. EP1175383B1 (2018)
7. Fang, B., Druckenbrodt, C., Akhondi, S.A., He, J., Baldwin, T., Verspoor, K.: ChEMU-Ref: a corpus for modeling anaphora resolution in the chemical domain. In: Proceedings of the 16th Conference of the European Chapter of the Association for Computational Linguistics. Association for Computational Linguistics, April 2021
8. Fang, B., et al.: ChEMU-ref dataset for modeling anaphora resolution in the chemical domain (2021). https://doi.org/10.17632/r28xxr6p92
9. He, J., et al.: Overview of ChEMU 2020: named entity recognition and event extraction of chemical reactions from patents. In: Arampatzis, A., et al. (eds.) CLEF 2020. LNCS, vol. 12260, pp. 237–254. Springer, Cham (2020). https://doi.org/10.1007/978-3-030-58219-7_18
10. Hu, M., Cinciruk, D., Walsh, J.M.: Improving automated patent claim parsing: dataset, system, and experiments. arXiv preprint arXiv:1605.01744 (2016)
11. Krallinger, M., Leitner, F., Rabal, O., Vazquez, M., Oyarzabal, J., Valencia, A.: CHEMDNER: the drugs and chemical names extraction challenge. J. Cheminform. **7**(S1), S1 (2015)
12. Lupu, M., Mayer, K., Kando, N., Trippe, A.J.: Current Challenges in Patent Information Retrieval, vol. 37. Springer, Heidelberg (2017). https://doi.org/10.1007/978-3-662-53817-3
13. Muresan, S., et al.: Making every SAR point count: the development of Chemistry Connect for the large-scale integration of structure and bioactivity data. Drug Discov. Today **16**(23-24), 1019–1030 (2011)
14. Nguyen, D.Q., et al.: ChEMU: named entity recognition and event extraction of chemical reactions from patents. In: Jose, J.M., et al. (eds.) ECIR 2020. LNCS, vol. 12036, pp. 572–579. Springer, Cham (2020). https://doi.org/10.1007/978-3-030-45442-5_74
15. Nguyen, N., Kim, J.D., Tsujii, J.: Overview of BioNLP 2011 protein coreference shared task. In: Proceedings of BioNLP Shared Task 2011 Workshop, pp. 74–82 (2011)

16. Ohta, T., Tateisi, Y., Kim, J.D., Mima, H., Tsujii, J.: The GENIA corpus: an annotated research abstract corpus in molecular biology domain. In: Proceedings of the Second International Conference on Human Language Technology Research, pp. 82–86 (2002)
17. Park, K.D., et al.: Alpha-aminoamide derivative compound and pharmaceutical composition comprising same. European patent no. EP3202759A1 (2017)
18. Senger, S., Bartek, L., Papadatos, G., Gaulton, A.: Managing expectations: assessment of chemistry databases generated by automated extraction of chemical structures from patents. J. Cheminform. **7**(1), 1–12 (2015)
19. Verspoor, K., et al.: ChEMU dataset for information extraction from chemical patents (2020). https://doi.org/10.17632/wy6745bjfj
20. Yoshikawa, H., et al.: Detecting chemical reactions in patents. In: Proceedings of the The 17th Annual Workshop of the Australasian Language Technology Association, pp. 100–110. Australasian Language Technology Association, Sydney, Australia, 4–6 December 2019. https://www.aclweb.org/anthology/U19-1014
21. Zhai, Z., et al.: Improving chemical named entity recognition in patents with contextualized word embeddings. In: Proceedings of the 18th BioNLP Workshop and Shared Task. pp. 328–338. Association for Computational Linguistics, Florence, Italy, August 2019. https://doi.org/10.18653/v1/W19-5035. https://www.aclweb.org/anthology/W19-5035

The 2021 ImageCLEF Benchmark: Multimedia Retrieval in Medical, Nature, Internet and Social Media Applications

Bogdan Ionescu[1(✉)], Henning Müller[2], Renaud Péteri[3], Asma Ben Abacha[4],
Dina Demner-Fushman[4], Sadid A. Hasan[12], Mourad Sarrouti[4], Obioma Pelka[5],
Christoph M. Friedrich[5], Alba G. Seco de Herrera[7], Janadhip Jacutprakart[7],
Vassili Kovalev[6], Serge Kozlovski[6], Vitali Liauchuk[14], Yashin Dicente Cid[13],
Jon Chamberlain[7], Adrian Clark[7], Antonio Campello[9], Hassan Moustahfid[8],
Thomas Oliver[8], Abigail Schulz[8], Paul Brie[10], Raul Berari[10], Dimitri Fichou[10],
Andrei Tauteanu[10], Mihai Dogariu[1], Liviu Daniel Stefan[1],
Mihai Gabriel Constantin[1], Jérôme Deshayes[11], and Adrian Popescu[11]

[1] University Politehnica of Bucharest, Bucharest, Romania
bogdan.ionescu@upb.ro
[2] University of Applied Sciences Western Switzerland (HES-SO),
Sierre, Switzerland
[3] La Rochelle University, La Rochelle, France
[4] National Library of Medicine, Bethesda, MD, USA
[5] University of Applied Sciences and Arts Dortmund, Dortmund, Germany
[6] Belarussian Academy of Sciences, Minsk, Belarus
[7] University of Essex, Colchester, UK
[8] NOAA/US IOOS, Silver Spring, MD, USA
[9] Wellcome Trust, London, UK
[10] teleportHQ, Cluj-Napoca, Romania
[11] Université Paris-Saclay, CEA, List, 91120 Palaiseau, France
[12] CVS Health, Wellesley, MA, USA
[13] University of Warwick, Coventry, UK
[14] United Institute of Informatics Problems, Minsk, Belarus

Abstract. This paper presents the ideas for the 2021 ImageCLEF lab that will be organized as part of the Conference and Labs of the Evaluation Forum—CLEF Labs 2021 in Bucharest, Romania. ImageCLEF is an ongoing evaluation initiative (active since 2003) that promotes the evaluation of technologies for annotation, indexing and retrieval of visual data with the aim of providing information access to large collections of images in various usage scenarios and domains. In 2021, the 19th edition of ImageCLEF will organize four main tasks: (i) a *Medical* task addressing visual question answering, a concept annotation and a tuberculosis classification task, (ii) a *Coral* task addressing the annotation and localisation of substrates in coral reef images, (iii) a *DrawnUI* task addressing the creation of websites from either a drawing or a screenshot by detecting the different elements present on the design and a new (iv) *Aware* task addressing the prediction of real-life consequences of online photo sharing. The strong participation in 2020, despite the COVID pandemic,

© Springer Nature Switzerland AG 2021
D. Hiemstra et al. (Eds.): ECIR 2021, LNCS 12657, pp. 616–623, 2021.
https://doi.org/10.1007/978-3-030-72240-1_72

with over 115 research groups registering and 40 submitting over 295 runs for the tasks shows an important interest in this benchmarking campaign. We expect the new tasks to attract at least as many researchers for 2021.

Keywords: User awareness · Medical image classification · Medical image understanding · Coral image annotation and classification · Recognition of hand drawn website UIs · ImageCLEF benchmarking · Annotated data

1   Introduction

The ImageCLEF evaluation campaign was started as part of the CLEF (Cross Language Evaluation Forum) in 2003 [6,7]. It has been held every year since then and delivered many results in the analysis and retrieval of images [12,15]. Medical tasks started in 2004 and have in some years been the majority of the tasks in ImageCLEF [10,11]. The objectives of ImageCLEF have always been the multilingual or language-independent analysis of visual content. A focus has often been on multimodal data sets, so combining images with structured information, free text or other information that helps in the decision making, usually based on real user needs [14].

Since 2018, ImageCLEF uses the crowdAI (now migrated to AIcrowd[1]) platform to distribute the data and receive the submitted results. The system allows having an online leader board and gives the possibility to keep data sets accessible beyond competition, including a continuous submission of runs and addition to the leader board.

Over the years, ImageCLEF and also CLEF have shown a strong scholarly impact that was captured in [20,21]. This underlines the importance of evaluation campaigns for disseminating best scientific practices. In the ImageCLEF 2020 campaign [11], 115 teams registered, 40 teams completed the tasks and submitted over 295 runs, despite the outbreak of the COVID-19 pandemic and lockdown during the benchmark. Although the number of registrations was lower than in 2019, the rate of the participants actually submitting runs increased by over 8%.

In the following, we introduce the four tasks that are planned for 2021[2], namely: ImageCLEFmedical, ImageCLEFcoral, ImageCLEFdrawnUI and the new ImageCLEFaware. Figure 1 captures with a few images the specificity of the tasks.

2   ImageCLEFmedical

The *concept detection task* concentrates on developing systems that are capable of predicting Unified Medical Language System (UMLS®) Concept Unique

---

[1] https://www.aicrowd.com/.
[2] http://clef2021.clef-initiative.eu/.

Identifiers (CUIs) on a given image. In 2021 the task will include a larger data set compared to 2020 [17]. The distributed corpus will be an extension of the Radiology Objects in Context (ROCO) [18] data set that originates from image-caption pairs extracted from the PubMed Central Open Access subset. The development data includes radiology images grouped into 7 sub-classes denoting the imaging acquisition technique with a corresponding set of concepts. In 2021, the data set will be manually curated to reduce the data variability, something that participants had asked for in previous editions. The automatically predicted concepts can be further adopted as first steps towards the *Medical Visual Question Answering (VQA-Med)* task.

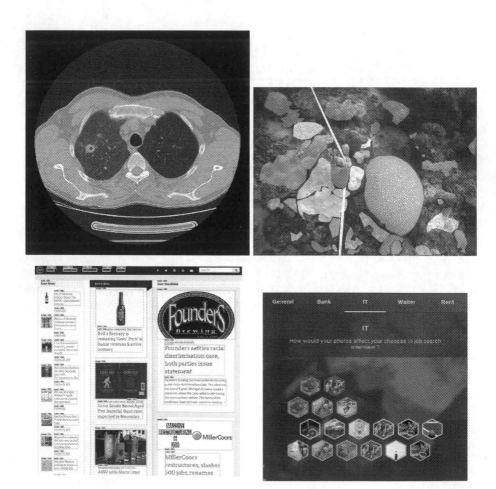

Fig. 1. Sample images from (left to right, top to bottom): ImageCLEFmedical with *(a slice of a chest CT with tuberculosis)*, ImageCLEFcoral with *(an example of an annotated coral reef image)*, ImageCLEFdrawnUI with recognition of UI elements from website screenshots, and ImageCLEFaware with an example of user photos and predicted influence when searching for an job in IT.

The Medical Visual Questions Answering task (VQA-Med [2]) will focus in 2021 on the most commonly performed radiology exams such as chest x-rays and will include two subtasks on visual question generation (VQG) and visual question answering (VQA). In this context, participants will be encouraged to use available resources in addition to the provided data in order to build robust VQG and VQA models. An additional objective will be to combine the concept detection task with the VQA task by using a common subset of radiology images.

The ImageCLEF tuberculosis task [13] will focus in 2021 on a larger data set than in 2020 and also on a larger number of concepts to extract for structured report generation. As in previous editions the task will use 3D Computed Tomography (CT) data of the chest. Lung masks will be supplied [8] and as in 2020 the report generation will be on a lung basis, so separate for left and right lung.

3   ImageCLEFcoral

The increasing use of structure-from-motion photogrammetry for modelling large-scale environments has driven the development of next-generation visualisation and analysis techniques. The main goal of the ImageCLEFcoral task since its first edition is to address this particular issue for monitoring coral reef structure and composition, in support of their conservation. In this third edition, it follows a similar format as in the previous editions [3,4] containing the same two subtasks with a few modifications. The two tasks are: *coral reef image annotation and localisation* and *coral reef image pixel-wise parsing*.

In the *coral reef image annotation and localisation* subtask, the participants are asked to annotate types of benthic fauna (substrate such as hard coral, soft coral, sponge, algae, etc.) in coral reef images using bounding boxes. In the *coral reef image pixel-wise parsing* subtask, participants need to submit a series of boundary image coordinates which form a single polygon around each identified substrate (see Fig. 1). In both tasks, the participants will also identify the substrate type annotated in each coral reef image. The performance of the submitted algorithms will be evaluated using the PASCAL VOC style metric of intersection over union (IoU) and the mean of pixel-wise accuracy per class.

Previous editions of ImageCLEFcoral in 2019 and 2020 showed improvements in task performance and promising results on cross-learning between images from different geographical regions. In 2021, the task continues to explore how cross-learning can improve performance by offering supplemental data sets the participants may wish to use, as well as increased training data for the task itself. In addition, the training and test data form the complete set of images required to form a 3D reconstruction of the environment. This allows the participants to explore novel probabilistic computer vision techniques based around image overlap and transposition of data points.

4   ImageCLEFdrawnUI

The increasing importance of User Interfaces (UIs) for companies highlights the need for novel ways of creating them. Currently, this activity can be slow and error prone due to the constant communication between the specialists involved in this field, e.g. designers and developers. The use of machine learning and automation can speed up this process and ease access to the digital space for companies who could not afford it with today's tools. A first step to build a bridge between developers and designers is to infer the intent from a hand drawn UI (wireframe) or from a web screenshot. This is done by detecting atomic UI elements, such as images, paragraphs, containers or buttons.

Inspired by recent progress of machine learning usage for UI creation [1,5], the previous edition of drawnUI challenged the participants to perform object detection on hand-drawn representations of websites (wireframes). The participant submissions offered promising results [9] and encouraged further extension of the task at hand.

In the 2021 edition, two tasks are proposed to the participants, both requiring them to detect rectangular bounding boxes corresponding to the UI elements from the images. The first task, *wireframe annotation*, is a continuation of the previous edition, where 1,000 more wireframes are added to the existing 3,000 images of the data set. These new images contain a bigger proportion of the rare classes to tackle the long tail problem found in the previous edition. For the second task we present the new challenge of *screenshot annotation*, where 10,000 screenshots of real websites were compiled into a data set by utilizing an in-house parser. Due to the nature of the web, the data set is noisy, e.g., some of the annotations correspond to invisible elements, while other elements have missing annotations. The training set will be provided without cleaning and will contain 8,000 images. The remaining images will be cleaned manually and split into validation and test subsets.

The performance of the algorithms will be evaluated using the standard Mean Average Precision over IoU 0.50 and recall over IoU 0.50.

5   ImageCLEFaware

Images constitute a large part of the content shared on social networks. Their disclosure is often related to a particular context and users are often unaware of the fact that, depending on their privacy status, images can be accessible to third parties and be used for purposes which were initially unforeseen. For instance, it is common practice for employers to search information about their future employees online. Another example of usage is that of automatic credit scoring based on online data. Most existing approaches that propose feedback about shared data focus on inferring user characteristics and their practical utility is rather limited. We hypothesize that user feedback is more efficient if conveyed through the real-life effects of data sharing. The objective of the task is to automatically score photographic user profiles in a series of situations with strong impact on her/his life. While potentially affected by bias, the proposed task mirrors common practices related to the reuse by third parties of user data shared on social networks and it is important for users to be made aware of such reuses.

This is the first edition of the task. A data set of 500 user profiles with 100 photos per profile will be created and annotated with an "appeal" score for a series of real-life situations via crowdsourcing. Participants to the experiment were asked to provide a global rating of each profile in each situation modeled using a 7-points Likert scale ranging from "strongly unappealing" to "strongly appealing". The averaged "appeal" score will be used to create a ground truth composed of ranked users in each modeled situation. User profiles are created by repurposing a subset of the YFCC100M dataset [19]. The set is split into train/validation/test and participants is provided with the train and validation parts along with the associated rankings. Participants are required to provide an automatic ranking for the test subset. The objective of the task is to produce an automatic ranking that is as closely correlated as possible to the manual ranking. Correlation is measured using a classical measure such as the Pearson correlation coefficient. More details about the constitution of the datasets and a first solution to solve the task are available in [16].

In accordance with GDPR, data minimization is applied and participants receive anonymized only the information necessary to carry out the task in an anonymized form. Resources include (i) anonymized visual concept ratings for each situation modeled; (ii) automatically extracted predictions for the images that compose the profiles. The final objective of the task is to integrate the most promising of the developed algorithms into YDSYO[3], a mobile app that provides situation-related feedback to users.

6   Conclusions

In this paper, we present an overview of the upcoming ImageCLEF 2021 campaign. ImageCLEF has organized many tasks in a variety of domains over the past 18 years, from general stock photography, medical and biodiversity data to multimodal lifelogging. The focus has always been on language independent or multi-lingual approaches and most often on multimodal data analysis. 2021 has a set of interesting tasks that are expected to again draw a large number of participants. As in 2020, the focus for 2021 has been on the diversity of applications and on creating clean data sets to provide a solid basis for the evaluations of machine learning approaches.

Acknowledgement. Part of this work is supported under the H2020 AI4Media "A European Excellence Centre for Media, Society and Democracy" project, contract #951911.

---

[3] https://ydsyo.app.

References

1. Beltramelli, T.: pix2code: generating code from a graphical user interface screenshot. In: Proceedings of the ACM SIGCHI Symposium on Engineering Interactive Computing Systems, pp. 1–9 (2018)
2. Ben Abacha, A., Datla, V.V., Hasan, S.A., Demner-Fushman, D., Müller, H.: Overview of the VQA-med task at imageCLEF 2020: visual question answering and generation in the medical domain. In: CLEF 2020 Working Notes. CEUR Workshop Proceedings, CEUR-WS.org, Thessaloniki, Greece, 22–25 September 2020
3. Chamberlain, J., Campello, A., Wright, J.P., Clift, L.G., Clark, A., García Seco de Herrera, A.: Overview of ImageCLEFcoral 2019 task. In: CLEF2019 Working Notes. CEUR Workshop Proceedings, Lugano, Switzerland, vol. 2380. CEUR-WS.org (2019). http://ceur-ws.org
4. Chamberlain, J., Campello, A., Wright, J.P., Clift, L.G., Clark, A., García Seco de Herrera, A.: Overview of the ImageCLEFcoral 2020 task: automated coral reef image annotation. In: CLEF2020 Working Notes. CEUR Workshop Proceedings, Thessaloniki, Greece, 22–25 September 2020, vol. 1166. CEUR-WS.org. http://ceur-ws.org
5. Chen, C., Su, T., Meng, G., Xing, Z., Liu, Y.: From UI Design Image to GUI Skeleton: a Neural Machine Translator to Bootstrap Mobile GUI Implementation. In: International Conference on Software Engineering, vol. 6 (2018)
6. Clough, P., Müller, H., Sanderson, M.: The CLEF 2004 cross-language image retrieval track. In: Peters, C., Clough, P., Gonzalo, J., Jones, G.J.F., Kluck, M., Magnini, B. (eds.) CLEF 2004. LNCS, vol. 3491, pp. 597–613. Springer, Heidelberg (2005). https://doi.org/10.1007/11519645_59
7. Clough, P., Sanderson, M.: The CLEF 2003 cross language image retrieval task. In: Proceedings of the Cross Language Evaluation Forum (CLEF 2003) (2004)
8. Dicente Cid, Y., Jiménez del Toro, O.A., Depeursinge, A., Müller, H.: Efficient and fully automatic segmentation of the lungs in CT volumes. In: Goksel, O., Jiménez del Toro, O.A., Foncubierta-Rodríguez, A., Müller, H. (eds.) Proceedings of the VISCERAL Anatomy Grand Challenge at the 2015 IEEE ISBI, pp. 31–35. CEUR Workshop Proceedings, CEUR-WS.org, May 2011. http://ceur-ws.org
9. Fichou, D., et al.: Overview of ImageCLEFdrawnUI 2020: the detection and recognition of hand drawn website UIs task. In: CLEF2020 Working Notes, CEUR Workshop Proceedings, Thessaloniki, CEUR-WS. org (2020)
10. Ionescu, B., et al.: ImageCLEF 2019: multimedia retrieval in medicine, lifelogging, security and nature. In: Crestani, F., et al. (eds.) CLEF 2019. LNCS, vol. 11696, pp. 358–386. Springer, Cham (2019). https://doi.org/10.1007/978-3-030-28577-7_28
11. Ionescu, B., et al.: Overview of the ImageCLEF 2020: multimedia retrieval in medical, lifelogging, nature, and internet applications. In: Arampatzis, A., et al. (eds.) CLEF 2020. LNCS, vol. 12260, pp. 311–341. Springer, Cham (2020). https://doi.org/10.1007/978-3-030-58219-7_22
12. Kalpathy-Cramer, J., et al.: Evaluating performance of biomedical image retrieval systems: overview of the medical image retrieval task at ImageCLEF 2004–2014. Computer. Med. Imaging Graph. **39**(0), 55–61 (2015)
13. Kozlovski, S., Liauchuk, V., Dicente Cid, Y., Tarasau, A., Kovalev, V., Müller, H.: Overview of ImageCLEFtuberculosis 2020 - automatic CT-based report generation. In: CLEF2020 Working Notes. CEUR Workshop Proceedings, Thessaloniki, Greece, 22–25 September 2020. CEUR-WS.org http://ceur-ws.org

14. Markonis, D., et al.: A survey on visual information search behavior and require-ments of radiologists. Methods Inf. Med. **51**(6), 539–548 (2012)
15. Müller, H., Clough, P., Deselaers, T., Caputo, B. (eds.): ImageCLEF - Experimen-tal Evaluation in Visual Information Retrieval. The Springer International Series On Information Retrieval, vol. 32. Springer, Heidelberg (2010). https://doi.org/10.1007/978-3-642-15181-1
16. Nguyen, V.K., Popescu, A., Deshayes-Chossart, J.: Unveiling real-life effects of online photo sharing. arXiv preprint arXiv:2012.13180 (2020)
17. Pelka, O., Friedrich, C.M., García Seco de Herrera, A., Müller, H.: Overview of the ImageCLEFmed 2020 concept prediction task: Medical image understanding. In: CLEF2020 Working Notes. CEUR Workshop Proceedings, vol. 1166. CEUR-WS.org, Thessaloniki, Greece, 22–25 September 2020
18. Pelka, O., Koitka, S., Rückert, J., Nensa, F., Friedrich, C.M.: Radiology objects in context (ROCO): a multimodal image dataset. In: Stoyanov, D., et al. (eds.) LABELS/CVII/STENT 2018. LNCS, vol. 11043, pp. 180–189. Springer, Cham (2018). https://doi.org/10.1007/978-3-030-01364-6_20
19. Thomee, B., et al.: Yfcc100m: the new data in multimedia research. Commun. ACM **59**(2), 64–73 (2016)
20. Tsikrika, T., de Herrera, A.G.S., Müller, H.: Assessing the scholarly impact of ImageCLEF. In: Forner, P., Gonzalo, J., Kekäläinen, J., Lalmas, M., de Rijke, M. (eds.) CLEF 2011. LNCS, vol. 6941, pp. 95–106. Springer, Heidelberg (2011). https://doi.org/10.1007/978-3-642-23708-9_12
21. Tsikrika, T., Larsen, B., Müller, H., Endrullis, S., Rahm, E.: The scholarly impact of CLEF (2000–2009). In: Forner, P., Müller, H., Paredes, R., Rosso, P., Stein, B. (eds.) CLEF 2013. LNCS, vol. 8138, pp. 1–12. Springer, Heidelberg (2013). https://doi.org/10.1007/978-3-642-40802-1_1

BioASQ at CLEF2021: Large-Scale Biomedical Semantic Indexing and Question Answering

Anastasia Krithara[1(✉)], Anastasios Nentidis[1,2], Georgios Paliouras[1],
Martin Krallinger[3], and Antonio Miranda[3]

[1] National Center for Scientific Research "Demokritos", Athens, Greece
{akrithara,tasosnent,paliourg}@iit.demokritos.gr
[2] Aristotle University of Thessaloniki, Thessaloniki, Greece
nentidis@csd.auth.gr
[3] Barcelona Supercomputing Center, Barcelona, Spain
{martin.krallinger,antonio.miranda}@bsc.es

Abstract. This paper describes the ninth edition of the BioASQ Challenge, which will run as an evaluation Lab in the context of CLEF2021. The aim of BioASQ is the promotion of systems and methods for highly precise biomedical information access. This is done through the organization of a series of challenges (shared tasks) on large-scale biomedical semantic indexing and question answering, where different teams develop systems that compete on the same demanding benchmark datasets that represent the real information needs of biomedical experts. In order to facilitate this information finding process, the BioASQ challenge introduced two complementary tasks: (a) the automated indexing of large volumes of unlabelled data, primarily scientific articles, with biomedical concepts, (b) the processing of biomedical questions and the generation of comprehensible answers. Rewarding the most competitive systems that outperform the state of the art, BioASQ manages to push the research frontier towards ensuring that the biomedical experts will have direct access to valuable knowledge.

Keywords: Biomedical information · Semantic indexing · Question answering

1 Introduction

BioASQ[1] is a series of international challenges (shared tasks) and workshops focusing on biomedical semantic indexing and question answering. The BioASQ challenges [8] are structured into complementary tasks and sub-tasks so that participating teams can focus on tasks relevant to their area of expertise, including hierarchical text classification, machine learning, information retrieval and multi-document summarization amongst many other areas.

---

[1] http://www.bioasq.org.

D. Hiemstra et al. (Eds.): ECIR 2021, LNCS 12657, pp. 624–630, 2021.
https://doi.org/10.1007/978-3-030-72240-1_73

As BioASQ consistently rewards highly precise biomedical information access systems developed by teams around the world, ensures that the biomedical experts eventually have more and more direct access to valuable knowledge that will help them avoid costly mistakes and provide high quality health services. BioASQ has reportedly had a very large impact, both in research and in industry; it has vastly helped advance the field of text mining in bioinformatics and has enabled researchers and practitioners to create novel computational models for life and health sciences. In addition a unique dataset of 3743 realistic questions and answers has been generated. The BioASQ challenge has been running on an annual basis since 2012, with more than 70 teams from 20 countries participating in its tasks. The workshop has been taking place in the CLEF conference till 2015. In 2016 and 2017 it took place in ACL, in conjunction with BioNLP. In 2018, it took place in EMNLP as an independent workshop. In 2019 the workshop was again an independent workshop in ECML conference. Last year (2020) the BioASQ workshop was part of CLEF.

2   BioASQ Evaluation Lab 2021

The BioASQ challenge assesses the performance of information systems in supporting the following tasks that are central in the biomedical question answering process: (a) the indexing of large volumes of unlabeled data, primarily scientific articles, with biomedical concepts (in English and Spanish), (b) the processing of biomedical questions and the generation of answers and supporting material. Both these tasks have been running since the first year of BioASQ. Since last year the semantic indexing of articles has been extended to the Spanish biomedical literature, by introducing the MESINESP task. This year, a new task is introduced, called BioASQ Synergy, which will allow biomedical experts to pose unanswered questions for developing problems, such as COVID-19. Therefore, the ninth BioASQ challenge will consist of the four tasks described in this section.

2.1   Task 9a: Large-Scale Biomedical Semantic Indexing

BioASQ Task A requires systems to automatically assign MeSH terms to biomedical articles added to the MEDLINE database, thus assisting the indexing of biomedical literature. In effect, this is a classification task that requires documents to be automatically classified into a hierarchy of classes. Systems participating in Task A are given newly published MEDLINE articles, before the NLM curators have assigned MeSH terms to them. The systems assign MeSH terms to the documents, which are then compared against the terms assigned by the NLM curators. As the manual annotations become gradually available, the scores of the systems are updated. In this manner, the evaluation of the systems is fully automated on the side of BioASQ and thus can run on a weekly basis throughout the year. The performance of the systems taking part in task 9a is assessed with a range of different measures. Some of them are variants of standard information retrieval measures for multi-label classification problems (e.g. precision, recall, f-measure, accuracy). Additionally, measures that use the MeSH hierarchy to provide a more refined estimate of the systems' performance are used. The official measures for identifying the winners of the task are micro-averaged F-measure (MiF) and the Lowest Common Ancestor F-measure (LCA-F) [2]. As this task can been considered as a extreme multi-label classification problem, additional evaluation measures are currently been considered to be used.

2.2   Task MESINESP9: Medical Semantic Indexing in Spanish

Since last year, the semantic indexing task has been extended for medical content published in Spanish. In this task, the participants are asked to classify new IBECS[2] and LILACS[3] documents in Spanish, before curators annotate them manually. The classes come from the MeSH hierarchy through the Health Sciences Descriptors (DeCS[4]) vocabulary. As new manual annotations become available, they are used to evaluate the classification performance of participating systems. The data from last year will be used as training/development, and three subsets for the test phase will be given to the participants, indexed with DeCS terms: Literature, medical Wikipedia, and Patent summaries. The BioASQ Task MESINESP is co-organized with the Barcelona Supercomputing Center. The provided dataset contains 369,368 records from 26,609 different journals. The responses of the systems in this task are evaluated with the same variety of flat evaluation measures used for task 9a [2], with the micro-averaged F-measure (MiF) as the official one.

2.3   Task 9b: Biomedical Question Answering

BioASQ task 9b takes place in two phases. In the first phase, the participants are given English questions formulated by biomedical experts. For each question, the participating systems have to retrieve relevant MEDLINE documents, relevant snippets (passages) of the documents, relevant concepts (from five designated ontologies), and relevant RDF triples (from the Linked Life Data platform). This is also a classification task that requires questions to be classified into classes from multiple hierarchies. Subsequently, in the second phase of task 9b, the participants are given some relevant documents and snippets that the experts themselves have identified (using tools developed in BioASQ [6]). In this phase, they are required to return 'exact' answers (e.g., names of particular diseases or genes, depending on the type of the question) and 'ideal' answers (a paragraph-sized summary of the most important information of the first phase for each question, regardless of its type).

---

[2] IBECS includes bibliographic references from scientific articles in health sciences published in Spanish journals. http://ibecs.isciii.es.

[3] LILACS is the most important and comprehensive index of scientific and technical literature of Latin America and the Caribbean. It includes 26 countries, 882 journals and 878,285 records, 464,451 of which are full texts https://lilacs.bvsalud.org.

[4] http://decs.bvs.br/I/decsweb2019.htm.

A training dataset of 3,743 biomedical questions will be available for participants of task 9b to train their systems and about 500 new biomedical questions, with corresponding golden annotations and answers, will be developed for the five testsets of task 9b. The responses of the systems are evaluated both automatically and manually by the experts employing a variety of evaluation measures [3]. In phase A, on the retrieval of relevant material, both ordered and unordered measures are calculated but the official evaluation is based on the Mean Average Precision (MAP). For the exact answers in phase B, different evaluation measures are used depending on the type of the question. For yes/no questions the official evaluation measure is the macro-averaged F-Measure on questions with answers *yes* and *no*. For factoid questions, where the participants are allowed to return up to five answers, the Mean Reciprocal Rank (MRR) is used. For List questions, the official measure is the mean F-Measure. Finally, for ideal answers, even though automatic evaluation measures are provided and semi-automatic measures [7] are also considered, the official evaluation is based on manual scores assigned by experts estimating the readability, recall, precision and repetition of each response provided by the participating systems.

2.4   BioASQ Synergy Task

The current BioASQ task B is structured in a sequence of phases. First comes the annotation phase; then with a partial overlap runs the challenge; and only when this is finished does the assessment phase start. This leads to minimal interaction between the experts and the participating systems, which is acceptable due to the nature of the questions that are generated. Namely, we are looking for interesting research questions that have a clear, undisputed answer.

This model is less suitable to developing biomedical research topics, such as the case of COVID-19, where new issues appear every day and most of them remain open for some time. A more interactive approach is needed for such cases, aiming at a synergy between the biomedical experts and the automated question answering systems. We envision such an approach as a continuous dialog, where experts issue open questions to the systems and the systems respond to the questions. Then, the experts assess the responses, and their assessment is fed back to the systems, in order to help improving them. Then, the process continues iteratively with new feedback and new system predictions. Figure 1 sketches this vision, which could take the form of a new BioASQ task, namely the BioASQ Synergy task. This new task will allow biomedical experts to pose unanswered questions for developing problems, such as COVID-19. Participating systems will attempt to provide answers, together with supporting material (relevant documents and snippets), which will in turn be assessed by the experts and fed back to the systems, together with new questions. Through this process, we aim to facilitate the incremental understanding of COVID-19 and contribute to the discovery of new solutions. At the same time, we are adapting the BioASQ infrastructure and expand the community to address new developing public health issues in the future. In each round of this task, we consider material from the current version of the COVID-19 Open Research Dataset (CORD-19).

Fig. 1. A continuous dialog between the experts and the systems is taking place.

Additionally, we expect the questions provided by experts to not have definite answers and, as a consequence, the answers to the questions to be more volatile. The evaluation of the systems will be based on the measures used in Task 9b. Nevertheless, as this is a new task, additional evaluation measures are examined, in order to capture the iterative nature of the task.

2.5   BioASQ Datasets and Tools

BioASQ uses for its tasks the real stream of articles provided by MEDLINE, while at the same time it employs a team of trained experts, who provide annually a set of 500 questions from their specialized field of expertise. Thus, in its eight years of operation, BioASQ has evaluated hundreds of systems from research teams around the world on hundreds of thousands of fresh biomedical publications. The dataset for the semantic indexing task include more than 14M articles from PubMed. Since last year, a dataset of Spanish semantically indexed articles has been created, which includes 369,368 records. Furthermore, a set of 3743 realistic questions and answers have been generated, constituting a unique resource for the development of question answering systems. This year, with the new Synergy task, an additional dataset with COVID-19 related questions and answers will be created. In addition, BioASQ has created a lively ecosystem, supported by tools and systems that facilitate research, such as the BioASQ Annotation Tool [6] for dataset development on question answering and a range of evaluation measures for automated assessment of system performance in all tasks. All software and data that are produced are open to the public[5]. It is worth mentioning, that this year we plan to create a repository, through which, several participating systems will also be available. This will allow new participants and teams, to build on existing models.

---

[5] https://github.com/bioasq.

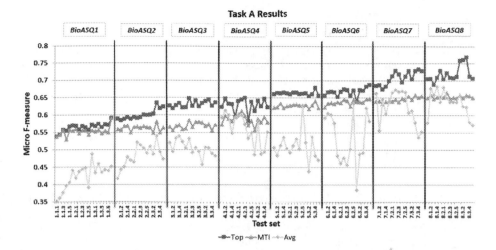

Fig. 2. Performance of the participating systems in task a, on semantic indexing. Each year, the participating systems push the state-of-the-art to higher levels

3   The Impact of BioASQ Results

BioASQ has reportedly had a very large impact, both in research and in industry; it has vastly helped advance the field of text mining in bioinformatics and has enabled researchers and practitioners to create novel computational models for life and health sciences. By bringing people together who work on the same benchmark data, BioASQ significantly facilitates the exchange and fusion of ideas and eventually accelerates progress in the field. For example, the Medical Text Indexer (MTI) [5], which is developed by the NLM to assist in the indexing of biomedical literature, has improved its performance by almost 10% in the last 8 years (Fig. 2). NLM has announced that improvement in MTI is largely due to the adoption of ideas from the systems that compete in the BioASQ challenge [4]. Recently, MTI has reached a performance level that allows it to be used in the fully automated indexing of articles of specific types [1].

Acknowledgments. Google is a proud sponsor of BioASQ in 2020. BioASQ is also sponsored by the Atypon Systems inc. BioASQ is grateful to NLM for providing the baselines for task 9a and to the CMU team for providing the baselines for task 9b. The MESINESP task is sponsored by the Spanish Plan for advancement of Language Technologies (Plan TL) and the Secretaría de Estado para el Avance Digital (SEAD). BioASQ is also grateful to LILACS, SCIELO and Biblioteca virtual en salud and Instituto de salud Carlos III for providing data for the MESINESP task.

References

1. Incorporating values for indexing method in medline/pubmed xml. https://www.nlm.nih.gov/pubs/techbull/ja18/ja18_indexing_method.html. Accessed 01 Oct 2019
2. Kosmopoulos, A., Partalas, I., Gaussier, E., Paliouras, G., Androutsopoulos, I.: Evaluation measures for hierarchical classification: a unified view and novel approaches. Data Min. Knowl. Discov. **29**(3), 820–865 (2015)
3. Malakasiotis, P., Pavlopoulos, I., Androutsopoulos, I., Nentidis, A.: Evaluation measures for task b. Tech. rep., BioASQ (2018). http://participants-area.bioasq.org/Tasks/b/eval_meas_2018
4. Mork, J., Aronson, A., Demner-Fushman, D.: 12 years on-is the NLM medical text indexer still useful and relevant? J. Biomed. Semant. **8**(1), 8 (2017)
5. Mork, J., Jimeno-Yepes, A., Aronson, A.: The NLM medical text indexer system for indexing biomedical literature (2013)
6. Ngomo, A.C.N., Heino, N., Speck, R., Ermilov, T., Tsatsaronis, G.: Annotation tool. Project deliverable D3.3 (2013). http://www.bioasq.org/sites/default/files/PublicDocuments/2013-D3.3-AnnotationTool.pdf. Accessed 02 2013
7. ShafieiBavani, E., Ebrahimi, M., Wong, R., Chen, F.: Summarization evaluation in the absence of human model summaries using the compositionality of word embeddings. In: Proceedings of the 27th International Conference on Computational Linguistics, pp. 905–914. Association for Computational Linguistics, Santa Fe (August 2018). https://www.aclweb.org/anthology/C18-1077
8. Tsatsaronis, G., et al.: An overview of the BIOASQ large-scale biomedical semantic indexing and question answering competition. BMC Bioinform. **16**, 138 (2015). https://doi.org/10.1186/s12859-015-0564-6

Advancing Math-Aware Search: The ARQMath-2 Lab at CLEF 2021

Behrooz Mansouri[1]($\boxtimes$), Anurag Agarwal[1], Douglas W. Oard[2], and Richard Zanibbi[1]

[1] Rochester Institute of Technology, Rochester, NY, USA
{bm3302,axasma,rxzvcs}@rit.edu
[2] University of Maryland, College Park, MD, USA
oard@umd.edu

Abstract. ARQMath-2 is a continuation of the ARQMath Lab at CLEF 2020, with two main tasks: (1) finding answers to mathematical questions among posted answers on a community question answering site (Math Stack Exchange), and (2) formula retrieval, where formulae in question posts serve as queries for formulae in earlier question and answer posts; the relevance of retrieved formulae considers the context of the posts in which query and retrieved formulae appear. The 2020 Lab created a large new test collection and established strong baselines for both tasks. Plans for ARQMath-2 includes extending the same test collection with additional topics, provision of standard components for optional use by teams new to the task, and post-hoc evaluation scripts to support tuning of new systems that did not contribute to the 2020 judgment pools.

Keywords: Community Question Answering · Formula retrieval · Mathematical Information Retrieval · Math-aware search

1 Introduction

The ARQMath lab [15] was established to support research on search using mathematical notation. With a number of Math Information Retrieval (MIR) systems having been introduced recently [4,7,10,13,16], a standard MIR benchmark is essential for understanding the behavior of their retrieval models and implementations. To that end, the first ARQMath produced a new collection, assessment protocols, parsing and evaluation tools, and a benchmark containing over 70 annotated topics for each of two tasks: math question answer retrieval, and formula retrieval.[1]

Effective question answering systems for math would be highly valuable for both math Community Question Answering (CQA) forums, and more broadly for the Web at large. Community Question Answering sites for mathematics such as Math Stack Exchange[2] (MSE) and Math Overflow [12] are widely-used resources.

---

[1] https://www.cs.rit.edu/~dprl/ARQMath.
[2] https://math.stackexchange.com.

© Springer Nature Switzerland AG 2021
D. Hiemstra et al. (Eds.): ECIR 2021, LNCS 12657, pp. 631–638, 2021.
https://doi.org/10.1007/978-3-030-72240-1_74

This indicates that there is great interest in finding answers to mathematical questions posed in natural language, using *both* text and mathematical notation. Moreover, a recent study found that retrieval effectiveness for mathematical queries submitted to a general-purpose search engine was much lower than for other queries [6].

ARQMath is the first shared-task evaluation of question answering for math. Using formulae and text in posts from Math Stack Exchange (MSE), participating systems are given a question, and asked to return potential answers. Relevance is determined by how well returned posts answer the provided question. Table 1 (left column) shows an example topic from Task 1, showing one answer assessed as relevant, and another assessed as non-relevant. The goal of Task 2 in ARQMath is retrieval of *visually distinct* formulae in decreasing relevance order, where the relevance of a visually distinct formula is the highest relevance of any assessed instance of that formula when judged in context. This task is illustrated in the right column of Table 1.

Before ARQMath, early benchmarks for math-aware search were developed through the National Institute of Informatics (NII) Testbeds and Community for Information Access Research (at NTCIR-10 [1], NTCIR-11 [2] and NTCIR-12 [14]). The Mathematical Information Retrieval (MathIR) at NTCIR included tasks for both structured "text + math" queries and isolated formula retrieval, using collections created from arXiv and Wikipedia. ARQMath complements the NTCIR test collections by introducing additional test collections based on naturally occurring questions, by assessing formula relevance in context, and by substantially increasing the number of topics.

ARQMath-2 will re-use the ARQMath 2020 collection, which consists of MSE posts from 2010 to 2018. ARQMath-1 topics disproportionately sampled commonly asked questions; in ARQMath-2 we plan to better balance topic development to include a greater range of novel questions. To facilitate participation of new teams we will provide some standard components (e.g., for computing formula similarity) that can easily be integrated with existing systems for ranked retrieval. ARQMath scoring in 2020 was designed for systems that had contributed to the judgment pools, but we are reworking the evaluation scripts to generate comparable scores for unjudged runs to support training and tuning learning to rank systems. We summarize the existing data and tools, the first edition of the ARQMath task, and planned changes for ARQMath-2 in the remainder of the paper.

2   The ARQMath Test Collection

The collection to be searched is comprised of question and answer posts from Math Stack Exchange (MSE). These postings are freely available as data dumps from the Internet Archive. The collection contains posts published from 2010 to 2018, a total of 1 million questions and 1.4 million answers. In ARQMath-1, posts from 2019 were used as a basis for topic construction. For ARQMath-2, posts from 2020 will be used for that purpose. The first criterion for selecting

Table 1. Example ARQMath queries and results.

Question answering (task 1)	Formula retrieval (task 2)
QUESTION (TOPIC A.4) I have the sum $$\sum_{k=0}^{n} \binom{n}{k} k$$ I know the result is $n2^{n-1}$ but I don't know how you get there. How does one even begin to simplify a sum like this that has binomial coefficients.	FORMULA QUERY (TOPIC B.4) $$\sum_{k=0}^{n} \binom{n}{k} k$$
RELEVANT (✓) You have to take the derivative of $$\sum_{i=0}^{n} \binom{n}{k} x^k = (1+x)^n$$ and then set x=1 in $$\sum_{i=0}^{n} k \binom{n}{k} x^{k-1} = n(1+x)^{n-1}$$	RELEVANT (✓) ... which can be obtained by manipulating the second derivative of $$\sum_{k=0}^{n} \binom{n}{k} z^k$$ and let $z = p/(1-p)$ ...
NON-RELEVANT (X) By your example, it seems that you're computing all the combinations of k elements of a set X having n elements. Intuitively, you wrote all possible strings, without considering the order (i.e. ab=ba as string) with the elements of X. Observe also that $\sum_{k=0}^{n} \binom{n}{k} = 2^n$, i.e. all the possible subsets of X.	NON-RELEVANT (X) Yes, it is in fact possible to sum this. The answer is $$\sum_{k=0}^{n} \binom{n}{k} \binom{m}{k} = \binom{m+n}{n}$$ assuming that $n \leq m$. This comes from the fact that ...

a topic is that the question contains at least one formula; with that constraint, nearly 240K questions are available for ARQMath-2 topic development.

Formulae. In the Internet Archive version of the collection, formulae are located between two '\$' or '\$\$' signs, or inside a 'math-container' tag. For ARQMath, all posts (and all MSE comments on those posts) have been processed to extract formulae, assigning a unique identifier to each formula instance. Each formula is represented in three ways to facilitate participation by teams without specialized expertise in mathematical notation processing: (a) as LaTeX strings, (b) as (appearance-based) Presentation MathML, and (c) as (operator tree) Content MathML.

The open source LaTeXML[3] tool used for converting LaTeX to MathML fails on some MSE formulae. Moreover, producing Content MathML from LaTeX requires inference, and is thus potentially errorful. As a result, the coverage

---

[3] https://dlmf.nist.gov/LaTeXML/.

of Presentation MathML for detected formulae in the ARQMath-1 collection was 92%, and the coverage for Content MathML was 90%. For ARQMath-2 we reduced the error rate to less than a percent for both representations, thus reducing the need for participating systems to fall back to processing the LaTeX string.

Files. As with any CQA task, the ARQMath collection contains more than just question and answer posts. We distribute the collection as four main files:

– **Posts.** The post file contains a unique identifier for each question or answer post, along with additional information such as creation date and creator (see Users below). Question posts contain both a title and a body (with the body holding the question itself) while answer posts have a body and the unique identifier of the associated question.
– **Comments.** Any post can have one or more comments, each having a unique id and the unique identifier of the associated post.
– **Votes.** This file provides information about positive or negative reactions to a post. Interestingly, no participating team in ARQMath-1 found this information to be helpful in their ranking algorithm.
– **Users.** Each poster or a question or an answer has a unique User ID and a reputation score.

Table 2. Relevance scores, ratings, and definitions for tasks 1 and 2.

TASK 1: QUESTION ANSWERING		
SCORE	RATING	DEFINITION
3	High	Sufficient to answer the complete question on its own
2	Medium	Provides some path towards the solution. This path might come from clarifying the question, or identifying steps towards a solution
1	Low	Provides information that could be useful for finding or interpreting an answer, or interpreting the question
0	Not relevant	Provides no information pertinent to the question or its answers. A post that restates the question without providing any new information is considered non-relevant
TASK 2: FORMULA RETRIEVAL		
SCORE	RATING	DEFINITION
3	High	Just as good as finding an exact match to the query formula would be
2	Medium	Useful but not as good as the original formula would be
1	Low	There is some chance of finding something useful
0	Not relevant	Not expected to be useful

3 Previous ARQMath Edition

The ARQMath-1 lab was part of the 2020 Conference and Labs of the Evaluation Forum (CLEF) [5,15].

3.1 Finding Answers to Math Questions

The primary task for ARQMath 2020 was answer retrieval, in which participants were presented with a question that had actually been asked on MSE in 2019, and were asked to return a ranked list of up to 1,000 answers from prior years (2010–2018). Participating teams ranked answer posts for 100 topics, 74 of which were assessed and used for the evaluation of participating systems. System results ('runs') were evaluated using the nDCG$'$ measure (read as "nDCG-prime") introduced by Sakai and Kando [11] as the primary measure for the task. This measure is simply Normalized Discounted Cumulative Gain (nDCG), but with unjudged documents removed before scoring. Table 2 summarizes the graded relevance scale used for assessment. Two additional measures, mAP$'$ and P@10, were also reported using binarized relevance judgments.

Five teams participated in ARQMath-1 task 1. Teams submitted up to 5 runs, with at least one designated as primary. For each primary run, for 5 additional organizer-provided baseline runs, and for any manual runs among those not designated as primary, the pooling depth was set to 50. A pool depth of 20 was used for other runs. The highest nDCG$'$ value (0.345) was achieved by the MathDowsers [9] team, while the highest mAP$'$ and P@10 was achieved by an oracle baseline built using links to related posts in the MSE collection (which were not available to the participating teams).

3.2 Formula Search

Formula search was run as an experimental task in ARQMath-1. The intent of the formula search task was similar to the Wikipedia Formula Browsing Task from NTCIR-12 [14], but with two novel innovations. First, relevance is defined differently: in NTCIR-12, formula queries were compared by assessors with retrieved formula instances, in isolation (i.e., the relevance of a retrieved formula was judged without access to the context in which that formula was found). In ARQMath, by contrast, both the formula query and a retrieved formula instance were presented to the assessor in context (in the question post and in an answer post, respectively). Second, in NTCIR-12 systems could receive credit for finding formula instances, whereas in ARQMath systems received credit for finding *visually distinct* formulae. In other words, an NTCIR-12 system that found identical formulae in two different documents and returned that formula twice would get credit (or be penalized twice), whereas an ARQMath system would receive credit (or be penalized) only once for each visually distinct formula that was retrieved. We implemented this by deduplicating submitted ranked lists based on the linearized Symbol Layout Trees produced from Presentation MathML by Tangent-S [3] where possible, and by comparing LaTeX strings otherwise.

Notably, the NTCIR-12 formula browsing task test collection had only 20 formula queries (plus 20 modified versions of the same formulae with wildcards added), whereas ARQMath-1 generated relevance judgments for 74 queries (45 of which were used for evaluation, with both those and the remaining 29 available for training future systems).

Table 2 also summarizes the graded relevance scale used for assessment. In this case, however, assessors are asked to assess formula instances, drawing upon the context provided by the question post from which the formula query was selected and a specific answer post in which the formula was found. The relevance of a *visually distinct* formula is then computed as the maximum over all assessed instances of that visually distinct formula. For efficiency reasons, we limit the number of instances of any visually distinct formula that were assessed to 5.

Four teams participated in ARQMath-1 Task 2, with submission and pooling protocols similar to those for Task 1. The single baseline system provided by the organizers (Tangent-S [3]) achieved the highest nDCG' value, while the DPRL team [8] obtained the highest mAP' and P@10 scores.

4   Changes for ARQMath-2

ARQMath-2 will include the same two tasks as ARQMath-1, with formula retrieval (Task 2) being promoted from an experimental task to a full task now that the evaluation details have been fully worked out.

For ARQMath-1 we restricted our selection of question posts for topic construction to those with at least one related post link to a question in the collection to be searched.[4] We did this to minimize the risk of investing assessment effort on topics that yielded no relevant documents. For ARQMath-2 we plan to remove this restriction, and instead guard against wasted assessment effort by doing a limited amount of pre-assessment for the results of an ARQMath-1 baseline system.

The scoring scripts for ARQMath-1 were designed to score participating systems, but to support training of ARQMath-2 systems we need to change the order of some of the processing. Rather than deduplicating by clustering submitted runs, we will instead cluster all formula instances in the collection, and then score every run using that single clustering. This will permit accurate *post hoc* assessment. We also plan to extend the number of submitted formula instances beyond 1000 so that adequately deep lists of visually distinct formulae will remain after deduplication. As with all of the tools and collections used in the lab, the new Task 2 scoring script will be available on the AQRMath GitHub page.[5]

---

[4] These links were not available to participants, although they were used to construct the oracle baseline system.

[5] https://github.com/ARQMath/ARQMathCode.

5   Conclusion

The ARQMath-2 lab at CLEF 2021 will be the second in what we plan to be a three-year series of labs aiming to advance the state-of-the-art for math-aware IR. As in the first edition, we have chosen to focus on answer retrieval for math questions as the first task, and formula search for the second. The same Math Stack Exchange collection will be used, both because the first task models an actual employment scenario, and because we expect that the continuity provided by that consistency will facilitate training and refinement of increasingly capable systems.

Acknowledgements. This material is based upon work supported by the Alfred P. Sloan Foundation under Grant No. G-2017-9827 and the National Science Foundation (USA) under Grant No. IIS-1717997.

References

1. Aizawa, A., Kohlhase, M., Ounis, I.: NTCIR-10 math pilot task overview. In: NTCIR (2013)
2. Aizawa, A., Kohlhase, M., Ounis, I., Schubotz, M.: NTCIR-11 math-2 task overview. In: NTCIR (2014)
3. Davila, K., Zanibbi, R.: Layout and semantics: combining representations for mathematical formula search. In: Proceedings of the 40th International ACM SIGIR Conference on Research and Development in Information Retrieval (2017)
4. Fraser, D., Kane, A., Tompa, F.W.: Choosing math features for BM25 ranking with Tangent-L. In: Proceedings of the ACM Symposium on Document Engineering (2018)
5. Mansouri, B., Agarwal, A., Oard, D., Zanibbi, R.: Finding old answers to new math questions: the ARQMath lab at CLEF 2020. In: Jose, J.M., et al. (eds.) ECIR 2020. LNCS, vol. 12036, pp. 564–571. Springer, Cham (2020). https://doi.org/10.1007/978-3-030-45442-5_73
6. Mansouri, B., Zanibbi, R., Oard, D.W.: Characterizing searches for mathematical concepts. IEEE (2019)
7. Mansouri, B., Rohatgi, S., Oard, D.W., Wu, J., Giles, C.L., Zanibbi, R.: Tangent-CFT: an embedding model for mathematical formulas. In: Proceedings of the ACM SIGIR International Conference on Theory of Information Retrieval (2019)
8. Mansouri, B., Oard, D.W., Zanibbi, R.: DPRL systems in the CLEF 2020 ARQMath lab. In: International Conference of the Cross-Language Evaluation Forum for European Languages (2020)
9. Yin Ki, N.G., et al.: Dowsing for answers with Tangent-L. In: International Conference of the Cross-Language Evaluation Forum for European Languages (2020)
10. Pfahler, L., Morik, K.: Semantic search in millions of equations. In: Proceedings of the 26th ACM SIGKDD International Conference on Knowledge Discovery & Data Mining (2020)
11. Sakai, T., Kando, N.: On information retrieval metrics designed for evaluation with incomplete relevance assessments. Inf. Retr. **11**, 447–470 (2008)
12. Tausczik, Y.R., Kittur, A., Kraut, R.E.: Collaborative problem solving: a study of MathOverflow. In: CSCW (2014)

13. Yasunaga, M., Lafferty, J.D.: TopicEq: a joint topic and mathematical equation model for scientific texts. In: Proceedings of the AAAI Conference on Artificial Intelligence (2019)
14. Zanibbi, R., Aizawa, A., Kohlhase, M., Ounis, I., Goran, T., Davila, K.: NTCIR-12 MathIR task overview. In: NTCIR (2016)
15. Zanibbi, R., Oard, D.W., Agarwal, A., Mansouri, B.: Overview of ARQMath 2020: CLEF lab on answer retrieval for questions on math. CLEF 2020. LNCS, vol. 12260, pp. 169–193. Springer, Cham (2020). https://doi.org/10.1007/978-3-030-58219-7_15
16. Zhong, W., Rohatgi, S., Wu, J., Giles, C.L., Zanibbi, R.: Accelerating substructure similarity search for formula retrieval. In: Jose, J.M., et al. (eds.) ECIR 2020. LNCS, vol. 12035, pp. 714–727. Springer, Cham (2020). https://doi.org/10.1007/978-3-030-45439-5_47

The CLEF-2021 CheckThat! Lab on Detecting Check-Worthy Claims, Previously Fact-Checked Claims, and Fake News

Preslav Nakov[1]([✉]), Giovanni Da San Martino[2], Tamer Elsayed[3],
Alberto Barrón-Cedeño[4], Rubén Míguez[6], Shaden Shaar[1], Firoj Alam[1],
Fatima Haouari[3], Maram Hasanain[3], Nikolay Babulkov[5], Alex Nikolov[5],
Gautam Kishore Shahi[7], Julia Maria Struß[8], and Thomas Mandl[9]

[1] Qatar Computing Research Institute, HBKU, Ar-Rayyan, Qatar
{pnakov,SShaar,fialam}@hbku.edu.qa
[2] University of Padova, Padova, Italy
dasan@math.unipd.it
[3] Qatar University, Doha, Qatar
{telsayed,200159617,maram.hasanain}@qu.edu.qa,
200159617@student.qu.edu.qa
[4] DIT, Università di Bologna, Forlì, Italy
a.barron@unibo.it
[5] Sofia University, Sofia, Bulgaria
babulkov@uni-sofia.bg, alex.nikolov@checkstep.com
[6] Newtral Media Audiovisual, Madrid, Spain
ruben.miguez@newtral.es
[7] University of Duisburg-Essen, Duisburg, Germany
gautam.shahi@uni-due.de
[8] University of Applied Sciences Potsdam, Potsdam, Germany
struss@fh-potsdam.de
[9] University of Hildesheim, Hildesheim, Germany
mandl@uni-hildesheim.de

Abstract. We describe the fourth edition of the CheckThat! Lab, part of the 2021 Cross-Language Evaluation Forum (CLEF). The lab evaluates technology supporting various tasks related to factuality, and it is offered in Arabic, Bulgarian, English, and Spanish. Task 1 asks to predict which tweets in a Twitter stream are worth fact-checking (focusing on COVID-19). Task 2 asks to determine whether a claim in a tweet can be verified using a set of previously fact-checked claims. Task 3 asks to predict the veracity of a target news article and its topical domain. The evaluation is carried out using mean average precision or precision at rank k for the ranking tasks, and F_1 for the classification tasks.

Keywords: Fake news · Fact-checking · Disinformation · Misinformation · Check-worthiness estimation · Verified claim retrieval · COVID-19

© Springer Nature Switzerland AG 2021
D. Hiemstra et al. (Eds.): ECIR 2021, LNCS 12657, pp. 639–649, 2021.
https://doi.org/10.1007/978-3-030-72240-1_75

1   Introduction

The mission of the CheckThat! lab is to foster the development of technology that would enable the automatic verification of claims. Automated systems for claim identification and verification can be very useful as supportive technology for investigative journalism, as they could provide help and guidance, thus saving time [20,32,34,58]. A system could automatically identify check-worthy claims, make sure they have not been fact-checked already by a reputable fact-checking organization, and then present them to a journalist for further analysis in a ranked list. Additionally, the system could identify documents that are potentially *useful* for humans to perform manual fact-checking of a claim, and it could also estimate a *veracity score* supported by evidence to increase the journalist's understanding and the trust in the system's decision.

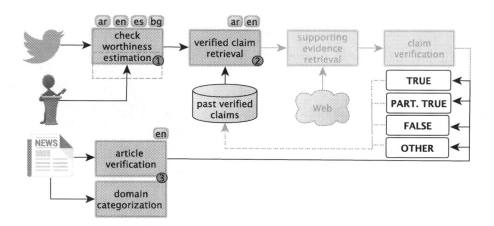

Fig. 1. The full verification pipeline. The lab covers three tasks from that pipeline: 1. check-worthiness estimation, 2. verified claim retrieval, and 3. fake news detection.

CheckThat! at CLEF 2021 is the fourth edition of the lab. The 2018 edition [43] of CheckThat! focused on the identification and verification of claims in political debates. The 2019 edition [18,19] featured political debates and isolated claims, in conjunction with a closed set of Web documents to retrieve evidence from. In 2020 [8], the focus was on social media—in particular on *Twitter*— as information posted on this platform is not checked by an authoritative entity before publication and such information tends to disseminate very quickly. Moreover, social media posts lack context due to their short length and conversational nature; thus, identifying a claim's context is sometimes key for enabling effective fact-checking [14].

In the new 2021 edition of the CheckThat! lab, we feature three tasks: 1. check-worthiness estimation, 2. detecting previously fact-checked claims, and 3. predicting the veracity of news articles and their domain. In these tasks, we focus on (*i*) *tweets*, (*ii*) *political debates and speeches*, and (*iii*) news articles. Moreover, besides English and Arabic, we extend our language coverage to Spanish and Bulgarian. We further add a new task on multi-class fake news detection for news articles and domain classification, which can help direct the article to the right fact-checking expert.

2   Description of the Tasks

The lab is organized around three tasks, each of which in turn has several subtasks. Figure 1 shows the full `CheckThat!` verification pipeline, with the three tasks we target this year highlighted.

2.1   Task 1: Check-Worthiness Estimation

Given a piece of text (e.g., a tweet or a sentence in a debate), detect whether it is worth fact-checking. In order to determine what is worth fact-checking, we either resort to the judgments of professional fact-checkers or we ask human annotators to answer several auxiliary questions [2,3], such as "does it contain a verifiable factual claim?", "is it harmful?" and "is it of general interest?", before deciding on the check-worthiness label.

– **Subtask 1A: Check-worthiness of tweets.** Given a tweet, predict whether it is worth fact-checking. This is a classification task, focusing on COVID-19 (and some other topics), and it is offered in Arabic, Bulgarian, English, and Spanish. The participants are free to work on any language(s) of their interest, and they can also use multilingual approaches that make use of all datasets for training.
– **Subtask 1B: Check-worthiness of debates/speeches.** Given a political debate/speech, produce a ranked list of its sentences, ordered by their check-worthiness. This is a ranking task, and it is only offered in English.

2.2   Task 2: Detecting Previously Fact-Checked Claims

Given a check-worthy claim in the form of a tweet, and a set of previously fact-checked claims, rank the previously fact-checked claims in order of usefulness to fact-check the input claim.

– **Subtask 2A: Detect previously fact-checked claims from tweets.** Given a tweet, detect whether the claim the tweet makes was previously fact-checked with respect to a collection of fact-checked claims. The task is offered in Arabic and English. This is a ranking task, where the systems are asked to produce a list of top-n candidates.
– **Subtask 2B: Detect previously fact-checked claims in political debates/speeches.** Given a claim in a political debate or a speech, detect whether the claim has been previously fact-checked with respect to a collection of previously fact-checked claims. This is a ranking task, and it is offered in English only.

2.3 Task 3: Fake News Detection

Given the text of a news article, determine whether the claims made in the article are true, partially true, false or other (e.g., claims in dispute or unchecked) and also detect the topical domain of the article [52,53].

- **Subtask 3A: Multi-class fake news detection of news articles.** This task is a four-class classification problem, offered in English. Given the text of a news article, determine whether the claims made in the article are *true*, *partially true*, *false*, or *other*.
- **Subtask 3B: Given the text of a news article, determine the topical domain of the article.** This is a classification task to determine the topic of a news article [54], and it is offered in English.

3 Datasets

3.1 Task 1: Check-Worthiness Estimation

- **Subtask 1A: Check-worthiness for tweets.** For **English** we have 900 labeled examples from 2020, which we use for training, and we add 200 more examples for testing. For **Arabic**, we have 7,500 labeled examples, and we add 2,500 new tweets for testing. For **Bulgarian**, we have a new dataset of 2,000 tweets for training and 200 for testing. For **Spanish**, we have a new dataset of 3,700 tweets for training and 500 for testing, coming from 300 Spanish political accounts. The datasets for Arabic, Bulgarian, and English focus on COVID-19 and have annotations for some auxiliary questions.
- **Subtask 1B: Check-worthiness for debates/speeches.** We have a dataset of 70 debates/speeches and 64,000 sentences for training from 2020, and we add a new test set of 20 new debates/speeches and 20,000 new sentences (all in English).

3.2 Task 2: Detecting Previously Fact-Checked Claims

- **Subtask 2A: Detecting previously fact-checked claims from tweets.** For English, we have 1,200 annotated examples from Snopes from CLEF-2020, to which we add new development and test datasets from PolitiFact, to perform evaluation in a cross-domain setup. For Arabic, we have claims from two popular Arabic fact-checking platforms [28], and we are extending our claims collection with data from additional trusted Arabic fact-checking websites. We collect corresponding tweets either from fact-checking sources which usually present a list of tweets that contain a paraphrase of the target claim, or by interactive search over Twitter or existing tweet datasets, e.g., ArCOV-19 [27].
- **Subtask 2B: Detecting previously fact-checked claims in political debates/speeches.** We have 1,000 annotated claims for training [50], and a new set of 200 examples for testing.

3.3   Task 3: Fake News Detection

– **Subtask 3A: Multi-class fake news categorization of news articles.**
We collected 4,000 news articles for training and 500 news articles for testing; this is work in collaboration with a fact-checking organization. This task is offered in English only.

– **Subtask 3B: Topical domain identification of news articles (English):** We are annotating a subset of the articles from subtask 3A with their domain, to be used for training and testing. This task is also offered in English only.

4   Evaluation

For the ranking tasks, as in the two previous editions, we use *Mean Average Precision* (MAP) as the official evaluation measure; we further calculate and report reciprocal rank, and $P@k$ for $k \in \{1, 3, 5, 10, 20, 30\}$. For the classification tasks, we use accuracy and F1 measure.

5   Previously on CheckThat!

Three editions of CheckThat! have been held so far, and some of the tasks in the 2021 edition are reformulated from previous editions. Hence, considering the most successful approaches applied in the past is a good starting point to address the new challenges. Below we discuss some relevant tasks from previous years.

5.1   CheckThat! 2020

Task 1$_{2020}$. *Given a topic and a stream of potentially-related tweets, rank the tweets by check-worthiness for the topic* [30,51]. The most successful runs adopted state-of-the-art transformers models. The top-ranked teams for the English version of this task used BERT [15] and RoBERTa [46,59]. For the Arabic version, the top systems used AraBERT [36,59] and the multilingual BERT [29].

Task 2$_{2020}$. *Given a check-worthy claim and a dataset of verified claims, rank the verified claims, so that those that verify the input claim (or a sub-claim in it) are ranked on top* [51]. The most effective approaches fine-tuned BERT and its variants. For example, the top-ranked run fine-tuned RoBERTa [10].

Task 4$_{2020}$. *Given a check-worthy claim on a specific topic and a set of potentially-relevant Web pages, predict the veracity of the claim* [30]. Two runs were submitted to the task [57], using a scoring function that computes the degree of concordance and negation between a claim and all input text snippets for that claim.

Task 5$_{2020}$. *Given a debate segmented into sentences, together with speaker information, prioritize sentences for fact-checking* [51]. Only one out of 8 runs outperformed a strong bi-LSTM baseline [38].

5.2   CheckThat! 2019

Task 1 $_{2019}$. Given a political debate, interview, or speech, segmented into sentences, rank the sentences by the priority with which they should be fact-checked [5]. The most successful approaches used neural networks for the individual classification of the instances. For example, Hansen et al. [26] learned domain-specific word embeddings and syntactic dependencies and applied an LSTM classifier.

Task 2 $_{2019}$. Given a claim and a set of potentially relevant Web pages, identify which of the pages (and passages thereof) are useful for assisting a human in fact-checking the claim. Finally, determine the factuality of the claim [31]. The most effective approach used textual entailment and external data [21].

5.3   CheckThat! 2018

Task 1 $_{2018}$ [4] was identical to Task 1_{2019}. The best approaches used *pseudo-speeches* as a concatenation of all interventions by a debater [62], and represented the entries with embeddings, part-of-speech tags, and syntactic dependencies [25].

Task 2 $_{2018}$. Given a check-worthy claim in the form of a (transcribed) sentence, determine whether the claim is likely to be true, half-true, or false [9]. The best approach retrieved relevant information from the Web, and fed the claim with the most similar Web-retrieved text to a convolutional neural network [25].

6   Related Work

There has been work on checking the factuality/credibility of a claim, of a news article, or of an information source [6, 7, 35, 37, 42, 45, 49, 61]. Claims can come from different sources, but special attention has been given to those from social media [23, 40, 55, 60]. Check-worthiness estimation is still a fairly-new problem especially in the context of social media [20, 32–34]. A lot of research was done in fake news detection for news articles, which is mostly approached as a binary classification problem [47].

CheckThat! is related to several other initiatives at SemEval on determining rumour veracity and support for rumours [17, 22], on stance detection [41], on fact-checking in community question answering forums [39], on propaganda detection [16], and on semantic textual similarity [1, 44]. It is also related to the FEVER task [56] on fact extraction and verification, as well as to the Fake News Challenge [24], and the FakeNews task at MediaEval [48].

7   Conclusion

We have presented the 2021 edition of the CheckThat! Lab, which features tasks that span the full verification pipeline: from spotting check-worthy claims to checking whether they have been fact-checked elsewhere before. We further feature a fact-checking task, and we also check the class and the topical domain of news articles. Last but not least, in-line with the general mission of CLEF, we promote multi-linguality by offering our tasks in different languages.

Acknowledgments. The work of Tamer Elsayed and Maram Hasanain is made possible by NPRP grant #NPRP-11S-1204-170060 from the Qatar National Research Fund (a member of Qatar Foundation). The work of Fatima Haouari is supported by GSRA grant #GSRA6-1-0611-19074 from the Qatar National Research Fund. The statements made herein are solely the responsibility of the authors.

This research is also part of the Tanbih mega-project, developed at the Qatar Computing Research Institute, HBKU, which aims to limit the effect of "fake news", propaganda, and media bias.

References

1. Agirre, E., et al.: SemEval-2016 task 1: Semantic textual similarity, monolingual and cross-lingual evaluation. In: Proceedings of the 10th International Workshop on Semantic Evaluation, SemEval 2016, pp. 497–511 (2016)
2. Alam, F., et al.: Fighting the COVID-19 infodemic in social media: a holistic perspective and a call to arms. ArXiv preprint 2007.07996 (2020)
3. Alam, F., et al.: Fighting the COVID-19 infodemic: modeling the perspective of journalists, fact-checkers, social media platforms, policy makers, and the society. ArXiv preprint 2005.00033 (2020)
4. Atanasova, P., et al.: Overview of the CLEF-2018 CheckThat! lab on automatic identification and verification of political claims. Task 1: Check-worthiness. In: Cappellato, L., Ferro, N., Nie, J.Y., Soulier, L. (eds.) Working Notes of CLEF 2018-Conference and Labs of the Evaluation Forum. CEUR Workshop Proceedings. CEUR-WS.org (2018)
5. Atanasova, P., Nakov, P., Karadzhov, G., Mohtarami, M., Da San Martino, G.: Overview of the CLEF-2019 CheckThat! lab on automatic identification and verification of claims. Task 1: Check-worthiness. In: Cappellato, L., Ferro, N., Losada, D., Müller, H. (eds.) Working Notes of CLEF 2019 Conference and Labs of the Evaluation Forum. CEUR Workshop Proceedings. CEUR-WS.org (2019)
6. Ba, M.L., Berti-Equille, L., Shah, K., Hammady, H.M.: VERA: a platform for veracity estimation over web data. In: Proceedings of the 25th International Conference on World Wide Web, WWW 2016, pp. 159–162 (2016)
7. Baly, R., et al.: What was written vs. who read it: news media profiling using text analysis and social media context. In: Proceedings of the 58th Annual Meeting of the Association for Computational Linguistics, ACL 2020, pp. 3364–3374 (2020)
8. Barrón-Cedeño, A., et al.: Overview of CheckThat! 2020 - automatic identification and verification of claims in social media. In: Proceedings of the 11th International Conference of the CLEF Association: Experimental IR Meets Multilinguality, Multimodality, and Interaction, CLEF 2020, pp. 215–236 (2020)
9. Barrón-Cedeño, A., et al.: Overview of the CLEF-2018 CheckThat! lab on automatic identification and verification of political claims. Task 2: Factuality. In: Cappellato, L., Ferro, N., Nie, J.Y., Soulier, L. (eds.) Working Notes of CLEF 2018-Conference and Labs of the Evaluation Forum. CEUR Workshop Proceedings. CEUR-WS.org (2018)

10. Bouziane, M., Perrin, H., Cluzeau, A., Mardas, J., Sadeq, A.: Buster.AI at Check-That! 2020: Insights and recommendations to improve fact-checking. In: Cappellato, L., Eickhoff, C., Ferro, N., Névéol, A. (eds.) CLEF 2020 Working Notes. CEUR Workshop Proceedings, CEUR-WS.org (2020)

11. Cappellato, L., Eickhoff, C., Ferro, N., Névéol, A. (eds.): CLEF 2020 Working Notes. CEUR Workshop Proceedings, CEUR-WS.org (2020)

12. Cappellato, L., Ferro, N., Losada, D., Müller, H. (eds.): Working Notes of CLEF 2019 Conference and Labs of the Evaluation Forum. CEUR Workshop Proceedings. CEUR-WS.org (2019)

13. Cappellato, L., Ferro, N., Nie, J.Y., Soulier, L. (eds.): Working Notes of CLEF 2018-Conference and Labs of the Evaluation Forum. CEUR Workshop Proceedings. CEUR-WS.org (2018)

14. Cazalens, S., Lamarre, P., Leblay, J., Manolescu, I., Tannier, X.: A content management perspective on fact-checking. Proceedings of the International Conference on World Wide Web, WWW 2018, pp. 565–574 (2018)

15. Cheema, G.S., Hakimov, S., Ewerth, R.: Check_square at CheckThat! 2020: Claim detection in social media via fusion of transformer and syntactic features. In: Cappellato, L., Eickhoff, C., Ferro, N., Névéol, A. (eds.) CLEF 2020 Working Notes. CEUR Workshop Proceedings, CEUR-WS.org (2020)

16. Da San Martino, G., Barrón-Cedeno, A., Wachsmuth, H., Petrov, R., Nakov, P.: SemEval-2020 task 11: detection of propaganda techniques in news articles. In: Proceedings of the 14th Workshop on Semantic Evaluation, SemEval 2020, pp. 1377–1414 (2020)

17. Derczynski, L., Bontcheva, K., Liakata, M., Procter, R., Wong Sak Hoi, G., Zubiaga, A.: SemEval-2017 task 8: RumourEval: determining rumour veracity and support for rumours. In: Proceedings of the 11th International Workshop on Semantic Evaluation, SemEval 2017, pp. 69–76 (2017)

18. Elsayed, T., et al.: CheckThat! at CLEF 2019: automatic identification and verification of claims. In: Advances in Information Retrieval, pp. 309–315 (2019)

19. Elsayed, T., et al.: Overview of the CLEF-2019 CheckThat! lab: automatic identification and verification of claims. In: Crestani, F., et al. (eds.) CLEF 2019. LNCS, vol. 11696, pp. 301–321. Springer, Cham (2019). https://doi.org/10.1007/978-3-030-28577-7_25

20. Gencheva, P., Nakov, P., Màrquez, L., Barrón-Cedeño, A., Koychev, I.: A context-aware approach for detecting worth-checking claims in political debates. In: Proceedings of the International Conference Recent Advances in Natural Language Processing, RANLP 2017, pp. 267–276 (2017)

21. Ghanem, B., Glavaš, G., Giachanou, A., Ponzetto, S., Rosso, P., Rangel, F.: UPV-UMA at CheckThat! lab: verifying Arabic claims using cross lingual approach. In: Cappellato, L., Ferro, N., Losada, D., Müller, H. (eds.) Working Notes of CLEF 2019 Conference and Labs of the Evaluation Forum. CEUR Workshop Proceedings. CEUR-WS.org (2019)

22. Gorrell, G., et al.SemEval-2019 task 7: rumourEval, determining rumour veracity and support for rumours. In: Proceedings of the 13th International Workshop on Semantic Evaluation, SemEval 2019, pp. 845–854 (2019)

23. Gupta, A., Kumaraguru, P., Castillo, C., Meier, P.: TweetCred: real-time credibility assessment of content on twitter. In: Aiello, L.M., McFarland, D. (eds.) SocInfo 2014. LNCS, vol. 8851, pp. 228–243. Springer, Cham (2014). https://doi.org/10.1007/978-3-319-13734-6_16

24. Hanselowski, A., et al.: A retrospective analysis of the fake news challenge stance-detection task. In: Proceedings of the 27th International Conference on Computational Linguistics, COLING 2018, pp. 1859–1874 (2018)

25. Hansen, C., Hansen, C., Simonsen, J., Lioma, C.: The Copenhagen team participation in the check-worthiness task of the competition of automatic identification and verification of claims in political debates of the CLEF-2018 fact checking lab. In: Cappellato, L., Ferro, N., Nie, J.Y., Soulier, L. (eds.) Working Notes of CLEF 2018-Conference and Labs of the Evaluation Forum. CEUR Workshop Proceedings. CEUR-WS.org (2018)

26. Hansen, C., Hansen, C., Simonsen, J., Lioma, C.: Neural weakly supervised fact check-worthiness detection with contrastive sampling-based ranking loss. In: Cappellato, L., Ferro, N., Losada, D., Müller, H. (eds.) Working Notes of CLEF 2019 Conference and Labs of the Evaluation Forum. CEUR Workshop Proceedings. CEUR-WS.org (2019)

27. Haouari, F., Hasanain, M., Suwaileh, R., Elsayed, T.: ArCOV-19: the first Arabic COVID-19 Twitter dataset with propagation networks. arXiv preprint arXiv:2004.05861 (2020)

28. Haouari, F., Hasanain, M., Suwaileh, R., Elsayed, T.: ArCOV19-rumors: arabic COVID-19 Twitter dataset for misinformation detection. arXiv preprint arXiv:2010.08768 (2020)

29. Hasanain, M., Elsayed, T.: bigIR at CheckThat! 2020: Multilingual BERT for ranking Arabic tweets by check-worthiness. In: Cappellato, L., Eickhoff, C., Ferro, N., Névéol, A. (eds.) CLEF 2020 Working Notes. CEUR Workshop Proceedings, CEUR-WS.org (2020)

30. Hasanain, M., et al.: Overview of CheckThat! 2020 Arabic: automatic identification and verification of claims in social media. In: Cappellato, L., Eickhoff, C., Ferro, N., Névéol, A. (eds.) CLEF 2020 Working Notes. CEUR Workshop Proceedings, CEUR-WS.org (2020)

31. Hasanain, M., Suwaileh, R., Elsayed, T., Barrón-Cedeño, A., Nakov, P.: Overview of the CLEF-2019 CheckThat! lab on automatic identification and verification of claims. Task 2: evidence and factuality. In: Cappellato, L., Ferro, N., Losada, D., Müller, H. (eds.) Working Notes of CLEF 2019 Conference and Labs of the Evaluation Forum. CEUR Workshop Proceedings. CEUR-WS.org (2019)

32. Hassan, N., Li, C., Tremayne, M.: Detecting check-worthy factual claims in presidential debates. In: Proceedings of the 24th ACM International on Conference on Information and Knowledge Management, CIKM 2015, pp. 1835–1838 (2015)

33. Hassan, N., Tremayne, M., Arslan, F., Li, C.: Comparing automated factual claim detection against judgments of journalism organizations. In: Computation+Journalism Symposium, pp. 1–5 (2016)

34. Hassan, N., et al.: ClaimBuster: the first-ever end-to-end fact-checking system. Proc. VLDB Endow. **10**(12), 1945–1948 (2017)

35. Karadzhov, G., Nakov, P., Màrquez, L., Barrón-Cedeño, A., Koychev, I.: Fully automated fact checking using external sources. In: Proceedings of the International Conference Recent Advances in Natural Language Processing, RANLP 2017, pp. 344–353 (2017)

36. Kartal, Y.S., Kutlu, M.: TOBB ETU at CheckThat! 2020: prioritizing English and Arabic claims based on check-worthiness. In: Cappellato, L., Eickhoff, C., Ferro, N., Névéol, A. (eds.) CLEF 2020 Working Notes. CEUR Workshop Proceedings, CEUR-WS.org (2020)

37. Ma, J., et al.: Detecting rumors from microblogs with recurrent neural networks. In: Proceedings of the International Joint Conference on Artificial Intelligence, IJCAI 2016, 3818–3824 (2016)

38. Martinez-Rico, J., Araujo, L., Martinez-Romo, J.: NLP&IR@UNED at CheckThat! 2020: a preliminary approach for check-worthiness and claim retrieval tasks using neural networks and graphs. In: Cappellato, L., Eickhoff, C., Ferro, N., Névéol, A. (eds.) CLEF 2020 Working Notes. CEUR Workshop Proceedings, CEUR-WS.org (2020)

39. Mihaylova, T., Karadzhov, G., Atanasova, P., Baly, R., Mohtarami, M., Nakov, P.: SemEval-2019 task 8: fact checking in community question answering forums. In: Proceedings of the 13th International Workshop on Semantic Evaluation, SemEval 2019, pp. 860–869 (2019)

40. Mitra, T., Gilbert, E.: CREDBANK: a large-scale social media corpus with associated credibility annotations. In: Proceedings of the Ninth International AAAI Conference on Web and Social Media, ICWSM 2015, pp. 258–267 (2015)

41. Mohammad, S., Kiritchenko, S., Sobhani, P., Zhu, X., Cherry, C.: SemEval-2016 task 6: detecting stance in tweets. In: Proceedings of the 10th International Workshop on Semantic Evaluation, SemEval 2016, pp. 31–41 (2016)

42. Mukherjee, S., Weikum, G.: Leveraging joint interactions for credibility analysis in news communities. In: Proceedings of the 24th ACM International Conference on Information and Knowledge Management, CIKM 2015, pp. 353–362 (2015)

43. Nakov, P., et al.: Overview of the CLEF-2018 lab on automatic identification and verification of claims in political debates. In: Working Notes of CLEF 2018 - Conference and Labs of the Evaluation Forum, CLEF 2018 (2018)

44. Nakov, P., et al.: SemEval-2016 Task 3: Community question answering. In: Proceedings of the 10th International Workshop on Semantic Evaluation, SemEval 2015, pp. 525–545 (2016)

45. Nguyen, V.H., Sugiyama, K., Nakov, P., Kan, M.Y.: FANG: leveraging social context for fake news detection using graph representation. In: Proceedings of the 29th ACM International Conference on Information & Knowledge Management, CIKM 2020, p. 1165–1174 (2020)

46. Nikolov, A., Da San Martino, G., Koychev, I., Nakov, P.: Team_Alex at CheckThat! 2020: identifying check-worthy tweets with transformer models. In: Cappellato, L., Eickhoff, C., Ferro, N., Névéol, A. (eds.) CLEF 2020 Working Notes. CEUR Workshop Proceedings, CEUR-WS.org (2020)

47. Oshikawa, R., Qian, J., Wang, W.Y.: A survey on natural language processing for fake news detection. In: Proceedings of the 12th Language Resources and Evaluation Conference. pp. 6086–6093. LREC '20 (2020)

48. Pogorelov, K., et al.: FakeNews: corona virus and 5G conspiracy task at MediaEval 2020. In: MediaEval 2020 Workshop (2020)

49. Popat, K., Mukherjee, S., Strötgen, J., Weikum, G.: Credibility assessment of textual claims on the web. In: Proceedings of the 25th ACM International Conference on Information and Knowledge Management, CIKM 2016, pp. 2173–2178 (2016)

50. Shaar, S., Babulkov, N., Da San Martino, G., Nakov, P.: That is a known lie: detecting previously fact-checked claims. In: Proceedings of the 58th Annual Meeting of the Association for Computational Linguistics, ACL 2020, pp. 3607–3618 (2020)

51. Shaar, S., et al.: Overview of CheckThat! 2020 English: automatic identification and verification of claims in social media. In: Cappellato, L., Eickhoff, C., Ferro, N., Névéol, A. (eds.) CLEF 2020 Working Notes. CEUR Workshop Proceedings, CEUR-WS.org (2020)

52. Shahi, G.K.: AMUSED: An annotation framework of multi-modal social media data. arXiv preprint arXiv:2010.00502 (2020)
53. Shahi, G.K., Dirkson, A., Majchrzak, T.A.: An exploratory study of COVID-19 misinformation on Twitter. arXiv preprint arXiv:2005.05710 (2020)
54. Shahi, G.K., Nandini, D.: FakeCovid - a multilingual cross-domain fact check news dataset for COVID-19. In: Workshop Proceedings of the 14th International AAAI Conference on Web and Social Media (2020)
55. Shu, K., Sliva, A., Wang, S., Tang, J., Liu, H.: Fake news detection on social media: a data mining perspective. SIGKDD Explor. Newsl. **19**(1), 22–36 (2017)
56. Thorne, J., Vlachos, A., Christodoulopoulos, C., Mittal, A.: FEVER: a large-scale dataset for fact extraction and VERification. In: Proceedings of the Conference of the North American Chapter of the Association for Computational Linguistics: Human Language Technologies, NAACL 2018, pp. 809–819 (2018)
57. Touahri, I., Mazroui, A.: EvolutionTeam at CheckThat! 2020: integration of linguistic and sentimental features in a fake news detection approach. In: Cappellato, L., Eickhoff, C., Ferro, N., Névéol, A. (eds.) CLEF 2020 Working Notes. CEUR Workshop Proceedings, CEUR-WS.org (2020)
58. Vasileva, S., Atanasova, P., Màrquez, L., Barrón-Cedeño, A., Nakov, P.: It takes nine to smell a rat: Neural multi-task learning for check-worthiness prediction. In: Proceedings of the International Conference on Recent Advances in Natural Language Processing, RANLP 2019, pp. 1229–1239 (2019)
59. Williams, E., Rodrigues, P., Novak, V.: Accenture at CheckThat! 2020: If you say so: Post-hoc fact-checking of claims using transformer-based models. In: Cappellato, L., Eickhoff, C., Ferro, N., Névéol, A. (eds.) CLEF 2020 Working Notes. CEUR Workshop Proceedings, CEUR-WS.org (2020)
60. Zhao, Z., Resnick, P., Mei, Q.: Enquiring minds: Early detection of rumors in social media from enquiry posts. In: Proceedings of the 24th International Conference on World Wide Web, WWW 2015, pp. 1395–1405 (2015)
61. Zubiaga, A., Liakata, M., Procter, R., Hoi, G.W.S., Tolmie, P.: Analysing how people orient to and spread rumours in social media by looking at conversational threads. PLoS ONE **11**(3), e0150989 (2016)
62. Zuo, C., Karakas, A., Banerjee, R.: A hybrid recognition system for check-worthy claims using heuristics and supervised learning. In: Cappellato, L., Ferro, N., Nie, J.Y., Soulier, L. (eds.) Working Notes of CLEF 2018-Conference and Labs of the Evaluation Forum. CEUR Workshop Proceedings. CEUR-WS.org (2018)

eRisk 2021: Pathological Gambling, Self-harm and Depression Challenges

Javier Parapar[1]([envelope])[iD], Patricia Martín-Rodilla[1][iD], David E. Losada[2][iD], and Fabio Crestani[3][iD]

[1] Information Retrieval Lab, Centro de Investigación en Tecnoloxías da Información e as Comunicacións (CITIC), Universidade da Coruña, A Coruña, Spain
{javierparapar,patricia.martin.rodilla}@udc.es
[2] Centro Singular de Investigación en Tecnoloxías Intelixentes (CiTIUS), Universidade de Santiago de Compostela, Santiago, Spain
david.losada@usc.es
[3] Faculty of Informatics, Universitá della Svizzera italiana (USI), Lugano, Switzerland
fabio.crestani@usi.ch

Abstract. eRisk, a CLEF lab oriented to early risk prediction on the Internet, started in 2017 as a forum to foster experimentation on early risk detection. After four editions (2017, 2018, 2019 and 2020), the lab has created many reference collections in the field and organized multiple early risk detection challenges using those datasets. Each challenge focused on a specific early risk detection problem (e.g., depression, anorexia or self-harm). This paper describes the work done so far, discusses the main lessons learned over the past editions and the plans for the eRisk 2021 edition, where we introduced pathological gambling as a new early risk detection challenge.

1 Introduction

As a part of CLEF (Conference and Labs of the Evaluation Forum), the eRisk lab is a forum for exploring the evaluation methodology and effectiveness metrics related to early risk detection on the Internet (with past challenges particularly focused on health and safety). Over the past editions [5–8], a number of testbeds and tools have been developed under the eRisk's umbrella. eRisk's dataset building methodology and the evaluation strategies proposed are general and, thus, potentially applicable to multiple application domains.

This lab brings together different research disciplines (e.g. information retrieval, computational linguistics, machine learning or psychology) to address the posed problems in an interdisciplinary way. Furthermore, effective solutions to eRisk tasks are potentially applicable to socially important concerns. For example, systems may send warning alerts when an individual starts broadcasting suicidal thoughts or threats of self-harm on Social Media. Previous editions of eRisk proposed shared tasks focused on specific health and security problems, such as depression, anorexia or self-harm detection.

© Springer Nature Switzerland AG 2021
D. Hiemstra et al. (Eds.): ECIR 2021, LNCS 12657, pp. 650–656, 2021.
https://doi.org/10.1007/978-3-030-72240-1_76

eRisk takes an iterative approach, where risk prediction is seen as a sequential process of accumulation of evidence. The constant production of data in a given data source (e.g. Social Media entries) needs to be automatically analyzed by the systems designed by eRisk participants. Within this process, the algorithms need to estimate when and if there is enough aggregated evidence about a certain type of risk. The shared tasks represent a successful methodology for improving results collaboratively about different types of risks. On each shared task, the participants have access to a temporally organized dataset where they have to balance between making *early* alerts (e.g., based on few social media entries) or *not-so-early* (late) alerts (e.g., evaluating a wider range of entries and only emit alerts after analyzing a larger number of pieces of evidence).

2 Previous Editions of eRisk

eRisk, a CLEF lab for research on early risk prediction on the Internet, started in 2017 as a forum to set the experimental foundations of early risk detection. After four editions (2017, 2018, 2019 and 2020), the lab has created many reference collections in the field and organized several early risk detection challenges using those datasets. Each challenge focused on a specific early risk detection problem, such as depression, anorexia and self-harm.

In the first edition (2017) [5], eRisk focused on the detection of early signs of depression, trying to explore the relationship between the use of language in social networks and early signs of depression. It was the first edition of such an innovative evaluation scheme and, thus, eRisk 2017 was very demanding for both the participants and the organizers. Temporal data chunks were released sequentially (one chunk per week). After each release, the participants had to send their predictions about the users in the collection. Only 8 of the 30 participating groups completed the tasks by the required deadline. These teams proposed more than 30 different interdisciplinary approaches to the problem (variants or runs). The evaluation methodology and metrics were those defined in [4].

In 2018, eRisk [6] included two shared tasks: 1) a continuation of 2017's task on early detection of depression and 2) a task on early detection of signs of anorexia. Both tasks followed a similar organization and the same evaluation methods of eRisk 2017. eRisk 2018 had 11 final participants (out of 41 registered), proposing 45 runs for Task 1 and 35 runs for Task 2.

In 2019, we organized three tasks [7], Task 1 as a continuation of 2018 task on early detection of signs of anorexia and Task 2, a new one on early detection of signs of self-harm. Furthermore, a new task, Task 3, was introduced oriented to automatically filling a depression questionnaire based on user interactions in social media. Note that Task 3 does not address early detection but another complex task (depression level estimation). For eRisk 2019, 14 participants (out of 62 registered teams) actively participated in the three tasks and submitted 54, 33 and 33 system variants (runs), respectively for each task.

Finally, the last edition of eRisk (2020) [8] continued the task of early detection of self-harm (task 1) and the task of measuring the severity of the signs of depression (depression level estimation, task 2). Task 1 had 12 final participants who submitted 46 different variants, while task 2 had six active participants who proposed 17 different system variants (runs).

Over these four years, eRisk has received a steady number of active participants, slowly placing the lab as a reference forum for early risk research.

2.1   Early Risk Prediction Tasks

Most of the proposed shared tasks were oriented to the early prediction of risk in different challenges (depression, anorexia, self-harm) whereas one specific task addresses the estimation of the level of depression.

Regarding the former group of tasks, all of them followed the same organization: the teams had to sequentially (following chronological order) process social media writings –posts or comments– intending to detect signs of risk as soon as possible. The resulting algorithms represent effective solutions for monitoring social network activity. A summary of the main statistics of the collections used in the early risk detection task over the years is shown in Table 1.

Reddit was the social media platform used as a source for all shared tasks in the different editions. It is important to highlight that Reddit's terms of use permit to extract data for research purposes. Reddit does not permit the unauthorized commercial use of its contents or redistribution, except as permitted by the doctrine of fair use. eRisk's research activities are an example of fair use.

Commonly, users in Reddit present a highly active profile, with a large thread of submissions (covering several years). Regarding psychological disorders, there are specific subcommunities (*subreddits*) about depression, anorexia, and self-harm, just to name a few. We used these valuable sources for building the eRisk test collections (as we described in [4].), creating collections of writings (posts or comments) published by *redditors*. Redditors are classified into two classes: the positive class (e.g., depressed) and the negative class (control group).

Following the method proposed by Coppersmith and colleagues [3], the positive class was obtained using a retrieval approach for identifying *redditors* diagnosed with the condition at hand (e.g. depressed). This was based on searches for self-expressions related to medical diagnoses (e.g. "Today, I was diagnosed with depression"). Many *redditors* are active on subreddits related to psychological disorders and, often, they tend to be very explicit about their medical condition. Next, we manually reviewed the retrieved results to verify that the expressions about diagnosis look really genuine. For example, expressions such as "I am anorexic", "I have anorexia" or "I think I have anorexia" were not considered as explicit expressions of a diagnosis. We only included a user into the positive set when there was a mention of a diagnosis that was clear and explicit (e.g., "Last month, I was diagnosed with anorexia nervosa", "After struggling with anorexia for a long time, last week I was diagnosed"). Our confidence in the reliability of these labels is high. This semi-automatic extraction method has been successful in retrieving information about people diagnosed with a specific disorder. In 2020, we introduced the use of Beaver, a new tool for labelling positive and negative cases [9].

For evaluating early detection, the first editions of eRisk considered a new measure called ERDE (Early Risk Detection Error) [4]. This measure acted as a complement of standard classification metrics, which ignore the delay in making predictions. ERDE takes into account the correctness of the (binary) decision and the delay, which is measured by counting the number (k) of writings seen before making the decision. From the 2019 edition, eRisk also incorporated a ranking-based approach to evaluate the participants: a user ranking was produced after each round of writings (ranked by decreasing estimated risk) and these rankings were evaluated under standard information retrieval metrics (e.g., P@10 or NDCG). The ranking-based evaluation is fully detailed in [7]. Since eRisk 2019, we also adopted $F_{latency}$, an alternative evaluation metric for early risk prediction that was proposed by Sadeque and colleagues [10].

2.2   Severity Level Estimation Task

One specific task in 2019 and 2020 was dedicated to estimating the severity level of depression. Depression Level Estimation Task explores the viability and possible approaches for automatically estimating the occurrence and intensity of multiple well-known symptoms of depression. In these tasks, the participants had access to the full history of writings of a number of redditors, and each group had to design an automatic method that reads the history of each user and fills a standard depression questionnaire based on the evidence found in the user's writings. The questionnaire included 21 questions (with four possible responses corresponding with different severity levels) about the intensity of depression signals and symptoms (e.g., loss of energy, sadness, and sleeping problems). The questionnaire is derived from the Beck's Depression Inventory (BDI) [2].

The ground truth for this task was a collection of questionnaires directly filled by social media users, together with their history of writings. Due to the specific nature of the task, it was necessary to introduce evaluation metrics for evaluating the participants' estimations. We considered four metrics [7]: Average Closeness Rate (ACR), Average Hit Rate (AHR), Average DODL (ADODL) and Depression Category Hit Rate (DCHR).

2.3   Results

Yearly reports with a full description and critical analysis of eRisk results have been published since 2017 [5–8]. The early risk prediction tasks have involved a wide range of participants and variants. Most of the approaches are based on traditional classification workflows (centred on obtaining effective classifiers from the training data). In general, the participants paid less attention to the accuracy-delay tradeoff. In terms of performance, the results show some differences between challenges, with, for example, more effective results in anorexia detection than those in depression. The performance figures showed how participants managed to improve the detection accuracy edition by edition. This encourages us to keep fostering research on text-based early risk screening from social media. Furthermore, given the effectiveness achieved by some participants,

Table 1. Statistics of the train and test collections used in the early prediction tasks.

	Training stage		Test stage	
	eRisk 2017 - Depression task			
	Depressed	*Control*	*Depressed*	*Control*
Num. subjects	83	403	52	349
Num. submissions (posts & comments)	30,851	264,172	18,706	217,665
Avg num. of submissions per subject	371.7	655.5	359.7	623.7
Avg num. of days from first to last submission	572.7	626.6	608.31	623.2
Avg num. words per submission	27.6	21.3	26.9	22.5
	eRisk 2018 - Depression task			
	Depressed	*Control*	*Depressed*	*Control*
Num. subjects	135	752	79	741
Num. submissions (posts & comments)	49,557	481,837	40,665	504,523
Avg num. of submissions per subject	367.1	640.7	514.7	680.9
Avg num. of days from first to last submission	586.43	625.0	786.9	702.5
Avg num. words per submission	27.4	21.8	27.6	23.7
	eRisk 2018 - Anorexia task			
	Anorexia	*Control*	*Anorexia*	*Control*
Num. subjects	20	132	41	279
Num. submissions (posts & comments)	7,452	77,514	17,422	151,364
Avg num. of submissions per subject	372.6	587.2	424.9	542.5
Avg num. of days from first to last submission	803.3	641.5	798.9	670.6
Avg num. words per submission	41.2	20.9	35.7	20.9
	eRisk 2019 - Anorexia task			
	Anorexia	*Control*	*Anorexia*	*Control*
Num. subjects	61	411	73	742
Num. submissions (posts & comments)	24,874	228,878	17,619	552,890
Avg num. of submissions per subject	407.8	556.9	241.4	745.1
Avg num. of days from first to last submission	$\approx$800	$\approx$650	$\approx$510	$\approx$930
Avg num. words per submission	37.3	20.9	37.2	21.7
	eRisk 2019 - Self-harm task			
	Self-harm	*Control*	*Self-harm*	*Control*
Num. subjects	–	–	41	299
Num. submissions (posts & comments)	–	–	6,927	163,506
Avg num. of submissions per subject	–	–	169.0	546.8
Avg num. of days from first to last submission	–	–	$\approx$495	$\approx$500
Avg num. words per submission	–	–	24.8	18.8
	eRisk 2020 - Self-harm task			
	Self-harm	*Control*	*Self-harm*	*Control*
Num. subjects	41	299	104	319
Num. submissions (posts & comments)	6,927	163,506	11,691	91,136
Avg num. of submissions per subject	169.0	546.8	112.4	285.6
Avg num. of days from first to last submission	$\approx$495	$\approx$500	$\approx$270	$\approx$426
Avg num. words per submission	24.8	18.8	21.4	11.9

it appears that automatic or semi-automatic screening tools that estimate the onset of certain risks are within reach.

The difficulty in finding and adjusting metrics for these innovative tasks has also motivated us to incorporate new metrics for eRisk. Some eRisk participants [10,11] were also active in proposing new forms of evaluation, which is another valuable result of the lab.

Regarding depression level estimation, the results suggest that automatic analysis of the user's writings might be a complementary approach for extracting some signals or symptoms related to depression. Some participants had a hit rate of 40% (i.e., 40% of the BDI questions were answered by the systems with the exact same response given by the real user). This has still much room for improvement, but, in any case, it suggests that the participants were able to extract some signal from the noisy Social Media data.

3   Conclusions and Future Work

The results achieved so far encourage us to continue with the lab in 2021 and further explore the relation between text-based screening from social media and early risk. For eRisk 2021, our plan is twofold:

- Firstly, expanding the range of target domains for early risk detection from social networks. Specifically, eRisk 2021 presents as Task 1 the early detection of risks in pathological gambling, a growing psychological disorder. Pathological gambling (ICD-10-CM code F63.0) is also called ludomania and usually referred to as *gambling addiction* (it is an urge to gamble independently of its negative consequences). According to the World Health Organization [1], in 2017, adult gambling addiction had prevalence rates ranged from 0.1% to 6.0%. Following our usual methodology, we will collect and release data in a sequential way. The participating systems will interact with a server prepared for this task in order to collect data and send results.
- Secondly, we will establish an (at least) three year cycle per task, where we will not release training data in the first year (as it happened in the first edition of self-harm). The objective is to foster research on methods that do not solely depend on the existence of training. Then, in the second edition, we will see how the performance of the systems can be improved with training data. Finally, in the third edition, we will see how participants manage to improve and refine their models after two years of experience.
- Following the scheme suggested above, in 2021, we present the third edition of two already existing tasks: a shared task will be organized on early detection of self-harm (2021's Task 2), and a task on estimating the severity of the signs of depression (2021's Task 3, based on standard depression questionnaire).

Acknowledgements. This work was supported by projects RTI2018-093336-B-C21, RTI2018-093336-B-C22 (Ministerio de Ciencia e Innvovación & ERDF). The first and second authors thank the financial support supplied by the Consellería de Educación, Universidade e Formación Profesional (accreditation 2019–2022 ED431G/01, ED431B

2019/03) and the European Regional Development Fund, which acknowledges the CITIC Research Center in ICT of the University of A Coruña as a Research Center of the Galician University System. The third author also thanks the financial support supplied by the Consellería de Educación, Universidade e Formación Profesional (accreditation 2019–2022 ED431G-2019/04, ED431C 2018/29) and the European Regional Development Fund, which acknowledges the CiTIUS-Research Center in Intelligent Technologies of the University of Santiago de Compostela as a Research Center of the Galician University System.

References

1. Abbott, M.: The epidemiology and impact of gambling disorder and other gambling-related harm. In: WHO Forum on Alcohol, Drugs and Addictive Behaviours, Geneva, Switzerland (2017)
2. Beck, A.T., Ward, C.H., Mendelson, M., Mock, J., Erbaugh, J.: An inventory for measuring depression. JAMA Psychiatry **4**(6), 561–571 (1961)
3. Coppersmith, G., Dredze, M., Harman, C.: Quantifying mental health signals in Twitter. In: ACL Workshop on Computational Linguistics and Clinical Psychology (2014)
4. Losada, D.E., Crestani, F.: A test collection for research on depression and language use. In: Fuhr, N., et al. (eds.) CLEF 2016. LNCS, vol. 9822, pp. 28–39. Springer, Cham (2016). https://doi.org/10.1007/978-3-319-44564-9_3
5. Losada, D.E., Crestani, F., Parapar, J.: eRISK 2017: CLEF lab on early risk prediction on the Internet: experimental foundations. In: Jones, G.J.F., et al. (eds.) CLEF 2017. LNCS, vol. 10456, pp. 346–360. Springer, Cham (2017). https://doi.org/10.1007/978-3-319-65813-1_30
6. Losada, D.E., Crestani, F., Parapar, J.: Overview of eRisk: early risk prediction on the Internet. In: Bellot, P., et al. (eds.) CLEF 2018. LNCS, vol. 11018, pp. 343–361. Springer, Cham (2018). https://doi.org/10.1007/978-3-319-98932-7_30
7. Losada, D.E., Crestani, F., Parapar, J.: Overview of eRisk 2019 early risk prediction on the Internet. In: Crestani, F., et al. (eds.) CLEF 2019. LNCS, vol. 11696, pp. 340–357. Springer, Cham (2019). https://doi.org/10.1007/978-3-030-28577-7_27
8. Losada, D.E., Crestani, F., Parapar, J.: Overview of eRisk 2020: early risk prediction on the Internet. In: Arampatzis, A., et al. (eds.) CLEF 2020. LNCS, vol. 12260, pp. 272–287. Springer, Cham (2020). https://doi.org/10.1007/978-3-030-58219-7_20
9. Otero, D., Parapar, J., Barreiro, Á.: Beaver: efficiently building test collections for novel tasks. In: Proceedings of the Joint Conference of the Information Retrieval Communities in Europe (CIRCLE 2020), Samatan, Gers, France, July 6–9, 2020 (2020). http://ceur-ws.org/Vol-2621/CIRCLE20_23.pdf
10. Sadeque, F., Xu, D., Bethard, S.: Measuring the latency of depression detection in social media. In: Proceedings of the Eleventh ACM International Conference on Web Search and Data Mining. WSDM 2018, pp. 495–503. ACM, New York (2018)
11. Trotzek, M., Koitka, S., Friedrich, C.: Utilizing neural networks and linguistic metadata for early detection of depression indications in text sequences. IEEE Trans. Knowl. Data Eng. **32**, 588–601 (2018)

Living Lab Evaluation for Life and Social Sciences Search Platforms - LiLAS at CLEF 2021

Philipp Schaer[1]([⊠]) [iD], Johann Schaible[2] [iD], and Leyla Jael Castro[3] [iD]

[1] TH Köln - University of Applied Sciences, Cologne, Germany
philipp.schaer@th-koeln.de
[2] GESIS - Leibniz Institute for the Social Sciences, Cologne, Germany
johann.schaible@gesis.org
[3] ZB MED - Information Centre for Life Sciences, Cologne, Germany
ljgarcia@zbmed.de

Abstract. Meta-evaluation studies of system performances in controlled offline evaluation campaigns, like TREC and CLEF, show a need for innovation in evaluating IR-systems. The field of academic search is no exception to this. This might be related to the fact that relevance in academic search is multi-layered and therefore the aspect of user-centric evaluation is becoming more and more important. The Living Labs for Academic Search (LiLAS) lab aims to strengthen the concept of user-centric living labs for the domain of academic search by allowing participants to evaluate their retrieval approaches in two real-world academic search systems from the life sciences and the social sciences. To this end, we provide participants with metadata on the systems' content as well as candidate lists with the task to rank the most relevant candidate to the top. Using the STELLA-infrastructure, we allow participants to easily integrate their approaches into the real-world systems and provide the possibility to compare different approaches at the same time.

Keywords: Evaluation · Living labs · Academic search · CLEF

1 Introduction and Background

Scientific information and knowledge is growing at an exponential rate [15]. This includes not only the traditional journal publication but also a vast amount of preprints, research data sets, code, survey data, and many others research objects. This heterogeneity and mass of documents and data sets introduces new challenges to the disciplines of information retrieval (IR), recommender systems, digital libraries or more generally the field of academic search systems. Progress in these fields is usually evaluated by means of shared tasks that are based on the principle of Cranfield/TREC-style studies. Typical shared tasks at CLEF and TREC are based on the offline computation of results/runs missing a valuable link to real-world environments [7]. Most recently the TREC-COVID

© Springer Nature Switzerland AG 2021
D. Hiemstra et al. (Eds.): ECIR 2021, LNCS 12657, pp. 657–664, 2021.
https://doi.org/10.1007/978-3-030-72240-1_77

[16] evaluation campaign run by NIST attracted a high number of participants and showed the high impact of scientific retrieval tasks in the community.

TREC-COVID showed the massive retrieval performance that recent deep learning approaches are capable of; however, classic vector-space retrieval using the SMART system was also highly successful[1]. This can be attributed to the limitations of the test collection based evaluation approach of TREC-COVID and the general need for innovation in the field of academic search and IR. Meta-evaluation studies of system performances in controlled offline evaluation campaigns, like TREC and CLEF, show a need for innovation in evaluating IR-systems [1,17]. The field of academic search is no exception to this. The central concern of academic search is to find both relevant and high-quality documents. The question of what constitutes relevance in academic search is multi-layered [4] and an ongoing research area.

To compensate for these shortcomings, e.g., lack of extensive training corpora, the living labs concept was introduced. It is meant to carry out online evaluations within a fixed methodological, organizational, and technical framework and open them up to other actors. As in a laboratory TREC environment, the aim is to prevent as many disturbing influences as possible while at the same time preserving the advantages of evaluation in live systems. For example, in the context of online IR experiments, document inventories that change over time can cause problems. Furthermore, it must be ensured that all experimental rankings have the chance to be calculated and displayed regardless of the system performance. These and other factors can be taken into account in living labs and thus form a bridge between structured, but also rigid, laboratory evaluation and free, but also less planned and controlled online evaluation. The best-known case of a living lab became known in 2014 as the "Facebook Experiment" [9]. Even though this experiment was pervasive and did not serve the system's direct evaluation, it shows the possibilities that living labs and online experiments offer. Unfortunately, these experiments are limited by the actual access to the systems itself. As long as one is not the operator of a large-scale platform, one is most likely unable to perform such experiments. Therefore previous attempts such as Living Labs for Information Retrieval (LL4IR) and Open Search initiatives [2] were established at CLEF or TREC to bring together IR researchers and platform operators. Likewise, the NewsREEL workshop series was an attempt to do the same for recommendation systems [10]. In summary, the living lab evaluation paradigm represents a user-centered study methodology for researchers to evaluate the performance of retrieval systems within real-world applications. As such, it offers a more realistic experiment and evaluation environment than offline test collections, and therefore should be further investigated to raise IR-evaluation to the next level.

Fuhr [5] argues that evaluation initiatives should take a leading role in improving the current IR evaluation practice. We want to move beyond the traditional offline evaluation setup and bring together industry and practice evaluation techniques into the academic realm. Therefore, utilizing online eval-

---

[1] https://ir.nist.gov/covidSubmit/archive.html.

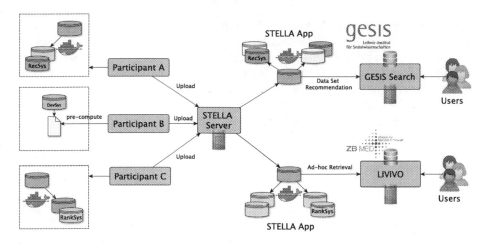

Fig. 1. Schematic representation of the two core tasks: Adhoc search and dataset recommendation in the two academic search systems GESIS Search and LIVIVO. Participants can upload pre-computed results or share their systems in form of Docker containers for both tasks to the STELLA Server, which distributes the experimental data and systems to the STELLA App on premise of GESIS Search and LIVIVO. This app curates the evaluation process by offering A/B-testing or interleaving setups. The results of the runs are aggregated and displayed in a dashboard on the STELLA Server.

uations, taking the actual user into account, would be a step forward towards improving the evaluation landscape. Following these lines, the primary motivation behind the LiLAS (Living Labs for Academic Search) lab at CLEF 2021 is to learn more about

- the potentials and limitations of different styles of living labs for search evaluation. Here we would like to compare pre-computed results and those provided by our live evaluation framework STELLA [3] which incorporates interactions with end-users.
- the reproducibility of click-based evaluations in the academic domain.
- the validity and expressiveness of click-based and relevance assessment-based evaluation metrics on small to medium-scale academic platforms.

After LiLAS ran as a workshop lab at CLEF 2020 [12,13], in 2021 a full evaluation lab will take place. This lab's unique selling point is that we offer two tasks to test this approach in two different academic search domains and evaluation setups.

2   Evaluation Infrastructure and Submission Types

Based on previous work done in campaigns such as LL4IR at CLEF and Open Search at TREC, we built a living lab evaluation infrastructure named STELLA currently integrated into two academic search systems to allow a more realistic evaluation setup [3]. In addition to the previous labs, where pre-computed results were submitted, we now offer participants the possibility to submit Docker containers that can be run within STELLA. This simple but yet powerful mechanism enhances the evaluation state of the art. Figure 1 shows the schematics of STELLA in the context of this evaluation lab, which we describe in the following.

LiLAS offers two different evaluation tasks: *Academic ad-hoc retrieval* for the multi-lingual and multi-source Life Science search portal LIVIVO and *research data recommendation* within the Social Science portal GESIS Search. For both tasks, participants are invited to submit

- **Type A.** *pre-computed runs* based on previously compiled queries (ad-hoc search) or documents (research data recommendations) from server logs (comparable to the CLEF LL4IR or TREC Open Search labs [8]) or
- **Type B.** *Docker containers* of full running retrieval/recommendation systems that run within our evaluation framework called STELLA.

For type A, participants pre-compute result files following TREC run file syntax and submit them for integration into the live systems. For type B, participants encapsulate their retrieval system into a Docker container following some simple implementation rules inspired by the OSIRRC workshop at SIGIR 2019. We release datasets containing queries and metadata of documents and data sets from the two systems mentioned above for training purposes. We offer a list of candidate documents and candidate research data for each query and seed document, respectively, so participants focus on the actual ranking approaches behind the ad-hoc search and recommendation task.

3   Task 1: Ad-Hoc Search Ranking

Motivation. Finding the most relevant publications to a query remains a challenge in scholarly Information Retrieval systems, even more in multi-lingual and cross-domain environments.

Task Description. The participants are asked to define and implement their ranking approach for a multi-lingual candidate documents list. A good ranking should present users with the most relevant documents regarding a query on top of the result set. Regardless of the language used to pose the query, the retrieval can include candidate documents in multiple languages. Participants can submit type A and type B results. Type A rankings will be based on the most common queries in LIVIVO (see below), while Type B submissions should rank candidate documents for any incoming query.

Dataset and Lab Data. LIVIVO[2] is a search portal developed by ZB MED - Information Centre for Life Sciences[3], providing comprehensive access to literature in life sciences, including resources from medicine, health, environment,

---

[2] https://livivo.de.
[3] https://zbmed.de.

agriculture, and nutrition. LIVIVO corpus consists of about 80 million documents from more than 50 data sources in multiple languages (e.g., English, German, French) covering various scholarly publication types (e.g., conferences, preprints, peer-review journals). We provide LiLAS participants with a set of common queries with their corresponding candidate documents (and metadata), in which participants will rank according to their relevance regarding the query. We also provide participants with logs regarding which users have accessed documents and in what order (e.g., click-through rate, if available).

Evaluation. Participating approaches will be evaluated in the LIVIVO production system on gains, losses, and ties regarding user preferences (e.g., click-through rate per query and candidates list). We will follow a Team Draft Interleaving (TDI) approach [11,14] where LIVIVO and participants rankings are interleaved and presented together. This way, we will be able to compare all participating systems against each other.

4   Task 2: Research Data Recommendations

Motivation. Research data is of high importance in scientific research, especially when making progress in experimental investigations. However, finding useful research data can be difficult and cumbersome, even if using dataset search engines, such as Google Dataset Search[4]. Therefore, one possible solution is to recommend "appropriate" research data sets to users based on research articles, i.e., publications, of the users' interest.

Task Description. The main task here is to provide recommendations of research data that are *relevant* to the publication the user is currently viewing. For example, the user is interested in the impact of religion on political elections. She finds a publication regarding that topic, which has a set of research data candidates covering the same topic. The task is to rank the most relevant candidates to the top. Participants can submit type A and type B results. Whereas the pre-computed type A results comprise recommendations only for publications and research data existing in the provided lab data, the Docker variant in type B will also compute recommendations for publications and research data that have recently been added to the real-life search system.

Dataset and Lab Data. The data for this task is taken from the academic search system *GESIS Search*[5] [6]. Besides social science literature (107k publications), it also provides research data (77k) on social science topics, out of which the participants are given the metadata to all publications and all contained research data. The publications are mostly in English and German and are annotated with further textual metadata like title, abstract, topic, persons, and others. Metadata on research data comprises (among others) a title, topics, datatype, abstract, collection method and universe, temporal and geographical

---

[4] https://datasetsearch.research.google.com/.
[5] https://search.gesis.org/.

coverage, primary investigators, as well as contributors in English and/or German. The set of research data candidates for each publication, which is given to the participants as well, is computed based on context similarity between publications and research data.

Evaluation. With an A/B-testing, the GESIS Search users will be shown the recommendations separated by the users' session-id. This means, for each session-id, STELLA selects one recommendation approach out of all participants. This way, we are able to compare all participating systems against each other without confusing the user with different recommendations for the same publication. In both type A and type B, the participating approaches will be evaluated in the GESIS Search productive system, where the top-k (with $3 \leq k \leq 10$) recommendations are shown to the user. The evaluation itself is performed using implicit and explicit feedback. For the implicit feedback, we calculate the click-through-rate (CTR) as well as the bounce rate once a user clicks on a recommended dataset. The explicit feedback is gathered via options, such as a *thumbs up* and *thumbs down*, in which the users can indicate whether the recommendation was relevant to them or not.

5   Conclusion

Academic Search is a timeless research domain and a very recent topic, as shown by TREC-COVID. We want to support the latest research in this field by bringing together real-world platforms and academic researchers on a joint living lab research infrastructure. As the search for scientific material is more than just "10 blue links", we see the demand for domain-specific retrieval tasks, which comprises document, dataset as well as bibliometric-enhanced retrieval. To allow academic researchers to go beyond proprietary web-search platforms like Google Scholar (or Google Dataset Search) or digital libraries like the ACM Digital Library, we focus on mid-size scientific search systems. The two tasks we run in 2021 are a starting point and are designed to be as open as possible by offering the possibility to submit both pre-computed and Docker-based results and systems. In the future, STELLA can be exploited and integrated into other academic search systems enabling online evaluations in different domains.

References

1. Armstrong, T.G., Moffat, A., Webber, W., Zobel, J.: Improvements that don't add up: ad-hoc retrieval results since 1998. In: Proceeding of the 18th ACM Conference on Information and Knowledge Management, CIKM 2009, pp. 601–610. ACM, Hong Kong (2009). https://doi.org/10.1145/1645953.1646031
2. Balog, K., Schuth, A., Dekker, P., Schaer, P., Tavakolpoursaleh, N., Chuang, P.Y.: Overview of the trec 2016 open search track. In: Proceedings of the Twenty-Fifth Text REtrieval Conference (TREC 2016). NIST (2016)

3. Breuer, T., Schaer, P., Tavakolpoursaleh, N., Schaible, J., Wolff, B., Müller, B.: STELLA: towards a framework for the reproducibility of online search experiments. In: Clancy, R., Ferro, N., Hauff, C., Lin, J., Sakai, T., Wu, Z.Z. (eds.) Proceedings of the Open-Source IR Replicability Challenge Co-Located with 42nd International ACM SIGIR Conference on Research and Development in Information Retrieval, OSIRRC@SIGIR 2019, Paris, France, July 25, 2019. CEUR Workshop Proceedings, vol. 2409, pp. 8–11. CEUR-WS.org (2019). http://ceur-ws.org/Vol-2409/position01.pdf

4. Carevic, Z., Schaer, P.: On the connection between citation-based and topical relevance ranking: results of a pretest using iSearch. In: Proceedings of the First Workshop on Bibliometric-Enhanced Information Retrieval Co-Located with 36th European Conference on Information Retrieval (ECIR 2014), Amsterdam, The Netherlands, April 13, 2014. CEUR Workshop Proceedings, vol. 1143, pp. 37–44. CEUR-WS.org (2014). http://ceur-ws.org/Vol-1143/paper5.pdf

5. Fuhr, N.: Some common mistakes in IR evaluation, and how they can be avoided. SIGIR Forum 51(3), 32–41 (2018). https://doi.org/10.1145/3190580.3190586

6. Hienert, D., Kern, D., Boland, K., Zapilko, B., Mutschke, P.: A digital library for research data and related information in the social sciences. In: 19th ACM/IEEE Joint Conference on Digital Libraries, JCDL 2019, Champaign, IL, USA, June 2–6, 2019, pp. 148–157. IEEE (2019). https://doi.org/10.1109/JCDL.2019.00030

7. Hopfgartner, F., et al.: Continuous evaluation of large-scale information access systems: a case for living labs. Information Retrieval Evaluation in a Changing World. TIRS, vol. 41, pp. 511–543. Springer, Cham (2019). https://doi.org/10.1007/978-3-030-22948-1_21

8. Jagerman, R., Balog, K., de Rijke, M.: Opensearch: lessons learned from an online evaluation campaign. J. Data Inf. Qual. 10(3), 13:1–13:15 (2018). https://doi.org/10.1145/3239575

9. Kramer, A.D.I., Guillory, J.E., Hancock, J.T.: Experimental evidence of massive-scale emotional contagion through social networks. Proc. Natl. Acad. Sci. 111(24), 8788–8790 (2014). https://doi.org/10.1073/pnas.1320040111

10. Lommatzsch, A., Kille, B., Hopfgartner, F., Ramming, L.: Newsreel multimedia at mediaeval 2018: news recommendation with image and text content. In: Working Notes Proceedings of the MediaEval 2018 Workshop. CEUR-WS (2018)

11. Radlinski, F., Kurup, M., Joachims, T.: How does clickthrough data reflect retrieval quality? In: Proceeding of the 17th ACM Conference on Information and Knowledge Mining - CIKM 2008, p. 43. ACM Press, Napa Valley (2008). https://doi.org/10.1145/1458082.1458092

12. Schaer, P., Schaible, J., Garcia Castro, L.J.: Overview of LiLAS 2020 – living labs for academic search. In: Arampatzis, A., et al. (eds.) CLEF 2020. LNCS, vol. 12260, pp. 364–371. Springer, Cham (2020). https://doi.org/10.1007/978-3-030-58219-7_24

13. Schaer, P., Schaible, J., Müller, B.: Living labs for academic search at CLEF 2020. In: Jose, J.M., et al. (eds.) ECIR 2020. LNCS, vol. 12036, pp. 580–586. Springer, Cham (2020). https://doi.org/10.1007/978-3-030-45442-5_75

14. Schuth, A., Balog, K., Kelly, L.: Extended overview of the living labs for information retrieval evaluation (LL4IR) CLEF lab 2015. In: Cappellato, L., Ferro, N., Jones, G.J.F., SanJuan, E. (eds.) Working Notes of CLEF 2015 - Conference and Labs of the Evaluation forum, Toulouse, France, September 8–11, 2015. CEUR Workshop Proceedings, vol. 1391. CEUR-WS.org (2015). http://ceur-ws.org/Vol-1391/inv-pap8-CR.pdf

15. de Solla Price, D.J.: Little Science, Big Science. Columbia University Press, New York (1963)
16. Voorhees, E.M., et al.: TREC-COVID: constructing a pandemic information retrieval test collection. CoRR abs/2005.04474 (2020). https://arxiv.org/abs/2005.04474
17. Yang, W., Lu, K., Yang, P., Lin, J.: Critically examining the "neural hype": weak baselines and the additivity of effectiveness gains from neural ranking models. In: Proceedings of the 42nd International ACM SIGIR Conference on Research and Development in Information Retrieval - SIGIR 2019, pp. 1129–1132. ACM Press, Paris (2019). https://doi.org/10.1145/3331184.3331340

Doctoral Consortium Papers

Automated Multi-document Text Summarization from Heterogeneous Data Sources

Mahsa Abazari Kia[✉]

School of Computer Science and Electronic Engineering, University of Essex, Essex, UK
ma19194@essex.ac.uk

We are currently witnessing an exponential increase of data which emanate from varied sources such as different types of records in companies, online social networks, videos, unstructured text in web pages, and others. It is very challenging to process this sparse, noisy and domain specific data. For instance, BT, a technology company in the UK and the PhD project sponsor, has a significant workforce of field engineers, desk-based agents, and customer support services who generate, collect and manage large volumes of temporally organized unstructured and semi-structured information every day. The problem that they face is effectively and efficiently answering client questions regarding order status live. The main challenge in my PhD is to propose computational models that could effectively and efficiently distil relevant information for the user who could answer the client's questions from various technical order record documents which are very noisy and follow no structural pattern. To this end, what would be useful is to automatically summarize and derive meaningful information in the form of short answers to queries from this vast source of distributed occurring data. The solution that my thesis proposes is based on a computational model that jointly learns extractive and abstractive summarization techniques with a temporal structure. Besides, the model interplays with a question-answering framework to help answer questions.

The information about orders at BT are in structured and free text format which is captured by and stored in different internal systems. These are being used by teams handling the orders. This volume of text about orders is an invaluable source of information which needs to be effectively and efficiently summarized in a way containing the information most relevant to:

- *'When' is the next action on the order.*
- *'What' is the current stage of the order.*
- *'Why' is it in this stage.*

It will help the desk agents to have a clear picture of the latest status of the order journey at the point in time t, instead of checking the order information from several places for the time that a customer calls in to find out about the progress of their order. In other words, we would like to generate summaries at the point in time t which can help humans comprehend the text content effectively and efficiently.

BT orders are structured in such a way that there is an update at regular intervals of time. These updates are required to be input to the summarizer as data over time. It means that summaries at time t are required to contain an update to the previous summary at

© Springer Nature Switzerland AG 2021
D. Hiemstra et al. (Eds.): ECIR 2021, LNCS 12657, pp. 667–671, 2021.
https://doi.org/10.1007/978-3-030-72240-1_78

time $t - 1$. The summary S will contain the latest important information about an order including order progress information and answers for WH questions that are mentioned earlier. For this reason, we consider the setup mentioned above as a temporal question based multi-document summarization where input is a sequence $S = <d_1, ..., d_n>$ of time-stamped documents d_t covering some information for a specific order at BT.

In general, there are two different approaches for automatic text summarization: extractive and abstraction. Extractive summarization methods work by identifying important sections of the text. In contrast, abstractive summarization methods aim at producing important material in a new way.

The fundamental question surrounding my thesis revolves around proposing novel computational multi-document text summarization models that, 1) consider timestamps in noisy and sparse orders when generating summaries, 2) answer questions about the order progress including the three WH questions using an integrated abstractive and extractive approach. Since the BT orders information are written by different people with different roles, some noise and inconsistencies are introduced. Therefore, regenerating sentences with an abstractive technique would enhance the quality of the summary. Using a joint abstractive and extractive approach takes advantages of both approaches can produce high-quality summaries.

The summarization setting in our problem scenario is different from traditional summarization in such a way that it aims to capture only the latest relevant information about the orders so that desk agents could easily follow the latest order status. My other goal is to also generalize my novel approaches to other domains such as news, TREC datasets, scientific datasets, and others which largely fall under single document text summarization. This would help make my framework useful to others applying both single and multi-document summarization who wish to use other kinds of datasets. This is another fundamental challenge in my thesis.

Figure 1 shows the high-level model architecture for generating summaries and in the following sections I present details on these components.

1   Temporal Summarization

Three different approaches are proposed for generating temporal summaries.

Text Summarization Using Topic Modeling Over Time: Text summarization using topic modeling over time will generate the summary at time t regarding the evolution of topics and we could have a summary that contains the latest important sentences about important topics in order notes. So, applying topic modeling over time to text summarization, considering sentence diversity using semantic spaces such as sentence embeddings from BERT and maximum separation, as in maximum-margin setup, between topics could lead us to generate qualitative temporal summaries.

Unsupervised Temporal Abstractive Summarization: MeanSum [1] proposed an end-to-end, neural model architecture to perform unsupervised abstractive summarization, which could be used as a base method for our temporal summarization.

Adding temporal component, improving the sentence representation and making structural changes in MeanSum model which could process time-stamped documents.

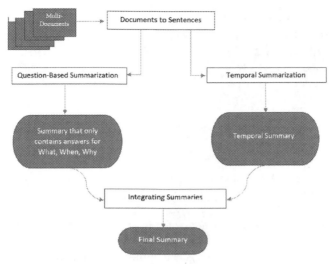

Fig. 1. A high-level architecture of my model.

Appling the updates to the summary (from Time $t - 1$ to t), would be ideal for our problem scenario due to the lack of training data.

Unsupervised Temporal Extractive Summarization: Tuning an unsupervised summarizer based on modern language models (which are recent trends in text summarization) for generating temporal summaries is another probable solution for this problem scenario. A BERT extractive summarizer is one of the unsupervised summarizers that could be utilized as a base for generating temporal extractive summaries.

2 Question-Based Summarization

Most of the techniques for answer extraction are supervised and due to the lack of training data in BT data, unsupervised approaches are more suitable. Giveme5W1H [2] is an open-source system that extracts phrases answering the journalistic 5W1H questions describing a news article's main event, i.e., who did what, when, where, why, and how? we need the sentences containing answers. Ranking and selecting the best answers (sentences) for When, What, and Why questions based on their date-time.

3 Merging Summaries

After obtaining temporal summary and question-based extractive summary our next goal is merging and aggregating these two summaries considering coherency, removing redundancy and temporal order. To this end, the main challenge is to find the correct position for placing question-based summary sentences considering their date-time. Another challenge lies in tuning the appropriate length of the summary using the development set.

Recall-Oriented Understudy for Gisting Evaluation (ROUGE) measures summary quality by counting overlapping units such as the n-gram, word sequences, and word pairs between the system summary and the reference summary. There are automatic evaluation methods ROUGE-N which is an n-gram recall between a candidate summary and a set of reference summaries [3]. ROUGE-N is computed as follows:

$$ROUGE - N = \frac{\sum\limits_{S \in REF} \sum\limits_{gram_n \in S} Count_{match}(gram_n)}{\sum\limits_{S \in REF} \sum\limits_{gram_n \in S} Count(gram_n)}$$

Since no benchmark is available, we can use KL-Divergence (Kullback–Leibler) Optimization [4] for evaluating the results for BT data in two steps:

- Discovering topics and their distribution for main document and summary document and computing KL-Divergence between them
- Doing summarization and KL-Divergence optimization at the same time

There are substantial challenges to the problem mentioned above because documents related to each order are stored in different internal systems, i.e., they are distributed in nature and they were produced by different teams and engineers which incorporates a considerable amount of incoherence and different distributions of the vocabulary use. In other words, we will have a heterogeneous set of documents where the main topic for the documents is unrelated, but they contain some information that is related to the order progress. Furthermore, there is no labeled data in this use case. We must consider temporal information and summarize order documents in a way that it contains information relevant to three WH questions.

Given the recent progress in automated text summarization, extractive techniques are still attractive as they are less complex, less expensive, and generate grammatically and semantically correct summaries [5]. However, these methods suffer from the inherent drawbacks of discourse incoherence and long, redundant sentences [6]. On the other hand, due to the difficulty of natural language understanding and generation most previous research on document summarization is more focused on extractive methods and most recent abstractive work has focused on headline generation tasks. Regarding the challenges for this use case and drawbacks for both extractive and abstractive methods, I would like to combine abstractive and extractive techniques to generate temporal summaries that contain answers for WH questions. Proposing a hybrid multi-document text summarization technique with contextualized language representations could generate accurate and coherent summaries since it can overcome natural language understanding challenges. What makes my work more unique is that it is going to be used by the company to solve real-life applied problem towards the end of my PhD which potentially could generate economic impact and help its users.

References

1. Chu, E., Liu, P.J.: MeanSum: a neural model for unsupervised multi-document abstractive summarization. arXiv preprint arXiv:1810.05739 (2018)

2. Hamborg, F., Breitinger, C., Schubotz, M., Lachnit, S., Gipp, B.: Extraction of main event descriptors from news articles by answering the journalistic five W and one H questions. In: Proceedings of the 18th ACM/IEEE on Joint Conference on Digital Libraries, pp. 339–340 (2018)
3. Song, S., Huang, H., Ruan, T.: Abstractive text summarization using LSTM-CNN based deep learning. Multimed. Tools Appl. **78**(1), 857–875 (2018). https://doi.org/10.1007/s11042-018-5749-3
4. Hu, Z., Hong, L.J.: Kullback-Leibler divergence constrained distributionally robust optimization. Available at Optimization Online (2013)
5. Nallapati, R., Zhai, F., Zhou, B.: Summarunner: a recurrent neural network based sequence model for extractive summarization of documents. In: Thirty-First AAAI Conference on Artificial Intelligence (2017)
6. See, A., Liu, P.J., Manning, C.D.: Get to the point: summarization with pointer-generator networks, Vancouver, Canada, pp. 1073–1083 (2017)

Background Linking of News Articles

Marwa Essam[(✉)]

Computer Science and Engineering Department, Qatar University, Doha, Qatar
me1709534@qu.edu.qa

Abstract. Nowadays, it is very rare to find a single news article that solely contains all the information about a certain subject or event. Very recently, a number of methods were proposed to find background articles that can be linked to a query article to help readers understand its context, whenever they are reading it. These methods, however, are still far from reaching an optimal performance. In my thesis, I propose techniques that aim to improve the background linking process for online news articles. For example, I propose to exploit different techniques to construct representative search queries from the query article, that be can effectively employed to retrieve the required background links in an ad-hoc setting. Moreover, I aim to study how to train neural models that can learn the background relevance between pairs of articles. Through the proposed techniques, I aim to experiment with the possible criteria that may distinguish useful background articles from non-relevant ones, such as their semantic and lexical similarities, and the granularity of the topics discussed in each. Defining these criteria will enable understanding the notion of background relevance, and accordingly allow for effective background links retrieval.

Keywords: Document linking · Background knowledge · Event extraction · Online news analysis

1 Introduction

Recently, online news articles have become a valuable source of information for many users on the web. Nonetheless, all the information regarding any subject or event rarely exists in a single news article. Most often, authors of news articles assume that readers have some background knowledge on the subject they are reading, and they leave it up to the readers to seek knowledge for what they did not understand elsewhere. In this context, it becomes vital to develop techniques to link news articles using the background knowledge they provide to one another. This way, when a reader reads one article, she can directly follow background links to other articles that can help her understand the content of the article at hand, and gain more context knowledge on its subject.

To solve the news background linking problem, I propose techniques that attempt to analyze the input (query) article to reveal its influential keywords, salient information, and events mentioned, to effectively identify the required

© Springer Nature Switzerland AG 2021
D. Hiemstra et al. (Eds.): ECIR 2021, LNCS 12657, pp. 672–676, 2021.
https://doi.org/10.1007/978-3-030-72240-1_79

background links. Furthermore, I will analyze some labeled articles, released for this research direction, in order to deeply understand the notion of background relevance, and extend my proposed techniques accordingly. Specifically, I aim to tackle the following research questions: **RQ1:** What criteria in both the query and its candidate background articles affect the background retrieval relevance?, **RQ2:** Can the background linking problem be effectively treated as an *ad-hoc retrieval problem*?, **RQ3:** For query articles that are mainly triggered by the occurrence of a specific event in time (i.e., *event-triggered*), can the event's related information (who did what, when, where, why, and how) be extracted and utilized to follow the context of the mentioned event, and accordingly retrieve background links?, **RQ4:** Can we *learn* an effective model that predicts the relevance of a background article to the reader of a query article?

2   Related Work

The news background linking problem was very recently introduced to the research community as a new task in TREC 2018 [16]. The task then continued with a follow-up in TREC 2019 [17], and TREC 2020. A number of teams participated in this task proposing different methods to solve the problem. Some methods addressed the news background linking problem following an ad-hoc search approach, in which, an input query article was analyzed to construct a search query and the retrieval goal was to find relevant background articles. To construct a search query from the query article, teams used different methods for selecting the query terms including: the whole article as a query [2,10], the query article's title [2,9], the terms with the highest tf-idf scores [19], the lead terms in the query article [19], the terms that are part of extracted named entities [2], and key-phrases extracted using a graph-based text analysis method [2]. Upon the retrieval of an initial set of background links, some methods further adopted query expansion to increase the effectiveness of the retrieved set of articles [3,11]. A number of methods suggested to learn a function that can compute the usefulness of a background article to a query article [7,15]. To train the models, different features from both the query document and the candidate background document were extracted. Surprisingly, the published results in both 2018 and 2019 showed that simply using the full article as a search query in an ad-hoc setting achieved the best performance among all the methods submitted to TREC [16,17]. I believe, however, that, for long articles, this method will be inefficient, since the retrieval model will consider all words in the query article even if it is irrelevant. Furthermore, the effectiveness reported by this method is still far from being optimal (ndcg@5 of 0.461 and 0.606 in TREC 2018 and TREC 2019 respectively), which leaves a big room for improvement.

3   Proposed Methodology

In this section, I describe my proposed solutions to address each research question that I listed in the introduction.

- **RQ1. Notion of Background Relevance:** To address RQ1, I aim to manually analyze a sample of the query articles and their corresponding background links (released by TREC) to determine what affects the judgment of background relevance. As a preliminary work, I started the manual analysis process, where I qualitatively analyzed 25 randomly selected query articles from the TREC 2018 dataset, as well as a sample of their corresponding background links [6]. Overall, I annotated 227 articles. My analysis drawn many useful insights about the notion of background relevance. For instance, I found that event-triggered articles are harder to process than other articles, with most of their corresponding background links mentioning the event or the context at which it occurs. I further found that the highly relevant background articles must discuss the subtopics that are mentioned in the query article in more detail, and, at the same time, introduce new subtopics that add to the readers' knowledge on the context of the query article's main topic. I additionally found that, in general, query articles and their corresponding background articles do not exhibit high lexical similarity. While this preliminary analysis was useful, I will still explore more potential background relevance factors, such as whether the query article is reporting hard or soft news, and whether the article is a story report, a feature detailed article, an editorial, or an opinion article. Furthermore, I propose to ask readers (of different backgrounds and expertise) to extract parts of the query articles that they do not understand, or would want more information about, and analyze those specific parts with respect to the relevant background articles to determine possible linkage points, and, moreover, explore options of diversifying the result set to suit different types of news readers.
- **RQ2. Ad-hoc Retrieval:** To address RQ2, I intend to study if I can effectively construct a search query using keywords extracted from the query news article, and use this search query to retrieve the background links as in traditional ad-hoc retrieval task. As my preliminary work in this direction, I employed graph decomposition techniques to extract weighted terms from the query article, and used them as a search query to retrieve the required background links [5]. I participated in TREC 2019 with runs that used this graph-based method, and my best submitted run was ranked second, indicating the potential effectiveness of this approach. My next step will be to study more recent and effective techniques for keyword extraction such as the supervised keyword extraction frameworks (e.g., [4]). I further aim to divide the query article into segments, where each segment consists of one or more consecutive paragraphs that represent a subtopic of the article, and analyze each subtopic independently, and in context, for keyword extraction. This is based on the assumption that a term in a specific paragraph may not have high weight if it is considered with respect to the whole article, but might be a good representative of the subtopic, hence may lead to useful background articles that contain more details on that subtopic. A search query can then be constructed by computing an overall weight for each term that combines both its subtopic keyword weight, and its subtopic offset in the query article. To ensure that relevant background articles are retrieved during the ad-hoc

retrieval process in case the authors of the query and the background articles use different vocabulary, I aim to experiment with different methods for query expansion [1,12] to expand the extracted search query with keywords that might lead to the required background links.

- **RQ3. Event Extraction:** To address RQ3, I aim to experiment with open-domain event extraction techniques to extract the key sentences that contain answers to the 5W1H questions of events[8] from the *event-triggered* query articles, and form an event descriptor through the concatenation of these key sentences that can be employed to find other articles that discuss the context of the mentioned event. More specifically, I propose to rerank candidate background articles (obtained for example by searching the articles collection using the lead paragraph of the query article as a search query) given its context similarity to the extracted query event-descriptor. During my manual annotation of event-triggered query articles, I noticed that a background article may discuss the context of the query article's event without specifically mentioning it, and that this discussion may be in any part of the background article. Accordingly, I propose to split the candidate background articles into passages (e.g., sections or paragraphs), and compute the similarity between each passage and the query event descriptor (e.g., using cosine similarity of its corresponding embedding-vectors), then compute an aggregated reranking score for each candidate article given the scores of its passages.

- **RQ4. Supervised Learning:** News background linking can be perceived as a classification task, where the goal is to check if a candidate article is a background of a query article or not. Accordingly, to address RQ4, I propose to use a supervised model to rerank a set of articles that I will initially retrieve given the most effective ad-hoc retrieval based method. Since the research in news background linking is still in its preliminary stage, training data is limited. Therefore, in this work, I plan to experiment with fine-tuning pre-trained supervised models (such as monoBERT [13]) for news background linking. Recently, substantial work has shown that models trained on a large corpus can learn universal language representations, which are beneficial for tackling different downstream tasks via fine-tuning [14]. As the input to most of the pre-trained models for Information Retrieval is limited in size, I aim to explore with different representations of both the query and candidate background articles, before passing it to the reranker model. One proposed idea is to use extractive summarization methods on the news articles to extract its most representative sentences [18] to pass to the reranking model. Another idea is to chunk both the query and the candidate articles into passages and feed pairs of passages from both articles to the reranker model, then compute an aggregated score for the candidate article.

4   Experimental Evaluation

I aim to evaluate my proposed techniques using the Washington Post dataset released by TREC for the news background linking task. The dataset, first released in the 2018 News track, has around 600k news articles. 50 Query articles from the dataset were selected for the task in TREC 2018, 57 in TREC 2019, and 60 in TREC 2020. For evaluation, I plan to compute precision, recall, F1, and nDCG scores.

References

1. Azad, H.K., Deepak, A.: A new approach for query expansion using wikipedia and wordnet. Inf. Sci. **492**, 147–163 (2019)
2. Bimantara, A., et al.: htw saar @ TREC 2018 news track (2018)
3. Ding, Y., Lian, X., Zhou, H., Liu, Z., Ding, H., Hou, Z.: ICTNET at TREC 2019 news track (2019)
4. Duari, S., Bhatnagar, V.: Complex network based supervised keyword extractor. Expert Syst. Appl. **140**, 112876 (2020)
5. Essam, M., Elsayed, T.: bigIR at TREC 2019: Graph-based analysis for news background linking (2019)
6. Essam, M., Elsayed, T.: Why is that a background article: a qualitative analysis of relevance for news background linking. In: Proceedings of the 29th ACM International Conference on Information & Knowledge Management, pp. 2009–2012 (2020)
7. Foley, J., Montoly, A., Pena, M.: Smith at TREC2019: Learning to rank background articles with poetry categories and keyphrase extraction (2019)
8. Hamborg, F., Breitinger, C., Gipp, B.: Giveme5w1h: a universal system for extracting main events from news articles. In: Proceedings of the 13th ACM Conference on Recommender Systems, 7th International Workshop on News Recommendation and Analytics (INRA 2019), September 2019
9. Lopez-Ubeda, P., Diaz-Galiano, M.C., Valdivia, M.T.M., Urena-Lopez, L.A.: Using clustering to filter results of an information retrieval system (2018)
10. Lu, K., Fang, H.: Leveraging entities in background document retrieval for news articles (2019)
11. Missaoui, S., MacFarlane, A., Makri, S., Gutierrez-Lopez, M.: DMINR at TREC news track (2019)
12. Nasir, J.A., Varlamis, I., Ishfaq, S.: A knowledge-based semantic framework for query expansion. Inf. Process. Manag. **56**(5), 1605–1617 (2019)
13. Nogueira, R., Cho, K.: Passage re-ranking with BERT. arXiv preprint arXiv:1901.04085 (2019)
14. Qiu, X., Sun, T., Xu, Y., Shao, Y., Dai, N., Huang, X.: Pre-trained models for natural language processing: a survey. arXiv preprint arXiv:2003.08271 (2020)
15. Qu, J., Wang, Y.: UNC SILS at TREC 2019 news track (2019)
16. Soboroff, I., Huang, S., Harman, D.: TREC 2018 news track overview. In: TREC (2018)
17. Soboroff, I., Huang, S., Harman, D.: TREC 2019 news track overview. In: TREC (2019)
18. Xiao, W., Carenini, G.: Extractive summarization of long documents by combining global and local context. arXiv preprint arXiv:1909.08089 (2019)
19. Yang, P., Lin, J.: Anserini at TREC 2018: Centre, common core, and news tracks (2018)

Multidimensional Relevance
in Task-Specific Retrieval

Divi Galih Prasetyo Putri[✉]

Department of Informatics, Systems, and Communication (DISCo), Information
and Knowledge Representation, Retrieval, and Reasoning (IKR3) Lab, University
of Milano-Bicocca, Edificio U14, Viale Sarca, 336, 20126 Milan, Italy
d.putri@campus.unimib.it
http://www.ir.disco.unimib.it/

Abstract. Several criteria of relevance have been proposed in the literature. However, relevance criteria are strongly related to the search task. Thus, it is important to employ the criteria that are useful for the considered search task. This research explores the concept of multidimensional relevance in a specific search-task. Firstly, we want to investigate search tasks and the related relevance dimension. Then, we intend to explore the approaches that can be used to combine more than one relevance dimension. The goal of this study is to improve the retrieval system in a specific task.

Keywords: Multidimensional relevance · Relevance dimension · Search task

1 Motivation

Relevance, as the core notion in Information retrieval, is a complex subject. The multidimensionality of relevance has been discussed for a long time by the research community. Topicality is the basic relevance criterion, but it constitutes just one facet of relevance and it is not sufficient [3]. The overall relevance score is based on the computation of the considered criteria or the relevance dimensions. Many aspects can impact the considered criteria such as context and situation. For example in blog post retrieval task [22,23] and microblog retrieval task [13], the characteristic of the content affects the definition of relevance. Credibility has been used in addition to topicality to assess relevance because User-Generated Content (UGC) is not always trustworthy. Moreover, the search intent or task behind a search process also influences relevance where different importance for each dimension can be applied. Thus, it is essential to pay attention to the process of defining the considered relevance dimensions in order to design an information retrieval system. Another important process is to model and aggregate the relevance dimensions. The model has to consider the weighted preference over the relevance dimension in a specific search task. This research will focus on task-specific search and explore both aspects. First, we analyze

D. Hiemstra et al. (Eds.): ECIR 2021, LNCS 12657, pp. 677–681, 2021.
https://doi.org/10.1007/978-3-030-72240-1_80

the relevance dimensions that can be useful for specific search tasks. Then, we intend to explore the approaches to combine several relevance dimensions.

2   Related Work

Topical relevance is not the only dimension of relevance. In [6], the authors point out several criteria based on document properties that can be exploited to assess document relevance, including novelty, informativeness, and credibility. Several works address the criteria of relevance in a specific context, such as e-commerce [2], legal search [20] and health-information search [16]. Each of them tends to favor different criteria of relevance. In [2], the authors found that most e-commerce users consider accuracy and availability when assessing relevance. Besides topical relevance, six additional criteria are addressed in the context of legal search, including algorithmic relevance, bibliographic relevance, cognitive relevance, situational relevance and domain relevance [20]. In Microblog retrieval, several criteria of relevance have been introduced; they include credibility [10,13,21], informativeness [5,10], and interestingness [1,15,18]. While in health information search [16], the combination of topicality and understandability could improve the effectiveness of the retrieval results.

Several approaches can be used to combine more than one relevance dimension to estimate the overall relevance score. Most approaches are based on mathematical aggregation functions [7,8,12,14]. Another study tried to optimize the importance of the considered relevance dimension by applying multi-objective technique in learning-to-rank setting [9]. Recent work adopted the quantum theory to model multidimensional relevance [19].

3   Proposed Research and Methodology

3.1   How Search Task Affects the Considered Relevance Dimensions?

In [17], the objective was to investigate the impact of different relevance dimensions on different search tasks in Microblog. Given the nature of social media platform, Microblog contains a wide variety of topics. The availability of the information enables the user to perform many search tasks. We hypothesised that particular relevance dimensions need to be considered depending on the search task. In this work, we considered four relevance dimensions that have been introduced in the literature related to Microblog search, namely informativeness, interestingness, credibility, and opinionatedness. To evaluate the possible impact that each of the aforementioned relevance dimensions has on the considered tasks, we made a comparative evaluation of a baseline implementing relevance as topicality, and a system that assesses relevance by combining topicality with just an additional dimension at a time. We used a simple approach via linear combination to combine the relevance dimensions. We reported the result obtained on two different search tasks, disaster-related retrieval task and opinion retrieval task. Each task has different search objectives. In the disaster-related retrieval task, the relevant document should be helpful for emergency relief operations. In the opinion retrieval task, the aim is to understand other user's thoughts on a specific topic. The result shows that informativeness, interestingness, and credibility are useful for disaster-related retrieval. In the case of opinion retrieval, informativeness and interestingness do not positively affect the retrieval system's result. Instead, credibility and opinionatedness are important. We can conclude that some specific dimensions may impact a given search task while others could not be considered. In particular, this indicates that each search task has different criteria that define relevance. Moreover, the same impactful relevance dimension can have different importance (weight) in other search tasks.

3.2 How to Model Multidimensional Relevance Using Deep Neural Ranking?

In the previous work, we only employ a simple linear combination strategy. We propose to study other approaches to combine the relevance dimensions and model the importance. Following the success of the neural ranking approaches in information retrieval, we wish to model the concept of multidimensional relevance via a multi-task neural network. In Multi-task Learning (MTL), several tasks can be learned concurrently to enable sharing information between tasks [4]. The model can benefit from having more training data and reducing overfitting in one task. This concept supports the fact that task-specific retrieval tends to have limited data. The main focus or the *primary task* in this approach is the information retrieval task and the *auxiliary task* that will provide additional knowledge is the prediction task of the considered relevance dimension other than topicality. The closest approach to ours is proposed in [11], where the vector representation is learned simultaneously between information retrieval task and query classification task in a multi-task setting. We plan to work on the customer health search (CHS) task[1,2]. In CHS, credibility and understandability are considered as important criteria of relevance. We will use a simple neural ranking model and learn the model jointly with the prediction task of only one additional relevance dimension (credibility or understandability) to get a better insight into the potential benefit of the multi-task model. However, it could be extended such that it also considers more complex neural ranking models.

3.3 How to Model Multidimensional Relevance for Task-Specific Retrieval?

The ranking approaches based on deep learning can be data-hungry. However, labeled data for specific task retrieval is limited and can be too small in size. In addition, the importance of each dimension and the interaction between dimensions is hard to model in the Learning-to-Rank approach. Thus, we also plan to examine the Multi-Criteria Decision Making (MCDM) approach to perform

---

[1] https://clefehealth.imag.fr/?page_id=189.

[2] https://trec-health-misinfo.github.io/.

aggregation of several relevance criteria. MCDM has been used in the context of personalized IR [8,14]. As shown in both works, the interaction between relevance dimensions and the importance can be modelled in the MCDM approach. We plan to extend this idea for task-specific retrieval. Specific-task retrieval can be similar to personalized IR in terms of preference over relevance dimensions, where different search tasks might prefer different relevance dimensions. In personalized IR, the weight of each dimension can be obtained explicitly from the user's preference or implicitly from the user search history. While the importance of each relevance dimensions can be unknown and not easy to define in the specific-task retrieval. First, we are interested in studying how effective the existing MCDM approach is within a specific search task. Then, we have to consider the uncertainty of the weight or importance of different relevance dimensions in different search tasks.

4   Research Issues for Discussion

We found several problems and challenges in our proposed approach and current works. Labeled dataset on specific-task retrieval is limited. Moreover, we need additional assessment besides topical relevance assessment (In the case of CHS: credibility and understandability assessment). Even the assessment that is available on the existing dataset is incomplete. Our challenge is to consider this problem in the proposed approaches and evaluation methods. We also want to discuss how to improve our proposal.

References

1. Alhadi, A.C., Gottron, T., Kunegis, J., Naveed, N.: LiveTweet: microblog retrieval based on interestingness and an adaptation of the vector space model. In: TREC (2011)
2. Alonso, O., Mizzaro, S.: Relevance criteria for e-commerce: a crowdsourcing-based experimental analysis. In: Proceedings of the 32nd International ACM SIGIR Conference on Research and Development in Information Retrieval, pp. 760–761 (2009)
3. Boyce, B.: Beyond topicality: a two stage view of relevance and the retrieval process. Inf. Process. Manag. **18**(3), 105–109 (1982)
4. Caruana, R.: Multitask learning. Mach. Learn. **28**(1), 41–75 (1997)
5. Choi, J., Croft, W.B., Kim, J.Y.: Quality models for microblog retrieval. In: Proceedings of the 21st ACM International Conference on Information and Knowledge Management, pp. 1834–1838. ACM (2012)
6. Cooper, W.S.: On selecting a measure of retrieval effectiveness. J. Am. Soc. Inf. Sci. **24**(2), 87–100 (1973)
7. da Costa Pereira, C., Dragoni, M., Pasi, G.: Multidimensional relevance: a new aggregation criterion. In: Boughanem, M., Berrut, C., Mothe, J., Soule-Dupuy, C. (eds.) ECIR 2009. LNCS, vol. 5478, pp. 264–275. Springer, Heidelberg (2009). https://doi.org/10.1007/978-3-642-00958-7_25
8. da Costa Pereira, C., Dragoni, M., Pasi, G.: Multidimensional relevance: prioritized aggregation in a personalized information retrieval setting. Inf. Process. Manag. **48**(2), 340–357 (2012)

9. van Doorn, J., Odijk, D., Roijers, D.M., de Rijke, M.: Balancing relevance criteria through multi-objective optimization. In: Proceedings of the 39th International ACM SIGIR conference on Research and Development in Information Retrieval, pp. 769–772 (2016)
10. Huang, H., et al.: Tweet ranking based on heterogeneous networks. In: Proceedings of COLING 2012, pp. 1239–1256 (2012)
11. Liu, X., Gao, J., He, X., Deng, L., Duh, K., Wang, Y.Y.: Representation learning using multi-task deep neural networks for semantic classification and information retrieval. In: Proceedings of the 2015 Conference of the North American Chapter of the Association for Computational Linguistics: Human Language Technologies, pp. 912–921 (2015)
12. Marrara, S., Pasi, G., Viviani, M.: Aggregation operators in information retrieval. Fuzzy Sets Syst. **324**, 3–19 (2017)
13. Massoudi, K., Tsagkias, M., de Rijke, M., Weerkamp, W.: Incorporating query expansion and quality indicators in searching microblog posts. In: Clough, P., et al. (eds.) ECIR 2011. LNCS, vol. 6611, pp. 362–367. Springer, Heidelberg (2011). https://doi.org/10.1007/978-3-642-20161-5_36
14. Moulahi, B., Tamine, L., Yahia, S.B.: Toward a personalized approach for combining document relevance estimates. In: Dimitrova, V., Kuflik, T., Chin, D., Ricci, F., Dolog, P., Houben, G.-J. (eds.) UMAP 2014. LNCS, vol. 8538, pp. 158–170. Springer, Cham (2014). https://doi.org/10.1007/978-3-319-08786-3_14
15. Naveed, N., Gottron, T., Kunegis, J., Alhadi, A.C.: Searching microblogs: coping with sparsity and document quality. In: Proceedings of the 20th ACM International Conference on Information and Knowledge Management, pp. 183–188. ACM (2011)
16. Palotti, J., Goeuriot, L., Zuccon, G., Hanbury, A.: Ranking health web pages with relevance and understandability. In: Proceedings of the 39th International ACM SIGIR conference on Research and Development in Information Retrieval, pp. 965–968 (2016)
17. Putri, D.G.P., Viviani, M., Pasi, G.: Social search and task-related relevance dimensions in microblogging sites. In: Aref, S., et al. (eds.) SocInfo 2020. LNCS, vol. 12467, pp. 297–311. Springer, Cham (2020). https://doi.org/10.1007/978-3-030-60975-7_22
18. Tao, K., Abel, F., Hauff, C., Houben, G.-J.: Twinder: a search engine for twitter streams. In: Brambilla, M., Tokuda, T., Tolksdorf, R. (eds.) ICWE 2012. LNCS, vol. 7387, pp. 153–168. Springer, Heidelberg (2012). https://doi.org/10.1007/978-3-642-31753-8_11
19. Uprety, S., Su, Y., Song, D., Li, J.: Modeling multidimensional user relevance in IR using vector spaces. In: The 41st International ACM SIGIR Conference on Research & Development in Information Retrieval, pp. 993–996 (2018)
20. Van Opijnen, M., Santos, C.: On the concept of relevance in legal information retrieval. Artif. Intell. Law **25**(1), 65–87 (2017)
21. Vosecky, J., Leung, K.W.-T., Ng, W.: Searching for quality microblog posts: filtering and ranking based on content analysis and implicit links. In: Lee, S., Peng, Z., Zhou, X., Moon, Y.-S., Unland, R., Yoo, J. (eds.) DASFAA 2012. LNCS, vol. 7238, pp. 397–413. Springer, Heidelberg (2012). https://doi.org/10.1007/978-3-642-29038-1_29
22. Weerkamp, W., De Rijke, M.: Credibility improves topical blog post retrieval. In: Proceedings of ACL-08: HLT, pp. 923–931 (2008)
23. Weerkamp, W., de Rijke, M.: Credibility-inspired ranking for blog post retrieval. Inf. Retr. **15**(3–4), 243–277 (2012)

Deep Semantic Entity Linking

Pedro Ruas[(⊠)] [iD]

LASIGE, Faculdade de Ciências, Universidade de Lisboa, 1749-016 Lisbon, Portugal
psruas@fc.ul.pt

Abstract. Named entity linking systems are an essential component in text mining pipelines, mapping entity mentions in the text to the appropriate knowledge base identifiers. However, the current systems have several limitations affecting their performance: the lack of context of the entity mentions, the incomplete disambiguation graphs and the lack of approaches to deal with unlinkable entity mentions. The PhD project will focus on solving the aforementioned challenges in order to develop a NEL model which outperforms state-of-the-art performance in Biomedical and Life Sciences domains.

Keywords: Named Entity Linking · Text mining · NIL entities · Multilingual corpora · Graph-based models

1 Introduction

In text mining pipelines, named entity linking (NEL) systems map the entity mentions recognised by named entity recognition tools to the appropriate knowledge base (KB) concepts. These play an important role in several tasks, such as automatic population and curation of KBs [6], improvement of question answering [22] and search engines [15], and identification of diseases in electronic health records [11]. The simplest approach to the NEL problem consists in choosing the KB concept with the most similar label for each entity mention using string matching techniques, which is very limited since it does not consider the context of the mention. At the contrary, language models pre-trained with large amounts of text, like BERT [4] or ELMo [17], learn contextualised representations of words able to express their meaning according to their local context. Graph-based NEL models consider the global context of the mentions, building a disambiguation graph with mentions and the respective KB candidates as nodes and then attempting to maximise the coherence between the disambiguation candidates. Those based on Personalized PageRank algorithm are one of the state-of-the-art approaches in NEL [7]. However, the main limitation of graph-based approaches is incomplete graphs (e.g., graphs with few edges between nodes) affecting their precision, which is usually caused by a lack of domain

Supported by FCT through the DeST: Deep SemanticTagger project, ref. PTDC/CCI-BIO/28685/2017, PhD Scholarship, ref. 2020.05393.BD, LASIGE ResearchUnit, ref. UIDB/00408/2020 and ref. UIDP/00408/2020.

knowledge in the KB. Also, when the KB is incomplete, a NEL system is not able to associate some entity mentions with the respective KB concepts (unlinkable or NIL entities), which leads to a low recall [21]. Wu et al. [23] divided the approaches to NIL entity clustering in three categories: string matching, hierarchical agglomerative clustering and graph-based. These approaches only attempt to group different mentions of the same NIL entity, but none of them attempts to disambiguate it, even if it is not a perfect disambiguation. The main challenges associated with NEL systems that the PhD proposal intends to address are the lack of mention context to determine local similarity, the incompleteness of disambiguation graphs on graph-based models, and the absence of approaches to link NIL entities to KBs.

The main objectives of the PhD proposal are the development of a NEL system that outperforms state-of-the-art approaches in Biomedical and Life Sciences domains in terms of recall, by creating deep semantic links between NIL entities and concepts of a given KB (NIL entity linking), and in terms of precision, by completing disambiguation graphs with relations extracted from text and with the output of the NIL entity linking model, and by improving the local similarity determination with contextualised embedding representations for entity mentions, their context and respective KB candidates.

2   Research Methodology

2.1   Improvement of the Disambiguation Graph of a Graph-Based NEL Model

Usually, the output of NEL improves RE systems. The hypothesis here is that, at the contrary, RE improves the performance of NEL: RE captures relations between entities that are expressed in text but not in the KB, which complete the disambiguation graph with edges. The goal is to develop a graph-based NEL model that integrates the output of RE systems to improve the disambiguation graph (REEL). The novelty is the use of RE systems to improve NEL systems, and not the other way around as it usually happens. This methodology could originate a feedback cycle in which NEL performance impacts RE output, which then improves NEL performance and so forth. RE tools, like BO-LSTM [10], extract the relations between entities in the text and will add them as edges to the disambiguation graph. This module evaluates the impact of denser disambiguation graphs on the performance of the PPR algorithm. The work relative to this module has been executed and published in a journal paper [19].

2.2   Improvement of a Local NEL Model

The hypothesis is that pre-trained language models improve the determination of local similarity between entity mention and KB candidates through contextualised word embeddings. The goal is to develop a local NEL model that goes beyond string similarity methods, leveraging contextualised word embeddings.

The precision of the model should increase compared with a string matching based approach. The first step is the generation of a KB candidates list for each mention resorting to abbreviation expansion, string matching and synonyms lookup, and then pre-trained language models are explored, like BERT [4], ClinicalBERT [1], or BioBERT [13] to create contextualised embeddings for mentions, as well their KB candidates. The comparison of mention embeddings with KB candidate embeddings will return a similarity score that will be further used to filter out less relevant candidates from the respective candidates lists.

2.3 Development of a NIL Entity Linking Model

The basis for this module is the framework by Qi et al. [18] to originate embeddings for multi-word expressions, leveraging the sememes associated with the constituent words. The hypothesis here is that, analogously, the meaning of a NIL entity is expressed through the KB concepts associated with its words. The goal is to develop an attention-based model to find the most relevant KB candidate concept for the respective NIL entity in order to disambiguate it. The model converts NIL entities into deep semantic links to the KB, which are added to the disambiguation graph in Subsect. 2.1. The first step is to build a word-concept dictionary to allow candidate retrieval for NIL entities: a key is a word present either in a KB concept designation or definition, and its values are the KB concept identifiers where that word appears. For each of the words of a NIL entity, the associated KB concepts are retrieved from the dictionary. Both words and candidates are represented by embeddings, the input to the attention model. The second step is the development of an attention-based model to find the most relevant KB candidate concept, and its schema is represented in Fig. 1.

2.4 Evaluation

The evaluation of the improved graph-based model REEL (Subsect. 2.1) consists of the comparison of its performance with two baseline approaches: string matching and PPR-SSM [9]. The performance of these models (F1-score, precision, recall) is measured in two gold standard datasets: BC5CDR Corpus [14] and CRAFT corpus [2]. The evaluation of the improved local model (Subsect. 2.2) consists of the comparison of its performance (F1-score, precision, recall) with a string matching baseline approach in the following datasets: NCBI Disease Corpus [5], BC5CDR Corpus, and CRAFT corpus, MedMentions [16]. The evaluation of the NIL entity linking model (Subsect. 2.3) includes two different steps. The first step involves a specific silver standard built from existing NEL datasets. To build the dataset, existing annotations are converted into NIL annotations, by associating each entity to the label of the direct ancestor of the gold label. The performance of two models (accuracy), string matching (baseline) and NIL entity linking model, is measured in the referred dataset. In the second step, deep semantic links, i.e. the output generated by the NIL entity linking model, are added to the disambiguation graph (nodes and respective edges) of PPR-SSM [9]). The performance of two models, PPR-SSM and improved PPR-SSM, is measured (F1-score, precision, recall) in NCBI Disease

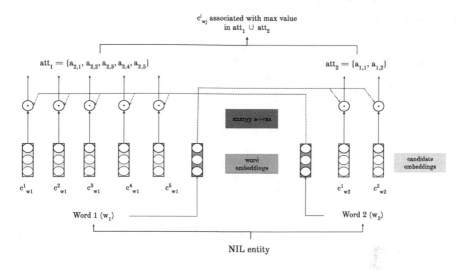

Fig. 1. Attention model schema. A NIL entity with two words is tokenized, word 1 has five KB candidates associated, whereas word 2 has two candidates. Word and candidate embeddings are the input for the attention model. The attention weights of word 1 candidates (att_1) are based on the energy scores computed from the embeddings for word 2, and vice-versa. At the end, the candidate associated with the highest attention weight in both att_1 and att_2 disambiguates the NIL entity.

Corpus, BC5CDR Corpus, CRAFT corpus, and MedMentions dataset. The three referred modules are then integrated into a unique hybrid NEL model, which is evaluated in several datasets [5, 14] and, additionally, in a new parallel, multilingual dataset. Since there is no Portuguese biomedical NEL dataset available, the goal is to build one containing biomedical and clinical text in Portuguese, English and Spanish. The documents are retrieved from SciELO[1] and PubMed[2] repositories, automatic NER and NEL tools, like MER [3], recognise medical diagnostic entities present in the documents and link them to terms of the *International Classification of Diseases 10 - Clinical Modification* (ICD10-CM), and then there is a manual validation of the obtained annotations by crowdsourcing and by expert analysis over a selected subset of the documents. The performance of the hybrid model (F1-score, precision, recall), as well of other SOTA approaches (BERT-Based Biomedical Entity Normalization [8] or TaggerOne [12]) is measured on the referred datasets. Preliminary work relative to the development of the parallel, multilingual dataset has been done and published in a workshop paper [20].

---

[1] https://scielo.org/.
[2] https://pubmed.ncbi.nlm.nih.gov/.

References

1. Alsentzer, E., et al.: Publicly available clinical BERT embeddings. In: Proceedings of the 2nd Clinical Natural Language Processing Workshop, pp. 72–78. Association for Computational Linguistics, Minneapolis, Minnesota (2019). https://doi.org/10.18653/v1/w19-1909
2. Ide, N., Pustejovsky, J. (eds.): Handbook of Linguistic Annotation. Springer, Dordrecht (2017). https://doi.org/10.1007/978-94-024-0881-2
3. Couto, F.M., Lamurias, A.: MER: a shell script and annotation server for minimal named entity recognition and linking. J. Cheminform. **10**(1), 58 (2018). https://doi.org/10.1186/s13321-018-0312-9
4. Devlin, J., Chang, M.W., Lee, K., Toutanova, K.: BERT: Pre-training of Deep Bidirectional Transformers for Language Understanding, October 2018. http://arxiv.org/abs/1810.04805
5. Doğan, R.I., Leaman, R., Lu, Z.: NCBI disease corpus: a resource for disease name recognition and concept normalization. J. Biomed. Inform. **47**, 1–10 (2014). https://doi.org/10.1016/j.jbi.2013.12.006
6. Dredze, M., Mcnamee, P., Rao, D., Gerber, A., Finin, T.: Entity disambiguation for knowledge base population. In: 23rd International Conference on Computational Linguistics, pp. 277–285, August 2010. https://doi.org/10.3115/1119176.1119181
7. Guo, Z., Barbosa, D.: Robust named entity disambiguation with random walks. Semantic Web **9**(4), 459–479 (2018). https://doi.org/10.3233/SW-170273
8. Ji, Z., Wei, Q., Xu, H.: BERT-based Ranking for Biomedical Entity Normalization (2019). http://arxiv.org/abs/1908.03548
9. Lamurias, A., Ruas, P., Couto, F.M.: PPR-SSM: personalized PageRank and semantic similarity measures for entity linking. BMC Bioinform. **20**(1), 1–12 (2019). https://doi.org/10.1186/s12859-019-3157-y
10. Lamurias, A., Sousa, D., Clarke, L.A., Couto, F.M.: BO-LSTM: classifying relations via long short-term memory networks along biomedical ontologies. BMC Bioinform. **20**(10) (2019). https://doi.org/10.1186/s12859-018-2584-5
11. Leaman, R., Khare, R., Lu, Z.: Challenges in clinical natural language processing for automated disorder normalization. J. Biomed. Inform. **57**, 28–37 (2015). https://doi.org/10.1016/j.jbi.2015.07.010
12. Leaman, R., Lu, Z.: TaggerOne: joint named entity recognition and normalization with semi-Markov Models. Bioinformatics **32**(18), 2839–2846 (2016). https://doi.org/10.1093/bioinformatics/btw343
13. Lee, J., Yoon, W., Kim, S., Kim, D., Kim, S., So, C.H., Kang, J.: BioBERT: a pre-trained biomedical language representation model for biomedical text mining. Bioinformatics **36**, 1–7 (2019). https://doi.org/10.1093/bioinformatics/btz682
14. Li, J., et al.: BioCreative V CDR task corpus: a resource for chemical disease relation extraction. Database J. Biol. Databases Curation **2016**, 1–10 (2016). https://doi.org/10.1093/database/baw068
15. Meij, E., Balog, K., Odijk, D.: Entity linking and retrieval for semantic search. In: WSDM 2014 - Proceedings of the 7th ACM International Conference on Web Search and Data Mining, New York, New York, USA, February 2014, p. 683 (2014). https://doi.org/10.1145/2556195.2556201
16. Mohan, S., Li, D.: Medmentions: a large biomedical corpus annotated with UMLS concepts (2019)
17. Peters, M., Neumann, M., Iyyer, M., Gardner, M., Clark, C., Lee, K., Zettlemoyer, L.: Deep Contextualized Word Representations, pp. 2227–2237 (2018). https://doi.org/10.18653/v1/n18-1202

18. Qi, F., Huang, J., Yang, C., Liu, Z., Chen, X., Liu, Q., Sun, M.: Modeling semantic compositionality with sememe knowledge. In: Proceedings of the 57th Annual Meeting of the Association for Computational Linguistics, Florence, Italy, July 28 - August 2, 2019, pp. 5706–5715. Association for Computational Linguistics (2019). https://doi.org/10.18653/v1/p19-1571

19. Ruas, P., Lamurias, A., Couto, F.M.: Linking chemical and disease entities to ontologies by integrating PageRank with extracted relations from literature. J. Cheminform. **12**(1), 1–11 (2020). https://doi.org/10.1186/s13321-020-00461-4

20. Ruas, P., Lamúrias, A., Couto, F.M.: Towards a multilingual corpus for named entity linking evaluation in the clinical domain. In: CEUR Workshop Proceedings, vol. 2619, pp. 2–4 (2020)

21. Shen, W., Wang, J., Han, J.: Entity linking with a knowledge base: issues, techniques, and solutions. IEEE Trans. Knowl. Data Eng. **27**(2), 443–460 (2015). https://doi.org/10.1109/TKDE.2014.2327028.   http://ieeexplore.ieee.org/xpls/abs_all.jsp?arnumber=6823700

22. Sorokin, D., Gurevych, I.: Mixing context granularities for improved entity linking on question answering data across entity categories. In: 7th Joint Conference on Lexical and Computational Semantics (*SEM), pp. 65–75. Association for Computational Linguistics (2018)

23. Wu, G., He, Y., Hu, X.: Entity linking: an issue to extract corresponding entity with knowledge base. IEEE Access **6**(c), 6220–6231 (2018). https://doi.org/10.1109/ACCESS.2017.2787787. http://ieeexplore.ieee.org/document/8246707/

Deep Learning System for Biomedical Relation Extraction Combining External Sources of Knowledge

Diana Sousa(✉)

LASIGE, Faculdade de Ciências, Universidade de Lisboa, Lisbon, Portugal
dfsousa@lasige.di.fc.ul.pt

Abstract. Successful biomedical relation extraction can provide evidence to researchers about possible unknown associations between entities, advancing our current knowledge about those entities and their inherent processes. Multiple relation extraction approaches have been proposed to identify relations between concepts in literature, namely using neural networks algorithms. However, the incorporation of semantics is still scarce. This project proposes that using external semantic sources of knowledge along with the latest state-of-the-art language representations can improve the current performance of biomedical relation extraction both in English and non-English languages. The goal is to build a relation extraction system using state-of-the-art language representations, such as BERT and ELMo, with semantics retrieved from external sources of knowledge, such as domain-specific ontologies, graph attention mechanisms, and semantic similarity measures.

Keywords: Biomedical relation extraction · Deep learning · Semantics

1 Motivation

The volume of unstructured textual information currently available widely surpasses the ability of analysis by a researcher, even if restring it to a domain-specific topic. Biomedical literature is the standard method that researchers use to share their findings mainly in the form of articles, patents and other types of written reports [8]. Thus, scientific articles are the primary source of knowledge for biomedical relations, including human phenotypes and other biomedical entities, such as genes and diseases. Processing the amount of information available is only feasible using text mining techniques.

Deep learning is widely used to solve problems such as speech recognition, visual object recognition, and object detection. However, deep learning methods

This work was supported by FCT through funding of DeST: Deep Semantic Tagger project, ref. PTDC/CCI-BIO/28685/2017 (http://dest.rd.ciencias.ulisboa.pt/), LASIGE Research Unit, ref. UIDB/00408/2020 and ref. UIDP/00408/2020, and PhD Scholarship, ref. SFRH/BD/145221/2019.

D. Hiemstra et al. (Eds.): ECIR 2021, LNCS 12657, pp. 688–693, 2021.
https://doi.org/10.1007/978-3-030-72240-1_82

that effectively identify and extract relations between biomedical entities in the text are still scarce [12]. Lately, efforts regarding new pre-trained language representation models have been proposed with BERT [6,23], and applied to the biomedical domain with BioBERT [11], achieving promising results. These pre-trained models can act as information layers for a biomedical RE deep learning model that uses not only the training data but also external sources of knowledge like domain-specific ontologies combined with graph attention mechanisms or semantic similarity measures. External sources of knowledge, such as the Gene Ontology (GO) [2] and the Human Phenotype Ontology (HPO) [15], can provide highly valuable information for the detection of relations between entities in the text [10], each containing several thousands of terms and annotations.

To the best of our knowledge, there is no deep learning RE system that includes in their data representations the information encoded in ontologies combined with other types of semantics to identify and extract relations between biomedical entities in articles.

2   Background and Related Work

Using different sources of information to support automated extracting of relations between biomedical concepts contributes to the development of our understanding of biological systems [22]. Researchers have proposed several RE approaches to identify relations between concepts in biomedical literature, namely, using neural network algorithms. The use of multichannel architectures composed of multiple data representations, as in deep neural networks, leads to state-of-the-art results. The right combination of data representations can eventually lead us to even higher evaluation scores in RE tasks.

Semantic resources such as knowledge bases and graphs can contain highly structured background data, particularly for the biomedical domain [13]. These resources play a fundamental role in the way we store, organize and retrieve information. Biological knowledge bases are commonplace for researchers and clinicians to access all types of biomedical data retrieved from biomedical literature [1]. Researchers can explore these resources regarding information retrieval systems, so one can rely on more than the literature itself to train a RE model. By integrating semantic resources, we feed the training process with extra, highly relevant information about each entity in the relation and the connections that entity establishes within the known semantic universe. Using heterogeneous graphs attention mechanisms to represent indirect relations between different type entities, such as genes and diseases in the biomedical domain, can be a viable additional external source of knowledge to preexisting deep learning RE systems [24]. Thus, enabling us to find representations of an indirect relation between two entities using knowledge graphs. The knowledge graphs to implement heterogeneous graphs attention mechanisms could be ontologies representing the entities of interest and their semantic relationships in a given domain. An ontology is a structured way of providing a common vocabulary in which shared knowledge is represented [7]. Word embeddings can learn how to detect relations between entities but manifest difficulties in grasping each entity's semantics and their specific domain. Domain-specific ontologies provide and formalize this knowledge. Biomedical ontologies are usually structured as a directed acyclic graph, where each node corresponds to an entity and the edges correspond to known relations between those entities. Thus, a structured representation of the semantics between entities and their relations, an ontology, allows us to use it as an added feature to a machine learning classifier.

3   Research Questions and Methodology

This doctoral proposal can be divided into three main research questions (RQ):

- **RQ1:** Can the latest advances in language representations be used to create a state-of-the-art RE deep learning system? (Subsect. 3.1)
- **RQ2:** Can we use biomedical semantics as an add-on for RE systems? (Subsect. 3.2)
- **RQ3:** How can we evaluate RE systems regarding the biomedical domain in English and non-English languages? (Subsect. 3.3).

The RE systems will go through ongoing evaluation as new information is added, using different benchmark datasets: the semantic relations between pairs of nominals corpus SemEval-2010 Task 8 [9], the drug-drug interactions corpus SemEval-2013 task-9 [17], and the Phenotype-Gene Relations corpus [19]. This project will use three distinct state-of-the-art evaluation metrics: recall, precision, and F-measure to compare the results obtained with different datasets and approaches.

3.1   Deep Learning System

Each set of biomedical entities has distinct textual characteristics, inherent to unique contexts. Each entity will be identified with a domain-specific Named-Entity Recognition (NER) system [25]. Regarding Named-Entity Linking (NEL), entities such as genes, chemicals, diseases, and proteins, will be matched to an identifier through the corresponding ontology. These tasks need to be optimized to perform RE.

The RE system between the linked identified entities is going to be built using bidirectional Long Short-Term Memory (LSTM) networks, a deep learning method that deals with long sentences of words, with a similar architecture to Reccurrent Neural Networks (RNN), based on the work of Lamurias et al. [10] (BO-LSTM system). These models use different types of information, known as channels, such as word embeddings, part-of-speech tags, grammatical relations, and WordNet hypernyms [4] to maximize performance. Each of these channels has different types of input information and is responsible for one of the model layers. All of these layers can be connected to a softmax layer outputting the probabilities of each class.

3.2 Semantics as an Add-on for RE Systems

Taking advantage of semantics can provide supplementary information that may not be present in the training data. Ontologies formalize existing knowledge about entities such as genes [2], and diseases [16]. By representing each entity as the sequence of its ancestors, it is possible to detect new relations between entities that were not evident by only using the training data. Also, a new word embedding layer is going to be built, taking advantage of semantics/attention mechanisms. Word embeddings usually represent a variable-length sentence into a fixed-length vector, where each element of the vector encodes some semantics of the original sentence. The innovation resides in adding the ontology semantics of the identified entity to each vector, as well a graph attention mechanism, and test the use of semantic similarity measures. This work will explore some avenues, such as creating an annotation vector, along with the pre-existing entity vector, that expresses ascendants, descendants, and their connections to be fed to the model, including cross-domain relationships already established as for different types of biomedical entities.

3.3 Evaluation Tactics of RE Systems to the Biomedical Domain

Apart from the standard evaluation tactic reported, some paths can facilitate the evaluation of different approaches, including the development of an improved automated corpus creation based on the PGR corpus for system assessment [19]. Improving automating corpus creation is of interest to create training data for the developed systems since some biomedical relations do not have gold standard corpus available to use to test the quality of these systems. Leveraging on previous work [19] it is possible to generate multiple silver standard corpus for different entities with good enough results. These results have been demonstrated to be sufficient for training deep learning-based systems [20], and constitute a solid contribution to the Information Retrieval (IR) field. Also, apply domain-specific ontologies of non-biomedical topics, for example, the Planteome, a plant ontology [5], using benchmark datasets. Finally, making use of the translation of some ontologies like the HPO, and the DECS ontology [3] (i.e., Health Sciences Descriptors in Portuguese and Spanish) linked to English mesh terms [14], will allow us to study the effect of different languages in the system.

This thesis's early contributions consist on four publications, including a book chapter about neural networks [22], a conference paper describing the integration of multiple ontologies into a deep learning system [18], a journal paper describing improving accessibility and distinction between negative results in biomedical RE using the PGR dataset [21], and a journal paper on an approach to create biomedical training corpora using distant supervision and crowdsourcing [20].

4 Research Issues for Discussion

I seek suggestions and comments on how to improve this proposal. I am specifically interested in discussing how to integrate external knowledge into a relation extraction system effectively in a seamless and generalizable way.

References

1. Arnaboldi, V., Raciti, D., Van Auken, K., Chan, J.N., Müller, H.M., Sternberg, P.W.: Text mining meets community curation: a newly designed curation platform to improve author experience and participation at WormBase. Database 2020 (2020)
2. Ashburner, M., et al.: Gene ontology: tool for the unification of biology. Nat. Genet. **25**(1), 25–29 (2000)
3. Campanatti-Ostiz, H., Andrade, C.: Health sciences descriptors in the Brazilian speech-language and hearing science. Pro-fono: revista de atualizacao cientifica **22**(4), 397 (2010)
4. Ciaramita, M., Altun, Y.: Broad-coverage sense disambiguation and information extraction with a supersense sequence tagger. In: Proceedings of the 2006 Conference on Empirical Methods in Natural Language Processing, pp. 594–602. Association for Computational Linguistics (2006)
5. Cooper, L., et al.: The planteome database: an integrated resource for reference ontologies, plant genomics and phenomics. Nucleic Acids Res. **46**(D1), D1168–D1180 (2018)
6. Devlin, J., Chang, M.W., Lee, K., Toutanova, K.: Bert: pre-training of deep bidirectional transformers for language understanding. In: Proceedings of the 2019 Conference of the North American Chapter of the Association for Computational Linguistics: Human Language Technologies, Volume 1 (Long and Short Papers), pp. 4171–4186 (2019)
7. Gruber, T.R., et al.: A translation approach to portable ontology specifications. Knowl. Acquisition **5**(2), 199–221 (1993)
8. Hearst, M.A.: Untangling text data mining. In: Proceedings of the 37th Annual Meeting of the Association for Computational Linguistics on Computational Linguistics, pp. 3–10. Association for Computational Linguistics (1999)
9. Hendrickx, I., et al.: SemEval-2010 task 8: multi-way classification of semantic relations between pairs of nominals. In: Proceedings of the 5th International Workshop on Semantic Evaluation, pp. 33–38. Association for Computational Linguistics (2010)
10. Lamurias, A., Sousa, D., Clarke, L.A., Couto, F.M.: BO-LSTM: classifying relations via long short-term memory networks along biomedical ontologies. BMC Bioinform. **20**(1), 1–12 (2019)
11. Lee, J., et al.: BioBERT: a pre-trained biomedical language representation model for biomedical text mining. Bioinformatics **36**(4), 1234–1240 (2020)
12. Li, F., Zhang, M., Fu, G., Ji, D.: A neural joint model for entity and relation extraction from biomedical text. BMC Bioinform. **18**(1), 198 (2017)
13. Li, Z., Lian, Y., Ma, X., Zhang, X., Li, C.: Bio-semantic relation extraction with attention-based external knowledge reinforcement. BMC Bioinform. **21**, 1–18 (2020)
14. Papagiannopoulou, E., et al.: Large-scale semantic indexing and question answering in biomedicine. In: Proceedings of the Fourth BioASQ workshop, pp. 50–54 (2016)
15. Robinson, P.N., Mundlos, S.: The human phenotype ontology. Clin. Genet. **77**(6), 525–534 (2010)
16. Schriml, L.M., et al.: Disease ontology: a backbone for disease semantic integration. Nucleic Acids Res. **40**(D1), D940–D946 (2012)

17. Segura-Bedmar, I., Martínez, P., Herrero-Zazo, M.: SemEval-2013 task 9: Extraction of drug-drug interactions from biomedical texts (DDIExtraction 2013). In: Second Joint Conference on Lexical and Computational Semantics (* SEM), Volume 2: Proceedings of the Seventh International Workshop on Semantic Evaluation (SemEval 2013), pp. 341–350 (2013)

18. Sousa, D., Couto, F.M.: BiOnt: deep learning using multiple biomedical ontologies for relation extraction. In: Jose, J.M., et al. (eds.) ECIR 2020. LNCS, vol. 12036, pp. 367–374. Springer, Cham (2020). https://doi.org/10.1007/978-3-030-45442-5_46

19. Sousa, D., Lamurias, A., Couto, F.M.: A silver standard corpus of human phenotype-gene relations. In: Proceedings of the 2019 Conference of the North American Chapter of the Association for Computational Linguistics: Human Language Technologies, Volume 1 (Long and Short Papers), pp. 1487–1492 (2019)

20. Sousa, D., Lamurias, A., Couto, F.M.: A hybrid approach toward biomedical relation extraction training corpora: combining distant supervision with crowdsourcing. Database 2020 (2020)

21. Sousa, D., Lamurias, A., Couto, F.M.: Improving accessibility and distinction between negative results in biomedical relation extraction. Genom. Inform. 18(2), e20 (2020)

22. Sousa, D., Lamurias, A., Couto, F.M.: Using neural networks for relation extraction from biomedical literature. In: Cartwright, H. (ed.) Artificial Neural Networks. MMB, vol. 2190, pp. 289–305. Springer, New York (2021). https://doi.org/10.1007/978-1-0716-0826-5_14

23. Vaswani, A., et al.: Attention is all you need. In: Advances In Neural Information Processing Systems, pp. 5998–6008 (2017)

24. Wu, Z., Pan, S., Chen, F., Long, G., Zhang, C., Philip, S.Y.: A comprehensive survey on graph neural networks. IEEE Trans. Neural Netw. Learn. Syst. (2020)

25. Yadav, V., Bethard, S.: A survey on recent advances in named entity recognition from deep learning models. In: Proceedings of the 27th International Conference on Computational Linguistics, pp. 2145–2158. Association for Computational Linguistics, Santa Fe (2018)

Workshops

Second International Workshop on Algorithmic Bias in Search and Recommendation (BIAS@ECIR2021)

Ludovico Boratto[1]([envelope]) [ORCID], Stefano Faralli[2] [ORCID], Mirko Marras[3] [ORCID],
and Giovanni Stilo[4] [ORCID]

[1] EURECAT, Centre Tecnòlogic de Catalunya, Barcelona, Spain
ludovico.boratto@acm.org
[2] University of Rome Unitelma Sapienza, Rome, Italy
stefano.faralli@unitelmasapienza.it
[3] École Polytechnique Fédérale de Lausanne (EPFL), Lausanne, Switzerland
mirko.marras@epfl.ch
[4] University of L'Aquila, L'Aquila, Italy
giovanni.stilo@univaq.it

Abstract. Providing efficient and effective search and recommendation algorithms has been traditionally the main objective for the industrial and academic research communities. However, recent studies have shown that optimizing models through these algorithms may reinforce the existing societal biases, especially under certain circumstances (e.g., when historical users' behavioral data is used for training). Identifying and mitigating data and algorithmic biases thus becomes a crucial aspect, ensuring that these models have a positive impact on the stakeholders involved in the search and recommendation processes. The BIAS 2021 workshop aims to collect novel contributions in this emerging field, providing a common ground for researchers and practitioners.

Keywords: Bias · Algorithms · Search · Recommendation · Fairness

1 Motivations and Topics of Interest

Both *search* and *recommendation* algorithms provide a user with a ranking of results that aims to match their needs and interests. Despite the (non-)personalized perspective that characterizes each class of algorithms, both learn patterns from data which often conveys biases in terms of *unbalances* and *inequalities*.

In most cases, the trained models and, by extension, the final ranking, capture and unfortunately strengthen these biases in the learned patterns [3]. When a bias impacts on human beings as individuals or as groups characterized by certain legally-protected sensitive attributes (e.g., their race, gender or religion), the inequalities reinforced by search and recommendation algorithms even lead to *severe societal consequences*, such as discrimination and unfairness [5].

© Springer Nature Switzerland AG 2021
D. Hiemstra et al. (Eds.): ECIR 2021, LNCS 12657, pp. 697–700, 2021.
https://doi.org/10.1007/978-3-030-72240-1_83

Being able to *detect*, *characterize*, and *mitigate* biases while preserving effectiveness is thus a timely goal for modern search and recommendation algorithms. Challenges that arise in real-world applications are focused, among others, on controlling the effects of popularity biases in order to improve users' perceived quality of the results [1,6,7], supporting consumers and providers by means of rankings that ensure a multi-sided fairness [4,8], and explaining why a model provides biased results and how their effects can be transparently mitigated.

Given the growing importance of these topics, the European IR community is more and more eager to delve into them and, as a consequence, can strongly benefit from a *dedicated event*. Therefore, BIAS 2021[1] is the ECIR's workshop aimed at collecting new contributions in this vibrant research field and providing a common ground for interested researchers and practitioners. Specifically, BIAS 2021 is the second edition of this successful series of dedicated events, which saw a constant participation of 70+ attendants and resulted in proceedings collected in a Springer volume [2] in the context of the first edition in 2020[2]. The workshop and the related initiatives are being supported by the ACM Conference on Fairness, Accountability, and Transparency (ACM FAccT) Network.

The workshop contributions include studies related to data and algorithmic bias and fairness in search and recommendation, focused (but not limited) to:

- *Data Set Collection and Preparation*:
  - Managing imbalances and inequalities within data sets;
  - Devising collection pipelines that lead to fair and less unbiased data sets;
  - Collecting data sets useful for studying biased and unfair situations;
  - Designing procedures for creating data sets for research on bias.
- *Countermeasure Design and Development*:
  - Conducting exploratory analysis that uncover biases;
  - Designing treatments that mitigate biases (e.g., popularity bias);
  - Devising explainable search and recommendation models;
  - Providing treatment procedures whose outcomes are easily interpretable;
  - Balancing inequalities among different groups of users or stakeholders.
- *Evaluation Protocol and Metric Formulation*:
  - Conducting quantitative experimental studies on bias and unfairness;
  - Defining objective metrics that consider fairness and/or bias;
  - Formulating bias-aware protocols to evaluate existing algorithms;
  - Evaluating existing strategies in unexplored domains;
  - Comparative studies of existing evaluation protocols and strategies.
- *Case Study Exploration*:
  - E-commerce platforms;
  - Educational environments;
  - Entertainment websites;
  - Healthcare systems;
  - Social media;
  - News platforms and digital libraries;
  - Job and dating portals.

---

[1] https://biasinrecsys.github.io/ecir2021/.
[2] http://bias.disim.univaq.it.

2   Scientific Objectives

The workshop has the following main objectives:

1. Raise awareness on algorithmic bias issues within the IR community;
2. Identify social and human dimensions affected by algorithmic bias in IR;
3. Solicit contributions from researchers who are facing algorithmic bias in IR;
4. Get insights on existing approaches, recent advances, and open issues;
5. Familiarize the IR community with existing practices from the field;
6. Uncover gaps between academic research and real-world needs in the field.

Moreover, the workshop scientific objectives include:

- Collecting research papers with new contributions on emerging aspects in this research area, falling into one of the following categories:
  - Full papers of 12 pages, references included.
  - Reproducibility papers of 12 pages, references included.
  - Short or position papers of 6 pages, references included.
- Fostering a vivid discussion among workshop participants and speakers on algorithmic bias in IR, depicting the state of the art and future research.
- Strengthening the community working on algorithmic bias, fostering ideas and sparks for challenges, and shaping collaborations in future initiatives.
- Collecting the extended versions of the most relevant workshop papers, to publish them into a top-tier journal special issue, after the event.

3   Organizing Team

Ludovico Boratto is Senior Research Scientist in the Data Science and Big Data Analytics research group at Eurecat, Barcelona (Spain). His research interests focus on recommender systems and their impact on the different stakeholders, both considering accuracy and beyond-accuracy evaluation perspectives. He has a wide experience in workshop organizations, with 10+ events organized at ECIR, IEEE ICDM, ECML-PKDD, and ACM EICS and is currently giving tutorials on algorithmic bias in recommender systems at UMAP and ICDM 2020.

Stefano Faralli is Assistant Professor at University of Rome Unitelma Sapienza, Rome, Italy. His research interests include Ontology Learning, Distributional Semantics, Word Sense Disambiguation/Induction, Recommender Systems, Linked Open Data. He co-organized the International Workshop: Taxonomy Extraction Evaluation (TexEval) Task 17 of Semantic Evaluation (SemEval-2015), the International Workshop on Social Interaction-based Recommendation (SIR 2018), and the ECIR 2020 BIAS workshop.

Mirko Marras is Postdoctoral Researcher at the Digital Vocation, Education and Training (D-VET) & Machine Learning for Education (ML4ED) Laboratory of the Swiss Federal Institute of Technology in Lausanne - EPFL (Switzerland).

His research interests focus on data mining and machine learning for education, with attention to issues related to bias and fairness. He took a leading role when chairing the first edition of the BIAS 2020 workshop and is giving tutorials on algorithmic bias in recommender systems at UMAP and ICDM 2020.

Giovanni Stilo is Assistant Professor at the Department of Information Engineering, Computer Science and Mathematics of the University of L'Aquila. His research interests focus on machine learning and data mining, and specifically temporal mining, social network analysis, network medicine, semantics-aware recommender systems, and anomaly detection. He has organized several international workshops, held in conjunction with top-tier conferences (ICDM, CIKM, and ECIR), with the ECIR 2020 BIAS workshop being one of them.

References

1. Abdollahpouri, H., Burke, R., Mobasher, B.: Controlling popularity bias in learning-to-rank recommendation. In: Proceedings of the Eleventh ACM Conference on Recommender Systems, pp. 42–46. ACM (2017)
2. Boratto, L., Faralli, S., Marras, M., Stilo, G. (eds.): BIAS 2020. CCIS, vol. 1245. Springer, Cham (2020). https://doi.org/10.1007/978-3-030-52485-2
3. Boratto, L., Fenu, G., Marras, M.: the effect of algorithmic bias on recommender systems for massive open online courses. In: Azzopardi, L., Stein, B., Fuhr, N., Mayr, P., Hauff, C., Hiemstra, D. (eds.) ECIR 2019. LNCS, vol. 11437, pp. 457–472. Springer, Cham (2019). https://doi.org/10.1007/978-3-030-15712-8_30
4. Burke, R., Sonboli, N., Ordonez-Gauger, A.: Balanced neighborhoods for multi-sided fairness in recommendation. In: Conference on Fairness, Accountability and Transparency, pp. 202–214 (2018)
5. Hajian, S., Bonchi, F., Castillo, C.: Algorithmic bias: from discrimination discovery to fairness-aware data mining. In: Proceedings of the 22nd ACM SIGKDD International Conference on Knowledge Discovery and Data Mining, San Francisco, CA, USA, 13–17 August 2016, pp. 2125–2126. ACM (2016)
6. Jannach, D., Lerche, L., Kamehkhosh, I., Jugovac, M.: What recommenders recommend: an analysis of recommendation biases and possible countermeasures. User Model. User-Adap. Inter. **25**(5), 427–491 (2015). https://doi.org/10.1007/s11257-015-9165-3
7. Kamishima, T., Akaho, S., Asoh, H., Sakuma, J.: Correcting popularity bias by enhancing recommendation neutrality. In: RecSys Posters (2014)
8. Zheng, Y., Dave, T., Mishra, N., Kumar, H.: Fairness in reciprocal recommendation: a speed-dating study. In: Adjunct Publication of the 26th Conference on User Modeling, Adaptation and Personalization, pp. 29–34. ACM (2018)

The 4th International Workshop on Narrative Extraction from Texts: Text2Story 2021

Ricardo Campos[1,2](✉) ⓘ, Alípio Jorge[1,3] ⓘ, Adam Jatowt[4] ⓘ, Sumit Bhatia[5] ⓘ,
and Mark Finlayson[6] ⓘ

[1] LIAAD - INESCTEC, Porto, Portugal
ricardo.campos@ipt.pt, amjorge@fc.up.pt
[2] Ci2 - Smart Cities Research Center - Polytechnic Institute of Tomar, Tomar, Portugal
[3] FCUP, University of Porto, Porto, Portugal
[4] University of Innsbruck, Innsbruck, Austria
adam.jatowt@uibk.ac.at
[5] IBM Research AI, New Delhi, India
sumitbhatia@in.ibm.com
[6] Florida International University, Miami, USA
markaf@fiu.edu

Abstract. Narrative extraction, understanding and visualization is currently a popular topic and an important tool for humans interested in achieving a deeper understanding of text. Information Retrieval (IR), Natural Language Processing (NLP) and Machine Learning (ML) already offer many instruments that aid the exploration of narrative elements in text and within unstructured data. Despite evident advances in the last couple of years the problem of automatically representing narratives in a structured form, beyond the conventional identification of common events, entities and their relationships, is yet to be solved. This workshop held virtually on April 1st, 2021 co-located with the 43rd European Conference on Information Retrieval (ECIR'21) aims at presenting and discussing current and future directions for IR, NLP, ML and other computational fields capable of improving the automatic understanding of narratives. It includes a session devoted to regular, short and demo papers, keynote talks and space for an informal discussion of the methods, of the challenges and of the future of the area.

1 Motivation

Narratives have long been studied in the computational field as a sequence or chain of events (happening) communicated by word (oral and written) and/or visually (through images, videos or other forms of representations). Over the years several methods borrowed from different computational areas, including Information Retrieval (IR), Natural Language Processing (NLP) and Machine Learning (ML) have been applied as a means to better understand the constituents of a narrative, their actors, events, entities and their relationship on time and space. Industries such as finance [1], business [5], news outlets [10], and health care [12] have been the main beneficiaries of the investment in this kind of technology. The ultimate goal is to offer users the chance to more quickly

© Springer Nature Switzerland AG 2021
D. Hiemstra et al. (Eds.): ECIR 2021, LNCS 12657, pp. 701–704, 2021.
https://doi.org/10.1007/978-3-030-72240-1_84

understand the information conveyed in economic and financial reports, patient records, and to offer them more appealing and alternative formats of exploring common narratives through interactive visualizations [4]. Timelines [13] and infographics for instance, can be employed to represent in a more compact way automatically identified narrative chains in a cloud of news articles [9] or keywords [3], assisting human readers in grasping complex stories with different moments and a network of characters. Also, the automatic generation of text [14] shows impressive results towards computational creativity but still needs to develop means for controlling the narrative intent of the output and a profound understanding of their methods by humans (explainable AI) and of the challenges associated with it, such as bias on text, transparency and trust.

The Text2Story workshop, now in its fourth edition, aims to provide a common forum to consolidate the multi-disciplinary efforts and foster discussions to identify the wide-ranging issues related to the narrative extraction task. In the three first editions [2, 6, 7], we had an approximate number of 140 accumulated participants, 70 of which in the last edition as the result of moving to an online format due to the Covid-19 pandemics [11]. In addition to this, we also hosted the Text2Story Special Issue on IPM Journal [8] demonstrating the growing activity of this research area. In this year's edition, we welcomed contributions from interested researchers on all aspects related to narrative understanding, including the extraction and formal representation of events, entities, temporal aspects and their intrinsic relationships. In addition to this, we seek contributions related to alternative means of presenting the information and on the formal aspects of evaluation, including the proposal of new datasets. A list of all the topics can be found on the Text2Story webpage [https://text2story21.inesctec.pt/].

2   Scientific Objectives

The workshop has the following main objectives: (1) raise awareness within the IR community to the problem of narrative extraction and understanding; (2) shorten the gap between academic research, practitioners and industry; (3) obtain insight on new methods, recent advances and challenges, as well on future directions; (4) share experiences of research projects, case studies and scientific outcomes, (5) identify dimensions potentially affected by the automatization of the narrative process.

3   Organizing Team

Ricardo Campos is an assistant professor at the Polytechnic Institute of Tomar. He is an integrated researcher of LIAAD-INESC TEC, the Artificial Intelligence and Decision Support Lab of U. Porto, and a collaborator of Ci2.ipt, the Smart Cities Research Center of the Polytechnic of Tomar. He is PhD in Computer Science by the University of Porto (U. Porto). He has over ten years of research experience in IR and NLP. He is an editorial board member of the IPM Journal (Elsevier), co-chaired international conferences and workshops, being also a PC member of several international conferences. More in http://www.ccc.ipt.pt/~ricardo.

Alípio M. Jorge works in the areas of data mining, ML, recommender systems and NLP. He is a PhD in Comp. Science (CS) by the University of Porto (UP). He is an Associate Professor of the dep. of CS of the UP since 2009 and is the head of that dep. Since 2017. He is a researcher and the coordinator of LIAAD-INESC TEC, having also coordinated the MSc in Computer Science from 2010 to 2013. He has projects in web automation, recommender systems, IR, text mining and decision support for the management of public transport. He represents Portugal in the Working Group on Artificial Intelligence at the European Commission and is the coordinator for the Portuguese Strategy on Artificial Intelligence "AI Portugal 2030".

Adam Jatowt is Full Professor at the University of Innsbruck. He has received his Ph.D. in Information Science and Technology from the University of Tokyo, Japan in 2005. His research interests lie in an area of IR, knowledge extraction from text and in digital history. Adam has been serving as a PC co-chair of IPRES2011, SocInfo2013, ICADL2014, JCDL2017 and ICADL2019 conferences and a general chair of ICADL2020, TPDL2019 and a tutorial co-chair of SIGIR2017. He was also a co-organizer of 3 NTCIR evaluation tasks and co-organizer of 16 international workshops at WWW, CIKM, ACL, ECIR, IUI, SOCINFO, TPDL and DH conferences.

Sumit Bhatia is a Research Staff Member at IBM Research AI, India. He received his Ph.D. from the Pennsylvania State University in 2013. His doctoral research focused on enabling easier information access in online discussion forums followed by a post-doc at Xerox Research Labs on event detection and customer feedback monitoring in social media. With primary research interests in the fields of Knowledge Management, IR and Text Analytics, Sumit is a co-inventor of more than a dozen patents. He has served on program committees of multiple conferences and journals including WWW, CIKM, ACL, EMNLP, NAACL, TKDE, TOIS, WebDB, JASIST, IJCAI, and AAAI.

Mark Finlayson is Eminent Scholar Chaired Associate Professor of Comp. Science and Interim Associate Director of the School of Comp. And Inf. Sciences at Florida International University in Miami, FL, USA. He received his Ph.D. from the Massachusetts Institute of Technology (MIT) in 2012. He served as a Research Scientist at the MIT Computer Science and AI Laboratory for 2 ½ years before coming to FIU. His research spans the study of narrative across AI, NLP, cognitive science, and the digital humanities. He has served on the organizing committees for numerous narrative-focused workshops. He regularly serves on the technical program committees for major AI and NLP conferences.

Acknowledgements. Ricardo Campos and Alípio Jorge were financed by the ERDF – European Regional Development Fund through the North Portugal Regional Operational Programme (NORTE 2020), under the PORTUGAL 2020 and by National Funds through the Portuguese funding agency, FCT - Fundação para a Ciência e a Tecnologia within project PTDC/CCI-COM/31857/2017 (NORTE-01-0145-FEDER-03185). This funding fits under the research line of the Text2Story project.

References

1. Athanasakou, V., et al.: Proceedings of the 1st Joint Workshop on Financial Narrative Processing and MultiLing Financial Summarisation (FNP-FNS 2020) co-located to Coling 2020, Barcelona, Spain, pp. 1–245 (2020). Accessed 12 Dec

2. Campos, R., Jorge, A., Jatowt, A., Bhatia, S.: The 3rd international workshop on narrative extraction from texts: Text2Story 2020. In: Jose, J., et al. (eds.) Advances in Information Retrieval. ECIR 2020. LNCS, vol. 12036, pp. 648–653. Springer, Cham (2020). https://doi.org/10.1007/978-3-030-45442-5_86

3. Campos, R., Mangaravite, V., Pasquali, A., Jorge, A.M., Nunes, C., Jatowt, A.: A text feature based automatic keyword extraction method for single documents. In: Pasi, G., Piwowarski, B., Azzopardi, L., Hanbury, A. (eds.) ECIR 2018. LNCS, vol. 10772, pp. 684–691. Springer, Cham (2018). https://doi.org/10.1007/978-3-319-76941-7_63

4. Figueiras, A.: How to tell stories using visualization: strategies towards Narrative Visualization. Ph.D. Dissertation. Universidade Nova de Lisboa, Lisboa, Portugal (2016)

5. Grobelny, J., Smierzchalska, J., Krzysztof, K.: Narrative gamification as a method of increasing sales performance: a field experimental study. Int. J. Acad. Res. Bus. Soc. Sci. **8**(3), 430–447 (2018)

6. Jorge, A., Campos, R., Jatowt, A., Nunes, S.: First international workshop on narrative extraction from texts (Text2Story'18). In: Pasi, G., Piwowarski, B., Azzopardi, L., Hanbury, A. (eds.) ECIR 2018. LNCS, vol. 10772, pp. 833–834. Springer, Cham (2018)

7. Jorge, A.M., Campos, R., Jatowt, A., Bhatia, S.: The 2nd international workshop on narrative extraction from text: Text2Story 2019. In: Azzopardi, L., Stein, B., Fuhr, N., Mayr, P., Hauff, C., Hiemstra, D. (eds.) Advances in Information Retrieval. ECIR 2019. LNCS, vol. 11438, pp. 389–393. Springer, Cham (2019). https://doi.org/10.1007/978-3-030-15719-7_54

8. Jorge, A., Campos, R., Jatowt, A., Nunes, S.: Special issue on narrative extraction from texts (Text2Story): preface. IPM J. **56**(5), 1771–1774

9. Liu, S., et al.: TIARA: interactive, topic-based visual text summarization and analysis. ACM Trans. Intell. Syst. Technol. **3**(2), 28 pages (2012). Article 25

10. Martinez-Alvarez, M., et al.: First international workshop on recent trends in news information retrieval (NewsIR'16). In: Ferro, N., et al. (eds.) Advances in Information Retrieval, ECIR 2016. LNCS, vol. 9626, pp. 878–882. Springer, Cham (2016). https://doi.org/10.1007/978-3-319-30671-1_85

11. Nunes, S., et al.: ECIR 2020 workshops: assessing the impact of going online. SIGIR Forum **54**(1), 1–11 (2020)

12. Özlem, U., Amber, S., Weiyi, S.: Chronology of your health events: approaches to extracting temporal relations from medical narratives. Biomed. Inf. **46**, 1–4 (2013)

13. Pasquali, A., Mangaravite, V., Campos, R., Jorge, A.M., Jatowt, A.: Interactive system for automatically generating temporal narratives. In: Azzopardi, L., Stein, B., Fuhr, N., Mayr, P., Hauff, C., Hiemstra, D. (eds.) ECIR 2019. LNCS, vol. 11438, pp. 251–255. Springer, Cham (2019). https://doi.org/10.1007/978-3-030-15719-7_34

14. Wu, Y.: Is automated journalistic writing less biased? An experimental test of auto-written and human-written news stories. J. Pract. **14**(7), 1–21 (2019)

Bibliometric-Enhanced Information Retrieval: 11th International BIR Workshop

Ingo Frommholz[1(✉)], Philipp Mayr[2,3], Guillaume Cabanac[4], and Suzan Verberne[5]

[1] School of Mathematics and Computer Science, University of Wolverhampton, Wolverhampton, UK
ifrommholz@acm.org
[2] GESIS – Leibniz-Institute for the Social Sciences, Cologne, Germany
philipp.mayr@gesis.org
[3] Institute of Computer Science, University of Göttingen, Göttingen, Germany
[4] Computer Science Department, University of Toulouse, IRIT UMR 5505, Toulouse, France
guillaume.cabanac@univ-tlse3.fr
[5] LIACS, Leiden University, Leiden, The Netherlands
s.verberne@liacs.leidenuniv.nl

Abstract. The Bibliometric-enhanced Information Retrieval (BIR) workshop series at ECIR tackles issues related to academic search, at the intersection of Information Retrieval, Natural Language Processing and Bibliometrics. BIR is a hot topic investigated by both academia and the industry. In this overview paper, we summarize the 11th iteration of the workshop and present the workshop topics for 2021.

Keywords: Academic search · Information retrieval · Digital libraries · Bibliometrics · Scientometrics

1 Motivation and Relevance to ECIR

Bibliometric-enhanced IR is a hot topic with growing recognition in the information retrieval as well as the scientometrics community in recent years. This is motivated by the exploding number of scholarly publications and the need to satisfy scholars' specific information needs to find relevant research contribution for their own work. As a very recent example, the COVID-19 crisis and the large number of scientific publications triggered by it has made the effective and efficient scholarly search for and discovery of high-quality publications, for instance in pre-print repositories to ensure the quick dissemination of crucial research results, a priority. Bibliometric-enhanced information retrieval tries to provide solutions to the peculiar needs of scholars to keep on top of the research in their respective fields, utilising the wide range of suitable relevance signals

© Springer Nature Switzerland AG 2021
D. Hiemstra et al. (Eds.): ECIR 2021, LNCS 12657, pp. 705–709, 2021.
https://doi.org/10.1007/978-3-030-72240-1_85

that come with academic scientific publications, such as keywords provided by authors, topics extracted from the full-texts, co-authorship networks, citation networks, and various classification schemes of science. Bibliometric-enhanced IR systems must deal with the multifaceted nature of scientific information by searching for or recommending academic papers, patents, venues (i.e., conferences or journals), authors, experts (e.g., peer reviewers), references (to be cited to support an argument), and datasets.

The purpose of the BIR workshop series founded in 2014 [3] is to tackle these challenges by tightening up the link between IR and Bibliometrics. We strive to bring the 'retrievalists' and 'citationists' [4] active in both academia and industry together. The success of past BIR events (Table 1) evidences that BIR@ECIR is a much needed scientific event for the different communities involved to meet and join forces to push the knowledge boundaries of IR applied to literature search and recommendation.

Table 1. Overview of the BIR workshop series and CEUR proceedings

Year	Conference	Venue		Papers	Proceedings
2014	ECIR	Amsterdam,	NL	6	Vol-1143
2015	ECIR	Vienna,	AT	6	Vol-1344
2016	ECIR	Padua,	IT	8	Vol-1567
2016	JCDL	Newark,	US	$10 + 10^a$	Vol-1610
2017	ECIR	Aberdeen,	UK	12	Vol-1823
2017	SIGIR	Tokyo,	JP	11	Vol-1888
2018	ECIR	Grenoble,	FR	9	Vol-2080
2019	ECIR	Cologne,	DE	14	Vol-2345
2019	SIGIR	Paris,	FR	$16 + 10^b$	Vol-2414
2020	ECIR	Lisbon (Online),	PT	9	Vol-2591
2021	ECIR	Lucca (Online),	IT	9	TBA

[a]With CL-SciSumm 2016 Shared Task; [b]With CL-SciSumm 2019 Shared Task

2 Objectives and Topics

The call for papers for the 2021 workshop (the 11th BIR edition) addressed current research issues regarding 3 aspects of the search/recommendation process:

1. User needs and behaviour regarding scientific information, such as:
   - Finding relevant papers/authors for a literature review.
   - Measuring the degree of plagiarism in a paper.
   - Identifying expert reviewers for a given submission.
   - Flagging predatory conferences and journals.

- Information seeking behaviour and HCI in academic search.
2. Mining the scientific literature, such as:
   - Information extraction, text mining and parsing of scholarly literature.
   - Natural language processing (e.g., citation contexts).
   - Discourse modelling and argument mining.
3. Academic search/recommendation systems, such as:
   - Modelling the multifaceted nature of scientific information.
   - Building test collections for reproducible BIR.
   - System support for literature search and recommendation.

At the time of writing, three keynote speakers accepted our invitation to give an invited talk during the workshop: Ludo Waltman, Lucy Lu Wang and Jimmy Lin.

Ludo Waltman is professor and deputy director at the Centre for Science and Technology Studies (CWTS) at Leiden University. He leads the Quantitative Science Studies (QSS) research group at CWTS, which does research in the fields of bibliometrics and scientometrics. Ludo is coordinator of the CWTS Leiden Ranking, a bibliometric ranking of major universities worldwide.

Lucy Lu Wang is a postdoctoral investigator at the Allen Institute for AI (AI2) in the Semantic Scholar research group. Lucy works in the areas of knowledge representation and biomedical ontologies, natural language processing applications for biomedical and scientific text, open access, and meta-science. She is one of the authors of the COVID-19 open research dataset (CORD-19).

Jimmy Lin is a professor and the David R. Cheriton Chair in the David R. Cheriton School of Computer Science at the University of Waterloo, Canada. His main work is at the intersection of information retrieval, natural language processing, databases and data management. He has spearheaded the development of a search engine that provides access to over 45,000 scholarly articles about COVID-19 in the Allen Institute for AI's CORD-19 research dataset.

3   Target Audience

The target audience of the BIR workshops are researchers and practitioners, junior and senior, from Scientometrics as well as Information Retrieval and Natural Language Processing. These could be IR/NLP researchers interested in potential new application areas for their work as well as researchers and practitioners working with bibliometric data and interested in how IR/NLP methods can make use of such data. The 10th anniversary edition in 2020 ran online with an audience peaking at 97 online participants [1]. In December 2020, we published our third special issue emerging from the past BIR workshops [2].

4   Peer Review Process and Workshop Format

Our peer review process is supported by Easychair. Each submission is assigned to 2 to 3 reviewers, preferably at least one expert in IR and one expert in Bibliometrics or NLP. The programme committee for 2021 consists of peer reviewers from all participating communities. Accepted papers are either long papers (15-min talks) or short papers (5-min talks). Two interactive sessions close the morning and afternoon sessions with posters and demos, allowing attendees to discuss the latest developments in the field and opportunities (e.g., shared tasks such as CL-SciSumm). These interactive sessions serve as ice-breakers, sparking interesting discussions that, in non-pandemic times, usually continue during lunch and the cocktail party. The sessions are also an opportunity for our speakers to further discuss their work.

As a follow-up of the workshop, the co-chairs will write a report summing up the main themes and discussions to *SIGIR Forum* [1, for instance] and BCS Informer[1], as a way to advertise our research topics as widely as possible among the IR community.

5   Next Steps

Research on scholarly document processing has for many years been scattered across multiple venues such as ACL, SIGIR, JCDL, CIKM, LREC, NAACL, KDD, and others. Our next strategic step is the Second Workshop on Scholarly Document Processing (SDP)[2] that will be held in June 2021 in conjunction with the 2021 Conference of the North American Chapter of the Association for Computational Linguistics (NAACL). This workshop and initiative will be organized by a diverse group of researchers (organizers from BIR, BIRNDL, Workshop on Mining Scientific Publications/WOSP and Big Scholar) which have expertise in NLP, ML, Text Summarization/Mining, Computational Linguistics, Discourse Processing, IR, and others.

Acknowledgement. The organizers wish to thank all those who contributed to this workshop series: the researchers who contributed papers, the many reviewers who generously offered their time and expertise, and the participants of the BIR and BIRNDL workshops. Since 2016, we maintain the Bibliometric-enhanced-IR Bibliography that collects scientific papers which appear in collaboration with the BIR/BIRNDL organizers.

References

1. Cabanac, G., Frommholz, I., Mayr, P.: Report on the 10th anniversary workshop on bibliometric-enhanced information retrieval (BIR 2020). In: SIGIR Forum, vol. 54, no. 1 (2020). https://doi.org/10.1145/3451964.3451974

---

[1] BIR 2020 appeared in https://irsg.bcs.org/informer/category/spring-2020/.
[2] https://sdproc.org/2021/.

2. Cabanac, G., Frommholz, I., Mayr, P.: Scholarly literature mining with information retrieval and natural language processing: preface. Scientometrics **125**(3), 2835–2840 (2020). https://doi.org/10.1007/s11192-020-03763-4
3. Mayr, P., Scharnhorst, A., Larsen, B., Schaer, P., Mutschke, P.: Bibliometric-enhanced information retrieval. In: de Rijke, M., et al. (eds.) ECIR 2014. LNCS, vol. 8416, pp. 798–801. Springer, Cham (2014). https://doi.org/10.1007/978-3-319-06028-6_99
4. White, H.D., McCain, K.W.: Visualizing a discipline: an author co-citation analysis of Information Science, 1972–1995. J. Am. Soc. Inf. Sci. **49**(4), 327–355 (1998). https://doi.org/b57vc7

MICROS: Mixed-Initiative ConveRsatiOnal Systems Workshop

Ida Mele[1]([⊠])(iD), Cristina Ioana Muntean[2](iD), Mohammad Aliannejadi[3](iD), and Nikos Voskarides[3](iD)

[1] IASI-CNR, Rome, Italy
ida.mele@iasi.cnr.it
[2] ISTI-CNR, Pisa, Italy
cristina.muntean@isti.cnr.it
[3] University of Amsterdam, Amsterdam, The Netherlands
{m.aliannejadi,n.voskarides}@uva.nl

Abstract. The 1st edition of the workshop on *Mixed-Initiative ConveRsatiOnal Systems* (MICROS@ECIR2021) aims at investigating and collecting novel ideas and contributions in the field of conversational systems. Oftentimes, the users fulfill their information need using smartphones and home assistants. This has revolutionized the way users access online information, thus posing new challenges compared to traditional search and recommendation. The first edition of MICROS will have a particular focus on *mixed-initiative conversational systems*. Indeed, conversational systems need to be proactive, proposing not only answers but also possible interpretations for ambiguous or vague requests.

Keywords: Conversational search · Mixed-initiative interaction · Interactive recommendation

1 Motivation and Topics of Interest

The increasing popularity of personal assistant systems as well as smartphones has drawn attention to conversational systems with many application scenarios ranging from simple ones (e.g., checking the weather forecast) to more complex ones (e.g., performing e-commerce transactions). Moreover, thanks to the recent advances in automatic speech recognition and voice generation, conversational assistants, such as Apple Siri or Microsoft Cortana, are widely being used in chatbots and smart-home devices as well as in wearable devices and smartphones.

Users employ conversational systems to seek information in an interactive way, often through voice interfaces. Information-seeking conversations can be categorized into two main classes: (i) search and (ii) recommendation. In *conversational search*, answering users' requests poses several challenges. First, the system must understand the user requests (a.k.a. questions, queries, or utterances) and return a ranked list of documents (results). The very top results (e.g., 1 or 2) must be potentially useful as the system replies vocally and thus it

© Springer Nature Switzerland AG 2021
D. Hiemstra et al. (Eds.): ECIR 2021, LNCS 12657, pp. 710–713, 2021.
https://doi.org/10.1007/978-3-030-72240-1_86

is impossible for the user to browse the list of results as in Web search. Another important challenge in conversational search is that (complex) information needs are not expressed with a single request; rather, the user formulates multiple subsequent questions that can be related to each other. In these multi-turn conversations, the current request may not be self-explanatory as the context is missing from the current question, but it was implied or explicitly mentioned in previous turns [6]. In particular, the subjects can be pronouns referring to topics mentioned in the previous requests and/or answers [1,4,6]. Moreover, during the conversation, there might be slight or significant topic changes that need to be detected by the system [1,4,6]. Furthermore, the users' requests can be vague, ambiguous, or misleading. Since the requests are formulated in natural language, they are prone to the ambiguity and polysemy of words, the presence of acronyms, mistakes, and grammar misuses. In such cases, the system can take the initiative by asking clarifying questions or by proposing keywords that disambiguate the request [2,3].

In *conversational recommendation*, the system interacts with the user asking for her opinion about some items [5]. Preference elicitation introduces numerous challenges, such as modeling users' preference upon receiving their feedback and selecting the next question in a conversation to optimize the information gain. At the same time, the system should avoid any bias in the user's feedback.

We envision that advanced, flexible, and mixed-initiative interactions are very important in conversational systems as they allow the systems to identify the correct intent behind the user's requests and needs.

The workshop topics include but are not limited to:

1. Applications of conversational search and recommendation systems
   - Large-scale retrieval candidate responses (e.g., documents, passages) in conversational search
   - Conversational and question-based recommendation systems
   - Tracking information-need evolution during the conversation (e.g., context changes)
   - Processing and rewriting of natural language conversational queries
   - Relevance feedback in conversational search.
2. Mixed-initiative interaction systems, such as clarification and preference elicitation in conversational systems
   - Dialogue schema for conversational search
   - Conversational navigation of search results
   - Conversation history understanding and query modeling
   - Pro-active search and recommendation interactions in conversational search.
3. Deep learning and reinforcement learning for conversational search
   - Conversational question answering
   - Result summarization, explanation, and presentation in conversational search
   - Balance and bias for more inclusive conversational systems.

4. Multi-modal interactions for conversational interfaces (e.g., speech-only and small-screen interfaces)
   - Voice-based search engine operations
   - User intent and dialog state tracking in conversational search
   - Personalization and user models for conversational search.
5. Specialized applications and use cases for conversational search (e.g., health, finance, travel)
6. Knowledge graph presentation in conversational search
7. Data creation and curation for conversational search
8. Evaluation metrics for effectiveness, engagement, satisfaction of conversational systems.

2   Scientific Objectives

The goal of the MICROS workshop is to collect and discuss novel approaches, evaluation techniques, datasets, and domain-specific applications of conversational systems. The workshop aims at bringing together academic and industry researchers to create a forum for interacting and discussing the latest developments and new directions of research in the area of search- and recommendation-oriented conversational systems. These discussions are open to the whole audience and lead by experienced researchers from both academia and industry who actively participate in the workshop as keynote speakers and panelists.

A particular focus of MICROS is on mixed-initiative interactions. This novel and still under-explored topic represents an important development in conversational systems. As a matter of fact, the interaction between the user and the system should go beyond the usual *"user asks, system responds"* paradigm. Especially for those scenarios where the user requests are too generic, ambiguous, and may lack explicit subjects or context. The conversational system lacking enough confidence in identifying the topic of interest would take the initiative by asking the user to clarify her request, or proposing possible interpretations, or inferring the user's crisp opinion and interest.

3   Organizing Team

- **Ida Mele** is currently a researcher at IASI-CNR, Rome (Italy). She got her Ph.D. in Computer Engineering from Sapienza University of Rome. She has co-authored papers in peer-reviewed international conferences and top-tier journals. She has also served as PC member and reviewer for international conferences and journals. Her research interests are Web Mining, Information Retrieval, Recommendation Systems, and Social Media. Her current research focuses on conversational search and, in particular, on passage retrieval and re-ranking for multi-turn conversational searches.

- **Cristina Ioana Muntean** is a Researcher at ISTI-CNR, Pisa (Italy). Her main research interests are in Information Retrieval and Machine Learning with applications to Web search and social media. She is particularly interested in passage retrieval and conversational search using neural and classic IR models. She is an active member in the SIGIR, ECIR, CIKM, and TheWebConf communities, as author and part of the program committees.
- **Mohammad Aliannejadi** is a post-doctoral researcher at the University of Amsterdam (The Netherlands). His research interests include single- and mixed-initiative conversational information access and recommender systems. Previously, he completed his Ph.D. at Università della Svizzera italiana (Switzerland), where he worked on novel approaches of information access in conversations. He has been an active member of the community, publishing and serving as a PC member in major venues and journals of the field.
- **Nikos Voskarides** is a PhD candidate at the University of Amsterdam (The Netherlands). He is an active member of the community, publishing and serving as a PC member at major conferences such as SIGIR, ACL, EMNLP, ECIR and AKBC. His current research focuses on information retrieval for knowledge graphs and conversational search.

References

1. Aliannejadi, M., Chakraborty, M., Ríssola, E.A., Crestani, F.: Harnessing evolution of multi-turn conversations for effective answer retrieval. In: CHIIR 2020: Conference on Human Information Interaction and Retrieval, Vancouver, BC, Canada, pp. 33–42. ACM (2020)
2. Aliannejadi, M., Kiseleva, J., Chuklin, A., Dalton, J., Burtsev, M.: ConvAI3: generating clarifying questions for open-domain dialogue systems (ClariQ). In: SCAI: Workshop on Search Oriented Conversational AI, at EMNLP 2020 (2020)
3. Aliannejadi, M., Zamani, H., Crestani, F., Croft, W.B.: Asking clarifying questions in open-domain information-seeking conversations. In: SIGIR 2019: International ACM SIGIR Conference on Research and Development in Information Retrieval, Paris, France, pp. 475–484. ACM (2019)
4. Mele, I., Muntean, C.I., Nardini, F.M., Perego, R., Tonellotto, N., Frieder, O.: Topic propagation in conversational search. In: SIGIR 2020: 43rd International ACM SIGIR Conference on Research and Development in Information Retrieval, pp. 2057–2060. Association for Computing Machinery, New York (2020)
5. Radlinski, F., Balog, K., Byrne, B., Krishnamoorthi, K.: Coached conversational preference elicitation: a case study in understanding movie preferences. In: SIGdial 2019: Annual SIGdial Meeting on Discourse and Dialogue, Stockholm, Sweden, pp. 353–360. ACL (2019)
6. Voskarides, N., Li, D., Ren, P., Kanoulas, E., de Rijke, M.: Query resolution for conversational search with limited supervision. In: SIGIR 2020: 43rd International ACM SIGIR Conference on Research and Development in Information Retrieval. ACM (2020)

ROMCIR 2021: Reducing Online Misinformation through Credible Information Retrieval

Fabio Saracco[1]([✉])([iD]) and Marco Viviani[2]([✉])([iD])

[1] IMT School for Advanced Studies, Piazza S. Ponziano, 6, 55100 Lucca, Italy
fabio.saracco@imtlucca.it
[2] University of Milano-Bicocca (DISCo – IKR3 Lab),
Edificio U14, Viale Sarca, 336, 20126 Milan, Italy
marco.viviani@unimib.it
https://networks.imtlucca.it/
http://www.ir.disco.unimib.it/people/marco-viviani

Abstract. The Reducing Online Misinformation through Credible Information Retrieval (ROMCIR) 2021 Workshop, as part of the satellite events of the 43rd European Conference on Information Retrieval (ECIR), is concerned with providing users with access to genuine information, to mitigate the information disorder phenomenon characterizing the current online digital ecosystem. This problem is very broad, as it concerns different information objects (e.g., Web pages, online accounts, social media posts, etc.) on different platforms, and different domains and purposes (e.g., detecting fake news, retrieving credible health-related information, reducing propaganda and hate-speech, etc.). In this context, all those approaches that can serve, from different perspectives, to tackle the credible information access problem, find their place.

Keywords: Information disorder · Credibility · Information retrieval

1 Motivations and Topics of Interest

Nowadays, we are more and more aware of the problems that can arise from coming into contact with different kinds of misleading contents that are propagated online, especially through social media platforms [5,7]. Fake news can, for example, influence public opinion in political and financial choices [3]; fake reviews can promote substandard products or, on the contrary, destroy florid economic activities by means on discredit campaigns [9]; unverified medical information can lead people to follow behaviors that can be harmful to their own health and

Supported by the IMT School for Advanced Studies Lucca, the University of Milano-Bicocca (DISCo – IKR3 Lab), and the scheme 'INFRAIA-01-2018-2019: Research and Innovation action', Grant Agreement n. 871042 'SoBigData++: European Integrated Infrastructure for Social Mining and Big Data Analytics'.

D. Hiemstra et al. (Eds.): ECIR 2021, LNCS 12657, pp. 714–717, 2021.
https://doi.org/10.1007/978-3-030-72240-1_87

to that of society as a whole (let us think, for example, of the risk of following negationism hypotheses in the context of the recent COVID-19 pandemic) [6]. Access to unverified information is made easier and easier to the fact that, from a technological point of view, information is produced at a speed and volume never seen before, almost without any trusted traditional intermediary [1,2]. Faced with this huge amount of information, and the uncertainty associated with its degree of veracity, human cognitive abilities are not always sufficient to take well-informed decisions [4].

For the above-mentioned reasons, the central topic of the workshop concerns providing access to users to credible and/or verifiable information, to mitigate the so-called *information disorder* phenomenon [8]. By "information disorder", we mean all forms of communication pollution, encompassing *dis-*, *mis-*, and *mal*-information. Misinformation is the spread of false content resulting from the spreader's ignorance, disinformation is a form of intentional sharing of false content to produce harm, while malinformation spreads information that is based on reality, having the same harmful intent (e.g., the despicable act of revenge porn). In this context, it is clear that the problem of guaranteeing access to genuine information online is very broad, as it concerns different information objects (e.g., Web pages, online accounts, social media posts, etc.), different online platforms (e.g., Web portals, social networking services, question-answering systems, etc.), and different domains and purposes (e.g., detecting fake news, retrieving credible health-related information, reducing propaganda and hate-speech, etc.). Hence, all those approaches that can serve, from different perspectives, to tackle the credible information access problem, find their place in ROMCIR. Specifically, the topics of interest include, but are not limited to:

- Access to/retrieval of credible information;
- Bias evaluation and detection;
- Bot/spam/troll detection;
- Computational fact-checking;
- Crowdsourcing for information credibility assessment;
- Deep fake analysis and detection;
- Disinformation/misinformation/malinformation analysis and detection;
- Evaluation strategies to assess information credibility;
- Fake news/fake reviews detection, propaganda identification and analysis;
- Filter bubbles, echo chambers, and information polarization online;
- Harassment/bullying/hate-speech detection;
- Security, privacy, and information credibility;
- Sentiment/emotional analysis, and stance detection;
- Trust, reputation, and information credibility;
- Understanding and guiding the societal reaction in the presence of dis-/mis-/mal-information.

Both theoretical studies, model-driven, and data-driven approaches, supported by publicly available datasets, are more than welcome.

2   Scientific Objectives

The key goal of the workshop is to encourage a discussion between researchers also belonging to different disciplines, and propose innovative solutions, about the problem of guarantee to users access to credible information that does not distort their perception of reality. In recent years, despite numerous approaches have been proposed to tackle the considered issue in different contexts, and for different purposes, we are still a long way from having found completely effective and domain-independent solutions.

The problem is still of great interest with respect to many open issues, such as the access to and retrieval of credible information, the early detection of dis-/mis-/mal-information, the development of solutions that can be understood by final users (explainable AI), the study of the problem in the health-related field, the relationship between security, privacy and credibility in information access and dissemination.

In this scenario, the role of researchers working in the fields of Information Retrieval, Social Computing, Social Sciences, and other related research areas, is crucial to investigate such open issues, providing users with automatic but understandable tools to help them come into contact with genuine information.

3   Organizing Team

The ROMCIR 2021 organizing team is composed of the following people with respect to their distinct roles.

3.1   Co-chairs

– **Fabio Saracco**. He is Assistant Professor (RTDa) at IMT School For Advanced Studies since May 2016, where he works in the NETWORKS research unit guided by Prof. Garlaschelli. Fabio's research is devoted to the theoretical development of tools for the analysis of complex networks. Recently these techniques were applied in the context of Online Social Network in the activities of the TOFFEe (TOol for Fighting FakEs) projecy, funded by the IMT School For Advanced Studies and leaded by Prof. Rocco De Nicola, and in those of the European Project SoBigData++ (GA. 871042). *Website*: https://www.imtlucca.it/en/fabio.saracco.
– **Marco Viviani**. He is Assistant Professor (RTDb) at the University of Milano-Bicocca, Department of Informatics, Systems, and Communication (DISCo). He works in the Information and Knowledge Representation, Retrieval and Reasoning (IKR3) Lab. He has been co-chair of several special tracks and workshops at international conferences, also related to the assessment of information credibility, and general co-chair of MDAI 2019. His main research activities include Information Retrieval, Social Computing, User Modeling, Trust and Reputation Management. *Website*: http://www.ir.disco.unimib.it/people/marco-viviani.

3.2   Publicity Chair

– **Marinella Petrocchi**, Institute of Informatics and Telematics (IIT) – CNR, Pisa, Italy. *Website*: https://www.iit.cnr.it/marinella.petrocchi.

3.3   Program Committee

– **Rino Falcone**, Inst. of Cognitive Sciences and Technologies (ISTC) – CNR, Rome, Italy
– **Carlos A. Iglesias**, Universidad Politècnica de Madrid, Madrid, Spain
– **Petr Knoth**, The Open University, London, UK
– **Udo Kruschwitz**, University of Regensburg, Regensburg, Germany
– **Yelena Mejova**, ISI Foundation, Turin, Italy
– **Preslav Nakov**, Qatar Computing Research Institute, HBKU, Doha, Qatar
– **Symeon Papadopoulos**, Inf. Tech. Inst. (ITI), Thessaloniki, Greece
– **Marinella Petrocchi**, Inst. of Inf. and Telematics (IIT) – CNR, Pisa, Italy
– **Barbara Poblete**, University of Chile, Santiago, Chile
– **Adrian Popescu**, CEA LIST, Gif-sur-Yvette, France
– **Paolo Rosso**, Universitat Politècnica de València, València, Spain
– **Fabio Saracco**, IMT School for Advanced Studies, Lucca, Italy
– **Marco Viviani**, University of Milano-Bicocca, Milan, Italy
– **Xinyi Zhou**, Syracuse University, Syracuse, NY, USA
– **Arkaitz Zubiaga**, Queen Mary University of London, London, UK.

Acknowledgements. We would like to thank the authors of the submitted articles for their interest in the considered problem, the members of the Program Committee for their valuable contribution to the success of the ROMCIR 2021 Workshop, and the Keynote Speakers for the interest aroused in new research directions. F.S. acknowledge also support from the European Project SoBigData++ (GA. 871042).

References

1. Carminati, B., Ferrari, E., Viviani, M.: Security and trust in online social networks. Synth. Lect. Inf. Secur. Priv. Trust **4**(3), 1–120 (2013)
2. Eysenbach, G.: Credibility of health information and digital media: new perspectives and implications for youth. In: Metzger, M.M., Flanagin, A.J. (eds.) Digital Media, Youth, and Credibility, pp. 123–154. The MIT Press (2008)
3. Lazer, D.M., et al.: The science of fake news. Science **359**(6380), 1094–1096 (2018)
4. Metzger, M.J., Flanagin, A.J.: Credibility and trust of information in online environments: the use of cognitive heuristics. J. Pragmatics **59**, 210–220 (2013)
5. Pasi, G., Viviani, M.: Information credibility in the social web: contexts, approaches, and open issues. arXiv preprint arXiv:2001.09473 (2020)
6. Tagliabue, F., Galassi, L., Mariani, P.: The "pandemic" of disinformation in COVID-19. SN Compr. Clin. Med. **2**(9), 1287–1289 (2020)
7. Viviani, M., Pasi, G.: Credibility in social media: opinions, news, and health information—a survey. WIREs Data Mining Knowl. Disc. **7**(5), e1209 (2017)
8. Wardle, C., Derakhshan, H.: Information disorder: toward an interdisciplinary framework for research and policy making. Council Europe Rep. **27**, 1–107 (2017)
9. Wu, Y., Ngai, E.W., Wu, P., Wu, C.: Fake online reviews: literature review, synthesis, and directions for future research. Decision Support Syst. **132**, 113280 (2020)

Tutorials

Adversarial Learning for Recommendation

Vito Walter Anelli$^{(\boxtimes)}$, Yashar Deldjoo, Tommaso Di Noia,
and Felice Antonio Merra

Polytechnic University of Bari, Bari, Italy
{vitowalter.anelli,yashar.deldjoo,tommaso.dinoia,
feliceantonio.merra}@poliba.it

Abstract. Modern recommender systems (RSs) utilize a variety of machine learning (ML) models to provide users with relevant, personalized suggestions about products in a vast catalog. Notwithstanding the great success of ML models to make recommendations, they are often no-robust to adversarial actors, e.g., competitors, that might act to alter recommendations toward a malicious outcome. While the injection of hand-engineered fake profile, i.e., shilling attacks, [1, 2] has been the core of investigation between years 2000 and 2015, the last years have been characterized by the rise of Adversarial Machine Learning (AML) techniques, i.e., ML-based approaches for attacking and defending RSs. In this tutorial, we present an overview of more than 75 publications on AML applications in RSs reviewed in our recent survey [3]. In particular, we introduce a twofold categorization of AML uses in RSs: the one based on the study of adversarial attacks, and defenses, against either the model parameters [5], content data [4], or user-item interactions [6]; the other one related to the use of Generative Adversarial Networks (GAN) to propose novel recommender models [7]. All the material is publicly available at github.com/sisinflab/amlrecsys-tutorial.

Keywords: Adversarial machine learning · Recommender systems

References

1. Anelli, V.W., Deldjoo, Y., Di Noia, T., Di Sciascio, E., Merra, F.A.: SAShA: semantic-aware shilling attacks on recommender systems exploiting knowledge graphs. In: Harth, A., Kirrane, S., Ngonga Ngomo, A.-C., Paulheim, H., Rula, A., Gentile, A.L., Haase, P., Cochez, M. (eds.) ESWC 2020. LNCS, vol. 12123, pp. 307–323. Springer, Cham (2020). https://doi.org/10.1007/978-3-030-49461-2_18
2. Deldjoo, Y., Di Noia, T., Di Sciascio, E., Merra, F.A.: How dataset characteristics affect the robustness of collaborative recommendation models. In: ACM SIGIR (2020)
3. Deldjoo, Y., Di Noia, T., Merra, F.A.: A survey on adversarial recommender systems: from attack/defense strategies to generative adversarial networks. In: ACM Computing Surveys (2021). https://doi.org/10.1145/3439729
4. Di Noia, T., Malitesta, D., Merra, F.A.: Taamr: targeted adversarial attack against multimedia recommender systems. In: DSN Workshops, pp. 1–8. IEEE (2020)

© Springer Nature Switzerland AG 2021
D. Hiemstra et al. (Eds.): ECIR 2021, LNCS 12657, pp. 721–722, 2021.
https://doi.org/10.1007/978-3-030-72240-1

5. He, X., He, Z., Du, X., Chua, T.: Adversarial personalized ranking for recommendation. In: SIGIR, pp. 355–364. ACM (2018)
6. Li, B., Wang, Y., Singh, A., Vorobeychik, Y.: Data poisoning attacks on factorization-based collaborative filtering. In: NIPS, pp. 1885–1893 (2016)
7. Wang, J., et al.: IRGAN: a minimax game for unifying generative and discriminative information retrieval models. In: SIGIR, pp. 515–524. ACM (2017)

Operationalizing Treatments Against Bias - Challenges and Solutions

Ludovico Boratto[1(✉)] [iD] and Mirko Marras[2] [iD]

[1] EURECAT - Centre Tecnológic de Catalunya, Barcelona, Spain
ludovico.boratto@acm.org
[2] École Polytechnique Fédérale de Lausanne (EPFL), Lausanne, Switzerland
mirko.marras@acm.org

Abstract. The objective of this tutorial is to provide attendees with an overview on concepts, methodologies, and tools used to understand and mitigate bias and discrimination against individuals or demographics groups (e.g., based on gender, race, or religion), when machine learning is applied to generate rankings of results. Tutorial description, lecture slides, code, and Jupyter notebooks showcased in this tutorial can be retrieved at https://biasinrecsys.github.io/ecir2021-tutorial/.

Keywords: Bias · Fairness · Rankings · Recommender systems

1 Tutorial Description

Over the technologies getting attention in recent years, ranking and recommender systems are playing a key role in today's online platforms, influencing how and what information individuals access. However, the adoption of machine learning in information retrieval has shown biased and even discriminatory impacts in various domains. Given that bias is becoming a threat to information seeking, uncovering, characterizing, and counteracting biases, while preserving the effectiveness of the system, is proving to be essential. The core of the problem deals with the study of interdisciplinary concepts, the design of bias-aware algorithmic pipelines, and the materialization and mitigation of biased effects.

This tutorial provides a timely perspective to consider while inspecting information retrieval outputs, leaving attendees with a solid understanding on how to integrate bias-related countermeasures in their research pipeline. The first part introduces real-world examples of how a bias can impact on our society, the conceptual foundations underlying the study of bias and fairness in algorithmic decision-making, and the strategies to plan, uncover, assess, reduce, and evaluate a bias in an information retrieval system. The second part provides practical case studies to attendees, where they are engaged in uncovering sources of bias and in designing countermeasures for rankings of results. By means of use cases on personalized rankings, the presented algorithmic approaches would help academic researchers and industrial practitioners to better develop systems that tackle bias constraints. Finally, this tutorial identifies the current challenges in bias-aware research and new directions in the context of information retrieval.

© Springer Nature Switzerland AG 2021
D. Hiemstra et al. (Eds.): ECIR 2021, LNCS 12657, p. 723, 2021.
https://doi.org/10.1007/978-3-030-72240-1

Tutorial on Biomedical Text Processing Using Semantics

Francisco M. Couto[✉]📷

LASIGE, Faculdade de Ciências, Universidade de Lisboa, Lisbon, Portugal

Abstract. Exploring the vast amount of rapidly growing biomedical text is of utmost importance, but is also particularly challenging due to the highly specialized domain knowledge and inconsistency of the nomenclature.

This introductory tutorial will be a hands-on session to explore the semantics encoded in biomedical ontologies to process text using shell scripting with minimal software dependencies. Participants will learn how to process OWL, retrieve synonyms and ancestors, perform entity linking, and construct large lexicons.

Keywords: Semantic indexing · Ontologies · Controlled vocabularies · Information retrieval · Text mining · Shell scripting · Bioinformatics

A major problem with biomedical text is the inconsistency of the nomenclature used for describing biomedical concepts and entities [1]. To address this, text mining tools have been taking advantage of the vast number of biomedical ontologies to improve their performance [5]. This tutorial will present how we can select an ontology that models a given domain and identify the official names and synonyms of biomedical entities [4]. This tutorial will use two ontologies, one about human diseases and the other about chemical entities of biological interest. The semantics encoded in those ontologies will be explored to find the ancestors and related classes of a given entity. Participants will learn how to apply semantic similarity to address ambiguity in the entity linking process [3]. After constructing large lexicons that include all the entities of a given domain, participants will learn how to recognize them in biomedical text [2].

References

1. Barros, M., Couto, F.M.: Knowledge representation and management: a linked data perspective. Yearb. Med. Inform. **25**(01), 178–183 (2016)
2. Couto, F.M., Lamurias, A.: MER: a shell script and annotation server for minimal named entity recognition and linking. J. Cheminformatics **10**(1), 1–10 (2018). https://doi.org/10.1186/s13321-018-0312-9

Supported by FCT Through Funding of the DeST: Deep Semantic Tagger Project, Ref. PTDC/CCI-BIO/28685/2017, and LaSIGE Research Unit, Ref. UIDB/00408/2020 and Ref. UIDP/00408/2020.

D. Hiemstra et al. (Eds.): ECIR 2021, LNCS 12657, pp. 724–725, 2021.
https://doi.org/10.1007/978-3-030-72240-1

3. Couto, F., Lamurias, A.: Semantic similarity definition. In: Ranganathan, S., Nakai, K., Schönbach, C., Gribskov, M. (eds.) Encyclopedia of Bioinformatics and Computational Biology, vol. 1. Elsevier, Oxford (2019)
4. Couto, F.M.: Data and Text Processing for Health and Life Sciences. AEMB, vol. 1137. Springer, Cham (2019). https://doi.org/10.1007/978-3-030-13845-5
5. Lamurias, A., Couto, F.: Text mining for bioinformatics using biomedical literature. In: Ranganathan, S., Nakai, K., Schönbach, C., Gribskov, M. (eds.) Encyclopedia of Bioinformatics and Computational Biology, vol. 1. Elsevier, Oxford (2019)

Large-Scale Information Extraction Under Privacy-Aware Constraints

Rajeev Gupta[✉] and Ranganath Kondapally

Microsoft R&D, Hyderabad, India
{rajeev.gupta, rakondap}@microsoft.com

Abstract. Emails are personal and due to privacy and legal considerations, no other human except the receiver can view them.. This poses interesting and complex challenges from scalable information extraction point of view: extracting information under privacy aware constraints where there is little data to learn from but need highly accurate models to run on large amount of data across different users. Anonymization is typically used to convert private data into publicly accessible data. But this may not always be feasible and may require complex differential privacy guarantees to be safe from any potential negative consequences. Other techniques involve building models on a small amount of *eyes-on* data and a large amount of *eyes-off* data. In this tutorial, we explain the concepts of scalable IE from emails under privacy-aware constraints and the techniques extend to other forms of private data.

Around 270 billion emails are sent and received per day and more than 60% of them are business to consumer (B2C) emails. To extract information from B2C emails, one needs to classify and cluster them into possible templates, build models to extract information from them, and monitor the models to maintain a high precision and recall. How are the IE techniques for private eyes-off data different compared to that for eyes-on HTML data? How to get labeled data in a privacy preserving manner? How to build scalable extraction models across a number of sender domains using different ways to represent the information? In this tutorial we address all these questions from various *research to production* perspectives. As part of hands-on exercise, we use publicly available data sets to first classify the *hotel confirmation* emails and extract various fields from those (e.g., check-in date, hotel address, etc.) under simulated privacy constraints. We use Python Jupiter notebooks and various machine learning algorithms for the same.

Keywords: Emails · Privacy & legal constraints · Scalable information extraction · Eyes-off data processing · Rule learning · Semi-supervised machine learning

© Springer Nature Switzerland AG 2021
D. Hiemstra et al. (Eds.): ECIR 2021, LNCS 12657, p. 726, 2021.
https://doi.org/10.1007/978-3-030-72240-1

Reinforcement Learning for Information Retrieval

Alexander Kuhnle[1], Miguel Aroca-Ouellette[1], Murat Sensoy[1], John Reid[1], and Dell Zhang[1,2]([✉]) [ID]

[1] Blue Prism AI Labs, 338 Euston Road, London NW1 3BG, UK
{alexander.kuhnle,miguel.aroca,murat.sensoy,john.reid}@blueprism.com
[2] Birkbeck, University of London, Malet Street, London WC1E 7HX, UK
dell.z@ieee.org

Abstract. Reinforcement Learning (RL) is an area of machine learning which is concerned with optimal decision making over time in a dynamic environment. Recent years have witnessed rapid development and great success of methods combining RL with deep neural networks, e.g., in AlphaGo. Unsurprisingly, many Information Retrieval (IR) researchers and practitioners have become interested in applying RL techniques to solve challenging decision making problems in IR systems. The growing popularity of RL in the field of IR is attributed to not only the technology push but also the demand pull. Because of the wide usage of web and mobile apps, modern IR systems for search, recommendation, and advertising have become more personalized and interactive. In these scenarios, traditional IR approaches which assume user preferences to be static and maximize immediate user satisfaction no longer work well. RL is a promising approach to tackling the problems of personalization and interactivity by capturing a user's evolving interests and optimizing their long-term engagement. This *full-day* tutorial aims to give IR researchers and practitioners who have no or little experience with RL an opportunity to learn about the fundamentals of modern RL techniques together with their recent IR applications in a practical *hands-on* setting. It consists of two main parts. First, we will introduce the most important RL concepts and algorithms, including Markov Decision Process (MDP), Exploitation vs Exploration, Q-Learning, Deep Q-Network (DQN), Policy Gradient (REINFORCE), and Actor-Critic. Second, we will describe how these techniques (especially DQN and REINFORCE) could be utilized to address some representative IR problems like "learning to rank" and discuss the recent developments as well as the outlook for research. The tutorial mixes presentations of theory with practical sessions of examples/exercises (as Python Jupyter notebooks on Google Colab). We hope that in this format the tutorial will equip the participants with a good knowledge of RL which can help them better understand the latest IR publications involving RL and enable them to tackle their own IR problems in practice using RL. Please refer to the tutorial website (https://rl-starterpack.github.io/) for more information.

Keywords: Reinforcement learning · Information retrieval

D. Hiemstra et al. (Eds.): ECIR 2021, LNCS 12657 p. 727, 2021.
https://doi.org/10.1007/978-3-030-72240-1

IR from Bag-of-words to BERT and Beyond Through Practical Experiments
An ECIR 2021 Tutorial with PyTerrier And OpenNIR

Sean MacAvaney[1(✉)], Craig Macdonald[2], and Nicola Tonellotto[3]

[1] IR Lab, Georgetown University, Georgetown, Washington DC, USA
`sean@ir.cs.georgetown.edu`
[2] School of Computing Science, University of Glasgow, Glasgow G12 8QQ, UK
`craig.macdonald@glasgow.ac.uk`
[3] Information Engineering Department, University of Pisa, Pisa, Italy
`nicola.tonellotto@unipi.it`

Abstract. Advances from the natural language processing community have recently sparked a renaissance in the task of adhoc search. Particularly, large contextualized language modeling techniques, such as BERT [1], have equipped ranking models with a far deeper understanding of language than the capabilities of previous bag-of-words (BoW) models. Applying these techniques to a new task is tricky, requiring knowledge of deep learning frameworks, and significant scripting and data munging. In this full-day tutorial, we build up from foundational retrieval principles to the latest neural ranking techniques. We provide background on classical (e.g., BoW), modern (e.g., Learning to Rank) and contemporary (e.g., BERT, doc2query) search ranking and re-ranking techniques. Going further, we detail and demonstrate how these can be easily experimentally applied to new search tasks in a new declarative style of conducting experiments exemplified by the PyTerrier [2] and OpenNIR [3] search toolkits. This tutorial is interactive in nature for participants; it is broken into sessions, each of which mixes explanatory presentation with hands-on activities using prepared Jupyter notebooks running on the Google Colab platform. At the end of the tutorial, participants will be comfortable accessing classical inverted index data structures, building declarative retrieval pipelines, and conducting experiments using state-of-the-art neural ranking models.

Keywords: Declarative experimentation · Neural ranking · BERT

D. Hiemstra et al. (Eds.): ECIR 2021, LNCS 12657, pp. 728–729, 2021.
https://doi.org/10.1007/978-3-030-72240-1

References

1. Devlin, J., Chang, M.W., Lee, K., Toutanova, K.: Bert: pre-training of deep bidirectional transformers for language understanding. In: NAACL-HLT (2019)
2. Macdonald, C., Tonellotto, N.: Declarative experimentation in information retrieval using PyTerrier. In: ICTIR (2020)
3. MacAvaney, S.: OpenNIR: A complete neural ad-hoc ranking pipeline. WSDM (2020)

Search Among Sensitive Content

Graham McDonald[1]([⊠]) and Douglas W. Oard[2]

[1] University of Glasgow, Glasgow, UK
graham.mcdonald@glasgow.ac.uk
[2] University of Maryland, College Park, MD, USA
oard@umd.edu

Keywords: Sensitive information · Sensitivity-aware IR · Information leakage

Information retrieval (IR) systems provide access to large amounts of content, some of which may be personal, confidential, or otherwise sensitive. While some information protection is legislated, e.g., through the European Union's General Data Protection Regulation (GDPR) or disclosure exemptions in Freedom of Information Acts; other cases are regulated only by social expectations. Information retrieval research has traditionally focused on finding indexed content. However, the increased intermixing of sensitive content with content that can properly be disclosed now motivates research on systems that can balance multiple interests: serving the searcher's interest in finding content while serving other stakeholders' interests in appropriately protecting their sensitive information.

If the content requiring protection were marked, protecting it would be straightforward. There are, however, many cases in which sensitive content must be discovered before it can be protected. Discovering such sensitivities ranges in complexity from detection of personally identifiable information (PII), to automated text classification for sensitive content, to human-in-the-loop techniques for identifying sensitivities that result from the context in which the information was produced.

Once discovered, IR systems can use the results of sensitivity decisions to filter search results, or such systems can be designed to balance the risks of missing relevant content with the risks of disclosing sensitive content. Optimising sensitivity-aware IR systems' performance depends on how well the sensitivity classification works, and requires development of new evaluation measures. Moreover, the evaluation of such IR systems requires new test collections that contain (actual or simulated) sensitive content, and when actual sensitive content is used secure ways of evaluating retrieval algorithms (e.g., algorithm deposit or trusted online evaluation) are needed. Where untrusted data centres provide services, encrypted search may also be needed. Many of these components rely on algorithmic privacy guarantees, such as those provided by k-anonymity, L-diversity, t-closeness or differential privacy.

This tutorial will introduce these challenges, review work to date on each aspect of the problem, describe current best practices, and identify open research questions. Resources and outputs from the tutorial can be found on the tutorial website: https://search-among-sensitive-content.github.io.

© Springer Nature Switzerland AG 2021
D. Hiemstra et al. (Eds.): ECIR 2021, LNCS 12657, p. 730, 2021.
https://doi.org/10.1007/978-3-030-72240-1

Fake News, Disinformation, Propaganda, Media Bias, and Flattening the Curve of the COVID-19 Infodemic

Preslav Nakov[1]([⊠]) and Giovanni da San Martino[2]

[1] Qatar Computing Research Institute, HBKU, Doha, Qatar
pnakov@hbku.edu.qa
[2] University of Padova, Padua, Italy
dasan@math.unipd.it

Keywords: Fake news · Fact-checking · Disinformation · Misinformation · Check-worthiness estimation · Verified claim retrieval · COVID-19

Tutorial Description

The rise of social media has democratized content creation and has made it easy for anybody to share and to spread information online. On the positive side, this has given rise to citizen journalism, thus enabling much faster dissemination of information compared to what was possible with newspapers, radio, and TV. On the negative side, stripping traditional media of their gate-keeping role has left the public unprotected against the spread of disinformation, which could now travel at breaking-news speed over the same democratic channel. This situation gave rise to the proliferation of false information specifically created to affect individual people's beliefs, and ultimately to influence major events such as political elections; it also set the dawn of the Post-Truth Era, where appeal to emotions has become more important than the truth. More recently, with the emergence of the COVID-19 pandemic, a new blending of medical and political misinformation and disinformation has given rise to the first global infodemic. Limiting the impact of these negative developments has become a major focus for journalists, social media companies, and regulatory authorities.

The tutorial offers an overview of the emerging and inter-connected research areas of fact-checking, misinformation, disinformation, "fake news", propaganda, and media bias detection, with focus on text and on computational approaches. It further explores the general fact-checking pipeline and important elements thereof such as check-worthiness estimation, spotting previous fact-checked claims, stance detection, source reliability estimation, and detecting malicious users in social media. Finally, it covers some recent developments such as the emergence of large-scale pre-trained language models, and the challenges and opportunities they offer.

Tutorial website: https://propaganda.math.unipd.it/ecir21-tutorial

© Springer Nature Switzerland AG 2021
D. Hiemstra et al. (Eds.): ECIR 2021, LNCS 12657, p. 731, 2021.
https://doi.org/10.1007/978-3-030-72240-1

Author Index

Printed in the United States
by Baker & Taylor Publisher Services